WINFIELD AND JOLOWICZ ON TORT

AUSTRALIA AND NEW ZEALAND
The Law Book Company Ltd.
Sydney : Melbourne : Perth

CANADA AND U.S.A.
The Carswell Company Ltd.
Agincourt, Ontario

INDIA
N. M. Tripathi Private Ltd.
Bombay
and
Eastern Law House Private Ltd.
Calcutta and Delhi
M.P.P. House
Bangalore

ISRAEL
Steimatzky's Agency Ltd.
Jerusalem : Tel Aviv : Haifa

PAKISTAN
Pakistan Law House
Karachi

WINFIELD AND JOLOWICZ

ON

TORT

THIRTEENTH EDITION

BY

W. V. H. ROGERS, M.A.

of Gray's Inn, Barrister;
Professor of Law in the University of Leeds

LONDON
SWEET & MAXWELL
1989

First Edition   (1937) The Author
Second Edition   (1943) The Author
Third Edition   (1946) The Author
Fourth Edition   (1948) The Author
Fifth Edition   (1950) The Author
Sixth Edition   (1954) T. Ellis Lewis
Seventh Edition   (1963) J. A. Jolowicz and T. Ellis Lewis
Eighth Edition   (1967) J. A. Jolowicz with T. Ellis Lewis
Ninth Edition   (1971) J. A. Jolowicz with T. Ellis Lewis
                            and D. M. Harris
Tenth Edition   (1975) W. V. H. Rogers
Eleventh Edition   (1979) W. V. H. Rogers
Twelfth Edition   (1984) W. V. H. Rogers
Reprinted   (1986)
Thirteenth Edition   (1989) W. V. H. Rogers

Published by
Sweet & Maxwell Limited of
South Quay Plaza, 183 Marsh Wall, London E14 9FT
Computerset by MFK Graphic Systems (Typesetting) Limited
Reproduced, printed and bound in Great Britain by
BPCC Hazell Books Ltd
Member of BPCC Ltd
Aylesbury, Bucks, England

British Library Cataloguing in Publication Data
Rogers, W. V. H. (William Vaughan Horton)
Winfield and Jolowicz on tort. – 13th ed.
1. England. Torts. Law
344.2063

ISBN 0–421–37620–1
ISBN 0–421–37630–9 pbk

PREFACE TO THIRTEENTH EDITION

THE preface to the twelfth edition said that its preparation had been dominated by the extension of the duty of care in negligence after *Anns* v. *Merton* and referred to the note of caution sounded by Robert Goff L.J. (as he then was). Since then the courts (and particularly the House of Lords and Privy Council) have gone a long way to demolishing the structure which was run up after *Anns*. What decision of the House of Lords has, without Parliamentary intervention, fallen further and faster than *Junior Books* v. *Veitchi*, of which by 1988 a Lord Justice of Appeal could say that he found it difficult to see that future citation from it could ever serve any useful purpose? The resurgence of a form of common law fundamentalism is not surprising when we see that what Mr. Weir has called the "why-nottery" of the post-*Anns* era could lead to its being seriously argued in *C.B.S. Songs* v. *Amstrad* that the law of *negligence* was a proper mechanism to deal with the loss of revenue to recording companies caused by the sale of tape-to-tape domestic audio systems. While there is considerable room for debate whether the "fundamentalist" answers are necessarily good ones (particularly in the area of economic loss) it is at least satisfying that the doctrinal issues are now being articulated (or perceived?) and not simply ignored. That said, in the context of defective premises heterodoxy has been grievously wounded but not slain in *D. & F. Estates* v. *Church Commissioners* and there is plenty of further litigation and uncertainty waiting in the wings.

To compensate for the substantial quantity of new material (particularly on negligence and the Consumer Protection Act 1987) there has been some pruning and the text of this edition is about twenty pages shorter than its predecessor. However, I believe there are more words to a page and the end result is probably longer. The decision to have yet another review of defamation law (along with privacy) may justify what might otherwise appear to be a self-indulgent retention of discussion of the Faulks proposals.

Most of the text was delivered just before Christmas 1988. The publishers were kind enough to let me include a mention of further developments at proof stage so that, for example, it has been possible to take account of *Smith* v. *Eric S. Bush*.

Once again I must express my thanks to Mrs. C. J. Taylor, Secretary of the Faculty of Law, who has displayed her customary efficiency, dedication and good humour in a more than usually difficult period; and to the publishers, who have remained patient and helpful in the face of my delays and the removal of their entire enterprise to a new base.

W.V.H.R.

LEEDS
June, 1989

CONTENTS

TABLE OF CASES

xiii

TABLE OF STATUTES

CHAPTER 1

MEANING AND FUNCTIONS OF THE LAW OF TORT

MEANING OF THE LAW OF TORT

NUMEROUS attempts have been made to define "a tort" or "tortious liability," with varying degrees of lack of success. Winfield's definition is discussed below but that was primarily a formal one designed to distinguish tortious liability from other traditional legal categories such as contract or trust. Such distinctions do not often arise in a practical form[1] but an attempt at formal definition is not without value whether or not one accepts the continuing usefulness of the traditional legal classifications.[2] The primary need of the reader, however, must be a statement of what a book of this kind is about. We should begin, therefore, with description rather than with definition and must be content for the moment to sacrifice accuracy and completeness for the sake of simplicity. Having given a very broad description of the purposes of the law of tort we can then return to the problem of formal definition and, finally, look at what is currently the most controversial matter in relation to the practical operation of the law—the relationship of parts of the tort system with certain other legal and social institutions pursuing similar ends.

Aims of the law of tort

It is not possible to assign any one aim to the law of tort, which is not surprising when one considers that the subject comprehends situations as disparate as A carelessly running B down in the street and C calling D a thief; or E giving bad investment advice to F and G selling H's car when he has no authority to do so. At a very general level, however, we may say that tort is concerned with the allocation or prevention of losses, which are bound to occur in our society. It is obvious that in any society of people living together numerous conflicts of interest will arise and that the actions of one man or group of men will from time to time cause or threaten damage to others. This damage may take many forms—injury to the person, damage to physical property, damage to financial interests, injury to reputation and so on—and whenever a man suffers damage he is inclined to look to the law for redress. But the granting of redress by the law means that some person or group of

---

[1] In some instances it might have been better if the courts had paid a little *more* attention to these distinctions: see, in particular, m the law governing the liability of the vendor of defective premises (*post*, p. 229).

[2] See *post*, p. 7.

1

persons will be required by the law to do or refrain from doing something. This redress may take various forms. In the great majority of tort actions coming before the courts, the plaintiff is seeking monetary compensation (damages) for the injury he has suffered and this fact strongly emphasises the function of tort in allocating or redistributing loss. In many cases, however, the plaintiff is seeking an injunction to prevent the occurrence of harm in the future and in this area the "preventive" function of tort predominates.[3] Whichever aim is pursued, however, the law clearly cannot decree that whenever a man suffers loss he should automatically be entitled to redress from the author of that loss. If, for example, A begins to trade in a commodity in a district in which B has previously had a monopoly, A can clearly foresee that if he adopts superior methods of business he will cause loss to B, indeed it might be said in one sense that his purpose was to cause loss to B, but he is clearly not liable to compensate B for this loss. Indeed, the law takes quite the opposite stance by providing that many agreements between traders to restrict competition are unlawful.[4] There must be some reason in any given case for calling on the law to provide the redress sought, to shift the loss. In fact, the law cannot even go so far as to order every person whose action may be regarded as morally culpable to make redress to those who suffer by it: "Acts or omissions which any moral code would censure cannot in a practical world be treated so as to give a right to every person injured by them to demand relief. In this way rules of law arise which limit the range of complainants and the extent of their remedy."[5] The somewhat paradoxical conclusion follows that the law of tort is as much about *non*-liability as it is about liability.[6]

It is the business then of the law of tort to determine when the law will and when it will not grant redress for damage suffered or threatened, and the rules for liability whereby it does this are the subject of this book. We may say, therefore, that if a plaintiff has suffered damage in circumstances covered by the rules for liability stated in a book on the law of tort, then, assuming the rules to be correctly stated, the plaintiff has been the victim of a tort; by this we mean no more than that a tort is a wrong the victim of which is

---

[3] The injunction is the primary remedy for, say, nuisance and the so-called "economic torts." In many cases the plaintiff may claim both an injunction and damages, but the functions of allocating loss and preventing loss are often inextricably intermingled even if only one remedy is sought. The award of damages against a defendant may make him take greater care in the future; and if the plaintiff obtains an injunction against the publication of a potentially profitable but libellous book by the defendant the law has in effect allocated a financial loss to the defendant.

Allocation and prevention of loss does not complete the tally of the aims of the law of tort. Libel, for instance, has a powerful punitive flavour in fact if not in theory and some tort actions (*e.g.* trespass) are often brought only as an indirect method of obtaining a declaration of rights: see further Williams and Hepple, *Foundations of the Law of Tort,* pp. 23–26. There are at least four possible bases of the action for damages in tort—appeasement, justice (*i.e.* the moral principle that one who by his fault has caused damage ought as a matter of justice to make compensation), deterrence and compensation—and each of these will be found to receive different emphasis according to the particular branch of the law under consideration. No one theory adequately explains the whole of the law. Linden, *Canadian Tort Law,* Chap. 1, ascribes to tort law the function of "Ombudsman," stressing the publicity produced by certain tort claims against Government and corporations: see further *post,* p. 27.

[4] Restrictive Trade Practices Act 1976; Resale Prices Act 1976; Art. 85 of the Treaty of Rome.

[5] *Donoghue* v. *Stevenson* [1932] A.C. 562, 580, *per* Lord Atkin.

[6] Jolowicz, "The Law of Tort and Non-Physical Loss" (1972) 12 J.S.P.T.L. 91.

entitled to redress.[7] It should be emphasised, however, that the law of tort, like other branches of private law, is concerned with questions of *liability*. An action founded upon tort is an action between persons, either natural or artificial (*i.e.* corporations), and the outcome can only be that one of them, the defendant, is or is not liable to do or refrain from doing something at the suit of the other. If there is no defendant whose liability can be established according to the principles of the law, then the plaintiff is left without redress so far as the law of tort is concerned. It does not follow, however, that he is without other forms of redress. The act or omission of the other party may be some other sort of wrong for which a remedy may lie in contract or quasi-contract or according to the rules of equity governing breach of trust, matters which are briefly considered in the next section. Alternatively, the victim may be able to look for compensatory redress to someone other than the author of his loss, for example to an insurance company with which he has entered into a contract of loss insurance or to the Welfare State. The relationship, present and future, between the law of tort and those sources of compensation must be considered at length in the concluding part of this chapter.

Definition of tortious liability[8]

Tortious liability arises from the breach of a duty primarily fixed by law; *this duty is towards persons generally and its breach is redressible by an action for unliquidated damages.*

At the risk of repetition, we must again stress that in framing this definition Winfield was not seeking to indicate what conduct is and what is not sufficient to involve a person in tortious liability, but merely to distinguish tort from certain other branches of law. As we shall see, it cannot be accepted as entirely accurate but it has the merit of comparative brevity and contains elements which deserve continuing emphasis. It must also be emphasised that the number of cases in which it will be essential to classify the plaintiff's claim as tort, contract, trust, etc., will be comparatively small. A cause of action in modern law is merely a factual situation the existence of which enables the plaintiff to obtain a remedy from the court[9] and he is not required to head his statement of claim with a description of the branch of the law on which he relies,[10] still less with a description of a particular category (*e.g.* negligence, trespass, sale) within that branch. But statutes and rules of procedure sometimes distinguish between, say, contract and tort with reference to matters such as limitation of actions,[11] service of

---

[7] See *S.C.M. (United Kingdom) Ltd.* v. *Whittall and Son Ltd.* [1971] 1 Q.B. 337, 347–348, *per* Winn L.J.
[8] For other definitions, see Winfield, *Province of the Law of Tort* (1931), Chap. XII; Williams and Hepple, *Foundations of the Law of Tort,* (2nd ed.), p. 27. For a collection and discussion of English and American definitions, see Prosser, *Torts* (5th ed.) Chap. 1. Winfield's definition is preferred, with qualification, by Clerk and Lindsell, *Torts* (16th ed.), para. 1–01.
[9] *Letang* v. *Cooper* [1965] Q.B. 232–244, *per* Diplock L.J.
[10] *Drane* v. *Evangelou* [1978] 1 W.L.R. 455 is an example.
[11] In contract time runs from the date of the breach, in tort it *usually* runs from the date when damage is suffered: see *post*, p. 718.

process[12] and costs[13] and the court cannot then avoid the task of classification.[14]

Contract and tort[15]

The first point that must be made is that from a practical lawyer's point of view there may be a considerable overlap in any factual situation between the law of contract and the law of tort. For example, a claim for damages arising from a defective product may involve a complex web of issues under the Sale of Goods Act, the law of misrepresentation and collateral warranty, the tort of negligence, the Consumer Protection Act 1987 and a chain of contractual indemnities among retailer, middleman and manufacturer.[16] It is unlikely that any legal system can ever cut loose from general conceptual classifications such as "contract" and "tort"[17] but the student will quickly come to recognise that the boundary must sometimes be crossed in the solution of a problem. Secondly, while it has long been trite law that a defendant may be liable on the same facts in contract to A and in tort to B (notwithstanding privity of contract)[18] it is now recognised that there may be concurrent contractual and tortious liability to the same plaintiff, though he may not, of course, recover damages twice over.

It has been said that it is "a clearly established principle that where under the general law a person owes a duty to another to exercise reasonable care and skill in some activity, a breach of that duty gives rise to a claim in tort notwithstanding the fact that the activity is the subject-matter of a contract between them. In such a case, the breach of duty will also be a breach of contract. The classic example of this situation is the relationship between doctor and patient,"[19] to which might be added that of carrier and passenger. If one or other of the claims presents the plaintiff with an advantage he may elect to present that which is more favourable to him,[20] though as far as the substance of the duty is concerned there may be no difference between

[12] See Rules of the Supreme Court, Ord. 11.

[13] At one time the County Courts Act contained different financial limits of contract and tort for the purposes of recovery of costs and this led to a very large number of cases in which the sole issue was whether the claim sounded in contract or tort. The present legislation draws no distinction.

[14] The distinction may still arise for pleading purposes: if the plaintiff sues for breach of contract he should plead the contract and the consideration therefor.

[15] "Never did a Name so obstruct a true understanding of the Thing. To such a plight has it brought us that a favourite mode of defining a Tort is to declare merely that it is not a Contract. As if a man were to define Chemistry by pointing out that it is not Physics or Mathematics": Wigmore, *Select Cases on the Law of Torts*, vii.

[16] See, *e.g. Lambert* v. *Lewis* [1982] A.C. 225.

[17] *cf.* Jolowicz, *The Division and Classification of the Law,* and Lord Roskill in *Junior Books Ltd.* v. *Veitchi Co. Ltd.* [1982] 3 W.L.R. 477, 493–494.

[18] *Donoghue* v. *Stevenson* [1932] A.C. 562.

[19] *Forsikringsaktieselskapet Vesta* v. *Butcher* [1988] 3 W.L.R. 565, 571, *per* O'Connor L.J. The example of the doctor refers, of course, to a "private" patient. See also *Midland Bank Trust Co. Ltd.* v. *Hett, Stubbs & Kemp* [1979] Ch. 384 (solicitor and client, a context in which the rule was formerly that a claim lay in contract only: *Groom* v. *Crocker* [1939] 1 K.B. 194); *Central Trust Co.* v. *Rafuse* (1986) 31 D.L.R. (4th) 481.

[20] See, *e.g. Midland Bank Trust Co. Ltd.* v. *Hett, Stubbs & Kemp, supra* (limitation, though on the facts the judge concluded that neither claim was time-barred). But for criticism, see Kaye, "The Liability of Solicitors" (1984) 100 L.Q.R. 680.

them. For example, a doctor's duty in tort is to exercise proper professional care and skill and the implied term in his contract is the same[21]: he does not impliedly warrant that he will effect a cure, though theoretically he may do so by an express promise to that effect.[22] Where, however, the law of contract imposes a duty lower than one of reasonable care, the courts are reluctant to allow the contractual allocation of responsibility to be overridden by the law of tort. In *Tai Hing Cotton Mill Ltd.* v. *Liu Chong Hing Bank Ltd.*[23] the plaintiffs' employee had forged some 300 cheques totalling HK$5.5 million. A forgery is a nullity and the plaintiffs claimed a declaration that the defendant bank was not entitled to debit those cheques to their account and was therefore required to reimburse the plaintiffs. It was established law that a customer's duty in contract to a bank was (*a*) not to draw cheques in such a manner as to facilitate forgery and (*b*) to notify the bank immediately of any forgery of which he became aware, but on the facts neither of these duties had been broken. The bank, however, contended that the plaintiffs were negligent, and hence in breach of a tort duty to them, in that their internal system of financial control was too lax to detect or prevent forgeries. This was rejected by the Privy Council. Lord Scarman went so far as to say that there was no "advantage ... in searching for a liability in tort where the parties are in a contractual relationship," a proposition which, taken literally, would deny the concurrence of contract and tort, but in view of the other authorities on this point it is unlikely that it will be treated as having so broad an effect. Rather, it stands for the proposition that the law will not recognise a duty of care in tort when that same duty of care has been rejected or excluded by the court as an implied term in the type of contract which the parties have made.[23a]

To say that contract and tort may co-exist on the same facts does not tell us how we distinguish between them. It was Winfield's view that tortious duties exist by virtue of the law itself and are not dependent upon the agreement or consent of the persons subjected to them. I am under a duty not to assault you, not to slander you, not to trespass on your land, because the law says I am under such a duty and not because I have agreed with you to undertake such a duty. Winfield therefore considered that tortious liability could for this reason be distinguished from contractual liability and from liability on bailment, neither of which can exist independently of the parties' or at least of the defendant's agreement or consent. There are, however, several instances of what is undoubtedly tortious liability for the existence of which some prior consent on the part of the defendant is essential. The liability of

---

[21] The implied term in a contract for the supply of a service where the supplier is acting in the course of a business (which includes a profession) is found in s.13 of the Supply of Goods and Services Act 1982, restating the common law. Where goods are transferred under such a contract there may be strict liability as to that element, on the analogy of sale.

[22] *Thake* v. *Maurice* [1986] Q.B. 644 shows that a court will require very clear evidence to establish such a warranty against a doctor. *cf. Greaves & Co. (Contractors) Ltd.* v. *Baynham Meikle & Partners* [1974] 1 W.L.R. 1261 (architect).

[23] [1986] A.C. 80. See also *Canadian Pacific Hotels Ltd.* v. *Bank of Montreal* (1987) 40 D.L.R. (4th) 385.

[23a] See *National Bank of Greece S.A.* v. *Pinios Shipping Co. No. 1* [1989] 1 All E.R. 213; *Bank of Nova Scotia* v. *Hellenic Mutual War Risks Assoc., The Times,* April 20, 1989; *Reid* v. *Rush & Tompkins* [1989] N.L.J. 680.

the occupier of premises to his visitor, for example, which is now governed by the Occupiers' Liability Act 1957, is based upon breach of a duty of care owed by the occupier to persons whom he has permitted to enter upon his premises. The duty owed to trespassers, *i.e.* persons who enter without his consent, is not the same.[24] Again, the duty of care owed by a person who gives gratuitous advice upon a serious occasion is, doubtless, a tortious one,[25] but its existence is dependent upon the adviser's agreement to give the advice and, perhaps, upon his agreement to undertake legal responsibility for it.[26]

If it is not true that all tortious duties arise independently of the will of the defendant, it is equally not true that contractual duties are always dependent upon that will. Not only is there the obvious point that the duty not to break one's contracts is itself a duty imposed by the law, but it is also the case that contractual liability may exist even in the absence of any true consent between the parties. Whether or not there is a contract normally depends upon the outward manifestations of agreement by the parties, not on their subjective states of mind.[27]

A slightly better mode of differentiation between tortious and contractual liability, it is suggested, is to be found in the proposition that in tort the content of the duties is fixed by the law whereas the content of contractual duties is fixed by the contract itself. If I consent to your entry upon my premises then the duty which I owe to you is the duty fixed by the Occupiers' Liability Act, *i.e.* by the law itself, but whether, for example, my duty is to deliver to you 10 or 20 tons of coal can only be discovered from the contract between us. Even this distinction, however, is by no means always valid for today in many cases the content of contractual duties is also fixed by the law. Statute provides, for example, that certain quite specific obligations shall be contained in contracts for the sale or hire-purchase of goods[28] and it is now no longer true, as once, perhaps, it was, that implied terms in a contract, in the absence of a statutory rule, are always to be based upon the presumed intention of the parties.[29] Conversely, there are tortious duties which are subject to variation by agreement, whether or not that agreement amounts in law to a contract between the parties.[30]

At the risk of abandoning the limits of formal definition, a more satis-factory basis for distinguishing between contract and tort may be sought in considering the aims of the two heads of liability. Tort, as we have seen, aims principally at the prevention or compensation of harms whereas the "core"

---

[24] But since Winfield wrote, the duty owed to trespassers has risen: see *post*, p. 225.
[25] But the relationship between adviser and advised has been described as "equivalent to contract": *Hedley Byrne & Co.* v. *Heller & Partners Ltd.* [1964] A.C. 465, 530, *per* Lord Devlin.
[26] This depends upon the effect of the Unfair Contract Terms Act 1977: see *post*, p. 286.
[27] See, *e.g. Smith* v. *Hughes* (1871) L.R. 6 Q.B. 597, 607, *per* Blackburn J.; Treitel, *The Law of Contract*, (7th ed.), p. 1. Winfield would have no doubt replied that the objective approach was taken merely for reasons of evidential and commercial convenience.
[28] Sale of Goods Act 1979; Unfair Contract Terms Act 1977.
[29] *Lister* v. *Romford Ice & Cold Storage Co. Ltd.* [1957] A.C. 535, 594, *per* Lord Tucker; *Liverpool City Council* v. *Irwin* [1977] A.C. 239, 257, 258, *per* Lord Cross.
[30] Occupiers' Liability Act 1957, s.2(1); *Ashdown* v. *Samuel Williams Ltd.* [1957] 1 Q.B. 409. This case would be decided differently, since the Unfair Contract Terms Act 1977, but is still illustrative of the general principle of law.

of contract is the idea of enforcing certain promises.[31] This difference of function has two principal consequences: first, that a mere failure to act will not usually be actionable in tort, for that would be to set at naught the rule that even a positive promise will not give rise to legal liability unless it is intended as legally binding and supported by consideration or the formality of a deed; secondly, that damages cannot be claimed in tort for a "loss of expectation," as opposed to "out of pocket" losses, or, as it is sometimes expressed, damages in contract put the plaintiff in the position he would have been in had the contract been performed, whereas damages in tort put him in the position he would have been in had the tort not been committed. Of course, like many fundamental but dimly-perceived distinctions this one often breaks down or is ignored in practice. Thus tort-type losses are usually also recoverable in contract if contract there be[32] and, as we have seen, given suitable damage there is no difficulty about the concurrence of liability in contract and tort on the same facts, the plaintiff having the benefit of whichever is the more favourable to him on the particular facts.[33]

There was a period, however, in which it seemed that the boundary between the two categories might be breaking down.[34] In *Junior Books* v. *Veitchi Co. Ltd.*[35] a sub-contractor was held liable in tort to a building owner for negligent installation of a floor which was defective but not dangerous, despite the fact that the most natural description of the situation was not that the defendant had damaged the plaintiff's property but that he had failed to fulfil an undertaking (by contract to the head contractor) to provide a floor of adequate quality. However, predictions that we were heading towards a situation in which plaintiffs could sue in tort because they had not got what they paid for and that every breach of contract which might with reasonable care have been avoided was also a tort to any person foreseeably affected thereby have now been shown to be unfounded, and *Junior Books* has been interpreted as a decision very much on its own facts, namely, the peculiar relationship between a building owner and a sub-contractor nominated by him, a relationship which, but for the technical point of privity,[36] is all but contractual.[37] Indeed, the House of Lords has reaffirmed, in the context of

---

[31] See Reynolds, "Tort Actions in Contractual Situations" (1985) 11 N.Z.U.L.R. 215, 231. Great play is often made with the fact that "contract" in the guise of *assumpsit* grew out of "tort" in the form of trespass on the case, but this does not show that there is any necessary connection between the two, still less that lawyers thought there was: it merely shows a readiness to adapt what lay to hand to meet the serious formal and procedural deficiencies of the "contractual" actions of covenant and debt.

[32] *Godley* v. *Perry* [1960] 1 W.L.R. 9 is a good example. The plaintiff's complaint was not "my catapult doesn't work" (contract) but "it broke and put my eye out" (tort). Curiously, the recent expansion of tort beyond its "negative" function of redressing harms has been accompanied by a sustained academic attack on the alleged "positive" function of contract in enforcing promises, most notably by Atiyah in *The Rise and Fall of Freedom of Contract* and *Promises, Morals and Law*. See Burrows, "Contract, Tort and Restitution" (1983) 99 L.Q.R. 217.

[33] *Ante*, p. 4.

[34] The movement has not all been on the tort side, for there has been increasing use of the concept of promissory estoppel so that certain promises are now binding without compliance with the requirements of consideration and the proposition that estoppel can only be used as a shield, not as a sword, while broadly true, needs qualification: see Treitel, *Law of Contract* (7th ed.), Chap. 3.

[35] [1983] 1 A.C. 520. See also *Ross* v. *Caunters* [1980] Ch. 297, *post*, p. 96.

[36] Though the parties have deliberately chosen *not* to make a contract between themselves when they could have done so.

[37] See *post*, p. 89.

buildings, that the mere fact that the work is defective does not give rise to damage actionable in tort.[38]

The point that the court may impose tort liability where the loss is fundamentally contractual where there is a very close relationship between the parties is also relevant to the validity of the second element of Winfield's definition, that the duty in tort is owed to persons generally. The reference now is, of course, to the primary duty, *i.e.* the duty not to trespass, not to slander and so on, for breach of which tortious liability is imposed. The breach of such a duty gives rise to a remedial duty, *i.e.* a duty to make redress, and this is always owed to a specific person or persons whatever the source of the liability. Winfield would now be forced to retreat from the claim that if the primary duty is towards a specific person or specific persons it cannot arise from tort,[39] but there is probably still some substance in his contention that the element of generality was an important factor in the definition and, while not capable of precise definition, was sufficiently workable in the majority of cases. However, even leaving aside recent developments, it appears that everything depends upon the level of abstraction at which the duty is expressed. It can, no doubt, be truly stated that by virtue of the law of tort I am under a duty not to convert to my own use the goods of anybody else, while my contractual duty to deliver goods which I have sold is owed only to the person to whom I have sold them. But this is to compare two statements at different levels. Just as I have a general duty not to commit the tort of conversion, so I have a general duty not to commit breaches of contract. If, on the other hand, we descend to the particular, then just as my duty to deliver certain goods is owed only to their buyer, so also my duty not to convert certain goods to my own use is owed only to the person in possession, or having the immediate right to possession, of them.

Quasi-contractual liability

We may here conveniently make use of the idea of the primary duty to mark off from the law of tort one other branch of law, namely, quasi-contractual liability. This signifies liability imposed upon a particular person to pay money to another person on the ground of unjust enrichment.[40] A good example is the liability to repay money which has been paid under a mistake of fact. I owe you £10. I pay the £10 to your twin brother, whom I mistake for you, and he honestly believes that he is entitled to the money. Now he is, of course, legally bound to repay the money to me and so is under a remedial duty. But it cannot be said that this remedial duty is the result of the breach of some primary duty, as would be the case in tortious and, indeed, also in contractual liability. It would be meaningless to say that your twin brother was under a duty not to accept the money from me or that he

---

[38] *D. & F. Estates Ltd.* v. *Church Commissioners* [1988] 3 W.L.R. 368, *post*, p. 230.
[39] The *Midland Bank Trust Co.* case, *supra*, provides a clear example.
[40] See Winfield, *op. cit.*, Chap. VIII; Winfield, *Law of Quasi-Contract*; Jackson, *History of Quasi-Contract*; Goff and Jones, *Law of Restitution*, 3rd ed.

was ever under a relevant duty of any kind save the remedial duty to return the money to me because otherwise he would be unjustly enriched at my expense. The remedial duty in tort always springs from the breach of a primary duty of some kind. But in quasi-contract there is no primary duty whatsoever.

The third element of Winfield's definition is that breach of the duty is redressible by an action for unliquidated damages. Here again is a ground for distinguishing quasi-contractual liability for a quasi-contract claim rests upon the extent to which the defendant has been unjustly enriched, not the extent to which the plaintiff has suffered loss, and hence it is not a claim for *damages* at all. In other contexts, however, the distinction between liquidated and unliquidated damages must be made clear. Where the plaintiff in an action sues for a predetermined and inelastic sum of money, he is claiming liquidated damages. But where he seeks to recover such an amount as the court, in its discretion, is at liberty to award, he is claiming unliquidated damages, and this is so even where he has specified a particular sum of money in his pleadings.[41] The action for unliquidated damages is one pretty sure test of tortious liability and it has some show of express judicial approval.[42] But we hasten to add that it is not an infallible test[43] and that it is by no means the only remedy for a tort, and that, for some torts, it is not even the primary remedy.[44] Nevertheless, the possibility of bringing such an action is not fettered by any of the conditions which attach to other remedies and the courts must at least hear what the plaintiff in an action for damages has got to say, even if they come to the conclusion that the defendant has, in the circumstances of the case, nothing to which he need answer.[45]

Tort and crime distinguished

It would appear then that the possibility of an action for unliquidated damages is one of the factors in tortious liability. And this serves to distinguish it from *criminal liability*. A crime is a wrong the sanction of which involves punishment.[46] What then is punishment? Death, imprisonment

---

[41] The award cannot be of a sum greater than the amount claimed if an amount is specified in the pleadings, but leave to amend the statement of claim can be granted even after verdict: McGregor, *Damages*, (15th ed.), p. 1120.

[42] *Hulton* v. *Hulton* [1917] 1 K.B. 813, 820, 822–823, 824, *cf. Re Great Orme Tramways Co.* (1934) 50 T.L.R. 450; *Att.-Gen.* v. *Canter* [1938] 2 K.B. 826; affirmed [1939] 1 K.B. 326 (action to recover penalty under Income Tax Acts not a cause of action in tort); *Philip Morris Ltd.* v. *Ainley* [1975] V.R. 345. Salmond and Heuston, *Torts*, 19th ed., p. 10. Prosser, *Torts*, 5th ed., p. 2.

[43] Williams and Hepple, *op. cit.*, p. 23.

[44] For the other remedies which may be available in a case of tort, see *post*, Chap. 23.

[45] Winfield, pp. 231–233.

[46] Kenny, *Outlines of Criminal Law*, (16th ed.), p. 539. The relevant chapter is omitted from later editions. Kenny added that the sanction must be remissible (*i.e.* capable of forgiveness) by the Crown alone, if remissible at all. Winfield suggested that this leads to the vicious circle: "What is a crime? Something that the Crown alone can pardon. What, then, is it that the Crown alone can pardon? A crime." *Province of the Law of Tort*, pp. 196–197. See, generally, Smith and Hogan, *Criminal Law*, (6th ed.), Chap. 2; Kenny, *op. cit.* pp. 538–547; Winfield, *op. cit.* Chap. VIII; Allen, *Legal Duties*, pp. 221–252 (The Nature of Crime). Glanville Williams, "The Definition of a Crime" (1955) 8 *Current Legal Problems* 107, argues that the whole of the law of procedure must be taken into account in a definition of a crime. See also Jolowicz, *Lectures on Jurisprudence*, pp. 347–358.

(provided it is not merely imprisonment which is terminable by the act of the prisoner himself), and pecuniary fines.[47] Now it will be instantly perceived that death and imprisonment have nothing in common with the unliquidated damages which are claimed in an action in tort. But the distinction between crime and tort became much less obvious when the criminal courts in 1972 were given power to order an offender to pay compensation to his victim, a power which has since been widened. Indeed, "power" is a slightly mis-leading expression, for the court is now required to give reasons, on passing sentence, if it does not make a compensation order.[48] A magistrates' court is not to order compensation in excess of £2,000[49] and losses resulting from road accidents are generally excluded but the compensation which may be awarded may include a sum for bereavement[50] or anxiety and distress.[51] A compensation order should only be made where the convicted person's responsibility is clear[52] but civil liability is not a precondition,[53] so that an order might be made where, for example, there was no civil liability for breach of statutory duty.[54] This summary procedure is obviously unsuitable for cases where there are complex questions of quantification of the loss and a civil action may offer the plaintiff other advantages,[55] but in minor matters a compensation order is obviously a much more sensible course than requir-ing the victim to take separate civil proceedings. In this respect the dis-tinction between crime and tort has become more blurred, though since tort originated in trespass, which to our eyes was in medieval times quasi-criminal, tort may only be returning to its roots. Furthermore, the compen-satory sums awarded under these provisions are, until the court specifies their exact amount, quite uncertain and are therefore just as "unliquidated" as are damages in tort. But there is one peculiarity which marks them off from damages in tort. In every case they are obtainable only as a result of a process the primary purpose of which, when it is initiated, is the imposition of punishment, or something in the nature of punishment. In crime, the award of compensation is ancillary to the criminal process: in tort it is normally its very object.[56]

---

[47] There are, of course, now several other methods of dealing with offenders: see generally the Powers of Criminal Courts Act 1973.
[48] Powers of the Criminal Courts Act 1973, s.35(1), as substituted by the Criminal Justice Act 1988. For a full account of the theoretical relationship between crime and compensation, see Ashworth, "Punishment and Compensation" (1986) 6 O.J.L.S. 86.
[49] The majority of awards are in any case for less than £100.
[50] Powers of the Criminal Courts Act 1973, s.35(1).
[51] Bond v. Chief Constable of Kent [1983] 1 W.L.R. 40.
[52] R. v. Chappell (1984) 128 S.J. 629: R. v. Horsham JJ., ex p. Richards [1985] 1 W.L.R. 986.
[53] R. v. Chappell, supra. Where civil liability is established in subsequent proceedings sums recovered as compensation are to be brought into account: Powers of the Criminal Courts Act 1973, s.38(2).
[54] See Chap. 7.
[55] e.g. a lower burden of proof than that necessary to establish the criminal guilt which is a precondition to a compensation order; a higher likelihood of recovery because the defendant may be cable to call on a policy of insurance; and, in suitable cases, exemplary damages.
[56] It is submitted that this distinction remains broadly valid even though (a) since 1982 it has been possible to award compensation in criminal proceedings without making any other order and (b) in a limited category of cases a civil court may award exemplary damages, the purpose of which may be to punish the defendant.

Tort and breach of trust distinguished

The test of an action for unliquidated damages might also be used to distinguish a tort from a *breach of trust*. If a trustee misappropriates property which he holds upon trust for a beneficiary, the beneficiary can claim compensation. But that compensation is measured by the loss which the trust property has suffered.[57] It is ascertainable before the beneficiary commences his action. It is, therefore, not an "unliquidated" sum of money. Indeed, it is not damages of any sort, liquidated or unliquidated. But a much better way of differentiating tort from breach of trust is to regard the whole law of trusts as a division of the law of property which is fairly detachable from other parts of our law. The administration of trusts has for centuries been within the province of a special court which is now represented by the Chancery Division of the High Court. Although questions relating to trusts do incidentally arise in the common law courts,[58] it is better to take advantage of the fact that they belong more properly to the jurisdictional *enclave* of Chancery and to leave them there. That course is more consistent with their history and with the opinion of any legal practitioner at the resent day.[59]

Tort and liability on bailment

A bailment is a delivery of goods on a condition, express or implied, that they shall be restored to the bailor, or according to his directions, as soon as the purpose for which they are bailed has been completed.[60] The person who delivers the goods is called a "bailor," the person to whom they are delivered is the "bailee." Common examples of bailment are hire of goods, such as hire of a car from a garage; gratuitous loan of goods, such as lending this book to a friend; and pawn or pledge. Now, supposing that the bailee misuses or damages the goods he is, of course, liable in a civil action to the bailor. Is this liability to be distinguished from liability in tort? Many bailments arise out of contract, but it is undoubtedly possible for bailment to exist without contract and where this is the case as in the gratuitous loan of something for the use of the borrower, what is the nature of the liability? Winfield's opinion was that the bailee's liability is not tortious because, he said, the duty arises from a relation, that of bailor and bailee, which is created by the parties. No one need be a bailee if he does not wish to be one and no one can have liability for the safe custody of goods thrust upon him against his will—a fact which is frequently ignored by pushing tradesmen who send goods to persons who have never asked for them.[61] It is certainly

---

[57] Lewin, *Law of Trusts*, (16th ed.), p. 670.
[58] A striking example is *Hawkesley* v. *May* [1956] 1 Q.B. 304.
[59] Winfield, *op. cit.* Chap. VI, for a fuller discussion of the relation of tort to breach of trust.
[60] Sir William Jones, *Treatise on the Law of Bailment* (1781), p. 1; Paton, *Bailment in the Common Law*, Chap. I; Palmer, *Bailment*, Chap. 1.
[61] See *post*, pp. 472–474 Winfield's view is set out in full in *Province of the Law of Tort*, Chap. 5, where he makes the point that bailment is more fittingly regarded as a distinct branch of the law of property under the title "Possession" than as appropriate to either the law of contract or the law of tort.

true that a man cannot be subjected to the duties of a bailee without his consent but as we have already seen, there are duties which are undoubtedly tortious and which can only exist if there has been some prior agreement between the parties so it may be argued that there is no good reason for distinguishing the common law duties of a bailee from duties of this kind. If the bailor's claim is necessarily founded upon some specific provision in a contract, then, no doubt, the bailee's liability is not tortious but contractual, but if the bailor's claim rests upon a breach by the bailee of one of the bailee's common law duties, then is not his liability as much attributable to the law of tort as is the claim of a visitor against the occupier of premises under the Occupier's Liability Act?[62] In practice, the principal argument against acceptance of Winfield's view is the tendency of the legislature to lay down rules by reference to the contract/tort distinction and no other. The courts are then forced to accommodate bailment to this distinction or render the legislation inoperative.[63]

Law of obligations?

At this stage we may, perhaps, claim to have given some reason why a book on the law of tort need not concern itself with quasi-contract, crime or breach of trust, and to have gone a little way towards distinguishing tortious from contractual liability. As to the last, we have seen that the boundaries between the two types of liability are by no means easy to state[64] and that there are plentiful opportunities for both forms of liability to co-exist on one and the same set of facts. The plaintiff in such a case cannot recover damages under different heads of legal liability. Would it not, therefore, be advantageous to bring tortious and contractual liability together in one book under some such title as "The Law of Obligations"? There is a great deal to be said for this and it will be essential in a study of a particular factual area of legal liability,[65] but to be logical, a general book on the law of obligations ought also to include both quasi-contract and trusts as well as the whole of contract and tort, and would become unmanageably large. The book would also have to contain a great deal of material having only indirect connection with problems of the incidence of liability. Books on contract or on trusts are, no doubt, concerned with the incidence of liability for loss or damage suffered, as are those on tort, but there, liability only forms a part, and sometimes a

---

[62] *Turner* v. *Stallibrass* [1898] 1 Q.B. 56, *per* Collins L.J. at p. 59; *Morris* v. *C. W. Martin & Sons Ltd.* [1966] 1 Q.B. 716; *Chesworth* v. *Farrar* [1967] 1 Q.B. 716; *Gilchrist Watt and Sanderson Pty. Ltd.* v. *York Products Pty. Ltd.* [1970] 1 W.L.R. 1262.

[63] See, *e.g. American Express Co.* v. *British Airways Board* [1983] 1 W.L.R. 701 (action "in tort" under the Post Office Act 1969) and *post*, p. 662.

[64] See p. 4, *ante*. With changes in the law a topic may "move" from contract into tort, an important example being the imposition of a tortious duty to take care in making statements in *Hedley, Byrne & Co. Ltd.* v. *Heller & Partners Ltd.* [1964] A.C. 465; *post*, Chap. 11.

[65] See, *e.g.* Miller and Lovell, *Product Liability*.

small part, of their subject-matter. Equally if not more important, are such questions as the ways in which a contract may be concluded or a trust set up, the various modes of discharge or dissolution and the nature of the property rights these institutions may create. But the central question for the law of tort is always that of liability, and it is this which really forms the link between the various topics covered in this book. We are not here concerned with the creation of legal relationships or rights of property, though it may be necessary to mention them incidentally from time to time.

FOUNDATION OF TORTIOUS LIABILITY

Winfield's definition of tortious liability has been criticised on the ground that it is formal, not material, and does nothing to indicate the lawfulness or otherwise of a given act. This, it seems, Winfield admitted for he agreed that the layman must be told that no one but a professional lawyer can say whether or not the loss inflicted on him by the action or inaction of a neighbour will entitle him to a remedy by civil action against that neighbour[66] and added, "a layman is not remarkable for wisdom if he imagines that he can safely say that he is entitled to sue his neighbour for tort or for breach of contract, or for any conceivable claim without consulting a professional lawyer first."

A satisfactory material definition of tort is almost certainly an impossibility, but Winfield did devote several pages of earlier editions of this work to discussion of a familiar controversy concerning the foundation of tortious liability which has some bearing on the problem of a material definition. Salmond had asked,[67] "Does the law of torts consist of a fundamental general principle that it is wrongful to cause harm to other persons in the absence of some specific ground of justification or excuse, or does it consist of a number of specific rules prohibiting certain kinds of harmful activity, and leaving all the residue outside the sphere of legal responsibility?" and had chosen the second alternative.[68] From the point of view of the practical lawyer concerned with the law at a particular moment there can be no doubt that the second view is the correct one: for example, a recording company was held to have no civil action in respect of "bootlegging" of its artists' performances where it was unable to prove any of the economic torts or the distinct tort of breach of statutory duty,[69] even though the defendants' conduct was criminal and no justification for it could be offered. Despite

---

[66] The question was put by Jenks, "The Province of Tort in English Law" (1932) 14 J.C.L. 207, 210.

[67] *Torts*, 2nd ed. (1910), pp. 8–9.

[68] To take two modern examples, in *Furniss* v. *Fitchett* [1958] N.Z.L.R. 396, 401, Barrowclough C.J. said, "The well known torts do not have their origin in any all embracing general principle of tortious liability." In *Bollinger* v. *Costa Brava Wine Co. Ltd.* [1960] Ch. 262, 283 Danckwerts J. said, "The substance of [the argument for the defendants] was that, before a person can recover for loss which he suffered from another person's act, it must be shown that his case falls within the class of actionable wrongs. But the law may be thought to have failed if it can offer no remedy for the deliberate act of one person which causes damage to the property of another."

[69] *R.C.A. Corp.* v. *Pollard* [1983] Ch. 135; *Dunlop* v. *Woolahra Municipal Council* [1982] A.C. 158; *Lonrho Ltd.* v. *Shell Petroleum Co. Ltd. (No. 2)* [1982] A.C. 173.

occasional judicial canvassing of the idea,[70] English law has not adopted what in the United States is known as the "prima facie tort theory" whereby "the intentional infliction of temporal damages is a cause of action, which, as a matter of substantive law, whatever may be the form of the pleading, requires a justification if the defendant is to escape."[71] Nevertheless, it should be noted that we have for a good many years had something very close to a generalised principle of liability in situations where the defendant's purpose is the infliction of physical harm on the plaintiff,[72] and despite the caution which now characterises the courts' attitude to the duty of care in negligence[73] it will be an unusual case in which the defendant is not liable where his act has caused foreseeable physical damage to the plaintiff or his property.

Winfield conceded the correctness of the "narrow" view as a practical, day-to-day matter, but he contended that from a broader outlook there was validity in the theory of a fundamental general principle of liability, for if we take the view, as we must, that the law of tort has grown for centuries, and is still growing, then some such principle seems to be at the back of it. It is the difference between treating a tree as inanimate for the practical purposes of the moment (e.g. for the purpose of avoiding collision with it, it is as lifeless as a block of marble) and realising that it is animate because we know that it has grown and is still growing. The caution and slowness which usually mark the creation of new rules by the judges tend to mask the fact that they have been created; for they have often come into existence only by a series of analogical extensions spread over a long period of time. To vary the metaphor, the process has resembled the sluggish movement of the glacier rather than the catastrophic charge of the avalanche. But when once a new tort has come into being, it might fairly seem to have done so, if the whole history of its development is taken into account, in virtue of the principle that unjustifiable harm is tortious.[74]

Where the courts hold that the harm is justifiable, there is, of course, no tort. And they may hold that it is justifiable for any one or more of several reasons. The plaintiff may be asking them to do what they think Parliament is more fitted to do; or he may be alleging a particular tort, without giving proof of some essential requisite of it; or he may be taking an exaggerated view of what is necessary to his own comfort or prosperity; or he may be demanding the creation of a remedy which would throw out of gear other parts of the law. But, subject to these restrictions and looking at the law of

---

[70] e.g. Mogul S.S. Co. v. McGregor, Gow & Co. (1884) 23 Q.B.D. 598, 663, per Bowen L.J. In Beaudesert Shire Council v. Smith (1966) 120 C.L.R. 145 the High Court of Australia stated that independently of the "nominate" torts, "a person who suffers harm or loss as the inevitable consequence of the unlawful, intentional and positive acts of another is entitled to recover damages from the other." This appears never to have been followed in Australia and even if "unlawful" be confined to breaches of statutory prohibitions it is not part of English law: Lonrho Ltd. v. Shell Petroleum Co. Ltd., supra, at p. 188.

[71] Aikens v. Wisconsin 195 U.S. 194 (1904), per Holmes J. See further Forkosch (1957) 42 Cornell Law Quarterly 465; Restatement, Torts, 2d., s.870.

[72] Wilkinson v. Downton [1897] 2 Q.B. 57; post, p. 68.

[73] See post, p. 76.

[74] Damage for which compensation is not recoverable is known as damnum sine injuria; where a tort is actionable per se (without proof of loss, e.g. trespass) there is said to be injuria sine damno.

torts in the whole of its development, Winfield still inclined to the first theory.

However, since the supporters of the second view do not deny that the law of tort is capable of development, or even that new heads of liability can come into existence, and since the supporters of the first view admit that no action will lie if the conduct which caused the harm was justifiable,[75] the difference between them is perhaps less than is sometimes supposed. Summing up his investigation into the controversy, Professor Glanville Williams says this[76]:

> "The first school has shown that the rules of liability are very wide. The second school has shown that some rules of absence of liability are also very wide. Neither school has shown that there is any general rule, whether of liability or of non-liability, to cover novel cases that have not yet received the attention of the courts. In a case of first impression— that is, a case that falls under no established rule or that falls equally under two conflicting rules—there is no ultimate principle directing the court to find for one party or the other. . . . Why should we not settle the argument by saying simply that there are some general rules creating liability . . . and some equally general rules exempting from liability. . . . Between the two is a stretch of disputed territory, with the courts as an unbiased boundary commission. If, in an unprovided case, the decision passes for the plaintiff, it will be not because of a general theory of liability but because the court feels that here is a case in which existing principles of liability may properly be extended."[77]

TORT AND OTHER COMPENSATION SYSTEMS

As will be seen, much of the law of tort in practice is concerned with the problem of accidental injury to the person or damage to property, and the general approach of the law to these problems rests on two broad principles. Both are subject to a very large number of exceptions and qualifications but by and large it is the case first that the victim of accidental injury or damage is entitled to redress through the law of tort if, and only if, his loss was caused

---

[75] "What is justifiable conduct? This, of course, is the whole question of tortious liability. If it means justifiable in law, the statement merely means that you must compensate for harms (and it will be noticed that what *kind* of harms is not specified) unless the law says you are not obliged to. In other words we still have to decide what losses the law deems worthy of compensation, and what are the circumstances producing such harm which will be considered sufficient to entail liability": Wright, "Introduction to the Law of Torts" (1944) 8 C.L.J. 240.

[76] "The Foundation of Tortious Liability" (1939) 7 C.L.J. 131; Salmond and Heuston, *Torts*, (19th ed.), pp. 18–21; Prosser, *Torts*, (5th ed.), pp. 3–4; Wright, *loc. cit.* at p. 240.

[77] "The truth is there is no single integrating principle of tort liability save one so broad that it answers nothing": Fleming James, "Tort Law in Midstream" (1959) 8 *Buffalo Law Review* 315, 320. "The law of tort has fallen into great confusion, but, in the main, what acts and omissions result in responsibility and what do not are matters defined by long-established rules of law from which judges ought not wittingly to depart and no light is shed upon a given case by large generalisations about them": *Victoria Park Recreation Grounds Co. Ltd.* v. *Taylor* (1937) 58 C.L.R. 479, 505, *per* Dixon C.J.

by the fault of the defendant or those for whose fault the defendant must answer, and secondly that the redress due from the defendant whose liability is established should be "full" or should, in other words, be as nearly equivalent as money can be to the plaintiff's loss. Nevertheless, even in those accidents which can be attributed to another's fault the role played by the law of tort should not be exaggerated. A century or so ago, the law of tort was probably the primary vehicle of compensation but poverty, ignorance or economic pressure deprived many injured persons of access to the law and threw them back on the Poor Law, charity or the assistance of a trade union or friendly society. In more recent times the development of insurance and social security have tended to relegate tort law to a secondary role[78] and the process may be carried further in the future with regard to personal injuries. We must, therefore, turn to look at some of these other sources of compensation and their relationship with the law of tort.

Damage to property

There is little in the way of state provision for loss or damage to property, which obviously occupies a much lower position of priority than personal injury.[79] Private insurance is, however, of very great significance in relation to property damage. Insurance takes two basic forms, "loss" or "first party" insurance and "liability" or "third party" insurance. Under the first, the owner of property has cover against loss or damage to that property from the risks described in the policy, such as fire, flood and theft, *whether or not the loss occurs through the fault of any other person.*[80] Under the second, the assured himself is covered against legal liability which he may incur to a third party and the establishment of such liability by the third party, not merely loss suffered by the third party, is an essential prerequisite to a claim on the policy. A good example of a policy combining both types of cover is a motor "comprehensive" policy,[81] which will (*a*) cover the assured against legal liability to other road users and passengers and (*b*) entitle the assured to claim from his insurer the cost of repairs should his vehicle be damaged or the value of the vehicle if it becomes a "write-off."[82]

Loss insurance is of very great significance in relation to damage to

---

[78] This type of phenomenon is not, of course, unique to the law of tort but lawyers tend to exaggerate the overall practical effect of legal liability. It is likely that regulatory controls like those in the Trade Descriptions Acts and Fair Trading Act and commercial self-interest are more powerful protectors of "consumers" than the law of contract.

[79] In an emergency such as flood or fire the social security authorities would assist with clothing, bedding and other immediate needs. Provision may sometimes be made on an ad hoc basis for widespread disasters.

[80] Indeed, the assured could normally claim on the policy even if the property was damaged through his own *negligence* (but not his own deliberate act). On the effect of a term that the assured shall take all reasonable care see *Fraser* v. *B.N. Furman (Productions) Ltd.* [1967] 1 W.L.R. 898 (a case of liability insurance).

[81] The majority of motor policies are compehensive, though all that is required by law is cover against liability for personal injuries and, from 1989, property damage to third parties. A standard householder's policy will also combine both loss and liability insurance.

[82] The fact that the accident is the assured's own fault will not prevent a claim under (*b*), though there will normally be conditions as to the use of the vehicle and its maintenance in a roadworthy condition, breach of which will entitle the insurer to repudiate liability. In no circumstances can the assured claim under (*a*) in respect of his own *injuries*, though many policies contain a limited element of "no-fault" loss insurance for injury to driver and passengers.

property. The annual number of road accidents cannot be stated with any precision, since a vast number of collisions involving only property damage are never reported to the police[83] but it can be confidently stated that the figure greatly exceeds the official figure, which has never passed 300,000[84] and it may well be that for every accident involving serious personal injury or death there are 10 or more of less severity. Many of these, however, involve substantial property damage leading to an insurance claim and there can be little doubt that the total cost of property damage in road accidents is the largest single item of loss caused by them.[85] The role of the law of tort in respect of damage to vehicles in road accidents is in fact small, for not only does the prevalence of loss insurance remove most of the vehicle owners' incentives to litigate but the "knock for knock" agreement prevents the operation of insurers' rights of subrogation. The effect of the knock for knock agreement[86] (to which most motor insurers are parties) is as follows. If there is an accident between car A and car B, caused by the fault of car A and leading to damage to both vehicles, the "normal" process would be that the insurers of car A would have to pay for the damage to car A (by virtue of the loss aspect of A's policy) and, if A were sued by B, for the damage to car B as well (by virtue of the liability aspect of A's policy). Alternatively, if B did not wish to sue A and insisted, as would be his contractual right, upon *his* insurers paying for the repairs to his car, B's insurers would then have the right to take over B's claim against A (subrogation) and recover an indemnity against A (or, in reality, his insurers) on this basis. The pursuit of such claims, often for very small amounts, would be wasteful and hence insurers who are party to the knock for knock agreement agree that each will bear its own loss in respect of the vehicle it insures.[87] The existence of the knock for knock agreement does not in law prevent a vehicle owner from bringing legal proceedings in respect of damage to the vehicle, even if he has already

---

[83] Even where personal injury is involved, between 15 and 30 per cent. may go unreported: Report of the Royal Commission on Civil Liability and Compensation for Personal Injury, Cmnd. 7054 (1978), Vol. 2, para. 182.

[84] Road accident statistics may be found in *Road Accidents*, an annual publication by H.M.S.O.

[85] The Royal Commission on Civil Liability, etc., estimated that the consequence of its proposal to remove most small road accident personal injury claims from the tort system would be a fall of about 14 per cent. in the element of insurance premiums covering personal injury to third parties but only a fall of about 4 per cent. in premiums as a whole.

The Secretary of State for Transport in a written answer (*Hansard*, H.C., Vol. 952, col. 216, June 21, 1978) gave the following estimate of the cost of road accidents in 1977:

	£ million
Lost output	284
Police and administration	75
Medical, etc.	42
Property damage	542
Pain, grief, suffering (notional)	347
	1290

The figure for property damage is, if anything likely to be an under-estimate since no insurance claim may be made in many minor cases. The inflation factor between 1977 and 1988 is approximately × 2.5.

[86] Which is set out in part in *Hobbs* v. *Marlowe* [1978] A.C. 16.

[87] For an example of a subrogation claim against an uninsured driver, see *Buckland* v. *Palmer* [1984] 1 W.L.R. 1109.

been indemnified by his insurers,[88] though in that event he would be obliged to reimburse his insurers from the damages recovered. In practice, however, it will be a comparatively rare case where a vehicle owner will consider it worthwhile to pursue a claim for damages where he has comprehensive insurance cover.[89] The widespread existence of loss insurance in respect of other types of property, even without any equivalent of the knock for knock agreement, similarly reduces the incidence of litigation, though if one is to judge by reported cases it seems quite common in the case of damage to ships, no doubt because their high earning capacity and capital value make it worthwhile for loss insurers to exercise their rights of subrogation.[90]

While by no means insignificant, therefore, the role of the law of tort in relation to property damage is largely supplementary to that of insurance. Logically, it is arguable that fault is here an even less suitable determinant of liability than in other areas, that when combined with the insurer's right of subrogation the system is economically wasteful and that the incidence of loss should be determined by asking who is best able to insure against the risk.[91] It is unlikely, however, that we can look for any substantial change in this area: state intervention would clearly not be justifiable, widespread public sympathy is unlikely to be raised for the victims of property damage and so long as some people carry no, or inadequate, loss insurance,[92] the idea that the person at fault should pay for the damage he causes will continue to exert a strong appeal.

Personal injuries and death

Every year in the United Kingdom perhaps 20,000 people die as a result of injury and close to three million are sufficiently seriously injured to lose four or more days' work. The most comprehensive readily available statistics are

[88] *Morley* v. *Moore* [1936] 2 K.B. 359. This would seem to be consistent with the general policy of the law in not treating loss insurance as diminishing the plaintiff's loss: see also *post*, p. 623. However, the rule in *Morley* v. *Moore* may be of less practical significance than it appears because most policies give the insurer the right to institute, conduct and settle legal proceedings in the name of the assured.
[89] Examples where he might pursue a claim are damage to commercial vehicles, where the "excess" might amount to hundreds of pounds, or where the assured had incurred substantial expense in hiring a substitute, a consequential loss covered by only some policies. In *Hobbs* v. *Marlowe, supra*, the plaintiff had been indemnified by his insurers for the damage to the vehicle but not for the cost (£63) of hiring a substitute. An action was brought against the defendant for the whole loss in order to evade the rule that costs of legal representation are not recoverable in the county court in respect of "small claims" (then less than £100). The county court judge awarded the plaintiff his whole loss, but exercised his discretion to refuse costs, a decision which was upheld by the House of Lords. See Birds (1978) 41 M.L.R. 201.
[90] Similar considerations will apply to, *e.g.* industrial premises: *Harbutt's "Plasticine" Ltd.* v. *Wayne Tank & Pump Co. Ltd.* [1970] 1 Q.B. 447 is an excellent example of a subrogation claim. For subsequent proceedings between the defendants and their liability insurers, see *Wayne Tank & Pump Co. Ltd.* v. *Employers' Liability Assurance Corpn. Ltd.* [1974] Q.B. 57. Insurance of houses and household goods is very common, but most people are probably seriously under-insured, a matter made worse by the standard "average" clause whereby the insurer may make a pro rata reduction in respect of one item even if that item is within the value limit of the policy. In practice the incidence of litigation over damage to houses and contents would be low even without insurance, for the vast majority of household losses must be caused: (*a*) by criminal acts; (*b*) by the negligence of the householder or his family; or (*c*) by pure accident.
[91] *cf.* Jolowicz, "Liability for Accidents" C.L.J. 50, though most of that discussion is directed towards personal injuries. See a variant of this by Lord Denning M.R. in *Lamb* v. *Camden L.B.C.* [1981] Q.B. 625, 637–638, though the learned judge is not perhaps entirely accurate in assuming that a standard household policy would cover the loss that was in issue in that case.
[92] Compulsion could hardly be justified.

to be found in the Report of the Pearson Commission[93] and these reflect the position in the mid-1970s. While there has been some decline in some classes of accidents (for example, injuries to car passengers—but not pedestrians—have declined quite sharply), the overall picture is not likely to be very different today. The vast majority of these deaths and injuries are accidental[94] and the largest categories are accidents on the road, at home and at work.[95] At prices prevailing in 1977 about £827 million per annum was paid in various forms of compensation for these injuries, a figure which represents well over £2 billion at today's values. Of this rather more than half comes from the social security system, with the balance being shared more or less equally between the tort system and other, predominantly private sources such as occupational sick pay and private insurance.[96] Overall, therefore, the tort system accounts for no more than a quarter of all compensation paid but the relationship would be rather different if one examined particular categories of accidents. In the field of motor accidents, tort payments considerably exceed social security payments though the position is reversed with regard to work and other accidents.[97] The ratio of tort to social security is not, of course, reflected in the proportion of beneficiaries of each system. The great majority of accident victims may expect to receive some sort of social security benefit[98] but the proportion of those who recover tort damages[99] is only about 6.5 per cent. though with considerable variations from one class of accident to another.[1] In a large number of cases of minor injury the victim will not think it worth his while to pursue a tort claim;

---

[93] Compensation for Personal Injuries Cmnd. 7054 (1978), Vol. 1,. Chap. 3.

[94] The Pearson Report attributed 720 deaths and 55,000 injuries per annum to criminal violence: Vol. 2, Chap. 12.

[95]

	Deaths	Injuries
Road	7696	403,000
Work	1300	720,000
Home	6200	
Other (e.g. occupiers' liability, transport other than road)	5220	approx. 2 million

No direct comparison for work injuries is possible because the figures in the Health and Safety Commission's Report are not prepared on the same basis.

No precise allocation could be made for injuries as between home and "other" but the Pearson Report estimates that the split is not far off equal: Vol. 1, para. 37.

[96] Pearson Report, Vol. 1, Table 4. But the insurance figure does not include life assurance, for which no estimates could be made.

[97] In the case of home accidents it would be a rare case where the accident could be attributed to the fault of another or, even if it could, where effective legal action could be taken.

[98] But not all: some benefits are confined to members of the working population. Serious injury such as loss of an arm in a road accident might lead to no benefit entitlement if there were no reduction in earning capacity.

[99] The interrelationship of social security benefits and tort damages is considered post, p. 622.

[1] Pearson Report, Vol. 1, Table 5 (i) (road accidents 10.5 per cent., work accidents 1.5 per cent., other 1.5 per cent.) cf. Harris et al., Compensation and Support for Illness and Injury (29 per cent. for road accidents, 19 per cent. for work accidents). According to the Civil Justic Review (1988), Cm. 394, about 340,000 accident victims per year may "claim" for tort, but in 1986 only 51,000 personal injury actions were started.

in many serious cases he will be unable to prove the breach of legal duty necessary to establish his claim against the defendant.[2]

This is not a book about the law of compensation as a whole, but the student of tort cannot ignore the operation of the non-tort sources and we must accordingly attempt a survey of them and of their relationship with the tort system. The reader should also remember that in dealing with personal injuries the cost of provision of medical services, though not "compensation," cannot be left out of account. It was estimated in 1977 that the cost attributable for the National Health Service and the personal social services (*e.g.* under the Chronically Sick and Disabled Persons Act 1970) to accidental death, injury and industrial disease was nearly 40 per cent. more than the social security payments made in respect of such losses, and employers' medical services added a further considerable sum to this.[3]

Private insurance, occupational pensions, etc.

Three main types of insurance give protection against accidental death or injury: life assurance, personal accident insurance and permanent health insurance. The first is without doubt the most important but unfortunately the Pearson Commission was unable to make any estimate of its total contribution to accident compensation.[4] Personal accident and permanent health insurance are a good deal less common, the Pearson Commission's personal injury survey finding that such cover was held by about 10 per cent. of the persons involved in the survey and contributed about £50 million per annum to accident compensation.[5] More significant are employers' occupational sick pay schemes. In fact, in 1983 sick pay from employers replaced social security payments as the method of short-term income replacement, though the employer is reimbursed by the state.[6] However, many employers' sick pay schemes go well beyond this statutory minimum, providing all or part of lost income for a maximum period which may be related to length of service but which rarely exceeds six months. In cases of death or long-term injury leading to premature retirement a payment may be made

---

[2] See, *e.g. Snelling* v. *Whitehead, The Times*, July 31, 1975. Where a claim is made, its chance of success in whole or in part is between 85 and 90 per cent., the greater the injury the greater the chance of a claim being made: Pearson Report, Vol. 1, Table 5, and Vol. 2, Chap. 18. It is interesting that of the persons in the Commission's personal injury survey only 33 per cent. attributed the accident in whole or in part to the fault of another person.

[3] Pearson Report, Vol. 2, Table 158.

[4] Apart from straightforward "term" life assurance under which the assured sum is payable on death within the assured period and "endowment" assurance taken out primarily as a means of saving, most house purchases on mortgage will involve a substantial element of life assurance, in the form of endowment or a "mortgage protection" policy. The aggregate sum assured by ordinary life policies in 1976 was £71,500 million and £9,560 million was assured by so-called "industrial" policies, (*i.e.* for small sums primarily intended to cover funeral costs): Pearson Report, Vol. 2, paras. 146–152.

[5] Personal accident insurance is usually short-term and usually provides fixed periodic payments and a lump sum related to degree of disability (*e.g.* the insurance tickets that may be purchased by a railway passenger). Permanent health insurance provides cover against loss of employment income (whether by accident or illness) and has been rapidly expanding, mainly through employers' "group" schemes: Pearson Report, Vol. 2, paras. 141–145; Table 158.

[6] *Infra.*

under an occupational pension scheme. The size of such payments is difficult to estimate but is probably small.[7]

The chance of receipt of any one or more of the above benefits is heavily influenced by the social class of the victim and the nature of his employment but it will readily be appreciated that many accident victims or their dependants stand to get very large sums from such sources and it may be asked to what extent such receipts are taken into account in assessing tort damages for loss of earnings.[8] The question is complex and will be considered in more detail later,[9] but the broad answer is that the courts will ignore all charitable and comparable payments, all proceeds of private insurance and all occupational pension scheme payments[10] but will make a deduction in respect of sick pay. Quite apart, therefore, from social security benefits, there is a strong possibility that some accident victims who are successful in a tort claim will receive considerably more than they have lost in income.

Social security payments

The present system of social security is extraordinarily complicated, there being about 30 different cash benefits which may properly be called "social security,"[11] and we can do no more here than touch on the principal benefits payable to accident victims.[12]

(1) *Non-industrial injuries*

Cases of injury falling outside the industrial injuries scheme are dealt with in the same way as sickness. The primary short-term benefit for sickness or injury is in fact now paid, at least in the first instance, by employers. From April 6, 1983 the former "sickness benefit" was replaced by the "statutory sick pay" scheme under which an employee unfit for work may claim from his employer a sum of up to £49.20 per week (depending upon his normal rate of pay) for up to 28 weeks. Employers may recoup statutory sick pay payments by deducting them from national insurance contributions due to the Inland Revenue, so that it is the administration rather than the ultimate source of the benefit which has been changed.[13] When the statutory sick pay

---

[7] £5 million in 1977. Pearson Report, Vol. 2, paras. 125–139. Miscellaneous payments by trade unions, friendly societies and charities probably account for a similar sum: *ibid.* Table 158.

[8] The question usually arises in this way because the payment of such benefits nearly always precedes the recovery of tort damages. If the issue arose of whether tort damages were to be taken into account in assessing payments under the insurance policy or the pension scheme, everything would depend upon the construction of the contract. Tort damages, however, would almost invariably have no effect on payments on life or personal accident policies.

[9] *Post*, pp. 622.

[10] Except, in this case, so far as loss of income is claimed for the period after the normal date of retirement.

[11] Definition is not easy. For example, the Criminal Injuries Compensation Scheme is completely outside the legal and administrative framework governing social security benefits. Yet it is a form of state assistance to victims of misfortune.

[12] See standard works such as Ogus and Barendt, *Law of Social Security.* There have been substantial changes since the rèsumè of the system by the Department of Health and Social Security in Vol. 1, Annex 4 of the Pearson Report. Rates are given here for illustrative purposes only and are those in effect at April 1988.

[13] Many employees will, in any event, be entitled under their contracts of employment to occupational sick pay for longer periods and at a higher rate than the statutory entitlement.

entitlement has been exhausted it is replaced by "invalidity benefit." This consists of invalidity pension at a flat rate of £41.15 per week, supplemented by £24.75 for an adult dependant and £8.40 for a child.[14] There may also be payable (a) an "invalidity allowance" of up to £8.65 per week according to the claimant's age and (b) an additional pension calculated upon his earnings since 1978. These benefits are only payable to persons who have a sufficient record of contributions to the National Insurance Scheme, but there is a non-contributory severe disablement allowance payable after 28 weeks' absence from work at the rate of £24.75 per week, with increases for dependants.

A wide range of more specialised benefits or concessions (such as tax relief), may be available to a person disabled as a result of a tort.[15] Nor should we forget those areas of the social security system which are not directed at sickness or injury. For example, the victim of an accident may recover from injury without any permanent disability but may have lost his job as a result of absence from work and hence may be eligible for unemployment benefit or the means-tested income support and housing benefit.

(2) *Industrial injuries*

The Workmen's Compensation Act 1897 introduced into English law the first important type of accident compensation not based on the law of tort. Under that Act, workers injured in various types of employment could recover compensation for personal injury "arising out of and in the course of employment." Unlike the modern system of industrial injury benefits, however, this compensation was payable by the employer and was recoverable by action in the courts. With the implementation of the Beveridge Report[16] the Workmen's Compensation Scheme was abolished and replaced by a system of benefits payable by the state for such accidents and diseases.[17] The industrial injuries scheme[18] now covers industrial injuries (including certain prescribed diseases) and provides for payment of "disablement benefit" to the injured worker.[19] The basic condition of award is that the injury was caused by accident "arising out of and in the course of employment." Injuries with short-term effects are excluded by the rule that disablement benefit is not payable for the first 13 weeks after the accident. It is most important to note that disablement benefit is not necessarily looked upon as a method of replacement of lost earnings but is based upon an objective assessment of disablement, fixed on a percentage basis either by regulations[20] or by a medical board. For example, the regulations provide

---

[14] Payments will be made for each child under the child benefit scheme, which is unconnected with sickness or accident.

[15] *e.g.* mobility allowance; assistance with buying a car; payments under the Vaccine Damage Payments Act 1979.

[16] Cmd. 6404 (1942).

[17] National Insurance (Industrial Injuries) Act 1946.

[18] Strictly, this is a misnomer since there is no separate fund nor even, now, a separate Act.

[19] Formerly, there was an equivalent "industrial death benefit" payable to dependants in fatal cases. This was abolished in 1988, such cases now falling within the ordinary widow's pension and allowance scheme.

[20] The regulations have been severely criticised as being based on an outdated method of assessing the effect of disability.

that loss of sight of one eye amounts to a 30 per cent. disablement so that the victim receives proportionate benefit even though his earnings may not be affected at all. Formerly, disablement of less than 20 per cent. attracted a lump sum gratuity but many of these cases were taken out of the system in 1986, thereby making tort claims more important in "minor" cases. Payments under the scheme take the form of a pension (maximum £67.20 per week) but may be substantially increased by additional benefits. There are additional payments of £24.75 for an adult dependant and £8.40 for each child and where the injured man is likely to be permanently unfit for work he may claim a "reduced earnings allowance."[21]

The reader may wonder why work-related injuries are not simply governed by the ordinary social security scheme. After all, if a man breaks his leg by falling downstairs at home his needs are not necessarily different from what they would be if he suffered the same misfortune at work.[22] Various arguments were in fact made for separate treatment in the Beveridge Report, but the principal reason is probably a feeling at that time that since work-related accidents had for 50 years received "preferential" treatment under the Workmen's Compensation Act this state of affairs should continue. In the early days this "industrial preference" was very considerable, for the victim of an industrial accident received, during the first six months of disablement, a flat rate "injury benefit" that was 73 per cent. higher than the flat rate of sickness benefit payable for non-industrial injury. However, by the late 1970s this differential had been eroded to less than 20 per cent. and as a result of an overall review[23] of the industrial injuries scheme, injury benefit was abolished in April 1983, so that short-term injuries at work are now compensated by statutory sick pay. Nevertheless, in longer-term cases the industrial preference remains, particularly in the availability of payments which are unrelated to continuing incapacity to work.

The question of offsetting social security payments against tort damages[24] is largely governed by statute and a distinction must be drawn between fatal accidents and others. In the case of fatal accidents all social security benefits are disregarded[25]; in other cases half of certain benefits receivable by the injured person in the five years succeeding the accident are brought into account.[26] As in the case of private insurance the possibility of "double recovery" by a combination of tort damages and social security benefits is

---

[21] Other increases are: (1) a constant attendance allowance (maximum £53.80 per week) and (2) where the need for such attendance is likely to be permanent, an exceptionally severe disablement allowance (£26.90 per week).

[22] Industrial injuries benefits are more expensive to administer than other aspects of social security because they involve not only determination of qualifying incapacity but also whether that incapacity results from an accident arising out of and in the course of employment, and this may be a complex issue: see Lewis, "Tort and Social Security: the Importance Attached to the Cause of Disability with Special Reference to the Industrial Injuries Scheme" (1980) 43 M.L.R. 514. The abolition of short-term injury benefit (*infra*) has removed the great majority of these causal determinations.

[23] See Cmnd. 8402 (1981).

[24] None of the benefits described above, except income support, is subject to any deduction by reason of a successful tort claim.

[25] Fatal Accidents Act 1976, s.4. See also *post*, p. 655.

[26] Law Reform (Personal Injuries) Act 1948, s.2(1). See also *post*, p. 622.

therefore very considerable, particularly given the prospective value of those benefits. A man with family responsibilities disabled at work early in his working life might receive (tax free) social security benefits amounting to some hundreds of thousands of pounds in current prices by the time he reached retirement age, yet in assessing his lost earnings for purposes of damages the offset would not amount to a tenth of this sum.[27]

The "fault principle"

Enough has been said to show that the overlap between the law of tort and private and public insurance is striking. Though overall the law of tort is by no means the most important vehicle for accident compensation, an accident victim who can make out a tort claim stands to recover very substantially more than one who cannot, partly because of the generous rules about deductibility of other compensation payments from tort damages and partly because tort damages, unlike social security payments, are subject to no financial limits and take into account matters like pain and suffering, loss of amenity,[28] loss of promotion prospects and extra expenses incurred as a result of the injury.[29] As we have seen, the plaintiff in a tort action must generally show that his injuries were caused by the defendant's fault and until comparatively recently it was taken as almost axiomatic that payment of much higher compensation to the victims of fault was justified, but the development of insurance, particularly in the form of the social security system, has led many commentators[30] to take a different view.

Since the law of tort is a system of establishing *liability* it is obvious that it could never have compensated all victims of misfortune. At the very least there must be some causal link between an activity of the defendant and the injury to the plaintiff. There is, however, no logically compelling reason why the law should have chosen fault as the determinant of this liability.[31] What justification, then, can be advanced for the adoption of the fault principle?

The principle that a person should be called upon to pay for damage caused by his fault may be thought to have an affinity with the criminal law (which the law of tort as a whole certainly did have much earlier in its history) in the sense that one of its purposes is deterrence, the prevention of harmful conduct. It is certainly true that at least some parts of the law dealing with premeditated conduct do help to serve this purpose as well as that of deciding whether or not redress for damage already suffered should

---

[27] Pearson Report, Vol. 1, para. 182.

[28] Industrial disablement benefit, *supra*, is, however, based upon loss of faculty.

[29] In *Cunningham* v. *Harrison* [1973] Q.B. 942, where the plaintiff had a life expectancy of 12 years, the total damages were £59,316, of which £24,700 were awarded for cost of nursing and attendance. The annual interest on the latter sum alone would considerably exceed the annual amount payable (£728) in respect of a non-industrial injury attendance allowance at the time the Pearson Commission reported.

[30] Lord Parker C.J. in (1965) 18 *Current Legal Problems* 1 was one of the earliest critics of the present system. The leading academic monograph is Atiyah, *Accidents, Compensation and the Law*, (4th ed.); see also Elliott and Street, *Road Accidents* (1968); and Ison, *The Forensic Lottery* (1967).

[31] Earlier law was perhaps more inclined to admit specific defences than to postulate a general requirement of fault.

be ordered: newspaper editors, for example, take steps to avoid publication of defamatory matter, and trade union officials have recognised the efficiency of the "economic" torts as an instrument for controlling conduct by demanding, and receiving, statutory exemption from some of them so as to secure for themselves greater freedom of industrial action.[32] It is, however, much more doubtful whether there is any effective deterrent force in those parts of the law relating to accidental injury, where liability is based upon negligence. There are a number of reasons for this. First, a generalised instruction to people to take care, which is all that the law gives, is of little practical use in guiding their behaviour in a given situation.[33] Certain driving practices, for example driving at 60 m.p.h. down a crowded shopping street, could be recognised as negligent by ordinary people without any judicial assistance but the majority of cases do not present such clear-cut issues and the number of variable factors is so great that one case is hardly even of persuasive value in another.[34] The force of this criticism probably varies from one type of accident to another. It is particularly strong in the case of road accidents, where the activity is, in the case of an experienced driver, largely instinctive and where a momentary lapse of attention can lead to catastrophic results with few realistic possibilities of taking other precautions to minimise or avoid the risk.[35] Where, however, the accident arises from an alleged defect in a system of work or the organisation of a business, it is possible that a tort judgment may play a part in exposing the risk and leading others to take measures to prevent recurrence, whether voluntarily or at the insistence of their insurers.[36]

The second reason why the deterrence argument is of limited validity relates to the sources from which damages are in fact paid. If it were the case that tort damages were paid out of the tortfeasor's own resources it could hardly be denied that the threat of legal liability would deter[37] but in practice damages are, far more often than not, paid by an insurer rather than by the tortfeasor himself,[38] which undoubtedly blunts the deterrent edge. Liability insurance is now actually compulsory so far as concerns road accidents

---

[32] See *post*, pp. 527–534.

[33] See *Brown* v. *National Coal Board* [1962] A.C. 574, 594–599, 595, *per* Lord Radcliffe.

[34] Statutory duties are often (but not always) more precise in this respect. Breach of such duties often gives rise to civil liability (see *post*, Chap. 7) but does not generally do so in the field of road traffic. Cases where it is held that merely exceeding the statutory speed limit does not automatically amount to civil negligence are commonplace.

[35] But car users can wear safety belts and it is interesting that the courts held that failure to take this preliminary precaution amounted to contributory negligence even before their use became compulsory: *post*, p. 162.

[36] This argument would be particularly applicable to work accidents, defective products and medical misadventures. The Pearson Commission received conflicting evidence on this point: Vol. 1, paras. 906–910, 1342–1343. The Robens Committee (*Safety and Health at Work* Cmnd. 5034 (1972)) concluded that in industrial accidents, the existence of the tort action might actually militate against improved safety procedures, which might be withheld for fear that their introduction would be taken as an admission that the previous procedures were deficient. *cf.* the view of an underwriting manager in *Accident Compensation after Pearson* at p. 130. As to disclosure of accident inquiry reports, see *Waugh* v. *B.R.B.* [1980] A.C. 521.

[37] Damages would usually be much larger than any fine likely to be imposed by a criminal court for comparable conduct.

[38] But at least 78 organisations carried their own risks and dealt with 29,070 claims in 1973. These were mostly public bodies (the Crown, nationalised industries, transport undertakings) but included 17 large private sector organisations.

affecting third parties[39] and most work accidents[40] and to meet the problem of the uninsured driver there is an agreement under which the Motor Insurers' Bureau (*i.e.* the road traffic insurers acting collectively) satisfies claims.[41] It is true that the defendant has had to pay in advance for his insurance cover and that he may have to pay more in the future if the insurer considers that he or his employees are more than ordinarily likely to cause further accidents, but the link between the fault and the obligation to find the money to pay for its consequences in the individual case is nonetheless tenuous. And where the defendant is in the business of supplying goods or services to the public the link may be still more tenuous, for the cost of obtaining insurance cover will be reflected in the price charged to the public or in a reduced profit margin so that those who actually pay it are either the consumers or the shareholders or both[41a]. Theoretically, of course, a very bad accident record will lead to such a rise in insurance premiums that the assured will be priced out of business or off the road[42] and to some extent the law of tort therefore operates as a "general" or "market" deterrent though the practical reality of this is a matter open to debate and it has been argued that strict liability would be a superior mechanism.[43]

Deterrence is not only produced of course by the threat of direct imposition of a financial penalty. It is perfectly possible that a person may be induced to take greater care by the harm to his reputation which may be caused by a successful tort suit against him.[44] Again, this effect would probably only be produced in certain fields of liability such as professional negligence, injuries caused by defective products and work injuries. While

---

[39] Road Traffic Act 1988, s.143, replacing earlier legislation and, from the end of 1988, extended to cover property damage as well as personal injury.

[40] Employers' Liability (Compulsory Insurance) Act 1969, s.1.

[41] There is a supplementary agreement covering claims by uninsured drivers. See Hepple and Matthews, *Tort, Cases and Materials* (3rd ed.). The agreements are not strictly enforceable by the plaintiff, but the Bureau will never take the point. For a similar "back-up" fund for financial loss in the investment context, see Financial Services Act 1986, s.54.

[41a] See Lord Griffiths in *Smith* v. *Eric S. Bush* [1989] 2 W.L.R. 790 "There was once a time when it was considered improper even to mention the possible existence of insurance cover in a lawsuit. But those days are long past ... The result of denying a Surveyor, in the circumstance of this case, the right to exclude liability, will result in distributing the risk of his negligence among all house purchasers through an increase in his fees to cover insurance, rather than allowing the whole of the risk to fall upon the one unfortunate purchaser."

[42] There is little precise information on the extent to which employers' liability premiums are "risk-rated." It is well known that motor premiums are, but except in extreme cases (such as drunken driving), the rating is done in a fairly arbitrary manner. Premiums on a new sports car for a man under 25 will be very high but not high enough to keep him off the road if he can afford the car in the first place. Most foreign "no-fault" accident compensation schemes provide for premium or contribution rating according to risk (see the Pearson Report, Vol. 3) but the British industrial injuries scheme carries no element of risk rating whatsoever: the risk of injury in mining and quarrying is nearly 50 times greater than in banking, but employers and workers in both industries pay exactly the same national insurance contributions. The major objection to risk rating is that it complicates administration: see the Pearson Report, Vol. 1, paras. 898–905, 940–948.

[43] The theory of general or market deterrence has been most fully expounded by Calabresi, *The Costs of Accidents*. In its pure form the theory seeks to reduce the number of accidents by allocating the cost of those accidents to the activity which creates them. A tort system based upon fault will only allocate a proportion of accident costs in this way. "Fault uses that market in an expensive and unstable way to reduce fault-caused accidents, while from the standpoint of market deterrence, we want to use the market in an efficient and stable way to reduce accident costs whether they are fault-caused or not": Calabresi in *Crisis in Car Insurance* (ed. Keeton, O'Connell and McCord), p. 250.

[44] See Linden (1973) 51 Can. Bar Rev. 155.

experience shows that a powerful force of public opinion can be mobilised against a drug company which was alleged to have produced a drug which had injured children it is very unlikely that people would take much interest in a road accident caused by one of its delivery vans. In any event, a large corporate defendant which has the wherewithal is capable of avoiding much adverse publicity by an out-of-court settlement and the speed with which substantial compensation has been offered in the wake of recent mass disasters suggests that in practice the victim's chances of recovery are in direct proportion to the scale of the accident and, hence, the amount of public attention it receives.

We may conclude, therefore, that the prospect of tort liability will have some influence on conduct but that this influence is probably very limited. Even it it had a greater deterrent effect it would not necessarily justify a *fault-based* system, for strict liability would, presumably, have just as great an effect.

The other argument in favour of a tort system based on fault is still more difficult to assess but cannot be dismissed out of hand on that basis. It is that the notion of individual or corporate responsibility is a powerful and perhaps intuitive factor in people's attitudes to accidents and that there is a deep-seated idea that those who are at fault should be "held accountable" or should "pay" (even if in fact the source of that payment is an insurance company).[45] It may be objected that this view is essentially punitive and confuses the functions of tort and criminal law,[46] but public opinion does not make such convenient distinctions. Certainly such demands come to the fore in public debates over "disasters" like thalidomide, the *Herald of Free Enterprise* or the King's Cross fire, though it must be said that in this context they are often hopelessly confused with demands for no-fault compensation. Certainly a tort suit can establish the causation of an accident and "point the finger," but it must be said that in disaster cases the customary public inquiry is likely to do this job far better.[47] For other types of accident there are already fairly comprehensive criminal sanctions on careless conduct on the road and in industry and these may be regarded as an adequate way for the law to mark its disapproval of damage-causing conduct. But there are other areas in which the criminal law hardly operates (*e.g.* injuries caused by negligent medical treatment) and in which the abolition of tort liability would require very careful consideration of what alternative investigative machinery would be necessary to establish causation and, where necessary, attribute blame.[48] When all is said and done, however, there is a powerful

---

[45] On punitive damages in "products liability" actions in the U.S.A., see Owen (1976) 74 Mich.L.Rev. 1257. In *Grimshaw* v. *Ford Motor Co.* (1981) 174 Cal.Rptr. 348, a jury awarded $125 million in respect of injuries suffered in a road accident as a result of the design of the petrol tank of the Ford Pinto (reduced on appeal to $3.5 million). Though there is strict "products liability" in the U.S.A. the jury heard evidence that Ford had considered the risk inherent in the tank design and had decided that a change would not be worthwhile. The damages were overtly punitive (though they could not be awarded in this country, see *post*, p. 602).
[46] But see *ante*, p. 10 for the growth of compensation orders in criminal courts.
[47] If the inquiry attributes blame a settlement is likely to follow as a matter of course, the only issue being quantum of damages in individual cases.
[48] Of course, professional disciplinary and complaints procedures for doctors already exist quite independently of the law of tort. The problem is the activation of such machinery and its effectiveness. In the medical context, see Ham *et al.*, *Compensation and Accountability* (1988).

objection to raising the allocation of responsibility justification for tort in the simple and undoubted fact that the current tort rules have the effect of ignoring massive disproportions between the defendant's negligence and the consequences for which he is obliged to pay, for a momentary lapse of concentration or judgment can lead to liability in damages amounting to hundreds of thousands of pounds.

In trying to seek these justifications of the fault system we have already exposed some of its weaknesses. There are, however, other, independent criticisms.

First, the tort system based upon fault is undoubtedly expensive to administer when compared with, say, social security. The Pearson Commission estimated that in the tort system the cost of operation was about 85 per cent. of the value of compensation paid through the system, whereas the corresponding figure for social security was about 11 per cent. In other words, using tort it cost about £171 million to transfer £202 million while social security transferred £421 million at a cost of about £46 million.[49] The very great cost of the tort system is not entirely caused by its fault basis, however, since disputes about the medical prognosis of the plaintiff and quantum of damages outnumber disputes about liability.[50]

Secondly, there is the problem of delay. The median period from the date of claim to the date of its disposal in the Commission's survey was only 9½ months[51] which, given the availability of social security benefits, may be thought to be a not unreasonable period; but the delay was longer in more serious cases and well over half the payments in excess of £5,000 were made more than two years after the date of claim.[52] The Pearson Commission concluded that delay was:

> ". . . the most important reason for dissatisfaction with the legal system . . . delay is sometimes justifiable[53]; but it can often aggravate pressure on the plaintiff to settle prematurely, and can be a source of worry and distress. Nor is it necessarily in the interests of the defendant. The problem of delay is also linked with the medical condition sometimes known as 'compensation neurosis.' "

Thirdly, the unpredictability of the result of cases based upon fault liability may put plaintiffs under pressure to settle their claims for amounts less

---

[49] The figures, however, favour social security because they conceal the fact that the cost of collection of contributions falls outside the account, *i.e.* on the employer.

[50] Pearson Report, Vol. 2, Table 116 (cases where period from claim to disposal was greater than three months). The Civil Justice Review ((1988) Cm. 394) estimated that in actions proceeding to trial in the High Court costs amounted to between 50 and 70 per cent of damages received. County court proceedings, though cheaper in absolute terms, are, because of the low jurisdiction limit, more expensive in relative terms of costs to sums insured.

[51] *cf.* the survey in Harris, *Compensation, supra* (16 months). However, the Civil Justice Review (n.50 *supra*), using a survey based on cases where legal proceedings had been started, found medians for High Court (London) cases of 26 months from first advice to settlement and 35 months from first advice to trial.

[52] Pearson Report, Vol. 2, Tables 114, 115.

[53] *e.g.* so that an accurate medical prognosis may be made.

than they would receive if their claim went successfully to trial. The vast majority of personal injury claims are settled without trial, most of them without even the issue of a writ.[54] It is true that of plaintiffs who make a claim some 86 per cent. will receive some payment but, though there is no clear statistical evidence on the point, many of those payments will be for substantially less than would be awarded if the matter went to trial. Since there is always *some* risk that the plaintiff's claim will founder in whole or in part at the trial, the defendant's insurers are in a position to exploit this factor by making a discount in the amount they offer in settlement.[55] This element of risk, leading to pressure to settle, is of course present in virtually all litigation but it is peculiarly powerful in the case of personal injuries because a very large part of the plaintiff's future wealth may be at stake. His position of inequality is exacerbated by the fact that even if he wins at the trial on liability he may face a large bill for costs if the defendant's insurers have made an accurately-calculated payment into court.[56] Not surprisingly, perhaps, small claims may be over-compensated: their "nuisance value" may make insurers willing to buy off plaintiffs with fairly generous offers. Undercompensation in serious cases may also be contributed to by the present practice on assessment of damages but this is not a problem which flows from fault liability, nor even from the tort system: its origin is the inveterate rule that damages may only be awarded in the form of a lump sum with the consequent difficulty of predicting what will, or would have, happened in the future to the plaintiff's health, his employment, the rate of inflation and return on investments, and countless other factors.

These criticisms do not complete the tally of objections to the present law of tort so far as it concerns personal injury accidents,[57] but similar considerations apply in other jurisdictions and the last decades have seen widespread debate and the advocacy (and in some cases implementation) of a bewildering variety of what may loosely be called "no-fault systems."

Any reform of the law governing compensation for personal injuries might adopt one of two basic solutions—an extension of strict liability, (*i.e.* liability imposed without proof of fault), which would retain the law of tort though in a different form; and the "insurance" technique (whether private

---

[54] Pearson Report, Vol. 2, Table 104. 86 per cent. are settled without issue of a writ and of the remainder, only 1 per cent. reach court, some of them being settled before conclusion of the trial. For this reason, reform of civil procedure can have only a limited impact. Implementation of the proposals of the Civil Justice Review (n.50, *supra*) would mean that the overwhelming majority of personal injury cases proceeding to trial would be handled by the county court.

[55] See Harris, *Compensation, supra*, Chap. 3, and Phillips and Hawkins, "Some Economic Aspects of the Settlement Process: A Study of Personal Injury Claims" (1976) 39 M.L.R. 497. At a fairly early stage in the thalidomide saga, where there were considerable potential disputes both as to law and fact, leading counsel advised some of the parents to accept an offer by the manufacturers to pay 40 per cent. of the damages the court would award: see *S. v. Distillers & Co. (Biochemicals) Ltd.* [1970] 1 W.L.R. 114.

[56] The defendant may pay a sum into court in satisfaction of the claim. If the plaintiff does not accept it and the action goes to trial, the judge is not informed of the payment and, if his award does not exceed the amount paid in, the plaintiff bears the costs of the action from the date of the payment.

[57] Other criticisms voiced to the Pearson Commission were that the system was difficult for the injured person to understand and operate (Vol. 1, para. 250); that the adversarial nature of the system had a damaging effect on family relations, friendships and employment relations (para. 260); and that the system could be unfair to the tortfeasor, particularly where his reputation was affected by allegations made in litigation (para. 256).

or public), which would mean the abolition or by-passing of the law of tort in whole or in part.

Strict liability and no-fault compensation

Despite the continuing dominance of fault liability the English law of tort does contain certain limited principles of strict liability with regard to personal injuries. Some of these are of common law origin and of respectable antiquity,[58] others have been the creation of modern statutes and have either been limited in their practical importance[59] or of rather haphazard application.[60] It is unlikely that any consistent policy has been followed in the creation of these areas of strict liability, though it is perhaps possible to discern behind them some very hazy idea of unusual or increased risk. However, the strictness of the liability varies considerably along a spectrum from near-absolute liability to little more than a reversed burden of proof, and in nearly every case the defendant may plead the contributory fault of the plaintiff as a defence or in diminution of damages. While there may be some merit in a system of strict liability for unusual risks it can hardly make much contribution to the accident compensation problem as a whole when common risks are left to the law of negligence.[61] As a result of an EEC initiative one such risk has been brought into the strict liability fold, namely losses caused by defective products, though the liability is by no means absolute and may, indeed, be only a modified form of fault.[62] French law has always had an element of strict liability for motor accidents because of the provision in Article 1384 of the Code Civil governing damage caused by a "thing" in one's custody, but the law of July 5, 1985[63] goes further by allowing victims (other than drivers) to recover damages even though they themselves are at fault. Only if the victim's fault is "inexcusable" and is the sole cause of the accident is he barred. Ordinary contributory negligence remains relevant, however, to claims by drivers or to claims for property damage.[64] The exclusion of contributory negligence is very important because its retention would require the same kind of investigation into the facts of the accident as does the present law, and hence lose much of the advantage of strict liability. By contrast, our legislation on product liability retains contributory negligence. Theoretically, negligence could be replaced across the board by substituting for the question "Whose fault was it that this

---

[58] *e.g.* the rule in *Rylands* v. *Fletcher, post*, Chap. 15, though it is not beyond doubt whether this applies to personal injuries.

[59] The liability under the Nuclear Installations Act 1965 (*post*, p. 449) is probably the strictest known to English law.

[60] See, *e.g.* the many statutory duties arising under industrial safety legislation, some of which are considered *post*, Chap. 8.

[61] See Spencer, "Motor Cars and the Rule in *Rylands* v. *Fletcher* [1983] C.L.J. 65, who, while conceding that social security may be a better method of handling road accidents than liability in tort, concludes that this is a case where the best is the enemy of the good.

[62] See *post*, Chap. 10.

[63] Loi no. 85–677.

[64] Art. 12 puts the onus upon the liability insurer to make an offer of amends to the victim within eight months and there are stiff financial penalties for failure to do so or for making an inadequate offer.

accident occurred?" the question "Whose risk was it that this accident might occur?" The answer to this question would be found in the economics and practicability of insurance. It should be recognised by the law that the normal sequel to the imposition of liability is that persons potentially subject to liability will protect themselves against its consequences by insurance. It should also be recognised by the law that where no one is liable for a given injury then the victim must bear his loss himself unless he has insured against the risk that it might occur.[65] The question "Whose risk was it that this accident might occur?" can thus be translated into "Should the risk of this kind of accident be disposed of by liability insurance, or, is it right, against the background of insurance, that the victim should bear his own loss or pay for his own insurance against it?" In short, the law could be reformed by the abolition or virtual abolition of liability for fault, and a thoroughgoing reappraisal made of the scope and function of strict liability,[66] but it seems unlikely that this will occur.

The alternative approach is to abandon tort liability and create direct compensation rights. This can be done either by ad hoc compensation schemes for particular types of accidents or by a broader extension of social security rights.

The Workmen's Compensation Scheme, abolished in England in 1948 (but still existing in various forms in the United States and Australia) was an early form of ad hoc no-fault compensation, though it involved adversarial litigation between the claimant and his employer, who was liable to pay the compensation. No-fault schemes have, however, proliferated and about half the states in the United States operate them in the field of road accidents.

The schemes vary greatly in the amount and range of benefits and in the extent to which they limit the right to claim tort damages from an insurer, but they all fall within the following general pattern.[67] The motorist is required to buy from an insurer no-fault cover up to the limit required by the local legislation. Any person injured as a result of the operation of the vehicle (including the driver) may then claim against the insurer for medical expenses, substitute services and loss of wages[68] up to the statutory limit. No scheme covers non-pecuniary loss such as pain and suffering, but this is still covered by the tort system. To discourage small claims, some states ban tort claims for non-pecuniary loss unless the case passes a "threshold" defined by severity of injury or amount of medical expenses. Various attempts have been made to introduce a federal no-fault scheme but none has so far

---

[65] This self-evident truth appears sometimes to be overlooked. See, *e.g. S.C.M. (United Kingdom) Ltd. v. W. J. Whittall and Son Ltd.* [1971] 1 Q.B. 337, 344, where the Court of Appeal held that the defendants were not liable for the plaintiff's loss of profits caused by their negligence and Lord Denning M.R. said that the risk should be borne by the whole community who suffer the losses rather than the defendant who may or may not be insured against the risk. The result of the decision was, however, that the plaintiff, not the whole community, had to carry the loss.

[66] See Jolowicz, "Liability for Accidents" [1968] C.L.J. 50. It will, of course, be a difficult and possibly a continuing, but not an impossible, task to determine the appropriate allocation of strict liability.

[67] Pearson Report, Vol. 3, Chap. 3 and Annex 2; and see Fleming, *Torts* (7th ed.), Chap. 20, s.2 and Malkin, "Victoria's Transport Accident Reforms" (1987) 16 M.U.L.R. 254.

[68] In some states there is a percentage and/or period limit upon such claims. In death cases funeral expenses may be claimed.

succeeded. Experience with no-fault has varied from state to state. In Massachusetts there was a sudden and very large drop in the number of claims on insurers leading to a refund of 25 per cent. of premiums but there is evidence that in that state there had previously been an unusually high number of fraudulent small claims under the tort system.[69] Elsewhere, the financial effect of the no-fault is difficult to assess because of the effect of inflation and the continued existence of large numbers of tort claims above the no-fault limit,[70] but the general experience has been that there has been some reduction in the cost of motor insurance as a result of no-fault schemes, while a modicum of basic compensation has been awarded to a large number of victims who would have recovered nothing under a pure tort system. Comparable plans have also been implemented in some Australian states though administration is in the hands of public bodies rather than insurance companies on the American pattern. The most ambitious is that of the Northern Territory, which abolishes all tort claims for pecuniary loss in return for instalment payments up to 85 per cent. of average wages. Non-pecuniary loss claims are preserved unless the plaintiff elects to receive benefits under the scheme, which are measured by degree of resulting disability. One rather extraordinary hybrid is that in New South Wales[71] under which tort liability for transport accidents is abolished to be replaced by scheme benefits but these are only payable where the accident was the fault of someone other than the victim.[72] In effect, though tort has nominally been abolished, the substance of it has been removed to the jurisdiction of an administrative tribunal and, because of the financial limits on benefits, compensation in the most severe cases has been reduced.

In England, selective compensation from public funds is most clearly exemplified by industrial injuries benefits.[73] This country, however, provides another instance of such compensation (though not in respect of "accidents"), quite independent of the social security system, in the form of the Criminal Injuries Compensation Scheme. The Scheme was instituted on a non-statutory basis but was put into statutory form by the Criminal Justice Act 1988. It is administered by the Criminal Injuries Compensation Board and the moneys are provided by Parliament. Compensation is payable in respect of injuries suffered from what may, for brevity's sake, be called crimes of violence[74] or from the apprehension of offenders. However, conduct is treated as a crime for this purpose notwithstanding that the wrongdoer may not be convicted by reason of age, insanity or diplomatic immunity. The claimant presents his case to the Board (most cases are dealt

---

[69] Pearson Report, Vol. 3, para. 265.

[70] Michigan has one of the most generous no-fault schemes but the number of motor tort cases filed in 1975–76 was 10,079 compared with 13,118 in 1972, the last full year before the introduction of the no-fault schemes.

[71] Transport Accidents Compensation Act 1987.

[72] Reduction for contributory negligence is retained.

[73] See ante, pp. 22–23. The first scheme of this kind was that set up in the German Empire under Bismarck's Industrial Accident Insurance Law of 1884.

[74] For the statutory definition see s.109 of the Criminal Justice Act 1988. The rather surprising inclusion of trespassing on a railway (s.109(3)(m)) stems from R. v. Criminal Injuries Compensation Board, ex p. Webb [1986] Q.B. 184.

with "on paper") and the compensation is calculated in a manner approximately equivalent to the assessment of damages in a tort action. The principal differences are that (*a*) as far as loss of earnings is concerned it is conclusively presumed that the claimant's earning capacity was not more than one-and-a-half times the gross average industrial wage and (*b*) there is a more extensive reduction of compensation in respect of benefits coming to the victim from other sources (for example, social security payments and pensions).[75] The Board has power to refuse or reduce an award because of the claimant's conduct in connection with the injury or his criminal convictions or unlawful conduct (whether before or after the time of the injury). Since its inception in 1964 the Scheme has paid more than £310 million in compensation (over £48 million in 1987) and the annual number of awards rose from about 14,000 in 1978 to about 22,000 in 1987.[76] Administrative costs, at about 10.5 per cent., compare well with tort, but because most cases involve an element of inquiry, are somewhat above those for most social security benefits. We have already seen that the offender himself may be ordered to pay compensation directly to the victim[77] but under section 115 of the Criminal Justice Act 1988 the Board also has a statutory right of recourse against the offender, which it may exercise if it has reason to believe that the offender is able to pay the whole or a substantial part of the award. The Scheme has been subjected to severe criticism in that it lacks theoretical foundation and is merely an attempt to single out yet another group of unfortunates for special treatment,[78] but the Scheme can be defended on at least two grounds. First, it may be argued that the state has a more direct responsibility here than for accidental injury because of its responsibility for maintaining law and order.[79] Secondly, the Scheme can be seen as supplementary to the law of tort.[80] Persons entitled to compensation under the Scheme are generally also entitled to damages at law, it being inconceivable that the victim of a crime of violence is not also the victim of a tort. It is, however, equally obvious that the tort remedy in such cases will usually be valueless to the victim for the simple reason that even if the assailant is identified and sued to judgment the chances of his being able to pay substantial damages are negligible.[81] In short, the Scheme merely guarantees payment to those who are the victims of tort.[82] In any event, the Scheme is now firmly embedded in public expectations.

Though nearly all ad hoc, selective no-fault schemes have been created in the context of transport accidents or criminal injuries, there are instances of

---

[75] See further, *post*, p. 622. 94 per cent. of awards are for less than £5,000 but an award of £400,000 was made in 1987, £310,000 of which was for services, nursing and other costs.

[76] Applications, however, rose in the same period from about 20,000 to 42,000. A substantial backlog of cases has built up. See the 23rd Report of the Board: Cm. 265 (1987).

[77] See *ante*, p. 10.

[78] Atiyah, *Accidents, Compensation and the Law*, (4th ed.).

[79] *cf.* the limited precedent of the Riot Damages Act 1886.

[80] There is some analogy with the Motor Insurers' Bureau agreements: *ante*, p. 26.

[81] Indeed, the intervention of the state in fining or imprisoning the offender may reduce the victim's chances of being able to execute his judgment.

[82] Yet another ad hoc scheme, prompted by the fact that most of the potential tort defendants had gone into liquidation, is found in the Pneumoconiosis, etc., (Workers' Compensation) Act 1979.

their application to other types of case, for example, the medical accident scheme which operates in Sweden[83] and the rising cost of doctors' liability insurance in the face of increased claims and damages awards has brought calls for a similar system here.[84]

Much more far reaching than anything we have discussed so far is the scheme now operating in New Zealand. The origin of the scheme is the Report of the Woodhouse Commission, which had been appointed to deal only with compensation for work injuries but which felt unable to limit itself to its terms of reference and proposed an all-embracing no-fault system of compensation financed by the state and based on the five guiding principles of community responsibility, comprehensive entitlement, "real" compensation (including non-pecuniary loss), the promotion of rehabilitation and administrative efficiency. Most of the proposals were implemented by the Accident Compensation Act 1972 which was consolidated and amended by the Accident Compensation Act 1982.[85] The scheme is administered by an Accident Compensation Commission, the day-to-day handling of claims being dealt with by the 50 branches of the State Insurance Office, whose staff had experience of operating the previous workmen's compensation legislation. All cases considered not to qualify are referred to the compensation division of the Accidents Compensation Commission and an applicant dissatisfied with a decision of that division may apply for a review. An appeal from a review lies to the Accident Compensation Appeal Authority, whence there is a further appeal on a question of law or of general or public importance to the Supreme Court. A final appeal, on a question of law, lies to the Court of Appeal.

The scheme is financed from three sources: for injuries to employed or self-employed persons a risk-rated levy is imposed upon employers and the self-employed; for motor accidents there is a levy on vehicles (with the possibility of penalty rates for bad risks); for other cases (e.g. pensioners and housewives injured elsewhere than on the road) compensation is financed out of general taxation.

Compensation is payable in respect of "personal injury by accident"

---

[83] See Brahams (1988) 138 N.L.J. 14. But the scheme by no means guarantees compensation since it does not apply if the injury constitutes an unavoidable complication of a measure which was justified from a medical viewpoint.

[84] It is estimated that the number of claims may have risen by 800 per cent. since the mid-1970s: *The Independent*, March 25, 1988. A doctor's "premium" to the medical protection societies has risen to well over £1,000 and one of them is proposing risk-rating by specialism (*e.g.* much higher payments by those practising gynaecology/obstetrics). However, the government has proposed that the present system under which liability is shared between the medical protection societies and health authorities should be scrapped, so that health authorities would pick up the bill for damages. This will very substantially reduce "premiums" except for those operating exclusively in the private sector: *The Times*, March 27, 1989.

[85] For descriptions of the Scheme, see the Pearson Report, Vol. 3, Chap. 10; Harris, "Accident Compensation in New Zealand: A Comprehensive Insurance System" (1974) 37 M.L.R. 361; Palmer, "Compensation for Personal Injury: A Requiem for the Common Law in New Zealand" (1973) 21 Amer.Jo. of Comp. Law 1. Extended commentaries on the Act in operation are Palmer, *Compensation for Incapacity*; Ison, *Accident Compensation*; and Blair, *Accident Compensation in New Zealand* (2nd ed.). In Australia a National Committee of inquiry in 1974 proposed a scheme that would cover all incapacity, whether caused by accident or illness but the proposal was lost with a change of government in 1975.

which is defined to include an occupational disease.[86] Rights of action in tort are abolished. In a case of total incapacity for work compensation is at the rate of 80 per cent. of earnings before tax, subject to a statutory maximum payment.[87] Where incapacity is only partial but leads to a loss of earning capacity, compensation is payable at the rate of 80 per cent. of that loss. In fatal cases compensation is payable to dependants of the victim on a scale related to degree of dependence so that, for example, a dependent widow receives three-fifths of the compensation which would have been payable if the deceased had lived but had been permanently and totally incapacitated and a totally dependent minor receives one-fifth. When compared with the general flat rate benefits payable under the New Zealand social security scheme, the compensation payable under the Accidents Compensation Act is certainly generous but in comparing it with the British social security system it should be borne in mind that payments in respect of loss of earnings under the Act are taxable, whereas most British benefits directly relevant to an accident victim are not. A comparison with common law damages for pecuniary loss is more difficult to make. On the one hand, the recipient of damages has the advantage of a lump sum which may enable him to make a "fresh start"; on the other hand the recipient of compensation under the scheme has the assurance of regular compensation for the greater part of his loss (unless he is a very high income earner) and security from inflation. In its treatment of non-pecuniary loss, however, the New Zealand scheme is a good deal less generous than the common law would be to a successful plaintiff. A lump sum not exceeding $17,000 (about £6,000) is payable in respect of permanent loss or impairment of bodily function,[88] together with a further lump sum not exceeding $10,000 (about £3,500) in respect of loss of amenities of life, disfigurement and pain and suffering. It must be emphasised that subject to the fixed statutory percentages in the case of impairment of function the Accidents Compensation Commission adopts the principle of "steering by the maximum," or reserving the top figures for the very worst cases, so that the sums recovered are very much lower than would be awarded at common law.[89] This low priority accorded to non-pecuniary loss is a feature of most of the radical proposals for reform put forward in recent years.[90] It is no doubt true that "loss" of this description is very different from the loss of something having an obvious monetary value and that damages are awarded at common law more by way of "solace for

---

[86] The decisions cited by Sutcliffe, "Precedent and Policy in Accident Compensation" (1977) 7 N.Z.U.L.R. 305, are an important corrective to the view that the scheme has done away with fine lines and arbitrary distinctions. Potentially one of the most difficult problems is the line between medical misadventure (which is "accident") and a result within the ordinary risks of treatment (which is not).

[87] About £290 in 1986.

[88] Percentages of the maximum are fixed for the most common impairments.

[89] See the examples in the Pearson Report, Vol. 3, paras. 879–880. In one case a 74-year-old pensioner who sustained a skull fracture received no compensation because any pain and suffering and loss of enjoyment of life experienced when in hospital and during subsequent recovery was of insufficient degree to justify an award. Compare this with *Frangoulis* v. *Ichard* [1977] 2 All E.R. 461 where £1,000 was awarded as general damages for fracture of clavicle and two ribs with no significant permanent effects. The only aggravating factor was that the plaintiff suffered loss of enjoyment of his holiday.

[90] See the works by Atiyah and Ison, *supra*, n. 30.

unpleasantness and misfortune" than by way of replacement of something of which a person has been deprived. It is also true that it is difficult to find a basis for the assessment of some types of non-pecuniary damage.[91] On the other hand, there is no *a priori* reason for saying that those who suffer pain or loss of amenity are undeserving of such solace as the payment of money can bring them. The reply of the radical reformers is that compensation of this kind should be given to none until such time as the basic income losses of all can be restored through the chosen compensation system.

REPORT OF THE PEARSON COMMISSION

The merits and demerits of the various approaches to the problem received detailed consideration in the Report of the Royal Commission on Civil Liability and Compensation for Personal Injury, the Pearson Report.[92] The Commission was appointed in 1973 as a result of widespread public concern with accident compensation generated by the thalidomide affair, in which some 400 children in the United Kingdom[93] were born with deformities caused by the taking by their mothers of the drug thalidomide between 1958 and 1961.[94] Its terms of reference were to consider

" . . . to what extent, in what circumstances and by what means compensation should be payable in respect of death or personal injury (including ante-natal injury) suffered by any person:

  (a) in the course of employment;
  (b) through the use of a motor vehicle or other means of transport;
  (c) through the manufacture, supply or use of goods or services;
  (d) on premises belonging to or occupied by another; or
  (e) otherwise through the act or omission of another where compensation under the present law is recoverable only on proof of fault or under the rules of strict liability; having regard to the cost and other implications of the arrangements for the recovery of compensation, whether by way of compulsory insurance or otherwise."

The Commission's inquiry lasted for nearly five years, during which it received oral or written evidence from over 800 individuals and organisations. Members of the Commission visited nine countries with social and political backgrounds comparable to our own and the headquarters of three international organisations with an interest in the accident problem.

---

[91] See *post*, pp. 614–616.
[92] Cmnd. 7054 (1978).
[93] The number worldwide is thought to be 8,000–10,000.
[94] The long-drawn-out litigation between the manufacturers of the drug (Distillers Co. Ltd.) and the parents of the children was eventually settled in 1973 on the basis that Distillers would pay £6 million as a lump sum and put £2 million a year for seven years into a trust fund. To offset tax liability on the payments from the fund the Government made a single payment of £5 million. Distillers have never admitted negligence. The legal consequences ranged beyond accident compensation: see the *Sunday Times* cases arising from an article containing allegations about the development and marketing of the drug: [1974] A.C. 273 and (1979) 2 E.H.R.R. 245.

For the purposes of this chapter the crucial and principal point of the Report is that it did *not* recommend the creation of a comprehensive scheme of state compensation on the lines of the New Zealand Accident Compensation Act. The Report states that consideration of a comprehensive scheme was precluded by the terms of reference, particularly paragraph (e), which excluded the bulk of accidents in the home. This interpretation is somewhat surprising in view of the fact that the Woodhouse Commission in New Zealand had been appointed to consider only compensation for industrial accidents but had not thereby felt constrained from venturing into much wider areas.[95] There is, however, some internal evidence in the Report that this attitude to the terms of reference may conceal some disagreement among the members of the Commission as to the desirability of a comprehensive state scheme. The final chapter of the Report[96] speaks of three schools of thought on the ultimate objectives of compensation. One school would welcome the extension of no-fault compensation (and, by implication, of state-financed no-fault compensation) to all accidents and, in the long run, to sickness.[97] Others hoped that there would always be a role for tort damages because they were able to deal more discriminatingly than social security payments with individual losses and embodied a recognition of the principle of responsibility. A third group thought that it would be better to assess the consequences of the Commission's limited proposals before trying to judge in which direction it would be appropriate to move next.

It is not, therefore, surprising that what the Report proposed was adjustments of the compromise arrived at with the birth of the welfare state rather than any radical change. The Report contained no less than 188 recommendations,[98] nearly all of which now seem fated to gather dust.[99] Some of them will be mentioned at relevant points in this book, but despite the unlikelihood of implementation it is still worthwhile to look briefly at what were perhaps the two major recommendations, governing road accidents and damages for tort.

For road accidents the Commission proposed payment by way of social

---

[95] Even the Pearson Commission strayed outside its terms of reference at one point in proposing a non-taxable disability income of £4 a week for all severely handicapped children. They commented (Vol. 1, para. 1489), "Recent legislation and practice relating to the compensation and care of severely handicapped children suggest that Government policy is based on the principle that they are to be treated alike, without regard to the cause of their condition. We decided to follow suit. It would not be sensible to allow the constraints of our terms of reference to prevent us from seeking the right solution."

[96] Chap. 33, "Concluding Reflections."

[97] The Commission estimated that at 1977 prices full implementation of its proposals for limited no fault would add £51 million a year, or about 9 per cent., to total payments from tort and social security in respect of injury. Extension of that no-fault compensation to all injuries would add about £250 million a year. Extension to all illness would add a further £2,000 million a year, an 80 per cent. addition to the total cost of social security and compensation for illness and injury: Vol. 1, paras. 1691, 1711.

[98] There is a substantial literature on the Report. See, *e.g. Accident Compensation after Pearson*, especially Atiyah, "What Now?" at pp. 227–255; Fleming, "The Pearson Report: Its 'Strategy' " (1979) 42 M.L.R. 249; Marsh, "The Pearson Report" (1979) 95 L.Q.R. 513; Tunc (1978) 30 *Revue International de Droit Comparè*.

[99] In fact it is doubtful if any legislative action can really be said to be directly traceable to the Pearson Report. The Vaccine Damage Payments Act 1979 was certainly prompted by the Report but is quite different in its nature from the Commission's recommendation. Most of the changes in the law of damages found in the Administration of Justice Act 1982 were anticipated by the Law Commission in Law Comm. No. 56.

security benefits (financed by a levy on petrol) at the same rates as under the industrial injuries scheme in respect of injury and death suffered as the result of the use of a motor vehicle on land to which the public has access. The right to sue in tort would remain.[1] Since benefits under the industrial injuries scheme were higher than those for non-industrial injuries the Commission in effect accepted the survival of the so-called "industrial preference" but revealed a curiously ambivalent attitude in its comment that "this does not mean we endorse the preference in principle. Although Beveridge concluded that an element of industrial preference should remain it seemed to us that his arguments carried a good deal less weight now, especially as the scheme has been applied to all industries, whether dangerous or not."[2]

In proposing an ad hoc arrangement for road accidents the Commission followed a long-standing and international tradition among reformers of accident compensation. It justified singling out this type of accident in the following way:

"First, motor vehicle injuries occur on a scale not matched by any other category of accidental injury within our terms of reference, except work injuries (which are already covered by a no-fault scheme). Secondly— and here they are to be distinguished from work injuries—they are not confined to any particular group of victims. Thirdly, they are particularly likely to be serious,[3] so that they highlight the difficulties of compensating for prolonged incapacity. Fourthly, road transport itself is an essential part of everyday life, of fundamental importance to the economy as a whole and to the mobility of individuals."[4]

The possibility of the creation of limited state-financed no-fault compensation schemes to cover other types of accident within its terms of reference was considered by the Commission but in nearly all cases there were substantial practical objections. In the case of accidents arising from the provision of services, for example, there would be enormous difficulties in deciding the scope of the scheme and in the collection of finance if any attempt were to be made at hypothecation, rather than finance out of general revenue; in other cases, while it might be possible to identify those on whom the burden of finance should fall, the cost of administration of the system would be out of all proportion to the number of cases involved. However, the road accident proposals have been subject to fierce attack for their failure to give full recognition to the savings that could be made from

[1] However, as a result of the Commission's general proposals for full offsets of social security benefits many small tort suits would disappear: *infra*.

[2] Vol. 1, para. 290. Recent developments have significantly eroded the industrial preference (*ante*, p. 23), but there seems no prospect of the removal of the core of it—the special treatment for long-term disablement.

[3] Road accidents were found to account for one in eight of all injuries, but for one in three of all accidental deaths.

[4] Vol. 1, para. 996. The Civil Justice Review (n.50, *supra*) suggests consideration of a no-fault scheme for minor motor accidents, though it accepts that it would probably raise motor insurance premiums.

abolition of the tort action and their tendency to create a further ad hoc privileged class in an already complicated system.[5] Indeed, one could argue that the proposals would build on an already existing privilege since however inadequate the tort system may be as a method of ensuring compensation, it seems that it provides it for a greater proportion of victims in road accident cases than in others.[6]

Given its overall commitment to the retention of a "mixed" system of compensation there is much of interest in the Commission's proposals with regard to the interrelation of tort damages[7] and social security payments, particularly the question of offsetting the latter against the former, for "the time has come for full co-ordination of the compensation provided by tort and social security. An injured person, or his dependants, should not have the same need met twice, not only because it is inequitable, but because it is wasteful.[8] The Commission's proposal was that all social security benefits paid or payable to the plaintiff as a result of the injury for which damages were awarded should be deducted in assessing those damages. The effect of this, in combination with a proposal to stop recovery of non-pecuniary loss suffered in the first three months after injury[9] would be to remove a large number of small claims from the system and increase the proportion of claimants for whom the social security system provides incomplete compensation—high earners. Indeed, when one adds certain other proposals designed to produce more realistic assessments of damages for long-term losses the effect of implementation would be startling in depressing the awards to low earners and inflating those of high earners.[10] While fully consistent with the purpose of avoiding duplication of compensation and with the objective of tort, "which is to restore an injured person as closely as possible to the position which he was in before he was injured,"[11] such a result would present grave political difficulties to implementation, no matter what the complexion of the Government.

The Pearson Report can be defended as a realistic medium-term strategy,[12] recognising and encouraging the progressive and inevitable shift of tort towards the role of a more and more junior partner in compensating accidental misfortune,[13] though it is perhaps a matter for debate how far a Royal Commission should go in pursuit of this sort of delicate balancing and assessment of what "the market will bear." That it has not been implemented and probably never will be may be attributed principally to two

---

[5] See especially Atiyah in *Accident Compensation after Pearson*.
[6] *Ante*, p. 19, n. 1.
[7] The Commission's proposals on *methods* of assessment of tort damages are mentioned *post*, p. 617.
[8] Vol. 1, para. 475.
[9] Vol. 1, para. 388.
[10] Taking two men aged 35, married with two children, both permanently incapacitated, one earning £60 per week, the other £240 per week the Commission calculated total damages for pecuniary loss under the existing system as £28,570 and £97,700 respectively. Under their proposals, the figure would be £2,000 and £126,000: Vol. 1, Chap. 15, Table 13.
[11] Vol. 1, para. 706.
[12] See Lord Allen of Abbeydale in *Accident Compensation after Pearson*, pp. 3–8.
[13] The Commission contemplated a long-term reduction in the proportion of tort compensation to social security, from about 1:2, to about 1:4.

factors. First, the cornerstone of the Report may be said to be the continuation and improvement of the industrial injuries scheme and its "extension" to road accidents. In fact, the D.H.S.S.'s own review led to the scheme changing course to concentrate on longer-term and more severe cases of disablement and hence the reduction of its overall importance in compensation for misfortune. What had been envisaged as a model for other areas ceased to be so when even its traditional role was cut back. Secondly, even if this had not happened, it is a fact that virtually all accident victims receive some form of social security benefit and the Commission's proposals for upgrading certain areas (bought, it should be remembered, by severe pruning of tort claims in less serious cases) did not involve the sort of dramatic increase in compensation or coverage which might have caught the public imagination.

The second point is one that really lies at the heart of the "compensation debate." Reformers have concentrated upon the relative equity between "fault" and "non-fault" victims and have advocated moderate automatic benefits to which the abolition of the costs (including transfer costs) of the tort system could make a major contribution. The price of this might be a reduction in compensation for non-pecuniary loss to those who can at present prove fault and for pecuniary loss in the case of high income earners, but the reformers would respond that as to the first income support should occupy a higher place in the scale of priorities and as to the second this category can protect themselves by insurance. A decent meal for all is preferable to a banquet for some. However, public debate over medical negligence and some mass-disaster cases suggests that expectations of the "proper" level of compensation are at a level well beyond that which could be financed without additional taxation.[14] This may be irrational and retributive, but it cannot be ignored if any reform is to be effected. Even if this difficulty can be got over, however, there remains the problem of the scope of no-fault compensation. The Pearson Commission's reasons for singling out the victims of road accidents for preferential treatment would by no means commend universal assent[15] and the savings stemming from the abolition of tort liability will not go very far if spread across the whole spectrum of accident compensation. A comparatively high proportion of road accident victims recover tort damages so that there would be a substantial sum (perhaps £500 million a year) available to finance a road scheme. However, road accidents comprise less than 20 per cent. of all accidents and the only other area in which tort damages play a major role is that of accidents at work, the number of which is rather greater, but in which the proportion of tort recoveries is lower. The result is that a comprehensive accident scheme would have to fund compensation for about half of its

---

[14] Until 1982 the law allowed no damages at all for non-pecuniary loss in cases of bereavement. A conventional sum of £3,500 was introduced by the Administration of Justice Act of that year but in the *Herald of Free Enterprise* settlement negotiations (1987) even offers well above this figure were widely criticised as too low. See also the Pearson Commission, Vol. 1, Chap. 8, on the widespread view that social security benefits do not really constitute "compensation."

[15] See, *e.g.* Harris *et al*, *Compensation and Support for Illness and Injury*; Stapleton, *Disease and the Compensation Debate*.

claimants without any significant saving from the abolition of tort liability. Indeed, it is widely felt among reformers that a rational compensation system cannot even confine its coverage to *accident* victims[16] since the needs of a person under disability are not mitigated by the fact that it has arisen from illness or congenital cause rather than by accident. On this view, even the comprehensive New Zealand scheme suffers from the vice of cause-related compensation.[17] But if we bring in illness, we enter a wholly different statistical dimension, since it is generally thought that the contribution of accidents to all forms of disability is not more than about 10 per cent.[18] Reform in this area is as much about politics as principle, and the present system contains a whole range of firmly entrenched misconceptions about the nature and quantum of compensation, not to mention vested interests (of particular classes of victims as well as of personal injury lawyers). If there were no social security system and all persons suffering disability for non-fault reasons were condemned to utter destitution, it might be possible to raise a sufficient head of steam for a new and comprehensive approach. But the basic social security system does exist and reform[19] may well be perceived by the public as "fine tuning" brought about at the price of taking away existing rights and there are no votes in that. There is perhaps more chance of the introduction of limited ad hoc no-fault schemes but these are likely to make comprehensive change even more difficult by creating further enclaves of preferential treatment.

---

[16] *Ibid.*

[17] Though the Woodhouse Report contemplated that the scheme might in due course be extended to illness. The abortive Australian scheme of 1974/1975 (see *supra*, n. 85) would have covered illness.

[18] See the Pearson Report, Vol. 2, p. 12. Though tort is certainly applicable to man-made disease its contribution to compensation is necessarily very limited, because of the difficulties of proof of causation: see Stapleton, *op. cit.*

[19] See the (uncosted) proposals in Harris (*supra*, n. 1) Chap. 12, which broadly involve (1) abolition of tort; (2) abolition of benefit entitlement by reference to cause of disability; (3) a shift to greater use of employers' sick pay in short-term cases; (4) concentration of social security benefits upon long-term disability.

CHAPTER 2

GENERAL CHARACTERISTICS OF TORTIOUS LIABILITY

TRESPASS AND CASE

Forms of action

THE chief source of our law of tort is the common law as opposed to the statute law. This, of course, signifies that it is for the most part based on decided cases and owes its development to the activity of the judges more than to the activity of Parliament. It also means that the law of tort has grown up, like other branches of our law, behind a screen of legal procedure. Until the mid-nineteenth century, the question which arose when a plaintiff sued a defendant for some alleged injury was not "Has the defendant broken some duty which he owed to the plaintiff?" but "Has the plaintiff any form of action against the defendant, and, if so, what form?" If he could not fit his claim into one of the recognised forms of action, he had no legal grievance. An action was usually commenced by a royal writ issued from the Chancery, which is in this sense signified not a court of law, but a government depart-ment, one of whose functions was the creation and issue of these writs.[1] It was known also as the *officina brevium* which has been conveniently tran-slated as "the writ-shop," for a plaintiff could not get a writ without paying for it. For a very considerable period of our legal history the shape of the law was no more than a classification of writs.

The writs that remedied the injuries which in modern time are called torts were principally the writ of trespass and the writ of trespass on the case or "case."[2] Trespass in common parlance now signifies unauthorised entry on another person's land, but in law it has a wider signification. The writ of trespass lay for injuries to land or to goods, or to the person. But it was limited to injuries which were direct and immediate such as those sustained by a person struck by a log which is thrown into the highway. It did not extend to indirect or consequential injuries, such as those sustained by a person who stumbled over the log while it lay in the highway. But these indirect injuries came to be remediable through the action on the case. These two classes of action, "trespass" and "case," existed side by side for

---

[1] For the modern form of writ, see R.S.C., Ord. 6, r. 1. Writs are issued out of the Central Office or a district registry of the Supreme Court.

[2] See Milsom, "Not doing is no Trespass" [1954] C.L.J. 105; "Trespass from Henry III to Edward III" (1958) 74 L.Q.R. 195, 407, 561.

centuries and to them we owe most of our law of tort. There were, however, definite distinctions between these two forms of action and until the nineteenth century it was vital for a plaintiff to choose correctly between them.[3] Only after the reforms of that century had broken up the cast-iron moulds of procedure did it cease to be necessary "to canvass the niceties of the old forms of action. Remedies now depend upon the substance of the right, not on whether they can be fitted into a particular framework."[4] Nevertheless a knowledge of the forms of action is still necessary for the understanding of the old authorities and of the classification of much of the modern law. Moreover in some instances the existence and nature of tortious liability depend upon the form of action which would have been appropriate under the old procedure. Maitland's famous phrase, "The forms of action we have buried, but they still rule us from their graves,"[5] has been repeated often enough to become a *clichè*. One does not venture to polish any aphorism of Maitland's but we shall see that in some respects it may be questioned whether the forms of action have not been buried alive.[6]

Forms of liability

There are different ways in which liability in tort may arise:

(*a*) Liability may be imposed as a legal consequence of a person's act, or of his omission if he is under a legal duty to act. Liability may also be imposed upon one person as the legal consequence of the act or omission of another person with whom he stands in some special relationship such as that of master and servant. This is known as vicarious liability and is the subject of a separate chapter.[7]

(*b*) In some cases liability is based upon fault; sometimes an intention to injure is required but more often negligence is sufficient. In other cases, which are called cases of strict liability, liability is in varying degrees independent of fault.

(*c*) Whereas most torts require damage resulting to the plaintiff which is not too remote a consequence of the defendant's conduct, a few, such as trespass in some, or perhaps all, of its various forms and libel, do not require proof of actual damage.

INTENTION OR NEGLIGENCE OR THE BREACH OF STRICT DUTY

Intention

Some torts require intention on the part of the wrongdoer. It is, of course,

---

[3] See Pritchard, "Trespass, Case and the Rule in *Williams* v. *Holland*" [1964] C.L.J. 234.
[4] *Nelson* v. *Larholt* [1948] 1 K.B. 339, 343, *per* Denning J. See also *Dies* v. *British and International Mining and Finance Corporation* [1939] 1 K.B. 724, 738, *per* Stable J.; *Abbott* v. *Sullivan* [1952] 1 K.B. 189, 200, *per* Denning L.J.
[5] *Equity*, p. 296.
[6] *e.g.* the distinction between trespass to land and private nuisance still turns upon the old distinction between trespass and case. See, *e.g. Esso Petroleum Co. Ltd.* v. *Southport Corporation* [1956] A.C. 218, where the judgment of Devlin J. at first instance is also reported. For proceedings in the Court of Appeal see [1954] 2 Q.B. 182.
[7] *Post*, Chap. 21.

impossible for the law to do more than to infer a man's intention, or indeed any other mental state of his, from his conduct.[8] The law may frequently attribute to him an intention which a metaphysician would at most consider very doubtful. Centuries ago, Brian C.J. said: "It is common knowledge that the thought of man shall not be tried, for the Devil himself knoweth not the thought of man."[9] On the other hand, Bowen L.J. in 1885, had no doubt that "the state of a man's mind is as much a fact as the state of his digestion."[10] There is no contradiction in these dicta. All that Brian C.J. meant was that no one can be perfectly certain of what passes in the mind of another person. But Brian would certainly not have dissented from the proposition that in law what a man thinks must be deduced from what he says and does; and that is all that Bowen L.J. meant.

Given this basic premise that intention can only be inferred from conduct we are still left with the problem of defining intention. Everyone agrees that a person intends a consequence if it is his desire or motive to bring it about, but beyond that it is probably not possible to lay down any universal definition for the purposes of tort. In crime, the law now is that the jury is entitled (but not, it seems, required) to infer intention where the defendant was aware that the harm was "virtually certain" to result from his act.[11] There has been much less discussion of intention in tort and there are probably at least two reasons for this (apart from the relative infrequency of cases on intentional torts). First, since the abolition of the forms of action the plaintiff will often be able to fall back upon a wider principle of liability for negligence: if I strike you, then provided I cause you hurt and that hurt could have been foreseeable to a reasonable man then my conduct amounts to the tort of negligence even if the court is in doubt whether I acted intentionally.[12] Secondly, while the criminal law may insist that the defendant's intention must extend to all the elements and consequences of his act making up the definition of the crime, the law of tort may separate the initial interference with the victim from the consequences of that interference (remoteness of damage[13]) and while intention or foresight may be necessary as to the former it may not be as to the latter. Thus if A strikes B intending some slight harm but B suffers greater harm (because, for example, he falls as a result of the blow) A is responsible for the greater harm if it is a direct consequence of the blow: he need not even foresee the possibility of the greater harm, let alone intend it.[14] Indeed, the defendant is liable for the greater harm even if it is the result of some unusual susceptibility of the plaintiff, a principle developed primarily in the context of negligence[15] but applying with even more force to intentional wrongdoers.[16]

---

[8] Including his conduct in the witness box.
[9] Year Book Pasch. 17 Edw. 4, fol. 2, pl. 2.
[10] *Edgington* v. *Fitzmaurice* (1885) 29 Ch.D. 459, 483.
[11] *R.* v. *Nedrick* [1986] 1 W.L.R. 1025 (intent in murder).
[12] It is implicit in *Williams* v. *Humphrey, The Times*, February 20, 1975, that an intentional blow may lead to liability in trespass and negligence at the same time.
[13] See *post*, Chap. 6.
[14] *Williams* v. *Humphrey, The Times*, February 20, 1975.
[15] See *post*, p. 147.
[16] See *Allan* v. *New Mount Sinai Hospital* (1980) 109 D.L.R. (3d) 634.

In one tort, conspiracy to injure, intention has the very narrow meaning of single-minded desire to do harm[17] so that the defendant does not "intend" even what he foresees as a certainty if his purpose is to advance his own interests. Some torts in the area of unlawful interference with economic interests may require that the plaintiff is the "target" of the defendant's actions, though it has been said that "if an act is done deliberately and with knowledge of its consequences [the actor] cannot sensibly say that he did not 'intend' the consequences or that the act was not 'aimed' at the person who, it is known, will suffer them."[18] In the context of trespass to land it has been said that indifference to a risk that trespass will occur by animals in the defendant's charge amounts to intention[19] and it is thought that the same approach should be taken in all the trespass torts: if D throws his coffee dregs out of the window of his office knowing that others may be passing, that should be trespass if anyone is hit, whether the street is so crowded that it is a virtual certainty or is comparatively unfrequented.[20]

Negligence

"Negligence" may signify full advertence to one's conduct and its consequences. More usually, however, it signifies inadvertence by the defendant, a simple example being the motorist who falls asleep at the wheel. It may be that the word should be used only in the latter sense[21] but a defendant clearly cannot escape liability because he adverted to the risk if the case is one where even inadvertence would saddle him with liability. An illustration of full advertence is *Vaughan* v. *Menlove*[22] where the defendant had been warned that his haystack was likely to overheat and to take fire, which might spread to the land of his neighbour. He said he would chance it,[23] and he was held liable for the damage which occurred when the stack actually took fire.

We are concerned at this point with negligence merely as a state of mind. But it also has the further meaning of an independent tort, with the specific name of "negligence." Its treatment as such must be postponed until we come to deal with specific torts.[24]

Breach of strict duty

In some torts, the defendant is liable even though the harm to the plaintiff occurred without intention or negligence on the defendant's part. Thus it was laid down in the celebrated case of *Rylands* v. *Fletcher*[25] that "if a person

---

[17] The same is probably now true for all forms of conspiracy. See *post*, p. 519.
[18] *Bourgoin S.A.* v. *Ministry of Agriculture, Fisheries and Food* [1986] Q.B. 716, 777, *per* Oliver L.J.
[19] See *League Against Cruel Sports* v. *Scott* [1986] Q.B. 240, 252.
[20] But *cf.* the American *Restatement of Torts* 2d, s.8A ("substantial certainty"). As to "transferred intent" (where A strikes at B, misses and hits C instead) see *post*, p. 71, n. 47.
[21] See the comments of Lord Reid in *I.C.I.* v. *Shatwell* [1965] A.C. 656, 672.
[22] (1837) 3 Bing N.C. 468.
[23] He was insured.
[24] *Post*, Chap. 5.
[25] (1868) L.R. 3 H.L. 330, 340.

brings or accumulates on his land anything which, if it should escape, may cause damage to his neighbours, he does so at his peril. If it does escape and cause damage, he is responsible, however careful he may have been, and whatever precautions he may have taken to prevent damage." This is sometimes styled "absolute" liability, but the epithet is misplaced, as there are possible defences even to torts of this kind, *e.g.* the act of God excludes liability under the rule in *Rylands* v. *Fletcher*.[26] Liability in nuisance *may* be strict where the defendant himself or someone for whom he is responsible has created the nuisance.[27] Liability for breach of a statutory duty is not, as a rule, dependent on proof of negligence,[28] and where an Act requires something to be done without qualification contravention of the statute automatically establishes liability.[29]

"Reasonable" and "reasonable man"

It is convenient to insert here an explanation of the terms "reasonable" and "reasonable man." They recur so frequently in the law of tort, and indeed in every branch of the law,[30] that their meaning must be grasped at the outset of this exposition. As to the law of tort, reasonableness is an essential ingredient in the law of negligence, whether that word be used to indicate an independent tort or a mental element in the commission of certain other torts; and more will be said of this in the chapter on negligence.[31] But there are many other torts in which, in one way or another, the idea appears. If any broad sense can be extracted from the various significations of "reasonable conduct" it might be described as the behaviour of the ordinary man in any particular event or transaction, including in such behaviour obedience to the special directions (if any) which the law gives him for his guidance in that connection. This is, of course, an abstraction. Lord Bowen visualised the reasonable man as "the man on the Clapham omnibus"; an American writer as "the man who takes the magazines at home, and in the evening pushes the lawn mower in his shirt sleeves."[32] He has not the courage of Achilles, the wisdom of Ulysses or the strength of

---

[26] (1926) 42 L.Q.R. 37; *post,* Chap. 16.

[27] *Rapier* v. *London Tramways Co.* [1893] 2 Ch. 588, 599, *per* Lindley L.J.; *Sedleigh-Denfield* v. *O'Callaghan* [1940] A.C. 880, 904. "Negligence is not a necessary condition of a claim in nuisance": *per* Lord Wright. See *post,* pp. 380–385.

[28] *Galashiels Gas Co.* v. *O'Donnell* [1949] A.C. 275, 282, *per* Lord Morton, 286, *per* Lord MacDermott (absolute duty to maintain lift—Factories Act 1937, ss.22(1) and 152(2)); *Carroll* v. *Barclay (Andrew) & Sons Ltd.* [1948] A.C. 477, 487, *per* Lord Normand (absolute obligation to fence dangerous machinery). But a statute may prescribe that reasonable care is all that is required, or that something shall be done so far as is reasonably practicable: *post,* pp. 199–200.

[29] *John Summers & Sons Ltd.* v. *Frost* [1955] A.C. 740. Liability under the Nuclear Installations Act 1965 will exist even if the damage is attributable to an act of God, but not if it is attributable to hostile action in the course of armed conflict: *ibid.* s.13(4).

[30] (1931) 45 Harv.L.Rev.: 125–126, Eldredge, *Modern Tort Problems,* pp. 1–24.

[31] *Post,* Chap. 5.

[32] Cited by Greer L.J. in *Hall* v. *Brooklands Auto Racing Club* [1933] 1 K.B. 205, 224. Eldredge, *Modern Tort Problems,* p. 3, "The reasonable man is a fiction—he is the personification of the court and jury's social judgment." Despite the inveterate use of the masculine gender, there is no doubt that the personification includes the reasonable woman.

Hercules, nor has he "the prophetic vision of a clairvoyant."[33] He will not anticipate folly in all its forms, but he never puts out of consideration the teachings of experience and so will guard against the negligence of others when experience shows such negligence to be common.[34] He is a reasonable man but he is neither a perfect citizen nor a "paragon of circumspection."[35] This is good so far as it goes, but it must be added that where a person exercises any calling, the law requires him, in dealing with other people in the course of that calling, to exhibit the degree of skill or competence which is usually associated with its efficient discharge.[36] Nobody expects the man on the Clapham omnibus to have any skill as a surgeon, a lawyer, a docker, or a chimney-sweep unless he is one; but if he professes to be one, then the law requires him to show such skill as any ordinary member of the profession or calling to which he belongs, or claims to belong, would display.

The description of "reasonable" just given is, and can only be, a rough approximation to exactness. As was indicated in it, if the law gives special directions for the guidance of the ordinary man, he must regulate his conduct by them if his conduct is to be regarded as reasonable. Now these directions are often so precise and technical that a man, if he is to ascertain and act upon them, strikes one as anything but a commonplace person, and seems to need the Clapham lawyer at his elbow on many occasions. Here the judicial method, being what it is, shows two rather conflicting tendencies. One is to get as near exactness as may be in the rules relating to what is regarded as reasonable. The other is to recognise that complete exactness is neither attainable nor desirable.[37] Nor is this all. The judge has to decide what "reasonable" means, and it is inevitable that different judges may take variant views on the same question with respect to such an elastic term.[38] An extreme example of this was a case in which "reasonable cause" was an element and the very same act was held by an appellate criminal court to be a felony punishable with penal servitude for life, and by an appellate civil court to be not even a tort.[39] But conflicts of this sort are very unusual, and

---

[33] *Hawkins* v. *Coulsdon & Purley U.D.C.* [1954] 1 Q.B. 319, 341, *per* Romer L.J. *Pace* Lord Bramwell, who occasionally attributed to the reasonable man the agility of an acrobat and the foresight of a Hebrew prophet. For a somewhat far-fetched claim, see *Smith* v. *Southwark Offset, The Times,* December 20, 1974.

[34] *L.P.T.B.* v. *Upson* [1949] A.C. 155, 173, *per* Lord Uthwatt; p. 176, *per* Lord du Parcq; *Lang* v. *London Transport Executive* [1959] 1 W.L.R. 1168, 1175, *per* Havers J. See the *Restatement of Torts,* 2d, ss.289, 290, "What is customarily regarded as requisite for the protection of others, rather than that of the average man in the community."

[35] *A.C. Billings & Sons Ltd.* v. *Riden* [1958] A.C. 240, 255, *per* Lord Reid. For a brilliant caricature of "this excellent but odious creature" see Sir Alan Herbert, *Uncommon Law,* pp. 1–5.

[36] General and approved practice may, however, fall below the standard of the reasonable man, and if so, it is not a good defence, *post,* p. 116.

[37] The latter tendency is dominant at the present day, but with the diminishing use of juries in civil cases and the expansion of law reporting, there is a danger that judges' decisions of fact may come to be treated as laying down detailed rules of law: *Qualcast (Wolverhampton) Ltd.* v. *Haynes* [1959] A.C. 743, especially *per* Lord Somervell at pp. 757–758, *per* Lord Denning at pp. 759–761.

[38] *Glasgow Corpn.* v. *Muir* [1943] A.C. 448, 457, *per* Lord Macmillan, who deals with some of the attributes of a reasonable man. Though invested with power to decide what is reasonable, it does not follow that the judge will always behave like a reasonable man himself: *O'Connor* v. *State of South Australia* (1976) 14 S.A.S.R. 187.

[39] *R.* v. *Denyer* [1926] 2 K.B. 258; *Hardie & Lane Ltd.* v. *Chilton* [1928] 2 K.B. 306. This conflict was resolved in *Thorne* v. *Motor Trade Association* [1937] A.C. 797. *cf.* the differing views expressed in the Court of Appeal and in the House of Lords in *Woods* v. *Duncan* [1946] A.C. 401.

although we shall find the reasonable man doing some things which a moralist would regard as quixotic and a good many other things which he would condemn as slovenly or even cowardly, yet the law upon the whole strikes a fair average between these extremes.

Several other phrases will be encountered in the law reports which have sometimes, but not always, a meaning equivalent to "reasonable." Such are "fair," "just," "natural justice." Like certain other phrases (*e.g.* "judicial discretion"), they show that although law and ethics are distinct topics, it is impossible to make or to administer a civilised system of law without taking account of current ethical ideas.[40]

MOTIVE AND MALICE

Motive may be conveniently treated here. It signifies the reason for conduct. Unfortunately it has become entangled with the word "malice" which is used quite differently in the law of tort. It may mean what the layman usually takes it to be—"evil motive"; or it may signify doing an act wilfully without just cause or excuse.[41] This latter meaning has really nothing to do with motive but refers to intention, a term which ought to be confined to advertence to conduct and its consequences, and which is quite colourless as to the motive which influences the actor; we are not concerned with it here.

Motive generally irrelevant

As to motive in its proper meaning, the general rule is that, if conduct is presumptively unlawful, a good motive will not exonerate the defendant, and that, if conduct is lawful apart from motive, a bad motive will not make him liable.

We shall see that there are several exceptions to the second part of this rule. To the first part of it, defences like necessity and private defence are exceptions, for they depend to a certain extent on a good motive on the part of the defendant.

The general irrelevancy of evil motive was affirmed by the House of Lords in *Bradford Corporation* v. *Pickles*.[42] Pickles was annoyed at the refusal of the Corporation of Bradford to purchase his land in connection with the scheme of water supply for the inhabitants of the town. In revenge, he sank a shaft on his land. The water which percolated through his land in unknown

---

[40] Winfield, "Ethics in English Case Law" (1931) 45 Harv.L.Rev. 112–135, reprinted in *Select Legal Essays* (1952), pp. 266–282.

[41] Bayley J. in *Bromage* v. *Prosser* (1825) 4 B. & C. 247, 255; Bowen L.J. in *Mogul Steamship Co. Ltd.* v. *McGregor, Gow & Co.* (1889) 23 Q.B.D. 598, 612; Lord Watson, in *Allen* v. *Flood* [1898] A.C. 1, 94, Fridman, "Malice in the Law of Torts" (1958) 21 M.L.R. 484. In earlier times one of the meanings of malice was "harmfulness" quite independently of any human mental element, *e.g.* in Paynel, *Salerne's Regim.* (a book on health A.D. 1528), "such wyne doth alay the malice of ye meate."

[42] [1895] A.C. 587; *Crofter Hand Woven Harris Tweed Co.* v. *Veitch* [1942] A.C. 435, 442, *per* Viscount Simon L.C. See also *Perera* v. *Vandiyar* [1953] 1 W.L.R. 672.

and undefined channels from the land of the corporation on a higher level was consequently discoloured and diminished when it passed again to the lower land of the corporation. For this injury Pickles was held not liable. "It is the act," said Lord Macnaghten, "not the motive for the act that must be regarded. If the act, apart from motive, gives rise merely to damage without legal injury, the motive, however, reprehensible it may be, will not supply that element."[43] Three years later this was again emphasised by the House of Lords in *Allen* v. *Flood*[44] and, for better or worse,[45] it remains the general rule today. As we shall see, however, there are certain exceptional cases in which the evil motive of the defendant, if proved, will tip the scales of liability against him.

---

[43] [1895] A.C. 587, 601. See further as to this case, *post*, pp. 391–393.
[44] [1898] A.C. 1.
[45] Gutteridge, "Abuse of Rights" 5 C.L.J. 22; Allen, *Legal Duties*, pp. 95–118; Ames in *Selected Essays on the Law of Torts*, pp. 150–161; Holmes, *ibid*. pp. 162–175; Roscoe Pound, *Spirit of the Common Law*, pp. 202–203; Friedmann, *Legal Theory*, (5th ed.), p. 554. See also *ante*, p. 13.

CHAPTER 3

NOMINATE TORTS

IN the course of English legal history certain forms of tortious liability have gained specific names, such as assault, battery, libel, slander, nuisance and negligence. The fact that they acquired such names was due to mere accidents of terminology traceable probably to their frequent occurrence. In the following chapters it is proposed to deal with these particular torts. But it is important to remember that they do not exhaust the content of tortious liability. Outside these nominate torts there are wrongs which are well known to exist but which have no compendious name; beyond these again are wrongs which may possibly be torts, but of which it is impossible to say whether they are such or not. Thus, as a family group, torts may be divided into those which received names soon after birth, those which seem to be awaiting baptism in their riper years and those whose paternity is uncertain enough to make it doubtful whether they ought to be included in the family at all.

It is also important to remember that these nominate torts are not exclusive of one another and that there is no reason why a given set of facts should not contain the elements of several of them. Since the plaintiff does not, today, have to specify the particular tort on which he wishes to rely,[1] all that is necessary for his success is that the facts of his case should include those essential to liability under one tort, without at the same time including any which are fatal to that liability. But the whole sequence of events leading up to the plaintiff's damage may include the essentials of more than one tort, and where this is so the position is simply that there is more than one reason why the plaintiff should succeed.[2] It is not, however, in accordance with the principles of the common law to analyse rights as something separate from the remedy given to the plaintiff, so that although we have abolished the procedural restrictions of the *forms* of action, it is still necessary for the plaintiff to establish a *cause* of action. It is not therefore correct to say that a person has a basic right not to have untruths told about himself, for he is only able to restrain the publication of such untruths if the circumstances in which they are disseminated fall within a specific tort such as passing off, injurious falsehood or defamation.[3]

---

[1] R.S.C., Ord. 18, r. 7; *Leakey* v. *National Trust* [1980] Q.B. 485, 514 (statement of claim expressed to be founded on nuisance but containing allegation of failure to take due care); *Hesperides Hotels Ltd.* v. *Muftizade* [1979] A.C. 508.

[2] *Letang* v. *Cooper* [1965] 1 Q.B. 232, 242–244, where Diplock L.J. states that a "cause of action" is simply a factual situation the existence of which entitles one person to obtain from the court a remedy against another person.

[3] *Kingdom of Spain* v. *Christie, Manson & Woods Ltd.* [1986] 1 W.L.R. 1120, 1129.

On the other hand, though a case may sometimes be so clear that it is unnecessary for the plaintiff, through his counsel at the hearing, to identify which of the particular torts do, in his opinion, entitle him to a remedy, it is normally prudent for him to do so. Judges are presumed to know the law, but they are entitled to and should receive the assistance of counsel. Furthermore, though there is today considerable latitude to a party to amend his pleadings even at the trial, no one is allowed to lead evidence of facts which he has not pleaded.[4] It is therefore necessary for counsel for the plaintiff, in settling the statement of claim, to plead all the facts which are essential to the particular tort or torts on which he intends to rely. He cannot, however, simply plead all the facts which led up to the plaintiff's injury for this would be to go back to the creation of the world. He is bound to select from the whole complex of facts those which are relevant to his client's claim in point of law. And this, of course, he cannot do save by reference to particular torts. Suppose that the defendant has said of the plaintiff, a shopkeeper, that the plaintiff habitually sells goods which he knows to have been stolen. Here the defendant's words prima facie fall under the tort known as "slander of title" or "injurious falsehood"[5] and also within that form of the tort of defamation known as "slander actionable per se."[6] Now it is not normally an essential of the tort of defamation that the defendant should have used the words maliciously, but this is an essential of slander of title. If, therefore, the plaintiff wishes to make use in argument of that tort he must allege in his pleading that the defendant acted with malice. Otherwise,.even though the defendant was in fact malicious, he will be precluded from proving this at the trial and so will fail to bring his case within slander of title. He will thus lose the advantage of an alternative line of argument which, on the facts as they actually occurred, should have been open to him.

We may say, therefore, that the law of tort is divided over the various nominate torts which we are now to consider, but life itself is not similarly divided. The law of tort may say, "If A, B and C, then liability in negligence" and also "If A, B and D, then liability in nuisance." Life may produce A, B, C, D, E, F, G, H. If it does, and assuming E, F, G and H to be legally irrelevant, the plaintiff should plead and prove "A, B, C, D." If he does he is entitled to succeed under the rules both of negligence and of nuisance. But this conclusion cannot, of course, be reached by one who is not familiar with the essentials of each particular tort.

The grouping of particular torts which have acquired names in any sort of classification is of no value except for purposes of exposition. And even for that it cannot possibly be scientifically complete. Following his definition of tortious liability, Winfield made the liability of the defendant and not the right of the plaintiff the root of his classification, while the modern tendency is to adopt the other course. The order followed in the succeeding chapters adheres strictly to neither course but has as its principal aim no more than

---

[4] *Farrell* v. *Secretary of State for Defence* [1980] 1 W.L.R. 172.
[5] *Post*, p. 289.
[6] *Post*, p. 301.

the avoidance, so far as possible, of repetition and of references forward to later chapters. The object is comprehensibility and the convenience of the reader who wants to begin at the beginning and go on to the end. The result is neither "historical" nor "scientific." If it is convenient, that is enough.

CHAPTER 4

TRESPASS TO THE PERSON[1]

IN its original legal meaning "trespass" signified no more than "wrong,"[2] and in early times the great bulk of trespasses were dealt with in the local courts. A trespass which was also a breach of the king's peace, however, fell within the jurisdiction of the king's courts, and in course of time the allegation that the trespass was committed *vi et armis* came to be used as common form in order to preserve the jurisdictional propriety of an action brought in those courts, whether or not there was any truth in it.[3] In its developed form the writ of trespass covered injuries to land, to goods and to the person, but the first two are today more conveniently considered in separate chapters.

There is no doubt that as a matter of history trespass to the person might be committed negligently, *i.e.* inadvertently as well as by intention,[4] though this is probably not the law in England today. We return to this point at the end of the chapter,[5] but for the moment we shall treat trespass to the person as requiring intention. There are three main forms, namely, assault, battery and false imprisonment[6] and their common element is that the wrong must be committed by "direct means."[7] Where, however, physical harm is intentionally inflicted by "indirect" means there may be liability under the so-called "rule in *Wilkinson* v. *Downton*," which is discussed later.

Civil actions for trespass to the person are not common, bearing in mind the volume of offences against the person handled by the criminal courts. No doubt this has always been so, for in trivial cases the plaintiff is likely to hesitate at the risks of civil litigation once tempers have cooled, and in serious cases the defendant may well not be worth pursuing. Furthermore, even in serious cases the existence of the Criminal Injuries Compensation Scheme[8] and the power of the criminal court to make direct compensation orders against defendants[9] nowadays do much to remove the incentive to

---

[1] See Weir, *Casebook on Tort*, (6th ed.), Chap. 8, Introduction.
[2] Milsom, *Historical Foundations of the Common Law*, (2nd ed.), p. 285; Milsom, "Trespass from Henry III to Edward III" (1958) 74 L.Q.R. 195, 407, 561.
[3] See, *e.g.* the case of 1317, cited by Milsom, *op. cit.* p. 289.
[4] *Weaver* v. *Ward* (1616) Hob. 134; *Dickenson* v. *Watson* (1681) T. Jones 205; *Dodwell* v. *Burford* (1670) 1 Mod. 24; *Gibbon* v. *Pepper* (1695) 2 Salk. 637; 1 Ld.Raym. 38; 4 Mod. 404; *Scott* v. *Shepherd* (1773) 2 W.Bl. 892.
[5] See *post*, p. 70.
[6] Trespass to the person was also the parent of some torts, now abolished, which protected family and service relationships: see *post*, p. 496.
[7] Explained *ante*, p. 42.
[8] See *ante*, p. 32.
[9] See *ante*, p. 10.

bring a civil action.[10] If reported cases are anything to go by, actions for trespass to the person tend to arise from allegedly improper police conduct[11] and to serve more as a vindication of personal liberty than as a vehicle for compensating harm. However, bearing in mind the possibility of aggravated and exemplary damages, judgments in these cases may be very substantial.[12]

ASSAULT AND BATTERY[13]

Battery is the intentional and direct application of force to another person.
Assault is an act of the defendant which causes to the plaintiff reasonable apprehension of the infliction of a battery on him by the defendant.

In popular language the word "assault" is used to describe either or both of these torts, but in this chapter it will be used in its strict sense. So, to throw water at a person is an assault but if any drops fall upon him it is battery[14]; riding a horse at a person is an assault but riding it against him is a battery. Pulling away a chair, as a practical joke, from one who is about to sit on it is probably an assault until he reaches the floor, for while he is falling he reasonably expects that the withdrawal of the chair will result in harm to him. When he comes in contact with the floor, it is a battery. Throwing over a chair on which another person is actually sitting is either a battery or one of the forms of residuary trespass to the person; either way the defendant is liable.[15]

Meaning of force

Any physical contact with the body of the plaintiff (or with his clothing) is sufficient to amount to "force": there is a battery when the defendant shoots the plaintiff from a distance just as much as when he strikes him with his fist. Mere passive obstruction, however, is not a battery[16] and the requirement that the wrong be direct means that there is no battery if I daub with filth a towel which I hope that you will use, and you unwittingly do so and befoul your face.[17] Whether the infliction of such things as heat or light or blowing smoke upon a person would be held to be battery is uncertain,[18] but there is

---

[10] But not all incentive, for common law damages may be more generous than either form of compensation. Trindade, "Intentional Torts: Some Thoughts on Assault and Battery" (1982) 2 O.J.L.S. 211 surveys the relationship of the common law and the schemes.

[11] The number of civil actions against the Metropolitan police force rose from 50 in 1973 to 126 in 1987 and of the latter 62 were successful (whereas only 3 to 4 per cent. of complaints to the Police Complaints Authority are substantiated: *The Times*, April 14, 1987).

[12] See, *e.g. White* v. *Commissioner of Metropolitan Police, The Times*, April 24, 1982.

[13] Weir, *Casebook on Tort*, (6th ed.), pp. 305–313.

[14] *Pursell* v. *Horne* (1838) 3 N. & P. 564; and, as Pollock noted (*Torts* (15th ed.), p. 159), there is much older authority in Reg.Brev. (ed. 1687), 108b (*de liquore calido super aliquo projecto*).

[15] *Per* Gibbs C.J. in *Hopper* v. *Reeve* (1817) 7 Taunt. 698, 700.

[16] *Innes* v. *Wylie* (1844) 1 C. & K. 257, 263, *per* Lord Denman. *cf. Bruce* v. *Dyer* (1966) 58 D.L.R. (2d) 211 and *Fagan* v. *Metropolitan Police Comr.* [1969] 1 Q.B. 439.

[17] This is a battery according to the *Restatement of Torts*, 2d, s.18, *comment*, but U.S. law has abandoned the requirement that the injury be "direct."

[18] See Trindade & Cane, *The Law of Torts in Australia*, p. 38. Photographing a person is not an assault: *Murray* v. *Ministry of Defence* [1985] 12 N.I.J.B. 12.

no doubt that if injury is thereby caused it would be actionable on the principle of *Wilkinson* v. *Downton*.[19] If, however, there is "force" in the technical sense, no physical hurt is necessary, for all forms of trespass are actionable *per se*. Where there is consent to the contact there is no battery[20] and the same is true if the plaintiff, though not in fact consenting, so conducts himself as to lead the defendant reasonably to believe that consent exists.[21]

Life, however, would be difficult if all bodily contact were actionable unless it could be brought within these categories or some other, specific defence and the courts have struggled to find some further ingredient to distinguish battery from legally unobjectionable conduct. In *Cole* v. *Turner*[22] Lord Holt C.J. said that "the least touching of another in anger is a battery" but this would be too narrow, for an unwanted kiss is as much actionable as a blow and "anger" might well be an inapt description of the defendant's motive. In *Collins* v. *Wilcock*[23] Robert Goff L.J. made an interesting attempt to rationalise the authorities on the basis that, quite apart from specific defences such as lawful authority in effecting an arrest or the prevention of crime, bodily contact was not actionable if it was generally acceptable in the ordinary conduct of daily life. This is more satisfactory than the somewhat artificial approach whereby a person is deemed to consent to the multitude of minor contacts, including deliberate contacts, which take place in, for example, a crowded underground station during the rush hour.[24] However, the Court of Appeal in *Wilson* v. *Pringle*[25] while not wholly rejecting this approach, has laid down that a battery involves a "hostile" touching, though this seems to mean little more than that the defendant wilfully interferes with the plaintiff in a way to which he is known to object. The actual decision was that the trial judge had been wrong to grant summary judgment under Order 14 of the Rules of the Supreme Court (which is based upon there being no triable defence to the plaintiff's claim) where the defendant, a schoolboy, had on his own admission pulled the plaintiff's bag from his shoulder and thereby caused him to fall to the ground and injure himself: such horseplay, it seems, may or may not be battery, according to whether the tribunal of fact can discern the ingredient of "hostility."[26]

Whatever the true explanation, it remains the law that touching another in the course of conversation or in order to draw his attention to something is

---

[19] *Post*, p. 68.

[20] It may be that the plaintiff has to prove absence of consent: *post*, p. 683.

[21] See, *e.g.* *O'Brien* v. *Cunard S.S. Co.* 28 N.E. 266 (1891).

[22] (1704) 6 Mod. 149.

[23] [1984] 1 W.L.R. 1172.

[24] Winfield seems to have thought that even these contacts amounted to technical batteries, for he said that "every day scores of trivial assaults and batteries are committed which never find their way into the law courts owing to the rough common sense and humour of mankind. It is not so much *de minimis non curat lex* as *de minimis non agit sapiens*".

[25] [1987] Q.B. 237. Weir, *Casebook on Tort* (6th ed.), p. 309; Glazebrook [1986] C.L.J. 379.

[26] Consider *Nash* v. *Sheen* [1953] C.L.Y. 3726 (hairdresser's application of "tone rinse" without consent a trespass). *cf.* the *Restatement*, 2d, s.18, which defines battery as a contact which is harmful or offensive to personal dignity.

no battery. Even some persistence may be justifiable, for "the lost or distressed may surely be permitted a second touch, or possibly even more on a reluctant or impervious sleeve or shoulder, as may a person who is acting reasonably in the exercise of a duty. In each case, the test must be whether the physical contact so persisted in has in the circumstances gone beyond generally accepted standards of conduct."[27] Medical treatment of an unconscious person has traditionally been regarded as lawful on the basis of implied consent (or perhaps necessity)[28] but in *Wilson* v. *Pringle* the court seems to have regarded such action as within the category of what was "acceptable in the ordinary conduct of everyday life" which it had rejected as an adequate test on the facts of the case before it. However, the court's remarks in this context are *obiter* and in *T.* v. *T.* the more traditional view was adopted that surgery, whether or not it can properly be described as "hostile" is a battery unless there is consent, express or implied.[29]

For battery there must be a voluntary act by the defendant intended to bring about the contact with the plaintiff. I do not commit battery against you if X seizes my arm and uses it like a club—here X and X alone is liable. But the act need be intentional only as to the contact and intention to bring about the harmful consequence is not required: if D pushes P into a swimming pool and injury occurs, then, assuming D's act to be "hostile," there is liability for the injury even though it was neither desired nor even foreseen by D.[30]

Assault

Assault of course requires no contact because its essence is conduct which leads the plaintiff to *apprehend* the application of force. In the majority of cases an assault precedes a battery, perhaps by only a very brief interval, but there are examples of battery in which the plaintiff has no opportunity of experiencing any apprehension *before* the force is applied, *e.g.* a blow from behind inflicted by an unseen assailant.[31] Just as there can be a battery without an assault, so also there can be an assault without a battery, as where the defendant has no intention of carrying through his threatening gesture but knows that the plaintiff is unaware of this. Similarly if the blow is intercepted or prevented by some third person. In *Stephens* v. *Myers*[32] the

---

[27] *Collins* v. *Wilcock, supra,* at p. 1178; *Wiffin* v. *Kincard* (1807) 2 Bos. & Pul. 471; *Coward* v. *Baddeley* (1859) 4 H. & N. 478.

[28] *Post,* p. 706.

[29] [1988] 2 W.L.R. 189. Since in this case the patient was permanently mentally handicapped with a mental age of three the judge regarded implied consent as "wholly unrealistic." However, the H.L. has now held that treatment in such a case can be justified on the ground of necessity: *Re F* [1989] N.L.J. 789.

[30] *Wilson* v. *Pringle* [1987] Q.B. 237, 249; *Williams* v. *Humphrey, The Times,* February 20, 1975. Of course in a very large number of cases there will be a concurrent liability in negligence, as in the latter case. *cf. Lambertson* v. *U.S.* 528 F. 2d 441 (1976) (battery claim barred by statute; could not be "dressed up" as negligence).

[31] A Biblical instance in point is the slaying of Sisera by Jael, the wife of Heber the Kenite. She drove a tent-peg through his head while he was asleep.

[32] (1840) 4 C. & P. 349.

plaintiff was in the chair at a parish meeting. The defendant, who sat at the same table some six or seven places away from the plaintiff, became vociferous and by a large majority it was resolved that he be expelled. He said he would rather pull the plaintiff out of the chair than be ejected and he advanced with clenched fist upon the plaintiff, but was stopped by the church-warden who sat next but one to the plaintiff. He was held to be liable for assault. If, however, the plaintiff has no reasonable belief that the defendant has present ability to effect his purpose there is no assault even if the conduct is intimidating or even frightening, as where pickets who made violent threats and gestures were held back by a police cordon and those who wished to work went through the gates in vehicles.[33] Where this ability is present, however, it is irrelevant that the plaintiff is courageous and is not frightened by the threat or that he could easily defeat the defendant's attack.

Though assault involves no contact it is often said that some bodily movement is required and that threatening words alone are not therefore actionable. In fact, the "authorities" on the point are only *dicta* and go both ways[34] and it is thought that there is much to be said for dropping the supposed limitation. This is not to say that threats on the telephone would be actionable for there must be a threat of an immediate battery, not a battery at some time in the future. Where there is a menacing gesture that would suffice for assault words accompanying it may negative the inference that it is so intended, as where the defendant laid his hand upon his sword and said, "If it were not assize time, I would not take such language from you"; as it was assize time, he was held not to have committed an assault.[35] Similarly it would be no assault if a landowner were to insist that a trespasser leave his land and show that he would use reasonable force in the event of a refusal; but the highwayman could not defend an action for assault by showing that he offered the plaintiff the opportunity to escape violence by handing over his money.

Pointing a loaded pistol at a person is of course an assault, but despite a curious statement to the contrary[36] it is submitted that the law is exactly the same if the pistol is unloaded unless the person at whom it is pointed knows this (or unless his distance from the weapon is so great that any reasonable person would have believed that he was out of range, in which event there would be no assault even if it were loaded).[37] Assault involves reasonable apprehension of impact of something on one's body, and unless some such factor as is mentioned above is present that is exactly what occurs when a firearm is pointed at one by an aggressor.

---

[33] *Thomas* v. *N.U.M. (South Wales Area)* [1986] Ch. 20; cf. *Smith* v. *Superintendent of Woking Police Station* [1983] Crim.L.R. 323.

[34] Not assault: *Meade's Case* (1823) 1 Lew C.C. 184. Assault: *R.* v. *Wilson* [1955] 1 W.L.R. 493. The Canadian case of *R.* v. *Byrne* (1968) 3 C.C.C. 179 supports the *Meade* view. See Williams in [1957] Crim.L.R. 219: "If a highwayman, visibly armed, says: 'Your money or your life,' should he escape the consequences of the law of assault merely because he does not trouble to point his pistol at his victim?"

[35] *Turbervell* v. *Savadge* (1669) 1 Mod. 3. cf. *R.* v. *Light* (1857) Deers & B. 332, where the physical act was perhaps rather more immediate.

[36] *Blake* v. *Barnard* (1840) 9 C. & P. 626, 628.

[37] See the Restatement, 2d, s.29 and *Logdon* v. *D.P.P.* [1976] Crim.L.R. 121.

Offences Against the Person Act 1861

Assault and battery are crimes as well as torts, and the Offences against the Person Act 1861[38] makes criminal proceedings in certain circumstances a bar to any subsequent civil proceedings. By sections 42 to 45, where a person is prosecuted before a court of summary jurisdiction and, after a hearing on the merits,[39] either the summons is dismissed and a certificate of dismissal is granted by the magistrates or he is convicted and has served his imprisonment or paid the whole amount awarded against him,[40] no further proceedings, civil or criminal, for the same cause, shall lie at the instance of anyone against that person. The Act is only a defence (a) if the proceedings are instituted by or on behalf of the party aggrieved, and not by someone else; (b) if the summons is dismissed on the merits of the case and not for some technical defect; or (c) if the proceedings are summary and not by way of indictment. The Act does not prevent proceedings against anyone other than the defendant, so that the conviction of a servant for an assault committed in the course of his employment is no bar to an action against his master.[41] Quite apart from the statutory provision there is a common law principle, founded upon public policy, whereby a person will not be allowed, in a civil action, to mount a collateral attack upon the final decision of a criminal court of competent jurisdiction. Thus where at his trial X contended that his confession was involuntary because he had been beaten up by Y but the trial judge found that it was voluntary, X's subsequent attempt to bring an action for battery against Y was dismissed as an abuse of the process of the court.[42] However, this principle would not prevent the commencement of a civil action merely because the defendant had been acquitted in a criminal court: apart altogether from substantive differences between the statutory crime and the tort, the burdens of proof are different and a verdict of acquittal in the criminal case is quite consistent with a finding of liability in the civil action.

FALSE IMPRISONMENT[43]

This is the *infliction of bodily restraint which is not expressly or impliedly authorised by the law.*

Both "false" and "imprisonment" are somewhat misleading terms. "False" does not here necessarily signify "mendacious" or "fallacious," but

---

[38] 24 & 25 Vict. c. 100. See North, "Civil and Criminal Proceedings for Assault" (1966) 29 M.L.R. 16. Alternative routes to compensation for the victim of crime are mentioned *ante,* pp. 10, 32.

[39] *Reed* v. *Nutt* (1890) 24 Q.B.D. 669 (prosecutor obtained summons, did not attend to give evidence, magistrates dismissed summons, and granted defendant certificate of dismissal. Held, certificate invalid, not having been given after a hearing on the merits, and therefore, no bar to an action); *Ellis* v. *Burton* [1975] 1 All E.R. 395 (guilty plea).

[40] It has been held in the county court that these actions afford no defence to a person who has been convicted and bound over in his own recognisances: *Gibbons* v. *Harris* [1956] C.L.Y. 8611; *Toomey* v. *Condon* (1962) 112 L.J. 497.

[41] *Dyer* v. *Munday* [1895] 1 Q.B. 742.

[42] *Hunter* v. *Chief Constable of West Midlands* [1982] A.C. 529.

[43] It is a crime as well as a tort.

is used in the less common sense of "erroneous" or "wrong."[44] And it is quite possible to commit the tort without "imprisonment" of a person in the common acceptation of that term. In fact neither physical contact nor anything resembling a prison is necessary. If a lecturer locks his class in the lecture-room after the usual time for dismissal has arrived, that is false imprisonment; so, too, if a man be restrained from leaving his own house or any part of it,[45] or be forcibly detained in the public streets.[46] "Imprisonment," says the old *Termes de la Ley*,[47] "is the restraint of a man's liberty whether it be in the open field, or in the stocks or cage in the street, or in a man's own house, as well as in the common gaol. And in all these places the party so restrained is said to be a prisoner, so long as he hath not his liberty freely to go at all times to all places whither he will, without bail or mainprize."[48] This definition (with due elimination of the archaisms in it) was accepted by the Court of Appeal in *Meering* v. *Grahame-White Aviation Co. Ltd.*[49]

There is no false imprisonment where the plaintiff consents to the defendant's order, but he is not to be taken as consenting simply because he does not resist by force.[50] A difficult line must be drawn between consent on the one hand and peaceful but unwilling submission to express or implied threats of force or asserted legal authority (whether valid or not) on the other.[51]

Knowledge of plaintiff [52]

It had been held in *Grainger* v. *Hill*[53] that imprisonment is possible even if the plaintiff is too ill to move in the absence of any restraint. In *Meering's* case the court went much further by holding that the tort is committed even if the plaintiff did not know that he was being detained.[54] The facts were that

---

[44] Salmond and Heuston, *Torts,* (19th ed.), p. 137, n. 50.

[45] *Warner* v. *Riddiford* 4 C.B.(N.S.) 180 (1858).

[46] Blackstone, Comm., iii, 127. *cf.* the wedding guest detained by Coleridge's Ancient Mariner:
"He holds him with his glittering eye—
The wedding-guest stood still,
And listens like a three years' child,
The Mariner hath his will."
Would restraint by post-hypnotic suggestion suffice? There seems to be no reason why it should not be false imprisonment if the victim would not have assented to it.

[47] Its first edition was about 1520.

[48] A person bailed is theoretically in the custody of his sureties; a person mainprized (now wholly obsolete) is at large.

[49] (1920) 122 L.T. 44, 51, 53.

[50] Resistance to arrest is generally unwise, because the arrest may turn out to be lawful.

[51] See Prosser, *Torts,* (5th ed.), pp. 50–51. Thus there is no false imprisonment when the plaintiff complies with a police request to accompany them to the police station, but the tort is committed if the "request" is made in such a manner as to lead the plaintiff to believe he has no choice in the matter.

[52] There appears to be no authority on the state of mind of the defendant. Historically, there is something to be said for the view that negligence should suffice (*e.g.* locking a room without checking whether there is anyone inside: see Street, *Torts,* (8th ed.), p. 28) but false imprisonment is a species of trespass to the person and intention is probably now required for all forms of this wrong. However, if damage is suffered, an action on the case for negligence will lie and being deprived of one's liberty for a substantial period is surely damage? *cf. Sayers* v. *Harlow U.D.C.* [1958] 1 W.L.R. 623.

[53] (1838) 4 Bing.N.C. 212.

[54] *Contra* the *Restatement of Torts,* 2d, ss.35, 42. But the *Restatement* imposes liability if the plaintiff is harmed by the confinement and gives a wide meaning to harm.

the plaintiff, being suspected of stealing a keg of varnish from the defendants, his employers, was asked by two of their police to go with them to the company's office. He assented and at his suggestion they took a short cut there. On arrival he was taken or invited to go to the waiting-room, the two policemen remaining in the neighbourhood. In an action for false imprisonment the defence was that the plaintiff was perfectly free to go where he liked, that he knew it and that he did not desire to go away. But it was held by a majority of the Court of Appeal that the defendants were liable because the plaintiff from the moment that he came under the influence of the police was no longer a free man. Atkin L.J. said: "It appears to me that a person could be imprisoned without his knowing it. I think a person can be imprisoned while he is asleep, while he is in a state of drunkenness, while he is unconscious, and while he is a lunatic.[55] . . . Of course the damages might be diminished and would be affected by the question whether he was conscious of it or not." The learned Lord Justice's ground for this opinion was that, although a person might not know he was imprisoned, his captors might be boasting elsewhere that he was.[56] This point might be regarded as more relevant to defamation than to false imprisonment, but Atkin L.J.'s view has been approved, *obiter*,[57] by the House of Lords in an appeal from Northern Ireland, *Murray* v. *Ministry of Defence*[58] though with the rider that a person who is unaware that he has been falsely imprisoned and has suffered no harm can normally[59] expect to recover no more than nominal damages. The curious old case of *Herring* v. *Boyle*[60] where it was held that there was no false imprisonment of a schoolboy wrongfully kept at school during holidays, in the absence of evidence that he was aware of the restraint, must be regarded as wrongly decided. The basis of the law as stated in *Meering* and *Murray* is no doubt that personal liberty is supremely important so that interference with it must be deterred even where there is no consciousness nor harm.

Restraint must be complete

The tort is not committed unless motion be restrained in every direction. In *Bird* v. *Jones*[61] the defendants wrongfully enclosed part of the public footway on Hammersmith Bridge, put seats in it for the use of spectators of a regatta on the river, and charged for admission to the enclosure. The plaintiff insisted on passing along this part of the footpath, and climbed over the fence of the enclosure without paying the charge. The defendants refused to let him go forward, but he was told that he might go back into the

---

[55] Even if it be accepted that the tort is committed in these cases, did not Meering consent to remaining in the room?
[56] (1920) 122 L.T. 44, 53–54.
[57] Because on the facts the plaintiff was aware she was under restraint.
[58] [1988] 1 W.L.R. 692.
[59] Perhaps this is intended as a reference to the possibility of exemplary damages where there is arbitrary, oppressive or unconstitutional action: *post*, p. 603.
[60] (1834) 1 Cr. M. & R. 377.
[61] (1845) 7 Q.B. 742; Weir, *Casebook on Tort*, (6th ed.), p. 296.

carriage way and cross to the other side of the bridge if he wished. He declined to do so and remained in the enclosure for half an hour. The defendants were held not to have committed false imprisonment.[62]

Means of escape

If a person has the means of escape, but does not know it, it is submitted that his detention is nevertheless false imprisonment unless any reasonable man would have realised that he had an available outlet. Thus, if I pretend to turn the key of the door of a room in which you are and take away the key, it would seem unreasonable if you made no attempt to see whether the door was in fact locked. A more difficult case is that in which you have a duplicate key in your pocket but have forgotten its existence. A reasonable man may suffer from a lapse of memory.

Defences

Most of the defences depend upon conditions which in general negate liability in tort.[63] Some particular cases may be mentioned here.

(1) *Reasonable condition*[64]

It is no tort to prevent a man from leaving your premises because he will not fulfil a reasonable condition subject to which he entered them. In *Robinson* v. *Balmain Ferry Co. Ltd.*[65] the plaintiff paid a penny for entry to the defendants' wharf from which he proposed to cross the river by one of the defendants' ferry-boats. A boat had just gone and, as there was not another one for 20 minutes, the plaintiff wished to leave the wharf and was directed to the turnstile which was its exit. There he refused to pay another penny which was chargeable for exit, as was stated on a notice-board, and the defendant declined to let him leave the wharf unless he did pay. The Judicial Committee held that this was not false imprisonment. "There is no law requiring the defendants to make the exit from their premises gratuitous to people who come there upon a definite contract which involves their leaving the wharf by another way. ... The question whether the notice which was affixed to these premises was brought home to the knowledge of the plaintiff is immaterial, because the notice itself is immaterial."[66] And the court regarded the charge of a penny for exit as reasonable. It must be stressed that it was crucial to the decision in this case that the plaintiff had

---

[62] But if the plaintiff suffers damage (*e.g.* misses an important appointment), an action on the case might lie.
[63] *Post*, Chap. 26. See too *Liversidge* v. *Anderson* [1942] A.C. 206 (Reg. 18B of the Defence (General) Regs. 1939). *cf. Kuchenmeister* v. *Home Office* [1958] 1 Q.B. 496 (Aliens Order 1953); *Buxton* v. *Jayne* [1960] 1 W.L.R. 783 (Lunacy Act 1890).
[64] See Trindade and Cane, *Law of Torts in Australia*, pp. 49–52.
[65] [1910] A.C. 295; Weir, *Casebook on Tort* (6th ed.), p. 300. Amos, "A Note on Contractual Restraint of Liberty" (1928) 44 L.Q.R. 464.
[66] [1910] A.C. 295, 299; *cf.* Viscount Haldane L.C. in *Herd* v. *Weardale Steel Co. Ltd.* [1915] A.C. 67, 72.

contracted to leave the wharf by a different route. Nonetheless, the decision is a strong one because it amounts, in effect, to recognising extra-judicial imprisonment as a method of enforcing contractual rights.[67]

A similar case, but one containing a further difficulty, is *Herd* v. *Weardale, etc., Co. Ltd.*[68] A miner, in breach of his contract of employment with the defendants, refused to do certain work allotted to him in the mine, and demanded to be taken to the surface by the lift five hours before his shift expired. He was not allowed to leave for 20 minutes. The essential difference between this case and *Robinson's* was that the conduct of the defendants was an omission rather than a positive act of restraint. Since false imprisonment is a form of trespass it might have been held that this was a sufficient answer to the claim[69] but the House of Lords seems to have accepted that breach of a contractual duty to bring the miner to the surface might have founded the action. On the facts, however, there was no breach of such a duty.

(2) *Imprisonment and arrest*

A lawful sentence of imprisonment passed by a court provides a complete defence to an action for false imprisonment[70] and, whatever may be the position as to judicial review, a change in the conditions in which the prisoner is kept gives rise to no action for false imprisonment.[71] However, in a case involving detention in a police cell it has been said that keeping a person in conditions threatening his health would render the detention unlawful.[72]

A lawful arrest is, of course, no false imprisonment and it follows that a person who arrests another in pursuance of a valid warrant cannot be sued.[73] The law concerning arrest without warrant is mainly contained in the Police and Criminal Evidence Act 1984. Only an outline is given here and more detail must be sought in books on constitutional law or civil liberties.

[67] A right denied in *Bahner* v. *Marwest Hotel* (1970) 12 D.L.R. (3d) 646. The plaintiff in *Robinson's* case was, after a short time, allowed to leave by squeezing past the turnstile. Could the defendants have kept him there indefinitely?

Winfield also put the cases of a person getting on the wrong bus and not being allowed to leave without paying the minimum fare; and of a student who mistakenly enters the wrong lecture-room and is not allowed by the lecturer to leave until the end of the hour on the ground that he will interrupt the discourse (though one would have thought, that the effort of keeping him there would cause a good deal more interruption). He suggested that in each case the decision must turn upon whether (*a*) the mistake was a reasonable one, and (*b*) the condition as to exit was a reasonable one.

Tan Keng Fen in "A Misconceived Issue in the Tort of False Imprisonment" (1981) 44 M.L.R. 166 argues that neither *Robinson's* case nor *Herd* v. *Weardale Steel Co.*, *infra*, supports the view stated in the text, and that a person may always withdraw his consent to restraints upon his liberty, though he may not demand instant release if that would be unduly inconvenient. However, he admits that the *result* of neither case is easily reconcilable with this view.

[68] [1915] A.C. 67. *cf. Whittaker* v. *Sandford* 85 A. 399 (1912).
[69] Though not, of course, if damage had been alleged.
[70] For excess of jurisdiction, see p. 664, *post*. See the Criminal Justice Act 1988 for provision for compensation for erroneous convictions.
[71] *Williams* v. *Home Office (No. 2)* [1981] 1 All E.R. 1211; *R.* v. *Board of Visitors, Gartree Prison, ex p. Sears, The Times*, March 20, 1985.
[72] *Middleweek* v. *Chief Constable of Merseyside, The Times*, August 1, 1985.
[73] See *post*, p. 666.

First, the common law gives the police no power to detain for questioning[74] or to detain otherwise than by way of arrest,[75] but section 1(2) of the 1984 Act gives a police officer power to stop and search any person or vehicle for stolen or prohibited[76] goods if he has reasonable grounds to believe that such goods will be found. As to arrest, the "core" provision is section 24, which is a modified form of the law previously contained in the Criminal Law Act 1967; before that Act, the law of arrest turned on the now defunct distinction between felonies and misdemeanours. An arrest may be made without a warrant for an "arrestable" offence which means (*a*) offences for which the sentence is fixed by law,[77] (*b*) those for which a person may on a first conviction be sentenced to imprisonment for five years or more and (*c*) offences specifically listed in section 24(2) of the Act, for example offences under the customs and excise legislation and taking a motor vehicle without authority. In addition, the power of arrest applies to attempts and conspiracies in relation to such offences and to inciting, abetting or procuring them. A fundamental distinction is drawn between the powers of private citizens and the wider powers granted to police officers. *Anyone* (including, of course, a police officer) may arrest without warrant anyone who is in the act of committing an arrestable offence or anyone whom he has reasonable grounds for suspecting to be committing such an offence.[78] This power does not allow arrest where the offence has been completed, but under section 24(5), where an arrestable offence has been committed, any person may arrest without warrant anyone who is guilty of the offence or anyone whom he has reasonable grounds for suspecting to be guilty of it. In other words, where the offence has been committed there may be a defence even if the arrester "gets the wrong man." The powers of a police officer are, however, wider in two respects. First, he may arrest without warrant anyone whom he suspects on reasonable grounds to have committed an offence even though the offence has not in fact been committed.[79] Secondly, a police officer may arrest without warrant anyone who is or whom he has reasonable grounds for suspecting to be about to commit an arrestable offence.[80]

A further provision, which largely though not entirely[81] replaces numerous statutory powers of arrest, gives a police officer, who has reasonable grounds for suspecting that a non-arrestable offence has been committed or is being committed or attempted, power to arrest the suspected person if it appears to him that service of a summons is impracticable or inappropriate

---

[74] A person who voluntarily attends at a police station for questioning cannot be detained there unless he is lawfully arrested: Police and Criminal Evidence Act 1984, s.29.

[75] But in *Murray* v. *Ministry of Defence* [1988] 1 W.L.R. 692 it is suggested that there may be power to restrain the movement of A for a short time if reasonably necessary to effect the lawful arrest of B.

[76] *i.e.* offensive weapons or things used for offences of dishonesty.

[77] *e.g.* murder.

[78] s.24(4).

[79] s.24(6). There is therefore preserved the somewhat anomalous rule in *Walters* v. *W.H. Smith & Son Ltd.* [1914] 1 K.B. 595 whereby the liability of a private person for false imprisonment may depend upon the outcome of a criminal trial (not necessarily of the person arrested) which takes place after the arrest was made. A private person arresting on suspicion of an arrestable offence must prove not only reasonable grounds for his suspicion but also that the arrestable offence in question has been committed by someone.

[80] s.24(7).

[81] Various powers are preserved in Sched. 2 of the Act.

because any of the "general arrest conditions" is satisfied.[82] These conditions cover various circumstances such as where the suspected person's name or address for service is unknown (or the officer reasonably doubts whether the name and address given is the real one) or there are reasonable grounds for believing that he will cause injury or damage.[83]

In addition to these powers under the 1984 Act any person may use such force including detention,[84] as is reasonable in the circumstances[85] in the prevention of crime, or in effecting or assisting in the lawful arrest of offenders, suspected offenders or persons unlawfully at large[86]; and there still exists a common law power to arrest to prevent an imminent breach of the peace.

The burden of proof of justifying an arrest is upon the person effecting it and if he fails to do so he is liable for false imprisonment and, where there has been a threatened or actual use of force, no matter how minor, for assault or battery as well. Many powers of arrest depend on reasonable grounds for suspicion[87] and in this connection it is obviously necessary first to establish that the arrester actually did suspect the plaintiff[88] but there must also be an objective basis for that state of mind. Reasonable suspicion is less than prima facie proof, if only because the latter must be based on admissible evidence, whereas suspicion can take into account other matters as well[89] and Lord Devlin has said that "suspicion in its ordinary meaning is a state of conjecture or surmise where proof is lacking: 'I suspect but I cannot prove.' Suspicion arises at or near the starting point of an investigation of which the obtaining of prima facie proof is at the end."[90] Though in no way binding on the courts,[91] the Code of Practice promulgated for the purposes of section 1(2) of the Police and Criminal Evidence Act 1984 draws a distinction between "mere suspicion," which is "a hunch or instinct which cannot be explained or justified to any objective observer," and "reasonable suspicion" with "some concrete basis . . . related to the individual person concerned, which can be considered or evaluated by an objective third person." According to the Code reasonable suspicion cannot be supported simply on the basis of a "higher than average chance that the person has committed . . . an offence, for example because he belongs to a group within

---

[82] s.25(1).

[83] See s.25(3).

[84] *Albert* v. *Lavin* [1982] A.C. 546.

[85] Clearly there must be some proportionality between the force and the crime prevented, but the issue is treated as one of fact: *Att.-Gen. for Northern Ireland's Reference (No. 1 of 1975)* [1977] A.C. 105. This is open to criticism, *inter alia*, on the ground that it gives insufficient guidance to persons using force. See generally Doran (1987) 7 L.S. 291. Compare Art. 2 of the European Convention on Human Rights, which allows fatal force where "absolutely necessary" to prevent unlawful violence, to effect a lawful arrest or quell riot or insurrection.

[86] Criminal Law Act 1967, s.3. See also Public Order Act 1986.

[87] Certain powers of entry and search require that there be "reasonable grounds to believe," which seems to be a higher standard.

[88] *Siddique* v. *Swain* [1979] R.T.R. 474.

[89] *Hussain* v. *Chong Fook Kam* [1970] A.C. 943, 949. Weir, *Casebook on Tort* (6th ed.), p. 338.

[90] *Ibid.* at p. 948; *Dumbell* v. *Roberts* [1944] 1 All E.R. 326; *Dallison* v. *Caffery* [1965] 1 Q.B. 348.

[91] A failure by a police officer to comply with any of the Codes of Practice does not of itself render him liable to any criminal or civil proceedings but may be treated by the court as relevant to any question arising in such proceedings: s.67(10), (11).

which offenders of a certain kind are relatively common." In *Dallison* v. *Caffery*[92] where a theft had undoubtedly been committed, the defendant police officer had received trustworthy information that the plaintiff had been identified as the man responsible and it was held that therefore the arrest was justified. In *Hogg* v. *Ward*,[93] on the other hand, a police constable was held liable for arresting the plaintiff on a mistaken charge of theft made by the owner of some harness because the constable ought to have known, from the plaintiff's open use of the property and his immediate statement of facts which raised a reasonable inference that he had acquired it honestly, that arrest was not justifiable in the circumstances.

The existence of reasonable grounds for suspicion gives the police officer a discretion whether or not to arrest, and like other public officers invested with a discretion he must exercise it in good faith and without taking into account irrelevant matters.[94] Reasonable suspicion is a condition precedent of the rightfulness of an arrest, but it is not conclusive. However, in *Holgate-Mohammed* v. *Duke*[95] it was held that the constable's belief that the plaintiff would be more likely to confess by being questioned at the police station was a legitimate reason for exercising the discretion to arrest and did not render the arrest unlawful.[96]

(a) *Information of charge*

It was established at common law in *Christie* v. *Leachinsky*[97] that in ordinary circumstances a person arrested must be informed of the ground on which he is arrested: the officer is not entitled to remain silent or to fabricate a "holding charge." The law is now to be found in section 28 of the Police and Criminal Evidence Act 1984 and the position with regard to arrest by a police officer is as follows: where a person is arrested otherwise than by being informed that he is under arrest (for example, where he is physically seized) he must as soon as practicable[98] be informed that he is under arrest even if the fact is obvious and also of the ground for the arrest, again even if it is obvious. The only qualification to these duties is that they do not apply if it was not reasonably practicable for the information to be given because the plaintiff escaped from custody before it could be given. Where the arrest is by a private individual he does not have to inform the plaintiff of the fact of the arrest or of the ground where it is obvious. As to what is required by way

---

[92] *Supra*, decided under the common law where the test was whether there was reasonable and probable cause for the arrest.

[93] (1858) 27 L.J.Ex. 443. See also *Holtham* v. *Metropolitan Police Commissioner, The Times*, January 8, 1987 (emergence of new factor during investigation required police to re-examine the suspicion to see whether it could be reasonably maintained).

[94] That is to say, according to the principles laid down in *Associated Provincial Picture Houses Ltd.* v. *Wednesbury Corp.* [1948] 1 K.B. 223.

[95] [1984] A.C. 437.

[96] Using detention to question the suspect was described by the Royal Commission on Criminal Procedure as "one of the primary purposes of detention upon arrest." Cmnd. 8092 (1981), para. 3.66.

[97] [1947] A.C. 573.

[98] *Quaere* whether this is more onerous than "reasonably practicable." In *Murray* v. *Ministry of Defence* [1988] 1 W.L.R. 692 where the arrest was under emergency legislation it was held lawful to postpone the words of arrest until the premises had been searched, for fear of violent resistance from other persons.

of information the cases before the Act will no doubt be of persuasive value: technical or precise language need not be used[99] but sufficient detail should be given to enable him to understand the factual as well as the legal nature of what he is accused of, so that, for example, "you are under arrest for burglary" is insufficient without information of when and where.[1]

(b) *Detention after arrest*

Where the arrest is by a private individual the arrested person must be taken before a magistrate or a police officer, not necessarily forthwith, but as soon as is reasonably possible. For example, a person arrested in the street by a store detective on suspicion of shoplifting may be taken back to the store while the matter is reported to the store manager, and may be detained there while the police are sent for.[2] It is unlikely that he would be allowed to take the suspect to the suspect's house to see whether any of the stolen property is there, though it was held that a police office could do so.[3]

The position after a police arrest was radically modified by the Police and Criminal Evidence Act 1984. By section 30 a person arrested otherwise than at a police station must be taken to a police station as soon as practicable after his arrest, unless his presence elsewhere is necessary in order to carry out such investigations as it is reasonable to carry out immediately.[4] The time for which and the conditions in which he may be held are then governed by Part IV of the Act and since section 34(1) provides that a person "shall not be kept in police detention" except in accordance with Part IV a contravention presumably creates a case of false imprisonment. These provisions are much too detailed to examine here but very broadly the position is as follows. The custody officer at the police station may detain the arrested person without charging him[5] for up to 24[6] hours. If he has not then been charged, further detention of another 12 hours may be authorised by an officer of the rank of superintendent or above if he has reasonable grounds for believing that—

(*a*) the detention ... without charge is necessary to secure or preserve evidence relating to an offence for which [the suspect] is under arrest or to obtain such evidence by questioning him;

(*b*) an offence for which he is under arrest is a serious arrestable offence[7]; and

---

[99] *Ibid.* Hence "you are under arrest for killing X" would be sufficient; and if the ground given was "the murder of X" the arrest is valid even if the charge is eventually manslaughter.
[1] *R.* v. *Telfer* [1976] Crim.L.R. 562.
[2] *John Lewis & Co. Ltd.* v. *Tims* [1952] A.C. 676.
[3] *Dallison* v. *Caffery* [1965] 1 Q.B. 348.
[4] Thus preserving *Dallison* v. *Caffery, supra.*
[5] Though if there is sufficient evidence to charge him it must be done forthwith.
[6] These time periods are approximate: s.45(2).
[7] See s.116.

(c) the investigation is being conducted diligently and expeditiously.

Detention without charge beyond 36 hours up to a maximum of 96 hours can only be authorised by a magistrates' court[8] the requirements being the same as those for further detention authorised by a superintendent. No further detention without charge is allowed and the suspect must either be released or charged, in which latter event he must be brought before a magistrates' court as soon as practicable (and in any event not later than the first sitting after he has been charged) so that the decision may be taken whether he should be remanded in custody or bailed.

Various matters ancillary to detention are dealt with in Part V. Contravention of the provisions on searches and fingerprinting will presumably lead to liability for battery but will not render the detention unlawful, but it is by no means clear that there is any civil sanction attached to the provisions dealing with the suspect's right to have someone informed of his arrest or access to legal advice.[9]

Awards of damages for false imprisonment by the police can be very substantial even without the addition of aggravated or exemplary[10] damages.[11] Where the unlawful detention is continuing the plaintiff may seek a writ of habeas corpus: this is not often used but it has certainly not fallen into disuse.[12] A person who is unlawfully detained may use self-help to escape, including reasonable force[13] though this is a risky course since the power of arrest is likely to depend not only upon the commission of an offence but, in the alternative, upon a reasonable suspicion thereof. Hence, even an innocent man who forcibly resists arrest may be liable in tort for battery if the arrester had reasonable grounds for his suspicion.[14]

Distinction from abuse of procedure

A defendant may be liable for false imprisonment even though he did not personally detain the plaintiff, so long as he acted through an intermediary who exercised no independent discretion of his own. In *Austin* v. *Dowling*[15] a police inspector refused to take the responsibility of arresting B on a charge made by A, but finally did arrest B when A signed the charge sheet. It

---

[8] s.43.
[9] Clayton and Tomlinson, *Civil Actions Against the Police*, p. 313, suggest an action for breach of statutory duty.
[10] See *post*, p. 602.
[11] Clayton and Tomlinson, *loc. cit.*, pp. 369–373 where a number of awards equivalent to some hundreds of pounds an hour are noted.
[12] *R.* v. *Holmes, ex p. Sherman* [1981] 2 All E.R. 612.
[13] Though it is a question of fact, one might ask what force is reasonable to avoid a few hours in police custody?
[14] In the criminal law the defendant's mistaken belief in circumstances which, if they existed, would make his resistance lawful may provide him with a defence even if the mistake is unreasonable (*Beckford* v. *The King* [1988] A.C. 130) but the civil law is probably less generous: *post*, p. 704.
[15] (1870) L.R. 5 C.P. 534. *cf. Pike* v. *Waldrum* [1952] 1 Lloyd's Rep. 431. See also Weir, *Casebook on Tort*, (6th ed.), pp. 302–303; Kodilinye (1979) 28 I.C.L.Q. 766.

was held that A could be liable for false imprisonment. There can, however, be no false imprisonment if a discretion is interposed between the defendant's act and the plaintiff's detention. If, for example, A makes a charge against B before a magistrate and the magistrate then decides to order the arrest of B, A has set in motion not a ministerial but a judicial officer exercising a discretion of his own and A cannot be liable for false imprisonment.[16] He may, however, be liable for abuse of legal procedure, an entirely different matter which is considered in detail in a later chapter. For the present it is sufficient to note that whereas in false imprisonment the plaintiff need prove no more than his detention, leaving it to the defendant to prove its lawfulness if he can,[17] in malicious prosecution, the best known form of abuse of procedure, the plaintiff must prove that the defendant (a) instituted a prosecution of him which (b) ended in his favour and (c) was instituted without reasonable and probable cause and (d) was malicious. It is true the plaintiff may still succeed in the absence of both (a) and (b) if he was actually arrested[18] but he must still prove as distinct matters both absence of reasonable and probable cause and also malice.

INTENTIONAL PHYSICAL HARM OTHER THAN TRESPASSES TO THE PERSON[19]

An act wilfully done which is calculated to cause, and actually does cause, physical harm to another person is a tort although it may not, according to current practice, be treated either as a trespass to the person or as any other specific tort.

This statement of principle is quite modern and its limits have not been explored in the law courts. It was laid down by Wright J. in *Wilkinson* v. *Downton*,[20] where A, by way of practical joke, falsely told the plaintiff, a married woman, that her husband had met with an accident whereby both his legs were broken. She believed this and was so violently upset by the consequent nervous shock that she had a serious illness. A was held liable. Some attempt was made by counsel to base the claim on deceit as a tort, but the learned judge indicated that this would have been an extension of that tort, presumably because it is necessary that there the injured party should be intended to *act* upon the false statement and should have acted upon it, and here the plaintiff could scarcely be said to have acted in any way by falling ill.[21] Wright J. preferred the following ground: "The defendant has ... wilfully done an act calculated to cause harm to the plaintiff—that is to say, to infringe her legal right to personal safety, and has in fact thereby caused physical harm to her. That proposition without more appears to me

---

[16] *Austin* v. *Dowling, supra,* at p. 540, *per* Willes J.; *Sewell* v. *National Telephone Co. Ltd.* [1907] 1 K.B. 557.
[17] *Ante,* p. 64.
[18] *Melia* v. *Neate* [1863] 3 F. & F. 757; *Roy* v. *Prior* [1971] A.C. 470. See *post,* Chap. 19.
[19] Weir, *Casebook on Tort,* (6th ed.), p. 290.
[20] [1897] 2 Q.B. 57.
[21] The plaintiff recovered in deceit the sum of 1s. 10½ d. for railway fares. *cf. Beaulne* v. *Ricketts* 96 D.L.R. (3d) 550 (1979).

to state a good cause of action there being no justification alleged for the act."[22]

Since *Wilkinson* v. *Downton* no other example of the principle in that case has appeared in the English reports, except *Janvier* v. *Sweeney*,[23] in which on similar facts *Wilkinson's* case was approved by the Court of Appeal. There is no ground for thinking that the principle is limited to harm arising from a *statement, e.g.* if I scare a person into nervous shock by dressing up as a ghost.[24] Nor need the principle be confined to nervous shock.[25] If I suddenly shout at a child who is descending a narrow staircase, intending the child to fall, I am surely liable if it does so and breaks its neck. Indeed, there seems no reason why the same principle should not extend to damage to property, so that I would also be liable for the child's clothing damaged in the fall.[26] The administration of a noxious drug to an unwitting victim may be another illustration of this tort, although it would not be the tort of battery for there is no application of force (if accompanied by false representations, it might also be the tort of deceit). The principle would also extend to the intentional infection of another person with disease. If the disease is a venereal one contracted from cohabitation, the position is doubtful, although it is hard to see why fraudulent concealment by the person suffering from the disease should not negative the victim's consent to cohabitation and thus make the infection a tortious battery.[27]

The extent of the defendant's liability for a wilful and unjustifiable act of this nature is not quite clear. "Calculated to cause harm" is ambiguous, since it could refer to harm actually contemplated by the defendant or to harm which a reasonable person would foresee as a probable result.[28] In some cases it may be that actual intention or recklessness by the defendant at least as to the broad nature of the harm suffered is necessary[29]; but there are other cases falling under this head where the act would, even if done negligently, entail liability for any consequences which could be foreseen by a reasonable man.[30]

---

[22] [1897] 2 Q.B. 57, 58–59.

[23] [1919] 2 K.B. 316. *cf. Bunyan* v. *Jordan* (1937) 57 C.L.R. 1 (High Court of Australia). See also Fleming, *The Law of Torts*, (7th ed.), pp. 30–33.

[24] *cf. Blakeley* v. *Shortal's Estate* 20 N.W. 2d 28 (1945) (defendant cut his throat in plaintiff's kitchen).

[25] However, in the U.S.A. *Wilkinson* v. *Downton* has been generalised into a principle of liability for shock or distress caused by extreme and outrageous conduct. See Prosser, *Torts*, (5th ed.), pp. 54–64. Damages have been recovered in many cases even though there has been no physical hurt or mental trauma amounting to illness. No Commonwealth court appears to have gone so far; for an argument that they should do so, see Trindade (1986) 6 O.J.L. S.219.

[26] There would be no trespass to goods because there is no "direct" injury: see *post*, p. 468. But to extend this principle to *all* harms would subvert the limitations on the economic torts (*post*, Chap. 18): See Fleming, *The Law of Torts*, (7th ed.), p. 32, n. 54.

[27] *Post*, p. 686.

[28] In *Janvier* v. *Sweeney, supra*, the jury specifically found that the defendant knew that injury might be caused. The report of *Wilkinson* v. *Downton* does not set out the findings of the jury but at [1897] 2 Q.B. 59 Wright J. says: "This wilful *injuria* is in law malicious, although no malicious purpose to cause the harm which was caused . . . is imputed to the defendant. . . . It is difficult to imagine that such a statement . . . could fail to produce grave effects under the circumstances . . . and therefore an intention to produce such an effect must be imputed."

[29] Required by the *Restatement of Torts*, 2d, s.46.

[30] See, *e.g.* the example given above of frightening a child by making a loud noise and *cf. Slatter* v. *British Railways Board* (1966) 110 S.J. 688. Further, there seems reason to think that inadvertent infection with disease could be actionable as negligence: Clerk and Lindsell, *Torts*, (16th ed.), para. 10–74.

TRESPASS TO THE PERSON AND NEGLIGENCE

It is unlikely that it was ever the law that a person could be liable in trespass if he was wholly without fault.[31] However, it certainly was once the law that if the defendant committed a "direct" wrong against the plaintiff he was liable unless he established some justification or excuse (which included, in our terminology, that he had exercised all due care).[32] Since a party was generally required to plead only those matters in respect of which the burden of proof lay on him, a declaration[33] which alleged that "the defendant struck the plaintiff" was perfectly good. If the plaintiff proved this by evidence he did not necessarily win the action for the defendant might be able to show, for example, that the blow was a blameless accident or that it was inflicted in the course of effecting a lawful arrest; but failure to plead and prove such matters meant that the plaintiff won—it was not incumbent upon him to show intention or negligence in the defendant. In contrast, in an action on the case, or negligence as we would call it, the plaintiff bore the burden of showing that the defendant's conduct failed to come up to the standard required by law. To this rule about the burden of proof in trespass, collisions on the highway were an exception.[34] The origin of this rule is obscure and Winfield, in common with most other writers, regarded it as both exceptional and historically unjustifiable.[35] Nevertheless, in *National Coal Board* v. *Evans*[36] Cohen L.J. said he could see no logical reason for restricting it to highway accidents, and in *Fowler* v. *Lanning*[37] Diplock J. held generally that the burden of proving negligence in actions for unintentional trespass to the person lay upon the plaintiff.[38] Accordingly, the plaintiff's statement of claim, which recorded laconically that "the defendant shot the plaintiff" was struck out as disclosing no cause of action since it lacked an allegation of intention or negligence. Some years later, the relationship between trespass and negligence came before the Court of Appeal in the context of limitation of actions. In *Letang* v. *Cooper*[39] the defendant drove his car over the legs of the plaintiff, who was sunbathing on a piece of grass outside an hotel where cars were parked. She did not issue a writ until more than three years had elapsed and this meant that a claim in negligence was statute-barred[40] but she argued that she had an alternative claim in trespass, which was not. This

---

[31] Winfield, "The Myth of Absolute Liability" (1926) 42 L.Q.R. 37; *cf.* Milsom (1958) 74 L.Q.R. at pp. 582–583. See also Winfield and Goodhart, "Trespass and Negligence" (1933) 49 L.Q.R. 359; *Fowler* v. *Lanning* [1959] 1 Q.B. 426, 433, *per* Diplock J.

[32] *Weaver* v. *Ward* (1616) Hob. 134; *Stanley* v. *Powell* [1891] 1 Q.B. 86.

[33] Nowadays the statement of claim.

[34] *Holmes* v. *Mather* (1875) L.R. 10 Ex. 261; *Southport Corporation* v. *Esso Petroleum Co. Ltd.* [1956] A.C. 218, 225–227, *per* Devlin J., affd. by the House of Lords, *ibid.*

[35] Winfield and Goodhart, *loc. cit.*, p. 376. The question could still be the subject of dispute in South Australia in 1980: *Lord* v. *The Nominal Defendant* (1980) 24 S.A.S.R. 458.

[36] [1951] 2 K.B. 861, 875.

[37] [1959] 1 Q.B. 426; Weir, *Casebook on Tort* (6th ed.), p. 285. See (1959) 75 L.Q.R. 161; Glanville Williams [1959] C.L.J. 330; Dworkin (1959) 22 M.L.R. 538.

[38] The same result had been reached in Massachusetts as long ago as 1850 (*Brown* v. *Kendall* 6 Cush. (60 Mass.) 292. *cf.* *Kopka* v. *Bell Telephone Co. of Pennsylvania* 91 A. (2d) 232 (1952).

[39] [1965] 1 Q.B. 232; Weir, *Casebook on Tort* (6th ed.), p. 288; Dworkin (1965) 28 M.L.R. 92.

[40] Limitation Act 1939, s.2(1), as amended by the Law Reform (Limitation of Actions, etc.) Act 1954, s.2(1). The result would not necessarily be the same today on this point: Limitation Act 1980, s.11.

argument succeeded before Elwes J. but was rejected by the Court of Appeal. One reason, which need not detain us, was that an action for trespass to the person fell within the terms of the Act,[41] but the court went a good deal further. According to Diplock L.J., a cause of action is simply a factual situation the existence of which entitles a person to obtain a remedy from the court and an action founded upon a failure to take reasonable care is an action for negligence notwithstanding that it can also be called an action for trespass to the person,[42] in particular, the plaintiff must show damage and has the burden of proof of negligence.[43] Lord Denning M.R. expressed his agreement with *Fowler* v. *Lanning* but added, "I would go this one step further: when the injury[44] is not inflicted intentionally, but negligently, I would say the only cause of action is negligence and not trespass."[45] In *Wilson* v. *Pringle*[46] the Court of Appeal referred to the necessity for the touching in trespass to be "deliberate" and that is really the only view reconcilable with the requirement of hostility emphasised in that case. The net result appears to be that in England the action for unintentional trespass to the person has disappeared. To classify liability in this way according to the mental state of the defendant rather than solely according to the direct- ness of the injury is, it is submitted, a welcome rationalisation of the law[47] but it is one which has not found favour everywhere.[48]

---

[41] It has since been held that the Act covers even intentional trespass: *Long* v. *Hepworth* [1968] 1 W.L.R. 1299.

[42] [1965] 1 Q.B. 232, 242–244. As to this reasoning, see Jolowicz [1964] C.L.J. 200.

[43] Of course, the circumstances of the act may in themselves be strong evidence of negligence: for the maxim *res ipsa loquitur*, see *post*, p. 125.

[44] By "injury" his Lordship must be taken to have meant the physical contact, for it is not necessary that the defendant should have intended the harmful consequences: *Williams* v. *Humphrey, The Times*, February 20, 1975; *Wilson* v. *Pringle* [1987] Q.B. 237, 249.

[45] [1965] 1 Q.B. 232, 240.

[46] [1987] Q.B. 237.

[47] Aside from the burden of proof issue, the assimilation of unintentional trespass into negligence has a limited practical impact. (1) Plaintiffs have lost the somewhat theoretical right to sue for unintentional "battery" in the absence of damage, but we are not likely to lose much sleep over that. The victim of a negligent false imprisonment (assuming *Letang* v. *Cooper* to apply to that tort) might have more cause for complaint—see the example in Trindade and Cane, *The Law of Torts in Australia*, p. 266, of the man locked in a bank vault for 18 hours—but it is at least arguable that being deprived of your liberty for a substantial period is damage. (2) Trespass has no "duty" element and duty, as the next chapter shows, is a central element of negligence. But duty serves two functions, (a) to eliminate certain claims on grounds of policy and (b) to limit the range of liability to plaintiffs who are foreseeable victims. As to the first, it is hard to believe that in those cases where negligence rejects a claim this policy could have been evaded by framing the case as trespass. As to the second, it is not surprising that the trespass cases were not concerned with it, bearing in mind that the injury had to be direct and the defendant could escape by showing that he was not at fault in causing it. However, the criminal law has a well-developed doctrine of transferred intent, *i.e.* if A aims a blow at B and hits C he is liable for a battery of C *even if the striking of C is unforeseeable*. In the U.S. this is firmly embedded in tort law, too (see Prosser, "Transferred Intent" (1967) 45 Texas L.Rev. 650), and it was applied by the Northern Ireland Court of Appeal to a civil action in *Livingstone* v. *Ministry of Defence* [1984] N.I. 356 (D fired baton round and hit P; liable for battery even if he had intended to hit another person unless he could show justification). (3) It is submitted that the definition of "fault" in the Law Reform (Contributory Negligence) Act 1945, s.4, is amply wide enough to include cases which might formerly have been classified as unintentional trespass to the person (as to intentional acts, see *post*, p. 159).

[48] Particularly in Australia, where there is still support for the view that not only may there be a negligent trespass properly so called but the defendant has the burden of showing he was not at fault; *McHale* v. *Watson* (1964) 111 C.L.R. 384; *Venning* v. *Chin* (1974) 10 S.A.S.R. 299; *Shaw* v. *Hackshaw* [1983] 2 V.R. 65. All these cases went to the High Court of Australia ((1966) 115 C.L.R. 199, (1975) 49 A.L.J.R. 378, (1985) 56 A.L.R. 417) but in none of them was it necessary for that court to decide the point. In Canada among cases contrary to *Fowler* v. *Lanning* are *Larin* v. *Goshen* (1975) 56 D.L.R. (30) 719 and *Bell Canada* v. *Cope (Sarnia) Ltd.* (1980) 11 C.C.L.T. 170.

CHAPTER 5

NEGLIGENCE[1]

As was stated earlier, negligence may mean a mental element in tortious liability or it may mean an independent tort. In this chapter we are concerned with negligence as an independent tort.[2]

Negligence as a tort is the breach of a legal duty to take care which results in damage, undesired by the defendant, to the plaintiff. Thus its ingredients are: (*a*) a legal duty on the part of A towards B to exercise care in such conduct of A as falls within the scope of the duty; (*b*) breach of that duty; (*c*) consequential damage to B. Because the concept of foreseeability plays a part in all of these elements they cannot always be kept apart, and it has been said that "they are simply three different ways of looking at one and the same problem."[3] In considering them separately, therefore, it must be borne in mind that their separation is, to some extent at least, artificial, though it does accord with the way in which most cases are handled by the courts[4].

DUTY TO TAKE CARE[5]

It is not for every careless act that a man may be held responsible in law, nor even for every careless act that causes damage. He will only be liable in negligence if he is under a legal duty to take care. It may be objected that "duty" is not confined to the law of negligence and that it is an element in every tort, because there is a legal duty not to commit assault or battery, not to commit defamation, not to commit nuisance and so forth. But all that "duty" signifies in these other torts is that you must not commit them: they have their own, detailed, internal rules which define the circumstances in which they are committed and duty adds nothing to those. But in the tort of negligence, breach of "duty" is the chief ingredient of the tort; in fact there is no other except damage to the plaintiff. A general liability for carelessly causing harm to others would, at least as things are perceived by the courts, be too onerous for a practical system of law and we shall see that there are

[1] Smith, *Liability in Negligence* (1984); Buckley, *Modern Law of Negligence* (1988).
[2] For history, see Winfield, "The History of Negligence in the Law of Torts" (1926) 42 L.Q.R. 184 (*Select Legal Essays* 30); Fifoot, *History and Sources of the Common Law*, Chap. 8.
[3] *Roe* v. *Minister of Health* [1954] 2 Q.B. 66, 86, *per* Denning L.J. Compare the speech of Lord Reid in *Home Office* v. *Dorset Yacht Co. Ltd.* [1970] A.C. 1004 with those of the other judges.
[4] See, *e.g.* Bingham L.J. in *Attia* v. *British Gas plc* [1988] Q.B. 304, 318–319.
[5] Weir, *Casebook on Tort* (6th ed.), Chap. 1.

important areas of activity and important types of loss where the law of negligence does not intervene. Duty is the primary control device which allows the courts to keep liability for negligence within acceptable limits, and the controversies which have centred around the criteria for the existence of a duty reflect differences of opinion as to the proper ambit of the law of negligence.

The concept of duty has sometimes shown signs of becoming an arcane mystery but much difficulty will be avoided if it is grasped at the outset that duty is fulfilling two functions. If we ask "Is there a duty of care not to inflict economic loss?" or "Is there a duty to prevent third parties inflicting harm on another?" we are concerned with mapping out the areas in which the law of negligence will operate and identifying those in which there are features (fairness, practicability,[6] risk of untoward consequences[7]) which suggest that the law should not give a remedy for negligent conduct or at least should do so only to a limited extent. If a duty does exist in this general sense then there may be an issue on the facts of the particular case whether in all the circumstances it was owed to the particular plaintiff. For example, the House of Lords in *Donoghue* v. *Stevenson*[8] was concerned with the general question whether a manufacturer owed a duty of care to the ultimate user of his products and the conclusion was that he did. If, however, the product had been stolen from his factory and taken to Australia where, many years later, it caused injury to P, then it might be a difficult question to determine whether a duty was owed to P, that is to say, whether P was a foreseeable victim of the initial negligence in manufacture. This is the second sense of duty[9] but if there is no duty in the first, general sense we never get to the second question. Unless we keep this fundamental distinction in mind we have no means of explaining those situations in which foreseeable damage goes without legal redress.

Establishing categories of duty

It would be wrong to envisage negligence as a sea of non-liability surrounding areas of liability. If anything, the true picture is the reverse, for as Lord Goff has said,[10] "the broad general principle of liability for foreseeable damage is so widely applicable that the function of the duty of care is not so much to identify cases where liability is imposed as to identify those where it is not," a proposition which it is thought *as a practical matter* has survived the subsequent attacks on the decision in which it has its origin[11]; but the fact

---

[6] See, *e.g. Yuen Kun Yeu* v. *Att.-Gen. of Hong Kong* [1988] A.C. 175, *post*, p. 76.
[7] See, *e.g. Rowling* v. *Takaro Properties Ltd.* [1988] 2 W.L.R. 418, *post*, p. 102; *Rondel* v. *Worsley* [1969] 1 A.C. 191, *post*, p. 105.
[8] [1932] A.C. 562, *post*, p. 74.
[9] Earlier editions of this work referred to the first question as that of "notional duty" and to the second as "duty in fact." It is arguable that the second question is an unnecessary stage in the argument: see *post*, p. 83.
[10] *Smith* v. *Littlewoods Organisation Ltd.* [1987] A.C. 241, 280.
[11] Lord Goff was referring to the speech of Lord Wilberforce in *Anns* v. *Merton London Borough* [1978] A.C. 758, 752: see below.

that in the type of case before the court failure to take care is foreseeably likely to cause injury to others is not and never has been enough. What was said by du Parcq L.J. in 1946 is as true now as it was then (even though the range of recognised duties has increased substantially in the intervening years), namely, that "it is not true to say that whenever a person finds himself in such a position that unless he does a certain act another person may suffer, or that if he does something another person will suffer, it is his duty in the one case to be careful to do the act and in the other case to be careful not to do the act."[12] On the facts the defendant, an employer of a pantomime artiste, was not liable for failing to take steps to provide secure locks on the theatre dressing rooms because there was no duty to guard employees' property against theft.

Many duties of care have been established time out of mind (for example, the duties owed by drivers to other road users and of employers in respect of the safety of their workers). Others are of more recent vintage but nonetheless firmly fixed in the law (for example, the duty of a person giving information or advice). Since in a novel case the court must take a decision as to whether a new duty should be recognised,[13] is there any principle to guide it in this task? Three periods in the history of the law must be distinguished.

(1) Law before Anns v. Merton

The first attempt to formulate a general principle was made by Brett M.R. in *Heaven* v. *Pender*[14] but by far the most important generalisation is that of Lord Atkin in *Donoghue* v. *Stevenson*.[15] A manufacturer of ginger beer sold to a retailer ginger beer in an opaque bottle. The retailer resold it to A, who treated a young woman of her acquaintance with its contents. These included the decomposed remains of a snail which had found its way into the bottle at the factory.[16] The young woman alleged that she became seriously ill in consequence and sued the manufacturer for negligence. The doctrine of privity of contract prevented her bringing a claim founded upon breach of a warranty in a contract of sale but a majority of the House of Lords held that the manufacturer owed her a duty to take care that the bottle did not contain noxious matter and that he would be liable in tort if that duty was broken. Lord Atkin said[17]:

---

[12] *Deyong* v. *Shenburn* [1946] K.B. 227, 233.

[13] An extreme view was sometimes advanced that liability for negligence could only exist where there was a duty recognised by previous judicial decision. See Landon (1941) 57 L.Q.R. 183: "Negligence is not actionable unless the duty to be careful exists. And the duty to be careful exists where the wisdom of our ancestors has deemed that it shall exist." There are echoes of this in the dissent of Viscount Dilhorne in *Home Office* v. *Dorset Yacht Co. Ltd.* [1970] A.C. 1004 but it is quite inconsistent with the law since 1932. To emphasise the need for respect for precedent, as the courts now do (*post*, p. 76) is not at all the same thing as saying that new duties cannot be created. *Mills* v. *Winchester Diocesan Board* [1989] 1 All E.R. 317, 332.

[14] (1883) 11 Q.B.D. 503, 509.

[15] [1932] A.C. 562; Weir, *Casebook on Tort* (6th ed.), p. 21. For the history of litigation and of Mrs. Donoghue, see A. Rodger, Q.C., "Mrs. Donoghue and Alfenus Varus" [1988] C.L.P.1.

[16] The case came before the House of Lords from Scotland as what in modern English procedural terms would be called a preliminary issue of law and no trial of the truth of the averments ever appears to have taken place: see Heuston (1957) 20 M.L.R. 2.

[17] [1932] A.C. 562, 580.

"In English law there must be, and is, some general conception of relations giving rise to a duty of care, of which the particular cases found in the books are instances. The liability for negligence, whether you style it such or treat it as in other systems as a species of 'culpa,' is no doubt based upon a general public sentiment of moral wrongdoing for which the offender must pay. But acts or omissions which any moral code would censure cannot in a practical world be treated so as to give a right to every person injured by them to demand relief. In this way rules of law arise which limit the range of complainants and the extent of their remedy. The rule that you are to love your neighbour becomes, in law, you must not injure your neighbour; and the lawyer's question, Who is my neighbour? receives a restricted reply. *You must take reasonable care to avoid acts or omissions which you can reasonably foresee would be likely to injure your neighbour. Who, then, in law is my neighbour? The answer seems to be—persons who are so closely and directly affected by my act that I ought reasonably to have them in contemplation as being so affected when I am directing my mind to the acts or omissions which are called in question.*"[18]

There could be no denying that *Donoghue* v. *Stevenson* established that manufacturers owed a duty to ultimate consumers of their wares[19] but for a long time there was a marked judicial reluctance to accept that what we may call the "neighbour principle" had much relevance to determining whether a duty of care might exist in other areas of activity, though it might determine the spatial and temporal limits of such duties as were held to exist.[20] Still less did it have any impact where, before 1932, duties had been specifically rejected. There continued to be no duty of care in making statements or in disposing of tumbledown houses—words were not like deeds and a dwelling was inherently different from a ginger beer bottle. Certainly new "duty situations" continued to be recognised, for as Lord Macmillan had said in *Donoghue* v. *Stevenson*, "the categories of negligence are never closed"[21] but little reliance was placed upon this generalised concept.[22]

(2) *Law as stated in Anns* v. *Merton*

In *Home Office* v. *Dorset Yacht Co. Ltd.*[23] Lord Reid had suggested that the time had come to regard the "neighbour principle" of *Donoghue* v. *Stevenson* as applicable in all cases where there was no justification or valid explanation for its exclusion. The suggestion was taken up by the House of Lords in *Anns* v. *Merton London Borough*,[24] in particular in the speech of

---

[18] Emphasis added.

[19] A duty which was stated with greater precision in a subsequent passage: see *post*, p. 239.

[20] *i.e.* duty in the second sense above.

[21] [1932] A.C. 562, 619.

[22] Thus in the Court of Appeal in *Home Office* v. *Dorset Yacht Co. Ltd.* [1969] 2 Q.B. 412 no reference was made to *Donoghue* v. *Stevenson*.

[23] [1970] A.C. 1004, 1027.

[24] [1978] A.C. 728. Weir, *Casebook on Tort* (6th ed.), p. 61. Robert Goff L.J. in *Paterson Zochonis & Co. Ltd.* v. *Merfarken Packaging Ltd.* [1986] 3 All E.R. 522 (decided in 1982) referred to this case as the "coming of age of the law of negligence."

Lord Wilberforce, who said[25] that the matter should be approached in two stages. First, one must ask whether there was a sufficient relationship of "proximity or neighbourhood" between plaintiff and defendant such that in the defendant's reasonable contemplation carelessness on his part might cause damage to the plaintiff. If so, a prima facie duty of care arose. Then, at the second stage, it was necessary to consider whether there were any considerations which ought to "negative, or to reduce or limit" that duty.[26] The enthusiasm with which some judges took up this elegant rationalisation of the law and used it to attack previously well-entrenched principles of non-liability produced a remarkably swift reaction so that within a decade it could be said that it no longer represented the correct general approach to the establishment of a duty of care.[27] One of the most radical manifestations of this expansive reliance on *Anns* was *Junior Books Ltd.* v. *Veitchi Co. Ltd.*[28] where a majority of the House of lords in dealing with a loss which, at least on one view, was economic in nature, imposed a liability which appeared to conflict with hitherto well-established principles.[29]

(3) *Present law*

After a comment by the House of Lords in *Governors of the Peabody Donation Fund* v. *Sir Lindsay Parkinson Ltd.*[30] deprecating the tendency to treat the *Anns* formula as being of a "definitive character" the reaction may fairly be regarded as dating from the decision of the House in *Leigh and Sillavan Ltd.* v. *Aliakmon Shipping Co. Ltd.*,[31] another "economic loss" case, in which it upheld a long-established principle whereby a person could only claim in respect of loss caused to him by reason of damage to property if he had either ownership or possession of the property at the time when the damage occurred. In coming to this conclusion it was observed that the *Anns* formula did not provide a universally applicable test of the existence and scope of a duty of care and that in any event Lord Wilberforce had been dealing "with the questions of the existence and scope of a duty of care in a novel type of factual situation which was not analogous to any factual situation in which the existence of such a duty had already been held to exist."[32] A "novel" problem was presented to the Privy Council in *Yuen Kun Yeu* v. *Attorney-General of Hong Kong.*[33] A statutory officer, the Commissioner of Deposit-taking Companies, registered as a deposit-taker a company which subsequently went into liquidation with the result that the

[25] At pp. 751–752.
[26] Whether as to its scope or the class of persons to whom it was owed or the damages to which a breach of it might give rise.
[27] The actual decision concerned liability for defective premises. Even in this respect it has come under attack: *post*, p. 230.
[28] [1983] 1 A.C. 520.
[29] See the dissenting speech of Lord Brandon at p. 551. The case is dealt with more fully, *post*, p. 89.
[30] [1985] A.C. 210, 240.
[31] [1986] 785, *post*, p. 86. See also the Privy Council decision in *Candlewood Navigation Corp. Ltd.* v. *Mitsui O.S.K. Lines* [1986] A.C. 1.
[32] *Supra*, at p. 815, *per* Lord Brandon, with whose speech all members of the House concurred.
[33] [1988] A.C. 175, Weir, *Casebook on Tort* (6th ed.), p. 29.

plaintiffs lost the money they had deposited with it. They alleged that the Commissioner knew or ought to have known that the affairs of the company were being conducted fraudulently and speculatively; that he failed to exercise his statutory powers of supervision so as to secure that the company complied with its obligations; and that he should either never have registered the company or have revoked its registration. On a preliminary issue of law and assuming these allegations to be well-founded, the Privy Council upheld the judgment of the Hong Kong Court of Appeal in favour of the Commissioner. It is hard to take exception to the decision itself, for the facts were replete with characteristics which have been relied upon in many other cases as justifying denial of a duty. The loss was economic in nature; the plaintiffs were unascertained members of a huge class of persons depositing money with Hong Kong financial institutions and had no "special relationship" with the Commissioners; the loss had been directly inflicted by the wrongful act of a third party and there is no general duty to confer protection against such loss; the Commissioner had neither the legal power nor the resources to control the day-to-day running of the many companies subject to his jurisdiction so that no duty which could fairly and practicably be imposed on him would be likely to forestall fraud by those determined to practise it; and the failure of the legislature to impose a civil sanction in the legislation[34] was at least a pointer towards rejecting a common law duty of care.[35] No doubt a court faithfully applying *Anns* v. *Merton* might have rejected a duty at the second stage on all or any of these grounds[36] but the Privy Council held that it was not necessary to pass beyond the first stage because these were matters which on the proper interpretation of *Anns* were part of the notion of "proximity." There were, said the court, two possible interpretations of the first stage of the *Anns* formula: the first was that proximity meant merely reasonable foreseeability of injury, all matters of "policy" then being relegated to the second stage; the other, which was favoured by the Privy Council,[37] was that proximity included other factors which should enter into the decision whether a duty of care should be imposed, the "whole concept of necessary relationship between the plaintiff and the defendant," in particular the closeness and directness of that relationship. The effect of this seems to be that proximity differs according to the type of case.[38] Where the defendant has inflicted physical harm on the plaintiff or his property by an act, a duty may readily be established by showing foreseeability alone; where, however, there is failure to act or the loss is economic in nature or arises from the making of a statement, the court

---

[34] The legislation was subsequently amended to give the Commissioner immunity from civil suit. (For comparable English provisions see the Financial Services Act 1986, s.187(1) and the Banking Act 1987, s.1(4)).

[35] However, this factor had not inhibited the court in *Anns* v. *Merton* from finding a common law duty superimposed upon a statutory *power*.

[36] As, indeed, Huggins V.-P. and Fuad J.A. in the Hong Kong Court of Appeal had done: [1986] L.R.C. (Comm.) 300. See also *Mills* v. *Winchester Diocesan Board* [1989] 2 All E.R. 317.

[37] Adopting the view of Gibbs C.J. in the High Court of Australia in *Sutherland Shire Council* v. *Heyman* (1985) 60 A.L.R. 1.

[38] See generally Kidner, "Resiling from the *Anns* principle: the Variable Nature of Proximity in Negligence" (1987) 7 L.S. 319.

may insist upon a substantially closer relationship between the parties. The
second stage of the exercise is not wholly defunct, for it is accepted that there
may be cases in which the relationship is a close one but in which there are
special policy factors which rebut the initial inclination towards a duty.
These cases, however, will be rare: the example given by the Privy Council is
Rondel v. *Worsley*,[39] dealing with the liability of a barrister for negligence in
the conduct of proceedings in court. The court is certainly concerned with
the question of whether it is fair and reasonable to impose a duty of care but
it seems that this can be decided, in the generality of cases without proceeding to the second stage — though it must be said that the criteria for the
application of the second stage are elusive.[39a]

These points may be illustrated by a subsequent decision of the House of
Lords, *Hill* v. *Chief Constable of West Yorkshire*.[40] A 20-year-old student
was murdered by one Sutcliffe, known as the "Yorkshire Ripper." He had
committed a number of other similar offences in the area over a period of
years and the estate of the deceased brought an action against the defendant
police authority,[41] which, it was alleged, had been guilty of negligence in the
investigations into the previous offences and had thereby failed to catch
Sutcliffe and prevent the murder of the deceased. The House of Lords
upheld a decision striking out the claim as disclosing no cause of action.[42]
The claim was based upon failure to control another person so as to prevent
him doing harm to a third party and there was insufficient proximity between
the parties to take the case out of the general rule denying a duty in such a
situation. A duty might arise, for example, between a gaoler and persons in
the immediate vicinity of a prison who suffered damage during an escape[43]
but the deceased was a member of the public at large and any risk the alleged
negligence presented to her was no different from that presented to many
thousands of young women who might be Sutcliffe's victims. It was, therefore, unnecessary to go to the second stage mentioned in *Anns*[44] but the
House of Lords went on to say that the application of that stage was capable
of constituting a separate and independent ground for denial of a duty.
While the imposition of a duty of care might in the general run of cases be for
the public benefit in increasing safety, there were risks that to do so in this
area might lead to the police carrying on some investigations in a detri-
mentally "defensive" way, to the courts being asked to adjudicate on mat-

---

[39] [1969] 1 A.C. 191; *post*, p. 104.

[39a] In *Caparo Industries pl.c.* v. *Dickman* [1989] 2 W.L.R. 316 Bingham L.J. suggests that the requirement
that it be just and reasonable to impose a duty "covers very much the same ground as had Wilberforce's
second stage test in *Anns*." This may well accord with what Lord Wilberforce intended but it is hard to
reconcile with *Yuen Kun Yeu*.

[40] [1989] A.C. 53. See also *Ryeford Homes Ltd.* v. *Sevenoaks D.C.* [1989] N.L.J. 255 (no duty of care in
granting planning permission; no proximity; and even if proximity council had overriding duty to the
public); *Mills* v. *Winchester Diocesan Board* [1989] 2 All E.R. 317 (Charity Commissioners).

[41] Rather unusually, civil actions against Sutcliffe had already been brought by some of his victims.

[42] The last edition of this work, written at the flood-tide of the expansion of negligence which followed *Anns*,
asked, "how long before we get a successful claim against the police for failing to prevent a crime?" Now we
have the answer.

[43] *cf. Home Office* v. *Dorset Yacht Co. Ltd.* [1970] A.C. 1004 (escape of borstal boys).

[44] The analogy between the police and the Commissioner of Deposit Taking Institutions in *Yuen Kun Yeu's*
case is obvious.

ters of police policy and discretion for which they were ill-suited and to the diversion of large amounts of police resources to defending such actions.[45] Lord Templeman pointed out that the estate was not really seeking compensation (any damages would have been given to charity) but to obtain an investigation into the shortcomings of the force, and in his view "the efficiency of a police force can only be investigated by an inquiry instituted by the national or local authorities which are responsible to the electorate for that efficiency."[46]

To a certain extent the differences between the approach in these cases on the one hand and the *Anns* formula on the other is verbal, a matter of emphasis. It is pointed out in *Yuen Kun Yeu* v. *Attorney-General of Hong Kong*[47] that "foreseeability of harm is a necessary ingredient of a [proximity] relationship, but it is not the only one. Otherwise there would be liability in negligence on the part of one who sees another about to walk over a cliff with his head in the air, and forbears to shout a warning." This is of course correct, but even on the assumption that Lord Wilberforce in *Anns* meant proximity to mean no more than foreseeability it is most unlikely that he would have found liability in such a case. He would no doubt have replied that the second stage considerations were not merely matters arising from the facts of a particular case but might be identifiable in a whole range of cases of a particular type and lead to denial of liability in all of them.[48] Whether one says that there is no proximity between a defendant and a person whom he fails to rescue (or upon whom he inflicts economic loss) or that the law has concluded that in the generality of cases it is socially undesirable to hold liable those who are simply inactive (or who inflict non-physical harm) might be argued not to matter. Perhaps what was wrong with *Anns* was less the formula itself than the way in which it was applied, particularly in striking down prior established immunities or restriction with little regard for previous case law. If the first stage was comparatively easy to pass (as it was if based on nothing more than foreseeability) there was a risk that the bounds of liability would be unreasonably[49] extended,[50] particularly

---

[45] [1989] A.C. 53, 63, *per* Lord Keith.

[46] *Ibid.* at pp. 64–65. "The present action could not consider whether the training of the West Yorkshire police force is sufficiently thorough, whether the selection of candidates for appointment or promotion is defective, whether rates of pay are sufficient to attract recruits of the required calibre, whether financial restrictions prevent the provision of modern equipment and facilities, or whether the Yorkshire police force is clever enough if not, what can and ought to be done about it. The present action could only investigate whether an individual member of the police force conscientiously carrying out his duty was negligent when he was bemused by contradictory information or overlooked significant information or failed to draw inferences which later appeared to be obvious. That kind of investigation would not achieve the object which Mrs. Hill desires." This view is correct on the facts, but in some circumstances a defective "system" can constitute negligence; *post*, p. 193.

[47] [1988] A.C. 175, 192.

[48] Which was, broadly, the approach of the approach of the Privy Council in *Candlewood Navigation Corp. Ltd.* v. *Mitsui O.S.K. Ltd.* [1986] A.C. 1, 25.

[49] The reaction against *Anns* coincided with increased public debate over the burden of liability insurance, particularly on the professions. However, this has been focussed primarily upon the medical profession and there has never been any doubt that a doctor owes a duty of care to his patient.

[50] See Lord Templeman's acid comment in *C.B.S. Songs Ltd.* v. *Amstrad Consumer Electronics plc* [1988] A.C. 1013, 1059: "The pleading assumes that we are all neighbours now, Pharisees and Samaritans alike, that foreseeability is a reflection of hindsight and that for every mischance in an accident-prone world someone solvent must be liable in damages."

if judges were reluctant (as some were) to engage in the overt discussion of policy issues which the second stage demanded. This attitude is manifest in the speech of Lord Scarman in *McLoughlin* v. *O'Brian*[51] in which, refusing to impose any limit other than that of mere foreseeability for "nervous shock," he said that "the policy issue as to where to draw the line is not justiciable. The problem is one of social, economic and financial policy. The considerations relevant to a decision are not such as to be capable of being handled within the limits of the forensic process."[52]

The effect of the reaction against *Anns* is not that the categories of negligence are closed but the creation of a new duty is likely to involve a much more gradual, step-by-step process with greater emphasis on analogy with previous decisions,[53] which is why it is all the more important that we should look more closely at some prominent areas in which "proximity" is by no means the same thing as foreseeability.[54] As Lord Devlin said in *Hedley, Byrne & Co. Ltd.* v. *Heller & Partners Ltd.*,[55] itself one of the landmark decisions on the extension of the duty of care, "new categories in the law do not spring into existence overnight." Three points of a general nature must, however, be made.

First, the law in a novel situation is no more easily determined or certain than it was under *Anns*: it is true that we have abandoned an apparently exclusive reliance on the uncertain criterion of the individual judge's view of policy[56] but the criteria of proximity are sometimes themselves almost as vague.[57] Secondly, it should not be thought that the role of policy in the broad sense has been reduced in importance as a result of the relegation of the second stage in *Anns* to a limited role: to require, for example, a link closer than mere foreseeability of harm where the case involves information or advice is neither more nor less than a statement of judicial policy that words should be treated differently from deeds because, for example, the range of persons who may be affected by reliance on them is so great as to create a risk of imposing an unreasonable burden on their originator. "Policy," whether concealed in the language of proximity, or free-standing in the comparatively rare cases to which the *Anns* second stage is now said to be applicable, means simply that the court must decide (subject to the doctrine of precedent) whether there should be a duty, taking into account the established framework of the law and also the implications that a decision one way or the other may have for the operation of the law in our

---

[51] [1983] 1 A.C. 410, 431.

[52] Lord Edmund-Davies at p. 427 described this proposition as "as novel as it is startling." However, reluctance to embark on policy discussions is understandable. Judicial pronouncements on what is or is not socially desirable regularly draw forth criticism (usually misconceived) alleging political bias, isolation or lack of "accountability."

[53] Ironically, Lord Wilberforce himself adopted just such an "incremental" approach to nervous shock in *McLoughlin* v. *O'Brian, supra*, n. 51.

[54] See below.

[55] [1964] A.C. 465, 525.

[56] Oliver L.J. in *Leigh and Sillavan Ltd.* v. *Aliakmon Shipping Co. Ltd.* [1985] 1 Q.B. 310, 374.

[57] The process of finding a duty has been described as "intensely pragmatic": *Rowling* v. *Takaro Properties Ltd.* [1988] A.C. 473, 501.

society.[58] This is an inescapable part of the judicial process and it is better to recognize it as such than to cloud the issue by saying that "policy need not be invoked where reason and good sense will . . . point the way"[59] for in the last analysis these apparently contrasted concepts are surely one and the same thing. Finally, we may perhaps be allowed a word in favour of the *Anns* formulation. The process of finding a duty of care has been described as requiring an inductive analysis of the existing authorities in the area to identify their common factors followed by the framing of a general proposition of law which is capable of being applied to the facts before the court[60] but where it is sought to extend the law into a new area the court must exercise a conscious choice in the matter and it would be surprising if the judge were to approach this matter without *any* general conception, however vague, of what *ought* to give rise to a duty of care.[61] If *Anns* meant to equate proximity with foreseeability it can be argued that it did offer just such a general conception which, for all its dangers, was certainly more comprehensible than the case law which has taken its place.

Duty to this plaintiff

Though the order is not perhaps logical, it is desirable before turning to examine some of the categories where a duty of care is denied or restricted, to say some more about the other sense of duty. After all, the great majority of the negligence cases coming before the courts involve physical injury or damage and in them the matters discussed in the previous section rarely arise[62]: no-one would think of opening in a running-down case by citing authorities to show that a duty of care was owed by drivers to pedestrians. But even though the general proposition is obvious it is, as we have seen, still necessary that on the particular facts the defendant owed a duty to the *plaintiff*. In such a case the test is whether injury to the plaintiff would have been in the contemplation of a reasonable man.[63] Despite the reference in *Donoghue* v. *Stevenson* to "neighbours" the test is not one of physical closeness[64] but of foresight, for my neighbours are "persons who are so closely and directly affected by my act that I ought reasonably to have them

---

[58] Civil law systems generally know no concept of duty of care, but they certainly take policy factors into account and may reach the same answer as English law: see Markesinis, "The Not-So Dissimilar Tort and Delict" (1977) 93 L.Q.R. 78; Lawson and Markesinis, *Tortious Liability for Unintentional Harm in the Common Law and the Civil Law*, Vol. 1, Chap. 2; Lord Goff in *Smith* v. *Littlewoods Organisation Ltd.* [1987] A.C. 241, 271, 280. His Lordship described the judicial function in this context as "an educated reflex to facts." See generally, Bell, *Policy Arguments in Judicial Decisions* (1983).

[59] Lord Morris in *Home Office* v. *Dorset Yacht Co. Ltd.* [1970] A.C. 1004, 1039, cited with approval by the House of Lords in *Curran* v. *Northern Ireland Co-ownership Housing Association Ltd.* [1987] A.C. 718.

[60] See Lord Diplock in *Home Office* v. *Dorset Yacht Co. Ltd.* [1970] A.C. 1004.

[61] *Ibid.*

[62] But occasionally they do: drivers owe a duty to passengers but there may be no duty between a driver and passenger jointly engaged in a criminal enterprise: *post*, p. 697.

[63] It is true that in *Donoghue* v. *Stevenson* Lord Atkin went on to formulate the content of the duty of a manufacturer with some precision (see, *post*, p. 239) but the modern tendency is to say that at bottom the question is one of reasonable foreseeability and Lord Atkin's words are not to be read as if they were a statute: *M/S Aswan Engineering Establishment Co.* v. *Lupdine Ltd.* [1987] 1 W.L.R. 1, 23.

[64] One is tempted to say "proximity" but now that that has been elevated to the status of a legal "code word" it is better avoided.

in contemplation." Sometimes plaintiff and defendant may be physically close but there is no duty because, for example, the latter has no reason to expect the former's presence; conversely, there may be a duty even though goods are negligently manufactured in Newcastle and cause damage in Southampton. In other cases, the physical propinquity of the parties or lack of it will be a factor to be taken into account in determining what a reasonable man would have had in contemplation.[65]

Negligence "in the air" or towards some other person is not enough: the plaintiff cannot build on a wrong to someone else.[66] The point is graphically illustrated by the famous United States case of *Palsgraf* v. *Long Island Railroad*.[67] The facts as presented to the New York Court of Appeals,[68] were that the defendants' servants negligently pushed X, who was attempting to board a moving train, and caused him to drop a package containing "fireworks." The resulting explosion knocked over some scales, many feet away, which struck the plaintiff, injuring her. By a majority the court reversed a decision for the plaintiff. It might well have been that the defendants' servants were negligent with regard to the man carrying the package, at least as far as his property was concerned, but there was nothing in the appearance of the package to suggest even to the most cautious mind that it would cause a violent explosion. In the words of Cardozo C.J.:

"If no hazard was apparent to the eye of ordinary vigilance, an act innocent and harmless, at least to outward seeming, with reference to her, did not take to itself the quality of a tort because it happened to be a wrong, though apparently not one involving the risk of bodily insecurity, with reference to someone else . . . The orbit of the danger as disclosed to the eye of reasonable vigilance would be the orbit of the duty."

On this side of the water, *Bourhill* v. *Young*[69] the case of the pregnant fishwife who sustained nervous shock at witnessing the aftermath of a road accident, is to the same effect. As Lord Russell of Killowen put it, a duty of care "only arises towards those individuals of whom it may reasonably be anticipated that they will be affected by the act which constitutes the alleged breach."[70]

When we say that the plaintiff must be a foreseeable victim we do not mean that he need be identifiable by the defendant. It is enough that he

---

[65] Or, if one prefers, what the court thinks is a fair limit to the defendant's responsibility.
[66] *Bourhill* v. *Young* [1943] A.C. 92, 108, *per* Lord Wright.
[67] 248 N.Y. 339; 162 N.E. 99 (1928).
[68] There is much doubt as to what actually happened.
[69] [1943] A.C. 92. For a case decided before the concept of duty became clear and which seems to have allowed A to build upon a wrong to B, see *Smith* v. *L. & S.W. Ry.* (1870) L.R. 6 C.P. 14.
[70] [1943] A.C. 92, 102. For the problem of nervous shock, see *post*, p. 106. The plaintiff heard the accident but did not see it and was in no physical danger from it. Since she viewed the scene after the corpse had been removed some interval of time must have elapsed and, while nowhere stated in the speeches, it may be that the judges regarded the plaintiff as having to some extent brought her injury upon herself.

should be one of a class within the area of foreseeable injury.[71] In *Haley* v. *London Electricity Board*[72] the defendants, with statutory authority, excavated a trench in the street. They took precautions for the protection of passers-by which were sufficient for normal-sighted person, but the plaintiff, who was blind, suffered injury because the precautions were inadequate for him. It was held that the number of blind persons who go about the streets alone was sufficient to require the defendants to have them in contemplation and to take precautions appropriate to their condition.

For convenience we often categorise duties by reference to relationships. For example, we say that manufacturers owe duties to ultimate consumers, drivers to other road users and so on. This does no harm (indeed, it is necessary in so far as we must identify those areas in which a duty of care is rejected or limited) provided it is remembered that it is normally not the existence of the relationship alone which makes the plaintiff the defendant's neighbour, but the fact that the defendant ought to have the plaintiff in contemplation[73] when directing his mind to the acts or omissions which are called in question, *i.e.* the alleged acts of negligence themselves. It follows that the test can only be applied *ex post facto*. It also follows that it is impossible always to keep separate from each other questions of the existence of a duty, of the breach of that duty and of remoteness of damage. The foresight of the reasonable man is of critical importance in the first two questions and plays a not insignificant role in the third, and it has been said that "it is, on final analysis, the need for care lest someone be injured that both creates the duty and determined what amounts to a breach of it."[74] Indeed, it can be argued that the only necessary function performed by the duty of care concept in the present law is to deal with those cases where liability is denied not because of lack of foreseeability but for reasons of legal policy and that in all other cases (the great majority) everything can be handled by asking whether the defendant behaved with the prudence of a reasonable man.[75] However, the fact remains that the existence of a duty of care, breach of that duty and remoteness of damage are regularly treated as separate ingredients of the tort of negligence and this continues to have advantages from the point of view of exposition.[76] In some cases there is no doubt whatever that the defendant's conduct was negligent towards

---

[71] If A damages property in B's custody he is in breach of a duty of care to any persons unknown who have sufficient interest in the goods to bring a claim (see *post* Chap. 17) even if B has represented that he is the only such person: *Awad* v. *Pillai* [1982] R.T.R. 266. *cf.* Palmer and Murdoch (1983) 46 M.L.R. 73 and *post*, p. 486.

[72] [1965] A.C. 778; Weir, *Casebook on Tort* (6th ed.) p. 125.

[73] Of course, the existence of the relationship may be a necessary pre-condition to liability under a particular heading, *e.g.* the relationship of occupier and visitor under the Occupiers' Liability Act 1957: *post*, Chap. 7.

[74] *Voli* v. *Inglewood Shire Council* [1963] Qd.R. 256, 257, *per* Windeyer J. (Aust.H.Ct.). See Fleming, "Remoteness and Duty" (1953) 31 Can. Bar Rev. 486; Fleming James, "The Scope of Duty in Negligence Cases" (1953) 47 North Western Univ.L.Rev. 778.

[75] For the former "controversy" on this subject see Winfield, "Duty in Tortious Negligence" in *Select Legal Essays* and Lawson, "Duty of Care in Negligence: a Comparative Study" (1947) 22 Tulane L.Rev. 111–130. "The two sides were never at issue; they were arguing about different things": Clerk and Lindsell, *Torts* (16th ed.), para. 10–169.

[76] *cf.* Clerk and Lindsell, *Torts* (16th ed.), para. 10–171, which is strongly critical of the confusing conceptualisation of the elements of negligence.

someone; what is seriously in issue is whether the defendant was negligent towards the plaintiff and this is most conveniently considered in terms of duty; in other cases there is no doubt that if the defendant was negligent at all then he was negligent towards the plaintiff, and these cases are most conveniently discussed in terms of breach. If there is a duty and a breach then the extent of the liability to *that plaintiff* will be considered as a matter of remoteness.

Some categories of restricted duty

(1) *Economic loss*[77]

Much of the controversy about the role of the duty of care in negligence has arisen in cases which have involved the problem of "economic loss." The expression is liable to mislead: if a car is destroyed, that is "economic" in the sense that the owner's assets are thereby diminished,[78] but in legal terms it is classified as damage to property and the owner is entitled to its value as damages. Even if the loss is unquestionably only financial in nature no difficulty is felt about allowing its recovery if it is a consequence of physical injury or damage to the plaintiff's property: for example, the plaintiff in *Donoghue* v. *Stevenson* could have recovered lost earnings and medical expenses and a company whose machinery was damaged by negligence would recover lost profits while the machinery was out of action.[79] Where, however, this link of physical harm[80] is absent, liability has generally been denied[81] unless there is some further factor. The point is neatly illustrated by *Spartan Steel & Alloys Ltd.* v. *Martin & Co. (Contractors) Ltd.*[82] A power cut caused by the defendants' negligence caused material to solidify in the plaintiff's furnace. The plaintiffs recovered the reduction in the value of the solidified "melt" (which had undergone a chemical change from partial processing) and the profits they would have made from its sale as an ingot, but they recovered nothing for the loss of profits on four further melts which could have been processed before the electricity was restored, for this was not a consequence of any damage to their property but simply of the

[77] Atiyah, "Negligence and Economic Loss" (1967) 83 L.Q.R. 248; Cane, "Physical and Economic Loss" (1979) 95 L.Q.R. 117; McGrath, "The Recovery of Pure Economic Loss" (1985) 3 O.J.L.S. 350.

[78] Even pain and suffering and loss of amenities are economic in the sense that the court can only award monetary damages for their infliction, though they do not have a market value like property.

[79] It is assumed in both cases that the loss is not "too remote" in the sense considered in the next chapter and that the plaintiff has acted reasonably to mitigate his loss—*e.g.* in the second example, by hiring a replacement machine if one is available. As to the first point, where A damaged B's ship and this led to oil spillage which damaged C, a voluntary payment by B to C was not recoverable by B in his action against A in the absence of an assignment of C's claim against A: *Esso Petroleum Co. Ltd.* v. *Hall Russell & Co. Ltd.* [1988] 3 W.L.R. 730.

[80] Nearly all the case law is about property damage, but the same applies to personal injury cases. Apart from the common law action *per quod* (*post*, p. 496) and the Fatal Accidents Act, A cannot sue B for loss which A suffers by reason of B's injury of C. Scots law is the same: *Robertson* v. *Turnbull* 1982 S.C.(H.L.) 1.

[81] It must be stressed that we are speaking only of negligence. There is no such restriction in the case of some intentional torts, *e.g.* deceit or inducing breach of contract.

[82] [1973] Q.B. 27; Weir, *Casebook on Tort* (6th ed.), p. 36. Among many other cases see *Weller & Co. Ltd.* v. *Foot and Mouth Disease Research Institute* [1966] 1 Q.B. 560 (loss caused to auctioneers when cattle sales suspended during outbreak of "foot and mouth") and *Electrochrome Ltd.* v. *Welsh Plastics Ltd.* [1968] 2 All E.R. 205.

interruption of the electricity supply.[83] In duty language the defendants owed the plaintiffs a duty in respect of damage to their property but did not owe them any duty with respect to mere loss of profits unconnected therewith.[84] Of course, property damage *was* the source of the whole of the plaintiffs' loss but with regard to the lost profits it was a consequence of damage to the property of the electricity undertaking and they had suffered no loss other than the cost of repairing the cable and, perhaps, loss of income during the interruption. In other words, the plaintiff may only sue for damage to property or for loss consequent on that damage if at the time when it was inflicted he was the owner of the property or was in possession[85] of it[86]: it is not enough that he has merely contractual rights in it which are rendered less valuable as a result of the damage or that he has a contractual obligation in respect of it which becomes more onerous.[87] The point was affirmed after a period of doubt in *Candlewood Navigation Corporation Ltd. v. Mitsui O.S.K. Lines Ltd.*[88] The first plaintiffs were owners of the *Ibaraki Maru*, which was damaged by the negligence of the defendants' vessel, the *Mineral Transporter*. However, the first plaintiffs had let the *Ibaraki Maru* to the second plaintiffs on a "bareboat charter," the effect of which in law was to put the second plaintiffs in possession of her. The second plaintiffs then relet the vessel to the first plaintiffs on a time charter, a transaction which does not confer possession.[89] The second plaintiffs were entitled to recover the cost of repairs from the defendants but the first plaintiffs failed in their claim to (*a*) Yen 544,000 a day in hire which they had to pay even while the vessel was out of action and (*b*) profits which they lost through being unable to make use of the vessel. It was of course argued that since the first plaintiffs were in fact owners, although not in possession at the time, that gave them title to sue but this was rejected because both the items of loss were suffered in their capacity as charterers, not as owners. The position would have been different if, say, the second plaintiffs had not been obliged to repair the vessel and had redelivered it in damaged condition.[90] It

---

[83] Hence the result would presumably have been different had the supply been speedily restored but it had taken hours to clean the furnace; spilling petrol across a highway requiring it to be cleaned was held to be property damage in *Att.-Gen. for Ontario* v. *Fatehi* (1984) 15 D.L.R. (4th) 1323 (S.C.C.)

[84] Lord Denning M.R. hesitated about classifying such cases as belonging to duty or remoteness, but it is submitted that the problem only arises if one fails to keep separate the two meanings of duty: D may owe P a duty with respect to loss "A" but not loss "B." *cf. Attia* v. *British Gas* [1988] Q.B. 304, 319.

[85] The common law always equated possession with ownership for the purpose of title to sue for damage to goods: hence a bailee could sue for the full value of the goods bailed to him (even though his interest was limited) whether or not he would be responsible to the owner for the loss. The *amount* which a bailee can recover may now be restricted by a statute: *post*, p. 481. For a marginal case on possession see *Nacap Ltd.* v. *Moffat Plant Ltd.* 1987 S.L.T. 221.

[86] This is the reason why if an insurer insures A's property and B negligently destroys it the insurer cannot sue the wrongdoer in its own name, though it may be subrogated to A's rights: *Simpson & Co.* v. *Thompson* (1877) 3 App.Cas. 279 (where the right of subrogation was no use since the owner of the damaged ship and the owner of the negligent ship were one and the same person, who could not sue himself).

[87] *Cattle* v. *Stockton Waterworks* (1875) L.R. 10 Q.B. 453. But it has been held in the U.S.A. that fishermen may sue one who pollutes the sea and deprives them of their catch: *Union Oil Co.* v. *Oppen* 501 F.2d. 558 (1974), described as a "special rule" in *State of Louisiana* v. *M/V Testbank* 752 F. 2d. 1019 (1985).

[88] [1986] A.C. 1. Jones (1986) 102 L.Q.R. 13; Tettenborn [1986] C.L.J. 13.

[89] In non-marine terms, a bareboat charter is like hiring a self-drive van; a time (or voyage) charter is like engaging a removal firm.

[90] The Privy Council reserved its opinion on the position if the second plaintiffs had failed to repair in breach of contract.

will be observed that there was nothing unforeseeable about loss to the charterers in these circumstances[91] and that the defendants escaped part of the liability which they would otherwise have incurred had the first plaintiffs been in possession of the vessel, for the lost profits would then have been a consequence of damage to "their" property. However, this is an area where all parties are presumably well able to protect themselves by assessing risks and translating them into contract safeguards and hire rates,[92] and the present law provides a certain, if apparently arbitrary, rule which is understood by the maritime community[93] and by reference to which disputes can be settled without recourse to litigation. A change in the law might involve great difficulty in "drawing the line": if a time charterer can sue what about sub-charterers or even persons with contractual interests in goods delayed while the vessel is repaired.[94] This is a variant of the "floodgates" (or "where is to end?") argument which is often deployed in economic loss cases, the spectre of a liability in Cardozo C.J.'s famous words, "in an indeterminate amount for an indeterminate time to an indeterminate class"[95] and which is typified by cases involving the cutting of public utility supplies. In fact, the risk in such cases has probably been exaggerated because individual losses are likely to be comparatively small and in the absence of the institution of the "class action" in English law will probably not be brought to court.[96] Furthermore, the physical consequences of an accident may be very wide ranging[97] and in that context the courts do not deny a remedy because it will be available to many rather than to a few.[98] In any event, the non-recovery of economic loss is not restricted to cases where there is a risk of widespread liability. This is demonstrated by the decision of the House of Lords in *Leigh and Sillavan Ltd.* v. *Aliakmon Shipping Co. Ltd.*[99] The plaintiffs were buyers of steel coils which were carried by the defendant shipowners from Korea to England under a contract made between the shipowners and the Korean sellers. The coils were badly stored and damaged in transit. The

---

[91] A shipowner using his vessel to carry his own goods would be the exception rather than the rule in modern conditions.

[92] See Gaskell, "Economic Loss in the Maritime Context" [1985] L.M. & C.L.Q. 96, written before the decision of the Privy Council in the *Candlewood* case but containing a full examination of the issues.

[93] And recognised by courts in other common law jurisdictions: see, *e.g. State of Louisiana* v. *M/V Testbank* 752 F. 2d. 1019 (1985); *Getty Refining* v. *M.T. Fadi B.* 766 F. 2d. 829 (1985).

[94] Where owners of cargo have to make, after a collision, a "general average" contribution to the ship in which their goods are carried (*i.e.* share rateably in expenditure necessary to meet the emergency) they may recover this from the wrongdoer even though their goods are not damaged: *Morrison S.S. Co. Ltd.* v. *Greystoke Castle* [1947] A.C. 265. This may rest upon a special rule about general average or upon a concept of joint venture. Lord Roche (at p. 280) thought that if a lorry belonging to A were damaged due to the negligence of B then C, whose goods were on the lorry but were not damaged, could sue B for the expense of transhipment.

[95] *Ultramares Corp.* v. *Touche* 174 N.E. 441, 444 (1931). On the availability of insurance see Alexander in (1972–1973) 12 J.S.P.T.L. 119 and the report of the discussion *ibid.* at pp. 173–176.

[96] See *New Zealand Forest Products* v. *Att.-Gen* [1985] L.R.C.(Comm.) 558.

[97] See Fleming James in (1972–1973) 12 J.S.P.T.L. 105, who instances damage from nuclear installations (for which, however, there are special statutory provisions: see *post*, p. 449) and the London and Chicago fires. See also *The Grandcamp* [1961] 1 Lloyd's Rep. 504.

[98] But Parliament sometimes restricts liability (see, *e.g.* the provisions in the Merchant Shipping Act limiting liability in accordance with the defendant's ship's tonnage).

[99] [1986] A.C. 786. Clarke [1986] C.L.J. 382; Markesinis [1986] C.L.J. 384. *Mitsui & Co. Ltd.* v. *Flota Mercante Grancolombiana S.A.* [1988] 1 W.L.R. 1145.

plaintiffs were obliged to pay the Korean sellers the contract price because the "risk" had passed to them upon shipment in Korea; but "property" (which for this purpose may be equated with ownership) did not pass to them until they paid, some time after the gods were landed in England. The plaintiffs' action against the shipowners failed in the House of Lords. Looked at only through the spectacles of tort the result looks hard to defend.[1] However, a number of further matters must be taken account of before the decision is dismissed in this way. First, the facts of the case are atypical, for in the majority of cases the property in the goods passes to the buyer by endorsement to him of the bill of lading and when that happens he takes over, by virtue of section 1 of the Bills of Lading Act 1855, the rights of the seller under the contract of carriage—in other words, there is a statutory exception to the rule of privity of contract and there is no need for tort law to operate.[2] On the facts, however, because unexpected circumstances rendered the buyers unable to pay for the goods on arrival they took possession of them not as principals but as agents for the sellers, who retained a right of disposal.[3] Secondly, it is not wholly true to say that the shipowners evaded their proper responsibilities because the sellers (owners when the damage was done) could still have sued and in such an action it would be irrelevant that they had already been paid by the buyers, though any damages would be held by them on behalf of the buyers.[4] It is true that the sellers in such circumstances might have little incentive to sue, but as the House of Lords pointed out, it would have been open to the buyers to have protected themselves by requiring the sellers to exercise this right on their account or taking an assignment from them.[5] Far more important, however, from the point of view of the general law is a further point which is applicable beyond the particular maritime context of this case. The carriage of the goods was under a contract effected between the sellers and the shipowners. Commercial contracts are likely to contain detailed exemptions and limitations for the purpose of allocating particular risks between the parties,[6] and allowing a right of action in negligence to a third party[7] runs the risk that this

[1] See the interesting judgment of Robert Goff L.J. in the Court of Appeal ([1985] Q.B. 350, 399) where, without suggesting the imposition of a wide or indeterminate liability for economic loss, he proposed a theory of recovery for "transferred loss," *i.e.* when A owes a duty in tort not to damage B's property and commits a breach of that duty in circumstances in which the loss foreseeably falls on C by reason of the contract between B and C, then A would be liable in tort to C. *cf.* the German law theory of *Drittschadensliquidation*, discussed by Markesinis, "An Expanding Tort Law—The Price of a Rigid Contract Law" (1987) 103 L.Q.R. 354, 368.
[2] Alternatively, there may be an implied contract between the buyer and the shipowner if he takes delivery from him and pays the freight: *Brandt* v. *Liverpool, etc. Steam Navigation Co. Ltd.* [1924] 1 K.B. 575.
[3] What started as an ordinary c. + f. contract was varied to a sale ex-warehouse performed when the buyers eventually paid.
[4] *The Albazero* [1977] A.C. 774, which deals with the seller's position against the carrier when property *has* passed.
[5] [1986] A.C. 786, 819. It must also be remembered that in this sort of transaction there will almost always be an insurance policy for the benefit of the person having the risk and the "real" plaintiff may be the insurer exercising rights of subrogation (see, *e.g. Mitsui & Co. Ltd.* v. *Flota Mercante Grancolombiana S.A.* [1989] 1 All E.R. 951). That is supposed to be legally irrelevant but may have significance in a court's perception of what appears a "hard case."
[6] Indeed, the content of the contract in question was largely prescribed by statute: the Hague Rules, operating under the Carriage of Goods by Sea Act.
[7] Or, indeed, between the original parties: see *ante*, p. 5.

allocation can in effect be disturbed.[8] There have been suggestions that where A's duty of care has its origin in a contract between him and B, the ultimate aim of which is to confer a benefit on C (in the *Aliakmon* case the delivery of the goods to C) then C can be in no better position than B would have been, even though C's action is in tort,[9] but this was rejected by the House of Lords on the ground that the complex contractual provisions could not be synthesised into anything resembling a duty of care.[10] Rather than import the terms of an alien contract into the tort duty, the tort duty is rejected altogether.

The law is, therefore, fairly clear[11] when physical damage is caused by A to B's property and this leads to economic loss to C.[12] But there is no blanket rule forbidding recovery of economic loss in negligence. So much was clearly established by the House of Lords in *Hedley, Byrne & Co. Ltd.* v. *Heller & Partners.*[13] The case was primarily important for establishing that there might be a duty to take care in making statements but the loss in question there (and, indeed, in the majority of negligent misstatement cases) was of an economic nature. Lord Devlin[14] castigated the supposed general rule against non-recovery of economic loss, saying that it was absurd that the interposition of some physical damage should make a difference; but the predominant view was that this case established a special rule for misstatements and had no effect on liability for negligent acts. Liability for misstatements is particularly likely to give rise to a wide-ranging liability but to meet this by barring claims for economic loss would have been to strangle the duty at birth and a different control device was used—the requirement that there should be a "special relationship" between the parties. However, the decision in *Ross* v. *Caunters*[15] was made not on the basis of *Hedley, Byrne*

---

[8] Under the Bills of Lading Act, *supra*, the buyer takes over the seller's *contractual* rights.

[9] See, *e.g. Junior Books Ltd.* v. *Veitchi Co. Ltd.* [1983] 1 A.C. 520, 534 (*per* Lord Fraser) and perhaps at p. 564 (*per* Lord Roskill); the *Aliakmon* case in the Court of Appeal, [1983] Q.B. 350, 399, *per* Robert Goff L.J. An interesting variant of this is in *Norwich City Council* v. *Harvey* [1989] 1 All E.R. 1180, where the exclusion clause was in the contract between *B* and C. See further, p. 687, *post.*

[10] [1986] A.C. 786, 818.

[11] But see Griew (1986) 136 New L.J. 1201, who points out that a literal interpretation of s.3 of the Latent Damage Act 1986 (*post*, p. 721) would reverse the *Aliakmon* rule in some cases. The section provides in effect, that where A causes damage to B's property and B disposes of it to C, then C has a cause of action against A (running, for limitation purposes, from the date on which B's accrued), provided that B had not become aware of the damage when he was owner. This would not apply to the *Aliakmon* case itself, where the damage was discovered long before B parted with ownership. But it would apply where, *e.g.* C acquired the goods by endorsement of the bill of lading to him before they were landed. This would be inconvenient, for it would allow C to evade the contractual limitations to which he would be subject under the Bills of Lading Act. The legislative history of s.3 revolves around latent damage to buildings and the law of limitation against successive owners and it is unlikely to have occurred to anyone that it would be relevant in the *Aliakmon* situation. However, it refers to "property" not "land."

[12] The decision of the High Court of Australia in *The Willemstad* (1976) 11 A.L.R. 227 (see Cane (1977) 93 L.Q.R. 333; Rogers [1978] C.L.J.; Thompson (1977) 40 M.L.R. 714) appears now to be in the limbo reserved for cases without a *ratio*. D by negligent navigation damaged X's pipeline supplying oil to P's terminal across the bay. Hardly any of P's oil was lost, but P had to spend a lot of money transporting it while the pipeline was out of action. P recovered from D. There is a bewildering array of reasoning in the High Court of Australia. The Privy Council, in the *Candlewood* case, (*ante*, p. 85) declined to identify a *ratio* for it, but specifically rejected the view that it turned on the plaintiff being an individual or a member of a limited class of persons likely to be affected.

[13] [1964] A.C. 465, *post*, p. 273.

[14] *Ibid.* at pp. 516–517.

[15] [1980] Ch. 297. Cane (1980) 96 L.Q.R. 182; Dias [1980] C.L.J. 45. For a further aspect of this case, see *post*, p. 96.

but of the general law governing negligent conduct. The defendant solicitors were negligent in arranging the witnessing of a will so that the plaintiff lost her legacy and she was allowed to recover damages for this. Clearly, there was no problem of a wide-ranging liability: the defendants could be liable only to the plaintiff[16] and their contemplation of her was "actual, nominate and direct. It was contemplation by contract, though of course the contract was with the third party, the testator."[17]

Then came the remarkable case of *Junior Books Ltd.* v. *Veitchi Co. Ltd.*,[18] which threatened to revolutionise the law of negligence, soon fell from judicial favour,[19] but the effects of which may not be wholly spent. The defenders were engaged as subcontractors to lay a floor in the pursuer's factory. There was no contractual relationship between the parties and the main contractors were not involved in the proceedings. The pursuers alleged that the floor was defective (though not dangerous), that this was caused by the negligence of the defenders and that they had suffered damage totalling some £207,00, being the cost of replacing the floor and various other items of consequential loss. On a preliminary issue of law, the majority[20] of the House of Lords held that the pursuers' allegations disclosed a cause of action in negligence. Some saw in this the beginnings of a major extension of liability for economic loss, but by subsequent interpretation it has been largely relegated to the status of a decision on its own special facts. It has even been said that the case involved damage to the pursuers' property.[21] Certainly the pursuers were owners of the floor,[22] but to say that this meant there was damage to their property is tantamount to saying that supply of an article which is shoddy and breaks is actionable in negligence and that is not the law.[23] Alternatively, the defenders could be regarded as having damaged the pursuers' *building* by installing the defective floor, but it does not seem that the House of Lords thought it was deciding the case on this basis. A more satisfactory approach, it is suggested, is that of the Court of Appeal in

---

[16] There is no doubt that there was a breach of contract against the testator but it was assumed that the estate could have recovered only nominal damages. *cf. Abrahams* v. *Nelson Hurst & Marsh, The Times*, June 9, 1989.

[17] [1980] Ch. 297, 308. *cf. Abrahams* (n. 16): duty of insurance broker to client's client?

[18] [1983] 1 A.C. 520. Jaffey [1983] C.L.J. 39; Palmer and Murdoch (1983) 46 M.L.R. 213. During its brief reign this case generated a very large literature about economic loss. See, *inter alia*, Smith and Burns, "*Donoghue* v. *Stevenson*—the Not So Golden Anniversary" (1983) 46 M.L.R. 147 and Furmston (ed.), *The Law of Tort, Policies and Trends in Liability for Damage to Property and Economic Loss.*

[19] According to Purchas L.J. in *Greater Nottingham Cooperative Society Ltd.* v. *Cementation Piling and Foundations Ltd.* [1989] Q.B. 71, 96, *Junior Books* "intrepid progress towards Pandora's box [has] been subsequently set in retreat by the prudent withdrawal along that path in the ensuing authorities in the House of Lords." Dillon L.J. in *Simaan General Contracting Co.* v. *Pilkington Glass Ltd. (No. 2)* [1988] Q.B. 758, 784, was more forthright: "I find it difficult to see that future citation from the *Junior Books* case can ever serve any useful purpose."

[20] Lord Brandon dissented. He was a member of the Board in the *Candlewood* case and delivered the single opinion in the *Aliakmon* case. His dissent in *Junior Books* has been said to enunciate with cogency and clarity the fundamental principles applicable where there is no contract and no relationship as "uniquely proximate" as that in *Junior Books: D & F Estates Ltd.* v. *Church Commissioners* [1988] 3 W.L.R. 368, 381, *per* Lord Bridge.

[21] *Tate & Lyle Ltd.* v. *G.L.C.* [1983] 2 A.C. 509, 530, *per* Lord Templeman. But his Lordship at p. 535 seems to envisage "damage to property" as including interference with a contractual right. The *Tate & Lyle* case actually involved public nuisance and where that tort is committed by obstruction of the highway or navigable waters it has always been recognised as covering economic loss: *Rose* v. *Miles* (1815) 4 M. & S. 101.

[22] *Leigh and Sillavan Ltd.* v. *Aliakmon Shipping Co. Ltd.* [1986] A.C. 785, 817.

[23] See *post*, p. 246.

Muirhead v. *Industrial Tank Specialities Ltd.*,[24] which was a claim against a manufacturer of electric pumps (supplied to the plaintiffs by an intermediary) which failed to function properly and caused, *inter alia*, economic loss to the plaintiff.[25] In rejecting the plaintiff's claim for this loss the Court of Appeal laid great stress on the very close relationship which had existed between the parties in *Junior Books*: though there was no contract between them, the defenders, as nominated sub-contractors, would have been chosen by the pursuers (no doubt after direct negotiations between them) and therefore could be regarded as having given an undertaking to the pursuers upon which they had relied, even though the defenders' contractual relationship was with the main contractors. As in *Hedley, Byrne*, there is a relationship which is not contractual but which may be regarded as "equivalent to contract" and that may justify the imposition of liability for a loss of a type which is readily remediable in contract but rarely so in tort. To say that there is a difference between contract and tort is not the same as saying that there is no "debatable land" between them. Even this view is not without its difficulties (in particular the fact that it involves imposing a contract-type liability between the parties who have structured their relationships in such a way as not to create a contract[26]) but in any event it seems that the requirements of undertaking and reliance will be strictly insisted upon. As *Muirhead* clearly shows it is not satisfied by the existence of the relationship of manufacturer and ultimate user even though the latter no doubt "relies" on the former's producing a good quality product: something more is required, like compliance by the manufacturer with a request for an assurance of suitability—though at that point where would be very likely to be a collateral contract anyway.[27] In *Simaan General Contracting Co.* v. *Pilkington Glass Ltd. (No. 2)*[28] the plaintiffs were main contractors for the construction of a building in Abu Dhabi belonging to Sheikh Al-Oteiba. The erection of curtain walling was sub-contracted to Feal and green glass panels were supplied, on the instructions of the Sheikh, by Pilkingtons to Feal. These were not a uniform shade and the Sheikh withheld payment of part of the contract price from the plaintiffs. The plaintiffs' action in tort against Pilkingtons failed in the Court of Appeal. Whatever might be the position between the Sheikh and Pilkingtons on the basis of *Junior Books*, there was no sufficiently close relationship between the plaintiffs and Pilkingtons: they had had no technical discussions about the glass and Feal had been instructed to order it from Pilkingtons for one reason only, namely, that the Sheikh insisted on it.

Great stress was laid by the judges in the *Simaan* case upon the risk of a direct tort action disturbing the allocation of contractual responsibility down the chain of contracts and sub-contracts in a complex building project. For a

---

[24] [1986] Q.B. 507; Rogers [1986] C.L.J. 13.
[25] On the damage in this case and in other product liability cases, see further, *post*, p. 24.
[26] See Robert Goff L.J. at [1986] Q.B. 528. There is no legal reason why a building contract should not involve direct contracts with those who are normally sub-contractors.
[27] See, *e.g. Shanklin Pier* v. *Detel Products Ltd.* [1951] 2 K.B. 854.
[28] [1988] Q.B. 758.

similar reason liability in tort was rejected in *Greater Nottingham Cooperative Society Ltd.* v. *Cementation Piling and Foundations Ltd.*[29] where the relationship between the parties was so close there actually was a contract between them. The contract contained an express warranty by the defendants to exercise skill and care in the design of pile-driving operations and the selection of materials therefor, but said nothing about the *conduct* of those operations and the defendants were not liable in tort for economic loss resulting from their negligence in that respect. The case is in no way inconsistent with the proposition that a tort duty may exist between parties who have a contractual relationship: it merely warns against using tort to subvert the parties' contractual allocation of risks. If the defendants had damaged the plaintiffs' property[30] they would have been liable in tort as well as in contract,[31] but the terms of the contract negatived the exceptional circumstances needed for liability for economic loss. The existence of a contract between A and B was regarded in *Pacific Associates Inc.* v. *Baxter*[32] as a reason for denying a tort duty in respect of economic loss in C, the agent of A for the supervision of the A–B contract. By accepting the terms of the contract offered by A and in the absence of any direct undertaking of responsibility by C, B must be taken to have agreed to look for redress to A under the terms of the contract.

The requirement of undertaking and reliance may be a little more lax in cases of negligent misstatement, for there is still room for the existence of a duty to a class of persons.[33] This may not be a true theoretical difference for the defendant may be regarded as giving his undertaking to any persons who, he knows, will act upon his statement, but as a practical matter it may be easier to establish liability. This is dealt with later.[34]

The above account assumes that the distinction between physical damage and economic loss can be easily drawn, but this will not always be the case. Difficulties have arisen where a part of a complex product fails causing damage to the product as a whole[35] and many cases about defective premises in the 1970s and 1980s assumed without very much argument that the cost of repairing a defectively constructed building was recoverable in tort though it now seems that some of them may have been wrongly decided.[36]

(2) *Failure to act*

One must take care not to cause injury to others, but there is no general

---

[29] [1989] Q.B. 71.

[30] Physical damage was done to property next door. The defendants' liability to indemnify the plaintiffs for their liability to the neighbour was not disputed, but this obligation of the defendant arose from the Civil Liability (Contribution) Act 1978, not the common law.

[31] What Woolf L.J. at p. 106 referred to as their "normal" liability in tort. Of course an exclusion clause in the contract might negative this, too.

[32] [1989] 2 All E.R. 159.

[33] *Candlewood Navigation Corp. Ltd.* v. *Mitsui O.S.K. Lines Ltd.* [1986] A.C. 1, 24.

[34] *Post*, Chap. 11. The pumps in the *Muirhead* case bore an inaccurate statement about their voltage range, but the case was not run as one of negligent misstatement because the plaintiff has not relied on the voltage plates.

[35] See *post*, p. 246.

[36] *D. & F. Estates Ltd.* v. *Church Commissioners* [1988] 3 W.L.R. 368; *post*, p. 229.

duty to act for the benefit of others. The rule is that I must not *harm* my neighbour (misfeasance), not that I am required to save him (nonfeasance). "The very parable of the good Samaritan ... which was invoked by Lord Atkin in *Donoghue* v. *Stevenson* ... illustrates, in the conduct of the priest and the Levite who passed by on the other side, an omission which was likely to have as its reasonable and probable consequence damage to the health of the victim of the thieves, but for which the priest and the Levite would have incurred no civil liability in English law."[37] Harsh this basic rule may be,[38] but its existence is not surprising in view of the fact that long before the development of the tort of negligence the law had attached the label "contract" to duties to act for the benefit of others and, moreover, had insisted that a contractual duty could arise only on the basis of a promise, express or implied, supported by consideration or seal.[39] However, these conceptual lines are not always clear and it is by no means easy to state with precision the limits of the basic rule.[40] Further, there is dissatisfaction in some quarters with the basic morality of the present law.[41]

The first point is that an apparent omission may be treated as simply an item in a chain of active negligent conduct: no one would seriously argue that a driver's failure to brake at a junction constituted an omission in the sense here discussed[42]; and a doctor's failure to inform his patient of the nature and (where called for) risks of treatment is as much actionable as the negligent administration of the treatment itself.[43] However, even where there is a "true" omission there may be a relationship such that the law will impose a duty to act affirmatively to protect the plaintiff. Thus an occupier of land is obliged not merely to take care not to run over his visitor but to take steps to ensure that the premises are reasonably safe for the purposes for which he

---

[37] *Home Office* v. *Dorset Yacht Co. Ltd.* [1970] A.C. 1004, 1060, *per* Lord Diplock.

[38] But if the law were otherwise, real-life cases would tend to raise rather less straightforward issues than the classic example of an adult who watches a child drown in a foot of water: what do we do when the defendant is one of a large number of people who could have assisted; or when the defendant, perhaps unreasonably, perceives the danger of undertaking the rescue to be greater than it actually is?

[39] "The heart of the nonfeasance rule consists in the peremptory refusal to attach legal sanctions to gratuitous undertakings to confer a benefit on a promisee, as there is no more sacrosanct axiom in our jurisprudence than that a promise without consideration will not be enforced": Fleming, The Law of Torts (5th ed.), p. 147 (wording modified in the 7th ed., p. 136).

[40] Bowman and Bailey, "Negligence in the Realms of Public Law—A Positive Obligation to Rescue?" [1984] P.L. 277; Smith and Burns, "*Donoghue* v. *Stevenson*—the Not So Golden Anniversary" (1983) 46 M.L.R. 147.

[41] See, *e.g.* Linden, "Rescuers and Good Samaritans" (1971) 34 M.L.R. 241; Weinrib, "The Case for a duty to Rescue" (1981) 90 Yale L.J. 247; Markesinis, "Negligence, Nuisance and Affirmative Duties of Action" (1989) 105 L.Q.R. 104. Lord Goff in *Smith* v. *Littlewoods Organisation Ltd.* [1987] A.C. 241, 271, while accepting the rule, says that it may one day have to be reconsidered.

[42] Rigby, L.J. in *Kelly* v. *Metropolitan Ry. Co.* [1895] 1 Q.B. 944, 947, said of a driver's failure to shut off steam so that his train ran into a dead-end, "the proper description of what was done is that it was a negligent act in so managing the train as to allow it to come into contact with the dead-end." The other members of the court inclined to the view that there was an omission, but came to what must be the correct conclusion on the point in issue: that the action lay in tort as well as contract.

[43] But it is not necessarily enough that the defendant has done something active to make the harm possible. In *C.B.S. Songs Ltd.* v. *Amstrad Consumer Electronics p.l.c.* [1988] A.C. 1013 the defendants produced tape recorders which made it easy to copy copyright material. The House of Lords emphatically denied that they were under any duty of care to the owners of the copyright material. The rights of the owners were to be found in the copyright legislation and nowhere else and that had not been infringed.

enters[44]; the Supreme Court of Canada has held that a (non-contractual) carrier is obliged to take steps to save a passenger who falls overboard from the boat in which he is being carried[45]; and an employer must look after an injured worker.[46] It is impossible to catalogue the factors pointing towards such a duty of affirmative action, though the fact that there is some benefit accruing to the defendant will certainly incline the court towards imposing one.[47] Benefit should not, however, be necessary. Neglect by a parent of a young child gives rise to criminal liability and it is hard to see why there should not be a tort duty, too, albeit that the absence of liability insurance would make many actions futile.[48] A school is certainly under a duty to protect its pupils against danger,[49] though this may rest on the idea of undertaking and reliance discussed below,[50] as may other cases where a defendant has been liable when he has had charge of a person unable to look after himself.[51] These cases concern relationships between the plaintiff and the defendant, but the relationship between the defendant and a third party may impose on the defendant a duty to protect the plaintiff from injury (even deliberate injury) by the third party.[52] For this reason a school authority was liable for letting a small child out of school in circumstances where it was foreseeable that he would cause an accident in which a driver was killed trying to avoid him,[53] and Borstal authorities were responsible for damage done by escaping inmates in the immediate vicinity.[54] Where the

---

[44] Since the occupier expressly or impliedly invites his visitor on to the premises it may be objected that the case is not one of pure omission. But since *British Railways Board* v. *Herrington* [1972] A.C. 877 (see now Occupiers' Liability Act 1984, *post*, p. 225) the occupier has been under a limited duty even to uninvited entrants.

[45] *Horsley* v. *Maclaren* [1971] 2 Lloyd's Rep. 410.

[46] *Kasapis* v. *Laimos* [1959] 2 Lloyd's Rep. 378. But he has no duty to safeguard the employee's property against theft (*Deyong* v. *Shenburn* [1946] 1 K.B. 236) nor to advise him to insure himself against accidental injury: *Reid* v. *Rush & Tompkins* [1989] N.L.J. 680.

[47] Eldredge, *Modern Tort Problems*, p. 14, It may be that there is also a general principle that he who creates a danger, albeit innocently, must take steps to remedy it: *Johnston* v. *Rea Ltd.* [1962] 1 Q.B. 373; *McKinnon* v. *Burtatowski* [1969] V.R. 899.

[48] The High Court of Australia in *Hahn* v. *Conley* (1971) 126 C.L.R. 276 took a narrow view of the duty of a parent, saying that it did not arise from the relationship as such but from the assumption of responsibility on the particular occasion (*e.g.* by taking the child on the highway). However, the decision was heavily influenced by a desire to avoid the consequences of the contribution legislation: *post*, p. 593.

[49] See Clerk and Lindsell, *Torts*, 16th ed., para. 10–91.But the school's duty does not extend to taking out personal accident insurance cover for the pupil nor even to advising the parent to take that step: *Van Oppen* v. *Bedford School* [1989] 1 All E.R. 273. A university, even in the United States, fertile home of tort duties, incurs no liability for failing to control the private lives of its students, allowing them to be seduced, become associated with criminals, or become drug users: *Hegel* v. *Langsam* 273 N.E. 2d. 351 (1971).

[50] See *post*, p. 95. But the duty to disclose in insurance law does not sound in damages: *Banque Keyser Ullman S.A.* v. *Skandia (U.K.) Insurance Co. Ltd.* [1988] 2 Lloyd's Rep. 513; *Bank of Nova Scotia* v. *Hellenic Mutual War Risks Asscn.*, *The Times*, April 20, 1989.

[51] *Bryson* v. *Northumbria Police Authority* [1977] 2 C.L. 176.

[52] A court in *Munro* v. *Porthkerry Holiday Estates* (1984) 81 L.S.Gaz. 2450 appears to have accepted that a person selling excessive quantities of alcohol to a customer might owe a duty to him, though on the facts there was no breach of duty (*cf. Jorden House* v. *Menow* (1973) 38 D.L.R. (3d) 105, where he also put the plaintiff out of the premises). Could he be under a duty to a third party injured by the drunk? Robert Goff L.J. in *Paterson Zochonis & Co. Ltd.* v. *Merfarken Packaging Ltd.* [1986] 3 All E.R. 522, 540, relying on *Ontario Hospital Services Commission* v. *Borsoski* (1974) 54 D.L.R. (3d) 339, thought there might be liability on a person who entrusted a car to a drunk but that a dealer who sold a car to a person whom he knew to be an alcoholic would not be liable for an accident caused by intoxication a few weeks later.

[53] *Carmarthenshire C.C.* v. *Lewis* [1955] A.C. 549. As to a parent's duty, see further, *post*, p. 672.

[54] *Home Office* v. *Dorset Yacht Co. Ltd.* [1970] A.C. 1004. Weir, *Casebook on Tort* (6th ed.), p. 53. See also *Holgate* v. *Lancashire Mental Hospital Board* [1937] 4 All E.R. 19, though Lord Diplock in the *Dorset Yacht* case at pp. 1062–1063 reserved his opinion on this case.

defendant has control of *both* the plaintiff and the third party (for example, in a case where there is an assault by a prison inmate upon a fellow-prisoner[55]) the case for the imposition of a duty is particularly strong.

Where, however, the defendant has a "special relationship" with neither the author nor the victim of the harm there is generally no duty to act.[56] We have already seen the point in the refusal to hold the police liable to the victim of a notorious criminal for their alleged inefficiency in failing to catch him.[57] Similarly, a property owner has been held not to be under a general duty to keep his premises lockfast so as to prevent them being used as a means of access to adjoining property by thieves[58] or so as to prevent vandals gaining access and causing damage to adjoining property.[59] The imposition of such a duty is regarded as an unreasonable burden upon a landowner[60] and, at least in the case of theft, the primary obligation to protect his property should, in the courts' view, rest upon the neighbour.[61] However, this does not mean that a landowner can never be under a duty to take steps for the protection of his neighbour, for the occupation of land is a source of obligation as well as of rights and he must not allow it to become a danger to others.[62] If an occupier returned home to find a burglar in the act of boring through his wall into the adjoining jeweller's shop, he would be under a duty to take whatever steps were reasonable to ensure that the boring ceased[63] and an occupier who was aware that his premises presented some unusual hazard which might be triggered off by vandals (for example, large quantities of inflammable material) might be required to take reasonable steps to guard them.[64] From an analytical point of view the House of Lords in *Smith*

---

[55] *Ellis* v. *Home Office* [1953] 2 All E.R. 149. It must be stressed that in all these cases the liability is not vicarious—the injury must be attributable to the defendant's negligence in failing to prevent it: *Smith* v. *Leurs* (1945) 70 C.L.R. 256.

[56] An established business relationship between an insurer and insured does not alter the rule that silence is not misrepresentation and does not give rise to a duty to disclose for the purposes of an action in tort; the legal remedy is avoidance of the contract: *Banque Keyser Ullman S.A.* v. *Skandia (U.K.) Insurance Co. Ltd.* [1988] 2 Lloyd's Rep. 513.

[57] *Hill* v. *Chief Constable of West Yorkshire* [1988] 2 W.L.R. 1049, *ante*, p. 78. An interesting case which raises a comparable problem with the added complication of medical ethics is *Tarasoff* v. *University of California* 551 P. (2d.) 334 (1976) (psychiatrist knowing murderous propensities of his patient).

[58] *P. Perl (Exporters)* v. *Camden London Borough* [1984] Q.B. 342; Jones (1984) 47 M.L.R. 223. Contrast *Stansbie* v. *Troman* [1948] 2 K.B. 48 (*post*, p. 155) where a decorator was held liable for a burglary when he left unlocked the premises he was decorating. His duty to the householder arose from his undertaking (implied, no doubt, from his contract on the facts) to keep the premises safe. He would not have been liable to an adjoining householder if the burglar had bored through from the premises first entered.

[59] *Smith* v. *Littlewoods Organisation Ltd.* [1987] A.C. 241; *King* v. *Liverpool City Council* [1986] 1 W.L.R. 890. A person who leaves an unlocked vehicle in a private drive is not liable for damage caused to another by wrongful interference with the vehicle by a third party (*Bohdal* v. *Streets* [1984] Tas.R. 83) and in *Denton* v. *United Omnibus Co., The Times*, May 6, 1986, a bus company was not liable for damage caused by someone who drove a bus away. Most American cases accord, even though there is evidence there that stolen vehicles have a much higher accident rate: Prosser, *Torts*, (5th ed.), pp. 313–314.

[60] See Lord Goff's example at p. 277 in the *Littlewoods* case, *supra*, of the family going on holiday who forget to lock their front door.

[61] In many cases the contest would effectively be between the defendant's liability insurer and the neighbour's loss insurer.

[62] See *Goldman* v. *Hargrave* [1967] 1 A.C. 645, *post*, p. 399.

[63] *Smith* v. *Littlewoods Organisation Ltd.* [1987] A.C. 241, 265, *per* Lord Mackay.

[64] *Ibid.* at p. 251, *per* Lord Griffiths. "So far as Littlewoods knew, there was nothing significantly different about these empty premises from tens of thousands of such premises up and down the country. People do not mount 24-hour guards on empty properties and the law would impose an intolerable burden if it required them to do so save in the most exceptional circumstances."

v. *Littlewoods Organisation Ltd.*[65] did not speak with on voice on the subject of damage caused by third parties. Lord Goff laid stress upon the general rule of non-liability for omissions and the requirement of finding special circumstances to take the case out of that rule, but other members of the House based their opinions on the proposition that while there is a duty upon a landowner to ensure that his property does not become a source of danger to others, wilful human conduct is not normally sufficiently likely to require the defendant to contemplate it as a reasonable probability rather than a mere remote possibility[66]: almost anything is foreseeable in the literal sense but that degree of likelihood is not sufficient to require action by the landowner. In most cases there is likely to be no practical difference between the two approaches,[67] but the majority view, with its greater emphasis upon factual matters of degree, may make it more difficult, on appeal, to attack a finding in the plaintiff's favour.

A difficult area is that concerned with failure by a defendant to carry out some service which he has, without contract, undertaken to perform for the plaintiff. Suppose, for example, that the defendant sees the plaintiff drowning and goes to his assistance[68] but then, though there is no danger to himself, abandons the venture. He has certainly failed to exercise reasonable care, but it may be argued that no *act* of his has caused the plaintiff any damage[69] and the complaint against him is that he failed to confer a promised benefit upon the plaintiff. At the risk of being accused of conceptualism, we might say that "you made me worse" sounds properly in tort but "you failed to save me" is essentially a contractual allegation and there is no contract. However, there should be no great difficulty when the defendant's failure to carry through the rescue deprives the plaintiff of the assistance of others or, in some cases, of the opportunity to take alternative steps to protect himself.[70] Liability then arises from reliance upon the defendant's undertaking to carry the task through, which may be express or implied from a consistent course of conduct.[71] However, there are cases which have imposed liability

---

[65] *Ibid.*

[66] "Unless the needle that measures the probability of a particular result flowing from the conduct of a human agent is near the top of the scale it may be hard to conclude that it has risen sufficiently from the bottom to create the duty reasonably to foresee it": *ibid.* at p. 261, *per* Lord Mackay.

[67] Lord Keith at p. 249 felt able to agree with both Lord Goff and Lord Mackay.

[68] If the defendant does nothing, he clearly cannot be liable. *Quaere* if he is a lifeguard?

[69] Distinguish the case of the rescuer who bungles the job and actually injures the plaintiff, who might otherwise have escaped unharmed. "Both priest and levite ensured performance of any common law duty of care to the stricken traveller when, by crossing to the other side of the road they avoided any risk of throwing up dust in his wounds": Deane J. in *Jaensch* v. *Coffey* (1984) 54 A.L.R. 417, 440.

[70] *Semble, Wood* v. *Thurston, The Times,* May 25, 1951; *Barnett* v. *Chelsea and Kensington Hospital Management Committee* [1969] 1 Q.B. 420; *Zelenko* v. *Gimbel Bros.* 287 N.Y.S. 134 (1935) (P taken ill in D's store. D put P in sick room and left her there for six hours without treatment, whereby she died. D liable for P's death). The much battered case of *East Suffolk Rivers Catchment Board* v. *Kent* [1941] A.C. 74 might have been regarded as supporting this analysis, but the House of Lords has held that it turned on a different point: *post,* p. 100.

[71] See *Bird* v. *Pearce* (1979) L.G.R. 753 (collision caused by temporary obliteration of "stop" lines; reasonable to expect drivers to rely on system of precedence apparently in force along the road); *Sutherland Shire Council* v. *Heyman* (1985) 60 A.L.R. 1, 47, *per* Brennan J; *McDonogh* v. *Commonwealth* (1985) 73 A.L.R. 148 (though the precise point at issue there would not arise in England since the

and which are not explicable in terms of reliance. In *Ross* v. *Caunters*[72] the plaintiff was permitted to recover damages from the defendant solicitors when their negligence caused her legacy under a will to fail, despite the absence of any allegation of reliance by her. Most important, however, was the decision in *Anns* v. *Merton London Borough*,[73] which has already been encountered in connection with the establishment of duties in general.

The defendant authority had a statutory power (but not a duty) to inspect dwellings in the course of construction in its area. According to the plaintiff's statement of claim[74] the authority had failed to carry out an inspection or had carried one out negligently, with the result that the foundations of the block of flats in which he was a long leaseholder were inadequate and structural movement had occurred.[75] There was no evidence of reliance by the plaintiffs upon any inspection and it was therefore argued that the authority had merely failed to protect the plaintiff from someone else's negligence. However, pointing out that statutory powers were subject to judicial control (via judicial review) in a way in which the powers of a natural person were not, Lord Wilberforce replied that "their immunity from attack, in the event of failure to inspect . . . though great,[76] is not absolute. And because it is not absolute, the necessary premise for the proposition, 'if no duty to inspect, then no duty to take care in inspection' vanishes."[77] The connection between the public law control of a discretion and the imposition of a duty to act to protect another has not been obvious to all[78] but the majority of the House of Lords seems to have contemplated a liability even for *failure* to inspect. Lord Salmon (who would not have gone so far) said that the plaintiff's loss was

Highways Act 1961); *Maxey* v. *Canada Permanent Trust Co.* (1984) 9 D.L.R. (4th) 380). Perhaps, in a non-personal injury context, this is the explanation of the old case of *Wilkinson* v. *Coverdale* (1793) 1 Esp. 75 (*cf. Thorne* v. *Deas* 4 Johns. 84 (U.S.) (1809)). But once, as here, we combine this principle with recovery of economic loss, what is left of the special requirements of contract, for do not promisees rely on promisors fulfilling their undertakings? That the requirements of contract are not so easily sidestepped is indicated in the somewhat esoteric and extremely complex environment of the marine reinsurance market in *General Accident, etc. Corpn.* v. *Tanter* [1985] 2 Lloyd's Rep. 529. A broker's indication that he would use his best endeavours to ensure that a syndicate's risk would be reduced from its original level was held by the trial judge to be non-contractual. On this basis, the Court of Appeal thought there would be no alternative liability in tort. "The complaint cannot without abuse of language be expressed by saying that the partially signed down slip was an injurious object which caused the syndicate economic loss; or that allowing the risk to attach with the slip only partially signed down was an injurious act. In reality, the fault of the brokers lay in a continuing failure to perform a positive undertaking. Once any contractual background is subtracted, I do not see how such a right of action can be sustained without holding that if the relationship between the parties is of the right kind English law recognises the enforceability of a gratuitous promise.": *ibid.* at p. 538, *per* Mustill L.J.

[72] [1980] Ch. 297; *Gartside* v. *Sheffield, Young & Ellis* [1983] N.Z.L.R. 37. The loss was, of course, economic: *ante*, p. 88. An Australian court rejected *Ross* v. *Caunters* in *Seale* v. *Perry* [1982] V.R. 193 but in *Hawkins* v. *Clayton* (1988) 78 A.L.R. 69 a majority of the High Court of Australia held that a solicitor who had custody of a will and was aware of the testator's death was under a duty to the estate to seek out the executor.

[73] [1978] A.C. 728; *ante*, p. 75. Weir, *Casebook on Tort* (6th ed.), p. 61.

[74] The case was decided on the pleadings as a preliminary issue of law.

[75] As to the builder's liability, see *post*, p. 229.

[76] This is a reference to a further difficult aspect of the case, the extent to which the law of negligence applies to "discretionary" functions.

[77] [1978] A.C. 728, 755.

[78] See Mason J. in *Sutherland Shire Council* v. *Heyman* (1985) 60 A.L.R. 1, 31: "although a public authority may be under a public duty, enforceable by mandamus, to give proper consideration to the question whether it should exercise a power, this duty cannot be equated with, or regarded as the foundation for imposing, a duty of care on the public authority in relation to the exercise of the power. Mandamus will compel proper consideration by the authority of its discretion, but that is all."

caused "not by any reliance placed by the plaintiffs on the council or the building inspector but by the fact that if the inspection had been carefully made, the defects in the foundations would have been rectified. ... *In the present case reliance is not even remotely relevant.*"[79] This, like other aspects of *Anns* has come in for criticism, though it must still be taken to represent the law in Britain.

In *Curran* v. *Northern Ireland Co-ownership Housing Association Ltd.*,[80] *Anns* was distinguished because the defendants were not a body carrying out inspections to safeguard public health and safety but one giving grants for housing improvement. Although they were required by the relevant legislation to satisfy themselves that the dwelling would attain a certain standard of fitness when the work was completed, this was for the protection of the public revenue, not of the recipients of the grants and their successors in title.[81] However, Lord Bridge also remarked that the courts should be wary of extending the cases in which a statutory body might be held to be under a duty to control the activities of third parties and that *Anns* tended to "obscure the important distinction between misfeasance and nonfeasance."[82] He also referred with approval to the judgment of Brennan J. in the High Court of Australia in *Sutherland Shire Council* v. *Heyman*,[83] another case of alleged negligent inspection pursuant to statutory powers, in which the court, after full consideration of the authorities, declined to follow *Anns*. Having accepted that there might be liability where reliance on the carrying out of a careful inspection could be shown, Brennan J. declined to find a duty where reliance was absent, for in that case, while "the Council's actions did nothing to minimise the risk of defective footings, ... they did not create or increase that risk. The Council's omission to exercise its powers of inspection more rigorously do not make it liable for the builder's negligence."[84] However, Mason J. in the same case suggested that when a public authority is involved, there may be a "general reliance" by the public which requires neither specific conduct on the part of the defendant nor acts of detrimental reliance by the plaintiff.[85] For example, the public might rely upon a statutory aviation authority to supervise the safety of aircraft even though they are unaware of the details of the authority's powers and could not take any alternative step themselves.[86] Whether or not this represents English law one cannot say, but since *Anns* has not been overruled it is difficult to accept the "rigorous" view of Brennan J., whatever its logical

[79] [1978] A.C. 728, 769, emphasis added.
[80] [1987] A.C. 718.
[81] Other important decisions cutting down *Anns* in the building context are *Governors of the Peabody Donation Fund* v. *Sir Lindsay Parkinson & Co. Ltd.* [1985] A.C. 210 and *Investors in Industry Ltd.* v. *South Bedfordshire D.C.* [1986] Q.B. 1034. As a result of these, the local authority is not liable to the original builder who is himself in breach of building regulations. See *post*, p. 232.
[82] [1987] A.C., 718, 724, 726.
[83] (1985) 60 A.L.R. 1.
[84] *Ibid.* at p. 49.
[85] *Ibid.* at p. 30. This is taken up in *Parramatta C.C.* v. *Lutz* (1988) 12 N.S.W.L.R. 293 (failure by council to exercise powers of demolition of dangerous premises. McHugh J.A. thought that such cases might be based upon a"right of control" by the authority (cf. p. 93 *ante*) but he thought this approach different from and inconsistent with, that of "general reliance").
[86] But what if the plaintiff is wholly unaware of the existence of the authority?

attraction. Reliance is very briefly touched on by the Privy Council in *Christchurch Drainage Board* v. *Brown*.[87] The case arose from the failure of a statutory drainage board to warn the plaintiffs of the risk of flooding on the site on which their house was to be built,[88] despite the fact that the board habitually checked flood levels when building permits were referred to it. Dealing with a submission that the plaintiffs had not relied upon the board, the Privy Council replied that "in circumstances such as these reliance cannot be required from the ignorant." However, it may be that the correct explanation of the case is that the permit was passed on by an intermediate public body which was aware of the board's practice and in the circumstances this might be treated as replacing or equivalent to reliance by the plaintiffs. Overall, it seems that the English courts are still reluctant to countenance arguments by a public authority fulfilling a statutory function that a member of the public has not relied upon discharge of that function, even though the net effect is to impose a duty where Parliament has declined to impose one.

(3) *Negligence and public law.*[89]

Aside from the question of nonfeasance there are further complexities involved in the relationship between statutory functions and the common law of negligence.[90] The straightforward application of the principle that you must take reasonable care not to injure persons foreseeably likely to be affected by your acts has been thought to involve the risk that the law of negligence might unduly hamper the discretionary functions of public bodies and the public law concept of *ultra vires* has been to some extent superimposed upon the common law of negligence. This originated in the speech of Lord Diplock in *Home Office* v. *Dorset Yacht Co. Ltd.*[91] The facts which the House of Lords was required to assume for an appeal on a preliminary issue of law were that some Borstal trainees had been working under an "open regime" on an island in Portsea Harbour and during the night some of them escaped owing to the negligence of Borstal Officers. The boys went aboard a yacht moored nearby and caused it to collide with the plaintiff's yacht, doing considerable damage. From one aspect the case involved the question whether there could be a duty to prevent others doing harm,[92] but it was also strenuously argued for the Home Office that the imposition of a duty of care

---

[87] *The Times*, October 26, 1987.

[88] The board seems to have been under a *duty* to check the drains, etc., but this did not extend to the risk of flooding. The board's liability was for common law negligence.

[89] Aronson and Whitmore, *Public Torts and Contracts*; Harlow *Compensation and Government Torts*; Craig, "Negligence in the Exercise of a Statutory Power" (1979) 84 L.Q.R. 428; Oliver, "*Anns v. London Borough of Merton* Reconsidered" (1980) 33 C.L.P. 269; Todd, "The Negligence Liability of Public Authorities: Divergence in the Common Law" (1986) 102 L.Q.R. 370; Bailey and Bowman, "The Policy/Operational Dichotomy—A Cuckoo in the Nest" [1986] C.L.J. 430.

[90] Whether a public authority owes a statutory duty remediable by the action of breach of statutory duty is a question of the construction of the statute: *post*, Chap. 7.

[91] [1970] A.C. 1004; Hamson, "Escaping Borstal Boys and the Immunity of Office" [1968] C.L.J. 273. For the basis upon which the Home Office granted *ex gratia* compensation in such cases, see Harlow, *op. cit.*, p. 154.

[92] See *ante*, p. 93.

might lead to excessive caution in the administration of Borstal institutions and thus hamper the training of young delinquents; in particular, experience had shown that the duty to train such people was better carried out by using activities outside rather than within the confines of an institution. According to Lord Diplock[93] the correct way to deal with this was to recognise the significance of the public law doctrine of *ultra vires*:

> "According to this concept Parliament has entrusted to the department or authority charged with the administration of the statute the exclusive right to determine the particular means within the limits laid down by the statute by which its purpose can best be fulfilled. It is not the function of the court, for which it would be ill-suited, to substitute its own view of the appropriate means for that of the department or authority by granting a remedy by way of a civil action at law to a private citizen adversely affected by the way in which the discretion has been exercised. Its function is confined in the first instance to deciding whether the act or omission complained of fell within the statutory limits imposed upon the department's or authority's discretion."

Suppose, therefore, that the plaintiff's property has been damaged by escaping inmates, that there is no evidence as to how they escaped, but that it can be shown that the level of escapes from "open" institutions is 10 times that from "closed" ones. On this view, the plaintiffs' action for negligence does not even get off the ground unless he first shows that the decision to operate the Borstal system in this way is impliedly beyond the power given by Parliament. The usual bases upon which *ultra vires* may be established are (*a*) illegality (the power claimed does not exist) (*b*) irrationality (the decision is so unreasonable that no reasonable authority could have arrived at it) or (*c*) procedural impropriety (bias or the taking into account of irrelevant considerations). The second is much the most likely to be relevant where a tort claim arises out of an administrative decision to adopt a particular policy,[94] but it would require more to be shown than that there was a higher risk, even a substantially higher risk, of loss or damage to neighbouring landowners. This approach was reinforced by its adoption in *Anns* v. *Merton London Borough*.[95] As we have seen, the case was based upon an alleged failure to exercise, or to exercise properly, powers of inspection under the Public Health Act 1936.[96] While holding that the plaintiffs' statement of claim disclosed a cause of action in negligence, the House of Lords made it clear that the plaintiff would not succeed simply by showing that the level of inspection carried out by the authority was insufficient to detect bad workmanship. An authority entrusted with statutory powers of inspection would

---

[93] [1970] A.C. 1004, 1067. But the other judges utilised the general concepts of negligence law: see *post*, p. 101.

[94] But the third was in issue in *City of Kamloops* v. *Nielsen* (1984) 10 D.L.R. (4th) 641; see also *Potter* v. *Mole Valley D.C.* (1983) 80 L.S.Gaz. 158.

[95] [1978] A.C. 728; Weir, *Casebook on Tort* (6th ed.), p. 61.

[96] For an alternative system of supervision, see Part II of the Housing and Building Control Act 1984.

have numerous and fluctuating calls upon its resources and it might take a proper, reasoned decision to direct resources from building inspections to what it considered were more urgent tasks by, for example, reducing the frequency of inspections or the methods by which inspections were carried out.[97] Indeed, it might, for good reasons,[98] stop inspections altogether.[99] The general idea is simple enough and it would be hard dispute it: the allocation of resources to, *inter alia*, building inspection is not generally "justiciable" in the sense that the court is not a suitable body to decide it. However, this gives rise to some formidable legal difficulties.

First, if, as the cases suggest, the plaintiff wishing to attack a decision of policy on the ground that it amounts to negligence is required to show that it is *ultra vires* as a preliminary to establishing breach of a duty of care,[1] much the most likely way of doing so is by showing that the policy is "irrational." However, having done this, it is not at all clear what he must then go on to do to establish the breach of duty: establishing the precondition seems to prove his case.[2] Secondly, the usual procedure for judicial review of administrative action is not by ordinary suit but by application under R.S.C. Order 53. A claim for damages may be made in Order 53 proceedings, but there are various restrictions upon the procedure, in particular a requirement of leave and a short time limit. It is regrettably unclear how far a claim like that in *Anns* is caught by Order 53, but if it is it may prevent the plaintiff with practical difficulties.[3]

Perhaps the most serious problem is that of the extent of the *ultra vires* precondition to a negligence claim. Lord Wilberforce in *Anns* drew a distinction between "policy" and "operational" matters, saying that the law of negligence would more easily operate on the latter than on the former.[4] The

---

[97] However, authorities may now charge for such inspections. *cf. Cynat Products Ltd.* v. *Landbuild, etc., Ltd.* [1984] 3 All E.R. 513, 523 (approval for purposes of building regulations).

[98] If the authority decided to cease inspections altogether to avoid liability, such a decision would be *ultra vires*. Lord Salmon at [1978] A.C. 762 doubted whether non-inspection, as opposed to careless inspection, could lead to liability, but *cf.* Lord Wilberforce at p. 760.

[99] The House distinguished its own decision in *East Suffolk Rivers Catchment Board* v. *Kent* [1941] A.C. 74, when an action failed against a public authority which sent an inexperienced man to repair a sea wall, with the result that the plaintiff's land remained flodded much longer than it need have done. According to *Anns*, the authority's devision to devote small resources to the repair of the breach was one made in the proper exercise of its discretion and hence not negligent. This may be true (see Bowman and Bailey, [1984] P.L. 277) but it is doubtful if it was the court's *ratio* (see the 11th ed. of this work at p. 80).

[1] Establishing such a breach, is of course, essential. Under our law an *ultra vires* act does not of itself give rise to a claim for damages.

[2] Subject, of course, to causation.

[3] According to *O'Reilly* v. *Mackman* [1983] 2 A.C. 236, 285, Ord. 53 covers the protection of rights to which a person is entitled "under public law." In *Cocks* v. *Thanet D.C.* [1983] 2 A.C. 286 this was held to include a situation where, as a precondition to establishing a private right of action under a statute, the plaintiff was required to impugn an adverse decision of the defendants as to his status. However, the H.L. has subsequently held that *Cocks* v. *Thanet* was concerned with a case where the defendants' decision prevented the plaintiff from establishing a "new" private law right; it did not operate where the defendants had deprived him of a pre-existing private law right: *Wandsworth London Borough* v. *Winder* [1985] A.C. 461. On the facts, the decision is not surprising since the person alleging *ultra vires* was *defendant* to an ordinary action brouht by the council. In *Davy* v. *Spelthorne B.C.* [1984] A.C. 262 the Ord. 53 procedure was said to have no application to the plaintiff's claim for negligent msistatement, the public law element being "peripheral"; and in *R.* v. *Secretary of State for the Home Office ex p. Dew* [1987] 1 W.L.R. 881 an application under Ord. 53 in respect of alleged negligence by prison authorities in failing to provide medical treatment was held to be misconceived.

[4] [1978] A.C. 728, 754.

general distinction between the two categories is clear enough[5] though, as Lord Wilberforce admitted, the two shade into each other and even "operational" functions may have built into them a large element of discretion. It is not, however, wholly clear what is the *consequence* of the distinction. It is tempting to assume that policy matters are subject to the precondition of establishing *ultra vires* (that is to say, they are generally non-justiciable) whereas operational matters are not, but a subsequent passage in Lord Wilberforce's speech appears to be inconsistent with this. Referring to an inspector conducting an inspection on behalf of the council, he says,

"but this duty, heavily operational though it may be, is still a duty arising under the statute. There may be a discretionary element in its exercise—discretionary as to the time and manner of inspection and the techniques to be used. A plaintiff complaining of negligence must prove, the burden being on him, that action taken was not within the limits of a discretion bona fide exercised, *before he can begin to rely upon a common law duty of care.*"[6]

Now since all activities of public authorities are carried out under statute[7] and virtually any conscious act by a public authority employee involves an element of discretion[8] this would lead to the extraordinary result that a showing of *ultra vires* would be a necessary precondition of a claim if, say, a school teacher let a young child out unsupervised. In practice, the courts seem to have treated operational matters as governed solely by the private law principles of negligence which, of course, contain ample flexibility to deal with "discretion" by a public employee.[9] Indeed, there have been cases which could well have been treated as involving "policy" issues in which singularly little attention has been paid to *Anns*.[10] It has been forcefully argued[11] that the policy/operational distinction has shown itself to be unworkable and that while it is certainly true that a court dealing with a claim against a public authority exercising statutory functions must be cautious not

---

[5] For "policy" decisions see, *e.g. Allison* v. *Corby D.C.* [1980] R.T.R. 111; *D.H.S.S.* v. *Kinnear, The Times*, July 7, 1984; *West* v. *Buckinghamshire C.C.* (1984) 83 L.G.R. 449. In *Vicar of Writtle* v. *Essex C.C.* (1979) L.G.R. 656 the defendants might have been allowed to place the pyromaniac juvenile in non-secure accommodation for his benefit, but could not rely on that point when he was so placed as a result of their failure to put his record before the right persons. *cf.* Lord Diplock in the *Dorset Yacht* case at [1970] A.C. 1079.

[6] [1978] A.C. 728, 755. Emphasis added.

[7] Certain functions of the Crown are carried out under the prerogative, but that, too, is subject to judicial review in so far as the subject matter is justiciable: *C.C.S.U.* v. *Minister for the Civil Service* [1985] A.C. 374.

[8] Even, *e.g.* the decision on what research to undertake before answering an enquiry.

[9] See, *e.g. post*, p. 119. In *Rigby* v. *Chief Constable of Northamptonshire* [1985] 1 W.L.R. 1242 Taylor J. treated the decision to retain "old" C.S. gas canisters with a higher fire risk than newer versions as a policy matter. But firing one when there was no fire engine in the vicinity was held negligent without reference to public law.

[10] Perhaps the best example is *Page Motors Ltd.* v. *Epsom and Ewell B.C.* (1982) 80 L.G.R. 337 (failure to move gipsies from council land) which cannot turn on any distinction between nuisance and negligence; see also *Bird* v. *Pearce* (1979) 77 L.G.R. 753 and *Simkiss* v. *Rhondda B.C.* (1983) 81 L.G.R. 460. For application of *Anns* see *Fellowes* v. *Rother D.C.* [1983] 1 All E.R. 513.

[11] Bailey and Bowman, "The Policy/Operational Dichotomy—A Cuckoo in the Nest" [1986] C.L.J. 430.

to trespass on the authority's legitimate area of discretion and policy-making, no special rules of law are necessary to ensure this.[12] If it is to have any field of operation it could perhaps be confined to cases, like *Anns*, where there would be no duty of care without the statutory power in question.[13] It may be that the courts are already abandoning it in favour of a careful examination of the issues in individual cases. Thus the decision of an adjudication officer on the payment of unemployment benefit is presumably "operational"[14] but in *Jones* v. *Department of Employment*[15] the Court of Appeal declined to impose a duty of care because adequate remedies to correct errors were provided by the statutory appeal procedure.[16] In *Rowling* v. *Takaro Properties Ltd.*[17] the Privy Council was concerned with an action for negligence arising out of the refusal of a New Zealand minister to allow the issue of shares to a foreign company, a refusal which had been struck down on judicial review. On the facts, the court came to no conclusion on whether a duty of care existed, since even if it did, the minister's mistaken construction of his statutory powers was not negligent. However, having said that the policy/operational distinction could not be relied on to provide a "touchstone of liability" and that there were difficulties in applying it to the activity in which the minister had been engaged, the Privy Council inclined to the view that there would have been no duty even if the function were properly classified as operational. As in the *Jones* case, there was an adequate alternative remedy (judicial review) which could be speedily set in train, but perhaps decisive was the danger that if a duty were imposed it might lead to excessive caution by the administration, to the unnecessary obtaining of legal advice and hence to unnecessary delay: the cure would be worse than the disease.

(4) *Liability of lawyers*

Professional men of all descriptions have become increasingly exposed to negligence and in some spheres liability insurance premium have risen far faster than other costs,[18] though this probably has more to do with an

---

[12] After all, a judgment or policy which turns out with hindsight to be "mistaken" is not necessarily negligent.

[13] Bailey and Bowman, *loc. cit.* Such an approach would be an answer to a claim by an authority that lack of resources allowed it to adopt a "policy" of letting maintenance of vehicles or buildings decline to a dangerous level.

[14] It is not judicial.

[15] [1988] 2 W.L.R. 493; *Calveley* v. *Chief Constable of Merseyside* [1989] 2 W.L.R. 624 (police disciplinary procedure); *Mills* v. *Winchester Diocesan Board* [1989] 2 All E.R. 317 (Charity Commissioners).

[16] "It cannot be right in law that the isolated adjudication officer should have so many hundreds, possibly thousands, of neighbours to whom the common law says he owes a duty of care when Parliament has provided a whole scheme of legislation to protect the so-called neighbours against a mistake by the adjudication officer": *Jones* at p. 510, *per* Caulfield J. *cf.* the position of a legal representative: below. For another example of rejection of a duty of care on the basis that there was an alternative remedy (although the state of the law on that remedy was "lamentable") see *C.B.S. Songs Ltd.* v. *Amstrad Consumer Electronics plc* [1988] A.C. 1013.

[17] [1988] A.C. 473. Bradgate (1988) 51 M.L.R. 382; Craig (1988) 104 L.Q.R. 185.

[18] From less than £100 p.a. a few years ago, doctors' subscriptions to the medical defence societies have risen to over £1,000. Despite the element of immunity enjoyed by the Bar, some commercial chambers suffered a 1,800 per cent. increase in premiums in 1985 and even criminal chambers had average increases of 50–80 per cent.: (1985) 135 N.L.J. 1132.

increase in litigation consciousness than changes in the rules of law.[19] However, certain special features of legal practice, particularly with regard to litigation, have produced a more restricted liability for lawyers.[20]

For many years, a barrister was held to be not liable to his client for negligence and the rule was regarded as resting on the ground that no contractual relation exists between a barrister and his client.[21] This reason certainly became inadequate after *Hedley, Byrne* v. *Heller* and the whole matter has had to be re-examined in a series of decisions in the House of Lords and the Court of Appeal.

It is clear that no special rule applies to a lawyer engaged in "pure paperwork" or advice unconnected with litigation. The solicitor who mishandles a conveyance or a company merger or the tax counsel who drafts an instrument which exposes the settlor to an untoward fiscal liability is as liable for negligence as anyone else, though it should not be assumed that merely because he turns out to be "wrong" he has been negligent: many legal points are matters of opinion on which differing views may legitimately be held and no one can anticipate all the actions of the courts in developing the law. Where litigation is involved, however, there are policy factors which make the law more complicated.

First, although a lawyer engaged in litigation enjoys a degree of immunity from suit, in many cases it will be unnecessary to consider the precise scope of this because of a procedural rule whereby an action for negligence will be struck out as an abuse of the process of the court if it involves an attack on the decision of a court of competent jurisdiction.[22] In *Somasundaram* v. *M. Julius Melchior & Co.*[23] the plaintiff, who had been gaoled for an assault upon his wife, sued his solicitors, alleging that they were guilty of negligence in advising him to change his plea to guilty. The Court of Appeal upheld the striking out of the action and found it unnecessary to decide whether the solicitors' immunity from suit extended to the advice given. Since the plaintiff would, in order to establish damage, have to show that a plea of not guilty would have led to a verdict of acquittal in the criminal trial, his civil action was in effect an attack upon the correctness of the result of that trial and the criminal appeal system, not the civil courts, is the proper vehicle for such an attack.[24]

In some cases, however, this point will not be relevant: for example, the prior decision may have been quashed on appeal or there may be no final decision adverse to the plaintiff. In that case, counsel is immune from an

---

[19] But the developments in the law of defective premises in the 1970s (*post*, p. 229) must be regarded as the prime cause of the increased expenses of architects, engineers and surveyors.

[20] For comparative law, see Hill, "Litigation and Negligence" (1986) 60 J.L.S. 183.

[21] *Swinfen* v. *Lord Chelmsford* (1860) 5 H. & N. 890; *Kennedy* v. *Brown* (1863) 13 C.B.(N.S.) 677. See Roxburgh, "*Rondel* v. *Worsley*: The Historical Background" (1968) 84 L.Q.R. 178; Baker, "Counsellors and Barristers" [1969] C.L.J. 205.

[22] The principle is not new, but its relevance to a tort action where there had been prior criminal proceedings was made clear in *Hunter* v. *Chief Constable of West Midlands* [1982] A.C. 529, *ante* p. 58.

[23] [1989] 1 All E.R. 129.

[24] The matter needs, however, to be considered by the House of Lords because this principle was not relied on in the leading case of *Rondel* v. *Worsley* [1969] 1 A.C. 191 even though it would have been a short answer to the claim.

action for negligence in respect of the actual conduct of the case in court or
for pre-trial work where the act in question was so intimately connected with
the conduct of the case in court that it could fairly be regarded as a preliminary decision affecting the way the case would be conducted when it came to a
hearing. In *Saif Ali* v. *Sydney Mitchell & Co.*,[25] where the House of Lords
adopted this test[26] the court held, by a majority, that an allegation of failure
to advise resetting the claim in the plaintiff's personal injury action so as to
add additional defendants disclosed a cause of action.[27] A decision made,
out of court, not to call a witness must be as subject to immunity as a decision
not to ask a particular question in court, and in the *Somasundaram* case the
Court of Appeal took the view, *obiter*, that advice as to a plea was immune,
but beyond this it is not easy to identify conduct which will or will not be
immune.[28] It will certainly not be easy to bring within the immunity advice
not to take proceedings.[29] Though the issue has not been directly before an
English court, it is clear that the same immunity attaches to a solicitor acting
as an advocate in court,[30] though care must be taken in such a case to
determine whether the alleged negligence truly relates to his conduct *qua*
advocate.[31] It is not, however, clear whether the solicitor's immunity in
respect of preparatory work is as extensive as that of counsel, anomalous as
any such distinction may be,[32] though it must be borne in mind that where
the solicitor has sought the opinion of counsel he will normally have fulfilled
his duty of care if he relies on that.[33] Claims against advocates will generally
be brought by their own clients, but the immunity also extends to claims
against them by opposing parties in the litigation.[34]

The law is, therefore, that there is a substantial degree of immunity from
suit, though it is not complete. According to the House of Lords in *Rondel* v.

[25] [1980] A.C. 198; Zander (1979) 42 M.L.R. 319; *Giannarelli* v. *Wraith* (1988) 81 A.L.R. 417.
[26] Which was borrowed from the New Zealand case of *Rees* v. *Sinclair* [1974] 1 N.Z.L.R. 180.
[27] The issue arose as a result of a third party claim against counsel by the solicitors who were the original
defendants to the action. However, solicitors are normally entitled to rely on the advice of counsel: see
below.
[28] In *Rees* v. *Sinclair* itself, *supra*, a decision not to advance issues of misconduct in matrimonial proceedings
was held to be immune. Bridge L.J. in *Saif Ali* in the Court of Appeal thought that the facts fell within the
test: [1978] Q.B. 95, 106.
[29] But the arguments of policy (see below) apply to some extent to advice not to sue: counsel should not give
his assistance to the presentation of an obviously unfounded claim. In *Biggar* v. *Macleod* [1978] 2 N.Z.L.R.
9 a decision to compromise an action was held within the area of immunity.
[30] *Saif Ali* v. *Sydney Mitchell & Co.* [1980] A.C. 198, 215, 224, 227; *Giannarelli* v. *Wraith* (1988) 81 A.L.R.
417. A solicitor-advocate may act under contract but the Supply of Goods (Exclusion of Implied Terms)
Order 1982 (S.I. 1982 No. 1771) provides that the Supply of Goods and Services Act 1982, s.13 (implied
terms of reasonable care and skill) does not apply to "the services of an advocate in court or before any
tribunal, inquiry or arbitrator and in carrying out preliminary work directly affecting the conduct of the
hearing." However, s.44A(3) of the Solicitors Act 1974, inserted by Part I of the Administration of Justice
Act 1985, gives the Council of the Law Society power to take steps where the services provided by a
solicitor are not of the quality reasonably to be expected.
[31] In *Rondel* v. *Worsley* [1969] 1 A.C. 191 Lord Upjohn suggested that even if a solicitor were immune in
respect of conduct in court this would not save him if his mistake were the result of a failure properly to
instruct himself. *Rees* v. *Sinclair*, *supra* was decided in the context of a "fused" profession but another
jurisdiction with a fused profession has rejected immunity: *Demarco* v. *Ungaro* (1979) 95 D.L.R. (3d) 385.
[32] *Somasundaram* v. *M. Julius Melchior & Co.* [1989] 1 All E.R. 129, 136.
[33] *Ibid.*; *Ward* v. *Chief Constable of Avon* [1987] 10 C.L. 306.
[34] *Orchard* v. *S.E. Electricity Board* [1987] Q.B. 565; *cf. Al-kandari* v. *J.R. Brown & Co.* [1988] 2 W.L.R. 671
(in giving undertaking as to custody of passport solicitor had stepped outside his role as client's representative in litigation). As to the court's power to order a solicitor guilty of serious misconduct to pay costs, see
ibid. at p. 675 and R.S.C., Ord. 62, r. 8.

Worsley[35] the immunity rests upon the demands of public policy in connection with the administration of justice: in order to fulfil his duty to the *court* the advocate must be relieved of even the possibility that actions for negligence might be brought against him by disgruntled clients. This is not based upon a desire to protect the advocate from the consequences of any negligence on his part but to ensure that he will not be deflected from his duty by fear of an action by a client who, for example, takes as incompetence a proper decision not to call a witness or not to press questioning of a witness to the limit.[36] It may be replied that such conduct on the advocate's part would not constitute professional negligence, but the fact that he may win the case brought against him by his client does not remove the "nuisance" factor in litigation—the expense and possible damage to reputation inherent even in a successfully defended action—and so the possibility of his being deflected from his duty is still there. However, in the absence of any empirical evidence, it is hard to judge the force of this argument[37]: the contention that negligence liability encourages doctors to practise "defensive medicine" has not led English courts to give them immunity from suit, though the point is being increasingly made in some quarters when reform of the compensation system is discussed. A further reason advanced in *Rondel v. Worsley* for the immunity of the advocate is the undesirability of retrying, in the action against the advocate, the issues which arose in the original litigation out of which the action arose.[38] As we have seen, this has now been elevated from being a reason for immunity to an independent bar even where there might be no immunity. However, speculative issues as to what might have been the result of litigation cannot be entirely avoided. There is, for example, no doubt that a solicitor is liable in negligence for letting a limitation period expire but success in such an action requires that the plaintiff establish at least a reasonable prospect of success had his claim proceeded.

The significance of the public interest in the due administration of justice extends a good deal further than the immunity of advocates. For example, judges and witnesses have a wide immunity from negligence, defamation and other torts[39] and a litigant owes no duty of care to his opponent as to the

---

[35] [1969] 1 A.C. 191; Jolowicz [1967] C.L.J. 10 and [1968] C.L.J. 23; Miller (1981) 97 L.Q.R. 12.

[36] "Far more cases have been lost by going on too long than by stopping too soon. But the client does not know that. To him brevity may indicate incompetence or negligence": [1969] 1 A.C. 191, 228, *per* Lord Reid.

[37] The lack of such evidence was one reason for the rejection of immunity in Ontario: *Demarco v. Ungaro* (1979) 95 D.L.R. (3d) 385. Another was the absence of the "cab-rank" principle whereby counsel must take any case within his field of competence, but even in England the cab-rank rule is not of much significance in civil litigation: *Saif Ali v. Sydney Mitchell & Co.* [1980] A.C. 198, 2212, 230. Lord Diplock in *Saif Ali* expressed some regret that the House had not received "a more radical submission that the immunity . . . ought no longer to be upheld."

[38] [1969] 1 A.C. 191, 230, 248–250. See also *Calveley v. Chief Constable of Merseyside* [1989] 2 W.L.R. 624.

[39] See *post*, p. 663. The advocate's immunity is closely connected with this: *Saif Ali v. Sydney Mitchell & Co.* [1980] A.C. 198, 222; *Evans v. London Hospital Medical College* [1981] 1 W.L.R. 184.

manner in which the litigation is conducted, for the proper remedies for misconduct in that sphere lie in the court rules and procedures.[40]

We have seen that outside the context of litigation lawyers are subject to the same principles as the members of other professions. Although his contract, if any, is only with his client, it was held in *Ross* v. *Caunters*[41] that a lawyer dealing with a will may owe a duty of care to an intended beneficiary, but that was rather a special case where there was no possible conflict of interest. As was admitted in the case, the solicitor's duty is to do all he properly can for his client and he is not guardian of the interests of third parties except to the limited extent of being required to use due care to carry out those instructions of his client which are intended to benefit others.[42] He owes no duty to the third parties actively to represent and advance their interests.[43] Thus in *Clarke* v. *Bruce Lance & Co.*[44] the defendants in 1973 drew up a will for the testator which left a filling station to the plaintiff. Some five years later they acted for the testator again in granting an option (at a fixed price) over the filling station to an existing tenant, who was virtually certain to exercise it.[45] The plaintiff's claim for negligence was struck out: if the defendants owed him any duty of care they could find themselves in the intolerable position of having to seek to dissuade their client (the testator) from carrying through a transaction. If, on the other had, the transaction was improvident that might be a breach of contract to the testator and the estate (and, indirectly the plaintiff as a beneficiary) had its remedy by that route.[46]

(5) *Nervous shock*[47]

The first point to make here is that damages may not be recovered solely on the basis that, as a result of negligence, the plaintiff has suffered the sensations of fear or mental distress or grief.[48] But shock which produces

---

[40] *Business Computers International Ltd.* v. *Registrar of Companies* [1988] Ch. 229 (winding up order [subsequently set aside] made against company when service of process against it had been made at wrong address). See also, in very different context, *Hanratty* v. *Lord Butler of Saffron Walden* (1971) 115 S.J. 386 (no cause of action against the Home Secretary for negligence in advising the Crown on the exercise of the prerogative of mercy).

[41] *Ross* v. *Caunters* [1980] Ch. 297, discussed *ante*, p. 96: Luntz, "Solicitor's Liability to Third Parties" (1983) 3 O.J.L.S. 284.

[42] [1980] Ch. 297, 322.

[43] See *Sutherland* v. *Public Trustee* [1980] 2 N.Z.L.R. 536.

[44] [1988] 1 W.L.R. 881.

[45] The option was not exercisable until the death of the testator's widow, which had not occurred at the time of the proceedings.

[46] To allow an action for negligence might have led to double liability: [1988] 1 W.L.R. 881, 889.

[47] Teff (1983) 99 L.Q.R. 100; Trindade [1986] C.L.J. 476.

[48] Hence if a police investigation is conducted without due care the suspect cannot found a claim in negligence upon anxiety, vexation or injury to reputation: *Calveley* v. *Chief Constable of Merseyside* [1989] 2 W.L.R. 624. *Whitmore* v. *Euroway Express Coaches, The Times*, May 4, 1984 is out of line with the other accident cases, though in the arbitrations pursuant to the Zeebrugge disaster settlement "pathological grief" was accepted as legal damage: *The Times*, April 29, 1989. But where there is some more tangible injury the law will take account of such matters as part of the assessment of "pain and suffering" (*post*, p. 610) and they may form part of aggravated damages or the general damages recoverable for torts actionable *per se*. There is also a growing tendency to allow damages for mental distress in certain types of contract cases. Where a tort causes a death a limited number of persons may now claim a statutory sum for bereavement: *post*, p. 650.

some recognisable medical condition[49] (whether physical, like heart failure
or abortion, or mental, like neurosis) is a different matter.[50] An early view
that such damage was not compensable at all[51] was soon discarded, but the
courts, still fearful of the wide-ranging liability and fraudulent claims which
might be associated with shock cases, remained reluctant to apply the
ordinary principles of liability without qualification.[52] As Lord Macmillan
said, "in the case of mental shock there are elements of greater subtlety than
in the case of an ordinary physical injury and those elements may give rise to
debate as to the precise scope of legal liability."[53] In *Dulieu* v. *White* it was
held that shock was actionable only if it arose from the plaintiff's reasonably
sustained fear for his own safety.[54] This would have kept liability within
narrow bounds and provided a fairly simple rule but the majority of the
Court of Appeal in *Hambrook* v. *Stokes Bros.*[55] found it unsatisfying and
decisively rejected it. That was a case in which a mother suffered shock from
an apprehension of injury to her children from whom she had just parted and
the court rejected the *Dulieu* v. *White* limitation because it would favour a
plaintiff who thought only of her own safety and deny a remedy to a mother
who, like Mrs. Hambrook, was "courageous and devoted to her child."[56]
However, it was made clear that liability would only arise if the shock
resulted from what the victim saw or realised by her own unaided senses, and
not from what someone else told her.[57] The subsequent decision of the
House of Lords in *Bourhill* v. *Young*[58] hardly clarified the law. Some of the
speeches showed signs of wishing to revive the *Dulieu* v. *White* limitation in
another form, *viz.* by confining liability for *shock* to those within the area of
foreseeable *physical harm*, but while such an approach would be consistent
with the result of the case it does not seem to be its *ratio decidendi*,[59] and the
speeches certainly did not produce a clear conclusion on the status of
Hambrook v. *Stokes*. Little would be gained by examining the subsequent
authorities, though their general tenor was to reject any "area of impact"
limitation while remaining loyal to the "unaided senses" requirement.[60] The

---

[49] *Hinz* v. *Berry* [1970] 2 Q.B. 40; *McLoughlin* v. *O'Brian* [1982] 2 W.L.R. 982, 999.

[50] Bingham L.J. in *Attia* v. *British Gas plc* [1988] Q.B. 304, 317, describes the expression "nervous shock" as "misleading and inaccurate" and prefers "psychiatric damage." But the traditional expression serves a purpose in reminding us that this head of negligence requires something in the way of a reaction to an *event*. The spouse of a brain-damaged accident victim may (foreseeably) succumb to psychiatric illness from the strain of caring for the victim, but no case thus far has said that he or she has a cause of action.

[51] See *Victorian Railway Commissioners* v. *Coultas* (1888) 13 App.Cas. 222.

[52] Less difficulty was felt where shock was the result of an intentional act and, as we have seen, it was in a case of shock that Wright J. laid down his general principle about wilful acts calculated to cause harm: *Wilkinson* v. *Downton* [1897] 2 Q.B. 57, *ante*, p. 68.

[53] *Bourhill* v. *Young* [1943] A.C. 92, 103.

[54] [1901] 2 K.B. 669.

[55] [1925] 1 K.B. 141.

[56] *Ibid.* at p. 151, *per* Bankes L.J. *cf.* Havard, "Reasonable Foresight of Nervous Shock" (1956) 19 M.L.R. 478, 482, where it is observed that from the medical point of view the most likely cause of illness through shock is fear for one's own safety, "one reason for this being that the very excessive discharge (through the 'autonomic nervous system') which it initiates is directed solely towards protecting him from immediate danger to his own personal safety." The court in *Hambrook* v. *Stokes* was not, of course, denying that there was liability where the plaintiff feared only for his own safety.

[57] [1925] 1 K.B. 141, 152, *per* Bankes L.J.; *ibid.* at p. 159, *per* Atkin L.J.

[58] [1943] A.C. 92; see also, *ante*, p. 82.

[59] Goodhart, "The Shock Cases and Area of Risk" (1953) 16 M.L.R. 14; *cf. McLoughlin* v. *O'Brian* [1983] 1 A.C. 410, 436, *per* Lord Bridge.

[60] *Schneider* v. *Eisovitch* [1960] 2 Q.B. 430 was an exception.

law must now be sought in the decision of the House of Lords in *McLoughlin* v. *O'Brian*.[61] A road accident caused by the defendants' negligence killed the plaintiff's young daughter and caused injuries of varying severity to others of her children and to her husband. At the time the plaintiff was at home two miles away. An hour later the accident was reported to her by a friend, who drove her to the hospital in Cambridge, where she was told of the death and saw the injured members of her family in circumstances which, it was found, were "distressing in the extreme and were capable of producing an effect going well beyond that of grief and sorrow."[62] The House of Lords unanimously allowed an appeal by the plaintiff against the decision of the Court of Appeal upholding dismissal of her claim for nervous shock. Unfortunately, here unanimity ends.

In the view of Lord Bridge (with whom Lord Scarman agreed[63]), the law should eschew any rigid lines designed to keep liability for nervous shock within bounds and should adopt the test of reasonable foreseeability for shock claims just as for other sorts of accident. This would undoubtedly introduce an element of uncertainty and throw upon the defendant the burden of meeting borderline claims that would have been entirely excluded by earlier tests, but this risk was not unreasonable given that the defendant was *ex hypothesi* at fault, that there was no real evidence of the prospect of a crushing number of claims and that all previous attempts at "drawing the line" had produced arbitrary results.[64] Some indication of how Lord Bridge contemplates the test of reasonable foreseeability being applied can, however, be gathered from his opinion. He clearly considered the result in *Bourhill* v. *Young* to be as correct today as it was in 1942 and endorsed the statement of Lord Porter in that case[65] that "the driver of a car ... is entitled to assume that the ordinary frequenter of the streets has sufficient fortitude to endure such incidents as may from time to time be expected to occur in them, including the noise of a collision and the sight of injury to others, and is not to be considered negligent towards one who does not possess the customary phlegm"; but it seems he would impose liability where the witness was a near relation[66] or when the accident was unusually horrific.[67] However, he would go well beyond the previous law in abandoning any requirement that the accident be perceived by the unaided senses of the person suffering shock.

---

[61] [1983] 1 A.C. 410; Owen [1983] C.L.J. 41; Hutchinson & Morgan (1982) 45 M.L.R. 694; Teff (1983) 99 L.Q.R. 100; Weir, *Casebook on Tort*, (6th ed.), p. 69.

[62] [1983] 1 A.C. 410, 417.

[63] Lord Scarman's remarks on the place of "policy" in judicial decisions are considered *ante*, p. 80.

[64] [1983] 1 A.C. 410, 442. See also Lord Scarman, *ibid*. at p. 431: "Principle requires the judges to follow the logic of the 'reasonably foreseeable test' so as, in circumstances where it is appropriate, to apply it untrammelled by spatial, physical or temporal limits. Space, time, distance, the nature of the injuries sustained and the relationship of the plaintiff to the immediate victim of the accident are factors to be weighed, but not legal limitations, when the test of reasonable foreseeability is to be applied."

[65] [1943] A.C. 92, 117. See also Deane J. in *Jaensch* v. *Coffey* (1984) 54 A.L.R. 417, 464.

[66] See his implicit approval of the result in *Hambrook* v. *Stokes* [1925] 1 K.B. 141 and *Hinz* v. *Berry* [1970] 2 Q.B. 40.

[67] Thus at p. 442 he regarded *Chadwick* v. *British Transport Commission* [1967] 1 W.L.R. 912 as correctly decided, but not on the narrow basis that the plaintiff was engaged in rescue work. See also *Mount Isa Mines Ltd.* v. *Pusey* (1970) 125 C.L.R. 383.

"Take the case of a mother who knows that her husband and children are staying at a certain hotel. She reads in her morning newspaper that it has been the scene of a disastrous fire. She sees in the paper a photograph of unidentifiable victims trapped on the top floor waving for help from the windows. She learns shortly afterwards that all her family have perished. She suffers an acute psychiatric illness. That her illness in these circumstances was a reasonably foreseeable consequence of the events resulting from the fire is undeniable."

In contrast Lord Wilberforce considered that the plaintiff's appeal could be allowed without significantly extending previously accepted principles in nervous shock cases[68]: the plaintiff was a close relative of those involved in the accident[69]; her shock resulted from the distressing scenes which she had witnesssed herself[70]; and, while she did not witness the accident itself, existing authority allowed recovery on the basis of witnessing the "immediate aftermath."[71] Lord Edmund Davies did not structure his speech in favour of allowing the appeal so closely to the previous legal principles and he disclaimed the possibility of "indicating with clarity where the limit of liability should be drawn in such cases as the present,"[72] but the general tenor of his speech seems to be in favour of drawing the limits of liability more narrowly than does Lord Bridge and he expressly rejected as a sole test of liability for nervous shock the reasonable foreseeability of injury by shock.[73] It would, however, be unsafe to conclude that he would have drawn the bounds of liability at precisely the same point as Lord Wilberforce.[74] The fifth judge, Lord Russell, adopted the test of reasonable foreseeability but gave no express guidance on how that test should be applied, for "to attempt in advance solutions, or even guidelines, in hypothetical cases may well . . . in this field, do more harm than good."[75]

It is not easy to discern a clear *ratio* in *McLoughlin* v. *O'Brian*[76] and a further difficulty arises from the fact that the decision was given at a time when there was a very general expansion of the tort of negligence, which is no longer the case. However, it is thought that lower courts are likely to follow the principles set out by Lord Bridge and to take guidance from his

---

[68] He thought the plaintiff's case was covered either by "the existing law, or the existing law with only such circumstantial extension as the common law process may legitimately make": [1983] 1 A.C. 410, 423.

[69] His Lordship thought such a relationship was not an absolute requirement but that cases involving less close relationships "must be very carefully scrutinised": *ibid.* at p. 422.

[70] "Whether some equivalent of sight or hearing, *e.g.* through simultaneous television, would suffice may have to be considered": *ibid.* at p. 423.

[71] *Benson* v. *Lee* [1972] V.R. 879; *Marshall* v. *Lionel Enterprises Inc.* (1971) 25 D.L.R. (3d) 141; *Fenn* v. *City of Peterborough* (1976) 73 D.L.R. (3d) 177; *Chadwick* v. *British Transport Commission* [1967] 1 W.L.R. 912.

[72] [1983] 1 A.C. 410, 426.

[73] *Ibid.* at p. 426.

[74] He does, however, draw an analogy between the plaintiff and a rescuer: see *ibid.* at p. 424.

[75] What would potential litigants think of this remark?

[76] See also the extended discussion on rather similar facts by the High Court of Australia in *Jaensch* v. *Coffey* (1984) 54 A.L.R. 417. Bingham L.J. in *Attia* v. *British Gas plc* [1988] Q.B. 304, 319 thought that Lords Bridge and Scarman were in the minority in *McLoughlin* because Lord Russell thought that "policy" as well as foreseeability might be relevant. But it is not entirely clear whether Lord Russell was referring to duties of care in general or to the particular context of nervous shock.

examples of the proper application of the foreseeability test, bearing in mind that the bounds of what is foreseeable are likely to be altered by progressive medical awareness of mental illness.[77] In *Attia* v. *British Gas plc*[78] the Court of Appeal was faced with a novel claim for shock arising from the destruction of the plaintiff's home by the defendant's negligence. In refusing to uphold the dismissal of the plaintiff's claim on a preliminary issue of law and ordering the action to be tried, the court necessarily rejected the proposition that liability for nervous shock could never arise in such circumstances (whether because of a direct rule of law to that effect or because shock resulting from property damage was so unlikely as always to be beyond the contemplation of the reasonable man). However, the case is not like other nervous shock decisions in that the shock was a consequence of a tort to the plaintiff which had already caused her actionable damage (*viz.*, the destruction of her property).[79] Indeed, at least two of the judges considered that the proper analysis of the facts was in terms of remoteness of damage, not of duty.[80] Nevertheless, it is hard to see how the plaintiff's case would have been any the less deserving or the shock any less foreseeable if "her home" had been the sole property of her husband.

If liability for nervous shock is not to be confined to apprehension of physical injury[81] can it be extended even to cases where there is no "accident?" Other common law jurisdictions have had to deal with actions for the negligent publication in a newspaper of a report of the death of the plaintiff's husband and children,[82] and for a negligent medical diagnosis which led to the break-up of the plaintiff's marriage and consequent mental trauma.[83] In these cases the statements causing shock were false and it has been said that there is no duty to break bad news gently,[84] but this may go too far if the circumstances are such that the impact of the news is needlessly exacerbated.[85]

(6) *Other areas of immunity or limited duty; obsolete immunities*

The preceding pages do not by any means provide a complete coverage of all the situations in which the demands of justice and policy require denial of a duty of care or restriction of a duty within narrower limits than would be

---

[77] [1983] 1 A.C. 410, 443.

[78] [1988] Q.B. 304.

[79] If a person is killed a surviving relative may have a cause of action under the Fatal Accidents Act and it might therefore be thought that a case like *Hinz* v. *Berry* [1970] 2 Q.B. 40 raises the same point. However, the statutory action is "parasitic" upon that of the deceased (see *post*, p. 649) and without the statute the relative would have no claim.

[80] Dillon L.J. at p. 312 and Bingham L.J. at p. 319 (perhaps also Woolf L.J. at pp. 315–316).

[81] The plaintiff may sue if he suffers shock as a result of fear for his own safety or that of a third party. Can he sue if he suffers shock from the defendant's carelessly putting *himself* in danger? Deane and Dawson JJ. in *Jaensch* v. *Coffey* thought not: (1984) 54 A.L.R. 417, 458–466.

[82] *Guay* v. *Sun Publishing Co.* [1953] 4 D.L.R. 577 (not liable: see MacIntyre (1953), 31 Can. Bar Rev. 773; *cf.* (1975) *Barnes* v. *Commonwealth* (1937) 37 S.R.N.S.W. 511; *Johnson* v. *State* 334 N.E. 2d 590). See also *D.* v. *N.S.P.C.C.* [1978] A.C. 171.

[83] *Molien* v. *Kaiser Foundation Hospitals* 616 P. 2d 813 (1980).

[84] *Mount Isa Mines Ltd.* v. *Pusey* (1970) 125 C.L.R. 383, 407, *per* Windeyer J.

[85] *cf. Furniss* v. *Fitchett* [1958] N.Z.L.R. 396.

provided by reasonable foreseeability of harm. Some others are considered at various points in this book[86] but no "catalogue" is feasible for, although we are no longer in an era of rapid expansion, there is no telling what novel claims will be presented to the courts. In any event, many of the immunities with which a lawyer of a previous generation would have been familiar have been swept away, a process in which Parliament, as well as the courts, has played a substantial part.[87]

BREACH OF DUTY[88]

Criterion of "the reasonable man"

The defendant must not only owe the plaintiff a duty of care, he must be in breach of it. The test for deciding whether there has been a breach of duty is laid down in the oft-cited dictum of Alderson B. in *Blyth* v. *Birmingham Waterworks Co.*[89] "Negligence is the omission to do something which a reasonable man, guided upon those considerations which ordinarily regulate the conduct of human affairs, would do, or doing something which a prudent and reasonable man would not do."

The general characteristics of the reasonable man have already been described.[90] Since he is an abstraction, the standard of reference he provides can be applied to particular cases only by the intuition of the court. The standard is objective and impersonal in the sense that it eliminates the personal equation and is independent of the idiosyncrasies of the particular person whose conduct is in question, but it cannot eliminate the personality of the judge. "It is . . . left to the judge to decide what, in the circumstances of the particular case, the reasonable man would have in contemplation, and what, accordingly, the party sought to be made liable ought to have foreseen."[91] In the following pages we describe some of the factors taken into account by the judges in reaching their conclusions.

"Reasonable" varies with the circumstances

There can be no doubt that the general standard is objective and the question is not "did the defendant do his best?" but "did he come up to the standard of the reasonable man?" Nevertheless, the law cannot be understood unless we bear in mind that it judges conduct by the particular

---

[86] For example, negligent misstatement (Chap. 11) and judicial immunity (*post*, p. 663). Some immunities from suit (for example, that of foreign sovereigns) are only aspects of wider rules not particularly connected with tort.

[87] *e.g.* straying animals (Chap. 16); non-repair of highways (*post*, p. 418); defective premises *post*, p. 229; and an occupier's duty to trespassers (*post*, p. 225).

[88] Weir, *Casebook on Tort*, (6th ed.), Chap. 2.

[89] (1856) 11 Ex. 781, 784.

[90] *Ante*, pp. 46–48.

[91] *Glasgow Corporation* v. *Muir* [1943] A.C. 448, 457, *per* Lord Macmillan. Weir, *Casebook on Tort*, (6th ed.), p. 116. Bannerman, "Negligence—The Reasonable Man and the Application for the Objective Test in Anglo-American Jurisprudence" (1969) 6 U.G.L.J. 69.

circumstances in which the defendant finds himself and in some circumstances actually modifies the objective standard. An example of the latter category is *Goldman* v. *Hargrave*[92] where, in dealing with the liability of the defendant for failing to extinguish a fire started on his land by natural causes, the Privy Council held that the standard was what it was reasonable to expect of him in his individual circumstances. "Less must be expected of the infirm than of the able-bodied . . . [and the defendant] should not be liable unless it is clearly proved that he could, and reasonably in his individual circumstances should, have done more."[93] This, however, was a case in which the defendant was making no unusual use of his land and had a risk thrust upon him: the test would be unsuitable for a case in which the danger arose from the defendant's activity.[94] The law is fairly ready to modify the objective standard where *contributory* negligence is in issue (that is to say, where it is asserted that the plaintiff's injury is in part attributable to his own fault and damages should be reduced accordingly)[95] and there is some authority, at least in the case of children, that a similar allowance should be made when the negligence involved is that of the *defendant*.[96] However, the courts will probably be wary of being too lenient to defendants, particularly where they are likely to be insured.[97]

It might be expected that the particular circumstances of the relationship between the plaintiff and the defendant might also lead the courts to modify the content of the defendant's duty as, for example, where the plaintiff submitted himself to treatment by someone whom he knew to be of limited competence. However, in *Nettleship* v. *Weston*[98] the Court of Appeal came to the rather remarkable conclusion that a learner driver was required, even *vis-à-vis* his instructor, to come up to the standard of an ordinary, competent driver. The Court of Appeal was heavily influenced by the presence of compulsory insurance[99] but the High Court of Australia has described the result as "contrary to common sense and the concept of what is reasonable in the circumstances" and has refused to follow the case.[1] A similar problem is raised by a passenger who knowingly takes a lift with a drunken driver: English courts adopt the objective standard and reduce the damages for contributory negligence.[2]

As to the circumstances in which the defendant acts, no reasonable man

---

[92] [1967] 1 A.C. 645, 663; *post*, p. 399.

[93] But the case does not mean that the court has to engage in a detailed assessment of financial resources: *Leakey* v. *National Trust* [1980] Q.B. 485.

[94] See, *e.g.* the cases on professional negligence, *post*, p. 114.

[95] See *post*, p. 161.

[96] See *post*, p. 671. As to insane persons, see *post*, p. 678.

[97] A finding of contributory negligence bears more harshly upon a plaintiff than does a finding of liability on an insured defendant.

[98] [1971] 2 Q.B. 691 (Weir, *Casebook on Tort* (6th ed.), p. 92). *cf. Phillips* v. *William Whiteley Ltd.* [1938] 1 All E.R. 566 (jeweller piercing ears is not bound to take the same precautions as a surgeon, but such as may reasonably be expected of a jeweller. But in the AIDS era, high standards should be required even of a jeweller).

[99] See Lord Denning M.R. at p. 700. Salmon L.J., however, would have come to the opposite conclusion but for a prior conversation about insurance between the parties.

[1] *Cook* v. *Cook* (1986) 68 A.L.R. 353 (though on the facts the defendant was in breach of duty even by learner's standards). See also the division of opinion over negligent misstatement: *post*, p. 277.

[2] See *post*, p. 689.

handles a stick of dynamite and a walking-stick in the same way. But that is not an admission that there are different degrees of negligence in the law of torts in the sense that negligence may possibly be "gross" or "ordinary" or "slight."[3] Either there is a breach of duty or there is not. It does not, however, follow that every error of judgment or mistake amounts to negligence.[4] There must be a falling below the standard of care called for by the circumstances and these may allow for an excusable "margin of error," particularly where the defendant has to deal with an emergency or take quick decisions or exercise judgment on a matter on which opinions may differ. For example, "serious and dangerous foul play" on the football field amounts to negligence but it does not follow that the same is true of every infringement of the technical rules of the game, nor can the plaintiff, who has entered voluntarily into the game, expect other players to behave as if they were taking a walk in the countryside.[5]

Since the standard is that of the hypothetical reasonable man, in applying this standard it is necessary to ask what, in the circumstances, the reasonable man would have foreseen.[6] This question is not always susceptible of only one possible answer. "What to one judge may seem far-fetched may seem to another both natural and probable."[7] Nevertheless, in most cases the courts can apply the standard of care of the reasonable man with some confidence for it is to be assumed that the judges who staff them have the qualities of that hypothetical creature well in mind. In some cases, however, the question of the foreseeability of an event will depend upon whether or not a particular item of knowledge is to be imputed to the reasonable man and in these cases it is of particular importance to remember that what is in question is *foreseeability*, not *probability*. The *probability* of a consequence does not depend upon the knowledge or experience of anybody, but its reasonable *foreseeability* can only be discovered if it is first decided what knowledge and experience is to be attributed to the reasonable man in the circumstances.

In *Roe* v. *Minister of Health*[8] R. was, in 1947, a patient in a hospital and

---

[3] See, *e.g. Caswell* v. *Powell Duffryn Associated Collieries Ltd.* [1940] A.C. 152, 175, *per* Lord Wright: "Generally speaking in civil cases 'gross' negligence has no more effect than negligence without an opprobrious epithet." It is true that in *Rondel* v. *Worsley* [1969] 1 A.C. 191, 287, Lord Upjohn said that a barrister's liability in non-contentious work (see *ante*, p. 105) required "*crassa negligentia* or gross negligence by some really elementary blunder" but it is submitted that this merely means that he is not negligent merely because his opinion is wrong or he overlooks a relevant authority.

[4] *Whitehouse* v. *Jordan* [1981] 1 W.L.R. 246 has, it is hoped, ended an unfortunate practice of speaking as if an "error of judgment" *could not* be negligence.

[5] *Condon* v. *Basi* [1985] 1 W.L.R. 866; Hudson (1986) 102 L.Q.R. 11. In accepting (*a*) that the plaintiff's voluntary participation is a factor in determining the content of the duty of care and (*b*) that a higher degree of care may be required in the First Division than in a local league this case appears to depart from *Nettleship* v. *Weston*, though that decision is not mentioned. For the relationship between the standard of care and the defence of *volenti non fit injuria*, see *post*, p. 692.

[6] As we have already seen, this question is also of importance to the existence of a "duty in fact" (*ante*, p. 81). It may again be of critical importance to the problem of remoteness of damage: *Overseas Tankship (U.K.) Ltd.* v. *Morts Dock & Engineering Co. Ltd. (The Wagon Mound)* [1961] A.C. 388 (*post*, p. 140).

[7] *Glasgow Corp.* v. *Muir* [1943] A.C. 448, 457, *per* Lord Macmillan. For a high degree of prescience see *Bohlen* v. *Perdue* [1976] 1 W.W.R. 364.

[8] [1954] 2 Q.B. 66. Weir, *Casebook on Tort* (6th ed.), p. 139; *cf. Bailey* v. *Rolls-Royce Ltd.* [1984] I.C.R. 688 ("likely" in statutory provision).

Dr. G., an anaesthetist, administered a spinal anaesthetic to him in prep-aration for a minor operation. The anaesthetic was contained in a glass ampoule which had been kept before use in a solution of phenol and unfortunately some of the phenol had made its way through an "invisible crack" into the ampoule. It thus contaminated the anaesthetic, with the result that R. became permanently paralysed from the waist down. Dr. G. was aware of the consequences of injecting phenol, and he therefore sub-jected the ampoule to a visual examination before administering the anaes-thetic, but he was not aware of the possibility of "invisible cracks." Had he been aware of this possibility, the danger to R. could have been eliminated by adding a powerful colouring agent to the phenol so that contamination of the anaesthetic could have been observed. It was held that he was not negligent in not causing the phenol to be coloured because the risk of invisible cracks had not been drawn to the attention of the profession until 1951 and "care has to be exercised to ensure that conduct in 1947 is only judged in the light of knowledge which then was or ought reasonably to have been possessed. In this connection the then-existing state of medical litera-ture must be had in mind."[9] But the then-existing state of medical literature did not make R.'s injury any less *probable* than it would have been after 1951.

Professional and industry standards

The proposition that the defendant must have failed to behave reasonably in the circumstances means that a passer-by who renders emergency first-aid after an accident is not required to show the skill of a qualified surgeon.[10] Perhaps less obviously, a householder who does some small job of repair or replacement about his house is not required to show the skill which might be required of a professional carpenter working for reward—he need only do his work with the skill of a reasonably competent carpenter doing the work in question.[11] Where, however, anyone practices a profession or is engaged in a transaction in which he holds himself out as having professional skill, the law expects him to show the amount of competence associated with the proper discharge of the duties of that profession, trade or calling, and if he falls short of that and injures someone in consequence, he is not behaving reasonably. Thus, where a brewing company owned a ship which was regularly used for the carriage of their stout from Dublin to Liverpool and Manchester, it was held that the Board of Directors of the company must exercise the same degree of care and skill in the management of the ship as would any other shipowner.[12] "The law must apply a standard which is not

[9] [1954] 2 Q.B. 66, 92, *per* Morris L.J.; *Graham* v. *Co-operative Wholesale Society Ltd.* [1957] 1 W.L.R. 511; *Jones* v. *Dennison* [1971] R.T.R. 174. See also *Dwan* v. *Farquhar* [1988] 1 Qd. R. 234 (journal article in March 1983 adverting to possible transmission of AIDS by blood transfusions; transfusion in May 1983; no negligence).

[10] A ship's master who diagnoses insanity in a crew member is required to act only as a prudent master armed with the ship's medical guide: *Ali* v. *Furness, Withy, The Financial Times*, April 22, 1988.

[11] *Wells* v. *Cooper* [1958] 2 Q.B. 265. Even this, however, is an objective standard, which may be higher than the defendant's "best."

[12] *The Lady Gwendolen* [1965] P. 294 ("actual fault" under the Merchant Shipping Act 1894, s.503); *Griffiths* v. *Arch Engineering Co. Ltd.* [1968] 3 All E.R. 217.

relaxed to cater for their factual ignorance of all activities outside brewing: having become owners of ships, they must behave as reasonable shipowners."[13] The rule *imperitia culpae adnumeratur* is just as true in English law as in Roman law.[14]

The objective standard therefore appears to make no allowance for the fact that everyone must learn to some extent by practical experience of the job, a point which was pressed upon the Court of Appeal in *Wilsher* v. *Essex Area Health Authority*,[15] where one of the doctor-defendants was junior and of limited experience. The majority of the court, however, rejected the argument that what was expected of an individual doctor was what was reasonably to be required of a person of *his* qualifications and experience, for that would entail that "the standard of care which the patient is entitled to demand [would] vary according to the chance of recruitment and rostering."[16] Rather, the standard was to be set by reference to the *post* held by the defendant in the unit in which he operated.[17] A junior member of the team could not be expected to show the skill of a consultant, but subject to that no allowance would be made for the inexperience of the individual any more than for his domestic circumstances or his financial worries, either of which might equally contribute to an error.[18] This approach may also govern the reverse case, where the defendant has *more* skill and experience than most members of the profession. It is surely beyond argument that a City law firm[19] must show more expertise in offshore tax havens or company flotations than, say, a firm in rural Dorset (though a member of the latter should at least possess an acute sense of when he was getting out of his depth). In practice, however, there is likely to be a contract in a case raising this point, which may well make the court more ready to conclude that the plaintiff has "bought" the extra skill for the (no doubt higher) price.[20]

The content of the duty of professional men is a large subject and must be sought in specialised works[21] but it is necessary to say something about the courts' approach to the setting of standards. There is no reason in principle why a professional man should not by *contract* promise to produce a result rather than merely exercise skill and care to do so,[22] but in the absence of an

---

[13] [1965] P. 294 350, *per* Winn L.J.

[14] Buckland and McNair, *Roman Law and Common Law* (2nd ed.), pp. 259–260.

[15] [1987] Q.B. 730. The case was reversed by the House of Lords but not on this point: [1988] A.C. 1074.

[16] [1987] Q.B. 730, 750, *per* Mustill L.J. Unlike the situation in *Nettleship* v. *Weston* there is no voluntary relationship here.

[17] The case was not presented on the basis that the hospital authority had failed in *its* duty (see *post* p. 565). This might cover some cases in which the individual doctor was not liable.

[18] "If this test appears unduly harsh . . . the inexperienced doctor called on to exercise a specialist skill will, as part of that skill, seek the advice and help of his superiors when he does or may need it. If he does seek such help, he will often have satisfied the test, even though he may himself have made a mistake": [1987] Q.B. 730, 774, *per* Glidewell L.J. Despite the headnote it is not entirely clear that Glidewell L.J. was not imposing an even more severe standard than Mustill L.J.

[19] The collective description is important: the client deals with the firm and the level of service should not vary as he is moved from one partner or assistant to another.

[20] See *Duchess of Argyll* v. *Bueselinck* [1972] 2 Lloyd's Rep. 172, 183, *obiter, per* Megarry J. The Supply of Goods and Services Act 1982, s.13 implies a term of reasonable care and skill, but "reasonable," in contract as in tort, varies with the circumstances.

[21] Dugdale and Stanton, *Professional Negligence*; Jackson and Powell, *Professional Negligence* (2nd ed.); Partlett, *Professional Negligence*; Charlesworth and Percy, *Negligence*, (7th ed.).

[22] *Greaves & Co.* v. *Baynham Meikle* [1975] 1 W.L.R. 1095.

express promise the courts will be reluctant to hold that he has impliedly given such an undertaking. In *Thake* v. *Maurice*[23] a statement by a surgeon that a vasectomy (carried out with all due care) would be "irreversible" was held by a majority of the Court of Appeal not to be the sort of clear and unequivocal promise necessary to amount to a contractual warranty of permanent sterility.[24] In practice, however, many claims brought against professional men are based on failure to carry out fairly simple, even mechanical, functions and proof of the failure itself will virtually guarantee success in these cases whether the action is framed in contract or tort: there must be a very limited range of circumstances in which a solicitor could show that failing to issue proceedings within the limitation period was "not his fault." Nevertheless, in theory the standard is one of reasonable care.

There is no doubt that the question of what amounts to reasonable care is to be determined by a legal standard framed by the court, not by the profession or industry in question. "Neglect of duty does not cease by repetition to be neglect of duty"[25] and the courts have not hesitated to hold that a general practice amounts to negligence in law though the cases in which they have done so have been overwhelmingly in an industrial[26] rather than a professional context.[27] Considerable deference is, however, paid to the practices of the professions (particularly the medical profession) as established by expert evidence and the court should not attempt to put itself into the shoes of the surgeon or other professional man.[28] This means that if it is shown that the defendant did comply with professional standards the court is very likely indeed to find for him,[29] for "when the court finds a clearly established practice 'in like circumstances' the practice weighs heavily in the scale on the side of the defendant and the burden of establishing

---

[23] [1986] Q.B. 644.

[24] But note that on the facts the trial judge came to the opposite conclusion (*ibid.* at p. 658) and Kerr L.J. thought he was entitled to do so. See also *Eyre* v. *Measday* [1986] 1 All E.R. 488; *Worster* v. *City and Hackney Health Authority, The Times*, June 22, 1987.

[25] *Bank of Montreal* v. *Dominion Guarantee, etc., Co. Ltd.* [1930] A.C. 659, 666, *per* Lord Tomlin; *Re The Herald of Free Enterprise, The Independent*, December 18, 1987 (not a tort case).

[26] *Lloyds Bank Ltd.* v. *Savory* [1933] A.C. 201; *Markland* v. *Manchester Corporation* [1934] 1 K.B. 566; *Barkway* v. *South Wales Transport Co. Ltd.* [1950] A.C. 185; *Paris* v. *Stepney B.C.* [1951] A.C. 367; *General Cleaning Contractors* v. *Christmas* [1953] A.C. 180; *Morris* v. *West Hartlepool Steam Navigation Co. Ltd.* [1956] A.C. 552; *Cavanagh* v. *Ulster Weaving Co. Ltd.* [1960] A.C. 145; *MacDonald* v. *Scottish Stamping and Engineering Co.*, 1972 S.L.T.(Notes) 73.

[27] In *Edward Wong Finance Co. Ltd.* v. *Johnson Stokes & Master* [1984] A.C. 296 the Privy Council held that following the customary "Hong Kong" style of conveyancing completion amounted to negligence, though the risk could have been avoided by changes in practice which would not wholly undermine the institution. A startling transatlantic example of striking down professional standards is *Helling* v. *Carey* 519 P. 2d 981 (1974) because the complaint was not that the omission of the precaution rendered the treatment dangerous but that it did not ensure detection of a rare pathological condition.

[28] See, *e.g. Sidaway* v. *Bethlem Royal Hospital and Maudsley Hospital* [1985] A.C. 871, *post*, p. 685, dealing with the giving of information to patients.

[29] *Vancouver General Hospital* v. *McDaniel* (1934) 152 L.T. 56, 57, *per* Lord Alness (methods of preventing infection in hospital); *Whiteford* v. *Hunter* [1950] W.N. 533; *Wright* v. *Cheshire C.C.* [1952] 2 All E.R. 789; *Rich* v. *L.C.C.* [1953] 1 W.L.R. 895; *Simmons* v. *Pennington & Sons* [1955] 1 W.L.R. 183.

negligence, which the plaintiff has to discharge, is a heavy one."[30] Where the defendant has not so complied that is not of itself negligence for "otherwise all inducement to progress . . . would then be destroyed"[31] but it may raise an inference of negligence against him and it has been held that it reverses the burden of proof and requires him to justify his conduct.[32] "Keeping up to date" is obviously a central element in the attainment of a proper standard of care, for in most professions and trades each generation convicts its predecessor of ignorance and there is a steady rise in the standard of competence incident to them. This was given detailed consideration in the context of an employer's duty to guard his workers against the risk of deafness in *Thompson* v. *Smiths Shiprepairers (North Shields) Ltd.*[33] Basing himself upon the proposition that the employer should take reasonable care to keep up to date with devices available to protect hearing but must not be blamed for failing to plough a lone furrow, Mustill J. held that even though the availability of effective ear-protectors had been announced in *The Lancet* in 1951, the defendants were not in breach of their duty until the publication in 1963 of a government pamphlet on the subject.[34]

One further problem arises on "general and approved practice," as it is often known, namely, that there may be no uniformity within the profession as to what is proper. The law here is clearly that the defendant is not negligent if he acts in accordance with a practice accepted at the time as proper by *a* responsible body of professional opinion skilled in the particular form of treatment, even though there is a body of competent professional opinion which might adopt a different technique.[35] It is not the court's function to choose between the schools of professional thought. Though originating in the context of medical negligence, this test is of general application to professional men,[36] and in the medical context it is not confined to "therapeutic" treatment. Hence in *Gold* v. *Haringey Health Authority*[37] a doctor was not negligent in failing to warn the plaintiff of the failure rate for female sterilisation when the expert witnesses testified that

---

[30] *Morris* v. *West Hartlepool Steam Navigation Co. Ltd.* [1956] A.C. 552, 579, *per* Lord Cohen; *Brown* v. *Rolls-Royce Ltd.* [1960] 1 W.L.R. 210. Lord Dunedin in *Morton* v. *Dixon (William) Ltd.* 1909 S.C. 807 said, "where the negligence of the employer consists of what I may call a fault of omission, I think it absolutely necessary that the proof of that fault of omission should be one of two kinds—either to show that the thing which he did not do was a thing which was commonly done by other persons in like circumstances, or to show that it was a thing which was so obviously wanted that it would be folly in anyone to neglect to provide it."

[31] *Hunter* v. *Hanley* 1955 S.C. 200, 206, *per* Lord Clyde.

[32] The Statements of Standard Accounting Practice drawn up by the professional bodies are strong evidence of proper standards and consequently a departure from them requires to be justified: *Lloyd Cheyham & Co. Ltd.* v. *Littlejohn & Co.* [1987] B.C.L.C. 303. *Clark* v. *MacLennan* [1983] 1 All E.R. 416 (medical negligence) was criticised by Mustill L.J. in *Wilsher* v. *Essex Area Health Authority* for its reliance on *McGhee* v. *N.C.B., ante,* p. 115.

[33] [1984] Q.B. 405.

[34] Is a lawyer liable for professional negligence if he does not have LEXIS? It is thought not (or not yet, or not all lawyers!). Is one who has it negligent if he fails to consult it?

[35] *Bolam* v. *Friern Hospital Management Committee* [1957] 1 W.L.R. 582, 587 (the direction to the jury in this case has become known as the "*Bolam* test"); *Whitehouse* v. *Jordan* [1981] 1 W.L.R. 246; *Maynard* v. *West Midlands Regional Health Authority* [1984] 1 W.L.R. 634; *Sidaway* v. *Bethlem Royal Hospital* [1985] A.C. 871.

[36] *Gold* v. *Haringey Health Authority* [1988] Q.B. 481.

[37] *Supra.* See Grubb [1988] C.L.J. 12; Montgomery (1988) 51 M.L.R. 245. On the scope of the duty to warn of risks of treatment, see further *post,* p. 685.

although they would have given such a warning a substantial body of doctors (perhaps as many as 50 per cent.) would not have done so.

Many matters other than general practice may be adverted to for guidance on the standard which the court should adopt as the measure of reasonable care. For example, the Highway Code does not of itself give rise to any liability but it is specifically provided that a failure to observe it may be relied upon to establish (or negative) any liability which is in question in a civil action.[38] As to criminal law, it may be said that (putting aside cases where statute gives rise to a direct civil liability, which are dealt with in Chapter 7) failure to comply with it is normally good evidence of negligence but it is not possible to lay down any hard and fast rule. There are circumstances for example, in which it would not be negligent to exceed the statutory speed limit. Equally, it is not difficult to imagine a case in which statutory requirements are met but the court would find that there is common law negligence. With regard to the latter type of case, however, a distinction must be drawn between activities like driving, or operating a factory, where there must be room for varying standards to meet varying circumstances, and matters such as the legally permissible level of toxic materials in products. For example, if statutory regulations lay down the amount of lead which may be incorporated in petrol the court cannot hold it negligent to incorporate this amount even in the face of evidence that this amount is harmful: to do so would be tantamount to declaring that if the speed limit on a stretch of road were 30 m.p.h. it was nonetheless *always* (and not merely in unusual conditions like ice or fog) negligent to exceed 20 m.p.h.[39]

Factors of the objective standard

The standard of reasonable care is set by law but its application in a particular case is a question of fact in the sense that propositions of good sense which are applied by one judge in one case should not be regarded thereafter as propositions of law.[40] If that were the case, the system would collapse under the weight of accumulated precedent. On the other hand situations do tend to repeat themselves and it is permissible to look at decisions of the courts to see how the standard of the reasonable man should be applied.[41] The result is that in each case a balance must be struck between the magnitude of the risk and the burden to the defendant in doing (or not doing) what it is alleged he should (or should not) have done. "The law in all cases exacts a degree of care commensurate with the risk."[42] In some cases,

---

[38] Road Traffic Act 1988, s.38(7); *Powell* v. *Phillips* [1972] 3 All E.R. 864. Fire Safety and Safety of Places of Sport Act 1987, s.6. As to codes of practice under the Health and Safety at Work (etc.) Act 1974, see *post*, p. 188.

[39] See *Albery and Budden* v. *B.P. Oil* [1980] J.P.L. 586.

[40] *Qualcast (Wolverhampton) Ltd.* v. *Haynes* [1959] A.C. 743; *Foskett* v. *Mistry* [1984] R.T.R. 1.

[41] *Hazell* v. *British Transport Commission* [1958] 1 W.L.R. 169. See generally Charlesworth, *Negligence* (7th ed.); Bingham, *All the Modern Cases on Negligence*.

[42] *Read* v. *J. Lyons & Co. Ltd.* [1974] A.C. 156, 173, *per* Lord Macmillan. "As the danger increases, so must the precautions increase." *Lloyds Bank Ltd.* v. *Railway Executive* [1952] 1 All E.R. 1248, 1253, *per* Denning L.J.; *Miller* v. *Evans* [1975] R.T.R. 70; *cf. Goldman* v. *Hargrave* [1967] 1 A.C. 645, 663, *per* Lord Wilberforce.

where there is only a remote possibility of injury, no precautions need be taken for "one must guard against reasonable probabilities, not fantastic possibilities,"[43] but this means no more than that if the risk is very slight the defendant may have behaved reasonably though he did nothing to prevent the harm.[44] If his act was one for which there was in any case no justification he may still be liable so long only as the risk of damage to the plaintiff is not such that a reasonable man would brush it aside as far-fetched.[45] Theoretically at least, in every case where a duty of care exists the courts must consider whether the risk was sufficiently great to require of the defendant more than he has actually done.

(1) *Magnitude of the risk*

Two elements go to make up the magnitude of the risk, the likelihood that injury will be incurred[46] and the seriousness of the injury that is risked. In *Bolton* v. *Stone*[47] the plaintiff was standing on the highway in a road adjoining a cricket ground when she was struck by a ball which a batsman had hit out of the ground. Such an event was foreseeable and, indeed, balls had to the defendant's knowledge occasionally been hit out of the ground before. Nevertheless, taking into account such factors as the distance from the pitch to the edge of the ground, the presence of a seven foot fence and the upward slope of the ground in the direction in which the ball was struck, the House of Lords considered that the likelihood of injury to a person in the plaintiff's position was so slight that the cricket club was not negligent in allowing cricket to be played without having taken additional precautions such as increasing the height of the fence. As Lord Reid said, "I think that reasonable men do in fact take into account the degree of risk and do not act upon a bare possibility as they would if the risk were more substantial."[48] On the other hand, in *Hilder* v. *Associated Portland Cement Manufacturers Ltd.*[49] the plaintiff's husband was riding his motor-cycle along a road outside a piece of open land, occupied by the defendants, where children were permitted to play football, when a ball was kicked into the road and caused him to have an accident. The conditions were such that the likelihood of injury to passers-by was much greater than in *Bolton* v. *Stone* and accordingly the defendants were held liable for having permitted football to be played on their land without having taken any additional precautions.

The relevance of the seriousness of the injury was recognised by the House of Lords in *Paris* v. *Stepney Borough Council*[50] after having been

---

[43] *Fardon* v. *Harcourt-Rivington* (1932) 146 L.T. 391, 392, *per* Lord Dunedin.
[44] *Bolton* v. *Stone* [1951] A.C. 850, 886–889, *per* Lord Radcliffe.
[45] *The Wagon Mound (No. 2)* [1967] 1 A.C. 617, 643–644, *per* Lord Reid.
[46] *i.e.* the foreseeable, not the objective, likelihood. See *supra*.
[47] [1951] A.C. 850. Weir, *Casebook on Tort* (6th ed.), p. 107. *cf. Miller* v. *Jackson* [1977] Q.B. 966, on somewhat similar facts. The substantial claim was for an injunction and this was refused. But a majority of the Court of Appeal held the cricket club guilty of negligence and nuisance.
[48] *Ibid.* at p. 865; *Brewer* v. *Delo* (1967) 117 New L.J. 575. *Mays* v. *Essex C.C.*, *The Times*, October 11, 1975. *cf. The Wagon Mound (No. 2)* [1967] 1 A.C. 617, 642, *per* Lord Reid.
[49] [1961] 1 W.L.R. 1434.
[50] [1951] A.C. 367; *Pentney* v. *Anglian Water Authority* [1983] I.C.R. 464.

denied by the Court of Appeal in the same case.[51] In that case the plaintiff, a one-eyed man employed by the defendants, was working in conditions involving some risk of eye injury, but the likelihood of injury was not sufficient to call upon the defendants to provide goggles to a normal two-eyed workman. In the case of the plaintiff, however, goggles should have been provided for, whereas the risk to a two-eyed man was of the loss of one eye, the plaintiff risked the much greater injury of total blindness.

In assessing the magnitude of the risk it is important to notice that the duty of care is owed to the plaintiff himself and therefore that if he suffers from some disability which increases the magnitude of the risk to him that disability must be taken into account so long as it is or should be known to the defendant.[52] If it is unknown and could not reasonably have been known to the defendant then it is, of course, irrelevant.[53]

(2) *The importance of the object to be attained*

Asquith L.J. summed it up by saying that it is necessary to balance the risk against the consequences of not taking it. "As has often been pointed out, if all the trains in this country were restricted to a speed of five miles an hour, there would be fewer accidents, but our national life would be intolerably slowed down. The purpose to be served, if sufficiently important, justifies the assumption of abnormal risk."[54] In *Watt* v. *Hertfordshire County Council*[55] W., a fireman, was injured by the movement of a heavy jack when travelling with it in a lorry not specially equipped for carrying it. A woman had been trapped under a heavy vehicle and the jack was urgently required to save her life. It was held that the fire authorities had not been negligent for the risk involved to W. was not so great as to prohibit the attempt to save life. But if the same accident had occurred in a commercial enterprise W. could have recovered. "The commercial end to make profit is very different from the human end to save life or limb."[56] A fire authority has been held liable for damage caused by a fire engine which went through a red light on the way to a fire[57] for there is no special exemption from the law of negligence for

---

[51] [1950] 1 K.B. 320.
[52] *Paris* v. *Stepney Borough Council* [1951] A.C. 367; *Haley* v. *London Electricity Board* [1965] A.C. 778; *Baxter* v. *Woolcombers* (1963) 107 S.J. 553 (plaintiff's low intelligence relevant to standard of care due to him but not to question of contributory negligence); *Thorne* v. *Northern Group Hospital Management Committee* (1964) 108 S.J. 484.
[53] *Bourhill* v. *Young* [1943] A.C. 92, 109–110, *per* Lord Wright. See also *Darvill* v. *C. & J. Hampton Ltd.* (1972) 12 K.I.R. 275, though the decision went on the pleadings.
[54] *Daborn Bath Tramways* [1946] 2 All E. R. 333, 336 (left-hand drive ambulance during emergency period of war not negligent in turning right without giving a signal). *cf. Quinn* v. *Scott* [1965] 1 W.L.R. 1004 (National Trust negligent in not felling dangerous tree near highway. Safety of public must take precedence over preservation of the amenities). The fact that the defendants in *Bolton* v. *Stone* were playing cricket must have had some influence upon the decision. It by no means follows that the same risk could be taken for a less worthy end. See also the discussion of the nature of the duty owed by a public authority, *ante*, p. 98.
[55] [1954] 1 W.L.R. 835. Weir, *Casebook on Tort* (6th ed.), p. 110.
[56] *Ibid.* at p. 838, *per* Denning L.J.
[57] *Ward* v. *L.C.C.* [1938] 2 All E.R. 341; *Wardell-Yerburgh* v. *Surrey C.C.* [1973] R.T.R. 462. But in proceedings of an entirely different type the Court of Appeal refused to declare unlawful a fire authority order stating that drivers were allowed to go through red lights: *Bucocke* v. *G.L.C.* [1971] 1 Ch. 655.

them, the police or other emergency services.[58] However, the question of whether the defendant behaved like a reasonable man admits of a flexible response which may take account of the emergency in which the defendant acts.[59]

(3) *Practicability of precautions*

The risk must be balanced against the measures necessary to eliminate it, and the practical measures which the defendant could have taken must be considered.[60] In *Latimer* v. *A.E.C.*[61] a factory floor became slippery after a flood. The occupiers of the factory did everything possible to get rid of the effects of the flood, but nevertheless the plaintiff was injured and then sought to say that the occupiers should have closed down the factory. The House of Lords held that the risk of injury created by the slippery floor was not so great as to justify, much less require, so onerous a precaution. On the other hand, the greater the risk, the less weight will be given to the factor of cost, and in any case the courts will not view with favour a defence based simply upon the cost, in terms of money, of the required precaution.[62]

Evidence of negligence

The Civil Evidence Act 1968 reversed the common law rule that a conviction might not be used as evidence in civil proceedings[63] and provides that if a person is proved to have been convicted of an offence then he shall be taken to have committed that offence unless the contrary is proved. It follows that a plaintiff in an action for negligence may be entitled to succeed simply on proof that the defendant has been convicted of an offence in respect of conduct which is now complained of as negligent[64] unless the defendant can

---

[58] Even though they may be exempt from *criminal* liability for, *e.g.* exceeding the speed limit. *Gaynor* v. *Allen* [1959] 2 Q.B. 403.

[59] *Marshall* v. *Osmond* [1983] Q.B. 1034; *cf. Rigby* v. *Chief Constable of Northamptonshire* [1985] 1 W.L.R. 1242, where, on the facts, the defendants were negligent even allowing for the emergency.

[60] See *Haley* v. *London Electricity Board* [1965] A.C. 778; *Stokes* v. *Guest, Keen and Nettlefold (Bolts and Nuts) Ltd.* [1968] 1 W.L.R. 1776; *Moore* v. *Poyner* [1975] R.T.R. 127; *Wooler* v. *London Transport Board* [1976] R.T.R. 206; *Idnani* v. *Elisha* [1979] R.T.R. 488; *Stockley* v. *Knowsley M.B.C.* (1986) 279 E.G. 677.

[61] [1953] A.C. 643; *Jones* v. *Barclays Bank* [1949] W.N. 196; *Whiteford* v. *Hunter* [1950] W.N. 533; *McCarthy* v. *Coldair Ltd.* [1951] 2 T.L.R. 1226 *cf. Bolton* v. *Stone* [1951] A.C. 850, 867, *per* Lord Reid: "I think that it would be right to take into account not only how remote is the chance that a person might be struck but also how serious the consequences are likely to be if a person is struck; but I do not think that it would be right to take into account the difficulty of remedial measures." The risk involved in taking a precaution may actually outweigh the advantages of taking it: *Morris* v. *West Hartlepool Steam Navigation Co. Ltd.* [1956] A.C. 552; *Bolam* v. *Friern Hospital Management Committee* [1957] 1 W.L.R. 582.

[62] *Morris* v. *Luton Corporation* [1946] 1 All E.R. 1, 4, *per* Lord Greene M.R. The report of the case at [1946] K.B. 116 is incomplete. *cf. Hicks* v. *British Transport Commission* [1958] 1 W.L.R. 493, 505, *per* Parker L.J.; *Aiken* v. *Port of London Authority* [1962] 2 Lloyd's Rep. 30. See also *Henderson* v. *Carron* (1889) 16 R. (Ct. of Sess.) 633; *Christmas* v. *General Cleaning Contractors* [1952] 1 K.B. 141, 149, *per* Denning L.J. affirmed [1953] A.C. 180); *H. & A. Scott Ltd.* v. *J. Mackenzie Steward & Co. Ltd.* 1972 S.L.T.(Notes) 69. There may be situations in which an activity must be abandoned altogether if adequate safeguards cannot be provided. In *Goldman* v. *Hargrave* [1967] 1 A.C. 645, 663–664, the Privy Council treated the question of the actual monetary cost of the precautions as a material factor, but the case must be read in the light of its particular facts. *Ante*, p. 112.

[63] *Hollington* v. *F. Hewthorn & Co. Ltd.* [1943] K.B. 587.

[64] *Wauchope* v. *Mordecai* [1970] 1 W.L.R. 317.

discharge the burden of proving that he was not negligent.[65] The Act thus shifts the legal burden of proof on to the defendant once his conviction is proved.[66] In the absence of proof of a relevant conviction, however, the legal burden of proof rests throughout with the plaintiff, and if at the conclusion of the evidence it has not been proved on a balance of probabilities[67] that the defendant was negligent, then the plaintiff fails.[68] If a case is tried by a jury, however, it is necessary to distinguish between the question whether there is evidence of negligence—which must be answered by the judge—and whether negligence is actually proved—which is for the jury. If the judge considers that no evidence of negligence exists he must not allow the case to go to the jury. "A scintilla of evidence, or a mere surmise[69] that there may have been negligence on the part of the defendants, clearly would not justify the judge in leaving the case to the jury."[70] So too, if the plaintiff's evidence is equally consistent with the absence as with the presence of negligence on the part of the defendant, the case ought not to go to the jury.[71] On the other hand, if there is evidence from which negligence could be reasonably inferred, the judge must not withhold the case from the jury merely because in his view negligence has not been established.

This division of function came to be important, and at one time a large percentage of the appeals in negligence litigation was upon the question whether the judge had been right in allowing the case to go to the jury or in withholding it from them. So far as cases tried by jury are concerned there has been no change in the law, but today jury trials in negligence cases are exceedingly rare.[72] Though the position is also theoretically the same in actions tried by judge alone—the position is simply that the judge must answer both questions—in practice the distinction between the two questions is obscured. At the conclusion of the evidence the judge answers the single question, Has the plaintiff proved that the defendant was negligent? The result is a difference in the approach taken by appellate courts to trials by jury and to trials by judge alone. In the former, unless the jury's verdict is perverse, an appellate court will interfere only on the ground of error on the part of the judge in allowing the case to go to the jury, in

---

[65] For differing views concerning the extent of this burden, see *Stupple* v. *Royal Insurance Co. Ltd.* [1971] 1 Q.B. 50, 71–73, *per* Lord Denning M.R. (with whom Winn L.J. substantially agreed, *ibid.* at pp. 74–75) and *ibid.* at pp. 75–76, *per* Buckley L.J. See also *Hunter* v. *Chief Constable of W. Midlands* [1982] A.C. 529, 544, disapproving dicta of Lord Denning M.R. in the Court of Appeal. Care must be taken to distinguish between the effect of s.11 and the effect of s.13, by virtue of which proof of conviction of an offence is *conclusive* evidence that the convicted person did commit the offence if the question is relevant to an issue arising in an action for libel or slander. See *post*, p. 324.
[66] *Stupple* v. *Royal Insurance Co. Ltd., supra.*
[67] This is the normal standard of proof in civil cases. The more serious the allegation, (*e.g.* an allegation of fraud) the higher the degree of probability that is required: *Hornal* v. *Neuberger Products Ltd.* [1957] 1 Q.B. 247.
[68] *Brown* v. *Rolls-Royce Ltd.* [1960] 1 W.L.R. 210. Note the distinction drawn by Lord Denning between the legal and the provisional burdens of proof; *ibid.* at pp. 215–216. *Henderson* v. *Henry E. Jenkins & Sons* [1970] A.C. 2182, 301, *per* Lord Pearson.
[69] For the distinction between conjecture and inference, see *Jones* v. *G.W. Ry.* (1931) 142 L.T. 194, 197, *per* Lord Buckmaster at p. 202, *per* Lord Macmillan and compare this case with *Wakelin* v. *L. & S.W. Ry* (1886) 12 App.Cas. 41.
[70] *Toomey* v. *L.B. & S.C. Ry.* (1857) 3 C.B.(N.S.) 146, 150. *per* Williams J.
[71] *Cotton* v. *Wood* (1860) 8 C.B.(N.S.) 568.
[72] *Post*, p. 614.

admitting or rejecting certain evidence, or in his direction to the jury. In an appeal from the decision of a judge alone, on the other hand, though the appellate court will accept the judge's findings of primary fact, it will decide for itself the conclusions or inferences to be drawn from them.[73]

The decline in the use of juries has thus led to a corresponding decline in importance of the question whether there is evidence of negligence, and this question is not really raised even when the defendant submits, at the conclusion of the plaintiff's evidence, that there is no case for him to answer. If the trial is by judge alone, then, because of the obvious inconvenience of asking the judge for an opinion before the evidence is complete, the defendant must elect to call no evidence at the same time that he makes his submission.[74] Since the defendant is bound by his election the case thus falls to be decided once and for all on the evidence presented.[75] In a trial by jury the judge probably has a discretion whether or not to put the defendant to his election,[76] but even if he does not the result is much the same. In *Payne* v. *Harrison*[77] the trial judge rejected the submission that there was no case to answer and the defendant proceeded to call his evidence, which, as it happened, proved the relevant negligence beyond doubt. His appeal on the ground that the judge had been wrong to reject his submission failed on the ground, *inter alia*, that the defendant, having chosen to call evidence, could not subsequently ask to have that evidence ignored.

It is not enough, of course, that there is evidence of negligence on the part of someone. There must be evidence of negligence on the part of the defendant, and this sometimes causes difficulty where the acts of more than one person are in question. In *Bray* v. *Palmer*[78] the plaintiffs' motor-cycle and the defendant's motor-car came into head-on collision in the middle of the road. The plaintiffs' evidence was in direct conflict with the defendant's, and the trial judge held that although the accident was due exclusively to the negligence of one side or the other, he was unable to decide between them. He therefore dismissed both the plaintiffs' claim and the defendant's counterclaim. The Court of Appeal took the view that a not unlikely inference was that both parties were equally to blame and ordered a new trial. They indicated, however, that the judge's decision as it stood was tantamount to a denial of justice,[79] and that he should have formed some conclusion on the matter one way or the other. In point of fact, in cases of this kind where there is really no evidence to enable the court to distinguish between two drivers

---

[73] *Watt* v. *Thomas* [1947] A.C. 484; *Benmax* v. *Austin Motor Co. Ltd.* [1955] A.C. 370; Goodhart, "Appeals on Questions of Fact" (1955) 71 L.Q.R. 402. A good many cases even in the House of Lords are today concerned almost exclusively with inferences and conclusions of fact, *i.e.* whether or not the primary facts proved amount to negligence. For an example, see *Whitehouse* v. *Jordan* [1981] 1 W.L.R. 246.

[74] *Alexander* v. *Rayson* [1936] 1 K.B. 169; *Parry* v. *Aluminium Corporation Ltd.* [1940] W.N. 44.

[75] If after a submission of no case the judge decides in favour of the defendant the Court of Appeal may, if it is so minded, reverse the decision and enter judgment for the plaintiff without affording the defendant an opportunity to call his evidence; *Goulding* v. *Ministry of Works* (1955), unreported, cited Salmond and Heuston, *Torts* (19th ed.), p. 266.

[76] *Young* v. *Rank* [1950] 2 K.B. 510.

[77] [1961] 2 Q.B. 403.

[78] [1961] 1 W.L.R. 1455.

[79] [1953] 1 W.L.R. 1455, 1459, *per* Jenkins L.J.

involved in an accident, the correct inference will commonly be that both drivers were equally to blame.[80] In the Canadian case of *Cook* v. *Lewis*,[81] however, no similar inference was possible. A and B were out shooting and fired simultaneously in the direction of C, who was injured, but it was impossible for C to prove which of them had injured him. The case had to be sent for retrial, but on the issue of substance the Supreme Court of Canada expressed the view that C could recover. They adopted the principle that where two defendants have committed acts of negligence in circumstances that deprive the plaintiff of the ability to prove which of them caused his damage, the burden is cast upon each of the defendants to exculpate himself, and if both fail to discharge this burden, then both are liable. It has been argued, however, that this principle does not form part of English law because it conflicts with the basic rule that the plaintiff must prove his case on a balance of probabilities, and if it is no more likely that one defendant was negligent than that the other was negligent then no case is proved against either.[82] The only qualification is said to be that if a plaintiff sues two defendants[83] and his difficulties in proving which of them was negligent are due to their failure to call available evidence, adverse inferences may be drawn. But if all available evidence is called and the natural inference is that the accident was due to negligence on the part of one or other of the defendants but not of both, then the plaintiff will fail.[84]

---

[80] *Baker* v. *Market Harborough Industrial Co-operative Society; Wallace* v. *Richards Ltd.* [1953] 1 W.L.R. 1472; *France* v. *Parkinson* [1954] 1 W.L.R. 581; *W. & M. Wood (Haulage) Ltd.* v. *Redpath* [1967] 2 Q.B. 520. *Davison* v. *Leggett* (1969) 133 J.P. 552 appears to take the matter very far but see the comments on it in *Knight* v. *Follick* [1977] R.T.R. 316. *cf. Nesterczuk* v. *Mortimore* (1965) 39 A.L.J.R. 288 (Aust.H.Ct.), and see *The Anneliese* [1970] 2 All E.R. 29 for the position under the Maritime Conventions Act 1911, s.1(1)(*a*).

[81] [1951] S.C.R. 830; (1952) 1 D.L.R. 1; noted by Glanville Williams (1953) 31 Can. Bar Rev. 315–317; (1953) 72 *Law Notes* 194. Hogan, "*Cook* v. *Lewis* Re-examined" (1961) 24 M.L.R. 331. See also *Summers* v. *Tice* (1948) 5 A.L.R. 2d 91; and, in the criminal law, *cf. R.* v. *Dyos* [1979] Crim.L.R. 660.

[82] It would be exceedingly difficult to apply the principle of *Cook* v. *Lewis* to a situation involving numerous possible defendants. In product liability litigation in California, a principle akin to that of *Cook* v. *Lewis* has been carried to extraordinary lengths, including the apportionment of liability among multiple defendants according to "market shares": *Sindell* v. *Abbott Laboratories* 607 P. 2d. 924 (1980).

[83] Where the defendant is in law responsible for the negligence of all the possible tortfeasors, the plaintiff is not required to lay his finger on the exact person in all the chain who was responsible. It is enough if he has proved that someone for whom the defendant must answer has been negligent: *Grant* v. *Australian Knitting Mills* [1936] A.C. 85, 101, *per* Lord Wright; *Cassidy* v. *Ministry of Health* [1951] 2 K.B. 343; *Rob* v. *Minister of Health* [1954] 2 Q.B. 66; *Walsh* v. *Holst & Co. Ltd.* [1958] 1 W.L.R. 800.

[84] *Baker* v. *Market Harborough Industrial Co-operative Society* 1953] 1 W.L.R. 1472, 1475, *per* Somervell L.J.; *Salt* v. *Imperial Chemical Industries* [1958] C.L.Y. 2251; *Wotta* v. *Haliburton Oil Well Cementing Co.* [1955] 2 D.L.R. 785; *Nesterczuk* v. *Mortimore* (1965) 39 A.L.J.R. 288 (Aust.H.Ct.). *cf. Roe* v. *Minister of Health* [1954] 2 Q.B. 66, 82, *per* Denning L.J. The learned Lord Justice's judgment in *Baker* v. *Market Harborough Industrial Co-operative Society, supra*, is equivocal on this point. If in an action against two defendants the plaintiff makes out a prima facie case that one or both of them was negligent, then he is entitled to have the case tried out between all the parties: *Hummerstone* v. *Leary* [1921] 2 K.B. 664. The plaintiff in a case like *Cook* v. *Lewis* might at one time have sought support from *McGhee* v. *N.C.B.* [1973] 1 W.L.R. 1, although that decision was by no means on all fours. However, *McGhee* now seems to be treated as a decision on the facts: *post*, p. 134.

Res ipsa loquitur[85]

In order to discharge the burden of proof placed upon him it is usually necessary for the plaintiff to prove specific acts or omissions on the part of the defendant which will qualify as negligent conduct. Sometimes, however, the circumstances are such that the court will be prepared to draw an inference of negligence against the defendant without hearing detailed evidence of what he did or did not do. Thus, for example, the presence of an unlighted vehicle on the road at night will, if there is no other lighting, be regarded as prima facie evidence of negligence on the part of the driver.[86] It is important to appreciate, however, that this means no more than that, in the absence of an explanation from the defendant, the plaintiff has discharged his burden of proof. The inference of negligence is by no means irrebuttable,[87] and the nature of the evidence required from the defendant in rebuttal will depend in each case on the strength of the inference against him and the standard of care called for in the circumstances.

The position has, however, been complicated and obscured by the use in many cases of the maxim *res ipsa loquitur*. As Morris L.J. has said, the maxim "possesses no magic qualities: nor has it any added virtue, other than that of brevity, merely because it is expressed in Latin. When used on behalf of a plaintiff it is generally a short way of saying: 'I submit that the facts and circumstances which I have proved establish a prima facie case of negligence against the defendant. ... ' There are certain happenings that do not normally occur in the absence of negligence, and upon proof of these a court will probably hold that there is a case to answer."[88] In other words the maxim does no more than express in three words what has just been said. Nevertheless, it has given rise to a disproportionate amount of discussion and perhaps also to the development of detailed rules which do more than realise its simple underlying basis.

(1) *Conditions for application*[89]

The principal requirement is that the mere fact of the accident having happened should tell its own story and raise the inference of negligence so as

---

[85] Ellis Lewis, "A Ramble with *res ipsa loquitur*" (1951) 11 C.L.J. 74; O'Connell, "*Res ipsa loquitur*: The Australian Experience" [1954] C.L.J. 118; Underhay (1936) 14 Can. Bar Rev. 287; Baker (1950) 24 Australian L.J. 194; Prosser (1949) 37 California L.Rev. 183; Atiyah, "*Res ipsa loquitur* in England and Australia" (1972) 35 M.L.R. 337. The principle appears as early as *Christie* v. *Griggs* (1809) 2 Camp. 79; its Latin form is much later. It is untraceable in the civil law, although Prof. Buckland and Mr. Ashton-Cross state that phrases like "*res loquitur ipsa*" and "*res ipsa dixit*" occur in Cicero and other lay literature.

[86] *Hill-Venning* v. *Beszant* [1950] 2 All E.R. 1151; *Parish* v. *Judd* [1960] 1 W.L.R. 867; *Moore* v. *Maxwells of Emsworth Ltd.* [1968] 1 W.L.R. 1077.

[87] It was rebutted in the second and third of the cases cited in the last note.

[88] *Roe* v. *Minister of Health* [1954] 2 Q.B. 66, 87–88, *per* Morris L.J., *ibid.* at p. 80, *per* Somervell L.J.; *Ballard* v. *North British Ry.*, 1923 S.C. (H.L.) 43, 53, *per* Lord Dunedin, at p. 56, *per* Lord Shaw; *Easson* v. *L.N.E. Ry.* [1944] K.B. 421, 425, *per* du Parq L.J.; *Barkway* v. *South Wales Transport Co. Ltd.* [1950] 1 All E.R. 392, 403, *per* Lord Radcliffe; *Anchor Products Ltd.* v. *Hedges* (1966) 115 C.L.R. 493 (Aust.H.Ct.); *Lloyde* v. *West Midlands Gas Board* [1971] 1 W.L.R. 749.

[89] It is unnecessary specifically to plead the maxim: *Bennett* v. *Chemical Construction (G.B.) Ltd.* [1971] 1 W.L.R. 1571.

to establish a prima facie case against the defendant. The story must be clear and unambiguous; if it may tell one of half a dozen stories the maxim is inapplicable.[90] This single requirement is, however, commonly divided into two on the basis of Erle C.J.'s famous statement in *Scott* v. *London and St. Katherine Docks Co.*[91]

> "There must be reasonable evidence of negligence. But where the thing is shown to be under the management of the defendant or his servants, and the accident is such as in the ordinary course of things does not happen if those who have the management use proper care, it affords reasonable evidence, in the absence of explanation by the defendants, that the accident arose from want of care."

The two requirements are thus (i) that the "thing" causing the damage be under the control of the defendant or his servants,[92] and (ii) that the accident must be such as would not in the ordinary course of things have happened without negligence.

(a) **Control.** The point of this requirement is that the happening of the accident must be evidence of negligence on the part of the defendant or of someone for whose negligence he is responsible. A mere right to control, as opposed to actual control, is therefore sufficient[93] and it is not always necessary that all the circumstances be under the defendant's control.[94] But if the events leading up to the accident were, or might well have been, under the control of others besides the defendant, then the mere happening of the accident is insufficient evidence against the defendant.[95] In *Gee* v. *Metropolitan Ry.*[96] the plaintiff leant lightly against the door of an underground train not long after it had left a station. The door flew open, causing the plaintiff to

---

[90] *Carruthers* v. *MacGregor*, 1927 S.C. 816, 823, *per* Lord Murray; *Cole* v. *De Trafford* [1918] 2 K.B. 528; 11 C.L.J. 82–83. Even so simple a situation as the presence of a carton of yoghurt on a supermarket floor can produce differing judicial inferences. In *Ward* v. *Tesco Stores Ltd.* [1976] 1 W.L.R. 810 (noted by Manchester (1977) 93 L.Q.R. 13) Lawton and Megaw L.JJ. considered this established a prima facie case of negligence by the defendant's staff but Ormrod L.J. dissented because in his view the presence of the yoghurt on the floor did not establish that it had been there for any significant length of time, a vital element in an allegation of negligence. See also *Richards* v. *W.F. White & Co.* [1957] 1 Lloyd's Rep. 367 and *Dulhunty* v. *J.B. Young Ltd.* (1975) 7 A.L.R. 409.

[91] (1865) 3 H. & C. 596 (six bags of sugar fell on plaintiff whilst lawfully passing doorway of defendant's warehouse. Defendants called no evidence. Held, sufficient evidence of negligence). This passage has been said to be "the foundation of all subsequent authority": *Moore* v. *R. Fox & Sons* [1956] 1 Q.B. 596, 611, *per* Evershed M.R. See also *Britannia Hygienic Laundry Co.* v. *Thornycroft & Co.* (1926) 95 L.J.K.B. 237; *Halliwell* v. *Venables* (1930) 143 L.T. 215; *Ellor* v. *Selfridge & Co. Ltd.* (1930) 46 T.L.R. 236; *Mahon* v. *Osborne* [1939] 2 K.B. 14; *Easson* v. *L.N.E. Ry.* [1944] K.B. 421; *Barkway* v. *South Wales Transport Co.* (1950) 94 S.J. 95; *Bolton* v. *Stone* [1951] A.C. 850, 859.

[92] It is sufficient if an independent contractor employed by the defendant has control, provided that the circumstances are such that the defendant will be liable for the negligence of his independent contractor or the circumstances are such that he should supervise the contractor (*Kealey* v. *Heard* [1983] 1 W.L.R. 573). *Walsh* v. *Holst & Co. Ltd.* [1958] 1 W.L.R. 800.

[93] *Parker* v. *Miller* (1926) 42 T.L.R. 408.

[94] *McGowan* v. *Stott* (1930) 143 L.T. 217; *Chaproniére* v. *Mason* (1905) 21 T.L.R. 633; *Grant* v. *Australian Knitting Mills* [1936] A.C. 85; *Moore* v. *R. Fox & Sons* [1956] 1 Q.B. 596.

[95] The true principle therefore appears to be not that the plaintiff must show any positive control in the defendant but rather that outside interference is unlikely: *Lloyde* v. *West Midlands Gas Board* [1971] 1 W.L.R. 749.

[96] (1873) L.R. 8 Q.B. 161; *Burns* v. *N.B. Ry.* 1914 S.C. 754; *Brookes* v. *L.P.T.B.* [1974] 1 All E.R. 506.

fall out, and it was held that there was evidence of negligence against the railway company. On the other hand, in *Easson* v. *L.N.E. Ry.*[97] where the plaintiff, a boy aged four, fell through a door of a corridor train about seven miles from its last stopping place it was held that the defendants did not have sufficient control over the door for *res ipsa loquitur* to apply. "It is impossible to say that the doors of an express corridor train travelling from Edinburgh to London are continuously under the sole control of the railway company. . . . Passengers are walking up and down the corridors during the journey and get in and out at stopping places."[98] The fact that the door came open could as well have been due to interference by a passenger as to the negligence of the defendants' servants.

(b) **Accident must be such as could not in the ordinary course of things have happened without negligence.** The question here is whether the fact of the accident itself justifies the inference of negligence and this means not only that all the circumstances must be considered, but that they must be considered in the light of common experience and knowledge. In effect the judge takes judicial notice of the common experience of mankind.[99] It is common experience which shows that a barrel will not fall from an upstairs window on to a passer-by in the street if those in charge take proper care[1] or that two railway trains belonging to the same company will not collide without negligence on the part of the company or its servants.[2] So also, if a vehicle strikes a person on the pavement[3] or moves on to the wrong side of the road into the path of oncoming traffic,[4] there is a prima facie case of negligence against the driver: and this is not displaced merely by proof that the defendant's vehicle skidded.[5] Indeed, an unexplained and violent skid is itself evidence of negligence.[6] On the other hand, the mere fact that a fire spread from an ordinary domestic grate is not sufficient[7] for "everyone knows fires occur through accidents which happen without negligence on anybody's part."[8] Similarly, it is well known that losses occur in commodity futures trading without any negligence by brokers.[9]

---

[97] [1944] 2 K.B. 421; *Lloyde* v. *West Midlands Gas Board* [1971] 1 W.L.R. 749.
[98] [1944] K.B. 421, 424, *per* Goddard L.J. See too *O'Connor* v. *British Transport Commission* [1958] 1 W.L.R. 346 and *McLeod* v. *Glasgow Corp.* 1971 S.L.T.(Notes) 64.
[99] Ellis Lewis, *loc. cit.* at p. 80.
[1] *Byrne* v. *Boadle* (1863) 2 H. & C. 722; *aliter* where an armchair falls from an hotel window, because the hotel does not have "control": *Larson* v. *St. Francis Hotel* 188 P. 2d 513 (1948).
[2] *Skinner* v. *L.B. & S.C. Ry.* (1850) 5 Ex. 787. Of the many other cases see, *e.g. Chaproniére* v. *Mason* (1905) 21 T.L.R. 633 (stone in bun); *Fosbroke-Hobbes* v. *Airwork Ltd.* [1937] 1 All E.R. 108 (aeroplane crashing immediately after take-off); *Grant* v. *Australian Knitting Mills* [1936] A.C. 85 (excess of sulphites in woollen pants); *Colvilles Ltd.* v. *Devine* [1969] 1 W.L.R. 475 (explosion in hose carrying oxygen).
[3] *Ellor* v. *Selfridge & Co. Ltd.* (1930) 46 T.L.R. 236; *Watson* v. *Thomas S. Witney & Co. Ltd.* [1966] 1 W.L.R. 57.
[4] *Richley (Henderson)* v. *Faull* [1965] 1 W.L.R. 1454.
[5] *Laurie* v. *Raglan Building Co. Ltd.* [1942] 1 K.B. 152. This, it is submitted, is all that is meant by Lord Greene M.R.'s statement (*ibid.* at p. 154) that "the skid itself is neutral." If the vehicle's presence in the wrong place is due to a skid and the skid is proved to have occurred without negligence then there is, of course, no negligence: *Hunter* v. *Wright* [1938] 2 All E.R. 621; *Brown* v. *De Luxe Car Services* [1941] 1 All E.R. 383.
[6] *Hurlock* v. *Inglis* (1963) 107 S.J. 1023; *Richley (Henderson)* v. *Faull, supra.*
[7] *Sochacki* v. *Sas* [1947] 1 All E.R. 344.
[8] *Ibid.* at p. 345, *per* Lord Goddard C.J.
[9] *Stafford* v. *Conti Commodity Services Ltd.* [1981] 1 All E.R. 691; *Merrell Lynch Futures Inc.* v. *York House Trading* (1984) 7 L.S.Gaz. 2544.

If it is the common experience of mankind which enables the inference of negligence to be drawn from the fact of the accident having happened then it might be thought that in cases outside the range of common experience, such as those involving surgical operations, *res ipsa loquitur* could not apply. This was the view of Scott L.J. in *Mahon* v. *Osborne*,[10] where a swab was left in the body of a patient after an abdominal operation, but the modern trend is to permit the maxim to be used. A plaintiff is entitled to say, "I went into hospital to be cured of two stiff fingers. I have come out with four stiff fingers, and my hand is useless. That should not have happened if due care had been used. Explain it, if you can."[11] And there seems no reason why the plaintiff should not call expert witnesses to show that the accident would not have occurred without negligence. Otherwise he may find himself put to an impossible burden of proof and in the result fail to establish what in truth is a valid claim simply because the judge lacks the experience to draw the appropriate inferences.[12]

(c) **Absence of explanation.** It is sometimes said that there is a third requirement for the application of the maxim, namely, that there must be no evidence of the actual cause of the accident. All this seems to mean, however, is that, if the facts are sufficiently known, the question ceases to be whether they speak for themselves, and the only question is whether on the facts as established, negligence is to be inferred or not.[13] The mere fact that the plaintiff attempts, and fails, to prove some specific act of negligence on the part of the defendant does not, of itself, deprive him of the benefit of the maxim[14] and, of course, even its actual exclusion does not necessarily lead to the conclusion that the defendant was not negligent. In *Barkway* v. *South Wales Transport Co. Ltd.*[15] B. was travelling as a passenger in the defendants' omnibus and was killed when it veered across the road and fell over an embankment. A great deal of evidence was given by the defendants and it was established that the cause of the accident was a defect in one of the tyres which might have been discovered beforehand if the defendants had required their drivers to report occurrences which could result in "impact fractures." The House of Lords held that as the cause of the accident was known *res ipsa loquitur* did not apply, but that on the facts the negligence of the defendants was established.

(2) *Effect of the maxim*

It may well be that the correct analysis of the effect of the maxim *res ipsa*

---

[10] [1939] 2 K.B. 14. Goddard L.J., dissenting, thought that *res ipsa loquitur* could be used.
[11] *Cassidy* v. *Ministry of Health* [1951] 2 K.B. 343, 365, *per* Denning L.J.; *Roe* v. *Minister of Health* [1954] 2 Q.B. 66; *Saunders* v. *Leeds Western Health Authority* (1985) 129 S.J. 225 (anaesthesia).
[12] See *Fish* v. *Kapur* [1948] 2 All E.R. 176 where, however, the plaintiff's expert witnesses helped to negative the inference of negligence.
[13] *Barkway* v. *South Wales Transport Co. Ltd.* [1950] 1 All E.R. 392; *Bolton* v. *Stone* [1951] A.C. 850, 859, *per* Lord Porter.
[14] *Anchor Products Ltd.* v. *Hedges* (1966) 115 C.L.R. 493.
[15] [1950] 1 All E.R. 392.

loquitur is that it entitles (but does not require) the tribunal of fact to find for the plaintiff. This may be easier to understand if we postulate a trial by jury which, of course, is now practically extinct in negligence cases in England. In such a case, if the plaintiff successfully raises a plea of *res ipsa loquitur* the judge must obviously reject a submission by the defendant that there is no case to go to the jury. It would not seem to follow, however, that if the defendant gives no evidence and yet the jury were to give a verdict in his favour, the verdict is necessarily perverse. The inference of negligence raised by the mere fact of the accident may sometimes be irresistible, but it will not always be so.[16] In theory the same should be true in cases of trial by judge alone. The judge may hold that *res ipsa loquitur* applies, reject a submission of no evidence and yet, without further evidence from the defence, give judgment for the defendant. In practice, however, it is impossible for a judge sitting alone to distinguish so sharply between his functions as judge of law and judge of fact. If he is not prepared to hold that, in the absence of some evidence from the defendant, the plaintiff has sufficiently proved negligence by proving the fact of the accident alone, he will not hold that *res ipsa loquitur* applies in the first place. But if he holds that it does apply then that will compel, rather than merely justify, a decision for the plaintiff in the absence of rebutting evidence.[17]

A burden is therefore cast upon the defendant by the application of the maxim. But the question remains of what the defendant must do to discharge it. The view has been advanced in some cases that the actual burden of proof on the issue of negligence shifts, so that the defendant is required to show on a balance of probabilities that the accident was not attributable to his fault: "when a balance has been tilted one way, you cannot redress it by adding an equal weight to each scale. The depressed scale will remain down."[18] Now, however, the Privy Council has unanimously approved the view that there is no shift in the formal burden of proof.[19] This remains throughout upon the plaintiff, so that at the end of the day the court must ask itself what is the effect of the rebutting evidence by the defendant upon the cogency of the initial inference of negligence which arose from the mere happening of the accident." The *res*, which previously spoke for itself, may be silenced, or its voice may, on the whole of the evidence, become too weak or muted."[20] Certainly, the defendant will be exonerated if he shows how the accident actually occurred and if this true explanation is consistent with due

---

[16] See *Davies* v. *Bunn* (1936) 56 C.L.R. 246, 267–268, *per* Evatt J.

[17] See, *e.g.* Lord Pearson in *Henderson* v. *Henry E. Jenkins & Sons* [1970] A.C. 282, 301: "the issue will be decided in the plaintiff's favour unless the defendants by their evidence provide some answer which is adequate to displace the prima facie inference."

[18] *Barkway* v. *South Wales Transport Co. Ltd.* [1948] 2 All E.R. 460, 471, *per* Asquith L.J.; *Moore* v. *R. Fox & Sons* [1956] 1 Q.B. 596.

[19] *Ng* v. *Lee* [1988] R.T.R. 298. In *Henderson* v. *Jenkins, supra,* at p. 479 Lord Donovan used the metaphor of the scales to the opposite effect from Asquith L.J. in *Barkway*: "it was for the [defendants] to show that the accident was just as consistent with their having exercised due diligence as with their having been negligent. In that way, the scales which had been tipped in the plaintiff's favour by the doctrine . . . would be once more in the balance, and the plaintiff would have to begin again and prove negligence in the usual way."

[20] Megaw L.J. in *Lloyde* v. *West Midlands Gas Board* [1971] 1 W.L.R. 749, 755, approved in *Ng* v. *Lee, supra.*

care on his part[21]; and if he cannot do this he will still escape liability if he shows that in no respect was there any lack of care on his part or on the part of persons for whom he is responsible.[22] But the evidence which he is able to call may still leave open a reasonable inference that there was negligence (for example, the provision of a good quality control system in a factory does not remove the possibility that an employee tampered with it[23]) and the standard of care called for by the activity of the defendant may dispose the court to require him to rebut even unlikely possibilities. In *Henderson* v. *Henry E. Jenkins & Sons*,[24] where the plaintiff's husband was killed by a heavy lorry whose brakes failed on a steep hill, the defendants pleaded that the brake failure was due to a latent defect in the main brake fluid pipe. They proved that they had cleaned and carried out visual inspections of the pipe at the proper intervals and that the cause of its failure was corrosion in a part of the pipe which could only be inspected by removing the pipe itself from the vehicle. Notwithstanding that neither the manufacturers of the vehicle nor the Ministry of Transport recommended removal of the pipe for inspection in normal circumstances, it was held by a majority of the House of Lords that the defendants had not done sufficient to rebut the inference that they had been negligent: they should have gone on to show that nothing had occurred in the life of the vehicle which would cause abnormal corrosion or call for special inspection or treatment. The strength of the inference of negligence raised by the extensive corrosion of the pipe, and the extremely high standard of inspection and maintenance required of a person who sends a heavy lorry on a journey involving the descent of a steep hill justify the heavy burden placed on the defendants in this case. In other circumstances the inference will be rebutted more easily, but in each case the question is the same: has the defendant rebutted the inference of negligence raised against him by the plaintiff's evidence?

CONSEQUENT DAMAGE

The third ingredient of the tort of negligence is that the plaintiff's damage must have been caused by the defendant's breach of duty and must not be too remote a consequence of it. Discussion of this ingredient thus involves consideration of remoteness of damage, a topic relevant in all torts and not only in the tort of negligence. It is in cases of negligence, however, that problems of remoteness of damage most commonly arise, and these can only be dealt with against the background of the tort of negligence as a whole. Although a topic of general importance throughout the law, therefore, remoteness of damage will be dealt with in the next chapter.

---

[21] *Barkway* v. *South Wales Transport Co. Ltd.* [1948] 2 All E.R. 460, 471, *per* Asquith L.J.; *Colvilles Ltd.* v. *Devine* [1969] 1 W.L.R. 475.

[22] *Woods* v. *Duncan* [1946] A.C. 401; *Walsh* v. *Holst & Co. Ltd.* [1958] 1 W.L.R. 800; *Swan* v. *Salisbury Construction Co. Ltd.* [1966] 1 W.L.R. 204. Something more than a bare statement to this effect by the defendant himself is necessary: *Ludgate* v. *Lovett* [1969] 1 W.L.R. 1016.

[23] See *post*, p. 245.

[24] [1970] A.C. 282.

Chapter 6

CAUSATION, REMOTENESS OF DAMAGE AND CONTRIBUTORY NEGLIGENCE[1]

EVEN if the plaintiff proves every other element in tortious liability he will lose the action or, in the case of torts actionable *per se*, fail to recover more than nominal damages if the defendant has not caused his loss or, even if there is the required causal link, if the harm the plaintiff has suffered is too remote a consequence of the defendant's conduct.[2] Causation and remoteness may arise in the context of any tort (or indeed in contract) but the overwhelming majority of cases concern negligence. Causation and remoteness are concerned with the question whether damages may be recovered for particular items of the plaintiff's loss. As such they are logically distinct from and anterior to the question of measure of damages, which is concerned with the calculation of the amount of pecuniary compensation which the defendant must pay in respect of those items of the plaintiff's loss for which he is responsible.[3] Measure of damages will therefore be dealt with at a later stage.[4]

CAUSATION IN FACT[5]

Before one reaches the question of remoteness it must be decided whether the defendant's breach of duty was, *as a matter of fact*, a cause of the damage.[6] Although the question of factual causation has exercised philosophers and more than one approach is possible,[7] for the practical purposes

---

[1] Weir, *Casebook on Tort* (6th ed.), Chaps. 4 and 5, s.1.

[2] As it is sometimes put, "if the damage is too remote."

[3] *The Argentino* (1881) 13 P.D. 191, 196, *per* Lord Esher M.R. "Measure of damages" is sometimes used where remoteness is meant, *e.g. The Wagon Mound (No. 2)* [1967] 1 A.C. 167, 638, *per* Lord Reid, but it must be admitted that the two questions sometimes run into each other. If we classify an issue as one of remoteness we generally require that the consequence in question be foreseeable but we do not require foreseeability as to the *measure* of damages. Thus if I drive carelessly and cause injury to X, it must be foreseeable that my driving will injure X if I am to be held liable; but I am liable for X's full loss of income even though it exceeds what I could have foreseen. Yet with regard to damage to profit-earning chattels some cases have taken a different line and required foreseeability of the *amount* of the loss; *post*, p. 147. The line between remoteness and measure of damages is peculiarly difficult to draw where the plaintiff could have reduced the damage if he had had more financial resources: *post*, p. 148.

[4] See Chap. 23.

[5] See generally Hart and Honoré, *Causation in the Law* (2nd ed.).

[6] If it was, then remoteness is a limiting factor and may be said to be concerned with whether the defendant's breach will be treated as an *effective* cause in law. Care must therefore be taken to note in what sense the court is using the language of "causation." Suppose A leaves a loaded gun in an unlocked cupboard. B steals it and uses it to murder C. A court is likely to say that B, but not A, is responsible for C's death (*post*, p. 153) and it may speak in terms of B's act being "the cause" of the death. But A's breach of duty (if such it was) was *a* cause in the sense used in this section. If all remoteness issues could be dealt with as questions of foreseeability the potential confusion would not occur, but they cannot.

[7] Hart and Honoré, *op. cit.*, n. 4 esp. Part I. Glanville Williams, "Causation in the Law" [1961] C.L.J. 62; Fraser and Howarth, "More Concern for Cause" (1984) 4 L.S. 131.

of the law that most generally accepted by the courts is the so-called "but-for" test. If the result would not have happened but for a certain event then that event is a cause; contrariwise, if it would have happened anyway, the event is not a cause.[8] On this basis, of course, every result has an infinite number of causes but the objection that this is "Adam-and-Eve" causation is misplaced, for the function of the test is merely to act as a preliminary filter and eliminate the irrelevant rather than to allocate legal responsibility—that is the next stage. The application of the test is neatly illustrated by *Barnett* v. *Chelsea and Kensington Hospital Management Committee*.[9] Three night-watchmen, one of whom was the plaintiff's husband, called early in the morning at the defendant's hospital and complained of vomiting after drinking tea. The nurse on duty consulted a doctor by telephone and he said that the men should go home and consult their own doctors later in the morning. Later the same day the plaintiff's husband died of arsenical poisoning and the coroner's verdict was one of murder by persons unknown. In failing to examine the deceased the doctor was in breach of his duty of care, but this breach was not a cause of the death because, even if the deceased had been examined and treated with proper care, the probability was that it would have been impossible to save his life. The plaintiff's claim therefore failed.[10] It should be noted that the court is not concerned with what did happen but with what would have happened if the defendant's breach of duty had been removed from the set of events surrounding the accident and replaced by rightful conduct on his part. The burden of showing that the damage would thereby have been avoided is, however, squarely upon the plaintiff and if he fails to discharge it on the balance of probabilities he fails. In *Wilsher* v. *Essex Area Health Authority*[11]; the plaintiff, born prematurely, succumbed to RLF, a retinal condition causing serious damage to his sight. A possible cause, or contributing cause, of this was an excess of oxygen caused by a mistaken placing of a catheter[12] but the conflicting expert evidence at the trial identified a number of other possible causes and the failure of the trial judge to consider whether the mistake was more likely as a cause than these others[13] meant there had to be a retrial on the causation issue.

For a brief period it looked as if the courts might be developing a principle whereby damages might be recovered for the value of the chance that the defendant's conduct caused the plaintiff's loss. Damages based upon a

[8] "Subject to the question of remoteness, causation is a question of fact. If the damage would not have happened but for a particular fault, then that fault is the cause of the damage; if it would have happened just the same, fault or no fault, the fault is not the cause of the damage. It is to be decided by the ordinary plain common sense of the business": *Cork* v. *Kirby Maclean Ltd.* [1952] 2 All E.R. 402, 406–407. For comparative law see Hart and Honorè, *op. cit.*, n. 5, *supra*, Part III and Lawson and Markesinis, *Tortious Liability for Unintentional Harm in the Common Law and the Civil Law,* Vol. 1, Chap. 3, s.1.
[9] [1969] 1 Q.B. 428.
[10] See also *McWilliams* v. *Sir William Arrol & Co. Ltd.* [1962] 1 W.L.R. 295 (death by falling; breach of employer's duty to provide safety harness; evidence showed that deceased would not have used it).
[11] [1988] A.C. 1074 Boon (1988) 51 M.L.R. 508.
[12] A further point on breach of duty is discussed in the Court of Appeal but not dealt with by the House of Lords: *ante*, p. 115.
[13] Indeed, he had placed the onus squarely on the defendants to show that it was probably not a cause. In a vaccine damage case the burden of proof of causation is not discharged by showing that there is a respectable body of opinion that the vaccine may cause such damage: *Loveday* v. *Renton, The Times*, March 31, 1988.

"chance" are, after all, well enough known in the law of torts: a plaintiff who has suffered no present loss of income may recover a sum in respect of the risk that his injuries may at some time disadvantage him in the labour market[14] and it has been commonplace in cases of head injury to award something for the risk that epilepsy may develop.[15] But we are now concerned not with what may happen at some time in the future as a result of the plaintiff's injury but with the question whether the plaintiff has suffered injury from the defendant's act at all. One is a case of quantification, the other of causation and the House of Lords has held that the requirement of proof of causation cannot be sidestepped in this way. In *Hotson* v. *East Berkshire Health Authority*[16] the defendants failed correctly to diagnose the plaintiff's condition after a fall and there developed a serious disability of the hip joint. On the facts, there was a 75 per cent. risk that this disability would have developed even if the plaintiff had been treated properly but the trial judge (and the Court of Appeal) held that he was entitled to damages representing 25 per cent. of his full loss. This was reversed by the House of Lords: the judge's findings of fact amounted to a conclusion that on a balance of probabilities the disability would have occurred anyway and that the fall was therefore the sole cause of the loss. On this basis, there was no foundation for awarding damages for loss of the chance of recovery. Equally, however, had the plaintiff shown on a slight balance of probabilities that he would have recovered if given proper treatment then he would recover his damages in full.[17]

It is true that the "chance" doctrine is not specifically rejected in all circumstances in the case. Lord Mackay thought it would be unwise "to lay it down as a rule that a plaintiff could never succeed by proving loss of a chance in a medical negligence case" and Lord Bridge, while referring to "formidable difficulties" in connection with the doctrine, thought the appeal was not a suitable occasion for reaching a settled conclusion whether it could ever be applied. However, the result of *Hotson* (not to mention the further insistence on proof on a balance of probabilities in *Wilsher*) seems to leave no

---

[14] *Post*, p. 621.

[15] Though since the Administration of Justice Act 1982 such a case might be more suitable for the award of provisional damages: *post*, p. 629.

[16] [1987] A.C. 750. Stapleton, "The Gist of Negligence, Part II" (1988) 104 L.Q.R. 389.

[17] *Ibid*. at p. 783, *per* Lord Bridge and at p. 793, *per* Lord Ackner. But in assessing damages for future loss in a personal injuries case the court is required to make a discount for the "vicissitudes of life," *i.e.* scale down the damages to take account of other risks which might have affected the plaintiff if he had not been injured (*post*, p. 618). *Hotson* cannot be intended to affect this. Further, according to *Davies* v. *Taylor* [1974] A.C. 207 where the plaintiff claims loss of support from the death of a deceased spouse he is not required to prove on a balance of probabilities that that support would have continued had the death not occurred, merely that there was a reasonable chance that it would have continued, the damages being scaled down accordingly. Of course, it is possible to argue that this case concerned quantification, not causation, but the line is a fine one. See also contract cases such as *Chaplin* v. *Hicks* [1911] 2 K.B. 786. Such matters were examined fully at first instance by Simon Brown J. ([1985] 1 W.L.R. 1036) but are hardly touched on in the House of Lords.

discernible scope for it.[18] However, the origin of the doctrine that had appealed to the lower courts in these cases is a third decision of the House, *McGhee* v. *N.C.B.*[19] The pursuer developed dermatitis and alleged that it had been caused by the defenders' failure to provide washing facilities at the work place. The defenders admitted negligence in failing to provide these facilities but medical knowledge about the causes of dermatitis was such that it was not possible to say that had washing facilities been provided the pursuer would have escaped the disease. Indeed, it was not even possible to put a figure on the increased risk; all that could be said was that the absence of the facilities had materially increased the risk. On these facts the pursuer was held entitled to succeed in the absence of proof by the defenders that their breach of duty was not causative and there seems little doubt that the decision was motivated as much by policy as by logic for as Lord Wilberforce candidly said, "if one asks which of the parties, the workman or the employers, should suffer from this inherent evidential difficulty, the answer as a matter of policy or justice should be that it is the creator of the risk who, *ex hypothesi*, must be taken to have foreseen the possibility of damage, who should bear its consequences."[20] The case was certainly not on all fours with *Wilsher* v. *Essex Area Health Authority*,[21] but in the latter it is treated as laying down no new principle of law as to causation and the burden of proof. *McGhee* is no more than a "robust and pragmatic" decision that it was legitimate to infer from the primary facts that the defenders' breach of duty probably made some contribution to the development of the disease[22] and that was enough to entitle the pursuer to win, whether or not a factor for which the defenders were not responsible was also in operation.

It is implicit in *McGhee's* case that an event may have two causes and that the author of each cause is responsible for the whole loss resulting from the event. This is also the case *even where each cause would in itself have been sufficient to produce the result*, as where A and B both fatally wound C at the same moment.[23] The "but-for" test is inadequate here, for it gives the result, contrary to common sense, that neither is a cause, but however we justify it[24]

---

[18] A variant of such a doctrine had motivated the dissenting judgment of Russell L.J. in *Cutler* v. *Vauxhall Motors* [1971] 1 Q.B. 418. P had to have an operation for a pre-existing varicose condition because this was desirable as a result of an ulcer caused by D. He would, on a balance of probabilities, have required the operation in four or five years anyway. Russell L.J. thought the plaintiff should have a proportion of the loss attributable to the operation because it was only a probability that he would have required it anyway. The majority view, that he should get nothing in respect of the operation, would now seem to be confirmed.

[19] [1973] 1 W.L.R. 1. Weinrib, "A Step Forward in Factual Causation" (1975) 38 M.L.R. 518.

[20] [1973] 1 W.L.R. 1, 6. Establishing causation in cases of disease and impairment can present formidable difficulties: see, *e.g. Thompson* v. *Smith's Shiprepairers (North Shields) Ltd.* [1984] Q.B. 405 and see generally Stapleton, *Disease and the Compensation Debate.*

[21] In *McGhee* there was no doubt that the defenders' dust caused the dermatitis; what was in doubt was whether the defenders' failure to provide the facilities to remove it was a causative factor. In *Wilsher* there were at least four agents other than the oxygen administered by the defendants which could have been responsible.

[22] See [1988] A.C. 1074, 1090, *per* Lord Bridge.

[23] On one view of the facts *Roberts* v. *J.W. Ward & Son* (1981) 126 S.J. 120 involved two errors by the defendants which were both fatal to the plaintiff's contract but only one of which was negligent. The Court of Appeal said that in this event the defendants would not be allowed to set up their innocent error to escape the consequences of their negligence.

[24] See Wright, "Causation in Tort Law" (1985) 73 Cal.L.Rev. 1735.

both tortfeasors are held fully liable for the loss, subject to the contribution legislation.[25]

Matters of factual causation become more complex when the plaintiff is affected by two successive acts or events. In *Baker v. Willoughby*,[26] as a result of the defendant's negligence, the plaintiff suffered an injury to his left leg and, taking both past and future losses into account, the judge assessed his damages, on a basis of full liability,[27] at £1,600. Before the trial, however, and while the plaintiff was working at a new job he had taken up after his accident he was the victim of an armed robbery in the course of which he suffered gunshot wounds to his left leg of such severity that the leg had to be amputated. The defendant therefore argued that his liability was limited to the loss suffered before the date of the robbery; all loss suffered thereafter was merged in and flowed from the robbery.[28] This argument succeeded before the Court of Appeal but was rejected by the House of Lords because it produced a manifest injustice. Even if the robbers could have been successfully sued to judgment,[29] they would only have been liable for depriving the plaintiff of an already damaged leg[30] and the plaintiff would therefore have been left uncompensated in the period after the robbery for the "difference" between a sound leg and a damaged one. The defendant's argument was said to contain a fallacy in its assertion that the injury to the leg was obliterated by the subsequent amputation because, as Lord Reid put it,[31] a man "is not compensated for the physical injury: he is compensated for the loss which he suffers as a result of that injury. His loss is not in having a stiff leg: it is his inability to lead a full life, his inability to enjoy those amenities which depend on freedom of movement and his inability to earn as much as he used to earn or could have earned if there had been no accident. In this case the second injury did not diminish any of these. So why should it be regarded as having obliterated or superseded them?" In other words, the

---

[25] *Post*, Chap. 22. But if only one cause operates, though the other would inevitably have done the same thing a little later (D kills P, who has a terminal illness), the tendency is to say that the first is a cause and here the defendant is liable, but the damages are to be discounted to take account of the fact that the threat of the second reduces "value": *Smith* v. *Cawdle Fen Comrs.* [1938] 4 All E.R. 64, 71; *Dillon* v. *Twin State Gas and Electric Co.* 163 Atl. 111 (1932). A criminal court would give the same answer as to causation but the device of mitigating liability by reducing damages is not open to it.

[26] [1970] A.C. 467; McGregor, "Successive Causes of Personal Injury" (1970) 33 M.L.R. 378; Strachan, "The Scope and Application of the 'But For' Causal Test" (1970) 33 M.L.R. 386; Goodhart (1970) 86 L.Q.R. 291; Cohn (1970) 86 L.Q.R. 449.

[27] The plaintiff was guilty of contributory negligence assessed at 25 per cent.

[28] Note that it is not wholly true that the plaintiff would have lost his leg even if he had suffered the accident for which the defendant was responsible because he had had to change his employment as a result of his original injury. But while the original injury was in this sense a cause of the shooting it could not possibly be contended that the defendant was liable for the loss arising from the shooting: *Carslogie Steamship Co. Ltd.* v. *Royal Norwegian Government* [1952] A.C. 292, *post*, p. 150.

[29] The speeches do not disclose whether the plaintiff had made any claim under the Criminal Injuries Compensation Scheme.

[30] *Performance Cars Ltd.* v. *Abraham* [1962] 1 Q.B. 33; *Baker* v. *Willoughby* [1970] A.C. 467, *per* Lord Reid; *ibid.* at p. 495, *per* Lord Pearson. An argument that the robbers would in theory be liable for the whole of the plaintiff's loss because they had deprived him of his right of action against the defendant was rejected (*ibid.* at p. 496, *per* Lord Pearson); *cf. Griffiths* v. *Commonwealth* (1983) 50 A.C.T.R. 7. In any case, to have held that the plaintiff had a complete remedy against the robbers would have brought him little comfort.

[31] [1970] A.C. 467, 492.

plaintiff's loss after the removal of the leg was to be regarded as having two concurrent causes.[32]

The decision in *Baker* v. *Willoughby*, however, received a hard knock in *Jobling* v. *Associated Dairies Ltd.*[33] The defendant's breach of duty caused the plaintiff to suffer injury to his back and this left him with a continuing disability. Three years later, and before trial, the plaintiff was diagnosed as suffering from a condition (myelopathy), unrelated to the accident, and arising after the accident,[34] which of itself rendered him totally unfit for work. The defendants naturally contended that the onset of the myelopathy terminated their liability for the effects of the back injury; in reply, the plaintiff argued that the case should be governed by *Baker* v. *Willoughby*. A unanimous House of Lords found for the defendants. The myelopathy was one of the "vicissitudes of life" for the *chance* of which the courts regularly made discounts in the assessment of damages for future loss of earnings[35] and it followed inevitably that it must be taken into account when it had actually occurred before the trial:

> "When the supervening illness or injury which is the independent cause of loss of earning capacity has manifested itself before trial, the event has demonstrated that, even if the plaintiff had never sustained the tortious injury, his earnings would now be reduced or extinguished. To hold the tortfeasor, in this situation, liable to pay damages for a notional continuing loss of earnings attributable to the tortious injury, is to put the plaintiff in a better position than he would be in if he had never suffered the tortious injury."[36]

This approach is totally inconsistent with the theory of the concurrent effect of consecutive causes advanced in *Baker* v. *Willoughby*[37] and that case can no longer be regarded as a general authority on causation.[38] Whether it is an authority on successive *tortious* injuries remains unclear. Lord Russell was prepared to suggest that it might have been correctly decided on the basis that a subsequent tortious injury was not to be regarded as within the "vicissitudes" principle, and hence should not be regarded as removing the effects of the first injury,[39] and Lord Keith would, though not for the same reasons, draw a similar distinction between tortious and non-tortious inju-

---

[32] If the plaintiff had died of natural causes before the trial it is clear that neither the defendant nor the robbers could have been liable to his dependants. If he had died from the gunshot wounds the robbers would have been liable to his dependants under the Fatal Accidents Act, *post,* Chap. 24.

[33] [1982] A.C. 794; Evans (1982) 45 M.L.R. 329; Borrowdale, "Vicissitudes in Anglo-Australian Perspective" (1983) 32 I.C.L.Q. 651.

[34] It had been conceded that if the myelopathy had been existing but dormant at the time of the accident it would have to be taken into account in assessing damages.

[35] See *post,* Chap. 23.

[36] [1982] A.C. 794, 820, *per* Lord Bridge.

[37] Is it also inconsistent with the proposition that *simultaneous* sufficient causes may have concurrent effect?

[38] [1982] A.C. 794, 802, 809, 815, 821.

[39] *Ibid.* at p. 810. See also *Penner* v. *Mitchell* [1978] 5 W.W.R. 328 and *Hodgson* v. *General Electricity Co. Ltd.* [1978] 2 Lloyd's Rep. 210. But while it may be true that tortious injury is generally less likely than illness, it is much more likely than some types of illness. It is hard to see the justification for dissecting the "accident" side of life's vicissitudes but not the "illness" side.

ries.[40] However, Lord Bridge, while recognising the force of the argument that the plaintiff should not be under-compensated by reason of the chance that he is the victim of two torts rather than one, pointed out that the distinction between tortious and non-tortious causes was implicitly rejected in *Baker* v. *Willoughby*.[41] Accordingly, inferior courts find themselves for the time being in the unenviable position of having to decide whether *Baker* v. *Willoughby* is a decision on its own facts without any discernible binding *ratio* or whether it does represent the principle governing successive tortious injuries.[42]

Another area where "but-for" causation raises difficulties is that of failure to comply with statutorily prescribed standards of competence (perhaps involving testing and licensing). In *The Empire Jamaica*[43] a collision was caused by the negligence of the officer of the watch on board the ship of that name. There was no doubt that the owners were vicariously liable for this, but under the Merchant Shipping Act[44] they were entitled to limit their liability if the collision was without *their* "actual fault." The only fault attributable to the owners was that contrary to relevant legislation the officer did not hold the necessary mate's certificate. The evidence showed that if the owners had made application for exemption from the legislation it would probably have been granted, but all the judges treated as the crucial point the fact that the owners had every reason to believe the officer to be experienced and competent and his lack of a certificate was therefore a merely incidental matter which was in no way a cause of the collision. Of course, if the owners had had no previous knowledge of him and had engaged him without a certificate that might have been very cogent evidence of negligence on their part, but on the facts the absence of a certificate merely prevented them from adducing it as virtually conclusive evidence that they had *fulfilled* their duty—it did not preclude them from showing that they had done so in other ways. Ultimately, the matter is one of statutory interpretation rather than causation and it is open to the legislature by clear words to render it irrelevant that the unqualified person is competent or that a qualified person would have acted in the same way.[45]

Enough has been said to demonstrate that factual causation may involve much more than the simple application of the "but-for" test and that there are problems which perhaps can only be dealt with by drawing arbitrary lines or by reference to policy. However, in the majority of cases factual causation is easily enough established and it is on the assumption that it has been established that the ensuing discussion of remoteness of damage proceeds.

---

[40] [1982] A.C. 794, 815.

[41] *Ibid.* at pp. 819, 821. Lord Edmund-Davies would seem to agree with Lord Bridge, for he says he "can formulate no convincing juristic or logical principles supportive of the decision" in *Baker* v. *Willoughby*.

[42] Lord Wilberforce pays a good deal of attention to the fact that compensation is not merely a matter of tort damages and that the plaintiff's position with regard to other sources of money may determine whether he is under or over-compensated. With respect, however, this is the general problem of offsets and deductions of collateral benefits (see *post* Chap. 23) and raises no more problems in multiple causation cases than in those where the chain of causation is clear.

[43] [1957] A.C. 386.

[44] See now The Merchant Shipping Act 1979, containing a different formula.

[45] *John Pfeiffer Pty.* v. *Canny* (1981) 36 A.L.R. 466.

REMOTENESS

Theoretically the consequences of any conduct may be endless, but no defendant is responsible *ad infinitum* for all the consequences of his wrongful conduct, however remote in time and however indirect the process of causation, for otherwise human activity would be unreasonably hampered.[46] The law must draw a line somewhere, it cannot take account of everything that follows a wrongful act, some consequences must be abstracted as relevant not on grounds of pure logic, but simply for practical reasons.[47] Bacon's rendering of the maxim *in jure non remota causa sed proxima spectatur* has often been cited. "It were infinite for the law to consider the causes of causes, and their impulsions one of another: therefore it contenteth itself with the immediate cause, and judgeth of acts by that without looking to any further degree."[48] Of course this does not tell us what is an "immediate" cause, and we shall see that the common law has probed the matter more deeply than the maxim does. But any student who expects a scientific analysis of causation will be grievously disappointed. Up to a certain point the common law does touch upon metaphysics. But no test of remoteness of causation put forward by Anglo-American courts would satisfy any metaphysician. On the other hand, no test suggested by metaphysicians would be of any practical use to lawyers. "Causation is to be understood as the man in the street, and not as either the scientist or the metaphysician would understand it."[49] "The choice of the real or efficient cause from out of the whole complex of the facts must be made by applying common sense standards."[50] The rather unscientific way in which lawyers are apt to approach the problem is shown in their use of metaphors about causation, such as chains, rivers, transmission gears, conduit pipes, nets, insulators,[51] or phrases expressive of it, such as "*causa causans* and *causa sine qua non*," "direct cause and intervening cause," "effective cause and ineffective cause," "*nova causa interveniens*"; but all these merely conceal the puzzle and do not solve it. In fact, neither metaphor nor catchword will release judges from the effort or agony of deciding each case on its merits with such help as they can get from some very general principles. This may not be systematic, but what is often forgotten by critics is that the judges would do no better if they tried to be more exact. For, as Lord Sumner said,

[46] A Frenchman, in celebrating the restoration of Alsace to France in 1919, fired a revolver which burst and injured him. His claim that his injuries were due to the outbreak of war in 1914 was rejected by the Metz Pensions Board as too remote: *The Times,* February 6, 1933. For Continental law, see Hart and Honorè, *op. cit.*, Pt. III. Social security law may be concerned with issues which are very similar to remoteness of damage: for example, where industrial injury benefit is payable in respect of an accident "arising out of and in the course of employment."

[47] *Liesbosch Dredger* v. *Edison SS.* [1933] A.C. 449, 460, *per* Lord Wright.

[48] *Maxims of the Law* (1630) Reg. 1. For other views of Bacon's meaning, see Beale in *Selected Essays in the Law of Torts* (1924) pp. 730 *et seq.,* and McLaughlin in (1925–26) 39 Harv.L.Rev. 156, n. 30; and for some criticisms of Bacon, see Jeremiah Smith (1925–26) 39 Harv.L.Rev. 652–654.

[49] *Yorkshire Dale Steamship Co. Ltd.* v. *Minister of War Transport* [1942] A.C. 691, 706, *per* Lord Wright.

[50] *Ibid.* at p. 706.

[51] Goodhart, *Essays in Jurisprudence,* p. 131, n. 8.

"The object of a civil inquiry into cause and consequence is to fix liability on some responsible person and to give reparation for damage done. . . . The trial of an action for damage is not a scientific inquest into a mixed sequence of phenomena, or an historical investigation of the chapter of events. . . . It is a practical inquiry."[52]

Such principles as we have are no earlier than the nineteenth century.[53] Until then no one seems to have made use of Bacon's maxim,[54] and the courts either took refuge in scraps of scholastic logic about *causa causans* and *causa causata*,[55] or indulged in the mistiest generalities, such as "he that does the first wrong shall answer for all consequential damages"[56] or "the damages must be the legal and natural consequence"[57] of the wrongful act. Then the phrase "natural and proximate consequence" creeps in.[58] "Proximate" was a misplaced adjective, for it suggested that the event which occurs immediately before the harm suffered by the plaintiff is always to be selected by the law as the determined cause of that harm. But that is not necessarily so. If A throws a lighted squib into a crowd and it falls upon B who, in alarm, at once throws it away and it falls upon C, who does the like, and the squib ends its journey by falling upon D, exploding and putting out his eye, here A's act is held to be the proximate cause of the damage, though in fact it was the act farthest from the damage, not the one nearest to it.[59]

Since 1850 two competing views of the test of remoteness of consequence have been current in the law.[60] According to the first, *consequences are too remote if a reasonable man would not have foreseen them*[61]; according to the second, if a reasonable man would have foreseen any damage to the plaintiff as likely to result from his act, then *he is liable for all the direct consequences of it suffered by the plaintiff, whether a reasonable man would have foreseen them or not*. To put the second view another way, reasonable foresight is relevant to the question, "Was there any legal duty owed by the defendant to the plaintiff to take care?" It is irrelevant to the question, "If the defendant broke a legal duty, was the consequence of this breach too remote?" What ought to have been reasonably contemplated "goes to culpability, not to compensation."[62]

---

[52] *Weld-Blundell* v. *Stephens* [1920] A.C. 956, 986. See, too, Goddard L.J. in *Duncan* v. *Cammell, Laird Ltd.* (1944) 171 L.T. 186, 199, quoting Lord Wright in *Liesbosch Dredger* v. *Edison S.S.* [1933] A.C. 449, 460.

[53] Two important U.S. studies on the topic are in *Selected Essays on the Law of Torts*, (1924) pp. 649–730 (Jeremiah Smith), pp. 730–755 (Joseph H. Beale).

[54] Beale, *op. cit.*, p. 732.

[55] *Earl of Shrewsbury's Case* (1610) 9 Rep. 46, 50b.

[56] *Roswell* v. *Prior* (1700) 12 Mod. 636, 639; *Scott* v. *Shepherd* (1773) 2 W.Bl. 892, 898, 899.

[57] *Vicars* v. *Wilcocks* (1806) 8 East 1, 3.

[58] *e.g. Ward* v. *Weeks* (1830) 7 Bing. 211, 212.

[59] *Scott* v. *Shepherd* (1773) 2 W.Bl. 892. Nor would it be correct to think that there must be some close temporal connexion between the act and the damage. A coroner's verdict found a death in 1982 to be due to enemy action in 1949 (*Daily Telegraph*, December 3, 1982). A tort claim after such a period might run foul of the Limitation Act and/or the principle that there is only one cause of action for one injury, but would not, it is thought, fail simply because the death was too remote.

[60] Both have been described by a great variety of phrases and in *H.M.S. London* [1914] P. 72, 77–78, Evans P. collected eight specimens. See Lord Sumner's criticism of some of them in *Weld-Blundell* v. *Stephens* [1920] A.C. 956, 983–984.

[61] First propounded by Pollock C.B. in *Rigby* v. *Hewitt* (1859) 5 Ex. 240, 243; *Greenland* v. *Chaplin* (1850) 5 Ex. 243, 248.

[62] *Weld-Blundell* v. *Stephens*, *supra*, at p. 984, *per* Lord Sumner.

In 1921, in the case known as *Re Polemis*,[63] the Court of Appeal apparently settled English law in favour of the second rule. A chartered vessel was unloading in Casablanca when stevedores, who were servants of the charterers, negligently let a plank drop into the hold. Part of the cargo was a quantity of benzine in tins, which had leaked, and a rush of flames at once followed, totally destroying the ship. The charterers were held liable for the loss[64]—nearly £200,000—the Court of Appeal holding that they were responsible for all the direct consequences of the negligence, even though they could not reasonably have been anticipated. None of the court except Scrutton L.J. defined "direct" consequence. He said that damage is indirect if it is "due to the operation of independent causes having no connection wih the negligent act, except that they could not avoid its results."[65] It is important to note that in *Re Polemis* it was foreseeable that the ship would suffer some damage from the dropping of the plank and the initial breach of duty was therefore established. The case is no authority on the "unforeseeable plaintiff,"[66] despite some passages which might suggest the contrary.[67]

In *The Wagon Mound*[68] the Judicial Committee of the Privy Council, through Viscount Simonds, expressed its unqualified disapproval of *Re Polemis* and refused to follow it. O.T. Ltd. were charterers by demise[69] of *The Wagon Mound*, an oil-burning vessel which was moored at the C. Oil Co.'s wharf in Sydney harbour for the purpose of taking on fuel oil. Owing to the carelessness of O.T. Ltd.'s servants a large quantity of fuel oil was spilt on to the water, and after a few hours this had spread to M.D. Ltd.'s wharf about 600 ft. away, where another ship, the *Corrimal,* was under repair. Welding operations were being carried out on the *Corrimal*, but when M.D. Ltd.'s manager became aware of the presence of the oil he stopped the welding operations and inquired of the C. Oil Co. whether they might safely be continued. The result of this inquiry, coupled with his own belief as to the non-inflammability of fuel oil in the open, led him to give instructions for the welding operations to continue, though with all precautions to prevent inflammable material from falling into the oil. Two days later the oil caught fire and extensive damage was done to M.D. Ltd.'s wharf.

Two findings of fact are important: (*a*) It was unforeseeable that fuel oil spread on water would catch fire[70]; (*b*) some foreseeable damage was caused to M.D. Ltd.'s wharf from the spillage of the oil in that the oil had got onto

---

[63] [1921] 3 K.B. 560. Weir, *Casebook on Tort* (6th ed.), p. 183. Davies, "The Road from Morocco" (1982) 45 M.L.R. 534.

[64] A fire exception clause in the charter did not help them because it did not cover negligence.

[65] [1921] 3 K.B. 560, 577.

[66] *Ante*, p. 81.

[67] And in the earlier case of *Smith* v. *L. & S.W. Ry.* (1870) L.R. 6 C.P. 14.

[68] [1961] A.C. 388. Weir, *Casebook on Tort* (6th ed.), p. 185. For a list of articles see Dias in [1962] C.L.J. 178, n. 2 and [1967] C.L.J. 63, n. 4.

[69] That is, they were in full possession of it with their own crew.

[70] This finding was reached after the learned judge had heard expert evidence on the matter, but this evidence, it is submitted, should not have influenced him. What was in issue was the foresight of the reasonable man in the position of O.T. Ltd., or rather of its servants. What "a distinguished scientist" could have foreseen was irrelevant. In *Overseas Tankship (U.K.) Ltd.* v. *Miller Steamship Co. Pty. Ltd. (The Wagon Mound) (No. 2)* [1967] A.C. 617, an action by the owners of the *Corrimal* for damage caused to their ship by the same fire, the Privy Council, on somewhat different evidence, held that the damage was foreseeable. See *post*, p. 382.

the slipways and interfered with their use. The case was dealt with, there-fore, on the footing that there was a breach of duty and direct damage, but that the damage caused was unforeseeable. At the trial and on appeal to the Full Court of the Supreme Court of New South Wales it was held, following *Re Polemis,* that O.T. Ltd. were liable,[71] but the Privy Council reversed their decision[72] and held that *Re Polemis* should no longer be regarded as good law. "It is the foresight of the reasonable man which alone can determine responsibility. The *Polemis* rule by substituting 'direct' for 'rea-sonably foreseeable' consequence leads to a conclusion equally illogical and unjust."[73]

Notwithstanding the fact that *Re Polemis* is a decision of the Court of Appeal and was clearly affirmed by the same court in 1951[74] the technical point of precedent was side-stepped or ignored and there is no doubt that *The Wagon Mound* represents the law in England.[75] However, whether this has made very much difference to the results of cases is debatable in view of the subsequent decisions. The essence of *The Wagon Mound* is that in negligence foreseeablility is the criterion not only for the existence of a duty of care but also for remoteness of damage, and the Privy Council clearly attached importance to the supposed illogicality of using different tests at different stages of the inquiry in any given case:

> "If some limitation must be imposed upon the consequences for which the negligent actor is to be held responsible—and all are agreed that some limitation there must be—why should that test (reasonable fore-seeability) be rejected which, since he is judged by what the reasonable man ought to foresee, corresponds with common conscience of man-kind, and a test (the 'direct' consequence) be substituted which leads to nowhere but the never-ending and insoluble problems of causation."[76]

It might have been thought from this that the effect of *The Wagon Mound* was restricted to actions for negligence, or at least to cases in which foresee-ability of damage is relevant to liability.[77] In *The Wagon Mound (No. 2),*[78] however, the Privy Council held that foreseeability is the test for remoteness of damage in cases of nuisance also, and, though they pointed out that liability in many cases of nuisance depends on fault and thus on foreseeabil-ity, they stated that the same test must apply even where this is not so. There

---

[71] For the proceedings before Kinsella J., see [1958] 1 Lloyd's Rep. 775 and for those before the full court, see [1959] 2 Lloyd's Rep. 692.

[72] So far as the cause of action in negligence was concerned; the action was remitted to the full court on the issue of nuisance, but was not proceeded with. In *The Wagon Mound (No. 2), supra,* the Privy Council held that the test of reasonable foreseeability applies also to a cause of action in nuisance. See *post,* p. 382.

[73] [1961] A.C. 388, 424.

[74] *Thurogood* v.*Van den Burghs and Jurgens* [1951] 2 K.B. 537.

[75] For decisions recognising this, see the 12th ed. of this work, p. 131, nn. 77–79.

[76] *The Wagon Mound* [1961] A.C. 388, 423, *per* Viscount Simonds.

[77] Their Lordships expressly reserved the question of remoteness of damage under "the so-called rule of 'strict liability' exemplified in *Rylands* v. *Fletcher*" ((1868) L.R. 3 H.L. 330, *post,* p. 440).

[78] [1967] 1 A.C. 617. See Dias, "Trouble on Oiled Waters: Problems of *The Wagon Mound (No. 2)*" [1967] C.L.J. 62.

now seems every likelihood that foreseeability will be held to be the test of remoteness in some other torts as well, whether or not it is the test of liability.[79]

If the "foresight of the reasonable man" is to be used as a test of remoteness in torts of strict liability some adjustment will have to be made. If a man may be liable notwithstanding that he neither could nor should have foreseen any harmful consequences of his act whatever, it is meaningless to say that the extent of his liability is limited to what he ought reasonably to have foreseen. In *Galashiels Gas Co. Ltd.* v. *O'Donnell*,[80] for example, the defendants had a lift at their gas works and the lift, so far as anyone could discover, was in perfect condition both before and after the accident. Nevertheless, on a single isolated occasion something went wrong for reasons no one could ascertain and as a result the plaintiff's husband was killed. The defendants were held liable for breach of an absolute statutory duty,[81] but how can it realistically be said that they could have foreseen the death of the deceased? What can be said—and this seems now to be the meaning of "reasonably foreseeable" in such cases—is that a reasonable man, told of the way in which the lift went wrong, would not be surprised to learn that the deceased had been killed.[82]

Even in cases where liability is based upon negligence, foreseeability as a test of remoteness is heavily qualified by the fact that neither the precise extent of the damage nor the precise manner of its infliction need be foreseeable. So much, indeed, has been expressly stated by Lord Denning M.R.:

> "It is not necessary that the precise concatenation of circumstances should be envisaged. If the consequence was one which was within the general range which any reasonable person might foresee (and was not of an entirely different kind which no one would anticipate) then it is within the rule that a person who has been guilty of negligence is liable for the consequences."[83]

In *Hughes* v. *Lord Advocate*[84] employees of the Post Office opened a manhole in the street and in the evening left the open manhole covered by a canvas shelter, unattended and surrounded by warning paraffin lamps. The plaintiff, a boy aged eight, took one of the lamps into the shelter and was

[79] As to deceit, see *post*, p. 271.
[80] [1949] A.C. 275.
[81] Factories Act 1937, s.22(1), now the Factories Act 1961, s.22(1).
[82] See Dias, *loc. cit.*, at pp. 68, 77–82. *cf. Millard* v. *Serck Tubes Ltd.* [1969] 1 W.L.R. 211 where the Court of Appeal held that once a part of machinery is found to be "dangerous" within s.14(1) of the Factories Act 1961, which means that it is a *foreseeable* cause of injury, and it is unfenced in breach of the section, it matters not that the plaintiff's injury occurred in an unforeseeable way, so long as the injury would not have occurred if the duty to fence had been fulfilled. The judgments, which refer to no decisions on remoteness of damage, provide admirable, if unintentional, examples of the operation of the rule in *Re Polemis* at its most straightforward.
[83] *Stewart* v. *West African Terminals Ltd.* [1964] 2 Lloyd's Rep. 371, 375; *Bradford* v. *Robinson Rentals Ltd.* [1967] 1 W.L.R. 337, 344–345, *per* Rees J. See also *Donaghey* v. *Boulton & Paul Ltd.* [1968] A.C. 1, and *McGovern* v. *B.S.C.* [1986] I.C.R. 608, dealing with liability for breach of statutory duty.
[84] [1963] A.C. 837. Weir, *Casebook on Tort*, (6th ed.), p. 196. *cf. Doughty* v. *Turner Manufacturing Co. Ltd.* [1964] 1 Q.B. 518. See further, Kidner, "Remoteness of Damage" (1989) 9 L.S. 1.

playing with it there when he stumbled over it and it fell into the manhole. A violent explosion followed and the plaintiff himself fell into the hole, sustaining terrible injuries from burns. It was quite unpredictable that a lamp might explode, but the Post Office men were in breach of duty leaving the manhole unattended because they should have appreciated that boys might take a lamp into the shelter and that, if the lamp fell and broke, they might suffer serious injury from burning. So the lamp, a known source of danger, caused injury through an unforeseeable sequence of events, but the defendants were nevertheless held liable.

On facts such as these, therefore, the rejection of *Re Polemis* has made no difference so far as the actual result is concerned. *The Wagon Mound* does, however, introduce the requirement that the foreseeable damage must be of the same "kind" as the damage which actually occurred. In point of fact even under *Re Polemis* it was probably necessary to distinguish between three very broad "kinds" of damage, namely injury to the person, damage to property and pure financial loss,[85] but *The Wagon Mound* certainly demands a more elaborate classification of "kinds" of damage than that: in the case itself damage to the plaintiffs' wharf was foreseeable and damage to the plaintiffs' wharf occurred. It follows that, in the Privy Council's judgment, a distinction must be taken between damage by fouling, which was foreseeable, and damage by fire, which occurred. The difficulty is to know how narrowly the kind of damage in question in any given case must be defined.[86] In *Tremain* v. *Pike*[87] the rat population on the defendant's farm was allowed to become unduly large and the plaintiff, a herdsman on the farm, contracted leptospirosis, otherwise known as Weil's disease, in consequence. Even on the assumption that the defendants had been negligent in failing to control the rat population,[88] Payne J. held that the plaintiff could not succeed. Weil's disease is extremely rare and is caused by contract with rat's urine, and in the learned judge's opinion it was therefore both unforeseeable and "entirely different in kind" from such foreseeable consequences as the effects of a rat-bite or food poisoning from contaminated food: the plaintiff could not simply say that rat-induced disease was foreseeable and rat-induced disease occurred.[89]

If *Tremain* v. *Pike* is rightly decided then a fairly high degree of precision in classifying kinds of damage is required.[90] It is respectfully suggested,

[85] This is based on the "interest theory" which, though not the subject of any judicial decision has the support of Lord Wright: *Bourhill* v. *Young* [1943] A.C. 92, 110; "*Re Polemis*" (1951) 14 M.L.R. 393, 400.

[86] The point if very clearly made in Morris, *Torts*, (2nd ed.), pp. 164–165, commenting on *Hines* v. *Morrow* 236 S.W. 183 (1922). See also *Crossley* v. *Rawlinson* [1982] 1 W.L.R. 369 (plaintiff fell while running to put out fire caused by defendant's negligence; not enough that plaintiff might foreseeably be injured, must ask whether injury by *falling* foreseeable).

[87] [1969] 1 W.L.R. 1556; (1970) 86 L.Q.R. 151. *cf. Bradford* v. *Robinson Rentals Ltd.* [1967] 1 W.L.R. 337; *Malcolm* v. *Broadhurst* [1970] 3 All E.R. 508.

[88] The defendant's negligence in this respect was not actually made out.

[89] His Lordship's suggested method of avoiding the question about what is meant by difference in kind by asking instead the direct question whether on the facts leptospirosis was reasonably foreseeable, succeeds only by assuming one particular answer to the question: [1969] 1 W.L.R. 1556, 1561. *cf.* the opinion of Edmund Davies L.J. in *Draper* v. *Hodder* [1972] 2 Q.B. 556 that the foreseeable risk of the infant plaintiff being injured by being bowled over by the dogs would justify the imposition of liability where the dogs *attacked* him.

[90] Fridman and Williams, "The Atomic Theory of Negligence" (1971) 45 A.L.J. 117.

however, that the case is out of line with the general trend of decisions since *The Wagon Mound*. Apart from the tendency in some cases to give a broad definition of foreseeable consequences,[91] it is clear that two other principles have survived *The Wagon Mound*: the so-called "egg-shell skull" rule[92] and the principle that the defendant is not relieved of liability because the damage was more extensive than might have been foreseen.[93] Furthermore, the House of Lords, in emphasising the difference between the rules of remoteness in contract and in tort has given to the word "foreseeable" a meaning which is far removed from "probable" or "likely." The rule in tort, Lord Reid has said, imposes a much wider liability than that in contract; "the defendant will be liable for any type of damage which is reasonably foreseeable as liable to happen *even in the most unusual case*, unless the risk is so small that a reasonable man would in the whole circumstances feel justified in neglecting it."[94]

As this passage indicates, foreseeability is a relative, not an absolute, concept. In *The Wagon Mound* the Privy Council accepted and based its reasoning on the trial judge's finding that the defendant did not know and could not reasonably be expected to have known that furnace oil was capable of being set afire when spread on water.[95] In *The Wagon Mound (No. 2)*, however, somewhat different evidence was presented[96] and in the Privy Council the trial judge's finding to similar effect, not being a primary finding of fact but an inference from other findings, was rejected. There was, it was held, a real risk of fire such as would have been appreciated by a properly qualified and alert chief engineer and this, given the fact that there was no justification for discharging oil into Sydney Harbour in any case, was sufficient to fix liability on the defendants. In other words, the mere fact that the damage suffered was unlikely to occur does not relieve the defendant of liability if his conduct was unreasonable—a proposition very little different from that contained in *Re Polemis* itself. On the facts of that case, notwithstanding the arbitrator's finding that the spark which caused the explosion was not reasonably foreseeable, there was, surely, a "real risk" that the vapour in the hold might be accidentally ignited and there was, of course, no justification for dropping the plank into the hold.

---

[91] See *ante*, p. 142. But *cf. Attia* v. *British Gas* [1988] Q.B. 304, 319, *per* Bingham L.J., equating duty and remoteness.

[92] See *post*, p. 147.

[93] See *post*, p. 147.

[94] *C. Czarnikow Ltd.* v. *Koufos* [1969] 1 A.C. 350, 385; *ibid.* at p. 411, *per* Lord Hodson; *ibid.* at p. 422, *per* Lord Upjohn. Emphasis added. In *Emeh* v. *Kensington and Chelsea and Westminster A.H.A.* [1985] Q.B. 1012 congenital abnormality (a risk of 0.5 per cent. to 0.25 per cent. on the evidence) was held not to be too remote a consequence of a negligent sterilisation.
The loss in *Czarnikow* v. *Koufos* was of profit on a sale. But what happens if, by a breach of contract, the defendant causes damage to the person or property of the plaintiff? According to Lord Denning M.R. in *Parsons (H.) (Livestock) Ltd.* v. *Uttley Ingham & Co. Ltd.* [1978] Q.B. 791 the test is then, notwithstanding *Czarnikow* v. *Koufos*, the same as in tort. Scarman and Orr L.JJ. thought that in contract, whether the loss was financial or physical, the test was whether the *type* of loss was within the presumed contemplation of the parties. Whether this view is reconcilable with *Victoria Laundry (Windsor) Ltd.* v. *Newman Industries Ltd.* [1949] 2 K.B. 528 remains to be seen. In many cases the plaintiff will have concurrent actions in contract and tort and it is not very clear why the *Parsons* case was not also pleaded in tort. See further Hamson, "Contract and Tort: Measure of Damages" [1968] C.L.J. 14 and (on the *Parsons* case) Hadjihambis (1978) 41 M.L.R. 483.

[95] [1961] A.C. 388, 413.

[96] See Lord Reid's explanation of this, [1967] 1 A.C. 617, 640–641, and Dias, [1967] C.L.J. at pp. 63–65.

Competing rules compared

It seems, therefore, that *The Wagon Mound* has made little difference to the law in terms of practical result, and, indeed, Viscount Simonds indicated that this would probably be so in *The Wagon Mound* itself.[97] That case has, however, undoubtedly produced a change of principle and it is right, therefore, to conclude with some brief discussion of its merits as compared with those of *Re Polemis*. Much has been written on this subject[98] but two points only can be considered here:

(1) **Simplicity.** The Privy Council laid much stress upon the difficulties of the directness test. If foreseeability is treated as a question of fact to be decided once and for all at the trial, then, no doubt, the task of the appellate courts is made easier by the change, but the application of the law to the facts is made correspondingly more difficult.[99] If, on the other hand, questions of foreseeability are open in the appellate courts—and *The Wagon Mound (No. 2)* indicates that they are—then there seems no reason for supposing that the foreseeability test is any easier than directness. On the contrary, not only does the change from the one to the other raise the question of the meaning of "kind" of damage but it "gets rid of the difficulties of determining causal connection by substituting the difficulty of determining the range and extent of foresight of the hypothetical reasonable man."[1] The fact is that the issue of remoteness of damage is not susceptible to short cuts. "There is no substitute for dealing with the particular facts, and considering all the factors that bear on them, interlocked as they must be. Theories . . . have not improved at all on the old words 'proximate' and 'remote' with the idea they convey of some reasonable connection between the original negligence and its consequences, between the harm threatened and the harm done."[2]

(2) **Fairness.** According to the Privy Council the test of directness works unfairly: "It does not seem consonant with current ideas of justice or morality that for an act of negligence, however slight or venial, which results in some trivial foreseeable damage the actor should be liable for all consequences however unforeseeable and however grave, so long as they can be said to be 'direct.' "[3] It is no doubt hard on a negligent defendant that he should be held liable for unexpectedly large damages, but it is not clear that the final outcome is any fairer if the plaintiff is left without redress for damage which he has suffered through no fault of his own. Bearing in mind that negligence involves the creation of an *unreasonable* risk of causing some foreseeable damage to the plaintiff it might be thought that even though "justice" may be impossible of achievement where unforeseeable damage

---

[97] [1961] A.C. 388, 422; *cf.* Davies (1982) 45 M.L.R. 534, 551.
[98] See *ante* p. 140, n. 68.
[99] This must be a matter for concern not only to trial judges but also to counsel and solicitors when consulted about the settlement of an action.
[1] Walker, "Remoteness of Damage and *Re Polemis*" [1961] S.L.T. 37.
[2] Prosser, "Palsgraf Revisited" (1953) 52 Michigan L.Rev. 1, 32.
[3] [1961] A.C. 388, 422.

occurs,[4] greater injustice is produced by *The Wagon Mound* than by *Re Polemis*.[5]

Rules as to remoteness

The preceding account of *The Wagon Mound* should not mislead one into thinking that foreseeability is all there is to the law of remoteness. Sometimes policy comes to the surface and a loss is dismissed as too remote simply because the court does not think it reasonable or desirable to impose it on the defendant. Thus in *Pritchard* v. *J.H. Cobden Ltd.*[6] it was held that where the plaintiff's marriage broke up as a result of his injuries, orders for financial provision made against him by the divorce court could not be the subject of a claim against the tortfeasor: quite apart from the point that redistribution of assets on divorce could not be regarded as a "loss," acceptance of such claims would risk confusion in the judicial process and be open to abuse. There are also a number of commonly-recurring situations in which principles have developed which are qualifications of foreseeability and we must now turn to these.

(1) *Intended consequences*

Intended consequences are never too remote.[7] "The intention to injure the plaintiff ... disposes of any question of remoteness of damage."[8] However, the liability of an intentional wrongdoer is not *limited* to the intended consequences and it will extend at least to such as are foreseeable. *Scott* v. *Shepherd*[9] may be regarded as a classical instance of this. The man who first threw the squib certainly intended to scare somebody or other. With equal certainty he did not, in common parlance, "intend" to hurt the plaintiff, much less to destroy his eye. But he was nevertheless held liable to the plaintiff, because the law insists, and insists quite rightly, that fools and mischievous persons must answer for consequences which common sense would unhesitatingly attribute to their wrongdoing.[10] Indeed, the intentional wrongdoer's liability may extend beyond the foreseeable because intentional torts have not necessarily been affected by *The Wagon Mound*.[11] An intentional departure from the terms of a bailment, for example, may make the bailee subject to the liability of an insurer.[12]

[4] Prosser, "Palsgraf Revisited" (1953) 52 Michigan L.Rev. 1, 17.

[5] *cf.* Glanville Williams, "The Risk Principle" (1961) 77 L.Q.R. 179–180. See, too, Weir (1961) 35 Tulane L.Rev. 619, 626, and the observations of Walsh J., the trial judge in *The Wagon Mound (No. 2)* [1963] 1 Lloyd's Rep. 402, 412.

[6] [1988] Fam. 22, not following *Jones* v. *Jones* [1985] Q.B. 704. See also *Meah* v. *McCreamer (No. 2), post*, p. 148.

[7] The *Restatement of Torts*, 2d, ss.870, 915, qualifies the rule by adding, "except where the harm results from an outside force the risk of which is not increased by the defendant's act." But this exception is unreal, for all the illustrations are explicable on some other ground, (*e.g. volenti non fit injuria*) or are merely cases in which all the consequences were not intended. See also Glanville Williams. "The Risk Principle" (1961) 77 L.Q.R. 179, 200–202; Hart and Honoré, *Causation in the Law* pp. 170–171.

[8] *Quinn* v. *Leatham* [1901] A.C. 495, 537, *per* Lord Lindley.

[9] *Ante*, p. 139.

[10] See also *ante*, p. 44.

[11] See, *e.g. Doyle* v. *Olby (Ironmongers) Ltd.* [1969] 2 Q.B. 158 and *post*, p. 271.

[12] But a trespasser to land is not liable for unintended, indirect and unforeseen damage: *Mayfair Ltd.* v. *Pears* [1987] 1 N.Z.L.R. 459 (fire in wrongfully parked car).

(2) *Unintended consequences*

(a) *Existing states of affairs*

(i) **Pecuniary amount of the damage**. If the defendant injures a high income earner or a piece of property with a high intrinsic value (such as an antique vase) he cannot argue that he had no reason to expect the amount of the loss to be so great.[13] Such an issue is treated as belonging to the realm of assessment of damages rather than of remoteness, so that foreseeability is irrelevant.[14] The law is not, however, so clearly committed to this stand where the loss claimed is not "intrinsic" but arises from the fact that the damage to the plaintiff's goods renders him unable to earn profits with them.[15] Support can be found in the cases (none of them decisive, at least for the purposes of negligence[16]) for both views: on the one hand that foreseeability is irrelevant,[17] on the other, that the defendant's liability is limited to "ordinary" or "foreseeable" losses.[18]

(ii) **Extent of the damage.** If the accident occurs in a foreseeable way the defendant will be liable even though the damage is much greater in extent than would have been anticipated.[19] It has sometimes been suggested that the "egg-shell skull" rule (see below) is an example of this principle, but this does not seem correct.[20]

(iii) **The "egg-shell skull" principle.** *The Wagon Mound* has not displaced the principle that the defendant must take his victim as he finds him.[21] It has for long been the law that "if a man is negligently run over or otherwise negligently injured in his body, it is no answer to the sufferer's claim for

[13] The point is perhaps so obvious that the only express authority for it appears to be the celebrated dictum of Scrutton L.J. in *The Arpad* [1934] P. 189, 202, though that case had nothing to do with negligence and the judgment was a dissenting one!

[14] Fleming, *Torts*, (7th ed.), p. 185, neatly says that it is concerned not with responsibility for unexpectable consequences, but for the unexpectable cost of expected consequences. But in *B.D.C. Ltd.* v. *Hofstrand Farms Ltd.* (1986) 26 D.L.R. (4th) 1 the Supreme Court of Canada said, *obiter*, that if D were liable in tort for failure to deliver P's package and had notice that P would suffer some loss, he would not be liable for a loss of extraordinary magnitude, of the risk of which he had no notice. The contract rule is applied even though the action is in tort: what goes for damage does not necessarily apply to economic loss. *cf.* the *Parsons* case, *supra*, n. 94.

[15] The case of a plaintiff who is disabled from performing particular contracts, (*e.g.* a musician) is perhaps analogous: see *The Arpad*, *supra*, at p. 221, *per* Greer L.J.

[16] *The Arpad*, *supra*, denying lost profits on the sale of a cargo, was a case of conversion.

[17] *The Star of India* (1876) 1 P.D. 466; *Liesbosch Dredger* v. *S.S. Edison* [1933] A.C. 449, 463–464 ("The measure of damages is the value of the ship to her owner as a going concern at the time and place of the loss. In assessing that value regard must naturally be had to her pending engagements, either profitable or the reverse." This case is, of course, best known on the different point relating to the plaintiff's impecuniosity, *post*, p. 148.

[18] *The Argentino* (1889) 14 App.Cas. 519, 523; *The Arpad*, *supra*; *The Daressa* [1971] 1 Lloyd's Rep. 60. See further McGregor, *Damages*, (15th ed.), pp. 124–126.

[19] One of the few clear examples of this is *Vacwell Engineering* v. *B.D.H. Chemicals* [1971] 1 Q.B. 88 (minor explosion foreseeable; huge explosion took place because plaintiffs put number of ampoules in same sink). See also *Bradford* v. *Robinson Rentals Ltd.* [1967] 1 W.L.R. 337 (exposure causing frostbite) and *Richards* v. *State of Victoria* [1969] V.R. 136 (blow causing brain damage). *cf. supra*, n. 14.

[20] The suggestion seems to be made by Lord Wright in the *Liesbosch* case, *supra*, at p. 461 and by Lord Parker C.J. in *Smith* v. *Leech Brain & Co. Ltd.* [1962] 2 Q.B. 405, 415. But the law does not regard personal injury as indivisible (see *ante*, p. 143) and damage in the form of cancer triggered off by a burn (as in *Smith* v. *Leech Brain*) seems different in kind from the burn.

[21] But not his family: *McLaren* v. *Bradstreet* (1969) 113 S.J. 471. *cf. Nader* v. *Urban Transport Authority* [1985] 2 N.S.W.L.R. 501.

damages that he would have suffered less injury . . .[22] if he had not had an unusually thin skull or an unusually weak heart."[23] This principle survives *The Wagon Mound* and is as applicable to "nervous shock" as to any other type of injury.[24] It also applies where the immediate cause of the loss is voluntary conduct by the plaintiff (for example, the commission of a crime) to which his personality may have predisposed him but which would not have occurred but for his injury.[25] The plaintiff's weakness cuts both ways, however: his damages are likely to be less than those of a "normal" person suffering the same injury to reflect the greater risk to which he is exposed by the normal vicissitudes of life. The same (or a similar)[26] principle operates when the plaintiff's injury is exacerbated by a combination of his abnormality and some external force which foreseeably and naturally intervenes after the accident, *e.g.* medical treatment to which he is allergic.[27]

   (iv) Plaintiff's impecuniosity. In *Liesbosch Dredger* v. *Edison S.S.*[28] the *Edison*, by negligent navigation, fouled and sank the dredger *Liesbosch*, whose owners were under contract with a third party to complete a piece of work within a given time. They were put to much greater expense in fulfilling this contract because they were too poor to buy a substitute for the dredger. The House of Lords held that they could recover as damages the market price of a dredger comparable to the *Liesbosch* and compensation for loss in carrying out the contract between the date of the sinking and the date on which the substituted dredger could reasonably have been available for work, for the measure of damages in such cases is the value of the ship to her owner as a going concern at the time and place of the loss, and, in assessing that value, regard must naturally be paid to her pending engagements[29]; but the claim for extra expenses due to poverty was rejected, because the plaintiff's want of means was an extraneous matter which made this special loss too remote. Lord Wright (with whose speech the rest of the House concurred) distinguished *Re Polemis* (then the leading case on remoteness)

[22] The missing words are "or no injury at all." Kennedy J. went too far here, for there must be a breach of duty owed to the plaintiff and if no damage at all could have been foreseen to a person of normal sensitivity and the plaintiff's abnormal sensitivity was unknown to the defendant, then he is not liable: *Bourhill* v. *Young* [1943] A.C. 92, 109–110, *per* Lord Wright; *Cook* v. *Swinfen* [1967] 1 W.L.R. 457.

[23] *Dulieu* v. *White* [1901] 2 K.B. 669, 679, *per* Kennedy J.

[24] *Brice* v. *Brown* [1984] 1 All E.R. 997. For other cases in which the thin-skull rule has been applied *post-Wagon Mound*, see *Smith* v. *Leech Brain & Co. Ltd.* [1962] 2 Q.B. 405; *Warren* v. *Scruttons* [1962] 1 Lloyd's Rep. 497; *Lines* v. *Harland and Wolff* [1966] 1 Lloyd's Rep. 400; *Boon* v. *Thomas Hubback* [1967] 1 Lloyd's Rep. 281; *Wieland* v. *Cyril Lord Carpets Ltd.* [1969] 3 All E.R. 1006; *Malcolm* v. *Broadhurst* [1970] 3 All E.R. 508. See also Linden, "Down with Foreseeability! Of Thin Skulls and Rescuers" (1969) 47 Can. Bar Rev. 545; Rowe, "The Demise of the Thin Skull Rule?" (1977) 40 M.L.R. 377. Goodhart, "Liability and Compensation" (1960) 76 L.Q.R. 567, 577, suggests that though it is unusual to find a man with an egg-shell skull "it is not so extraordinary as to make the consequences unforeseeable." *cf.* Williams, "The Risk Principle" (1961) 77 L.Q.R. 179; James, "*Polemis*: The Scotch'd Snake" [1962] J.B.L. 146.

[25] *Meah* v. *McCreamer* [1985] 1 All E.R. 367, though the point is only referred to in subsequent proceedings: [1986] 1 All E.R. 943.

[26] It has been said that this is a logical corollary of the egg-shell skull principle: *Stephenson* v. *Waite Tileman Ltd.* [1973] N.Z.L.R. 152.

[27] *Robinson* v. *Post Office* [1974] 1 W.L.R. 1176; Dias [1975] C.L.J. 15. As to whether negligent treatment amounts to a *novus actus interveniens*, see *post*, p. 153.

[28] [1933] A.C. 448; Weir, *Casebook on Tort*, (6th ed.), p. 563. See the observations of Viscount Simonds on this case: *The Wagon Mound* [1961] A.C. 388.

[29] [1933] A.C. 448, 463–464. See *supra*, n. 17.

on the ground that the injuries there suffered were the "immediate physical consequences of the negligent act," and he added:

> "Nor is the appellants' financial disability to be compared with that physical delicacy or weakness which may aggravate the damage in the case of personal injuries, or with the possibility that the injured man in such a case may be either a poor labourer or a highly paid professional man. *The former class of circumstances goes to the extent of actual physical damage and the latter goes to interference with profit-earning capacity; whereas the appellants' want of means was, as already stated, extrinsic.*"[30]

It is not possible to give any logical reason for regarding the plaintiff's impecuniosity as extrinsic but taking into account his physical disability and the rule has been said to be one of policy.[31] The decision is one of the House of Lords and has never been overruled, but nevertheless there are great difficulties in reconciling it with other principles of law[32] and in stating how far it represents current practice. In the first place, impecuniosity *may* excuse a failure to mitigate loss, for the plaintiff is required to do what is reasonable in his circumstances.[33] Unfortunately, while there is undoubtedly a theoretical distinction between the concepts of remoteness and mitigation,[34] judges have admitted that no one has ever satisfactorily shown where the line between the two is to be drawn.[35] If the failure of a personal injuries plaintiff to take medical treatment is a failure to mitigate loss, why was not the failure to buy a replacement dredger in *The Liesbosch* in the same category? Furthermore, losses which are incurred as a result of the plaintiff's impecuniosity may not necessarily be treated as too remote in contract, though there the law seems not to be that the defendant takes the plaintiff as he finds him but that such a loss is recoverable if it satisfies the ordinary test of remoteness.[36] In any event, there now appears to be a strong tendency to cut down the scope of the *Liesbosch* rule. Perhaps most important is the insistence that there is a distinction between a plaintiff's failure to act as a result of personal financial stringency and a reasoned commercial

---

[30] *Ibid.* at p. 461. Emphasis supplied. The principle has even been applied to a case of fraud: *Clements* v. *Bawns Shipping Co.* (1948) 81 Ll.L.R. 232.

[31] See Lord Wright, *Legal Essays and Addresses*, p. 113. *cf.* the principle of contract law that impecuniosity is not a frustrating event. The *Liesbosch* rule might also have some affinity with the former rule that damages are not recoverable for non-payment of money. Where special loss is within the contemplation of the parties this is no longer the law: *Wadsworth* v. *Lydall* [1981] 1 W.L.R. 598.

[32] See Davies, "Economic Stringency and the Recovery of Damages" [1982] J.B.L. 21; Burrows, *Remedies for Torts and Breach of Contract*, pp. 78–82.

[33] *Clippens Oil Co.* v. *Edinburgh and District Water Trustees* [1907] A.C. 291, 303, *obiter per* Lord Collins; *Dodd Properties Ltd.* v. *Canterbury City Council* [1980] 1 W.L.R. 433, 453, 459. The remark in *Martindale* v. *Duncan* [1973] 1 W.L.R. 574, 577 seems insupportable.

[34] And a practical one, for the plaintiff must show that the loss is not too remote but the defendant (despite the contrary suggestion in *Selvangayagam* v. *University of West Indies* [1983] 1 W.L.R. 585) must show that the plaintiff unreasonably failed to mitigate: McGregor, *Damages* (15th ed.), pp. 1134–1136.

[35] See in particular Oliver J. in *Radford* v. *De Froberville* [1977] 1 W.L.R. 1262, 1268; and the caustic remarks of the Court of Appeal in *Compania Financiera "Soleada" S.A.* v. *Hamoor Tanker Corp. Inc.* [1981] 1 W.L.R. 274.

[36] See the *Compania Financiera* case, *supra*, at pp. 282, 285.

decision not to incur expenditure, into which the plaintiff's financial position enters as but one factor. *The Liesbosch* may bar the claim in the first case, but not in the second. Thus in *Dodd Properties Ltd.* v. *Canterbury City Council*[37] the plaintiffs were allowed to delay repairing their premises (which were still usable) and claim from the defendants the higher cost of repair at the date of trial because the defendants' liability to pay would not be determined until then. Donaldson L.J. commented that in modern terms the decision in *The Liesbosch* might even be seen as turning on the point that the higher loss incurred by the plaintiffs was not foreseeable.[38] In the High Court of Australia it has been said that "reliance upon the regular receipt of income in the ordering of a natural person's financial affairs . . . is so much a feature of ordinary life that it would misapply [*The Liesbosch*] to suggest that where the cessation of regular receipts of income is occasioned by a tortious deprivation of earning capacity and impecuniosity and financial loss follow, the impecuniosity and financial loss are causally unrelated to the tort."[39] *The Liesbosch* is being attenuated[40] but it is still sometimes applied without qualification[41] and it needs consideration by the House of Lords.

(b) Intervening acts or events

Everyone agrees that a consequence is too remote if it follows a "break in the chain of causation" or is due to a *nova causa interveniens*. This means that although the defendant's breach of duty is a cause of the plaintiff's damage in the sense that it satisfies the "but-for" test of causation in fact, nevertheless in the eyes of the law some other intervening event is regarded as the sole cause of that damage. Three classes of case fall to be considered, namely (a) where a natural event occurs independently of the act of any human being; (b) where the event consists of the act or omission of a third party; (c) where the event consists of the act or omission of the plaintiff himself. It should not be thought, however, that in any of these cases the law will be particularly astute to attribute the plaintiff's damage to a single cause. There is no objection to a finding that the separate torts of two independent actors were both causes of the damage, and where this is so the plaintiff may recover in full from either of them.[42] Nor is there any objection to a finding that the defendant's breach of duty and the plaintiff's own fault were both causes of the plaintiff's damage. On the contrary, such a finding is a condition precedent to the operation of the law of contributory negligence.[43]

---

[37] [1980] 1 W.L.R. 433; *Perry* v. *Sidney Phillips & Son* [1982] 1 W.L.R. 1297 (a claim in tort and contract); *London Congregational Union* v. *Harriss* [1985] 1 All E.R. 335 (reversed in part without reference to this point [1988] 1 All E.R. 15).

[38] [1980] 1 W.L.R. 433, 459. So, in *Archer* v. *Brown* [1985] Q.B. 401, where the plaintiff's financial position was known to the defendant, liability was imposed. See also *Att.-Gen.* v. *Geothermal Produce (N.Z.) Ltd.* [1987] 2 N.Z.L.R. 348.

[39] *Fox* v. *Wood* (1981) 35 A.L.R. 607, 613, *per* Brennan J. Hence a personal injury plaintiff without adequate sick-pay should be able to recover the cost of borrowing to tide him over. See also *Jarvis* v. *T. Richards & Co.* (1980) 124 S.J. 793.

[40] *Perry* v. *Sidney Phillips & Sons, supra*, at p. 1307.

[41] *Ramwade* v. *J.W. Emson & Co.* [1987] R.T.R. 72.

[42] *Grant* v. *Sun Shipping Co. Ltd.* [1948] A.C. 549. For contribution between tortfeasors, see *post*, Chap. 22.

[43] *Post*, pp. 159–161.

(i) **Intervening natural event.** It is, of course, impossible for anything to happen in the physical world without the operation of natural forces, but sometimes the plaintiff suffers damage as the immediate result of a natural event which occurs independently of the defendant's breach of duty but which would have caused the plaintiff no damage if the breach of duty had not occurred. In such a case, if the breach of duty has neither increased the likelihood that the plaintiff will suffer damage nor rendered him more susceptible to damage, it will not be treated as a cause of the damage. Thus, in *Carslogie Steamship Co. Ltd.* v. *Royal Norwegian Government*[44] the plaintiff's ship was damaged in a collision for which the defendant's ship was wholly responsible. After temporary repairs which restored the ship to a seaworthy condition she set out on a voyage to the United States, a voyage which she would not have made had the collision not occurred. During her crossing of the Atlantic she suffered extensive damage due to heavy weather, and on her arrival in the United States the collision damage was permanently repaired at the same time that the heavy weather damage was dealt with. It was held in the House of Lords that the plaintiffs were not even entitled to damage for the loss of the use of their ship while the collision damage was being repaired because that time was used also for the repair of the heavy weather damage. There was no question of the defendants being liable for the heavy weather damage itself: that damage "was not in any sense a consequence of the collision, and must be treated as a supervening event occurring in the course of a normal voyage."[45] It was true that with the benefit of hindsight it was possible to say that if the collision had not taken place the storm damage also would not have taken place because the vessel would not have been there at that time, but no reasonable man would have said that such damage was within the likely or foreseeable risk created by the defendant's negligence.[46]

(ii) **Intervening act of a third party.** If the defendant's breach of duty has done no more than provide the occasion for an entirely independent act by a third party and that act is the immediate cause of the plaintiff's damage, then it will amount to a *nova causa interveniens* and the defendant will not be liable.[47] This, however, may not be the case if the act of the third party was not truly independent. In *The Oropesa*[48] a collision occurred between the ship of that name and another ship, the *Manchester Regiment*, for which both ships were to blame. The *Manchester Regiment* was severely damaged and her master decided to cross to the *Oropesa* in one of the ships's boats to

---

[44] [1952] A.C. 292; *Cutler* v. *United Dairies (London) Ltd.* [1933] 2 K.B. 297; *Vinney* v. *Star Paper Mills Ltd.* [1965] 1 All E.R. 175.

[45] [1952] 1 All E.R. 20, *per* Viscount Jowitt. Not all of his Lordship's speech is reported in the Law Reports. It seems that if the supervening event had been detention caused by an outbreak of war, the defendants would have been liable: *Monarch S.S. Co.* v. *Karlshamns Oljifabriker* [1949] A.C. 196.

[46] Distinguish the situation where the vessel is rendered less able to ride out the storm because of the damage inflicted on it by the defendant.

[47] *Weld-Blundell* v. *Stephens* [1920] A.C. 956; *Harnett* v. *Bond* [1925] A.C. 669; *S.S. Singleton Abbey* v. *S.S. Paludina* [1927] A.C. 16.

[48] [1943] P. 32; Weir, *Casebook on Tort*, (6th ed.), p. 199; *The City of Lincoln* (1890) 15 P.D. 15; *Summers* v. *Salford Corp.* [1943] A.C. 283, 296–297, *per* Lord Wright.

discuss salvage arrangements with the master of the *Oropesa*. The boat overturned in heavy seas before reaching the *Oropesa* and nine of the men on board, one of whom was the plaintiff's son, were drowned. The question was whether his death was caused by the negligence of the *Oropesa*,[49] or whether the master's action in taking to the boat constituted *a nova causa interveniens*. It was held that that action could not be severed from the circumstances affecting the two ships, that the "hand of the casualty lay heavily" upon the *Manchester Regiment,* and so that it was caused by and flowed from the collision.[50] "To break the chain of causation it must be shown that there is something which I will call ultroneous, something unwarrantable, a new cause which disturbs the sequence of events, something which can be described as either unreasonable or extraneous or extrinsic."[51]

In *The Oropesa,* the action of the master was not itself tortious: he was not guilty of a breach of duty to the deceased in ordering him into the boat, but that fact is not itself decisive one way or another. A wholly unpredictable but non-tortious intervention may break the chain of causation in one case while in another even deliberate tortious conduct may not do so, though as a general proposition it is probably correct to say that the further along the scale from innocent mistake to wilful wrongdoing the third party's conduct moves the more likely it is to terminate the defendant's liability.[52] The matter is what in former times would have been regarded as a jury question (though according to modern practice on appeal from trial by judge alone it is a question which the appellate court considers itself in as good a position to answer as the trial judge[53]) and there have been calls for "common sense rather than logic"[54] and a "robust and sensible approach."[55] The student is only likely to get a "feel" for the current application of the law by reading cases, but two multiple collision cases, one on each side of the line, may be used for illustration. In *Rouse* v. *Squires*[56] D1, driving negligently, jack-knifed his lorry across a motorway; a following car collided with the lorry, and, some minutes later D2's lorry, also being driven negligently, collided with the other vehicles, killing P, who was assisting at the scene. The Court of Appeal, reversing the trial judge, held that D1's negligence was an operative cause of P's death,[57] for if:

"a driver so negligently manages his vehicle as to cause it to obstruct the highway and constitute a danger to other road users, including those

---

[49] It is irrelevant to this question that the negligence of the *Manchester Regiment* leading to the collision may also have been a cause of the death.
[50] [1943] P. 32, 37, *per* Lord Wright.
[51] *Ibid.* at p. 39, *per* Lord Wright.
[52] *Knightley* v. *Johns* [1982] 1 W.L.R. 349, 365.
[53] See *ante*, p. 123.
[54] *Knightley* v. *Johns, supra,* at p. 367.
[55] *Lamb* v. *Camden London Borough* [1981] Q.B. 625, 647; and see Sir Robin Cooke, "Remoteness of Damages and Judicial Discretion" [1978] C.L.J. 288.
[56] [1973] Q.B. 889; *Lloyds Bank Ltd.* v. *Budd* [1982] R.T.R. 80.
[57] For which D1 was held 25 per cent. to blame under the Law Reform (Married Women and Tortfeasors) Act 1935.

who are driving too fast or not keeping a proper lookout, but not those who deliberately or recklessly drive into the obstruction, then the first driver's negligence may be held to have contributed to the causation of an accident of which the immediate cause was the negligent driving of the vehicle which because of the presence of the obstruction collides with it."[58]

In contrast, in *Knightley* v. *Johns*[59] D1's negligent driving caused the blocking of a busy tunnel. After a good deal of confusion as to the location of the accident, D2, a police inspector, took charge but did not immediately close the tunnel as he should have done. He then ordered P, a constable, to drive back against the traffic for that purpose. While doing so P was struck and injured by D3, who was driving too fast into the tunnel. The Court of Appeal set aside a judgment for P against D1.[60] While it might be natural, probable and foreseeable that the police would come to deal with the accident in the tunnel and that there might be risk-taking[61] and even errors on their part, there had in fact been so many errors before the plaintiff was ordered to ride back down the tunnel[62] that the subsequent collision with D3 was too remote a consequence of D1's original negligence.

If the plaintiff's injury is exacerbated by negligent medical treatment, can the defendant be liable for that? A decision of the House of Lords on the Workmen's Compensation Act suggests not[63] but it is not decisive[64] and it is submitted that the better view is that the original injury should be regarded as carrying a risk of medical error, including negligence, so that it should not necessarily be treated as a *novus actus interveniens*. Where, however, efficient medical services are available, the initial injury should not be regarded as carrying the risk of treatment which is wholly inept or extravagant.[65]

Most difficulty arises in the case of acts of a third party which are wilfully wrong towards the plaintiff, for it is especially here that the straightforward and literal application of the test of reasonable foreseeability (at least as it has been applied to personal injury cases) leads to an unacceptably wide-ranging liability. "In general . . . even though A is in fault, he is not responsible for injury to C which B, a stranger to him, deliberately chooses to do. Though A may have given the occasion for B's mischievous activity, B then

---

[58] [1973] Q.B. 889, 898, *per* Cairns L.J.
[59] [1982] 1 W.L.R. 349.
[60] However, D2 and D3 were liable to P. In many cases, provided all defendants are claim-worthy, these issues will essentially be related to contribution among defendants and will be of no direct concern to the plaintiff.
[61] Taking risks to save others from danger does not normally break the chain of causation: see *post*, p. 695.
[62] See in particular [1982] 1 W.L.R. 349, 365–366.
[63] *Hogan* v. *Bentinck Collieries* [1949] 1 All E.R. 588.
[64] McGregor, *Damages* (15th ed.), pp. 96–97.
[65] The law was stated in this way by the High Court of Australia in *Mahony* v. *Kruschich (Demolitions) Pty.* (1985) 59 A.L.R. 722. This would accord with the view of causation taken by the English law of murder. Should tort be less generous? In *Prendergast* v. *Sam & Dee Ltd.*, *The Independent*, March 17, 1988, D1, a doctor, wrote an unclear prescription; D2, a pharmacist, misread it, though he should have been put on inquiry. D2's act did not break the chain of causation and the relative responsibility was assessed as 25 per cent. to D1 and 75 per cent. to D2. Affirmed, February 22, 1989 (LEXIS).

becomes a new and independent cause."[66] Much of the case law in this area analyses the problem in terms of the existence of a duty of care to prevent wilful injury by a third party and this problem has already been mentioned.[67] It has been suggested that "the question of the existence of duty and that of whether damage brought about by the act of a third party is too remote are simply two facets of the same problem"[68] but where the defendant has caused some initial injury to the plaintiff before the intervention of the third party the cases have continued to look at the question as one of remoteness. Not surprisingly, however, there is the same reluctance to find the defendant liable for the wilful wrongdoing of others. It has been said that the conduct of the third party must be something very likely to happen if it is not to break the chain of causation[69] but if anything, this formulation, whether it is to be regarded as a separate test to be applied *after* that of reasonable foreseeability,[70] or as representing what the hypothetical reasonable man would contemplate[71] probably understates the burden on the plaintiff and "there may be circumstances in which the court would require a degree of likelihood amounting almost to inevitability before it fixes the defendant with responsibility for the act of a third party over whom he has and can have no control."[72] In *Lamb* v. *Camden London Borough*[73] the defendants' negligence caused the plaintiff's house to be damaged and become unoccupied but they were not liable for the further damage done by the depredations of squatters, notwithstanding a finding by the Official Referee that squatting was "foreseeable." On the other hand, in *Ward* v. *Cannock Chase District Council* on rather similar facts, but where the defendants had been guilty of wilful delay in effecting repairs and where the risk of vandal damage was rather higher, they were found liable for the further loss.[74] The consequence of all this may be, of course, that precisely the same physical act may or may not break the chain of causation depending on the mental state of the actor: further negligence may be within the risk created by the defendant when wilful conduct may not.[75] So also, the intervening deliberate act of a child may not break the chain when that of an adult would.[76]

The above principles are applicable where there are no special circumstances imposing upon the defendant a duty to take care to guard against the

---

[66] *Weld-Blundell* v. *Stephens* A.C. 956, 986, *per* Lord Sumner.

[67] *Ante*, p. 94.

[68] *Perl* v. *Camden London Borough* [1984] Q.B. 342, *per* Oliver L.J.

[69] *Home Office* v. *Dorset Yacht Co. Ltd.* [1970] A.C. 1004, *per* Lord Reid. Note, however, that the majority of the House of Lords regarded this case as about duty, not causation.

[70] *Lamb* v. *Camden London Borough* [1981] Q.B. 625, 647, *per* Watkins L.J.

[71] *Ibid.* at pp. 644, 647, *per* Oliver L.J. Lord Mackay in *Smith* v. *Littlewoods Organisation Ltd.* [1987] A.C. 241, would appear to agree, despite the remark at p. 263E.

[72] *Lamb* v. *Camden London Borough*, *supra*, at p. 647, *per* Oliver L.J.

[73] Weir, *Casebook on Tort*, (6th ed.), p. 203; Murdoch (1982) 98 L.Q.R. 22.

[74] [1986] Ch. 546. But the defendants were not liable for theft of the plaintiff's goods, perhaps because he could have taken steps himself to secure those. Note that this case shows (at p. 558) that Lord Denning M.R. was wrong in *Lamb's* case to assume that plaintiffs will have insurance against these losses.

[75] *Watson* v. *Kentucky & Indiana Bridge R.R.* 126 S.W. 146 (1916) is a good example. D negligently derailed a petrol tanker. X struck a match and caused an explosion. New trial ordered for failure to leave to jury issue of D's liability upon conflicting testimony that X acted negligently or maliciously. See also *Philco Radio, etc., Corp.* v. *J. Spurling Ltd.* [1949] 2 K.B. 33.

[76] See McGregor, *Damages* (15th ed.), pp. 88–89.

wrongdoing of the third party. If such a duty exists, it would be futile to classify the damage as too remote merely because it was wilfully inflicted. A driver who knocks down a pedestrian would not be liable for theft of the pedestrian's wallet while he was lying injured; but a bailee, who is under a duty (normally, but not necessarily, arising from a contract) to safeguard his bailor's goods, is as liable where, by his default, they are stolen by a burglar as he is where they are destroyed in a fire. In *Stansbie* v. *Troman*[77] a decorator was at work in a house and left it for two hours to get wallpaper. He was alone and had been told by the householder to close the front door whenever he left the house. Instead of doing so he left the door unlocked and during his absence a thief entered the house and stole a diamond bracelet and some clothes. The Court of Appeal held that the decorator was liable for the loss.[78] Similarly, in *Haynes* v. *Harwood*[79] the defendants were held liable when the plaintiff was injured by their horses which had been left unattended in the street and caused to bolt by a mischievous boy. It was negligent to leave the horses unattended precisely because children might interfere.[80]

(iii) Intervening act of the plaintiff. Where it is the plaintiff's own act or omission which, in combination with the defendant's breach of duty, has brought about his damage, then the problem is generally seen as one of contributory negligence. Before there can be any question of contributory negligence, however, it is necessary that both the plaintiff's lack of care and the defendant's breach of duty shall be found to have been causes of the plaintiff's damage and in some cases, especially those in which the plaintiff seeks to recover for damage suffered in a second accident, the defendant has been exonerated on the ground that the plaintiff's conduct amounted to a *nova causa interveniens*. In *McKew* v. *Holland & Hannen & Cubitts (Scotland) Ltd.*[81] the pursuer had suffered an injury in an accident for which the defenders were liable and as a result he occasionally lost control of his left leg which gave way under him. Some days after this accident he went to inspect a flat which was approached by a steep stair between two walls and without a handrail. On leaving the flat he started to descend the stair holding his young daughter by the hand and going ahead of his wife and brother-in-law who had accompanied him. Suddenly he lost control of his left leg, threw his daughter back in order to save her, and tried to jump so as to land in an upright position instead of falling down the stairs. As a result he sustained a severe fracture of his ankle. The House of Lords agreed that the pursuer's act of jumping in the emergency in which he found himself did not break the chain of causation, but that it had been broken by his conduct in placing himself unnecessarily in a position where he might be confronted by just

---

[77] [1948] 2 K.B. 48, criticised by Lord Denning M.R. in *Lamb's* case, *supra*, at p. 638 but approved by Lord Goff in *Smith* v. *Littlewoods, supra,* at p. 272. The defendant was not a bailee.
[78] But even in these cases the loss must be within the ambit of the duty. Would the defendant have been liable for malicious damage? For the seizure of the house by squatters?
[79] [1935] 1 K.B. 147; *Davies* v. *Liverpool Corp.* [1949] 2 All E.R. 175.
[80] [1935] 1 K.B. 147, 153, *per* Greer L.J. Would the defendant have been liable if an adult had caused the horses to bolt?
[81] [1969] 3 All E.R. 1621 (H.L.Sc.); *The San Onofre* [1922] P. 243. *cf. Wieland* v. *Cyril Lord Carpets Ltd.* [1969] 3 All E.R. 1006.

such an emergency, when he could have descended the stair slowly and carefully by himself or sought the assistance of his wife or brother-in-law.

The basis of the decision of the House of Lords in this case was that the pursuer's conduct amounted to a *nova causa interveniens* because, even though it may have been foreseeable, it was unreasonable in the circumstances.[82] If he had had no reasonable alternative to acting as he did his conduct would not have broken the chain of causation.[83] But even where a reasonable alternative exists the court should be slow to stigmatise the plaintiff's behaviour as unreasonable merely because he does not take the course which is cheapest for the defendant. In *Emeh* v. *Kensington and Chelsea and Westminster Area Health Authority*[84] the defendants negligently performed a sterilisation operation on the plaintiff and she became pregnant again, though she did not discover this until 20 weeks into the pregnancy. The Court of Appeal rejected the argument that her refusal to have an abortion broke the chain of causation between the negligence and the child's birth. As Slade L.J. put it, "save in the most exceptional circumstances, I cannot think it right that the court should ever declare it unreasonable for a woman to decline to have an abortion, in a case where there is no evidence that there were any medical or psychiatric grounds for terminating the particular pregnancy."[85]

An interesting question arises if, as a result of depression traceable to his injuries, the victim of a tort commits suicide. Can the tortfeasor be liable for his death? An affirmative answer was given at first instance in *Pigney* v. *Pointer's Transport Services*[86] and the case is a strong one because at that time suicide was a crime and the deceased was not insane within the M'Naghten Rules. The case was decided under the *Re Polemis* but it is thought that the result should be the same under *The Wagon Mound*.[87]

CONTRIBUTORY NEGLIGENCE[88]

If the plaintiff's injuries have been caused partly by the negligence of the defendant and partly by his own negligence,[89] then, at common law, the

---

[82] [1969] 3 All E.R. 1621, 1623, *per* Lord Reid.

[83] A rescuer will not be regarded as acting unreasonably because he takes a risk: *post*, p. 695.

[84] [1985] Q.B. 1012; *Scuriaga* v. *Powell* (1979) 123 S.J. 406.

[85] [1985] Q.B. 1012, 1024. See also *The Calliope* [1970] P. 172 (maritime collision caused by negligence of plaintiff and defendant; plaintiff vessel sustaining further damage in turning because of Chief Officer's negligence; turning maneouvre difficult but not unreasonable and did not break chain of causation; defendant liable for further damage, subject to further apportionment for contributory negligence: *post*, p. 166.

[86] [1957] 1 W.L.R. 1121.

[87] See particularly Williams, "The Risk Principle" (1961) 77 L.Q.R. 179, 196: "Either the victim's suicide was a normal reaction to his injuries, or it was abnormal. If it was normal, it should be taken as reasonably foreseeable; if it was abnormal, it comes within the thin skull rule as applied to psychic states." Liability was denied on the basis of *The Wagon Mound* in *Swami* v. *Lo* (1979) 105 D.L.R. (3d) 451, but imposed in *Cotic* v. *Gray* (1981) 124 D.L.R. (3d) 641 where, however, there was a pre-accident neurosis. *cf.* the dictum of Lord Denning M.R. in *Hyde* v. *Tameside A.H.A.*, *The Times*, April 16, 1981.

[88] Weir, *Casebook on Tort*, (6th ed.), Chap. 5, s.1.

[89] The burden of proving the plaintiff's negligence lies with the defendant: *Heranger (Owners)* v. *S.S. Diamond* [1939] A.C. 94, 104, *per* Lord Wright; *Fitzgerald* v. *Lane* [1988] 3 W.L.R. 356.

plaintiff can recover nothing. This rule of "contributory negligence"[90] first appeared at the beginning of the nineteenth century, though the general idea is traceable much earlier.[91] In *Butterfield* v. *Forrester*,[92] A wrongfully obstructed a road by putting a pole across it. B, riding violently on the road in the dusk, was overthrown by the pole and injured. The pole was discernible at a distance of 100 yards. It was held that A was not liable to B. Bayley J. said: "If he had used ordinary care he must have seen the obstruction; so that the accident appeared to happen entirely from his own fault"; and Lord Ellenborough C.J. added: "One person being at fault will not dispense with another's using ordinary care of himself."

The common law rule produced hardship where one of the two negligent parties suffered the greater loss although his negligence was not the major cause of the accident. Accordingly, the courts modified the defence of contributory negligence by the so-called rule of last opportunity. This enabled the plaintiff to recover notwithstanding his own negligence, if upon the occasion of the accident the defendant could have avoided the accident while the plaintiff could not.[93] The authorities were confused, and confusion was made worse confounded by the extension of the rule, in *British Columbia Electric Ry.* v. *Loach*,[94] to cases of "constructive last opportunity." This meant that if the defendant would have had the last opportunity but for his own negligence, he was in the same position as if he had actually had it, and the plaintiff again recovered in full. There are cogent reasons for denying that either of these rules was derived from those concerning remoteness of damage[95] but they seem on the whole to have been regarded by the courts as if they were, and it is perhaps fair to say that in the result the ultimate question was, "Who caused the accident?"

Whether it is based upon remoteness of damage or not, if it means that in every case the person whose negligence came last in time is solely responsible for the damage, the rule of last opportunity is clearly illogical. It is not surprising, therefore, that when apportionment of the damages between plaintiff and defendant became possible in cases of maritime collision under the Maritime Conventions Act 1911,[96] the rule began to receive adverse criticism. In *Admiralty Commissioners* v. *S.S. Volute*[97] the House of Lords held that even where the defendant's negligence was subsequent to that of

---

[90] There is a wealth of literature on the topic, the most useful work being Glanville Williams, *Joint Torts and Contributory Negligence*, Pt. II.

[91] Thus the strict liability of an innkeeper for the safe-keeping of his guest's goods was negatived if the goods were stolen by the guest's own fault: *Sanders* v. *Spencer* (1567) 3 Dyer 266b. See also Holdsworth, *A History of English Law*, (7th ed.), Vol. 3, p. 378.

[92] (1809) 11 East 60.

[93] The authority usually regarded as supporting the rule of last opportunity is *Davies* v. *Mann* (1842) 10 M. & W. 546. Plaintiff fettered the fore feet of his donkey and negligently turned it loose on the highway. Defendant, driving his wagon and horses faster than he should have done, collided with and killed the donkey. Defendant liable because by the exercise of ordinary care he might have avoided the consequences of plaintiff's negligence. Neither in this case nor in *Butterfield* v. *Forrester*, *supra*, was the phrase "contributory negligence" used. *Davies* v. *Mann* was approved by the House of Lords in *Radley* v. *L. & N.W. Ry.* (1876) 1 App.Cas. 759.

[94] [1916] 1 A.C. 719.

[95] Glanville Williams, *op. cit.*, pp. 236–255.

[96] s.1.

[97] [1922] 1 A.C. 129, 144–145.

the plaintiff, nevertheless the plaintiff's negligence was still contributory to the collision if there is not "a sufficient separation of time, place, or circumstance" between the plaintiff's negligence and the defendant's negligence to make the defendant's negligence the sole cause of the collision.

The Law Reform (Contributory Negligence) Act 1945[98] applied the principle on which the Maritime Conventions Act 1911[99] was based to contributory negligence on land and today, therefore, the damages may be apportioned wherever both parties have been negligent and both have contributed to the damage. It is still open to the court to conclude that the fault of only one party was the sole effective cause of the loss[1] but all the refinements of "last opportunity" have gone.

Present law—the Act of 1945

Section 1(1) of the Act of 1945 provides as follows: "Where any person suffers damage as the result partly of his own fault and partly of the fault of any other person or persons, a claim in respect of that damage shall not be defeated by reason of the fault of the person suffering the damage, but the damages recoverable in respect thereof shall be reduced to such extent as the court thinks just and equitable having regard to the claimant's share in the responsibility for the damage."[2] By section 4, damage includes loss of life and personal injury.[3] There is no doubt that it also includes injury to property for that was so before the Act. By the same section "fault" means negligence, breach of statutory duty or other act or omission which gives rise to a liability in tort or would, apart from the Act, give rise to the defence of contributory negligence.

The words "negligence, breach of statutory duty or other act or omission which gives rise to liability in tort" apply to the "original" liability-creating fault of the defendant but the whole definition applies to the conduct of the plaintiff.[4] The scope of the Act is therefore wide, but not unlimited, for it

---

[98] The common law rule of "all or nothing" was more tenacious in the U.S.A., but there was a fundamental shift after the 1960s and by 1981 some 38 states had some form of apportionment.

[99] The Act of 1911 is unaffected by the Act of 1945.

[1] See *post*, p. 160.

[2] The section does not operate to defeat any defence arising under a contract (though such defences will be limited in scope after the Unfair Contract Terms Act 1977), nor can the amount of damages recoverable exceed the limit fixed by any contract or enactment applicable to the claim: s.1(2) and (6). The court must find and record the total damages which would have been recoverable had the claimant not been at fault; if the case is tried with a jury, they assess the total amount of the damages and also the extent to which they are to be reduced. The Act binds the Crown: Crown Proceedings Act 1947, s.4(3). The Act must be pleaded: *Fookes* v. *Slaytor* [1978] 1 W.L.R. 1293.

[3] It probably includes physical and economic damage, all damages which might have been awarded at common law apart from the plaintiff's own fault, including physical injury resulting from shock: Glanville Williams, *op. cit.* pp. 116–118, 317. In *Drinkwater* v. *Kimber* [1952] 2 Q.B. 281 it was held that a claim for contribution which could not succeed under the Law Reform (Married Women and Tortfeasors) Act 1935 could not be brought within the 1945 Act because the damages which the tortfeasor had to pay to the victim were not "damage" within that Act. The contribution legislation was made to apply to such facts by the Law Reform (Husband and Wife) Act 1962.

[4] *Forsikringsaktieselskapet Vesta* v. *Butcher* [1988] 3 W.L.R. 565, 573, *per* O'Connor L.J. *cf. Rowe* v. *Turner Hopkins & Partners* [1980] 2 N.Z.L.R. 550, 555 where the first limb is said to apply to the conduct of the defendant and the second limb to the conduct of the plaintiff, but in *Vesta* O'Connor L.J. referred to this as a construction "which for practical purposes coincides with my own."

does not apply to intentional interference with goods[5] nor to deceit.[6] After some hesitation, the courts seem now to accept that the Act may be applicable to cases of intentional trespass to the person, given sufficiently serious conduct on the part of the plaintiff.[7] The Act does not apply to claims for breach of contract where the defendant's liability arises from some contractual provision which does not depend on negligence on his part (for example, the implied terms to be found in sections 12–15 of the Sale of Goods Act 1979) or from a contractual obligation which is expressed in terms of taking care but which does not correspond to a common law duty to take care which would exist in the given case independently of contract.[8] Where, however, the defendant's liability, though framed in contract, is the same as his liability in the tort of negligence independently of the existence of any contract, the Act is applicable.[9] This would be the case, for example, in a claim for personal injuries by a patient against a doctor giving private treatment, by passenger against carrier or by visitor against occupier.[10] What if the defendant is liable in tort to the plaintiff but the plaintiff has committed a breach of contract which cannot be framed as a liability in tort (for example, breach of a strict repairing covenant in a lease)? The 1945 Act is inapplicable because the plaintiff's conduct is not "contributory negligence," but it has been held that the court has power to apportion, based on causation.[11]

Causation

In the majority of cases the plaintiff's negligence will have contributed to the accident which led to his injury (as where a driver or pedestrian fails to keep a proper look-out or an employee omits to turn off a machine before cleaning it) but this is not necessary for a finding of contributory negligence: what is essential is that the plaintiff's conduct contributes to his *damage*. Thus there may be a reduction where a motor cyclist fails to wear a crash helmet,[12] where a passenger in a car does not wear his seat belt,[13] or where a

[5] Torts (Interference with Goods) Act 1977, s.11. But under s.47 of the Banking Act 1979 a collecting banker sued for conversion of a cheque in circumstances in which s.4 of the Cheques Act 1957 would be applicable has "a defence of contributory negligence." It is thought this means that the 1945 Act applies.

[6] This would seem to follow from such cases as *Redgrave* v. *Hurd* (1881) 20 Ch.D. 1 and no distinction can be drawn between rescission and damages: the plaintiff's fault would not "apart from the Act give rise to the defence of contributory negligence." As to negligent misstatement, see *post*, p. 287.

[7] *Murphy* v. *Culhane* [1977] Q.B. 96; *Barnes* v. *Nayer, The Times*, December 19, 1986; *Wasson* v. *Chief Constable, R.U.C.* (1987) 6 B.N.I.L. 140; *Tumelty* v. *M.o.D.* (1988) 4 B.N.I.L. 140; *contra, Horkin* v. *Melbourne Football Club* [1983] V.R. 153. See Hudson, "Contributory Negligence as a Defence to Battery" (1984) 4 L.S. 332. *cf. Lane* v. *Holloway* [1968] 1 Q.B. 379 and see *post*, p. 701.

[8] *Forsikringsaktieselskapet Vesta* v. *Butcher, supra*, n. 4. It seems that in contract the matter is to be dealt with as one of causation, so that the plaintiff recovers his whole loss unless his fault is the substantial cause of the accident, in which case he recovers nothing. In *Lambert* v. *Lewis* [1982] A.C. 268 a party's negligence was held to be the effective cause of his loss rather than the breach of warranty of the dealer who had supplied him, thus preventing recovery of a contractual indemnity.

[9] *Forsikringsaktieselskapet Vesta* v. *Butcher, supra*, n. 4.

[10] *Sayers* v. *Harlow U.D.C.* [1958] 1 W.L.R. 623. Hence the plaintiff guilty of a small degree of contributory negligence cannot avoid a reduction by pleading his claim only in contract.

[11] *Tennant Radiant Heat Ltd.* v. *Warrington Development Corporation* [1988] 11 E.G. 71.

[12] *O'Connell* v. *Jackson* [1972] 1 Q.B. 270; *Capps* v. *Miller* [1989] 2 All E.R. 333.

[13] *Froom* v. *Butcher* [1976] Q.B. 286, *post*, p. 167. *cf. Kaye* v. *Alfa-Romeo* (1984) 134 New L.J. 126 (defective seat belt; bad driving as contributory negligence).

man rides in a dangerous position on the outside of a dust cart,[14] or rides with a driver whom he knows to have taken substantial quantities of alcohol.[15] It is, however, essential that the plaintiff's lack of care should be a contributory factor to his damage, that is to say, the injury to him must at least be within the broad scope of the risk created by his negligence. In *Jones* v. *Livox Quarries Ltd.*,[16] the plaintiff was riding on the towbar at the back of a "traxcavator" vehicle in order to return from his place of work to the canteen when the driver of another vehicle negligently drove into the back of the traxcavator and caused him injury. Though the obvious danger arising from riding on the towbar was that of being thrown off, it was held that the risk of injury from the traxcavator being run into from behind was also one to which the plaintiff had exposed himself and his damages were reduced accordingly. The result would have been otherwise if, for example, he had been hit in the eye by a shot from a negligent sportsman.[17] In that case his presence on the towbar would have been only part of the history.[18]

The power to apportion damages under the Act has certainly meant that we are freed from some of the artificiality of the old law and there is no longer the same temptation to avoid finding a small element of contributory negligence on the part of the plaintiff.[19] However, we should guard against the asumption that merely because the acts of the plaintiff and the defendant combine in a factual sense to cause the injury that the case is one for apportionment, for the intention of the Act was to alter only the legal consequences of contributory negligence and not the general rules for determining whether a case of contributory negligence exists.[20] Thus it is still perfectly possible for a court to come to the conclusion that as a matter of legal cause the fault of the plaintiff is so overwhelming that he must bear the whole loss. In *Stapley* v. *Gypsum Mines Ltd.*[21] Lord Porter said[22]:

"I agree, indeed, with the opinion which has been commonly held since

[14] *Davies* v. *Swan Motor Co.* [1949] 2 K.B. 291. The fact that the contributory negligence need not contribute to the accident means that it is very difficult to distinguish it from the duty to mitigate damage (*post*, p. 609). Before the Act, the courts seem to have regarded contributory negligence as something that related to the occurrence of the initial injury and mitigation as relating to the time after that occurrence. Failure to mitigate would debar the plaintiff from any recovery for additional loss suffered by reason of that failure but would have no effect on his other loss. The Act probably does not apply to failure to mitigate, but for a powerful argument that it should see Williams, *op. cit.*, Chap. 11.

[15] *Owens* v. *Brimmell* [1977] Q.B. 859; Symmons (1977) 40 M.L.R. 350. See also *Gregory* v. *Kelly* [1978] R.T.R. 426 (knowledge of defective brakes).

[16] [1952] 2 Q.B. 608.

[17] For a somewhat more colourful example, see *Moor* v. *Nolan* (1960) 94 I.L.T.R. 153.

[18] [1952] 2 Q.B. at p. 616, *per* Denning L.J. See also *ibid.* at p. 612, *per* Singleton L.J., at p. 618, *per* Hodson L.J.

[19] *Boy Andrew (Owners)* v. *St. Rognvald (Owners)* [1948] A.C. 140, 155, *per* Lord Porter; *Sayers* v. *Harlow U.D.C.* [1958] 1 W.L.R. 623, 630, *per* Lord Evershed M.R.

[20] *Davies* v. *Swan Motor Co.* [1949] 2 K.B. 291, 310, *per* Bucknill L.J., at p. 322, *per* Denning L.J. This was the view of Lord Simon, the promoter of the Act, expressed extra-judicially: Salmond and Heuston, *Torts*, (19th ed.), p. 579, n. 21.

[21] [1953] A.C. 663 (two miners abandoned attempt to bring down unsafe part of roof; one of them killed in subsequent fall; widow suing employers as vicariously responsible for fault of other miner). This case provoked much judicial disagreement during its passage. The decision that the fault of both men contributed to the accident was followed on somewhat similar facts in *I.C.I. Ltd.* v. *Shatwell* [1965] A.C. 565 but the House of Lords in that case was able to come to a different conclusion by the application of the defence of *volenti non fit injuria*: *post*, p. 688.

[22] [1953] A.C. 663, 677 (a dissenting speech); see also *ibid.* at pp. 681, 684, 687, *per* Lords Reid, Tucker and Asquith respectively.

the decision of *Admiralty Commissioners* v. *S.S. Volute (Owners)*,[23] viz., that the abolition of the rule that any contributory negligence, however small, on the part of a plaintiff defeated his claim, has no effect on causation. It enables the court (be it judge or jury) to seek less strenuously to find some ground for holding the plaintiff free from blame or for reaching the conclusion that his negligence played no part in the ensuing accident inasmuch as owing to the change in the law the blame can now be apportioned equitably between the two parties. What was the cause of an event, however leads to an inquiry of the same nature as existed before the change."

The application of this principle is typified in a series of cases where employers were guilty of breaches of strict statutory duty but the breaches were brought about solely by the failure of the plaintiffs, experienced workmen, to carry out clear safety procedures in which they had been properly instructed.[24]

Duty of care

The existence of a duty of care is, of course, essential to a cause of action for negligence, but for contributory negligence it is quite unnecessary that the plaintiff should owe a duty to the defendant.[25] All that is required is that the plaintiff should have failed to take reasonable care for his own safety.[26]

Standard of care

The standard of care expected of the plaintiff is in general the same as that in negligence itself[27] and is in the same sense objective and impersonal,[28] though some concession is made towards children[29] and probably towards other persons suffering from some infirmity or disability[30] rendering them unable to come up to the normal standard.[31] Putting aside such exceptional

---

[23] [1922] 1 A.C. 129.

[24] *Rushton* v. *Turner Bros.* [1960] 1 W.L.R. 96; *Ginty* v. *Belmont Building Supplies Ltd.* [1959] 1 All E.R. 414; *Horne* v. *Lec Refrigeration Ltd.* [1965] 2 All E.R. 898; *Jayes* v. *I.M.I. (Kynoch)* [1985] I.C.R. 155 ("crazy thing to do"); *cf. Ross* v. *Associated Portland Cement Manufacturers Ltd.* [1964] 1 W.L.R. 768. For civil liability for breach of statutory duty in factories, etc., see *post,* Chaps. 7 and 8.

[25] Nevertheless, it will often be the case, as where there is a collision between two vehicles, that the plaintiff does owe a duty of care to the defendant. A duty is essential if the defendant wishes to counterclaim against the plaintiff in respect of his own damage.

[26] *Nance* v. *British Columbia Electric Ry.* [1951] A.C. 601, 611, *per* Viscount Simon. See *Davies* v. *Swan Motor Co.* [1949] 2 K.B. 291 for a full discussion. *cf. Dawrant* v. *Nutt* [1961] 1 W.L.R. 253 and see Dias [1961] C.L.J. 17.

[27] *Billings & Sons Ltd.* v. *Riden* [1958] A.C. 240, *Bittner* v. *Tait-Gibson Optometrists Ltd.* (1964) 44 D.L.R. (2d) 113, Ontario C.A. "Fault" in the Act of 1945 does not include some fault falling short of negligence: *Jones* v. *Price* [1963] C.L.Y. 2316. See also *Clayards* v. *Dethick* (1848) 12 Q.B. 439; *Sayers* v. *Harlow U.D.C.* [1958] 1 W.L.R. 623.

[28] *Ante,* p. 111.

[29] Below.

[30] Not self-induced intoxication: *Owens* v. *Brimmell* [1977] Q.B. 859.

[31] *Daly* v. *Liverpool Corp.* [1939] 2 All E.R. 142; *M'Kibbin* v. *Glasgow Corp.* 1920 S.C. 590. The proposition is, indeed, implicit in *Haley* v. *London Electricity Board* [1965] A.C. 778 since a sighted person would have had no difficulty in avoiding the danger. On the other hand, an infirm person may act in such an unpredictable way that there is no breach of duty by the defendant: *Bourhill* v. *Young* [1943] A.C. 92, 109; *Barnes* v. *Flucker* 1985 S.L.T. 142.

cases, a "person is guilty of contributory negligence if he ought reasonably to have foreseen that, if he did not act as a reasonable, prudent man, he might be hurt himself; and in his reckonings he must take into account the possibility of others being careless."[32] The degree of want of care which will constitute contributory negligence varies with the circumstances: the law certainly does not require the plaintiff to proceed on his way like a timorous fugitive constantly looking over his shoulder for threats from others.[33] For example, it is not the law that a pedestrian is guilty of contributory negligence if he crosses the road without using an "authorised" crossing.[34]

As with any other aspect of the law of negligence the standard of care demanded may be adjusted to meet changing conditions; for example, in *Froom* v. *Butcher*[35] the Court of Appeal held that non-use of a car seat belt generally constituted contributory negligence some seven years before Parliament made the wearing of belts compulsory.[36] Now that there is legislation requiring belts to be worn the correctness of this decision becomes even more obvious, though the details of the relationship between the requirements of the criminal law and the civil consequences will need to be worked out.[37]

Dilemma produced by negligence

Where the defendant's negligence has put the plaintiff in a dilemma, the defendant cannot escape liability if the plaintiff, in the agony of the moment, tries to save himself by choosing a course of conduct which proves to be the wrong one, provided the plaintiff acted in a reasonable apprehension of danger and the method by which he tried to avoid it was a reasonable one.[38] If those conditions are satisfied he committed no contributory negligence.[39]

---

[32] *Jones* v. *Livox Quarries Ltd.* [1952] 2 Q.B. 608, 615, *per* Denning L.J. See also *Grant* v. *Sun Shipping Co.* [1948] A.C. 549, *per* Lord du Parcq. *cf. Hawkins* v. *Ian Ross (Castings) Ltd.* [1970] 1 All E.R. 180. Equally, however, the defendant should bear in mind the possibility that his activity may distract persons from looking after their own safety. A bizarre example is *Edwards* v. *Tracy Starr's Shows (Edmonton) Ltd.* (1984) 13 D.L.R. (4th) 129 (patron of "burlesque show" falling over unseen obstruction).

[33] A worker is not normally put on inquiry as to whether his employer has fulfilled his duties under statutes and regulations governing industrial safety: *Westwood* v. *Post Office* [1974] A.C. 1.

[34] *Tremayne* v. *Hill* [1987] R.T.R. 131.

[35] [1976] Q.B. 286. As to apportionment in such cases see *post*, p. 167. *cf. Gibson* v. *British Insulated Callender's Construction Co.* 1973 S.L.T. 1.

[36] In 1976 the position as to a seat belt was that "everyone is free to wear it or not, as he pleases. Free in this sense, that if he does not wear it, he is free from any penalty by the magistrates. Free in the sense that everyone is free to run his head against a brick wall, if he pleases. . . . But it is not a sensible thing to do. If he does it it is his own fault; and he has only himself to thank for the consequences": [1976] Q.B. 286, 293.

[37] In *Froom* v. *Butcher* the court said that it is no excuse that the plaintiff sincerely believes that wearing a belt is more dangerous than not wearing one, but that an unduly fat man or pregnant woman might be spared a finding of contributory negligence. However, the last two categories are not exempted as such from the criminal law: under S.I. 1982 No. 1203, reg. 5(*d*) exemption is granted to "the holder of a . . . certificate . . . signed by a registered medical practitioner to the effect that it is inadvisable on medical grounds for him to wear a seat belt." It is thought that, *e.g.* a pregnant woman who had no certificate might still escape a finding of contributory negligence. Contrariwise, it is thought that some exempted persons (*e.g.* a taxi driver, see reg. 5(*i*)) might still be found to be contributorily negligent. It has been held that where a vehicle is not required by law to be fitted with belts it is a question of fact whether failure to fit them amounts to contributory negligence: *Hoadley* v. *Dartford District Council* [1979] R.T.R. 359.

[38] Glanville Williams, *op. cit.*, pp. 360–364.

[39] The rule is equally applicable in favour of the defendant where there is contributory negligence on the part of the plaintiff which has forced the dilemma upon him instead of upon the plaintiff: *Swadling* v. *Cooper* [1931] A.C. 1, 9; *McLean* v. *Bell* (1932) 147 L.T. 262, 263.

A famous illustration of the principle is *Jones* v. *Boyce*,[40] where the plaintiff was a passenger on the top of the defendant's coach and, owing to the breaking of a defective coupling rein, the coach was in imminent peril of being overturned. The plaintiff, seeing this, jumped from it and broke his leg. In fact the coach was not upset. Lord Ellenborough C.J. directed the jury that if the plaintiff acted as a reasonable and prudent man would have done, he was entitled to recover, although he had selected the more perilous of the two alternatives with which he was confronted by the defendant's negligence; and the jury gave a verdict for the plaintiff. But where all that the plaintiff is threatened with is mere personal inconvenience of a trifling kind, he is not entitled to run a considerable risk in order to get rid of it; *e.g.* if the door of a railway-carriage in which he is travelling is so ill-secured that it keeps flying open, but he can avoid the draught by sitting elsewhere, it is his own fault if he falls out in trying to shut it (after several earlier unsuccessful attempts) while the train is in motion.[41]

Children

While it is not possible to specify an age below which, as a matter of law, a child cannot be guilty of contributory negligence,[42] age of the child is a circumstance which must be considered in deciding whether it has been guilty of contributory negligence.[43] In *Yachuk* v. *Oliver Blais Co. Ltd.*, Y.,[44] a boy aged nine years, bought from O.B. Co. some gasoline (highly inflammable liquid), falsely stating that his mother wanted it for her car. In fact, he used it to play with, and, in doing so, was badly burnt by it. It was held by the Judicial Committee that O.B. Co. were negligent in supplying gasoline to so young a boy and that Y. had not been guilty of contributory negligence for he neither knew nor could be expected to know the properties of gasoline. Although Lord Denning M.R. has said that a child should not be found guilty of contributory negligence "unless he or she is blameworthy,"[45] it is not thought that the characteristics of the particular child other than its age are to be considered. The question is whether an "ordinary" child of the plaintiff's age—not a "paragon of prudence" nor a "scatter-brained" child—would have taken any more care than did the plaintiff.[46]

---

[40] (1816) 1 Stark. 493; *The Bywell Castle* (1879) 4 P.D. 219; *United States of America* v. *Laird Line Ltd.* [1924] A.C. 286; *Admiralty Commissioners* v. *S.S. Volute* [1922] 1 A.C. 129, 136; *Sayers* v. *Harlow U.D.C.* [1958] 1 W.L.R. 623. See, too, Lord Blackburn in *Stoomvaart Maatschappij Nederland* v. *P. & O.S.N. Co.* (1880) 5 App.Cas. 876, 891, and Brett L.J. in *Woodley & Co.* v. *Michell & Co.* (1883) 11 Q.B.D. 47, 52–53.

[41] *Adams* v. *L. & Y. Ry.* (1869) L.R. 4 C.P. 739; *cf. Sayers* v. *Harlow U.D.C.* [1958] 1 W.L.R. 623.

[42] *cf. Gough* v. *Thorne* [1966] 1 W.L.R. 1387, 1390, *per* Lord Denning M.R., and *Ducharme* v. *Davies* [1984] 1 W.W.R. 699. "The descending line measuring reasonable expectation of care rapidly approaches zero as the age diminishes, but the line is apparently asymptotic": *Beasley* v. *Marshall* (1977) 17 S.A.S.R. 456, 459, *per* Bright J.

[43] Clerk and Lindsell, *Torts*, (16th ed.), para. 1–149. *cf.* Glanville Williams, *op. cit.*, p. 355; *Whitehouse* v. *Fearnley* (1964) 47 D.L.R. (2d) 472; *Lynch* v. *Nurdin* (1841) 1 Q.B. 29; *Culkin* v. *McFie & Sons Ltd.* [1939] 3 All E.R. 613; *Jones* v. *Lawrence* [1969] 3 All E.R. 267; *Minter* v. *D. & H. Contractors, The Times*, June 30, 1983. A comparison of *Jones* v. *Lawrence* with *McKinnel* v. *White* 1971 S.L.T. (Notes) 61 suggests that standards may be more severe north of the border.

[44] [1949] A.C. 386; *French* v. *Sunshine Holiday Camp (Hayling Island) Ltd.* (1963) 107 S.J. 595.

[45] *Gough* v. *Thorne, supra*, at p. 1390. *Jones* v. *Lawrence, supra*, refers to the need for culpable want of care by the child for his own safety.

[46] [1966] 1 W.L.R. 1387, 1391, *per* Salmond L.J. *cf. Beasley* v. *Marshall* (1977) S.A.S.R. 456, 458.

If the injury is due partly to the negligence of the child's parent or guardian in failing to look after it and partly to the negligence of the defendant the child may still recover his whole loss against the defendant, for he is not "identified" with the negligence of his parent or guardian[47] and the case follows the normal rule that a plaintiff may sue and execute judgment against either of two concurrent tortfeasors for the whole sum.[48] In practice, however, the impact of this rule was substantially changed by the introduction of contribution between concurrent tortfeasors,[49] for the defendant may now join the negligent parent or guardian as a third party and hold him responsible for a proportion of the damages.[50] If the parent or guardian is insured[51] this may be a matter of indifference, but if he is not, the result, for obvious practical reasons, is likely to be a settlement which makes a deduction for his share in the blame for the accident.[52]

Workmen[53]

It has been suggested that in actions by workmen against their employers for injuries sustained at work the courts are justified in taking a more lenient view of careless conduct on the part of the plaintiff than would otherwise be justified, and that it is not for every risky thing which a workman in a factory may do that he is to be held to have been negligent. Regard must be had to the dulling of the sense of danger through familiarity, repetition, noise, confusion, fatigue and preoccupation with work.[54] Where, however, the operation leading up to the accident is divorced from the bustle, noise and repetition that occurs in such places as factories these considerations cannot apply and, indeed, it may be that they are only relevant where the workman's cause of action is founded upon his employer's breach of statutory duty.[55]

It was settled by the House of Lords in 1939 that contributory negligence is a defence to an action for breach of statutory duty,[56] and the general principles of contributory negligence are the same as where the cause of

---

[47] The contrary view was exploded in *Oliver* v. *Birmingham, etc., Omnibus Co. Ltd.* [1933] 1 K.B. 35, following *The Bernina* (1888) 13 App.Cas. 1. *cf.* the position of master and servant, *post*, p. 165. A minor exception to the non-identification rule is found in the Congenital Disabilities (Civil Liability) Act 1976: *post*, p. 669.

[48] *Post*, p. 590.

[49] Law Reform (Married Women and Tortfeasors) Act 1935. See *post*, p. 593.

[50] *McCallion* v. *Dodd* [1966] N.Z.L.R. 710. For the parental duty of care, see *ante*, p. 93.

[51] As where the plaintiff is a passenger in his father's car.

[52] It was this that led the High Court of Australia to a surprisingly narrow view of the parental duty of care in *Hahn* v. *Conley* [1971] 45 A.L.J.R. 631.

[53] Fagelson, "The Last Bastion of Fault" (1979) 42 M.L.R. 646.

[54] *Flower* v. *Ebbw Vale Steel, Iron and Coal Co. Ltd.* [1934] 2 K.B. 132, 139–140, *per* Lawrence J., cited with approval by Lord Wright, [1936] A.C. 206, 214; *Caswell* v. *Powell Duffryn Collieries Ltd.* [1940] A.C. 152, 166, *per* Lord Atkin; *ibid.* at pp. 176–179, *per* Lord Wright; *Grant* v. *Sun Shipping Co.* [1948] A.C. 549, 567, *per* Lord du Parcq; *Hawkins* v. *Ian Ross (Castings) Ltd.* [1970] 1 All E.R. 180.

[55] *Staveley Iron & Chemical Co.* v. *Jones* [1956] A.C. 627, 642, *per* Lord Reid, at pp. 647–648, *per* Lord Tucker; *Hicks* v. *British Transport Commission* [1958] 1 W.L.R. 493; *Quintas* v. *National Smelting Co.* [1961] 1 W.L.R. 401, 411, *per* Willmer L.J. *cf. ibid.* at pp. 408–409, *per* Sellers L.J. Disobedience is not necessarily contributory negligence: *Westwood* v. *Post Office* [1974] A.C. 1.

[56] *Caswell* v. *Powell Duffryn Associated Collieries Ltd.* [1940] A.C. 152 (Factories Act); *Sparks* v. *Edward Ash Ltd.* [1943] K.B. 223 (Pedestrian Crossing Places Regulations). For the action for breach of statutory duty, see *post*, Chap. 7.

action is founded upon negligence. In practice, however, especially where the statute creates an absolute obligation to secure the existence of a certain state of affairs, e.g. that dangerous parts of machinery shall be securely fenced,[57] questions of contributory negligence may be treated rather differently. It has often been stated that statutes such as the Factories Act exist to protect workmen from the consequences of their own carelessness,[58] and the courts will therefore be slow to hold a workman guilty of contributory negligence where the defendant is in breach of his statutory duty.[59] Furthermore, even if the workman's negligence involves him in a breach of his own statutory duty his claim is not defeated by the maxim *ex turpi causa non oritur actio*.[60] On the other hand, given the nature of some statutory duties, it can happen that the defendant's breach is brought about wholly and exclusively by the plaintiff's own breach of his duty, and in such a case the plaintiff can recover nothing.[61]

Contributory negligence of the plaintiff's servants or agents[62]

As between the plaintiff and the defendant each is identified with any third person for whom he is vicariously responsible. The rule that the negligence of a servant in the course of his employment is imputed to his master applies whether the master is the plaintiff or the defendant. But the contributory negligence of an independent contractor for whom the plaintiff is not responsible does not affect the plaintiff's action. If X has charge of the person or property of A, A is not for that reason identified with X, hence if an accident happens owing to the negligence of X and a third person, Y, A may sue Y and recover in full, even though X could not.[63]

Apportionment of damages[64]

In a case of contributory negligence the damages recoverable by the plaintiff are to be reduced "to such extent as the court thinks just and equitable having regard to the claimant's share in the responsibility for the damage."[65] This may seem simple enough at first sight, though the problem

[57] Factories Act 1961, s.14(1).
[58] *Staveley Iron & Chemical Co.* v. *Jones* [1956] A.C. 627, 648, *per* Lord Tucker; *Hutchinson* v. *L. & N.E. Ry.* [1942] 1 K.B. 481. *cf. Mullard* v. *Ben Line Steamers Ltd.* [1970] 1 W.L.R. 1414.
[59] See, *e.g. John Summers & Sons Ltd.* v. *Frost* [1955] A.C. 740. Nevertheless, cases in which workmen are held partly and even substantially to blame for their own injuries are exceedingly common. See, *e.g. Cork* v. *Kirby Maclean Ltd.* [1952] 2 All E.R. 402; *Jones* v. *Richards* [1955] 1 W.L.R. 444; *Williams* v. *Sykes & Harrison Ltd.* [1955] 1 W.L.R. 1180; *Hodkinson* v. *H. Wallwork & Co. Ltd.* [1955] 1 W.L.R. 1195 (plaintiff 90 per cent. to blame); *Quinn* v. *Horsfall & Bickham Ltd.* [1956] 1 W.L.R. 652; *Uddin* v. *Associated Portland Cement Manufacturers Ltd.* [1965] 2 Q.B. 582; *Thornton* v. *Swan Hunter (Shipbuilders) Ltd.* [1971] 1 W.L.R. 1759.
[60] *National Coal Board* v. *England* [1954] A.C. 403. See *post*, pp. 697–701.
[61] See the cases cited *supra*, n. 24.
[62] Williams, *op. cit.*, pp. 428–456.
[63] See also *ante*, p. 164 (parent and child).
[64] Gravells "Three Heads of Contributory Negligence" (1977) 93 L.Q.R. 581; Payne, "Reduction of Damages for Contributory Negligence" (1955) 18 M.L.R. 344; Williams, *op. cit.*, Chaps. 16–19.
[65] Law Reform (Contributory Negligence) Act 1945, s.1(1). The equivalent provision in the Maritime Conventions Act 1911, s.1(1) laid down that "the liability to make good the damage or loss shall be in proportion to the degree in which each vessel was in fault." For apportionment under the Civil Liability (Contribution) Act 1978, see *post*, p. 593.

may be complex when there are successive accidents which are causally connected with one another,[66] and in the majority of cases the judges give little by way of reason for their assessments of the extent to which the plaintiff's damages should be reduced. The matter is commonly treated as one of fact, and appellate courts will only vary an assessment in extreme cases unless the trial judge can be said to have erred in principle or failed to take some relevant factor into account.[67]

Broadly speaking, two principal criteria of "responsibility" suggest themselves, causation and blameworthiness or culpability.[68] If the plaintiff's lack of care for his own safety is to be taken into account at all, it is, as we have seen, necessary that his own negligence should have been a cause of his damage, but as a basis for apportionment causation has been severely criticised:

> "To attempt to apportion damages by reference to degree of participation in the chain of causation is a hopeless enterprise, for it has no necessary connection with anything that would appeal to the ordinary person as being just and equitable."[69]

Nevertheless there is high authority for the view that both causation and blameworthiness must be taken into account.[70] It would seem, however, that no hard-and-fast rule can be laid down. Degrees of causation may be impossible of rational assessment, but concentration exclusively upon comparative blameworthiness will tend in some cases to defeat the purpose of the Contributory Negligence Act. Where the defendant's liability is based upon breach of a strict common law or statutory duty he may have been guilty of no blameworthy behaviour at all, in which case if comparative blameworthiness were the sole criterion, even slight contributory negligence would prevent the plaintiff from recovering any damages.[71] Naturally the

---

[66] In *The Calliope* [1970] P. 172 Brandon J. held that where the first accident is caused partly by the negligence of the defendant and partly by the negligence of the plaintiff and then the plaintiff suffers further, consequential, damage which is caused partly by the first accident and partly by his own further negligence, there must be a sub-apportionment of responsibility for that consequential damage.

[67] Of the many authorities, see *The Macgregor* [1943] A.C. 197, 200–201, *per* Lord Wright; *Brown* v. *Thompson* [1968] 1 W.L.R. 1003, 1009–1011, *per* Winn L.J.; *The Jan Laurenz* [1973] 1 Lloyd's Rep. 329; *Hannam* v. *Mann* [1984] R.T.R. 252 (only when "clearly wrong"). Nevertheless appellate courts, and especially the House of Lords, have from time to time varied apportionments of damages quite freely: *Stapley* v. *Gypsum Mines Ltd.* [1953] A.C. 663; *National Coal Board* v. *England* [1954] A.C. 403; *Davison* v. *Apex Scaffolds Ltd.* [1956] 1 Q.B. 551; *Quintas* v. *National Smelting Co.* [1961] 1 W.L.R. 401; *Kerry* v. *Carter* [1969] 1 W.L.R. 1372; *Jennings* v. *Norman Collison Ltd.* [1970] 1 All E.R. 1121.

[68] Culpability should be measured by the degree of departure from the standard of the reasonable man rather than by *moral* blameworthiness. "A drunken motorist is to be disciplined not for his intoxication but for his negligence": Fleming, *Law of Torts,* (7th ed.); *Pennington* v. *Norris* (1956) 96 C.L.R. 10.

[69] Glanville Williams, "The Two Negligent Servants" (1954) 17 M.L.R. 66, 69. "Causation itself is difficult enough; degrees of causation would really be a nightmare": Chapman (1948) 64 L.Q.R. 28.

[70] *Davies* v. *Swan Motor Co.* [1949] 2 K.B. 291, 326, *per* Denning L.J.; *Stapley* v. *Gypsum Mines Ltd.* [1953] A.C. 663, 682, *per* Lord Reid; *The British Aviator* [1965] 1 Lloyd's Rep. 271; *The Miraflores and The Abadesa, supra,* especially *per* Lord Pearce at p. 845; *Brown* v. *Thompson, supra,* at p. 1008, *per* Winn L.J.

[71] Denning J. seems to have accepted the logic of this in *Lavender* v. *Diamints Ltd.* [1948] 2 All E.R. 249, 252, but the Court of Appeal held that the plaintiff was not guilty of contributory negligence at all: [1949] 1 K.B. 585.

courts have been unwilling to reach such a conclusion; on the contrary, as has been stated, the protection intended to be given by strict statutory duties must not be emasculated by the "side-wind of apportionment."[72]

It has been persuasively argued, therefore, that once the liability of the defendant has been established, regard should be had only to the plaintiff's conduct in assessing the extend to which the damages should be reduced.[73] Comparative blameworthiness cannot be assessed when the defendant's liability is not based upon moral fault, but "the legal effects of contributory negligence follow only from morally culpable conduct."[74] This may, in fact, very possibly explain the way in which judges often approach the problem of apportionment, but it is not in truth always possible to ignore the nature of the defendant's liability. In *Quintas* v. *National Smelting Co.*[75] Devlin J. held that the defendants had not been guilty of negligence but had broken their statutory duty and assessed the plaintiff's contributory negligence at 75 per cent. The Court of Appeal, by a majority, held that the defendants were not guilty of breach of statutory duty but had been guilty of negligence and therefore reduced Devlin J.'s assessment to 50 per cent.:

"The respective responsibilities of the parties, and what is just and equitable having regard thereto, can only properly be assessed when it has been found what the plaintiff in fact did and what the defendants failed in their duty to do. The nature and extent of the defendants' duty is, in my view, highly important in assessing the effect of the breach or failure of duty on the happening of the accident giving rise to the plaintiff's claim and on the conduct of the plaintiff. There is an interaction of factors, acts and omissions to be considered."[76]

Comparative blameworthiness becomes even more difficult where the plaintiff's conduct in no way contributes to the accident but consists in failure to take some safety precaution which would have eliminated or reduced his damage, for example failing to wear a car safety belt. What the courts have done here is to lay down a "ready made" range of reductions which will operate regardless of whether the defendant's driving was slightly or grossly negligent and of whether the failure to wear the belt was "entirely inexcusable or almost forgivable."[77] If the plaintiff's injuries would have

---

[72] *Mullard* v. *Ben Line Steamers Ltd.* [1970] 1 W.L.R. 1414, 1418, *per* Sachs L.J. *McGuinness* v. *Key Markets Ltd.* (1973) 13 K.I.R. 249.

[73] Payne, *loc. cit.*

[74] *Ibid.* at p. 347.

[75] [1960] 1 W.L.R. 217; [1961] 1 W.L.R. 401. See also the example given by Lord Pearce in *The Miraflores and The Abadesa* [1967] 1 A.C. 826, 845.

[76] [1961] 1 W.L.R. 401, 408, *per* Sellers L.J. It may be relevant, also, whether the plaintiff's claim is founded upon negligence or nuisance: *Trevett* v. *Lee* [1956] 1 W.L.R. 113, 122, *per* Evershed M.R. It may also be argued that a breach of statutory duty may not be blameworthy and yet amount to contributory negligence. On the interpretation of s.4 of the 1945 Act now adopted (*ante*, p. 158) it may not matter whether such a breach would have amounted to contributory negligence at common law. *cf. Laszczyk* v. *National Coal Board* [1954] 1 W.L.R. 1426.

[77] *Froom* v. *Butcher* [1976] Q.B. 286, 296. These are not rigid rules: (*Salmon* v. *Newland, The Times*, May 16, 1983) but they should generally be followed: *Capps* v. *Miller* [1989] 2 All E.R. 333.

been altogether avoided by wearing the belt there should be a reduction of 25 per cent., but if he would still have been injured, but less severely, the reduction should be only 15 per cent.[78] The court will not encourage attempts to reduce these figures by speculative evidence as to what injuries would have been suffered if the plaintiff *had* been wearing a belt.[79]

The result is, therefore, that there is no single principle for the apportionment of damages in cases of contributory negligence, and certainly no mathematical approach is possible.[80] No doubt the extent of the plaintiff's lack of care for his own safety must be a major factor in all cases, but the court is directed by the statute to do what is "just and equitable."[81] The matter is thus one for the discretion of the court,[82] and, though the discretion must be exercised judicially, it is both unnecessary and undesirable that the exercise of the discretion be fettered by rigid rules requiring the court to take some aspects of the given case into account and to reject others.[83]

Multiple defendants

Where the acts of two or more defendants combine to injure the plaintiff each is liable to the plaintiff for the whole amount of the loss, though as between the defendants the court has a statutory power to apportion liability.[84] Both matters are usually settled in the same proceedings, but there are two stages. First the court must determine liability and decide what deduction if any is to be made for the plaintiff's contributory negligence. This is done by comparing the plaintiff's conduct on the one hand with the totality of the tortious conduct on the other: the question at this stage is not "what is the relative share of responsibility of each and every party?" but "how far is the plaintiff the author of his own loss?" The respective shares of the resulting liability are then determined in the contribution proceedings, which are no concern of the plaintiff's.[85] Hence if, at the first stage, the court concludes that the plaintiff is 50 per cent. responsible there is judgment against both defendants for 50 per cent. of the damage. If the defendants'

---

[78] *Ibid.* But note that the reduction is to be made only in respect of the category of injury causally related to the lack of a belt. If head injuries would have been avoided by wearing a belt there should be a reduction of 25 per cent. in respect of them, but no reduction in respect of a broken leg which would have occurred anyway. It seems that in a serious road accident it may be difficult to determine whether the injuries result from the plaintiff being thrown into contact with the facia or from the facia being forced back upon him. In *Owens* v. *Brimmell* [1977] Q.B. 859, Watkins J. found each possibility equally likely and therefore made no reduction on account of failure to wear a belt. A reduction of 20 per cent. was, however, made because the plaintiff knew that the defendant was under the influence of drink and hence was guilty of contributory negligence in being in the car in the first place. Symmons (1977) 40 M.L.R. 350.

[79] *Patience* v. *Andrews* [1983] R.T.R. 447.

[80] *Connor* v. *Port of Liverpool Stevedoring Co.* [1953] 2 Lloyd's Rep. 604; *Williams* v. *Port of Liverpool Stevedoring Co.* [1956] 1 W.L.R. 551.

[81] See, *e.g. Ashton* v. *Turner* [1981] 1 Q.B. 137, 149 (no duty of care owed by get-away driver to co-criminal, but if such a duty were owed co-criminal should be held guilty of 50 per cent. contributory negligence).

[82] Where there is a jury it is a question for the jury: s.1(6) of the Act of 1945.

[83] However, subject to the *de minimis* principle, a court which has found *some* contributory negligence has no power to disregard it if it thinks it just and equitable so to do: *Boothman* v. *British Northrop Ltd.* (1972) 13 K.I.R. 112. A reduction as low as 10 per cent. was made in *Capps* v. *Miller* [1989] 2 All E.R. 333 (helmet worn but improperly fastened; not possible to assess extent to which injury caused by helmet coming off).

[84] See Chap. 22.

[85] The position is different under the Maritime Conventions Act 1911: see *The Miraflores and The Abadesa* [1967] 1 A.C. 826, as explained in *Fitzgerald* v. *Lane* [1988] 3 W.L.R. 356.

responsibility *inter se* is equal then, assuming both to be solvent, each one will finally bear 25 per cent. of the loss. If, however, the court concludes that the plaintiff is only one third to blame, then the correct judgment is for two-thirds of the damage against both defendants, even though the plaintiff is as much at fault as either defendant.[86]

---

[86] *Fitzgerald* v. *Lane, supra.*

CHAPTER 7

BREACH OF STATUTORY DUTY[1]

EXISTENCE OF LIABILITY

THIS chapter is not concerned with statutes which have as their principal objective the imposition of tort liability[2] nor with the circumstances in which the courts may pay regard to a statutory requirement or standard in deciding whether the defendant's conduct amounts to negligence.[3] What it is concerned with is when a court will conclude that a statute which is primarily regulatory or criminal in its purpose should be treated as giving rise to a civil action at the suit of a person who is injured as a result of non-compliance with it. Fundamentally, the question is one of interpretation of the particular statute but enough case law has accumulated around the subject to require treatment in a book on torts.

Before looking at the approach of the courts to this question of interpretation something should be said about the nature of the action for breach of statutory duty. In purely numerical terms, the most important area of operation of the tort of breach of statutory duty is that concerned with industrial safety and there is, of course, no doubt that an employer owes his employee a duty of care for the purposes of the tort of negligence. The English view is that liability for breach of statutory duty is a wholly separate tort superimposed on this, but this is not the approach of all common law countries, nor, indeed, of all the cases here. In *Lochgelly Iron & Coal Co.* v. *M'Mullan*[4] an action was brought under the Coal Mines Act 1911[5] in respect of an accident caused by the collapse of a roof in a mine and it became necessary to decide whether breach of the statutory duty amounted to "personal negligence" for the purposes of the Workmen's Compensation Act 1925. The House of Lords held that it did and that the action was in substance one for negligence, the only important difference being that "whereas at the ordinary law the standard of the duty must be fixed by the verdict of the jury,[6] the statutory duty is conclusively fixed by the statute."[7]

---

[1] Stanton, *Breach of Statutory Duty in Tort*; Buckley, "Liability in Tort for Breach of Statutory Duty" (1984) 100 L.Q.R. 204; Williams, "The Effect of Penal Legislation in the Law of Tort" (1960) 23 M.L.R. 233; Weir, *Casebook on Tort*, (6th ed.), Chap. 3.
[2] *e.g.* the Occupiers' Liability Act 1957 (Chap. 9) and the Consumer Protection Act 1987, Pt. I (Chap. 10).
[3] See *ante*, p. 118.
[4] [1934] A.C. 1.
[5] Now the Mines and Quarries Act 1954.
[6] Now, of course, the judge.
[7] [1934] A.C. at p. 23, *per* Lord Wright.

This view approximates to that taken in the majority of jurisdictions in the United States that, in accident cases, breach of a statute is negligence *per se* and is tantamount to saying that the statute "concretises" the common law duty by putting beyond controversy the question whether reasonable care in the circumstances required that a particular precaution be taken. Other American states adopt the view that the statutory standard is compelling evidence of what reasonable care demands but in the last resort does not bind the court, a view taken since 1983 in Canada.[8] There are attractions in these views where a common law duty exists, for they relieve the court of the task of searching for a legislative intention on civil liability, but where there is no common law duty it would amount to rejecting statute as a source of civil liability, a view which is inconsistent with English law as it stands.[9] In any event, even where there is a common law duty the overwhelming weight of authority is to the effect that the action for breach of statutory duty is a separate tort. There have been many decisions in which a defendant has been acquitted of negligence but held liable on the same facts for breach of statutory duty[10] and, contrariwise, cases in which the defendant has fulfilled his statutory duty but has nevertheless been held guilty of negligence,[11] for the statutory duty may be higher or lower than that imposed by the common law. Furthermore, it does not seem satisfactory or even sensible to describe as a failure to take care the breach of such duties as the unqualified obligation that dangerous parts of machinery shall be "securely fenced."[12] Dealing with regulations[13] governing pedestrian crossings Lord Wright in *L.P.T.B.* v. *Upson*[14] expressed the approach of the English courts as follows:

> "A claim for damages for breach of a statutory duty intended to protect a person in the position of the particular plaintiff is a specific common law right which is not to be confused in essence with a claim for negligence ... I have desired before I deal specifically with the regulations to make it clear how in my judgment they should be approached, and also to make it clear that a claim for their breach may stand or fall independently of negligence. There is always a danger if the claim is not sufficiently specific that the due consideration of the claim for breach of statutory duty may be prejudiced if it is confused with the claim in negligence."

---

[8] *R.* v. *Saskatchewan Wheat Pool* (1983) 143 D.L.R. (3d) 9; Matthews (1984) 4 O.J.L.S. 429; Rogers [1984] C.L.J. 23. However, U.S. federal law does recognise the concept of breach of statutory duty as a distinct tort. The implication of tort causes of action from the Constitution and civil rights legislation has been particularly important since *Bivens* v. *Six Unknown Agents* 403 U.S. 388 (1971).

[9] See, *e.g. Ashby* v. *White* (1703) 2 Ld.Raym. 938; *Monk* v. *Warbey* [1935] 1 K.B. 75; *Sephton* v. *Lancashire River Board* [1962] 1 W.L.R. 623; *Ekland* v. *Scripglow Ltd.* [1982] F.S.R. 431.

[10] See, *e.g. Kelly* v. *W.R.N. Contracting Ltd.* [1968] 1 W.L.R. 921; *Denyer* v. *Charles Skipper and East Ltd.* [1970] 1 W.L.R. 1087. The statute might expressly or impliedly abolish the common law liability but there is no presumption that such is its effect.

[11] See, *e.g. Kilgollan* v. *William Cooke & Co.* [1956] 1 W.L.R. 527; *Bux* v. *Slough Metals Ltd.* [1973] 1 W.L.R. 1358. *cf. Quintas* v. *National Smelting Co.* [1961] 1 W.L.R. 401, in which Sellers and Danckwerts L.JJ. held the defendants liable for negligence, but not for breach of the Factories Act, and Willmer L.J. thought they were not liable for negligence, but were in breach of the Act.

[12] Factories Act 1961, s.14(1). See *John Summers Ltd.* v. *Frost* [1955] A.C. 740, *post*, p. 199.

[13] The action for breach of statutory duty applies to subordinate legislation as much as to statutes proper.

[14] [1949] A.C. 155, 168–169.

The question, then, is when a private right of action in tort[15] will be inferred from the existence of the statutory duty. When Parliament has clearly stated its intention one way or the other no difficulty arises[16] but all too often this is not the case. Until the nineteenth century the view seems to have been taken that whenever a statutory duty is created, any person who can show that he has sustained harm from its non-performance can bring an action against the person on whom the duty is imposed.[17] During the first half of the nineteenth century, however, a different view began to be taken,[18] and in *Atkinson* v. *Newcastle Waterworks Co.*[19] the Court of Appeal's doubts about the old rule were so strong as to amount to disapproval of it. With the vast increase in legislative activity, the old rule was perceived to carry the risk of liability wider than the legislature could have contemplated, particularly in relation to public authorities. Since that time, therefore, the plaintiff has generally been required to point to some indication in the statute that it was intended to give rise to a civil action.

Where, as is normally the case, the only express sanction contained in the statute is a criminal penalty, the law was stated by the House of Lords in *Lonrho Ltd.* v. *Shell Petroleum Co. Ltd. (No. 2)*[20] to be that there is no civil action unless *either* the obligation or prohibition was imposed for the benefit or protection of a particular class of individuals "as in the case of the Factories Acts and similar legislation" *or* the statute created a public right and the plaintiff suffered "special damage peculiar to himself" from interference with that right. The first category may be regarded as summarising those matters which have led the courts to the conclusion that a civil action lies, and these are considered in more detail below. The second category is obscure. It bears some resemblance to the principle upon which an individual can sue for public nuisance (one of the cases cited being on that tort[21]) but the principal authority cited by Lord Diplock concerned not an action for damages but whether a member of the public could, without the assistance of the Attorney-General, seek an injunction to restrain an interference with public rights.[22] However, it was said in *Lonrho* that "a mere prohibition on members of the public generally from doing what it would otherwise be lawful for them to do is not enough" to create a public right for this purpose. In other words, even if this category creates an independent head of breach of statutory duty a plaintiff who has failed to show that the criminal statute

---

[15] The action is properly an action in tort, even though the duty arises from statute: *American Express Co.* v. *British Airways Board* [1983] 1 W.L.R. 701 (action "in tort" within s.29(1) of the Post Office Act 1969); *Philip Morris Ltd.* v. *Ainley* [1975] V.R. 345.

[16] See, *e.g.* Mines and Quarries Act 1954, s.159; Resale Prices Act 1964, s.4(2); Guard Dogs Act 1975, s.5; Safety of Sports Grounds Act 1975, s.13; Building Act 1984, s.38; Telecommunications Act 1984, s.18(6)(a); Fire Safety and Places of Sport Act 1987, s.12.

[17] "Where-ever a statute enacts anything, or prohibits anything, for the advantage of any person, that person shall have remedy to recover the advantage given him, or to have satisfaction for the injury done him contrary to the law by the same statute; for it would be a fine thing to make a law by which one has a right, but no remedy in equity": *Anon.* (1704) 6 Mod. 26, *per* Holt C.J. Com.Dig.tit. "Action upon Statute," F; *Ashby* v. *White* (1703) 2 Ld. Raym. 938; *Couch* v. *Steel* (1854) 3 E. & B. 402.

[18] *Doe d. Murray* v. *Bridges* (1831) 1 B. & Ad. 847.

[19] (1877) 2 Ex.D. 441.

[20] [1982] A.C. 173; Weir, *Casebook on Tort* (6th ed.), p. 153.

[21] *Benjamin* v. *Storr* (1874) L.R. 9 C.P. 400.

[22] *Boyce* v. *Paddington B.C.* [1903] 1 Ch. 109.

infringed by the defendant gives him a direct right of action (the first category) is not very likely to succeed by this route either.[23]

On the question of whether the statute confers a private right of action, "the only rule which in all circumstances is valid is that the answer must depend on a consideration of the whole Act and the circumstances, including the pre-existing law, in which it was enacted."[24] Unfortunately, statutes all too rarely contain very much in the way of a clear indication on this matter and various presumptions have been developed by the courts. First, it is said that where a duty is imposed by statute but no sanction of any kind is provided, there is a presumption that a person injured by it has a right of action.[25] It has, however, been pointed out that in some cases this could lead to surprising results for it is precisely those duties of a "politically sensitive" nature involving wide discretion which are likely to be couched in these terms.[26] In the great majority of cases, however, some sanction, whether criminal or administrative, will be contained in the statute and it has been said that "where an Act creates an obligation, and enforces the performance in a specified manner, we take it to be a general rule that performance cannot be enforced in any other manner."[27] Where the statute provides its own administrative machinery for redress (for example, by appeal to the Minister) the court may adopt this approach[28] but the authorities are by no means consistent.[29] Nor has the existence of the general remedy of judicial review of administrative action necessarily deterred the courts from finding a duty actionable by an individual.[30] Reluctance to impose liability against public bodies is probably based upon a fear of overturning, by this route, the general principle that *ultra vires* action does not of itself give rise to a claim for damages. In *Bourgoin S.A.* v. *Ministry of Agriculture, Fisheries and Food*[31] the plaintiffs were French importers of turkeys into the United Kingdom and their licence to import was revoked by the defendants as part

---

[23] Another of the law's mysteries is the case of *Emperor of Austria* v. *Day and Kossuth* (1861) 3 De. G.F. & J. 217. The plaintiff obtained an injunction to restrain the printing of forged Austrian bank notes here on the grounds of an "injury to property." The House of Lords has said that a cause of action in private law which attracted only an injunction against future harm but not damages for harm already suffered, would be "wholly novel" (*Garden Cottage Foods Ltd.* v. *Milk Marketing Board* [1984] A.C. 130) but it is not obvious what the cause of action in the *Emperor of Austria* case was. Browne-Wilkinson V.-C. followed the case in *Kingdom of Spain* v. *Christie Manson & Woods Ltd.* [1986] 1 W.L.R. 1120, but Hoffmann J. in *Associated Newspapers* v. *Insert Media Ltd.* [1988] 1 W.L.R. 509 declined to accept that it could extend to restrain "unfair trading" which was not actionable as one of the economic torts.

[24] *Cutler* v. *Wandsworth Stadium Ltd.* [1949] A.C. 398, 407, *per* Lord Simonds; *ibid.* at p. 412, *per* Lord Normand; *Ministry of Housing* v. *Sharp* [1970] 2 Q.B. 223, 272, *per* Salmon L.J.

[25] *Doe d. Murray* v. *Bridges* (1831) 1 B. & Ad. 847, 859, *per* Lord Tenterden C.J.; *Square* v. *Model Farm Dairies (Bournemouth) Ltd.* [1939] 2 K.B. 365, 375, *per* Slesser L.J.; *Cutler* v. *Wandsworth Stadium Ltd.* [1949] A.C. 398, 407, *per* Lord Simonds; *Att.-Gen.* v. *St. Ives R.D.C.* [1960] 1 Q.B. 312; *Reffell* v. *Surrey C.C.* [1964] 1 W.L.R. 358; *Thornton* v. *Kirklees B.C.* [1979] Q.B. 626; *cf. Wyatt* v. *Hillingdon B.C.* [1978] 76 L.G.R. 727.

[26] Stanton, *op. cit.*, p. 36.

[27] *Doe d. Murray* v. *Bridges* (1831) 1 B. & Ad. 847, 859, *per* Lord Tenterden C.J.

[28] *Wyatt* v. *Hillingdon B.C.* (1978) 76 L.G.R. 727 (Chronically Sick and Disabled Persons Act 1970).

[29] *Meade* v. *Haringey B.C.* [1979] 1 W.L.R. 637 (but this was a claim for an injunction and *cf. Watt* v. *Kesteven C.C.* [1955] 1 Q.B. 408). An actionable statutory duty was found in another education case, *Reffell* v. *Surrey C.C.* [1964] 1 W.L.R. 358, but that was concerned with safety.

[30] *Thornton* v. *Kirklees M.B.C.* [1979] Q.B. 626 (Housing (Homeless Persons) Act 1977). However, since *Cocks* v. *Thanet D.C.* [1983] 2 A.C. 286 such claims involving the exercise of discretion would have to be brought under R.S.C., Ord. 53 (*ante*, p. 100).

[31] [1986] Q.B. 716; Cripps [1986] C.L.J. 165.

of a campaign to prevent the spread of "Newcastle disease." This action was declared by the European Court of Justice to be a contravention of Article 30 of the EEC Treaty.[32] The defendants thereupon issued a new licence but the plaintiffs claimed damages for loss of trade in the intervening period. The House of Lords had held in *Garden Cottage Foods Ltd.* v. *Milk Marketing Board*[33] that directly applicable provisions of the Treaty might give rise to a civil action for damages but that case was concerned with Article 86 (abuse of a dominant market position). Article 30 was also directly applicable, but the majority of the Court of Appeal held that the EEC Treaty did not require a national court to impose a liability in damages for its breach. The acts in question in the *Garden Cottage* case were such as were likely to be committed by non-governmental bodies and the Article created essentially private law rights. In contrast, Article 30 was concerned with the acts of a public officer and if the duty in question had been imposed by domestic legislation it was axiomatic that no action for damages would have lain.[34] The Treaty conferred private rights in the sense that it conferred *locus standi* upon a person affected by breach of Article 30 to seek judicial review, but it did not require any radical departure from the pattern of English remedies for *ultra vires* acts.

The *Bourgoin* case was decided on a preliminary issue of law so there had been no trial on the facts. However, an alternative basis of the plaintiff's claim was that the defendants had been guilty of the common law tort of "misfeasance in a public office."[35] This tort requires either malice[36] or knowledge that the act is invalid and must necessarily injure the plaintiff. It is not confined to statutory duties as such,[36a] but the mental element required means that it is much narrower in its scope than any broad principle of liability for *ultra vires* acts.

The unreliability of reasoning based upon the enforcement procedures contained in the statute is demonstrated by *Groves* v. *Wimborne*.[37] The statute[38] made an occupier of a factory, who did not properly fence dangerous machinery, liable to a fine of £100; and it provided that the whole or any part of the fine might be applied, if the Secretary of State should so determine, for the benefit of the person injured by the occupier's neglect. A boy employed in the factory of the defendant was caught by an unfenced cogwheel and his arm had to be amputated. The Court of Appeal held that he

---

[32] Which deals with quantitative restrictions on imports between member states.

[33] [1984] A.C. 130, *post*, p. 496.

[34] [1986] Q.B. 716, 789, *per* Nourse L.J. See also *Calveley* v. *Chief Constable of Merseyside* [1989] 2 W.L.R. 624 (notice under police discipline regulations; breach of requirement giving rise only to judicial review).

[35] Having been recognised by the Privy Council in *David* v. *Abdul Cader* [1963] 1 W.L.R. 834 the tort was described by the same court as "well established" in *Dunlop* v. *Woollahra Municipal Council* [1982] A.C. 158.

[36] As in *Roncarelli* v. *Duplessis* (1959) 16 D.L.R. (2d) 689. In *Calveley's* case, *supra*, the H.L. left open the possibility that the tort might be committed where the act was done "without reasonable cause." But the making of a malicious report during the course of an investigation was not an act done by the officer by virtue of the power conferred or given by his office (though it might be defamation).

[36a] See *Jones* v. *Swansea C.C.* [1989] N.L.J. 503 (local authority landlord refusing consent for change of use of leased premises).

[37] [1898] 2 Q.B. 402.

[38] Factory and Workshop Act 1878.

was entitled to recover damages in a civil action. The court reasoned that there was no *certainty* that any part of the fine would be awarded to the victim and, even if it were awarded, its upper limit of £100, it was said, made it incredible that Parliament would have regarded that as a sufficient and exclusive compensation for mutilation or death. Nevertheless, since Parliament had expressly adverted to the matter of compensation and the common law of negligence applied to the relationship between employer and employee,[39] there was some force in the argument that no civil claim was intended.[40] Perhaps a court today would be more ready to take the view that the alternative remedy excluded a civil action, but *Groves* v. *Wimborne* is nonetheless the progenitor of a long line of authority giving a civil remedy for breach of industrial safety legislation.

By far the most common sanction provided for non-performance of a statutory duty is a criminal penalty. No doubt it was this that led Lord Diplock in the *Lonrho* case to say that it was in these cases that the plaintiff might establish that a civil action would lie if the legislation was passed for the benefit of a particular class of individuals. In principle, however, the "class-protection" argument would seem open even if some non-criminal sanction were imposed by the Act in question. Atkin L.J. once denied the validity of this test for, as he said, "it would be strange if a less important duty, which is owed to a section of the public, may be enforced by action, while a more important duty owed to the public at large cannot."[41] However, it is firmly established in the law and was applied in *Rickless* v. *United Artists Corporation*[42] to confer a right of action upon a performer, parts of whose films had been made up, without his consent, into a new production, contrary to the Dramatic and Musical Performers' Protection Act 1958. The decision is a strong one because there were indications in the wording of the Act, in its history and in its relationship with the general law that no civil action lay.[43] On the other hand, bookmakers were not a class of persons intended to be protected by a provision in the Betting and Lotteries Act 1934 requiring the occupier of a dog track to provide space for them, the purpose of the statute being the regulation of dog racing[44]; and in *Atkinson* v. *Newcastle Waterworks Co.*[45] an Act requiring a water company to keep pipes, to which fire-plugs were fixed, charged with a certain pressure of water, was construed as in the nature of a bargain between the company and Parliament for the supply of water to the city rather than as creating a duty actionable by householders. The court regarded as startling the proposition

---

[39] Though to a more limited extent than today because of the doctrine of "common employment": see *post*, p. 185.

[40] Contrast *Atkinson* v. *Newcastle Waterworks Co.* (1877) 2 Ex.D. 441, where certain provisions of the statute provided that the penalty was payable to the aggrieved individual. It was conceded by the plaintiff that in these cases no civil remedy could arise: *ibid.* at p. 447.

[41] *Phillips* v. *Britannia Hygienic Laundry Co.* [1923] 2 K.B. 832, 841.

[42] [1988] Q.B. 40. The law has been modified by the Copyright, Designs and Patents Act 1988.

[43] But the Court of Appeal would have found in favour of the plaintiffs even if there had not been a dictum the same way in *Lonrho Ltd.* v. *Shell Petroleum Co. Ltd. (No. 2)* at [1982] A.C. 187. The maximum fine under the statute was £400; the award was $1,000,000 plus a percentage of the profits of the film. *cf. Groves* v. *Wimborne, supra.*

[44] *Cutler* v. *Wandsworth Stadium Ltd.* [1949] A.C. 398.

[45] (1877) 2 Ex.D. 441. *cf. Read* v. *Croydon Corp.* [1938] 4 All E.R. 631.

that the water company should become virtually insurers of the safety from fire, so far as water can produce that safety, of all the houses in the district. This is a variant of the "floodgates" argument familiar in the law of negligence and the courts in this context, too, are reluctant to impose civil liabilities where there is a very large number of potential claimants and the risk of crushing liability. Nonetheless, at least one "class"—that of employees for the purpose of industrial safety legislation—is very large indeed.

Sometimes an indication may be found in the wording of the statute itself as to whether a civil remedy is intended.[46] A common form of words in statute creating offences is that "nothing in this Act shall be taken to prejudice any liability or remedy to which a person guilty of an offence thereunder may be subject in civil proceedings," but such words do not create civil liability, they merely preserve whatever liability (*e.g.* for negligence or trespass) may exist apart from the statute.[47] It has also been said that, although the point is far from decisive, it is easier to spell out a civil right if Parliament has expressly stated that something is unlawful and then provided a penalty, rather than merely saying that "it is an offence to do such-and-such"[48] but this is a very tenuous basis for imposing civil liability. More important is the relationship of the claimed civil right of action with the general law.

Some decisions are capable of supporting the thesis that a court will not impose civil liability when the common law already contains adequate remedies to enforce private rights. Thus in *McCall* v. *Abelesz*[49] the Court of Appeal, in denying that the crime of harassment of tenants in section 30 of the Rent Act 1965[50] gave rise to civil liability, laid stress upon the fact that many acts of harassment by a landlord must inevitably involve trespass or breach of contract.[51] This, of course, leaves the question of what is "adequate": Atkin L.J. in *Phillips* v. *Britannia Hygienic Laundry Co.*,[52] in rejecting the contention that the regulations governing the construction and use of motor vehicles gave rise to civil liability, spoke of highway accidents being "already well provided for" by the common law, but that is a view that would not necessarily command widespread assent today. In any event, this approach has never prevented the courts from holding that an action lies for breach of industrial safety legislation, notwithstanding the existence of the employer's duties at common law. More convincing (though once again industrial accident cases may have to be treated as an exception to it) is the view that the courts will, in the absence of clear indications to the contrary,

---

[46] In *Keating* v. *Elvan Reinforced Concrete Co. Ltd.* [1968] 1 W.L.R. 722, the fact that the Public Utilities Street Works Act 1950 contained provisions creating civil liabilities in favour of public authorities was regarded as a reason for holding that it gave no right of action to individuals.

[47] *McCall* v. *Abelesz* [1976] Q.B. 585.

[48] *Rickless* v. *United Artists Corp.* [1988] Q.B. 40, 51, where, however, the court concluded that a civil action lay despite the latter form of words being used.

[49] [1976] Q.B. 585; *cf. Warder* v. *Cooper* [1970] Ch. 495, which may not survive *McCall* v. *Abelesz.*

[50] For the present law, which does give rise to tort liability, see the Housing Act 1988, Pt. I, Ch. IV.

[51] But any statutory remedy would not be redundant. Acts like cutting off main services could only be actionable in contract and exemplary damages may be recovered in tort, but not in contract: *post*, p. 605.

[52] [1923] 2 K.B. 832. *Square* v. *Model Farm Dairies Ltd.* [1939] 2 K.B. 365.

lean against a statutory duty which would contradict the general pattern of liability in a particular area of activity but will find one which will support or supplement it. This would explain why the courts have consistently rejected[53] road traffic legislation as a direct source of civil liability, for the effect would have been to introduce isolated pockets of strict liability into an area generally governed by negligence. At the same time, however, it would support the decision in *Monk* v. *Warbey*.[54] The defendant permitted his car to be driven by an uninsured driver and thereby committed an offence against section 35 of the Road Traffic Act 1930.[55] Owing to the negligence of that driver the plaintiff was injured but could recover no damages against him as he was destitute of means. It was held that the plaintiff could claim this loss against the defendant owner.[56] The damage was, of course, financial in nature[57] and such damage was not then and is not now so easily recoverable at common law as physical injury, but the Act did not derogate from the basic common law principle that only victims of *negligence* on the highway should recover: rather it supported that principle by creating machinery whereby judgments in favour of such victims might be more readily satisfied.[58]

The law on inferring civil actions from statutory duties is not very satisfactory and Lord Denning M.R. commented with perhaps a little pardonable exaggeration that the legislature "has left the courts with a guess-work puzzle. The dividing line between the pro-cases and the contra-cases is so blurred and so ill-defined that you might as well toss a coin to decide it."[59] As Lord du Parcq pointed out[60] the draftsmen of Acts of Parliament are aware of the principles—and lack of principles—applied by the courts to fill the gaps·left in legislation, and it can be argued, therefore, that the silence of a statute on the question of civil remedies for its breach is a deliberate invitation to the courts to decide the question for themselves. Certainly it should not be assumed that where the statute is silent this is because its promoters have not adverted to the point—much more likely that it would be politically inconvenient to attempt to answer the question one way or the

---

[53] *Phillips* v. *Britannia Hygienic Laundry*, *supra*; *Badham* v. *Lambs Ltd.* [1946] K.B. 45; *Clarke* v. *Brims* [1947] K.B. 497; *Coote* v. *Stone* [1971] 1 W.L.R. 279. The only exception appears to be *L.P.T.B.* v. *Upson* [1949] A.C. 155 (breach of the Pedestrian Crossing Regulations). Conversely, the fact that the common law afforded no remedy to a highway user for injury caused by straying animals (but see now the Animals Act 1971, s.8(1), *post*, p. 457) did not lead the courts to grant a civil remedy for the statutory *offence* of allowing animals to stray on to the highway: *Heath's Garage Ltd.* v. *Hodges* [1916] 2 K.B. 370.

[54] [1935] 1 K.B. 75.

[55] See now the Road Traffic Act 1988, s.143.

[56] The court must look at the realities of the matter, and it is not necessary to show that the driver will *never* pay; *Martin* v. *Dean* [1971] 2 Q.B. 208.

[57] The defendant, who had no reason to doubt the driver's competence, had not in any legally relevant sense caused the plaintiff to be injured.

[58] See [1935] 1 K.B. 75, 86. Where the lack of insurance has no connection with the loss suffered, *Monk* v. *Warbey* does not apply: *Daniels* v. *Vaux* [1938] 2 K.B. 203; nor where there is no criminal liability under the Road Traffic Act: *Goodbarne* v. *Buck* [1940] 1 K.B. 771; *Gregory* v. *Ford* [1951] 1 All E.R. 121. *Monk* v. *Warbey* is now of less significance to plaintiffs since a claim against the uninsured driver will be met by the Motor Insurers Bureau (*ante*, p. 26). But the Bureau may still require the plaintiff to obtain and assign to it a judgment against any person liable.

[59] *Ex p. Island Records* [1978] Ch. 132, 134–135.

[60] *Cutler* v. *Wandsworth Stadium Ltd.* [1949] A.C. 398, 411; *Solomons* v. *R. Gertzenstein Ltd.* [1954] 2 Q.B. 243, 267, *per* Romer L.J.

other. If this is so, then the pretence of seeking for the non-existent intention of Parliament should be abandoned. Not only does it involve an unnecessary fiction, but it may lead to decisions being made on the basis of insignificant details of phraseology instead of matters of substance. If the question whether a person injured by breach of statutory duty is to have a right of action for damages is in truth a question to be decided by the courts, then it should be acknowledged as such and some useful principles of law developed, if that is possible.[61] If it is not, then at least a clear overall presumption might help.[62] At least it can be said that there are numerous decisions on particular statutes so that in many cases it is already settled that a right of action does or does not exist.[63] Even where a right of action has been held to exist, however, it is not enough for the plaintiff simply to prove breach of the statute. There are other elements in the tort which we must now consider. We may, however, note that where the statute creates a criminal offence the victim may choose to seek a compensation order from the criminal court, a procedure which is not dependent upon the establishing of a civil right of action. Though applicable to all criminal offences outside the road traffic field, this mechanism has so far been of limited importance in the type of case considered in this chapter but its role in compensating losses may be expected to increase.[64]

ELEMENTS OF THE TORT

Duty must be owed to the plaintiff

Some statutory duties are so expressed as to limit the classes of person for whose benefit they exist, and where this is so it is a question of the construction of the statutory provision in question whether the plaintiff is a member of the protected class. If he is not, then his action for breach of statutory duty cannot succeed. In *Hartley* v. *Mayoh & Co.*,[65] for example, a fireman was electrocuted while fighting a fire at the defendants' factory. His widow relied, *inter alia*, upon a breach by the defendants of their obligations under certain statutory regulations, but these existed only for the protection of "persons employed," and firemen did not come within this description. The claim for breach of statutory duty therefore failed.

Injury must be of the kind which the statute is intended to prevent

If the object of the statute was to prevent mischief of a particular kind, one

---

[61] For a case decided by reference to principle and policy rather than the supposed intention of Parliament, see *Hargreaves* v. *Bretherton* [1959] 1 Q.B. 45 (no action in tort for perjury).

[62] The Law Commission suggested a general presumption in favour of actionability: Law Com. No. 21 (1969). Stanton, *loc. cit.*, pp. 54–55 argues for a presumption the other way.

[63] Professor Glanville Williams' statement that when legislation concerns industrial welfare it results in absolute liability while in all other cases it is ignored ((1960) 23 M.L.R. 233), an admitted oversimplification, is perhaps less true now than when it was written. It is also the case that many statutory duties are less than absolute: *Ministry of Housing* v. *Sharp* [1970] 2 Q.B. 223 and *post*, p. 180.

[64] For the powers of the criminal court, see *ante*, p. 10.

[65] [1954] 1 Q.B. 383; *Wingrove* v. *Prestige & Co.* [1954] 1 W.L.R. 524; *Herbert* v. *Harold Shaw Ltd.* [1959] 2 Q.B. 138. *cf. Lavender* v. *Diamints Ltd.* [1949] 1 K.B. 585; *Canadian Pacific Steamships Ltd.* v. *Bryers* [1958] A.C. 485; *Smith* v. *Supreme Wood Pulp Co. Ltd.* [1968] 3 All E.R. 753.

who suffers from its non-observance loss of a different kind cannot twist its remedy into an action for his own recoupment. In *Gorris* v. *Scott*[66] the defendant, a shipowner, was under a statutory duty to provide pens for cattle on his ship in order to lessen the risk of murrain among them. The plaintiff's sheep were swept overboard in consequence of lack of such pens. The defendant was held not liable, because it was no part of the purpose of the statute to protect cattle against the perils of the sea.[67] The modern tendency is, however, not to apply this decision too strictly,[68] and it has been said that if the plaintiff's damage is of the kind that the statute was designed to prevent, then it does not matter that it occurred in a way not contemplated by the statute.[69] On the other hand the House of Lords has affirmed that a workman who is injured by a dangerous part of machinery which flies out of a machine and hits him cannot base a claim on the statutory obligation that dangerous parts of machinery "shall be securely fenced."[70] The object of this provision, it has been said is "to keep the worker out, not to keep the machine or its product in."[71] It is only if he comes into contact with the dangerous part of the machine, therefore, that the workman can rely upon breach of the obligation to fence, and an injury caused in a different way is not covered.

Defendant must be guilty of a breach of his statutory obligation

Two points must be noted here. In the first place, many statutes and statutory regulations have strictly defined spheres of application, and outside their proper sphere they are irrelevant. To take a typical example, the Shipbuilding and Ship-repairing Regulations 1960, which lay down an elaborate code of safety precautions to be observed in the construction and repair of ships, do not in general apply to the construction and repair of ships not exceeding 100 feet in length; and many actions for injury caused by acts or omissions which would have amounted to breaches of the Factories Acts had they occurred in a factory have failed on the ground that the place where they in fact occurred was not a factory as defined.[72] In *Chipchase* v. *British Titan Products Co.*[73] a workman was injured when he fell from a platform

---

[66] (1874) L.R. 9 Exch. 125; Weir, *Casebook on Tort*, (6th ed.), p. 194; *Larrimore* v. *American National Insurance Co.* 89 P. 2d 340 (1939); *Bailey* v. *Ayr Engineering Co. Ltd.* [1959] 1 Q.B. 183.

[67] This decision may easily be misunderstood unless it is realised that the plaintiffs made no claim whatever apart from the statute. If, quite apart from this statutory duty, the defendant had been negligent so that the sheep would have been washed overboard, pens or no pens, then the plaintiffs could have recovered either for breach of contract or for the tort of negligence. As it was, they relied on the statutory obligation and on nothing else.

[68] *Grant* v. *National Coal Board* [1958] A.C. 649; *Gatehouse* v. *John Summers & Sons Ltd.* [1953] 1 W.L.R. 742; *Littler* v. *G.L. Moore (Contractors) Ltd.* [1967] 1 W.L.R. 1241; *Donaghey* v. *Boulton & Paul Ltd.* [1968] A.C. 1; *McInally* v. *Frank B. Price & Co. (Roofings) Ltd.* 1971 S.L.T.(Notes) 43.

[69] *Donaghey* v. *Boulton & Paul Ltd.*, *supra*, at p. 26, *per* Lord Reid. Note the similarity to the development at common law subsequent to *The Wagon Mound*.

[70] Factories Act 1961, s.14; *Close* v. *Steel Co. of Wales Ltd.* [1962] A.C. 367 (Lords Denning and Morris dissenting on this point); *Sparrow* v. *Fairey Aviation Co. Ltd.* [1964] A.C. 1019.

[71] *Nicholls* v. *F. Austin (Leyton) Ltd.* [1946] A.C. 493, 505, *per* Lord Simonds.

[72] An example is *Longhurst* v. *Guildford, etc., Water Board* [1963] A.C. 265.

[73] [1956] 1 Q.B. 545. *cf. Blamires* v. *Lancashire & Yorkshire Ry.* (1873) L.R. & Ex. 283; *Thomas Stone Shipping Ltd.* v. *Admiralty* [1953] P. 117; *Butt* v. *Inner London Authority* (1968) 118 New L.J. 254.

nine inches wide and six feet above the ground. Statutory regulations required that "every working platform from which a person is liable to fall more than six feet and six inches shall be . . . at least 34 inches wide"[74] and it was argued that the case was so nearly within the regulations that the court ought to take them into account. The argument was rejected and the defendants were held not liable either for breach of statutory duty, for there was none, or for negligence at common law.

The second point which it is necessary to make is that the measure of the defendant's obligation in every case must be found in the statute itself and that no single standard of conduct exists. In some cases the statute imposes an unqualified obligation, *i.e.* an absolute duty, that a certain state of affairs shall exist, and in such cases the non-existence of that state of affairs constitutes the breach.[75] In *John Summers & Sons Ltd.* v. *Frost*,[76] for example, a workman in a factory was injured when his thumb came into contact with a revolving grinding wheel. The Factories Act required[77] that "every dangerous part of any machinery . . . shall be securely fenced," and there was a hood over the grinding wheel which covered most of it. There was, however, a part of the wheel unguarded and if this had not been so the grinding wheel could not have been used. It was held that there had been a breach of the statutory obligation that dangerous parts be "securely fenced," and that it was no answer that secure fencing of a grinding wheel would render it unusable. In other cases,[78] however, the obligation may be qualified by some such words as "so far as is reasonably practicable," and where this is so, it has been said, the obligation adds little to that which exists at common law.[79] Again, the obligation may be "to take such steps as may be necessary"[80] and this, it appears, falls somewhere between the duty that a given state of affairs shall exist and a duty that it shall exist "so far as is reasonably practicable." That the necessary steps were not reasonably practicable will be no answer to an allegation of breach of this duty, but there will be no breach if the necessity of the steps was not and could not have been known before the event.[81]

---

[74] Building (Safety, Health and Welfare) Regulations 1948, reg. 22(*c*). Now Construction (Working Places) Regulations 1966, reg. 26(1).

[75] *Galashiels Gas Co.* v. *Millar* [1949] A.C. 275. "The fact that the rung gave way establishes . . . beyond question that the ladder was not in an efficient state and was not in good repair at that time"; *Cole* v. *Blackstone & Co.* [1943] K.B. 615, *per* Macnaghten J.; *Reffell* v. *Surrey C.C.* [1964] 1 W.L.R. 358.

[76] [1955] A.C. 740; *Davies* v. *Owen* [1919] 2 K.B. 39.

[77] Factories Act 1937, s.14(1). Now the Factories Act 1961, s.14(1).

[78] Including other sections of the Factories Act itself.

[79] *Levesley* v. *Thomas Firth & John Brown Ltd.* [1953] 1 W.L.R. 1206, 1210, *per* Denning L.J. referring to the Factories Act 1937, s.26(1) (now the Factories Act 1961, s.29(1)); *cf. Trott* v. *W. E. Smith* [1957] 1 W.L.R. 1154; *Jenkins* v. *Allied Ironfounders Ltd.* [1970] 1 W.L.R. 304. For cases where a duty of care which would not have existed at common law was created by statute, see *Sephton* v. *Lancashire River Board* [1962] 1 W.L.R. 623; *Ministry of Housing* v. *Sharp* [1970] 2 Q.B. 223. Where the duty is to the effect that something shall be done "so far as is reasonably practicable" it is for the defendant to prove the impracticability, not for the plaintiff to prove that it was reasonably practicable: *Nimmo* v. *Alexander Cowan & Sons Ltd.* [1968] A.C. 107.

[80] *e.g.* Mines and Quarries Act 1954, s.48.

[81] *Brown* v. *National Coal Board* [1962] A.C. 574; [1961] 1 Q.B. 603 (C.A.); Hamson [1961] C.L.J. 20; [1962] C.L.J. 26; *Tomlinson* v. *Beckermet Mining Co. Ltd.* [1964] 1 W.L.R. 1043; *John G. Stein & Co. Ltd.* v. *O'Hanlon* [1965] A.C. 890.

Breach of duty must have caused the damage

In an action for breach of statutory duty, as in an action for common law negligence, the plaintiff bears the burden of proving the causal connection between the breach of duty and the damage.[82] There is, however, one rather special kind of case, peculiar to actions for breach of statutory duty, which must be mentioned, namely that in which the act or omission of the plaintiff himself has the legal result that both plaintiff and defendant are in breach of the same duty.

In *Ginty* v. *Belmont Building Supplies Ltd.*[83] the plaintiff was an experienced workman in the employment of the defendants who were roofing contractors. Statutory regulations binding upon both parties required that crawling boards should be used for work done on fragile roofs and, although boards had been provided by the defendants, the plaintiff neglected to use them and fell through a roof in consequence. In law both plaintiff and defendants were in breach of their statutory duties, but Pearson J. held that the plaintiff's claim failed altogether because the defendants' breach consisted of and was co-extensive with his own wrongful act.[84] In other words, there was no wrongful act but the plaintiff's own, and "it would be absurd if, notwithstanding the employer having done all he could reasonably be expected to do to ensure compliance, a workman, who deliberately disobeyed his employer's orders and thereby put the employer in breach of a regulation, could claim damages for injury caused to him solely by his own wrongdoing."[85]

Although the result reached in *Ginty* v. *Belmont Building Supplies Ltd.* has been judicially described as "obvious,"[86] the scope of the decision is restricted. If the plaintiff establishes the defendant's breach of duty and that he suffered injury as a result, he establishes a prima facie case against the defendant. The defendant will escape liability only if he can rebut that prima facie case by proof that the only act or default of anyone which caused the breach was that of the plaintiff himself.[87] It follows that where some fault is to be attributed to the defendant, as where an employer calls upon a workman to do a job beyond his proper competence,[88] fails to provide adequate instructions or supervision,[89] is responsible for some independent

---

[82] *Bonnington Castings Ltd.* v. *Wardlaw* [1956] A.C. 613; *McWilliams* v. *Sir William Arrol & Co.* [1962] 1 W.L.R. 295 (H.L.); *Wigley* v. *British Vinegars Ltd.* [1964] A.C. 307; *Lineker* v. *Raleigh Industries* [1980] I.C.R. 83. For the contrary view, overruled by later cases, see *Vyner* v. *Waldenberg Bros. Ltd.* [1946] K.B. 50. It is enough if the plaintiff establishes on a balance of probabilities that the breach of duty contributed materially to the damage: *ibid.*; *McGhee* v. *N.C.B.* [1973] 1 W.L.R. 1, *ante*, p. 134.

[83] [1959] 1 All E.R. 414; *Manwaring* v. *Billington* [1952] 2 All E.R. 747.

[84] [1959] 1 All E.R. 414, 424. *cf. P.O.* v. *Hampshire C.C.* [1980] Q.B. 124.

[85] *Boyle* v. *Kodak Ltd.* [1969] 1 W.L.R. 661, 665–666, *per* Lord Reid. "To say you are liable to me for my own wrongdoing is neither good morals nor good law": *ibid.* at p. 673, *per* Lord Diplock.

[86] *Donaghey* v. *Boulton & Paul Ltd.* [1968] A.C. 1, 24, *per* Lord Reid.

[87] *Boyle* v. *Kodak Ltd.* [1969] 1 W.L.R. 661, 672–673, *per* Lord Diplock.

[88] *Byers* v. *Head Wrightson & Co. Ltd.* [1961] 1 W.L.R. 961; *Ross* v. *Associated Portland Cement Manufacturers Ltd.* [1964] 1 W.L.R. 768 (H.L.).

[89] *Jenner* v. *Allen West & Co. Ltd.* [1959] 1 W.L.R. 554; *Ross* v. *Associated Portland Cement Manufacturers Ltd., supra*; *Boyle* v. *Kodak Ltd.* [1969] 1 W.L.R. 661.

fault,[90] or encourages him in his own breach of statutory duty,[91] then the plaintiff is entitled to recover some damages, even though they may be substantially reduced on account of his contributory negligence.

DEFENCES

Volenti non fit injuria[92]

It was for long thought that this defence was not available in actions for breach of statutory duty.[93] In 1964, however, the House of Lords held that this is only so where a workman sues his employer for breach of the employer's statutory duty.[94] In all other cases the defence is available,[95] subject to express contrary provision.

Contributory negligence

Before the Law Reform (Contributory Negligence) Act 1945 the contributory negligence of the plaintiff was a complete defence to an action for breach of statutory duty[96] and now, therefore, it is a reason for reducing the damages which he may recover. This matter has already been considered.[97]

Delegation

It is clear that in the ordinary way it is no defence for a person subjected to a statutory duty to claim that he has delegated the duty or its performance to another person.[98] In some cases, however, it seems to have been thought that delegation may be a defence where performance of the tasks necessary to secure compliance with the statutory obligation has been delegated to the plaintiff himself.[99] Nevertheless, although some specific requirements for the defence of delegation were laid down,[1] in no case did the plaintiff

---

[90] *McMath* v. *Rimmer Bros. (Liverpool) Ltd.* [1962] 1 W.L.R. 1; *Leach* v. *Standard Telephones & Cables Ltd.* [1966] 1 W.L.R. 1392. *Donaghey* v. *Boulton & Paul Ltd.* [1968] A.C. 1; *Keaney* v. *British Railways Board* [1968] 1 W.L.R. 879. It appears that the fault for which the employer is responsible need not be such as to suffice as an independent ground of action.

[91] *Barcock* v. *Brighton Corp.* [1949] 1 K.B. 339; *Laszczyk* v. *National Coal Board* [1954] 1 W.L.R. 1426.

[92] *Post*, pp. 682–697.

[93] *Baddeley* v. *Granville (Earl)* (1887) 19 Q.B.D. 423; *Wheeler* v. *New Merton Board Mills* [1933] 2 K.B. 669; *Alford* v. *N.C.B.* [1952] 1 All E.R. 754, 757, *per* Lord Normand.

[94] *Imperial Chemical Industries Ltd.* v. *Shatwell* [1965] A.C. 656.

[95] *Imperial Chemical Industries Ltd.* v. *Shatwell, supra,* concerned an action by a workman against his employer on the ground of a fellow employee's breach of statutory duty, but the generalisation is implicit in the reasoning of the House of Lords.

[96] *Caswell* v. *Powell Duffryn Associated Collieries* [1940] A.C. 152.

[97] *Ante,* pp. 166–167. A possible technical explanation of the result in *Ginty* v. *Belmont Building Supplies Ltd.* [1959] 1 All E.R. 414, *ante,* p. 181 (if one be needed), is that in that case the odd situation prevailed that the accident was caused *wholly* by the fault of the plaintiff *and wholly* by the (identical) fault of the defendant while the Act of 1945 governs the case where "any person suffers damage as the result *partly* of his own fault *and partly* of the fault of any other person." So the Act did not apply and at common law a person whose own fault was a cause of his injury can recover nothing: [1959] 1 All E.R. 414, 424, *per* Pearson J.

[98] *Gray* v. *Pullen* (1864) 5 B. & S. 970; *Whitby* v. *Burt, Boulton & Hayward Ltd.* [1947] K.B. 918. See *post,* p. 584.

[99] See, *e.g. Vincent* v. *Southern Ry.* [1927] A.C. 430; *Smith* v. *Baveystock & Co.* [1945] 1 All E.R. 531; *Vyner* v. *Waldenberg Bros.* [1946] K.B. 50; *Gallagher* v. *Dorman, Long & Co.* [1947] 2 All E.R. 38; *Barcock* v. *Brighton Corp.* [1949] 1 K.B. 339.

[1] See, *e.g.* *Beale* v. *Gomme Ltd.* (1949) 65 T.L.R. 543; *Manwaring* v. *Billington* [1952] 2 All E.R. 774.

actually fail in his action on the express ground that the defendant's statutory duty had been delegated to him[2] and the doctrine has now fallen into disrepute. In *Ginty* v. *Belmont Building Supplies Ltd.*,[3] in a passage subsequently approved by the Court of Appeal,[4] Pearson J. doubted its soundness. "There has been a number of cases . . . in which it has been considered whether or not the employer delegated to the employee the performance of the statutory duty. In my view, the law which is applicable here is clear and comprehensible if one does not confuse it by seeking to investigate this very difficult and complicated question whether or not there was a delegation. In my view, the important and fundamental question in a case like this is not whether there was a delegation, but simply the usual question: Whose fault was it? . . . If the answer to that question is that in substance and reality the accident was solely due to the fault of the plaintiff, so that he was the sole author of his own wrong, he is disentitled to recover."[5] It is submitted, therefore, that there is no special defence of delegation of a statutory duty and, indeed, that any other view would conflict with the general principle that no duty can be delegated.[6]

---

[2] The judgment of Lord Goddard in *Smith* v. *Baveystock & Co.* [1945] 1 All E.R. 531, 533–534 may be an exception, but *cf.* the judgment of du Parcq L.J. at p. 535 and see Pearson J.'s explanation of the case in *Ginty* v. *Belmont Building Supplies Ltd.* [1959] 1 All E.R. 414, 425. In *Barcock* v. *Brighton Corp.* [1949] 1 K.B. 339, Hilbery J. seems to have held that the defence of delegation defeated the claim for breach of statutory duty, but he held the defendants liable at common law.

[3] [1959] 1 All E.R. 414, 423–424.

[4] *McMath* v. *Rimmer Bros. Ltd.* [1962] 1 W.L.R. 1, 6. See also *Jenner* v. *Allen West & Co.* [1959] 1 W.L.R. 554.

[5] "Fault is not necessarily equivalent in this context to blameworthiness. The question really is whose conduct caused the accident": *Ross* v. *Associated Portland Cement Manufacturers Ltd.* [1964] 1 W.L.R. 768, 777, *per* Lord Reid.

[6] *Ibid.* at p. 776, *per* Lord Reid.

CHAPTER 8

EMPLOYERS' LIABILITY[1]

INTRODUCTORY

SINCE 1948, when the National Insurance (Industrial Injuries) Act 1946[2] came into force, there has been in operation a national insurance system under which benefits are payable to the victims of industrial accidents and to sufferers from certain prescribed industrial diseases. Both employer and workman make national insurance contributions and, generally speaking, any person employed under a contract of service or apprenticeship is entitled to the benefits provided by the Act. The scope of the scheme and benefits thereunder have already been outlined.[3] Benefits are payable in respect of personal injury by accident "arising out of and in the course of insurable employment." An accident arising in the course of the employment is deemed in the absence of evidence to the contrary, to have arisen out of that employment.[4] If the employee was, at the time of the accident, disobeying any statutory or other regulations applicable to his employment, or disobeying his master's orders, the accident is nevertheless deemed to arise out of and in the course of the employment, provided (*a*) the accident would be deemed so to have arisen if there had been no disobedience, and (*b*) the act was done for the purpose of, and in connection with, the employer's trade or business.[5] The employee is insured against injuries sustained while travelling to and from work in transport provided by his employer[6] or while acting in an emergency (actual or supposed) on his employer's premises, for instance, averting damage by fire. The legislation is administered by the Department of Social Security and not by the ordinary courts. Claims under the Act are not a matter for the employer, they are made against the state, and their validity depends in no way upon proof of the fault or breach of duty of the employer.

The Act of 1946 replaced the Workmen's Compensation Acts, the first of which was enacted in 1897, and these Acts too, though in a different way,

---

[1] See Munkman, *Employer's Liability*, (10th ed.) *passim*.
[2] The principal Act is now the Social Security Act 1975.
[3] See *ante*, pp. 22–23.
[4] Social Security Act 1975, s.50(3), heavily amended.
[5] s.52.
[6] s.53.

provided compensation to an injured workman without requiring him to prove the fault or breach of duty of his employer. It has thus been possible since 1897 for an injured workman to receive some compensation independently of the ordinary law governing the civil liability of his employer, and it is probable that in cases of long-term disability the compensation that he would receive in this way substantially exceeds the damages he could recover in a successful action against his employer.[7] However, under the law now in force the workman is entitled to retain his benefits under the scheme and also to bring an action for damages against his employer.[8] There has thus always been a strong incentive for a workman whose case offers reasonable prospects of success to bring an action against his employer, and today those prospects have been considerably enhanced by the abolition of the rule that contributory negligence is a complete defence[9] and of the doctrine of common employment.[10] Actions by workmen against their employers are, in fact, amongst the most numerous to be dealt with by the courts.[11]

The recorded history of employers' liability does not start until 1837,[12] and then it began by denying the workman a remedy. *Priestley* v. *Fowler*,[13] decided in that year, is generally regarded as the *fons et origo* of the doctrine of common employment, which held that the employer was not liable to his employee for injury caused by the negligence of another employee, but the case really went further than that. It came close to denying that an employer might be liable to his workmen on any grounds,[14] and there can be no doubt that the judges of the first half of the nineteenth century viewed with alarm the possibility of widespread liability for industrial accidents.[15] Nevertheless, by 1858, if not earlier, common employment was recognised to be an exception to the ordinary principle that a master is liable for the tort of his servant done in the course of the servant's employment.[16] It was said to rest upon the theory that the contract of service contained an implied term to the effect that the servant agreed to run the risks naturally incident to the employment, including the risk of negligence on the part of his fellow employees,[17] but it did not follow that he agreed to take the risk of negligence on the part of the employer himself. If the employer had been negligent the workman's claim was still defeated if he had been guilty of

---

[7] See, *ante*, p. 24.

[8] The damages recoverable for loss of earnings are subject to a deduction of one-half of the value of the insurance benefits for a period: Law Reform (Personal Injuries) Act 1948, s.2. See *post* p. 622. There is no deduction in fatal accident cases: *post*, p. 655.

[9] Law Reform (Contributory Negligence) Act 1945, *ante*, pp. 158–169.

[10] *Post*, p. 187.

[11] Under the Employers' Liability (Compulsory Insurance) Act 1969 all employers other than the nationalised industries, local authorities and the police are compelled to maintain insurance against their liability to their workmen. Such insurance was, of course, extremely common before the Act. For criticism of the Act, see Hasson (1979) 3 I.L.J. 79.

[12] Munkman, *Employer's Liability at Common Law* (10th ed.), p. 3.

[13] (1837) 3 M. & W. 1; *Farwell* v. *Boston and Worcester Railroad Corp.* (1842) 4 Metcalf 49; 149 R.R. 262.

[14] "The mere relation of the master and the servant can never imply an obligation on the part of the master to take more care of the servant than he may reasonably be expected to do of himself": *per* Lord Abinger C.B. at p. 6; *Seymour* v. *Maddox* (1851) 16 Q.B. 327.

[15] Striking instances are the judgments of Pollock C.B. in *Vose* v. *Lancs. & Yorks. Ry.* (1858) 27 L.J.Ex. 249 and of Bramwell B. in *Dynen* v. *Leach* (1857) 26 L.J.(N.S.) Ex. 221.

[16] *Post*, Chap. 21.

[17] *Bartonshill Coal Co.* v. *Reid* (1858) 3 Macq. 266.

contributory negligence,[18] or even if he merely knew of the danger,[19] but something of a general principle had emerged. If the workman was injured by the employer's own negligence he could recover,[20] but if he was injured by the negligence of a fellow employee he could not.[21]

During the second half of the nineteenth century judicial opinion veered in favour of the workman, and efforts began to be made to limit the scope of common employment. The doctrine was not finally abolished, however, until 1948[22] and, though much restricted in scope before that date,[23] the harshness of the law was chiefly modified by the evasion of common employment through the development of the rule that an employer was liable for an injury to his workman caused by his own negligence or breach of statutory duty.[24] So far as the latter is concerned, no particular difficulty existed: if a duty is placed directly upon the employer by statute, then he does not discharge that duty by entrusting its performance to another.[25] But how can an employer be personally negligent unless he actually takes a hand in the work himself, a physical impossibility where the employer is not a human individual but, as was increasingly the case during the nineteenth century and is now the general rule, a limited company with independent legal personality? Such an employer could only act through its servants, and if they were negligent the doctrine of common employment applied and relieved the employer of liability.[26]

The answer to this difficulty was found in the concept of duties personal to the employer, for the careful performance of which the employer remained responsible even though the tasks necessary to discharge the duties were entrusted to a servant:

> "It is quite clear," said Lord Herschell,[27] "that the contract between employer and employed involves on the part of the former the duty of taking reasonable care to provide proper appliances, and to maintain them in a proper condition, and so to carry on his operations as not to subject those employed by him to unnecessary risk. Whatever the dangers of the employment which the employed undertakes, amongst

---

[18] *Senior* v. *Ward* (1859) 1 El. & El. 385.

[19] *Alsop* v. *Yates* (1858) 2 L.J.Ex. 156; *Williams* v. *Clough* (1858) 3 H. & N. 258. In *Smith* v. *Baker & Sons* [1891] A.C. 325, the House of Lords finally held that mere knowledge did not defeat the workman's claim: *post*, pp. 690–691.

[20] Early cases include *Brydon* v. *Stewart* (1855) 2 Macq. 30; *Tarrant* v. *Webb* (1856) 25 L.J.C.P. 261; *Roberts* v. *Smith* (1857) 26 L.J.Ex. 319. *cf. Dynen* v. *Leach* (1857) 26 L.J.(N.S.) Ex. 221.

[21] The negligent employee was, of course, liable, but he was seldom worth suing.

[22] Law Reform (Personal Injuries) Act 1948, s.1(1). Contracting out of the Act is forbidden: *ibid.* s.1(3). The abolition of the doctrine extends only to personal injuries and Lord Denning M.R. has suggested that it survives for the purposes of defamation: *post*, p. 315.

[23] See, *e.g. Radcliffe* v. *Ribble Motor Services* [1939] A.C. 215; *Graham* v. *Glasgow Corp.* [1947] A.C. 368; *Lancaster* v. *L.P.T.B.* [1948] 2 All E.R. 796 (H.L.).

[24] It was settled in *Groves* v. *Wimborne* [1898] 2 Q.B. 402 that common employment afforded no defence in an action brought against the employer for breach of his statutory duty. The Employers' Liability Act 1880 (repealed by the Law Reform (Personal Injuries) Act 1948, s.1(2)) also excluded the defence in a limited number of defined cases.

[25] *Ante*, p. 182.

[26] Subject to the Employers' Liability Act 1880 it was no answer to the defence of common employment that the negligent servant was the plaintiff's superior: *Wilson* v. *Merry* (1868) L.R. 1 H.L.(Sc.) 326.

[27] *Smith* v. *Baker* [1891] A.C. 325, 362.

them is certainly not to be numbered the risk of the employer's negligence and the creation or enhancement of danger thereby engendered."[28]

Later, in the famous case of *Wilsons and Clyde Coal Co.* v. *English,*[29] Lord Wright redefined the employer's duty as threefold: "the provision of a competent staff of men, adequate material, and a proper system and effective supervision."[30] The duty is not absolute, for it is fulfilled by the exercise of due care and skill. "But it is not fulfilled by entrusting its fulfilment to employees, even though selected with due care and skill."[31]

Before the abolition of common employment, therefore, it was important to maintain carefully the distinction between a breach of the employer's personal duty, for which he was liable, and the mere negligence of a fellow employee, for which he was not[32]:

> "There is a sphere in which the employer must exercise his discretion and there are other spheres in which foremen and workmen must exercise theirs. It is not easy to define these spheres, but where the system or mode of operation is complicated or highly dangerous or prolonged or involves a number of men performing different functions, it is naturally a matter for the employer to take the responsibility of deciding what system shall be adopted. On the other hand, where the operation is simple and the decision how it shall be done has to be taken frequently, it is natural and reasonable that it should be left to the foreman or workmen on the spot."[33]

With the abolition of the doctrine of common employment in 1948,[34] the employer became liable as much for the negligence of a fellow servant of the plaintiff acting in the course of his employment as for breach of his personal duty, and it thus became unnecessary always to distinguish between the two kinds of wrongdoing. Nevertheless the concept of the employer's personal duty was not destroyed, and the employer is today liable either vicariously or for breach of his personal duty.[35] Additionally, in many forms of employment there are numerous and detailed statutory duties which are imposed directly upon employers and these have the effect of increasing his overall liability for injury suffered by his workmen. Vicarious liability is the subject of a separate chapter and here we shall consider the employer's personal duty to his employees, but in view of the mass of statutory duties in existence, to consider the common law alone would give a false picture of the

---

[28] *cf.* the views of Lord Bramwell, dissenting, at pp. 345–346.

[29] [1938] A.C. 57.

[30] *Ibid.* at p. 78, citing Lord MacLaren in *Bett* v. *Dalmeny Oil Co.* (1905) 7 F. 787, quoted with approval by Lord Shaw in *Butler* v. *Fife Coal Co.* [1912] A.C. 149, 173–174.

[31] *Ibid. per* Lord Wright.

[32] See, *e.g. Speed* v. *Thomas Swift* [1943] K.B. 557; *Winter* v. *Cardiff R.D.C.* [1950] 1 All E.R. 819.

[33] [1950] 1 All E.R. 819, 822–823, *per* Lord Oaksey.

[34] Law Reform (Personal Injuries) Act 1948, s.1(1).

[35] See *Staveley Iron & Chemical Co.* v. *Jones* [1956] A.C. 627; Weir, *Casebook on Tort*, (6th ed.), p. 238.

present law of employer's liability. We shall also, therefore, consider some of the more significant of these duties and their effect upon employer's liability as a whole.

It is also necessary to make some mention of the Health and Safety at Work, etc., Act 1974, though the impact of this upon the matters discussed in this chapter has so far been slight. The Report of the Committee on Safety and Health at Work[36] made severe criticisms of the existing industrial safety legislation which, in their view, required a determined effort at revision, harmonisation and up-dating. This aim is pursued by the Act, which gives power to repeal existing statutes and replace them by provisions in regulations.[37] The regulations will continue to give rise to civil liability,[38] but until they are drafted and put into effect, the present statutory and regulatory provisions will remain in force. An important development is the introduction by the Act of a generalised duty upon employers to ensure, so far as is reasonably practicable, the health, safety and welfare at work of all his employees. This duty is in some respects reminiscent of the employer's common law duty of care towards his workers,[39] though the duty under the Act is supported only by penal sanctions and does not give rise to any civil liability.[40]

COMMON LAW

Since the employer is now liable to his employee for an injury caused by a fellow employee, it might be thought that there is no longer value in retaining the concept of the employer's personal duty.[41] The enormous majority of workmen are in the service of corporate employers who are in reality not capable of negligence, or anything else, so why not treat every case as one of vicarious liability? One answer to this may be that habits of thought acquired under the rule of common employment have survived its abolition, but in fact the concept of the personal duty continues to serve a useful purpose. In many cases it is obviously much more convenient to say that a given state of affairs or a given event proves a breach by the employer of his personal duty than to say that some employee must somehow have been negligent for that state of affairs to exist or for that event to come about. If a workman is injured because no one has taken the trouble to provide him with an obviously necessary safety device, it is sufficient and in general satisfactory to say that the employer has not fulfilled his duty.[42] It is

---

[36] Cmnd. 5034 (1972); Simpson (1973) 36 M.L.R. 192. The Committee also proposed a more far-reaching inquiry into the basis of compensation for work-accidents, which was taken up in the terms of reference of the Pearson Commission, *ante*, Chap. 1.

[37] See the *Encyclopedia of Health and Safety at Work, Law and Practice*, Vol. 1. Note that the regulation-making power allows the Secretary of State wide powers to modify existing provisions.

[38] s.47(2) (except in so far as the Regulations provide otherwise).

[39] See s.2. *R.* v. *Swan Hunter Shipbuilders Ltd.* [1981] I.C.R. 831.

[40] s.47(1). For "approved codes of practice" and their relevance in *criminal* proceedings, see ss.16 and 17. Such codes will no doubt be admissible as evidence of what is "reasonable" or "practicable" in civil actions.

[41] See *Sullivan* v. *Gallagher & Craig* 1960 S.L.T. 70, 76, *per* Lord Justice-Clerk Thomson.

[42] See *Commonwealth* v. *Introvigne* (1982) 41 A.L.R. 577 (accident at school).

unnecessarily complicated to say that someone whose duty it was to provide the device in question, or someone whose duty it was to see that there was someone else to consider what safety devices were required and to provide them, must have been negligent and therefore that the employer is liable. Again, in many cases the only person involved in the sequence of events leading up to the accident is the plaintiff himself and yet his employer is liable, *e.g.* because the plaintiff should not have been left alone to do the job. In terms of vicarious liability this would have to be explained by saying that some other employee had somehow failed in his duty of organising the work. It is simpler, and no less accurate, to say that the employer himself was in breach of his duty.[43]

It is not only for its convenience, however, that the continued use of the employer's personal duty is justified. True vicarious liability exists only where a servant has committed a tort in the course of his employment,[44] but the employer's liability is not so restricted, so that there are cases in which the workman's injury is attributable to the negligence of an independent contractor and yet the employer is liable for breach of his personal duty to the workman.[45] Moreover, though employer's liability is most commonly dealt with as a matter of tort, it is also a matter of contract,[46] and the workman's contract of service is made with his employer, not with his fellow employees. Duties which exist by virtue of express or implied terms in the contract of employment must, therefore, be duties owed by the employer himself. Theoretically at least, the employer's vicarious liability for his servants' negligence which is a liability in tort, must be distinct.[47]

Nature of employer's duty

We have already noticed Lord Wright's threefold division of the employer's duty—"the provision of a competent staff of men, adequate material and a proper system and effective supervision"[48]—and it is convenient to adhere approximately to this in an exposition of the law. In truth, however, there is but one duty, a duty to take reasonable care so to carry on operations as not to subject the persons employed to unnecessary risk[49]:

> "In case there is any doubt about the meaning of 'unnecessary' I would
> ... take the duty as being a duty not to subject the employee to any risk
> which the employer can reasonably foresee, or, to put it slightly lower,
> not to subject the employee to any risk which the employer can reason-
> ably foresee and which he can guard against by any measure, the

---

[43] *McCafferty* v. *Metropolitan Police Receiver* [1977] 1 W.L.R. 1073 is a good example of this approach.
[44] *Post*, Chap. 21.
[45] *Post*, p. 195.
[46] *Matthews* v. *Kuwait Bechtel Corp.* [1959] 2 Q.B. 57; *Reid* v. *Rush & Tompkins* [1989] N.L.J. 680.
[47] See Jolowicz [1959] C.L.J. 163, 164–165.
[48] *Wilsons and Clyde Coal Co.* v. *English* [1938] A.C. 57, 78; *ante*, p. 187.
[49] *i.e.* risk of injury: it is not the employer's duty to insure his servant nor to advise him to insure himself: *Reid* v. *Rush & Tompkins, supra.*

convenience and expense of which are not entirely disproportionate to the risk involved."[50]

In many respects, therefore, the duty is similar to the duty of care in the tort of negligence generally, but expressed in terms appropriate to the relationship of employer and employee.[51] As we shall see, the duty of the employer cannot, as can an ordinary duty of care, always be discharged by the employment of an independent contractor,[52] but it is nevertheless a duty of care, not an absolute duty,[53] and it is for the plaintiff to prove its breach. If a workman cannot prove negligence, whether by direct evidence or with the aid of the maxim *res ipsa loquitur,* an action based upon breach of the employer's personal duty must fail. With this in mind we can consider the various branches of the employer's common law duty to his workmen.

(1) *Competent staff of men*

The duty to take reasonable care to provide a competent staff of men is still extant, but it is of comparatively little importance since the abolition of common employment. If, however, an employer engages a person with insufficient experience or training for a particular job and as a result a workman is injured, it may well be that there is a breach of this branch of the employer's duty.[54]

In one situation of a slightly different kind, however, this branch of the employer's liability retains its importance. If one employee is injured by the violent horseplay of another, or is actually assaulted by him, it is most unlikely that the employer will be liable vicariously, for the horseplay or the attack will not have been done in the course of the employment.[55] It may be, however, that the employer should have known of his employee's playful or vicious propensities and have taken steps to prevent them from resulting in injury to another. In that case he may be liable for breach of his personal duty.[56]

---

[50] *Harris* v. *Brights Asphalt Contractors* [1953] 1 Q.B. 617, 626, *per* Slade J.; *Parker* v. *Vickers* [1979] C.L.Y. 1876.

[51] The special relationship of employer and worker may impose positive duties of assistance or protection: thus an employer may be obliged to provide medical assistance in cases of illness or injury in no way attributable to him (*Kasapis* v. *Laimos* [1959] 2 Lloyd's Rep. 378) or to warn his workers to be medically examined if he learns that past working conditions, which were then regarded as proper, have caused a danger of disease (*Wright* v. *Dunlop Rubber Co.* (1971) 11 K.I.R. 311).

[52] *Post,* pp. 195–197.

[53] *Winter* v. *Cardiff* R.D.C. [1950] 1 All E.R. 819, 823, *per* Lord MacDermott; *Davie* v. *New Merton Board Mills* [1959] A.C. 604.

[54] See *Butler* v. *Fife Coal Co.* [1912] A.C. 149. So regarded, a case of this kind would not give rise to the question whether negligence is to be judged subjectively or objectively. If a man who has never previously operated a crane is put in charge of one and an accident results, despite the exercise by him of all the care of which he is, subjectively, capable, there might be difficulties in saying that the employer is vicariously liable for his negligence. In a question whether the employer is personally in breach of his duty no such difficulty exists.

[55] *O'Reilly* v. *National Rail and Tramway Appliances Ltd.* [1966] 1 All E.R. 499. cf. *Harrison* v. *Michelin Tyre Co. Ltd.* [1985] I.C.R. 696, doubted in *Aldred* v. *Nacano* [1987] I.R.L.R. 292.

[56] *Hudson* v. *Ridge Manufacturing Co.* [1957] 2 Q.B. 348; *Veness* v. *Dyson, Bell & Co.* [1965] C.L.Y. 2691. cf. *Smith* v. *Crossley Bros.* (1951) 95 S.J. 655; *Coddington* v. *International Harvester Co. of Great Britain Ltd.* (1969) 6 K.I.R. 146.

(2) *Adequate plant and equipment*

The employer must take reasonable care to provide his workmen with the necessary plant and equipment, and is therefore liable if an accident is caused through the absence of some item of equipment which was obviously necessary or which a reasonable employer would recognise to be needed.[57] He must also take reasonable care to maintain the plant and equipment in proper condition, and the more complex and dangerous that machinery the more frequent must be the inspection.[58] What is required in each case, however, is reasonable care according to the circumstances, and in some cases it may be legitimate to rely upon the workman himself to rectify simple defects in the plant he is using.[59] The duty extends to the installation of necessary safety devices on dangerous machinery[60] and the provision of protective equipment when required,[61] but the employer does not warrant the safety of plant and equipment. At common law, therefore, he is not liable if an accident is caused by some latent defect in equipment which could not have been discovered by the exercise of reasonable care on the part of persons for whose negligence he is answerable.[62] By the Employer's Liability (Defective Equipment) Act 1969,[63] however, if an employee is injured in the course of his employment in consequence of a defect in equipment provided by his employer and the defect is due to the fault of a third party, whether identified or not, then the injury is deemed to be also attributable to the negligence of the employer. Today, therefore, if a workman can show, for example, that a tool he was using was defective in such a way that there must, on a balance of probabilities, have been negligence or other fault in its manufacture, and that his injury was caused by that defect, then the employer as well as the manufacturer will be liable to him, whether or not the employer was in any way to blame.[64] The principal advantage of this from the workman's point of view is that he is relieved of any need to identify and sue the manufacturer of defective equipment provided by his employer. Since the coming into force of the Consumer Protection Act 1987, the

---

[57] *Williams* v. *Birmingham Battery and Metal Co.* [1892] 2 Q.B. 338; *Lovell* v. *Blundells & Crompton & Co.* [1944] 1 K.B. 502; *Ross* v. *Associated Portland Cement Manufacturers Ltd.* [1964] 1 W.L.R. 768. It is not always necessary, however, for the employer to adopt the latest improvements: *Toronto Power Co.* v. *Paskwan* [1915] A.C. 734, *per* Sir Arthur Channell. See also *O'Connor* v. *B.T.C.* [1958] 1 W.L.R. 346.

[58] *e.g. Murphy* v. *Phillips* (1876) 35 L.T. 477; *Baxter* v. *St. Helena Hospital Management Committee, The Times*, February 14, 1972. Even inspection may not always be sufficient: *Barkway* v. *S. Wales Transport Co.* [1950] A.C. 185; *Pearce* v. *Round Oak Steel Works Ltd.* [1969] 1 W.L.R. 595.

[59] Munkman, *op. cit.*, p. 117; *Bristol Aeroplane Co.* v. *Franklin* [1948] W.N. 341; *Richardson* v. *Stephenson Clarke Ltd.* [1969] 1 W.L.R. 1695.

[60] *Jones* v. *Richards* [1955] 1 W.L.R. 444; *Lovelidge* v. *Anselm Odling & Sons Ltd.* [1967] 2 Q.B. 351. See also *Naismith* v. *London Film Productions* [1939] 1 All E.R. 794.

[61] *Qualcast Ltd.* v. *Haynes* [1959] A.C. 743, *per* Lord Denning. But see *Brown* v. *Rolls-Royce* [1960] 1 W.L.R. 210. See also *McGhee* v. *N.C.B.* [1973] 1 W.L.R. 1 (washing facilities).

[62] *Davie* v. *New Merton Board Mills* [1959] A.C. 604. *cf. Taylor* v. *Rover Co. Ltd.* [1966] 1 W.L.R. 1491; *Pearce* v. *Round Oak Steel Works Ltd., supra.*

[63] The Act came into force on October 25, 1969, its main purpose being to reverse on its facts the result of *Davie* v. *New Merton Board Mills Ltd., supra.* "Equipment" has been held to include a 90,000 ton ship: *Coltman* v. *Bibby Tankers Ltd.* [1988] A.C. 276.

[64] *Clarkson* v. *Jackson, The Times*, November 21, 1984. The employer is entitled to raise the defence of contributory negligence against the workman and may seek to recover indemnity or contribution from the person to whose fault the defect is attributable. He cannot, however, contract out of the liability imposed by the Act.

manufacturer is subject to a stricter liability, but this does not affect the employer's position under the 1969 Act: if there is no negligence the employer is not liable even though the manufacturer may be.[65]

(3) Safe place of work

Though not expressly mentioned by Lord Wright in *Wilsons and Clyde Coal Co.* v. *English*,[66] it is clear that the employer's duty of care extends to the place of work[67] and in some cases may even also apply to the means of access to the place of work.[68] No particular difficulty exists where the place of work is in the occupation or control of the employer, but it must be recalled that the duty is one of reasonable care only and thus that the employer is not obliged to take unreasonable precautions even against foreseeable risks.[69] At one time, however, it was thought that because an employer had no control over premises in the occupation of a third party he could owe no duty in respect of those premises,[70] but it is now clear that this is wrong.[71] The duty of care remains, but what is required for its performance may well be different where the place of work is not under the employer's control:

"The master's own premises are under his control: if they are dangerously in need of repair he can and must rectify the fault at once if he is to escape the censure of negligence. But if a master sends his plumber to mend a leak in a private house, no one could hold him negligent for not visiting the house himself to see if the carpet in the hall creates a trap. Between these extremes are countless possible examples in which the court may have to decide the question of fact: Did the master take reasonable care so to carry out his operations as not to subject those employed by him to unnecessary risk? ... So viewed, the question whether the master was in control of the premises ceases to be a matter of technicality and becomes merely one of the ingredients, albeit a very

---

[65] See *post*, p. 250.

[66] [1938] A.C. 57; *ante*, p. 187.

[67] *e.g. Cole* v. *De Trafford (No. 2)* [1918] 2 K.B. 535, *per* Scrutton L.J.; *Davidson* v. *Handley Page* [1945] 1 All E.R. 235, 236, *per* Lord Greene M.R. At the lowest, the employer's duty to his employee in respect of premises occupied by the employer must be the common duty of care under the Occupiers' Liability Act 1957, but probably it is stricter than that duty: *post*, pp. 196–197.

[68] *Ashdown* v. *Samuel Williams & Sons* [1957] 1 Q.B. 409, 430–432, *per* Parker L.J.; *Smith* v. *National Coal Board* [1967] 1 W.L.R. 871. The employer can be subject to no duty of care so far as the means of access consists of a public highway, but if the employee has to cross private property, whether the employer's own or that of a third party, the duty should exist.

[69] *Latimer* v. *A.E.C.* [1953] A.C. 643; *Thomas* v. *Bristol Aeroplane Co.* [1954] 1 W.L.R. 694. Nor is he liable for a defect which would not have been revealed by inspection: *Bevan* v. *Milford Haven Dry Dock Co.* [1962] 2 Lloyd's Rep. 281; *O'Reilly* v. *National Rail and Tramway Appliances Ltd.* [1966] 1 All E.R. 499.

[70] *Taylor* v. *Sims and Sims* [1942] 2 All E.R. 375; *Cilia* v. *H.M. James & Sons* [1954] 1 W.L.R. 721. *cf. Hodgson* v. *British Arc Welding Co.* [1946] K.B. 302. In any case the duty in respect of a safe system of work (*post*, pp. 193–194) continues: *General Cleaning Contractors* v. *Christmas* [1953] A.C. 180.

[71] *Wilson* v. *Tyneside Window Cleaning Co.* [1958] 2 Q.B. 110; *Smith* v. *Austin Lifts* [1959] 1 W.L.R. 100; *Clay* v. *A.J. Crump & Sons Ltd.* [1964] 1 Q.B. 533.

important one, in a consideration of the question of fact whether, in all the circumstances, the master took reasonable care."[72]

(4) *Safe system of working*

This, the most frequently invoked branch of the employer's duty, is also the most difficult to define,[73] but it includes:

" ... the physical lay-out of the job—the setting of the stage, so to speak—the sequence in which the work is to be carried out, the provision in proper cases of warnings and notices and the issue of special instructions. A system may be adequate for the whole course of the job or it may have to be modified or improved to meet the circumstances which arise; such modifications or improvements ... equally fall under the head of system."[74]

The employer's duty in respect of the system of working is most evident where the work is of regular or routine nature, but its application is not limited to such cases. Even where a single act of a particular kind is to be performed, the employer may have an obligation to organise the work if it is of a complicated or unusual kind or if a large number of men are involved.[75] In each case it is a question of fact whether a reasonable employer would have left it to his men to decide for themselves how the job should be done.[76]

In devising a system of working the employer must take into account the fact that workmen are often heedless of their own safety,[77] and this has two consequences. First, the system should so far as possible minimise the danger of a workman's own foreseeable carelessness. Secondly, the employer must also exercise reasonable care to see that his system of working is complied with by those for whose safety it is instituted and that the necessary safety precautions are observed.[78] As Lord Denning has

---

[72] *Wilson* v. *Tyneside Window Cleaning Co.* [1958] 2 Q.B. 110, 121–122, *per* Pearce L.J.; *Kilbride* v. *Scottish & Newcastle Breweries* 1986 S.L.T. 642. The employer's duty extends similarly to the plant and equipment of a third party: *Biddle* v. *Hart* [1907] 1 K.B. 649; *Gledhill* v. *Liverpool Abattoir Utility Co.* [1957] 1 W.L.R. 1028.

[73] On the extent to which the employer must take steps to guard against the deliberate acts of "outsiders" see *Charlton* v. *Forrest Printing Ink Co. Ltd.* [1980] I.R.L.R. 331; *Longworth* v. *Coppas* 1985 S.L.T. 111.

[74] *Speed* v. *Thomas Swift & Co.* [1943] K.B. 557, 563–564, *per* Lord Greene M.R. For the relevance of general practice in industry, see *ante*, p. 114.

[75] *Winter* v. *Cardiff R.D.C.* [1950] W.N. 193, 200, *per* Lord Reid; *Byers* v. *Head Wrightson & Co.* [1961] 1 W.L.R. 961; *Boyle* v. *Kodak Ltd.* [1969] 1 W.L.R. 661. The fact that an untrained young man with indifferent English is a member of a team may call for special precautions by the employer: *Hawkins* v. *Ian Ross (Castings) Ltd.* [1970] 1 All E.R. 180, 186, *per* Fisher J. *cf. Brennan* v. *Techno Constructions* [1962] C.L.Y. 2069; *Vinnyey* v. *Star Paper Mills Ltd.* [1965] 1 All E.R. 175.

[76] Since the abolition of common employment the employer is liable vicariously for the negligence of the person in charge of the operation, but this cannot assist the plaintiff if he was himself in charge or if no workman was guilty of negligence.

[77] *General Cleaning Contractors* v. *Christmas* [1953] A.C. 180, 189–190, *per* Lord Oaksey; *Smith* v. *National Coal Board* [1967] 1 W.L.R. 871, 873, *per* Lord Reid; *Kerry* v. *Carter* [1969] 1 W.L.R. 1372.

[78] *General Cleaning Contractors* v. *Christmas* [1953] A.C. 180; *Clifford* v. *Charles H. Challen & Son* [1951] 1 K.B. 495; *Crookall* v. *Vickers-Armstrong Ltd.* [1955] 1 W.L.R. 659; *Nolan* v. *Dental Manufacturing Co.* [1958] 1 W.L.R. 936. *cf. Woods* v. *Durable Suites* [1953] 1 W.L.R. 857; *Bux* v. *Slough Metals Ltd.* [1973] 1 W.L.R. 1358.

pointed out,[79] however, this is not a proposition of law but a proposition of good sense, so that proof that a workman was never actually instructed to wear necessary protective clothing is not itself proof of negligence.[80] The employer's personal duty is not confined to devising a safe system, it extends to its implementation, so that the employer is liable even if the system itself is safe but A fails to follow it and causes injury to B.[81]

Scope of duty

The employer's duty of care concerns not only the actual work of his employees, but also all such acts as are normally and reasonably incidental to a man's day's work,[82] and the mere fact that an employee disobeys an order does not necessarily deprive him of the protection of his employer's duty, though he may, of course, be guilty of contributory negligence.[83] The special duty we are now considering arises only when the relationship of master and servant exists and so an independent contractor employed to do work in a factory, or a visitor, cannot rely upon it. Such a person will, however, generally be owed some other duty of care.[84] It is important to notice that although the employer's duty springs from the relationship of master and servant generally, the duty is owed individually to each workman, so that circumstances concerning the particular workman which are known or which ought to be known to the employer will affect the precautions which the employer must take in order to fulfil his duty. Thus in *Paris* v. *Stepney Borough Council*[85] the plaintiff had only one eye and it was therefore held that he should have been provided with goggles even though the risk involved in his work was not so great as to require the provision of goggles to a normal two-eyed man doing a similar job. Conversely, "an experienced man dealing with a familiar and obvious risk may not reasonably need the same attention or the same precautions as an inexperienced man who is likely to be more receptive of advice or admonition."[86]

Strictness of the duty

As has been emphasised in the foregoing paragraphs and has been constantly reiterated by the courts, the employer's duty is a duty of care only

[79] *Qualcast (Wolverhampton) Ltd.* v. *Haynes* [1959] A.C. 743, 760.
[80] *Ibid.* "I deprecate any tendency to treat the relation of employer and skilled workman as equivalent to that of a nurse and imbecile child": *Smith* v. *Austin Lifts* [1959] 1 W.L.R. 100, 105, *per* Viscount Simmonds. In *Smith* v. *Scot Bowyers* [1986] I.R.L.R. 315 it was held to be enough to inform workers about the availability of replacement boots; it was not necessary to inspect boots in use from time to time. *Osarak* v. *Hawker Siddeley Water Engineering Ltd.*, *The Times*, October 28, 1982, is an entertaining case, turning on safe system at common law and s.23 of the Offices, Shops and Railway Premises Act 1963.
[81] *McDermid* v. *Nash Dredging and Reclamation Co. Ltd.* [1987] A.C. 906.
[82] *Davidson* v. *Handley Page Ltd.* [1945] 1 All E.R. 235.
[83] *Rands* v. *McNeil* [1955] 1 Q.B. 253 (but no breach of duty on the facts).
[84] *e.g.* under the Occupiers' Liability Act 1957. *cf.* as to volunteer workers, Munkman, *op. cit.*, pp. 630–633.
[85] [1951] A.C. 367. *cf. James* v. *Hepworth & Grandage Ltd.* [1968] 1 Q.B. 94.
[86] *Qualcast (Wolverhampton) Ltd.* v. *Haynes* [1959] A.C. 743, 754, *per* Lord Radcliffe. Note that it is not the nature of the duty that changes, only the result of its application to the facts: *McPhee* v. *General Motors Ltd.* (1970) 8 K.I.R. 885.

and, though a high standard is required, there are limits to the protection which the employer must provide, even against foreseeable risks to his employee.[87] In *Withers* v. *Perry Chain Co.*[88] the plaintiff had previously contracted dermatitis from contact with grease in the course of her work and was therefore given by her employers the driest work they had available. This work she accepted without protest but nevertheless she again contracted dermatitis and sued her employers on the ground that, knowing that she was susceptible to dermatitis, they should not have permitted her to do work carrying a risk of causing that disease. Her action was dismissed by the Court of Appeal because the employers had done everything they reasonably could have done to protect the plaintiff short of refusing to employ her at all. "In my opinion there is no legal duty on an employer to prevent an adult employee from doing work which he or she is willing to do. If there is a slight risk . . . it is for the employee to weigh it against the desirability, or perhaps the necessity, of employment. The relationship of master and servant is not that of a schoolmaster and pupil. . . . It cannot be said that an employer is bound to dismiss an employee rather than allow her to run a small risk."[89]

Independent contractors

It might be supposed, therefore, that an employer who entrusts some task to a third party (not a servant), whose competence he has taken reasonable care to ascertain, has thereby discharged his own duty of reasonable care. To state the law in this way, however, would be to deny the *ratio decidendi* of *Wilsons and Clyde Coal Co.* v. *English*[90] that the employer's duty is personal and is not discharged simply by the appointment of a competent person to carry out the necessary tasks. In that case the defendant employers were held liable in respect of an injury sustained by a miner because the system of working was not reasonably safe. The system had been devised by the manager of the mine, a fellow servant of the plaintiff, to whom the employers were obliged by statute[91] to leave the matter, but yet, despite the existence of common employment and despite the fact that the employers personally had done everything they possibly could, they were held to be in breach of their duty to the plaintiff. Their duty was "the employer's personal duty, whether he performs or can perform it himself, or whether he does not perform it or cannot perform it save by servants or agents. A failure to perform such a duty is the employer's personal negligence."[92] The employer's liability, therefore, not being a vicarious liability, was not defeated by the doctrine of common employment.

---

[87] See, *e.g. Latimer* v. *A.E.C.* [1953] A.C. 643. For the standard of care in negligence generally see *ante*, pp. 111–121.
[88] [1961] 1 W.L.R. 1314.
[89] *Ibid*. at p. 1320, *per* Devlin L.J. See also *Foufoulas* v. *F.G. Strang Pty. Ltd.* (1970) 44 A.L.J.R. 361.
[90] [1938] A.C. 57; *ante*, p. 187.
[91] Coal Mines Act 1911, s.2(4).
[92] [1938] A.C. 57, 83–84, *per* Lord Wright. See also *per* Lord Thankerton at pp. 64–65; *per* Lord Macmillan at p. 75; *per* Lord Maugham at pp. 87–88.

There can be little doubt that the concept of the employer's personal duty was developed in order to reduce the hardship created by the doctrine of common employment. In practical effect, however, it extends to cases which never were covered by that doctrine, for it involves the proposition that the employer's duty is not so much a duty to take reasonable care as a duty that care be taken. It thus carries the implication that the employer is liable in respect of matters covered by the personal duty for damage caused by the negligence of others, in particular independent contractors. A man can be liable vicariously only for the torts of his servants done in the course of their employment, but a duty that care be taken is not fulfilled if anyone concerned is guilty of a failure to take care.[93] This view of the law is confirmed by the decision in *McDermid* v. *Nash Dredging and Reclamation Co. Ltd.*[94] The defendands were a wholly owned subsidiary of S, a Dutch company, and their function was to employ British staff engaged in S's dredging work in Sweden. While the plaintiff, an employee of the defendants, was aboard a tug owned by S he was seriously injured as a result of the negligence of the skipper (an employee of S) in putting the engines astern without warning to the plaintiff. Whether the case was looked at as one of failing to devise a safe system (for which finding the Court of Appeal thought there was scope on the evidence) or failing to follow a system in itself safe (as the trial judge thought) the defendants were liable because they had delegated the performance of their duty to take care for the plaintiff's safety to S and its employees on the tug and they could not escape their liability when that duty was not fulfilled. Given the connection between the defendants and S the decision is not surprising,[95] for if the law were otherwise the plaintiff's rights would be at risk from the chances of corporate organisation,[96] but it does not mean that the employer is liable whenever his employee is injured at work as a result of the negligence of a third party. To hold otherwise would be inconsistent with the decision in *Davie* v. *New Merton Bord Mills*[97] where the House of Lords specifically rejected the argument that the employer was in breach of his personal duty by reason of the negligence of the manufacturers of a standard tool which, because of an undiscoverable latent defect, injured the plaintiff employee. So far as injury resulting from defective equipment is concerned, the result of *Davie's* case was reversed by the Employer's Liability (Defective Equipment) Act 1969,[98] but the underlying *ratio* of the case remains. This, it is submitted, is that the employer is only responsible for the negligence of someone other than his servant if it can fairly be said that he has delegated the performance of his duty of care to employees to that

---

[93] See *post*, pp. 582.

[94] [1987] A.C. 906; Weir, *Casebook on Tort* (6th ed.), 260; *Kondis* v. *State Transport Authority* (1984) 55 A.L.R. 225.

[95] The tug was skippered turn and turn about by an employee of S and an employee of the defendants. Had the accident occurred on the next shift there could have been no disputing the defendants' liability.

[96] No proceedings were brought against S because of the difficulties of effecting service against a Dutch company in respect of a claim arising in Sweden and because of a practice of the legal aid authorities not to support claims against a foreign defendant in respect of a foreign tort. Had S been sued, they might have been entitled to limit their liability under the Merchant Shipping Act.

[97] [1959] A.C. 604; Weir, *Casebook on Tort* (6th ed.), p. 255.

[98] See *ante*, p. 191.

person. In *Davie's* case itself the employers had discharged their duty by buying from a reputable supplier a standard tool whose latent defect they had no means of discovering.[99] Similarly, if a lorry driver delivering goods to a factory were negligently to run into and injure a workman, the workman's employer would not be liable: the lorry driver (and *his* employer) cannot reasonably be described as the independent contractor of the employer, his negligence does not negative the exercise of care in the employer's personal duty for it is unrelated to any aspect of that duty, and the employer has delegated nothing to him. But if, for example, a gas fitter negligently installs a gas appliance at the employer's premises with the result that a workman is injured by an explosion, it is submitted that the employer's personal duty with regard to the safety of the place of work has not been fulfilled and he is liable,[1] whether or not the workman is entitled to rely upon the Act of 1969.[2]

BREACH OF STATUTORY DUTY[3]

The employer's common law duty to his workman exists by virtue of the relationship of master and servant and therefore applies wherever that relationship exists, but no similar generalisation is possible in the case of duties imposed by statute. The application of those duties is governed purely and simply by the statute which creates them. Nevertheless the number of statutory duties which affect the employer's liability to his workman in one way or another is now so great that for the enormous majority of workmen it is no longer true to say simply that their employer's duty is the common law duty described above. That duty always exists, but in factories, in mines and quarries, on building sites, and in most other forms of employment,[4] a host of specific obligations are superimposed upon it by statute and statutory regulations. It would be out of the question in a book of this kind, however, to consider in detail even a limited number of these obligations[5] and the purpose of the following paragraphs is to do no more than show how a few of the more important of them operate in relation to employer's liability. For

[99] The House of Lords in *Davie* approved the decision of Finnemore J. in *Mason* v. *Williams & Williams Ltd.* [1955] 1 W.L.R. 549, where the judge had not been "embarrassed by the citation of authority": [1959] A.C. 604, 617, *per* Viscount Simmonds.

[1] *Sumner* v. *William Henderson & Sons Ltd.* [1964] 1 Q.B. 450. The judgment of Phillimore J. was later set aside ([1963] 1 W.L.R. 823) but for procedural reasons only.

[2] Under the Hague-Visby Rules, the carrier of goods by sea must "exercise due diligence to make the ship seaworthy," and there may be an analogy between this duty and the employer's. In a question concerning the carrier's liability a distinction apparently exists between the manufacturer of the ship, for whose negligence the carrier is not liable, and the repairer of the ship, for whose negligence the carrier is liable. See *Angliss (W.) & Co. (Australia) Ptd.* v. *P. & O. Steam Navigation Co.* [1927] 2 K.B. 456 and *Riverstone Meat Co. Pty.* v. *Lancashire Shipping Co.* [1961] A.C. 807 (Weir, *Casebook on Tort* (6th ed.), p. 261). In the latter case it was regarded as almost self-evident that the carrier is in general liable for the negligence of independent contractors.

[3] For the action for breach of statutory duty in general, see *ante*, Chap. 7. For the Health and Safety at Work, etc., Act 1974, see *ante*, p. 188.

[4] See, *e.g.* Offices, Shops and Railway Premises Act 1963. The principal statute for agricultural employment, the Agriculture (Safety, Health and Welfare) Act 1956 is little more than a framework for making regulations and some of its functions in this respect are superseded by regulations made under the Health and Safety at Work, etc., Act 1974: see S.I. 1975 No. 46.

[5] See further *Encyclopedia of Health and Safety at Work, Law and Practice.*

the solution of any particular problem there is no alternative to an examination of the relevant legislation itself.

Factories

The earlier legislation[6] is now consolidated in the Factories Act 1961,[7] Part II of which deals with "Safety (General Provisions)."[8] A great variety of matters are dealt with in this Part of the Act[9] but the majority of actions are based either upon the sections dealing with the fencing of machinery or upon those dealing with the condition of the factory premises.

Sections 12 to 16 cover the fencing of machinery, and the general rule is laid down that flywheels and moving parts of prime movers,[10] transmission machinery,[11] and "every dangerous part" of other machinery,[12] shall be securely fenced. The obligation imposed is to fence, rather than to make safe[13] and it has therefore been said that something is only "part of machinery" within the meaning of the Act if it is something to which a reasonable person would think of applying a fence.[14] Accordingly, a fan in a factory vehicle may require to be fenced, but the vehicle itself does not, even though it may be dangerous to pedestrians when in motion.[15] In deciding whether a part of machinery is dangerous, a question around which a substantial body of case law has developed, the basic question is whether it is foreseeably likely to cause injury, and in assessing this not only the careful but the careless and inattentive workman must be borne in mind.[16] This does not mean, however, that it must be foreseen that a workman will act with total disregard for his own safety.[17] The fencing provided must be of substantial

---

[6] Chiefly the Factories Acts of 1937, 1948 and 1959.

[7] The duties created by the Act are for the most part imposed upon the occupier of the factory, not upon the employer as such, but in the vast majority of cases the occupier and the employer are one and the same.

[8] This is the most important Part of the Act for present purposes, but it does not follow that no action for damages can be brought for breach of a section in some other Part of the Act: *Nicholson* v. *Atlas Steel Foundry & Engineering Co.* [1957] 1 W.L.R. 613; *Thornton* v. *Fisher & Ludlow Ltd.* [1968] 1 W.L.R. 655, both concerning sections contained in Pt. I, "Health (General Provisions)"; *Reid* v. *Westfield Paper Co.* [1957] S.C. 218, concerning a section contained in Pt. III, "Welfare (General Provisions)." For power to substitute regulations for the provisions of the Act, see *ante*, p. 188.

[9] *e.g.* hoists and lifts, lifting tackle, cranes, dangerous fumes, steam boilers and means of escape in case of fire.

[10] s.12(1). For definition of "prime mover," see s.176(1).

[11] s.13(1). For definition of "transmission machinery," see s.176(1).

[12] s.14(1). There is no duty to fence the dangerous parts of machinery constructed in the factory and not part of the equipment used in the processes of the factory: *Parvin* v. *Morton Machine Co.* [1952] A.C. 515; *Ballard* v. *Ministry of Defence* [1977] I.C.R. 513. *Aliter* where the machinery though not yet in use, has been installed in the factory where it is to be used: *Irwin* v. *White, Tomkins & Courage Ltd.* [1964] 1 W.L.R. 387.

[13] Though the requirements of the Act are satisfied if the machinery is as safe by position or construction as it would be if fenced: *infra*, n. 18.

[14] *Mirza* v. *Ford Motor Co. Ltd.* [1981] I.C.R. 757, 763, *per* Ormrod L.J. There is, however, some difficulty in reconciling this approach with *John Summers & Sons Ltd.* v. *Frost* [1955] A.C. 740, *infra*, n. 20.

[15] See *British Railways Board* v. *Liptrot* [1969] 1 A.C. 136, overruling *Cherry* v. *International Alloys Ltd.* [1961] 1 Q.B. 136; *Mirza* v. *Ford Motor Co.*, *supra* (hook attached to hoist).

[16] See, *e.g. Hindle* v. *Birtwistle* [1897] 1 Q.B. 192; *Walker* v. *Bletchley Flettons Ltd.* [1937] 1 All E.R. 170; *Mitchell* v. *North British Rubber Co.* [1945] S.C. 69; *John Summers & Sons* v. *Frost* [1955] A.C. 740; *Close* v. *Steel Co. of Wales* [1962] A.C. 367; *Cross* v. *Midland and Low Moor Iron and Steel Co. Ltd.* [1965] A.C. 343; *F.E. Callow (Engineers) Ltd.* v. *Johnson* [1971] A.C. 335.

[17] *Higgins* v. *Harrison* (1932) 25 B.W.C.C. 113; *Carr* v. *Mercantile Produce Co.* [1949] 2 K.B. 601; *Pearce* v. *Stanley-Bridges Ltd.* [1965] 1 W.L.R. 931.

construction and, subject to certain restricted exceptions,[18] must be kept in position while the parts required to be fenced are "in motion or use."[19] The duty to fence is absolute, in the sense that difficulty or even impossibility of complying and at the same time leaving the machine in a usable condition affords no defence,[20] but the requirement that the fencing be "secure" does not mean that it must protect the workman against every possible kind of injury. In the first place there is no duty to guard against an unforeseeable danger such as might be caused by a machine going wrong in a way which could not be reasonably anticipated.[21] Secondly, the duty to fence applies only to parts of the machinery, not to material or components upon which the machine is performing some operation.[22] Thirdly, there is no duty that the fencing shall protect the workman from being struck by something ejected from the machine, whether part of the material on which the machine is working[23] or part of the machine itself.[24] "Fencing, in my opinion, means the erection of a barricade to prevent any employee from making contact with the machine, not an enclosure to prevent broken machinery from flying out."[25] But if a workman is injured by coming into contact with a part of machinery which is required to be fenced, then, unless the accident was due entirely to his own fault,[26] he is automatically entitled to recover. The liability of the occupier of the factory for breach of his obligation to

---

[18] Parts which are in such a position or of such construction as to be as safe as if they were securely fenced need not be fenced: ss.12(3), 13(1), 14(1): *Atkinson* v. *L.N.E.R.* [1926] 1 K.B. 313; *Hodkinson* v. *Henry Wallwork* [1955] 1 W.L.R. 1195. Operations at unfenced machinery are permitted only in the exceptional cases allowed for by s.16 of the Act and the Operations at Unfenced Machinery Regulations 1938 to 1976.

[19] s.16. These words have given rise to considerable trouble. See, *e.g. Richard Thomas & Baldwins Ltd.* v. *Cummings* [1955] A.C. 321; *Knight* v. *Leamington Spa Courier Ltd.* [1961] 2 Q.B. 253; *Stanbrook* v. *Waterlow & Sons Ltd.* [1964] 1 W.L.R. 825; *Mitchell* v. *W.S. Westin Ltd.* [1965] 1 W.L.R. 297; *Horne* v. *Lec Refrigeration Ltd.* [1965] 2 All E.R. 898.

[20] *Davies* v. *Thomas Owen & Co.* [1919] 2 K.B. 39; *John Summers & Sons Ltd.* v. *Frost* [1955] A.C. 740. S.161 of the Factories Act provided a defence in criminal (but *not* civil) proceedings to an employer who could show that he had used due diligence and that another person had committed the offence. This has now been repealed for most purposes. As to the Health and Safety at Work, etc., Act 1974, see ss.36 and 15(6).

[21] *Eaves* v. *Morris Motors* [1961] 2 Q.B. 385; *cf. Rogers* v. *George Blair & Co.* (1971) 11 K.I.R. 391. But if a part of machinery is dangerous, in the sense that it is a foreseeable cause of injury, and is unfenced, then it is irrelevant that the plaintiff's accident occurred in an unforeseeable way: *Millard* v. *Serck Tubes Ltd.* [1969] 1 W.L.R. 211.

[22] *Bullock* v. *G. John Power (Agencies)* [1956] 1 W.L.R. 171; *Kilgollan* v. *William Cooke Ltd.* [1956] 1 W.L.R. 527; *Eaves* v. *Morris Motors* [1961] 2 Q.B. 385. Such issues must, however, be approached in a practical manner: *Wearing* v. *Pirelli Ltd.* [1977] 1 W.L.R. 48 (breach of s.14 where injury arose from high speed revolving drum even though only contact was with the rubber—the raw material—stretched around the drum). There is no duty to prevent a tool which the workman is holding from coming into contact with the machine and thus causing an injury: *Sparrow* v. *Fairey Aviation Co. Ltd.* [1964] A.C. 1019. In considering whether a part is dangerous regard must be had to the operation of the machine in the normal course of working. So a part may be dangerous even though the danger only arises through the juxtaposition of the part and the material on which the machine is working: *Cross* v. *Midland Low Moor Iron Steel Co. Ltd.* [1965] A.C. 343; *F.E. Callow (Engineers) Ltd.* v. *Johnson* [1971] A.C. 335. *cf. Pearce* v. *Stanley-Bridges Ltd.* [1965] 1 W.L.R. 931; *Hindle* v. *Joseph Porritt & Sons Ltd.* [1970] 1 All E.R. 1142.

[23] *Nicholls* v. *Austin (Leyton) Ltd.* [1946] A.C. 493.

[24] *Carroll* v. *Andrew Barclay & Sons* [1948] A.C. 477; *Close* v. *Steel Co. of Wales* [1962] A.C. 367. But see the powerful dissenting judgment of Lord Denning in the latter case.

[25] *Carroll* v. *Andrew Barclay & Sons, supra,* at p. 486, *per* Lord Porter.

[26] *Rushton* v. *Turner Bros.* [1960] 1 W.L.R. 96; *Horne* v. *Lec Refrigeration Ltd.* [1965] 2 All E.R. 898; *Jayes* v. *I.M.I. (Kynock) Ltd.* [1985] I.C.R. 155.

fence is independent of any fault on his part and exists even though the workman at the time of his accident was engaged "on a frolic of his own."[27]

Safety of the factory premises is dealt with chiefly by sections 28 and 29, the former covering specific matters such as the construction and maintenance of floors and the provision of handrails for staircases, while the latter deals generally with the safety of workplaces and means of access thereto.[28] The sections impose duties of two main kinds; the unqualified obligation, for example, that "all ladders shall be soundly constructed and properly maintained,"[29] and the qualified obligation, for example, that safe means of access[30] shall, "so far as is reasonably practicable," be provided and maintained.[31] If a rung of a ladder breaks then, without more, a breach of duty is established,[32] but the absence of "safe means of access" does not always involve a breach, for it must have been "reasonably practicable" to provide and maintain it.[33] In other words, liability depends upon whether the risk in question is sufficiently great to call for the measures necessary to eliminate it.[34] On the other hand, the burden of proving that the measures necessary were not "reasonably practicable" rests with the defendant,[35] and therefore a workman who proves that he suffered injuries because of the absence of a safe means of access establishes at least a prima facie case. It is true that the House of Lords has more than once observed that after all the evidence has been produced the initial burden of proof is rarely of importance,[36] but the fact remains that in the absence of evidence that the measures necessary were not reasonably practicable, the plaintiff is entitled to succeed. He is thus in a stronger position when attempting to negotiate an agreed settlement of his claim and in the early stages of litigation even if not in the

---

[27] Uddin v. Associated Portland Cement Manufacturers Ltd. [1965] 2 Q.B. 582; Allen v. Aeroplane and Motor Aluminium Castings Ltd. [1965] 1 W.L.R. 1244; see also Westwood v. Post Office [1974] A.C. 1. cf. Napieralski v. Curtis (Contractors) Ltd. [1959] 1 W.L.R. 835. Carelessness of his own safety will, of course, lead to a reduction of the workman's damages on the ground of contributory negligence.

[28] s.29(1). s.29(2) deals with the specific case of a man working at a place from which he is liable to fall more than six feet six inches.

[29] s.28(5). "Maintained" means "maintained in an efficient state, in efficient working order, and in good repair." See Latimer v. A.E.C. [1953] A.C. 643.

[30] Including means of access passing over articles being repaired or manufactured in the factory, such as ships: Gardiner v. Admiralty Commissioners [1964] 1 W.L.R. 590.

[31] s.29(1). A third type of duty is contained in s.28(4): "All openings in floors shall be securely fenced, except in so far as the nature of the work renders such fencing impracticable." A precaution may be "practicable" without being "reasonably practicable," and may be "impracticable" without being actually impossible: Jayne v. National Coal Board [1963] 2 All E.R. 220; and a precaution may be "practicable" even though the risks inherent in setting up the precaution exceed the probable benefit to be gained from it: Boyton v. Willment Bros. [1971] 1 W.L.R. 1625, obiter. See also, on the difference between such duties and the common law, Wallhead v. Ruston and Hornsby Ltd. (1973) 14 K.I.R. 285. For discussion of the correct approach to the problem of "obstructions," see Marshall v. Ericsson Telephones Ltd. [1964] 1 W.L.R. 1367. A screw on the floor has been held to be an obstruction: Gillies v. Glynwed Foundries 1977 S.L.T. 97.

[32] Cole v. Blackstone & Co. [1943] K.B. 615.

[33] See especially Levesley v. Firth & Brown Ltd. [1953] 1 W.L.R. 1206; Braham v. J. Lyons & Co. Ltd. [1962] 1 W.L.R. 1048; Jenkins v. Allied Ironfounders Ltd. [1970] 1 W.L.R. 304. The last-named is a case on s.28(1) which also contains the words "so far as is reasonably practicable."

[34] McCarthy v. Coldair Ltd. [1951] 2 T.L.R. 1226; and see Thompson v. Bowaters United Kingdom Paper Co. [1975] K.I.L.R. 47. Where there is a safe route and the workman unpredictably chooses another and unsafe route, there is no breach of the subsection: Donovan v. Cammell Laird & Co. [1949] 2 All E.R. 82.

[35] Nimmo v. Alexander Cowan & Sons Ltd. [1968] A.C. 107; Gibson v. British Insulated Callender's Construction Co. Ltd. 1973 S.L.T. 2; Bowes v. Sedgefield D.C. [1981] I.C.R. 234.

[36] Dorman Long (Steel) Ltd. v. Bell [1964] 1 W.L.R. 333, 335, per Lord Reid; Jenkins v. Allied Ironfounders Ltd. [1970] 1 W.L.R. 304, 312, per Lord Guest.

appellate courts, if he can rely upon the section than if he has to shoulder the burden of proving negligence at common law.

As with the sections prescribing the duty to fence dangerous machinery, the application of these sections has inevitably developed a fair degree of technicality. Until 1959 there was no general duty with regard to the safety of a man's place of work, as opposed to the means of access to that place, and a good many cases therefore turned upon the distinction between the two.[37] Now, however, this defect in the law has been remedied and the subsection reads: "There shall, so far as is reasonably practicable, be provided and maintained safe means of access to every place at which any person has at any time to work, and every such place shall, so far as is reasonably practicable, be made and kept safe for any person working there."[38] Nevertheless cases such as *Davies* v. *De Havilland Aircraft Co.*,[39] in which it was held that no duty under the section was owed to a workman walking along a passage to the canteen for his mid-morning break, are not decided differently today.[40] Equally the duties in respect of the things specified in section 28 apply only to those things and not to other things, however similar they may be and however reasonable it may appear that a similar duty should exist. A plankway between gantries 100 feet above the ground, for example, is not a "floor" and therefore the widow of a workman who was killed when he fell through an aperture in the plankway could not rely upon the requirement that "all openings in floors shall be securely fenced."[41] In a case of this kind the question is not one of what is reasonable, but whether the words used in the section are "apt to cover or describe the circumstances in question in any particular case."[42]

Mines and quarries

The previous legislation is now collected together, in a modified form, in the Mines and Quarries Act 1954 and in regulations made under the Act,[43] Part III of the Act dealing with safety in mines and Part V with safety in quarries. Almost every aspect of safety is dealt with in the Act or regulations, and it is a feature of the legislation that many duties are imposed directly upon individuals such as managers, inspectors and shotfirers. It is, however, expressly provided that the owner of the mine shall be liable for the breach of such a duty by one of his servants.[44] It is also a feature of the legislation that although it contains numerous unqualified obligations, there

---

[37] *e.g. Lovell* v. *Blundells & Crompton & Co.* [1944] K.B. 502; *Hopwood* v. *Rolls-Royce Ltd.* (1947) 176 L.T. 514; *Dorman Long & Co.* v. *Hillier* [1951] 1 All E.R. 357.
[38] s.29(1).
[39] [1951] 1 K.B. 50; *Rose* v. *Colvilles Ltd.* 1950 S.L.T.(Notes) 72; *Dryland* v. *London Electrical Manufacturing Co.* (1949) 99 L.J. 665.
[40] *Cockady* v. *Bristol Siddeley Engines Ltd.* (1965) 115 L.J. 661.
[41] s.28(4); *Tate* v. *Swan Hunter & Wigham Richardson Ltd.* [1958] 1 W.L.R. 39.
[42] *Bath* v. *B.T.C.* [1954] 1 W.L.R. 1013, 1015, *per* Somervell L.J. (dry dock not an "opening" in a floor); *Kimpton* v. *Steel Co. of Wales* [1960] 1 W.L.R. 527 (three steps wedged into a platform not a "staircase").
[43] Especially the Miscellaneous Mines Regulations 1956. As with the Factories Act, the 1954 Act may be replaced by regulations made under the Health and Safety at Work, etc., Act 1974.
[44] s.159.

is a general provision that in any case[45] it shall be a defence to prove that it was "impracticable to avoid or prevent the contravention."[46] The burden of proving the impracticability rests squarely on the defendant and he must do more than prove that he took all reasonable care,[47] but at least it seems likely that no such decision as *John Summers & Sons* v. *Frost*[48] need be reached under the Act of 1954. In what follows, therefore, the existence of this general defence must be borne in mind.

One of the most important topics dealt with by the Act is the security from falls of the roads and working places in a mine, and numerous detailed rules concerning support are laid down. Under earlier legislation[49] there was also the general obligation that "the roof and sides of every travelling road and working place shall be made secure ... " and it has been held that this created an absolute duty.[50] Now, however, in place of this impersonal obligation the manager of the mine is personally subjected to the duty to take such steps as may be necessary for keeping the road or working place secure,[51] and in order to determine what steps may be necessary to achieve this result, he must also take the necessary steps to secure that he is in possession of all relevant information.[52] This imposes a less than absolute duty, and there is no breach if the manager has merely failed to take steps the necessity for which could not have been discovered until after the accident.[53] On the other hand, the duty that all parts and working gear of machinery used in the mine "shall be of good construction, suitable material, adequate strength and free from patent defect, and shall be properly maintained"[54] does create an absolute duty[55] and therefore as soon as there is a patent, *i.e.* observable, defect, there is a breach. It makes no difference that at the time of the accident the defect had not in fact and could not have been observed.[56] Similarly, the duty imposed upon the manager of a quarry "to secure that any quarrying operations ... are so carried on as to avoid danger from falls"[57] means that he must achieve the result that no fall shall produce any

---

[45] Both actions for damages and prosecutions.

[46] s.157. The equivalent provision in the Coal Mines Act 1911, s.102(8), contained the words "not reasonably practicable" and the standard of liability has thus presumably been raised.

[47] *Sanderson* v. *N.C.B.* [1961] 2 Q.B. 244. Impracticability must be proved by evidence, "not deduced by casual inference": *per* Holroyd Pearce L.J., *ibid.* at p. 252. The defence may succeed, however, if the precaution required by a regulation is impracticable even though the work could have been done in a different way altogether so as not to invoke the regulation in question at all: *Morris* v. *N.C.B.* [1963] 1 W.L.R. 1382.

[48] [1955] A.C. 740, *ante*, p. 199. S.82(1) of the Act of 1954 provides that "every fly-wheel and every other dangerous exposed part of any machinery ... shall be securely fenced."

[49] Coal Mines Act 1911, s.49.

[50] *Lochgelly Iron and Coal Co.* v. *M'Mullan* [1934] A.C. 1.

[51] s.48(1).

[52] s.48(2).

[53] *Brown* v. *N.C.B.* [1962] A.C. 574. See also *John G. Stein & Co. Ltd.* v. *O'Hanlon* [1965] A.C. 890; *Tomlinson* v. *Beckermet Mining Co. Ltd.* [1964] 1 W.L.R. 1043; *Soar* v. *National Coal Board* [1965] 1 W.L.R. 886; *Aitken* v. *N.C.B.* 1973 S.L.T.(Notes) 48. If insecurity is shown it is for the defendant to prove performance of the requirements of the section: *Sinclair* v. *National Coal Board* 1963 S.L.T. 296; *Beiscak* v. *National Coal Board* [1965] 1 W.L.R. 518; *Hill* v. *N.C.B.* 1976 S.L.T. 261.

[54] s.81(1).

[55] *Hamilton* v. *N.C.B.* [1960] A.C. 633.

[56] *Sanderson* v. *N.C.B.* [1961] 2 Q.B. 244.

[57] s.108(1).

danger.[58] The nature of the duty in each case depends purely and simply upon the way it is expressed in the appropriate section of the Act.

EMPLOYERS' LIABILITY

Despite the view sometimes expressed that an action for breach of statutory duty is identical with an action for negligence,[59] in the context of employers' liability the two are kept wholly distinct and some judges have even expressed concern lest the employer's common law duty be so enlarged that it becomes indistinguishable from a duty created by statute.[60] Nevertheless the subject-matter of both kinds of duty, so far as the law of tort is concerned, is the same, namely, the employer's liability to pay damages to his injured workman. It is the combined effect of the common law duty and such statutory duties as apply which governs the liability of the employer in any given case.[61]

At common law the employer's duty is a duty of care and it follows that the burden of proving negligence rests with the plaintiff workman throughout the case.[62] It has even been said that if he alleges a failure to provide a reasonably safe system of working the plaintiff must plead, and therefore prove, what the proper system was and in what relevant respects it was not observed.[63] It is true that the severity of this particular burden has been somewhat reduced,[64] but it remains clear that for a workman merely to prove the circumstances of his accident will normally be insufficient.[65] Where a statutory duty applies, on the other hand, the employer's duty is often absolute, so that no question of negligence arises at all, and even where it is qualified by such words as "so far as reasonably practicable" it is for the employer to prove that it was not reasonably practicable to avoid the breach.[66] It follows that the existence of a relevant statutory duty will almost invariably ease the task of the workman in establishing his employer's liability.

There is nothing intrinsically wrong in a system of law which sometimes imposes liability upon an employer without requiring the workman to prove negligence and sometimes does not. The common law generally requires proof of negligence as a precondition to liability, but the legislature, it may be said, has seen fit in specific cases to modify the common law and relieve the workman of this burden. "The Factories Acts and the elaborate regulations made under them testify to the care with which the common law has

---

[58] *Brazier* v. *Skipton Rock Co.* [1962] 1 W.L.R. 471; *Sanderson* v. *Millom Hematite Ore & Iron Co. Ltd.* [1967] 3 All E.R. 1050.

[59] *Ante*, pp. 170–171.

[60] *Latimer* v. *A.E.C. Ltd.* [1953] A.C. 644, 658, *per* Lord Tucker.

[61] This is, of course, a truism for any branch of the law of tort, but it is of particular significance here owing to the enormous number of statutory duties which exist.

[62] *Brown* v. *Rolls-Royce Ltd.* [1960] 1 W.L.R. 210 provides a striking example.

[63] *Colfar* v. *Coggins & Griffith (Liverpool)* [1945] A.C. 197, 203, *per* Viscount Simon L.C.

[64] *Dixon* v. *Cementation Co.* [1960] 1 W.L.R. 746.

[65] The workman may be entitled to rely upon the maxim *res ipsa loquitur* (*ante*, pp. 125–130, but cases in which it is of assistance are comparatively rare. See, *e.g.* the doubts expressed in *Moore* v. *R. Fox & Sons* [1956] 1 Q.B. 596.

[66] *Ante*, p. 200.

been altered, adjusted and refined in order to give protection and compensation to the workman."[67] It is legitimate to inquire, however, whether the statutory modifications of the common law duty of care were really enacted with an eye to actions for damages by injured workmen and whether the combination of common law and statutory duties does in fact produce a coherent body of law.[68]

A comprehensive answer to these questions would require an examination of the whole mass of statutes and statutory regulations which impose specific duties upon employers, but it is perhaps not unfair to express some doubts about the matter without undertaking this mammoth task. Although by now Parliament may be assumed to know the way in which the courts will treat breaches of the duties it creates, it can safely be said that the primary object of most of the legislation in question is not the modification of the law of employers' liability. It is to secure, so far as the enactment of specific duties can do so, the maximum protection for the workman against injury. This has, indeed, been expressly acknowledged in the House of Lords,[69] and the point emerges clearly from the change introduced by the Mines and Quarries Act 1954 in the obligation regarding the security of the roads and working places of a mine.[70] Formerly, the duty was expressed impersonally and was unqualified, but now the manager of the mine is directed to take such steps as may be necessary. "This was no doubt inserted as the result of the disaster in 1951 at the Knockshinnoch Colliery, when the duties were so distributed among the officials that 'what was everybody's business was nobody's business.' So in 1954 Parliament declared that it is the duty of the *manager* to see to the security of the road."[71] It can scarcely be argued that the purpose of the change was to modify the law governing the employer's liability for damages even though this was its incidental effect.[72]

The result of incorporating into the law of employer's liability the manifold duties enacted for the purpose of preventing accidents has inevitably been the creation of technical and often irrational distinctions, and it is the existence of these distinctions which gives rise to dissatisfaction with this branch of the law. We have already noticed, for example, that the duty created by the Factories Act that dangerous parts of machinery shall be

---

[67] *Davie* v. *New Merton Board Mills* [1959] A.C. 604, 627, *per* Viscount Simonds.

[68] See the remarks of Ormrod L.J. in *Mirza* v. *Ford Motor Co. Ltd.* [1981] I.C.R. 757, 761: "Counsel for defendants habitually stress the criminal character of the Factories Act 1961 and its manifold regulations, and argue for the strict construction appropriate to a criminal statute. Counsel for plaintiffs tend to approach this legislation as if it were a vehicle for the introduction of strict or no fault liability on the part of employers and argue . . . that it is immaterial that a liberal construction will produce serious anomalies or create grave practical difficulties. Factory inspectors will not prosecute and employers just have to pay up if accidents happen. Both these approaches rely to a considerable extent on rhetoric. The Factories Acts were and are, in form, criminal statutes, but they have been adapted by generations of judges into a code of civil liability . . . and should, therefore, be construed as such. They do not, however, establish a system of strict liability to employees for accidents occurring in factories in connection with machinery."

[69] *Gill* v. *Donald Humberstone & Co. Ltd.* [1963] 1 W.L.R. 929, 933–934, *per* Lord Reid; at pp. 941–942, *per* Lord Devlin. See also *Alford* v. *N.C.B.* [1952] 1 All E.R. 754, 757, *per* Lord Normand; *Brown* v. *N.C.B.* [1962] A.C. 574, 594, *per* Lord Radcliffe.

[70] *Ante*, p. 202.

[71] *Brown* v. *N.C.B., supra*, at p. 597, *per* Lord Denning.

[72] It is not denied that a change may sometimes be made with this object. The purpose of adding the duty that places of work shall be safe, so far as reasonably practicable, to the section dealing with means of access to those places was presumably to avoid discussion of the distinction between the two. See *ante*, p. 200.

securely fenced does not extend to protecting the workman from injuries caused by material or even fragments of the machine itself which are ejected from it.[73] From the point of view of accident prevention it may be impracticable to legislate against this kind of thing,[74] but that is a poor reason for requiring a workman so injured to prove negligence while allowing his fellow workman, injured by direct contact with a dangerous part, an automatic right to damages.[75] Yet over and over again one will find in this branch of the law that the all-important question of the burden of proof turns upon a point of the purest technicality, for which no justification in terms of principle or expediency is to be found. It is, no doubt, too late now for the courts themselves to rid the law of these technicalities, but if the law of employers' liability were more generally realised to consist of both the common law and the statutory duties and their combined effect considered as a whole, the birth of still more technical distinctions might be avoided.[76] Some amelioration may come about as the result of the gradual replacement of the present legislation by regulations made under the Health and Safety at Work, etc., Act 1974,[77] particularly since that Act allows distinctions to be made between the defences available in criminal prosecutions and civil actions[78] but it seems unlikely that the "conflict" between penal and compensation purposes will ever be eradicated.[79]

---

[73] *Ante*, p. 199.
[74] In *Eaves* v. *Morris Motors Ltd.* [1961] 2 Q.B. 385, 400, Pearson L.J. suggested that the reason why no regulations have been made for the fencing of dangerous materials (Factories Act 1961, s.14(6)) lies in the difficulty of drafting general provisions for the fencing of such things.
[75] This is the effect of *Close* v. *Steel Co. of Wales* [1962] A.C. 367. See the criticism of Lord Hailsham L.C. in *F.E. Callow (Engineers) Ltd.* v. *Johnson* [1971] A.C. 335, 342–343.
[76] Perhaps Lord Hailsham's speech in *F.E. Callow (Engineers) Ltd.* v. *Johnson, supra*, marks the beginning of a somewhat less technical approach to this part of the law. *cf.* however, the concurring speech of Lord Donovan, *ibid.* at p. 355 and the dissenting speech of Viscount Dilhorne, *ibid.* at pp. 354–355.
[77] See *ante*, p. 188, but this is proceeding very slowly.
[78] s.47(2), (3).
[79] See also Hepple and Matthews, *Tort, Cases and Materials*, (3rd ed.), Chap. 11, Part 6.

CHAPTER 9

LIABILITY FOR LAND AND STRUCTURES[1]

INTRODUCTION

THE greater part of this chapter concerns the liability of an occupier of premises for damage done to visitors to the premises and the main source of the law is the Occupiers' Liability Act 1957. Where things done on the premises affect other premises, that is the province of the law of nuisance, which is dealt with in Chapter 14. "Liability for premises," though it would be a neat antithesis to the "liability for products" in the next chapter would not, however, be an exact description, for the rules now to be discussed are not limited to immovable property like open land, houses, railway stations and bridges, but have been extended to movable structures like ships, gangways and scaffolding. Technically, a claim by a passenger in a vehicle against its owner[2] in respect of a collision caused by the defective condition of the vehicle[3] could be framed as one falling within the scope of this chapter, though most lawyers would probably conceive it more as a case of common law negligence. No real difficulties arise over the borderline between these two heads of liability because the duty under the Act is for most purposes identical to the ordinary duty in negligence; and the courts are in any event quite ready to accept that the law of negligence can operate concurrently with the statutory liability.[4] Henceforth we shall use the expression "premises" because that does cover the vast majority of cases.

Common law before the Occupiers' Liability Act 1957

At common law the duties of an occupier were cast in a descending scale to four different kinds of persons and a brief account is necessary to gain a full understanding of the Act. The highest degree of care was owed by the occupier to one who entered in pursuance of a contract with him (*e.g.* a guest in an hotel): in that case there was an implied warranty that the premises were as safe as reasonable care and skill could make them.[5] A lower duty was

---

[1] North, *Occupiers' Liability* (1971) is the leading treatment.
[2] If the defect was caused by the manufacturer or a previous owner the case would fall under the principles considered in Chap. 10. The present chapter deals with cases where the defendant has control of the structure when the damage occurs.
[3] Before the Act of 1957 is was clear that at common law the special rules of occupiers' liability had no relevance to the way the vehicle was driven: *Haseldine* v. *Daw* [1941] 2 K.B. 343, 353, 373.
[4] See *post*, p. 208.
[5] But where the use of the premises was merely ancillary to the main purpose of the contract the occupier warranted that he, and perhaps his independent contractor, had taken reasonable care to see that the premises were safe.

owed to the "invitee," that is to say, a person who (without any contract) entered on business of interest both to himself and the occupier (*e.g.* a customer coming into a shop to view the wares): he was entitled to expect that the occupier should prevent damage from unusual danger, of which he knew or ought to have known.[6] Lower still was the duty to the "licensee," a person who entered with the occupier's express or implied permission but without any community of interest with the occupier: the occupier's duty towards him was to warn him of any concealed danger or trap of which he actually knew.[7] Finally, there was the trespasser, to whom under the original common law there was owed only a duty to abstain from deliberate or reckless injury.[8] With regard to lawful visitors the tripartite classification into contractual entrants, invitees and licensees did not provide a complete picture of the law for the courts sometimes showed themselves willing to confine these categories to cases arising from the static condition of the premises, and to treat accidents arising from an activity on the premises as governed by the general law of negligence. As Denning L.J. graphically put it:

> "If a landowner is driving his car down his private drive and meets someone lawfully walking upon it, then he is under a duty to take reasonable care so as not to injure the walker; and his duty is the same, no matter whether it is his gardener coming up with his plants, a tradesman delivering his goods, a friend coming to tea, or a flag seller seeking a charitable gift."[9]

The law was widely thought to be unsatisfactory and to have ossified in the form in which it was stated in *Indermaur* v. *Dames*[10] at a time when the general law of negligence was undeveloped. It was, therefore, referred to the Law Reform Committee in 1952 and as a result of the Committee's Report[11] the Occupiers' Liability Act 1957 was passed.

Modern Law: The Occupier's Liability Act 1957

Scope of the Occupers' Liability Act 1957

The Act abolished the common law distinction between invitees and licensees and substituted for it a single common duty of care owed by the

---

[6] *Indermaur* v. *Dames* (1866) L.R. 1 C.P. 274; affirmed (1867) L.R. 2 C.P. 311.
[7] But the later cases held that if the occupier knew the factual situation the test of his appreciation that it constituted a danger was objective. This blurred the distinction between invitees and licensees.
[8] *Robert Addie & Sons (Collieries) Ltd.* v. *Dumbreck* [1929] A.C. 358.
[9] *Slater* v. *Clay Cross Co. Ltd.* [1956] 2 Q.B. 264, 269.
[10] *Supra.*
[11] Cmnd. 9305, 1954; Odgers [1955] C.L.J. 1; Heuston (1955) 18 M.L.R. 271; Bowett, "Law Reform and Occupier's Liability" (1956) 19 M.L.R. 172. The principal criticisms and recommendations of the Committee are summarised in the twelfth edition of this work, pp. 204–206.

occupier to his "visitors."[12] The definition of "occupier" remains the same as at common law, and "visitors" are those persons who would at common law have been treated as either invitees or licensees.[13] The law therefore continues to treat contractual entrants as a separate category, but this is now of less significance than formerly: if there is an express provision in the contract warranting the safety of the premises, that will govern the case,[14] but if, as is usual, the contract is silent on the matter the Act provides that there shall be implied into the contract a term that the occupier owes the entrant the common duty of care.[15]

We saw how the courts utilised the concept of the "activity duty" to blur the distinction between invitees and licensees at common law and it may be asked whether this concept has survived the Act. On the one hand, it is enacted that the rules provided by the Occupiers' Liability Act "shall have effect, in place of the rules of the common law, to regulate the duty which an occupier of premises owes to visitors in respect of dangers due to the state of the premises *or to things done or omitted to be done on them*."[16] On the other hand, it is also enacted that those rules "shall regulate the nature of the duty imposed by law *in consequence of a person's occupation or control of premises*,"[17] and the "activity duty" does not seem to be aptly described in this way. It arises, generally speaking, by the application of the ordinary principles of negligence and applies equally to occupiers and non-occupiers.[18] It seems that the first provision is not to be read literally as covering all conduct of an occupier on his own premises so that, for example, the Act was regarded as irrelevant when the defendant failed to warn his children against playing with lighted candles,[19] and in *Ogwo* v. *Taylor*[20] a claim arising out of the defendant's negligence in setting fire to his house was decided on the basis of common law negligence. Defects in the premises which were not created by the occupier but which he has failed to remedy must be within the Act and the Act alone if there is no other relationship between him and the plaintiff,[21] for it is then only his role as occupier that puts the defendant under any duty to make the premises safe. The intermediate case is where

---

[12] In the United States, a trend towards the same "unitary" approach to occupiers' liability began with *Rowland* v. *Christian* 443 P. 2d 561 (1968). But this now seems to have stopped. Prosser, *Torts* (5th ed.), p. 433 comments that this "may reflect a ... fundamental dissatisfaction with certain developments in accident law which accelerated during the 1960s—the reduction of whole systems of legal principle to a single, perhaps simplistic, standard of reasonable care, the sometimes blind subordination of other legitimate social objectives to the goals of accident prevention and compensation and the commensurate shifting of the decisional balance of power to the jury."

[13] s.1(2).

[14] In the great majority of personal injury cases an express provision can now only be effective if it favours the entrant: a term reducing the occupier's duty below the common duty of care will usually be void under s.2 of the Unfair Contract Terms Act 1977: *post*, p. 220.

[15] s.5(1). A contractual entrant may frame his claim in the alternative as a non-contractual visitor: *Sole* v. *W. J. Hallt* [1973] Q.B. 574.

[16] s.1(1).

[17] s.1(2).

[18] *Riden* v. *Billings & Sons* [1957] 1 Q.B. 46, 56, *per* Denning L.J., affirmed [1958] A.C. 240. *Ogwo* v. *Taylor* [1988] A.C. 431, 434, *per* Dillon L.J., affirmed *ibid.* p. 441.

[19] *Jauffar* v. *Akhbar*, The Times, February 10, 1984.

[20] [1988] A.C. 431. The case was in fact pleaded in the alternative under both heads: see the decision of the Court of Appeal *ibid.*, p. 434.

[21] If there is (*e.g.* employer and employee), the plaintiff may rely upon both the Act and any duty incident to that relationship.

the defendant by some positive act creates a danger affecting the condition of the premises and here the matter is probably covered both by the Act and by the law of negligence. The issue is rarely likely to be of very much practical significance[22] for there can be little if any difference between the duty of care in negligence and the common duty of care as applied to current activities.[23] From a pleading point of view the answer would seem to be to plead the Act and negligence as alternatives wherever there is any doubt.

As before, the occupier's duties apply not only to land and buildings but also to fixed and movable structures,[24] and they govern his liability in respect of damage to property as well as injury to the person, including the property of persons not themselves visitors.[25] The Act also made certain alterations in the liability of a landlord to the visitors of his tenants though these have now been replaced by further legislation.[26]

Occupier

The duty under the Act is imposed upon the "occupier," but the important question is not so much "Who occupies the premises?," using the word "occupy" in its normal sense, as "Who has control over them?" The word occupier is simply a convenient one to denote a person who has a sufficient degree of control over premises to put him under a duty of care towards those who come lawfully upon the premises.[27] An owner in possession is, no doubt, an "occupier"; an owner who has demised the premises to another and parted with possession is not.[28] But an absentee owner may "occupy" through his servant and remain subject to the duty[29] and he may also be subject to it though he has contracted to allow a third party to have the use of the premises.[30] On the other hand, it is not necessary that an "occupier" should have any estate in land[31] or even exclusive occupation.[32] There may

---

[22] The issue arose in a curious form in *New Zealand Insurance Co.* v. *Prudential Insurance Co.* [1976] 1 N.Z.L.R. 84 where an indemnity policy set different limits for occupiers' liability and general public liability. Though the court discussed the various academic views on the scope of the Act, it declined to give any firm opinion.

[23] In *Ogwo* v. *Taylor, supra*, in the Court of Appeal, Neill L.J. implied at p. 439 that on the facts the common law duty might be *higher* than that under the Act. In *Ferguson* v. *Welsh* [1987] 1 W.L.R. 1553, 1561, Lord Keith remarked that the plaintiff's "alternative case, based on the ordinary common law duty of care, does not raise any considerations of a different nature to those applicable to the statutory case."

[24] s.1(3)(*a*). *Bunker* v. *Charles Brand & Son Ltd.* [1969] 2 Q.B. 480; *Hollingworth* v. *Southern Ferries* [1977] 2 Lloyd's Rep. 70; *cf. Wheeler* v. *Copas* [1981] 3 All E.R. 405.

[25] s.1(3)(*b*). See further *post*, p. 224.

[26] *Post*, p. 237.

[27] *Wheat* v. *Lacon & Co. Ltd.* [1966] A.C. 552, 577, *per* Lord Denning.

[28] A landlord may, nevertheless, be liable if the conditions of s.4 of the Defective Premises Act 1972 are fulfilled. See *post*, p. 237.

[29] *Wheat* v. *Lacon & Co. Ltd., supra.*; Weir, *Casebook on Tort* (6th ed.), p. 82. A company can only occupy through its servants: *ibid.* at p. 571, *per* Viscount Dilhorne; *Stone* v. *Taffe* [1974] 1 W.L.R. 1575; *Yeats* (1976) 39 M.L.R. 95.

[30] *Wheat* v. *Lacon & Co. Ltd., supra; Fisher* v. *C.H.T. Ltd. (No. 2)* [1966] 2 Q.B. 475. See also, *e.g. Hawkins* v. *Coulsdon & Purley U.D.C.* [1954] 1 Q.B. 319; *Greene* v. *Chelsea Borough Council* [1954] 2 Q.B. 127, where requisitioning authorities were held to occupy requisitioned houses which were being lived in by persons they had placed in them. *cf. Kearney* v. *Eric Waller Ltd.* [1967] 1 Q.B. 29.

[31] *Humphreys* v. *Dreamland (Margate) Ltd.* (1930) 144 L.T. 529.

[32] *Hartwell* v. *Grayson Rollo and Clover Docks Ltd.* [1947] K.B. 901; *Donovan* v. *Cammell Laird & Co.* [1949] 2 All E.R. 82. A local authority which has made a compulsory purchase order and served a notice of entry becomes an occupier when the former owner vacates the premises, and it is unnecessary that there should be any actual or symbolic taking of possession: *Harris* v. *Birkenhead Corp.* [1976] 1 W.L.R. 279.

thus be more than one "occupier" of the same structure or part of the structure.[33] The foundation of occupier's liability is occupational control, *i.e.* control associated with and arising from presence in and use of or activity in the premises."[34] Whether this exists is a question of degree: a contractor undertaking a large building development would be an occupier of the site, but a decorator painting a house would not.[35] Such occupational control may perfectly well be shared between two or more people, but where this is so, though each is under the same common duty of care, it does not follow that what that duty requires of each of them is necessarily itself the same.[36]

Visitors

The common duty of care is owed by the occupier to his "visitors" and they are those persons who would at common law have been treated as invitees or licensees.[37] For all practical purposes, therefore, the distinction between invitees and licensees was abolished.[38] A visitor is generally a person to whom the occupier has given express or implied permission to enter and the principal category opposed to visitor is that of trespasser, whose rights are governed not by the Act of 1957 but by the Occupiers' Liability Act 1984.[39] However, the Act of 1957 extends the concept of visitor to include persons who enter the premises for any purpose in the exercise of a right conferred by law, for they are to be treated as permitted by the occupier to be there for that purpose, whether they in fact have his permission or not.[40] The occupier therefore owes the common duty of care to firemen attending a fire, to policemen executing a search warrant and to members of the public entering recreation grounds under rights guaranteed by law.[41] On the other hand, it has been held that despite the wide wording of the Act, a person using a public[42] or private[43] right of way is not a visitor for the purposes of the Act. The user of a private right of way is now owed a duty under the Occupiers' Liability Act 1984,[44] but that aside, the owner of the highway[45] or servient tenement has no obligation to the user to maintain its safety, as opposed to not creating dangers on it.[46] Persons exercising access rights under the

---

[33] *Wheat* v. *Lacon & Co. Ltd.*; *Fisher* v. *C.H.T. Ltd. (No. 2), supra*; *AMF International Ltd.* v. *Magnet Bowling Ltd.* [1968] 1 W.L.R. 1028.

[34] *Wheat* v. *Lacon & Co. Ltd., supra* at p. 589, *per* Lord Pearson.

[35] *Page* v. *Read* (1984) 134 N.L.J. 723.

[36] *Wheat* v. *Lacon*, at p. 581, *per* Lord Denning; at pp. 585–586, *per* Lord Morris; at p. 587, *per* Lord Pearce.

[37] s.1(2).

[38] Following the recommendation of the Law Reform Committee: Cmnd. 9305 (1954), para. 78(1). "It is true that this is not done in so many words, but no significance is to be attached to this omission. A legal distinction is abolished by depriving it of legal consequences": Payne, (1958) 21 M.L.R. 359, 360.

[39] *Post*, p. 225.

[40] s.2(6). For powers of entry of public officials see Cmnd. 8092–1 (1981), Appendix 4.

[41] The balance of authority at common law was against the existence of a special category of persons entering as of right. The firemen and policemen in our examples were probably to be treated as invitees, the users of the recreation ground as licensees: see further the sixth edition of this work, pp. 692–696 and Cmnd. 9305 (1954), paras. 37–38.

[42] *Greenhalgh* v. *British Railways Board* [1969] 2 Q.B. 286.

[43] *Holden* v. *White* [1982] 2 Q.B. 679.

[44] See *post*, p. 225.

[45] A highway authority may have a duty to maintain a highway under the Highways Act 1980: *post*, p. 418.

[46] But see Clerk & Lindsell, *Torts* (16th ed.), para. 13–12 where it is argued that *Thomas* v. *British Railways Board* [1976] Q.B. 912 may support a duty at common law in some of these cases.

National Parks and Access to the Countryside Act 1949 are not visitors[47] but a duty is owed to them under the Act of 1984.[48]

Implied permission

It is a question to be decided on the facts of each case whether the occupier has impliedly given permission to a person to enter upon his structure, and the onus of proving an implied permission rests upon the person who claims that it existed.[49] The simplest example of implied permission is also the commonest in practice. Any person who enters the occupier's premises for the purpose of communicating with him[50] will be treated as having the occupier's tacit permission unless he knows or ought to know that he has been forbidden to enter,[51] *e.g.* by a notice "no canvassers, hawkers or circulars."[52] The occupier may, of course, withdraw this licence by refusing to speak or deal with the entrant, but if he does so the entrant has a reasonable time in which to leave the premises before he becomes a trespasser.[53] Other cases depend very much upon their particular facts and it is difficult to state any general rule. This much, however, is clear in principle: the facts must support the implication from the occupier's conduct that he has permitted entry,[54] not merely tolerated it, for knowledge is not tantamount to consent and failure to turn one's premises into a fortress does not confer a licence on anyone who may seek to take advantage of one's inaction.[55] This said, it must, however, be admitted that in some cases the courts have gone to surprising lengths in implying licences in the teeth of the facts. The classic example is *Lowery* v. *Walker*.[56] For 35 years the public had used a short cut across a farmer's field to a railway station. He had often interfered with them in doing so, but had never taken legal proceedings

---

[47] s.1(4).

[48] *Post*, p. 225.

[49] *Edwards* v. *Railway Executive* [1952] A.C. 737.

[50] Not necessarily in connection with business of the occupier: *Brunner* v. *Williams* [1975] Crim.L.R. 250.

[51] *Robson* v. *Hallett* [1967] 2 Q.B. 393; *Christian* v. *Johanesson* [1956] N.Z.L.R. 664; Cmd. 9305 (1954), para. 67. *cf. Dunster* v. *Abbott* [1954] 1 W.L.R. 58, 59–60, *per* Denning L.J.; and *Great Central Ry.* v. *Bates* [1921] 3 K.B. 578. The policeman in the last case, despite some unguarded dicta of Lord Sterndale M.R., was not acting in the execution of his duty: du Parcq J. in *Davis* v. *Lisle* [1936] 2 K.B. 434, 439–440. Nor would he now be assisted by the Occupiers' Liability Act 1957, s.2(6) (see *ante*, p. 216).

[52] *Quaere* as to the effect of "Private" or "Keep Out" in such cases: *cf. Christian* v. *Johanesson, supra*, at p. 666. Dismissive words may sometimes be abuse rather than revocation of the licence: *Snook* v. *Mannion* [1982] Crim.L.R. 601.

[53] *Robson* v. *Hallett, supra*; *Kay* v. *Hibbert* [1977] Crim.L.R. 226.

[54] *Edwards* v. *Railway Executive* [1952] A.C. 737; *Phipps* v. *Rochester Corp.* [1955] 1 Q.B. 450, 455; *Faulkner* v. *Willetts* [1982] R.T.R. 159. It is what may properly be inferred that counts, not the occupier's actual intention. Where O licenses A to enter his land to do work, A may have ostensible authority to invite B to enter as a sub-contractor even though the contract between O and A forbids this: *Ferguson* v. *Welsh* [1987] 1 W.L.R. 1553.

[55] "Repeated trespass of itself confers no licence; the owner of a park in the neighbourhood of a town knows probably only too well that it will be raided by young and old to gather flowers, nuts or mushrooms whenever they get an opportunity. But because he does not cover his park wall with a *chevaux de frise* or post a number of keepers to chase away intruders how is it to be said that he has licensed that which he cannot prevent?": *Edwards* v. *Railway Executive, supra*, at p. 746, *per* Lord Goddard C.J.

[56] [1911] A.C. 10; *Cooke* v. *Midland G.W. Ry. of Ireland* [1909] A.C. 229 (the facts must be supplemented from the report of the case in the lower courts: [1908] 2 Ir.R. 242). More easily supportable are the decisions in: *Oldham* v. *Sheffield Corp.* (1927) 136 L.T. 681; *Coleshill* v. *Manchester Corp.* [1928] 1 K.B. 776; *Purkis* v. *Walthamstow B.C.* (1934) 151 L.T. 30; *Phipps* v. *Rochester Corp.* [1955] 1 Q.B. 450.

against them to stop them trespassing, because most of them were customers for his milk. The House of Lords upheld a finding that they were licensees, not trespassers, and that one of them who was mauled by a savage horse, which the farmer had turned into the field without notice, could recover against him. A number of decisions in this category concern children, and it has been suggested that it might be rather easier to imply a licence in favour of a child; but there seems no good reason why this should be so and such a view seems inconsistent with *Edwards* v. *Railway Executive.*[57] The plaintiff, a boy of nine, got through a fence dividing a recreation ground from a railway, climbed up the embankment to fetch a ball on the other side of the railway line and was injured by a passing train. For many years children had climbed through the fence by breaking the wire to slide down the embankment. The Railway Executive knew this and had repaired the fence whenever damage had been observed. It was held that there was no evidence of any licence to enter the railway land.

In many cases the court has been astute to find an implied licence because of the severity of the law relating to liability to trespassers. The trespasser's position has now been improved[58] and it is likely that implied permission will be rather less readily found,[59] but the courts will still have to grapple with the problem of the implied licence, for the duty owed to a trespasser is by no means identical with that owed to a visitor under the Occupiers' Liability Act.[60]

The duty owed to a visitor does not extend to anyone who is injured by going where he is expressly or impliedly warned by the occupier not to go, as where a man falls over a cliff by getting on the wrong side of railings erected by the proprietor who has also put up a notice of the danger of going near the cliff[61]; or where a tradesman's boy deliberately chooses to go into a pitch dark part of the premises not included in the invitation and falls downstairs there.[62] Further the duty does not protect a visitor who goes to a part of the premises where no one would reasonably expect him to go.[63] A person who has two pieces of land and invites the public to come on one of them, can, if he chooses, limit the invitation to that one of the two pieces; but if the other piece is contiguous to the first piece, he may be held to have invited the public to come to both pieces.[64] Again, the plaintiff cannot succeed if,

---

[57] [1952] A.C. 737.

[58] See *post*, pp. 225–227.

[59] "The 'licence' treated as having been granted in such cases was a legal fiction employed to justify extending to meritorious trespassers, particularly if they were children, the benefit of the duty which at common law an occupier owed to his licensees . . . ": *British Railways Board* v. *Herrington* [1972] A.C. 877, 933, *per* Lord Diplock.

[60] But if what is in issue is a breach of statutory duty there is no universal rule that the plaintiff is disentitled to recover if he is a trespasser, for everything depends on the construction of the statute in question: *Westwood* v. *Post Office* [1974] A.C. 1.

[61] *Anderson* v. *Coutts* (1894) 58 J.P. 369.

[62] *Lewis* v. *Ronald* (1909) 101 L.T. 534; distinguished in *Prole* v. *Allen* [1950] 1 All E.R. 476.

[63] *Mersey Docks and Harbour Board* v. *Procter* [1923] A.C. 253, where there was a great difference of opinion as to the application of this principle to the facts; *cf. Walker* v. *M.R. Co.* (1886) 55 L.T. 489; *Lee* v. *Luper* [1936] 3 All E.R. 817; *Gould* v. *McAuliffe* [1941] 2 All E.R. 527; *Periscinotti* v. *Brighton West Pier* (1961) 105 S.J. 526.

[64] *Pearson* v. *Coleman Bros.* [1948] 2 K.B. 359, 375, *per* Lord Greene M.R.

although rightly on the structure, he makes a use of it alien to the invitation. "When you invite a person into your house to use the staircase you do not invite him to slide down the bannisters."[65] So, where a stevedore in loading a ship was injured by making use of the hatch covers for loading, although he knew that a statutory regulation forbade this practice in his own interests, it was held that he had no remedy.[66] In fact, in all these cases the plaintiff ceases to be a visitor and becomes a mere trespasser.[67] Where, however, the negligence of the occupier causes the visitor to take an involuntary step outside the area in which he is permitted to be, he does not thereby cease to be a visitor to whom a duty of care is owed,[68] and the position is probably the same even if the involuntary step is not caused by the occupier's negligence.[69] A person may equally exceed his licence by staying on premises after the occupier's permission has expired but the limitation of time must be clearly brought home to him. Thus a person on licensed premises who remained there when drinks were being consumed long after closing time was held to continue to be a visitor in the absence of evidence that he knew of instructions from the brewers to their manager forbidding this practice.[70]

Although it has been said that "infancy as such is no more a status conferring rights, or a root of title imposing obligations on others to respect it, than infirmity or imbecility"[71] the above principles have been applied with some degree of allowance for the proclivities of young children. The common duty of care, like the common law before it, requires that the occupier must be prepared for children to be less careful than adults[72] but the special characteristics of children are relevant also to the question of whether they enjoy the status of visitor. In *Glasgow Corporation* v. *Taylor*[73] it was alleged that a child aged seven had died from eating poisonous berries which he had picked from a shrub in some public gardens under the control of the corporation. The berries looked like cherries or large blackcurrants and were of a very tempting appearance to children. They thus constituted an "allurement" to the child. The corporation was aware of their poisonous nature, but nevertheless the shrub was not properly fenced from the public nor was any warning given of its deadly character. It was held that these facts disclosed a good cause of action. Certainly the child had no right to take the berries nor even to approach the bush, and an adult doing the same thing might well have become a trespasser, but since the object was an "allurement" the very fact of its being left there constituted a breach of the

---

[65] Scrutton L.J. in *The Carlgarth* [1927] P. 93, 110. In any case, the common duty of care only applies where the visitor is using the premises for the purpose for which he is invited or permitted to be there: s.2(2), *infra*.

[66] *Hillen* v. *I.C.I. (Alkali) Ltd.* [1936] A.C. 65.

[67] *Ibid.* at pp. 69–70, *per* Lord Atkin.

[68] *Braithwaite* v. *S. Durham Steel Co.* [1958] 1 W.L.R. 986.

[69] This provoked a difference of opinion in the High Court of Australia in *Public Transport Commission (N.S.W.)* v. *Perry* (1977) 14 A.L.R. 273. *Quaere* as to the plaintiff whose initial entry is involuntary. He cannot be sued for trespass, but that does not necessarily make him a visitor.

[70] *Stone* v. *Taffe* [1974] 1 W.L.R. 1575. The manager, as agent of the brewers, had authority to invite the plaintiff on to the premises in the first place.

[71] *Glasgow Corp.* v. *Taylor* [1922] 1 A.C. 44, 67, *per* Lord Sumner.

[72] s.2(3)(a).

[73] [1922] 1 A.C. 44.

occupier's duty.[74] On the other hand, there is nothing insidious about a hole in the ground,[75] or a sound, stationary vehicle,[76] or a pile of soil left against a wall,[77] for the danger is as obvious to the child as to anyone else. In the case of very young children, however, there exists a dilemma to which Hamilton L.J. drew attention in *Latham* v. *R. Johnson & Nephew Ltd.*[78]:

> "The child must take the place as he finds it and take care of himself; but how can he take care of himself? If his injury is not to go without legal remedy altogether by reason of his failure to use a diligence which he could not possibly have possessed, the owner of the close might be practically bound to see that the wandering child is as safe as in a nursery."

One escape from this was the concept of the conditional licence, whereby the occupier was treated as giving his permission to enter only if the child were accompanied by a person in charge capable of seeing and avoiding obvious perils and thus of placing both himself and his charge in the position of an ordinary licensee both able and bound to look after himself. Though this was favourably received in several cases and apparently accepted by the Court of Appeal in *Bates* v. *Stone Parish Council*,[79] it gave rise to difficulties: if the child were unaccompanied, he must inevitably be a trespasser, no matter how concealed and insidious the danger; what must be the qualification of the companion; and what degree of infancy calls for the imposition of the condition? The modern practice since *Phipps* v. *Rochester Corporation*[80] seems to be to deal with the matter by taking into account, in measuring the duty of the occupier, his reasonable expectations of the habits of prudent parents in relation to their offspring. This is dealt with below.[81] It must, however, be said that since the Occupiers' Liability Act 1984 there is likely to be very little practical difference between the duties owed to a young child who is a trespasser and one who is a lawful visitor.

Common duty of care

The common duty of care, owed to all visitors and also where the duty of the occupier depends upon a term to be implied in a contract, is defined as "a duty to take such care as in all the circumstances of the case is reasonable to see that the visitor will be reasonably safe in using the premises for the purposes for which he is invited or permitted to be there."[82] The question

---

[74] See also *Lynch* v. *Nurdin* (1841) 1 Q.B. 29; *Holdman* v. *Hamlyn* [1943] K.B. 664. The "allurement" doctrine did not legalise an initial entry to the occupier's land (*Edwards* v. *Railway Executive* [1952] A.C. 737) but seems to have covered interference with things left on the highway, as in *Lynch* v. *Nurdin*.
[75] *Perry* v. *Thomas Wrigley Ltd.* [1955] 1 W.L.R. 1164.
[76] *Donovan* v. *Union Cartage Co. Ltd.* [1933] 2 K.B. 71.
[77] *Latham* v. *R. Johnson & Nephew Ltd.* [1913] 1 K.B. 398.
[78] *Ibid.* at p. 414.
[79] [1954] 1 W.L.R. 1249.
[80] [1955] 1 Q.B. 450.
[81] *Post*, p. 215.
[82] s.2(2). *Ferguson* v. *Welsh* [1987] 1 W.L.R. 1553.

whether the occupier has fulfilled his duty to the visitor is thus dependent upon the facts of the case,[83] and, though the purpose of the visit may be a relevant circumstance, it can no longer be conclusive as it so often was before when it governed the status of the entrant. All the circumstances must be taken into account. If, for example, the owner of an inn permits the resident manager to accept paying guests, both are "occupiers" in relation to such guests, but while the owner may be liable for injury caused to them by a structural defect such as the collapse of a staircase, the manager alone would be liable for injury caused by a defect in his own furnishings, such as a dangerous hole in the carpet of the living room.[84]

The Act itself gives some guidance in applying the common duty of care, and it is laid down[85] that the relevant circumstances include the degree of care and of want of care that may be looked for in the particular visitor, "so that (for example) in proper cases:

(a) an occupier must be prepared for children to be less careful than adults; and

(b) an occupier may expect that a person, in the exercise of his calling, will appreciate and guard against any special risks ordinarily incident to it, so far as the occupier leaves him free to do so."

As to paragraph (a), it reflects the fact that in some circumstances it will be reasonable for the occupier to expect children to be on his premises unaccompanied, but it is submitted that the law is still as it was stated before the Act by Devlin J. in *Phipps* v. *Rochester Corporation*,[86] namely that one of the circumstances which must be taken into account in measuring the occupier's obligation is the degree of care for their children's safety which the occupier may assume will be exercised by the parents.[87] The plaintiff, a boy aged five, was out blackberrying with his sister, aged seven, and they walked across a large open space which formed part of a housing estate being developed by the defendants. The defendants had dug a long deep trench in the middle of the open space, a danger which was quite obvious to an adult. The plaintiff fell in and broke his leg. On the facts it was held that a prudent parent would not have allowed two small children to go alone on the open space in question or, at least, he would have satisfied himself that the place held no dangers for the children. The defendants were entitled to assume that parents would behave in this way and therefore, although the plaintiff was a licensee, the defendants were not in breach of their duty to him. Devlin J.'s judgment squarely placed the primary responsibility for the safety of small children upon their parents:

---

[83] For a case in which the House of Lords gave full consideration to the application of the duty to the facts before them, see *Wheat* v. *Lacon & Co. Ltd.* [1966] A.C. 552. The similarity of the duty to the common law duty of care is demonstrated in *Simms* v. *Leigh Rugby Football Club Ltd.* [1969] 2 All E.R. 923.

[84] *Wheat* v. *Lacon & Co. Ltd., supra*, at pp. 585–586, *per* Lord Morris; 587, *per* Lord Pearce.

[85] s.2(3).

[86] [1955] 1 Q.B. 450. Weir, *Casebook on Tort* (6th ed.), p. 127.

[87] See also *O'Connor* v. *British Transport Commission* [1958] 1 W.L.R. 346.

"It is their duty to see that such children are not allowed to wander about by themselves, or at least to satisfy themselves that the places to which they do allow their children to go unaccompanied are safe for them to go to. It would not be socially desirable if parents were, as a matter of course, able to shift the burden of looking after their children from their own shoulders to those who happen to have accessible bits of land."[88]

It is for this reason that a person who owns a mountain is not obliged to fence it off or to put up warning notices.[89] The occupier will have discharged his duty if the place is reasonably safe for a child who is accompanied by the sort of guardian whom the occupier is in all the circumstances entitled to expect him to have with him. If the child is in fact accompanied by a guardian, then the question will be whether the occupier ought to have foreseen that the source of the child's injury would be a danger to the child, bearing in mind the guardian's responsibility for the child's safety. There seems no reason, at least in theory, why the child's injury should not in an appropriate case be attributed both to the occupier's breach of his common duty of care and to the negligence of the guardian. In such a case the occupier would be liable in full to the child, but presumably could recover contribution from the guardian.[90]

Paragraph (b) clearly preserves such decisions as *Bates* v. *Parker*,[91] to the general effect that "where a householder employs an independent contractor to do work, be it of cleaning or repairing, on his premises, the contractor must satisfy himself as to the safety or condition of that part of the premises on which he is to work."[92] In *Roles* v. *Nathan*[93] two chimney sweeps were killed by carbon monoxide gas while attempting to seal up a "sweep hole" in the chimney of a coke-fired boiler, the boiler being alight at the time, but the occupier was not held liable for their deaths, partly at least on the ground that paragraph (b) applied.[94] As Lord Denning M.R. said, "When a householder calls in a specialist to deal with a defective installation on his premises, he can reasonably expect the specialist to appreciate and guard against the dangers arising from the defect."[95] But the result might no doubt have been different if, for example, the stairs leading to the cellar where the boiler was had given way,[96] for that would not have been a special risk ordinarily incidental to the calling of a sweep. In any case, it is important to

[88] [1955] 1 Q.B. 450, 472.
[89] *Simkiss* v. *Rhondda B.C.* (1983) 81 L.G.R. 460.
[90] Civil Liability (Contribution) Act 1978, *post*, p. 000. See *McCallion* v. *Dodd* [1966] N.Z.L.R. 710.
[91] [1953] 2 Q.B. 231; *Christmas* v. *General Cleaning Contractors* [1952] 1 K.B. 141; affirmed [1953] A.C. 180; Weir, *Casebook on Tort*, (6th ed.), p. 104; Cmd. 9305 (1954), para. 77(iii); *Roles* v. *Nathan* [1963] 1 W.L.R. 1117, 1123, *per* Lord Denning M.R.
[92] *Ibid.* at p. 235, *per* Lord Goddard C.J.
[93] *Supra*; Weir, *Casebook on Tort*, (6th ed.), p. 130.
[94] [1963] 1 W.L.R. 1117, 1123–1125, *per* Lord Denning M.R. Pearson L.J. dissented on the interpretation of the evidence but not on the law. Harman L.J., while not differing from Lord Denning, preferred to base his judgment in favour of the defendant upon the fact that the sweeps had been actually warned of the danger.
[95] [1963] 1 W.L.R. 1117, 1123; *Clare* v. *Whittaker & Son (London) Ltd.* [1976] I.C.R. 1; *Kealey* v. *Heard* [1983] 1 W.L.R. 573.
[96] *Ibid.*; *Bird* v. *King Line* [1970] 2 Lloyd's Rep. 349.

note that the fact that the plaintiff is an expert is only a factor to be taken into account in determining whether there has been a breach of duty: his calling is not in itself a defence. Thus an occupier who negligently starts a fire may be liable to a fireman injured by even an ordinary risk of fighting it if that risk is one which remains even when all proper skill is used.[97]

Specific aspects

Two specific aspects of the common duty of care are also dealt with. Regard is to be had to all the circumstances of the case, so that (for example):

(1) *Warning*

"(*a*) Where damage is caused to a visitor by a danger of which he had been warned by the occupier, the warning is not to be treated without more as absolving the occupier from liability, unless in all the circumstances it was enough to enable the visitor to be reasonably safe."[98]

In most cases, probably, a warning of the danger will be sufficient to enable the visitor to be reasonably safe and so amount to a discharge by the occupier of his duty of care, but if, for some reason, the warning is not sufficient then the occupier remains liable.[99] There are, after all, some situations in which a reasonable man incurs a known risk and the question now, therefore, is whether such a situation existed on the particular facts of the case. It is clear too, since a warning of the danger is not necessarily sufficient to constitute performance of the occupier's duty, that the decision in *London Graving Dock Co.* v. *Horton*[1] is no longer good law.[2] In that case, the House of Lords held that an invitee could not succeed if he had full knowledge of the nature and extent of the danger. Now, however, as in cases where he has actually received a warning, the question is whether a visitor with knowledge of the danger reasonably incurred it.[3]

(2) *Independent contractor*

"(*b*) where damage is caused to a visitor by a danger due to the faulty

---

[97] *Ogwo* v. *Taylor* [1988] A.C. 431; *Salmon* v. *Seafarers Restaurant Ltd.* [1983] 1 W.L.R. 1264. As to the position of "rescuers" generally, see *post*, p. 693. But where there is no negligence by the defendant in starting the fire, then he will only be liable for failing to call attention to unusual risks in the premises: *Bermingham* v. *Sher Bros.* (1980) 124 S.J. 117 (no duty on occupier of warehouse to provide means of egress which would remain safe throughout fire). Strictly, perhaps, only the second type of case falls within the Act, the other involving the common law, but if the plaintiff pleads both the Act and the common law nothing turns on the point.

[98] s.2(4)(*a*). The warning may be given by the occupier's agent: *Roles* v. *Nathan, supra.*

[99] See the different opinions expressed in the Court of Appeal about the warning given in *Roles* v. *Nathan, supra.*

[1] [1951] A.C. 737.

[2] *Roles* v. *Nathan, supra*, at p. 1124, *per* Lord Denning M.R.

[3] *Bunker* v. *Charles Brand & Son Ltd.* [1969] 2 Q.B. 480, 489, *per* O'Connor J. For contributory negligence in relation to the occupier's liability, see *post*, p. 219.

execution of any work of construction, maintenance or repair[4] by an independent contractor employed by the occupier, the occupier is not to be treated without more[5] as answerable for the danger if in all the circumstances he had acted reasonably in entrusting the work to an[6] independent contractor and had taken such steps (if any) as he reasonably ought in order to satisfy himself that the contractor was competent and that the work had been properly done."[7]

This is designed to afford some protection for the occupier who has engaged an independent contractor who has done the work in a faulty manner and was intended to reverse the decision of the House of Lords in *Thompson* v. *Cremin*[8] in so far as that laid down that an invitor was responsible for the shortcomings of his contractor. The paragraph is relevant not only to injuries to visitors entering after the contractor has completed the work, but also to injuries caused during the work by reason of the system adopted by the contractor.[9]

The operation of the paragraph is illustrated by two cases from the period before the Act. In *Haseldine* v. *Daw*[10] H was going to visit a tenant in a block of flats belonging to D and was injured when the lift fell to the bottom of its shaft as a result of the negligence of a firm of engineers employed by D to repair the lift. It was held that D, having employed a competent firm of engineers to make periodical inspections of the lift, to adjust it and report on it, had discharged the duty owed to H, whether H was an invitee or licensee. As Scott L.J. observed:

"the landlord of a block of flats, as occupier of the lifts, does not profess as such to be either an electrical or, as in this case, a hydraulic engineer. Having no technical skill he cannot rely on his own judgment, and the duty of care towards his invitees requires him to obtain and follow good technical advice. If he did not do so, he would, indeed, be guilty of negligence. To hold him responsible for the misdeeds of his independent contractor would be to make him insure the safety of his lift. That duty can only arise out of contract. . . . "[11]

In *Woodward* v. *Mayor of Hastings*,[12] on the other hand, a pupil at a

---

[4] A broad, purposive interpretation is required which will embrace demolition: *Ferguson* v. *Welsh* [1987] 1 W.L.R. 1553.
[5] For possible meanings of this cryptic phrase see North, *op. cit.*, p. 144.
[6] How can it ever be unreasonable to employ *a* (as opposed to *the*) contractor?
[7] s.2(4)(*b*); *O'Connor* v. *Swan & Edgar* (1963) 107 S.J. 215; *Gibson* v. *Skibs A/S Marina, etc.* [1966] 2 All E.R. 476. The burden of proving that the danger was due to the fault of an independent contractor rests with the occupier: *Christmas* v. *Blue Star Line* [1961] 1 Lloyd's Rep. 94; *A.M.F. International Ltd.* v. *Magnet Bowling Ltd.* [1968] 1 W.L.R. 1028, 1042–1043.
[8] [1953] 2 All E.R. 1181.
[9] *A.M.F. International Ltd.* v. *Magnet Bowling Ltd.* [1968] 1 W.L.R. 1028; *Ferguson* v. *Welsh* [1987] 1 W.L.R. 1553.
[10] [1941] 2 K.B. 343.
[11] *Ibid.* at p. 356. See also *per* Goddard L.J. at p. 374.
[12] [1945] K.B. 174.

school for which the defendants were responsible fell and was injured on an icy step which had been negligently left in a dangerous condition by a cleaner. Even assuming that the cleaner was an independent contractor, it was held that the defendants were liable and *Haseldine* v. *Daw* was distinguished. Technical knowledge was required in the maintenance and repair of a lift, but such considerations were not relevant in *Woodward's* case. "The craft of the charwoman may have its mysteries, but there is no esoteric quality in the nature of the work which the cleaning of a snow-covered step demands."[13]

Where an independent contractor has been employed, therefore, the question today is whether the occupier himself has done all that reasonable care requires of him. He must take reasonable steps to satisfy himself that the contractor he employs is competent, and, if the character of the work permits, he must take similar steps to see that the work has been properly done. In fact, where the work is especially complex, as with the construction of a large building or a ship, he may even have to cause the independent contractor's work to be supervised by a properly instructed architect or other professional man.[14] As the dictum of Scott L.J. indicates, there are many cases in which the technical nature of the work to be done will require the occupier to employ an independent contractor and he will be negligent if he attempts to do it himself. This does not mean, however, that a householder must not himself undertake some ordinary domestic repair such as the fixing of a new door handle. Provided that he does the work with the care and skill of a reasonably competent carpenter he has fulfilled his duty.[15]

Since the occupier may be responsible where he has notice of the contractor's incompetence or bad system of work, can he be liable to the contractor's employee who is injured thereby? An affirmative answer was given by a majority of the House of Lords in *Ferguson* v. *Welsh*,[16] but it would be surprising if this meant that an ordinary householder who happened to be aware that his contractor's system was unsafe was thereby under a duty to tell the contractor's workman how to do his work.[17]

Contributory negligence

In view of some doubts which existed as to whether the scheme of the Law

---

[13] *Ibid.* at p. 183, *per* du Parcq L.J.

[14] *A.M.F. International Ltd.* v. *Magnet Bowling Ltd.* [1968] 1 W.L.R. 1028, 1044, 1045–1047, *per* Mocatta J.; *Kealey* v. *Heard* [1983] 1 All E.R. 973. Mocatta J. also held that the negligence of the architect or other supervisor would not itself involve the occupier in liability for otherwise, in technical cases, the common duty of care would become equivalent to the obligation of an insurer. Negligence in supervision would not fall under s.2(4)(*b*), but it must be remembered that the purpose of s.2(4) is to insist that in determining whether the common duty of care has been discharged, regard is to be had to all the circumstances. Paragraphs (*a*) and (*b*) are introduced by the words "so that (for example)" and there is no reason for saying that an occupier is necessarily liable for the negligence of his independent contractor except when s.2(4)(*b*) applies.

[15] *Wells* v. *Cooper* [1958] 2 Q.B. 265; Weir, *Casebook on Tort*, (6th ed.), p. 134.

[16] [1987] 1 W.L.R. 1553.

[17] See, *per* Lord Goff at p. 1564. Like Lord Oliver, he considered that if there were special circumstances in which an occupier would be liable to the contractor's servant it would be *qua* joint tortfeasor rather than occupier.

Reform Contributory Negligence Act 1945[18] applied where an invitee was guilty of lack of care for his own safety it is perhaps surprising that the Occupiers' Liability Act does not expressly incorporate the Act of 1945. However, the point is probably implicit[19] and judges have in numerous cases applied the 1945 Act without hesitation to reduce damages.[20] Where the plaintiff's fault is extreme it may, of course, amount to the sole legal cause of his loss.[21]

Exclusion of liability

We have seen that the occupier may be able to discharge his duty by warning the visitor of the danger if the warning is enough to make the visitor reasonably safe. If he chooses to impose on the visitor's permission to enter a condition excluding or restricting his duty the answer will turn on whether or not the Unfair Contract Terms Act 1977 applies to the case. This Act, despite its short title, extends much further than the control of contractual exemption clauses. Section 2 provides that:

(1) A person cannot by reference to any contract term or to a notice[22] exclude or restrict his liability for death or personal injury resulting from negligence;

(2) in the case of other loss or damage, a person cannot so exclude or restrict his liability for negligence except in so far as the term or notice satisfies the requirement of reasonableness.[23]

The definition of "negligence" expressly includes the breach of the common duty of care imposed by the Occupiers' Liability Act 1957[24] but the prohibition on exclusion of liability applies only where the duty arises from things done in the course of a business or from the occupation of premises used for the business purposes of the occupier. A business probably requires at least some degree of regularity, so that an isolated transaction whereby access to land was granted for payment would probably not fall within the ban, but the Act contains an extended definition which makes the concept cover some activities which would not ordinarily be thought of as a business.[25] Activities

---

[18] See the twelfth edition of this work, p. 217.

[19] The statement of Diplock L.J.: "My neighbour does not enlarge my duty of care for his safety by neglecting it himself" (*Wheat* v. *Lacon & Co. Ltd.* [1966] 1 Q.B. 335, 372) which was approved by Viscount Dilhorne in the House of Lords [1966] A.C. 552, 576, is not inconsistent with this. The point is that a person cannot, by carelessness of his own safety, thereby put an occupier in breach of the common duty of care.

[20] See, *e.g. Woolins* v. *British Celanese Ltd.* (1966) 1 K.I.R. 438; *Stone* v. *Taffe* [1974] 1 W.L.R. 1575.

[21] See, *e.g. Brayshaw* v. *Leeds C.C.* [1984] 2 C.L. 234.

[22] Defined in s.14, *e.g.* a sign at the entry to the premises.

[23] See s.11.

[24] The Act does not prevent exclusion of a stricter duty: s.1(1)(*b*). By virtue of s.1(4) it is immaterial whether liability "arises directly or vicariously." This would probably cover any situations where the occupier is liable for the negligence of an independent contractor.

[25] By s.14 " 'business' includes a profession and the activities of any government department or local or public authority." The concept of business liability is relevant for various other purposes under the Unfair Contract Terms Act. For a full survey, see Benjamin's *Sale of Goods* (3rd ed.).

in aid of charity are an obvious example which would present the court with difficult questions of degree.[26] Since the owner of a farm or a commercial forest is clearly occupying his land in the course of a business, the effect of the Act as originally formulated was to cause restriction of public access and it was amended by section 2 of the Occupiers' Liability Act 1984, which provides that the:

"liability of an occupier of premises for breach of an obligation or duty towards a person obtaining access to the premises for recreational or educational purposes, being liability for loss or damage suffered by reason of the dangerous state of the premises, is not a business liability of the occupier unless granting that person such access for the purposes concerned falls within the business of the occupier."

Hence if a farmer has on his land a ruinous castle he may allow access on condition that he is not liable for death or personal injury caused by the state of the premises,[27] but the ancient monuments body English Heritage may not impose such a condition because admission for recreation or education is (probably) its business within the meaning of the Act. The liberty to exclude liability is, however, confined to damage suffered by reason of the dangerous state of the premises, so that if the visitor is knocked down by the farmer's tractor the exclusion, no matter how widely drawn, is ineffective. The Unfair Contract Terms Act does not abolish the defence of *volenti non fit injuria* but provides that a person's agreement to or awareness of an exempting condition or notice "is not of itself to be taken as indicating his voluntary acceptance of the risk."[28]

Where the Unfair Contract Terms Act does not apply because the premises are not occupied for business purposes the matter is still governed by section 2(1) of the 1957 Act, which provides that the occupier owes the common duty of care "except in so far as he is free to and does extend, restrict, modify or exclude his duty ... by agreement or otherwise." No contract is necessary for this purpose, for section 2(1) gives statutory force to the decision of the Court of Appeal, shortly before the Act, in *Ashdown* v. *Samuel Williams & Sons*[29]—though the actual decision would now go the other way, since the defendants were business occupiers. The plaintiff was a licensee on land belonging to the defendants when she was knocked down and injured by railway trucks which were being negligently shunted along a railway line on the land. Various notices had been posted by the defendants to the effect that every person on the land was there at his own risk and should have no claim against the defendants for any injury whatsoever, and it was found as a fact that they had taken reasonable steps to bring the

---

[26] See, *e.g. White* v. *Blackmore* [1972] 2 Q.B. 651.

[27] But if the farmer charges the public even a small sum for admission there is likely to be a business occupation.

[28] s.2(3). See further *post*, p. 687.

[29] [1957] 1 Q.B. 409; *White* v. *Blackmore* [1972] 2 Q.B. 651.

conditions contained in the notices to the plaintiff's attention. It was held, therefore, that the plaintiff could not recover. Despite criticism that the absence of a contract should have been fatal to the defence,[30] the decision seems to accord with general principle. If I can exclude you from my property altogether, why can I not permit you to enter upon any terms that I like to make? The result might, indeed, be construed as a contract whereby you give up what would otherwise be your legal rights in return for my allowing you to enter, but this construction is not essential to the validity of the conditions.[31] The occupier can (or at least could, as the law then stood) say simply: "You have your choice: stay out of my premises or enter them on my terms. You will be a trespasser unless you have my permission. I give it subject to your agreeing that I owe you no duty. If later you claim to have entered without so agreeing you must admit you have entered without my permission and you will indeed be a trespasser."[32]

It will be noticed that *Ashdown's* case was concerned not with the static condition of the land on which the plaintiff was a licensee but with the current activities of the occupier. Clearly, therefore, the power to exclude liability is not restricted to the static condition of the structure, but it is less easy to justify the existence of that power with regard to current activities. "There is much to be said for an occupier who is prepared to grant a gratuitous licence provided he is not put to trouble or expense in inspecting or maintaining his property: there is less to be said for one who claims a right to shoot, drive, shunt or blast without taking reasonable care."[33]

The occupier's power to exclude the common duty of care is, however, governed by the words "in so far as he is free to" do so. Clearly, therefore, the Occupiers' Liability Act does not enlarge the power which existed at common law. It is submitted, for example, that there could be no exclusion of liability to a person entering in exercise of a right conferred by law. Furthermore, the law's original level of duty to trespassers (not to injure them deliberately or recklessly) represented a minimum standard of conduct which could not be excluded, for A cannot lawfully license B to inflict a wilful injury upon him. However, the duty owed to trespassers is now much higher[34] and in practice in some cases approaches the level of the common duty of care. To make this the minimum standard would largely remove by the back door the freedom to exclude liability which Parliament has conferred. Perhaps there is much to be said for allowing non-business occupiers to exclude liability for all injury except that inflicted wilfully or recklessly. If it be objected that a lawful visitor may therefore be worse off than a trespasser entering without notice of the occupier's terms it may be replied that at least the visitor is, or ought to be, aware of these terms.

[30] See Gower (1956) 19 M.L.R. 536.
[31] It was rejected by Lord Greene M.R. in *Wilkie* v. *L.P.T.B.* [1947] 1 All E.R. 258, 260. *cf. Gore* v. *Van Der Lann* [1967] 2 Q.B. 31, and Odgers, "The Strange Case of Mrs. Gore" (1970) 86 L.Q.R. 69.
[32] On the other hand, as Lord Denning M.R. forcibly points out in *White* v. *Blackmore* [1972] 2 Q.B. 651, 665–666, this approach derogates severely from the purpose of s.2(4)(*a*) of the Act. Further, the duty to trespassers has risen since *Ashdown's* case: *infra.*
[33] Odgers [1957] C.L.J. 39, 54.
[34] See *post*, p. 225.

Effect of contract on occupier's liability to third parties

It was the opinion of the Law Reform Committee[35] that where a person contracts with the occupier for the use of premises on the footing that he is to be entitled to permit third persons to use them, the duty owed by the occupier to those third persons is the same as that owed to the other party to the contract.[36] This could lead to a person being deprived of his rights by a contract to which he was not a party and of whose provisions he was unaware. It is therefore provided by the Act that "where an occupier of premises is bound by contract to permit persons who are strangers to the contract[37] to enter or use the premises, the duty of care which he owes to them as his visitors cannot be restricted or excluded by that contract, but (subject to any provision of the contract to the contrary) shall include the duty to perform his obligations under the contract, whether undertaken for their protection or not, in so far as those obligations go beyond the obligations otherwise involved in that duty."[38] Furthermore, where a tenancy, including a statutory tenancy which does not in law amount to a tenancy, requires either the landlord or the tenant to permit persons to enter premises of which he is the occupier, the section applies as if the tenancy were a contract between the landlord and the tenant.[39]

This section has a twofold effect. The occupier cannot by contract reduce his obligations to visitors who are strangers to the contract to a level below that imposed by the common duty of care.[40] If, however, the contract requires him to take some precaution not required in the circumstances by that duty, the visitor shall have the benefit of that precaution. If, for example, A contracts with B to allow B and C to use his premises and the contract provides that the premises shall be lit during the hours of darkness, C has a right of action against A for injury due to A's failure to light the premises, whether or not such a failure would amount to a breach of the common duty of care.[41] It is provided, however, that the section shall not have the effect, unless the contract so provides, of making an occupier who has taken all reasonable care liable for dangers due to the faulty execution of any work of construction, maintenance or repair or other like operation by persons other than himself, his servants or persons acting under his direction and control.[42]

[35] On the authority of *Fosbroke-Hobbes* v. *Airwork Ltd.* [1937] 1 All E.R. 108.
[36] Cmd. 9305 (1954), para. 55. See, too, para. 79.
[37] Defined in s.3(3).
[38] s.3(1).
[39] s.3(4).
[40] It may be that as far as personal injuries are concerned much the same effect is achieved by s.2(1) of the Unfair Contract Terms Act 1977, *supra.* According to Law Com. No. 69, p. 133 "contract term" bears "its natural meaning of any term in any contract (and is not limited to the terms in a contract betweeen the instant parties)." However, the provisions of the Occupiers' Liability Act are more favourable to the plaintiff since (*a*) they are not confined to business occupation and (*b*) they extend to all types of loss or damage whereas the Unfair Contract Terms Act prohibition is a qualified one with regard to property damage.
[41] There is no general duty upon a landlord to light a common staircase at all times of darkness: *Irving* v. *L.C.C.* (1965) 109 S.J. 157.
[42] s.3(2). The wording of this subsection differs from that of s.2(4)(*b*), *ante*, p. 217 but the effect of the two subsections is probably the same and if s.2(4)(*b*) includes demolition (*Ferguson* v. *Welsh* [1987] 1 W.L.R. 1153) so should s.3(2).

It was formerly an open question whether the occupier, though unable to restrict his duty to third parties by a provision in the contract itself, could do so by publishing a notice as in *Ashdown* v. *Samuel Williams & Sons*.[43] Where the occupation is of a business nature it is now clear that such a notice is caught by the Unfair Contract Terms Act[44] and in other situations it is submitted that the case is one where the occupier is not "free to" restrict or exclude his duty of care for the alternative view would tend to defeat the object of section 3 of the Occupiers' Liability Act.[45]

Damage to property

The Act provides[46] that the rules which it enacts shall apply:

" . . . in like manner and to the like extent as the principles applicable at common law to an occupier of premises and his invitees or licensees would apply to regulate— . . . the obligations of a person occupying or having control over any premises or structure in respect of damage to property, including the property of persons who are not themselves his visitors."[47]

Clearly, therefore, where property lawfully on the premises is damaged by a structural defect of the premises,[48] whether it actually belongs to a visitor or not, the question in each case is whether the occupier has discharged the common duty of care. Where there has been a bailment, however, as where goods are deposited in a warehouse, the liability of the warehouse-keeper will not depend upon the common duty of care but upon his duty under the bailment or special contract. The rules contained in the Occupiers' Liability Act replace only the principles of the common law formerly applicable between the occupier and his invitee or licensee. They do not affect the relationship of bailor and bailee.[49] Where there is no bailment, the common law rule was that there was no duty on the occupier to protect the goods of his visitors from theft by a third party[50] and the Act has not changed this. A mere licence to put goods on land (as in the case of most car parks) does not make the occupier a bailee.[51]

---

[43] [1957] 1 Q.B. 409; *ante*, p. 221.

[44] *Ante*, p. 220.

[45] Clerk & Lindsell, *Torts*, (16th ed.), para. 13–29; North, *op. cit.*, pp. 151–152. *cf.* Payne, *loc. cit.*, at pp. 369–370. It must be admitted, however, that the Law Reform Committee seem to have been concerned only with the position of a person affected by an exempting term unknown to him: Cmnd. 9305 (1954), para. 55.

[46] s.1(3)(*b*), North, *op cit.* pp. 94–112 (based on the author's article, "Damage to Property and the Occupiers' Liability Act 1957" (1966) 30 Conv.(N.S.) 264).

[47] The last phrase would seem to allow an action by an owner who is not a visitor, as in *Drive Yourself Lessey's Pty. Ltd.* v. *Burnside* [1959] S.R.(N.S.W.) 390: but *cf.* North, *op. cit.* pp. 101–105.

[48] *e.g.* if, with your permission, I leave my car in the drive outside your house and a tile falls off the roof and damages it: *A.M.F. International Ltd.* v. *Magnet Bowling Ltd.* [1968] 1 W.L.R. 1028. Damages may be recovered not only in respect of actual damage to the property but also in respect of consequential financial loss: *ibid.* at pp. 1049–1051, *per* Mocatta J.

[49] *cf. Fairline Shipping Corp.* v. *Adamson* [1975] Q.B. 180.

[50] *Tinsley* v. *Dudley* [1951] 2 K.B. 18. See also *Ashby* v. *Tolhurst* [1937] 2 K.B. 242; *Deyong* v. *Shenburn* [1946] K.B. 227; *Edwards* v. *West Herts Group Hospital Management Committee* [1957] 1 W.L.R. 418.

[51] *Tinsley* v. *Dudley, supra*; *Hinks* v. *Fleet* [1986] 2 E.G.L.R. 243; *Chappell* v. *National Car Parks, The Times*, May 22, 1987.

LIABILITY TO TRESPASSERS

The duty of an occupier to a trespasser was unaffected by the Occupiers' Liability Act 1957.[52] The original common law rule was that the occupier was only liable to a trespasser in respect of some wilful act "done with deliberate intention of doing harm . . . or at least some act done with reckless disregard of the presence of the trespasser,"[53] but the law underwent substantial alteration and development by the House of Lords in 1972 in *British Railways Board* v. *Herrington*.[54] As a result of that case the occupier owed to the trespasser a "duty of common humanity" which, generally speaking, was lower than the common duty of care but substantially higher than the original duty. *Herrington's* case was applied by the Court of Appeal on a number of occasions without undue difficulty[55] but on a reference to the Law Commission that body decided that no sufficiently clear principle emerged from the case and recommended legislative action.[56] After a long delay, this was done by the Occupiers' Liability Act 1984.[57]

Though in this section we shall continue to speak of trespassers, for that is the commonest case, the Act in fact covers a rather wider field, for it applies to liability to persons other than the occupier's visitors. It therefore applies to persons exercising private rights of way[58] and persons exercising access rights under National Parks legislation[59] but not to persons using a public right of way,[60] whose rights, if any, must be sought in the highways legislation.[61] Section 1(3) provides that a duty is owed to the trespasser if:

"(*a*) [the occupier] is aware of the danger or has reasonable grounds to believe that it exists;
(*b*) he knows or has reasonable grounds to believe that the [trespasser] is in the vicinity of the danger concerned or that he may come into the vicinity of the danger . . . ; and
(*c*) the risk is one against which, in all the circumstances of the case, he may reasonably be expected to offer the other some protection."

The duty is to take such care as is reasonable in all the circumstances to see that the entrant does not suffer injury[62] on the premises by reason of the danger concerned[63] and it may, in appropriate circumstances, be discharged

---

[52] Contrast the Occupiers' Liability (Scotland) Act 1960. See *McGlone* v. *British Railways Board* 1966 S.C.(H.L.) 1.
[53] *Robert Addie & Sons (Collieries) Ltd.* v. *Dumbreck* [1929] A.C. 358, 365.
[54] [1972] A.C. 877.
[55] See, *e.g. Pannett* v. *P. McGuinness & Co. Ltd.* [1972] 2 Q.B. 599; *Melvin* v. *Franklins (Builders) Ltd.* (1973) 71 L.G.R. 142; *Harris* v. *Birkenhead Corp.* [1976] 1 W.L.R. 279.
[56] Law Com. No. 75.
[57] Jones (1984) 47 M.L.R. 713.
[58] *Ante*, p. 210.
[59] *Ante*, p. 211. But persons exercising other rights of access conferred by law (*e.g.* a police officer executing a search warrant) are visitors for the purposes of the 1957 Act.
[60] s.1(7).
[61] See *post*, p. 418.
[62] s.1(9).
[63] s.1(4).

by taking such steps as are reasonable to give warning of the danger concerned or to discourage persons from incurring the risk.[64] The defence of *volenti non fit injuria* is expressly preserved.[65] In some respects this approach is very close to that of the common duty of care and the ordinary negligence duty: in particular, the occupier incurs liability where he does not know but *ought* to know the facts which would signal to a reasonable man the presence of a trespasser or of the danger to him[66]; and the standard appears to be objective and not conditioned by the occupier's own resources, which was not true of the duty of common humanity.[67] However, it is submitted that the nature or character of the trespass is a matter which is very relevant in determining what the occupier may reasonably be expected to do: the very same precautions which should be taken for the benefit of a lawful visitor may in some cases be required to protect young trespassing children but it would be wholly unacceptable that they should be required for the benefit of a burglar or entrant intent on criminal damage.[68] Furthermore, while the giving of a prominent warning will not necessarily in all cases discharge the occupier's duty[69] it is more likely to do so than with regard to lawful visitors. The latter may have no choice but to encounter the risk and the warning must therefore in itself make them reasonably safe; the trespasser who continues to intrude after passing a prominent warning notice has himself to blame for any injury he may suffer.

A clear distinction (though probably of limited practical significance) between the 1984 Act and that of 1957 is that the former has no application when there is damage to property. If, therefore, P trespasses on D's property and he suffers injury when his car falls down a disused and concealed mine shaft, he may well be able to recover damages for his personal injuries but not for the loss of his car. However, the Act seems to leave the common law untouched on this point.[70] There can be little doubt that where an occupier is in breach of his duty of common humanity at common law his liability would extend beyond the personal injuries suffered by the trespasser to, say, the destruction of his clothing; and it has been said, *obiter*, that there can be liability even where no personal injury is involved—on the facts where the plaintiff's bees were foraging across land sprayed by the

---

[64] s.1(5).

[65] s.1(6).

[66] *cf. Herrington's* case [1972] A.C. 877, 941.

[67] [1972] A.C. 877, 899, 920–921, 942. It might be argued that the occupier's resources are to be taken into account as part of "all the circumstances of the case," but the same words appear in s.2(2) of the 1957 Act and it has not been suggested that the occupier's "personal equation" forms part of the standard of care owed to visitors.

[68] Deliberate or reckless infliction of harm going beyond what is permissible in defence of property (*post*, p. 703) would be another matter. Before the Act the burglar might conceivably have been defeated by the maxim *ex turpi causa non oritur actio* (*post*, p. 697) but the limits of this are not clear. Perhaps the Act should be treated as a complete statement of the law in this area.

[69] For example, where the likely trespassers are young children. But the principle that the occupier must be entitled to look to parents to take principal responsibility for the safety of their children (*ante*, p. 216) must apply here, too. The occupier of a natural hazard like a mountain or a river is no more required to fence it against trespassing children than against lawful visitors.

[70] s.1(1) provides that the Act is to replace the rules of the common law in respect of personal injury. s.1(8), preventing recovery in respect of "loss of or damage to property," applies only to breaches of duty under s.1.

defendant with a poisonous chemical.[71] It is not easy to apply the concept of "common humanity" to a situation where there is no personal injury or even no threat of personal injury, but it does seem that there may still be some scope for the duty of "common humanity" as stated in *British Railways Board* v. *Herrington*.[72]

Yet one more situation may leave scope for the common law. Suppose the defendant is not the occupier but the occupier's servant or a contractor or even a visitor to the premises. It is clear that the 1984 Act has no application to this situation and there was authority that as between the trespasser and the non-occupier, trespassory status as such[73] was irrelevant. In *Buckland* v. *Guildford Gas Light and Coke Co.*[74] the defendants had provided electric current for a farmer by high-voltage wires on poles over his fields, and the wires passed over and very close to the top of a tree which was easy to climb. The thirteen-year-old plaintiff was killed by electrocution after having climbed the tree. Morris J. held that the defendants were liable for they ought to have foreseen the danger and the general law of negligence, not the special rules as between occupier and trespasser, applied. However, the balance of the dicta in *Herrington's* case pointed towards the removal of any sharp distinction between occupiers and non-occupiers in this respect.[75] There is, therefore, a possibility that the duty of common humanity survives for this purpose, too.

LIABILITY OF VENDORS AND LESSORS[76]

Contractors

If A is working on B's land and causes injury to a visitor C it is the ordinary principles of negligence which apply, and not the Occupiers' Liability Act 1957. This was established as the law before the Act in *A.C. Billings & Sons Ltd.* v. *Riden*[77] but now the distinction between a duty at common law and the common duty of care under the Act will rarely be of importance.

---

[71] *Tutton* v. *A.D. Walter Ltd.* [1986] Q.B. 61; Spencer [1986] C.L.J. 15. The judge's decision, however, was that the categories of "visitor" and "trespasser" were inapt terms to be applied to the bees and the ordinary law of negligence applied.

[72] [1972] A.C. 877. For the details of this case, see the twelfth edition of this work. Briefly, the occupier was not obliged to institute checks for the presence of trespassers or dangers but a duty arose if on the facts of which he knew there was a likelihood of serious harm to the trespasser sufficient to make it inhumane to fail to take steps against it. But in determining the content of the duty the trespasser had to take the occupier as he found him with regard to the latter's knowledge, ability and resources.

[73] On the facts, a trespasser might of course be unforeseeable when a lawful visitor would not.

[74] [1949] 1 K.B. 410; *Davis* v. *St. Mary's Demolition and Excavation Co. Ltd.* [1954] 1 W.L.R. 592; *Creed* v. *McGeogh & Sons Ltd.* [1955] 1 W.L.R. 1005. None of these cases concerned the occupier's servant and any immunity attaching to the occupier clearly could not have been circumvented by the device of vicarious liability.

[75] Lord Wilberforce [1972] A.C. 877, 914 and Lord Pearson at p. 929. *cf.* Lord Diplock at p. 943. See also *Restatement* (2d) ss.383–386.

[76] Holyoak and Allen, *Civil Liability for Defective Premises.*

[77] [1958] A.C. 240. The case arose before the Act. *Johnson* v. *Rea Ltd.* [1961] 1 W.L.R. 1400 provides an interesting example, and perhaps an extension of the liability of a non-occupier for the condition of premises. It is, of course, possible for a contractor to be an occupier within the meaning of the Act: *A.M.F. International Ltd.* v. *Magnet Bowling Ltd.* [1968] 1 W.L.R. 1028.

Vendors and lessors

We are concerned here with the position of a vendor or lessor who creates a danger or defect in his premises and then sells or lets them to another who suffers damage from that danger or defect. The common law was at first perhaps unduly solicitous to the vendor or lessor; then, in the 1970s it swung sharply in favour of the purchaser or tenant but at the price of getting into a quite extraordinary state of complexity and uncertainty; there has now been something of a reaction but the law has still not settled down to a wholly clear pattern. Another strand in the problem is the liability of local authorities for faulty exercise of their statutory powers of approval and inspection and yet further problems have arisen on connection with limitation of actions, but this must be postponed until a later chapter.[78] One of the main characteristics of the cases in the middle period was a tendency to blur the distinction between contract and tort and even now any account of the law must examine a variety of contractual and tortious duties arising from statute and common law.

(1) *Vendor*

(a) Common law

There is, of course, a contract between vendor and purchaser of land but the implied contractual obligations as to quality are very much less extensive than they are in contracts for the sale of goods even if the vendor is a builder or developer, and hence "in the business" of selling houses. The basic rule is *caveat emptor* though this may be displaced by express terms in the contract or misrepresentations.[79] In one situation, however, there is a limited implied obligation, *viz.*, when there is a contract for the sale of a house to be built or completed by the vendor.[80] There is then a threefold implied warranty; that the builder will do his work in a good and workmanlike manner[81]; that he will supply good and proper materials; and that it will be reasonably fit for human habitation.[82] This warranty of course avails only the first purchaser from the builder and the limitation period (six years) will start to run when the defective work is done, not when it comes to the purchaser's notice. The latter rule is, however, somewhat mitigated by the fact that if the builder knowingly covers up defective work this will constitute concealment of the cause of action so that time will not run until the purchaser discovers, or could with reasonable diligence have discovered, the defect.[83] In practical terms, the N.H.B.C. insurance scheme, which is considered below, is a good deal more important than the implied contractual warranties.

---

[78] See *post*, Chap. 27.
[79] The Unfair Contract Terms Act 1977 does not extend to exclusion of contractual liability "in any contract so far as it relates to the creation or transfer of an interest in land" (Sched. 1, para. 1(*b*)) but s.3 of the Misrepresentation Act 1967 (as substituted by s.8 of the Unfair Contract Terms Act) does control exemption clauses dealing with misrepresentation in such contracts.
[80] Thus there is no implied warranty if the house is already completed before sale.
[81] s.13 of the Supply of Goods and Services Act 1982 seems to apply but not to add anything of substance.
[82] *Hancock* v. *B.W. Brazier (Anerley) Ltd.* [1966] 1 W.L.R. 1317.
[83] Limitation Act 1980, s.32(1)(*b*); *King* v. *Victor Parsons & Co.* [1973] 1 W.L.R. 29.

As for the law of tort, the original position was that if the builder was not himself the vendor he was liable for injury caused by negligent work, but if he was also vendor he enjoyed an immunity from suit once the property had been transferred. The rule, which may have been based on an unwillingness to allow contractual and tortious duties to exist concurrently, was established before *Donoghue* v. *Stevenson* and survived that decision.[84] This immunity was clearly removed from January 1, 1974 by section 3 of the Defective Premises Act 1972 which provides that "where work of construction, repair, maintenance or demolition or any other work[85] is done on or in relation to premises any duty of care owed because of the doing of the work, to persons who might reasonably be expected to be affected by defects in the state of the premises created by the doing of the work shall not be abated by the subsequent disposal of the premises." However, even before the Act was passed the Court of Appeal had declared, *obiter*, that the principle of *Donoghue* v. *Stevenson* applied as much to realty as to chattels.[86] This received the approval (albeit, again, strictly *obiter*) of a unanimous House of Lords[87] and has been applied in numerous cases so that there can be no doubt that it represents the law. But the question which gives rise to difficulty is "for what type of loss is the builder liable?" If the builder were liable only for personal injury and damage to other property caused by the collapse of his handiwork that would probably not impose a very serious burden on the trade as a whole[88] and would certainly present no doctrinal difficulty in law, but in reality the cases concerned *threatened* structural failure. This presented some difficulty because a house which threatens to collapse (or even one which *does* collapse, causing no injury to person or other property) is surely analogous to a manufactured article which is fragile and inferior in quality, matters which have always been looked on as the province of contract rather than tort.[89] In other words, the loss, though having physical symptoms in the form of, for example, cracks, was in its nature economic. This argument did not, however, find much favour and matters were confused by the intrusion of matters relating to the liability of local authorities in connection with building inspection. In *Anns* v. *Merton London Borough* Lord Wilberforce said that a cause of action against a local authority lay "when the state of the building is such that there is present or imminent danger to the health or safety of persons occupying it"[90] and that the measure of damages was "the amount of expenditure necessary to

---

[84] *Otto* v. *Bolton* [1936] 2 K.B. 46. Winfield in (1936) 52 L.Q.R. 313 suggested that if no one had ever sued in tort for injury arising from a ruinous house until after *Donoghue* v. *Stevenson* the "jerry-builder" would then have been held to be the "neighbour" of the injured person.

[85] To be construed *ejusdem generis*?

[86] *Dutton* v. *Bognor Regis U.D.C.* [1972] 1 Q.B. 373.

[87] *Anns* v. *Merton London Borough* [1978] A.C. 728, *ante*, p. 96. Weir, *Casebook on Tort*, (6th ed.), p. 60. The builder was not a party to the appeal, but the House of Lords thought it unreasonable "to impose liability in respect of defective foundations on the council, if the builder, whose primary fault it was, should be immune from liability": *ibid.* at p. 758.

[88] However, actions for personal injuries in respect of tumbledown houses are not unknown (see, *e.g. Otto* v. *Bolton* [1936] 2 K.B. 46; *Sharpe* v. *E.T. Sweeting & Son Ltd.* [1963] 1 W.L.R. 665) and the Ronan Point collapse suggests the possibility of large claims against builders of flats.

[89] See *Dutton* v. *Bognor Regis U.D.C.* [1972] 1 Q.B. 373, 414.

[90] [1978] A.C. 728, 760.

restore the [building] to a condition in which it was no longer such a danger."[91] These tests were taken up in *Batty* v. *Metropolitan Property Realisations Ltd.*[92] which involved a claim against a builder in respect of a house built on an unstable site, but a later decision, now clearly overruled, awarded damages to a corporate building developer which could not possibly have been under threat to its health or safety.[93] A return to principle is, however, indicated in *D. & F. Estates Ltd.* v. *Church Commissioners.*[94] The third defendants were main contractors for the construction of a block of flats, one of which was leased to the plaintiffs by the first defendants. The plasterwork in the flat had been incorrectly applied by a sub-contractor (who was not sued) and some of it fell down, necessitating, *inter alia*, replacement. The House of Lords found for the third defendants on the ground that having exercised reasonable care in the selection of the sub-contractor and having no notice of deficiencies during the course of his work they were not under any duty for the purposes of tort to supervise him.[95] Quite apart from this, however, the House of Lords considered that the cost of replacing the plasterwork was not recoverable in tort from the third defendants. Where a building was constructed so as to contain a defect which caused personal injury or damage to goods then an action would lie against the builder by a remote purchaser or even a visitor on the ordinary principle of *Donoghue* v. *Stevenson* but where no such loss occurred and the building merely became less valuable or required repairs, then the owner's loss was purely economic in nature and hence generally not recoverable in tort.[96] To hold otherwise would be to impose on the builder for the benefit of those with whom he had no contract the obligation of one who warranted the quality and fitness of his work. Carried to its limits, however, this approach would have involved overruling virtually every building case since *Dutton* v. *Bognor Regis U.D.C.*,[97] a course which the House of Lords was unwilling to take on the basis of the arguments advanced before them. It was, therefore, suggested that there might be cases of complex structures like buildings where it was proper to regard one element in the structure as distinct from another, so that damage to one part of a structure caused by a hidden defect in another part might qualify to be treated as damage to "other property": for example, if defective foundations caused cracking in the walls of the building. On this basis, however, it would have been entirely artificial to treat the defective plasterwork as distinct from the decorative surface placed upon it. Considerable difficulty may arise in applying the idea of distinct elements,[98] but even

---

[91] *Ibid.* at p. 759.
[92] [1978] Q.B. 554.
[93] *Acecrest Ltd.* v. *W.S. Hattrell & Partners* [1983] Q.B. 260, overruled in *Governors of Peabody Donation Fund* v. *Sir Lindsay Parkinson Ltd.* [1985] A.C. 210.
[94] [1988] 3 W.L.R. 368. Duncan Wallace Q.C., "Negligence and Defective Buildings" (1989) 105 L.Q.R. 46. The first rigorous analysis of the problem was by the High Court of Australia in *Sutherland Shire Council* v. *Heyman* (1985) 60 A.L.R. 1.
[95] As to liability for the negligence of an independent contractor, see *post*, p. 581. A contractor who has promised to produce a result may be liable in *contract* if a sub-contractor produces sub-standard work, but that would not have availed the plaintiffs.
[96] For the circumstances in which economic loss is recoverable in negligence, see *ante*, p. 84.
[97] *Supra.*
[98] Which may also apply to products: *post*, p. 247.

if it is accepted it is not wholly clear whether the resulting liability extends only to the further damage to the other part or covers also the cost of remedying the root of the problem (e.g. the defective foundations)[99]: if the latter is the law the decision may have made little practical difference.

Difficulty remains, however, in determining the status of the decision of the House of Lords in *Anns* v. *Merton London Borough*.[1] That case primarily concerned the liability of the local authority for negligence in carrying out a statutory inspection and the builder was not a party to the appeal. However, the court not surprisingly took the view that the builder's liability should be at least as extensive as that of the authority and a good deal of attention was therefore paid to it. Lord Wilberforce thought that the builder could be liable on two alternative grounds: (1) for breach of statutory duty in failing to comply with the building by-laws (now the building regulations[2]) and (2) for common law negligence. In either event, however, he seems to have been of the opinion[3] that the builder's liability (and that of the authority) arose only when the structure was in such a condition as to be a "present or imminent risk" to health or safety and the measure of damages was said to be the amount of expenditure necessary to restore the building to a condition in which it was no longer such a danger. From the point of view of a cause of action arising from a statute passed to protect public safety this approach may be logical, but as applied to common law negligence it has been described as "difficult to reconcile with any conventional analysis of the underlying basis of liability in tort for negligence".[4] In particular, the view that the cost of repair or demolition may be recovered where it is undertaken to avert the danger of personal injury seems impossible to reconcile with what Lord Bridge said in the *D. & F.* case.[5] However, a subsequent decision of the Court of Appeal proceeds on the basis that there may still be recovery for the cost of remedial work necessary to avoid injury as opposed to work which merely makes the building fit for its intended use.[6]

A further question is to whom is the duty of care owed? With regard to personal injury it seems clear that the answer must be "to any person who may reasonably be foreseen as likely to suffer injury in accordance with normal principles," such as residents in the building and visitors. In so far as a claim lies in respect of damage to the building itself, however, it has been said that at common law the duty is owed to "an owner or occupier who is

---

[99] Lord Oliver at [1988] 3 W.L.R. 391 seems clearly to incline to the view that the cost of repairing the foundations would be covered. *cf.* Lord Bridge at p. 386. Lords Ackner, Jauncey and Templeman agreed with both speeches. In any event, *Batty* v. *Metropolitan Realizations* seems doomed. There was nothing wrong with the house itself, the builder's default lying solely in his misjudgment of the suitablity of the site: [1988] 3 W.L.R. at 386, 394. From the owner's point of view, however, the distinction between a badly chosen site and badly built foundations may not be obvious.

[1] [1978] A.C. 728, *ante*, p. 96.

[2] As to this, see below.

[3] But *cf.* Lord Fraser in the *Pirelli General Cable Works Ltd.* v. *Oscar Faber & Partners* [1983] 2 A.C. 1, 17.

[4] *D. & F. Estates Ltd.* v. *Church Commissioners* [1987] 3 W.L.R. 368, 392, *per* Lord Oliver.

[5] See [1988] 3 W.L.R. at 385–386, despite the fact that at 382 he approved the dissenting speech of Lord Brandon in *Junior Books* v. *Veitchi*, which seems to accept *Anns* on this point.

[6] *D.o.E.* v. *Thomas Bates & Son Ltd.* [1989] 1 All E.R. 1075. The claim failed because the building was safe if only used below to design loading. See also *Bluett* v. *Woodspring D.C.* (1982) 266 E.G. 220 and *Ketteman* v. *Hansel Properties Ltd.* [1984] 1 W.L.R. 1274 (on appeal, but not on this point, [1987] A.C. 189).

such when the damage occurs."[7] Since damage might occur for this purpose before it became apparent this gave rise to difficulty, particularly where the property had been sold after the occurrence of non-apparent damage without warranty or misrepresentation, since the purchaser in such a case may have had no claim.[8] Now, however, section 3 of the Latent Damage Act 1986 goes some way to meet the problem. The effect of the section is that if the first purchaser (P1) from the builder had knowledge[9] of the damage during his ownership, his successor, P2, still has no claim. If, however, P1 had no such knowledge, then a fresh cause of action accrues to P2 on the date on which he acquires his interest in the property. For the purpose of calculating the period of limitation, however, the relevant starting time is when the property suffered the damage in the hands of P1.[10]

With regard to the liability of the local authority *Anns* is still the law. The former building by-laws have been replaced by building regulations made by central government but the local authority still has a duty to consider building plans for approval and has powers of inspection of work in progress[11] and the building regulations, like their predecessors, are still concerned with securing the health and safety of persons in or about buildings or who are affected by buildings.[12] Therefore, while a failure by the authority to discharge its statutory functions in relation to the building regulations may lead to liability to an occupier of the building whose safety is threatened, there is no such liability to the builder-developer himself. The point is illustrated by *Investors in Industry Commercial Property Ltd.* v. *South Bedfordshire District Council*.[13] The plaintiffs were developers of a site on which they erected four warehouses. The foundations were approved by local authority inspectors but were wholly inadequate and did not comply with the building regulations, with the result that the warehouses required complete reconstruction. It seems unlikely that *Anns* can ever now apply to a corporate plaintiff[14] but the Court of Appeal found it unnecessary to give a definitive answer on this because it was the developer's duty to ensure that the building was erected in accordance with the building regulations and "it cannot have been the intention of the legislature that, save perhaps in exceptional circumstances, a local authority could owe a duty" to a developer in breach of them.[15] The effect of the contrary view would be to shift responsibility from where it should properly lie, on the shoulders of the

[7] *Anns* v. *Merton London Borough* [1978] A.C. 728, 758.

[8] *Perry* v. *Tendring D.C.* (1984) 30 B.L.R. 118; *cf. Pirelli General Cable Works Ltd.* v. *Oscar Faber & Partners* [1983] 2 A.C. 1, 18.

[9] Which includes knowledge which he might reasonably have been expected to acquire.

[10] See further, *post*, p. 721.

[11] But under Pt. II of the Building Act 1984 an approved inspector may at the option of the person carrying out the work exercise supervision instead of the local authority.

[12] s.1(1) of the Building Act 1984. The other matters with which the regulations are concerned (convenience, conservation of energy, etc.) are hardly relevant in the context of tort. There is no statutory purpose of ensuring "value for money."

[13] [1986] Q.B. 1035.

[14] Which cannot be at any risk to its health or safety. *cf. Acecrest Ltd.* v. *W.S. Hattrell & Partners* [1983] Q.B. 260, overruled in *Governors of the Peabody Donation Fund* v. *Sir Lindsay Parkinson & Co. Ltd.* [1985] A.C. 210.

[15] [1986] Q.B. 1035, 1062.

developer's architects, engineers and contractors, against whom the developer has his contractual remedies.[16]

A rigorous application of the requirement of imminent danger to health or safety may provide local authorities with a measure of protection,[17] but given the financial instability of many builders, the local authority, which never dies or goes into liquidation and has effectively unlimited resources, must always be an attractive target for claims by disappointed houseowners.[18]

Finally, what of the houseowner himself? If he does work on his house in a negligent manner and this injures a subsequent owner then there would be liability in negligence.[19] If, however, he has not created the danger by his own action but knew or ought to have known about it at the time of sale it is unlikely that any liability would be imposed upon him. It is true that such a liability has been imposed upon a trader disposing of goods[20] but such a great departure from the principle of *caveat emptor* would, in the case of realty, be open only to the House of Lords[21] or the legislature.[22]

(b) Statute

Some years before *Dutton's* case started the revolution in the common law the issue of liability for defective premises was referred to the Law Commission and the result was the Defective Premises Act 1972,[23] which came into force on January 1, 1974. The provisions of the Act cannot be excluded or restricted by any agreement.[24]

Duty to build dwellings properly. Section 1 of the Act imposes upon persons who undertake work for, or in connection with, the provision of a dwelling[25] a statutory duty to see that the work taken on is done in a workmanlike or professional manner, with proper materials and so that as

---

[16] Still less is there a duty on the authority to intervene where the developer's advisers fail to comply with requirements imposed by the authority: see the *Peabody* case, *supra*.

[17] But it may lead to the limitation period against the local authority beginning to run later than that against the builder: *Jones* v. *Stroud D.C.* [1986] 1 W.L.R. 1141.

[18] In *Dennis* v. *Charnwood B.C.* [1983] Q.B. 409 Barrow-upon-Soar R.D.C. in 1955 negligently passed plans for the plaintiffs' house. The defendants succeeded to their liabilities in 1974 under the local government reorganisation. An action commenced in 1978 succeeded. Lawton L.J. commented that "a compulsory insurance scheme for builders of houses might provide better justice than the uncertainties of litigation," but the claim in *Dennis* would have been far outside the time limits of the current N.H.B.C. scheme (below) and it must be doubted whether such long-term cover would be actuarially acceptable.

[19] *Hone* v. *Benson* (1978) 248 E.G. 1013; Defective Premises Act 1972, s.3.

[20] *Andrews* v. *Hopkinson* [1957] 1 Q.B. 229 (dealer selling goods to a finance company to be let by it to the plaintiff on hire-purchase terms).

[21] See *Rimmer* v. *Liverpool City Council* [1985] Q.B. 1 (a landlord-tenant case).

[22] It may be of some significance that cl. 3 of the Defective Premises Bill would have made the "mere" vendor liable in respect of defects of which he knew, but this was rejected by Parliament.

[23] See Law Com. No. 40 (1970); Spencer, "The Defective Premises Act 1972—Defective Law and Defective Law Reform" [1974] C.L.J. 307, [1975] C.L.J. 48; North (1973) 36 M.L.R. 628; Samuels (1973) 37 Conv. 314; Holyoak & Allen, *op. cit.*, Chap. 3.

[24] s.6(3).

[25] Industrial and commercial premises are therefore outside the scope of this section. Such premises are also outside the scope of the N.H.B.C. scheme.

regards that work the dwelling will be fit for habitation when completed.[26] The range of persons on whom the duty is imposed therefore goes beyond the builder himself and includes the architect and surveyor and any sub-contractors involved,[27] though the manufacturer of standard components is not covered.[28] The duty is owed not only to the persons ordering the work but also to every person who then or later acquires an interest (whether legal or equitable) in the dwelling. The duty is therefore a statutory hybrid, having characteristics of both contract and tort: on the one hand, it covers mere defects of quality (provided they make the house unfit for human habitation) without any necessity for imminent danger of personal injury; on the other hand it may pass along a chain of purchasers notwithstanding the lack of privity between them and the builder.[29]

The operation of section 1 is, however, limited by two factors. First, the limitation period of six years begins to run when the dwelling is completed[30] whereas damage may "occur" for the purposes of the common law liability at a later time.[31] More important, however, is the fact that the Act has no application to dwellings protected by the N.H.B.C. scheme[32] because it was thought that the scheme generally provided purchasers with greater rights than did the Act. The scheme is operated by the National House-Building Council[33] and the great majority of builders participate in it.[34] Under the scheme the builder warrants[35] to the purchaser[36] that the house is soundly constructed and that he will remedy any defects. These obligations apply to the "Initial Guarantee Period," which is normally two years from purchase,

---

[26] This is in some ways stricter than a duty of care. It corresponds closely with the implied warranty at common law in a contract for the construction of a house (see *ante*, p. 228) and in that context it has been held that the warranty in relation to materials is strict: *Hancock* v. *B.W. Brazier (Anerley) Ltd.* [1966] 1 W.L.R. 1317; see also Supply of Goods and Services Act 1982, s.4. A sub-contractor may now also owe a duty of care at common law even in respect of defects of quality in the very limited circumstances in which *Junior Books Ltd.* v. *Veitchi Co. Ltd.* applies: *ante*, p. 98.

[27] See also s.2(4) (developers). But note the important provisions of s.1(2), (3), which will generally relieve a person of liability if he does the work properly in accordance with instructions given by another. This would appear to cover not only the builder on whom the client imposes detailed specifications, but also the sub-contractor who receives instructions from the builder. But "a person shall not be treated . . . as having given instructions for the doing of work merely because he has agreed to the work being done in a specified manner."

[28] He may, however, be liable under Pt. I of the Consumer Protection Act 1987 (*post*, p. 250) and if he were negligent he might be in breach of a common law duty. A builder held liable under s.1 might anyway seek a contractual indemnity from him. A local authority exercising powers of inspection probably cannot be said to "take on work for or in connection with the provision of a dwelling" but *cf.* the doubts of Lord Denning M.R. and Roskill L.J. in *Sparham-Souter* v. *Town and Country Developments (Essex) Ltd.* [1976] Q.B. 858, 870, 877.

[29] "The analogy is not with the common law of tort but with the rule contained in the Bills of Lading Act 1855 that a subsequent purchaser of goods carried by sea succeeds to the rights of the person who contracted with the carrier thereof": Weir, *Casebook on Tort*, (3rd ed.), p. 24.

[30] s.1(5).

[31] *Post*, p. 720.

[32] This is the "approved scheme" referred to by s.1 of the Act. "Section 1 gets all dressed up, and section 2 . . . leaves it virtually nowhere to go": Spencer, *loc. cit.*, p. 320.

[33] For a detailed account, see Holyoak & Allen, *op. cit.*, Chap. 3. Adams (1980) 130 N.L.J. 171, 195, 219, discusses the 1979 amendments to the scheme. Since 1983 a more limited version of the scheme has been available for conversions.

[34] If only because building societies may refuse to lend on non-N.H.B.C. new dwellings.

[35] These rights are additional to any other rights conferred by law.

[36] The benefit of this contract should be assigned by the purchaser to his successor in title, but the N.H.B.C. rules forbid the builder to take any privity objection. It was held in *Marchant* v. *Caswell & Redgrave Ltd.* (1976) 240 E.G. 127 that a second purchaser who had not taken an assignment might rely on s.78 of the Law of Property Act 1925.

but the builder also warrants that he will obtain N.H.B.C. insurance cover for the dwelling. This cover is in respect of major structural defects appearing within a further period of eight years,[37] though there are financial limits by reference to the price of the individual dwelling, the claims record against the individual builder and the total amount of claims received by the N.H.B.C. in one year.[38]

Finally, there are the building regulations themselves. In *Anns* v. *Merton London Borough* Lord Wilberforce said that the builder might be liable for breach of statutory duty by non-compliance with the building by-laws, the then equivalent of the building regulations[39] but the contrary view has been expressed.[40] A further statutory provision came, somewhat stealthily[41] on to the scene (or at least into the wings) in the shape of section 71 of the Health and Safety at Work, etc., Act 1974, which provided that a breach of duty imposed by the building regulations would be actionable as a breach of statutory duty. However, despite re-enactment 10 years later in section 38 of the Building Act 1984 this provision has yet to be brought into force. In any event, the absence of a full definition of "damage" may raise the same problems as those which have been discussed in connexion with the *D. & F.* case.

It cannot be pretended that the development of liability for defective premises provides a model in law reform techniques. As Roskill L.J. remarked in *Sparham-Souter* v. *Town and Country Developments (Essex) Ltd.*,[42] "in the [early 1970s] law reform was being pursued through two different channels—the Law Commission and Parliament on the one hand, and the courts on the other—without either apparently appreciating what developments the other was seeking to make." The common law developments had the effect of making the chosen parliamentary tool, the Defective Premises Act 1972, something of a dead letter.[43] The stance taken in *D. & F. Estates Ltd.* v. *Church Commissioners*,[44] may have brought this to an end, though that decision, too, is not without its difficulties. Referring to the way in which the common law duty had been extended more widely than the Act, Lord Bridge commented, "I cannot help feeling that consumer protection is an area of law where legislation is much better left to the legislators."[45]

---

[37] The N.H.B.C. also underwrites the builder's obligations during the Initial Guarantee Period and provides cover against the builder's failure to complete as a result of bankruptcy, liquidation or fraud.

[38] As a preliminary to the issue of its insurance cover, the N.H.B.C. may conduct spot checks on dwellings under construction, though a dwelling is not necessarily inspected on completion. Any liability for negligence in such inspections is probably effectively excluded by the Agreement: see Adams (1980) 130 New L.J. 219.

[39] [1978] A.C. 728, 759. *cf. Solomons* v. *R. Gertzenstein Ltd.* [1954] 2 Q.B. 243 (London Building Acts).

[40] *Worlock* v. *S.A.W.S.* (1982) 265 E.G. 774; *Perry* v. *Tendring D.C.* (1984) 30 Build.L.R. 118.

[41] Spencer, *loc. cit.*, at p. 48.

[42] [1976] Q.B. 858, 876.

[43] This was particularly because of the comparatively generous stance at first adopted on the running of the limitation period. This was checked by the *Pirelli* case, but under the Latent Damage Act 1986 the principle that time runs from discoverability of the damage, not necessarily from its occurrence, is restored, subject to a "long-stop" provision (see further *post*, p. 719).

[44] See *ante*, p. 230.

[45] [1988] 3 W.L.R. 368, 387.

(2) Lessor[46]

(a) Common law

A lease is a contract as well as an estate in land, but at common law the range of implied terms relating to the fitness of the premises is very limited. There is an implied warranty in the letting of furnished premises that they are fit for occupation at the commencement of the tenancy[47] and the House of Lords has held that in the case of a "high rise" block, obligations may be implied with regard to the maintenance of such necessary things as stairs and lifts.[48] These obligations sound in contract and hence avail only the tenant. As for tort, the lessor's position was equated with that of the vendor and he was immune from liability for negligence in respect of defects created by him before the demise.[49] This immunity has now died along with that of the vendor.[50]

(b) Statute

Sections 1 and 3 of the Defective Premises Act, which have been discussed above in relation to vendors, apply equally to lessors and the same problem of overlap with the common law duty of care arises here.[51] Statute, however, also imposes certain non-excludable obligations during the currency of the lease. By the Landlord and Tenant Act 1985, s.8, there is implied into contracts for the letting of a house at a very low rent an undertaking by the landlord that it is, and will be kept, fit for human habitation, but the rent limits are so low that the section is hardly ever applicable.[52] By section 11 of the same Act[52a] there is imposed upon the landlord in relation to leases for less than seven years an obligation to carry out certain repairs to the structure and to installations for sanitation and the supply of water, gas and electricity. Though primarily designed to allow the tenant to compel the landlord to do repairs, these provisions would also avail the tenant if, for example, he suffered personal injury as a result of the landlord's breach of obligation, but being contractual covenants their breach gave rise to no liability towards the tenant's family or visitors. This was first changed by section 4 of the Occupiers' Liability Act 1957, which imposed on the land-lord a tortious duty of care in respect of dangers arising from default in his

---

[46] Holyoak & Allen, op. cit., Chap. 7.
[47] Collins v. Hopkins [1923] 2 K.B. 617.
[48] Liverpool City Council v. Irwin [1977] A.C. 239. As to licences for occupation of business premises, see Wettern Electric Ltd. v. Welsh Development Agency [1983] Q.B. 796.
[49] Robbins v. Jones (1863) 15 C.B.(N.S.) 221. "Fraud apart, there is no law against letting a tumbledown house": ibid. at p. 240, per Erle C.J.
[50] Anns v. Merton London Borough [1978] A.C. 728 was a case of a long lease. But where the landlord did not create the defect, only the House of Lords can impose a duty: Rimmer v. Liverpool City Council [1985] Q.B. 1.; McNerny v. Lambeth B.C. [1989] N.L.J. cf. ante, p. 233.
[51] Ante, p. 229.
[52] Quick v. Taff-Ely B.C. [1986] Q.B. 809, 817.
[52a] Extended by s.116 Housing Act 1988 to cover parts of the building and installations outside the demised premises.

repairing obligations under the lease.[53] This was replaced and carried very much further by section 4 of the Defective Premises Act 1972. Where premises are let under a tenancy which puts on the landlord an obligation to the tenant for the maintenance or repair of the premises, the landlord owes to all persons who might reasonably be expected to be affected by defects in the state of the premises a duty to take such care as is reasonable in all the circumstances to see that they are reasonably safe from personal injury or damage to their property caused by a defect within the repairing obligation. The duty of care is owed if the landlord knows or ought to have known of the defect.[54] Most significant of all, a landlord who has a *power*, express or implied, to enter and repair is to be treated for the purposes of the section (but no other[55]) as if he were under an *obligation* to the tenant to repair.[56] The obvious beneficiaries of section 4 are the tenant's family and visitors, but other persons who might reasonably be expected to be affected include trespassers,[57] neighbours and passers-by[58] and even the tenant himself.[59] The tenant, however, is not owed any duty in respect of a defect arising from, or continuing because of, a failure to carry out an obligation expressly imposed on the tenant by the tenancy.[60]

---

[53] Whether those obligations arose from express covenants in the lease or from the equivalent statutory obligations existing before the Landlord and Tenant Act 1985. Care should be taken to note that we are now concerned with dangers arising on the premises which the landlord has demised. If he retains part in his own occupation, (*e.g.* staircases and lifts in a block of flats) he is liable for that *qua* occupier under the general provisions of the Occupiers' Liability Act: *ante*.

[54] s.4(2). Thus there may be liability if the landlord ought to have known even though s.11 of the Landlord and Tenant Act 1985 requires actual notice: *O'Brien* v. *Robinson* [1973] A.C. 912.

[55] Thus the tenant could not compel such a landlord to repair under s.17 of the Landlord and Tenant Act 1985.

[56] s.4(4). *Smith* v. *Bradford Metropolitan Council* (1982) 44 P.&C.R. 171; *Barrett* v. *Lounova Ltd.* [1989] 1 All E.R. 351. "Such a power apparently exists in any case in which the court thinks it is reasonable to imply it, and it is impossible to predict with certainty whether or not such a power will be implied in any given case": Spencer, *loc. cit.*, p. 77. Such a power is said to exist in the case of small houses let on periodic tenancies (*Mint* v. *Good* [1951] 1 K.B. 517, *post*, p. 404) though there will usually now be a statutory obligation in such cases.

[57] *cf.* the position of the tenant-occupier himself: *ante*, p. 225.

[58] In other words the section creates liability in nuisance, though it probably adds nothing to the common law in this respect: *post*, p. 403.

[59] But where there is an express or implied duty to repair the tenant will be better off suing on the contract.

[60] s.4(4). This clearly displaces the landlord's duty of care when the lease imposes upon the tenant the obligation to repair. What if the lease requires the tenant to give the landlord notice of the want of repair?

CHAPTER 10

LIABILITY FOR DEFECTIVE PRODUCTS[1]

THIS chapter is primarily concerned with the liability in tort of manufacturers (and certain other transferors) of defective products but since transfers of products normally take place pursuant to a contract, a realistic picture of the incidence of liability can only be obtained by bearing the relevant contractual principles in mind. Where a plaintiff is injured by a product transferred to him under a contract of sale[2] he may rely, subject to any valid exemption clause,[3] upon the seller's implied undertakings as to compliance with description, merchantable quality, fitness for purpose and compliance with sample under the Sale of Goods Act 1979. These undertakings give rise to what French law calls *obligations de resultat, i.e.* the seller is liable if the goods do not come up to the standard required by the Act even though he has taken all possible care that they should do so and is in no way to blame for the defect.[4] Though the purpose of these undertakings when they were being developed at common law[5] was probably to allow the buyer a remedy for the financial loss he suffered in acquiring goods of inferior quality,[6] it has been accepted for many years that they also allow recovery for consequential damage to other property and, most significantly, for personal injuries.[7] The existence of this strict liability in the seller (often, in modern conditions, a much larger organisation than the manufacturer[8]) means that as far as the purchaser is concerned his right of action in tort, dependent on proof of negligence, is often of academic interest and may only be utilised where the seller is insolvent or cannot, for some other reason, be successfully sued.[9]

---

[1] Miller, *Product Liability and Safety Encyclopaedia.*

[2] The duties of the creditor under a contract of hire purchase are for practical purposes the same as those of a seller: see the Supply of Goods (Implied Terms) Act 1973, as amended by the Consumer Credit Act 1974. The Supply of Goods and Services Act 1982 implies similar terms into other contracts for the transfer of goods (*e.g.* exchange) and hire of goods.

[3] If the purchaser is a "consumer" the clause will be void under s.6(2) of the Unfair Contract Terms Act 1977. Otherwise it will be subject to a test of reasonableness: *ibid.* s.6(3).

[4] He may, of course, have an indemnity under the contract of sale between him and his supplier, and so on up the chain to the manufacturer.

[5] The Sale of Goods Act 1893 (the fundamental structure of which is repeated in the 1979 Act) was a restatement of the common law.

[6] The use of "merchantable quality" to describe one of the obligations under s.14 of the Sale of Goods Act is revealing.

[7] *Godley* v. *Perry* [1960] 1 W.L.R. 9 is an excellent example. See also *Hyman* v. *Nye* (1880) 6 Q.B.D. 685; *Blandford* v. *Goole & Sheffield Transport Co.* [1910] 2 K.B. 94; *Grant* v. *Australian Knitting Mills Ltd.* [1936] A.C. 85; *Andrews* v. *Hopkinson* [1957] 1 Q.B. 229; *Vacwell Engineering Co. Ltd.* v. *B.D.H. Chemicals Ltd.* [1971] 1 Q.B. 88.

[8] Some retailers (*e.g.* Marks & Spencer, British Home Stores, Woolworth) affix their own brand name to all or some of their goods, though the goods are of course manufactured by specialist manufacturers. For the tort implications of this, see *post*, p. 251.

[9] There is nothing to prevent the plaintiff suing *both* seller (in contract) and manufacturer (in tort): *Grant* v. *Australian Knitting Mills Ltd.* [1936] A.C. 85.

Where a contractual action is successfully pursued then, in theory, the implied terms in the chain of contracts between manufacturer and retailer will lead to the manufacturer bearing the ultimate responsibility, but in practice this chain may be broken by the insolvency of a "middleman" or by some valid exemption clause.[10] The contractual liability outlined above is of no assistance to persons injured by the product who have not acquired any interests in it by contract—members of the purchaser's family,[11] passers-by[12] or donees from the buyer[13]—and it is this class of "ultimate consumers" who are most likely to seek to rely on tort.

LIABILITY AT COMMON LAW

Before *Donoghue* v. *Stevenson*,[14] was decided in 1932 it was doubtful whether the transferor of a product owed any duty to the ultimate transferee (in the absence of a contractual relationship between them) unless it belonged to the class of "dangerous chattels"[15] or was actually known to the transferor to be dangerous.[16] The classification of products into those which are dangerous and those which are not is, however, an unsatisfactory one and Scrutton L.J. confessed that he did not understand the difference "between a thing dangerous in itself, as poison, and a thing not dangerous as a class, but by negligent construction dangerous as a particular thing. The latter, if anything, seems to me the more dangerous of the two; it is a wolf in sheep's clothing instead of an obvious wolf."[17]

Donoghue v. *Stevenson* finally established, by a majority of three to two, that apart from contract and without reference to any special rule about dangerous chattels, there are circumstances in which a person owes a duty of care in respect of products. Lord Atkin laid down the following principle[18] for both Scots and English law:

"A manufacturer of products, which he sells in such a form as to show

---

[10] Or even as in *Lambert* v. *Lewis* [1982] A.C. 225, by a simple lack of records. These intermediate contracts will not be consumer transactions so that the exception clauses will be valid if shown to be reasonable under the Unfair Contract Terms Act 1977.

[11] But *cf. Jackson* v. *Horizon Holidays Ltd.* [1975] 1 W.L.R. 1468, doubted in *Woodar* v. *Wimpey* [1980] 1 W.L.R. 277.

[12] *Stennett* v. *Hancock* [1939] 2 All E.R. 578.

[13] *Donoghue* v. *Stevenson* [1932] A.C. 562; *Fisher* v. *Harrods* [1966] C.L.Y. 8148. Where the original buyer has resold the product to the plaintiff there will be no implied condition of merchantable quality or fitness for purpose in that contract unless the sale was in the course of a business: Sale of Goods Act 1979, s.14(2), (3).

[14] [1932] A.C. 562, *ante*, pp. 74–75.

[15] For the history, see Winfield, "Duty in Tortious Negligence" in *Select Legal Essays*, p. 70; Bohlen, "Liability of Manufacturers to Persons Other than their Immediate Vendors" (1929) 45 L.Q.R. 343. The "privity of contract fallacy" held that because the manufacturer (A) had a contract with the retailer (B) he could not owe a tort duty to the consumer (C).

[16] If the fraud of the transferor could be proved he would be liable for that: *Langridge* v. *Levy* (1837) 2 M. & W. 519; (1838) 4 M. & W. 337.

[17] *Hodge* v. *Anglo-American Oil Co.* (1922) 12 Ll.L.Rep. 183, 187.

[18] This is sometimes known as the "narrow rule" in *Donoghue* v. *Stevenson*. The "wide rule" about the duty of care in general has been considered *ante*, p. 74.

that he intends them to reach the ultimate consumer in the form in which they left him with no reasonable possibility of intermediate examination and with the knowledge that the absence of reasonable care in the preparation or putting up of the products will result in an injury to the consumer's life or property, owes a duty to the consumer to take that reasonable care."[19]

The category of dangerous chattels lingered on for some years but had expired by the 1950s. Now, apart from statute, there is no liability in tort for damage caused by products unless there is negligence and there is no class of product in respect of which there is no liability for negligence. There is simply the ordinary rule that the greater the risk the greater the precautions that must be taken to obviate it.[20] It is true that the law expects a great deal more care in the handling of a pound of dynamite than a pound of butter, but that is the result of the general law of negligence, not of the application of a special rule of law concerning dangerous things.

The liability under *Donoghue* v. *Stevenson* stands completely untouched by the enactment of the principle of strict liability in the Consumer Protection Act 1987[21] but in practice plaintiffs will be much more likely to rely upon the latter than upon the former. However, recourse to the common law will remain necessary in some cases, for example where the loss takes the form of damage to property not intended for private use[22] or where the special limitation period under the Act has expired.[23] We now turn to an examination of the common law as it has developed since *Donoghue* v. *Stevenson*.

Persons liable

The principle has been extended from manufacturers to include repairers,[24] fitters, erectors,[25] and assemblers.[26] Where a manufacturer of a finished article (such as a motor car) buys in components from another he is under a duty to consider their suitability and cannot rely blindly on the other to produce a good design.[27] A mere distributor or supplier has not actively created the danger in the same way as a manufacturer but he, too, may be under a duty to make inquiries or carry out an inspection of the product and if it is dangerous for some reason of which he should have known, his failure

---

[19] [1932] A.C. 562, 599. An American court had anticipated this by 16 years: *MacPherson* v. *Buick Motor Co.* (1916) 111 N.E. 1050.

[20] *Read* v. *J. Lyons & Co.* [1947] A.C. 156, 172–173, *per* Lord Macmillan; *ibid.* at pp. 180–181, *per* Lord Simonds.

[21] *Post*, p. 249.

[22] *Post*, p. 253.

[23] *Post*, p. 260.

[24] *Stennett* v. *Hancock* [1939] 2 All E.R. 578; *Haseldine* v. *Daw* [1941] 2 K.B. 343.

[25] *Brown* v. *Cotterill* (1934) 51 T.L.R. 21.

[26] *Howard* v. *Furness, Houlder Ltd.* [1936] 2 All E.R. 296.

[27] *Winward* v. *T.V.R. Engineering* (1986) (LEXIS, CA).

to warn of it will then amount to negligence.[28] In *Andrews* v. *Hopkinson*,[29] by arrangement with the plaintiff the defendant sold a second-hand car to a finance company and the company hired the car to the plaintiff under a hire-purchase agreement.[30] The car was some eighteen years old, and the defendant, who was a dealer in second-hand cars, had taken no steps to see that it was in a roadworthy condition although the car had been in his possession for a week. In fact the car had a defective steering mechanism which caused the plaintiff to have an accident a week after he took delivery of the car. Evidence showed that in an old car the danger spot is the steering mechanism and that the defect in question could have been discovered by a competent mechanic if the car had been jacked up. McNair J. held that the defendant was liable and said[31]:

> "Having regard to the extreme peril involved in allowing an old car with a defective steering mechanism to be used on the road, I have no hesitation in holding that the defendant was guilty of negligence in failing to make the necessary examination, or at least in failing to warn the plaintiff that no such examination had been carried out."[32]

Similarly suppliers may be liable if they carelessly represent the goods to be harmless without having made any adequate tests,[33] but it should not be thought that these cases impose a general duty on suppliers to subject all their goods to an exhaustive examination. The duty to examine will only arise if in all the circumstances they could reasonably be expected to carry out an examination. A second-hand car dealer may be expected to discover a patent defect in the steering mechanism of one of his cars, and a manufacturer and supplier of chemicals must take reasonable care to discover and give warning of industrial hazards arising out of the chemicals he supplies,[34] but a retail grocer, for example, cannot be expected to institute inspections to discover whether his tinned food is contaminated. He may be obliged to satisfy himself as to the reputation of his supplier[35] and he must certainly

---

[28] In the case of a gratuitous transfer, it is true that older authorities held that, unless the product was in the class of dangerous things, the transferor was liable only for willful or reckless conduct, *i.e.* when he actually knew of the danger: *Gautret* v. *Egerton* (1867) L.R. 2 C.P. 371, 375; *Coughlin* v. *Gillison* [1899] 1 Q.B. 145. But the validity of these cases is now very doubtful (see *Griffiths* v. *Arch Engineering Co. Ltd.* [1968] 3 All E.R. 217, 220; Marsh (1950) 66 L.Q.R. 39) and it is submitted that in the modern law the gratuitous nature of the transfer is simply a factor to be taken into account in assessing what is reasonable care by the transferor. *cf. Chaudhury* v. *Prabhakar*, [1989] 1 W.L.R. 29 (gratuitous agent inspecting property liable to principal, though the existence of a duty of care was conceded).

[29] [1957] 1 Q.B. 229. See, too, *White* v. *John Warwick & Co.* [1953] 1 W.L.R. 1285; *Griffiths* v. *Arch Engineering Co. Ltd.* [1968] 3 All E.R. 217.

[30] The finance company in a hire-purchase agreement gives the same implied warranties (now non-excludable) as to the condition of the goods as does a seller in a sale: see n. 2, *supra*.

[31] [1957] 1 Q.B. 229, 237. *cf. Rees* v. *Saville* [1983] R.T.R. 332 (duty of private purchaser; M.O.T. certificate).

[32] He was also prepared to hold the dealer liable on a collateral contract with the plaintiff.

[33] *Watson* v. *Buckley, Osborne, Garrett & Co.* [1940] 1 All E.R. 174 (distributors of a dangerous hair dye held liable because they advertised it as positively harmless and requiring no tests); *Devilez* v. *Boots Pure Drug Co.* [1962] C.L.Y. 2015; *Goodchild* v. *Vaclight* [1965] C.L.Y. 2669.

[34] *Vacwell Engineering Co. Ltd.* v. *B.D.H. Chemicals Ltd.* [1971] 1 Q.B. 88. An appeal from the judgment of Rees J. was settled: [1971] 1 Q.B. 111n. Note that the existence of a contractual liability did not prevent a concurrent claim in tort. This is still the law despite what is said in the *Tai Hing* case: *ante*, p. 5.

[35] *Fisher* v. *Harrods* [1966] C.L.Y. 8148.

follow proper practices in keeping his wares but otherwise unless the contamination was caused by his negligence or he actually knew of it, his only liability is to the actual purchaser under the contract of sale. If a third party becomes ill on eating the contaminated food, his remedy, if any, is against the manufacturer.

Given the potential liability for negligence of a supplier of goods (particularly second-hand goods) for failing to trace defects is there any way in which he can protect himself other than by carrying out an adequate inspection? It is clear that any exclusion clause in the contract of sale or otherwise will generally be void under the Unfair Contract Terms Act 1977,[36] but a suitable warning of possible defects may be regarded not as an attempt to exclude liability but as a discharge of the duty of care. In this respect, *Hurley* v. *Dyke*,[37] a claim arising before the Act, suggests that the supplier will be treated fairly leniently. The defendant, a garage owner, sold an old three-wheeler car by auction on terms that it was sold "as seen and with all its faults and without warranty." It was then resold by the purchaser to one Clay and eight days later it crashed because of corrosion in the chassis, injuring the plaintiff passenger. It was conceded before the House of Lords that the defendant's duty would be satisfied by giving adequate warning to his purchaser[38] and that if the defendant knew only that the car might be dangerous but had no knowledge of the specific defect the "all faults" terms on which it was sold would provide such a warning. The House seems to have thought these concessions rightly made and, no specific knowledge having been established, the plaintiff's claim failed. No concluded opinion was expressed on what the position would have been if the defendant had had knowledge of the defect but two judges said that it should not be assumed that on such facts he would be in breach of duty.[39]

Extension of subject-matter

The principle has been extended from articles of food and drink and includes, *inter alia*, kiosks,[40] tombstones,[41] hair dye,[42] industrial chemicals,[43] lifts,[44] motorcars[45] and pants.[46] Likewise the term "consumer" includes the ultimate user of the article[47] or anyone who is within physical proximity to

[36] *Ante*, p. 238.
[37] [1979] R.T.R. 265.
[38] *cf. Goodwear Treaders Ltd.* v. *D. & B. Holdings Ltd.* (1979) 98 D.L.R. (3d) 59 (suppliers of tyre held liable to third party when they knew that purchaser would ignore their warning of its unsuitability for his purpose).
[39] Viscount Dilhorne and Lord Scarman. *cf.* Lord Hailsham who thought (at p. 303) that the old decision in *Ward* v. *Hobbs* (1878) 4 App.Cas. 13 might have to be reconsidered in the light of developments in the law of negligence.
[40] *Paine* v. *Colne Valley Electricity Supply Co.* [1938] 4 All E.R. 803.
[41] *Brown* v. *Cotterill* [1934] 51 T.L.R. 21.
[42] *Watson* v. *Buckley* [1940] 1 All E.R. 174.
[43] *Vacwell Engineering Co. Ltd.* v. *B.D.H. Chemicals Ltd.* [1971] 1 Q.B. 88.
[44] *Haseldine* v. *Daw* [1941] 2 K.B. 343.
[45] *Herschtal* v. *Stewart & Ardern* [1940] 1 K.B. 155; *Andrews* v. *Hopkinson* [1957] 1 Q.B. 229.
[46] *Grant* v. *Australian Knitting Mills* [1936] A.C. 85.
[47] *Grant* v. *Australian Knitting Mills, supra*; *Griffiths* v. *Arch Engineering Co. Ltd.* [1968] 3 All E.R. 217; *Cassidy* v. *Imperial Chemical Industries Ltd. The Times*, November 2, 1972.

it.[48] The significance of *Donoghue* v. *Stevenson* in the creation of liability for defective buildings has already been considered.[49]

Possibility of alternative cause

In *Grant* v. *Australian Knitting Mills Ltd.*,[50] the Judicial Committee held that the defendants were liable to the ultimate purchaser of some pants which they had manufactured and which contained a chemical that gave the defendant a skin disease when he wore them. It was argued for the defendants that as they despatched the pants in paper packets of six sets there was greater possibility of intermediate tampering with the goods before they reached the user than there was with the sealed bottle in *Donoghue's* case, but the court held that "the decision in that case did not depend on the bottle being stoppered and sealed; the essential point in this regard was that the article should reach the consumer or user subject to the same defect as it had when it left the manufacturer."[51] Mere possibility of interference did not affect their liability. There must, however, be sufficient evidence that the defect existed when the article left the manufacturer's hands and that it was not caused later. In *Evans* v. *Triplex Safety Glass Co. Ltd.*,[52] the plaintiff bought a motor-car fitted with a "Triplex Toughened Safety Glass" windscreen of the defendants' manufacture. A year later, when the car was being used, the windscreen suddenly and for no apparent reason broke into many fragments and injured the occupants of the car. The defendants were held not liable for the following reasons: (a) the lapse of time between the purchase and the accident; (b) the possibility that the glass may have been strained when screwed into its frame; (c) the opportunity of intermediate examination by the intermediate seller and (d) the breaking of the glass may have been caused by something other than a defect in manufacture. Use of the article by the plaintiff for a purpose materially different from that for which the maker designed it or which he might reasonably be taken to have contemplated will also defeat a claim, but use for a different but similar purpose does not *ipso facto* absolve him from liability. The question here is one of fact and degree,[53] and it is suggested that the right thing to ask is whether the cause of the plaintiff's injury was the defect in the article or the plaintiff's own misuse of it.[54]

Intermediate examination

As originally formulated by Lord Atkin the principle applies where there

[48] *Brown* v. *Cotterill*, *supra* (child injured by falling tombstone); *Stennett* v. *Hancock* [1939] 2 All E.R. 578 (pedestrian hit by flange of lorry wheel). In *Lambert* v. *Lewis* [1978] 1 Lloyd's Rep. 610 manufacturers were held liable for a design defect in a vehicle coupling which caused a trailer to come adrift and injure the plaintiff. This was not challenged on appeal: [1982] A.C. 225.

[49] Chap. 9.

[50] [1936] A.C. 85.

[51] *Ibid.* at pp. 106–107.

[52] [1936] 1 All E.R. 283. *cf. Mason* v. *Williams & Williams Ltd.* [1955] 1 W.L.R. 549.

[53] *Davie* v. *New Merton Board Mills Ltd.* [1957] 2 Q.B. 368, 378–379, *per* Ashworth J. The manufacturers' liability was not in issue on appeal: [1959] A.C. 604.

[54] If both are causes, then damages should be reduced under the Law Reform (Contributory Negligence) Act 1945, as in *Griffiths* v. *Arch Engineering Co. Ltd.* [1968] 3 All E.R. 217.

is "no reasonable possibility of intermediate examination." These words have been the subject of much analysis, "almost as if they formed part of a statute"[55] but the better view is that they do not constitute an independent requirement which the plaintiff must satisfy but rather are to be taken into account in determining whether the injury to the plaintiff was foreseeable.[56] Even a probability of an intermediate examination will not exonerate the defendant unless it gives him reason to expect that it will reveal the defect and that this will result in the elimination of the defect or at least the plaintiff's being warned of it in such a way as to make him safe. In *Griffiths* v. *Arch Engineering Co. Ltd.*[57] the plaintiff borrowed from the first defendants a portable grinding tool which had been lent to them by its owners, the second defendants. The tool was in a dangerous condition because an incorrect part had been fitted to it at some time by a servant of the second defendants, and the plaintiff was injured in consequence. Although the first defendants had an opportunity of examining the tool, the second defendants had no reason to suppose that an examination would actually be carried out and they were liable to the plaintiff. The fact that the first defendants were also liable to the plaintiff meant not that the second defendants had a defence to the plaintiff's claim but that the case was one for ultimate apportionment of liability between the defendants.[58] On the other hand, in *Kubach* v. *Hollands*[59] a manufacturer sold a chemical to an intermediary with an express warning that it had to be tested before use. The intermediary was liable for the resulting injury, but the manufacturer was not and it would be difficult to do business on any other basis.[60] Prescription drugs will commonly have untoward side-effects upon a minority of users and a manufacturer will normally fulfil his duty under *Donoghue* v. *Stevenson* by giving adequate warning to the prescribing physician (who is far more likely than is the patient to be able to understand the warning): if the physician fails to heed the warning his default may properly be regarded as the sole cause of injury to the patient.[61]

Extension to containers, labels, etc.

The duty of reasonable care extends not only to the manufacture, erection or repair of the product itself but also to any container,[62] package or pipe,[63]

---

[55] *M/S Aswan Engineering Establishment Co.* v. *Lupdine Ltd.* [1987] 1 W.L.R. 1, 22, *per* Lloyd L.J.

[56] *Ibid.* at p. 23.

[57] [1968] 3 All E.R. 217; *Lambert* v. *Lewis* [1978] 1 Lloyd's Rep. 610 (point not involved on appeal, [1982] A.C. 225); *cf. Taylor* v. *Rover Co. Ltd.* [1966] 1 W.L.R. 1491.

[58] See now the Civil Liability (Contribution) Act 1978, *post*, p. 593. If the plaintiff himself neglects an opportunity of examination it may be a case for reduction of damages under the Law Reform (Contributory Negligence) Act 1945. If his default is so extreme as to break the chain of causation there may be a complete defence.

[59] [1937] 3 All E.R. 970.

[60] Similarly, one may sell an unroadworthy vehicle for scrap and if it is then used on the road that will be the purchaser's responsibility.

[61] See *Buchan* v. *Ortho Pharmaceuticals (Canada) Ltd.* (1986) 25 D.L.R. (4th) 658. But if there is no warning the court should assume, in the absence of evidence to the contrary, that the physician would have heeded one which had been given.

[62] *Donoghue* v. *Stevenson* [1932] A.C. 585, *per* Lord Atkin, who, at p. 595, disapproved of Horridge J.'s decision in *Bates* v. *Batey & Co.* [1913] 3 K.B. 351; *ibid.* at p. 604, *per* Lord Thankerton; *ibid.* at pp. 616–617, *per* Lord Macmillan.

[63] *Barnes* v. *Irwell Valley Water Board* [1938] 2 All E.R. 650.

in which it is distributed, and to the labels, directions or instructions for use that accompany it.[64]

Burden of proof

The duty owed is that of reasonable care[65] and the burden of proving negligence is on the plaintiff. In *Donoghue* v. *Stevenson*[66] itself Lord Macmillan said that in a case such as that there was no justification for applying the maxim *res ipsa loquitur*, but whether the maxim may be invoked or not, the question in each case is whether the plaintiff has given sufficient evidence to justify the inference of negligence against the defendant. He is not required to specify what the defendant did wrong[67] and, indeed, any other rule would stultify the principle of *Donoghue* v. *Stevenson*, for normally it will be impossible for a plaintiff to bring evidence of particular negligent acts or omissions occurring in the defendant's manufacturing processes. In *Mason* v. *Williams & Williams Ltd.*[68] the plaintiff was injured while using a cold chisel manufactured by the defendants and which was too hard for its purpose. Finnemore J. accepted that *res ipsa loquitur* could not be invoked but held that since the plaintiff had established that nothing had happened to the chisel after it left the defendants' factory which could have caused the excessive hardness, the defendants' negligence was established. It is suggested that the plaintiff will generally discharge his burden of proof by showing that the article was defective and that, on a balance of probabilities, the defect arose in the course of manufacture[69] by the defendant.[70] In many cases in practice this comes very close to the imposition of a strict liability, for even if the defendant gives evidence that the quality control system in his factory complies with approved practice, there is still the possibility—indeed it perhaps becomes stronger by this very evidence—that one of his servants was careless and prevented that system operating correctly, in which case he remains liable, though vicariously rather than for breach of his personal duty.[71]

---

[64] *Watson* v. *Buckley* [1940] 1 All E.R. 174; *Holmes* v. *Ashford* [1950] 2 All E.R. 76; *Vacwell Engineering Co. Ltd.* v. *B.D.H. Chemicals Ltd.* [1971] 1 Q.B. 88. Macleod (1981) 97 L.Q.R. 550. For a claim concerning instructions which was based on contract see *Wormell* v. *R.H.M. Agriculture (East) Ltd.* [1987] 1 W.L.R. 1091.

[65] A manufacturer is not liable on the ground only that an independent contractor employed by him had been negligent: *Taylor* v. *Rover Co. Ltd.* [1966] 1 W.L.R. 1491.

[66] [1932] A.C. 585, 622. The dictum was clearly *obiter*. *cf. Chaproniére* v. *Mason* (1905) 21 T.L.R. 633.

[67] *Grant* v. *Australian Knitting Mills Ltd.* [1936] A.C. 85, *ante*, p. 243. "If excess sulphites were left in the garment, that could only be because someone was at fault. The appellant is not required to lay his finger on the exact person in all the chain who was responsible, or to specify what he did wrong. Negligence is found as a matter of inference from the existence of the defects taken in conjunction with all the known circumstances": *ibid.* at p. 101, *per* Lord Wright. It may be observed that the phrase *res ipsa loquitur* appears nowhere in the opinion.

[68] [1955] 1 W.L.R. 549; *Davie* v. *New Merton Board Mills Ltd.* [1957] 2 Q.B. 368. *cf. Evans* v. *Triplex Safety Glass Ltd.* [1936] 1 All E.R. 283; *Moorhead* v. *Thomas Smith & Sons Ltd.* [1963] 1 Lloyd's Rep. 164.

[69] Or repair, etc., according to the business of the defendant.

[70] Whether this is described as the application of *res ipsa loquitur* or not seems to be a mere matter of terminology. See *ante*, pp. 125–126.

[71] See *Grant* v. *Australian Knitting Mills Ltd.* [1936] A.C. 85, 101; *Smedley's Ltd.* v. *Breed* [1974] A.C. 839 (a criminal prosecution under food hygiene statutes). *Daniels* v. *White & Sons* [1938] 4 All E.R. 258 is hard to reconcile with *Grant's* case (see Goodhart (1939) 55 L.Q.R. 6; Anon. (1939) 55 L.Q.R. 532) and MacKenna J. refused to follow it in *Hill* v. *J. Crowe (Cases)* [1978] 1 All E.R. 812.

Nature of the loss

Liability under *Donoghue* v. *Stevenson* clearly covers personal injury and damage to other property: if, for example, a defectively wired heater causes a fire which burns down the consumer's house he could sue for the value of the house. It does not, however, normally cover the financial loss caused by the failure of a product to fulfil the function for which it was acquired.[72] Such loss is properly claimable only in an action by the buyer against the seller under the Sale of Goods Act. In other words, *Donoghue* v. *Stevenson* is about *dangerous* products, not merely *defective* ones and a modern Mrs. Donoghue could not sue Stevenson if her bottle of "ginger beer" contained pure water. In *Muirhead* v. *Industrial Tank Specialities Ltd.*[73] the third defendants, French electrical manufacturers, were negligent in supplying (via an intemediary) pumps which were unsuitable for the range of English voltage, with the result that the plaintiff's stock of "farmed lobsters" died from lack of oxygen. The plaintiff succeeded in his claim for the value of the lobsters and certain consequential expenses in salvaging them for resale, but his claims for the cost of the pumps, for wasted expenditure in trying to make them work properly and for profits which could have been made from continuing operation of the lobster farm were all dismissed.[74] It is true that in *Junior Books* v. *Veitchi Co. Ltd.*[75] the House of Lords had held that an allegation that the defendants had, as sub-contractors, negligently installed a defective (but not dangerous) floor in the plaintiff's factory disclosed a cause of action in tort in respect of the cost of replacing the floor, but subsequent decisions (including *Muirhead*[76]) have made it plain that *Junior Books* does not create any general liability for economic loss between manufacturer and consumer. Even if the decision is not properly to be explained as one which involved physical damage to the plaintiff's property,[77] it is confined to unusual situations where the plaintiff can show a special relationship between himself and the defendant which amounted to reliance by the plaintiff on the defendant; while this requirement may sometimes[78] be satisfied as between a building owner and a nominated sub-contractor it is unlikely to be as between manufacturer and consumer, even if the manufacturer is aware of the destination of his product.[79]

The undoubted proposition that *Donoghue* v. *Stevenson* applies where the product causes damage to *other* property of the plaintiff causes some difficulty where failure of a component in a complex product causes damage to the product itself. If a replacement tyre bursts because of negligent

---

[72] For a general discussion of such loss, see *ante*, p. 84.

[73] [1986] Q.B. 507.

[74] The immediate suppliers, the first defendants, would have been liable in contract for all these items but they had gone into liquidation.

[75] [1983] 1 A.C. 520.

[76] See also *Simaan General Contracting Co.* v. *Pilkington Glass Ltd. (No. 2)* [1988] Q.B. 758.

[77] See *ante*, p. 89.

[78] By no means always: see *Greater Nottingham Co-operative Society Ltd.* v. *Cementation Piling & Foundations Ltd.* [1989] Q.B. 71 *ante*, p. 91.

[79] See the *Simaan* case *supra*, n. 76, where P ordered building components from D via a contract between A and D because the building owner required use of D's components. P's claim against D failed.

manufacture and causes my car to crash I can sue the tyre manufacturer for the cost of repairs to the car. Is the same true if the tyre is supplied new with the car? Or if, as is likely in modern conditions, the component parts of a product are made by A, B, C, D and so on while the "manufacturer" is in reality no more than a designer and assembler? Such points have been discussed in English cases but without very decisive answers. In *M/S Aswan Engineering Establishment Co.* v. *Lupdine Ltd.*[80] the plaintiffs lost a quantity of waterproofing compound when the pails in which it was contained collapsed because of the high temperatures to which they were exposed in Kuwait. An action against the manufacturer of the pails failed[81] on the ground that the circumstances in which the damage occurred was outside the range of what was reasonably foreseeable, but Lloyd L.J.[82] expressed the provisional view that had that not been the case the loss of the compound would have been damage to the property of the plaintiffs for which the manufacturer would have been liable. Nicholls L.J., on the other hand, inclined to the view that *Donoghue* v. *Stevenson* should not extend to making a container manufacturer liable for loss of contents, not so much because the contents are not in strict legal analysis "other property of the plaintiff" but because such a liability would be unreasonable. Suggestions that even where a product is entirely the work of one manufacturer failure of a component leading to damage to the product as a whole might fall within *Donoghue* v. *Stevenson* were in the past supported by reference to cases on defective premises. The House of Lords in *D. & F. Estates Ltd.* v. *Church Commissioners*[83] firmly held that no action in tort lay against a builder whose negligence caused plaster work to need to be replaced but, as we have seen,[84] left open the possibility that a failure of the foundations which caused the collapse of the building might be actionable, on the ground that separate parts of a complex structure might be treated as different items of the plaintiff's property.[85] If such an approach can be applied to complex chattels (and it is difficult to see why it cannot) there is still the possibility of tort liability if, say, a component of the pumps in *Muirhead* were to overheat and burn out the pumps themselves. On the other hand, the court also referred approvingly to the United States Supreme Court decision in *East River Steamship Corp.* v. *Transamerica Delaval Inc.*[86] denying a claim by tanker charterers against the manufacturer of turbines which caused the tankers to malfunction, in which the court remarked that:

"we [do not] find persuasive a distinction that rests on the manner in which the product is injured. We realise that the damage may be qualitative, occurring through a gradual deterioration or internal

---

[80] [1987] 1 W.L.R. 1.
[81] An action in contract against other defendants who had sold the compound and pails to the plaintiffs also failed.
[82] With whose judgment Fox L.J. agreed.
[83] [1988] 3 W.L.R. 368.
[84] *Ante*, p. 230.
[85] [1988] 3 W.L.R. 368, 386.
[86] 476 U.S. 858 (1986).

breakage. Or it may be calamitous. . . . But either way, since by definition no person or other property is damaged, the resulting loss is purely
economic. Even when the harm to the product itself occurs through an
abrupt, accident-like event, the resulting loss due to repair costs,
decreased value and lost profits is essentially the failure of the purchaser to receive the benefit of its bargain—traditionally the core
concern of contract law."[87]

A further possibility is that a dangerous defect is discovered in a product
before it has the opportunity to cause harm and is then repaired. Even
before *Junior Books* v. *Veitchi* there was some support for the view that the
plaintiff in such a case could recover the costs of repair but this approach was
flatly rejected in the *D. & F. Estates* case:

> "If the hidden defect in the chattel is the cause of personal injury or of
> damage to property other than the chattel itself, the manufacturer is
> liable. But if the hidden defect is discovered before any such damage is
> caused, there is no longer any room for the application of the *Donoghue*
> v. *Stevenson* principle. The chattel is now defective in quality, but is no
> longer dangerous. It may be valueless or it may be incapable of eco-
> nomic repair. In either case the economic loss is recoverable in contract
> by a buyer or hirer of the chattel entitled to the benefit of a relevant
> warranty of quality, but is not recoverable in tort by a remote buyer or
> hirer of the chattel."[88]

The post-*Junior Books* cases are part of a general pattern of restriction on
the reach of negligence law and represent an attempt to keep separate the
spheres of tort and contract law. In none of them, however, is there very
much discussion of the practical impact of placing upon the manufacturer a
liability for defects of quality and performance and it must be borne in mind
that if the plaintiff is a purchaser of the article and the usual chain of
contractual indemnities functions fully it is the manufacturer, as the originator of the defect, who carries responsibility, even if he is not negligent.
Certainly, the creation of a direct liability from manufacturer to consumer
might raise formidable difficulties. For example, how would a standard of
"defectiveness of quality" be set, since that is something which must be
related to the terms of the contract (in particular, the price) between the
manufacturer and the intermediary (the seller or some more remote person
in the distribution chain)? Further, what would be the effect of exclusions or
limitations of liability in the contract between the manufacturer and the
intermediary?[89] Perhaps these problems would be far from insuperable in

---

[87] See further Prosser, *Torts* (5th ed.), p. 708.

[88] [1988] 3 W.L.R. 368, 385, *per* Lord Bridge. But *cf.* the position as to buildings, since *Anns* v. *Merton
London Borough* has not been overruled: *ante*, p. 231.

[89] *e.g.* in *Junior Books* v. *Veitchi* Lord Fraser thought that the plaintiff in tort could be in no better position
than the purchaser from the manufacturer: [1983] 1 A.C. 520, 534.

the context of standard form transactions with little room for bargaining and judicial control of exemption clauses but in view of the present law it would be pointless to pursue them.

LIABILITY UNDER THE CONSUMER PROTECTION ACT 1987

Looked at against the background of the general law of tort the level of protection given to victims of dangerous goods by *Donoghue* v. *Stevenson* may be thought not unreasonable, though it may be hard to justify the strict liability in respect of death or personal injury[90] which the purchaser acquires by virtue of his contract of sale. Such a view is, however, out of accord with the spirit of a time in which the consumer interest has become one of the most important pressures for law reform. In the United States, liability for negligence was overtaken by judicial reform in favour of the consumer.[91] The first step was liability for express warranty, shorn of the restriction of privity of contract and based on advertising claims,[92] but this was soon overtaken by the idea of the *implied* warranty of safety.[93] The culmination was *Greenman* v. *Yuba Power Products Inc.*[94] in which the court abandoned the idea of warranty and imposed a straightforward strict liability in tort.[95] Various arguments have been advanced in favour of these developments[96] but the most commonly occurring ones are that the manufacturer, as creator of the risk, should bear its consequences[97]; that he is in the best position to insure that risk and to cover the cost of that insurance in his price[98]; that strict liability is even more of an incentive than fault to the taking of adequate precautions; and that strict tort liability only achieves in one action what the law of contract achieves in many cases by the chain of indemnities stretching back from the consumer-purchaser to the manufacturer.

In numerical terms the problem of injuries caused by product defects is small when compared with those attributable to other risks[99] and the difficulty of establishing a case under the law of negligence can be exaggerated,[1]

---

[90] As opposed to the liability for financial loss caused by the failure of the goods to function.

[91] See Miller & Lovell, *Product Liability* (1977).

[92] *Baxter* v. *Ford Motor Co.* 12 P. 2d 409 (1932). This has obvious affinities with the collateral contract.

[93] *Henningsen* v. *Bloomfield Motors* 161 A. 2d 69 (1960). *cf.* the alternative forms of art. 2–318 of the Uniform Commercial Code.

[94] (1963) 27 Cal.Rptr. 697.

[95] See *Restatement* 2d s.402A.

[96] See, *e.g.* Law Com. No. 82, Liability for Defective Products (1977), para. 38.

[97] But this argument proves too much—it would suggest strict liability for any injury caused in the production and distribution process, *e.g.* an accident to a worker in the factory or a crash caused by the driving of a delivery van. Liability under the Consumer Protection Act 1987 is confined to injuries caused by a defect in the product, which is by no means the same thing as injuries caused by the product.

[98] A sufficiently bad claims record should raise his premium costs to such a level that he is driven off the market: see the theory of "market deterrence" mentioned *ante*, p. 26.

[99] On the basis of its personal injury survey the Pearson Commission estimated that between 30,000 and 40,000 injuries per year (about 1 per cent. of all injuries) might be attributable to defective products other than drugs and that the risk of death was lower than for other categories of risk: Cmnd. 7054, Vol. 1, para. 1201. False claims may be common: See the baby food scare of 1989.

[1] See *supra*, n. 71. But tort compensation was recovered in only 5 per cent. of cases (half the rate for work accidents and one-fifth of the rate for road accidents) and the average payment was only half that for all personal injury accidents.

but there was a powerful tide in favour of change in the 1970s, prompted in part by the Thalidomide tragedy[2] and given impetus by pressure for harmonisation of laws within the EEC. The adoption by the Council of the EEC of a Directive on liability for defective products[3] meant that the United Kingdom was required, by virtue of its treaty obligations, to legislate to make our law accord with the Directive and this was done by Part I of the Consumer Protection Act 1987[4] which came into force on March 1, 1988,[5] and which expressly states that it is to "have effect for the purpose of making such provision as is necessary in order to comply with the . . . Directive and shall be construed accordingly."[6] The Act is too complicated to summarise accurately in one sentence and it is necessary to look at particular provisions in some detail, but very broadly its effect is to make the *producer* of a *product* (and certain others dealing with it) liable in damages for *personal injury* and *some property damage* caused by a *defect* in the product, *without the necessity for the plaintiff to show fault*, though *certain defences may be raised by the producer*. Liability is by no means absolute; how far it is properly described as "strict" is debatable but judgment on that must be suspended until the Act has been looked at more closely.

Who is liable?

Subject to a point discussed below, the Act does not impose liability on persons who merely supply goods, though it must again be emphasised that the supplier usually has a contractual liability which is more onerous than that imposed by the Act, albeit only to his immediate purchaser. The three principal categories of persons liable under the Act are listed in section 2(2) and the first is the producer of the product[7] who is further defined in section 1(2) as:

"(*a*) the person who manufactured it;

(*b*) in the case of a substance which has not been manufactured but has been won or abstracted, the person who won or abstracted it;

(*c*) in the case of a product which has not been manufactured, won or abstracted but essential characteristics of which are attributable to an industrial or other process having been carried out (for example, in relation to agricultural produce), the person who carried out that process."

---

[2] See Teff and Munro, *Thalidomide: The Legal Aftermath* (1976).

[3] A draft version of the Directive (different in a number of significant respects) was considered by the Law Commission (Law Com. No. 82 (1977)) and the Pearson Commission (see *supra*, n. 99).

[4] Miller, *Product Liability and Safety Encyclopaedia*, Division III; Fairest, *The Consumer Protection Act 1987*. For a highly critical account of the changes produced by the Directive, see Stapleton, "Products Liability Reform—Real or Illusory" (1986) 6 O.J.L. s.392. See also Newdick, "The Future of Negligence in Product Liability" (1987) 104 L.Q.R. 288 and "The Development Risk Defence" [1988] C.L.J. 455.

[5] The Act applies if the product was supplied to any person by the producer on or after that date.

[6] s.1(1). Surprisingly, perhaps, the Directive is not annexed to the Act. It can be found in the Official Journal of the European Communities, No. L 210/29.

[7] s.2(2)(*a*).

The first class within section 1(2) is self-explanatory, but it is important to note that if a product causes damage as a result of failure of a component part (for example, an aircraft which crashes because of a defective altimeter) then both the manufacturer of the component part and the final manufacturer/assembler are treated as producers and are liable under the Act.[8] Their liability is joint and several,[9] that is to say, each is liable in full to the plaintiff, though as between themselves the liability may be apportioned under the contribution legislation[10] and there may, of course, be contractual rights of indemnity. Paragraph (b) covers minerals and raw materials (oil, coal, cement). Paragraph (c), which covers things not falling within either of the two previous categories,[11] will raise some awkward questions of degree as to what is an "essential characteristic": the picking and packing of crops do not, presumably, bring this paragraph into play but the processing and freezing of poultry probably do. A further complication arises in relation to agricultural produce[12] and game, since by section 2(4) no liability is imposed upon a person who supplies these at a time when they have not undergone an industrial process. There is no definition of industrial, but on the assumption[13] that it excludes things done to crops or animals during growing or rearing and that it requires something on a fairly large scale, perhaps involving machinery, the upshot is that farmers, fishermen, etc., will not generally be exposed to liability under the Act. The relevant provisions, however, raise an almost infinite number of uncertainties of interpretation.[14] It should not be assumed that because the farmer escapes liability the Act is wholly inapplicable: if, say, bread were poisonous because of some pesticide which had come into contact with the growing corn, then the bakery would be liable even if it was not at fault in being unaware of the defect in its flour.

The second category in section 2(2) is the "own brander" or, as the Act puts it, "any person who by putting his name on the product or using a trade mark or other distinguishing mark in relation to the product, has held himself out to be the producer of the product." This provision may be of narrower effect than it has often been assumed to be, for it is not enough to put your name on the goods, you must do so in such a way as to hold yourself out as the producer: does anyone really believe that, for example, Marks & Spencer plc actually makes the products marketed under the "St. Michael" brand? The matter is, of course, fundamentally a question of fact but labelling which clearly states that the product is made *for* and not *by* the store will presumably exclude section 2(2).

Vast quantities of consumer goods are imported from abroad and the

---

[8] This is the effect of the definition of "product" in s.1(2), though this very important point could, perhaps, have been stated more clearly.

[9] s.2(5).

[10] *Post*, Chap. 22.

[11] If X extracts oil and Y refines it into petroleum, X falls within paragraph (b). Does Y fall within paragraph (a) or paragraph (c)? If (c), it is presumably irrelevant that it *has* been abstracted in another form.

[12] Defined in s.1(2) as "any produce of the soil, of stock-farming or of fisheries."

[13] Not necessarily well founded: see *Hansard*, H.L., Vol. 483, cols. 717 and 729.

[14] See Miller, *op. cit.*, n. 4, Division III, pp. 167–169.

third category in section 2(2) goes some way towards relieving the plaintiff from the problems of suing a foreign producer, for it imposes liability upon the person who has imported the product into the EEC from a place outside the EEC.[15] Hence, if A, a Belgian company, imports goods into Belgium from Japan and then sells them to B, who imports them into the United Kingdom, where they are sold to P, A (but not B) is liable under this head.[16]

This part opened by saying that the mere supply of goods to another did not of itself attract the operation of the Act, but under section 2(3) a supplier[17] who receives a request from the injured person to identify the producer (or other person liable under section 2(2)) is liable under the Act if he does not within a reasonable time either comply with the request or identify *his* supplier. The idea is to enable the plaintiff to trace "anonymous" goods back along the chain of distribution to a producer or importer who carries primary liability under the Act and anyone who breaks this chain[18] by his inability to identify his supplier is made liable as if he were the producer. Since in this way a wholesaler who is contractually remote from the plaintiff and who is in no way at fault with regard to the goods may incur heavy damages without hope of recourse, the importance of adequate record keeping can hardly be over-emphasised.

Products

A product is any goods or electricity[19] and "goods" is further defined as including "substances, growing crops[20] and things comprised in land by virtue of being attached to it and any ship, aircraft or vehicle."[21] Components of a building are, therefore, covered, so that a manufacturer of defective steel joists would be liable for injury caused by the collapse of a block of flats; but it is thought that the building as a whole is not "goods" and that a builder is not therefore responsible under the Act for shoddy workmanship,[22] though the law of negligence and the Defective Premises Act 1972 of course apply to these cases. It seems that information is not within the Act even though it is incorporated in tangible form in a book[23] but the same may not be true of computerised information, where the line between

---

[15] s.2(2)(c). However, the importing must be "in order to supply it to another." An airline which brings an American airliner to England to use it here is not liable under this paragraph: s.46(9).

[16] The conflict of laws is outside the scope of this book but it should be noted that under the Brussels Convention on Jurisdiction and Reciprocal Enforcement of Judgments P could sue A either here or in Belgium. If the latter, the Belgian judgment would be enforceable here. Fears were expressed in Parliament about the prospect of nominally capitalised "front" companies being used to import goods into the EEC. Such a company could be sacrificed and a judgment against it would exhaust the Act. However, the control of this sort of activity is a matter for company law, not tort.

[17] "Supply" is defined in s.46(1) and extends a good deal more widely than supply under a sale. But a finance company is not a supplier for the purposes of this Act; the "effective supplier" (*e.g.* the garage in a car hire purchase transaction) is: s.46(2).

[18] The request may be made to *any* supplier, not merely the one who directly supplied it to the plaintiff.

[19] s.1(2).

[20] The special treatment of unprocessed agricultural produce has already been mentioned.

[21] s.45(1).

[22] Even if this view is wrong, the same result will be reached in cases where the builder sells the house as a result of the combined effect of ss.4(1)(b), 46(3), 46(4).

[23] This was certainly the government's intention, though two remarkably opaque sub-clauses in the Bill which were designed to make this clear were removed.

"software" and "hardware" may be difficult to draw sensibly. If an airliner crashes because a component in an automatic landing device fails above a certain temperature there is clearly a defective product within the Act. Can the position really be any different if it is programmed so that it simply does not operate in certain, foreseeable conditions or if it gives the pilot a misleading indication?[24] Misleading instructions for use of a product are clearly not to be equated with "pure" information, for they may themselves render an otherwise perfect product defective.[25]

Damage

The Act applies to death or personal injury no matter how large or small the loss[26] but the position with regard to property damage is more restricted. First, there is no liability in respect of loss of or damage to the product itself or the whole or any part of any product which has been supplied with the product in question comprised in it.[27] If, therefore, my car radio catches fire as a result of faulty components and burns out the car, neither the car assembler nor the radio manufacturer is strictly liable,[28] but if the same thing were to happen with a replacement radio liability would be imposed on the manufacturer of that. Secondly, no liability arises unless the damages (apart from interest) would be at least £275.[29] Thirdly, the Act is inapplicable unless the property is of a description ordinarily intended for private use and is mainly so intended by the plaintiff.[30] The Act would, therefore, have no application to the *Muirhead* and *Aswan* cases.[31]

Defect

This is the core of the Act, the proposition that the damage must be caused wholly or partly by a defect in the product. Defect is defined in section 3 as being present where "the safety of the product is not such as persons generally are entitled to expect."[32] It is crucial to note that the standard is what persons generally are *entitled* to expect, a standard to be set by the court and which may be lower than what they do expect; public expectations may be unreasonably high, especially in a litigation conscious society. The

---

[24] It must, however, be confessed that the distinction between this and the book which contains misleading information is not easy to discern, still less to state. *cf. Brocklesby* v. *U.S.* 753 F. 2d 794 (1985), *post*, p. 283.

[25] See s.3(2)(*a*).

[26] The Act does not adopt the provisions of Art. 16 of the Directive whereby liability for death or personal injury caused by identical items with the same defect may be limited to 70 million ECU. There would be formidable practical difficulties in the application of such a provision.

[27] s.5(2).

[28] Compare the rather uncertain position at common law: *ante*, p. 247.

[29] s.5(4). It seems that Art. 9(2) of the Directive, from which this curious limit stems, is mandatory. It is a curiosity in English conditions, being well below the level at which most lawyers would probably advise embarking on litigation.

[30] s.5(3).

[31] *Ante*, pp. 246–247.

[32] It is further provided that "safety, in relation to a product, shall include safety with respect to products comprised in the product and safety in the context of risks of damage to property, as well as in the context of risks of death or personal injury."

simplest case is that of the so-called "production defect," the case where, despite quality controls, the production line turns out a sub-standard article. Subject to a point discussed below about the defence under section 4(1)(e), the plaintiff wins by showing that the sub-standard nature of the article made it dangerous and that it caused his damage. Although in many cases the mere existence of the defect would provide powerful indirect evidence of negligence the plaintiff is no longer required to rely on this. No doubt it will be argued that since "accidents will happen" the only thing that the public is entitled to expect is products made with all reasonable care and skill, but this would be little if at all different from the law of negligence, and it is most unlikely that the court would adopt a construction that would seem to deprive the Act of all its effect. Rather more complicated is what may be called the known inherent danger. Some products will not work effectively unless there is an element of risk in their design—carving knives which cut meat well are also more efficient at lopping off users' fingers. Other products could be made safer only by the expenditure of amounts of money which would be incompatible with the price range in the market at which the product is aimed—if all cars were required to be fitted with ABS brakes and four wheel drive there would be no cheap cars available to the public. In either case the court is required to come to a judgment on whether the risks associated with the product in its present form are outweighed by the benefits that it brings, and while scientific evidence is no doubt relevant and often helpful there is no escaping the fact that in the last resort the judgment is a "value" one: there is no scientific formula which will tell us whether the risk of allowing cars to be made without advanced braking systems is greater or less than the benefits obtained by having cheaper cars.[33] The necessity of adopting a cost-benefit approach was candidly admitted by the DTI explanatory note on the Directive, which commented, in relation to drugs—

> "The more active the medicine, and the greater its beneficial potential, the more extensive its effects are likely to be, and therefore the greater the chances of an adverse effect. A medicine used to treat a life threatening condition is likely to be much more powerful than a medicine used in the treatment of a less serious condition, and the safety that one is reasonably entitled to expect of such a medicine may therefore be correspondingly lower."

In cases of known, inherent dangers it is very arguable that the Act effects no practical change in the common law position,[34] despite the nominal shift from examining the conduct of the defendant to the safety of the product, for where the risk is known the real question will be, as it has always been, "was

[33] It is often asked whether cigarettes are "defective" within the Act (American litigation on the point has had mixed fortunes). Without wishing to pre-judge the issue, it is thought that the mere facts that the risk is considerable and the benefit not quantifiable in money are not decisive (consider also alcohol). *Volenti non fit injuria* is not, as such, a defence under the Act, though contributory negligence applies.

[34] This is not to say that the Act may not create a climate of opinion in which litigants are more ready to challenge the safety of designs.

it reasonable to market this design?"[35] A third category of case is where the product is thought to be safe at its launch but subsequent use reveals dangers which far outweigh its utility. Thalidomide, for example, was clearly defective by the criteria of the Act since it was dispensed to combat morning sickness in pregnant women but produced serious foetal deformities. However, the controversial "development risks" defence (discussed below) comes into play here.

Although section 3 provides that all the circumstances are to be taken into account in determining whether the product is as safe as persons generally are entitled to expect, it specifically draws attention to the following—

"(a) the manner in which, and the purposes for which, the product has been marketed, its get-up, the use of any mark in relation to the product and any instructions for, or warnings with respect to, doing or refraining from doing anything in relation to the product;

(b) what might reasonably be expected to be done with or in relation to the product; and

(c) the time when the product was supplied by its producer to another; and nothing . . . shall require a defect to be inferred from the fact alone that the safety of a product which is supplied after that time is greater than the safety of the product in question."

The demonology of American product liability law is full of cases (some apocryphal) of plaintiffs making startling uses of products and presenting exaggerated claims for protection against what might seem fairly obvious risks. Given the close resemblance of the concept of design defect with the common law of negligence and the absence here of trial by jury and (at least at present[35a]) of contingency fees there is little risk of these phenomena being repeated here, but circumstances of danger are so infinitely various that very little practical advice can be offered about instructions and labelling[36] beyond the general proposition that the manufacturer should err on the side of caution.[37]

The proposition that the safety of a product is to be judged by reference to standards prevailing when it was put into circulation (so that a 1988 car is not

---

[35] As in negligence, industry practice is likely to be an important but not ultimately controlling, factor. There is a good discussion in the context of American law in *Boatland of Houston* v. *Bailey* 609 S.W. (2d) 743 (1980) ("kill-switch" to immobilise power boat if operator thrown out). See also Henderson (1973) 73 Col.L.Rev. 1531 and (1976) 61 Cornell L.Rev. 541.

[35a] But see Cm. 571 (1989).

[36] These matters are obviously intimately connected with foreseeable use. By way of example—(1) Most perfume is highly inflammable, but should a manufacturer have to give warning of this? Yes, according to an American court in *Moran* v. *Fabergè* 332 A. (2d) 11 (1975)—plaintiff dowsing candle in perfume. (2) Sealing compounds are inflammable and contain warnings not to expose to naked flame. Should this extend to a warning to extinguish the pilot light on a stove? Yes, according to the Supreme Court of Canada, reversing an appeal court in *Lambert* v. *Lastoplex Chemicals* (1971) 25 D.L.R. (3d) 121, decided on a negligence standard.

[37] Provided, that is, he does not put in so much information that consumers are likely not to bother to read it! There is no blanket rule that the manufacturer may safely ignore a danger which is "obvious," for the product may foreseeably get into the hands of children or other incompetents and if a simple design change will reduce the danger to them, the law may require it: see Miller, *op. cit.*, n. 4, Division III, p. 171.

defective merely because subsequent models are produced with more advanced safety features) is an inevitable concomitant of the concept of "defect"[38] and if the rule were otherwise there might be a positive disincentive to an industry to introduce safety improvements. The "product" in question for this purpose is, of course, the individual item which causes the damage, not the product "line" or design—one cannot go on forever producing cars to 1988 standards when everyone else's safety standards have improved—but except in cases where legislative requirements are imposed (for example, as to the fitting of safety belts) it may be very difficult for the court to decide at what point a development becomes necessary to satisfy the requirement of safety, as opposed to being merely desirable. Furthermore, the plaintiff may face serious difficulties in assembling the required evidence of design standards.

Defences

Section 4 contains defences in the proper sense of that term, *i.e.* matters which must be raised and proved by the defendant. To the common law mind some of them are matters which might more naturally be regarded as casting a burden on the plaintiff but the Act is a consumer protection measure and the allocation of the burden is deliberate. Section 4 will, therefore, come into play if we postulate that the plaintiff has proved, directly or by getting the court to draw inferences—

(i) damage
(ii) attributable to a defect
(iii) in an article for which the defendant is responsible under the Act, as producer or otherwise.

The defences are—

(a) *That the defect is attributable to compliance with any requirement imposed by law*

Suppose that the law required all wine to contain sulphur dioxide. Suppose also that the ingredient was then found to be harmful. The producer would have a defence without reference to the "development risks" defence of section 4(1)(e). This defence does *not* mean that compliance with minimum legal standards automatically provides a defence. The hypothetical wine law forbids the addition of ingredients A, B and C. The producer adds ingredient X, widely thought to be beneficial, but then discovered to be harmful. Subject to section 4(1)(e), the producer is liable. Perhaps a more

---

[38] But Stapleton, *loc. cit.*, n. 4, (writing from the standpoint that the Act is a misguided and ineffective compensation measure which sticks much too closely to common law concepts) argues that reformers are illogical in readily accepting this proposition while at the same time rejecting (as many of them do) the "development risks" defence now enshrined in s.4(1)(e): "It is odd that risks discovered after circulation should be taken into account to show that a product was defective all along, but the development of better products after circulation should not be taken into account to demonstrate that the benefits of the product were all along less than supposed."

likely state of affairs is one where an ingredient is expressly permitted by law even though it is believed, or even known, to carry some risk of injury. Section 4(1)(*a*) does not provide a defence, but the legislative permission may provide almost conclusive evidence that the product is not defective.[39]

(*b*) *That the defendant did not at any time supply the product to another*

Being a supplier does not involve liability under the Act unless the "tracing" provision of section 2(3) comes into play. But even a producer is not liable if he has not supplied[40] the article to another. "Supply" is widely defined to include hiring out or lending but it does not cover merely putting goods in someone's hands for him to use, so if D produces a machine for internal use in the factory and this has a defect which injures workman P the Act does not apply.[41]

(*c*) *That any supply by the defendant was a "non-commercial" one within section 4(1)(c).*[42]

(*d*) *That the defect did not exist in the product when he put it into circulation.*[43]

The producer is not liable for defects which have arisen from interference, misuse or fair wear and tear but once the plaintiff has shown that the product was defective in the section 3 sense and has caused damage it is up to the producer to raise and prove such matters. Of course he may do so by indirect evidence (for example, by showing that a weakness in the wall of a burst tyre is reasonably consistent only with impact damage in use) but where the court is left in doubt the plaintiff should win.[44]

(*e*) *"That the state of scientific and technical knowledge at the relevant time*[45] *was not such that a producer of products of the same description as the product in question might be expected to have discovered the*

---

[39] *cf. Albery and Budden* v. *B.P. Oil, ante*, p. 118, a claim in negligence.

[40] See s.46.

[41] Miller, *op. cit.*, n. 4, points out that for the same reason the Act would have no application to an incident like the Bhopal disaster.

[42] This reads as follows—

"(i) that the only supply of the product to another by the person proceeded against was otherwise than in the course of a business of that person's; *and*

"(ii) that section 2(2) . . . does not apply to that person or applies to him by virtue only of things done otherwise than with a view to profit."

Hence a person donating a home-made pie to a church fete escapes liability. But if he *sold* it he would be liable if the cooking made him a "producer" within s.1(2)(c). A private seller of second-hand goods would escape the "tracing" liability under s.2(3) because s.2(2) does not apply to him.

[43] This is the position of defendants falling within s.2(2). There are, however, special provisions as to the relevant time in relation to electricity and to s.2(3) defendants.

[44] *cf.* the American case of *Scanlon* v. *General Motors* 326 A. (2d) (1974) where plaintiff failed because of inability to show that a "racing engine" was attributable to a defect in the vehicle when it left the manufacturer.

[45] Again, normally, the time when the produce is put into circulation, *supra*, n. 43.

defect if it had existed in his products while they were under his control."

This defence proved highly controversial during the passage of the Act but the government insisted on its inclusion. The first point is that the Directive merely allows the inclusion of such a defence[46] and the policy among member states has not been uniform: West Germany, for example, is to allow such a defence generally, but not for pharmaceuticals. Secondly, it is possible that the terms of section 4(1)(*e*) do not accord completely with Article 7(*e*) of the Directive, which provides "that the state of scientific and technical knowledge at the time when [the producer] put the product into circulation was not such as to enable the existence of the defect to be discovered,"[47] and it is certainly arguable that the Directive speaks in terms of scientific possibility, whereas section 4(1)(*e*), with its references to comparable producers and what might have been expected comes very close to a traditional negligence formula. Indeed, while the defence is almost always discussed in terms of unknown "design" defects, the paragraph can be read as being also applicable to production flaws where all practicable quality control measures are taken, which would amount to negligence with a reversed burden of proof, and on that basis, given the apparent readiness of the courts to infer negligence from the mere presence of a defect, the Act would not really have achieved anything at all.[48]

The argument in favour of section 4(1)(*e*), at least in so far as it applies to unknown design risks, is succinctly put in the D.T.I. Consultative Document on the Directive.

"Manufacturers . . . have argued that it would be wrong in principle, and disastrous in practice, for businesses to be held liable for defects that they could not possibly have foreseen. They believe that the absence of this defence would raise costs and inhibit innovation, especially in high risk industries. Many useful new products, which might entail a development risk, would not be put on the market, and consumers as well as businesses might lose out."

On the other hand, there is no such defence in contract law,[49] and it has been

---

[46] In any event, it is to be reviewed in 1995. See generally, Newdick [1988] C.L.J. 455.

[47] The European Commission has formally challenged s.4(1)(*e*) (*The Financial Times*, February 2, 1988). Ultimately, the matter can only be decided by the European Court of Justice but an English court must have regard to the Directive in interpreting the Act: n. 6, *supra*.

[48] Miller, *op. cit.*, n. 4, Division III, p. 178, suggests that the focus of s.4(1)(*e*) is on the individually defective product and that the defence is not therefore made out by showing that the best quality control systems will lead on average to a failure in, say 0.03 per cent. of cases. The defence is sometimes referred to as the "state of the art" defence. If production flaws do not fall within it, it is submitted that the alternative name, the "development risks" defence is the better one. "State of the art" is also liable to give rise to confusion because that concept is part of the notion of defect without reference to s.4(1)(*e*): the "state of the art" on carving knives is that they inevitably involve the risk of cutting fingers but they are not defective for that reason.

[49] *Henry Kendall & Sons* v. *William Lillico & Sons Ltd.* [1969] 2 A.C. 31; *Ashington Piggeries Ltd.* v. *Christopher Hill Ltd.* [1972] A.C. 441. However, this raises difficulties which have not been fully explored by the courts: Goode, *Commercial Law*, pp. 267–269.

suggested that another thalidomide-type tragedy might slip through the liability net under the Act, for which reason both the Law Commission and the Pearson Commission rejected any exemption for development risks.[50]

(f)

> "*That the defect*
>
> (i) *constituted a defect in a product ("the subsequent product") in which the product in question had been comprised; and*
>
> (ii) *was wholly attributable to the design of the subsequent product or to compliance by the producer of the product in question with instructions given by the producer of the subsequent product.*"

A Co. orders a consignment of standard tyres from B Co. and fits them to a high speed sports car model for which they are wholly unsuitable. The car is therefore "defective." If, as this paragraph seems to assume, the tyre is also thereby defective, B Co. has a defence to an action by an injured consumer. Where the component producer knows or ought to know that the final assembler intends, through inexperience, to make an unsuitable use of the component then an action in negligence might lie against the component producer at the suit of an injured consumer,[51] quite apart from any liability in contract to the assembler. The position is less clear where the assembler is aware of the danger and presses on regardless[52] but it is submitted that the component manufacturer must be entitled, after due warning to the assembler, to act on assurances by the latter and is not obliged to investigate compliance with those assurances.

Contributory negligence

The Consumer Protection Act applies the Law Reform (Contributory Negligence) Act 1945[53] by providing that when damage is caused partly by a defect in a product and partly by the fault of the person suffering the damage then the defect is to be treated as if it were the fault of every person liable for it under the Act.[54] In "deeming" fault to exist in the producer the Act recognises the difficulty of balancing blameworthy against non-blameworthy conduct, though it does not really solve the problem. However, there is plenty of experience under the Factories Act of applying apportionment of liability to strict liability situations and the courts should have no difficulty with this. Where the plaintiff's fault is extreme then it may amount to the sole cause in law and deprive him of damages altogether[55]; in many cases, exactly the same result may be reached by concluding that the plaintiff's use of the product is so unusual that it is not defective, even if it has caused damage.[56]

---

[50] See Law Com. No. 82, para. 105; Cmnd. 7054, Vol. 1, para. 1259.

[51] Whether the Act also applies in this situation would not seem to matter.

[52] Compare the cases on wilful wrongdoing by a third party: *ante*, p. 93.

[53] *Ante*, p. 158.

[54] s.6(4). Various other Acts are also applied by s.6, *e.g.* the Fatal Accidents Act 1976 and the Congenital Disabilities (Civil Liability) Act 1976.

[55] *Ante*, p. 160.

[56] This no doubt would be the answer to the (apocryphal) American case of the lady who used her microwave oven to dry her poodle.

Exclusion of liability

Section 7 enacts a simple rule invalidating any limitation or exclusion of liability "by any contract term, by any notice or by any other provision," no matter what the nature of the damage.[57] Of course, care must be taken to distinguish substance from form: "manufacturers will not be responsible unless this product is earthed" is not an exclusion of liability but a warning which goes to the safety of the product under section 3. Nor does section 7 invalidate the terms of contracts between, say, an assembler and component manufacturers allocating ultimate responsibility among themselves, though those contracts may be subject to judicial control under the Unfair Contract Terms Act 1977.

Limitation

This is dealt with in Chapter 27. At this stage, however, it is worth noting the "cut-off" provision whereby any liability is extinguished 10 years after the product has been put into circulation, thus smothering to some extent the risk of mass disaster litigation arising from defects which come to light only after many years.[58] This does not, however, affect the common law of negligence.

CONCLUSION

From a theoretical point of view, the Consumer Protection Act is one of the most important developments in English tort law for many years. However, liability is by no means absolute, the Act has a number of affinities with the common law and only time will tell, especially in relation to development risks, how far it will effect a substantial change in practice. One matter of great controversy is the cost of implementation. There is no doubt that in the United States strict product liability judgments became a serious burden on some sectors of manufacturing industry[59] but the cause of this lay not so much in the strict liability as in American practice on the use of juries, contingency fees and other matters. One estimate is that the implementation of the Directive will lead to an increase of no more than 25 per cent. in liability insurance premiums, which means, on average, an increase in unit costs of the order of 0.02 per cent.,[60] though there might be huge variations from one trade to another. In any event, greater "litigation consciousness" could wholly falsify these estimates.

---

[57] Contrast s.2 of the Unfair Contract Terms Act 1977, *post*, p. 687 which makes exclusion of liability for property damage caused by negligence subject to a reasonableness test.
[58] *e.g.* asbestosis.
[59] But there has been widespread state legislation in an effort to stem the tide: reduced limitation periods and "caps" on non-pecuniary loss damages have been popular devices.
[60] See North (1978) 128 New L.J. 315, 318 (based on the Law Commission/Pearson proposals, *i.e.* with no development risks defence).

It should also be noted that there is a further, modest element of strict liability in the consumer protection field. Since 1961 the Secretary of State has had power to make regulations imposing safety requirements for classes of goods and to make orders prohibiting the supply of goods which are not safe.[61] This power is now contained in Part II of the Consumer Protection Act 1987 (section 11) and contravention of the regulations is actionable[62] (as a breach of statutory duty) by any person affected thereby.[63] Part II is, however, primarily concerned with the enforcement of safety by criminal sanctions.

---

[61] Originally in the Consumer Protection Act 1961, succeeded by the Consumer Safety Act 1978.
[62] Except in so far as safety regulations provide otherwise.
[63] s.41. For the regulations, mostly made under the earlier Acts, see Miller, *op. cit.*, n. 4, Division IV.

CHAPTER 11

LIABILITY FOR STATEMENTS[1]

WORDS, especially if untrue, are capable of causing loss in several different ways. They may injure a man's reputation, if they are defamatory and published to a third party; they may cause direct injury by shock to the person to whom they are addressed; they may cause him to act in reliance upon them and suffer loss or damage as a result; or they may cause him to act in reliance upon them and so cause loss or damage to someone else. The first of these cases is covered by the tort of defamation which is the subject of a separate chapter[2] while the second is exemplified by *Wilkinson* v. *Downton,* to which we have already referred.[3] In this chapter we are concerned mainly with the other types of case.

Since the famous case of *Pasley* v. *Freeman*[4] in 1789, it has been the rule that A is liable in tort to B if he knowingly or recklessly (*i.e.* not caring whether it is true or false) makes a false statement to B with intent that it shall be acted upon by B, who does act upon it and thereby suffers damage. This is the tort of deceit (or "fraud"), and for liability in deceit the defendant must make the statement with knowledge of its falsity or at least reckless whether it is true or false.[5] It was for long thought that this meant that there could be no liability in tort for a false statement honestly made, however negligent its maker may have been and however disastrous its consequences: a careless man is not a dishonest one. Eventually however, the House of Lords held that there may in certain circumstances be a duty of care upon the maker of a statement,[6] and thus that a person may be liable for a false statement honestly but negligently made. Such liability cannot be brought under the tort of deceit—it is liability for negligence and not for fraud—but its existence has a profound bearing on liability for statements as a whole. As we have seen,[7] the plaintiff in an action for damages does not have to specify the particular tort on which he wishes to rely and all that is necessary is that he should prove the facts required for liability under at least one tort. If, therefore, there may be liability in negligence it may be of little more than academic interest that absence of fraudulent intent is fatal to a claim

---

[1] Allen, *Misrepresentation* (1988).
[2] *Post*, Chap. 12.
[3] [1897] 2 Q.B. 57, *ante*, p. 68. There seems no reason in principle why negligence by words leading directly to nervous shock should not be actionable, but cases will be rare. See *ante*, p. 110.
[4] (1789) 3 T.R. 51.
[5] *Derry* v. *Peek* (1889) 14 App.Cas. 337. In one instance, the law allows (but does not compel) the making of a false statement: Rehabilitation of Offenders Act 1974, s.4(2).
[6] *Hedley Byrne & Co. Ltd.* v. *Heller & Partners Ltd.* [1964] A.C. 465. See, too, the Misrepresentation Act 1967, s.2.
[7] *Ante*, pp. 50–51

founded on deceit. Nevertheless, the tort has not been abolished and the plaintiff may have good reason for seeking to establish a case of deceit.[8]

ESSENTIALS OF DECEIT

The five things that the plaintiff has to establish in a common law action of deceit may be summarised as follows[9]:

1. There must be a representation of fact made by words or conduct.

2. The representation must be made with the intention that it should be acted upon by the plaintiff, or by a class of persons which includes the plaintiff, in the manner which resulted in damage to him.

3. It must be proved that the plaintiff has acted upon the false statement.

4. It must be proved that the plaintiff suffered damage by so doing.[10]

5. The representation must be made with knowledge that it is or may be false. It must be wilfully false, or at least made in the absence of any genuine belief that it is true.

A false statement of fact

(1) *Representations*

The statement may, of course, be oral or written. It may also be implied from conduct. If the defendant deliberately acts in a manner calculated to deceive the plaintiff and the other elements of the tort are present, the defendant is as much liable for deceit as if he had expressly made a false statement of fact.[11] Deliberate concealment, too, amounts to deceit,[12] but subject to what is said below mere silence, however morally wrong, will not support an action for deceit.[13]

(2) *Promises and other statements of intention*

It is commonly said that mere promises are not statements of fact, but this

---

[8] A plaintiff who thinks he can prove dishonest behaviour is likely to allege it. Further, the plaintiff may have a reason for framing his claim as deceit, *e.g.* to obtain exemplary damages or the benefit of s.32 of the Limitation Act 1980. See *U.B.A.F. Ltd.* v. *European American Banking Corp.* [1984] Q.B. 713.

[9] *Bradford Building Society* v. *Borders* [1941] 2 All E.R. 205, 211, *per* Lord Maugham. There is no general liability for "fraud" in the sense of dishonesty unless it amounts to the tort of deceit or to equitable fraud. *Amalgamated Metal Trading Ltd.* v. *D.T.I.*, The Times, March 21, 1989. But it is also the case that a principal may recover damages for "fraud" in respect of a transaction into which his agent is bribed: *Mahesan* v. *Malaysia Government Officers' Co-operative Housing Society* [1979] A.C. 374.

[10] The damage is the gist of the action: *Smith* v. *Chadwick* (1884) 9 App.Cas. 187, 196, *per* Lord Blackburn; *Briess* v. *Woolley* [1954] A.C. 332.

[11] *Ward* v. *Hobbs* (1878) 4 App.Cas. 13, 26, *per* Lord O'Hagan; *Bradford Building Society* v. *Borders* [1942] 1 All E.R. 205, 211, *per* Lord Maugham; Salmond and Heuston *Torts*, 19th ed., p. 434. For a criminal case, see *R.* v. *Barnard* (1837) 7 C. & P. 784 and Smith, *The Law of Theft*, 5th ed.

[12] *Gordon* v. *Selico* (1984) 275 E.G. 899. But there is a difference between the concealing of a serious defect and doing minor acts to make a property more attractive to a purchaser.

[13] *Bradford Building Society* v. *Borders, supra*, at p. 211, *per* Lord Maugham, citing *Peek* v. *Gurney* (1873) L.R. 6 H.L. 377, 390, *per* Lord Chelmsford; *ibid.* at p. 403, *per* Lord Cairns. *cf.* the rule in s.551 of the *Restatement* 2d.

is misleading, for every promise involves a statement of present intention as to future conduct. "There must be a misstatement of an existing fact: but the state of a man's mind is as much a fact as the state of his digestion."[14] If, then, I make a promise believing that I shall fulfil it, the reason that I am not liable for deceit if I do not fulfil it is not that my promise was not a statement of fact but that the statement of fact involved in the promise was true.[15] If at the time I made it I had no intention of fulfilling my promise, I may be liable for deceit. So in *Edgington* v. *Fitzmaurice*[16] directors of a company were held liable for deceit in procuring the public to subscribe for debentures by falsely stating in a prospectus that the loan secured by the debentures was for the purpose of completing buildings of the company, purchasing horses and vans and developing the trade of the company; in fact the directors intended to use it for paying off pressing liabilities.[17]

(3) *Opinion*

A statement of opinion frequently carries within itself a statement of fact. A man who says "I believe X to be honest" is making a statement of fact as to his state of mind, and if it is untrue there is no reason why, if the other requirements of the tort are met, he should not be held liable for deceit. Often also an expression of opinion carries the implication that the person expressing it has reasonable grounds for it, and where this is not the case he may be guilty of a misstatement of fact.[18] On the other hand, there must be some latitude for "sales talk" and a seller's imprecise commendations of his wares do not give rise to liability merely because even the seller might, on careful reflection, think them exaggerated.[19]

(4) *Statements of law*

As a matter of general principle a misstatement of law ought to be a sufficient misstatement of fact for the purposes of deceit provided at least that the parties are not on an equal footing with respect to knowledge of the law or to general intelligence.[20] A great many statements which we should

---

[14] *Edgington* v. *Fitzmaurice* (1885) 29 Ch.D. 459, 483, *per* Bowen L.J.; *Clydesdale Bank Ltd.* v. *Paton* [1896] A.C. 381, 394, *per* Lord Herschell: *cf. ibid* at p. 397, *per* Lord Davey.

[15] *cf. British Airways Board* v. *Taylor* [1976] 1 W.L.R. 13 (Trade Descriptions Act; statement false because maker concealed risk that he might be unable to fulfil his promise).

[16] *Supra*; Weir, *Casebook on Tort*, (6th ed.), p. 488.

[17] There is said to be an exception to this, namely, that a purchaser may freely state his intention to pay no more than a certian sum or a vendor his intention to accept no less than a certain sum: Rolle Abr.101, pl. 16 (1598); *Vernon* v. *Keys* (1810) 12 East 632; affirmed *sub. nom. Vernon* v. *Keyes* (1812) 4 Taunt. 488. The exception must not, however, be carried too far: Pollock in 11 R.R.Pref. vi–vii, and *Torts*, (15th ed.), p. 213, n. 6; *Haygarth* v. *Wearing* (1871) L.R. 12 Eq. 320.

[18] *Brown* v. *Raphael* [1958] Ch. 636, a case of innocent misrepresentation in contract. *cf. Haycraft* v. *Creasy* (1891) 2 East 92 and see Pollock, *Torts*, (15th ed.), p. 212, n. 12.

[19] See the comments of Learned Hand J. in *Vulcan Metals Co.* v. *Simmons Mfg. Co.* 248 F. 853 (1918). Yet everything depends on the circumstances: see the words which were held to amount to the "higher" legal category of warranty in *Andrews* v. *Hopkinson* [1957] Q.B. 229.

[20] Direct authority for this proposition is lacking but the view stated in the text is shared by Clerk & Lindsell, *Torts*, (16th ed.), para. 18–09; Salmond and Heuston, *Torts* (19th ed.), p. 436; Fleming, *The Law of Torts*, (7th ed.), p. 601. A deliberate false statement of law is sufficient for the offence of obtaining property by deception: Theft Act 1968, s.15(4).

not hesitate to describe as statements of fact involve inferences from legal rules[21] and the distinction between law and fact is by no means as precise as might at first appear. So, in *West London Commercial Bank Ltd.* v. *Kitson,*[22] where directors of a company, knowing that the private Act of Parliament which incorporated the company gave them no legal power to accept bills of exchange, nevertheless represented to the plaintiff that they had such authority there was held to have been deceit:

> "Suppose I were to say I have a private Act of Parliament which gives me power to do so and so. Is not that an assertion that I have such an Act of Parliament? It appears to me to be as much a representation of a matter of fact as if I had said I have a particular bound copy of 'Johnson's Dictionary.' "[23]

If the representation is of a pure proposition of law and not a deduction from a rule of law there may be greater difficulty in treating it as a statement of fact, but there is no reason for holding that a solicitor, for example, can never be liable in deceit for a misstatement of law to his client.[24] It is not easy to see what argument can be produced the other way. To urge that everyone is presumed to know the law is to carry into the law of deceit a distinction between law and fact which, artificial enough in any event,[25] was never invented for the purpose of shielding swindlers. On the other hand, professional lawyers dealing with each other at arm's length would doubtless be deemed equal and if one falsely alleged to the other something purporting to be a pure proposition of law, this could scarcely ground an action for deceit.[26]

(5) *Duty to disclose*

The general rule is that there must be a statement or representation by words or conduct.[27] This does not mean that there must be a direct lie: *suppressio veri* may amount to *suggestio falsi* if it is "such a partial and

---

[21] "There is not a single fact connected with personal *status* that does not, more or less, involve a question of law. If you state that a man is the eldest son of a marriage, you state a question of law, because you must know that there has been a valid marriage, and that that man was the first-born son after the marriage. . . . Therefore, to state it is not a representation of fact seems to arise from a confusion of ideas. It is not the less a fact because that fact involves some knowledge or relation of law": *Eaglesfield* v. *Marquis of London-derry* (1876) 4 Ch.D. 693, 703, *per* Jessel M.R.

[22] (1884) 13 Q.B.D. 360.

[23] *Ibid.* at p. 363, *per* Bowen L.J.

[24] There is, of course, a contract between solicitor and client, and a solicitor may be liable for a negligent misstatement: *Otter* v. *Church, Adams, Tatham & Co.* [1953] Ch. 280.

[25] *Public Trustee* v. *Taylor* [1978] V.R. 289. For an extreme statement of the fiction, see *Rashdall* v. *Ford* (1866) L.R. 2 Eq. 750, 754–755, *per* Page-Wood V.C.

[26] One professional lawyer would not normally act in a professional capacity in reliance upon another's statement of law, and an action between such persons founded upon a false statement of law would therefore fail on the ground that the plaintiff did not rely upon the statement: *post,* pp. 268–270.

[27] In *Ward* v. *Hobbs* (1878) 4. App.Cas. 13, a failure to warn of a dangerous defect in goods sold was not deceit, though the result may have turned on the fact that the sale was "with all faults." But now it might amount to negligence: *Hurley* v. *Dyke* [1979] R.T.R. 265.

fragmentary statement of fact, as that the withholding of that which is not stated makes that which is stated absolutely false."[28] For example, where a husband whose income is £8,000 a year is under agreement to pay half to his wife and writes to her saying, "I send £3,000, half my income"—that would be a lie. It makes no difference if he sends her £3,000 and says nothing, for it would be an implied statement that it is half his income and he is guilty of deceit.[29] Sometimes, however, a man is under a legal duty to disclose facts and Lord Blackburn said that in such a case if he deliberately held his tongue with the intention of inducing the other party to act on the belief that he did not speak because he had nothing to say, that would be fraud.[30] However, the best known example of a duty to disclose arises in connection with insurance contracts and the Court of Appeal has rejected any right of action for damages in such a case: the legal remedy is avoidance of the contract.[31]

(6) Statements which prove to be false

Related to the above is the situation where A makes a true statement to B and then discovers, before B acts upon it, that it has become false. Does the law permit A to remain silent or does it compel him to correct B's false impression under pain of an action of deceit? It is submitted that the latter answer is in general correct. The tort of deceit is not complete when the representation is made. It only becomes complete when the misrepresentation—not having been corrected in the meantime—is acted upon by the representee.[32] The proper question in any case, therefore, is whether the statement was false when it was acted upon, not when it was made, and so a person whose true statement becomes false to his knowledge before it is acted upon should be liable in deceit if he does not correct it.[33]

Closely akin to this is another problem. Suppose that A's statement was false from the very beginning, but that when he made it he honestly believed it to be true and then discovers later and before B has acted upon it that it is false. Must he acquaint B with this? Here, again, equity has a decided answer, whereas the common law is short of any direct decision. In *Reynell* v. *Sprye*[34] a deed was cancelled by the Court of Chancery because A had not communicated the falsity of his belief.[35] As to the wider liability to an action

---

[28] *Peek* v. *Gurney* (1873) L.R. 6 H.L. 377, 403, *per* Lord Cairns. "Half the truth will sometimes amount to a real falsehood": *ibid.* at p. 392, *per* Lord Chelmsford. *Arkwright* v. *Newbold* (1881) 17 Ch.D. 301, 317–318; *Briess* v. *Woolley* [1955] A.C. 333.

[29] *Legh* v. *Legh* (1930) 143 L.T. 151, 152, *per* MacKinnon L.J.

[30] *Brownlie* v. *Campbell* (1880) 5 App.Cas. 925, 950.

[31] *Banque Keyser Ullmann S.A.* v. *Skandia (U.K.) Insurance Co. Ltd.* [1988] 2 Lloyd's Rep. 513 (a case of alleged negligence). However, duties of disclosure in connection with the issue of shares are imposed by Pts. IV and V of the Financial Services Act 1986 and these give rise to a duty to pay compensation for losses caused by breach.

[32] *Briess* v. *Woolley* [1954] A.C. 333, 353, *per* Lord Tucker; *ibid.* at p. 349, *per* Lord Reid; *Diamond* v. *Bank of London & Montreal* [1979] Q.B. 333 (service out of jurisdiction).

[33] See *Incledon* v. *Watson* (1862) 2 F. & F. 841; *With* v. *O'Flanagan* [1936] Ch. 575, 584, *per* Lord Wright; *Bradford Building Society* v. *Borders* [1941] 2 All E.R. 205, 220; *Jones* v. *Dumbrell* [1981] V.R. 199. *cf. Arkwright* v. *Newbold* (1881) 17 Ch.D. 301, 325, *per* Cotton L.J.; at p. 329, *per* James L.J.

[34] (1852) 1 De G.M. & G. 660, 708–709.

[35] See too, Jessel M.R. in *Redgrave* v. *Hurd* (1881) 20 Ch.D. 1, 12–13.

of deceit, it might be inferred from a dictum of Lord Blackburn that it exists.[36]

However we treat the question, there is no substantial difference between the two problems just put,[37] and the weight of the leading textbooks is decidedly in favour of the view that A is guilty of deceit in both of them if he withholds from B the further information.[38] This certainly ought to be the law where there is plenty of time to retract the statement and where the result of not doing so is certain to result in widespread loss or damage (as in the case of a company prospectus) or in physical danger or serious business loss to even one person.[39] But it must not be taken too far. As we have seen, a false statement of intention is a sufficient misrepresentation of fact to support an action of deceit, and the difference between a false statement of intention and a breach of a promise is that in the latter case the promisor believes what he says about his intention. The subsequent breach of promise shows, however, that at some time his intention must have changed, but it does not follow that his failure to inform the promisee of his change of intention is fraudulent. Suppose that B has booked (but not paid for) an unreserved seat on A's motor coach at 9 a.m., and that A tells him correctly that he intends to start the journey at 11 a.m. Suppose that A, finding that the vehicle is full by 10.30, starts then without informing B of his change of plans, because it would take nearly half an hour to find B. Here, A has certainly committed a breach of contract, but it is wrong to style his silence as to the changed circumstances deceit, even though it is admittedly intentional. It is really no more than a churlish indifference to a breach of contract.[40]

One more possible case of silence raises no difficulty. If A knowingly makes a false statement to B, but before B acts upon it subsequent events have turned the statement into a true one, this is not deceit. Thus in *Ship* v. *Crosskill*,[41] a false allegation in a prospectus, that applications for more than half the capital of the company had been subscribed, had become true before the plaintiff made his application for shares, and it was held that there was no misrepresentation for which relief could be given to him. "If false when made but true when acted upon there is no misrepresentation."[42]

Intent

The statement must be made with intent that the plaintiff shall act upon it.

[36] *Brownlie* v. *Campbell* (1880) 5 App.Cas. 925, 950.

[37] Except that in the latter case the statement was false from the moment it was made, while in the former it was not. Since it is impossible for a man to make a false statement of his intention while beilieving it to be true, it would appear that the qualification stated below has no application to the solution of the second problem put.

[38] Pollock, *Torts* (15th ed.), pp. 216–217; Salmond and Heuston, *Torts* (19th ed.), p. 435; Clerk & Lindsell, *Torts* (16th ed.), para. 18–27; Fleming, *The Law of Torts* (7th ed.), p. 599.

[39] It is submitted that the tort is not committed if there is no time for the statement to be retracted or corrected before it is acted upon.

[40] See Clerk & Lindsell, *Torts* (16th ed.), para. 18–06.

[41] (1870) L.R. 10 Eq. 73.

[42] *Briess* v. *Woolley* [1954] A.C. 333, 353, *per* Lord Tucker.

So long as that is satisfied, it need not be made to him either literally or in particular. In *Langridge* v. *Levy*,[43] the seller of a defective gun which he had falsely and knowingly warranted to be sound, was held liable to the plaintiff who was injured by its bursting, although it was the plaintiff's father to whom the gun had been sold, but who had acquainted the seller with the fact that he intended his sons to use it. If, however, the statement is made to a limited class of persons, no one outside that class can sue upon it. Thus a company prospectus was at common law ordinarily confined in its scope to the original shareholders. For false statements in it they could sue, but purchasers of the shares from them could not do so[44]; but circumstances might quite possibly make the prospectus fraudulent with respect even to them, as where it was supplemented by further lying statements intended to make persons who were not original allottees of the shares buy them in the market.[45] The intent need not be to cause damage to the plaintiff; it is enough that the plaintiff was intended to act on it and did act on it in the manner contemplated. The defendant is liable whether he actually intended damage to ensue or not.[46]

Plaintiff must rely on the statement

The plaintiff must be "taken in" by the misrepresentation: attempted fraud may be a crime, but it is not a tort.[47] If, however, the plaintiff does rely on the defendant's statement it is no defence that he acted incautiously and failed to take those steps to verify its truth which a prudent man would have taken.[48] In *Central Ry. of Venezuela* v. *Kisch*[49] directors of a company made deceitful statements in a prospectus and were held liable to a shareholder defrauded thereby, although the prospectus stated that certain documents could be inspected at the company's office and, if the shareholder had taken the trouble to do so, he would have discovered the fraud.[50] If the fraud is not

---

[43] (1837) 2 M. & W. 519; 4 M. & W. 337. See Clerk & Lindsell, *Torts* (16th ed.), para. 18–36. *cf. Gross* v. *Lewis Hillman Ltd.* [1970] Ch. 445.

[44] *Peek* v. *Gurney* (1873) L.R. 6 H.L. 377. But the statutory remedy under ss.150 and 166 of the Financial Services Act 1986 is not so limited. The question of to whom it was contemplated the false statement would be communicated is one of fact and if A makes a false statement to B with the intention that C will hear of it and act upon it, he cannot escape liability by telling B that it is for B's private use only: *Commercial Banking Co. of Sydney Ltd.* v. *R.H. Brown & Co.* [1972] 2 Lloyd's Rep. 360.

[45] *Andrews* v. *Mockford* [1896] 1 Q.B. 372.

[46] *Polhill* v. *Walter* (1832) 3 B. & Ad. 114; *Edgington* v. *Fitzmaurice* (1885) 29 Ch.D. 459, 482; *Brown Jenkinson & Co. Ltd.* v. *Percy Dalton (London) Ltd.* [1957] 2 Q.B. 621.

[47] For this purpose the knowledge of the plaintiff's agent is not to be imputed to the plaintiff; *e.g.* where a house-agent acting for the plaintiff knew that a prospective tenant of the plaintiff's house was a woman of immoral character, but the plaintiff was unaware of this: *Wells* v. *Smith* [1914] 3 K.B. 722. However, it is pointed out in Spencer Bower & Turner, *Actionable Misrepresentation* (3rd ed.), p. 216, that the rule can hardly be applied in this unqualified form to a corporation. It has been held in Australia that there may be fraud even though the victim is aware to some extent of the untruth of the statement, so long as he is not aware of the full extent of the untruth: *Gipps* v. *Gipps* [1978] 1 N.S.W.L.R. 454.

[48] It is sometimes said that there is no actionable deceit when the defect in what is sold is so obvious that any sensible purchaser would have discovered the untruth of the representation upon inspection (see Prosser, *Torts* (5th ed.), p. 750). It is doubtful if the English cases support such a proposition as a rule of law, as opposed to a common sense matter of evidence pointing to the conclusion that the plaintiff was not in fact misled.

[49] (1867) L.R. 2 H.L. 99.

[50] So too, *Dobell* v. *Stevens* (1825) 3 B. & C. 623; and see *Redgrave* v. *Hurd* (1881) 20 Ch.D. 1. It is not thought that the Law Reform (Contributory Negligence) Act 1945 has any application to cases of fraud.

obvious, it will not help that he inserted an express clause in a contract with the plaintiff that he must verify all representations for himself and not rely on their accuracy, for "such a clause might in some cases be part of a fraud, and might advance and disguise a fraud."[51]

It is rare for a person to enter upon a transaction solely on the basis of one factor and it is no bar to a claim for damages for deceit that the plaintiff was influenced by other things beside the defendant's misrepresentation.[52] Nor need the misrepresentation be even the decisive factor, so long as it has a real or substantial effect on the plaintiff's decision.[53] If, however, it is clear[54] that the plaintiff would have entered into the transaction anyway and his belief in the misrepresentation merely encouraged or confirmed him in this view, then he has not "relied" in the sense here required.[55] This is only another way of saying that the defendant has not caused the plaintiff's loss. The burden of proof of reliance is upon the plaintiff; but if the representation is such as would influence a reasonable person then the defendant may have to adduce evidence to rebut the inference that it was relied on.[56]

Ambiguity

In the case of an ambiguous statement the plaintiff must prove (*a*) the sense in which he understood the statement; (*b*) that in that sense it was false; and (*c*) that the defendant intended him to understand it in that sense or deliberately made use of the ambiguity with the express purpose of deceiving him.[57] It does not follow because the defendant uses ambiguous language that he is conscious of the way in which the plaintiff will understand it. Unless the defendant "is conscious that it will be understood in a different manner from that in which he is honestly though blunderingly using it, he is not fraudulent. An honest blunder in the use of language is not dishonest."[58] An ambiguous statement must therefore be taken in the sense in which the defendant intended it to be understood, and however reasonable a plaintiff may be in attaching the untrue meaning to the statement, there is no deceit unless the defendant intended his words to be taken in that sense. "The question is not whether the defendant in any given case honestly believed the representation to be true in the sense assigned to it by the court on an objective consideration of its truth or falsity, but whether he honestly

---

[51] S. Pearson & Son Ltd. v. Dublin Corporation [1907] A.C. 351, 360, per Lord Ashbourne; cf. Diamond v. Bank of London & Montreal [1979] Q.B. 333, 347.

[52] Edgington v. Fitzmaurice (1885) 29 Ch.D. 459.

[53] J.E.B. Fasteners Ltd. v. Marks Bloom & Co. [1983] 1 All E.R. 583, 589, per Stephenson L.J.

[54] "Can it be permitted to a party who has practised a deception, with a view to a particular end which has been attained by it, to speculate on what might have been the result if there had been a full communication of the facts?": Smith v. Kay (1859) 7 H.L.Cas. 750, 759, per Lord Chelmsford L.C.

[55] J.E.B. Fasteners Ltd. v. Marks Bloom & Co. [1983] 1 All E.R. 583. This is a case of negligent misrepresentation, but it is thought that causation must be the same whatever the form of the misrepresentation.

[56] Gould v. Vaggelas (1985) 56 A.L.R. 31.

[57] Smith v. Chadwick (1884) 9 App.Cas. 187, 201, per Lord Blackburn; Arkwright v. Newbold (1881) 17 Ch.D. 301, 324, per Cotton L.J.

[58] Angus v. Clifford [1891] 2 Ch. 449, 472, per Bowen L.J.; Smith v. Chadwick (1892) 20 Ch.D. 27, 79, per Lindley L.J.; Gross v. Lewis Hillman Ltd. [1970] Ch. 445.

believed the representation to be true in the sense in which he understood it albeit erroneously when it was made."[59]

In *Smith* v. *Chadwick*,[60] the prospectus of a company alleged that "the present value of the turnover or output of the entire works is over £1,000,000 sterling *per annum*." Did this mean that the works had *actually* turned out in one year, produce worth more than a million, or at that rate *per* year? If so, it was untrue. Or did it mean only that the works were *capable* of turning out that amount of produce? If so, it was true. The plaintiff failed to prove that he had interpreted the words in the sense in which they were false, so he lost his action. On the question of the actual meaning of the statement, the noble and learned Lords were evenly divided,[61] but there is no doubt that if an allegation is deliberately put forth in an ambiguous form with the design of catching the plaintiff on that meaning of it which makes it false, it is fraudulent and indeed is aggravated by a shabby attempt to get the benefit of a fraud without incurring the responsibility.[62]

Damage

The damage which the plaintiff must prove that he has suffered in consequence of acting upon the statement will usually be financial but it may consist of personal injury[63] or mental distress[64] or damage to property and it has also been held that loss of possession of a regulated tenancy under the Rent Acts, even without actual financial loss, will suffice.[65]

In principle the plaintiff is entitled, so far as money can do it, to be put into the position in which he would have been if the fraudulent statement had not been made, not that in which he would have been if it had been true,[66] and the defendant must make reparation for all the actual losses which flow from his deceit. Where the plaintiff has been induced to buy property by a fraudulent representation, therefore, he may recover the difference between the price he paid and the actual value of the property at the time of the sale. Events subsequent to the sale may have to be taken into account to determine the real value at the time of the sale, for a successful fraud may not be discovered for some time, during which the property may retain its

---

[59] *Akerhielm* v. *De Mare* [1959] A.C. 789, 805, *per* Lord Jenkins. This proposition is subject to the limitation that the meaning placed by the defendant on the representation may be so far removed from the sense in which it would be understood by any reasonable person as to make it impossible to hold that the defendant honestly understood the representation to bear the meaning claimed by him and honestly believed it in that sense to be true: *ibid*. Note that where liability for a negligent, as distinct from a fraudulent, misstatement is in issue, the important question concerns the sense in which the plaintiff, not the defendant, understood it: *W.B. Anderson & Sons Ltd.* v. *Rhodes (Liverpool) Ltd.* [1967] 2 All E.R. 850, 855–856, *per* Cairns J.

[60] (1884) 9 App.Cas. 187.

[61] Lord Selborne and Lord Bramwell thought that it had the first meaning, Lord Blackburn and Lord Watson that it had the second.

[62] *Ibid*. at p. 201, *per* Lord Blackburn.

[63] *Langridge* v. *Levy* (1837) 2 M. & W. 519; (1838) 4 M & W. 337; *Burrows* v. *Rhodes* [1899] 1 Q.B. 816. See also *Graham* v. *Saville* [1945] 2 D.L.R. 489; *Beaulne* v. *Ricketts* (1979) 96 D.L.R. (3d) 550 (bigamy).

[64] *Shelley* v. *Paddock* [1979] Q.B. 120; affm. [1980] Q.B. 348; *Saunders* v. *Edwards* [1987] 1 W.L.R. 1116.

[65] *Mafo* v. *Adams* [1979] 1 Q.B. 548.

[66] The rule thus differs from that governing the damages recoverable for a breach of contract and a plaintiff in deceit cannot normally recover in respect of prospective gains which he was expecting: *McConnel* v. *Wright* [1903] 1 Ch. 546, 554–555, *per* Collins M.R.; *Bango* v. *Holt* (1971) 21 D.L.R. (3d) 66; *State of S. Australia* v. *Johnson* (1982) 42 A.L.R. 161.

apparent or market value. Consequential loss may be recovered where this is not too remote, for example, where a fraudulently concealed danger in the property causes further damage.[67] In *Doyle* v. *Olby (Ironmongers) Ltd.*[68] the plaintiff recovered losses incurred in reasonably attempting to carry on the purchased business, these being regarded as directly attributable to the fraud.[69] The decision in the *Wagon Mound* apparently does not apply to deceit, so that damage is not too remote merely because it is unforeseeable.[70] On the other hand the plaintiff must, of course, give credit for any benefit he may have received from the transaction into which he entered as a result of the deceit.

The statement must be made with knowledge of its falsity or recklessly

This rule is the result of the decision in *Derry* v. *Peek*,[71] where the House of Lords made it clear that blundering but honest belief in an allegation cannot be deceit. For liability in deceit the defendant must either know his statement to be false or else must be reckless,[72] *i.e.* without knowing whether his statement is true or false he must be consciously indifferent whether it is the one or the other.[73]

The facts of *Derry* v. *Peek* were that the directors of a tramway company issued a prospectus in which they stated that they had parliamentary powers to use steam in propelling their trams. In fact the grant of such powers was subject to the consent of the Board of Trade. The directors honestly but mistakenly believed the giving of this consent to be a merely formal matter; it was, however, refused. The company was wound up in consequence and the plaintiff, who had bought shares in it on the faith of the prospectus, instituted an action for deceit against the directors. The House of Lords, reversing the decision of the Court of Appeal, gave judgment for the defendants, holding that a false statement made carelessly and without reasonable ground for believing it to be true could not be fraud, though it might furnish evidence of it. A careless man is not a dishonest man and no amount of argument will prove he is one.

[67] See, *e.g. Mullett* v. *Mason* (1866) L.R. 1 C.P. 559; *Nicholls* v. *Taylor* [1939] V.L.R. 119. In *Hornal* v. *Neuberger Products Ltd.* [1957] 1 Q.B. 247, the plaintiff was induced to buy a lathe by the fraudulent representation that it was fit for immediate use. Although it was worth in its actual condition what the plaintiff had paid for it, he was put to seven weeks' delay in preparing it for use and was awarded damages for this delay.

[68] [1969] 2 Q.B. 158; *Clark* v. *Urquhart* [1930] A.C. 28, 67–68; McGregor, *Damages* (15th ed.), p. 1095.

[69] Whether consequential losses were directly attributable provoked a difference of opinion in *Gould* v. *Vaggelas* (1985) 56 A.L.R. 31. Clearly, if events subsequent to the sale are taken into account in assessing the value of the property, one must take care in awarding consequential losses not to award damages twice over.

[70] But *cf. Gould* v. *Vaggelas, supra*, at p. 37 and *Archer* v. *Brown* [1985] Q.B. 401, 417. The *Wagon Mound* (*ante*, p. 140) was not cited in *Doyle* v. *Olby*. As to exemplary damages, see *post*, p. 604.

[71] (1889) 14 App.Cas. 337.

[72] It is vital to remember that in deceit, "reckless" does not have the extended meaning given to it in the criminal law by *R.* v. *Caldwell* [1982] A.C. 341.

[73] "A man may be said to know a fact when once he has been told it and pigeonholed it somewhere in his brain where it is more or less accessible in case of need. In another sense of the word a man knows a fact only when he is fully conscious of it. For an action of deceit there must be knowledge in the narrower sense; and conscious knowledge of falsity must always amount to wickedness and dishonesty": *Armstrong* v. *Strain* [1951] 1 T.L.R. 856, 871, *per* Devlin J. For recklessness, see *Angus* v. *Clifford* [1891] 2 Ch. 449, 471, *per* Bowen L.J.; *Derry* v. *Peek* (1889) 14 App.Cas. 337, 371, *per* Lord Herschell.

LIABILITY FOR NEGLIGENT MISSTATEMENT

Derry v. *Peek* settled that liability for deceit is liability for dishonest and not for careless statements, but for many years the case was treated as authority for more than that, for the House of Lords was taken to have held that there could be no tortious liability of any kind for a misstatement so long only as it was not dishonest. Earlier there had been at least one case in which damages for a negligent misstatement had been awarded,[74] but this was later held by the Court of Appeal to be inconsistent with and overruled by *Derry* v. *Peek*.[75] As late as 1950 Devlin J. was prepared to state categorically that "negligent misstatement can never give rise to a cause of action."[76] After *Donoghue* v. *Stevenson*[77] had been decided, more than one attempt was made to argue that the position had been changed,[78] but apart from evoking a notable dissenting judgment from Denning L.J.,[79] these attempts met with no success. Only Parliament it was thought, could introduce a duty to take care in making statements, as it did in the case of company directors by the Directors Liability Act 1890,[80] passed a year after the decision in *Derry* v. *Peek*. Other statutory duties of care in making statements also exist, the most important of which is contained in the Misrepresentation Act 1967.[81] On the other hand, as long ago as 1914, in *Nocton* v. *Lord Ashburton*,[82] the House of Lords itself pointed out that *Derry* v. *Peek* had not ruled out every form of liability independent of statute but that for fraud. Not only could there be liability in contract,[83] but it could exist in equity as well. A fiduciary relationship such as that between solicitor and client, is capable of giving rise to a duty of care in making statements for breach of which the plaintiff may recover compensation.

It is certain that *Nocton* v. *Lord Ashburton* was decided in equity and not at common law,[84] but fortunately for the subsequent development of the law the distinction between law and equity was blurred throughout the speeches of their Lordships and even an admittedly wrong order for an inquiry into damages—a common law remedy—was allowed to stand on the ground that its replacement by the correct order for equitable redress would not in the circumstances make any difference.[85] Strictly speaking, *Nocton* v. *Lord*

---

[74] *Cann* v. *Willson* (1888) 39 Ch.D. 39.

[75] *Le Lievre* v. *Gould* [1893] 1 Q.B. 491. See also *Angus* v. *Clifford* [1891] 2 Ch. 449; *Low* v. *Bouverie* [1891] 3 Ch. 82.

[76] *Heskell* v. *Continental Express Ltd.* [1950] 1 All E.R. 1033, 1042. The statement was approved by Cohen L.J., subject to the qualification that there could be liability where there is a contractual or a fiduciary relationship: *Candler* v. *Crane, Christmas & Co.* [1951] 2 K.B. 164, 198. See now *Hedley Byrne & Co. Ltd.* v. *Heller & Partners Ltd.* [1964] A.C. 465, 532, *per* Lord Devlin.

[77] [1932] A.C. 562.

[78] *Old Gate Estates Ltd.* v. *Toplis* [1939] 3 All E.R. 109; *Candler* v. *Crane, Christmas & Co.* [1951] 2 K.B. 164.

[79] *Candler* v. *Crane, Christmas & Co.*, *supra.*

[80] Its provisions are now contained in the Companies Act 1985.

[81] See *post*, p. 281.

[82] [1914] A.C. 932.

[83] This was always admitted.

[84] The clearest speech from this point of view is that of Lord Dunedin, but see also, *e.g. per* Viscount Haldane L.C., *ibid.* at pp. 946, 954, 957.

[85] *Per* Viscount Haldane L.C., *ibid.* at p. 958; *per* Lord Dunedin *ibid.* at p. 965. In *Woods* v. *Martins Bank Ltd.* [1959] 1 Q.B. 55, Salmon J. held that a fiduciary relationship existed and awarded the plaintiff damages for misstatement.

Ashburton decides only that where a relationship recognised by equity as fiduciary[86] exists, an equitable remedy may be given for misstatement, and it is probable that the House of Lords in that case did not consider that a common law duty of care could exist without a contract. Fifty years later, however, in *Hedley Byrne & Co. Ltd.* v. *Heller & Partners Ltd.*,[87] the House was able to rely on *Nocton* v. *Lord Ashburton* as showing that *Derry* v. *Peek* governed only liability in deceit and so that they were not precluded from holding that a tortious duty of care in making statements might exist. In the words of Lord Devlin[88]:

> "There was in *Derry* v. *Peek*, as the report of the case shows, no plea of innocent or negligent representation and so their Lordships did not make any pronouncement on that. I am bound to say that had there been such a plea I am sure that the House would have rejected it. As Lord Haldane said, their Lordships must 'be taken to have thought' that there was no liability in negligence.[89] But what your Lordships may be taken to have thought, though it may exercise great influence upon those who thereafter have to form their own opinion on the subject, is not the law of England. It is impossible to say how their Lordships would have formulated the principle if they had laid one down. They might have made it general or they might have confined it to the facts of the case. They might have made an exception of the sort indicated by Lord Herschell[90] or they might not. This is speculation. All that is certain is that on this point the House laid down no law at all."

The facts of *Hedley Byrne & Co. Ltd.* v. *Heller & Partners Ltd.*[91] were that the plaintiffs, who were advertising agents, were anxious to know whether they could safely give credit to a company, Easipower, on whose behalf they had entered into various advertising contracts, and they therefore sought bankers' references about Easipower. For this purpose the plaintiffs' bankers approached the defendants, who were Easipower's bankers, and on two occasions the defendants gave favourable references. These were passed on to the plaintiffs by their bankers and, although the defendants did not know who the plaintiffs were and had in fact marked their communications to the plaintiffs' bankers "Confidential. For your private use ... ," they did know that the inquiry was made in connection with an advertising contract. They must also have known that the references were to be passed on to a customer.[92] In reliance on these references the plaintiffs incurred expenditure

---

[86] See Sealy, "Some Principles of Fiduciary Obligation" [1963] C.L.J. 119, 137–140.
[87] [1964] A.C. 465; Weir, *Casebook on Tort* (6th ed.), p. 44.
[88] [1964] A.C. 465, 518–519.
[89] *Nocton* v. *Lord Ashburton* [1914] A.C. 932, 947.
[90] (1889) 14 App.Cas. 337, 360.
[91] [1964] A.C. 465. See Stevens, "*Hedley Byrne* v. *Heller*: Judicial Creativity and Doctrinal Possibility" (1964) 27 M.L.R. 121; Goodhart, "Liability for Innocent but Negligent Misrepresentations" (1964) 74 Yale L.J. 286; Honorè, "*Hedley Byrne & Co.* v. *Heller & Partners Ltd.*" (1965) 8 J.S.P.T.L.(N.S.) 284; Weir, "Liability for Syntax" [1963] C.L.J. 216; Gordon, "*Hedley Byrne* v. *Heller* in the House of Lords" (1964) 38 A.L.J. 39, 79.
[92] [1964] A.C. 465, 482, *per* Lord Reid; *ibid.* at p. 503, *per* Lord Morris.

on Easipower's behalf and, when Easipower went into liquidation, they suffered substantial loss. This loss they sought to recover from the defendants in an action based upon the defendants' alleged negligence in giving favourable references concerning Easipower.

At first instance McNair J. held that the defendants owed no duty to the plaintiffs, and this decision was affirmed in the Court of Appeal[93] both on the ground that the case was covered by authority[94] and also on the ground that it would not be reasonable to impose upon a banker an obligation to exercise care when informing a third party of the credit-worthiness of his client.[95] In the House of Lords the decision in favour of the defendants was affirmed, but none of their Lordships based his decision on a general rule of non-liability for negligent misstatement. On the contrary, Lords Reid, Devlin and Pearce held that, assuming the defendants to have been negligent, the only reason for exonerating them was that the references had been given "without responsibility."[96] Lord Hodson and, perhaps, Lord Morris considered that even without this denial of responsibility there was no duty of care on the facts, but nevertheless agreed that a duty of care in making statements was a legal possibility.

Before *Hedley Byrne* the position with regard to negligent misstatement was, in short, that there could be no liability apart from contract or fiduciary relation or, perhaps, in a case of physical damage to person or property. Now, at the least, it is clear that a duty of care may exist in other circumstances,[97] but the scope and extent of the duty cannot be stated with precision. As with *Donoghue* v. *Stevenson,* the implications of *Hedley Byrne* are very great, but its actual effect upon the law can only emerge with time.

It will have been observed that on the facts of *Hedley Byrne* not only did the loss result from a misstatement, not from an act, but that loss was pecuniary or economic not physical. At the time of the decision liability for such loss arising from negligence was severely restricted by the law and, despite a strongly worded rejection by Lord Devlin of a distinction between physical and economic damage,[98] the case was seen as an exception to a general rule.[99] Attempts to liberalise recovery for economic loss in general were mounted after *Hedley Byrne* but now seem to have been repelled.[1] While, therefore, it may be unduly cautious to say that such loss is not accepted in English law outside the *Hedley Byrne* type of liability,[2] that decision continues to look more like an exception than the rule in this respect. Indeed, the hall marks of *Hedley Byrne*—an undertaking by the defendant and reliance by the plaintiff, a "special relationship" between the

---

[93] [1962] 1 Q.B. 396.
[94] Especially *Le Lievre* v. *Gould* [1893] 1 Q.B. 491; *Candler* v. *Crane, Christmas & Co.* [1951] 2 K.B. 164.
[95] [1962] 1 Q.B. 396, 414, *per* Pearson L.J.
[96] See *post*, pp. 286–287.
[97] If ever it could be said that this liability was based on *obiter dicta* (see the 12th ed. of this work, p. 274, n. 96) that can no longer be the case after *Smith* v. *Eric S. Bush* [1989] 2 W.L.R. 790.
[98] [1964] A.C. 465, 516–517.
[99] See, *e.g. Weller* v. *Foot and Mouth Disease Research Institute Ltd.* [1966] 1 Q.B. 569.
[1] See *ante*, p. 84.
[2] *D. & F. Estates Ltd.* v. *Church Commissioners* [1988] 3 W.L.R. 368, 392, *per* Lord Oliver.

parties—have been adopted as justifications of exceptional recovery of economic loss where no statement of any kind has been involved.

Misstatement

In *Hedley Byrne* itself, Lord Morris said that he could see no essential reason in logic for distinguishing injury which is caused by reliance upon words from injury which is caused by, for example, reliance upon the safety for use of the contents of a bottle of hair wash or a bottle of some consumable liquid.[4] It is, of course, true that if a duty of care is assumed to exist then there is no logical reason for the distinction and it is also true that many cases of negligence which have never been regarded as raising the problem of misrepresentation nevertheless contain as an essential element in the sequence of events a misrepresentation, express or, more commonly, implied. No harm would have come to the pursuer in *Donoghue* v. *Stevenson*[5] if there had been no implied representation that the ginger beer was fit for human consumption.[6] Furthermore, there are cases, in which the distinction, between word and deed is for all practical purposes non-existent. Quite apart from contract, a doctor is as much liable for negligently advising his patient to take a certain drug as he is for negligently injecting the drug himself.[7] The fact remains, however, that if negligence in word were to be treated in precisely the same way as negligence in deed the result would be a liability far more extensive than the courts have hitherto been prepared to accept.[8] Whereas, speaking generally, foreseeability of harm, or at least of physical harm, is very often sufficient to establish a duty to act with reasonable care, it is clear from *Hedley Byrne* itself that for a duty of care in speech or writing something more is needed. Their Lordships were in general agreement that *Donoghue* v. *Stevenson* had little, if any, direct bearing on the problem of negligent misstatement and that a duty of care will exist in relation to statements only if there is a "special relationship" between the parties.[9] Without such a limitation there would be liability "in an indeterminate amount for an indefinite time and to an indeterminate class."[10] This

[3] See *ante*, p. 90.

[4] [1964] A.C. 465, 496. *cf.* the speeches of Lord Reid *ibid.* at pp. 482–483 and Lord Pearce, *ibid.* at p. 534, which recognise the necessity for distinguishing between word and deed. The explanation of the apparent disagreement seems to be that whereas Lord Morris is assuming duty to exist, Lords Reid and Pearce are concerned with that very question. See also *Mutual Life and Citizens' Assurance Co. Ltd.* v. *Evatt* [1969] A.L.R. 3, 9, *per* Barwick C.J. (reversed [1971] A.C. 793).

[5] [1932] A.C. 562.

[6] See also *Watson* v. *Buckley, Osborne Garrett & Co. Ltd.* [1940] 1 All E.R. 174; *Sharp* v. *Avery* [1938] 4 All E.R. 85; *Holmes* v. *Ashford* [1950] 2 All E.R. 76; *Devilez* v. *Boots Pure Drug Co.* (1962) 106 S.J. 552. An interesting American example is *Pease* v. *Sinclair Refining Co.*, 104 F. (2d) 183 (2nd Cir. 1939).

[7] This, it is submitted, is equivalent to the position as it was seen by Salmon J. in *Clayton* v. *Woodman & Son (Builders) Ltd.* [1962] 2 Q.B. 533. The Court of Appeal took a different view of the facts and held that the point decided by the learned judge did not arise: [1962] 1 W.L.R. 585. See also *The Apollo* [1891] A.C. 499 and the examples given by Denning L.J. in *Candler* v. *Crane, Christmas & Co.* [1951] 2 K.B. 164, 173, 179.

[8] Consider the familiar example of the marine hydrographer whose careless omission of a reef from his published chart leads to the loss of a ship: *Candler* v. *Crane, Christmas & Co.* [1951] 2 K.B. 164, 183, *per* Denning L.J.

[9] See too *W.B. Anderson & Sons Ltd.* v. *Rhodes (Liverpool) Ltd.* [1967] 2 All E.R. 850, 853, *per* Cairns J.

[10] *Ultramares Corp.* v. *Touche* 255 N.Y.Rep. 170 (1931), *per* Cardozo C.J. The clearest explanation of the reasons for a distinction between negligence in word and negligence in deed is in the speech of Lord Reid [1964] A.C. 465, 482–483. That a person's potential liability is very extensive may seem on the face of it a poor reason for relieving him of a duty of care, but it has a long history.

"floodgates" argument has been criticised but it still has its place[11] and perhaps nowhere more so than in the context of negligent misstatements.

Effect of Hedley Byrne[12]

The most significant consequence of the decision in *Hedley Byrne* was that it became possible for the courts to hold in certain circumstances that a special relationship exists and therefore that one person owes another a duty of care in the giving of information or advice.[13] The decision does not, however, specify exactly what those circumstances are, and we must look at subsequent case law to see how far the courts have gone in availing themselves of the opportunity created by the House of Lords for the expansion of liability for negligent misstatement.

Much of the reasoning in *Hedley Byrne* seems to be based upon the view that the duty of care arises from an undertaking, express or implied, by the defendant that he will exercise care in giving information or advice (a "voluntary assumption of responsibility"), and that this undertaking need not be supported by consideration.[14] However, liability of a rather similar nature was imposed in *Ministry of Housing and Local Government* v. *Sharp*,[15] where the defendants provided information pursuant to a *duty*, and in *Smith* v. *Eric S. Bush* Lord Griffiths said that "the phrase 'assumption of responsibility' can only have any real meaning if it is understood as referring to the circumstances in which the law will *deem* the maker of the statement to have assumed responsibility to the person who acts upon the advice."[15a] Thus where a surveyor carries out a valuation of an ordinary dwelling house on the instructions of a building society he thereby "assumes responsibility" to the intending purchaser who, as he knows, will rely upon his care and skill and no further undertaking, express or implied, by him is necessary.[15b] The assumption of responsibility is certainly voluntary in the sense that at common law the defendant can displace the duty by disclaimer, but this escape route is often barred by the Unfair Contract Terms Act 1977.[15c] In *Hedley Byrne* itself none of their Lordships was willing to lay down precise criteria for the existence of the special relationship and thus of the duty and, indeed, for the most part they preferred to rely upon broad statements of

---

[11] See *ante*, p. 86.

[12] The clearest discussion is Honorè, "Hedley Byrne & Co. Ltd. v. Heller & Partners Ltd." (1965) 8 J.S.P.T.L.(N.S.) 284.

[13] As in deceit there is a distinction between a statement and an unfulfilled promise: *General Accident, etc., Corp.* v. *Tanter* [1985] 2 Lloyd's Rep. 529.

[14] See *Carman Construction Ltd.* v. *Canadian Pacific Ry* (1982) 136 D.L.R. 193; Stevens, *loc. cit.* at p. 129, considers that the House of Lords has to some extent undermined the doctrine of privity of contract. But *Hedley, Byrne* is not excluded because the Service is not gratuitous: *Smith* v. *Eric S. Bush* [1989] 2 W.L.R. 790, 821,*per* Lord Jauncey.

[15] [1970] 2 Q.B. 223, *post*, p. 292. See also *Hull* v. *Canterbury Municipal Council* [1974] 1 N.S.W.L.R. 300.

[15a] [1989] 2 W.L.R. 790, 813 (emphasis added).

[15b] *Smith* v. *Eric S. Bush* [1989] 2 W.L.R. 790. But by obtaining and disclosing a valuation the building society does not in law assume responsibility for its accuracy: the lender owes a duty to take care to select a competent valuer but does not warrant the accuracy of the valuation. *cf. Harris* v. *Wyre Forest D.C.* [1989] 2 W.L.R. 790 (appeal heard with *Smith* v. *Bush*) where the valuer was a servant of the lender and the lender was vicariously liable for his negligence.

[15c] *Post*, p. 286.

general principle capable of being applied to a wide range of factual situations. Thus, for example, Lord Morris,[16] with the agreement of Lord Hodson,[17] said that:

" . . . it should now be regarded as settled that if someone possessed of a special skill undertakes, quite irrespective of contract, to apply that skill for the assistance of another person who relies upon such a skill, a duty of care will arise. The fact that the service is to be given by means of or by the instrumentality of words can make no difference. Furthermore, if in a sphere in which a person is so placed that others could reasonably rely upon his judgment or his skill or upon his ability to make careful inquiry, a person takes it upon himself to give information or advice to, or allows his information or advice to be passed on to, another person who, as he knows or should know, will place reliance upon it, then a duty of care will arise."

Though the formulations in the other speeches are not quite the same,[18] they are not inconsistent with this statement of the law and perhaps it may be said, therefore, that in general if there is a close relationship between the parties the foreseeability and reasonableness of the plaintiff's reliance upon the defendant's words are not only necessary but are also sufficient for the duty of care to arise.[19] In *Mutual Life and Citizens' Assurance Co. Ltd.* v. *Evatt,*[20] however, the majority of the Privy Council took a more restricted view.

The facts of *Evatt's* case were that the plaintiff, who was a policy holder in the defendant company, sought advice from the company as to the financial soundness of another company, "Palmer," with which it was closely associated. In reliance upon the information he was given the plaintiff refrained from realising his investment in Palmer and invested further sums in that company. The information he was given was incorrect and he lost his money. The case came before the Privy Council on a procedural question as to the

---

[16] [1964] A.C. 465, 502–503.

[17] *Ibid.* at p. 514

[18] *Ibid.* at p. 486, *per* Lord Reid; *ibid.* at p. 539, *per* Lord Pearce. Lord Devlin, *ibid.* at p. 530, was prepared to adopt any of the statements of the rule given by his brethren but preferred to say that the duty of care exists wherever there is a relationship "equivalent to contract," *i.e.* where there is an assumption of responsibility in circumstances in which but for the absence of consideration, there would be a contract. Lord Devlin's view does not, however, mean that to incur liability for negligent misstatement, the defendant must have intended to make a contract: *McInerny* v. *Lloyds Bank Ltd.* [1973] 2 Lloyd's Rep. 389, 400 (on appeal [1974] 1 Lloyd's Rep. 246). Lord Devlin probably had in mind the situation where there is direct advice from defendant to plaintiff, but the relationship between a mortgagor and a valuer (instructed by the mortgagee but paid for by the mortgagor) has been described as "akin to contract": *Smith* v. *Eric S. Bush, supra, per* Lord Templeman at p. 798.

[19] See Weir, "Liability for Syntax" [1963] C.L.J. 216, 217. The statement in the text is, it is submitted, consistent with the minority opinion in *Evatt's* case ([1971] A.C. 793, 811) even though their Lordships considered the appropriate question to be whether the advice was given on a business occasion (*ibid.* at p. 811). On the facts this comes to the same thing.

[20] [1971] A.C. 793; (1971) 87 L.Q.R. 147; Farmer [1971] C.L.J. 189; Rickford (1971) 34 M.L.R. 328; Hodgin, "Fortunes of Hedley Byrne" [1972] J.B.L. 23; Lindgren, "Professional Negligence in Words and the Privy Council" (1972) 46 A.L.J. 176; Stevens, "Two Steps Forward and Three Back! Liability for Negligent Words" (1972) 5 N.Z.U.L.R. 39; Harvey, "Negligent Statements—The Wilderness Revisited" (1970) 120 New L.J. 1155.

sufficiency of the plaintiff's declaration,[21] the objection to it being that it alleged neither that the defendant company was in the business of supplying information or advice nor that it had let it be known that it claimed to possess the necessary skill to do so and was prepared to exercise due diligence to give reliable advice. It was held by the majority that the omission was fatal.

An important premise from which the conclusion of the majority depends was that the imposition of a duty of care presupposes an ascertainable standard of skill, competence and diligence with which the adviser is, or has represented himself to be, acquainted: if he is not in the business of supplying information or advice he cannot reasonably be expected to know the standard to which he is required to conform and so he cannot be held to have accepted the responsibility of conforming to it.[22] As was pointed out in the minority opinion, however, a duty to take care is not the same as a duty to conform to a particular standard of skill, and there is no ground for saying that a specially skilled man must exercise care while a less skilled man need not do so. "One must assume a reasonable man who has that degree of knowledge and skill which facts known to the inquirer (including statements made by the adviser) entitled him to expect of the adviser, and then inquire whether a reasonable man could have given the advice which was in fact given if he had exercised reasonable care."[23] The view of the majority seems contrary to the very nature of a duty of care, while that of the minority shows how such a duty is to be applied in the special case of one person advising another. It is suggested, therefore, that *Evatt's* case should not be regarded as imposing a rigid limit on the scope of *Hedley Byrne* at least so far as English law is concerned,[24] and that it is preferable to adhere to a general statement such as that of Lord Morris which is capable of application to a wide range of circumstances.[25] It may be, however, that no duty should be imposed unless the defendant has held himself out in some way as possessing skill or knowledge relevant to the subject-matter of the plaintiff's inquiry.[26]

---

[21] The appeal was on the defendants' demurrer to the plaintiff's declaration in accordance with the old form of procedure then still current in New South Wales.

[22] [1971] A.C. 793, 802–808. Considerable reliance was placed on *Low* v. *Bouverie* [1891] 3 Ch. 82 which was not overruled by *Hedley Byrne*.

[23] [1971] A.C. 793, 812, *per* Lords Reid and Morris.

[24] So much is admitted in the opinion itself, [1971] A.C. 793, 809, where it is said that the absence of the missing characteristic of the relationship considered to be essential in the case under consideration would not in all circumstances be fatal, as, perhaps, where the adviser has a financial interest in the transaction upon which he gives advice. This would avoid a conflict with *W.B. Anderson & Sons Ltd.* v. *Rhodes (Liverpool) Ltd.* [1967] 2 All E.R. 850. See also *Walker, Hobson & Hill Ltd.* v. *Johnson* [1981] 2 N.Z.L.R. 532.

[25] In *Evatt's* case Lords Reid and Morris observe that it is quite common practice for businesses to perform gratuitous services for their customers with the object of retaining or acquiring their goodwill and that all concerned would be surprised to learn that in doing so the businesses come under no duty to exercise care: [1971] A.C. 793, 811. Whether or not such businesses could be held to be in the business of giving advice is unclear, but in view of the actual decision in *Evatt's* case it may be surmised that the majority of the Privy Council would consider that they were not, unless it was part of their business to give advice.

[26] This seems to be the view of Lords Morris, Hodson and Pearce in *Hedley Byrne*, and all cite with approval the statement of Lord Loughborough in *Shiells* v. *Blackburne* (1789) 1 H.Bl. 158 that "if a man gratuitously undertakes to do a thing to the best of his skill, where his situation or profession is such as to imply skill, an omission of that skill is imputable to him as gross negligence." The limitation was applied by Wilson J. in the Supreme Court of New Zealand in *Jones* v. *Still* [1965] N.Z.L.R. 1071. *cf.*, however, the decision of the same court in *Barrett* v. *J.R. West Ltd.* [1970] N.Z.L.R. 789, the opinion of Lords Reid and Morris in *Evatt's* case ([1971] A.C. 793, 812) and that of Barwick C.J. in the High Court of Australia [1969] A.L.R. 3.

Certainly this broader approach has recommended itself to judges at first instance,[27] in the Court of Appeal[28] and in the High Court of Australia,[29] though strictly perhaps it has not been necessary for them to choose between the majority and minority views in *Evatt's* case.[30] The issue was also really irrelevant when the House of Lords considered *Hedley, Byrne* in *Smith* v. *Eric S. Bush*.[30a] In fact, the extent of the practical difference between the two camps very much depends upon the way in which the court interprets the majority test in *Evatt* and its qualifications.[31] The majority in that case stressed, in relation to *Hedley Byrne*, the importance of reading judicial language in the light of the facts of the case, but exactly the same point applies to *Evatt* itself and it has accordingly been held that the expression "business or profession" is not meant to confine liability to those engaged in private enterprise or the pursuit of profit but may extend to a public authority supplying information.[32] It is thought that it is certainly too pessimistic to say that if the majority view in *Evatt* were to be accepted "the effect of *Hedley Byrne* would be so radically curtailed as to be virtually eliminated."[33]

Whatever the true view as to the formulation of the *Hedley Byrne* principle, one thing can be said with certainty, namely, that no duty will arise in respect of advice requested and given[34] on a purely social occasion for it is then neither foreseeable to the defendant that the plaintiff will rely upon it nor reasonable for the plaintiff to do so.[35] It should not, however, be assumed that the mere fact that the statement is made on a business occasion will necessarily give rise to a duty of care, for it may not be reasonable to rely

---

[27] *Argy Trading Development Co. Ltd.* v. *Lapid Developments Ltd.* [1977] 1 W.L.R. 444.

[28] *Esso Petroleum Co. Ltd.* v. *Mardon* [1976] Q.B. 801, 827; *Howard Marine and Dredging Co. Ltd.* v. *A. Ogden (Excavations) Ltd.* [1978] Q.B. 574. As a decision of the Privy Council, *Evatt's* case does not, of course bind an English court (though *cf.* the *Wagon Mound* saga). Of all the appellate judges who heard *Evatt's* case seven decided in favour of the plaintiff and six against. Moreover, the majority in the Privy Council "explained" certain passages in the speeches of Lords Reid and Morris in *Hedley Byrne* in a manner which those two learned Lords, who formed the minority in the Privy Council, were at pains to deny: [1971] A.C. 793, 813. It is of interest to note that the passage from the speech of Lord Morris, cited in the text, is one of those "explained" by the majority and that Lord Hodson, notwithstanding his agreement with and repetition of it in *Hedley Byrne*, shared in the majority opinion.

[29] *Shaddock* v. *Parramatta City Council* (1981) 36 A.L.R. 385, which contains a very full account of the problem.

[30] See, in particular, the differing views expressed in *Shaddock's* case about the extent to which the facts could be covered by the *Evatt* formula.

[30a] *Ante*, p. 276.

[31] *Viz.* that a duty may arise if the defendant holds himself out as possessing a skill equivalent to that of a "professional" or if he has a financial interest in the transaction. The former case in particular seems capable of almost infinite expansion.

[32] *Shaddock* v. *Parramatta City Council, supra.* In many such cases the public authority will be the only person with the information.

[33] *Esso Petroleum Co. Ltd.* v. *Mardon* [1976] Q.B. 801, 827, *per* Ormrod L.J. It should be noted that the narrower approach is more likely to confine liability to those who are insured.

[34] No doubt the sort of situation the courts have had in mind is that of a plaintiff "cadging" free advice from a professional man at a party. But if, say, an investment adviser were officiously to seek out someone in such a situation and suggest the purchase of particular shares, the "social occasion" might not protect him.

[35] In *Chaudhry* v. *Prabhakar*, [1989] 1 W.L.R. 29, liability was imposed upon a friend making an assessment of a used car for the plaintiff. A duty of care was, however, conceded and one judge doubted the correctness of the concession.

on an "off the cuff" response.[36] Nor would it normally be reasonable for a property developer to rely upon a city development plan as an assurance that the level of development specified therein was feasible; in any event, the relevant authority owes a duty to the public to ensure that its discretionary powers are exercised in the public interest, which must be allowed to prevail over the expectations of developers, except in so far as the plan is given effect by statute or by contract[37] (where that is possible).[38] We have seen that a surveyor engaged to value an ordinary dwelling house for a mortgagee owes a duty of care to the mortgagor (purchaser) but it does not follow that the same will apply to industrial or commercial property or even to "expensive" residential property.[38a] Despite caution *Hedley Byrne* has, however, been applied on many occasions. Thus it has been held that a dealer who also acted as a commission agent owed a duty of care to sellers of goods when he told them that a company on whose behalf he was purchasing those goods could safely be given credit.[39] Bankers advising third parties as to the credit of their customers are clearly within *Hedley Byrne* itself[40] (though the duty may be a low one in practice[41]); and whether or not a bank is obliged to explain to a customer the effect of a mortgage which he is about to grant to it, it is certainly obliged to use due care if it chooses to do so.[42] A duty of care is also owed by accountants who provide information to persons contemplating transactions with their employers.[43] In Australia, Canada and New Zealand it has been held that an estate agent acting for a vendor of property owes a duty to a potential purchaser of it to take reasonable care in providing information about it.[44] On the other hand, some allowance must be made for reasonable protection of one's own interests and an insurance adjuster

---

[36] See *Howard Marine* v. *Ogden, supra,* at pp. 591, 598; *John Bosworth Ltd.* v. *Professional Syndicated Developments Ltd.* (1979) 97 D.L.R. (3d) 112; *Shaddock's* case *supra,* at p. 395. An inquiry to a banker about an investment led to a difference of opinion in the Privy Council in *Royal Bank Trust Co. (Trinidad) Ltd.* v. *Pampellone* [1987] 1 Lloyd's Rep. 218. The majority took the view that the banker was merely undertaking to pass on such information as he possessed.

[37] See *San Sebastian Pty.* v. *Minister Administering the Environmental Planning, etc., Act* (1986) 68 A.L.R. 111. *cf. Meates* v. *Att.-Gen.* [1983] N.Z.L.R. 86. For other examples of the courts' refusal to interfere with discretionary public functions, see *ante,* p. 98.

[38] But public policy may equally prevent the authority contracting away its discretion: see, *e.g. Cory* v. *City of London Corp.* [1951] 2 K.B. 476.

[38a] *Smith* v. *Eric S. Bush* [1989] 2 W.L.R. 790, 811, 822.

[39] *W.B. Anderson Ltd.* v. *Rhodes (Liverpool) Ltd.* [1967] 2 All E.R. 850. See *supra,* n. 24, and *O'Leary* v. *Lamb* (1973) 7 S.A.S.R. 159.

[40] See also *Woods* v. *Martins Bank Ltd.* [1959] 1 Q.B. 55, approved in *Hedley Byrne.* But a bank which advised its client that a third person contracting with the client "ought to be satisfied" with the financial arrangement was not undertaking any duty of care with respect to the third person: *McInerny* v. *Lloyds Bank Ltd.* [1974] 1 Lloyd's Rep. 246.

[41] See *post,* p. 285.

[42] *Cornish* v. *Midland Bank plc* [1985] 3 All E.R. 513.

[43] *Candler* v. *Crane, Christmas & Co.* [1951] 2 K.B. 164 was overruled in *Hedley Byrne* and the dissenting judgment of Denning L.J. approved; *Haig* v. *Bamford* (1976) 72 D.L.R. (3d) 68 (Can.Sup.Ct.).

[44] *Dodds* v. *Millman* (1964) 45 D.L.R. (2d) 472; *Barrett* v. *J.R. West Ltd.* [1970] N.Z.L.R. 789; *Richardson* v. *Norris Smith Real Estate Ltd.* [1977] 1 N.Z.L.R. 152; *Bango* v. *Holt* (1971) 21 D.L.R. (3d) 66; *Roots* v. *Oentory Pty. Ltd.* (1983) 2 Qd.R. 745; *cf. Presser* v. *Caldwell* [1971] 2 N.S.W.L.R. 471. See also *Hodgson* v. *Hydro-Electric Commission of the Township of Nepean* (1972) 28 D.L.R. (3d) 174 (electricity authority giving estimate of heating costs, reversed on the facts, (1975) 60 D.L.R. (3d) 1). The vendor would, on normal principles, be liable as principal for the misrepresentations of the agent.

retained by insurers in dispute with the plaintiff does not owe him any duty of care[45]; nor does a merchant bank making representations on behalf of its client against the referral of a bid to the Monopolies Commission assume any responsibility towards its client's rival.[46] A number of decisions impose liability upon public authorities for negligence in supplying information or advice[47] as, for example, when a prospective purchaser of property is erroneously told that there are no planning proposals affecting it[48] or that it complies with public health or safety requirements.[49]

Negligent misstatement very often takes place in a contractual context, where one party is seeking to induce the other to enter into a contract with him, but the importance of *Hedley Byrne* in this situation has been very substantially reduced by the Misrepresentation Act 1967.[50] Section 2(1) provides that where a person has entered into a contract after a misrepresentation has been made to him by another party to the contract, then, if the representor would have been liable in damages if the representation had been made fraudulently, he shall be so liable unless he proves that he had reasonable grounds to believe and did believe up to the time the contract was made that the representation was true.[51] This is more favourable to the plaintiff than *Hedley Byrne* because there can be no argument to the effect that no duty is owed and the defendant bears the burden of proof, but there may still be situations in which the Act does not apply[52] and in which he will have to fall back on that decision. After early doubts,[53] the applicability of *Hedley Byrne* to pre-contractual negotiations is established[54] and the argument that the decision should not be allowed to subvert long-established principles of contract law loses a good deal of its force in England now that

---

[45] *Sulzinger* v. *C.K. Alexander Ltd.* (1971) 24 D.L.R. (3d) 137. The fact that a person is financially interested is escaping liability is not such a "financial interest" from which an undertaking of care can be implied: *Plummer-Allinson* v. *Spencer L. Ayrey Ltd.* [1976] 2 N.Z.L.R. 254.

[46] *Lonrho plc* v. *Fayed* [1988] 3 All E.R. 464 (on appeal on another point, [1989] 2 All E.R. 65). See also *Huxford* v. *Stoy Hayward, The Times*, January 11, 1989.

[47] But as to statements of policy see the *San Sebastian* case, *supra*, n. 37.

[48] *Shaddock* v. *Parramatta City Council* (1981) 36 A.L.R. 385; see also *Ministry of Housing and Local Government* v. *Sharp* [1970] 2 Q.B. 223 (plaintiff losing rights over land by negligent search by local authority); and *Culford* v. *E.C.G.D.* (1981) *The Times*, March 25, where the existence of a duty seems to have been conceded.

[49] *R.A. & T.J. Carll Ltd.* v. *Berry* [1981] 2 N.Z.L.R. 76. Among a number of Canadian decisions see, *e.g.* *Jung* v. *District of Burnaby* (1978) 91 D.L.R. (3d) 592; *Grand Restaurants of Canada Ltd.* v. *City of Toronto* (1981) 123 D.L.R. (3d) 349; *Bell* v. *City of Sarnia* (1987) 37 D.L.R. (4d) 438.

[50] Detailed discussion of this provision must be sought in works on the law of contract. For a very critical account see Atiyah and Treitel, "Misrepresentation Act 1967" (1967) 30 M.L.R. 369, Fairest [1967] C.L.J. 239 has an extremely lucid account for the student approaching the Act for the first time.

[51] Since the liability created by s.2(1) is, *ex hypothesi* non-contractual (a misrepresentation is not a term) the measure of damages is tortious, not contractual (*ante*, p. 270), but it was some time before the weight of the case law settled to this view.

[52] The most likely reason will be that the contractual negotiations break down so that the plaintiff will not have "entered into a contract" but he may still have suffered loss in reliance on the misrepresentation. The Act cannot be used to impose personal liability upon an agent: *Resolute Maritime* v. *Nippon Karji Kyokai* [1983] 1 W.L.R. 857. *cf. supra*, n. 44.

[53] *Oleificio Zucchi SpA* v. *Northern Sales Ltd.* [1965] 2 Lloyd's Rep. 496.

[54] *Esso Petroleum Co. Ltd.* v. *Mardon* [1976] Q.B. 801; *Howard Marine and Dredging Co. Ltd.* v. *A. Ogden & Son (Excavations) Ltd.* [1978] Q.B. 574; *Morrison-Knudson International Inc.* v. *The Commonwealth* (1972) 46 A.L.J.R. 265; *Box* v. *Midland Bank Ltd.* [1979] 2 Lloyd's Rep. 391; *Herrington* v. *Kenco Mortgage & Investments* (1981) 125 D.L.R. (3d) 377. *cf. Amalgamated Metal Trading Ltd.* v. *D.T.I., The Times*, March 21, 1989 (implied representation on entering contract only of honest intention to perform it).

the legislature has imposed a more onerous duty upon representors.[55] However, it should not be assumed that every pre-contractual statement, even in a business context, entitles the other party to take action upon it.[56] Despite the contrary view taken in Canada[57] it also seems to be clear law that a tort duty of care may exist in respect of statements after a contract has been made,[58] notwithstanding that the effect might be equivalent to a variation of the contractual duties. Of course, regard must be had to the terms of the contract, which may effectively exclude tort liability[59] or at least negative the implied assumption of responsibility which might otherwise arise from the statement being made in a "business" context.[60]

So far, we have been dealing with cases where there is more or less direct communication between plaintiff and defendant (including for this purpose communications by and to agents) but it may be asked whether there can be a "special relationship" between a defendant and a larger class of people or where, the information or advice having been given by A to B for a specific purpose it is passed on to C, who relies on it to his loss. It has been said that the information or advice must be "sought or accepted by a person on his own behalf or on behalf of an identified or identifiable class of persons,"[61] though it is clear that the actual name of the inquirer need not be known.[62] The notion of an "identifiable class" does not, however, seem to include

---

[55] Misrepresentation Act 1967, *supra*.

[56] In *Holman Construction Ltd.* v. *Delta Timber Co. Ltd.* [1972] N.Z.L.R. 1081 defendant responded to an invitation to tender for the supply of goods for use in a building contract and mistakenly quoted too low a price. Plaintiff relied on this by entering into the head contract at a price based on the erroneous tender. Defendant discovered his mistake and withdrew his tender before plaintiff could accept it. The learned judge dismissed plaintiff's claim on the basis that the doctrine of *Hedley Byrne* should not be allowed to subvert the established principles of offer and acceptance. For another approach, see *Drennan* v. *Star Paving Co.* (1958) 333 P. (2d) 757. The issue is a difficult one: from one point of view there is a reasonable reliance, but from another, one party is trying to get some of the advantages of a contract before he has committed himself to it.

[57] *J. Nunes Diamonds Ltd.* v. *Dominion Electric Co.* (1972) 26 D.L.R. (3d) 699; Symmons, "The Problem of the Applicability of Tort Liability to Negligent Mis-Statements in Contractual Situations" (1975) 21 McGill L.J. 79.

[58] This is implicit in the cases (particularly *Midland Bank* v. *Hett, Stubbs & Kemp* [1979] Ch. 384) which accepts the concurrence of contractual and tortious duties: *ante*, p. 4.

[59] It is submitted, with respect, that the decision in *Coates Patons (Retail) Ltd.* v. *Birmingham Corp.* (1971) 69 L.G.R. 356 (exemption clause applicable to contractual duty but not to concurrent tort duty, even though both duties were of reasonable care) is excessively mechanical. *cf. Lamport & Holt Lines Ltd.* v. *Cambro & Scrutton Ltd.* [1982] 2 Lloyd's Rep. 42, 46. There is, of course, now greater power to control unreasonable exemption clauses: see Unfair Contract Terms Act 1977, ss.2 & 3.

[60] Can the defendant be under a duty, after contract, to inform the plaintiff when a change of circumstances makes it dangerous to rely on information which was correct when given? See *Cherry* v. *Allied Insurance Brokers* [1978] 1 Lloyd's Rep. 274 (D, P's former broker, told P that G.A. Insurance Co. would not cancel old policy. P accordingly cancelled new policy with R. Co. G.A. then agreed to cancel old policy. Fire destroyed P's premises. D liable); *J. & J.C. Abrams Ltd.* v. *Ancliffe* [1978] 1 N.Z.L.R. 420, affmd. [1981] 1 N.Z.L.R. 244 (builder liable for failure to warn employer of inaccuracy of original estimate before employer irrevocably committed); *cf. Argy Trading Development Co. Ltd.* v. *Lapid Developments Ltd.* [1977] 1 W.L.R. 444, criticised by Gravells (1978) 94 L.Q.R. 334 (landlord may be under duty to give correct information about insurance at commencement of lease, but *Hedley Byrne* does not give rise to obligation to inform tenant when, later, cover lapses).

[61] *Evatt's* case, *supra*, at [1969] A.L.R. 11, *per* Barwick C.J. This "class" approach is valid for negligent misstatement cases even though it has been rejected as a test for negligent interference with contractual rights: *Candlewood Navigation* v. *Mitsui O.S.K. Lines* [1986] A.C. 1, 24. Lord Griffiths in *Smith* v. *Eric S. Bush.* [1989] 2 W.L.R. 970, 816, speaks of an identifiable person rather than of a class. In the context he seems primarily concerned that the duty owed by a building society surveyor to a purchaser of a dwelling should not extend to subsequent purchasers. Nevertheless, his Lordship expresses concern about the extension of liability beyond the immediate recipient.

[62] This follows from *Hedley Byrne* itself.

persons who rely on information published for general consumption—hence a marine hydrographer is not liable for omitting a reef and causing the wreck of an ocean liner[63] (even though the damage is physical[64]) and there is no special relationship between a manufacturer and a distributor of his products who reads his promotional literature.[65] Such restrictions may be justifiable to keep liability within acceptable (and insurable) bounds, but they cannot easily be reconciled with the concept of foreseeability as it is normally applied in the tort of negligence. Whether or not statements in a company prospectus[66] give rise to a duty of care to persons who buy shares on the market (as opposed to applying for an initial allotment),[67] the statutory liability under the Financial Services Act 1986 does extend this far and in any event is more favourable to the plaintiff than *Hedley Byrne* on the burden of proof.[68]

Accountants are particularly likely to raise problems of the range and scope of a duty of care. It has been held that an accountant may be liable in respect of auditing company accounts to someone whom he believes may be approached for financial support, even though that person in fact effects a takeover rather than making a loan.[69] In Canada in *Haig* v. *Bamford*[70] liability was imposed where the defendants were aware that the financial statement prepared by them was to be shown to a limited class of potential investors. Perhaps the most obvious question, which has had to wait a surprisingly long time for an answer, is of the duty, if any, owed by accountants carrying out a company's statutory audit. Obviously, a duty is owed to the company itself,[71] with which the auditors have a contract; but since the company's accounts are public documents and widely relied on by persons considering investment in the company, is a duty owed to them, too? According to the Court of Appeal in *Caparo Industries plc* v. *Dickman*[72] the

---

[63] This is Denning L.J.'s example in *Candler* v. *Crane, Christmas & Co.* [1951] 2 K.B. 164, 182–183. See also the *Restatement* 2d. s.552: "a limited group." *Foster Advertising* v. *Keenberg* (1987) 35 D.L.R. (4th) 521 (statement at press conference). One of the few cases imposing liability for general publication is *Sirois* v. *L'Association des Enseignants Francophones du Nouveau-Brunswick* (1984) 8 D.L.R. (4th) 279.

[64] But in *The Willemstad* (1976) 11 A.L.R. 227, *ante*, p. 88, producers of a navigation plotting chart were held liable at first instance. There was no appeal on the issue of duty by these defendants. In *Brocklesby* v. *U.S.* (1985) 753 F. 2d 794 the publisher of an inaccurate instrument approach chart for aircraft was held liable on strict products liability and negligence theories.

[65] *Lambert* v. *Lewis* [1982] A.C. 225, 264 (C.A.); reversed without consideration of this point, *ibid.* at p. 271. In fact, the distributor seems not to have relied on the literature: see [1978] 1 Lloyd's Rep. 610. It is not thought that any doubt was intended to be cast on the proposition that a consumer may sue for negligence in respect of inadequate instructions for the use of goods: *ante*, p. 245.

[66] Properly speaking, "prospectus" is now partly an anachronism since none is required in respect of shares to be listed on the Stock Exchange. However, the "listing particulars" required in such a case are a prospectus under another name.

[67] *cf. Peek* v. *Gurney, ante*, p. 268.

[68] See ss.150–152 of the Act. There is liability for loss arising from untrue or misleading statements in listing particulars (*supra*, n. 66) unless the person responsible for the particulars can show that he had reasonable grounds to believe they were true or not misleading. There are equivalent provisions for unlisted shares. See further, works on company law.

[69] *J.E.B. Fasteners Ltd.* v. *Marks, Bloom & Co.* [1981] 3 All E.R. 289. Affirmed [1983] 1 All E.R. 583. The plaintiffs in fact lost because they had not "relied" on the accounts (*ante*, p. 269) and this was the only issue on appeal. See also *Gordon* v. *Moen* [1971] N.Z.L.R. 526.

[70] (1977) 72 D.L.R. (3d) 68.

[71] *e.g.* the company might suffer loss because the auditors' report failed to reveal the activities of a fraudulent employee.

[72] [1989] 2 W.L.R. 316. *cf. Scott Group Ltd.* v. *McFarlane* [1978] 1 N.Z.L.R. 553 where at least one member of the N.Z.C.A. would have imposed such a duty.

answer is "no." A duty is, however, owed to individual shareholders even where they rely on the accounts to purchase more shares.[73] Accordingly, a different result will be reached according to whether an "investor" who buys shares in the company does or does not have a shareholding when the accounts are presented. The distinction may seem arbitrary, but this approach does enable liability to be confined to an ascertainable (though potentially very large) class of persons.[74]

Sometimes there will be no class of persons at all: even though the defendant may have been engaged to advise one person it may be in contemplation that the advice will be passed on to one individual. This was the case in *Smith* v. *Eric S. Bush* ,[75] where a surveyor providing a valuation on a house for a building society considering an advance on it was held liable to the *purchaser* for negligence in respect of his report which was passed on to the purchaser (having been paid for by him) and which stated that the house was a suitable security for the advance. It is not decisive that the purchaser could arrange his own survey[76] even though he is advised in the building society's leaflets[77] to do so and is told that the valuation is for the society's own use, for, at least at the lower end of the housing market, it is clear that buyers will rely on valuations notwithstanding such advice. Even an express disclaimer of responsibility has not always been effective to protect the defendant in such cases because of the impact of the Unfair Contract Terms Act 1977.[78] In cases of this type, liability may arise even if the purchaser has not seen any part of the valuation: in *Harris* v. *Wyre Forest District Council*[79] the purchaser received a mortgage offer of £8,505 on a house which he bought for £9,000 and was entitled thereby to assume that there was no serious defects which would have been revealed by a careful inspection.

As with any other head of negligence, there may be reasons of public policy which prevent a duty of care arising. *Hedley Byrne* has not affected the immunity from suit of a judge[80] but there is no reason for extending that immunity to a person appointed as a valuer[81] or to an architect granting certificates of completion of work under a building contract[82]: there is a difference between the judicial function and a duty to act fairly. Tradi-

[73] It was unsuccessfully argued that any duty owed to shareholders should extend only to the effect of the negligence upon the value of the shares they already held. *cf. Daniels* v. *Daniels* [1978] Ch. 406.

[74] It may be argued that only a major shareholder is likely to bring proceedings. But the legal system is becoming more familiar with centrally controlled multiple claims which have some of the characteristics of the American "class action."

[75] [1989] 2 W.L.R. 970. See also *Yianni* v. *Edwin Evans & Sons*. [1982] Q.B. 438; Brazier and Pople [1981] Conv. 435.

[76] There was expert evidence in *Yianni* v. *Evans* that the proportion of mortgagors having independent surveys was not more than 15 per cent. and perhaps less than 10 per cent.: [1982] Q.B. 438, 445.

[77] The plaintiff may well not read this material.

[78] *Post,* p. 286.

[79] [1989] 2 W.L.R. 970. Hence withholding the valuation report from the purchaser will not help. Building societies have offered three "levels": (1) a simple valuation without responsibility; (2) a "report" with responsibility by the surveyor; (3) a full structural survey. Since (2) is considerably more expensive than (1) and is said to involve no more detailed an inspection (see [1989] 2 W.L.R. 805) it serves little purpose.

[80] *Post*, p. 663, A sequestrator, though an officer of the court, is not immune from suit: *I.R.C.* v. *Hoogstraten* [1985] Q.B. 1007.

[81] *Arenson* v. *Casson Beckman Rutley & Co.* [1977] A.C. 405.

[82] *Sutcliffe* v. *Thackrah* [1974] A.C. 727.

tionally, an arbitrator[83] has been equated in this respect with a judge but dicta in *Arenson* v. *Casson Beckman Rutley & Co.*[84] cast doubt on the proposition that there is an all-embracing immunity[85] or even any immunity at all.[86]

Standard of duty

In *Hedley Byrne* and also in *Evatt's* there are references to a "duty of honesty" which, it is said, a person may incur even if he is not subjected to the duty which exists where there is a special relationship.[87] The meaning of this is not clear; it may be that the duty of honesty is the same as the duty to refrain from the tort of deceit[88] or it may mean something more so that, for example, a person subject to it must not give the impression that his advice is based on research into records when it is not, and must disclose any financial interest he may have in the advice he is giving.[89] The recognition of a duty of honesty in the first sense serves no useful purpose; but it is suggested that it is unnecessary in the second sense, too. The concept of reasonable care, correctly used, is adequate to enable the courts to impose more precisely the appropriate level of obligation by its use than by distinguishing the duty of care from the duty of honesty. The duty of care is not a duty to take every possible care; still less is it a duty to be right.[90] It is the familiar duty to take such care as, in all the circumstances, is reasonable. If it is unreasonable to expect a banker answering a query about a customer to spend time and trouble in searching records and so on, then a duty of reasonable care would not require him to do so. There is no need to say that the banker has no duty of care, only a duty not to tell lies.[91] Similarly, a surveyor conducting a valuation for mortgage purposes is not expected to go to the lengths required in a structural survey costing many hundreds of pounds; but if his inspection reveals grounds for suspicion he must take reasonable steps to follow the

---

[83] Whether appointed at common law or under the Arbitration Acts.

[84] [1977] A.C. 405. However, the immunity of arbitrators was accepted by both parties.

[85] Lord Salmon (*ibid.* at pp. 439–440) suggests that the issue may turn on the substance of the function. If the arbitrator has to receive submissions and evidence his function is judicial and he should be immune; but if the reality of his task is to act as a valuer, a formal appointment as arbitrator should not clothe him with immunity. *cf.* Lord Fraser at p. 442. See also *Palacath Ltd.* v. *Flanagan* [1985] 2 All E.R. 161 (surveyor appointed under rent review clause not discharging judicial function).

[86] See Lord Kilbrandon, *ibid.* at pp. 430–432, who points out that a judge, unlike an arbitrator, is neither selected nor remunerated by the parties; but the fact that the plaintiff has no choice but to rely on the defendant seems poor reason for denying a duty of care. Under s.4 of the Administration of Justice Act 1970 a judge of the Commercial Court may act as an arbitrator.

[87] *Hedley Byrne* [1962] 1 Q.B. 396, 414–415, *per* Pearson L.J. approved by Lords Reid, Morris and Hodson in the House of Lords: [1964] A.C. 465, 489, 503–504, 512; *Evatt's* case [1971] 793, 801, *per* Lord Diplock.

[88] In which case "we have travelled to the village church via the moon, because no one doubts that a person giving information to another owes a duty to abstain from deceit; at least, where he intends his information to be acted on": Honorè, *loc. cit.*, at p. 291. *cf.* Stevens, *loc. cit.*, at p. 146.

[89] Honorè, *loc. cit.*, at p. 291.

[90] *Evatt's* case [1971] A.C. 793, 812, *per* Lords Reid and Morris. For the special statutory provisions governing loss caused by inaccurate personal data held on a computer, see the Data Protection Act 1984, s.22.

[91] See *Hedley Byrne* [1962] 1 Q.B. 396, 414–415, *per* Pearson L.J. And see *Royal Trust Co. (Trinidad) Ltd.* v. *Pampellone* [1987] 1 Lloyd's Rep. 218, where even though there was no duty to consider the advisability of the plaintiff's investment, there was, it seems, a duty to convey accurately the information the defendants held.

trail even though he is working to a standard fee — he must "take the rough with the smooth" or decline to proceed.[92]

Disclaimer of responsibility

It must not be overlooked that, in the result, judgment in *Hedley Byrne* went to the defendants and this, at least in the opinion of the majority, was because they had supplied the information "without responsibility."[93] If it is the law that the duty arises from an undertaking to exercise care, it is not surprising that a defendant should incur no liability if he makes it clear from the outset that he accepts no responsibility for his statement. "A man cannot be said voluntarily to be undertaking a responsibility if at the very moment that he is said to be accepting it he declares that he is not."[94]

In effect, therefore, the liability created by the House of Lords would exist only if the defendant has been too careless of his own interests or too proud to protect himself by such a declaration. However, this situation has been radically altered by the Unfair Contract Terms Act 1977. By section 2(2) of the Act, a person cannot by means of any contract term or notice restrict his liability for loss or damage other than personal injury[95] caused by negligence in the course of a business[96] unless he shows that the term or notice is reasonable and section 1(1)(*b*) defines "negligence" as including the breach of any common law duty to take reasonable care or exercise reasonable skill. It may be objected that this is not apt to catch a statement given "without responsibility" since the defendant is then making it clear that he does not undertake a duty in the first place[97] but this objection is met by the provision in section 13 that section 2 also prevents "excluding or restricting liability by reference to terms and notices which exclude or restrict the relevant obligation or duty."[98] Of course, even under the Act the disclaimer may still be effective if it is reasonable in all the circumstances and the inquirer may not be able to expect the same standard of care in response to a gratuitous inquiry as he could expect if paying for the service.[99] Furthermore, while it will generally be unreasonable for a surveyor conducting a valuation for the purchase of a dwelling on mortgage to disclaim liability,[1]

---

[92] *Roberts* v. *J. Hampson & Co.* [1988] 2 E.G.L.R. 181; *Smith* v. *Eric S. Bush & Co.* [1989] 2 W.L.R. 790; *cf. Eley* v. *King & Chasemore, The Times*, April 24, 1989.

[93] Lord Hodson and, perhaps, Lord Morris woulld have reached the same conclusion even in the absence of the disclaimer: *ante*, p. 274.

[94] [1964] A.C. 465, 533, *per* Lord Devlin. But *cf.* Lord Griffiths' view of the basis of the duty in *Smith* v. *Eric S. Bush, ante*, p. 276.

[95] Personal injury is governed by s.2(1), which is still more onerous on the defendant.

[96] See s.14. It is not entirely clear that the statement in *Evatt's* case was made "in the course of a business" within the meaning of the Act: See *R. & B. Customs Brokers Co. Ltd.* v. *United Dominions Trust Ltd.* [1988] 1 W.L.R. 321.

[97] *Carman Construction Ltd.* v. *Canadian Pacific Ry.* (1982) 136 D.L.R. (3d) 193. But see p. 276, *ante.*

[98] *Smith* v. *Eric S. Bush* [1989] 2 W.L.R. 790.

[99] Note, however, that the disclaimer will commonly be a "notice" rather than a "contract term" and by s.11(3) "in relation to a notice ... the requirement of reasonableness ... is that it should be fair and reasonable to allow reliance on it, having regard to all circumstances obtaining when the liability arose or (but for the notice) would have arisen." *cf.* s.11(1), in relation to contract terms, which fixes the point of time as that when the contract was made.

[1] *Smith* v. *Eric S. Bush, supra.*

the position is probably different if industrial premises or a block of flats is involved for it may well then be reasonable to limit liability to the amount of the surveyor's insurance cover or even to exclude it altogether.[2]

Whether or not the Unfair Contract Terms Act is applicable the following qualifications would appear to apply to the power to disclaim responsibility:

(i) A person guilty of deceit will remain liable whatever he may have said by way of disclaimer.[3]

(ii) Words of exclusion should, following normal practice, be interpreted *contra proferentem*. There is no magic in a particular formula but it is submitted that the letters "E. & O.E." (Errors and Omissions Excepted) which are printed on many documents should not be treated as sufficient in themselves to exclude the duty of care. It is however, unlikely that a disclaimer would ever have been subjected to that form of strained interpretation which is now outdated even for true contractual exemption clauses[4]: the question in each case is whether the defendant has made it reasonably clear that he refuses to undertake responsibility for his statement.[5]

(iii) It is possible that the disclaimer must have been made before or at the time that the defendant supplies the information or advice,[6] but in view of the fact that the liability is non-contractual, it is submitted that the better view is that the defendant may withdraw his undertaking of responsibility before the plaintiff acts upon the information or advice.

Contributory negligence

Since it is a necessary part of the plaintiff's case to show that it was his reasonable reliance[7] on the misstatement that led to his loss[8] there is some difficulty in applying the Law Reform (Contributory Negligence) Act 1945[9] to a case of negligent misstatement. Woolf J. in *J.E.B. Fasteners Ltd.* v. *Marks, Bloom & Co.*[10] (where the issue did not in fact arise) commented that in a case of negligent auditing of accounts "if it is reasonable to rely on the accounts, it is difficult to envisage circumstances where as a matter of fact it would be negligent to do so without taking further steps to protect yourself from the consequence of relying on the auditor's certificate." The problem

---

[2] *Ibid*, at p. 810.

[3] [1964] A.C. 465, 540, *per* Lord Pearson. If the duty of honesty is different from the duty to abstain from deceit (*ante*) perhaps it might be excluded by the defendant stating that he does not propose to give an honest answer, but such a statement seems unlikely.

[4] See *Photo Production Ltd.* v. *Securicor Transport Ltd.* [1980] A.C. 827.

[5] See *Smith* v. *Eric S. Bush* in the C.A. ([1988] Q.B. 743) (applying the principle that general words of exclusion may suffice where negligence is the only type of liability in issue) and see *Hedley Byrne* [1964] A.C. 465, 492–493, 540.

[6] This, perhaps, is suggested by Lord Devlin at [1964] A.C. 533.

[7] *cf.* deceit, where the reliance need not be reasonable and contributory negligence does not apply: *ante* p. 268.

[8] *Shankie-Williams* v. *Heavy* (1986) 279 E.G. 316; *Markappa Inc.* v. *N.W. Spratt & Son* [1985] 1 Lloyd's Rep. 534.

[9] The *words* of the Act are certainly wide enough to comprehend this form of liability. One usually asks whether contributory negligence would have been a complete defence to the tort before 1945, a question which cannot be asked here for obvious reasons.

[10] [1981] 3 All E.R. 289, 297, *ante*, p. 269. An allegation of contributory negligence was also rejected on the facts in *Yianni* v. *Edwin Evans & Sons* [1982] Q.B. 438. *cf. Grand Restaurants of Canada Ltd.* v. *City of Toronto* (1981) 123 D.L.R. (3d) 349.

might not arise if the fault alleged against the plaintiff was subsequent to the point at which he had irrevocably committed himself to a transaction in reliance on the defendant's advice,[11] though such a situation might raise other, equally complex, problems about the distinction between contributory negligence and mitigation.

Lord Tenterden's Act

By the Statute of Frauds 1677 promises that are guarantees must be in writing and signed by the party to be charged or his agent in order to make them actionable. After *Pasley* v. *Freeman*[12] it appeared that the action of deceit provided a way for plaintiffs to evade the statute by alleging not that the defendant had given a guarantee but that he had fraudulently represented that a third party might safely be given credit. To block this evasion of the statute, the Statute of Frauds Amendment Act 1828 (commonly called Lord Tenterden's Act), s.6, was passed providing, in effect, that a false representation as to credit cannot be sued upon unless it is made in writing and signed by the party to be charged.[13]

The section clearly covers fraudulent representations as to a person's credit but it does not apply to an action between contracting parties in respect of advice negligently given.[14] "Section 6 appears to me, upon its plain meaning to be confined to actions brought upon misrepresentations as such, and not to bar redress for failure to perform any contractual or other duty."[15] The section was not considered in *Hedley Byrne* and rightly so, for it has no more place in actions for tortious negligence than it has in actions founded upon contract.[16] Nevertheless it is strange that what would be a defence in an action for fraud should not be one in an action for negligence.[17] It would be even stranger if a defendant against whom negligence is alleged could affirmatively set up his own fraudulent intent and plead the statute. Presumably, however, such a plea could be struck out on the general ground that no one should be allowed to take advantage of his own wrongful act.

Injury to third parties

It is not only the person who relies upon a statement who may suffer if the statement turns out to be untrue. Reliance on a statement made by A to B

---

[11] *e.g.* P buys a house in reliance on D's negligently conducted survey but P then negligently fails to notice warning signs so that the damage is greater than it would otherwise have been.
[12] (1789) 3 T.R. 51, *ante*, p. 262.
[13] Unlike the Statute of Frauds itself, there is no reference to signature by an agent. However, a company can only act by an agent, so the signature of its duly authorised agent is the signature of the company under the Act: *U.B.A.F. Ltd.* v. *European American Banking Corp.*, [1984] Q.B. 713; *cf. Hirst* v. *West Riding Union Banking Co. Ltd.* [1901] 2 K.B. 560.
[14] *Banbury* v. *Bank of Montreal* [1918] A.C. 626.
[15] *Ibid.* at p. 640, *per* Lord Finlay L.C.
[16] *W.B. Anderson & Sons Ltd.* v. *Rhodes (Liverpool) Ltd.* [1967] 2 All E.R. 850; *Evatt's* case [1969] A.L.R. 3.
[17] But it does apply to s.2(1) of the Misrepresentation Act 1967 because of the form of that provision: *U.B.A.F. Ltd.* v. *European American Banking Corp., supra*, n. 13.

may sometimes lead B to act in a manner detrimental to C but in respect of which C may have no redress against B, and the question then arises, if A's statement is false, whether C can sue A. A doctor employed by an insurance company may incorrectly inform the company that an applicant for life insurance is a bad risk, with the result that the company demands a higher premium than normal or refuses the applicant altogether; a newspaper may publish incorrectly that a trader has gone out of business with the result that the trader loses custom; a trader may circulate false information of a definite, factual nature that, because of technological development, his product is now twice as effective as his rival's. On these bare facts none of these statements is defamatory because there is no imputation of misconduct.[18] The third might constitute deceit but only as against purchasers of the product.[19]

The tort which has traditionally been applicable to these situations is "injurious falsehood" and we shall deal with this before considering the impact of the tort of negligence. Some specific tort, however, there must be: there is no general right to sue in respect of untruths or even to restrain the circulation of untruths.[20]

(1) *Injurious falsehood*[21]

The tort requires the making of a false statement, with "malice," to some person other than the plaintiff, as a result of which the plaintiff suffers damage.

(a) False statement to some person other than the plaintiff. The statement may be oral or written and even conduct conveying a false representation may be sufficient.[22] It is for the plaintiff to prove that the statement is false and there is no presumption in his favour.[23] If the statement is due to the plaintiff's own fault he has no claim.[24]

So long as the statement is made with the requisite intent there is no restriction about subject-matter. In one of the earliest cases the false statement was that the plaintiff was already married, whereby she lost a proposed marriage[25]; in the leading case of *Ratcliffe* v. *Evans*[26] an action succeeded in respect of a statement by a newspaper that the plaintiff had ceased to trade; and in an American case the defendant gave false information that the

---

[18] *Post,* p. 294.
[19] If the product was in fact just as good as the rival's and cost no more even these plaintiffs could not recover damages.
[20] *Kingdom of Spain* v. *Christie, Manson & Woods Ltd.* [1986] 1 W.L.R. 1120.
[21] The tort goes by various names. A common form of the tort is impugning the plaintiff's title to goods (*Green* v. *Button* (1835) 5 L.J.Ex. 81), hence the name "slander of title," which is misleading because (*a*) the tort has nothing in common with slander proper and (*b*) it is by no means confined to disparagement of title. The credit for "injurious falsehood" must go to Sir John Salmond, though he included the tort of "passing off" (*post,* p. 535) in it. "Injurious falsehood" has been adopted by the *Restatement* 2d.
[22] *Wilts. United Dairies* v. *Robinson & Sons* [1958] R.P.C. 94.
[23] *cf.* the position in defamation: *post,* p. 320.
[24] *Vacha* v. *Gillett* (1934) 50 Ll.L.R. 67, 74–75.
[25] *Sheperd* v. *Wakeman* (1662) 1 Sid. 79.
[26] [1892] 2 Q.B. 524; Weir, *Casebook on Tort* (6th ed.), p. 490; *Joyce* v. *Motor Surveys Ltd.* [1948] Ch. 252.

plaintiff was not a citizen, subjecting him to deportation proceedings.[27] The tort does not, however, extend to statements which have no connection with the plaintiff or his property: it is not this tort by A against C if A tells B lies to obtain property and thereby deprives C of the opportunity to bid for it.[28] A statement by one trader that his goods are superior to those of a rival (mere "puffing"), even if it is false and known to be so and causes damage to the other is not actionable, for courts of law cannot be converted into advertising agencies for trying the relative merits of rival productions.[29] However, this "privilege" is confined to those imprecise commendations which are a common part of advertising and to which a reasonable person does not attach very much importance. Accordingly, if the defendant chooses to frame his comparison in the form of scientific tests or other statements of ascertainable fact, he will be liable if they are proved untrue.[30]

 (b) Malice. This expression is never easy to define in the law of tort and perhaps nowhere more so than here. The requirement is fulfilled if the defendant knows that the statement is false or if he is reckless, *i.e.* makes the statement not caring whether it is true or false.[31] "Honest belief," said Scrutton L.J.,[32] "in an unfounded claim is not malice, but the nature of the unfounded claim may be evidence that there is not an honest belief in it. It may be so unfounded that the particular fact that it is put forward may be evidence that it is not honestly believed."[33] However, even if the defendant does believe the untrue statement there may still be malice if he is actuated by some indirect, dishonest or improper motive, which seems to mean the purpose of injuring the plaintiff rather than defending the defendant's own interests or pushing his own business.[34] But a mere careless statement

[27] *Al Raschid* v. *News Syndicate Co.* 191 N.E. 713 (1934) (the deportation proceedings were not "judicial proceedings" for the purpose of the tort of malicious prosecution).
[28] *Lonrho plc* v. *Fayed* [1988] 3 All E.R. 464 (though no claim for injurious falsehood appears to have been made; on appeal on another point, [1989] 2 All E.R. 65).
[29] *White* v. *Mellin* [1895] A.C. 154, 164–165; *Hubbuck & Sons Ltd.* v. *Wilkinson* [1899] 1 Q.B. 86. But for another possibility see the Trade Marks Act 1938, s.4.
[30] *De Beers Products Ltd.* v. *International General Electric Co. of New York Ltd.* [1975] 1 W.L.R. 972. Even imprecise assertions of superiority may be actionable if they denigrate the plaintiff's wares in a manner which a reasonable person would take seriously: *ibid.*; *White* v. *Mellin, supra,* at p. 171; *Alcott* v. *Miller's Karri and Jarrah Forests Ltd.* (1904) 91 L.T. 722. For the statutory remedy for unfounded claims of patent infringement see Clerk & Lindsell, *Torts* (16th ed.), para. 29–28.
[31] *Shapiro* v. *La Morta* (1923) 40 T.L.R. 39, 41, 201, 203; *Cellactite and British Uralite* v. *H. H. Robertson* [1957] C.L.Y. 1989. There may, however, be situations in which a person is justified in stating that which he knows or believes to be untrue: see the unusual case of *British Railway Traffic and Electric Co. Ltd.* v. *C.R.C. Co. Ltd.* [1922] 2 K.B. 260 though the statement there might perhaps be regarded as true in the context in which it was made. There might be occasions when a person would be protected, by analogy with the law of defamation, in carrying out a duty to pass on information which he does not believe to be true. The *Restatement* 2d. s.646 A applies the various heads of defamation qualified privilege to injurious falsehood.
[32] *Greers Ltd.* v. *Pearman & Corder Ltd.* (1922) 39 R.P.C. 406, 417 (assertion of trade mark infringement after years of disclaimer of right to exclusive use).
[33] If there is no belief in the truth of the statement it does not matter that the defendant's motive is only to advance his own interests: *Wilts. United Dairies* v. *Robinson* [1957] R.P.C. 220 (on appeal, but not on this point, [1958] R.P.C. 94). It is not thought that Roxburgh J. in *Joyce* v. *Motor Surveys Ltd.* [1948] Ch. 252 intended to cast any doubt on this proposition.
[34] *Dunlop* v. *Maison Talbot* (1904) 20 T.L.R. 579.

without such a motive, though damaging, is not actionable as injurious falsehood.[35]

(c) Damage. Save in cases falling within the provisions of section 3(1) of the Defamation Act 1952 proof of special damage is required[36] but this requirement is satisfied by proof of a general loss of business where the falsehood in its very nature is intended, or is reasonably likely, to produce and actually does produce in the ordinary course of things, such loss; for there are businesses, like those of an auctioneer or a publican, where the customers are often so fleeting in their patronage that it would be almost impossible for the plaintiff to name in particular such of them as have ceased to deal with him in consequence of the defendant's tort.[37] By section 3(1) of the Defamation Act 1952 it is no longer necessary to allege or prove special (*i.e.* actual) damage (*a*) if the words complained of are published in writing or other permanent form[38] and are calculated to cause pecuniary damage to the plaintiff, or (*b*) if the words complained of are calculated[39] to cause pecuniary damage to the plaintiff in respect of any office, profession, calling, trade or business held or carried on by him at the time of the publication.

(2) *Liability for negligence*

There is a close analogy between injurious falsehood and deceit, both being concerned with false statements and damage resulting from them and both requiring something more than mere negligence. Since the House of Lords in *Hedley Byrne* introduced liability for negligence into the "two party" situation analogous to deceit, it is not surprising that there will in some cases be liability for negligence in the "three party" situation, notwithstanding the requirement of malice in injurious falsehood. In one class of case this result was in effect achieved at an early date. A doctor called in to certify that a person should be admitted to a mental hospital was held to owe a duty of care to that person even though he is called in by and acts on behalf of another.[40] Denning L.J. said that there was liability in these cases "because the doctor knows that the certificate is required for the very purpose of deciding whether the man should be detained or not,"[41] though in view of the very serious invasion of liberty which would arise from erroneous certification, perhaps they should be regarded as *sui generis*.

---

[35] *Balden* v. *Shorter* [1933] Ch. 427; *Loudon* v. *Ryder (No. 2)* [1953] Ch. 423 (where no malice is proved but the defendant's claim is nevertheless wrongful, plaintiff may be entitled to a declaration as to his title); *McDonald's Hamburgers* v. *Burgerking (U.K.)* [1986] F.S.R. 45.

[36] *White* v. *Mellin* [1895] A.C. 154; *Royal Baking Powder Co.* v. *Wright & Co.* (1900) 18 R.P.C. 95, 99.

[37] *Ratcliffe* v. *Evans* [1892] 2 Q.B. 524, 533; *Leetham* v. *Rank* (1912) 57 S.J. 111; *Hargrave* v. *Le Breton* (1769) 4 Burr. 2422; *Evans* v. *Harries* (1856) 1 H. & N. 251; *Worsley & Co. Ltd.* v. *Cooper* [1939] 1 All E.R. 290.

[38] *Fielding* v. *Variety Incorporated* [1967] 2 Q.B. 841. Broadcasting is publication in permanent form (s.3(2)). If a plaintiff takes advantage of the section he cannot lead evidence of special damage: *Calvet* v. *Tomkies* [1963] 1 W.L.R. 1397.

[39] Which means "likely to": *Customglass Boats* v. *Salthouse Bros.* [1976] R.P.C. 589 (N.Z. Defamation Act 1954, s.5(1)).

[40] *Hall* v. *Semple* (1862) 3 F. & R. 33; *Everett* v. *Griffiths* [1921] A.C. 631; *Harnett* v. *Fisher* [1927] A.C. 573; *De Freville* v. *Dill* (1927) 96 L.J.K.B. 1056 (all decided under earlier statutes). See now The Mental Health Act 1983, Part II. No proceedings may be brought without leave of the court: *ibid.* s.139.

[41] *Candler* v. *Crane, Christmas & Co.* [1951] 2 K.B. 164, 183.

Ministry of Housing, etc. v. *Sharp*,[42] however, comes very close to the point here under consideration. An intending purchaser of land (B, in our notation above) caused the usual search to be made in the local land registry (A). A certificate was issued which, as a result of negligence, omitted a land charge in favour of the plaintiff (C). By statute, this freed the land from the obligation[43] and C lost the right represented by it. The Court of Appeal held that A owed a duty of care to C. It is tempting to regard this as a case where A's careless misstatements to B led B to act to the detriment of C, but it may well be that on the facts it was the issue of the certificate rather than the purchase of the land which caused the plaintiff's loss. In other words, it is the act of A, not the act of B in reliance on the statement of A, which caused C's damage.[44] Closer to our paradigm three-party situation is *Lawton* v. *B.O.C. Transhield Ltd.*[45] where a former employer of the plaintiff was held to be under a duty of care to him in giving a reference to a new employer, who dismissed him because of the contents of the reference.[46] The decision is surprising because it undercuts the protection which the concept of qualified privilege in the law of defamation[47] normally gives to the writer of a reference, but putting that point on one side, Tudor Evans J. recognised that the case could not fit squarely into the principle of *Hedley Byrne*.[48] Whether such cases are to be dealt with by an extension of *Hedley Byrne*[49] or under the general doctrine of *Donoghue* v. *Stevenson* as that applies to economic loss[50] matters little if it is borne in mind that *Hedley Byrne* liability is not a separate tort but the application of negligence law to a particular type of situation, and that the concepts of undertaking and reliance may form the basis upon which a court will deal with a claim for economic loss even where no misstatement is involved. The imposition of a duty of care should certainly not be undertaken with any less caution merely because the case involves a "three party" situation—it cannot be the law that A owes a duty to C whenever he should reasonably foresee loss to C resulting from his careless statement to B. Perhaps we have not yet reached the stage when a newspaper would be liable for negligently publishing a false story that a person has ceased to trade,[51] but it is hard to see any strong reason why there should be no duty of care where there is close proximity between the plaintiff and the defendant and the latter is aware of the precise purpose for which the

---

[42] [1970] 2 Q.B. 223.
[43] The case could not recur: see s.10 of the Land Charges Act 1975.
[44] But *cf. Ross* v. *Caunters* [1980] Ch. 297, 318.
[45] [1987] I.C.R. 7.
[46] On the facts, there was no breach of duty.
[47] That is to say, that an *honest* but inaccurate statement gives rise to no liability.
[48] This was also the view of Salmon L.J. on the facts of *Sharp's* case ([1970] 2 Q.B. 223, 278–280), but Lord Denning M.R. held that that case came "four square within the principles . . . in *Hedley Byrne*" at p. 268).
[49] Which seems to have been the view taken in *B.T. Australia Ltd.* v. *Raine & Horne Pty. Ltd.* [1981] 3 N.S.W.L.R. 221 (where trustee of a trust fund relies on a valuer, valuer owes duty to unit holders in the trust even though the only acts of reliance are by the trustee).
[50] The preference of Megarry V.-C. in *Ross* v. *Caunters* [1980] Ch. 297.
[51] *cf. Ratcliffe* v. *Evans* [1892] 2 Q.B. 524.

information is required by the third party, as, for example, in the case of a doctor carrying out an examination for an insurance company.[52]

[52] *cf.* Denning L.J.'s comment on the doctor examining an allegedly insane person, *supra*, n. 41. However, he thought that the doctor would not be liable in the insurance case: *ibid. cf. Nicholls* v. *Richmond* (1983) 145 D.L.R. (3d) 362. The fact that the doctor owes a contractual duty to the insurance company has not been a logically sufficient answer to such a claim since *Donoghue* v. *Stevenson*. If the doctor were liable for negligently certifying a fit plaintiff as unfit, would he also be liable to the insured where he negligently certified him fit when in fact he was suffering from a dangerous condition? See *Thomsen* v. *Davison* [1975] Qd.R. 93.

CHAPTER 12

DEFAMATION[1]

DEFINITION

Defamation is the publication of a statement which reflects on a person's reputation and tends to lower him in the estimation of right-thinking members of society generally or tends to make them shun or avoid him.

DEFAMATION is sometimes defined simply as the publication of a statement which tends to bring a person "into hatred, contempt or ridicule." But this is not quite exact, for a statement may possibly be defamatory even if it does not excite in reasonable people feelings quite so strong as hatred, contempt or ridicule[2]; and the definition is defective in omitting any reference to the alternative of "tending to shun or avoid." This addition is necessary, for falsely imputing insolvency or insanity to a man is unquestionably defamation, although, far from tending to excite hatred, contempt or ridicule, it would rouse only pity and sympathy in the minds of reasonable people,[3] who would nevertheless be inclined to shun his society. And Slesser L.J. took this view in *Youssoupoff* v. *Metro-Goldwyn-Mayer Pictures Ltd.*, where a cinematograph film falsely imputed that the plaintiff, a Russian princess, had been raped or seduced by the notorious monk, Rasputin, for this tended "to make the plaintiff be shunned and avoided and that without any moral discredit on her part."[4] A statement which disparages a man in his reputation in relation to his office, profession, calling, trade or business may be defamatory, *e.g.* the imputation of some quality which would be detrimental or the absence of some quality which is essential to the successful carrying on of his office, trade or profession, such as want of ability, incompetence and, of course, dishonest or fraudulent conduct.[5] Injurious statements which do not reflect on a person's reputation (*e.g.* that he has

---

[1] Gatley, *Libel and Slander* (8th ed.); Duncan and Neill, *Defamation* (2nd ed.); Carter-Ruck, *Libel and Slander*; Weir, *Casebook on Tort* (6th ed.), Chap. 14. The Reports of the Faulks Committee (Cmnd. 5909 (1975)) and the Porter Committee (Cmd. 7536 (1948)) are excellent sources of information.

[2] *e.g. Tournier* v. *National, etc., Bank of England* [1924] 1 K.B. 461; *Drummond-Jackson* v. *B.M.A.* [1970] 1 W.L.R. 691, 700, *per* Sir Gordon Willmer.

[3] *Pace* Juvenal: Nil habet infelix paupertas durius in se Quam quod ridiculos homines facit. (Sat.iii, 152–153.)

[4] (1934) 50 T.L.R. 581, 587. But would reasonable people shun the society of a woman who had the misfortune to be raped? (1935) 51 L.Q.R. 281–282. Slesser L.J. saw the difficulty but dismissed it with the remark: "It is to shut one's eye to realities to make these nice distinctions."

[5] *Turner* v. *Metro-Goldwyn-Mayer Pictures Ltd.* [1950] 2 All E.R. 449; *Angel* v. *H.H. Bushell & Co. Ltd.* [1968] 1 Q.B. 813; *Drummond-Jackson* v. *B.M.A.* [1970] 1 W.L.R. 688.

ceased to trade) are not defamatory but may be actionable if made maliciously.[6]

The words must tend to give rise to the feelings mentioned in the definition.[7] But on the part of whom? The answer is the reasonable man. This rules out on the one hand persons who are so lax or so cynical that they would think none the worse of a man whatever was imputed to him, and on the other hand those who are so censorious as to regard even trivial accusations (if they were true) as lowering another's reputation, or who are so hasty as to infer the worst meaning from any ambiguous statement. It is not these, but the ordinary citizen, whose judgment must be taken as the standard. He is neither unusually suspicious nor unusually naive and he does not always interpret the meaning of words as would a lawyer for he "is not inhibited by a knowledge of the rules of construction."[8] He may thus more freely read an implication into a given form of words, "and, unfortunately, as the law of defamation has to take into account, is especially prone to do so when it is derogatory."[9] The question, as Lord Atkin suggested, is "Would the words tend to lower the plaintiff in the estimation of right-thinking members of society generally?"[10] So, if the plaintiff can prove only that the statement tends to discredit him with one special class of persons, it is not defamatory unless reasonable people in general would take the same view.[11] Suppose that A is a member of a club which bans the wearing of coloured shirts and that B falsely accuses him of openly wearing one. That may tend to make A unpopular with members of the club, but B has committed no defamation; had A been accused of misappropriating the club funds, the case would have been otherwise; for while right-minded persons in general are indifferent to the hue of other people's underwear, they dislike dishonesty in any quarter; but there is nothing dishonest or dishonourable in openly breaking a club rule of this sort.[12] There will, of course, be many cases in which an implication of hypocrisy or disloyalty may be found in the allegation that the plaintiff does not follow the tenets of a group to which he claims to belong. To say of a man that he takes alcohol in moderation is not defamatory; but to say it of a temperance crusader may very well be. To say of a man that he has put in motion the proper machinery for suppressing crime, in that he has reported certain acts, wrongful in law, to the police,

---

[6] See *ante*, p. 289. For differing opinions as to whether disparaging of a man's dental technique was defamatory, see *Drummond-Jackson* v. *B.M.A.* [1970] 1 W.L.R. 688, 694, 699. An allegation that an airline is, without any fault on its part, peculiarly susceptible to hi-jacking would seem not to be defamatory at common law: *Sungravure Pty. Ltd.* v. *Middle East Airlines* (1975) 5 A.L.R. 147.

[7] Proof that they actually did give rise to it is unnecessary: *Hough* v. *London Express Newspaper* [1940] 2 K.B. 507, 515, *per* Goddard L.J.: "If words are used which impute discreditable conduct to my friend, he has been defamed to me, although I do not believe the imputation, and may even know that it is untrue."

[8] *Lewis* v. *Daily Telegraph Ltd.* [1964] A.C. 234, 258, *per* Lord Reid.

[9] *Ibid.* at p. 277, *per* Lord Devlin. This is in marked contrast with the old approach to slander typified by *Holt* v. *Astgrigg* (1608) Cro.Jac. 184, *post*, p. 302.

[10] *Sim* v. *Stretch* [1936] 2 All E.R. 1237, 1240.

[11] *cf.* Lord Hailsham in *Tolley* v. *Fry & Sons Ltd.* [1931] A.C. 333, 339; McCardie J. in *Myroft* v. *Sleight* (1921) 90 L.J.K.B. 883, 886, citing Farwell L.J. in *Leetham* v. *Rank* (1912) 57 S.J. 111; *Miller* v. *David* (1874) L.R. 9 C.P. 118.

[12] It is defamatory of a Muslim to say that he has insulted the Prophet because the reasonable man disapproves of any insult to religious beliefs: *Shah* v. *Akram* [1981] C.A., unreported.

cannot be defamatory,[13] though an additional comment that he had thereby behaved dishonourably could be.[14]

Libel and slander

Liability for defamation is divided into the two categories of libel and slander, and this division has important consequences. A libel consists of a defamatory statement or representation in permanent form; if a defamatory meaning is conveyed by spoken words or gestures it is slander. Examples of libel, as distinguished from slander, are a picture, statue, waxwork effigy, or any writing, print, mark or sign exposed to view. On the other hand, defamation in the manual language of the deaf and dumb, and mimicry and gesticulation generally (*e.g.* holding up an empty purse to indicate that the plaintiff has robbed the defendant[15]) would probably be slander, because the movements are more transient. These examples show that it is only broadly true to say that libel is addressed to the eye, slander to the ear. Moreover, broadcasting, both radio and television,[16] cable transmissions[17] and theatrical performances[18] are, by statute, treated as publication in permanent form, *i.e.* as libel.

It needs no demonstration that if an oral utterance is communicated orally it is a slander that is published, or that if a written statement is shown to a third person, it is a libel that is published. But further, if an oral statement by A is written down by B and shown by B to C, it is a libel, not a slander, that B has published. No doubt A's original uttering of the words to B may have been slander, but then the communication was oral; whereas disclosure of the writing by B to C is not oral. Conversely, if A writes to B a letter defamatory of X and B reads it aloud to C, it ought to be a slander that is published by B, not a libel; but the balance of authority is the other way, although it has very little reasoning in support of it.[19] If I dictate a defamatory letter to my typist the cause of action is slander as regards the publication to her.[20] If the typist reads it back to me or hands it back as a typed letter it would seem that *he or she* has not by that act published defamatory matter,[21] nor have I published it as a libel, since although I can be liable for a

<hr>

[13] *Byrne* v. *Deane* [1937] 1 K.B. 818, Greer L.J. dissenting. See also Donovan J.'s summing-up in *Grech* v. *Odhams Press Ltd.*, cited in [1958] 2 All E.R. 462, 464. *cf. Mawe* v. *Piggott* (1869) I.R. 4 C.L. 54.

[14] *Berry* v. *Irish Times* [1973] I.R. 368 ("20th Century felon setter") is a borderline case in this respect, though the majority of the court, in upholding the jury's verdict for the defendant, were not saying that the words could not as a matter of law be defamatory.

[15] Lord Ellenborough C.J. in *Cook* v. *Cox* (1814) 3 M. & S. 110, 114.

[16] Defamation Act 1952, ss.1, 16. For a consideration of television broadcasting in the absence of any statutory provision, see *Wainer* v. *Ripon* [1980] V.R. 129.

[17] Cable and Broadcasting Act 1984, s.28.

[18] Theatres Act 1968, s.4. Performances given on domestic occasions in private dwellings are excepted from this provision: *ibid.* s.7.

[19] In *Forrester* v. *Tyrrell* (1893) 9 T.L.R. 257, the C.A., following dicta in the *Case de Libellis Famosis* (1605) 5 Rep. 125a, and in *Lamb's Case* (1611) 9 Rep. 59b, held it to be libel. See too *Robinson* v. *Chambers* [1946] N.I. 148. In *Osborn* v. *Boulter* [1930] 2 K.B. 226, 231, 237 Scrutton and Slesser, L.JJ. were of opinion *obiter* that the reading back by a typist of a dictated statement, in the presence of a third party, was a slander; *contra*, Greer L.J. *ibid.* at p. 236. *Forrester* v. *Tyrrell* was not cited.

[20] It may be a publication on a privileged occasion and so protected on that ground; see *post*, p. 351.

[21] *Eglantine Inn Ltd.* v. *Smith* [1948] N.I. 29, 33. It is submitted that the dicta in *Osborn* v. *Thomas Boulter & Son* [1930] 2 K.B. 226 are concerned with the situation where defamatory matter is dictated and read back then and there from the notes in the presence of a third party, and not with the question of reading out a defamatory document.

publication of a libel through my agent, I can hardly publish it to *myself*. If the letter is sent out by me or by my typist on my behalf to a third party, I shall be liable for the libel published to the third party. In this connection it has been questioned whether defamatory matter on a gramophone record is, as such, libel or only potential slander.[22] If the test be, as we have suggested, "What is the mode of publication?" it seems to be potential slander.[23] Of course the record as such is in permanent form, but that does not settle the point, for matter on the record is not communicated to anyone until a needle is applied to the record, and then it takes the form of speech. No doubt the defamation may have been communicated to anyone who happened to be present while the speaker was consigning it to the record, but *then* the words were spoken and therefore slanderous; that, however, throws no light on what their reproduction by the needle would be.[24] The Court of Appeal in *Youssoupoff* v. *Metro-Goldwyn-Mayer Pictures Ltd.*[25] had no doubt that defamatory matter embodied in a "talking" cinematograph film was a libel:

> "There can be no doubt that, so far as the photographic part of the exhibition is concerned, that is a permanent matter to be seen by the eye, and is the proper subject of an action for libel, if defamatory. I regard the speech which is synchronised with the photographic reproduction and forms part of one complex, common exhibition as an ancillary circumstance, part of the surroundings explaining that which is to be seen."[26]

However, this reasoning does not help where there is nothing defamatory in the visual part of the exhibition nor, of course, where no visual image accompanies the recording.

Differences between slander and libel

Attempts have occasionally been made to justify the distinction between libel and slander (libel generally being more severe on the defendant) on the basis, for example, that libel has greater potential for harm and is more likely to be "premeditated." Such rationalisations are not wholly without merit but are open to powerful objections. First, the distinction seems to have appeared by historical chance rather than by design[27]; secondly, the distinction breaks down in relation to many modern inventions; and thirdly, the rationalisations fail to provide an answer consistent with the existing law even with regard to traditional methods of communication.[28] The Faulks

[22] Pollock, *Torts* (15th ed.), p. 176, n. 1. See further *Chicken* v. *Ham, Uncommon Law* (A.P.H.), 71.
[23] (1935) 51 L.Q.R. 281–283; 573–574. *Contra*, Landon, in Pollock, *Torts* (15th ed.), p. 176.
[24] *Semble*, matter confided to a parrot is slander when repeated by the bird to another person. *cf. Chicken* v. *Ham, supra*, at p. 75, *per* Lord Lick.
[25] (1934) 50 T.L.R. 581.
[26] *Ibid.* at p. 587, *per* Slesser L.J. It is submitted that a videotape should be equated with a film even though no image is visible unless it is played in a machine.
[27] See *post*, pp. 301–302.
[28] To write a letter which is seen by only one recipient is undoubtedly libel; to address a crowd of a thousand people at a public meeting is equally undoubtedly slander.

Committee recommended in 1975 that the distinction be abolished and fears that this might lead to a flood of petty actions for spoken words seem not to be borne out by experience in other parts of the world.[29]

For the time being at least, the distinction between libel and slander is still with us and has important consequences. First, though not directly relevant to the law of tort, libel is a crime as well as a tort.[30] Slander, as such, is not criminal, although spoken words may be punishable by common law or statute as being treasonable, seditious, blasphemous, tending to lead to breaches of the peace or the like. Secondly, libel is actionable *per se, i.e.* without proof of special damage. In slander, special damage must be proved except in the cases stated in the next section.

Special damage

"Special" damage is a phrase which has been rightly criticised as either meaningless or misleading and "actual" damage has been suggested as a more accurate expression.[31] But whatever be the adjective used, the wrong is not actionable unless the plaintiff proves loss of money or of some temporal or material advantage estimable in money. If there is only loss of the society of one's friends, that is not enough. Hence, while loss of your friend's hospitality is special damage, exclusion from the religious congregation to which you belong is not; for a dinner has temporal and material value, while spiritual communion has none in this connection.[32]

Where there is no need to prove special damage in defamation, the plaintiff can recover general damages for the injury to his reputation without adducing any evidence that it has in fact been harmed, for the law presumes that *some* damage will arise in the ordinary course of things. It is enough that the immediate tendency of the words is to impair his reputation. If the plaintiff contends that special damage has been suffered in addition to general damages, he must allege it in his pleadings and prove it at the trial, but even if he breaks down on this point, he can still recover general damages.[33]

Damage must of course not be too remote. The general principles as to

---

[29] Cmnd. 5909, Chap. 2. The same proposal had been made by a Select Committee of the House of Lords in 1843. The Porter Committee (Cmd. 7536) disagreed. The distinction has never existed in Scotland and has been abolished by statute in parts of Australia and in New Zealand.

[30] The law was reviewed by the House of Lords in *Gleaves* v. *Deakin* [1980] A.C. 477. There is no requirement that the libel should tend to a breach of the peace but it should be of a sufficiently serious nature to justify the use of the criminal process. Truth as such is not a defence, though s.6 of the Libel Act 1843 enables the defendant to plead it if "it was for the public benefit . . . that the matters charged should be published." No criminal proceedings may be brought in respect of a publication in a newspaper without leave of a High Court judge: Law of Libel Amendment Act 1888, s.8. In 1982 the Law Commission made provisional proposals for the replacement of criminal libel by a narrower offence of "criminal defamation," aimed at deliberate character assassination: Law Commission W.P. No. 84.

[31] Bower, *Actionable Defamation* (2nd ed.), Art. 13. See too, Bowen L.J. in *Ratcliffe* v. *Evans* [1892] 2 Q.B. 524. "Special damage" has other meanings with which the present meaning should not be confused: Jolowicz, "The Changing Use of 'Special Damage' and its Effect on the Law" [1960] C.L.J. 214.

[32] *Roberts* v. *Roberts* (1864) 5 B. & S. 384; *Davies* v. *Solomon* (1871) L.R. 7 Q.B. 112. It is a vexed question whether upon proof of the requisite special damage, the jury may award such general damages as may be awarded in cases of libel: see Gatley, *op. cit.*, p. 598. However, the Faulks Committee seems to have thought that they could: para. 86 of the Report.

[33] Gatley, *op. cit.*, pp. 451–453.

this have already been discussed,[34] and the only peculiarity in defamation is that illness arising from mental worry induced by slander not actionable *per se* is damage which is too remote,[35] although in slander actionable *per se*, libel, and other torts, that is not now the law provided the damage amounts to nervous shock.[36] The exception has been defended on the ground that otherwise the courts might be pestered with an infinity of trumpery or groundless actions.[37]

It was held in an old case[38] that if A slanders B so that B is wrongfully dismissed by C from C's employment, A is not liable to B, because the "special damage must be the legal and natural consequences of the words spoken," and that A is no more responsible for C's unlawful act than he would be if B's neighbours, believing A's lie to be true, were to duck B in a horse-pond. But this reasoning cannot now be regarded as law, for although the case has not been actually overruled (indeed, on the facts the decision may have been correct), yet the *ratio decidendi* encountered strong adverse criticism in later cases in the House of Lords and in other courts. In *Lynch* v. *Knight*,[39] Lord Wensleydale said: "To make the words actionable by reason of special damage, the consequence must be such as, taking human nature as it is, with its infirmities, and having regard to the relationship of the parties concerned, might fairly and reasonably have been anticipated and feared would follow from the speaking the words."[40] In other words, if A does an unlawful act to B, the chain of causation may possibly be severed by the unlawful act of C, but it does not follow that it must necessarily be severed thereby.[41]

"Unauthorised" repetition of the words by other persons will make the damage too remote.[42] But the defendant is responsible if there is a legal or moral duty to repeat them,[43] or he intends them to be repeated or, probably, the repetition is the natural and probable consequence of the original publication.[44]

Slander actionable per se

The exceptional cases in which slander is actionable without proof of special damage are:

[34] *Ante*, Chap. 6.
[35] *Allsop* v. *Allsop* (1860) 5 H. & N. 534.
[36] Gatley, *op. cit.*, p. 96.
[37] Wright J. in *Wilkinson* v. *Downton* [1897] 2 Q.B. 57, 60.
[38] *Vicars* v. *Wilcocks* (1806) 8 East 1.
[39] (1861) 9 H.L.C. 577, 600.
[40] See too, *Bowen* v. *Hall* (1881) 6 Q.B.D. 333, 339 and *cf. Longdon-Griffiths* v. *Smith* [1950] 2 All E.R. 662, 678 (not reported on this point in other reports).
[41] *Ante*, pp. 153–155. See too Gatley, *op. cit.*, pp. 98–100.
[42] *Ward* v. *Weeks* (1830) 7 Bing. 211; *Parkins* v. *Scott* (1862) 1 H. & C. 153.
[43] *Derry* v. *Handley* (1867) 16 L.T. 263.
[44] *Speight* v. *Gosnay* (1891) 60 L.J.Q.B. 231; *Ward* v. *Lewis* [1955] 1 W.L.R. 9; *Cellactite and British Uralite* v. *H.H. Robertson Co.* [1957] C.L.Y. 1989. For the application of a similar rule to libel, see *Weld-Blundell* v. *Stephens* [1920] A.C. 956, 987, 999; *Cutler* v. *McPhail* [1962] 2 Q.B. 292; *Sims* v. *Wren* [1984] 1 N.S.W.L.R. 317 (politician speaking slander at press conference liable for repetition as libel in media). See further Gatley, *op. cit.*, pp. 119–122.

(1) *Imputation of a criminal offence*

Imputation of a criminal offence punishable with imprisonment. There
must be direct imputation of the offence, not merely of suspicion of it,[45] and
the offence must be punishable by imprisonment in the first instance.[46] If the
slander goes into details of the offence charged, it is not actionable *per se* if
the details are inconsistent with one another, as in *Jackson* v. *Adams*,[47]
where the defendant said to the plaintiff, a churchwarden, "Who stole the
parish bellropes, you scamping rascal?" As the possession of the ropes was
vested in the churchwarden, theft of them by the plaintiff was impossible.[48]
But there is authority for the proposition that the basis of the rule, that
imputation of a criminal offence is actionable *per se*, is the probability of
social ostracism of the plaintiff and not his jeopardy of imprisonment[49]; this
seems inconsistent with *Jackson* v. *Adams*.

(2) *Imputation of disease*

*Imputation of a contagious or infectious disease likely to prevent other
persons from associating with the plaintiff*. There is some uncertainty about
this exception, nonetheless so because there is no reported English decision
on it later than 1844.[50] It has always included venereal disease and, in olden
times, plague and leprosy. Perhaps at the present day it covers any disease
which is infectious or contagious whether it be "owing to the visitation of
God, to accident, or to the indiscretion of the party therewith afflicted"[51];
for, although an accusation of smallpox was held in 1599 not to be actionable
at all, the decision turned upon a rule of interpretation now extinct.[52]

(3) *Imputation of unchastity*

Imputation of unchastity[53] *or adultery of any woman or girl*. This is a
statutory exception created by the Slander of Women Act 1891,[54] which also

---

[45] *Simmons* v. *Mitchell* (1880) 6 App.Cas. 156, P.C.
[46] *Hellwig* v. *Mitchell* [1910] 1 K.B. 609. It is not enough that imprisonment may be inflicted for non-payment
of a fine which has been imposed: *Ormiston* v. *G.W. Ry.* [1917] 1 K.B. 598.
[47] (1835) 2 Bing.N.C. 402.
[48] Perhaps this case would have been decided differently if the Theft Act 1968 had been law.
[49] *Gray* v. *Jones* (1939) 160 L.T. 361. In *D. & L. Caterers Ltd.* v. *D'Ajou* [1945] K.B. 364, the C.A. left open
the question whether a slander which imputes to a corporation an offence which, in the case of an
individual, is punishable with imprisonment is actionable *per se*. It is submitted that, as the law stands at
present, the answer ought to be in the negative, for if the basis of this species of slander actionable *per se* is
jeopardy of imprisonment, a corporation, being an artificial person, cannot be imprisoned; and if its basis
is the probability of social ostracism, a corporation cannot as such be subjected to *social* ostracism, though
ostracism of it as a trading body is possible. See Gatley, *op. cit.*, pp. 78–79.
[50] *Bloodworth* v. *Gray* 7 Man. & G. 334.
[51] Bacon, Abr. (7th ed.) vii, 266–267 (slander). The Porter Committee (Cmd. 7536), para. 45, suggested it
covered "such contagious skin complaints as are often caused by personal uncleanliness."
[52] *James* v. *Rutlech*, 4 Rep. 17a; ambiguous words were there interpreted *mitiori sensu, i.e.* in the sense more
favourable to the defendant. Hence at that time to charge a person with "pox" (which might mean venereal
disease or smallpox) was regarded as an accusation of the less repulsive ailment—smallpox. In *Villers* v.
Monsley (1769) 2 Wils. 403, there were *obiter dicta* that oral imputation of the itch was not actionable, but
the case itself was one of libel, not slander.
[53] Held in *Kerr* v. *Kennedy* [1942] 1 K.B. 409 to include an imputation of lesbianism.
[54] s.1.

provides that in this exception, "the plaintiff shall not recover more costs than damages, unless the judge shall certify that there was reasonable ground for bringing the action."[55]

(4) Imputation of unfitness or incompetence

Imputation of unfitness, dishonesty or incompetence in any office, profession, calling, trade or business held or carried on by the plaintiff at the time when the slander was published. This is by far the most important because the most frequently invoked exception. At common law its scope was severely restricted by the rule that the slander must be spoken of the plaintiff in the way of his office so that it was not, for example, slander actionable *per se* to say of a schoolmaster that he had committed adultery with one of the school cleaners.[56] Now, however, it is provided by section 2 of the Defamation Act 1952, "In an action for slander in respect of words calculated to disparage the plaintiff in any office, profession, calling, trade or business held or carried on by him at the time of publication, it shall not be necessary to allege or prove special damage whether or not the words are spoken of the plaintiff in the way of his office, profession, calling, trade or business." It is thought, therefore, that any words spoken of a man which are reasonably likely to injure him in his office, profession, calling, trade or business will be actionable *per se*.[57]

At common law a distinction was taken between profitable and purely honorary offices, and in the case of the latter slander was not actionable *per se* unless, if true, it would have been a ground for removing the plaintiff from his office.[58] The wording of section 2 of the Defamation Act 1952, however, appears to be wide enough to be interpreted so as to put an end to this distinction.[59]

(5) Reason for exceptions

Two questions may well be asked by the student. One is, "Why should some, but not all, slanders be actionable *per se*?" The other is, "Why has not the distinction been applied to libels?" The answers to both questions are historical.[60]

---

[55] See *Russo* v. *Cole* [1966] 1 W.L.R. 248.

[56] *Jones* v. *Jones* [1916] 2 A.C. 481; *De Stempel* v. *Dunkels* (1937) 54 T.L.R. 289; 55 T.L.R. 655; *Hopwood* v. *Muirson* [1945] K.B. 313 ("The slander was upon the solicitor as a man; not upon the man as a solicitor").

[57] It matters not how humble the office may be, so long as it is lawful (Gatley, *op. cit.*, p. 89, Clerk and Lindsell, *Torts* (16th ed.), para. 21–25) and a man may hold more than one office at the same time: *Bull* v. *Vazquez* [1947] 1 All E.R. 334. The exception does not include slander calculated to disparage the plaintiff in the performance of a duty compulsorily imposed upon citizens: *Cleghorn* v. *Sadler* [1945] K.B. 325 (firewatching in wartime).

[58] *e.g. Alexander* v. *Jenkinson* [1892] 1 Q.B. 797. To say of a justice of the peace, "He is an ass and a beetle-headed justice," was not actionable *per se*, for it imputes ignorance of the law and he need know none (cited in *How* v. *Prinn* (1702) 2 Salk. 695; Holt 652).

[59] Clerk and Lindsell, *Torts* (16th ed.), para. 21–28. *cf.* Gatley, *op. cit.*, p. 87; *Robinson* v. *Ward* (1958) 108 L.J. 491. A false charge of dishonesty even though not a ground for removal is in any case actionable *per se*: *Booth* v. *Arnold* [1895] 1 Q.B. 571.

[60] Holdsworth, "Defamation in the Sixteenth and Seventeenth Centuries" (1924) 40 L.Q.R. 302, 397; (1925) 41 L.Q.R. 13 esp. at 40 L.Q.R. 388–400; 41 L.Q.R. 14–17. Kaye, "Libel and Slander—Two Torts or One?" (1975) 91 L.Q.R. 524 modifies some of Holdsworth's conclusions.

As to the first, in early times, apart from some inadequate statutes, defamation was not actionable at common law, but was redressible only in the ecclesiastical or local courts. Eventually, the common law courts allowed an action on the case for defamatory words, whether written or spoken, and, just because it was an action on the case, damage had to be proved. In many cases, however, the allegation was of such a nature that it would have been foolish to require a proof of loss and damage came to be presumed. This is probably the origin of the exceptions (apart from the statutory one under the Slander of Women Act 1891) to the rule that slander requires proof of "special damage."[61] The category of slanders actionable *per se* seems to have accounted for a substantial majority of the reported cases in the seventeenth century[62] and, so popular did an action for defamatory words become that the courts seem to have felt that they were in danger of drowning in a flood of actions. The solution adopted was to dissect opprobrious epithets with the same care as if they had been technical terms in a conveyance of property— the so-called *mitiori sensu* rule which required that if at all possible the words must be construed in a non-defamatory sense.[63] This absurd rule was expunged from the law at the end of the seventeenth century, particularly by Holt C.J.

As to the second question, "Why is it unnecessary ever to prove special damage in libel?" Holdsworth's answer was that in *King* v. *Lake*[64] in 1670 the courts created a new tort of libel, influenced partly by the absurd technicalities which had invaded the action on the case for slander and partly by the demise of the Star Chamber, which had dealt with defamatory words as a crime. It seems likely, however, that what *King* v. *Lake* decided was not that all written words were actionable *per se* but merely that the method of publication in that case (printing of a petition and sending it to members of the House of Commons) was so presumptively damaging that it should be included in the category of defamation actionable *per se*.[65] The idea that there was a sharp distinction between libel (written) and slander (spoken) seems to be based on eighteenth-century interpretations of *King* v. *Lake* and was only firmly established in the law in 1812.[66]

ESSENTIALS OF DEFAMATION GENERALLY

Whether defamation consists of libel or slander the following requisites are common to both, and must be proved by the plaintiff:

---

[61] Kaye, *loc. cit.*, pp. 527–528. No satisfactory explanation can be given of why an accusation of crime is actionable *per se* only if the crime is punishable by imprisonment. Holdsworth suggested that it may have been connected with the division of offences cognisable by the common law courts and the ecclesiastical courts.

[62] Kaye, *loc. cit.*, pp. 527–528, who cites March's *Actions for Slander and Arbitrement.*

[63] The classic example is *Holt* v. *Astgrigg* (1608) Cro. Jac. 184 (statement that "Sir Thomas Holt struck his cook on the head with a cleaver, and cleaved his head; the one part lay on the one shoulder and another part on the other," not an accusation of homicide because it did not aver that the cook died).

[64] Hard. 470.

[65] Kaye, *loc. cit.*, pp. 531–532.

[66] *Thorley* v. *Lord Kerry*, 4 Taunt. 355. Kaye, *loc. cit.*, p. 539, comments that the libel-slander distinction was "based not on policy or rationalization but on the characteristic late eighteenth century tendency to follow the line of least resistance."

1. The words must be defamatory.
2. They must refer to the plaintiff.
3. They must be "maliciously" published.

Words must be defamatory

As we have seen, to be defamatory the words must tend to lower the plaintiff's reputation in the estimation of right-minded persons, or must tend to cause him to be shunned or avoided. For the issue to be decided, therefore, it is essential to know the very words on which the plaintiff founds his claim. A plaintiff is not entitled to bring a libel action on a letter which he has never seen and of the contents of which he is unaware but which he merely suspects to have been written and to contain words defamatory of him.[67]

(1) *Abuse*

It is commonly said that mere vulgar spoken abuse is neither defamation nor indeed any other tort[68] but this needs some explanation. Spoken words which are prima facie slanderous are not actionable if it is clear that they were uttered merely as general vituperation *and* were so understood by those who heard them.[69] This makes the manner in which the words were spoken very important in determining whether they were mere vituperation or slander. It is possible that the same word may or may not be slanderous according as it is said deliberately in cold blood, or is bawled out at the height of a violent quarrel.[70] "The manner in which the words were pronounced, and various other circumstances might explain the meaning of the word." So Sir James Mansfield C.J. in *Penfold* v. *Westcote*[71] where the defendant called out, "Why don't you come out you blackguard, rascal, scoundral [*sic*], Penfold, you are a thief," and it was left to the jury to say whether the general abusive terms accompanying "thief" reduced "thief" itself to mere abuse; and the jury gave a verdict for the plaintiff.

The speaker of the words must take the risk of his hearers construing them as defamatory and not simply abusive, and the burden of proof is upon him to show that a reasonable man would not have understood them in the former sense.[72]

If the words be written, not spoken, they cannot be protected as mere abuse,[73] for the defendant had time for reflection before he wrote and his

---

[67] *Collins* v. *Jones* [1955] 1 Q.B. 564.
[68] "For mere general abuse spoken, no action lies": Mansfield C.J. in *Thorley* v. *Kerry* (1812) 4 Taunt. 355, 365; Pollock C.B. and Wilde B. in *Parkins* v. *Scott* (1862) 1 H. & C. 153, 158, 159.
[69] Gatley, *op. cit.*, pp. 46, 62, 81–82. See too, Pound in *Selected Essays on the Law of Torts*, pp. 110–118.
[70] *Field* v. *Davis* [1955] C.L.Y. 1543 (defendant called plaintiff, who was a married woman, "a tramp." Held, this expression was capable of a defamatory meaning but considering the obvious temper of the defendant, it was understood by those who heard it as mere abuse). See also *Australian Newspaper Co. Ltd.* v. *Bennett* [1894] A.C. 284; *Gwynne* v. *Wairarapa Times-Age Ltd.* [1972] N.Z.L.R. 586.
[71] (1806) 2 B. & P. (N.R.) 335.
[72] Gatley, *op. cit.*, p. 46.
[73] Gatley, *op. cit.*, p. 82. But see Salmond and Heuston, *Torts* (19th ed.), p. 156.

readers may know nothing of any heated dispute or other circumstances which may have led him to write what he did; but it is quite possible for them to be not defamatory for some other reason.

Although there is no civil remedy for mere vituperation, a person may be bound over by justices of the peace to be of good behaviour if he utters rash, quarrelsome or unmannerly words which tend to a breach of the peace or which deter an officer from doing his duty.[74]

(2) *Function of jury*

In determining whether the words are defamatory, the functions of judge and jury must be carefully distinguished.[75] After fierce controversy, Fox's Libel Act 1792, which professed to be a declaratory Act, allotted to the jury in a criminal trial for libel the task of deciding whether the words are defamatory or not; the Act was necessary because judges had been usurping this function and had thereby warped criminal trials for seditious libels into modes for securing the conviction of political offenders. The provision of Fox's Act with respect to criminal libel has long been regarded as also applicable to civil actions for defamation.

(3) *Function of judge*

The power given to the jury by Fox's Act is not unlimited and the judge can exercise control in three ways.

First, if he decides to leave the case to the jury, he must tell them what defamation means in law.

Secondly, if he thinks that no reasonable man could regard the words as defamatory, he must withdraw the case from the jury.[76] "To put it from the point of view of an appellate court, the question of libel or no libel should have been left to the jury if it cannot be said that twelve men could not reasonably have come to the conclusion that the words were defamatory."[77] *Capital and Counties Bank Ltd.* v. *Henty*[78] is a leading case on this. Henty & Sons, a firm of brewers, were in the habit of receiving, in payment from their customers, cheques on various branches of the Capital and Counties Bank,

---

[74] Stone's *Justices' Manual*.

[75] Despite the general decline of jury trial in civil cases, the majority of actions for defamation are still tried by jury: see *Rothermere* v. *Times Newspapers Ltd.* [1973] 1 W.L.R. 448. For the recommendations of the Faulks Committee, see *post*, p. 356.

[76] *Turner* v. *Bowley* (1896) 12 T.L.R. 402; *Nevill* v. *Fine Art Insurance Co. Ltd.* [1897] A.C. 68; *Sim* v. *Stretch* [1936] 2 All E.R. 1237, H.L.; *Jones* v. *Skelton* [1963] 1 W.L.R. 1362, P.C. Only in a very clear case will the court dispose of the matter on an application to strike out the action: *Drummond-Jackson* v. *B.M.A.* [1970] 1 W.L.R. 688. The dissenting judgment of Lord Denning M.R. carries an important criticism of present-day practice. It seems that an interlocutory ruling refusing to hold that words are incapable of a defamatory meaning does not bind the trial judge to hold that they are so capable: *Morgan* v. *Odhams Press Ltd.* [1971] 1 W.L.R. 1239.

[77] *Turner* v. *Metro-Goldwyn-Mayer Pictures Ltd.* [1950] 1 All E.R. 449, 454, *per* Lord Porter; *Morris* v. *Sanders Universal Products* [1954] 1 W.L.R. 67. Words may still be capable of a defamatory meaning even though they make it clear that the law was on the plaintiff's side: *Clarke* v. *Associated Newspapers* [1955] C.L.Y. 1542.

[78] (1882) 7 App.Cas. 741.

which the bank cashed for the convenience of Hentys at a particular branch of which X was manager. In consequence of a squabble with X, Hentys sent a printed circular to a large number of their customers (who knew nothing of the squabble), "Henty & Sons hereby give notice that they will not receive in payment cheques drawn on any of the branches of the Capital and Counties Bank." The circular became known to other persons and there was a run on the bank, which sued Hentys for libel on the ground that the circular imputed insolvency. There was much difference of opinion in the courts below, and it was only after hearing the case twice argued that the House of Lords, by a majority of four to one, held that the circular, taken in conjunction with the circumstances of its publication, did not constitute evidence from which any reasonable person would infer such an imputation; that there was no case to go to the jury; and that the defendants were not liable. Lord Selborne L.C. said that the fact that some customers showed the circular to strangers was not the fault of Hentys, who had not authorised the communication,[79] and that where words in their natural meaning were not libellous, evidence must be brought to show that reasonable men might be led to understand them in a libellous sense. Both these propositions are unexceptionable and there are no doubt many reasons why a creditor may refuse to accept a cheque on a particular bank. Yet it might be thought that the first reason that would occur to any reasonable person would be that the bank was financially unsound. The decision has been subjected to considerable criticism[80] and Salmon L.J. has said that the principles, never better formulated than in *Henty's* case, were perhaps never worse applied.[81]

Generally the controversy is whether the words are capable of bearing a defamatory meaning at all, but in *Lewis* v. *Daily Telegraph Ltd.*[82] the defendants admitted that the words were defamatory. What they denied was that the words were defamatory in the particular sense alleged by the plaintiffs. The defendants had published a paragraph in their newspaper stating that officers of the City of London Fraud Squad were investigating the affairs of the plaintiff company and the plaintiffs alleged that these words carried the meaning that the company's affairs were conducted fraudulently or dishonestly. By a majority the House of Lords decided that the words were not capable of bearing that meaning.[83] As Lord Devlin pointed out, one cannot make a rule about the fundamental question—what is the meaning which the words convey to the ordinary man—but the ordinary sensible man is not capable of thinking that whenever there is a police

---

[79] 7 App.Cas. 746–747.
[80] Scrutton L.J. in *Youssoupoff* v. *Metro-Goldwyn-Mayer Pictures Ltd.* (1934) 50 T.L.R. 581, 594, thought that the law and the facts got pretty far apart from each other in *Henty's* case; and see *per* Goddard L.J. in *Hopwood* v. *Muirson* [1945] K.B. 313, 318.
[81] *Slim* v. *Daily Telegraph Ltd.* [1968] 2 Q.B. 157, 187.
[82] [1964] A.C. 234, Weir, *Casebook on Tort* (6th ed.), p. 455.
[83] See also *Mirror Newspapers Ltd.* v. *Harrison* (1982) 42 A.L.R. 487. *cf. Hayward* v. *Thompson* [1982] Q.B. 47.

inquiry there is guilt. Otherwise "it would be almost impossible to give accurate information about anything."[84]

Thirdly, if the words are obviously defamatory, the judge, although he cannot directly tell the jury that they are so, may nevertheless indicate to them that the evidence cannot bear any other interpretation. If, in spite of this, they find a verdict for the defendant, a new trial will be ordered on appeal.[85] But this is so stark an interference with the normal functions of a jury that the courts are very loth to make such an order, and examples of it in the reports are rare indeed.[86]

(4) *Innuendo*

The words of which the plaintiff complains may be either (*a*) defamatory in their natural and ordinary meaning or (*b*) defamatory only, or additionally to (*a*), in the light of facts and circumstances known to persons to whom the words were published.

As to (*a*) words can, of course, convey different meanings to different people[87] and the plaintiff is not obliged to give an interpretation of the words either in his statement of claim or in his evidence.[88] It is as defamatory of A to say that justice miscarried when he was acquitted of murdering X, as it is to say outright that he did murder X.[89] But it must be remembered that, as Lord Blackburn said, "there are no words so plain that they may not be published with reference to such circumstances, and to such persons knowing these circumstances, as to convey a meaning very different from that which would be understood from the same words used under different circumstances."[90] Or, we might add, at different periods of history, and this makes it hazardous to say dogmatically of any epithet that it is or is not, for all time and in all places and circumstances, defamatory. To call a man a "cony-catcher" would convey little to most people today but at one time it

---

[84] *Ibid.* at pp. 285–286. "A distinction needs to be drawn between the reader's understanding of what a newspaper is saying and judgments or conclusions which he may reach as a result of his own beliefs and prejudices. It is one thing to say that a statement is capable of bearing an imputation defamatory of the plaintiff because the ordinary reasonable reader would understand it in that sense, drawing on his own knowledge and experience of human affairs in order to reach that result. It is quite another thing to say that a statement is capable of bearing such an imputation merely because it excites in some readers a belief or prejudice from which they proceed to arrive at a conclusion unfavourable to the plaintiff. The defamatory quality of the published material is to be determined by the first, not the second proposition": *Mirror Newspapers Ltd.* v. *Harrison, supra, per* Mason J.

[85] *Levi* v. *Milne* (1827) 4 Bing. 195; Sankey L.J. in *Broome* v. *Agar* (1928) 138 L.T. 698, 701–702; Scrutton L.J. *ibid.* at p. 699, and in *Youssoupoff* v. *Metro-Goldwyn-Mayer Pictures Ltd.* (1934) 50 T.L.R. 581, 584; Lord Buckmaster in *Lockhart* v. *Harrison* (1928) 139 L.T. 521, 523.

[86] *Broome* v. *Agar* (1928) 138 L.T. 698.

[87] See *Slim* v. *Daily Telegraph Ltd.* [1968] 2 Q.B. 157, 171–177, *per* Diplock L.J. It is respectfully submitted that his Lordship overstates the difficulties when he insists that the legal process requires that a single "right" meaning be given to the words for the purposes of the action. Cannot a jury or a judge alone recognise and award damages upon the basis that the words may convey different meanings to different reasonable people? *cf. ibid. per* Lord Denning M.R. at pp. 168–169.

[88] *Cadam* v. *Beaverbrook Newspapers Ltd.* [1959] 1 Q.B. 413, 525, *per* Morris L.J.; *Lewis* v. *Daily Telegraph Ltd.* [1964] A.C. 234, 265, *per* Lord Morris; *Jones* v. *Skelton* [1963] 1 W.L.R. 1362, P.C.

[89] See *Loughans* v. *Odhams Press Ltd.* [1963] 1 Q.B. 299, as explained by Upjohn L.J. in *Grubb* v. *Bristol United Press Ltd.* [1963] 1 Q.B. 309, 331–333. *Hoare* v. *Silverlock* (1848) 12 Q.B. 624 is, perhaps, an extreme example.

[90] *Capital and Counties Bank* v. *Henty* (1882) 7 App.Cas. 741, 771.

was a well-known word for a swindler. Conversely, most people nowadays know what the Mafia is and so words alleging that a company is controlled by the Mafia are defamatory in their natural and ordinary meaning.[91] If the words are fairly capable of several meanings, some defamatory and some innocent, the case should be left to the jury.[92] But where the statement has only one reasonable meaning which is harmless, the court will not torture into it a defamatory meaning which no doubt is possible, but which can be reached only by inventing facts which are not disclosed and are in fact non-existent.

Where, however, the words are not defamatory in their natural and ordinary meaning, or where the plaintiff wishes to rely upon an additional defamatory meaning in which they were understood by persons having knowledge of particular facts,[93] then an innuendo is required. This is a statement by the plaintiff of the meaning which he attributes to the words,[94] and he must prove the existence of facts to support that meaning.[95] If such facts do not exist, the innuendo fails and may be struck out of the statement of claim,[96] though the plaintiff may still fall back on the natural and ordinary meaning of the words.[97] Separate causes of action exist in respect of that meaning and of each innuendo that is proved.[98]

One of the best-known cases of the successful use of the innuendo is *Tolley v. Fry & Sons Ltd.*[99] The plaintiff, a famous amateur golfer, was caricatured by the defendants, without his knowledge or consent, in an advertisement of their chocolate which depicted him with a packet of it protruding from his pocket. A caddy was represented with him, who also had a packet of chocolate the excellence of which he likened, in some doggerel verse, to the excellence of the plaintiff's drive. The plaintiff alleged in his innuendo that the defendants thereby meant that the plaintiff had agreed to let his portrait be exhibited for advertisement, that he had done this for gain, and that he had thus prostituted his reputation as an amateur golfer. The House of Lords held that the caricature, as explained by the evidence, was capable of

---

[91] *Associated Leisure Ltd.* v. *Associated Newspapers Ltd.* [1970] 2 Q.B. 450.

[92] *Cassidy* v. *Daily Mirror Newspapers Ltd.* [1929] 2 K.B. 331, 339–340, *per* Scrutton L.J.; *Newstead* v. *London Express Newspapers Ltd.* [1940] 1 K.B. 377, 396, *per* du Parcq L.J.; *English, etc. Society Ltd.* v. *Odhams Press Ltd.* [1940] 1 K.B. 440; *Sim* v. *Stretch* [1936] 2 All E.R. 1237, 1241 where Lord Atkin cited Brett L.J. in *Capital and Counties Bank* v. *Henty* (1880) 5 C.P.D. 514, 541: "It seems to me unreasonable that when there are a number of good interpretations, the only bad one should be seized upon to give a defamatory sense to the document." *Turner* v. *Metro-Goldwyn-Mayer Pictures Ltd.* [1950] 2 All E.R. 449, 454; *Pyke* v. *Hibernian Bank* [1950] I.R. 195; *Jones* v. *Skelton* [1963] 1 W.L.R. 1362, 1370, *per* Lord Morris.

[93] That is to say, so understood at the time they were published. Subsequent knowledge which makes the recipients look back on the words in a different light will not make them defamatory: *Grappelli* v. *Derek Block Holdings Ltd.* [1981] 1 W.L.R. 822. *cf.* Morgan [1981] C.L.J. 245.

[94] The plaintiff is bound by the meaning he attributes to the words in the innuendo as pleaded: *"Truth" (N.Z.) Ltd.* v. *Holloway* [1960] 1 W.L.R. 997, P.C.

[95] Since 1949 these facts must be pleaded with proper particularity: R.S.C., Ord. 82, r. 3(1).

[96] *Grubb* v. *Bristol United Press Ltd.* [1963] 1 Q.B. 309, applying *Capital and Counties Bank* v. *Henty* (1882) L.R. 7 App.Cas. 741. *cf. Loughans* v. *Odhams Press Ltd.* [1963] 1 Q.B. 299.

[97] *Lewis* v. *Daily Telegraph Ltd.* [1963] 1 Q.B. 340, affirmed [1964] A.C. 234.

[98] Common Law Procedure Act 1852; *Watkin* v. *Hall* (1868) L.R. 3 Q.B. 896; *Sim* v. *Stretch* [1936] 2 All E.R. 1237; *Grubb* v. *Bristol United Press Ltd., supra*; *Lewis* v. *Daily Telegraph Ltd., supra.* It is most important to distinguish carefully between these separate causes of action. There may be a defence to some but not to others. Nevertheless, Lord Devlin doubted the value of the rule: [1964] A.C. 234, 279.

[99] [1931] A.C. 333.

being thus construed; for golfers testified that any amateur golfer who assented to such advertisement might be called upon to resign his membership of any reputable club, and it also appeared from correspondence between the defendants and their advertising agents that they were quite alive to the possible effect of the advertisement on the plaintiff's amateur status.

This type of innuendo, the "true" innuendo, should be distinguished from the "false" innuendo in which the plaintiff does not rely upon extrinsic facts to support the defamatory meaning of the words, but merely states a particular inference which, he says, is to be drawn from the words themselves.[1] Here the plaintiff is not alleging a separate cause of action, but is relying upon the natural and ordinary meaning of the words.[2] For example, "if the defendant published of John Smith: 'His name is certainly not George Washington,' then, however much the defendant may argue that the words were a harmless truism concerned merely with nomenclature, the natural and ordinary implication of the words is that John Smith is untruthful; and presumably the jury would find that to be the ordinary meaning of the words."[3] The basic rule in such a case is that it is unnecessary to plead an innuendo explaining George Washington's reputation for truthfulness, but such a restrictive approach has led to difficulties: not only is the line between the true and false innuendo difficult to draw, but the defendant may be put in serious difficulty where, although the words clearly do not demand a true innuendo, their meaning is obscure or they are open to a number of interpretations.[4] The courts sought to meet this difficulty by stressing the desirability of pleading any meaning alleged by the plaintiff which was not immediately obvious on reading the words,[5] but this proved insufficient and the Court of Appeal in a series of decisions stated that unless the defamatory statement has only one meaning which is clear and explicit it is *necessary* for the fair trial of the action for the plaintiff to plead the meaning he ascribes to the

---

[1] Lord Devlin regrets the use of "true" and "false," but he agrees that there is a difference between the "legal" innuendo, which requires supporting facts, and the "popular" innuendo, which may not: *Lewis* v. *Daily Telegraph Ltd., supra*, at pp. 279–280.

[2] *Jones* v. *Skelton* [1963] 1 W.L.R. 1362, 1370–1371, *per* Lord Morris. *Taylor* v. *Beere* [1982] 1 N.Z.L.R. 81 which, like *Tolley* v. *Fry*, involves unauthorised publication of the plaintiff's likeness, illustrates the false innuendo.

[3] *Grubb* v. *Bristol United Press Ltd.* [1963] 1 Q.B. 309, 327, *per* Holroyd Pearce L.J. See also the examples given by Davies L.J., *ibid.* at pp. 336–337.

[4] "The time has surely come when specialist practitioners in the field of defamation must do some re-thinking about the desirability of pleading innuendoes far more freely than appears to have been done during the last 15 or 20 years.": *S. & K. Holdings Ltd.* v. *Throgmorton Publications Ltd.* [1972] 1 W.L.R. 1036, 1041, *per* Edmund Davies L.J.

[5] *Lewis* v. *Daily Telegraph, supra*; see also *Loughans* v. *Odhams Press Ltd.* [1963] 1 Q.B. 299; *Grubb* v. *Bristol United Press Ltd., supra*; *Drummond-Jackson* v. *B.M.A.* [1970] 1 W.L.R. 688, 694, *per* Lord Denning M.R.

words.[6] For pleading purposes, therefore, the distinction between true and false innuendoes has become blurred, though it has not entirely disappeared.[7]

(5) *Juxtaposition*

Mere juxtaposition to noxious matter may make an otherwise innocent representation defamatory. The most famous instance of this is *Monson v. Tussauds Ltd.*[8] where the defendants, who kept a waxworks exhibition, had exhibited a wax model of the plaintiff, with a gun, in a room adjoining the "Chamber of Horrors." The plaintiff had been tried for murder in Scotland and released on a verdict of "Not Proven" and a representation of the scene of the alleged murder was displayed in the Chamber of Horrors. The Court of Appeal considered that though in all the circumstances the case was not clear enough for the issue of an interlocutory injunction, the exhibition was capable of being found by a jury to be defamatory. On the other hand, the mere fact that an article about the plaintiff appeared in a newspaper where numerous articles attacking dishonest business men had appeared on other occasions was held incapable of carrying a defamatory inference.[9] If reliance is placed upon juxtaposition it must be shown that a reasonable man, seeing the two objects together, would draw from their relative positions an inference defamatory of the plaintiff.

(6) *Knowledge of defendant immaterial*

Subject to the provisions of the Defamation Act 1952,[10] it is immaterial whether the defendant knew, or did not know, of external facts which turn a presumptively innocent statement into a defamatory one. He must take the risk of that, and he is liable either way, provided the defamatory meaning which is alleged could reasonably have been put upon the words. In *Cassidy v. Daily Mirror Newspapers Ltd.*[11] the defendants published in their newspaper a photograph of one C. and Miss X together with the words, "Mr. C.,

---

[6] *Allsop v. Church of England Newspaper Ltd.* [1972] 2 Q.B. 161; *S. & K. Holdings Ltd. v. Throgmorton Publications Ltd., supra*; *D.D.S.A. Pharmaceuticals Ltd. v. Times Newspapers Ltd.* [1973] 1 Q.B. 21. In *Slim v. Daily Telegraph Ltd.* [1968] 2 Q.B. 157, 175, Diplock L.J. said that if a plaintiff sets out in his statement of claim particular defamatory meanings, then he is in effect estopped from contending at the trial that the words bear a more injurious meaning, but he may contend that they bear some other, less injurious but still defamatory, meaning. But if plaintiffs are to be encouraged, in the interests of clarity, to plead their interpretations of the natural and ordinary meanings of words, they should not be penalised by too severe an application of this rule. Otherwise the result will be that they will keep their options open by reverting to the old practice of pleading every possible defamatory meaning, however far-fetched, which the ingenuity of their counsel can devise. See also *ibid.* at pp. 184–186, *per* Salmon L.J.

[7] Thus in an action based on a popular innuendo in a newspaper or book it is unnecessary to specify persons to whom it was published, but in the case of a true innuendo it is necessary to specify such persons since there is no defamation unless the matter is published to a person with knowledge of the extrinsic facts: *Fullam v. Newcastle Chronicle Ltd.* [1977] 1 W.L.R. 651; *Grappelli v. Derek Block (Holdings) Ltd.* [1981] 1 W.L.R. 822. For possible exceptions, see *Fullam* at p. 659 and *Grappelli* at p. 830.

[8] [1894] 1 Q.B. 671; *Garbett v. Hazell, Watson and Viney Ltd.* [1943] 2 All E.R. 359.

[9] *Wheeler v. Somerfield* [1966] 2 Q.B. 94. In *Astaire v. Campling* [1966] 1 W.L.R. 34 it was held that a newspaper article identifying by name a "Mr. X" about whom derogatory articles had appeared in other newspapers was not capable of a defamatory meaning.

[10] *Post*, p. 313.

[11] [1929] 2 K.B. 331.

the race-horse owner, and Miss X, whose engagement has been announced." Mrs. C. was, and was known among her acquaintances, as the lawful wife of C., although she and C. were not living together. The information on which the defendants based their statement was derived from C. alone, and they had made no effort to verify it from any other source. Mrs. C. sued them for libel, the innuendo being that C. was not her husband but lived with her in immoral cohabitation. A majority of the Court of Appeal held that the innuendo was established and, the jury having found that the publication conveyed to reasonable persons an aspersion on the plaintiff's moral character, that she was entitled to damages.[12]

Words must refer to the plaintiff

If the plaintiff is mentioned by name, there is usually no difficulty about this, and it is to be observed that there is no requirement that the defendant should have intended to refer to the plaintiff. In *Hulton & Co.* v. *Jones*,[13] H. & Co. were newspaper proprietors and published in their paper a humorous account of a motor festival at Dieppe in which imputations were cast on the morals of one Artemus Jones, a churchwarden at Peckham. This person was intended to be, and was believed by the writer of the article and the editor of the paper to be, purely fictitious. In fact there was a barrister named Artemus Jones, who was not a churchwarden, did not live at Peckham and had taken no part in the Dieppe festival. He sued H. & Co. for libel, and friends of his swore that they believed that the article referred to him. The jury returned a verdict for the plaintiff and the House of Lords refused to disturb this. They held that if reasonable people would think the language to be defamatory of the plaintiff it was immaterial that the defendants did not intend to defame him. In *Newstead* v. *London Express Newspaper Ltd.*,[14] the Court of Appeal carried *Hulton* v. *Jones* farther in two directions. They held that (*a*) the principle applies where the statement truly relates to a *real* person, A, and is mistakenly but reasonably thought to refer to another real person, B; and (*b*) absence of negligence on the defendant's part is relevant only in the sense that it may be considered by the jury in determining whether reasonable people would regard the statement as referring to the plaintiff; otherwise it is no defence. In *Newstead's* case, the statement was that "Harold Newstead, thirty-year-old Camberwell man," had been convicted of bigamy. This was true of a Camberwell barman of that name, but it was untrue of the plaintiff, Harold Newstead, aged about thirty, who

---

[12] Followed in *Hough* v. *London Express Newspaper Ltd.* [1940] 2 K.B. 507, where it was pointed out that it need not be proved that reasonable persons actually did so understand the words; it is enough to prove that the words were published to persons having knowledge of the special facts, and so might understand the words in the secondary and defamatory sense: see Gatley, *op. cit.*, p. 48. Both cases were, however, criticised by Lord Denning M.R. in *Morgan* v. *Odhams Press Ltd.* [1970] 1 W.L.R. 820, 829, but, *semble*, only on the ground that the libel did not adequately refer to the plaintiff. See *post*, p. 311.

[13] [1910] A.C. 20. Applied by Scrutton and Slesser L.JJ. in *Youssoupoff* v. *Metro-Goldwyn-Mayer Pictures Ltd.* (1934) 50 T.L.R. 581, 582–583, 587. Weir, *Casebook on Tort* (6th ed.), p. 460. See now the Defamation Act 1952, *post*, p. 313.

[14] [1940] 1 K.B. 377. *cf. Shaw* v. *London Express Newspaper Ltd.* (1925) 41 T.L.R. 475, and see *Boston* v. *W.S. Bagshaw & Sons* [1966] 1 W.L.R. 1126, 1131, *per* Lord Denning M.R.; 1134, *per* Harman L.J.

assisted his father in a hairdressing business in Camberwell. The defendants were held liable.[15] Cases of this type may now be affected by the defence of "unintentional defamation" under section 4 of the Defamation Act 1952, which is considered below.

Material may be defamatory of the plaintiff even though it does not mention him by name and even if it contains no "key or pointer" indicating that it refers to him. Thus in *Morgan v. Odhams Press Ltd.*,[16] a newspaper article alleged that a girl had been kidnapped by a dog-doping gang. At the relevant time the girl had been staying at the plaintiff's flat and the plaintiff produced six witnesses who swore that they understood from the article that he was connected with the gang. A majority of the House of Lords held that these facts constituted sufficient material to leave the jury. The test of whether the words "refer to the plaintiff" in the special sense here used is whether a hypothetical, sensible reader, having knowledge of the special circumstances, would believe that the plaintiff was referred to, and due allowance must be made for the fact that such a reader will not give a sensational article in a popular newspaper the attention which a lawyer would bestow on a perusal of evidence.[17] Nor is it relevant that no person who actually read the defamatory words believed them true.[18]

Where a publication does not sufficiently identify the plaintiff he may nevertheless rely for identification on a subsequent publication by the same defendant.[19] It has been said that were the law otherwise, it would be open to a newspaper to publish a virulent libel without identifying the person defamed but adding a statement that the victim would be identified in a week's time.[20] However, the same result might be achieved by treating the second, identifying publication as a republication of the first or as an innuendo.

(1) *Defamation of a class*

The question whether an individual can sue in respect of words which are directed against a group, or body, or class of persons generally was considered by the House of Lords in *Knuppfer v. London Express Newspaper Ltd.*,[21] and the law may be summarised as follows: (*a*) The crucial question is whether the words were published "of the plaintiff" in the sense that he can

---

[15] But the damages were assessed at one farthing.

[16] [1971] 1 W.L.R. 1239; (1971) 87 L.Q.R. 452. *Astaire* v. *Campling* (*supra*, n. 9) was distinguished because in that case, although the article referred by name to the plaintiff, it did not itself defame him. *cf. Hayward* v. *Thompson, infra.*

[17] The minority in *Morgan* dissented because they thought there was no material in the article which a reasonable man could sensibly infer to apply to the plaintiff: they did not accede to the "key or pointer" argument which had found favour in the court below.

[18] At p. 1246, *per* Lord Reid, who refers to it as a proposition so obvious that no one has had the hardihood to dispute it. See also *Hough* v. *London Express Newspaper* [1940] 2 K.B. 507, 515.

[19] *Hayward* v. *Thompson* [1982] Q.B. 47, distinguishing *Grappelli* v. *Derek Block (Holdings) Ltd.* [1981] 1 W.L.R. 822, where the issue was not identification but the meaning of the words.

[20] *Hayward* v. *Thompson, supra*, at p. 72 *per* Sir Stanley Rees.

[21] [1944] A.C. 116; Weir, *Casebook on Tort* (6th ed.), p. 463; *Schloimovitz* v. *Clarendon Press, The Times*, July 6, 1973. The Porter Committee, paras. 30–32, did not recommend any general change in the existing law to deal with group defamation and the Faulks Committee did not consider the matter.

be said to be personally pointed at[22] rather than the application of any arbitrary general rule, subject to exceptions, that liability cannot arise from words published of a class.[23] (b) Normally where the defamatory statement is directed to a class of persons no individual belonging to the class is entitled to say that the words were written or spoken of himself. "No doubt it is true to say that a class cannot be defamed as a class, nor can an individual be defamed by a general reference to the class to which he belongs."[24] As Willes J. said in *Eastwood* v. *Holmes*, "If a man wrote that all lawyers were thieves, no particular lawyer could sue him unless there was something to point to the particular individual."[25] What the psalmist said in haste of all men was not defamatory even if it had been untrue. (c) Words which appear to apply to a class may be actionable if there is something in the words, or the circumstances under which they were published which indicates a particular plaintiff or plaintiffs.[26] (d) Again if the reference is to a limited class or group, *e.g.* trustees, members of a firm, tenants of a particular building, so that the words can be said to refer to each member, all will be able to sue.[27] (e) Whether there is any evidence on which the words can be regarded as capable of referring to the plaintiff is a matter of law for the judge.[28] If there is such evidence then it is a question of fact whether the words lead reasonable people who know the plaintiff to the conclusion that they do refer to him.[29]

Just as an innuendo may mark out the plaintiff as one member of a class, so it may show that the description of a single person, real or fictitious, refers to him. Thus in *J'Anson* v. *Stuart*,[30] a newspaper paragraph stated, "This diabolical character, like Polyphemus the man-eater, has but one eye, and is well known to all persons acquainted with the name of a certain noble circumnavigator." It was clear that the plaintiff was the person indicated on his giving proof that he had one eye and bore a name similar to that of Anson, the famous admiral.

---

[22] *cf. Braddock* v. *Bevins* [1948] 1 K.B. 586, 588–589. The law as to qualified privilege at elections as stated in this case has been altered by the Defamation Act 1952, s.10. *Plummer* v. *Charman* [1962] 1 W.L.R. 1469. As to evidence to identify the plaintiff as the person libelled, see *Jozwiak* v. *Sadek* [1954] 1 W.L.R. 275; *Bottomley* v. *Bolton* (1970) 115 S.J. 61.

[23] Indeed, it has been said to be misleading to speak of class defamation: *Orme* v. *Associated Newspapers Ltd. The Times*, February 4, 1981.

[24] Per Lord Porter in *Knuppfer* v. *London Express Newspaper Ltd., supra*, at p. 124.

[25] (1858) 1 F. & F. 347, 349.

[26] *Le Fanu* v. *Malcolmson* (1848) 1 H.L.C. 637; *Orme* v. *Associated Newspapers, supra*.

[27] *Browne* v. *D.C. Thomson* 1912 S.C. 359; *Foxcroft* v. *Lacey* (1613) Hob. 89. Seventeen men indicted for conspiracy, and A said, "These defendants are those that helped to murder Henry Farrer." *Held*, each of the 17 could bring a separate action against A. See also *Booth* v. *B.C.T.V. Broadcasting System* (1982) 139 D.L.R. (3d) 88; *Farnington* v. *Leigh, The Times*, December 10, 1987.

[28] In deciding this question the size of the class, the generality of the charge and the extravagance of the accusation may all be elements to be taken into consideration, but none of them is conclusive ... Each member of a body, however large [would be] defamed when the libel consisted in the assertion that no one of the members of a community was elected unless he had committed a murder": *Knuppfer's Case* [1944] A.C. 116, 124, *per* Lord Porter.

[29] A representative action will not assist plaintiffs in a "class" case: such an action does not get over the problem of insufficient identification and is anyway not generally available in a claim for tort damages: *E.E.T.P.U.* v. *Times Newspapers* [1980] Q.B. 585.

[30] (1787) 1 T.R. 748; *Jozwiak* v. *Sadek* [1954] 1 W.L.R. 275.

(2) *"Unintentional defamation" within the Defamation Act 1952, s.4*

It has been seen above that liability for an imputation defamatory of the plaintiff does not depend on the intention of the person responsible for the main publication[31] of the statement either with regard to reference to the plaintiff,[32] or with regard to knowledge of facts which make a statement innocent on the face of it defamatory of the plaintiff.[33] Defamation may thus be "unintentional," and in its result produce hardship, especially, perhaps, for the writers of fiction and their publishers. Either or both may find themselves at the mercy of any unscrupulous person whose name happens to be the same as that of a fictitious character.[34] Accordingly a change in the law was introduced by section 4 of the Defamation Act 1952. This provides a procedure whereby, in the case of words *published innocently* as defined by the section, a defendant may avoid liability to pay damages if he is willing to publish a reasonable correction and apology, and pay the plaintiff's costs and expenses reasonably incurred as a consequence of the publication in question. The section may be summarised as follows:

1. It applies only to words published innocently as defined by the section,[35] *i.e.* if and only if the following conditions are satisfied:

(*a*) "that the publisher did not intend to publish them of and concerning that other person, and did not know of circumstances by virtue of which they might be understood to refer to him[36]; or

(*b*) that the words were not defamatory on the face of them, and the publisher did not know of circumstances by virtue of which they might be understood to be defamatory of that person,[37] and in either case that the publisher exercised all reasonable care in relation to the publication[38]; and any reference in this subsection to the publisher shall be construed as including a reference to any servant or agent of his who was concerned with the contents of the publication."

2. A person who has published words alleged to be defamatory of another person may, if he claims that the words were published innocently in relation to that other person, make an offer of amends, which must be expressed to be made for the purposes of the section and must be accompanied by an affidavit specifying the facts relied upon by the person making it to show that the words in question were published innocently in relation to the aggrieved party.[39]

---

[31] See *post*, p. 317, for innocent dissemination by persons who take a subordinate part in the distribution of a libel.

[32] *Hulton* v. *Jones* [1910] A.C. 20; *Newstead* v. *London Express* [1940] 1 K.B. 377; *ante*, p. 310.

[33] *Cassidy* v. *Daily Mirror* [1929] 2 K.B. 331; *Hough* v. *London Express* [1940] 2 K.B. 507; *ante*, p. 309.

[34] Of course, mere coincidence of name does not mean that reasonable persons would think the plaintiff was referred to.

[35] s.4(5).

[36] *cf. Hulton* v. *Jones* [1910] A.C. 20; *Newstead* v. *London Express* [1940] 1 K.B. 377.

[37] *cf. Cassidy* v. *Daily Mirror* [1929] 2 K.B. 331; *Hough* v. *London Express* [1940] 2 K.B. 507.

[38] *Ross* v. *Hopkinson* [1956] C.L.Y. 5011 (plaintiff an actress using stage name of J. S. Defendant wrote book with minor character an actress called J. S. *Held*, that the defendant could have checked whether there was in fact an actress called J. S. and therefore he had not exercised all reasonable care). *cf. Solomon* v. *Simmons, The Times*, April 10, 1954.

[39] s.4(1) (2).

3. *An offer of amends* under the section is an offer—

(*a*) in any case to publish or join in the publication of a suitable correction and apology; and

(*b*) where copies of a document or record containing the words have been distributed by or with the knowledge of the person making the offer, to take such steps as are reasonably practicable on his part for notifying persons to whom copies have been so distributed that the words are alleged to be defamatory of the party aggrieved.[40]

4. *If the offer of amends is accepted by the party aggrieved, and duly performed*, no proceedings for libel or slander may be taken or continued by that party against the party making the offer in respect of the publication in question.[41]

5. *If the offer of amends is not accepted by the party aggrieved then it is a defence* in any proceedings by him for libel or slander to prove:

(*a*) that the words were *published innocently* in relation to the plaintiff[42];

(*b*) that the offer was made as soon as practicable after the defendant received notice that they were or might be defamatory of the plaintiff[43]; and

(*c*) that if the publication was of words of which the defendant was not the author that the words were written by the author without malice.[44] Moreover for the purposes of this defence no evidence, other than evidence of facts specified in the affidavit which accompanied the offer of amends, is admissible to prove that the words were published innocently.[45]

Words must be "maliciously" published

Publication is the communication of the words to at least one person other than the person defamed.[46] Communication to the plaintiff himself is not enough, for defamation is an injury to one's reputation, and reputation is what other people think of a man, and not his own opinion of himself.[47] It is normally said that the words must be published "maliciously," but this is purely formal. Though the word is usually inserted in the plaintiff's state-

[40] s.4(3).
[41] s.4(1)(*a*). The liability of any other person jointly responsible for the publication is unaffected.
[42] s.4(1)(*b*).
[43] *Ibid*. An offer made six weeks after complaint of the libel was received from the plaintiff was held to be too late in *Ross* v. *Hopkinson* [1956] C.L.Y. 5011.
[44] s.4(6). This requirement is exceedingly onerous and should be abrogated: Faulks Report, para. 281.
[45] s.4(2). The Faulks Committee thought the requirement of an affidavit an unnecessary complexity and that the defendant should not be limited to evidence of facts included or referred to in the document containing the offer of amends: para. 283 of the Report. For a quite different approach, which would extend the "offer of amends" to any defamer and allow it to be given in mitigation of damages, see "Reservation C" to the Report (Mr. M. Rubinstein and Miss Elizabeth Clarke).
[46] *Bata* v. *Bata* [1948] W.N. 366.
[47] In criminal libel publication to the prosecutor alone suffices, the traditional reason being that libel tends to a breach of the peace, but this will no longer suffice as an explanation: see *ante*, p. 298, n. 30. See also the offence under the Malicious Communications Act 1988, which presumably does not give rise to a civil action. In Scots law, publication to persons other than the pursuer is unnecessary even in civil proceedings but that is because the defamation is regarded by the system as an injury to a man's feelings as well as to his reputation: *Mackay* v. *M'Cankie* (1883) 10 Rettie 537.

ment of claim, no one takes any notice of it at the trial except for the purpose of inflating damages where there has been spite or deliberateness. As we shall see, however, malice in the sense of spite or evil motive—"express malice" as it is commonly called to distinguish it from merely formal malice—will defeat the defences of fair comment and qualified privilege.

The handing back by a printer to the author of a defamatory document printed in the ordinary course of business is not of *itself* a publication by the printer so as to make him liable[48]; nor is the handing back to the employer by a clerk or typist of a document copied or made to the employer's order a publication by the clerk or typist.[49] But there is, of course, publication *to* the typist or printer by the author when he hands the document over. Unless such communication is protected by qualified privilege,[50] it follows that if a manager of a company in the course of his duties dictates to a secretary a memorandum defamatory of a fellow-servant, not only is the manager liable for defamation but the company is also vicariously liable,[51] though it has been suggested that the doctrine of common employment ought to protect the company in such a case.[52] If the author intends further publication, as where he writes a letter to the editor of a newspaper, the author is liable in respect of that publication also.[53] Indeed, the author is probably liable for any repetition he has reason to expect.[54] A similar problem arises where the author intends no publication in the legal sense (*e.g.* where he sends a "defamatory" letter to the defamed person himself) but someone else gains access to the contents. Again the correct question would seem to be, "should the defendant reasonably have foreseen the possibility of the intervention of the third party?" though the courts may not in the context of defamation attribute to a defendant the somewhat exaggerated perception of future events that they do in actions for negligence. He will be liable if he leaves his correspondence about, if he inadvertently puts letters in the wrong envelopes, or if he speaks too loudly; but not if a thief or unauthorised person takes his letter. In *Huth* v. *Huth*,[55] the defamatory matter was in an unsealed letter sent through the post and the letter was opened and read by an

---

[48] *Eglantine Inn Ltd.* v. *Smith* [1948] N.I. 29.

[49] *Ibid.* at p. 33, *per* Andrews L.C.J.

[50] Which it very commonly will be: see *post*, p. 351. If the plaintiff comes across the memorandum by discovery in other proceedings an attempt to found a defamation action on it will be an abuse of the process of the court: *Riddick* v. *Thames Board Mills Ltd.* [1977] Q.B. 881. In so far as they concern defamation, the dicta in *Riddick* have not been affected by the qualifications imposed by the House of Lords in *Rank Film Distributors* v. *Video Information* [1982] A.C. 380.

[51] *Riddick* v. *Thames Board Mills Ltd., supra, per* Waller and Stephenson L.JJ.

[52] *Ibid. per* Lord Denning M.R. For the abolition of the doctrine in relation to personal injuries, see *ante*, p. 187.

[53] *Cutler* v. *McPhail* [1962] 2 Q.B. 292. The damage which flows from the original publication to the editor includes the damage caused by the re-publication in the paper, for that is what the author intended. Even if there has been a release of the separate cause of action arising from publication in the paper, therefore, the author remains liable. "It matters not whether the damages caused by the repetition of the libel are sued for as part of the damage flowing from the original publication to the editor, or separately as the damages flowing from the publication in the newspaper": *ibid.* at p. 299, *per* Salmon J.; *Gardiner* v. *Moore* [1969] 1 Q.B. 55.

[54] See *ante*, p. 299.

[55] [1915] 3 K.B. 32. *cf. Theaker* v. *Richardson* [1962] 1 W.L.R. 151 (husband opened sealed letter addressed to wife. Jury found publication). There, however, the facts were unusual and the Court of Appeal's decision, by a majority, was no more than that the jury's verdict was not perverse.

inquisitive butler. As it was no part of his duty to do this, there was no publication for which the defendant was responsible. No doubt the defendant did an unwise thing in not sealing the envelope, but the behaviour of the butler was not a direct consequence of his sending the letter. But there would have been a publication by the defendant if the letter, whether sealed or unsealed, had not been marked "private" and had been opened and read by the plaintiff's correspondence clerk in the course of his duty.[56] The court was much pressed with the argument that this letter was in exactly the same position as a postcard or a telegram. The legal presumption is that these are published on being sent through the Post Office without any proof that any one did in fact read them. It might be urged that a third person is no more entitled to read a postcard than an unsealed letter, and that the publication is due to the wrongful act of the third person just as much in the one case as in the other. But that is not the real basis of the distinction. What it really turns upon is practical necessity in the law of evidence. As the Court of Appeal pointed out in *Huth* v. *Huth*, the presumption as to postcards is based on the fact that it is practically impossible to *prove* that any third person did read it, although it is highly probable that someone did. Moreover, the presumption is a rebuttable one, although it is very difficult to conceive that such rebutting evidence could be given.[57]

If defamatory matter is imposed upon the defendant's property by the unauthorised act of a third person, is the defendant bound to remove the matter when he becomes aware of it and knows, or has reasonable grounds for suspecting, that it is defamatory? Certainly he must remove it where he can do so without any difficulty or expense: *e.g.* if it be a typed document affixed to a wall of his house, for otherwise he is a party to publication.[58] And, probably, the same is true even if the removal of that defamatory matter is more difficult, save, perhaps, in the unlikely event that it is so difficult that it can be achieved only by the virtual demolition and rebuilding of the wall.[59]

The statement must be intelligible to the recipient of it. There is no publication if it is in a foreign language which he does not understand,[60] or if he is too deaf to hear it, or too blind to read or, of course, if he does not realise that it refers to the plaintiff.[61]

(1) *Husband and wife*

Communication of defamatory matter by a husband to his wife, or vice versa, is not a publication, for what passes between them is protected on the

---

[56] [1915] 3 K.B. 32, 40, 43–44, *per* Lord Reading C.J., Swinfen Eady L.J.
[57] *Ibid.* at pp. 39–40, *per* Lord Reading C.J. The court will not take judicial notice of the fact that husbands read their wives' letters, but this may nevertheless be something which the defendant should anticipate in some cases: *Theaker* v. *Richardson* [1962] 1 W.L.R. 151, 157, *per* Holroyd Pearce L.J.
[58] *Byrne* v. *Dean* [1937] 1 K.B. 818.
[59] cf. *Byrne* v. *Dean, supra*, at p. 838, *per* Greene L.J.
[60] If he later deciphers the message with the aid of a dictionary is the situation covered by *Grappelli* v. *Derek Block (Holdings) Ltd., ante*, p. 307.
[61] *Fleetwood* v. *Curley* (1620) Hob. 267, 268; *Amann* v. *Damm* (1860) 8 C.B.N.S. 597, 600; *Sadgrove* v. *Hole* [1901] 2 K.B. 1.

ground that any other rule "might lead to disastrous results to social life."[62] But communication by a third party to one spouse of matter defamatory of the other spouse is publication; husband and wife are still, for some purposes of the law, one person, but not "for the purpose of having the honour and feelings of the husband assailed and injured by acts done or communications made to the wife."[63]

(2) *Distributors*

Every repetition of defamatory words is a fresh publication and creates a fresh cause of action.[64] This is strikingly illustrated by a libel in a newspaper or on a television show since there would, technically, be a separate publication to every person who read the newspaper or saw the programme, though in practice the plaintiff will normally sue in respect of the edition or broadcast.[65] Furthermore, the law spreads the net of liability very wide. Not only is the writer of the article liable, but so is the editor, the printer, the publisher, the proprietor of the paper, and, subject to what is said below, even the newsagent or boy who sells it in the street. Here, however, a distinction must be drawn between a mere distributor and a person who takes an active part in the production of the print. The proprietor, editor, printer or publisher is liable even if he was not negligent in embodying the libel in his journal.[66] He can, of course, set up any other defence appropriate to defamation—truth, fair comment, privilege; but he cannot successfully contend that he was not negligent except for the purpose of mitigating damages or, in appropriate cases, for the purposes of availing himself of the procedure and defence under section 4 of the Defamation Act.[67] Those who are concerned with the mere mechanical distribution of such matter—newsagents, libraries, booksellers (and presumably bookbinders and carriers)—are presumptively liable but have a good defence if they can prove (*a*) that they were innocent of any knowledge of the libel contained in the work; and (*b*) that there was nothing in the work or in the circumstances in which it came to them or was disseminated by them which ought to have led them to suppose that it contained a libel; and (*c*) that when the work was disseminated by them, it was not by any negligence on their part that they did not know it contained the libel. These requisites, which were laid down by Romer L.J. in *Vizetelly* v. *Mudie's Select Library Ltd.*,[68] were adopted by Scrutton L.J. in *Bottomley* v. *Woolworth & Co.*[69]; but in the later case of *Sun Life Assurance Co. of*

---

[62] *Wennhak* v. *Morgan* (1888) 20 Q.B.D. 635, 639, *per* Manisty J.

[63] *Wenman* v. *Ash* (1853) 13 C.B. 836, 844–845, *per* Maule J.; *Theaker* v. *Richardson, supra.*

[64] *Duke of Brunswick* v. *Harmer* (1849) 14 Q.B. 185; *"Truth" (N.Z.) Ltd.* v. *Holloway* [1960] 1 W.L.R. 997; *Cutler* v. *McPhail* [1962] 2 Q.B. 292. As to joinder and consolidations of actions, see Gatley, *op. cit.*, pp. 425–426, Law of Libel Amendment Act 1888, s.5; Defamation Act 1952, s.13.

[65] For exceptions (*e.g.* where there is an innuendo) see Duncan & Neil, *op. cit.*, pp. 38–39.

[66] *Cassidy's* case and *Newstead's* case, *ante*, pp. 309–310.

[67] See *ante*, p. 313. A mere witness of the publication may not even be subjected to interrogatories: *Ricci* v. *Chow* [1987] 1 W.L.R. 1658. *cf.* an innocent participant: *Norwich Pharmacal Co.* v. *Customs and Excise Comrs.* [1974] A.C. 133.

[68] [1900] 2 Q.B. 170, 180.

[69] (1932) 48 T.L.R. 521.

Canada v. *W.H. Smith & Son Ltd.*[70] the same judge thought that (*b*) and (*c*) might be combined into the single question, "Ought the defendant to have known that the matter was defamatory; *i.e.* was it due to his negligence in conducting his business that he did not know?"[71] In *Vizetelly's* case the proprietors of a circulating library were held liable because they took no steps to ascertain whether their books contained libels and had overlooked a publisher's request for the return of copies of the particular book. Contrast this with *Martin* v. *Trustees of the British Museum*,[72] where the defendants were held not liable for allowing readers in the British Museum to see books containing libellous matter, there being no negligence on the part of the defendants[73] and other cases in which judgments were given in favour of newsagents and booksellers who satisfied the three conditions stated above.[74] The law could scarcely be otherwise, for "a newspaper is not like a fire; a man may carry it about without being bound to suppose that it is likely to do an injury."[75]

While the defence of "innocent dissemination" gives a distributor a very substantial protection,[76] the fact that he is presumptively liable may lead him to refuse to distribute a journal, with or without threat of legal proceedings. In *Goldsmith* v. *Sperrings Ltd.*[77] the plaintiff, considering himself defamed by *Private Eye*, brought a criminal prosecution against the magazine in respect of one article and a civil action in respect of two others but he also sued 37 distributors of the magazine. Many settled by undertaking not to distribute *Private Eye* again, but some sought an order that the actions against them be stayed as an abuse of the process of the court. The majority of the Court of Appeal dismissed this application because, whilst it was undoubtedly an abuse of process to pursue by legal action a collateral advantage which the law would not allow, the plaintiff believed that the magazine was carrying on a defamatory campaign against him and the terms of the settlements were thus directly related to the grievance which had caused him to sue. His purpose was not to shut down *Private Eye* (though the proceedings might, conceivably, have had that effect) but to protect his reputation.[78]

The exclusion of the printer from the category of distributors puts him in a

---

[70] (1934) 150 L.T. 211.

[71] The authorities clearly accept that a publication may attain a "reputation for libel" so that a distributor virtually handles it at his peril. In *Goldsmith* v. *Sperrings Ltd.* [1977] 1 W.L.R. 478 Lord Denning M.R. gave his opinion that the distributor was not liable unless the plaintiff proved that the distributor knew or ought to have known that the publication contained a libel which could not be excused or justified. But the case involved interlocutory proceedings in which it had been conceded below that the plaintiff had a cause of action against the distributor and both Scarman and Bridge L.JJ. disclaimed any power to go into the issue of the nature of the liability in such circumstances.

[72] (1894) 10 T.L.R. 338.

[73] What is the position of the owner of a private library who lends a book to a friend, or who permits a guest to use the library? Or of a railway passenger who lends a fellow-traveller a magazine? Presumably, the same as that of a newsagent or bookseller. If this seems too onerous, we may perhaps be content with saying that actions are very unlikely to be brought in such circumstances.

[74] *Emmens* v. *Pottle* (1885) 16 Q.B.D. 354; *Weldon* v. *Times Book Club Co. Ltd.* (1911) 28 T.L.R. 143; *Bottomley* v. *Woolworth & Co. Ltd.* (1932) 48 T.L.R. 521.

[75] *Emmens* v. *Pottle, supra,* at p. 358, *per* Bowen L.J.

[76] Faulks Report, para. 297.

[77] [1977] 1 W.L.R. 478.

[78] The dispute between Sir James Goldsmith and *Private Eye* was subsequently compromised.

very difficult position and, while he may be able to extract a promise of indemnity from the publisher, he clearly cannot check what he prints for defamation.[79] Even more unhappy is the position of a broadcasting company in respect of a live television or radio transmission, particularly in respect of a discussion or "phone-in" programme. However, the apparent harshness of the law may be justified by the fact that in this situation the plaintiff is much less likely to have an effective remedy against someone else than in the case of a libel in a newspaper or book.[80]

(3) *Assent to publication*

If the plaintiff expressly or impliedly[81] assents to the publication of matter which is true on the face of it, the defendant is not liable[82]; and this is so even if it appears that some persons may interpret the statement in a sense much more prejudicial to the plaintiff than is warranted by the plain meaning of the words. After all, that is a possibility which the plaintiff ought to have considered before he assented to publication, and he cannot be heard to complain that words which, in their ordinary meaning, are true have been construed by third parties in a sense contemplated neither by him nor by the defendant. In *Cookson* v. *Harewood*,[83] the plaintiff sued the defendants for libel because they had published a true statement that the plaintiff had been warned off all pony racing courses under their control. The plaintiff had submitted to the rules of the Pony Turf Club which the defendants controlled, and one of these rules was that the stewards of the club might, in their absolute discretion, warn off any person. Warning off might be occasioned by mere negligence of the delinquent as well as by less reputable causes. The plaintiff contended that if, by innuendo, the jury interpreted the statement as meaning that he had been guilty of corrupt and fraudulent practices, then the defendants were liable. But the Court of Appeal held that this argument was unsound. Scrutton L.J. said[84]:

> "It has seemed to me all through this case that these questions about innuendoes are quite beside the mark. If you get a true statement and an authority to publish the true statement, it does not matter in the least what people will understand it to mean. The plaintiff had submitted to the jurisdiction [of the Pony Turf Club]. The stewards have authority to publish the decision in the Racing Calendar, and if it is defamatory, it

---

[79] In *Dering* v. *Uris* [1964] 2 Q.B. 669, where the jury awarded a halfpenny damages against the author, the printer had already settled by paying a substantial sum. The Faulks Committee recommended that printers should have the defence of innocent dissemination: para. 309.

[80] The Faulks Committee recommended no change in the law: para. 300, *cf. Kelly* v. *Hoffman* (1948) 61 A. 2d 143.

[81] See *Syms* v. *Warren* (1976) 71 D.L.R. (3d) 558.

[82] The Supreme Court of New Zealand has held that there is no assent to publication where the defamatory matter is first sent to the plaintiff himself and he, being under a duty to do so, sends it on to other persons: *Collerton* v. *MacLean* [1962] N.Z.L.R. 1045. A challenge to an M.P. to repeat a defamatory statement outside the protection of parliamentary privilege would not be consent for this purpose.

[83] [1932] 2 K.B. 478n.

[84] [1932] 2 K.B. 478n, 482.

does not matter in the slightest what exact shade of meaning you are to put upon the obviously defamatory statement."[85]

Judgment for the defendants was affirmed.

It should be observed that this defence, which has also been regarded as an instance of *volenti non fit injuria*,[86] has nothing whatever to do with the defence of qualified privilege. Emphasis of this is necessary because some expressions in *Chapman* v. *Ellesmere* might give the contrary impression.[87] As will be seen, when we come to deal with it, privilege, if it is established, negatives liability for any statement whether it is prima facie untrue or is untrue only by innuendo, and whether consent has been given to the publication or not; or, to put it in another way, privilege, truth and consent are three entirely separate defences. Another distinction between privilege and consent to publication is this: It is for the law to say whether privilege in any form exists. Parties cannot by mere agreement create it.[88] But they can, as they did in *Cookson* v. *Harewood*, agree that one of them shall be entitled to publish the truth about the other, and such an agreement will exclude liability for defamatory innuendoes which may be put upon a correct but bald statement of facts.

DEFENCES

In addition to the defence of assent to publication and the provisions of section 4 of the Defamation Act 1952, there are three specialised defences to an action for defamation. These are:
1.   Justification (or truth).
2.   Fair comment.
3.   Privilege, which may be (*a*) absolute or (*b*) qualified.

Justification (or truth)[89]

The plaintiff need not prove that the statement is false, for the law presumes that in his favour.[90] But the defendant can plead "justification"

---

[85] Approved by Lord Hanworth M.R. and Slesser L.J. in *Chapman* v. *Ellesmere* [1932] 2 K.B. 431, 451, 464, and *semble* by the Court of Appeal in *Pritchard* v. *Greyhound Racing Association Ltd.* (1933) 176 L.T.J. 393; (1934) 177 L.T.J. 90.

[86] Slesser L.J. in *Chapman* v. *Ellesmere* [1932] 2 K.B. 431, 463; *contra*, Romer L.J. *ibid.* at p. 474.

[87] [1932] 2 K.B. 431, 450–451, 468, *per* Lord Hanworth M.R., Slesser L.J.

[88] *cf.* Denning L.J. in *Russell* v. *Norfolk (Duke)* [1949] 65 T.L.R. 225, 232: "If the publication in the Racing Calendar is no wider than the occasion warrants, it is privileged. This might be the case even if the rules did not contain any provision on the matter, but any doubt is removed by the fact that the rules, to which the plaintiff has assented, empower the stewards to publish the decision in the Racing Calendar. That is, in effect, a consent by the plaintiff to this mode of publication, though consent cannot create a privilege where none would otherwise exist."

[89] The Faulks Committee proposed that "truth" should replace "justification."

[90] As a consequence of constitutional restrictions on defamation the plaintiff probably now bears the burden of proving falsity in the U.S.A.: see *Restatement* 2d, s.613, comment j. Consider the problems involved in rebutting a general charge of bad conduct.

(the technical name for truth here), and if he can establish it by evidence he has a good defence though he may have been actuated by ill-will or spite.[91] It is not that the law has any special relish for the indiscriminate infliction of truth on other people, but defamation is an injury to a man's reputation, and if people think the worse of him when they hear the truth about him that merely shows that his reputation has been reduced to its proper level. At the same time justification may be a dangerous plea if it is the only one which the defendant decides to adopt, for if he fails in it the jury are likely to regard his conduct as wanton and to return a verdict for heavier damages.[92] While there is no doubt that justification is a defence to an action for defamation, it has been held in interlocutory proceedings that it is not a defence if the statement is published as part of a conspiracy the object of which is to injure the plaintiff, for the tort of conspiracy may be committed without any act which is independently tortious.[93]

(1) *Must be true in substance*

Subject to the fact that the question whether a minor inaccuracy is sufficient to defeat the defence of justification is one for the jury,[94] it is a general principle that "the justification must be as broad as the charge, and must justify the precise charge."[95] To justify the repetition of a defamatory statement already made, therefore, the defendant must prove that the content of the statement was true, not merely that it was made. If I say to you, "Smith told me that Brown swindled his creditors," I can justify this only by proof that Brown did swindle his creditors; it is idle to show merely that Smith gave me the information.[96] It follows that although the defence of justification is distinct from the question whether words are defamatory, the two are interlocked to some extent.[97] In *Lewis* v. *Daily Telegraph Ltd.*,[98] for example, the defendants were clearly able to justify the literal meaning, admittedly itself defamatory, of their statement that the Fraud Squad was investigating the plaintiff company's affairs, and so once the House of Lords had held that the words were incapable of meaning that the plaintiffs had been guilty of fraud the case was at an end. In *Cadam* v. *Beaverbrook*

---

[91] But see the important exception in relation to "spent convictions" under the Rehabilitation of Offenders Act 1974: *post*, p. 354.

[92] *Simpson* v. *Robinson* (1848) 12 Q.B. 511; *Associated Leisure Ltd.* v. *Associated Newspapers Ltd.* [1970] 2 Q.B. 450. *cf. Broadway Approvals Ltd.* v. *Odhams Press Ltd. (No. 2)* [1965] 1 W.L.R. 805, 814, *per* Sellers L.J.; 825, *per* Davies L.J. *Loughans* v. *Odhams Press Ltd.* [1963] C.L.Y. 2007 is a remarkable case. The defendants published a statement which bore the meaning that the plaintiff had murdered a certain person. Although he had been acquitted by a criminal jury the defendants pleaded justification. The civil jury in the action for libel found that this defence succeeded.

[93] *Gulf Oil (Great Britain) Ltd.* v. *Page* [1987] Ch. 327. See further *post*, p. 514.

[94] *Alexander* v. *North-Eastern Ry.* (1865) 6 B. & S. 340.

[95] Odgers, *op. cit.*, p. 149; *Bishop* v. *Latimer* (1861) 4 L.T. 775.

[96] *"Truth" (N.Z.) Ltd.* v. *Holloway* [1960] 1 W.L.R. 997. If the action were brought by Smith on the innuendo that, Brown being notoriously honest, the words meant that Smith was an unreliable and dishonest person, proof that Smith did use the words could amount to justification. Note the distinction between the statement "It is rumoured that X is guilty of fraud" and the statement "It is rumoured that X is suspected of fraud": *Lewis* v. *Daily Telegraph Ltd.* [1964] A.C. 234, 283–284, *per* Lord Devlin.

[97] *Cadam* v. *Beaverbrook Newspapers Ltd.* [1959] 1 Q.B. 413, 423, *per* Hodson L.J.

[98] *Supra.* For the facts see *ante*, p. 305.

Newspapers Ltd.,[99] on the other hand, the defendants published a statement that a writ had been issued against the plaintiff for conspiracy to defraud and they sought to justify this by proving that such a writ had indeed been issued. On an interlocutory appeal the Court of Appeal held that it could not be said that proof of the issue of the writ could not justify some conceivable defamatory meaning that somebody might say was the ordinary meaning of the words, and the issue of justification must therefore be allowed to go to the jury. It must be for the jury to decide whether proof that the writ had been issued justified the natural and ordinary meaning of the words, whatever the jury itself might decide the natural and ordinary meaning to be.[1] The relationship between the plaintiff's statement of claim and the defence of justification has given rise to so much difficulty that pleading in libel actions has been fairly called an "artificial minuet"[2] but the following propositions have been established as a result of a cluster of cases in the Court of Appeal.

1. Just as the plaintiff must give particulars of any defamatory meaning which is not the plain, ordinary meaning of the words,[3] so must the defendant make clear and explicit the meaning he seeks to justify.[4] This, it will be observed, is not quite the same as requiring him to specify what the words do mean: he may give notice in his defence of his preparedness to justify two or three different meanings and he is not obliged to pick out one of those as his exclusive defence.

2. Where a defamatory statement contains more than one charge, the common law rule was that each must be justified. This was altered by section 5 of the Defamation Act 1952 so that "in an action . . . in respect of words containing two or more distinct charges . . . a defence of justification shall not fail by reason only that the truth of every charge is not proved if the words not proved to be true do not materially injure the plaintiff's reputation having regard to the truth of the remaining charges." To give a simple example, if D were to allege of P (i) that he had participated in genocide during a war and (ii) while so serving had made certain dishonest expenses claims, justification of (i) would entitle the jury to bring in a verdict for D on the whole article even if there was no evidence at all to justify (ii).[5] However, section 5 is only applicable where the action is brought in

---

[99] *Supra; Hennessy* v. *Wright* (1888) 57 L.J.Q.B. 594.

[1] The jury need not disentangle its verdict. Fox's Libel Act, *ante*, p. 304, gives the jury the right to give a general verdict for the plaintiff or the defendant as the case may be. See also *Barnes* v. *Hill* [1967] 1 Q.B. 579.

[2] *Polly Peck (Holdings) plc* v. *Trelford* [1986] Q.B. 1000, 1020, *per* O'Connor L.J.

[3] See *ante*, p. 308.

[4] *Lucas-Box* v. *News Group Newspapers Ltd.* [1986] 1 W.L.R. 147; *Viscount de L'Isle* v. *Times Newspapers Ltd.* [1988] 1 W.L.R. 49; *Prager* v. *Times Newspapers Ltd.* [1988] 1 W.L.R. 77.

[5] *cf.* Lord Denning M.R. in *Moore* v. *News of the World Ltd.* [1972] 1 Q.B. 441, 448: "That is a very complicated section, but it means that a defendant is not to fail simply because he cannot prove every single thing in the libel to be true." The section is, however, unclear on how far the judge can control the jury on the issue.

respect of the distinct charges, so if the plaintiff chooses to sue only in respect of one (and the initiative is his) the defendant cannot adduce evidence of justification relating to the other.[6]

3. The plaintiff is not, however, wholly free to pick and choose those items which he thinks the defendant will be unable to justify: the question of what is a distinct allegation is one of fact and degree and where a number of defamatory allegations in their context have a common sting the defendant is entitled to justify the sting.[7] The defendant is in any event entitled to use the whole publication to provide the context of the words complained of when the jury is considering their meaning: the "plaintiff is not permitted to use a blue pencil on words published of him so as to change their meaning and then prevent the defendant from justifying the words in their unexpurgated form."[8]

4. In accordance with the above principles, the defendant may justify a proportion of the defamatory words sued upon, but still fail on the plea. How far can the unsuccessful "partial justification" go in reduction of damages? The traditional rule has been that the defendant may adduce evidence of general bad reputation on the issue of damages but not of specific acts of misconduct[9]: the law must prevent the recovery of substantial damages by a person whose reputation is unworthy of protection but it would be oppressive to allow the defendant (perhaps a newspaper with large financial resources) to lengthen a trial with evidence of the plaintiff's past conduct.[10] On the other hand, the defendant is entitled to rely, in mitigation of damages, on any evidence which has been properly before the jury and this may include evidence of specific acts of misconduct advanced under an unsuccessful plea of justification.[11] What the court must not countenance is the pleading of such specific acts under the guise of a plea of justification with the sole purpose of mitigation of damages.[12]

(2) *Proof of justification*

The standard of proof of justification is the normal civil one of balance of probabilities, but as in other civil cases the seriousness of the defendant's allegation may be taken into account in determining whether he has discharged that burden.[13] Where the defamatory allegation was that the plaintiff had committed a criminal offence, the rule of the common law was that

[6] *Polly Peck (Holdings) plc* v. *Trelford* [1986] Q.B. 1000.
[7] *Ibid.*; *Khashoggi* v. *I.P.C. Magazines Ltd.* [1986] 1 W.L.R. 1412.
[8] *Polly Peck (Holdings) plc* v. *Trelford, supra*, at p. 1023. *cf. Bookbinder* v. *Tebbit* [1989] 1 All E.R. 1169 where a specific charge of misusing public funds was held not capable of being construed as a general charge of irresponsible squandering, so that the defendant was unable to rely on other alleged misconduct.
[9] *Plato Films* v. *Speidel* [1961] A.C. 1090.
[10] Which might unduly influence the jury.
[11] *Pamplin* v. *Express Newspapers Ltd. (No. 2)* [1988] 1 W.L.R. 116.
[12] *Atkinson* v. *Fitzwalter* [1987] 1 W.L.R. 201; *Prager* v. *Times Newspapers Ltd.* [1988] 1 W.L.R. 77.
[13] *Laurence* v. *Chester Chronicle, The Times*, February 8, 1986.

his criminal conviction was not even prima facie evidence of guilt for the purpose of the defamation proceedings, and this meant that the defendant had to prove the guilt of the plaintiff over again if the defence of justification was to succeed.[14] However, it was enacted by section 13 of the Civil Evidence Act 1968[15] that in an action for libel or slander in which the question whether a person committed a criminal offence is relevant, proof that he stands convicted of the offence is conclusive evidence that he did commit it. Furthermore, in many cases a claim for defamation in respect of an allegation of a crime for which the plaintiff has been convicted may be struck out as an improper collateral attack on the decision in the criminal proceedings.[16]

Fair comment

It is a defence to an action for defamation that the statement is a fair comment on a matter of public interest.

Honest criticism ought to be, and is, recognised in any civilised system of law as indispensable to the efficient working of any public institution or office, and as salutary for private persons who make themselves or their work the object of public interest. "Others abide our question, thou art free" may be true of Shakespeare in literature. In law it is not true of him or of anybody else. The defence has been recognised for a long time in English law,[17] and, although criticism of government and of public functionaries was not always so freely allowed as today,[18] it is now fully recognised as one of the essential elements of freedom of speech which is not to be whittled down by legal refinement.[19]

Requisites of fair comment

(a) Matter commented on must be of public interest

It is a question for the judge, not the jury, whether the matter is of public interest.[20] No principle for decision is laid down, the books contenting themselves with examples,[21] but the public interest is not confined within narrow limits and covers matters in which the public is legitimately *interested* as well as matters in which it is legitimately *concerned*.[22] It ranges from the behaviour of a Prime Minister or of a sanitary authority to the conduct of a

---

[14] This he did not always succeed in doing: *Hinds* v. *Sparks* [1964] Crim. L.R. 717; *Goody* v. *Odhams Press Ltd.* [1967] 1 Q.B. 333. *cf.* the observations of Greer L.J. in *Cookson* v. *Harewood* [1932] 2 K.B. 478n., 485.

[15] See *Levene* v. *Roxhan* [1970] 1 W.L.R. 1322.

[16] *Hunter* v. *Chief Constable of W. Midlands* [1982] A.C. 529.

[17] *e.g. Dibdin* v. *Swan* (1793) 1 Esp. 28.

[18] *Wason* v. *Walter* (1868) L.R. 4 Q.B. 73, 93–94, *per* Cockburn C.J.

[19] *Slim* v. *Daily Telegraph Ltd.* [1968] 2 Q.B. 157, 170, *per* Lord Denning M.R.; *Silkin* v. *Beaverbrook Newspapers Ltd.* [1958] 1 W.L.R. 743, 747, *per* Diplock J.; Faulks Committee Report, para. 151.

[20] *South Hetton Coal Co. Ltd.* v. *N.E. News Association* [1894] 1 Q.B. 133, 141, *per* Lopes L.J.

[21] Gatley, *op. cit.*, pp. 314–324; Clerk and Lindsell, *Torts* (16th ed.), para. 21–25.

[22] *London Artists Ltd.* v. *Littler* [1969] 2 Q.B. 375, 391, *per* Lord Denning M.R.

flower show and includes the conduct of every public man and every public institution[23] but it is not limited to what is sometimes called "public life."[24] The presentation of a new play or the sudden closure of one enjoying a successful run,[25] the publication of a book, the exhibition of a picture, the conduct of a newspaper,[26] the claim of a company to use a pedestrian way for vehicular traffic,[27] and even criticism publicly made[28] may all be the subject of fair comment.

(b) It must be an expression of opinion and not an assertion of fact

It is not always easy to draw this distinction. To describe the line,

"A Mr. Wilkinson, a clergyman,"[29]

as the worst in English poetry is obviously comment, for verification of it as a fact is impossible. But some cases are much nearer than that to the borderline between comment and fact. In *Dakhyl* v. *Labouchere*[30] the plaintiff described himself as "a specialist for the treatment of deafness, ear, nose, and throat diseases." The defendant described him as "a quack of the rankest species." Was this comment or an allegation of fact? It was held by the House of Lords that it might be comment.[31] Again, calling a man a fornicator or a swindler looks like a statement of fact, but what is calling him "immoral" or "a sinner"? Are immorality and sin facts or matters of opinion? To this there is no dogmatic answer. Every statement must be taken on its merits. The very same words may be one or the other according to the context. To say that "A is a disgrace to human nature," is an allegation of fact. But if the words were, "A murdered his father and is therefore a disgrace to human nature," the latter words are plainly a comment on the former.[32] Hence a critic should take pains to keep his facts and the comment upon them severable from one another, for if it is not reasonably clear that the matter purports to be comment, he cannot plead fair comment as a defence.[33]

(c) Comment must be "fair"

For comment to be fair it must first of all be based upon true facts in

---

[23] See *Kelly* v. *Sherlock* (1866) L.R. 1 Q.B. 686, 689, *per* Bramwell B.

[24] The former exclusion from fair comment of the affairs of private institutions as exemplified by *Gathercole* v. *Miall* (1846) 15 M. & W. 319 is, it is submitted, no longer law. This seems implicit in the decision of the Court of Appeal in *London Artists Ltd.* v. *Littler, supra.*

[25] *London Artists Ltd.* v. *Littler, supra.*

[26] *Kemsley* v. *Foot* [1952] A.C. 345.

[27] *Slim* v. *Daily Telegraph Ltd.* [1968] 2 Q.B. 157.

[28] *Turner* v. *M.G.M. Pictures Ltd.* [1950] 1 All E.R. 449, 463, *per* Lord Greene M.R.

[29] A parody of Wordsworth in Benson's *Life of Fitzgerald.*

[30] [1908] 2 K.B. 325n.

[31] See too, their decision in *Turner* v. *Metro-Goldwyn-Mayer Pictures Ltd.* [1950] W.N. 33 and *cf. London Artists Ltd.* v. *Littler* [1969] 2 Q.B. 375.

[32] Gatley, *op. cit.*, p. 297.

[33] *Hunt* v. *Star Newspaper Co. Ltd.* [1908] 2 K.B. 320, *per* Fletcher-Moulton L.J.; *London Artists Ltd.* v. *Littler* [1969] 2 Q.B. 375, 395, *per* Edmund Davies L.J. It is for the judge to rule whether words are capable of being regarded as comment and for the jury to decide whether they are: *Jones* v. *Skelton* [1963] 1 W.L.R. 1362, 1380, *per* Lord Morris.

existence when the comment was made.[34] You cannot invent untrue facts about a man and then comment upon them.[35] To this, however, there is one necessary exception, namely, that fair comment may be based upon an untrue statement which is made by some person upon a privileged occasion, *e.g.* a statement made by a witness in the course of judicial proceedings, and properly attributed to him.[36] Moreover if the comment is upon the statement of another person, even if the statement was not made on a privileged occasion, the statement need not always be proved to be true, for in some cases such proof is impossible. If A publishes a statement that "There are men on the planet Mars" and B criticises this allegation as unfounded, B's criticism may well be fair comment, for it is based on fact in the sense that it refers to an assertion actually made by A. B is not bound to prove that there are men on Mars—in fact it is the very thing that he denies. Suppose, however, that A's statement were false and defamatory of C, then if B repeats it with some comment of his own, and C sues B for defamation, B cannot successfully plead fair comment unless his comment is a repudiation of the lie; for any other kind of comment of his would be an acceptance of a lie put in circulation by A; *i.e.* comment based upon what is untrue.

It is not necessary, however, that all the facts upon which the comment is based should themselves be stated in the alleged libel. The question is whether there is a sufficient substratum of fact stated *or indicated* in the words which are the subject-matter of the action and whether the facts or subject-matter on which comment is made are indicated with sufficient clarity to justify comment being made. The substratum of fact, facts, or subject-matter may be indicated impliedly in the circumstances of the publication.[37] In *Kemsley* v. *Foot*[38] the defendant had published a newspaper article under the heading "Lower than Kemsley." The article was violently critical of the conduct of a newspaper not owned by the plaintiff and contained no reference to the plaintiff other than the heading. The House of Lords held that the defence of fair comment was open to the defendant as in the circumstances the conduct of the Kemsley Press in its publications was sufficiently indicated as the fact on which the comment was made, and if the jury found that the comment was such as an honest, though possibly prejudiced, man might make the defence of fair comment would be established.

(i) Comment and justification. The relation of justification (or truth) to fair comment must be carefully noted. We start with two propositions. First, justification and fair comment are totally independent defences; the defendant can, and often does, plead them alternatively, and it is quite possible for fair comment to succeed while justification fails. "It may be said in the

---

[34] *Cohen* v. *Daily Telegraph Ltd.* [1968] 1 W.L.R. 916.
[35] See the dictum of Kennedy J. in *Joynt* v. *Cycle Trade Publishing Co.* [1904] 2 K.B. 292, 294; approved in *Hunt* v. *Star Newspaper Co. Ltd.* [1908] 2 K.B. 309, 317, 320; *Silkin* v. *Beaverbrook Newspapers Ltd.* [1958] 1 W.L.R. 743, 746; *London Artists Ltd.* v. *Littler* [1969] 2 Q.B. 375. *cf. Lyon* v. *Daily Telegraph Ltd.* [1943] K.B. 746.
[36] *Mangena* v. *Wright* [1909] 2 K.B. 958; *Grech* v. *Odhams Press Ltd.* [1958] 1 Q.B. 310; [1958] 2 Q.B. 275, 285, *per* Jenkins L.J.
[37] *Kemsley* v. *Foot* [1952] A.C. 345, 356–357, *per* Lord Porter.
[38] [1952] A.C. 345; Weir, *Casebook on Tort* (6th ed.), p. 478.

appropriate circumstances that a man's conduct is discreditable and it may be a fair comment to make, although a jury is not prepared to find that the substance of the comment was true."[39] Secondly, it is impossible for the defendant to succeed in a plea of fair comment unless he is commenting on facts, *i.e.* on what is "true" in the qualified sense of that word stated above. No comment can be fair if it is upon something which the defendant has invented or distorted, and if the alleged facts relied upon as the basis for comment turn out to be untrue, a plea of fair comment avails the defendant nothing, even though they expressed his honest view.[40] Where the facts on which the comment is made are fully set out in the alleged libel, then, subject to section 6 of the Defamation Act 1952, each fact must be shown to be true to enable the defence of fair comment to succeed in relation to the comment.[41] And to that extent the defendant must prove the truth of facts, unless that much is conceded in his favour by the plaintiff; but his defence is still fair comment and not justification. Since 1952, however, the defence of fair comment does not fail by reason only that the truth of every allegation of fact contained in the alleged libel is not proved. It is enough "if the expression of opinion is fair comment having regard to such of the facts alleged or referred to in the words complained of as are proved."[42] It has been suggested that this may have a wider affect than section 5 (dealing with justification[43]) where the plaintiff sues only on part of an article.[44]

(ii) The "rolled-up" plea. In this connection the so-called "rolled-up" plea has caused much perplexity. By it the defendant alleges that "in so far as the words complained of consist of allegations of fact, they are true in substance and in fact, and in so far as they consist of expressions of opinion they are fair comments made in good faith and without malice upon the said facts, which are matters of public interest." The original object of this plea (which was sanctioned in 1890[45]) was to make it clear that the defendant proposed to prove the truth of the facts on which he had commented. As has just been said, no comment can be fair unless it is comment upon facts. The plea was

---

[39] *Broadway Approvals Ltd.* v. *Odhams Press Ltd. (No. 2)* [1965] 1 W.L.R. 805, 817–818, *per* Sellers L.J. See also *ibid.* at p. 823, *per* Davies L.J. If the statement is one of fact, fair comment is not of course available.

[40] *London Artists Ltd.* v. *Littler* [1969] 2 Q.B. 375, 395, *per* Edmund Davies L.J.

[41] *Kemsley* v. *Foot* [1952] A.C. 345, 358, 361–362. Where the facts are not published to the world at large, but are contained in the particulars delivered, they are not the subject-matter of the comment, but facts alleged to justify that comment. Since they are not published otherwise than in the particulars, which are privileged, it is unnecessary that the truth of all of them be proved and it is enough if the defendant establishes sufficient of the facts to support the comment in the eyes of the jury. "Twenty facts might be given in the particulars and only one justified, yet if that one fact were sufficient to support the comment so as to make it fair, a failure to prove the other nineteen would not of necessity defeat the defendant's claim": *ibid.* at p. 358, *per* Lord Porter.

[42] Defamation Act 1952, s.6. See *"Truth" (N.Z.) Ltd.* v. *Avery* [1959] N.Z.L.R. 274, where it was held: (*a*) that fair comment is a defence to comment only and not to defamatory statements of fact, and that s.6 has not altered the law in this respect; (*b*) that where there is any defamatory sting in any of the facts on which the comment is based these defamatory statements of fact can only be defended by a successful plea of justification with, now, the benefit of s.5 of the Defamation Act 1952; *Broadway Approvals Ltd.* v. *Odhams Press Ltd.* [1964] 2 Q.B. 683, 685–686, *per* Lawton J.; *Broadway Approvals Ltd.* v. *Odhams Press Ltd. (No. 2), supra,* at p. 818, *per* Sellers L.J.

[43] See *ante,* p. 322.

[44] *Polly Peck (Holdings) plc* v. *Trelford* [1986] Q.B. 1000, 1033.

[45] *Penrhyn* v. *Licensed Victuallers' Mirror* 7 T.L.R. 1; Gatley, *op. cit.,* pp. 437–438.

therefore one of fair comment and not of justification, and the sole reason
for its use was that it was difficult to frame the plea in any other way if facts
and comment were so mixed up in the defendant's imputation as to be
inextricable. But then it often occurred that the defamatory statement did
not happen to include all the facts upon which the defendant had made his
comment; of course it would be much tidier from the lawyer's point of view if
critics always took care to include all the facts, but when a man is uttering or
writing criticism he generally knows little about the law of defamation and
even less about the niceties of pleading in it. At any rate if he had not
included all the facts, and were sued for defamation, he would be compelled
to go outside his defamatory statement to collect the rest of the facts upon
which his comment was based. Therefore the concluding words of the above
plea, "they are fair comments made . . . *upon the said facts* which are matters
of public interest," could not, with respect to the italicised words, be
accurate. So the practice sprang up of omitting them and the plea simply
wound up, "they are fair comments made in good faith and without malice
on a matter of public interest." This was most unfortunate, for it gave rise to
the idea that the plea was one of justification and fair comment, "rolled-up"
together; and it took a decision of the House of Lords in *Sutherland* v.
Stopes[46] to remind the profession that it was still a plea of fair comment and
of nothing else. The result now is that the plea ought not to be used at all in
the mutilated form described above. A better plan, if all the facts are not
included in the defamatory statement, is not to make use of the rolled-up
plea, but to plead fair comment and then to set out particulars of the facts
upon which the defendant commented.[47] Where the rolled-up plea is used it
no longer has the advantage it had prior to 1949 that the defendant could not
be compelled to say what parts of the statement are allegations of fact and
what parts are comment.[48]

(iii) Fairness. Finally we must consider the "fairness" of the comment
itself. The principles upon which this is determined are not easy to state with
precision, but it is at least clear that for comment to be fair it is not necessary
that the jury should accept it as correct and therefore that the test is not what
the ordinary reasonable man would think about the subject-matter of the
comment. If the defendant was "an honest man expressing his genuine
opinion on a subject of public interest, then no matter that his words
conveyed derogatory imputations: no matter that his opinion was wrong or
exaggerated or prejudiced; and no matter that it was badly expressed so that

---

[46] [1925] A.C. 47.
[47] But see *London Artists Ltd.* v. *Littler* [1969] 2 Q.B. 375.
[48] See R.S.C., Ord. 82, r. 3(2), added in 1949, requiring the defendant where the rolled-up plea is used to
furnish particulars stating which of the words complained of he alleges are statements of fact and of the
facts and matters he relies on in support of the allegation that the words are true. This follows the
recommendation of the Porter Committee, Cmd. 7536, paras. 173–177. Particulars of the facts relied on
may also be ordered where the rolled-up plea is not used, but only an ordinary plea of fair comment:
Cunningham-Howie v. *Dimbleby Ltd.* [1951] 1 K.B. 360; *London Artists Ltd.* v. *Littler* [1969] 2 Q.B. 375,
391, *per* Lord Denning M.R.; *Lord* v. *Sunday Telegraph Ltd.* [1971] 1 Q.B. 235. As to the former practice,
see *Aga Khan* v. *Times Publishing Co.* [1924] 1 K.B. 675; *Tudor-Hart* v. *British Union* [1938] 2 K.B. 329.
The Faulks Committee recommended that the rolled-up plea should be abolished: para. 176.

other people read all sorts of innuendoes into it; nevertheless, he has a good defence of fair comment. His honesty is the cardinal test. He must honestly express his real view.[49] So long as he does this, he has nothing to fear, even though other people may read more into it."[50] On the other hand, criticism cannot be used as a cloak for mere invective, nor for personal imputations not arising out of the subject-matter or not based on fact.[51] "The question is not whether the comment is justified in the eyes of the judge or jury, but whether it is the honest expression of the commentator's real view and not mere abuse or invective under the guise of criticism."[52]

Mere violence in criticism does not make it unfair. Moderation here "is only used to express the idea that invective is not criticism. It certainly cannot mean moderate in the sense that that which is deemed by a jury, in the case of a literary criticism, extravagant and the outcome of prejudice on the part of an honest writer is necessarily beyond the limit of the fair comment." So Collins M.R., in *McQuire* v. *Western Morning News Co. Ltd.*,[53] where a critique of a play imputed that it was dull, vulgar and degrading, and the Court of Appeal, in giving judgment for the defendants, held that the case ought not even to have been left to the jury.[54] Nor need comment on a literary production be confined to criticism of it as literature. "It can be criticised for its treatment of life and morals as freely as it can for bad writing, *e.g.* it can be criticised as having an immoral tendency."[55]

To the general proposition that a man expressing an honest but unreasonable opinion will be protected by fair comment we must probably make two qualifications. First, where the plaintiff is charged with base, dishonourable or wicked motives, there is authority for the view that not only must the charge be an honest expression of the writer's opinion but there must be some foundation for that opinion. The true test was probably stated by Buckley L.J. in *Peter Walker Ltd.* v. *Hodgson*[56] to the effect that the defence was made out if the defendant showed that:

" . . . the imputation . . . although defamatory, and although not proved

---

[49] Hence, while evidence of the plaintiff's professional standing at the time of the comment may be relevant, evidence of it at the time of the trial is not: *Cornwell* v. *Myskow* [1987] 1 W.L.R. 630.

[50] *Slim* v. *Daily Telegraph Ltd.* [1968] 2 Q.B. 157, 170, *per* Lord Denning M.R.; *Silkin* v. *Beaverbrook Newspapers Ltd.* [1958] 1 W.L.R. 743, 747, *per* Diplock J.; *McQuire* v. *Western Morning News Co. Ltd.* [1903] 2 K.B. 100.

[51] *London Artists Ltd.* v. *Littler, supra*, at p. 399, *per* Widgery L.J. The rule that juries must not substitute their own views for those of the critic is a salutary one, but probably the more competent a jury is to judge the matter criticised, the harder it will be to observe the rule. A jury of law teachers, in considering the fairness of criticisms on this book, would have to make a considerable effort to restrain themselves from assessing it by their own opinions of the book.

[52] *Turner* v. *Metro-Goldwyn-Mayer Pictures Ltd.* [1950] 1 All E.R. 449, 461, *per* Lord Porter; *Cornwell* v. *Myskow* [1987] 1 W.L.R. 630.

[53] [1903] 2 K.B. 100, 110. *cf.* a reviewer's opinion that Keats' "Endymion" was a poem of "calm, settled, imperturbable idiocy." This is violent enough, but is not on that account unfair.

[54] A test given by Lord Esher M.R. in *Merivale* v. *Carson* (1887) 20 Q.B.D. 275, 281 was, "Would any fair man, however prejudiced he may be, however exaggerated or obstinate his views, have said that which this criticism said of the work which is criticised?" In *Turner* v. *Metro-Goldwyn-Mayer Pictures Ltd.* [1950] W.N. 83, 97, Lord Porter said he should adopt the words of Lord Esher except that he would substitute "honest" for "fair," lest some suggestion of reasonableness instead of honesty should be read in.

[55] *Kemsley* v. *Foot* [1952] A.C. 345, 356, *per* Lord Porter.

[56] [1909] 1 K.B. 239, 253, supported by Gatley, *op. cit.*, p. 310.

to have been founded in truth, yet was an imputation in a matter of public interest, made fairly and bona fide as the honest expression of the opinion which the defendant held on the facts truly stated, *and was in the opinion of the jury warranted by the facts, in the sense that a fair-minded man might upon these facts bona fide hold that opinion."*

While still, strictly, amounting to a defence of fair comment rather than of justification[57] this formulation is clearly narrower than the general rule and probably adds unnecessary complexity to the law.[58] Secondly, there are clearly circumstances in which one may repeat what one genuinely believes to be the opinion of another even though one does not hold that opinion oneself. By publishing a letter from a reader containing an honest opinion,[59] a newspaper becomes responsible for any libel therein but it is clearly not deprived of the defence of fair comment merely because the owner and editor do not agree with the sentiments in the letter.[60]

(d) The comment must not be malicious

Malice here means evil motive.[61] Until 1906 there was considerable doubt whether private spite on the critic's part could make his comment unfair.[62] In theory it is possible to judge a man's work fairly even if you hate him, though it is not easy in practice. However, in that year the Court of Appeal held, in the only successful libel action ever brought against the proprietors of *Punch*, that malice may negative fairness: *Thomas* v. *Bradbury, Agnew & Co. Ltd.*[63] In that case, the book reviewer of *Punch* showed both by his review of the plaintiff's book and by his demeanour in the witness-box and elsewhere personal hostility to the plaintiff, and judgment for £300 damages was affirmed.

---

[57] The dicta of Cockburn L.C.J. in *Campbell* v. *Spottiswoode* (1863) 3 B. & S. 769, 777 (Weir, *Casebook on Tort* (6th ed.), p. 474) are ambiguous and are capable of being read as meaning that the opinion must be "correct."

[58] The Faulks Committee recommended that cases of this type should no longer be governed by any special rule: para. 169.

[59] It seems a necessary inference from *Lyon* v. *Daily Telegraph* [1943] K.B. 746 that the newspaper is equally protected where there is no evidence as to the writer's state of mind. This would be consistent with the general rule that once the statement is shown to be comment it is up to the defendant to prove malice.

[60] The majority of the Supreme Court of Canada in *Chernesky* v. *Armadale Publishers Ltd.* (1978) 90 D.L.R. (3d) 321 (Rogers (1981) 10 Anglo-American L.R. 225) came to the somewhat surprising and inconvenient conclusion (speedily reversed by legislation in several provinces) that a newspaper could not rely on the defence of fair comment unless "it" shared the opinions in the letter. This would not be followed in England: Gatley, *op. cit.*, pp. 313–314. It is submitted that dicta in *Lyon* v. *Daily Telegraph* [1943] K.B. 746, 751 and *Slim* v. *Daily Telegraph* [1968] 2 Q.B. 157, 171 should not be taken as meaning that the newspaper necessarily shared the opinions in the letters.

[61] It is discussed more fully in relation to qualified privilege, *post*, pp. 351–353.

[62] Even now the point has not been settled by the House of Lords, but in *Broadway Approvals Ltd.* v. *Odhams Press Ltd. (No. 2)* [1965] 1 W.L.R. 805, 822, Davies L.J. considered a submission that the defence of fair comment might not be defeasible by express malice to be "a very remarkable one."

[63] [1906] 2 K.B. 627 (distinguished in *Longdon-Griffiths* v. *Smith* [1951] 1 K.B. 295); by R.S.C., Ord. 82, r. 6, first made in 1949 on the recommendation of the Report on Defamation, Cmd. 7536, paras. 182–187, where the defendant pleads fair comment or privilege "no interrogatories as to the defendant's sources of information or grounds of belief shall be allowed." In *Adams* v. *Sunday Pictorial Newspapers Ltd.* [1951] 1 K.B. 354, the C.A. held this also prohibits interrogatories as to the actual information and knowledge of the defendant.

We have seen that the defence of fair comment may be available to a publisher such as a newspaper, which does not share the view of the originator of the comment. But what is the position where the originator of the comment is actuated by malice but the other publisher is not? If the newspaper is vicariously liable for the originator it is clear that it cannot plead fair comment,[64] but in other situations the law cannot be stated with certainty. It was held in *Egger* v. *Viscount Chelmsford*[65] that in the case of qualified privilege one co-publisher is not "infected" with the malice of another, but the members of the court disagreed as to whether a similar principle could be applied to fair comment. Analytically, there is something to be said for imposing liability upon a newspaper which innocently publishes a malicious comment for "if a publication has been held not to be a fair comment, then all concerned in publishing it have published an unfair comment and no questions of individual malice or bona fides can arise,"[66] but this approach is inimical to free discussion in the press and the Faulks Committee recommended that it should be made clear that the newspaper could rely upon fair comment in such a situation.[67] In *Lyon* v. *Daily Telegraph Ltd.*[68] the defendants published a letter which was highly critical of the plaintiff's radio show. The letter was objectively within the bounds of fair comment but turned out to have come from a fictitious address. The points before the Court of Appeal were whether the fictitious name and address amounted to evidence of malice and whether the newspaper was required to verify the name and address of a correspondent, to both of which a negative answer was given. It was not necessary to decide the point we are now considering, but Scott L.J. said that it did not follow that because the writer of a letter was malicious, the newspaper could not rely on a defence of fair comment.[69]

(i) **Judge and jury.** If an allegation of malice is raised in answer to a plea of fair comment, the burden of proving malice rests with the plaintiff. The judge must not allow the case to go to the jury, therefore, unless he is satisfied that there is evidence to support a finding that the defendant was malicious.[70] It is probable that a similar rule also applies where the question is simply whether the words of the comment itself reveal its unfairness. If the judge has ruled that the matter is of public interest and if the words are comment, not statements of fact, the judge should not allow the case to go to the jury unless there is some evidence of unfairness.[71] Proof of malice is no

---

[64] *Gros* v. *Cook* (1969) 113 S.J. 408. However, there is much uncertainty over the scope of vicarious liability in this area: see Gatley, *op. cit.*, p. 409 and Rogers (1981) 10 Anglo-American L.R. 225, 232. Even if there is a wider responsibility for agents (as opposed to servants) in defamation than in most other torts it is not easy to say who is an agent for this purpose.

[65] [1965] 1 Q.B. 248 (see *post*, p. 353).

[66] *Ibid.* at p. 269 *per* Davies L.J.

[67] Para. 272 of the Report.

[68] [1943] K.B. 746.

[69] *Ibid.* at p. 752.

[70] See *Broadway Approvals Ltd.* v. *Odhams Press Ltd. (No. 2)* [1965] 1 W.L.R. 805.

[71] *McQuire* v. *Western Morning News Co. Ltd.* [1903] 2 K.B. 100; *Turner* v. *Metro-Golwyn-Mayer Pictures Ltd.* [1950] 1 All E.R. 449, 461–462, *per* Lord Porter; *Jones* v. *Skelton* [1963] 1 W.L.R. 1362, 1378, *per* Lord Morris, where, however, it is pointed out that considerations as to where the onus of proof lies are not often of great consequence when both parties have had every opportunity to adduce all the evidence they wish to call. *cf. Burton* v. *Board* [1929] 1 K.B. 301, 306, *per* Sankey L.J.

more than one special way of proving that the comment is unfair.[72] But questions of the unfairness of the comment are essentially questions of opinion to be formed on reading the passage complained of and the should, therefore, normally be left to the jury.[73]

(ii) **Fair comment and privilege.** It has been disputed whether fair comment is properly regarded (*a*) as a right which everyone has, or (*b*) as a species of qualified privilege[74] but the predominant view now is that fair comment is separate in its nature from qualified privilege.[75] There are two chief objections to the other view. First, so far as the contents of the statement go, mere honest belief in them on the part of the defendant is enough to preserve qualified privilege if the case is one that falls under qualified privilege at all; but the fact that a comment is based upon honest belief does not necessarily make it fair.[76] Secondly, malice, and nothing but malice, will rebut qualified privilege, whereas comment may be unfair in other ways than by being malicious: *e.g.* if it is upon matter which the law regards as not open to comment at all.

Privilege

In addition to the cases covered by the defence of fair comment the law recognises that there are other occasions on which freedom of communication without fear of an action for defamation is more important than the protection of a person's reputation. Such occasions are said to be "privileged,"[77] and the privilege may be either absolute or qualified. Absolute privilege covers cases in which complete freedom of communication is regarded as of such paramount importance that actions for defamation cannot be entertained at all: a person defamed on an occasion of absolute privilege has no legal redress, however outrageous the untrue statement which has been made about him and however malicious the motive of the maker of it. Qualified privilege, on the other hand, though it also protects the maker of an untrue defamatory statement, does so only if the maker of the statement acted honestly and without malice. If the plaintiff can prove "express malice"[78] the privilege is displaced and he may recover damages, but it is for him to prove malice, once the privilege has been made out, not for the defendant to disprove it. It is for the jury to decide whether malice has been proved, but it is for the judge to rule whether or not the occasion is a privileged one.[79]

---

[72] See the observations of Collins M.R. in *Thomas* v. *Bradbury, Agnew & Co. Ltd.* [1906] 2 K.B. 627, 638–641.

[73] This seems to have been the view of Diplock J. in *Silkin* v. *Beaverbrook Newspapers Ltd.* [1958] 1 W.L.R. 743, 749.

[74] *cf.* Lord Esher M.R. in *Merivale* v. *Carson* (1886) 13 Q.B.D. 275, 280 and Collins M.R. in *Thomas* v. *Bradbury, Agnew* [1906] 2 K.B. 627, 641.

[75] *Silkin* v. *Beaverbrook Newspapers Ltd., supra*, at p. 746. In *London Artists Ltd.* v. *Littler* [1968] 1 W.L.R. 607, Cantley J. dealt as separate issues with the two defences of privilege and fair comment. The unsuccessful defendant appealed only on the latter issue, a course which caused no difficulty in the Court of Appeal although it would have done if the court had regarded fair comment as a species of privilege.

[76] Blackburn J. in *Campbell* v. *Spottiswoode* (1863) 3 B. & S. 769, 781; and see *ante*, p. 329.

[77] The term "privilege" is open to criticism, but its use is inveterate.

[78] See *ante*, p. 315.

[79] *Adam* v. *Ward* [1917] A.C. 309.

(1) *Absolute privilege*

This includes:

(a) *Statements in Parliament*

The Bill of Rights 1688 provides that "the freedom of speech and debates or proceedings in Parliament ought not to be impeached or questioned in any court or place out of Parliament."[80] This has the effect not only of conferring absolute privilege upon statements in Parliament, but also of preventing a plaintiff from using statements in Parliament as evidence of malice in respect of statements made outside it.[81]

(b) *Reports, papers, votes and proceedings ordered to be published by either House of Parliament*

The Parliamentary Papers Act 1840,[82] by establishing this, put an end to a bitter and unedifying dispute between the House of Commons and the Law Courts.

(c) *Judicial proceedings*

Whatever is stated, whether orally or in documentary form, in a judicial proceeding is absolutely privileged. It does not matter how false or malicious the statement may be, and it does not matter who makes it—the judge,[83] the

---

[80] The Bill was declared to be law by 2 W. & M., c. 1 (1689). See *Dingle* v. *Associated Newspapers Ltd.* [1960] 2 Q.B. 405 (the case proceeded to the H.L. on another point [1964] A.C. 371). As to a letter by an M.P. to a Minister as a proceeding in Parliament, see *Re Parliamentary Privilege Act, 1770* [1958] A.C. 331, P.C. As to colonial legislatures, see *Chenard & Co.* v. *Joachim Arissol* [1949] A.C. 127, P.C.

[81] *Church of Scientology* v. *Johnson-Smith* [1972] 1 Q.B. 522. But if a member speaking outside Parliament says: "Every word I said about X in the House yesterday is true," X would probably be able to use the speech in the House to support the legal innuendo: Faulks Committee, para. 209. *Quaere* as to the position if the *defendant* sought to rely on his statements in Parliament in order to rebut an inference of malice in respect of a speech outside Parliament.

[82] Extracts or abstracts of such reports have, however, only qualified privilege under s.3, *post*, p. 338. Command papers as such do not enjoy absolute privilege, though they would almost inevitably attract qualified privilege at common law. The Faulks Committee rejected a proposal by the Law Officers to bring such papers within the 1840 Act: para. 225.

[83] *Glick* v. *Hinchcliffe* (1967) 111 S.J. 927 is a modern example. See further, *post*, p. 663 and *Royal Aquarium Society Ltd.* v. *Parkinson* [1892] 1 Q.B. 431, 451, *per* Lopes L.J.

jury, the parties, the advocates,[84] or the witnesses.[85] Protection does not, however, extend to an entirely irrelevant answer of a witness unprovoked by any question as if, for example, to counsel's question, "Were you at York on a certain day?" the witness replied, "Yes, and A B picked my pocket there."[86] But the privilege is given a wide application and extends to anything a witness might naturally and reasonably say when giving evidence with reference to the subject-matter of the proceedings; it is not limited by any technical considerations of relevance.[87]

Judicial privilege, in the wide sense explained above, applies not only to any ordinary law court but also whenever there is an authorised inquiry which, though not before a court of justice, is before a tribunal which has similar attributes,[88] e.g. a military court of inquiry, or the Disciplinary Committee of the Law Society,[89] but an industrial conciliation procedure does not have these attributes,[90] nor does an investigation by the Commission of the EEC into breaches of the competition provisions of the Treaty.[91]

Communication between solicitor and client. Any professional communication between solicitor and client is privileged, but apart from communications made in connection with litigation, which are absolutely privileged, it is uncertain whether the privilege is absolute or qualified.[92] The Court of Appeal in More v. Weaver[93] held that it was absolute, but the House of Lords in Minter v. Priest[94] found it unnecessary to decide the question and preferred to leave it open. On principle, no strong reason seems to have been

---

[84] Munster v. Lamb (1883) 11 Q.B.D. 588, 603–604, per Brett M.R. This privilege is different from, though related to, the immunity from suit for negligence enjoyed by the barrister in relation to his conduct of a case in court. A barrister is, of course, subject to the discipline of the General Council of the Bar and the Disciplinary Tribunal of the Senate of the Inns of Court and a solicitor to that of the Law Society, and any advocate may incur the penalties of contempt of court for insolence to the judge or the use of violent or abusive language to the jury: Borrie and Lowe, The Law of Contempt.

[85] Seaman v. Netherclift (1876) 2 C.P.D. 53. For a full historical review of the authorities, see Pigot C.B. in Kennedy v. Hilliard (1859) 10 Irish Common Law Reports 195. Where a solicitor is briefing the evidence of a witness to be given on an occasion of absolute privilege, the occasion of the briefing is covered by the same privilege: Thompson v. Turbott [1962] N.Z.L.R. 298; Lincoln v. Daniels [1962] 1 Q.B. 237, 257–262, per Devlin L.J. See also Evans v. London Hospital Medical College [1981] 1 W.L.R. 184. Much disquiet was caused by the allegations made by counsel and the bankrupt in the Poulson bankruptcy examination but the Faulks Committee refused to recommend any change in the absolute privilege in judicial proceedings. As the Committee pointed out, it is open to a person who considers himself defamed in the course of judicial proceedings to apply for leave to make a statement in open court: para. 198.

[86] Seaman v. Netherclift, supra, at pp. 56–57, per Cockburn C.J.

[87] Ibid. at p. 60, per Bramwell J.A. An attempt by a witness or counsel to introduce a "spent conviction" within the Rehabilitation of Offenders Act 1974 would be covered by absolute privilege, but a report of such an attempt might not be: see post, p. 354.

[88] Lord Esher M.R. in Royal Aquarium Society Ltd. v. Parkinson [1892] 1 Q.B. 431, 442. Applied in Smith v. National Meter Co. Ltd. [1945] 2 All E.R. 35. For a modern statement of the law see Trapp v. Mackie [1979] 1 W.L.R. 377 (H.L.(Sc.)).

[89] Addis v. Crocker [1961] 1 Q.B. 11. That the Committee sits in private makes no difference provided that its functions are otherwise similar to those of a court of justice. cf. Lincoln v. Danieals [1962] 1 Q.B. 237. Disciplinary proceedings before the Inns of Court themselves were held absolutely privileged in Marrinan v. Vibart [1963] 1 Q.B. 234, affd. [1963] 1 Q.B. 528, and no doubt the same is true of the present system of proceedings before a Disciplinary Tribunal of the Senate of the Inns.

[90] Tadd v. Eastwood [1985] I.C.R. 132.

[91] Hasselblad (G.B.) Ltd. v. Orbinson [1985] Q.B. 475. But as to another aspect of this case, see below.

[92] Distinguish this privilege in the law of defamation from the privilege in the law of evidence which enables a client to prevent his legal adviser from disclosing any professional communication. This point is clearly taken by Lord Atkin in Minter v. Priest [1930] A.C. 558, 578 et seq. See post, p. 337.

[93] [1928] 2 K.B. 520.

[94] [1930] A.C. 558. But the Faulks Committee thought the privilege was absolute: para. 183.

advanced for regarding the privilege as absolute. It ought to be only in the most exceptional cases that, in the interests of the public, privilege should be ranked as absolute, and surely a solicitor and his client are sufficiently protected if they are conceded qualified privilege for their transactions with each other.

The privilege has been regarded as *ejusdem generis* with "judicial privilege,"[95] but the affiliation is a loose one, for it is not confined to the walls of a law court and extends to communications which have nothing to do with litigation, *e.g.* the drawing of a client's will. One restriction on it is that the communication must be a professional one. First, the relationship of solicitor and client must be proved, and it is regarded as sufficiently established for this purpose if, though the solicitor does not ultimately accept a retainer, the statement were made in communications between him and a prospective client with a view to retainer.[96] Secondly, what passes between them when the relationship has been established is privileged if, within a very wide and generous ambit of interpretation, it is fairly referable to the relationship,[97] or (to put it in another way) if it consists of "professional communications passing for the purpose of getting or giving professional advice."[98] This would exclude a piece of gossip interjected by the client in a conversation on, say, land registration: *e.g.* "Have you heard that Jones has run off with Mrs. Brown?"[99] Another illustration is *Minter* v. *Priest*,[1] where the House of Lords held that conversations relating to the business of obtaining a loan for the deposit sum to be paid on the purchase of land fall under the professional work of a solicitor, but that conversations about speculation in land to enable the solicitor to share in the profits do not and that slanders of third persons uttered by the solicitor in the course thereof are not privileged.

(d) Communications made by one officer of state to another in the course of his official duty

In *Chatterton* v. *Secretary of State for India*,[2] the plaintiff was an officer in the Indian Staff Corps. The defendant, in the course of his duty, wrote to the Under-Secretary of State that the Commander-in-Chief in India and the Government of India recommended the removal of the plaintiff to the half-pay list as an officer, and the letter stated the reasons for the recommendation. The Court of Appeal held that an order dismissing the plaintiff's action for libel as vexatious had been rightly made, on the ground that it would be injurious to the public interest to allow such an inquiry, for it would tend to deprive officers of state of their freedom of action in matters concerning the public weal. If an action for defamation were permitted, it would place their official conduct at the mercy of a jury who might to that

---

[95] *More* v. *Weaver, supra*, at pp. 521, 523, *per* Scrutton L.J.
[96] *Minter* v. *Priest* [1930] A.C. 558.
[97] *Ibid.* at pp. 568, 586, *per* Lords Buckmaster and Thankerton.
[98] *Ibid.* at p. 581, *per* Lord Atkin.
[99] *More* v. *Weaver* [1928] 2 K.B. 520, 525, *per* Scrutton L.J.
[1] [1930] A.C. 558.
[2] [1895] 2 Q.B. 189.

extent substitute themselves for the officials in governing the country. The decision in *Isaacs & Sons Ltd.* v. *Cook*[3] shows that the fact that a report relates to commercial matters does not in itself preclude it from being one relating to state matters.[4]

The extent of this head of absolute privilege is, however, somewhat uncertain.[5] One High Court judge has suggested that it does not extend to officials below the rank of Minister, though they may, of course, have qualified privilege,[6] and in *Merricks* v. *Nott-Bower*[7] the Court of Appeal refused to strike out a claim for libel based on a report on two police officers written by a Deputy Commissioner of the Metropolitan Police to the Commissioner. In the words of Lord Denning M.R.,[8] "it is not so clearly the subject of absolute privilege that the courts ought to strike out the claim on that ground today." The position of reports made pursuant to military duty is also doubtful. In *Dawkins* v. *Lord Paulet*[9] a majority of the Court of Queen's Bench held that a report on a lieutenant-colonel made by a major-general to the adjutant-general of the Army was covered by absolute privilege, but Cockburn C.J. delivered a strong dissenting judgment and in *Dawkins* v. *Lord Rokeby*[10] the Exchequer Chamber congratulated themselves on the fact that the question was still open for consideration by the House of Lords.

The argument generally advanced for absolute rather than qualified privilege is to the effect that a man will perform his duties better by being released from the fear of being sued than by being given an easily substantiated defence if he is sued, but this is as true of the nationalised industries and private concerns as it is of the state. Absolute privilege should be reserved for those cases alone in which complete freedom of communication is so important that it is right to deprive the citizen of his remedy for all defamatory statements made about him including even those made maliciously. No one could claim that this is true of all communications between all servants of the Crown. It is respectfully submitted, therefore, that the caution of the Court of Appeal in *Merricks* v. *Nott-Bower*[11] was fully justified and that care should be taken not to extend absolute privilege further than can be shown to be really necessary. It is no less in the interest of the state that justice should be done to the citizen than that the machinery of government should be able to work without fear of legal action.

Distinct from absolute privilege in the law of defamation is evidentiary

---

[3] [1925] 2 K.B. 391.

[4] For a comparable principle whereby a foreign embassy document is subject to absolute privilege, see *Fayed* v. *Al-Tajir* [1987] 3 W.L.R. 102.

[5] *Fayed* v. *Al-Tajir, supra*, at p. 110. For particular cases covered by statute, see Parliamentary Commissioner Act 1967 s.10(5); Fair Trading Act 1973, s.82(2); Competition Act 1980, s.16(2).

[6] Henn-Collins J. in *Szalatnay-Stacho* v. *Fink* [1946] 1 All E.R. 303. The Court of Appeal ([1947] K.B. 1) made no reference to this point.

[7] [1965] 1 Q.B. 57.

[8] *Ibid.* at p. 68; *Richards* v. *Naum* [1967] 1 Q.B. 620.

[9] (1869) L.R. 5 Q.B. 94.

[10] (1873) L.R. 8 Q.B. 255, 272. On appeal the decision of the House of Lords was based on the ground that the defendant was a witness before a tribunal which must be regarded as a judicial body: (1875) L.R. 7 H.L. 744.

[11] [1965] 1 Q.B. 57.

privilege. For example, a solicitor cannot be compelled to answer questions about what passed between him and his client seeking legal advice, whether or not litigation was impending when the advice was given[12]: the confidentiality of the relationship outweighs the interests of justice in ensuring the availability of all relevant evidence. Again, disclosure of documents relevant to an action will be refused where to order their production would be against the public interest.[13] Evidentiary privilege has no direct connection with the law of defamation, though its application may hinder the plaintiff who brings proceedings for that (or any other) tort by depriving him of vital evidence.[14] However, the concept of "public interest" has been used to bar an action for defamation even though the case did not fall within the established heads of absolute privilege. In *Hasselblad (G.B.) Ltd.* v. *Orbinson*[15] the action was founded upon a letter of complaint written by the defendant to X about the plaintiffs' servicing policies and this was disclosed to the plaintiffs during an investigation into the trading practices of the plaintiffs by the Commission of the European Communities. The Court of Appeal held that the Commission's activities were more in the nature of administrative than judicial proceedings and that the absolute privilege attaching to the judicial process did not therefore apply. However, the majority of the court went on to hold that the action failed for the independent reason that there was a public interest in ensuring that the Commission should not be hindered in carrying out its duty of enforcing fair competition under the EEC Treaty and if complaints to the Commission could be subjected to the law of defamation the supply of information would soon dry up. This is a surprising decision because it is well established in English law that an informer[16] or complainant[17] outside the context of judicial proceedings enjoys only qualified privilege, but the court was influenced by the fact that the Commission was required to disclose to the plaintiffs the written evidence upon which it relied.

(e) Fair and accurate newspaper and broadcast reports of judicial proceedings in the United Kingdom

Section 3 of the Law of Libel Amendment Act 1888[18] provides that a fair and accurate report in any newspaper[19] of proceedings publicly heard before any court exercising judicial authority within the United Kingdom shall, if published contemporaneously[20] with such proceedings, be privileged; but

---

[12] See, *e.g. Re Sarah Getty Trust* [1985] Q.B. 956.
[13] See, *e.g. R.* v. *Lewes JJ., ex p. Home Secretary* [1973] A.C. 388; *Air Canada* v. *Secretary of State for Trade* [1983] 2 A.C. 394.
[14] As in *Minter* v. *Priest* [1930] A.C. 558.
[15] [1985] Q.B. 475.
[16] *Shufflebottom* v. *Allday* (1857) 5 W.R. 315.
[17] *Conerney* v. *Jacklin* (1985) 129 S.J. 285.
[18] Cited as amended by the Defamation Act 1952, s.8.
[19] By s.1 of this Act, the word "newspaper" shall have the same meaning as in the Newspaper Libel and Registration Act 1881 and covers publications at intervals not exceeding 26 days. *cf.* the definition of "newspaper" for the purpose of s.7 of the Defamation Act 1952—at intervals not exceeding 36 days.
[20] See Magistrates' Court Act 1980, s.8; Contempt of Court Act 1981, s.4; and *Bunker* v. *James* [1980] 26 S.A.S.R. 286.

that this shall not authorise the publication of any blasphemous or indecent matter.[21] The protection of the section is extended to broadcast reports from a broadcasting station within the United Kingdom.[22] After a long period of uncertainty it was at last decided in 1964 that the privilege created by the statute is absolute.[23] Qualified privilege would in any case exist at common law.[24]

(2) *Qualified privilege*

This includes—

(a) Fair and accurate reports of parliamentary proceedings

The long battle between reporters and Parliament on this matter belongs to Constitutional Law rather than to the Law of Tort. However, in 1868, *Wason* v. *Walter*[25] settled the privilege of faithful reports. The court regarded the privilege as on the same footing as reports of judicial proceedings: *i.e.* the advantage of publicity outweighed any private injury resulting from publication. This qualified privilege at common law is not limited to reports in newspapers and will cover other reports, *e.g.* broadcast reports. The publication by means of printing or broadcasting of extracts from or abstracts of reports, papers, votes or proceedings published by order of either House of Parliament is given the protection of qualified privilege by statute.[26]

In order to qualify as fair and accurate the report does not have to be a full précis of the debate: a "parliamentary sketch" may properly select those

---

[21] The report is still privileged even if it includes defamatory interruptions by A in proceedings between B and C, provided that they are connected in some way with the proceedings: *Farmer* v. *Hyde* [1937] 1 K.B. 728. See also *Burnett and Hallamshire Fuel Ltd.* v. *Sheffield Telegraph and Star Ltd.* [1960] 1 W.L.R. 502. (Report of opening speech by counsel or solicitor).

[22] Defamation Act 1952, s.9.

[23] *McCarey* v. *Associated Newspapers Ltd.* [1964] 1 W.L.R. 855 (the Court of Appeal subsequently ordered a new trial on the issue of damages only: [1965] 2 Q.B. 112). Though the ruling was given only at first instance, it is unlikely to be challenged and is in conformity with the opinion of most writers and of the Porter Committee (Cmd. 7536, para. 92). The Faulks Committee recommended that the matter be put beyond doubt by statute: para. 191.

[24] *Post*, pp. 339–340.

[25] L.R. 4 Q.B. 73. The decision was a strong piece of judicial legislation, for two earlier, but abortive, attempts had been made to get Parliament to sanction this privilege. It would have been hard indeed if the plaintiff had succeeded in his action, for he had procured a peer to present to the House of Lords a scandalously false attack on Sir Fitzroy Kelly, then newly appointed Chief Baron of the Court of Exchequer, and the Lord Chancellor had described the petition as a perpetual record of the plaintiff's falsehood and malignity. *The Times* newspaper accurately reported this proceeding and thereupon the plaintiff sued the publishers for libel. The action was dismissed. Sound broadcasting of parliamentary proceedings began on April 3, 1978. It no doubt attracts qualified privilege under *Wason* v. *Walter*. But the Faulks Committee recommended that *live* sound broadcasting (and the sound element of any live television coverage) should attract absolute privilege. See generally, Leopold, (1989) 9 L.S. 53.

[26] Parliamentary Papers Act 1840, s.3, as extended by s.9(1) of the Defamation Act 1952: *Mangena* v. *Lloyd* (1908) 98 L.T. 640; *Mangena* v. *Wright* [1909] 2 K.B. 958; *Associated Newspapers Ltd.* v. *Dingle* [1964] A.C. 371. The privilege extends to fair comment upon the extracts or abstracts, but if a newspaper "adds its own spice and prints a story to the same effect as the parliamentary paper, and garnishes and embellishes it with circumstantial detail, it goes beyond the privilege and becomes subject to the general law": *ibid.* at p. 411, *per* Lord Denning. The Defamation Act 1952, s.7 and Sched., give qualified privilege as regards publications in newspapers or by broadcasting to reports of proceedings in public of the legislatures of any part of Her Majesty's dominions outside Great Britain; *post*, p. 341.

portions of the debate which will be of interest to the public.[27] What matters is whether the report is fair and accurate in so far as the debate concerned the plaintiff's reputation.[28]

(b) Fair and accurate[29] reports of judicial proceedings which the public may attend[30]

This applies to the proceedings of any court of justice, high or low. "For this purpose," said Lord Campbell C.J.,[31] "no distinction can be made between a court of pie poudre and the House of Lords sitting as a court of justice." Nor, according to the better opinion, does it matter whether the court had jurisdiction or not, for it would be harsh to expect the reporter to be an infallible judge of a matter upon which the court itself is often in doubt.[32] Again, it is immaterial whether the proceedings are *ex parte* or interlocutory or are adjourned from time to time:

> "The privilege applies to a fair and correct account of proceedings published before the final decision is arrived at, if in the end there must be a final decision. ... If it were not so, the ridiculous result would follow that, where the trial of a case of the greatest public interest lasted fifty days, no report could be published until the case was ended."[33]

Reporters, therefore, need not wait until the final decision is rendered,[34] but they must recollect that any comment, as distinct from fair and accurate reproduction, before the decision is given runs the risk of interfering with the due administration of justice and attracting the penalties for contempt of court. This common law privilege is not limited to newspapers, but covers reports in pamphlets or in a broadcast or any other form of publication, and the report need not be contemporaneous.

Qualifications. The following points with respect to this species of privilege are noteworthy. First, if the proceedings are not public, it does not apply, for the ground of the privilege is that, if the public are entitled to be present in a court, they are also entitled to be informed of what goes on in

---

[27] *Cook* v. *Alexander* [1974] Q.B. 279.

[28] *Ibid.* at p. 291.

[29] *Mitchell* v. *Hirst, etc., Ltd.* [1936] 3 All E.R. 872; *Burnett and Hallamshire Fuel Ltd.* v. *Sheffield Telegraph and Star Ltd.* [1960] 1 W.L.R. 502.

[30] *Usill* v. *Hales* (1878) 3 C.P.D. 319. For an analysis of the reasons for the existence of this privilege, see *Webb* v. *Times Publishing Co.* [1960] 2 Q.B. 535, 557–562, *per* Pearson J. See also *Burnett and Hallamshire Fuel Ltd.* v. *Sheffield Telegraph and Star Ltd., supra.*

[31] *Lewis* v. *Levy* (1858) E.B. & E. 537, 554.

[32] The dictum of Lopes J. in *Usill* v. *Hales* (1878) 3 C.P.D. 319, 329 preferable to that of Lord Coleridge C.J. *ibid.* at p. 324.

[33] *Kimber* v. *Press Association Ltd.* [1893] 1 Q.B. 65, 71, *per* Lord Esher M.R.

[34] But under s.4 of the Contempt of Court Act 1981 the court has power to order the postponement of the report to avoid prejudice to the administration of justice.

their absence.[35] Secondly, the privilege presumably does not apply if publication is forbidden, either by law[36] or by an order of the court.[37] Thirdly, even at common law it is a criminal offence to publish obscene matter, so qualified privilege will not cover a report of that,[38] and this common law restriction was drawn tighter by the Judicial Proceedings (Regulation of Reports) Act 1926,[39] the object of which was to call a halt to the practice of some newspapers of reporting the more salacious details of a certain type of legal proceedings, for the mere purpose of inflating their circulation. Fourthly, qualified privilege does not attach automatically to all fair and accurate reports of proceedings in the courts of foreign countries. Such reports are only privileged if the public interest in this country requires their publication, as would be the case, for example, with a report of a decision of a United States court on an important question of commercial law or where the proceedings in the foreign court throw light upon or are connected with the administration of justice in England. But a report of a judicial proceeding wholly concerned with an alleged scandalous affair between Mrs. X and Mr. Y is unlikely to have a legitimate interest for the English public and is likely to appeal only to idle curiosity or a desire for gossip. It will not, therefore, be privileged.[40]

(c) Certain fair and accurate reports published in newspapers or broadcast from a station in the United Kingdom

Section 7 of the Defamation Act 1952[41] affords qualified privilege to the publication in a newspaper or in a broadcast for general reception of the reports or other matters specified in the Act. The reports or matters so privileged are divided into two categories, the first[42] comprising statements which are privileged "without explanation or contradiction," and the second[43] statements which are privileged "subject to explanation or contradiction." As regards statements in the second category, the defence of qualified privilege is lost if it is proved that the defendant has been requested by

[35] *Per* Romer L.J. in *Chapman* v. *Ellesmere* [1932] 2 K.B. 431, 475. The remarks of Greer L.J. in *Cookson* v. *Harewood, ibid.* at p. 485, are not really in conflict with this. In Scotland it has been held that the privilege extends to the publication of statements in pleadings which are not read out in open court but upon which the decision is founded: *Cunningham* v. *The Scotsman* 1987 S.L.T. 698. But this does not extend to the publication of pleadings which have been filed but which have not come before a court. *R. Lucas & Son (Nelson Mail) Ltd.* v. *O'Brien* [1978] 2 N.Z.L.R. 289. Reports of the findings or decision of a domestic tribunal if published in a newspaper may be privileged under the Defamation Act 1952, s.7, *infra.*
[36] *e.g.* Sexual Offences (Amendment) Act 1976, ss.4, 6; Magistrates' Courts Act 1980, s.8.
[37] *Brook* v. *Evans* (1860) 29 L.J. Ch. 616; Contempt of Court Act 1981, s.4.
[38] *Re the Evening News* (1887) 3 T.L.R. 255.
[39] Children and Young Persons Act 1933, ss.39, 49; Domestic and Appellate Proceedings (Restriction of Publicity) Act 1968, s.2; Children and Young Persons Act 1969, s.10; Magistrates' Courts Act 1980, s.71.
[40] *Webb* v. *Times Publishing Co.* [1960] 2 Q.B. 535; Payne, "Qualified Privilege" (1961) 24 M.L.R. 178. For the special case of international courts and courts exercising jurisdiction in the Commonwealth, see *post,* p. 341. Note that a newspaper is not privileged merely because its article is of great public interest: *post,* p. 345.
[41] ss.7, 9(2) (3), and the Sched. to the Act. This replaces the more restricted protection formerly given by the Law of Libel Amendment Act 1888, s.4. The provisions extend to cable programmes: Cable and Broadcasting Act 1984, s.28.
[42] See Pt. I, Sched. to the Defamation Act 1952.
[43] See Pt. II, Sched. to the Defamation Act 1952.

the plaintiff to publish in the newspaper in which (or, if by broadcast, in the manner in which) the original publication was made, a reasonable letter or statement by way of explanation or contradiction, and has refused or neglected to do so, or has done so in a manner not adequate or reasonable having regard to all the circumstances.[44] In neither case is protection given to the publication of any matter which is prohibited by law or of any matter which is not of public concern and the publication of which is not for the public benefit.[45]

The reports and other matters the publication of which is to have qualified privilege are listed in the Schedule to the Act[46] and cover:

(i) Statements privileged without explanation or contradiction.[47] (1) Fair and accurate reports of proceedings in public of legislatures of any part of Her Majesty's dominions outside Great Britain, of international organisations and international conferences of which the United Kingdom is a member, of international courts, of public inquiries appointed by the Government or legislature of any part of Her Majesty's dominions outside the United Kingdom.

(2) Fair and accurate reports of judicial proceedings of courts exercising jurisdiction throughout any part of Her Majesty's dominions outside the United Kingdom or of any proceeding before a British court-martial held outside the United Kingdom.[48]

(3) A fair and accurate copy of or extract from any register kept in pursuance of any Act of Parliament which is open to inspection by the public, or of any document which is required by the law of any part of the United Kingdom to be open to inspection by the public.

(4) A notice or advertisement published by or on the authority of any court within the United Kingdom or any judge or officer of such a court.

(ii) Statements privileged subject to explanation or contradiction.[49] (1) Fair and accurate reports of the findings or decisions (in relation to members or persons subject by contract to the control of the association) of certain associations or the committees or governing bodies thereof, *i.e.*

(a) an association formed in the United Kingdom for the purpose of

---

[44] s.7(2) of the Defamation Act 1952. *Khan* v. *Ahmed* [1957] 2 Q.B. 149 (a general letter demanding a full apology and withdrawal is not a request within the subsection. What is required is a special request that there should be published either a contradiction or an explanation in the words of the letter or in terms put forward by the person alleging that he has been libelled).

[45] s.7(3), *e.g.* reports of a torrent of abusive interruptions which have nothing to do with the purpose for which the meeting was summoned are not privileged (*Kelly* v. *O'Malley* (1889) 6 T.L.R. 62) nor remarks made at a company shareholders' meeting as to the guilt of a servant of the company and not relating to its financial affairs: *Ponsford* v. *Financial Times* (1900) 16 T.L.R. 249. See *Boston* v. *W.S. Bagshaw & Sons* [1966] 1 W.L.R. 1126, 1132, *per* Lord Denning M.R.

[46] For a proposed revision of the Schedule, see Appendix XI to the Faulks Report. Proposed for inclusion in Pt. I are, *inter alia*, reports of proceedings of the European Parliament, the Court of Justice and Commission of the European Communities, and of United Nations agencies; proposed for inclusion in Pt. II are, *inter alia*, reports of press conferences and of adjudications by the Take-Overs Panel, the Stock Exchange Council and the Press Council.

[47] Sched. to the Act, Pt. I, paras. 1–7.

[48] Such reports may also be privileged independently of s.7: *Webb* v. *Times Publishing Co.* [1960] 2 Q.B. 535, *ante*, p. 339.

[49] Sched. to the Act, Pt. II, paras. 8–12.

promoting or encouraging the exercise of or interest in any art, science, religion or learning, and empowered by its constitution to exercise control over or adjudicate upon matters of interest or concern to the association, or the actions or conduct of any persons subject to such control or adjudication;

(b) an association formed in the United Kingdom for the purpose of promoting or safeguarding the interests of any trade, business, industry or profession, or of the persons carrying on or engaged in any trade, business, industry or profession, and empowered by its constitution to exercise control over or adjudicate upon matters connected with the trade, business, industry or profession, or the actions or conduct of those persons;

(c) an association formed in the United Kingdom for the purpose of promoting or safeguarding the interests of any game, sport or pastime to the playing or exercise of which members of the public are invited or admitted and empowered by its constitution to exercise control over or adjudicate upon persons connected with or taking part in the game, sport or pastime.[50]

(2) Fair and accurate reports of the proceedings of any public meeting held in the United Kingdom. A public meeting is defined as "a meeting bona fide and lawfully held for a lawful purpose and for the furtherance or discussion of any matter of public concern, whether the admission to the meeting is general or restricted."[51]

(3) Fair and accurate reports of the proceedings at any meeting or sitting in any part of the United Kingdom of:

(a) any local authority or committee thereof;

(b) any justice or justices of the peace acting otherwise than as a court exercising judicial authority;

(c) any commission, tribunal, committee or person appointed for the purposes of any inquiry by Act of Parliament, by Her Majesty or by a Minister of the Crown;

(d) any person appointed by a local authority to hold a local inquiry in pursuance of any Act of Parliament;

not being a meeting or sitting admission to which is denied to representatives of newspapers and other members of the public.[52]

(4) Fair and accurate reports of proceedings at a general meeting of a public company.

(5) A copy or a fair and accurate report or summary of any notice or other matter issued for the information of the public by or on behalf of any

---

[50] The publication in *The Times* of the decision of the domestic tribunal in *Chapman* v. *Ellesmere* [1932] 2 K.B. 431 would now be covered.

[51] The meaning of "public meeting" may now be wider than before the Act, and a meeting may be "public" even though it is open only to members of the association holding the meeting and their guests: *Khan* v. *Ahmed* [1957] 2 Q.B. 149. Whether a meeting is a "public meeting" is a question of law for the judge to decide: *ibid*.

[52] See the Public Bodies (Admission to Meetings) Act 1960 as amended by the Local Government (Access to Information) Act 1985.

government department, officer of state, local authority, or chief officer of police.[53]

(d) Statements made by A to B about C (a) which A is under a legal, moral or social duty to communicate to B and which B has a corresponding interest in receiving; or (b) where A has an interest to be protected and B is under a corresponding legal, moral and social duty to protect that interest[54]

"If fairly warranted by any reasonable occasion or exigency, and honestly made, such communications are protected for the common convenience and welfare of society."[55] A very common example is that of a former employer giving the character of a servant to a prospective employer.

It was thought at one time that, so long as the recipient (who must be some person other than the plaintiff[56]) had an interest in hearing the statement, it was immaterial that the communicator had no interest in making it. But in *Watt* v. *Longsdon*,[57] the Court of Appeal dispelled this view and emphatically adopted the rule that reciprocity of interest is essential.[58] B was a foreign manager of the X Co. He wrote to the defendant, a director of the company, a letter containing gross charges of immorality, drunkenness and dishonesty on the part of the plaintiff, who was managing director of the company abroad. The defendant wrote a reply to B in which he stated his own suspicions of the plaintiff's immorality and asked B to get confirmation of B's own allegations in order that the defendant might communicate them to the plaintiff's wife whom the defendant stated to be an old friend of his. Then, without waiting for any corroboration of B's statement, the defendant showed B's letter to S, the chairman of the board of directors and largest shareholder in the company, and also to the plaintiff's wife. All the allegations against the plaintiff were false. He sued the defendant for libel (*a*) in writing what he did to B; (*b*) in communicating B's letter to S; (*c*) in communicating B's letter to the plaintiff's wife. The defendant pleaded qualified privilege. The Court of Appeal had little difficulty in holding that (*a*) the defendant's letter to B was privileged, because both B and the defendant had a common interest in the affairs of the company, and that entitled them to discuss the behaviour of the plaintiff as another employee of the company and to collect further information for the chairman of the company; (*b*) the defendant's communication of B's letter to S was privileged, because a duty to make it arose both from the fact of employment in

---

[53] *Boston* v. *Bagshaw & Sons* [1966] 1 W.L.R. 1126; *Blackshaw* v. *Lord* [1984] Q.B. 1.

[54] See Lord Greene M.R. in *De Buse* v. *McCarthy* [1942] 1 K.B. 156, 164; and in *Braddock* v. *Bevins* [1948] 1 K.B. 580, 589–593. The law relating to qualified privilege at elections as stated in *Braddock's* case has been altered by the Defamation Act 1952, s.10. *Plummer* v. *Charman* [1962] 1 W.L.R. 1469.

[55] Parke B. in *Toogood* v. *Spyring* (1834) 1 C.M. & R. 181, 193; cited by Scrutton L.J. in *Watt* v. *Longsdon* [1930] 1 K.B. 130, 143.

[56] *White* v. *Stone Ltd.* [1939] 2 K.B. 827.

[57] [1930] 1 K.B. 130; Weir, *Casebook on Tort* (6th ed.), p. 465.

[58] *Phelps* v. *Kemsley* (1942) 168 L.T. 18, 21. This does not mean that both parties must have a duty or both an interest: one may have an interest and the other a duty, as in the common case of a servant's character. See *Beach* v. *Freeson* [1972] 1 Q.B. 14. A privileged occasion will not protect an irrelevant defamatory matter in the publication: *Adam* v. *Ward* [1917] A.C. 309, 340; *R.* v. *Lancs C.C., ex p. Hook* [1980] Q.B. 603; *cf.* *Horrocks* v. *Lowe* [1975] A.C. 135, 151.

the same company and from the possibility that S might be asked by the plaintiff for a testimonial if the plaintiff were to seek another situation. But the court held that (c) the communication of the letter to the plaintiff's wife was not privileged. No doubt she had the strongest possible interest in hearing a statement about her husband's moral conduct; no doubt also there may be occasions on which a friend of the wife is under a duty, or has a corresponding interest, in informing her of statements about her husband— indeed each case must depend on its own circumstances, the nature of the information and the relation of the speaker to the wife.[59] But here the defendant had no sufficient interest or duty, for the information came from a very doubtful source and he had neither consulted the plaintiff nor obtained any confirmation of outrageous accusations before passing them to the wife.

(i) **Test of duty.** The determination of whether a duty to communicate the matter does or does not exist is a question for the judge. It is easy enough for him to decide where the duty is a legal one, but where it is alleged to be moral or social, what test is he to adopt? Naturally, no criterion of any affair of ethics or of social relations can be more than an approximate one, but unfortunately the authorities do not show complete agreement on even an approximate test. Lindley L.J. said in *Stuart* v. *Bell*[60]: "The question of moral or social duty being for the judge, each judge must decide it as best he can for himself. I take moral or social duty to mean a duty recognised by English people of ordinary intelligence and moral principle, but at the same time not a duty enforceable by legal proceedings, whether civil or criminal." If "all or, at all events, the great mass of right-minded men in the position of the defendant would have considered it their duty under the circumstances" to give the information, then the learned Lord Justice thought that the privilege arose. But Scrutton L.J. in *Watt* v. *Longsdon*[61] asked, "Is the judge merely to give his own view of moral and social duty, though he thinks that a considerable portion of the community hold a different opinion? Or is he to endeavour to ascertain what view the great mass of right-minded men would take?" It is suggested that the answer to this is that the judge's view, if, as is probable, it takes account of the arguments of counsel on each side, as well as of his own personal predilections, is the nearest approach that is possible to the ascertainment of public opinion. You cannot *subpoena* as witnesses a portion of the community in order to discover what they regard as a moral duty. At any rate, it is a fallacy to suppose that the mere existence of any relationship (*e.g.* host and guest) will suffice to raise the duty without weighing all the circumstances of the particular case before the court; and this seems to be the explanation of some decisions in which it looks as if facts which really constituted malice (*i.e.* abuse of the privilege) were regarded as showing that the privilege had never existed at all.[62]

[59] Scrutton L.J. [1930] 1 K.B. 130, 149–150.
[60] [1891] 2 Q.B. 341, 350. Cited by Scrutton and Greer L.JJ. in *Watt* v. *Longsdon* [1930] 1 K.B. 130, 144, 153. *cf. Phelps* v. *Kemsley* (1942) 168 L.T. 18. *Bridgman* v. *Stockdale* [1953] 1 W.L.R. 704 (statement by invigilator to the class at an examination on a trade course that a trainee had "cribbed" privileged on ground of common interest).
[61] [1930] 1 K.B. 130, 144; *Beach* v. *Freeson, supra*, at pp. 23–24, *per* Geoffrey Lane J.
[62] See *Angel* v. *H.H. Bushell & Co. Ltd.* [1968] 1 Q.B. 813, 830, *per* Milmo J.

In this privilege a distinction has been drawn between a statement which is made in answer to an inquiry and one which is merely volunteered. Certainly, where there has been a request for the information, that is useful evidence towards showing that the privilege exists, particularly if the case is on the border-line,[63] but it does not follow that because the information is given unasked there can be no privilege. A man is but a poor citizen, to say nothing worse of him, if he is deliberately silent when he sees the lives of the public likely to be imperilled or the property of another person in obvious danger of being stolen or destroyed by one whom he honestly believes to be a drunkard or a thief.[64] And decided cases show that something less than such urgency as this may be enough to establish privilege for a volunteered statement.[65]

(ii) **The press.** Since newspapers, other news media and journalists are perhaps the most frequent defendants in defamation actions, it may be asked, given the undoubted importance of a free and vigorous press,[66] whether the press stands in any peculiar position as regards qualified privilege at common law. The courts have consistently answered "no." The matter which is reported may be *of* very wide public interest, but the protection of privilege is not thrown about it unless its publication is *in* the public interest and the newspaper can be said to be fulfilling a duty in revealing it.[67] There is no defence of "fair information on a matter of public interest"[68] and it is not yet the law that privilege attaches to a statement or a matter of public interest believed by the publisher to be true and in relation to which he exercised reasonable care. In this respect English law stands in sharp contrast to that of the United States, which has been shaped by constitutional guarantees of free speech and a free press.[69] However, the Faulks Committee thought there was little or no evidence that the present law was unfair or that it deterred newspapers from performing their investigative and reporting functions.[70]

(iii) **Trade protection societies.** Two decisions on reports as to the financial stability of tradesmen must be distinguished. Trade protection societies are often formed for the purpose of supplying such information to inquirers, and

---

[63] *Macintosh* v. *Dun* [1908] A.C. 390, 399, *per* Lord Macnaghten.

[64] *Coxhead* v. *Richards* (1846) 2 C.B. 569, 609–610; *Boston* v. *W.S. Bagshaw & Sons* [1966] 1 W.L.R. 1126.

[65] Gatley, *op. cit.*, pp. 203 *et seq.*; *Beach* v. *Freeson*, *supra*.

[66] Freedom of expression has an international dimension too: Art. 10 of the European Convention on Human Rights.

[67] *London Artists Ltd.* v. *Littler* [1968] 1 W.L.R. 607 (not raised on appeal: [1969] 2 Q.B. 375); *Morosi* v. *Mirror Newspapers Ltd.* (1977) 2 N.S.W.L.R. 749; *Blackshaw* v. *Lord* [1984] Q.B. 1. See further Gatley, *op. cit.*, pp. 238–242. Because the applicability of common law privilege may be difficult to predict, the statutory privileges given by the Defamation Act 1952 are very important to the press.

[68] The decision in *Webb* v. *Times Publishing Co. Ltd.* [1960] 2 Q.B. 535 (*ante*, p. 340) is correct, but certain statements in it go too far.

[69] Where the plaintiff is a "public figure" there is no liability unless the defendant is shown to have been aware of or reckless as to the falsity of the statement: *N.Y. Times* v. *Sullivan* 376 U.S. 254 (1964). Where the plaintiff is a private person state law may impose a standard of negligence as to falsity: *Gertz* v. *Robert Welch* 418 U.S. 323 (1974).

[70] Paras. 211–215 of the Report. *cf. The Law and the Press* ("Justice,"); *Unfair Publication* (Australian Law Reform Commission, 1979).

the law has to steer some middle course between allowing third persons to help a tradesman to protect himself against dealing with insolvent persons and "safeguarding commercial credit against the most dangerous and insidious of all enemies—the dissemination of prejudicial rumour, the author of which cannot be easily identified, nor its medium readily disclosed."[71] In *Macintosh* v. *Dun*,[72] the defendants carried on business as a trade protection society under the title "The Mercantile Agency." X, one of the subscribers to the agency, asked for information about the credit of the plaintiffs, who were ironmongers. The agency replied unfavourably and, as it turned out, untruly. In an action for libel, the Judicial Committee of the Privy Council held that there was no privilege, for the defendants were only collectors of information which they were ready to sell to their customers, and it was immaterial whether the customer bought the information across the counter or whether he enjoyed the privilege of being enrolled as a subscriber and paid his fee in advance. In *London Association for Protection of Trade* v. *Greenlands Ltd.*,[73] the facts were much the same except that the appellants there did not trade for profit and that the secretary to their association collected and supplied the information about Messrs. Greenlands to X. The House of Lords held that the communication was privileged on the ground that the secretary, in supplying it, was acting, not as agent of the association as a whole but as the confidential agent of X; for if X had the right to make inquiries on his own account, he equally had the right to make them through an agent and the agent was under a duty to report to him. But had the association itself any such privilege? The question could not be directly decided by the House of Lords owing to procedural blunders in the court of first instance but it may be deduced from the speech of Lord Buckmaster[74] that the privilege exists if (*a*) the association consists of persons who are themselves interested in trade, and (*b*) it exercises control over the person who on their behalf procures the information and over the manner in which he procures it, and (*c*) it does not conduct its business purely for purposes of gain.[75] In *Macintosh* v. *Dun* not one of these conditions was satisfied; in the *Greenlands* case all were. The chances of an action for defamation being brought in respect of information held by credit bureaux are now increased by the Consumer Credit Act 1974 which gives the consumer the right to the disclosure of the name and address of any bureau to which his creditor has made inquiries and the right to require from that bureau a copy of the file on him.[76] The purpose of those provisions is to enable the consumer to correct wrong information but it is perfectly possible that he may decide to take

---

[71] Lord Buckmaster L.C. in *London Association, etc.* v. *Greenlands Ltd.* [1916] 2 A.C. 15, 26.

[72] [1908] A.C. 390.

[73] [1916] 2 A.C. 15.

[74] *Ibid.* at pp. 26–27.

[75] It may be that (*c*) is not always necessary. See *ibid.* at p. 42, *per* Lord Parker; *Watt* v. *Longsdon* [1930] 1 K.B. 130, 148, *per* Scrutton L.J.

[76] ss.157–160. Under s.160 the bureau may be required to provide the Director General of Fair Trading with a copy of the file. The publication to the Director would clearly attract qualified privilege since it would be done in pursuance of a statutory duty.

defamation proceedings against the bureau[77] or against the person who supplied the information to the bureau.[78]

(iv) Range of publication. This kind of qualified privilege may quite well exist where the people interested in the receipt of the information are very numerous.[79] Thus it would appear from *Chapman* v. *Ellesmere*[80] that the stewards of the Jockey Club had qualified privilege for statements published by them relating to the conduct of trainers and other persons connected with the running of horse-races under the rules of the club, for the stewards owe all persons interested in racing conducted under those rules a duty to give them such information[81]; but the medium of communication must be a proper one, and it was held in this case that, while publication in the Racing Calendar satisfied this condition because both the plaintiff and the defendants had agreed upon this, publication in *The Times* did not, because the racing community could be adequately informed of the decisions of the Jockey Club without broadcasting them to the public in general.[82] One occasion where a qualified privilege may have arisen at common law by virtue of interest is now limited by section 10 of the Defamation Act 1952, which provides that a defamatory statement published by or on behalf of a candidate in any election to a local government authority or to Parliament shall not be deemed to be published on a privileged occasion on the ground that it is material to a question in issue in the election, whether the person to whom it is published is qualified to vote at the election or not.[83]

---

[77] *i.e.* in respect of the publication to the creditor.

[78] The original Consumer Credit Bill contained a clause which would have given qualified privilege to a communication to or by a licensed credit bureau. The Faulks Committee accepted that statements *by* bureaux should be given statutory qualified privilege but did not think that the same automatic protection should be given to statements *to* them, though such statements might often attract qualified privilege at common law: para. 237.

[79] Even, very occasionally, the whole of the newspaper-reading public: *Adam* v. *Ward* [1917] A.C. 309. But see *infra*, n. 82.

[80] [1932] 2 K.B. 431; applied in *Russell* v. *Duke of Norfolk* [1949] 65 T.L.R. 225.

[81] The clearest statement on this point is that of Romer L.J. [1932] 2 K.B. 431, 473–474. Lord Hanworth M.R. at pp. 449–450 seems to have held the same view. *Contra* Slesser L.J. at pp. 465–467.

[82] Note that the parties' assent here was to the *mode* of exercising qualified privilege. Any expressions in the judgments which might indicate that the parties could *create* qualified privilege by agreement cannot be supported for it is the court alone which settles whether qualified privilege exists or not. As regards the publication in a newspaper of the findings or decisions of such a tribunal, qualified privilege now arises under s.7 of the Defamation Act 1952, and Sched., para. 8(*c*). "So far as I know, there is no authority in which a letter published in the press has been held to be privileged, except when it was published as a matter of duty, as in the case of *Adam* v. *Ward* ([1917] A.C. 309), or where it is published by a defendant in answer to a public attack which had been made upon him": *Cutler* v. *McPhail* [1962] 2 Q.B. 292, 296, *per* Salmon J. But if the subject-matter of the letter is comment on a matter of public interest then the defence of fair comment may be available.

[83] The section reverses the decision in *Braddock* v. *Bevins* [1948] 1 K.B. 580, 589–593 on this point; *Plummer* v. *Charman* [1962] 1 W.L.R. 1469. Electors (and perhaps some others) retain the privilege.

(e) Where A and B have a common interest in the statement made by A to B about the plaintiff[84]

It is impossible to classify the cases in which such a common interest arises. Whether it exists or not is a question of law for the judge and probably the principle upon which he ought to resolve it cannot be put more exactly than to say that "the law never sanctions mere vulgar curiosity or officious meddling in the concerns of others."[85] Nor will an honest belief that there is a common interest suffice to create it, if in law there is none.[86]

The common interest may be a pecuniary one, such as a communication made by an insurance company to its policy-holders about an agent of the company[87]; or it may be professional, such as a letter written by an auctioneer to other auctioneers in the area about a person who had "purchased" goods at an auction and removed them without paying,[88] or the "screening" of a barrister by the Benchers of his Inn of Court after he has been disbarred.[89] But a general interest in church architecture confers no privilege on the imputations of a clergyman on an architect employed to restore a church of which the clergyman was neither an incumbent, nor a patron, nor a parishioner.[90] Fair comment may of course be a defence in such a case provided its requisites are satisfied.

It would seem, although the English authorities are somewhat discordant, that a clergyman who prays for, or preaches at, another person for some sin which the clergyman expressly or impliedly alleges against him, has no privilege.[91] No doubt all men are sinners, but an admission of general iniquity is one thing, an accusation of personal sin is quite another, and the proper way for a pastor to rebuke it is in private and not in the pulpit, unless indeed public admonition of sin is one of the tenets of the particular form of worship which he professes and the plaintiff has become a member of his congregation on that understanding. If the imputation is true, of course, the plea of justification will be available. Whether fair comment can be pleaded presumably depends on the circumstances of the case; if the allegation of sin

---

[84] Lord Greene M.R. in *De Buse* v. *McCarthy* [1942] 1 K.B. 156, 164, 166–167 referred to the fact that this privilege has been stated as requiring a common interest "in the subject-matter" of the communication. He thought these words were too vague to be worth inclusion. He distinguished *Hunt* v. *Great Northern Ry.* [1891] 2 Q.B. 189 as a decision which brings out very clearly "the distinction between a case where there was an obvious interest to make the communication and an obvious interest to receive it, and one such as the present, where that cannot be said": *Bridgman* v. *Stockdale* [1953] 1 W.L.R. 704.

[85] Odgers, *Libel and Slander* (6th ed.), p. 232.

[86] *Ley* v. *Hamilton* (1935) 153 L.T. 384, 385; *Davidson* v. *Barclays Bank Ltd.* [1940] 1 All E.R. 316, 322, *per* Hilbery J.: "You cannot by making a mistake create the occasion for making a defamatory communication." For criticism of this case, see *Pyke* v. *Hibernian Bank* [1950] I.R. 195, 220–223, *per* Black J.

[87] *Nevill* v. *Fine Art and General Insurance Co.* [1897] A.C. 68; *Smythson Ltd.* v. *Cramp & Sons Ltd.* [1943] 1 All E.R. 322; the appeal to the H.L., [1944] A.C. 329, was upon a different point.

[88] *Boston* v. *W.S. Bagshaw & Sons* [1966] 1 W.L.R. 1126.

[89] Odgers, *op. cit.*, pp. 236–237. For other examples, see *Laughton* v. *Bishop of Sodor and Man* (1872) L.R. 4 P.C. 495; *Winstanley* v. *Bampton* [1943] K.B. 319; *Angel* v. *H.H. Bushell & Co. Ltd.* [1968] 1 Q.B. 813. It is doubtful how far professional communications about his client made by a solicitor to the opposing solicitor are privileged: *Groom* v. *Crocker* [1939] 1 K.B. 194.

[90] *Botterill* v. *Whytehead* (1879) 41 L.T. 588.

[91] *Greenwood* v. *Prist (or Prick)* (1584), cited in Cro.Jac. 91, 1 Camp. 270, and 13 St.Tr. 1387 (best report), is the other way, but it was declared not to be law in *Hearne* v. *Stowell* (1841) 11 A. & E. 726. Both Irish and Scots law support the statement in the text: *Magrath* v. *Finn* (1877) I.R. 11 C.L. 152; *Dudgeon* v. *Forbes* (1833) 11 S. 1014.

is based on a matter of fact which is fairly open to public comment (*e.g.* the behaviour of a public librarian in admitting books of a provocatively erotic character into the library) one does not see why this form of comment on it should be in any worse plight than, say, newspaper criticism; but purely private peccadilloes do not appear to be a fit matter for public comment at all.

(f) Statements in protection of oneself or of one's property[92]

An example of defence of one's property would be a master's warning to servants not to associate with a former fellow-servant whom he had dismissed for dishonesty.[93] Another illustration is *Osborn* v. *Boulter*,[94] where a publican complained to the brewers who supplied him with beer that it was of poor quality. They retorted that they had heard rumours that the poorness of the beer was due to the watering of it by the publican, and they published this statement to a third party. It was held to be privileged.[95] The case was regarded by the Court of Appeal as illustrative of the type of privilege which is based on the fact that A's statement to B is in protection of an interest of his own and B is under a corresponding duty to protect it.[96] But it falls just as well under this head, and indeed the reports and textbooks draw no very sharp lines of division between these and some other species of qualified privilege.

(g) Statements made to the proper authorities in order to procure the redress of public grievances

Such would be a complaint to the Post Office concerning the alleged delinquencies of a local postmaster,[97] or to the Home Secretary that a local magistrate had incited people to break the peace,[98] or to a bishop that a clergyman in his diocese was reputed to have had a fight with the local schoolmaster.[99] Probably a complaint to the Bar Council concerning the professional conduct of a barrister is also protected by qualified privilege

---

[92] *Turner* v. *M.G.M. Pictures Ltd.* [1950] 1 All E.R. 449, 470–471, *per* Lord Oaksey. "There is . . . an analogy between the criminal law of self-defence and a man's right to defend himself against written or verbal attacks. In both cases he is entitled to defend himself effectively, and he only loses the protection of the law if he goes beyond defence and proceeds to offence. That is to say, the circumstances on which he defends himself, either by acts or by words, negative the malice which the law draws from violent acts or defamatory words." See Gatley, *op. cit.*, pp. 218–221.

[93] *Somerville* v. *Hawkins* (1851) 10 C.B. 583.

[94] [1930] 2 K.B. 226, 233, *per* Scrutton L.J. "Brewers supplying beer and a licensee who receives it are quarrelling about its character. This is clearly a privileged occasion within the principle laid down in *Toogood* v. *Spyring* (1834) 1 Cr.M. & R. 181, because it is in the interest of one party to defend himself and the interest of the other to receive and consider the defence. The privilege is not lost where a man defending himself and making charges against another reads a letter to his servant on whose information he is making the charges and says, 'Is that correct?' Nor was it lost by dictating it to his clerk." *Meekings* v. *Henson* [1964] 1 Q.B. 472.

[95] *cf. Bennett* v. *Styrick* (1981) 125 D.L.R. (3d) 743 (attack rather than refutation of plaintiff's charge).

[96] *Ante,* pp. 343–345.

[97] *Woodward* v. *Lander* (1834) 6 C. & P. 548.

[98] *Harrison* v. *Bush* (1855) E. & B. 344.

[99] *James* v. *Boston* (1845) 2 C. & K. 4.

even though at that stage there are no proceedings before a disciplinary tribunal which would attract judicial privilege.[1] The grievance need not be one which especially affects the complainant. If it does, he will probably have an additional kind of qualified privilege—statements made in self-protection.[2]

The complaint, in order to be privileged, must be addressed to the right person, *i.e.* to someone who has some power of redressing the grievance. Meticulous selection of the proper official is not necessary. A petition for an inquiry into the conduct of a magistrate and for his removal from office was held to be correctly addressed to the Home Secretary; for, although power of removing a magistrate is with the Lord Chancellor, yet the memorial to the Home Secretary was in effect a petition to the Crown, who might direct the inquiry to be made by the Home Secretary, and the Lord Chancellor would then, if necessary, act upon the results of it.[3] On the other hand, the Home Secretary has no sort of control over a clerk to the justices of the peace, and it has been held that a petition to him alleging corruption on the part of that official is not privileged.[4]

An individual member of Parliament has no specific power to redress grievances but he clearly has an interest in receiving the complaints of his constituents about a wide variety of matters, including the conduct of public officials and professional men,[5] since he is in a position to pass these on to the proper quarters.[6]

(3) *Rebuttal of qualified privilege*

(a) *Range of publication*

Where a communication is made on a privileged occasion, the privilege is not lost merely because there is publication to a third person in the usual course of business, as where a letter sent by A to B is first dictated by A to his secretary and typed by her. "The person exercising the privilege is entitled to take all reasonable means of so doing, and those reasonable means may include the introduction of third persons, where that is reasonable and in the

---

[1] *Lincoln* v. *Daniels* [1962] 1 Q.B. 237, 269, *per* Danckwerts L.J.; Devlin L.J., *ibid*. at p. 264, expressly left the point open. Disciplinary jurisdiction is now exercised by the Senate of the Inns of Court.

[2] *Ante*, p. 349.

[3] *Harrison* v. *Bush* (1855) 5 E. & B. 344, 350–351. See also *Lincoln* v. *Daniels, supra.* If the recipient of the petition has an interest in the subject-matter of the complaint, qualified privilege may arise by virtue of common interest: *R.* v. *Rule* [1937] 2 K.B. 375; *De Buse* v. *McCarthy* [1942] 1 K.B. 156, 170.

[4] *Blagg* v. *Sturt* (1846) 10 Q.B. 899, (but *Gatley, op. cit.*, p. 223, suggests the case would now be decided differently). *Hebditch* v. *MacIlwaine* [1894] 2 Q.B. 54 is to the same effect, although, like so many cases on qualified privilege, it may be, and indeed was, treated under another head of qualified privilege.

[5] *R.* v. *Rule* [1937] 2 K.B. 375 (constable and justice of the peace); *Beach* v. *Freeson* [1972] 1 Q.B. 14 (solicitor). Would a complaint to an M.P. that a trader persistently infringed consumer protection legislation be privileged under this head? It is thought that it would.

[6] But the M.P. must pick the right person to whom to pass the complaint: *Beach* v. *Freeson, supra. cf.* the Faulks Report, para. 203.

ordinary course of business."[7] The law is the same where A sends a letter to B which is defamatory of B himself and, in the usual course of business, first dictates the letter to his secretary: B cannot sue in respect of the publication to the secretary.[8] If, however, the letter to B goes beyond a bona fide and warranted attempt to protect A's interest in a dispute with B the privilege will be lost.[9] Where publication to the intended recipients would itself be privileged it is possible to regard the publication to the secretary as governed by an "ancillary" privilege,[10] but this explanation will hardly serve for the case where the only publication apart from that to the secretary is that to the defamed person himself, for that publication, not being tortious, needs no privilege. Nonetheless the Court of Appeal in *Osborn* v. *Thomas Boulter & Sons*[11] assumed that there was some sort of privilege between defamer and defamed so that publication to the secretary could claim an "ancillary" privilege.[12] In some cases, of course, there may be an "original" privilege between the sender of the letter and his secretary based upon community of interest,[13] but the view that an original privilege arises automatically from a contract of employment has been rejected.[14]

(b) Express malice

As has been said above, a plea of qualified privilege can be rebutted by proof of express malice, and malice in this connection[15] may mean either (*a*) lack of belief in the truth of the statement or (*b*) use of the privileged occasion for an improper purpose. Lack of belief in the truth of the statement is generally conclusive as to malice, except in a case where a person is under a duty to pass on defamatory reports made by some other person.[16] Mere carelessness, however, or even honest belief produced by irrational

---

[7] *Edmonson* v. *Birch & Co. Ltd.* [1907] 1 K.B. 371, 380, *per* Collins M.R.; *Boxsius* v. *Goblet Freres* [1894] 1 Q.B. 842; *Roff* v. *British and French Chemical Manufacturing Co.* [1918] 2 K.B. 677; *Osborn* v. *Thomas Boulter & Son* [1930] 2 K.B. 226; *Bryanston Finance Ltd.* v. *de Vries* [1975] Q.B. 703. *Pullman* v. *Walter Hill & Co. Ltd.* [1891] 1 Q.B. 524, to the contrary, has been distinguished out of existence. For other cases see *Taylor* v. *Hawkins* (1851) 16 Q.B. 308 (witness present when servant dismissed for dishonesty); *Crisp* v. *Gill* (1857) 29 L.T.(o.s.) 82. As to whether there is a publication when the words are dictated to the secretary, see *ante*, p. 315.

[8] *Osborn* v. *Thomas Boulter & Son, supra.*

[9] *Bryanston Finance Ltd.* v. *de Vries* [1975] Q.B. 703 (attempt to exert pressure to settle dispute by threatening wide dissemination of libel).

[10] *Bryanston Finance Ltd.* v. *de Vries, supra,* at pp. 727, 736, even, it seems, if the intended further publications never take place.

[11] *Supra.*

[12] Winfield's own view (see the fifth edition of this book, p. 298) was to the effect that communication to the secretary was no publication if the communication to the addressee, being the person defamed was itself no publication. See also *Restatement*, 2d, s.577, comment (h); 604, comment (c).

[13] *e.g.* if A discovers that B, a notorious "asset stripper" is seeking to take over A's company, the publication of defamatory matter by A to his secretary C about B may be protected by the common interest which she and A have in the survival of the company as a going concern. But even if the common interest is present, it is hard to see how A can rely on it if, in dictating the letter, he has no purpose of informing his secretary.

[14] *Bryanston Finance Ltd.* v. *de Vries, supra, per* Lord Diplock and Lawton, L.J.; *contra,* Lord Denning M.R. Perhaps the view of Lord Diplock should be discounted as he dissented from the actual decision, but this would seem to be a rather narrow view of the *ratio* of a case.

[15] "Malice" is almost as unfortunate here as in the formal allegation of malicious publication (see *ante*, p. 314): a mere love of gossip will defeat the privilege, but this is not malice in the popular sense.

[16] *Horrocks* v. *Lowe* [1975] A.C. 135, 150, *per* Lord Diplock. *Stuart* v. *Bell* [1891] 2 Q.B. 341 is a good example of this type of case.

prejudice, does not amount to malice[17]: "despite the imperfection of the mental process by which the belief is arrived at it may still be 'honest'. The law demands no more."[18] Even an honest belief will not, however, protect the defendant if he uses the privileged occasion for some purpose other than that for which the privilege is accorded by law: if his dominant motive is spite or if he acts for some private advantage he will be liable.[19]

(c) Evidence of malice

The question of malice is one for the jury and may be left to them at large, provided, of course, that there is some evidence of it. It is not necessary for the judge to draw the attention of the jury to every possible item of evidence of malice; nor is it required that the jury be told that they may act on any single such item, even though there is also evidence to negative malice.[20]

Evidence of malice may be found in the publication itself. If the language used is utterly beyond or disproportionate to the facts, that may lead to an inference of malice,[21] but the law does not weigh words in a hair balance and it does not follow that merely because the words are excessive there is therefore malice.[22]

Malice may also be inferred from the relations between the parties before or after publication or from the conduct of the defendant in the course of the proceedings themselves, as, for example, where the defendant persisted in a plea of justification while nevertheless making no attempt to prove it.[23] But the mere pleading of justification is not itself evidence of malice even though the plea ultimately fails; on the contrary, it may point more to honesty than to malice.[24]

There may also be evidence of malice in the mode of publication and this is commonly illustrated by wider dissemination of the statement than is necessary, such as circulating it on a postcard instead of in an enclosed letter, or saying it at the top of one's voice so that bystanders who have no proper interest in it overhear.[25] An alternative way of reaching the same result is to

---

[17] *Horrocks* v. *Lowe*, *supra*. As in the tort of deceit, conscious indifference to the truth is here equivalent to knowledge of falsity, for it equally involves lack of honest belief.

[18] *Horrocks* v. *Lowe*, *supra*, at p. 150, *per* Lord Diplock.

[19] *Horrocks* v. *Lowe*, *supra*. Weir, *Casebook on Tort* (6th ed.), p. 469.

[20] *Boston* v. *W.S. Bagshaw & Sons* [1966] 1 W.L.R. 1126, not following a dictum of Lord Porter in *Turner* v. *M.G.M. Pictures Ltd.* [1950] 1 All E.R. 449, 455.

[21] *Spill* v. *Maule* (1869) L.R. 4 Ex. 232, 236; *Adam* v. *Ward* [1917] A.C. 309, 327, 330, 335; *Sun Life Assurance Co. of Canada* v. *Dalrymple* (1965) 50 D.L.R. (2d) 217, Sup.Ct.

[22] *Nevill* v. *Fine Art, etc., Co. Ltd.* [1895] 2 Q.B. 156, 170, *per* Lord Esher M.R. If in the course of the editing of a newspaper article certain vital matters were omitted or inserted so as to make the article more exciting or scandalous that might be evidence of malice, but "a newspaper would too readily be deprived of the privilege of fair comment if the editing of news by omissions or additions were of itself to be held more consistent with malice than with its absence": *Broadway Approvals Ltd.* v. *Odhams Press Ltd. (No. 2)* [1965] 1 W.L.R. 805, 815, *per* Sellers L.J. ("Malice is not established by forensic imagination, however eloquently and subtly expressed": *ibid.*).

[23] *Simpson* v. *Robinson* (1848) 12 Q.B. 511.

[24] *Broadway Approvals Ltd.* v. *Odhams Press Ltd. (No. 2)*, *supra*, at p. 825, *per* Davies L.J. A plea of justification should not, of course, be made unless the defendant has evidence of the truth of the statement, and if that evidence only comes to light at a later stage, leave to amend the defence by adding the plea may be given so long as the defendant has not been guilty of delay or failure to make proper inquiries at an earlier stage: *Associated Leisure Ltd.* v. *Associated Newspapers Ltd.* [1970] 2 Q.B. 450.

[25] *Sadgrove* v. *Hole* [1901] 2 K.B. 1; *Oddy* v. *Paulet* (1865) 4 F. & F. 1009; *Chapman* v. *Ellesmere* [1932] 2 K.B. 421, 474–475, *per* Romer L.J.

say that the privilege which covers publication by A to B does not in general cover the distinct, if contemporaneous, publication to C.[26]

(d) Privilege, agents and malice

When a defamatory communication is made by several persons on an occasion of qualified privilege, only those against whom express malice is actually proved are liable.[27] This may seem self-evident, but it was for long thought that where a defamatory communication was published by an agent, the agent's only protectton was by way of an ancillary privilege derived from his principal, so that the malice of the principal destroyed the protection of the agent.[28] However, in *Egger* v. *Viscount Chelmsford*,[29] the Court of Appeal declared this to be wrong. The malice of an agent may make the innocent principal liable in some cases on the ordinary principles of vicarious liability,[30] but the malice of the principal cannot do the same for the innocent agent.

The decision in *Egger* v. *Viscount Chelmsford* accords well with common sense—it would be absurd to hold a typist liable because her employer was malicious.[31] But there remains the difficulty that except where the agent has for some reason a privilege of his own (which Davies L.J. thought to be the case in *Egger* v. *Viscount Chelmsford* itself[32]) his protection can only be derived from the privilege of his principal. If, then, the malice of the principal does not destroy the protection of the agent, it follows that the derivative privilege survives the destruction of the privilege from which it is derived and has an independent existence of its own. In effect, therefore, the Court of Appeal created a new head of privilege, namely, publication by an agent in circumstances in which his principal has a prima facie privilege to make the defamatory communication.[33]

Apology

An apology for the defamatory statement by the defendant may mitigate damages and its absence may aggravate them,[34] but generally speaking it

---

[26] But on this approach, it may be that the privilege is destroyed even though there is no malice: *Cutler* v. *McPhail* [1962] 2 Q.B. 292; but cf. *Angel* v. *H.H. Bushell & Co. Ltd.* [1968] 1 Q.B. 813.

[27] *Longdon-Griffiths* v. *Smith* [1951] 1 K.B. 295; *Meekings* v. *Henson* [1964] 1 Q.B. 472.

[28] *Smith* v. *Streatfeild* [1913] 3 K.B. 764; *Adam* v. *Ward* [1917] A.C. 309, 320, *per* Lord Finlay L.C.; 340–341, *per* Lord Atkinson.

[29] [1965] 1 Q.B. 248; A similar issue arises in relation to fair comment: see *ante*, p. 331.

[30] *Fitzsimons* v. *Duncan and Kemp & Co. Ltd.* [1908] 2 I.R. 483; *Angel* v. *H.H. Bushell & Co. Ltd. supra*; *Gros* v. *Cook* (1969) 113 S.J. 408. For difficulties in this area see *ante*, p. 331.

[31] Even though she could recover a full indemnity under the Civil Liability (Contribution) Act 1978: *post*, p. 593.

[32] [1965] 1 Q.B. 248, 272.

[33] This goes further than the recommendations of the Porter Committee, which, in any event, were not accepted by Parliament, and, indeed, s.4(6) of the Defamation Act 1952 recognises and proceeds upon the principle of *Smith* v. *Streatfeild*. See further on *Egger* v. *Viscount Chelmsford*, Armitage [1965] C.L.J. 30. The Faulks Committee recommended that *Egger* v. *Viscount Chelmsford* be given statutory approval: Chap. 8 of the Report.

[34] *Fielding* v. *Variety Incorporated* [1967] 2 Q.B. 841. See the description of the defendants' conduct in *Blackshaw* v. *Lord* [1983] 2 All E.R. 311, 330.

does not affect his liability. Limited exceptions to this are to be found in section 4 of the Defamation Act 1952 (which has already been dealt with[35]) and under an Act of 1843, commonly called Lord Campbell's Act. Under Lord Campbell's Act, as amended by the Libel Act 1845, a newspaper which publishes a libel without malice and without gross negligence may plead in defence the publication of a full apology and payment of money into court by way of amends.[36] This provision has fallen into disuse, since it is generally more advantageous for the defendant to apologise to the plaintiff and pay money into court by way of satisfaction under the general provisions of Order 22 of the Rules of the Supreme Court.[37]

A full apology need not be an abject one, but it does at least require a complete withdrawal of the imputation and an expression of regret for having made it.[38] To say that a man has manners not fit for a pig and then to retract that by saying that his manners are fit for a pig would merely aggravate damages.

Where an action for defamation is settled, the parties may apply to make a statement in open court: this has the advantages that it is likely to come to the attention of the press and is subject to absolute privilege.[39]

THE REHABILITATION OF OFFENDERS ACT 1974[40]

Some mention must be made here of this important legislation, though it has many provisions unconnected with the law of defamation and a full account of it must be sought elsewhere.[41] The Act seeks to rehabilitate offenders by restricting or forbidding the disclosure of "spent convictions," which, broadly speaking, means convictions for offences in respect of which the offender has received a sentence not exceeding 30 months' imprisonment and where a specified time (the "rehabilitation period"—varying from five to 10 years, depending on the sentence) has elapsed since the conviction. A rehabilitated person is then to "be treated for all purposes in law as a person who has not committed or been charged with or prosecuted for or convicted of or sentenced for the offence ... the subject of that conviction."[42] However, this is severely limited with respect to proceedings for defamation by section 8(3) which provides that nothing shall prevent a defendant in such an action from "relying on any defence of justification or fair comment or of absolute or qualified privilege which is available to him or restrict the matters he may establish in support of any such defence." At this point, however, the Act introduces a novel concept into English law, for it goes on to provide that a defendant shall not be entitled to rely upon the defence of

---

[35] See *ante*, p. 313.
[36] s.2 of the Act of 1843; s.1 allows the defendant to offer an apology in mitigation of damages only.
[37] See Faulks Committee Report, para. 373 Ord. 22 applies to any action for debt or damages.
[38] See Gatley, *op. cit.*, pp. 484–486.
[39] R.S.C., Ord. 82, r. 5; *Barnet* v. *Crozier* [1987] 1 W.L.R. 272.
[40] The Act came into force on July 1, 1975.
[41] See Gatley, *op. cit.*, Chap. 17.
[42] s.4(1).

justification if the publication is proved to have been made with malice.[43] "Malice" here means that the publication is made with some spiteful, irrelevant or improper motive.[44]

FUTURE OF DEFAMATION

The law of defamation has come in for a good deal of criticism. Some of this has questioned the basic assumption upon which the law is based, namely that even where no financial loss is shown, reputation is to be protected by means of an action for damages, and sometimes heavy damages, more than might be awarded for a quite serious personal injury.[45] It may be replied to this that such an equation of two incommensurable interests is unhelpful[46] and that the law cannot ignore the fact that there are still people to whom honour is at least as important as life or limb.[47] However, it is not easy to escape the conclusion that in the present law there is a strong punitive element even in the avowedly compensatory awards of general damages. First, a plaintiff who is primarily interested in the standing of his reputation will, presumably, regard a full and prominent public retraction as the best way of restoring this whereas the award of even very large damages will not have this effect unless it is adequately published. Secondly, the defences available in a defamation action, while undoubtedly necessary to preserve a proper balance of free speech, may have the effect that a wholly unfounded and exceedingly damaging allegation may still result in a verdict for the defendant which on its face reveals nothing about the jury's opinion as to truth. Even where the plaintiff's reputation is finally vindicated it will only have been after protracted litigation, the expense of which is at least in part produced by that necessity to balance the protection of reputation and the right of free speech.[48] The risks of defamation litigation are enormous. It has

---

[43] s.8(5).

[44] *Herbage* v. *Pressdram Ltd.* [1984] 1 W.L.R. 1160. If the writer wishes to plead non-malicious justification, the provisions of s.13 of the Civil Evidence Act 1968 will still be available to him for the purpose of proving the offence and conviction but will not, of course, be finally determinative. The position of the writer of a reference after the Act is curious. He is not obliged to disclose a spent conviction of which he knows and incurs no liability to the addressee for failing to do so (s.4(2)). But the Act appears to allow him to choose to disclose and then plead non-malicious privilege or justification, though it remains to be seen how far such an answer may be non-malicious: see Gatley, *op. cit.*, pp. 360 and 363. In fact, however, the Rehabilitation of Offenders Act 1974 (Exceptions) Order 1975, S.I. No. 1023, as amended by S.I. 1986 No. 1249, has the effect of excluding from the protection of the Act members, or those who wish to be members, of a very wide range of professions and occupations.

The Act restricts the defence of privilege based upon a fair and accurate report of judicial proceedings if the report contains a reference to inadmissible evidence of a spent conviction: s.8(6), (7).

[45] See, *e.g.* the general damages award in the cases mentioned in n. 63, *infra*. As to the punitive damages, see *post*, p. 601.

[46] See *Blackshaw* v. *Lord* [1983] 2 All E.R. 311, 331, *per* Stephenson L.J. The plaintiff's award of £45,000 would have sufficed to buy him an annuity of £5,000 p.a.

[47] Captain Broome in *Cassell* v. *Broome* [1972] A.C. 1027 was no doubt one of them.

[48] The defendants' costs in *Orme* v. *Associated Newspapers Ltd.*, *The Times*, February 4, 1981 (the "Moonies" case) were of the order of £300,000.

The Press Council and the Broadcasting Complaints Commission may consider complaints of defamatory statements. The former requires a waiver of any claim at law; the latter is not to consider any complaint if the complainant has a legal remedy and "in the particular circumstances it is not appropriate for the Commission to consider a complaint about it": Broadcasting Act 1981, s.19(4).

been said that it is only the very rich, the very foolish, the very malicious or the very dedicated who will knowingly put themselves in a position in which they have to defend a libel action, even with the benefit of qualified privilege as a possible defence,[49] to which it may be added that something very similar might be said about plaintiffs.[50] How much more sensible, it may be argued, would be a system for defamation contained in the press whereby there was a speedy procedure for requiring a correction of a defamatory statement or the publication of a counter statement by the plaintiff, such as is allowed by the press laws of some European countries.[51] However, there are objections to the institution of such a remedy. From the plaintiff's point of view, in an imperfect world "mud sticks" and the possibility of being required to publish an apology and correction would not be a very powerful deterrent against the dissemination of careless or even deliberate falsehoods. As for the defendant, it would be a new and perhaps dangerous step to impose upon a newspaper a legal requirement[52] (which would presumably be backed by criminal sanctions) to publish a statement "extolling [the complainant's] non-existent virtue."[53]

It seems likely that the basic structure of the present law of defamation will be with us for the foreseeable future, but there is general agreement that that structure needs some widespread renovation and refurbishment.[54] The Faulks Committee proposed numerous reforms and many of these have been referred to at appropriate points in the text,[55] but despite the fact that many of them are non-controversial the report has now gathered dust for so long that there seems little prospect of legislation.[56] However, it is thought that it is worthwhile to devote some space to the most controversial of the Faulks proposals, that relating to trial by jury. At present either party to a defamation action is entitled to claim trial by jury unless the court is of the opinion that the trial "requires any prolonged examination of documents or accounts or any scientific or local investigation which cannot conveniently be made with a jury."[57] It is clear from this that Parliament still considers that

[49] *Hasselblad (G.B.) Ltd.* v. *Orbinson* [1985] Q.B. 475, 502, *per* Sir John Donaldson M.R.
[50] See, *e.g.* Sir Peter Hall's account in *The Independent*, November 30, 1987, of his reasons for withdrawing his action against *The Sunday Times*.
[51] The so-called "droit de rèponse": see the Faulks Committee Report paras. 618–624. See also the Illinois experimental Libel Dispute Resolution Program, reported in the A.B.A. Journal, August 1, 1987.
[52] Under Sched. II, Pt. II of the Defamation Act 1952, certain reports are privileged if the newspaper or broadcaster agree to publish a reasonable statement by way of explanation or contradiction, but there is no way of compelling publication. Under the Broadcasting Act 1980 the Broadcasting Complaints Commission may require a broadcaster to publish a summary of the complaint to it and its findings.
[53] The phrase is the Faulks Committee's. It is hard to see how any such procedure could work effectively if there had to be a determination of the truth of a response by the complainant.
[54] Diplock L.J. in *Slim* v. *Daily Telegraph Ltd.* [1968] 2 Q.B. 157, 159, commented that the law had passed beyond redemption by the courts.
[55] Three further matters are considered elsewhere: the proposal for a limited remedy for defamation of the dead (*post*, p. 644); the restriction on the ability of a corporation to sue for defamation (*post*, p. 674); and the proposal to abolish exemplary damages (*post*, p. 605).
[56] See the critical remarks in the preface to Gatley, *op. cit.*
[57] Supreme Court Act 1981 s.69(1). The formation of an opinion under s.69(1) is not a matter of discretion; but if the judge concludes that the case falls under s.69(1) there is still a discretion to order a jury under s.69(3): *Viscount de L'Isle* v. *Times Newspapers Ltd.* [1988] 1 W.L.R. 49. When the 1981 Act was a Bill it provided that jury trial should not be available where the likely length of the trial made it unsuitable for a jury. This was prompted by the six-month "Moonies case" (*Orme* v. *Associated Newspapers Ltd. The Times*, February 4, 1983), but was withdrawn in the face of vigorous opposition in the Commons.

in the ordinary way defamation actions should be tried by jury and it is not enough to displace this that the burden of costs will bear hardly on either party. For many years it has been argued that juries are largely responsible for the fact that the costs of defamation actions are generally much heavier than those of ordinary tort actions,[58] simply because the action must proceed at a slower pace. Even then, there are said to be complex cases where the jury are probably incapable of following the details of matters like company accounts.[59] Further, it is argued that awards of damages by juries are often excessive[60] and that there is a danger of the jury being unable to be completely impartial towards an "unconventional" party.[61] Some of these criticisms could be applied to trial by jury in criminal cases but the Faulks Committee, while entertaining "no dangerous, iconoclastic intentions towards the jury" in that sphere, concluded by a majority that the use of the jury should be curtailed in defamation actions. The jury received a substantial body of judicial support in the evidence given to the Committee[62] and the arguments most consistently advanced in favour of its retention were that it was better placed than a judge to determine the "ordinary meaning of words" and how damaging those words were to the plaintiff's reputation. The truth of such contentions is unprovable but, as the Committee pointed out, they seem to derive from a belief that judges are remote from the emotions, conventions, language and mode of life of the rest of the community.

The Faulks Committee did not recommend the abolition of jury trial for defamation, merely that defamation should be assimilated to the ordinary rule that the judge has a discretion to grant a jury on the application of either party, instancing as cases which might continue to be suitable for this mode of trial those which involved a matter of political, religious or moral controversy or where one of the parties had been outspokenly critical of the Bench. Where, however, juries continued to be used their powers in respect of damages would be confined to deciding whether they were to be substantial/

---

[58] Faulks Report, para. 490. Thus although a newspaper in a libel action is at risk of suffering heavier damages from a jury than would be awarded by a judge, a newspaper may press for a trial by jury to "raise the stakes" against the plaintiff, whose financial resources will usually be far smaller.

[59] See Lawton L.J's comments on *Associated Leisure Ltd.* v. *Associated Newspapers Ltd.* in the Faulks Report, para. 464.

[60] *e.g.* the £200,000 awarded by two juries in *Lewis* v. *Daily Telegraph* (plaintiff's appeal against an order for a retrial dismissed, [1964] A.C. 234). *cf.* the award of one farthing in *Newstead* v. *London Express* [1940] 1 K.B. 377. Under emergency legislation during World War II most defamation actions were tried by judge alone and the damages awarded were usually substantially less than would have been awarded by juries: Porter Committee, para. 157. On appeal the issue is not whether the appellate court considers the damages too high, but whether "twelve men with knowledge of the world and of the value of money today could reasonably have come to the figure": *Blackshaw* v. *Lord* [1983] 2 All E.R. 311, 337 *per* Dunn L.J.

[61] The possibility of an "unrepresentative" jury is not necessarily removed by the Juries Act 1974.

[62] Lord Gardiner, Viscount Dilhorne, Lord Salmon, Bean, Bristow and Shaw JJ. Lord Gardiner, then Lord Chancellor, said in the House of Lords in 1966 that he could hardly remember a single civil case in which he thought that the jury were wrong: H.L., Vol. 274, cols. 1441–1442.

moderate/nominal/or contemptuous, leaving the judge to fix the actual amount within the category.[63]

---

[63] To explain to a jury the difference between nominal and contemptuous damages would be easy enough. One wonders, however, how the judge would distinguish the other two categories without using actual figures.

The very large awards now being made even without proof of actual loss (£500,000 to Mr. Jeffrey Archer in 1987, £300,000 to Miss Koo Stark in 1988) have brought calls for the implementation of the Faulks proposal. Perhaps these awards might not have survived an appeal, but a newspaper, having been found to have behaved badly, may decide that an appeal will bring further odium upon it. There is, however, to be an appeal by *Private Eye* against the award of £600,000 to Mrs S. Sutcliffe in May 1989 and the Lord Chancellor has indicated that there will be a new review of libel law. For a proposal for a speedy procedure before a judge alone where the claimant wants only a correction and damages up to £5,000, see (1989) 139 N.L.J. 245.

CHAPTER 13

TRESPASS TO LAND[1]

TRESPASS DEFINED

TRESPASS to land is the name given to that form of trespass which is constituted by unjustifiable interference with the possession of land. Contrary to popular belief trespass is not criminal in the absence of some special statute which makes it so.[2] Since the decision in *Fowler* v. *Lanning*[3] it may be asked whether tortious liability for trespass to land, like that for trespass to the person, requires proof of intention or negligence on the part of the defendant. We must, however, be careful to define what that intention or negligence goes to, for it is clear law that an entry upon another's land is tortious whether or not the entrant knows that he is trespassing.[4] Thus it is no defence that the only reason for his entry was that he had lost his way or even that he genuinely but erroneously believed that the land was his.[5] It follows that the great majority of trespasses to land are, for legal purposes, self-evidently intentional—I intend to enter upon your land if I consciously place myself upon what proves to be your land, even though I neither knew nor could reasonably have known that it was not mine.[6] We are left with those cases where the defendant's entry was involuntary, whether caused by his fault or not. Where he is thrown or pushed on to the land he is not liable for trespass simply because there is no act on his part.[7] As for other

---

[1] Weir, *Casebook on Tort*, (6th ed.), Chap. 8, section 5.

[2] The familiar notice, "Trespassers will be prosecuted" is thus, normally, no more than a "wooden falsehood." The punitive element which originally attached to trespass finally disappeared in 1694 but it had fallen into obsolescence long before that date: Winfield, *Province of the Law of Tort*, p. 11. Under the Criminal Law Act 1977, it is a crime to (i) trespass with a weapon of offence; (ii) trespass on a foreign diplomatic mission; (iii) refuse to leave premises on being required to do so by a displaced residential occupier; (iv) enter premises by violence except as a displaced residential occupier. For the relationship between (iv) and the civil law, see *post*, p. 370. The crime of conspiracy to trespass is abolished by s.5(1) of the Act. Under s.39 of the Public Order Act 1986 it is an offence for two or more persons, having trespassed on land with the common purpose of residing there for any period, to refuse to obey the direction of a police officer to leave the land. For the reasons behind this offence, see *Wilts. C.C.* v. *Frazer* [1986] 1 W.L.R. 109.

[3] [1959] 1 Q.B. 426. See *ante*, p. 70.

[4] *Conway* v. *George Wimpey & Co. Ltd.* [1951] 2 K.B. 266, 273–274; *Jolliffe* v. *Willmett & Co.* [1971] 1 All E.R. 478.

[5] Hence the possibility, long appreciated, of using trespass as a means of testing title.

[6] By the Limitation Act 1623, s.5, if the defendant disclaims any title to the land and proves that his trespass was involuntary or negligent and that he had tendered sufficient amends before the action was brought, he has a defence to an action for trespass. But *Basely* v. *Clarkson* (1682) 3 Lev. 37 excludes from the scope of s.5 an intentional act done in ignorance that it is infringing the plaintiff's right. Hence the defence is extremely restricted. See Williams, *Liability for Animals*, p. 196.

[7] *Smith* v. *Stone* (1647) Style 65. Though he could, no doubt, be required to leave. In real life, such a situation is much more likely to result in a claim by the entrant for injury suffered on the land, as in *Public Transport Commission (N.S.W.)* v. *Perry* (1977) 14 A.L.R. 273.

situations it is clear that where land adjoining the highway is unintentionally entered, as a result, for example, of a motor accident, the plaintiff must prove negligence, a proposition established long before *Fowler* v. *Lanning*.[8] In *League against Cruel Sports* v. *Scott*[9] Park J. had to deal with trespass by hounds in pursuit of a stag and he concluded that the law was that the master of the pack was liable if he intended the hounds to enter the plaintiff's land or if, knowing that there was a real risk that they would enter, their entry was caused by his failure to exercise proper control on them.[10] The burden of proof of either condition is upon the plaintiff.[11]

Trespass is actionable *per se, i.e.* whether or not the plaintiff has suffered any damage.[12] This rule may seem harsh but in earlier times trespass was so likely to lead to a breach of the peace that even trivial deviations on to another person's land were reckoned unlawful. At the present day there is, of course, much greater respect for the law in general and appreciation of the security which it affords, and the theoretical severity of the rules as to land trespass is rarely exploited in practice. An action will not normally be brought for trespass without damage unless the plaintiff wishes to deter persistent trespassing or there are disputes over boundaries or rights of way.[13]

POSSESSION

Trespass to land, like the tort of trespass to goods which is considered in a later chapter, consists of interference with possession,[14] and it is necessary to say something here of this concept.[15] Our law has, however, not worked out a consistent theory of possession, and its meaning may turn upon the context in which it is used.[16]

Mere physical presence on the land or the use or *de facto* control of it does not amount to possession sufficient to bring an action of trespass. It is, for example, generally said that a lodger in another's house does not have possession,[17] nor does a servant occupying a room in his master's house[18] or a

---

[8] See, *e.g. River Wear Commissioners* v. *Adamson* (1877) 2 App.Cas. 743.

[9] [1986] Q.B. 240.

[10] Despite the reference to "knowing," this is a negligence standard, though it is not the *tort* of negligence since no damage is required.

[11] *cf. Fowler* v. *Lanning, ante,* p. 70.

[12] *Entick* v. *Carrington* (1765) 2 Wils. K.B. 275, 291, *per curiam*; Blackstone, Comm. iii, 209–210. If unintentional trespasses are to be relegated to the tort of negligence proof of damage would, of course, become essential.

[13] In the modern law an action for a declaration might be used to settle disputed rights.

[14] The distinction between the actions of trespass and trover is well settled: the former is founded on possession: the latter on property": *Ward* v. *Macauley* (1791) 4 T.R. 489, 490, *per* Lord Kenyon C.J.; *Smith* v. *Milles* (1786) 1 T.R. 475, 480, *per* Lord Ashhurst J.; *Thompson* v. *Ward* [1953] 2 Q.B. 153, 158–159, *per* Lord Evershed M.R.

[15] A more elaborate discussion of possession will be found in the 8th edition of this work. See further Pollock and Wright, *Essay on Possession in the Common Law;* Lightwood, *Possession of Land;* Paton, *Bailment,* pp. 6–25; Paton, *Jurisprudence* (3rd ed.), Chap. 22; Dias, *Jurisprudence* (3rd ed.), Chap. 12; Harris, "The Concept of Possession in English Law," *Oxford Essays in Jurisprudence,* p. 69.

[16] *Towers & Co. Ltd.* v. *Gray* [1961] 2 Q.B. 351, 361, *per* Lord Parker C.J.

[17] *Allan* v. *Liverpool Overseers* (1874) L.R. 9 Q.B. 180, 191–192, *per* Blackburn J., adopted by Davies L.J. in *Appah* v. *Parncliffe Investments Ltd.* [1964] 1 W.L.R. 1064, 1069–1070.

[18] *White* v. *Bayley* (1861) 10 C.B.(N.S.) 227; Weir, *Casebook on Tort* (6th ed.), p. 314.

guest in an hotel. On the other hand, a lessor of land gives up possession to his tenant so that the tenant alone can bring trespass during the currency of the lease—even against the lessor unless, of course, the lessor's entry was effected in accordance with the provisions of the lease.[19] Most of the cases on the distinction between a tenant and a licensee (who does not have possession) have arisen in the context of security of tenure under the Rent Acts, but it is clear that the matter is to be determined by the substance of the agreement between the parties rather than by the label which they have chosen to attach to their relationship[20] and the hallmark of a tenancy is the right in the tenant to "exclusive possession."[21] The lessor cannot bring proceedings for a wrongful entry during the currency of the lease except in so far as it has caused permanent damage to the land, leading to a reduction in the value of his reversion, such as would result from the cutting of trees or the pulling down of buildings.[22] It is not necessary that the plaintiff should have some lawful estate or interest in the land so that there is no doubt, for example, that a squatter occupying the land without any claim of right may have sufficient possession to bring trespass[23] and, generally speaking, a stranger who enters the land without the squatter's consent cannot rely in his defence upon another person's superior right (the *jus tertii*) unless he can prove that he acted with that person's authority.[24] This is not to say that legal title is irrelevant, for where the facts leave it uncertain which of several competing claimants has possession it is in him who can prove title, *i.e.* who can prove that he has the right to possess.[25] Indeed, it has been said that where an owner of land is suing for trespass against a person alleged to be in possession, even the slightest acts by the owner (or his predecessor in title) indicating his intention to take possession are enough to enable him to maintain the action. In *Ocean Estates Ltd.* v. *Pinder*[26] the plaintiffs had been freeholders of land since 1950 under a title traced back to 1937. They brought an action for damages for trespass against the defendant, who had since 1940 been engaged in a form of peripatetic vegetable growing on various parts of the land. During the earlier part of this period the plaintiffs' predecessors in title had been cultivating fruit trees on the land and in 1957, 1959 and 1960 a surveyor surveyed the land with a view to advising on its

---

[19] *Lane* v. *Dixon* (1847) 3 C.B. 776. *Aliter* if there was only an oral contract for a lease, unenforceable by virtue of the Law of Property Act 1925, s.40: *Delaney* v. *T.P. Smith Ltd.* [1946] K.B. 393; Weir, *Casebook on Tort* (6th ed.), p. 314. But a tenant in occupation under an unenforceable contract can certainly bring trespass against a stranger: *ibid.* at p. 397, *per* Tucker L.J.

[20] *Street* v. *Mountford* [1985] A.C. 809.

[21] That is to say, the right to exclude the landlord during the currency of the term except in so far as a right of entry is reserved for a limited purpose, *e.g.* to repair. See *Radaich* v. *Smith* (1959) 101 C.L.R. 209, 222, *per* Windeyer J., adopted in *Street* v. *Mountford, supra.*

[22] *Ward* v. *Macaulay* (1791) 4 T.R. 489; *Mayfair Property Co.* v. *Johnson* [1894] 1 Ch. 508; *Jones* v. *Llanrwst U.D.C.* [1911] 1 Ch. 393.

[23] Indeed, after 12 years he may acquire title to the property by "adverse possession."

[24] *Chambers* v. *Donaldson* (1809) 11 East 65; *Nicholls* v. *Ely Beet Sugar Factory* [1931] 2 Ch. 84. As to the *jus tertii* in relation to trespass to goods, see *post*, p. 480.

[25] "If there are two persons in a field, each asserting that the field is his, and each doing some act in assertion of the right of possession, and if the question is, which of those two is in actual possession, I answer the person who has the title is in actual possession and the other is a trespasser": *Jones* v. *Chapman* (1849) 2 Exch. 803, 821, *per* Maule-J.

[26] [1969] 2 A.C. 19; see also *Williams Bros. Direct Supply Ltd.* v. *Raftery* [1958] 1 Q.B. 159; *cf. Treloar* v. *Nute* [1976] 1 W.L.R. 1295.

development, though he recommended that it should be left in abeyance for the time being. The plaintiffs' action for trespass succeeded[27] and the defendant's contention that he had sufficient possession to acquire a title by adverse possession was rejected. Possession once acquired is not, however, determined by sending the defendant a letter demanding delivery-up of the land.[28] Some estate or interest in the land may also lead the court to find possession in the plaintiff in other circumstances. For example, it is probably still the law that a spouse who is occupying a matrimonial home along with the other spouse[29] does not have possession so as to maintain trespass,[30] but a spouse who has a share in the ownership would certainly have it.

Possession may obviously extend to things which are beyond a person's immediate physical control. I do not lose possession of my house and its contents when I leave them to go to the office and generally speaking a servant who is given charge of his master's premises will not acquire possession: the possession remains with the master, who alone can sue for trespass.[31]

Immediate right to possess: trespass by relation

The immediate right to possess, sometimes also known as constructive possession,[32] signifies the lawful right to retain possession when one has it or to acquire it when one has not. Without possession it is not sufficient to support an action of trespass[33] but, owing to the willingness of the courts to extend the superior protection afforded by the older law to possession as distinct from ownership, it has for long been the law that once a person entitled to immediate possession actually enters upon the land and so acquires possession, he is deemed to have been in possession from the moment that his right to it accrued.[34] This fiction, known as trespass by relation, has the result that he can sue for acts of trespass committed while he was actually out of possession and it also provides the foundation for the claim in respect of "mesne profits," that is, the claim for the damage suffered by a person as a result of having been kept out of the possession of his land.[35]

---

[27] Had the plaintiffs' action been for ejectment (post, p. 371) they would have had no need to show possession; but if the defendant had acquired possession their title would have been defeated by adverse possession.

[28] *Mount Carmel Investments Ltd.* v. *Peter Thurlow Ltd.* [1988] 1 W.L.R. 1078.

[29] cf. the position where the non-owning spouse has been deserted by the other: *National Provincial Bank Ltd.* v. *Ainsworth* [1965] A.C. 1175, 1232.

[30] But in Canada it has been held that members of the owner's family are "occupiers" for the purpose of suing for nuisance: *Devon Lumber Co. Ltd.* v. *MacNeill* (1987) 45 D.L.R. (4th) 300.

[31] *Lutan* v. *Cross* (1810) 2 Camp. 464. However, much depends on the facts: it would be surprising if, notwithstanding *White* v. *Bayley* (1861) 10 C.B.(N.S.) 227, an agricultural worker occupying a tied cottage could not, today, sue an intruder for trespass.

[32] For an explanation of this term, see *Alicia Hosiery Ltd.* v. *Brown Shipley & Co. Ltd.* [1970] 1 Q.B. 195, 207, *per* Donaldson J.

[33] It is, however, sufficient for an action of conversion and is explained more fully in connection with that tort, *post*, pp. 478–480. In view of *Ocean Estates* v. *Pinder* (*supra*, n. 26) there may be little practical consequence in the rule that a right to immediate possession does not support trespass to land, except in relation to a lessee holding over, as to which see *infra*, n. 38.

[34] See *Dunlop* v. *Macedo* (1891) 8 T.L.R. 43 and Clerk and Lindsell, *Torts* (16th ed.), para. 23–19.

[35] The action for mesne profits is explained *post*, p. 374.

INTERFERENCE

Interference with the possession of land sufficient to amount to trespass may occur in many ways. The most obvious example is unauthorised walking upon it or going into the buildings upon it, but it is equally trespass if I throw things on to your land[36] or allow my cattle to stray on to it from my land, and even if I do no more than place my ladder against your wall.[37] And if you have given me permission to enter your land and I act in excess of the permission or remain on your land after it has expired, then, again, I am a trespasser.[38] The one restriction is that for trespass the injury must be direct and immediate. If it is indirect or consequential, there may well be a remedy (usually for nuisance or for negligence), but whatever it is it will not be trespass. If I plant a tree on your land, that is trespass. But if the roots or branches of a tree on my land project into or over your land, that is a nuisance.[39]

Trespass on highway

It is obvious that a person who uses a highway for the purpose of travelling from one place to another commits no trespass against anyone, but it is not the case that a member of the public may do upon the highway whatever he pleases; apart from the criminal law and the law of public nuisance, if he does something going beyond the reasonable use of the highway for the purpose of passing along it and matters incidental thereto,[40] he commits trespass against the person in possession of the soil on which the highway rests.[41] In *Hickman* v. *Maisey*[42] the plaintiff, as the owner of land crossed by a highway, had possession of the soil underlying the highway. The defendant, a "racing tout," had for a considerable period of time walked to and fro on a 15-yard stretch of the highway for the purpose of observing and taking notes of trials of racehorses which were being conducted on the plaintiff's

---

[36] For a modern, power-assisted example, see *Rigby* v. *Chief Constable of Northamptonshire* [1985] 1 W.L.R. 1242.

[37] *Westripp* v. *Baldock* [1938] 2 All E.R. 779; affirmed [1939] 1 All E.R. 279; *Gregory* v. *Piper* (1829) 9 B. & C. 591; *Home Brewery Co. Ltd.* v. *William Davis & Co. (Leicester) Ltd.* [1987] Q.B. 339.

[38] *Hillen* v. *I.C.I. (Alkali) Ltd.* [1936] A.C. 65; *Canadian Pacific Ry.* v. *Gaud* [1949] 2 K.B. 239, 249, *per* Cohen L.J.; *ibid.* at pp. 254–55, *per* Singleton L.J.; *R.* v. *Jones* [1976] 1 W.L.R. 672. But a lessee holding over after the termination of his lease is no trespasser, for trespass can only be committed against the person in present possession of the land: *Hey* v. *Moorhouse* (1839) 6 Bing.N.C. 52. *cf. Minister of Health* v. *Bellotti* [1944] K.B. 298 (licensee holding over after termination of licence and after lapse of reasonable time, becomes a trespasser).

[39] *Smith* v. *Giddy* [1904] 2 K.B. 448, 451; *Davey* v. *Harrow Corp.* [1958] 1 Q.B. 60. As to removal of the intruding growth, see *post*, p. 636.

[40] See, *e.g. Harrison* v. *Duke of Rutland* [1893] 1 Q.B. 142, 145–147, *per* Lord Esher M.R.; *ibid.* pp. 152–154, *per* Lopes L.J.; *ibid.* at pp. 155–160, *per* Kay L.J.; *Iveagh* v. *Martin* [1961] 1 Q.B. 232, 273, *per* Paull J. In *Randall* v. *Tarrant* [1955] 1 W.L.R. 255 a car was parked in a narrow lane while some of its occupants trespassed in the adjoining field. It was held that the parked car did not constitute a trespass to the highway.

[41] At common law this is the person whose land abuts upon the highway. *cf. Tithe Redemption Commission* v. *Runcorn U.D.C.* [1954] Ch. 383, and Highways Act 1980, ss.263–265. Where the top surface is vested in a highway authority, there would seem no reason why that authority could not bring proceedings for trespass. *cf.* the view of Lord Denning M.R. in *Hubbard* v. *Pitt* [1976] Q.B. 142.

[42] [1900] 1 Q.B. 752; *Harrison* v. *Duke of Rutland, supra*: *Liddle* v. *Yorkshire (North Riding) C.C.* [1934] 2 K.B. 101, 125–127, *per* Slesser L.J.

land. It was held that he was a trespasser. As in all cases of trespass, however, only the person having possession can complain of it and, accordingly, the fact that a person on the highway is a trespasser upon it does not relieve lawful users of the highway of any duty of care they may owe to him in accordance with the ordinary law of negligence.[43]

Trespass to subsoil

Any intrusion upon the subsoil is just as much a trespass as entry upon the surface, and subsoil and surface may be possessed by different persons. If A is in possession of the surface and B of the subsoil, and I walk upon the land, that is a trespass against A, but not against B. If I dig holes vertically in the land, that is a trespass against both A and B. If I bore a tunnel from my land into B's subsoil, that is a trespass against B only.[44]

Interference with airspace

Lord Ellenborough once expressed the view that the invasion of the air space above a man's land could not be trespass unless there was some actual contact with the land itself.[45] Now, however, it is clear that this is incorrect, and in *Kelsen* v. *Imperial Tobacco Co.*[46] McNair J., after a full review of the authorities, held that an advertising sign erected by the defendants on their own property, which projected into the airspace above the plaintiff's shop, created a trespass. The issue arises not infrequently as a result of the operation of tower cranes on building sites, which swing over adjoining land. There is no doubt that this amounts to trespass[47] and the plaintiff will normally be entitled to an injunction[48] even though this state of the law allows him to take a "dog in the manger" attitude[49] and force the defendant to pay him a sum in excess of any damage he has suffered. The problem in these cases is in fact part of a wider one of access to neighbouring land for repair and construction work.[50]

Although an intrusion into air space at a relatively low height constitutes trespass, it must now be taken as settled that the landowner's rights in airspace extend only to such height as is necessary for the ordinary use and enjoyment of the land and structures on it, so that the flight of an aircraft "several hundred feet" above a house is not a trespass at common law.[51] But

---

[43] *Farrugia* v. *G.W. Ry.* [1947] 2 All E.R. 565.

[44] *Cox* v. *Glue* (1848) 5 C.B. 533.

[45] *Pickering* v. *Rudd* (1815) 4 Camp. 219, 220–221; *Clifton* v. *Viscount Bury* (1887) 4 T.L.R. 8. *cf. Kenyon* v. *Hart* (1865) 6 B. & S. 249, 252, *per* Blackburn J., *arguendo.* Lord Ellenborough considered that if the plaintiff suffered any damage from such an invasion, his remedy lay in an action on the case.

[46] [1957] 2 Q.B. 334.

[47] *Woollerton & Wilson Ltd.* v. *Richard Costain Ltd.* [1970] 1 W.L.R. 411; *Anchor Brewhouse Developments* v. *Berkley House (Docklands Developments)* (1987) 284 E.G. 625.

[48] In the *Woollerton & Wilson* case the injunction was suspended for long enough to allow the defendant to complete the works but this is very dubious: *Charrington* v. *Simons & Co. Ltd.* [1971] 1 W.L.R. 598; *John Trenberth Ltd.* v. *National Westminster Bank Ltd.* (1979) 39 P. & C.R. 104.

[49] *Anchor Brewhouse* case, *supra*, at p. 633.

[50] As to which, see Law Commission Report No. 151.

[51] *Bernstein* v. *Skyviews & General Ltd.* [1978] Q.B. 479. The maxim *cujus est solum ejus est usque ad coelum* is not, therefore, to be taken literally in municipal law, nor, for that matter in international law so far as concerns outer space: see Brownlie, *Basic Documents in International Law* (2nd ed.), p. 116.

if an aircraft, or anything from it, falls upon the land or comes into contact with a structure on it, that might be a trespass, no matter the height from which it fell.[52]

Quite apart from the position at common law, it is provided by statute that civil aircraft which fly at a reasonable height (having regard to wind, weather and all the circumstances of the case) do not commit trespass.[53] The protection conferred by the statute extends to any flight and is not to be limited by analogy with the common law bare right of passage along a highway.[54] A landowner is not, however, without protection from persistent aerial surveillance from a height outside his zone of user, for such conduct may constitute a nuisance.[55] The Civil Aviation Act also provides that if material loss or damage is caused to any person or property by, or by a person in, or an article or person falling from an aircraft while in flight, taking off[56] or landing, then, unless the loss or damage was caused or contributed to by the negligence of the person by whom it was suffered, damages are recoverable without proof of negligence or intention or other cause of action as if the loss or damage had been caused by the wilful act, neglect, or default of the owner of the aircraft.[57]

Continuing trespass

Trespass, whether by way of personal entry or by placing things on the plaintiff's land, may be "continuing" and give rise to actions *de die in diem* so long as it lasts. In *Holmes* v. *Wilson*,[58] highway authorities supported a road by wrongfully building buttresses on the plaintiff's land, and they paid full compensation in an action for trespass. They were nevertheless held liable in a further action for trespass, because they had not removed the buttresses. Nor does a transfer of the land by the injured party prevent the transferee from suing the defendant for continuing trespass.[59]

At one time it may have been the law that trespass did not lie for omission to remove something from the land which was lawfully there to begin with,[60] although if the thing did damage to the land after it ought to have been removed an action on the case would lie. However, more modern authority

---

[52] Unless the contact were without negligence. In view of s.76(2) of the Civil Aviation Act 1982, the matter is largely academic in relation to civil aircraft: *infra*, n. 57.

[53] Civil Aviation Act 1982 s.76(1) (replacing s.40(1) of the Civil Aviation Act 1949). Compliance with any Air Navigation Order and certain other provisions of the Act is a condition of this statutory exemption from liability. The section does not apply to military aircraft belonging to or exclusively employed in the service of Her Majesty. Civil aircraft belonging to or exclusively employed by the Crown were brought within the exemption by the Civil Aviation (Crown Aircraft) Order 1970 (S.I. No. 289). It is conceivable that s.76 confers a wider exemption than the common law and might, in certain circumstances, justify an entry even into the zone of normal user.

[54] *Bernstein* v. *Skyviews, supra.* Weir, *Casebook on Tort* (6th ed.), p. 317.

[55] See *post*, p. 555.

[56] This expression appears to be confined to the period after the pilot has come to the take-off position: *Blankley* v. *Godley* [1952] 1 All E.R. 436n.

[57] S.76(2). There is a proviso to the effect that if the owner's liability arises only by virtue of the section and if a legal liability to pay damages for the loss in question exists in some other person, then the owner is entitled to be indemnified by that other person.

[58] (1839) 10 A. & E. 503.

[59] *Hudson* v. *Nicholson* (1839) 5 M. & W. 437; followed in *Konskier* v. *Goodman Ltd.* [1928] 1 K.B. 421.

[60] *Shapcott* v. *Mugford* (1696) 1 Ld. Raym. 187, 188; trespass *vi et armis* does not apply to non-feasance.

imposes liability for trespass[61] and there is a close analogy with the situation where a visitor's stay exceeds the duration of his licence. However, there is no trespass if a man merely omits to restore land to the same condition (apart from removing anything which he has put on it) in which he found it, *e.g.* if he fails to fill up a pit which he has dug on his neighbour's land. He is, of course, liable in trespass for the original digging (but not for continuing trespass in allowing it to remain there) and, no doubt, for negligence if anyone falls into the pit.[62]

DEFENCES

Licence

For the purposes of trespass, the best definition of licence is that given by Sir Frederick Pollock. A licence is "that consent which, without passing any interest in the property to which it relates, merely prevents the acts for which consent is given from being wrongful."[63] In the law of real property it is important to distinguish a licence from interests in land like leases, easements or *profits á prendre,* existing at law. These confer rights *in rem, i.e.* rights which avail against persons generally, including, of course, the lessor or grantor himself, whereas a licence normally gives only a right *in personam* against the licensor. But the distinction seems to have little importance so far as defences to trespass are concerned. A man is not a trespasser if he is on land with the permission, express or implied,[64] of the possessor, and that is all that matters for present purposes.[65]

Revocation

A bare licence, *i.e.* one granted otherwise than for valuable consideration, may be revoked at any time, and so may many contractual licences, even though revocation may involve the licensor in liability for breach of contract.[66] After revocation the licensee becomes a trespasser, but he must

---

[61] *Konskier* v. *Goodman Ltd., supra; Restatement,* 2d, s.160; *cf. Penarth Dock Co.* v. *Pounds* [1963] 1 Lloyd's Rep. 359 (breach of contract); and see the remarks in *Clearlite Holdings Ltd.* v. *Auckland City Corp.* [1976] 2 N.Z.L.R. 729, 734. In *Konskier's* case it was held that there was a continuing trespass though negligence (case) would not lie for lack of a duty to the plaintiff.

[62] *Clegg* v. *Dearden* (1848) 12 Q.B. 576, 601. But a tenant who removes fixtures and does not make good may be liable for waste. This is a tort, but not one of much importance, since the landlord will normally rely on covenants in the lease: *Mancetter Developments Ltd.* v. *Garmanson Ltd.* [1986] Q.B. 1212.

[63] *Torts* (15th ed.), p. 284.

[64] See *Robson* v. *Hallett* [1967] 2 Q.B. 939, 950–951, *per* Lord Parker C.J.; *ibid.* at pp. 953–954, *per* Diplock L.J. For the purposes of the crime of burglary (of which trespassory entry is an ingredient) the question is whether the defendant honestly (not reasonably) believed in his right to enter: see the extraordinary case of *R.* v. *Collins* [1973] Q.B. 100. Implied licence is considered further at *ante,* p. 211.

[65] *Armstrong* v. *Sheppard and Short Ltd.* [1959] 2 Q.B. 384, 399, *per* Lord Evershed M.R.; Weir, *Casebook on Tort* (6th ed.), p. 331. Earlier editions of this work contained a full discussion of the difficult topic of licences (see the sixth edition, pp. 383–393) but the subject is today better left to books on real property. See Dawson and Pearce, *Licences.*

[66] *Thompson* v. *Park* [1944] K.B. 408. *cf. Kerrison* v. *Smith* [1897] 2 Q.B. 445; *King* v. *David Allen & Sons Ltd.* [1916] 2 A.C. 54.

be allowed a reasonable time in which to leave and to remove his goods.[67]
Some contractual licences are, however, irrevocable because revocation in
breach of contract would be prevented by the grant of an equitable remedy
to the licensee. A licence coupled with an interest is irrevocable because,
although the licence itself—the bare permission to enter—is only a right *in
personam,* it confers a right *in rem* to something when you have entered:

> "A licence to hunt in a man's park and carry away the deer killed to his
> own use; to cut down a tree in a man's ground, and to carry it away the
> next day to his own use, are licences as to the acts of hunting and cutting
> down the tree, but as to the carrying away of the deer killed and the tree
> cut down, they are grants."[68]

Until the tree or deer is carried away the licence is irrevocable.[69]

A contractual licence may also be irrevocable even if it is not coupled with
an interest, but the circumstances in which this will be so are not finally
settled. It seems, however, that the following conclusion is warranted by the
cases.[70] Whether a contractual licence is revocable is a question of construction of the contract in the light of relevant and admissible circumstances.[71] It
will be irrevocable if such is the intention of the parties, and this may be
inferred from the terms of the contract, the character of the transaction, and
the attendant circumstances that the licence is intended to endure for a
definite or ascertainable period.[72] Where it is granted for a limited period
and for a definite purpose, it will be irrevocable until the accomplishment of
the purpose.[73] If the licensee is prepared to observe the terms of the contract
the licensor may be restrained by injunction from revoking the licence[74] and
even where there is no opportunity to seek such a remedy (for example,
where the plaintiff is ejected from the cinema) the equitable right which the
licensee has destroys the defence of "trespasser" which the licensor could
otherwise plead to an action for assault.[75]

---

[67] *Cornish* v. *Stubbs* (1870) L.R. 5 C.P. 334; *Canadian Pacific Ry.* v. *The King* [1931] A.C. 414; *Minister of Health* v. *Bellotti* [1944] K.B. 289; *Robson* v. *Hallett, supra.*

[68] *Thomas* v. *Sorrell* (1672) Vaughan 330, 351, *per* Vaughan C.J.

[69] The court in *Wood* v. *Leadbitter* (1845) 13 M. & W. 838, 844–845; *Wood* v. *Manley* (1839) 11 A. & E. 34; *Jones & Sons Ltd.* v. *Tankerville* [1909] 2 Ch. 440, 442, *per* Parker J. cf. *Frank Warr & Co. Ltd.* v. *L.C.C.* [1904] 1 K.B. 713; *Clore* v. *Theatrical Properties Ltd.* [1936] 3 All E.R. 483.

[70] See especially *Hurst* v. *Picture Theatres Ltd.* [1915] 1 K.B. 1; Weir, *Casebook on Tort,* (6th ed.), p. 325; *Winter Garden Theatre (London) Ltd.* v. *Millennium Productions Ltd.* [1948] A.C. 173; *Bendall* v. *McWhirter* [1952] 2 Q.B. 466; *Hounslow* v. *Twickenham Garden Developments Ltd.* [1971] Ch. 233. cf. *Wood* v. *Leadbitter* (1845) 13 M. & W. 838; *Cowell* v. *Rosehill Racecourse Co. Ltd.* (1937) 56 C.L.R. 605.

[71] *Winter Garden* case [1946] 1 All E.R. 678, 680, *per* Lord Greene M.R.; *Re Spenborough U.D.C.'s Agreement* [1968] Ch. 139. cf. *Winter Garden* case [1948] A.C. 173, 193, *per* Lord Porter; Wade, "What is Licence" (1948) 64 L.Q.R. 57, 69.

[72] Walford (1947) 12 Conv.(N.S.) 126; Glanville Williams 30 Can. Bar Rev. 1006; Mitchell, "Learner's Licence" (1954) 17 M.L.R. 211–219.

[73] *Winter Garden* case [1948] A.C. 173, *per* Lord Porter; *ibid.* at p. 189, *per* Lord Simon. See *Munro* v. *Balnagown Estates Co.* 1949 S.L.T. 85.

[74] [1946] 1 All E.R. 678, 685, *per* Lord Greene M.R.; *Bendall* v. *McWhirter* [1952] 2 Q.B. 466, 478–483, *per* Denning L.J. In a proper case, revocation of the licence may be restrained even though performance has not yet commenced: *Verrall* v. *Great Yarmouth B.C.* [1981] Q.B. 202.

[75] Wade, *loc.cit.,* p. 76. *Errington* v. *Errington* [1952] 1 K.B. 290, 297–299 and *Bendall* v. *McWhirter* [1952] 2 Q.B. 466, 479–483, *per* Denning L.J. *Bendall* v. *McWhirter* has been overruled by *National Provincial Bank Ltd.* v. *Ainsworth* [1965] A.C. 1175 but, it is submitted, without affecting the statements in the text.

If a licence has been executed, it cannot be revoked in the sense that the licensee can be compelled to undo what he has lawfully done. If I allow you to post bills on my hoarding, I can cancel my permission, but I cannot force you to remove bills that you have already stuck there. So in *Liggins* v. *Inge*[76] where an oral licence had been given to lower a river bank and make a weir above the licensor's mill, it was held that the licensor could not sue the licensee for continuing the weir which the latter had erected. But the rule that an executed licence is irrevocable applies only where the licence can be construed as authorising the doing of exactly what has been done. It does not apply where there has been mere acquiescence in something which was never authorised before it was done.[77] Nor does it apply if its application would amount to the creation of an easement in favour of the licensee. An easement cannot be granted by parol and therefore, after the licence has been revoked, the plaintiff is prima facie entitled to an injunction restraining the continuation of the trespass.[78]

Justification by law

Acts which would otherwise be trespasses, whether to land, goods or the person, are frequently prevented from being so by the existence of some justification provided by the law. A person entering land in pursuance of arrangements made by a local authority for the public to have access to open country is not a trespasser so long as he complies with the specified conditions[79]; a landlord commits no trespass if he distrains for rent.[80] Most importantly there are innumerable instances in which officers of the law are authorised to enter land, to take goods or to arrest or restrain a person, but these belong more to public than to private law and only one or two illustrations can be given here.[81] The most important powers are those conferred on the police by the Police and Criminal Evidence Act 1984. Under section 17[82] a constable may enter and search premises (if need be, by force) for the purpose of arresting a person for an arrestable offence and for various other purposes (including those of saving life or limb or preventing serious damage to the property); and under section 18 there is power to enter premises after an arrest for an arrestable offence and search for evidence of that offence or connected or similar offences.[83] However, when

---

[76] (1831) 3 Bing. 682; *Davies* v. *Marshall* (1861) 10 C.B.(N.S.) 697. See Wade, *loc.cit.*, pp. 68–69.

[77] *Canadian Pacific Ry.* v. *The King* [1931] A.C. 414, 428–429 *per* Lord Russell.

[78] *Armstrong* v. *Sheppard & Short Ltd.* [1959] 2 Q.B. 384. The right to an injunction is not unqualified and an injunction may be refused on the ground that the injury is trivial: *ibid.*

[79] National Parks and Access to the Countryside Act 1949, s.60. See also Countryside Act 1968, ss.16–19.

[80] See Clerk and Lindsell, *Torts* (14th ed.), Chap. 16 (not in current ed.). For distress damage feasant (the seizure of an animal or chattel by the possessor of land when it is wrongfully on the land and causing damage to it) see Williams, *Animals,* Chaps. I–VIII and the seventh edition of this work, p. 383. In respect of animals, there is now a statutory right of detention and sale: see *post*, pp. 462–463.

[81] For a list in 1982, see Clerk and Lindsell, *Torts* (15th ed.), p. 1304. The statutory rights of entry of gas and electricity boards were held in *Groves* v. *Eastern Gas Board* [1952] 1 K.B. 77 to authorise forcible entry where necessary and to constitute a defence of justification in an action of trespass. By the Rights of Entry (Gas and Electricity Boards) Act 1954 these rights are (except in a case of emergency) to be exercised only by consent of the occupier or under a warrant.

[82] For search warrants, see ss.8–16.

[83] There is also a rather narrower power of entry and search under s.32, which extends to non-arrestable offences.

a constable is lawfully on the premises (for example, with the consent of the occupier or, it seems, pursuant to a lawful entry under section 18) he may seize anything which he reasonably believes to be evidence of *any* offence provided he has reasonable grounds to believe it would otherwise be concealed, destroyed, etc. A bailiff who enters private premises on civil process (*e.g.* to seize property in execution) commits no trespass, provided that he does not gain entry by breaking in.[84] Indeed a bailiff may even enter the house of a stranger to the debtor to execute process, but this he does at his peril. If the property of the debtor that he is to take or if the person whom he is to arrest is actually there, then he is justified, but otherwise he is a trespasser.[85] Nor is it only officers of the law who may be thus empowered. A private person may in certain circumstances arrest a criminal, and it is no trespass if he breaks into the house of another person in order to prevent him from murdering his wife,[86] or probably from committing other serious offences.[87]

Trespass ab initio

Where an entry upon land or other prima facie trespass is justified by the authority of the law itself, then, according to an ancient doctrine of the common law, if the actor abuses his authority he becomes a trespasser *ab initio*; his act is reckoned as unlawful from the very beginning, however innocent his conduct may have been up to the moment of the abuse.[88] The doctrine applies only if the authority is that of the law, not that of the other party concerned,[89] and the abuse must be by a positive act, not a mere omission.[90] The explanations of these restrictions on the doctrine are historical,[91] but they show that its purpose, derived from its origin in the law of distress, was to provide protection against abuses of authority.

Seen in this light it would seem to be unduly optimistic to suppose that the doctrine has outlived its usefulness,[92] even given the modern limitation that partial abuse of an authority does not render everything done under it unlawful. For example, in *Elias* v. *Pasmore*[93] police had lawfully entered the plaintiff's premises in order to arrest a man, and while there they seized a number of documents, some of them unlawfully. It was held that this did not render their original entry a trespass. However, in *Chic Fashions (West Wales) Ltd.* v. *Jones*[94] though no point involving trespass *ab initio* was in fact

---

[84] The bailiff may enter by opening an unlocked door, but may not break open a locked one: *Semayne's Case* (1604) 5 Co.Rep. 91a; *Southam* v. *Smout* [1964] 1 Q.B. 308; *Vaughan* v. *McKenzie* [1969] 1 Q.B. 557.

[85] *Southam* v. *Smout, supra.* "It is a case of justification not by faith but by works": *ibid.* at p. 327, *per* Harman L.J. *cf. Chic Fashions (West Wales) Ltd.* v. *Jones* [1968] 2 Q.B. 299.

[86] *Handcock* v. *Baker* (1800) 2 Bos. & P. 260.

[87] *Ibid.* at p. 265, *per* Chambre J. Such cases would now fall under s.3 of the Criminal Law Act 1967.

[88] *Six Carpenters' Case* (1610) 8 Co.Rep. 146a. The older cases are epitomised in Viner's *Abridgement,* Vol. XX (2nd ed.), pp. 499–504.

[89] *Delta Holdings Ltd.* v. *Magrum* (1975) 59 D.L.R. (3d) 126.

[90] *Ibid.*

[91] Holdsworth, H.E.L., vii, pp. 499–501.

[92] *Pace* the Court of Appeal in *Chic Fashions (West Wales) Ltd.* v. *Jones* [1968] 2 Q.B. 299.

[93] [1934] 2 K.B. 164; *Harvey* v. *Pocock* (1843) 11 M. & W. 740; *Canadian Pacific Wine Co. Ltd.* v. *Tuley* [1921] 2 A.C. 417.

[94] [1968] 2 Q.B. 299.

in issue, the three members of the Court of Appeal criticised the doctrine as offending against the principle that subsequent events cannot render unlawful an act which was lawful when it was done. This principle is, in general, a sound one, but it should not be over-stressed. Not only may subsequent events illuminate the intent with which an act was originally done and thus assist in determining its lawfulness or unlawfulness,[95] but there are, and should continue to be, cases in which, in effect, the law withholds judgment on the lawfulness of an act for a time and allows it to depend upon subsequent events.[96] The doctrine of trespass *ab initio* enables this to be done in the important area of the protection of a man's person, goods and land against abuse of official power.[97]

REMEDIES

The action for trespass, besides being used to remedy trespass as a pure tort, has also some varieties which are employed for the recovery of land and the profits thereof, and of these we shall speak in the next sections on ejectment and mesne profits.

Re-entry

The remedies for trespass as a pure tort need no special mention except the *right of re-entry*. The person entitled to possession can enter or re-enter the premises, but the Criminal Law Act 1977 makes it an offence punishable with imprisonment for anyone (other than a displaced residential occupier) to use or threaten violence for the purposes of securing entry to any premises occupied by another.[98] This replaces earlier criminal legislation in a series of Forcible Entry Acts, beginning in 1381. However, in *Hemmings* v. *Stoke Poges Golf Club*[99] the Court of Appeal held that whatever might be his criminal liability under the Statutes of Forcible Entry, a landowner was not civilly liable if he used no more force than necessary to remove the other

---

[95] This was one of the explanations of the doctrine of trespass *ab initio* itself given by Coke: 8 Co.Rep. 146b. Winfield ridiculed it (see the eighth edition of this book, p. 346) but even though it contains an element of fiction, it is submitted that it does have some merit.

[96] *Southam* v. *Smout* [1964] 1 Q.B. 308, *supra*, n. 85 provides one example, and there are others also. The power of a private person to arrest on reasonable suspicion of an arrestable offence exists only if the offence suspected has actually been committed (Police and Criminal Evidence Act 1984, s.24 *ante*, p. 63), and this cannot be known until further investigations have been carried out. If a person enters upon land under authority of the National Parks and Access to the Countryside Act 1949, s.60(1) (*ante*, p. 368) and then commits a breach of the restrictions contained in the Second Schedule, it seems that he becomes a trespasser *ab initio*: the subsection has effect subject to the provisions of the Sched. (s.60(4)) and the Sched. itself provides that s.60(1) "shall not apply to a person who" does any of the forbidden acts on the land.

[97] Lord Denning M.R., a member of the court in *Chic Fashions* subsequently referred to the doctrine with approval in *Cinnamond* v. *British Airports Authority* [1980] 1 W.L.R. 582.

[98] c. 45, s.6. The proposition in the text is a bare summary of a complex section. The crime is in one respect significantly wider than that under the Forcible Entry Acts for it was said that under those Acts the owner committed no offence in the use of force unless he had previously acquiesced in his dispossession: *McPhail* v. *Persons Unknown* [1973] Ch. 447.

[99] [1920] 1 K.B. 720, where the earlier authorities are considered.

party and his property. It is submitted that the law remains the same under the Criminal Law Act.[1]

Action for the recovery of land (Ejectment)

By the action of ejectment, or, as it should be called, the action for the recovery of land, a person dispossessed of land can recover it specifically. The story of this remedy is an old one and neatly exemplifies the use of fictions in the development of a legal system. It was originally a species of the action for trespass to land, and was invented for the benefit of the lease-holder, to whom the remedies of the freeholder were denied because he had mere "possession" of the land and not that blessed and superior "seisin" which gave the freeholder very adequate, if excessively dilatory, protection in the shape of the real actions. Then, by a notable paradox, the action of ejectment was seen to be so quick and efficient compared to the ponderous progress of the real actions that the freeholder adopted it by a series of fictions. If, for example, Smith, a freeholder, were seeking to recover the land from Brown, he was allowed to pretend that he had leased the land to John Doe, an imaginary person, and that John Doe had been ejected by another non-existent person, Richard Roe (the "casual ejector"). Then Smith began his action with Doe as the nominal plaintiff against Roe as the nominal defendant, but he first served on Brown a notice signed by "your loving friend, Roe," in which Roe informed Brown that Roe claimed no interest in the land and advised Brown to defend the action. The fictitious parties then disappeared and the stage was cleared for the proceedings between Smith and Brown. The title of the action was "*John Doe on the demise* [*i.e. lease*] *of Smith* v. *Brown*," or, more briefly, "*Doe* d. *Smith* v. *Brown*." It was useless for Brown to protest against these fictions; he was not allowed to defend the action unless he acquiesced in them.[2] The remarkable result was that the question of ownership of land was fought under the guise of an action of trespass.

These fictions have been long abolished,[3] and an action for the recovery of land differs in no formal respect from any other action. A special summary procedure has, however, been devised to enable a plaintiff to obtain an order for possession, and a writ for its enforcement, against persons in occupation of his land if they entered or remained there without his licence or consent, whether or not he is able to identify all, or even any, of those persons.[4] The plaintiff is not obliged to take steps to identify the persons in occupation.[5]

---

[1] But it is pointed out in Smith & Hogan, *Criminal Law* (6th ed.), p. 806 that if the landowner uses force the person being removed may, presumably, justify retaliatory force under s.3 of the Criminal Law Act 1967.

[2] Sometimes the fictitious names were more descriptive: *e.g. Fairclaim* v. *Shamtitle* (1762) 3 Burr. 1290.

[3] By the Common Law Procedure Act 1852. For the history of the matter, see Holdsworth, H.E.L., iii, pp. 213–217; vii, pp. 4–23. The best account is in Maitland, *Equity* pp. 352–355; reprinted separately as *Forms of Action* pp. 56–59. John Doe, however, continues to serve the law in another context: see *Barnett* v. *French* [1981] 1 W.L.R. 848, where his participation was singularly apt, the real defendant being the Department of the Environment.

[4] R.S.C., Ord. 113. The procedure is also available in the County Court. The court's jurisdiction extends to making an order for possession of the whole premises, not just that part presently under adverse occupation: *University of Essex* v. *Djemal* [1980] 1 W.L.R. 1301.

[5] R.S.C. App. A, Form 11A.

A rule that has been repeatedly asserted is that in an action of ejectment the plaintiff must recover by the strength of his own title and not by the weakness of the defendant's,[6] and since the action for the recovery of land has taken the place of ejectment the rule has been recognised by both the House of Lords[7] and the Judicial Committee of the Privy Council.[8] The defendant need only allege that he is in possession, and the plaintiff must, if he can do so, positively prove that his own title is better. But when we ask what exactly he must prove in order to establish his title, the law does not appear to require much. It has been said, indeed, that he must do more than set up mere *de facto* possession which, as we have seen, will usually enable him to sue for trespass as a tort,[9] but this distinction between the action of ejectment and the action for pure trespass is a tenuous one in view of other authorities, the most important of which is *Asher* v. *Whitlock,*[10] where it was held that if A takes possession of waste land without any other title than such seizure, he can maintain ejectment against B who subsequently enters on the land and who cannot show title or possession in anyone prior to A.[11] When, therefore, it is said that A's former possession raises only a presumption of title it must be confessed that this presumption is not easily upset.[12]

Jus tertii

It has already been noted that the defendant to an ordinary action of trespass cannot as a general rule set up the defence of *jus tertii.*[13] Is this rule applicable to the defendant to an action of ejectment? As the plaintiff there must prove his title, it would seem to be a corollary that if the evidence, whether it appear from the plaintiff's own case or be produced by the defendant, shows that some third person is entitled to the land, the plaintiff ought not to succeed; in other words, the defendant ought to be allowed to plead *jus tertii.* But whether this is the law has been greatly debated by various writers.[14] If, however, we limit ourselves to what has been actually decided by the courts, it appears that *jus tertii* is a defence. *Doe* d. *Carter* v. *Barnard*[15] is the leading authority to that effect. True, this decision received a glancing blow from Cockburn L.C.J. in *Asher* v. *Whitlock*[16] and a much harder knock from Lord Macnaghten in *Perry* v. *Clissold*[17] but the dicta of these learned judges were *obiter,* for in neither of these cases was *jus tertii*

---

[6] Lee C.J. in *Martin* d. *Tregonwell* v. *Strachan* (1742) 5 T.R. 107n. is said to have first formulated the rule: Wiren, "The Plea of *Jus Tertii* in Ejectment" (1925) 41 L.Q.R. 139, 145.
[7] *Danford* v. *McAnulty* (1883) 8 App.Cas. 456, 460, *per* Lord O'Hagan; *ibid.* at p. 462, *per* Lord Blackburn.
[8] *Emmerson* v. *Maddison* [1906] A.C. 569, 575, *per* Sir Alfred Wills.
[9] *Harper* v. *Charlesworth* (1825) 4 B. & C. 574, 589, *per* Bayley J.; *ibid.* at pp. 592–594, *per* Holroyd J.; Weir, *Casebook on Tort* (6th ed.), p. 313.
[10] (1865) L.R. 1 Q.B. 1. See, too, *Doe* d. *Hughes* v. *Dyeball* (1829) Moo. & M. 346.
[11] Approved by the Judicial Committee in *Perry* v. *Clissold* [1907] A.C. 73, 79.
[12] *Whale* v. *Hitchcock* (1876) 34 L.T. 136.
[13] *Ante*, p. 361.
[14] For full discussion of the question, see Wiren, *loc. cit.*; Hargreaves, "Terminology and Title in Ejectment" (1940) 56 L.Q.R. 376; Holdsworth, "Terminology and Title in Ejectment—A Reply," *ibid.* 479.
[15] (1849) 13 Q.B. 945.
[16] (1865) L.R. 1 Q.B. 1, 6.
[17] [1906] A.C. 73, 79–80.

raised, nor indeed could it have been raised on the facts. Both cases decide no more than that if the plaintiff in ejectment once had *de facto* possession of land, that raises a presumption of title in his favour which mere subsequent possession of the defendant will not defeat. Neither of them decides that the plaintiff's claim cannot be upset by proof of *jus tertii*; indeed, *Asher* v. *Whitlock* implies that it can be.

Moreover, the principle which is supported by *jus tertii*—that the plaintiff must win by his own strength and not by his opponent's weakness—is a sound one. What he is seeking to establish is ownership of the land and, if it appears to be in anyone else, why should the defendant be compelled to give up possession to *him?* Against this it has been urged that if the plaintiff can win (as undoubtedly he can) if he once had *de facto* possession and the defendant can show nothing but a later *de facto* possession on his own part, then the plaintiff ought to win in any event because the law greatly respects possession. But that is a two-edged argument, for if the law respects possession which the plaintiff once had, why should it not equally respect possession which the defendant now has? And it sounds odd to insist that, because C is the real owner of land, B, who is in wrongful (but legally protected) possession of it, ought to give it up to A who once had wrongful possession of it.[18]

Whether or not *jus tertii* is in general a defence in an action of ejectment, it cannot be relied upon where the defendant has acquired possession from the plaintiff himself or from one through whom the plaintiff claims. The rule that a tenant is estopped from denying his landlord's title is well known, but a licensee is similarly estopped from denying the title of his licensor,[19] and, indeed this rule of estoppel extends to anyone who is sued in ejectment by one from whom he derived his interest. "If a person obtains possession of land, claiming under a will or deed, he cannot afterwards set up another title to the land against the will or deed, though the deed or will did not operate to pass the land in question."[20]

---

[18] Winfield's account of this controversial topic has been left unchanged and it is not thought that either the dictum of Lord Diplock in *Ocean Estates Ltd.* v. *Pinder* [1969] 2 A.C. 19, 25 or the decision of the High Court of Australia in *Allen* v. *Roughley* (1955) 94 C.L.R. 98 (see Wade [1956] C.L.J. 177) would have led him to alter it. In that case Holdsworth's view that the plaintiff in ejectment must prove an absolutely good title and that therefore the *jus tertii* was a defence (H.E.L., vii, pp. 57–81) was rejected. But Winfield emphasises the strength of a case founded upon prior possession. Against a defendant in possession, however, the plaintiff must recover by the strength of his own title, and this he cannot do if the right to possession is proved to be in a third party. A plea of *jus tertii* is not made out merely by showing defects in the plaintiff's title. It must be proved that title is vested in some third party: Jolly, "The Jus Tertii and the Third Man" (1955) 18 M.L.R. 371. See further Salmond and Heuston, *Torts* (19th ed.), p. 55; Fleming, *Law of Torts* (7th ed.), pp. 44–45. *cf.* Clerk and Lindsell, *Torts* (16th ed.), para. 23–48. *Georgian Cottagers' Association Inc.* v. *Corp. of Township of Flos and Kerr* (1962) 32 D.L.R. (2d) 547 (Ontario). (Though *jus tertii* is not normally a defence against a plaintiff in possession, the defence is available where the plaintiff is in occupation of Crown land without the consent of the Crown. *cf. Harper* v. *Charlesworth* (1825) 4 B. & C. 574).

[19] *Doe d. Johnson* v. *Baytup* (1835) 3 Ad. & E. 188. A general denial in a pleading by a tenant does not amount to a sufficient denial of the landlord's title to cause a forfeiture of the lease: *Warner* v. *Sampson* [1959] 1 Q.B. 297.

[20] Lopes L.J. in *Dalton* v. *Fitzgerald* [1897] 2 Ch. 86, 93. Another exception to the permissibility of pleading *jus tertii* is suggested with some doubt in Salmond and Heuston, *Torts* (19th ed.), p. 56. "If the defendant's possession is wrongful as against the plaintiff, the plaintiff may succeed though he cannot himself show a good title." But assuming that this is the law, has it any necessary connection with *jus tertii*?

Mesne profits

The action for mesne profits is another species of the action for trespass and lies for the damage which the plaintiff has suffered through having been out of possession of his land. By Blackstone's time nothing but a shilling or some trivial sum was usually recoverable in the action of ejectment because it had been "licked into the form of a real action"[21] and its chief purpose had become the trial of the title to land.[22] If the claimant was successful, he got possession of the land but no compensation for having been kept out of it. The action for mesne profits enables the plaintiff to claim not only profits taken by the defendant during his occupancy, but also damages for deterioration and the reasonable costs of getting possession.[23] The Rules of the Supreme Court[24] enable a plaintiff in an action for the recovery of land to join with it a claim for mesne profits, and if he does so it is unnecessary for him to have entered the land before he sues.[25] If he prefers he can still bring the action for mesne profits separately but in that event he must first enter, for the action is one of trespass; trespass is a wrong to possession, and until he enters he has not got it. Once he has entered, however, then, by the fiction of trespass by relation[26] the plaintiff is deemed to have been in possession during the whole period for which he claims the mesne profits.[27]

---

[21] *Goodtitle* v. *Tombs* (1770) 3 Wils.K.B. 118, 120, *per* Wilmot C.J.

[22] Blackstone, Comm. iii, p. 205.

[23] "I have known four times the value of the mesne profits given by a jury in this sort of action of trespass": *Goodtitle* v. *Tombs* (1770) 3 Wils.K.B. 118, 121, *per* Gould J. And see *Doe* v. *Filliter* (1844) 13 M. & W. 47; *Hall & Co. Ltd.* v. *Pearlberg* [1956] 1 W.L.R. 244.

[24] Ord. 15, r. 1.

[25] If the plaintiff's title to the land has been extinguished by adverse possession, so is his claim for mesne profits: *Mount Carmel Investment Ltd.* v. *Peter Thurlow Ltd.* [1988] 1 W.L.R. 1078.

[26] *Ante*, p. 362.

[27] And it does not matter that he cannot bring evidence that he could have let the property to someone else: *Swordheath Properties Ltd.* v. *Tabet* [1979] 1 W.L.R. 285.

CHAPTER 14

NUISANCE[1]

INTRODUCTION

IN modern parlance, nuisance is that branch of the law of tort most closely concerned with "protection of the environment." Thus nuisance actions have concerned pollution by oil[2] or noxious fumes,[3] interference with leisure activities,[4] offensive smells from premises used for keeping animals[5] or noise from industrial installations.[6] Three important qualifications must be made, however, to this broad generalisation. First, there are areas of nuisance, such as obstruction of the highway or of access thereto,[7] which have no "environmental" flavour. Secondly, the prevailing stance of nuisance liability is that of protection of private rights in the enjoyment of land,[8] so that control of injurious activity for the benefit of the whole community is incidental.[9] Thirdly, the common law of nuisance has been supplemented and to a large extent replaced by an array of statutory powers designed to control environmental damage. A full account of these would be beyond the scope of a book on tort[10] but the reader's attention is directed to the following principal provisions:

(i) Under Part III of the Public Health Act 1936 various states of affairs[11] are "statutory nuisances."[12] A local authority which is satisfied that such a nuisance exists is under a duty to serve an abatement notice requiring the nuisance to be terminated and, if the notice is not

---

[1] Weir, *Casebook on Tort*, (6th ed.), Chap. 10; Buckley, *Law of Nuisance*.
[2] *Esso Petroleum Co. Ltd.* v. *Southport Corp.* [1956] A.C. 218.
[3] *St. Helen's Smelting Co.* v. *Tipping* (1865) 11 H.L.C. 642.
[4] *Bridlington Relay* v. *Yorkshire Electricity Board* [1965] Ch. 436.
[5] *Rapier* v. *London Tramways Co.* [1893] 2 Ch. 588.
[6] *Halsey* v. *Esso Petroleum Co. Ltd.* [1961] 1 W.L.R. 683.
[7] *Post*, p. 412.
[8] There is, however, a strong public law element in the shape of the power of public authorities to bring proceedings for an injunction to restrain a public nuisance: see below.
[9] Indeed, there may be circumstances in which the enforcement of private rights by injunction will bring positive hardship on the community at large: see *e.g. Bellew* v. *Cement Co. Ltd.* [1948] I.R. 62. The common law of nuisance has been a prominent topic for analysis by the economic approach to law. There is a large American literature on the topic. For an introduction see Ogus and Richardson, "Economics and the Environment" (1977) 36 C.L.J. 284.
[10] See *Encyclopedia of Environment Health Law and Practice*; Garner, *Control of Pollution Encyclopaedia*.
[11] *e.g.* premises in a state prejudicial to health or constituting a nuisance, accumulation or deposit prejudicial to health or constituting a nuisance.
[12] Where there is no allegation that the state of affairs is prejudicial to health there must be a nuisance in the common law sense, *i.e.* it must affect persons outside the premises: *National Coal Board* v. *Neath B.C.* [1976] 2 All E.R. 478. But see *post*, p. 394.

obeyed, to lay a complaint before a magistrates' court, which then
makes a nuisance abatement order.[13]

(ii) Under the Control of Pollution Act 1974 there are wide-ranging
powers to control disposal of waste of various kinds, principally by
means of a system of licensing. Parts of this Act give rise to civil
liability in damages and are considered in another section of this
book.[14]

(iii) Atmospheric pollution is controlled by a variety of powers in the
Clean Air Acts 1956[15] and 1968 and the Control of Pollution Act 1974.

(iv) Noise is now principally governed by Part III of the Control of
Pollution Act 1974, replacing the Noise Abatement Act 1960.[16]

The enforcement of these provisions is in the hands of public bodies[17]
(commonly the local authority) and they do not generally give rise to civil
liability. However, the principal remedy sought by most victims of nuisance
is an injunction to prevent its continuance and a complaint to the relevant
body under one of the above Acts will often be a considerably cheaper and
more expeditious way of getting redress than bringing a common law action
for an injunction, with the attendant delay and expense. The common law of
nuisance remains necessary where the plaintiff seeks damages or where for
some reason the public body is unable or unwilling to act,[18] but we are
witnessing here, as in other areas of tort, the steady ousting of private law by
public law.[19]

PUBLIC AND PRIVATE NUISANCES

Public nuisance

Nuisances are divided into public and private, although it is quite possible
for the same conduct to amount to both. A public nuisance is a crime, while a
private nuisance is only a tort. A public or common nuisance is one which
materially affects the reasonable comfort and convenience of life of a class of
Her Majesty's subjects who come within the sphere or neighbourhood of its
operation; the question whether the number of persons affected is sufficient
to constitute a class is one of fact in every case, and it is sufficient to show that

---

[13] Failure to obey the order is punishable by a fine which is increased each day the offence continues: s.95(1).
The local authority may abate the nuisance itself and recover its expenses in doing so: s.96. If the local
authority considers that summary proceedings are inadequate they may take proceedings in the High
Court: s.100.

[14] *Post,* p. 453.

[15] The best known provision is that of s.11, which allows a local authority to designate "smokeless zones"
(more properly known as smoke control areas).

[16] See *Hammersmith London Borough* v. *Magnum Automated Forecourts Ltd.* [1978] 1 W.L.R. 50 (injunction under Control of Pollution Act).

[17] But sometimes the statute provides for enforcement on complaint by a person aggrieved (*e.g.* s.59 of the
Control of Pollution Act, summary proceedings by occupier of premises affected by noise nuisance).

[18] See, *e.g. Tetley* v. *Chitty* [1986] 1 All E.R. 663, where the relevant public body was defendant.

[19] McLaren, "Nuisance Law and the Industrial Revolution" (1983) 3 O.J.L.S. 155 concludes that deficiences
of the law in dealing with pollution in the nineteenth century stemmed not from defects in principle
(indeed, judges were quite ready to reject the pleas of manufacturers) but from the disinclination of those
best able to take action to put the law in motion.

a representative cross-section of that class has been so affected for an injunction to issue.[20] It is one which is so widespread in its range or so indiscriminate in its effect that it would not be reasonable to expect one person as distinct from the community at large[21] to take proceedings to put a stop to it. This definition is vague and it has been rightly said that nuisance "covers a multitude of sins, great and small."[22] Public nuisances at common law include such diverse activities as carrying on an offensive trade, keeping a disorderly house, selling food unfit for human consumption, obstructing public highways, throwing fireworks about in the street and holding an ill-organised pop festival.[23]

Special or particular damage necessary for action for damages for public nuisance[24]

So long as the public only or some section of it is injured no civil action can be brought by a private individual for nuisance. Where a public highway is obstructed I cannot sue the obstructor for nuisance if I can prove no damage beyond being delayed on several occasions in passing along it and being obliged either to pursue my journey by a devious route or to remove the obstruction, for these are inconveniences common to everyone else.[25] The reason normally given for the rule is that it prevents multiplicity of actions, for if one were allowed to sue, a thousand might do so and this would lead to harsh results. If, for instance, a public body obstructed a highway temporarily for the purpose of draining, paving or lighting it and it was then discovered that owing to some technical error they had no authority to do so, they would be sufficiently punished by a criminal prosecution.[26] If, for some reason, a criminal prosecution is an inadequate sanction, the Attorney-General may, on the information of a member of the public, bring a civil action for an injunction (known as a "relator" action), but if he refuses to do so the courts are not at liberty to inquire into the propriety of his actions or to grant declarations at the suit of the individual instead of injunctions.[27] By statute, a local authority may bring proceedings for an injunction to restrain a public nuisance where they "consider it expedient for the promotion or protection of the interests of the inhabitants of their area."[28] Where, however, any person is injured in some way peculiar to himself, that is, if he can show that he has suffered some particular or special loss over and above the ordinary inconvenience suffered by the public at large, then he can sue in

---

[20] *Att.-Gen.* v. *P.Y.A. Quarries Ltd.* [1957] 2 Q.B. 169, 184, *per* Romer L.J. (quarrying blasting, stones and splinters projected from quarry, dust, noise and vibration) *R.* v. *Madden* [1975] 1 W.L.R. 1379 (hoax bomb alarm; see now Criminal Law Act 1977, s.51).

[21] *Ibid.* at pp. 190–191, *per* Denning L.J.

[22] *Southport Corp.* v. *Esso Petroleum Co. Ltd.* [1954] 2 Q.B. 182, 196, *per* Denning L.J.

[23] *Att.-Gen. for Ontario* v. *Orange Productions Ltd.* (1971) 21 D.L.R. (3d) 257.

[24] Kodilinye, "Public Nuisance and Particular Damage in Modern Law" (1986) 6 L.S. 182.

[25] *Winterbottom* v. *Lord Derby* (1867) L.R. 2 Ex. 316, 321–322. "Even if he chose to incur expense to remove it. There must be some damage to himself, his trade or calling": *per* Kelly C.B.

[26] *Winterbottom* v. *Lord Derby* (1867) L.R. 2 Ex. 316.

[27] *Gouriet* v. *Union of Post Office Workers* [1978] A.C. 435 (not a case of public nuisance).

[28] Local Government Act 1972, s.222.

tort, *e.g.* if he falls into a trench unlawfully opened in a street and breaks his leg. Particular damage[29] is not limited to special damage in the sense of pecuniary loss actually incurred, *e.g.* in an action for negligence.[30] It may consist of proved general damage, such as inconvenience and delay, provided it is substantial, direct and not consequential and is appreciably different in nature or extent to that in fact suffered by the general public, although in another sense it is "general" and not "special" to him.[31] "Direct" here means damage other or different from the damage caused to the rest of the public. It is narrower than when "direct" is used in determining whether damage is too remote.[32] The distinction between public and private nuisance and the meaning of particular damage is illustrated by *Tate & Lyle Industries Ltd.* v. *G.L.C.*[33] Ferry terminals constructed by the defendants in the Thames caused silting which obstructed large vessels' access to the plaintiffs' jetty and the plaintiffs had to spend large sums in dredging operations. Their claim in private nuisance was dismissed because the jetty itself was unaffected and they had no private rights of property in the river bed, but the silting had caused interference with the *public* right of navigation which the plaintiffs enjoyed along with all other river users and the expenditure incurred by the plaintiffs was damage sufficient to entitle them to bring an action for public nuisance.[34]

Private nuisance

Private nuisance may be described as *unlawful interference with a person's use or enjoyment of land, or some right over, or in connection with it.*[35] Generally, the essence of a nuisance is a state of affairs that is either continuous or recurrent, a condition or activity which unduly interferes with the use or enjoyment of land.[36] Not every slight annoyance, therefore, is actionable. Stenches, smoke, the escape of effluent and a multitude of

[29] *Rose* v. *Groves* (1843) 5 Man. & G. 613, 616. "It is not necessary to prove special damage in this action. It is sufficient to prove particular damage": *per* Cresswell J.

[30] See *post*, pp. 607–608.

[31] *Walsh* v. *Ervin* [1952] V.L.R. 361, 368–369, *per* Sholl J. reviewing the English authorities. Fleming, *The Law of Torts* (7th ed.), pp. 382–383. Particular damage includes injury to plaintiff's person, wife, servant, loss of custom, depreciation in the actual value of the property by reducing or cutting off the approach to it. *Boyd* v. *G.N. Ry.* (1895) 2 I.R. 555 (doctor held up at level crossing for 20 minutes, recovered). For an example of the narrower approach, requiring difference in kind, see *Hickey* v. *Electric Reduction Co. of Canada Ltd.* (1970) 21 D.L.R. (3d) 368.

[32] *Overseas Tankship (U.K.) Ltd.* v. *The Miller Steamship Co. Pty.* [1967] 1 A.C. 617, 636, P.C.

[33] [1983] 2 A.C. 509; Tromans [1984] C.L.J. 21.

[34] See also *Rose* v. *Miles* (1815) 4 M. & S. 101; *Iveson* v. *Moore* (1699) 1 Ld.Raym. 486; *News Group Newspapers Ltd.* v. *SOGAT '82* [1986] I.R.L.R. 337 (cost of "bussing-in" employees because of picketing). Note that in these cases the loss is "economic" but though that may be a bar to a claim for negligence (*ante*, p. 84) it is not so for public nuisance.

[35] Adopted by Scott L.J. in *Read* v. *Lyons & Co. Ltd.* [1945] K.B. 216, 236; by Lord Goddard C.J. in *Howard* v. *Walker* [1947] 2 All E.R. 197, 199; by Evershed J. in *Newcastle-under-Lyme Corp.* v. *Wolstanton Ltd.* [1947] Ch. 92, 107 (his dictum on this point was unaffected by the appeal [1947] Ch. 427, 467–468); and by Windeyer J. in *Hargrave* v. *Goldman* (1963) 37 A.L.J.R. 277, 283, affirmed [1967] 1 A.C. 645. For other definitions, see Pollock, *Torts* (15th ed.), p. 302; Salmond and Heuston, *Torts* (19th ed.), Street, *Torts* (8th ed.), pp. 312–315.

[36] It is not necessary that there be any physical emanation from the defendant's premises: *Thompson-Schwab* v. *Costaki* [1956] 1 W.L.R. 335; *Laws* v. *Florinplace Ltd.* [1981] 1 All E.R. 659 (sex shop; interlocutory injunction; triable issue of nuisance independently of risk of undesirable activities by customers). *cf. Stein & Tessler* v. *Gonzalez* (1985) 58 B.C.L.R. 110.

different things may amount to a nuisance *in fact* but whether they constitute an *actionable* nuisance will depend on a variety of considerations, especially the character of the defendant's conduct, and a balancing of conflicting interests. In fact the whole of the law of private nuisance represents an attempt to preserve a balance between two conflicting interests, that of one occupier in using his land as he thinks fit, and that of his neighbour in the quiet enjoyment of his land.[37] Everyone must endure some degree of noise, smell, etc., from his neighbour, otherwise modern life would be impossible and such a privilege of interfering with the comfort of a neighbour is reciprocal. It is repeatedly said in nuisance cases that the rule is *sic utere tuo ut alienum non laedas*, but the maxim is unhelpful and misleading. If it means that no man is ever allowed to use his property so as to injure another, it is palpably false.[38] If it means that a man in using his property may injure his neighbour, but not if he does so unlawfully, it is not worth stating, as it leaves unanswered the critical question of when the interference becomes unlawful.[39] In fact, the law repeatedly recognises that a man may use his own land so as to injure another without committing a nuisance. It is only if such use is unreasonable that it becomes unlawful.

Nuisance to servitudes

We have so far been considering private nuisance as the interference with a person's use or enjoyment of land, and we have seen that in determining liability, the nature and quality of the defendant's conduct is a factor of great importance. In addition to this situation, however, the tort of nuisance provides a remedy for the infringement of a servitude,[40] such as the obstruction of a right of way or the blocking of a right to light. In this type of nuisance, once the plaintiff has proved that he has suffered a substantial degree of interference,[41] the conduct of the defendant is in general irrelevant and the convenience of the locality, or the benefit of the activity in question to the community, or the care used by the defendant to avoid damage,[42] will not suffice to absolve him from liability. The plaintiff's right is paramount, and if the occupier of the servient tenement cannot prosecute his activities

---

[37] "A balance has to be maintained between the right of the occupier to do what he likes with his own, and the right of his neighbour not to be interfered with" *Sedleigh-Denfield* v. *O'Callaghan* [1940] A.C. 880, 903, *per* Lord Wright.

[38] *Bamford* v. *Turnley* (1862) 3 B. & S. 66, 79, 83–84. "Liability is imposed only in those cases where the harm or risk to one is greater than he ought to be required to bear under the circumstances:" *per* Bramwell B. Weir, *Casebook on Tort* (6th ed.), p. 365.

[39] The maxim has been described by Erle J. as an "ancient and solemn imposter:" *Bonomi* v. *Backhouse* (1858) E.B. & E. 622, 643. See also the comments of the same judge in *Brand* v. *Hammersmith Ry.* (1867) L.R. 2 Q.B. 223, 247. Holmes, *Harvard Essays*, pp. 162, 164 remarked that the "maxim teaches nothing but a benevolent yearning."

[40] *i.e.* easements, *profits á prendre* and natural rights.

[41] *Jackson* v. *Duke of Newcastle* (1864) 3 De G.J. & Sm. 275, 285, *per* Lord Hardwicke; *Colls* v. *Home and Colonial Stores Ltd.* [1904] A.C. 179, 182, *per* Lord Halsbury L.C.; *Warren* v. *Brown* [1900] 2 Q.B. 722; *Petley* v. *Parsons* [1914] 2 Ch. 653.

[42] The natural right of the riparian owner to the continued flow of a stream in its natural condition is an exception. "It is only for unreasonable and unauthorised use of this common benefit that an action would lie:" *Embrey* v. *Owen* (1851) 6 Ex. 353, 369, *per* Parke B. See generally *Swindon Waterworks Co.* v. *Wilts and Berks Canal Navigation Co.* (1875) L.R. 7 H.L. 697; *McCartney* v. *Londonderry and Lough Swilly Ry.* [1904] A.C. 301; Brett, "The Right to Take Flowing Water" (1950) 14 Conv.(N.S.) 154.

without infringing it, he must not perform them at all. This distinction led Lord Macnaghten in *Colls* v. *Home and Colonial Stores Ltd.*[43] to regard the action for interference with an easement as *sui generis*. The function of the action is to remedy the infringement of a right, not to compensate for the commission of a wrong.[44]

BASIC DIFFERENCES BETWEEN PUBLIC AND PRIVATE NUISANCE

Although claims (*a*) for a private nuisance, and (*b*) for particular damage resulting from a public nuisance have many features in common,[45] the rules relating to them are not identical. To succeed in private nuisance, the plaintiff must have an interest in land and consequently a non-occupier cannot recover damages for personal injuries,[46] whereas in public nuisance the plaintiff need have no interest in land and may recover for injury to the person or to property.

STANDARD OF LIABILITY IN NUISANCE[47]

One of the most difficult questions in the law of nuisance is the extent to which proof of fault on the part of the defendant is essential to liability.[48] Looking at the problem another way, can a plaintiff succeed in a claim in nuisance in circumstances in which a claim in negligence would be unsuccessful? If a plaintiff can prove his case in negligence, it may well be immaterial whether in addition the action of the defendant constitutes an actionable nuisance. On the other hand, if he cannot discharge the burden of proving negligence, his claim may fail unless (i) the facts bring him within the area of nuisance and (ii) the burden of proof in nuisance is less or at least different.

In attempting to determine the standard of liability in nuisance, it must always be borne in mind that the plaintiff has available two remedies which require different considerations. These are: (i) an injunction to restrain the defendant from commencing or continuing an activity causing or threatening an interference; (ii) an action for damages to compensate the plaintiff for the injury he has suffered. In the former the primary purpose of the remedy is to protect the plaintiff from further damage and the court is not principally concerned with the defendant's culpability.[49] As the Law Commission has

---

[43] [1904] A.C. 179.

[44] *Ibid.* at p. 186. Also *Price* v. *Hilditch* [1930] 1 Ch. 500, 507 *per* Maugham J.

[45] *Sedleigh-Denfield* v. *O'Callaghan* [1940] A.C. 880, 905, 907, 918; *Halsey* v. *Esso Petroleum Co. Ltd.* [1961] 1 W.L.R. 683, 699, *per* Veale J.

[46] *Post,* pp. 394–395.

[47] See generally: Friedmann, "Modern Trends in the Law of Torts" (1937) 1 M.L.R., pp. 39–48; Friedmann, "Negligence and the Overlapping of Torts" (1940) 3 M.L.R., pp. 305–309; Buxton, "The Negligent Nuisance" (1966) 8 U. Malaya L.R. 1, 2–6; Buxton, "Nuisance and Negligence Again" (1966) 29 M.L.R. 676; Newark, "The Boundaries of Nuisance" (1949) 65 L.Q.R. 480; Newark, "Trespass or Nuisance or Negligence" (1954) 17 M.L.R. 579. Eekelaar, "Nuisance and Strict Liability" (1973) 8 *Irish Jurist* 191.

[48] See, *e.g.* the differing views expressed in relation to nuisance by obstruction of the highway in *Dymond* v. *Pearce* [1972] 1 Q.B. 496.

[49] Though this may, of course, affect the terms of the injunction.

remarked, "consideration of the strictness of the duty is then out of place—all that the court is concerned with is the question, 'Should the defendant be told to stop this interference with the plaintiff's rights?' Whether or not the defendant knew of the smell or noise or the like when it first began to annoy the plaintiff does not matter; he becomes aware of it at the latest when the plaintiff brings his claim before the court."[50] Because the court is not directly concerned with the knowledge or culpability of the defendant liability appears to be strict. In an action for damages, on the other hand, the courts have traditionally been loth to penalise a defendant in the absence of fault, and so the nature and quality of the defendant's activities are of far greater importance. This distinction has not always been made by the courts and one must beware of accepting as law generalisations in injunction cases indicating that liability is strict.[51] The following discussion is concerned principally with liability for damages.

The first point is that we must draw a distinction between the *creation* or *adoption* of a nuisance by the defendant and the *continuance* of a nuisance[52] created by a third party or an act of nature. An occupier "continues" a nuisance, for the creation of which he is not responsible, if, once he knows or ought to know of its existence, he fails to take reasonable precautions to abate it and it is clear that he is not liable in damages if these conditions are not satisfied.[53] However, the decisions establishing this principle have no direct application to the situation where the occupier has himself, or through his servants or agents, created the nuisance and it is here that the law has fallen into complexity and confusion. Some of this is undoubtedly caused by loose use of the terminology of "negligence" and "strict liability" as if these were clearly defined standards and by a failure to accept that nuisance is far from being a self-contained tort with its own internal rules but rather a descriptive label for a particular dispute situation (disputes between neighbours) which may attract liabilities of differing stringency according to the facts.[54] Some cases have been judicially considered under the rubric "nuisance" even though they might well have been framed as actions under the rule in *Rylands* v. *Fletcher*[55]; others provide instances of the principle that an

---

[50] Report No. 32, "Civil Liability for Dangerous Things and Activities," p. 25.

[51] *e.g. Rapier* v. *London Tramways Co.* [1893] 2 Ch. 588, 560, *per* Lindley L.J.: "If I am sued for nuisance, and the nuisance is proved, it is no defence on my part to say, and to prove, that I have taken all reasonable care to prevent it." In its context, this statement means no more than that if the activity is unreasonably injurious when carried on with all care, it should not be carried on at all.

[52] *e.g. Noble* v. *Harrison* [1926] 2 K.B. 332, 338, *per* Rowlatt J.; *Barker* v. *Herbert* [1911] 2 K.B. 633, 636–637, *per* Vaughan Williams L.J. and *ibid.* at pp. 642–643, *per* Fletcher Moulton L.J.; *Sedleigh-Denfield* v. *O'Callaghan* [1940] A.C. 880, 904–908, *per* Lord Wright and *ibid.* at p. 913, *per* Lord Romer.

[53] This situation is discussed further *post*, p. 398. The burden of proof would appear to lie upon the plaintiff (*Sedleigh-Denfield* v. *O'Callaghan* [1940] A.C. 880, 887, 899, 908) and it is significant that in *Goldman* v. *Hargrave* [1967] 1 A.C. 645 the Privy Council thought it unnecessary to decide whether the cause of action lay in nuisance or negligence. See also *Smith* v. *Littlewoods Organisation Ltd.* [1987] A.C. 241, 274, *per* Lord Goff.

[54] Fleming, *The Law of Torts* (7th ed.), p. 396.

[55] In *Solloway* v. *Hampshire C.C.* (1981) 79 L.G.R. 449, 453, Dunn L.J. said that strict liability for nuisance is confined to "cases where there has been some non-natural user of the land as stated in *Rylands* v. *Fletcher*." If this means that all the requirements of *Rylands* v. *Fletcher* must be fulfilled it supports the argument above. If it means that there is strict liability in nuisance for any non-natural user one wonders what purpose *Rylands* v. *Fletcher* serves. See, *e.g. Midwood* v. *Manchester Corp.* [1905] 2 K.B. 597, where counsel for the plaintiffs relied on *Rylands* v. *Fletcher*. *Rylands* v. *Fletcher* is considered *post*, Chap. 15.

employer of an independent contractor may be responsible for the contractor's negligence because he owes a "non-delegable" duty.[56] There are in fact very few cases where nuisance liability has been imposed upon a defendant who has not been guilty of any negligence and which cannot be explained away on some such basis,[57] but despite a movement away from strict liability in this[58] and other areas and the lack of any apparent reason why rights of enjoyment over land should receive a higher level of protection than, say, rights of personal security on the highway, the courts have shown a singular reluctance to take the final step and assimilate nuisance with negligence with regard to the standard of liability.[59] The matter has certainly not been cleared up by the discussion of it by the Judicial Committee in *The Wagon Mound (No. 2)*,[60] though the general effect of that decision is probably to limit even further the scope of strict liability in nuisance.

The Wagon Mound (No. 2) was an action in negligence and nuisance against the same defendants as in *The Wagon Mound (No. 1)*[61] by the owners of the *Corrimal*, which was being repaired in MD Ltd.'s wharf and was badly damaged in the fire. In the Australian court,[62] Walsh J. held that the plaintiffs' claim in negligence failed because fire damage was not reasonably foreseeable, but that they succeeded in their claim in nuisance because in his view liability was not dependent on foreseeability. Both parties appealed to the Privy Council, who upheld the defendants' contention that foreseeability was a prerequisite to the claim in nuisance and also accepted the plaintiffs' contention that fire damage was reasonably foreseeable,[63] so that the plaintiffs succeeded.

Lord Reid referred to the argument of counsel for the plaintiffs that negligence is not an essential element in determining liability for nuisance and continued, in a passage which requires setting out in full[64]:

> "It is quite true that negligence is not an essential element in nuisance. Nuisance is a term used to cover a wide variety of tortious acts or omissions and in many negligence in the narrow sense is not essential. An occupier may incur liability for the emission of noxious fumes or

[56] *i.e.* the cases on withdrawal of support from neighbouring land: *post*, p. 397.

[57] For some possible contenders see *post*, p. 384.

[58] See the remarks of Lord Porter in *Longhurst* v. *Metropolitan Water Board* [1948] 2 All E.R. 834, 839 and of Lord Parker C.J. in *British Road Services* v. *Slater* [1964] 1 W.L.R. 504.

[59] *Paxhaven Holdings Ltd.* v. *A.G.* [1974] 2 N.Z.L.R. 185; *Clearlite Holdings Ltd.* v. *Auckland City Corp.* [1976] 2 N.Z.L.R. 729.

[60] [1967] 1 A.C. 617 *sub nom. Overseas Tankship (U.K.) Ltd.* v. *The Miller Steamship Co. Pty.*

[61] [1961] A.C. 388. See *ante*, pp. 140–142. This case was remitted to the Australian court for trial on the issue of nuisance, but the action was dropped.

[62] [1963] S.R.(N.S.W.) 948; [1963] 1 Lloyd's Rep. 402.

[63] In *The Wagon Mound (No. 1)* it had been found that fire damage was not reasonably foreseeable. In *The Wagon Mound (No. 2)*, Walsh J. found that it was foreseeable, though only as a remote possibility. The Privy Council stressed that in these circumstances it was not justifiable to neglect the risk, however small it was. It does not follow that whatever the circumstances may be, it is justifiable to neglect a risk of small magnitude. A reasonable man would only neglect such a risk if he had some valid reason for doing so: *e.g.* that it would involve considerable expense to eliminate the risk. There was no justification whatever for discharging the oil into the harbour. Not only was it an offence to do so, but it involved considerable financial loss. There could have been no question of balancing the advantages and disadvantages, it was their duty to stop the discharge immediately: [1967] 1 A.C. 617, 643.

[64] *Ibid.* at p. 639.

noise although he has used the utmost care in building and using his premises. The amount of fumes or noise which he can lawfully emit is a question of degree and he or his advisors may have miscalculated what can be justified. Or he may deliberately obstruct the highway adjoining his premises to a greater degree than is permissible, hoping that no one will object. On the other hand, the emission of fumes or noise or the obstruction of the adjoining highway may often be the result of pure negligence on his part: there are many cases (*e.g. Dollman* v. *Hillman*[65]) where precisely the same facts will establish liability both in nuisance and in negligence. And although negligence may not be necessary, fault of some kind is almost always necessary and fault generally involves foreseeability, *e.g.* in cases like *Sedleigh-Denfield* v. *O'Callaghan*[66] the fault is in failing to abate the nuisance the existence of which the defender is or ought to be aware as likely to cause damage to his neighbour."

With respect to a great master (though by adoption) of the common law it is unfortunate that such an important statement is expressed in difficult and ambiguous terms which are not defined and are hence open to a number of interpretations. First, it is true that the case was concerned with remoteness of damage[67] and establishes as a matter of precedent only that the test of remoteness in all cases of nuisance, as in negligence, is foreseeability of the kind of harm which in fact occurs. This has led one writer[68] to treat the above passage as concerned with remoteness and to argue that in those cases where "negligence in the narrow sense is not essential" the defendant will be liable if he can foresee some possibility of his activities interfering with his neighbour's land even though the much greater and unreasonable degree of interference which in fact occurs is not foreseeable.[69] This, however, is open to the objection that the passage of Lord Reid's speech is in response to the submission of counsel that in nuisance negligence is not an essential element in determining *liability*[70] and it seems odd to describe as "fault" the conduct of a defendant who is inflicting on his neighbour interference of a degree which is legally permissible and who is in no way to blame when that interference "escalates."[71]

An alternative (and, it is suggested simpler) view of the above passage is that Lord Reid is merely seeking to point out that the formulae of negligence are not suitable to expound liability in all cases of nuisance, for it will be

---

[65] [1940] 1 K.B. 229.

[66] [1940] A.C. 880.

[67] "The present case is one of creating a danger to persons or property in navigable waters (equivalent to a highway) and there it is admitted that fault is essential—in this case the negligent discharge of the oil": [1967] 1 A.C. 617, 639.

[68] Dias, "Trouble on Oiled Waters; Problems of The Wagon Mound (No. 2)" [1967] C.L.J. 62–82.

[69] *e.g.* D has premises run according to the best available system and which emits a trivial amount of fumes on to P's land; on the day in question the system goes catastrophically wrong as a result of an undiscoverable defect in the machinery and emits a seriously damaging quantity of fumes.

[70] [1967] 1 A.C. 617, 639.

[71] Dias describes his formulation as a category between strict liability and negligence (*loc. cit.*, p. 81) but it would in fact amount to a considerable degree of strict liability since there can be few industrial processes which do not involve some minor interference with neighbouring property.

noted that both of his examples concern conduct which is deliberate in the sense that the perpetrator knows he is interfering with his neighbour but believes (erroneously) that he is not going beyond the degree of interference which the law allows. To describe such conduct as "negligence" would be a misuse of language, which may be why he refers to "negligence in the narrow sense," but it certainly amounts to "fault" within the ordinary meaning of that word[72] and gives no support to the view that there may be a residual element of strict liability in cases of nuisance. In fact, Lord Reid's examples, though used in the context of a claim for damages, involve precisely the sort of "patent" nuisances which were in issue in the injunction cases responsible for so many of the misleading dicta in this area.[73] Neither throws any light on the "latent" nuisance, the case where an activity which is normally unobjectionable in law suddenly goes catastrophically wrong without any negligence, and it is submitted that in this situation the defendant is not liable. In short, there are not two separate categories of nuisance, one fault-based and the other strict, but one principle that the defendant is liable if his interference with his neighbour's land is of sufficient gravity to constitute a nuisance in law and if he is responsible for the interference in the sense that he knew or ought to have known of a sufficient likelihood of its occurrence to require him to take steps to prevent it.[74]

This view is advanced with some diffidence, though it is thought that no English case[75] is binding authority to the contrary. Perhaps the strongest argument against it comes from the cases dealing with the defence of statutory authority, which assume that there may be an element of strict liability at common law. However, cases of this type must be read in the light of the fact that at the time when the principles on statutory authority were being worked out the supply of public utility services was, apart from such authority, readily regarded as attracting strict liability under the rule in *Rylands* v. *Fletcher*.[76] Unfortunately, when the House of Lords examined the defence of statutory authority in *Department of Transport* v. *North West Water Authority*,[77] it was not necessary for it to go into the nature of the liability because the defendants did not contest that they would have been liable without negligence for the bursting of their water main had they not

---

[72] In an earlier edition of this work it was said that in such circumstances "a claim in negligence [might] well fail." In one sense this is correct but seems to have no practical significance since the abolition of the forms of action. See also Millner, *Negligence in Modern Law*, pp. 184 *et seq.* and Prosser, *Torts* (5th ed.), pp. 624–626.

[73] *e.g. Rapier* v. *London Tramways Co.*, *supra*, n. 51. See also *Home Brewery plc* v. *William Davis & Co. (Leicester) Ltd.* [1987] Q.B. 339 where the court accepted the necessity of foreseeable harm, but on the facts the harm was "inevitable."

[74] Though the application of other principles may introduce a stricter element of liability in individual cases: *supra*, nn. 55 and 56. There is also the so-called rule in *Wringe* v. *Cohen* [1940] 1 K.B. 229, widely regarded as anomalous: *post*, p. 416.

[75] There is no strict liability in Scots law: *R.H.M. (Bakeries) Ltd.* v. *Strathclyde Regional Council* 1985 S.L.T. 214. *cf. Clearlite Holdings Ltd.* v. *Auckland City Corp.* [1976] 2 N.Z.L.R. 729, 740: "There are academic writers, with one or two judicial adherents, who seem in favour of pressing for abolition of strict liability and for its substitution by the fault doctrine, but the current of judicial authority in the Commonwealth continues to run the other way." *Ilford U.D.C.* v. *Beal* [1925] 1 K.B. 671 perhaps supports the view in the text; *cf.* Street, *Torts* (8th ed.), p. 331.

[76] See *Green* v. *Chelsea Water Works Co.* (1894) 70 L.T.(N.S.) 547 and text to n. 55, *supra*.

[77] [1984] A.C. 336.

been acting in discharge of a statutory duty. It may well be that on such facts strict liability provides a desirable and efficient allocation of risks (though the defendants in fact escaped on the construction of their statutory authority[78]); what is argued here is not that strict liability is undesirable but that rational results are not likely to be achieved simply by attaching it to the range of liability situations we call nuisance. Further, in some contexts there would be acute difficulty in knowing when the strict liability would apply. Consider, for example, public nuisance on the highway, for it is now a century since the law decided that negligence should be the regime governing traffic accidents and great confusion would be caused if a different, stricter rule could be called in aid merely because a contributory factory in a particular case could, rather impressionistically,[79] be described as a "nuisance."[80]

If it be accepted that fault in the sense of negligence or deliberate or reckless act is generally necessary for liability in nuisance, we must still face the possibility that it differs from negligence on the burden of proof. According to Denning L.J. in *Southport Corporation* v. *Esso Petroleum Co. Ltd.*[81] "in an action for public nuisance, once the nuisance is proved and the defendant is shown to have caused it, then the legal burden is shifted on the defendant to justify or excuse himself." The implications of this view have not been explored in subsequent cases, though it has been suggested that it may also apply to some cases of private nuisance,[82] but it should be remembered that even if the view is ill-founded the fact that the nuisance emanates from property subject to the defendant's control will often be a pointer towards the application of the maxim *res ipsa loquitur* which, if it does not reverse the legal burden of proof, at least requires the defendant to advance evidence of sufficient strength to rebut the inference of negligence raised by the plaintiff.[83]

REASONABLENESS

The problems raised in the preceding section rarely arise in practice because the vast majority of nuisances are patent, but we now turn to the central issue of the whole law of nuisance, the question of the reasonableness of the

---

[78] s.18(2) of the Public Utilities Street Works Act 1950. But as to the liability of water undertakers to the general public, see the Water Act 1981, s.6: *post,* p. 436.

[79] A parked vehicle may be a nuisance and so, perhaps, may a moving one in a dangerous condition (*Tysoe* v. *Davis* [1984] R.T.R. 88) but no one would apply the label to a vehicle being *driven* carelessly.

[80] See further, *post,* p. 413.

[81] [1954] 2 Q.B. 182, 197. It may be argued that this passage is concerned with a quite different point, *viz.,* that once a substantial interference has been established the defendant bears the burden of showing that it is not of sufficient gravity in all the circumstances to constitute a legal nuisance (*post,* p. 386) but the context makes it clear that his Lordship was considering whether the defendants were responsible for a state of affairs which was undoubtedly of sufficient gravity to constitute a nuisance.

[82] *Radstock Co-operative & Industrial Society Ltd.* v. *Norton-Radstock U.D.C.* [1968] Ch. 605, 633–634, *per* Sachs L.J., dissenting. It is questionable whether the actual decision in this case can stand with *Goldman* v. *Hargrave* [1967] 1 A.C. 645, *post,* p. 399.

[83] *Ante,* p. 129. In *Southport Corp.* v. *Esso Petroleum Ltd., supra,* a majority of the Court of Appeal held that *res ipsa loquitur* applied, but the House of Lords ([1956] A.C. 218) held that this approach was not open on the pleading.

defendant's conduct "according to the ordinary usages of mankind living in
. . . a particular society."[84] It is vital to grasp at the outset that reasonableness
is being used here in a sense rather different from the law of negligence. It is
a comparatively simple proposition that you are liable for negligence if you
drive a car carelessly against a pedestrian in the street and it would be
ridiculous to say that there are some circumstances in which you may do so
and others in which you may not. In other words, our attention is concentrated on the relative issue of the characterisation of the defendant's conduct
and once we have determined this in the plaintiff's favour we immediately
progress to legal liability, treating the plaintiff's right to personal security as
absolute. Nuisance, however, generally approaches the issue from the other
end and we cannot make such a proposition as that you may not make a noise
which irritates your neighbour, for common sense tells one that such a rule
would be totally unworkable. Some intrusion by noise (or smells or dust,
etc.) is the inevitable price of living in an organised society in proximity to
one's neighbours, indeed "the very nuisance the one complains of, as the
ordinary use of his neighbour's land, he himself will create in the ordinary
use of his own and the reciprocal nuisances are of a comparatively trifling
character."[85] Accordingly, the protection of such interests must be
approached with an attempt to balance the competing rights of neighbours,
a process of compromise, a "rule of give and take, of live and let live."[86] It is
to this issue that we are directing our attention when we talk of the "reasonableness" of the defendant's conduct rather than to whether he took reasonable care in the negligence sense. "Reasonableness" signifies what is legally
right between the parties taking account of all the circumstances of the
case.[87] The difference between the two approaches is in some ways more
apparent than real and is perhaps the product of the fact that the majority of
nuisance actions involve deliberate interference by the defendant,[88] but for
practical purposes there is still a good deal of truth in the statement that
knocking a man down carelessly is a tort *simpliciter* while making a noise that
irritates him is only a tort *sub modo*. This is far short of saying that care is
irrelevant to liability for nuisance. It has been argued above that if the
defendant could not have expected any substantial degree of interference
with the plaintiff's property he cannot be liable. In the case of interference
which is patent, lack of care may, however, lead to liability for it is not
reasonable to expect the plaintiff to put up with interference which could be

---

[84] *Sedleigh-Denfield* v. *O'Callaghan* [1940] A.C. 880, 903, *per* Lord Wright.
[85] *Bamford* v. *Turnley* (1862) 3 B. & S. 62, 83, *per* Bramwell B.; Weir, *Casebook on Tort* (6th ed.), p. 365;
Kennaway v. *Thompson* [1981] Q.B. 88, 94.
[86] *Bamford* v. *Turnley* (1862) 3 B. & S. 62, 83.
[87] See Keeton, "Conditional Fault in the Law of Torts" (1959) 72 Harv. L.R. 432–433, n. 62; Fridman,
"Nuisance and the Reasonable Milkman" (1955) A.L.J. 435–436, based on *Munro* v. *Southern Dairies*
[1955] V.L.R. 332.
[88] All the circumstances of the case, including the utility of the defendant's activity must be taken into account
in determining whether his conduct is so unreasonable as to amount to a nuisance (see below) but such
matters may be equally relevant to determine whether his conduct constitutes legal negligence (*ante*,
p. 118). Indeed, where there is physical injury but no deliberate interference by the defendant one can
discern a strong tendency to run nuisance and negligence together: *Bolton* v. *Stone* [1951] A.C. 850;
Goldman v. *Hargrave* [1967] 1 A.C. 645.

reduced by the adoption of proper measures.[89] On the other hand, if, after balancing the competing interests of the parties, the court considers that the interference is excessive by any standards then the fact that the defendant has taken all reasonable care and reduced it to a minimum provides no defence—the irreducible minimum is itself the nuisance.[90]

No precise or universal formula is possible to determine reasonableness in the above sense. Whether an act constitutes a nuisance cannot be determined merely by an abstract consideration of the act itself, but by reference to all the circumstances of the particular case; the time and place of its commission, the seriousness of the harm, the manner of committing it, whether it is done maliciously or in the reasonable exercise of rights; and the effect of its commission, that is whether it is transitory or permanent, occasional or continuous; so that it is a question of fact whether or not a nuisance has been committed.[91] Certain of these factors will now be discussed in greater detail.

Extent of the harm and the nature of the locality[92]

In the leading case of *St. Helen's Smelting Co.* v. *Tipping,*[93] the plaintiff acquired an estate in a manufacturing area. Among the works situated nearby were those of a copper smelting company. The vapours emanating from these works proved injurious to the trees on the plaintiff's estate. In the House of Lords, Lord Westbury L.C. drew a distinction between nuisances producing material injury to property and nuisances causing sensible personal discomfort. In assessing whether the latter can constitute an actionable nuisance, it is necessary to take into account the nature of the locality. "If a man lives in a town, it is necessary that he should subject himself to the consequences of those operations of trade which may be carried on in his immediate locality, which are actually necessary for trade and commerce, and also for the enjoyment of property, and for the benefit of the inhabitants of the town and of the public at large."[94] Inevitably, therefore, interference which may be permissible in one area may not be permissible in another.[95]

---

[89] Compare *Leeman* v. *Montagu* [1936] 2 All E.R. 1677 (750 cockerels crowing between 2 and 7 a.m., no attempt to rearrange farm, held a nuisance) with *Moy* v. *Stoop* (1909) 25 T.L.R. 262 (crying children in day nursery, no lack of care, no nuisance). And see *Manchester Corp.* v. *Farnworth* [1930] A.C. 171, *Manners* v. *Chester* [1963] C.L.Y. 2561 and the cases on malicious activity, *post,* p. 391.

[90] *Rapier* v. *London Tramways Co.* [1893] 2 Ch. 588. Thus it must often be a pure gamble whether I act lawfully in opening a particular business in a street, for I will be liable, no matter how much care I have taken, if I make an error of judgment in deciding whether the business is offensive or not.

[91] *Bamford* v. *Turnley* (1862) 3 B. & S. 66, 79, *per* Pollock C.B.; *Stone* v. *Bolton* [1949] 1 All E.R. 237, 238–239, *per* Oliver J. (approved as to nuisance [1950] 1 K.B. 201 (C.A.), and on other grounds [1951] A.C. 850). For an interesting case involving dazzling glare produced by the defendant's building, see *Bank of New Zealand* v. *Greenwood* [1984] 1 N.Z.L.R. 525.

[92] Planning decisions as such are not conclusive one way or the other, though they may be relevant. In *Halsey* v. *Esso Petroleum Co. Ltd.* [1961] 1 W.L.R. 683, the plaintiff's house was in an area "zoned" as residential, while the defendant's depot was in an area "zoned" as industrial.

[93] (1865) 11 H.L.C. 642. Weir, *Casebook on Tort* (6th ed.), p. 368.

[94] (1865) 11 H.L.C. 642, 650; *Shoreham-by-Sea U.D.C.* v. *Dolphin Canadian Proteins Ltd.* (1972) 71 L.G.R. 261.

[95] "What would be a nuisance in Belgrave Square would not necessarily be so in Bermondsey": *Sturges* v. *Bridgman* (1879) 11 Ch.D. 852, 865, *per* Thesiger L.J.; *Polsue and Alfieri* v. *Rushmer* [1907] A.C. 121; *Andreae* v. *Selfridge & Co.* [1938] Ch. 11; *Milner* v. *Spencer* (1976) 239 E.G. 573.

On the other hand, in the case of "sensible injury to the value of the property,"[96] these considerations do not apply and the convenience of the locality for the particular trade in question cannot absolve a defendant from liability. The plaintiff therefore recovered damages.

It is easier to establish a nuisance causing material damage to property than one causing personal discomfort, for in the former case the damage is tangible and more easily observed and measured. In the case of non-tangible injuries, there must be something over and above the everyday inconveniences which are inevitable in the locality. "The law does not regard trifling inconveniences; everything is to be looked at from a reasonable point of view."[97] This distinction is not free from difficulties and its consequences do not seem to have been fully investigated by the courts,[98] but it was reiterated by Veale J. in *Halsey* v. *Esso Petroleum Co.*[99] The magnitude of the harm, therefore, and in some cases the nature of the locality are circumstances to be considered in determining whether the defendant has acted unreasonably.

Utility of the defendant's conduct

Since nuisance is the law of give and take the court is inevitably concerned to some extent with the utility or general benefit to the community of the defendant's activity. Thus we must all put up with the rattle of early morning milk deliveries, though probably not with the same amount of noise made by drunken neighbours.[1] This approach, however, will only justify an injurious activity up to a certain point, and that point is reached when serious damage is being done to the plaintiff's property or livelihood. In such a case the court will not accept the argument that the plaintiff should put up with the harm because it is beneficial to the community as a whole, for that would amount to requiring him to carry the burden alone of an activity from which many others benefit.[2] Nor have the courts in such cases shown willingness to adopt the device of awarding damages in lieu of an injunction, for that would amount to expropriation without the sanction of Parliament.[3] Indeed, in one case an Irish court enjoined a nuisance even though the order would have the effect of closing for three months the only cement factory in Ireland at a time when building was an urgent public necessity.[4]

---

[96] (1865) 11 H.L.C. 642, 651.

[97] *Ibid.* at p. 653.

[98] The *St Helen's* case gave no test for determining exactly whether a nuisance is one to property or is one causing personal discomfort, and the test which it did give for the latter is rather vague. Noises or smells primarily cause only personal discomfort, but they may make a hotel uninhabitable. It is uninjured as a building, but there is material injury to the business carried on in it. Is this an injury to property?

[99] [1961] 1 W.L.R. 683; and see *Miller* v. *Jackson* [1977] Q.B. 966, 986.

[1] This is demonstrated most clearly where the activity is actuated by malice, for malicious conduct can have no utility: see *post*, p. 391.

[2] See Bohlen, *Studies in the Law of Torts*, p. 429.

[3] *Shelfer* v. *City of London Electric Co.* [1895] 1 Ch. 287; *Munro* v. *Southern Dairies* [1955] V.L.R. 332; *cf. Bottom* v. *Ontario Leaf Tobacco Co.* [1935] 2 D.L.R. 699. In *Miller* v. *Jackson* [1977] Q.B. 966 Lord Denning M.R., dissenting, thought that public interest must prevail over private rights of property whether the issue was the existence of a legal nuisance or the grant of an injunction, but the Court of Appeal has rejected this: *Kennaway* v. *Thompson* [1981] Q.B. 88; Buckley (1981) 44 M.L.R. 212.

[4] *Bellew* v. *Cement Co.* [1948] Ir.R. 61. See further *post*, p. 637.

instance, the plaintiff, whilst standing on the highway, was injured by a cricket ball which had been hit from the defendant's adjacent cricket ground. At first instance Oliver J. held that a nuisance connotes some degree of continuity; it must "be a state of affairs, however temporary, and not merely an isolated happening."[18] In the Court of Appeal, Somervell L.J. regarded the gist of the alleged nuisance, not as the isolated act of hitting a ball into the highway, but the organising and carrying on of a game on property adjacent to the highway thereby endangering the public in the exercise of its right of passage.[19] The frequency of the escape,[20] and presumably the gravity of the harm caused, are important factors in determining whether a dangerous state of affairs existed on the defendant's land.[21] Even if the escape is isolated, if the harm caused by it is sufficiently grave that is evidence of a pre-existent dangerous state of affairs. In *Spicer* v. *Smee*[22] a fire which destroyed the plaintiff's bungalow was caused by defective electrical wiring installed in the defendant's adjacent bungalow. Atkinson J. held that there was a dangerous state of affairs on the defendant's property and held him liable in nuisance.[23] As Thesiger J. remarked in *S.C.M. (United Kingdom) Ltd.* v. *W.J. Whittall & Son Ltd.*, "while there is no doubt that a single isolated escape may cause the damage that entitles a plaintiff to sue for nuisance, yet it must be proved that the nuisance arose from the condition of the defendant's land or premises or property or activities thereon that constituted a nuisance."[24] Where the defendant's activity falls within the rule in *Rylands* v. *Fletcher* there is no difficulty in saying that an isolated escape is actionable without reference to a "state of affairs."[25]

Malice

Is malice material in nuisance? If A's use of his own property causes to B annoyance which does not amount to a nuisance, will the fact that A's acts are done solely for the purpose of annoying B convert them into a nuisance?

---

[18] [1949] 1 All E.R. 237, 238.

[19] [1950] 1 K.B. 201, 213: "Nuisance is the causing or permittting of a state of affairs from which damage is likely to result," *per* Jenkins L.J. at pp. 208–209. The element of nuisance was not discussed in the House of Lords, but Lord Reid reserved his opinion as to what constituted nuisance in cases of this character: [1951] A.C. 850, at p. 868. See also *Cunard* v. *Antifyre* [1933] 1 K.B. 331, 557, *per* Talbot J.; *Att.-Gen.* v. *P.Y.A. Quarries Ltd.* [1957] 2 Q.B. 169, 192, *per* Denning L.J.; *Hilder* v. *Associated Portland Cement Manufacturers Ltd.* [1961] 1 W.L.R. 1434 (football escaping on to road, liability in negligence, nuisance considered).

[20] Thus, *Castle* v. *St. Augustine's Links* (1922) 38 T.L.R. 615, where golf balls were repeatedly sliced on to the highway, is distinguishable, for there was substantial interference with the use of the road and a state of affairs which foreseeably threatened damage.

[21] Compare the facts of *Stone* v. *Bolton* with those of *Miller* v. *Jackson* [1977] Q.B. 966.

[22] [1946] 1 All E.R. 489.

[23] In *Sedleigh-Denfield* v. *O'Callaghan* [1940] A.C. 880, 895–896, Lord Atkin said that the defendants "created a state of things ... from which ... flooding on the plaintiff's ground might reasonably be expected to result," and were therefore liable in nuisance.

[24] [1970] 1 W.L.R. 1017, 1031. The learned judge continued: "I am satisfied that one negligent act that causes physical damage to an electric cable does not thereby constitute a nuisance." Nuisance was not considered on appeal by the Court of Appeal: [1971] 1 Q.B. 337. In *British Celanese Ltd.* v. *Hunt*, Lawton J. considered that an isolated escape is actionable as a nuisance but did not discuss the need for a pre-existing state of affairs, although on the facts set out there was such a state: [1969] 1 W.L.R. 959, 969. On this, see the comments of Thesiger J. in *S.C.M.* v. *Whittall, supra*, at p. 1031.

[25] This seems the explanation of *Midwood* v. *Mayor of Manchester* [1905] 2 K.B. 597.

In *Christie* v. *Davey*,[26] the defendant, exasperated by a considerable number of music lessons given by the plaintiff, a teacher of music whose residence was separated from that of the defendant only by a party-wall, interrupted the plaintiff's lessons by knocking on the party-wall, beating on trays, whistling and shrieking. North J. issued an injunction because the defendant had acted deliberately and maliciously for the purpose of annoying the plaintiff. The learned judge added: "If what has taken place had occurred between two sets of persons both perfectly innocent, I should have taken an entirely different view of the case."[27] Two years later, however, the House of Lords in *Bradford (Mayor of)* v. *Pickles*[28] asserted that a bad motive cannot make wrongful an act otherwise legal, and they reaffirmed this principle in *Allen* v. *Flood*[29]; but in neither decision was any reference made to *Christie* v. *Davey*.

In *Hollywood Silver Fox Farm Ltd.* v. *Emmett*,[30] Macnaghten J. followed *Christie* v. *Davey*. The defendant deliberately caused guns to be fired on his own land near the boundary of the plaintiff's land in order to scare the plaintiff's silver foxes during breeding-time. The vixens of these animals are extremely nervous during breeding-time and much damage was done in consequence of the defendant's act, which was motivated by pure spite.

Macnaghten J. considered that the intention of the defendant is relevant in determining liability in nuisance and granted an injunction and awarded damages to the plaintiff. It is submitted that this is the better view. The courts, in judging what constitutes a nuisance, take into consideration the purpose of the defendant's activity,[31] and acts otherwise justified on the ground of reciprocity, if done wantonly and maliciously with the object of injuring a neighbour are devoid of any social utility and cannot be regarded as "reasonable." The element of unreasonableness in nuisance as a tort had been recognised long before *Bradford* v. *Pickles* and that decision did not affect the principle of nuisances of this type,[32] *i.e.* those in which the law recognises that a certain amount of discomfort is inevitable in life owing to the activities of one's neighbours, but also expects that neighbours by their mutual forbearance will lessen this discomfort as much as they are reasonably able. The law of private nuisance gives to each party a qualified privilege of causing harm to the other. When the activity of one party is motivated principally by malice, his privilege is at an end and he is liable for the damage he has caused.

In both *Christie* v. *Davey*[33] and *Hollywood Silver Fox Farm Ltd.* v.

---

[26] [1893] 1 Ch. 316; *Palmar* v. *Loder* [1962] C.L.Y. 2233 (perpetual injunction granted to restrain defendant from interfering with plaintiff's enjoyment of her flat by shouting, banging, laughing, ringing door-bells or otherwise behaviour so as to cause a nuisance by noise to her).
[27] [1893] 1 Ch. 316, 326–327.
[28] [1895] A.C. 587, *ante*, p. 48.
[29] [1898] A.C. 1.
[30] [1936] 2 K.B. 468, 475; Weir, *Casebook on Tort* (6th ed.), p. 373: distinguished in *Rattray* v. *Daniels* [1959] 17 D.L.R. (2d) 134 (Alberta S.C.) (noise of bulldozer damaging mink in whelping season): for discussion on *Emmett's* case, see (1936) 52 L.Q.R. 460–461; (1957) 53 L.Q.R. 1–4.
[31] *Harrison* v. *Southwark and Vauxhall Water Co.* [1891] 2 Ch. 409, 414, *per* Vaughan Williams L.J.; *Bamford* v. *Turnley* (1862) 31 L.J.Q.B. 286, 294, *per* Bramwell B.; *Grant* v. *Fynney* (1872) L.R. 8 Ch.App. 8, 12, *per* Lord Selborne L.C.
[32] But in nuisances which are injuries to servitudes, malice is irrelevant to liability.
[33] [1893] 1 Ch. 316.

Emmett[34] the defendant interfered with a legally protected interest of the plaintiff and the issue was whether, in doing so, he had acted unreasonably. If, however, the defendant's activity has not infringed any such right or interest, the plaintiff has no cause of action and the defendant's motive is irrelevant. This was in fact the position in *Bradford* v. *Pickles*[35] itself, where the defendant deliberately drained his land so as to diminish the water supply reaching the land of the plaintiffs. His purpose was to coerce the plaintiffs into purchasing his land. It had previously been established that no interest in percolating waters exists until appropriation,[36] and as no interest or right could therefore have been infringed, the motive of the defendant was not material.[37] In other words, *Christie* v. *Davey* and the *Hollywood Silver Fox Farm* case represent the normal rule and *Bradford* v. *Pickles* turns on the peculiarity of the law governing percolating water.[38] This peculiarity has, however, given rise to difficulty where damage is caused by the pumping out of underground water. In *Langbrook Properties Ltd.* v. *Surrey County Council*[39] and *Stephens* v. *Anglia Water Authority*[40] such conduct by the defendants led to withdrawal of support and the collapse of the plaintiffs' neighbouring properties. Now it might be thought that *Bradford* v. *Pickles* simply involved a complaint that the plaintiff had been deprived of its water supply because the defendant had got to the water first and that the law would be different where foreseeable subsidence was caused. However, this is not so and it has been said that it is an inevitable logical consequence of *Bradford* v. *Pickles* that "the claim in that case would have no less failed if the defendant's activities had resulted in subsidence of buildings or even personal injury. As the law stands, the right of the landowner to abstract subterranean water flowing in undefined channels . . . appears . . . to be exercisable regardless of the consequences, whether physical or pecuniary, to his neighbours."[41] The plaintiff cannot escape this rule by framing his claim as negligence.[42]

SOURCE OF THE INTERFERENCE

Though there does not seem to be any necessity that a nuisance should emanate from land occupied by the defendant,[43] it has traditionally been

---

[34] [1936] 2 K.B. 468.

[35] [1895] A.C. 587; *Thomas* v. *Gulf Oil Refining* (1979) 123 S.J. 787.

[36] *Acton* v. *Blundell* (1843) 12 M. & W. 324; *Broadbent* v. *Ramsbotham* (1856) 11 Exch. 602; *Chasemore* v. *Richards* (1859) 7 H.L.C. 349. See Clayberg, "The Law of Percolating Waters" (1915) 14 Mich.L.R. 119.

[37] See Fridman, "Motive in the English Law of Nuisance" (1954) 40 Va.L.R. 583–595.

[38] In the case of water flowing in a defined channel a riparian owner can take water only for use on the adjoining land (see Clerk & Lindsell, *Torts* (16th ed.), para. 24–48). Water supplies, whether percolating or channelled, are now generally subject to licensing control by regional water authorities under statute.

[39] [1970] 1 W.L.R. 161.

[40] [1987] 1 W.L.R. 1381; Fleming (1988) 104 L.Q.R. 183.

[41] [1987] 1 W.L.R. 1381, 1387.

[42] *Langbrook Properties* case, *supra. cf. Re National Capital Commission and Pugliese* (1979) 97 D.L.R. (3d) 631 where the Supreme Court of Canada held that local legislation had impliedly altered the common law rule. This case at first instance ((1977) 79 D.L.R. (3d) 592)) reviews the rule in various parts of the common law world.

[43] *Post*, p. 396.

regarded as of the essence of nuisance that the interference emanates from *outside* the plaintiff's land,[44] though it has been held that where, by statute, a highway authority has control of a tree in the highway it is liable for damage caused by the tree to a neighbouring house, even though the house owner is, or is presumed to be, owner of the land of the highway on which the tree stands.[45] However, it has twice[46] been held in New Zealand that a defendant may incur liability in nuisance for acts committed on the plaintiff's land which interfere with the enjoyment of that land.[47] If these decisions were to be accepted in England the practical significance of this change would depend very much on the extent to which nuisance was regarded as imposing a stricter liability than negligence.[48]

WHO CAN SUE

Private nuisance

Private nuisance has traditionally been a remedy available only to a person who has suffered an interference with an interest in land. "It is clear that to give a cause of action for private nuisance, the matter complained of must affect the property of the plaintiffs."[49] "He alone has a lawful claim who has suffered an invasion of some proprietary or other interest in land."[50] The occupier of land can always maintain an action in respect of an interference to it, as can a tenant in possession,[51] even if there is only a weekly tenancy[52] or a tenancy at will.[53] The duration of the tenancy and the gravity

[44] *Salford City Council* v. *McNally* [1976] A.C. 379, 389; *N.C.B.* v. *Neath Borough Council* [1976] 2 All E.R. 478.

[45] *Russell* v. *Barnet London Borough* (1985) 83 L.G.R. 152. Scarman L.J. suggested a quasi-exception in *Hooper* v. *Rogers* [1975] Ch. 43: where plaintiff and defendant are co-occupiers of the land on which the nuisance originates and the plaintiff is in sole occupation of the land *affected* by the nuisance. The point was not in fact open to dispute by the defendant in the C.A.

[46] By the same judge, Mahon J.

[47] *Paxhaven Holdings Ltd.* v. *Att.-Gen.* [1974] 2 N.Z.L.R. 185; *Clearlite Holdings Ltd.* v. *Auckland City Corp.* [1976] 2 N.Z.L.R. 729; refusing to follow *Titus* v. *Duke* (1963) 6 W.I.R. 135. The *Clearlite* case contains a review of the authorities. Chambers [1978] N.Z.L.J. 172.

[48] It has been argued above that there is comparatively little foundation for the view that nuisance is stricter but Mahon J. in the *Clearlite* case imposed liability without fault. This approach gives force to the learned judge's argument that to confine nuisance to acts outside the land would be productive of anomalies: "If in the present case the contractors had been driving the same type of tunnel under the public street and parallel to the boundary of the plaintiff's premises, then the loss caused by any subsidence to the plaintiff's land would be recoverable from the contractor on the ground of public nuisance, and the same results would follow if similar damage occurred through the contractor mistakenly crossing the boundary. . . . In the latter case the loss . . . would be recoverable in an action for trespass. It seems in the highest degree illogical that the same damage could not be recovered from the same act merely because at the time of the commission of the act the tortfeasor is on the plaintiff's land pursuant to a licence granted to him by the plaintiff": [1976] 2 N.Z.L.R. 729, 739.

[49] *Southport Corp.* v. *Esso Petroleum Co.* [1953] 3 W.L.R. 773, 776, *per* Devlin J. *Tate & Lyle Industries Ltd.* v. *G.L.C.* [1983] 2 A.C. 509.

[50] *Read* v. *J. Lyons & Co. Ltd.* [1947] A.C. 156, 183, *per* Lord Simonds; *Sedleigh-Denfield* v. *O'Callaghan* [1940] A.C. 880, 902–903, *per* Lord Wright; *Cunard* v. *Antifyre Ltd.* [1933] 1 K.B. 551, 557, *per* Talbot J.; *Southport Corp.* v. *Esso Petroleum Co. Ltd.* [1954] 2 Q.B. 182, 193 *per* Veale J.; *Vaughn* v. *Halifax Dartmouth Bridge Commission* [1961] 29 D.L.R. (2d) 523. See West, "Nuisance or *Rylands* v. *Fletcher*" (1966) 30 Conv.(N.S.) 95, 101. Where there is a continuing nuisance (such as encroachment by tree roots) a person who is occupier at the time the action is brought may recover the cost of reinstatement even though the damage occurred before he acquired his interest and even though he was aware of the damage when he acquired his interest: *Masters* v. *Brent L.B.C.* [1978] Q.B. 841.

[51] *Inchbald* v. *Robinson* (1869) L.R. 4 Ch. 388.

[52] *Jones* v. *Chappell* (1869) L.R. 20 Eq. 539, 544.

[53] *Burgess* v. *City of Woodstock* [1955] 4 D.L.R. 615 (Ont.H.C.).

of the interference are factors to be considered in determining whether to
grant an injunction, but where there is a real injury to health and comfort it is
possible that even a weekly tenant will be granted an injunction as well as
damages.[54]

A person who has merely the use of land without either the possession of it
or any other proprietary interest in it, *e.g.* a licensee without possession,
such as a lodger or a guest, cannot sue in nuisance. For the same reason even
members of the occupier's family cannot maintain an action in nuisance[55]
although of course if they suffer personal injuries[56] it is always open to them
to sue in negligence. It may be, however, that a licensee with exclusive
possession has a sufficient interest in the land to be permitted to claim in
nuisance.

The owner of an incorporeal hereditament such as an easement or profit
can sue for disturbance of his right.[57]

A reversioner can bring an action in nuisance if he can show that there is a
likelihood that permanent injury will be caused to the property and his right
is then co-existent with that of the occupier. A permanent injury is one
which will continue indefinitely unless something is done to remove it,[58] for
example a building which infringes the right to ancient lights,[59] vibrations
causing structural damage,[60] or the keeping locked a gate across a path over
which the reversioner has a right of way[61]; but the emission of noise or fumes
or other invasions of a temporary nature, even if they cause the tenants to
leave, or reduce the letting value, will not suffice.[62]

It is doubtful whether there are any other persons who can maintain an
action in private nuisance. Pollock was of the opinion that in some instances
there may be a private nuisance where the plaintiff has no control, use or
enjoyment of immovable property; *e.g.* the owner or master of a ship lying in
a harbour might sue for a nuisance created by an occupier of the wharf or
shore which made the ship uninhabitable,[63] but it would seem that this would
be properly classified as a public nuisance.[64]

So long as private nuisance is confined to interference with the enjoyment
of land the insistence on the plaintiff having an interest in that land is
rational. However, it has been assumed on a number of occasions that

---

[54] *Jones* v. *Chappell, supra.*
[55] *Malone* v. *Laskey* [1907] 2 K.B. 144; *Oldham* v. *Lawson (No. 1)* [1976] V.R. 654. *Contra* is *Devon Lumber
Co. Ltd.* v. *MacNeill* (1987) 45 D.L.R. (4th) 300. The "right of occupation" conferred by the Matrimonial
Homes Act 1983 would not seem to be relevant to this situation, though one spouse exercising the right to
the exclusion of the other would have the right to sue in nuisance by virtue of *de facto* possession.
[56] *Malone* v. *Laskey* [1907] 2 K.B. 144, 153–154, *per* Fletcher Moulton L.J.; *Cunard* v. *Antifyre Ltd.* [1933] 1
K.B. 551.
[57] *Nicholls* v. *Ely Beet Sugar Factory Ltd.* [1936] 1 Ch. 343 (destruction of fish by pollution); *Weston* v.
Lawrence Weaver Ltd. [1961] 1 Q.B. 402 (physical damage to an easement of way without interference
with right of passage not actionable).
[58] *Jones* v. *Llanrwst U.D.C.* [1911] 1 Ch. 393, 404, *per* Parker J.
[59] *Jesser* v. *Gifford* (1767) 4 Burr. 2141.
[60] *Colwell* v. *St. Pancras B.C.* [1904] Ch. 707.
[61] *Kidgill* v. *Moor* (1850) 9 C.B. 364.
[62] *Simpson* v. *Savage* (1856) 1 C.B.(N.S.) 347; *Cooper* v. *Crabtree* (1882) 20 Ch.D. 589.
[63] *Torts* (15th ed.), p. 302.
[64] *Wagon Mound (No. 2)* [1967] 1 A.C. 617.

personal injuries are compensable in nuisance[65] and it certainly seems ano-malous that the occupier should be given such an advantage—if advantage it be[66]—over other persons injured by the nuisance.

Public nuisance

As we have seen, if a public nuisance has been committed, any person who has suffered special damage can sue in respect of it. It may, for instance, be the occupier of adjacent property[67] and it may be a user of the highway.[68]

WHO CAN BE SUED[69]

Creator of the nuisance

In general the person who creates the nuisance by some act of misfeasance as opposed to a mere non-feasance may always be sued in respect of it, whether or not he is in occupation of the land on which it originates,[70] and it is no defence that the land is now occupied by someone else and that he has no power to abate the nuisance without committing a trespass.[71] That may seem unfair, but he did the first wrong and he must answer for the damage resulting from it.[72]

Occupier

The occupier of the premises where the nuisance exists is in general liable during the period of his occupancy.[73] This is simple enough where he himself created the nuisance, but further questions arise where it originated (i) with someone else lawfully on the premises; or (ii) with a trespasser or as a result of an act of God; or (iii) with someone from whom the occupier acquired the property.

(1) *Persons lawfully on premises*

If a nuisance is caused by the servant of the occupier the latter is liable

---

[65] e.g. *Malone* v. *Laskey* [1907] 2 K.B. 141; *cf. Cunard* v. *Antifyre* [1933] 1 K.B. 551, 557 and *Halsey* v. *Esso Petroleum Co. Ltd.* [1961] 1 W.L.R. 683, 692.
[66] *Ante*, pp. 380–385.
[67] *Ante*, pp. 377–378 and *post*, pp. 412–413.
[68] e.g. *Holling* v. *Yorkshire Traction Co. Ltd.* [1948] 2 All E.R. 662; *Dollman* v. *Hillman Ltd.* [1941] 1 All E.R. 355; *Hilder* v. *Associated Portland Cement Manufacturers* [1961] 1 W.L.R. 1434.
[69] Friedmann (1943) 59 L.Q.R. 63–71 for an admirable analysis of the authorities.
[70] *Fennell* v. *Robson Excavations Pty. Ltd.* [1977] 2 N.S.W.L.R. 486 is most directly in point and reviews the authorities. See also *Southport Corp.* v. *Esso Petroleum Ltd.* [1954] 2 Q.B. 182, 204; [1956] A.C. 218, 225; *cf.* [1954] 2 Q.B. 196; [1956] A.C. 242.
[71] *Thompson* v. *Gibson* (1841) 7 M. & W. 456.
[72] Holt C.J., *Rosewell* v. *Prior* (1701) 12 Mod. 635, 639.
[73] Friedmann, "Incidence of Liability in Nuisance" (1943) L.Q.R. 63–71; *Sedleigh-Denfield* v. *O'Callaghan* [1940] A.C. 880; *Rigby* v. *Sun Alliance & London Insurance Ltd.* [1980] 1 Lloyd's Rep. 359 (relationship between insurance policies covering liability as "owner" and as "occupier."

according to the ordinary rules of vicarious liability. As a general rule, a principal cannot be held liable for the acts or defaults of an independent contractor employed by him, but there are certain exceptions to this rule. In some cases, for instance, the principal is said to be under a "non-delegable" duty to see that care is taken and if, in fact, damage is caused to a third party by the activity of the contractor, the principal will be liable, because he himself is thereby in breach of his duty of care.[74]

A person who engages in any activity which involves particular danger is under such a non-delegable duty of care[75] and this rule, of course, will cover some nuisance situations. Thus in *Bower* v. *Peate*[76] the defendant employed a contractor to do construction work on his land in the course of which the contractor undermined the support for the plaintiff's adjoining house. The defendant was held liable. In *Matania* v. *National Provincial Bank*[77] the occupier of the first floor of a building was liable to the occupier of the higher floors for a nuisance by dust and noise created by his independent contractor. In both cases the nature of the work was such that there was a special danger of a nuisance being caused by it. On the other hand, *Spicer* v. *Smee*[78] supports the view that it is the general rule in nuisance that the occupier is liable for his contractor's negligence.

A principal whose contractor interferes with or creates a danger on the highway may be liable to anyone who in consequence suffers special damage. In *Hole* v. *Sittingbourne Ry.*,[79] for instance, a railway company had authority to build a bridge across a navigable river provided that they did not impede navigation. The contractors whom they employed constructed it so imperfectly that it would not open to let boats through. The company were held liable to a user of the highway. In *Holliday* v. *National Telephone Co.*[80] the defendants were empowered by statute to lay telephone wires in the highway. One of their contractors in the course of the work negligently immersed a defective blowlamp in a pot of solder and the plaintiff was injured in the resultant explosion. The defendants were held liable. A person who has statutory authority to interfere with the highway owes a duty to the public to exercise his authority carefully, and he cannot delegate the performance of this duty to an independent contractor.[81]

In the above cases, however, the source of the danger was actually on the highway. It was clearly established by the Court of Appeal in *Salsbury* v. *Woodland*[82] that an occupier of land adjacent to the highway who commissions a contractor to do work *on* his land is not liable merely because as a result of the negligence of the contractor injury is caused to a user of the

---

[74] *Post*, pp. 581–586.

[75] *Ibid.*; *Honeywill and Stein Ltd.* v. *Larkin Bros.* [1934] 1 K.B. 191; *Rylands* v. *Fletcher* (1868) L.R. 3 H.L. 330; *Salsbury* v. *Woodland* [1970] 1 Q.B. 324.

[76] (1876) 1 Q.B.D. 321; *Dalton* v. *Angus* (1881) 6 App.Cas. 740.

[77] [1936] 2 All E.R. 633; *Duncan's Hotel (Glasgow) Ltd.* v. *J. & A. Ferguson Ltd.*, 1972 S.L.T. (Notes) 84.

[78] [1946] 1 All E.R. 489.

[79] (1861) 6 H. & N. 488; *Gray* v. *Pullen* (1864) 5 B & S. 970.

[80] [1899] 2 Q.B. 392.

[81] *Salsbury* v. *Woodland* [1970] 1 Q.B. 324, 345, *per* Harman L.J. *cf. Reid* v. *British Telecom, The Times*, June 27, 1987.

[82] *Supra.*

highway. It would be different if the work involved especial risk to the users of the highway, or if the work was done in response to a "positive and continuing duty"[83] to keep the premises in repair as in *Tarry* v. *Ashton*.[84] In that case the occupier of a public house adjoining the highway was liable when a heavy lamp attached to the building fell on a passer-by. Although the defendant had employed an independent contractor to maintain the lamp in good repair, it was held that because of the contractor's negligence the occupier had failed to discharge his duty. "That duty was imposed on him before the contractor came and after the contractor had gone."[85] There was no such continuing duty in *Salsbury* v. *Woodland* and the defendant was not liable for the negligence of a tree feller he had engaged to cut down a tree on his land adjacent to the highway.

An employer is never liable for "collateral" negligence on the part of an independent contractor.[86]

There is little authority on the position where the nuisance is created by a person who is licensed to be on the premises for his own purposes rather than to do work for the occupier. Probably, the occupier is not liable unless he had knowledge, or means of knowledge, of the nuisance and failed to take steps to control the licensee.[87]

(2) *Nuisances created by a trespasser or resulting from an act of nature*

An occupier is not liable for a state of affairs either created by a trespasser or resulting from an act of nature unless either he adopts the nuisance by using the state of affairs for his own purposes or he "continues" the nuisance. An occupier continues a nuisance if once he has actual or constructive knowledge of its existence he fails to take reasonably prompt and efficient steps to abate it. He cannot of course be liable unless he is in a position to take effective steps to abate the nuisance.[88] This principle was enunciated by the House of Lords in relation to a nuisance created by a trespasser in the leading case of *Sedleigh-Denfield* v. *O'Callaghan*.[89] The defendant occupied land on which there was a ditch. A trespasser laid a pipe in it with a grating designed to keep out leaves, but placed in such an ill-chosen position that it caused a blockage of the pipe when a heavy rainstorm occurred, and in consequence the plaintiff's adjacent land was flooded. The storm occurred nearly three years after the erection of the grating and during that period, the defendant's servant who was responsible for cleansing the ditch ought to have realised the risk of flooding presented by the obstruction. The defendant was held liable in nuisance. The House of Lords refused to draw any

---

[83] *Ibid.* at p. 339, *per* Widgery L.J.
[84] (1876) 1 Q.B.D. 314; *Wringe* v. *Cohen* [1940] 1 K.B. 229.
[85] *Post*, p. 582.
[86] *Post*, p. 585.
[87] *White* v. *Jamieson* (1874) L.R. 18 Eq. 303, which contains statements which might be regarded as placing a more onerous liability on the occupier, was in fact an action for an injunction.
[88] *Smeaton* v. *Ilford Corp.* [1954] Ch. 450, 462; *Goldman* v. *Hargrave* [1967] 1 A.C. 645.
[89] [1940] A.C. 880. "An absentee owner or occupier oblivious of what is happening under his own eyes is in no better position than a man who looks after his property:" at p. 887, *per* Lord Maugham; *Leanse* v. *Egerton* [1943] K.B. 323.

distinction in this connection between public and private nuisance.[90] The principle of *Sedleigh-Denfield* is not confined to cases where the trespasser interferes with the state of the land itself: a local authority was held liable for failing to take steps to remove from its land gypsies whose objectionable behaviour damaged the plaintiffs' business next door.[91] Something more, however, is required than a mere foreseeable possibility that intruders may gain access to the land and cause damage to the neighbouring owner.[92]

Although it had been held even before *Sedleigh-Denfield* v. *O'Callaghan* that an occupier can be liable for continuing a nuisance created by a third party,[93] until recent times it was considered that he was never under a duty to abate a natural nuisance.[94] This rule of immunity was however decisively rejected by the Judicial Committee in the important case of *Goldman* v. *Hargrave*.[95] A tall redgum tree growing in the centre of the defendant's land was struck by lightning and began to burn. The defendant properly requested a tree feller to come and cut down the tree. Until the time the tree was felled, the defendant's conduct in relation to the fire was not open to criticism. However, instead of extinguishing the fire immediately the tree was felled by inundating it with water, the defendant left the tree to burn itself out and took inadequate steps to prevent the fire from spreading. In fact, in consequence of a strengthening of the wind and an increase in temperature, the fire spread on to the plaintiff's property. It was found that the method adopted by the defendant involved a foreseeable risk of the revival and spread of the fire and the defendant was held liable. In an admirable judgment Lord Wilberforce rejected the traditional policy of regarding occupation of land as a source of privilege and immunity. "It is only in comparatively recent times that the law has recognised an occupier's duty as one of a more positive character than merely to abstain from creating, or adding to, a source of danger or annoyance."[96] The principle of *Goldman* v. *Hargrave* was formally accepted as part of English law by the Court of Appeal in *Leakey* v. *National Trust*,[97] which involved damage done by movement of the land itself. As regards such nuisances of omission, therefore, it is no longer relevant whether the state of affairs was originally

---

[90] As suggested by Bankes L.J. in *Job Edwards* v. *Birmingham Navigation* [1924] 1 K.B. 341. The actual decision in the case may be valid on other grounds, though dicta in *Sedleigh-Denfield's* case leave even that uncertain: [1940] A.C. 880, 893, 918–919.

[91] *Page Motors Ltd.* v. *Epsom and Ewell B.C.* (1982) 80 L.G.R. 337.

[92] *Smith* v. *Littlewoods Organisation Ltd.* [1987] A.C. 241, *ante*, p. 94.

[93] e.g. *Barker* v. *Herbert* [1911] 2 K.B. 633.

[94] *Giles* v. *Walker* (1890) 24 Q.B.D. 656; *Sparke* v. *Osborne* (1909) 7 C.L.R. 51; *Pontardawe U.D.C.* v. *Moore-Gwyn* [1929] 1 Ch. 656; *Neath R.D.C.* v. *Williams* [1951] 1 K.B. 115 (natural silting up of a watercourse—an interesting comparison with *Sedleigh-Denfield* v. *O'Callaghan, supra*). The rule of immunity did not extend to public nuisance: *Noble* v. *Harrison* [1926] 2 K.B. 332.

[95] [1967] 1 A.C. 645; Harris [1967] C.L.J. 24–27.

[96] *Ibid.* at p. 657. In the High Court of Australia, Windeyer J. said: "The tendency of the law in recent times has been to lessen the immunities and privileges of landowners and occupiers and to increase their responsibility to others for what happens on their land": [1964] A.L.R. 377, 392.

[97] [1980] Q.B. 485; Weir *Casebook on Tort* (6th ed.), p. 377; Buckley (1980) 96 L.Q.R. 185; Markisinis [1980] C.L.J. 259. Shaw L.J. agreed that *Goldman* v. *Hargrave* represented English law, but expressed substantial misgivings.

created by a third party or by nature.[98] Once the occupier becomes aware of the nuisance and fails to remedy it within a reasonable time, he may be liable for any damage it may cause, either to his neighbour[99] or the user of the highway. "The basis of the occupier's liability lies not in the use of his land; in the absence of 'adoption' there is no such use; but in the neglect of action in the face of something which may damage his neighbour."[1]

We have seen that in this nuisance situation, it is immaterial whether the cause of action is termed "nuisance" or "negligence"; the burden of proof on the plaintiff is the same.[2] In determining the standard of care required the court cannot disregard the fact that the occupier is confronted with a nuisance not of his own creation, and because of this the court is entitled to consider the occupier's individual circumstances. As Lord Wilberforce said in a passage of great clarity:

> "The law must take account of the fact that the occupier on whom the duty is cast has, *ex hypothesi,* had this hazard thrust upon him through no seeking or fault of his own. His interest, and his resources, whether physical or material, may be of a very modest character either in relation to the magnitude of the hazard, or as compared with those of his threatened neighbour. A rule which required of him in such unsought circumstances in his neighbour's interest a physical effort of which he is not capable, or an excessive expenditure of money, would be unenforceable or unjust. One may say in general terms that the existence of a duty must be based upon knowledge of the hazard, ability to foresee the consequences of not checking or removing it, and the ability to abate it. ... The standard ought to be to require of the occupier what is reasonable to expect of him in his individual circumstances."[3]

This subjective test is an exception to the general rule in negligence[4] and is

---

[98] But it is still the law that a lower occupier has no claim against the higher occupier for permitting the natural, unconcentrated flow of water to pass from the higher to the lower land. The lower occupier may put up barriers to prevent this, but his action in doing so must be a reasonable use of his land: *Home Brewery Co. Ltd.* v. *William Davis & Co. (Leicester) Ltd.* [1987] Q.B. 339.

[99] As a result of this principle the rule that the owner of a servient tenement subject to an easement of support owes no duty to incur expenditure has been outflanked: *Bradburn* v. *Lindsay* [1983] 2 All E.R. 408; Jackson [1984] Conv. 54. Yet in *Duke of Westminster* v. *Guild* [1985] Q.B. 668 a landlord was not liable in the absence of a covenant to repair when a defective drain on his premises prevented water escaping from the demised premises next door.

[1] [1967] 1 A.C. 645, 661. Contrast *Elston* v. *Dove* (1982) 43 A.L.R. 577 (in the absence of an easement or licence the occupier may remove a structure on his land which happens to remedy a natural deficiency of his neighbour's land).

[2] *Ante,* p. 381.

[3] [1967] 1 A.C. 645, 663. Lord Wilberforce proceeded to interpret some of the previous cases in this light. Thus in the *Job Edwards* case, to remove the hazard would have cost £1,000, therefore no liability. In *Pontardawe U.D.C.* v. *Moore-Gwyn,* the cost would have been between £300–£450: no liability. *cf. Leakey* v. *National Trust.* Individual circumstances are not confined to physical and financial resources: the defendants' responsibilities to the public at large were taken into account in *Page Motors Ltd.* v. *Epsom and Ewell B.C.* (1982) 80 L.G.R. 337.

[4] *Ante,* at p. 111.

But in applying this test "I do not think that, except perhaps in a most unusual case, there would be any question of discovery as to means of the plaintiff or the defendant, or evidence as to their respective resources. The question of reasonableness ... would fall to be decided on a broad basis, in which on some occasions, there might be included an element of obvious discrepancy of financial resources": *Leakey* v. *National Trust, supra,* at p. 527, *per* Megaw L.J.

carefully limited by Lord Wilberforce to cases where the defendant was not himself responsible for the creation of the source of danger.[5]

(3) *Predecessor in title*

Where the nuisance existed before the occupier acquired the property he will be liable if it can be proved that he knew, or ought reasonably to have known, of its existence; but not otherwise. In *St. Anne's Well Brewery Co.* v. *Roberts*,[6] X owned an ancient inn, one side of which was bounded by the old city wall of Exeter. Y owned part of the wall. On either side of X's kitchen fireplace, recesses had at some time unknown been formed by excavations in the wall. Part of the wall belonging to Y collapsed and demolished the inn. X sued Y who was held not liable because he neither knew of the defect nor could have discovered it by reasonable diligence.[7] It is arguable that the standard of care discussed in *Goldman* v. *Hargrave* should apply also to this situation.

Landlord

The basic rule is that a landlord is not liable for a nuisance on the premises, as he is not in occupation; the proper person to sue is the tenant.[8] But the landlord is liable in the following circumstances, which go a long way to displacing the basic rule.

(1) *If he has authorised nuisance*

The landlord is liable if he has expressly or impliedly authorised his tenant to create the nuisance. Where A let a field to B for working it as a lime quarry and B's acts in blasting the limestone and letting kiln smoke escape

[5] This may be a suitable point at which to make some mention of liability for damage done by encroachment by tree roots. It had been accepted before *Goldman* v. *Hargrave* that there might be liability whether the tree was planted or self-sown—indeed some cases (*e.g. Davey* v. *Harrow Corp.* [1958] 1 Q.B. 60) imposed liability in unqualified terms. However, in *Solloway* v. *Hampshire C.C.* (1981) 79 L.G.R. 449 the Court of Appeal held that an occupier of land containing a tree was only liable if he knew or ought to have known of the danger caused by it (see also *Leakey* v. *National Trust* at p. 522). Nothing seems to have turned on the point that the tree was in the highway (*cf.* Street [1982] Conv. 294). In *Solloway*, as in most other cases, the tree had been planted many years before by the defendant's predecessor in title. The position where the defendant himself without negligence plants a tree which becomes a nuisance is bound up with the question of strict liability for nuisance (*ante*, p. 380). *Butler* v. *Standard Telephones and Cables Ltd.* [1940] 1 K.B. 399 perhaps provides some support for strict liability, but there is no real discussion of the point and the trees in question (poplars) are notorious for causing subsidence.
[6] (1929) 140 L.T. 1. Followed in *Wilkins* v. *Leighton* [1932] 2 Ch. 106. *cf. Hall* v. *Duke of Norfolk* [1900] 2 Ch. 165 (present occupier held not liable for "continuing" an excavation made by his predecessor which eventually caused a subsidence).
[7] In *Broder* v. *Saillard* (1876) 2 Ch.D. 692, defendant was a tenant of premises the stables of which were erected upon an artificial mound of earth which adjoined the plaintiff's house, and into which rain and drainage from the stables penetrated and so caused the plaintiff's wall to be damp. Defendant was held liable although he had no knowledge of the nuisance, but one must assume that there had not been such reasonable diligence on the defendant's part with respect to leakage from a soil-pipe. In *Humphries* v. *Cousins* (1877) 2 C.P.D. 239, a drain which began on defendant's premises passed under other houses and received their drainage and then returned under defendant's premises and passed under plaintiff's house. The return drain beneath defendant's premises was decayed and allowed the drainage to escape which passed into plaintiff's premises. Defendant was ignorant even of the existence of the return drain. "It is probable, however, that the principle of *Rylands* v. *Fletcher*, though not referred to in the case, would justify the decision, as suggested in *Winfield on Torts*": *per* Lord Atkin in the *Sedleigh-Denfield* case, at p. 898.
[8] *Cheetham* v. *Hampson* (1791) 4 T.R. 318.

constituted a nuisance to C, A was held liable, for B's method of working the quarry was the usual way of getting lime and A was taken to have authorised it[9]; and a local authority was liable when it let land for go-karting and a nuisance was a natural and necessary consequence of that activity.[10] Here the liability of the landlord is not different from that of any principal who authorises his agent to commit a tort.[11] The tenant, of course, is also liable.[12] By way of contrast, a local authority which let a house to a "problem" family was not liable to be enjoined in respect of nuisance created by the family even though the authority could have terminated the lease for breaches of covenant: the authority had not expressly authorised the nuisance and it was caused solely by the acts of the tenants, not by any condition of the premises themselves.[13] A person does not authorise another to do an act merely because he has furnished him with the means of doing it or because he has sufficient control to stop him.[14]

(2) *If he knew of nuisance before letting*

If the landlord knowingly lets premises on which there is a nuisance for which the landlord was in some way himself responsible, he will remain liable for it. A person who creates a nuisance is of course always responsible even though he is no longer in occupation of the land on which the nuisance exists.[15] Moreover the tenant may be liable for adopting or continuing the nuisance.

(3) *If he ought to have known of nuisance before letting*

If he ought to have known of the nuisance at the date of the lease, the landlord is liable, but not if he had no reasonable grounds for suspecting its existence. This result has been attained gradually and by steps of doubtful consistency. In *Gandy* v. *Jubber*[16] the plaintiff was lamed by slipping through a defective iron grating over the area of a house in the occupation of X. She sued the defendant, who had originally let the premises to X. The court[17] was

---

[9] *Harris* v. *James* (1876) 45 L.J.Q.B. 545; *Sampson* v. *Hodson-Pressinger* [1981] 3 All E.R. 710 (*cf.* Owen [1982] C.L.J. 38); *Rich* v. *Basterfield* (1847) 4 C.B. 783 was regarded by Blackburn J. as a decision on the facts, and by Lush J. as hair-splitting: *Pwllbach Colliery Co.* v. *Woodman* [1915] A.C. 634, 639, "But permission to carry on a business is quite a different thing from permission to carry it on in such a manner as to create a nuisance, unless it is impossible in a practical sense to carry it on without committing a nuisance": *per* Lord Loreburn.

[10] *Tetley* v. *Chitty* [1986] 1 All E.R. 663.

[11] But an assignee of the reversion who takes with knowledge of the nuisance stands in the same position as the original landlord: *Sampson* v. *Hodson-Pressinger* [1981] 3 All E.R. 710.

[12] He may be able to recover a contribution or indemnity or recover damages for breach of covenant from the landlord: *ibid.*

[13] *Smith* v. *Scott* [1973] Ch. 314; criticised by Merritt [1973] J.P.L. 154. It was pointed out in the Court of Appeal in *Page Motors Ltd.* v. *Epsom and Ewell B.C.* (1982) 80 L.G.R. 337 that *Sedleigh-Denfield* v. *O'Callaghan* had not been considered in *Smith* v. *Scott*, but it would be a great step to apply that case to a defendant not in occupation. Contrast *Hilton* v. *James Smith & Sons (Norwood) Ltd.* (1979) 251 E.G. 1063 where the defendants were in occupation.

[14] See *C.B.S. Songs Ltd.* v. *Amstrad Consumer Electronics plc* [1988] A.C. 1013 (not a nuisance case).

[15] *Rosewell* v. *Prior* (1701) 12 Mod. 635; *Todd* v. *Flight* (1860) 9 C.B.(N.S.) 377.

[16] (1865) 5 B. & S. 78, 485; 9 B. & S. 15.

[17] 9 B. & S. 15; an undelivered judgment of the Exch. Chamber.

of the opinion that there was no tenancy between the defendant and X and held that, even if there were one, the defendant was not liable because it was not alleged that the grating was defective at the time of the letting. But the court also considered that, if there had been a tenancy, the defendant would have been liable for the nuisance provided (*a*) it had existed at the date of the creation of the tenancy, and (*b*) the defendant had had notice of it, and (*c*) it was such as to be in its very essence and nature a nuisance at the date of letting and was not merely some defect capable of being rendered a nuisance by the tenant after the tenancy had begun; *e.g.* a cellar with a flap is not an obvious nuisance; it may or may not be one according to whether the flap was improperly left open or carefully closed.[18] The court considered that if the above three conditions were fulfilled, the lessor ought to be liable because it is only just that the owner of property receiving rent should be thus answerable. A sweeping dictum in the later case of *Nelson* v. *Liverpool Brewery Co.*[19] might imply that unless the landlord actually knew of the nuisance he could not be liable for it; but still later dicta have narrowed it and probably the rule now is that the landlord is liable not only if he knew of the defect but also if he could have ascertained it with reasonable care, whether it was obvious or not.[20]

(4) *Where landlord reserves right to enter and repair or has implied right to do so*

The first point to make is that in this case the landlord will be liable to persons outside the premises (as well as to visitors therein) if he is in breach of section 4 of the Defective Premises Act 1972.[21] This duty is owed to "all persons who might reasonably be expected to be affected by defects in the state of the premises" and is a duty "to take such care as is reasonable in all the circumstances to see that they are reasonably safe from personal injury or from damage to their property" caused by the defects.[22] This provision would seem to make the common law in this area largely redundant as far as the landlord's liability is concerned, but the basis of liability in nuisance is so uncertain[23] that it is not inconceivable that a plaintiff might gain some advantage from relying on the common law and it is to that we now turn.

In *Wilchick* v. *Marks*[24] the plaintiff was walking along the highway when she was injured by the fall of a defective shutter from X's house. X had let the house to Y and both X and Y knew of the defect. There was no covenant on either side to repair. Both were held liable. Y was liable because he was the occupier and also because, if the rule were otherwise and the landlord

---

[18] *Ibid.* and Blackburn J. in 5 B. & S. 78, 90. *cf.* Lindley L.J. in *Gwinnell* v. *Eamer* (1875) L.R. 10 C.P. 658, 662.

[19] (1877) 2 C.P.D. 311. In any event the decision related to visitors *coming on* the premises and therefore belonged to a different branch of the law ("Liability for Land and Structures") *ante*, Chap. 9.

[20] *St. Anne's Well Brewery Co.* v. *Roberts* (1929) 140 L.T. 1; Goddard J. in *Wilchick* v. *Marks* [1934] 2 K.B. 56, 67–68; *Brew Bros Ltd.* v. *Snax (Ross) Ltd.* [1970] 1 Q.B. 612.

[21] A right to repair is equated with a duty to do so by s.4(4).

[22] See further, *ante*, p. 237.

[23] *Ante*, pp. 380–385.

[24] [1934] 2 K.B. 56.

happened to be abroad, the damage might be done before he could be notified of the risk and called upon to repair it. X was liable because he had reserved to himself the right to enter and do repairs (though he was under no obligation to do them) and to that extent he exercised a measure of control over the premises. In *Heap* v. *Ind, Coope and Allsopp Ltd.*[25] the landlord was held liable by the Court of Appeal to a passer-by where he had not covenanted to do repairs but had expressly reserved the right to enter for the purpose of viewing the condition and making the necessary repairs at the tenant's expense, although he did not know of the want of repair. The tenant was not sued but was clearly liable.[26] In *Mint* v. *Good*[27] the plaintiff was injured by the collapse of a wall on the highway, the wall being on premises which the defendant landlord had let to a weekly tenant, who was not sued in the action. The wall was found to be a nuisance due to its defective state of repair. The defendant had not contracted with the tenant to do repairs and had not reserved a right to enter on the property to do so. The Court of Appeal held that in a weekly tenancy such a right must be implied and the defendant was liable in nuisance. The Landlord and Tenant Act 1985 now provides that in any lease of a dwelling-house granted for a term of *less* than seven years or any lease which is determinable by the lessor in less than seven years, there is an implied covenant by the lessor to keep in repair the structure and exterior (including drains, gutters and external pipes), and certain installations within the dwelling-house. It renders ineffective any provision in a tenancy which seeks to place these burdens on the tenant.[28] The landlord's liability does not exempt the tenant; he is also liable even if he does not know of the defect provided he could have ascertained it if he had used reasonable care.[29]

(5) *Where covenant to repair*

Hitherto we have assumed that neither landlord nor tenant is under an express covenant to repair. Suppose that there is such a covenant, that it is not observed and that a nuisance consequently arises which causes an injury to a third person, how does that affect the position? As in the previous case there may now be liability under section 4 of the Defective Premises Act 1972 but, as we have said above, there may be circumstances in which a claim at common law may be more favourable to the plaintiff.[30]

If it is the tenant who has undertaken the repair, of course he is liable, but his liability is based on the fact that he is the occupier of the premises; any

---

[25] [1940] 2 K.B. 476.

[26] *Ibid.* at p. 482. MacKinnon L.J. refers to it as "an irrefragable claim."

[27] [1951] 1 K.B. 517; Weir, *Casebook on Tort* (6th ed.), p. 175. In the absence of evidence to the contrary, both parties must be taken to have contemplated that the landlord will do the necessary repairs: pp. 521–522, 527. Somervell L.J. was not prepared to hold the landlord liable because he had previously done the repairs: p. 523. See *Sleafer* v. *Lambeth B.C.* [1959] 1 Q.B. 43, at pp. 56–57.

[28] See *ante*, p. 236. The Act is extended by s.116 of the Housing Act 1988 to cover installations in a retained part of the premises which serve the demised part.

[29] Goddard L.J. in *Wilchick* v. *Marks* [1934] 2 K.B. 56. The dicta of Heath J. to the contrary in *Payne* v. *Rogers* (1794) 2 H.Bl. 350 are unsatisfactory.

[30] This is particularly so if the premises abut on the highway: see *Wringe* v. *Cohen, post*, p. 416.

additional obligation which he may have undertaken by contract with the landlord cannot affect his liability in tort to third parties. Does such an undertaking exempt the landlord from liability for the nuisance? In *Pretty* v. *Bickmore*[31] it was held that even if the landlord was aware of the nuisance he could not be liable where he had taken from his tenant a covenant to repair as he had done nothing to authorise the nuisance or its continuance. In the light of subsequent *obiter dicta*,[32] however, this view was of doubtful authority and was finally rejected by a majority of the Court of Appeal in *Brew Bros. Ltd.* v. *Snax (Ross) Ltd.*[33] The liability of the landlord now depends in part on whether the nuisance existed on the premises at the commencement of the tenancy. If it did and was such that the landlord knew or ought to have known of its existence at the commencement of the tenancy he is liable and the covenant to repair is irrelevant.[34] "If the nuisance arises after the lease is granted, the test of an owner's duty to his neighbour depends on the degree of control exercised by the owner in law or in fact for the purpose of repairs."[35] He cannot therefore be liable if he has no right to enter the premises to inspect and effect repairs,[36] but such a right is readily inferred by the courts, particularly in a weekly tenancy.[37] Indeed in *Mint* v. *Good*,[38] Denning L.J. doubted whether a landlord can now exempt himself from liability to passers-by by taking a covenant from a tenant to repair premises adjoining a highway.[39] If the landlord does have a sufficient degree of control, it is no defence that the tenant is under a duty to repair. As Sachs L.J. remarked in *Brew Brothers Ltd.* v. *Snax (Ross) Ltd.*,[40] there is no reason why liability to a third party should be "shuffled off merely by signing a document which as between owner and tenant casts on the latter the burden of executing remedial work. The duty of the owner is to ensure that the nuisance causes no injury—not merely to get somebody else's promise to take the requisite steps to abate it."[41]

If it is the landlord who has undertaken to repair, he is liable. Such was the decision in *Payne* v. *Rogers*,[42] where Heath J. said that if the tenant, and not the landlord, were held liable this would encourage circuity of action because the tenant would then be able to obtain an indemnity from the landlord. A more satisfactory explanation is that in such circumstances the

---

[31] (1873) L.R. 8 C.P. 401. The fact of the landlord's knowledge appears more clearly in the reports in 28 L.T. 704, *per* Honeyman J. and 21 W.R. 783. See, however, the comments of Sachs L.J. in *Brew Bros. Ltd.* v. *Snax (Ross) Ltd.* [1970] 1 Q.B. 612, 637.

[32] Brett J. in *Gwinnell* v. *Eamer* (1875) L.R. 10 C.P. 658, 661; Goddard J. in *Wilchick* v. *Marks* [1934] 2 K.B. 56, 67; the C.A. in *Wringe* v. *Cohen* [1940] 1 K.B. 229, 235–236, 246.

[33] [1970] 1 Q.B. 612.

[34] *Ibid.* at p. 638, *per* Sachs L.J., and at p. 644, *per* Phillimore L.J. Harman L.J. (at p. 643) appears to insist on actual knowledge.

[35] *Ibid.* at p. 638, following the judgment of Lord Denning and Birkett L.J. in *Mint* v. *Good* [1951] 1 K.B. 517, 529.

[36] *cf. post*, p. 706.

[37] *Mint* v. *Good* [1951] 1 K.B. 517, 523, *per* Somervell L.J.; at p. 527, *per* Denning L.J.; at p. 528, *per* Birkett L.J.

[38] [1951] 1 K.B. 517.

[39] *Ibid.* at p. 528.

[40] [1970] 1 Q.B. 612.

[41] *Ibid.* at pp. 638–639, following *Mint* v. *Good, supra*, at p. 527, *per* Denning L.J.

[42] (1794) 2 H.Bl. 350. See, too, dictum in *Nelson* v. *Liverpool Brewery Co.* (1877) 2 C.P.D. 311, 313.

landlord has control of the premises. He may not be in occupation but his covenant to repair gives him a right of access to the premises for the very purpose of preventing the injury which has occurred.[43] Moreover, in *Wringe* v. *Cohen* the Court of Appeal held that where premises on a highway become dangerous and constitute a nuisance, so that they collapse and injure a passer-by or an adjoining owner, the occupier or owner of the premises, if he has undertaken the duty to repair, is answerable, whether he knew or ought to have known of the danger or not.[44] A had let a house to B and the duty to keep it in repair was on A. A decayed gable-end fell from the house on to C's adjoining shop and destroyed its roof. It was held that A was liable to C in nuisance, whether A knew or ought to have known of the danger or not. It was conceded, however, that if the defect were due to either (*a*) a secret and unobservable operation of nature (*e.g.* subsidence under or near the foundations of the premises), or (*b*) the act of a trespasser, then neither landlord nor tenant would be liable, unless, with knowledge or means of knowledge, he were to allow the danger to continue.[45]

Where the landlord is under a duty to repair and injury to a third party has resulted from a breach of the duty, the tenant is also liable. In *Payne* v. *Rogers*,[46] Heath J. seemed to imply that in such circumstances the tenant cannot be liable, but in *St Anne's Well Brewery Co.* v. *Roberts,* this view was correctly rejected by Lawrence L.J. "Any bargain," said the learned judge, "made by the person responsible to his neighbour or to the public that another person should perform that obligation may give rise to rights as between the two contracting parties, but does not, in my judgment, in any way affect any right of third parties, who are not parties or privy to such contract."[47] If this were not so, it would result in the continuation of the fallacy finally exposed in *Donoghue* v. *Stevenson* that if A is injured by B and the cause of the injury is the breach of a contractual obligation owed by C to B, A cannot sue B in tort. The tenant of course will be able to obtain an indemnity from his landlord.[48]

DAMAGE

If the nuisance is a public one, it has long been settled that the plaintiff must prove damage.[49] In the case of a private nuisance, however, although it is said that damage must be proved, the law will often presume it. In *Fay* v. *Prentice*[50] a cornice of the defendant's house projected over the plaintiff's

[43] *cf.* Collins M.R. in *Cavalier* v. *Pope* [1905] 2 K.B. 757, 762.
[44] [1940] 1 K.B. 229. See further *post,* p. 416.
[45] [1940] 1 K.B. 233. See (1940) 56 L.Q.R. 1; Friedmann (1940) 3 M.L.R. 305–309; (1943) 56 L.Q.R. 63, 68.
[46] (1794) 2 H.Bl. 350.
[47] (1929) 140 L.T. 1, 8. The case was not one of landlord and tenant, but the C.A. in *Wringe* v. *Cohen* [1940] 1 K.B. 229, 145–246 apparently regarded the absence of knowledge on the part of the occupier as irrelevant in the *St. Anne's* case. But this was one more of the *obiter dicta* with which *Wringe's* case is replete, and it is contrary to the decision in the *St. Anne's* case.
[48] See Stallybrass (1929) 45 L.Q.R. 118–121.
[49] *Ante,* p. 377. Comyns, *Digest* (5th ed.), Action upon the Case for Nuisance (C.), and authorities there cited.
[50] (1845) 1 C.B. 828. Where tree roots abstract water from the soil, rendering it less able to support buildings thereon, there is damage even though the buildings have not yet subsided: *King* v. *Taylor* (1976) 238 E.G. 265.

garden so that rain-water dripped from it on the garden, and it was held that the law would infer injury to the plaintiff without proof of it. This inference appears to apply to any nuisance where the damage is so likely to occur that it would be superfluous to demand evidence that it has occurred. The inference cannot be made if the discomfort is purely personal, for personal sensitivity to smells, smoke and the like varies considerably and it is only fair that evidence of substantial annoyance should be required.

Again, no present damage need be proved where the nuisance is to an easement or *profit á prendre,* at any rate where the claim is for damages as distinct from a mandatory injunction.[51] As a series of such acts or the continuation of one particular act is evidence of acquiescence by the plaintiff in the annoyance, if no remedy were available in these circumstances for merely presumed damage the plaintiff would be barred by prescription after 20 years from suing at all.[52] If damage were not presumed, it might be difficult to establish that any one act had caused it. In these cases, however, although no present damage need be proved, probability that substantial damage will ensue must be shown; otherwise the law would be redressing merely fanciful claims.[53] In *Nicholls* v. *Ely Beet Sugar Factory Ltd.,*[54] large quantities of refuse and effluent were alleged to have been discharged from the defendants' beet sugar factory into the river in which the plaintiff owned two several and exclusive fisheries. The Court of Appeal held that there was no need for him to prove pecuniary loss, the injury being one actionable *per se,* although he lost his action on the ground that he had failed to show that the defendant had caused the injury.[55]

DEFENCES

Coming to nuisance no defence

It is usually said that it is no defence to prove that the plaintiff came to the nuisance or that the place is a convenient one for committing it. What this means is that if the annoyance is unreasonable in that particular district, then

---

[51] There substantial damage must be proved, at any rate in infringement of light: *Colls* v. *Home and Colonial Stores* [1904] A.C. 179. The decision might, however, be interpreted rather as defining the limits of the right of light than as laying down any rule with respect to the necessity of proving damage. It is arguable that what the H.L. actually decided was that the right exists only with respect to a particular amount of light.

[52] *cf.* Kelly C.B. in *Harrop* v. *Hirst* (1868) L.R. 4 Ex. 43, 45, 46–47; Lord Wright M.R. in *Nicholls* v. *Beet Sugar Factory Ltd.* [1936] Ch. 343, 349–350. Both these cases were applied in *Marriage* v. *East Norfolk Rivers Catchment Board* [1949] 2 K.B. 456, with respect to the date upon which the cause of action arose, but no opinion was expressed on this point on appeal: [1950] 1 K.B. 284.

[53] *Kensit* v. *G.E. Ry.* (1884) 27 Ch.D. 122.

[54] [1936] Ch. 343. *cf.* (1936) 52 L.Q.R. 463–465. See also *Pride of Derby and Derby Angling Association Ltd.* v. *British Celanese Ltd.* [1953] Ch. 149.

[55] Lord Wright M.R., at p. 349, adopted Sir Frederick Pollock's view (*Torts* (15th ed.), p. 283): "Disturbance of easements and the like, as completely existing rights of use and enjoyment, is a wrong in the nature of trespass, and remediable by action without any allegation of proof of specific damage; the action was on the case under the old forms of pleading, since trespass was technically impossible, though the act of disturbance might include a distinct trespass of some kind, for which trespass would lie at the plaintiff's option."

the plaintiff can recover even if it has been going on long before he came there. In *Bliss* v. *Hall*[56] the defendant had set up a tallow-chandlery which emitted: "divers noisome, noxious, and offensive vapours, fumes, smells and stenches" to the discomfort of the plaintiff, who had taken a house near it. It was held to be no defence that the business had been in existence for three years before the plaintiff's arrival, for he "came to the house . . . with all the rights which the common law affords, and one of them is a right to wholesome air."[57]

If, however, a man chooses to make his home in the heart of a coalfield or in a manufacturing district, he can expect no more freedom from the discomfort usually associated with such a place than any other resident. The oft-cited dictum that "What would be a nuisance in Belgrave Square would not necessarily be so in Bermondsey"[58] puts the matter concisely and needs only the addition that Belgrave Square may in course of time fall to the level of Bermondsey.[59] This test of the local standard does not apply to nuisance causing material damage to property.[60] It is confined to nuisance causing personal discomfort and even within this limit, it has much less to do with nuisances caused by the obstruction of ancient lights than those caused by noises and smells.[61]

Usefulness not in itself a defence[62]

The mere fact that a process or business is useful to persons generally, in spite of its annoyance to the plaintiff, is no defence. One who keeps a pigsty, a tannery, a limekiln or an iron-foundry is pursuing a laudable occupation and possibly one of great benefit to the public, yet that by itself will not excuse him. In *Adams* v. *Ursell*[63] a fried-fish shop was held to be a nuisance in the residential part of a street where it was carried on. It was argued unsuccessfully that an injunction would cause great hardship to the defendant and to the poor people who were his customers. The defendant could engage in his business in an area where it would not constitute a nuisance and indeed the injunction granted did not extend to the whole street.

No defence that it is due to many

It is no defence that the nuisance was created by independent acts of different persons, although the act of any one of them was not *per se*

---

[56] (1838) 4 Bing.N.C. 183 (followed, with some reluctance, by the majority of the Court of Appeal in *Miller* v. *Jackson* [1977] Q.B. 966.).

[57] *Per* Tindal C.J., *ibid.* at p. 186. So, too, *Elliotson* v. *Feetham* (1835) 2 Bing.N.C. 134.

[58] *Sturges* v. *Bridgman* (1879) 11 Ch.D. 852, 865. The American equivalents are apparently Palm Springs and Pittsburgh: Prosser, *Torts* (5th ed.), p. 633.

[59] As to the effect of a contract not to sue for annoyance see *Andreae* v. *Selfridge & Co. Ltd.* [1936] 2 All E.R. 1413 (this point was not raised on appeal: [1938] Ch. 1).

[60] *St. Helens Smelting Co.* v. *Tipping* (1865) 11 H.L.C. 642: see *ante*, p. 387.

[61] *Fishenden* v. *Higgs and Hill* (1935) 153 L.T. 128, 140, *per* Romer L.J.

[62] But usefulness is by no means irrelevant in determining whether a nuisance has been committed: *ante*, p. 388.

[63] [1913] 1 Ch. 269.

unlawful; *e.g.* where 100 people independently leave 100 wheelbarrows in a place and the obstruction consists in the accumulation of these vehicles and not in the presence of any one of them.[64] It may appear paradoxical that a defendant is held liable although *his* act alone would not be a tort, but the explanation lies in the fact that the standard of what is reasonable is governed by the surrounding circumstances, including the conduct of the others.[65]

Twenty years' prescription a defence

20 years' continuance will, by prescription, legalise a private nuisance but not a public one.[66] The period will not commence to run until the nuisance is known by the plaintiff to exist. The secret discharge of pollution upon his premises cannot be a root of prejudice to his rights until he knows of, or suspects, it.[67] This qualification is of especial importance where the nuisance has been in existence before the plaintiff came to it. In *Sturges* v. *Bridgman*[68] a confectioner had for more than 20 years used large pestles and mortars in the back of his premises which abutted on the garden of a physician, and the noise and vibration were not felt to be a nuisance during that period. In other words there had been no actionable interference with the physician's enjoyment of his own property. Then, however, the physician built a consulting room at the end of his garden and, for the first time, found that the noise and vibration materially interfered with the pursuit of his practice.[69] He was granted an injunction against the confectioner, whose claim to a prescriptive right failed because the interference had not been an actionable nuisance during the whole preceding period of 20 years.

Jus tertii

In *Nicholls* v. *Ely Beet Sugar Factory*[70] Farwell J. held that the defendant to an action for pollution of a private fishery could not plead *jus tertii* as a defence, *i.e.* that some third party had a better title to the land than the plaintiff, but the learned judge left it open whether this applied to nuisance

---

[64] *Thorpe* v. *Brumfitt* (1873) L.R. 8 Ch.App. 650, 656; *Lambton* v. *Mellish* [1894] 3 Ch. 163.
[65] Prosser, *Torts* (5th ed.), p. 354.
[66] For difficulties with respect to this rule; see Clerk and Lindsell, *Torts* (16th ed.), para. 24–80. The right to commit a private nuisance may be acquired by prescription as an easement in cases where such right is capable of being an easement, *e.g.* a right to discharge rain-water from your eaves on to your neighbour's land. To acquire a right by prescription there must be certainty and uniformity "for the measurement and determination of the user by which the extent of the prescriptive right is acquired": *per* Eve J. in *Hulley* v. *Silversprings Bleaching Co.* [1922] 2 Ch. 281. There are dicta that a right may be acquired by prescription to annoy your neighbour by smoke, smells and noise, although the quantity of the inconvenience is constantly changing. There is no reported case when such a right has arisen by prescription: *Waterfield* v. *Goodwin* (1957) 105 L.J. 332; *Khyatt* v. *Morgan* [1961] N.Z.L.R. 1020, 1024.
[67] *Liverpool Corp.* v. *Coghill & Son Ltd.* [1918] 1 Ch. 307.
[68] (1879) 11 Ch.D. 852, 863: "Acts which are neither preventable nor actionable cannot be relied on to found an easement"; *Whycer* v. *Urry* [1955] C.L.Y. 1939, C.A. (ophthalmic optician's work of too delicate a character in a business area to be protected by the law of nuisance).
[69] See *ante*, p. 407.
[70] [1931] 2 Ch. 84.

in general. It is true that at common law *jus tertii* might be pleaded in certain actions for conversion of goods but it was irrelevant where the action was based upon possession, *e.g.* trespass.[71] Since the right to sue in nuisance would seem to be based upon possession and nothing more it is submitted that *jus tertii* cannot afford a defence to any action in nuisance.[72]

Conduct permitted by statute

Many alleged nuisances are caused by public authorities acting under statutory powers and the defence of legislative authority is thus particularly important in this area. Everything of course depends on the construction of the particular statute in question and one must therefore be wary of laying down definite propositions.[73] Broadly, however, the position seems to be as follows.[74]

1. Since we are dealing with statutory powers the primary question where what is complained of is damage arising from the exercise of the powers (as opposed to some "collateral" damage[75])must be whether that exercise is *intra vires* the statute.[76] If it is, the plaintiff who suffers damage is left without redress unless the statute makes some provision for compensation.

2. Work causing substantial interference with neighbouring property will not normally be *intra vires* the statute unless that interference is the "inevitable" consequence of the work, *i.e.* unless it must arise even though the work is carried on with reasonable care and with approved techniques. The burden of showing inevitability is on the defendant.[77] Where the statute contains a "nuisance clause,"[78] then if the authority is merely permissive there may be liability even for the inevitable consequences of the works, but

---

[71] The position has now been substantially altered by the Torts (Interference with Goods) Act 1977 (*post*, pp. 480) but this has no application to land.

[72] In *Newcastle-under-Lyme Corp.* v. *Wolstanton Ltd.* [1947] Ch. 92, 109–110, Evershed J. expressed agreement with this view as expressed in a previous edition of this book, and the Court of Appeal's reversal of part of his decision was on grounds not affecting this dictum; [1947] Ch. 427, 467–468. In *Nicholl's* case, *supra*, Farwell J. agreed with, and considered himself bound by, *Fitzgerald* v. *Firbank* [1897] 2 Ch. 96, a decision of Kekewich J. affirmed by the C.A. Farwell J., however, admitted that the point about *jus tertii* was not raised in the C.A., but he assumed that it must have been present to that court. It is respectfully urged that Kekewich J.'s judgment, at p. 97, proceeded on the correct ground that *jus tertii* is irrelevant in an action for nuisance because the very nature of the tort makes it so; that in the C.A. counsel did not raise the point again; and that this was why no reference was made to it in the judgment of the C.A. *cf.* Scott L.J. in *Paine & Co. Ltd.* v. *St. Neots Gas Co.* [1939] 3 All E.R. 812, 816–817.

[73] Much difficulty in this area is also caused by a regrettable failure in the cases to draw any clear distinction between liability in nuisance and liability under *Rylands* v. *Fletcher: post*, p. 436.

[74] See *Marriage* v. *East Norfolk Rivers Catchment Board* [1950] 1 K.B. 284 and Fleming *The Law of Torts* (7th ed.), pp. 408–409.

[75] *e.g.* careless driving of a lorry on the way to the construction site or an industrial accident at the site.

[76] See the speech of Lord Diplock in *Home Office* v. *Dorset Yacht Co. Ltd.* [1970] A.C. 1004, 1064–1071, *ante*, p. 99.

[77] *Manchester Corp.* v. *Farnworth* [1930] A.C. 171. In *Allen* v. *Gulf Oil Refining Ltd.* [1981] A.C. 1001, 1017, Lord Edmund Davies said this issue was to be determined without regard to expense. *cf. Schenck* v. *The Queen* (1981) 131 D.L.R. (3d) 310.

[78] *e.g.* "Nothing in this Act shall exonerate the undertakers from any indictment, action, or other proceedings for nuisance in the event of any nuisance being caused by them".

this is not so if the undertaker is under a statutory duty to carry them out.[79] A more rational distinction is probably between statutes which require works to be done in a particular place and those which give the undertaker a wide discretion in this respect. In the former case, there is no liability provided that the work is undertaken with reasonable care[80]; in the latter, the undertaker may be liable if he chooses to carry out the works in a place where they cause a nuisance to neighbours when he could have carried them out elsewhere without such consequences.[81] Another type of case is where a power is given to effect a variety of works as and when the undertaker deems it necessary or expedient to do so (*e.g.* the powers given to land drainage authorities[82]). While no hard and fast line can be drawn between this and the previous situation it is obvious that if powers of this sort are read subject to an implied limitation that they are not to be exercised so as to cause any avoidable infringement of private rights the object of the legislation will be largely frustrated.[83] Accordingly, the court is not, under the guise of imposing liability for nuisance, to substitute its own discretion for that granted to the statutory undertaker by Parliament.[84]

Other defences

Other valid defences are: consent of the plaintiff[85]; contributory negligence subject to the provisions of the Law Reform (Contributory Negligence) Act 1945,[86] and in those cases where liability turns on negligence, inevitable accident would appear to be a defence.[87] Even where it is said that liability does not depend upon negligence, the act of a stranger, act of God and the "secret unobservable process of nature" are accepted as defences.[88]

---

[79] See the summary in *Dept. of Transport* v. *N.W. Water Authority* [1983] 3 W.L.R. 105 and in the H.L., [1984] A.C. 336. It might be argued that even without a nuisance clause the granting of merely permissive powers showed an intention not to take away any private rights, particularly since we are here commonly dealing with private Acts, to which the *contra proferentem* approach may fairly be applied, but this would be inconsistent with the authorities. Similarly, the absence of a provision for compensation in the Act is no more than a weak indication of an intention to preserve private rights: *Allen* v. *Gulf Oil Refining Ltd.* [1981] A.C. 1001, 1016.

[80] *Manchester Corp.* v. *Farnworth* [1930] A.C. 171; Weir, *Casebook on Tort* (6th ed.), p. 385; *Allen* v. *Gulf Oil Refining Ltd.* [1981] A.C. 1001.

[81] *Metropolitan Asylum District* v. *Hill* (1881) 6 App.Cas. 193. But if Parliament had specified the site there would have been no liability: *Allen* v. *Gulf Oil Refining Ltd., supra,* at p. 1014.

[82] Land Drainage Act 1930, as amended, particularly by the Land Drainage Act 1961 and the Water Act 1973.

[83] *Marriage* v. *East Norfolk Rivers Catchment Board* [1950] 1 K.B. 284, 308, *per* Jenkins L.J.

[84] See also *Buley* v. *British Railways Board* [1975] C.L.Y. 2458. Jenkins L.J. in *Marriage's* case, *supra,* speaks of liability in nuisance remaining (*a*) where the board's exercise of its discretion is capricious (*b*) where an act of negligence in the course of carrying out the work produces some unintended consequence. Note that in *Marriage's* case the statute contained provision for compensation for persons suffering damage by the exercise of the statutory powers.

[85] *Kiddle* v. *City Business Properties Ltd.* [1942] 1 K.B. 269. *Post,* at p. 432.

[86] *Trevett* v. *Lee* [1955] 1 W.L.R. 113, 122; *Gilson* v. *Kerrier R.D.C.* [1976] 1 W.L.R. 904.

[87] See *Southport Corp.* v. *Esso Petroleum Co. Ltd.* [1956] A.C. 218, 226, *per* Devlin J., citing Blackburn J. in *Fletcher* v. *Rylands* (1866) L.R. 1 Ex. 265, 286 and Lord Blackburn in *River Wear Commissioners* v. *Adamson* (1877) 2 App.Cas. 743, 767.

[88] *Post,* p. 417.

Highways[89]

"Nuisance may be defined, with reference to highways, as any wrongful act or omission upon or near a highway, whereby the public are prevented from freely, safely, and conveniently passing along the highway."[90] In considering the general law of nuisance we have to some extent considered its application to highways. We must now discuss some of the applicable rules in greater detail and also certain other matters which have not yet been mentioned.

Which obstructions are actionable

Every obstacle on the highway does not constitute an actionable nuisance, for the highway would be scarcely usable if it were. The law requires of users of the highway a certain amount of "give and take" and each person is deemed to assume the normal risks of passage along the highway by way of inconvenience and even danger.[91] It is only when the defendant creates a risk which in the circumstances is unreasonable that it becomes actionable. For this reason, the repair of the water, gas and electric mains which run under the street, of the surface of the street itself, and the building and alteration of the houses bordering on it, all constitute lawful occasions, either under statutory powers or by the common law, for temporary interference with its free passage and its amenities. And if shops and houses are to get any supplies, vehicles and persons must pause on the highway to deliver them. A temporary obstruction, provided it is reasonable in amount and duration, is permissible.[92] Whether it is so is a question of fact varying with the circumstances of each particular case. Nor is every permanent obstruction a nuisance.[93] These propositions are elementary but they need stating because it has been argued on the one hand that the highway can never be obstructed and on the other hand that obstruction can never give rise to an action for nuisance.[94]

In a number of cases the courts have been faced with problems arising from the parking or stopping of vehicles on the highway. If the vehicle is

[89] *Encyclopedia of Highway Law and Practice;* Hamilton, *Modern Law of Highways.* As to ferries see *Gravesham B.C.* v. *British Rail* [1978] Ch. 379.

[90] *Jacobs* v. *L.C.C.* [1950] A.C. 361, 375, *per* Lord Simonds.

[91] "Traffic on the highways, whether by land or sea, cannot be conducted without exposing those whose persons or property are near to it to some inevitable risk, and . . . those who go on the highway or have their property adjacent to it, may well be held to do so subject to their taking on themselves the risk of injury from that inevitable danger." *Fletcher* v. *Rylands* (1866) L.R. 1 Ex. 265, 286, *per* Blackburn J. See also the comments of the same judge in *River Wear Commissioners* v. *Adamson* (1877) 2 App.Cas. 743, 767.

[92] *Harper* v. *Haden & Sons Ltd.* [1933] Ch. 298, 304; *Amalgamated Theatres* v. *Charles S. Luney* [1962] N.Z.L.R. 226, S.C. (permit granted under a by-law by a local authority to a contractor to execute works on a highway which obstruct public right of passage may exempt him from criminal liability but not from civil liability to persons aggrieved by the nuisance); *Almeroth* v. *W.E. Chivers & Sons Ltd.* [1948] 1 All E.R. 53 (pedestrian on highway is not obliged to keep his eyes on the ground to see whether there is any obstruction there).

[93] *Att.-Gen.* v. *Wilcox* [1938] Ch. 934.

[94] *Fritz* v. *Hobson* (1880) 14 Ch.D. 542, 552.

left[95] in such a position that it is a foreseeable source of danger to other road users then there is clearly liability in nuisance and the defendant's conduct would anyway amount to negligence.[96] It has been said, however, that, quite apart from foreseeability of danger, the defendant will be liable in nuisance if he so leaves his vehicle as to constitute an obstruction of the highway even though it does not constitute a risk to other road users.[97] Whether or not this view represents the law, it may be doubted whether the distinction drawn between nuisance and negligence in relation to a stationary vehicle on the highway has any justification in the modern law. As Professor Newark has pointed out,[98] such cases are more conveniently dealt with in negligence.[99] It is only because the factual situation became common before the development of the law of negligence that it was incorporated into public nuisance. Whether or not the framing of a claim in nuisance gives the plaintiff any advantage[1] the duplication of action and the difficulty of drawing a line between nuisance on the highway and negligence give rise to confusion.[2] The situation was justifiably criticised by Adams J. in the New Zealand case of *Everitt* v. *Martin*.[3]

"It is well established," explained the learned judge, "that a duty rests on all users of the highway to exercise due care for the safety of other users; and, in regard to highway accidents arising out of the user of the highway and giving rise to claims for injury to persons or to chattels, the law of negligence is sufficient, and any liability, which can be legitimately founded on nuisance, can be equally well, and I think more conveniently, based on negligence. The breach, by act or omission, of the duty to exercise due care is indeed the foundation of the liability."[4]

---

[95] It is important to distinguish between the man who deliberately parks his vehicle and the man who stops temporarily, *e.g.* to deal with an emergency: *Dymond* v. *Pearce* [1972] 1 Q.B. 496, 504, *per* Edmund Davies L.J. Thus if the driver, on finding his lights are out, stops the vehicle, this is not of itself a nuisance, though it may be so if he leaves it on the highway for an unreasonable time or without giving warning of its presence there or if the vehicle became unlit because of some fault on his part: *Maitland* v. *Raisbeck* [1944] K.B. 689, explaining and distinguishing *Ware* v. *Garston Haulage Co. Ltd.* [1944] K.B. 30 (for criticism, see Laskin (1944) 22 Can. Bar Rev. 468–471; (1945) 23 Can. Bar Rev. 265); *Parish* v. *Judd* [1960] 1 W.L.R. 867.

[96] This is not to say that it makes no difference that the liability is founded on nuisance, for, a "nuisance situation" being shown, it may be that the burden of proof of lack of fault is on the defendant: *ante*, p. 385. It has been held that the statutory obligations in relation to the lighting of vehicles do not give rise to civil liability: *Clarke* v. *Brims* [1947] K.B. 497.

[97] *Dymond* v. *Pearce* [1972] 1 Q.B. 496. But see the contrary view of Edmund Davies L.J. at pp. 503 *et seq.* and *Mitchell* v. *Tsiros (No. 2)* [1982] V.R. 301.

[98] "The Boundaries of Nuisance" (1949) 65 L.Q.R. 480 at p. 485. See also Pritchard, "Trespass, Case, and the Rule in *Williams* v. *Holland*" [1964] C.L.J. 234, 237, 24.

[99] In fact, many cases involving a dangerous obstruction of the highway are not pleaded in nuisance at all: *e.g. Tart* v. *G.W. Chitty & Co. Ltd.* [1933] 2 K.B. 453; *Baker* v. *E. Longhurst & Sons Ltd.* [1933] 2 K.B. 461 (though horse and cart were moving); *Tidy* v. *Battman* [1934] 1 K.B. 319; *Henley* v. *Cameron* (1949) 118 L.J.K.B. 989; *Hill-Venning* v. *Beszant* [1950] 2 All E.R. 1151; *Moore* v. *Maxwells of Emsworth Ltd.* [1968] 1 W.L.R. 1077.

[1] See n. 96.

[2] See the cases in n. 95.

[3] [1952] N.Z.L.R. 298; *Mitchell* v. *Tsiros (No. 2)* [1982] V.R. 801.

[4] *Ibid.* at p. 300. Similarly C. A. Wright, "The Law of Torts: 1923–47" (1948) 26 Can. Bar Rev. 46, 78.

Access to and from highway

It is clear that the right of passage along the highway is a public right[5] and that interference with it is remediable by an action for public, not private, nuisance. As we have seen,[6] this means that the plaintiff can only sue if he has suffered damage over and above that suffered by the rest of the public. However, the owner of property adjoining the highway has a common law right of access to the highway[7] which is a private right remediable by an action of private nuisance, so that anything which prevents his access (as opposed to making it less convenient for his purposes[8]) enables the recovery of at least nominal damages.[9] The private right of access is subject to the public right of passage, which is the higher right,[10] but the right of passage of the public is also subject to the private right of access to the highway and is liable to be temporarily interrupted by the adjoining owner.[11] The conflict of these two rights is resolved on the ordinary principle that a reasonable exercise of both must be allowed.[12]

In some cases the gist of the plaintiff's complaint has been not so much that *his* access to and from the highway has been impeded but that the obstruction has prevented other people coming on to his premises and doing business with him. It seems that such a state of affairs is both a private and a public nuisance, though as far as the latter is concerned the loss of trade will amount to special damage.[13] Picketing in pursuance of a trade dispute is in certain circumstances made lawful by statute[14] but otherwise it is certainly capable of amounting to a nuisance if it involves violence or intimidation[15] and perhaps even if it is carried on so as to exert pressure to regulate and control access to and from the plaintiff's premises.[16] However, despite a suggestion in *Thomas* v. *National Union of Mineworkers*[17] there is no tort of "harassment" falling short of nuisance.[18]

Problems have also arisen with queues. A queue as such is perhaps not

---

[5] *Boyce* v. *Paddington B.C.* [1903] 1 Ch. 109, 114, *per* Buckley J.

[6] *Ante,* p. 377.

[7] The right is now heavily qualified by statute: see Cork [1952] J.P.L. 553–556.

[8] See *Att.-Gen.* v. *Thames Conservators* (1862) 1 H. & M. 1; *Tate & Lyle Ltd.* v. *G.L.C.* [1983] A.C. 509 (siltation prevented large vessels approaching plaintiffs' jetty; interference with public right of navigation rather than with private right).

[9] *Walsh* v. *Ervin* [1952] V.L.R. 361. *cf. Chaplin* v. *Westminster Corp.* [1901] 2 Ch. 329 (transference of goods across pavement into adjoining premises an aspect of public right of passage).

[10] *Vanderpant* v. *Mayfair Hotel Co.* [1930] 1 Ch. 138, 152–154, *per* Luxmoore J.

[11] *Marshall* v. *Blackpool Corp.* [1935] A.C. 16, 22, *per* Lord Atkin; *Farrell* v. *John Mowlem & Co. Ltd.* [1954] 1 Lloyd's Rep. 437, 439, 440, *per* Devlin J.; *Trevett* v. *Lee* [1955] 1 W.L.R. 113.

[12] See *supra,* p. 386.

[13] *Wilkes* v. *Hungerford Market Co.* (1835) 2 Bing.N.C. 281; *Lyons, Sons & Co.* v. *Gulliver* [1914] 1 Ch. 631; *Blundy, Clark & Co.* v. *L. & N.E. Ry.* [1931] 2 K.B. 342, 352, 362; *cf. ibid.* at p. 372; *Harper* v. *Haden & Sons Ltd.* [1933] Ch. 298, 306–307.

[14] See *post,* p. 533.

[15] *Messenger Newspapers Group Ltd.* v. *N.G.A.* (1982) [1984] I.R.L.R. 397; *News Group Newspapers Ltd.* v. *SOGAT '82* [1986] I.R.L.R. 337.

[16] *Mersey Dock & Harbour Co.* v. *Verrinder* [1982] I.R.L.R. 152; *Hubbard* v. *Pitt* [1976] Q.B. 142; but *cf.* Lord Denning M.R. in the latter case and *Ward Lock & Co. Ltd.* v. *Operative Printers' Assistants' Society* (1906) 22 T.L.R. 327.

[17] [1986] Ch. 20; Ewing [1985] C.L.J. 374; Weir, *Casebook on Tort* (6th ed.), p. 13.

[18] *Patel* v. *Patel, The Times,* August 21, 1987, though the facts were far removed from those in *Thomas's* case, being concerned with whether the defendant could be enjoined from entering an "exclusion zone" around the plaintiff's house.

unlawful even if its occupation of the pavement makes foot-passengers deviate or access to shops difficult. It is only when it is unreasonable that the proprietors of the establishment which causes it are liable for nuisance; *e.g.* where the queue was at times five deep, extended far beyond the theatre itself and remained there for very considerable portions of time, it was held to be a nuisance to the plaintiffs, whose premises were adjacent to the theatre.[19] The defendant is not liable if, although the queue was one of prospective customers at his shop, he was not responsible for it because other circumstances (*e.g.* shortage of supplies in consequence of war) were the primary cause of it; nor will he be liable unless the plaintiff can prove damage.[20] But the defendant is liable if the obstruction by means of the queue is due to an unusual method of conducting business; *e.g.* by the sale of ice-cream from a window of the shop instead of inside the shop.[21]

Damage on the highway from premises adjoining the highway

This area deserves special mention because the law is to some extent unsettled. It is clear that the mere fact that something (*e.g.* a tree, a clock, a sign, an awning or a corbel) projects over the highway from land or a building adjacent to it does not *per se* constitute an actionable nuisance. This must be so, for no conceivable damage is done to anyone and there is scarcely a garden or a building on the edge of the highway which would not have to be altered if the law were otherwise.[22] The rule is different where the projection is over private property because the rights of the proprietor of it are much wider than the limited right of the user of a highway.[23] If damage is done owing to the collapse of the projection on the highway or by some other mischief traceable to it, the occupier of the premises on which it stood is liable if he knew of the defect or ought, on investigation, to have known of it. At any rate that is the rule with respect to a thing that is naturally on the premises, *e.g.* a tree. In *Noble* v. *Harrison*[24] a branch of a beech tree growing on X's land overhung the highway and in fine weather suddenly broke and fell upon Y's vehicle passing along the highway. Neither X nor his servants knew that the branch was dangerous and the fracture was due to a latent

---

[19] *Lyons, Sons & Co.* v. *Gulliver* [1914] 1 Ch. 631 Phillimore L.J. dissenting. The C.A. approved *Barber* v. *Penley* [1893] 2 Ch. 447, where North J. examined the authorities in detail.

[20] *Dwyer* v. *Mansfield* [1946] K.B. 437.

[21] *Fabri* v. *Morris* [1947] 1 All E.R. 315.

[22] *Noble* v. *Harrison* [1926] 2 K.B. 332, 337.

[23] *Ibid.* at p. 340; and *Lemmon* v. *Webb* [1895] A.C. 1. But the context of these statements concerns the right of the neighbour to abate the nuisance by lopping the branches. There is no reason to think that the occupier is liable in damages for a collapse unless he has knowledge or means of knowledge of the defect. As to liability for encroachment by tree roots, see *ante,* p. 401; and for trespass by oversailing structures, see p. 364.

[24] [1926] 2 K.B. 332: applied in *Cunliffe* v. *Bankes* [1945] 1 All E.R. 459. See *Shirvell* v. *Hackwood Estates Co. Ltd.* [1938] 2 K.B. 577 and *Cunliffe* v. *Bankes* for remarks on care in looking after trees; *Brown* v. *Harrison* (1947) 177 L.T. 2281 (owner of tree in obvious state of decay held liable); *Quinn* v. *Scott* [1965] 1 W.L.R. 1004 (National Trust held liable in negligence in failing to fell a dangerous tree near a highway as they had means of knowing it was diseased); *British Road Services* v. *Slater* [1964] 1 W.L.R. 498 (liability of occupier of land for failing to remedy a nuisance which he inherited—projecting branch of tree in the verge of a highway—does not arise, although source of the nuisance is plain to be seen, until occupier becomes aware of its being a nuisance, or with ordinary care should have become aware of it).

defect undiscoverable by any reasonably careful inspection, and for this reason Y's action against X in nuisance failed.[25] In *Caminer* v. *Northern and London Investment Trust Ltd.*[26] the defendants in an action for (*a*) negligence or (*b*) nuisance were held not liable for either. They were lessees of land from which a tree fell on to a car driven by C, the plaintiff, on the highway. The fall of the tree was due to a disease of its roots of which there was no indication above ground. Evidence was also given that, if the tree had been trimmed or topped, it was unlikely that it would have fallen, but it did not appear to be dangerous to any of the witnesses called. On these facts, it was held by the House of Lords that the plaintiff had failed to prove that the defendants, as ordinary careful laymen (*i.e.* not experts), knew, or ought to have known, that the tree was dangerous and therefore they were not liable.

With respect to artificial things (*e.g.* a lamp) which project and do damage there is a conflict of judicial opinion as to the precise nature of the liability for it. According to one view the duty is no greater than that with respect to natural projections,[27] whilst according to another view it is a strict one analogous to that formulated in *Rylands* v. *Fletcher* which would make the occupier of the premises liable even in the absence of negligence.[28] Until *Wringe* v. *Cohen*,[29] however, the balance of authorities supported the view that an occupier could only be liable for damage caused by non-repair if, with actual or constructive knowledge of the condition, he failed to remedy it.[30] Vaughan Williams L.J. explained in *Barker* v. *Herbert*:

"There can be no liability on the part of the possessor of land in such a case, unless it is shown either that he himself, or some person for whose action he is responsible, created that danger which constitutes a nuisance to the highway, or that he neglected for an undue time after he became, or, if he had used reasonable care, ought to have become, aware of it, to abate or prevent the danger of nuisance."[31]

The occupier therefore could not be liable if he was justifiably unaware of the condition. In *Wringe* v. *Cohen*,[32] however, the Court of Appeal chose to rationalise the previous authorities and to formulate a rule of strict liability which was not warranted by them. "If, owing to want of repair, premises on

---

[25] A claim under the rule in *Rylands* v. *Fletcher* also failed: *post*, p. 431.
[26] [1951] A.C. 99. Note Lord Radcliffe's *caveat* at pp. 110–112.
[27] Blackburn J. in *Tarry* v. *Ashton* (1876) 1 Q.B.D. 314, 319; Wright J. in *Noble* v. *Harrison* [1926] 2 K.B. 332, 343–344. Both opinions were *obiter*.
[28] Lush and Quain JJ. in *Tarry's* case, *supra*, at p. 320; Rowlatt J., *obiter*, in *Noble's* case, *supra*, at p. 338.
[29] [1940] 1 K.B. 229; *ante*, p. 406.
[30] *Barker* v. *Herbert* [1911] 2 K.B. 633, 636, *per* Vaughan Williams L.J., at p. 643, *per* Fletcher Moulton L.J. See the comments of Branson J. in *Ilford U.D.C.* v. *Deal and Judd* [1925] 1 K.B. 671, 675 and contrast *Silverton* v. *Marriott* (1888) 59 L.T. 61 (defendant liable because failed to guard against danger of which aware); *St. Anne's Well Brewery Co.* v. *Roberts* (1929) 140 L.T. 1 (no difference between public and private nuisance); *Wilchick* v. *Marks* [1934] 2 K.B. 56, 67–68, *per* Goddard J.; *Palmer* v. *Bateman* [1908] 2 Ir.Rep. 393.
[31] [1911] 2 K.B. 633, 636–637.
[32] [1940] 1 K.B. 229.

a highway become dangerous and, therefore, a nuisance and a passer-by or an adjoining owner suffers damage by their collapse, the occupier, or owner if he has undertaken the duty of repair, is answerable whether he knew or ought to have known of the danger or not."[33] The unforeseeable act of a trespasser is a good defence and the Court of Appeal also held that the defendant would escape liability should the damage result from "a secret and unobservable operation of nature, such as subsidence under or near the foundations of the premises."[34]

As Professor Friedmann has pointed out, these exceptions seem to deprive the rule itself of much of its significance. "It can hardly be imagined that any damage caused neither by the act of a third person nor by a latent defect could be due to anything but knowledge or negligence of the occupier."[35] In subsequent cases the rule in *Wringe* v. *Cohen* has been interpreted restrictively. It might have been thought that an occupier whose tree projects over the highway would be in the same position as a defendant whose lamp overhangs the highway, although in the former case it would be easier for the defendant to argue that the injury was caused by a latent defect.[36] In *British Road Services* v. *Slater,*[37] however, Lord Parker C.J. refused to hold a non-negligent occupier liable for damage caused by an overhanging branch. In other cases attempts have been made to distinguish between inactivity *causing* the nuisance and the mere continuance of an inherited nuisance.[38]

In effect, it would seem that *Wringe* v. *Cohen* sets a standard somewhere between strict liability and ordinary fault liability. The plaintiff need only show that the defendant had control over the defective premises and that the injury resulted from their dangerous condition.[39] This gives rise to a presumption that the defendant has failed in his duty of inspection and repair which can only be rebutted by proof that the accident was inevitable, *i.e.* it was not, nor could have been, avoided by reasonable inspection. As Denning L.J. said in *Mint* v. *Good,*[40] the defendant "is liable when structures fall into dangerous disrepair, because there must be some fault on the part of

---

[33] *Ibid.* at p. 233.

[34] *Ibid.*

[35] "Nuisance, Negligence and the Overlapping of Torts" (1940) 3 M.L.R. 305, 309. See also *Sedleigh-Denfield* v. *O'Callaghan* [1940] A.C. 880 and Friedmann, "Incidence of Liability in Nuisance" (1943) 59 L.Q.R. 63. *cf.* Stephen J. in *Cartwright* v. *McLaine & Long Pty. Ltd.* (1979) 24 A.L.R. 97, 106 ("near absolute liability").

[36] This argument was accepted in the Irish case of *Lynch* v. *Dawson* [1946] Ir.Rep. 504 (plaintiff's lorry with high load ran in unusual circumstances into bough projecting from defendant's land. Defendant was liable even though he was justifiably unaware of the risk of an accident).

[37] [1964] 1 W.L.R. 498. Lord Parker refused to follow *Lynch* v. *Dawson, supra,* on the ground that *Sedliegh-Denfield* v. *O'Callaghan, supra,* had not been cited to the Irish Court, and said: "the present tendency of the law is not only to move further and further away from absolute liability but also more and more to assimilate nuisance and negligence" (at p. 504).

[38] *Cushing* v. *Peter Walker & Sons Ltd.* [1941] 2 All E.R. 693, 699, *per* Hallett J.; *Mint* v. *Good* [1951] 1 K.B. 517, 524, *per* Somervell L.J. It is suggested that this is not a valid distinction. The failure of the occupier to discover and remedy an inherited nuisance is equally the cause of the damage. It results just as much from the occupier's breach of his duty to inspect and repair as does, *e.g.* the negligent failure to discover a defective gable-end.

[39] But the evidence must show that the damage has occurred as a result of the want of repair of some structure for which the defendant was responsible: *Cartwright* v. *McLaine & Long Pty. Ltd.* (1979) 24 A.L.R. 97.

[40] [1951] 1 K.B. 517, 526.

someone or other for that to happen." From a substantive point of view, *Wringe* v. *Cohen* differs from ordinary liability in negligence because the occupier is liable for the default of his independent contractor.[41]

Condition of the highway

At common law a highway authority could not be liable for injury suffered by a user of the highway and resulting from the authority's failure to discharge its duty to keep the highway in repair.[42] This immunity did not extend to misfeasance on the highway nor to acts of repair improperly performed. The distinction between misfeasance and non-feasance and the rule of immunity were criticised and eventually the latter was abrogated by section 1 of the Highways (Miscellaneous Provisions) Act 1961[43] which came into force on August 3, 1964. The law is now to be found in the Highways Act 1980. In any action against a highway authority for damage resulting from its failure to maintain a highway maintainable at the public expense, it shall be a defence (without prejudice to any other defence such as voluntary acceptance of risk and contributory negligence) to prove that the authority had taken such care as in all the circumstances was reasonably required[44] to secure that the part of the highway to which the action relates was not dangerous for traffic. For the purpose of such a defence the court shall in particular have regard to:

1. the character of the highway, and the traffic which was reasonably to be expected to use it;

2. the standard of maintenance appropriate for a highway of that character and used by such traffic;

3. the state of repair in which a reasonable person would have expected to find the highway;

4. whether the highway authority knew, or could reasonably have been expected to know, that the condition of the part of the highway to which the action relates was likely to cause danger to users of the highway;

5. where the highway authority could not reasonably have been expected to repair that part of the highway before the cause of action arose, what warning notice of its condition had been displayed.[45]

The Act applies whether the plaintiff is suing in nuisance, negligence or for breach of a statutory duty.

The nature of the highway authority's liability has given rise to some

---

[41] *Tarry* v. *Ashton* (1876) 1 Q.B.D. 314. *cf. ante*, p. 397. It has been suggested ([1951] 1 K.B. 517, 526) that this more onerous liability may be justified by a desire to protect users of the public highway. But one of the oddities of *Wringe* v. *Cohen* is that the premises fell, not on to the highway, but on to adjoining premises.

[42] Clerk and Lindsell, *Torts* (16th ed.), para. 24–78.

[43] *Anns* v. *Merton London Borough* (*ante*, p. 96) suggests that the legislation may have been unnecessary: *Barratt* v. *North Vancouver* (1978) 89 D.L.R. (3d) 473.

[44] *Pridham* v. *Hemel Hempstead Corp.* (1970) 69 L.G.R. 523.

[45] Highways Act 1980, s.58. The source of the duty to maintain is s.41 and, perhaps, the common law (*Haydon* v. *Kent C.C.* [1978] Q.B. 343, 363, *per* Goff L.J. For the purpose of such a defence it shall not be relevant to prove that the highway authority had arranged for a competent person to carry out or supervise the maintenance of the part of the highway to which the action relates unless it is also proved that the authority had given him proper instructions with regard to the maintenance of the highway and that he carried out the instructions. This confirms *Hardaker* v. *Idle District Council* [1896] 1 Q.B. 335 (statutory duty non-delegable). *cf.* collateral negligence of independent contractor, *post*, p. 585.

disagreement. In *Griffiths* v. *Liverpool Corporation*[46] the plaintiff fell over a ridge of a flagstone which projected half an inch above the adjoining flagstone. It was found as a fact that the flagstone was a potential danger,[47] and the majority of the Court of Appeal held the defendants liable. Diplock and Salmon L.JJ. considered that the highway authority is under an absolute statutory duty to repair subject only to the defence provided in the Act, the onus as to which clearly falls on the authority. While this statutory defence is very similar to a plea of "no negligence" at common law it is not identical.[48] Sellers L.J., on the other hand, while accepting that the onus of proof lay upon the authority, took the view that the provisions of the Act "make negligence the essential and ultimate basis of a claim against a highway authority."[49] Whichever view is the correct one, *Griffiths'* case clearly establishes that once the plaintiff shows that he has suffered injury through the highway getting into disrepair so as to be a danger he has made out his case and the onus is thrown on to the authority. However, a different approach was taken in *Haydon* v. *Kent County Council*[50] where the allegation was of failure to maintain the highway.[51] The plaintiff slipped and was injured on a steep and icy footpath near her home. The highway authority, which did not rely on the defence provided by section 58,[52] argued that they were not in breach of their duty to maintain the highway under section 41 because, *inter alia,* their limited resources had required them to give first priority to the clearance of main motor highways. This was accepted by the majority of the Court of Appeal[53] which held that the plaintiff was required to show that having regard to the circumstances and the nature and importance of the way, sufficient time had elapsed to make it prima facie unreasonable for the authority to have failed to take remedial measures. Only then had she made out her case to a sufficient degree to require the authority to fall back upon the defence under section 58. It seems curious that the plaintiff should face a different burden according to whether his complaint is of non-repair or failure to maintain, a distinction which is far from clear in itself.

Whatever the true view as to the onus on the highway authority, it is clear that the plaintiff "must make out a case that the highway was not reasonably safe, that is, was dangerous to traffic."[54] There is an inevitable risk in

[46] [1967] 1 Q.B. 374. See [1967] C.L.J. 21; (1967) 83 L.Q.R. 4. Liverpool Corporation has been defendant in an unusual number of actions under the 1961 Act: see *Burnside* v. *Emerson* [1968] 1 W.L.R. 1490, 1492, *per* Lord Denning M.R.
[47] This finding, which the Court of Appeal felt with regret unable to disturb, is somewhat out of line with the later cases, *infra.*
[48] Thus proof that the accident would still have happened even if due care had been taken would not be a defence: [1967] 1 Q.B. 374, 391, 395. But for a possible qualification see *post,* p. 703.
[49] *Ibid.* at p. 386.
[50] [1978] Q.B. 343. See also *Burnside* v. *Emerson* [1968] 1 W.L.R. 1490.
[51] A failure to reduce the number of straying dogs is not a failure to maintain the highway: *Allison* v. *Corby D.C.* [1980] R.T.R. 111.
[52] [1978] Q.B. 343, 348. For the effect of industrial action, see *Bartlett* v. *Department of Transport* (1984) 83 L.G.R. 579.
[53] Goff and Shaw L.JJ. Lord Denning M.R. agreed with the decision to allow the authority's appeal but he considered that the removal of temporary obstructions like snow and ice was outside the scope of s.41 and within s.150 which, in his opinion, did not give rise to any civil liability.
[54] *Littler* v. *Liverpool Corp.* [1968] 2 All E.R. 343, 344, *per* Cumming-Bruce J., following *Meggs* v. *Liverpool Corp.* [1968] 1 W.L.R. 689.

travelling along the highway of unevenness in the pavement, and a highway is not to be criticised by the standards of a bowling green.[55] In *Littler* v. *Liverpool Corporation,*[56] Cumming-Bruce J. stated that the criterion to be applied in assessing whether any particular length of pavement is dangerous is that of reasonable foreseeability of danger:

> "A length of pavement is only dangerous if, in the ordinary course of human affairs, danger may reasonably be anticipated from its common use by the public. . . . It is a mistake to isolate and emphasise a particular difference in levels between flagstones unless that difference is such that a reasonable person who noticed and considered it would regard it as presenting a real source of danger."[57]

In relation to danger to vehicular traffic, it has been held that the highway authority must provide not merely for model drivers, but for the normal run of drivers to be found on the roads and that includes those who make the mistakes which experience and common sense teach are likely to occur.[58]

In *Scott* v. *Green & Sons,*[59] it was held that what is now section 180(6) of the Highways Act 1980, which imposes on an owner or occupier the duty to keep every vault arch and cellar under a street in good repair, does not give rise *per se* to a cause of action for breach of statutory duty. The statute does however give to the occupier sufficient control of any grating or flagstone over his cellar to enable him to effect repairs. Because of this, "he must use reasonable care to see that it is safe; and if he fails in his duty, he is liable in nuisance or negligence as the case may be.[60]

---

[55] *Littler* v. *Liverpool Corp., supra* at p. 345; *Ford* v. *Liverpool Corp.* (1972) 117 S.J. 167.
[56] [1968] 2 All E.R. 343.
[57] *Ibid.* at p. 345.
[58] *Rider* v. *Rider* [1973] Q.B. 505; *Tarrant* v. *Rowlands* [1979] R.T.R. 144.
[59] [1969] 1 W.L.R. 301.
[60] [1969] 1 W.L.R. 301, 302, *per* Lord Denning M.R.

CHAPTER 15

STRICT LIABILITY: RULE IN RYLANDS v. FLETCHER

HAVING considered the tort of nuisance, we now turn to a further tort which had its origins in nuisance but which has developed in such a way that it is now quite distinct from it. This is the rule in *Rylands* v. *Fletcher*.

THE RULE IN RYLANDS V. FLETCHER[1]

The facts of this case were as follows. B, a millowner, employed independent contractors, who were apparently competent, to construct a reservoir on his land to provide water for his mill. In the course of the work the contractors came upon some old shafts and passages on B's land. They communicated with the mines of A, a neighbour of B, although no one suspected this, for the shafts appeared to be filled with earth. The contractors did not block them up, and when the reservoir was filled the water from it burst through the old shafts and flooded A's mines. It was found as a fact that B had not been negligent, although the contractors had been. A sued B and the House of Lords held B liable.

The litigation originated in an unusual way. It began as an action upon the case (apparently for negligence) at Liverpool Assizes, and A secured a verdict, subject to the award of an arbitrator, who was afterwards empowered by a judge's order to state a special case instead of making an award. This he did, and so the case came before the Court of Exchequer which, by a majority, decided in favour of the defendant. The Court of Exchequer Chamber unanimously reversed this decision and held the defendant liable, and the House of Lords affirmed their decision. The judgment of the Exchequer Chamber was delivered by Blackburn J. and it has become a classical exposition of doctrine.[2] *"We think that the true rule of law is, that the person who for his own purposes brings on his lands and collects and keeps there anything likely to do mischief if it escapes, must keep it in at his peril,*

---

[1] (1865) 3 H & C. 774 (Court of Exchequer); (1866) L.R. 1 Ex. 265 (Court of Exchequer Chamber); (1868) L.R. 3 H.L. 330 (House of Lords) (Weir, *Casebook on Tort* (6th ed.), p. 391). See generally: Bohlen, *Studies in the Law of Torts* (1926), Chap. 7; Fridman, "The Rise and Fall of *Rylands* v. *Fletcher*" (1956) 34 Can. Bar Rev. 810–823; Erskine Blackburn , "The Rule in *Rylands* v. *Fletcher*" (1961) 4 Can. Bar J. 39–50; Simpson, "Legal Liability for Bursting Reservoirs: The Historical Context of *Rylands* v. *Fletcher*" (1984) 13 J.Leg.Stud. 209. Law Com. No. 32 (1970), *Civil Liability for Dangerous Things and Activities* (1970); Report of the Royal Commission on Civil Liability and Compensation for Personal Injury, Cmnd. 7054 (1978), Vol. 1, Chap. 31.
[2] (1866) L.R. 1 Ex. 265, 279–280.

and, if he does not do so, is prima facie *answerable for all the damage which is the natural consequence of its escape."*

This may be regarded as the "rule in *Rylands* v. *Fletcher*," but what follows is equally important:

> "He can excuse himself by showing that the escape was owing to the plaintiff's default; or perhaps that the escape was the consequence of *vis major*, or the act of God; but as nothing of this sort exists here, it is unnecessary to inquire what excuse would be sufficient. The general rule, as above stated, seems on principle just. The person whose grass or corn is eaten down by the escaping cattle of his neighbour, or whose mine is flooded by the water from his neighbour's reservoir, or whose cellar is invaded by the filth of his neighbour's privy, or whose habitation is made unhealthy by the fumes and noisome vapours of his neighbour's alkali works, is damnified without any fault of his own; and it seems but reasonable and just that the neighbour, who has brought something on his own property which was not naturally there, harmless to others so long as it is confined to his own property, but which he knows to be mischievous if it gets on his neighbour's, should be obliged to make good the damage which ensues if he does not succeed in confining it to his own property. But for his act in bringing it there no mischief could have accrued, and it seems but just that he should at his peril keep it there so that no mischief may accrue, or answer for the natural and anticipated consequences. And upon authority, this we think is established to be the law whether the things so brought be beasts, or water, or filth, or stenches."

The judgment for the plaintiff was upheld by the House of Lords, but Lord Cairns L.C. rested his decision on the ground that the defendant had made a "non-natural use" of his land, though he regarded the judgment of Blackburn J. as reaching the same result and said he entirely concurred in it.[3] It may well be true, therefore, that there were *two* rules in *Rylands* v. *Fletcher*, the fairly closely defined formulation of Blackburn J. and the more flexible one stated by Lord Cairns,[4] but the effect of the subsequent case law is to add the non-natural use requirement to Blackburn J.'s formulation, a development which has played a not insignificant part in the restriction of this form of strict liability.

Genesis of the principle

Such were the facts and decision in the case. Although Lord Cairns

[3] (1868) L.R. 3 H.L. 330, 338–340.
[4] *Porter (J.P.) Co. Ltd.* v. *Bell* [1955] 1 D.L.R. 62, 66; "The true situation seems to be that there is not one rule of *Rylands* v. *Fletcher* but two; and that Lord Blackburn's version or Lord Cairns' more flexible one is invoked according to the circumstances of the case in hand," *per* MacDonald J. "The complexity between a natural and non-natural user of land that has resulted from the words Lord Cairns used, and between dangerous and non-dangerous things, makes the application of the rule uncertain in some cases of fire and explosion": *Hargrave* v. *Goldman* [1963–1964] 37 A.L.J.R. 277, 283, *per* Windeyer J.

regarded the principles applicable as extremely simple,[5] it seems clear that the common law was faced by a new and important problem which could not be solved by merely applying the existing authorities.

This was not the first time that water had been collected in bulk, but hitherto those who indulged in the practice had generally been powerful bodies, like water or railway companies, who had acted under powers given them by legislation which at the same time made them liable for harm done by its escape. But here there was no statutory authority, and although there were several paths that seemed to lead to a solution, none of them went the whole way. Trespass did not really fit the case because the harm was consequential, not direct.[6] There was a finding that the contractors were at fault with regard to the old shafts, but it is not clear that they should have realised that their conduct would affect the plaintiff's land[7] and even if this had been the case there would have been a serious issue at that time[8] whether the defendant was liable for the negligence of his contractor. Nor was nuisance considered applicable, apparently on the basis that the defendant had no reason to foresee the injury.[9]

Look at the decision of the Exchequer Chamber how we may, it laid down a new principle. True, in the judgment itself it might appear that the court was making a pontifical statement of existing principle rather than laying down a new rule, for they regarded their own proposition as having been anticipated by Holt. C.J. some 160 years earlier in *Tenant* v. *Goldwin*,[10] and they cited as instances of it the rules relating to cattle-trespass, the escape of mischievous animals and nuisance by the escape of fumes. But in fact Holt C.J.'s decision related to the escape of filth and his formulation of principle was limited to that and to cattle-trespass; it was not nearly so sweeping as the rule expressed in *Rylands* v. *Fletcher*, which was reached by methods extremely characteristic of judicial development of the law—the creation of new law behind a screen of analogies drawn from existing law. And whatever views the Exchequer Chamber may have had about their decision, succeeding generations have regarded it as the starting-point of a liability wider than any that preceded it.[11]

Scope of extension

It seems unsound, then, to dismiss the rule as a convenient summary of the theory underlying several specific torts which had existed long before 1868,

---

[5] (1868) L.R. 3 H.L. 330, 338.
[6] (1865) 3 H. & C. 773, 792–793, *per* Martin B. But see the judgment of Bramwell B. at p. 790.
[7] See (1865) 3 H. & C. 773, 777–778, 799.
[8] Though not necessarily now: see *Dunne* v. *N.W. Gas Board* [1964] 2 Q.B. 806, 831.
[9] (1865) 3 H. & C. 773, 793.
[10] (1703) 2 Ld. Raym. 1089.
[11] *cf.* Newark, "The Boundaries of Nuisance" (1949) 65 L.Q.R. 480, 488. "What was novel in *Rylands* v. *Fletcher*, or at least clearly decided for the first time, was that as between adjacent occupiers an isolated escape is actionable."

or even as the old cattle-trespass rule raised to a high power.[12] The substantial advances which it made on the earlier law were two:

1. In the direction of *things* for the escape of which an occupier of land is subjected to strict liability.

2. In the direction of the *persons* for whose defaults in connection with such escape the occupier is vicariously responsible.

As to 1, the court took a rule of liability which had been more or less clearly perceived in connection with the escape of fire, cattle or unruly beasts, and extended it to the escape of mischievous things generally. As to 2, they held in effect that the occupier from whose land these things escaped and did damage is liable not only for the default of his servant, but also for that of an independent contractor and (as later decisions show) for that of anyone except a stranger.[13]

"Absolute" liability of a misnomer

It was unfortunate that Blackburn J. chose to describe liability under the rule as resting upon "an absolute duty to keep it [*sc.* the water] in at his peril."[14] Though stated as a rule of absolute liability, there "are so many exceptions to it that it is doubtful whether there is much of the rule left."[15] The liability may be strict, but it is not absolute as the exceptions to the rule indicated by Blackburn J. himself show. Recently, moreover, as we shall see, the courts have tended to erode and rationalise the rule so as to reduce the ambit of strict liability and to bring the rule more into line with the predominant modern philosophy of no liability without fault. As a result of this development the rule in *Rylands* v. *Fletcher* is sometimes unavailable at times when it is most needed, *i.e.* when the plaintiff cannot prove that the defendant was at fault.

SCOPE OF THE RULE

Like all broad formulations of principle, the rule in *Rylands* v. *Fletcher* had to be worked out in detail by later decisions, and it has been applied to a

---

[12] See Salmond and Heuston, *Torts* (19th ed.), p. 358. But it is difficult to agree with the statement as to the four historical grounds of the rule in *Rylands* v. *Fletcher*. In three of them (liability for trespass, fire and nuisance) it is too strong to say that absence of fault on the defendant's part was no defence. As to trespass and fire, see (1926) 42 L.Q.R. 44–51; as to nuisance, see Viner, Abr. Nuisance (H), Vol. xvi, pp. 27 *et seq.*, where several cases are cited which show that the defendant was not liable, because in effect he was "without fault." See, too, Rolle, Abr. Nusans, B 2, p. 137. As to instances of liability without proof of negligence, Lord Simon said it was "logically unnecessary and historically incorrect to refer to all these instances as deduced from one common principle": *Read* v. *Lyons* [1947] A.C. 156, 167.
[13] (1931) 4 Camb. L.J. 192–193.
[14] (1866) L.R. 1 Ex. 265, 279.
[15] *St. Anne's Well Brewery* v. *Roberts* (1928) 140 L.T. 1, 6, *per* Scrutton L.J.

remarkable variety of things.[16] Fire,[17] gas,[18] explosions,[19] electricity,[20] oil,[21] noxious fumes,[22] colliery spoil,[23] rusty wire from a decayed fence,[24] vibrations,[25] poisonous vegetation,[26] a flag-pole,[27] a "chair-o-plane"[28] and even (in a case of very questionable validity) noxious persons.[29] As we shall see below, there is no liability under the rule unless there is some "escape" from the defendant's land, but there is no necessity that the thing be *likely* to escape. What matters for this purpose is that *if* it escapes it is likely to do mischief[30] and this is the meaning to be given to "dangerous thing" in this context. Too much stress should not be laid upon Blackburn J.'s illustrations in support of the rule since new law was being created. He was certainly not purporting to compile a representative list of "extra-hazardous" activities[31]—though one of the fundamental problems about *Rylands* v. *Fletcher* is perhaps that the law has never made up its mind whether the rule is aimed at such activities.[32]

Escape necessary

Unless there is an "escape" of the substance from the land where it is kept, there is no liability under the rule[33]; this was the ground of the House of Lords' decision in *Read* v. *Lyons & Co. Ltd.*,[34] where the plaintiff was employed by the Ministry of Supply as an inspector of munitions in the defendants' munitions factory and, in the course of her employment there was injured by the explosion of a shell that was being manufactured. It was admitted that high explosive shells were dangerous. The defendants were held not liable. There was no allegation of negligence on their part and

---

[16] Neatly catalogued by Stallybrass in "Dangerous Things and the Non-Natural User of Land" (1929) 3 Camb. L.J. 382–385.

[17] *Post*, p. 448.

[18] *Batcheller* v. *Tunbridge Wells Gas Co.* (1901) 84 L.T. 765.

[19] *Miles* v. *Forest Rock, etc. Co.* (1918) 34 T.L.R. 500; *Rainham Chemical Works Ltd.* v. *Belvedere Fish Guano Co. Ltd.* [1921] 2 A.C. 465.

[20] *National Telephone Co.* v. *Baker* [1893] 2 Ch. 186; *Eastern and South African Telegraph Co. Ltd.* v. *Cape Town Tramways Companies Ltd.* [1902] A.C. 381; *Hillier* v. *Air Ministry* [1962] C.L.Y. 2084 (cows electrocuted by an escape of electricity from high-voltage cable laid under plaintiff's field, liability under *Rylands* v. *Fletcher*).

[21] *Smith* v. *G.W. Ry.* (1926) 135 L.T. 112.

[22] *West* v. *Bristol Tramways Co.* [1908] 2 K.B. 14.

[23] *Att-Gen.* v. *Cory Bros. Ltd.* [1921] 1 A.C. 521.

[24] *Firth* v. *Bowling Iron Co.* (1878) 3 C.P.D. 254.

[25] *Hoare & Co.* v. *McAlpine* [1923] 1 Ch. 167; *cf. Dodd Properties Ltd.* v. *Canterbury City Council* [1979] 2 All E.R. 118, 122.

[26] *Crowhurst* v. *Amersham Burial Board* (1878) 4 Ex.D. 5; *Ponting* v. *Noakes* [1894] 2 Q.B. 281.

[27] *Shiffman* v. *Grand Priory, etc.* [1936] 1 All E.R. 557 (*obiter*; it was decided on the ground of negligence).

[28] A species of centrifugal roundabout: *Hale* v. *Jennings Bros.* [1938] 1 All E.R. 579.

[29] *Att.-Gen.* v. *Corke* [1933] Ch. 89; but *cf. Smith* v. *Scott* [1973] Ch. 314, where it is suggested that this case could at least equally well have been decided on the basis that the landowner was in possession of the property and was himself liable for nuisances created by his licensees. A New Zealand court refused to follow *Corke's* case in *Matheson* v. *Board of Governors of Northcote College* [1975] 2 N.Z.L.R. 106 but accepted that the occupier could be liable for creating a nuisance. Liability in nuisance was imposed in similar circumstances in *Dunton* v. *Dover District Council* (1977) 76 L.G.R. 87.

[30] *Rylands* v. *Fletcher* (1866) L.R. 7 Ex. 265, 279; *Read* v. *Lyons* [1947] A.C. 156, 176; *cf. ibid.* at p. 186.

[31] *Read* v. *Lyons* [1945] K.B. 216, 247–248, *per* du Parcq L.J.

[32] *Post*, p. 441.

[33] *Read* v. *Lyons & Co. Ltd.* [1947] A.C. 156; Weir, *Casebook on Tort* (6th ed.), p. 400; *Howard* v. *Furness, etc., Lines Ltd.* [1936] 2 All E.R. 781.

[34] [1947] A.C. 156; (1947) 63 L.Q.R. 159–163.

STRICT LIABILITY: RULE IN RYLANDS V. FLETCHER

Rylands v. *Fletcher* was inapplicable because there had been no "escape" of the thing that inflicted the injury. "Escape" was defined as "escape from a place where the defendant has occupation or control over land to a place which is outside his occupation or control."[35] Viscount Simon stated that *Rylands* v. *Fletcher* is conditioned by two elements which he called (*a*) "the condition of 'escape' from the land of something likely to do mischief if it escapes," and (*b*) "the condition of 'non-natural' use of the land."[36] But the House of Lords emphasised that the absence of an "escape" was the basis of their decision. The rule is probably inapplicable to a deliberate release of the thing, the cause of action in that situation being trespass.[37]

Personal injuries

The House of Lords in *Read* v. *Lyons* also considered whether under the rule in *Rylands* v. *Fletcher* a plaintiff can recover damages for personal injuries. According to Lord Macmillan, the rule "derives from a conception of mutual duties of neighbouring landowners"[38] and is therefore inapplicable to personal injuries. "An allegation of negligence," he continued, "is in general essential to the relevancy of an action of reparation for personal injuries."[39] Viscount Simon and Lord Simonds reserved their opinions on this question,[40] and Lord Porter considered that opinions expressed supporting the application of the rule to personal injuries are an undoubted extension of it, "and may some day require examination."[41]

Lord Macmillan's view must however be considered in context. It is generally accepted that in the related tort of nuisance, an *occupier* can sue in respect of his personal injuries[42] and the same was established in the tort of cattle trespass.[43] Even after *Read* v. *Lyons*, therefore, there is no reason to doubt the correctness of decisions such as *Hale* v. *Jennings Bros.*[44] in which the Court of Appeal held that an occupier of land was entitled to damages for personal injuries under the rule in *Rylands* v. *Fletcher*. But before *Read* v. *Lyons*, the courts had gone further, holding that even a non-occupier may sue for personal injuries under the rule, and it is probably this development

---

[35] Viscount Simon [1947] A.C. 156, 168; *ibid.* at p. 177, *per* Lord Porter: "Escape from the place in which the dangerous object has been maintained by the defendant to some place not subject to his control"; at pp. 184–185, Lord Uthwatt shows that history supports the distinction between what happens within and what happens without a landowner's boundaries. But see comments of Law Com., No. 32 (1970), p. 16. The authorities clearly establish that it is not necessary for the defendant to have any property interest in the land; *Benning* v. *Wong* (1969) 122 C.L.R. 249, 294, *per* Windeyer J.

[36] [1947] A.C. 167, 173, *per* Lord Macmillan, "Escape . . . and not-natural use of the land, whatever precisely that may mean."

[37] *Rigby* v. *Chief Constable of Northamptonshire* [1985] 1 W.L.R. 1242 (firing of CS gas canister).

[38] [1947] A.C. 167, 173.

[39] *Ibid.* at pp. 170–171.

[40] *Ibid.* at pp. 168–169 and 180, respectively.

[41] *Ibid.* at p. 178. In the Court of Appeal, Scott L.J. considered that the rule in *Rylands* v. *Fletcher* is restricted to damage to land: [1945] K.B. 216, 236. Compare his earlier inconsistent judgment in *Hale* v. *Jennings Bros.* [1938] 1 All E.R. 579.

[42] *Ante*, p. 395.

[43] *Wormald* v. *Cole* [1954] 1 Q.B. 614; as to the present position see *post*, p. 461.

[44] *Supra* (tenant of stall at a fairground injured by escape of defendant's chair-o-plane).

that their lordships had in mind. In *Shiffman* v. *Order of St. John*,[45] for instance, the plaintiff was injured in Hyde Park when he was struck by a falling flag-pole belonging to the defendants. Although it was found that the defendants had been at fault, Atkinson J. considered that, irrespective of this, the defendants would have been liable under the rule in *Rylands* v. *Fletcher*.[46]

Judged from a strictly historical point of view, Lord Macmillan's approach is doubtless correct. It is, however, open to the criticism that it helps to preserve the anachronistic situation in which proprietary interests receive more protection than the interest in physical security. Perhaps because of this the courts have in subsequent cases generally declined to follow Lord Macmillan's view. In *Perry* v. *Kendricks Transport Ltd.*,[47] for instance, Parker L.J. did not "think it is open to this court to hold that the rule applies only to damage to adjoining land or to a proprietary interest in land and not to personal injury."[48] In *Weller* v. *Foot and Mouth Disease Research Institute*,[49] however, Widgery J. briefly held that the defendants could not be liable to the plaintiffs under the rule in *Rylands* v. *Fletcher*, because the plaintiffs, who were cattle auctioneers, had no interest in any land to which the virus could have escaped.[50] The plaintiffs' loss of business was pecuniary or economic damage. Widgery J.'s conclusion that the plaintiffs could not recover under the rule for economic injury alone seems perfectly correct at that time. But this was not due, it is suggested, to the absence of any proprietary interest on their part, but because of the restrictive attitude of the law towards the recovery of pecuniary loss which is not the consequence of a tangible, physical injury.[51] This does not in the least mean that in all cases a plaintiff cannot recover under the rule unless he proves interference to his proprietary interest. It is submitted with respect that Widgery J.'s view is inconsistent with the trend of modern authorities and should not be followed.

Land

The rule as originally formulated refers to a person who for his own purposes brings on to his lands and collects and keeps there anything likely to do mischief if it escapes. The words *for his own purposes* will be discussed later.[52] The rule is not confined to the case of adjacent freeholders. It

---

[45] [1936] 1 All E.R. 557. See also *Miles* v. *Forest Rock Granite Co. Ltd.* (1918) 34 T.L.R. 500 (C.A.). In *Wing* v. *L.G.O.* [1909] 2 K.B. 652, 665, Fletcher Moulton L.J. stated that the rule applies where "by excessive use of . . . [a] private right a person has exposed his neighbour's property or person to danger." It is clear from the context that this is not restricted to injury to an occupier. The previous authorities were not fully discussed by the House of Lords in *Read* v. *Lyons*.

[46] *Supra*, at p. 561.

[47] [1956] 1 W.L.R. 85; *Benning* v. *Wong* (1969) 122 C.L.R. 249.

[48] [1956] 1 W.L.R. 85, 92; Singleton L.J., at p. 87, assumed that an action for personal injuries was possible. See also *Dunne* v. *North Western Gas Board* [1964] 2 Q.B. 806, 836, *per* Sellers L.J.; *British Celanese Ltd.* v. *A.H. Hunt Ltd.* [1969] 2 All E.R. 1252, 1257, *per* Lawton J.; *Aldridge* v. *Van Patter* (1952) 4 D.L.R. 93, 105, *per* Spence J. See Salmond and Heuston, *Torts* (19th ed.), p. 364.

[49] [1966] 1 Q.B.569.

[50] *Ibid.* at p. 588.

[51] *Ante*, pp. 84–91.

[52] At p. 434.

applies, for instance, to a local authority which is required by statute to receive sewage into its sewers.[53] It applies where the defendant has a franchise, such as right to use land founded on a statute or upon private permission, *e.g.* for laying pipes to carry gas,[54] or cables for electricity.[55] One who uses land by permission of the tenant or occupier (*i.e.* a licensee) and brings on to it a dangerous thing is liable for its escape.[56] Although there are conflicting dicta it seems that an owner who is not in occupation of the land at the time when the thing escapes is liable if he has authorised the accumulation,[57] and that anyone who collects the dangerous thing and has control of it at the time of the escape would be liable,[58] perhaps even when he is carrying it along the highway and it escapes therefrom.[59]

Non-natural user

For some time before *Rylands* v. *Fletcher* the courts had been concerned with the extent of a person's liability for the escape of an accumulation of water from his land during the normal course of mining operations.[60] Their conclusions may be formulated as follows: if A conducts mining operations on his own land in such a way as to cause water to flood his neighbour's mine and the inundation is due to mere gravitation, A is not liable (or at least he is not strictly liable under *Rylands* v. *Fletcher*[61]), but if the flooding is due to A's accumulation of the water (*e.g.* by pumping), A is liable. This distinction was developed in *Rylands* v. *Fletcher* into the rule that as a prerequisite to liability the defendant must have brought onto the land something "which was not naturally there." As one author has put it, non-natural use was originally "an expression of the fact that the defendant has artificially introduced onto the land a new and dangerous substance."[62]

This term "natural" is inherently confusing for it has two distinct meanings. In its primary sense it signifies "that which exists in or by nature and is not artificial."[63] The term was used in this sense by Lord Cairns in *Rylands* v. *Fletcher*.[64] It also means, however, "that which is ordinary and usual, even

---

[53] *Smeaton* v. *Ilford Corp.* [1954] 1 Ch. 450, 469, 472.

[54] *Northwestern Utilities Ltd.* v. *London Guarantee Ltd.* [1936] A.C. 108, 118; *Read* v. *Lyons & Co. Ltd.* [1947] A.C. 156, 183. Lord Simonds did not consider it necessary to pronounce on these cases, but thought it possible that the rule extended to them.

[55] *Charing Cross Electricity Supply Co.* v. *Hydraulic Power Co.* [1914] 3 K.B. 772.

[56] *Rainham Chemical Works* v. *Belvedere Fish Guano Co.* [1921] 2 A.C. 465.

[57] *Rainham Case* [1921] 2 A.C. 465, 476, 489. *Contra, St. Anne's Well Brewery Co.* v. *Roberts* (1928) 140 L.T. 1, 5; Charlesworth, *Negligence* (7th ed.), p. 852.

[58] *Rainham Case* [1921] 2 A.C. 465, 479. *cf. Westhoughton Coal Co. Ltd.* v. *Wigan Coal Co. Ltd.* [1939] Ch. 800.

[59] *Powell* v. *Fall* (1880) 5 Q.B.D. 597; *Rigby* v. *Chief Constable of Northamptonshire* [1985] 1 W.L.R. 1242; *cf. Mitchell* v. *Mason* (1966) 10 W.L.R. 26. The history of *Rylands* v. *Fletcher* has seen a constant judicial oscillation between the view that it is a species of private nuisance and the view that it is a generalised conception of liability for "ultra-hazardous activities."

[60] *e.g. Smith* v. *Kenrick* (1849) 7 C.B. 515; *Baird* v. *Williamson* (1863) 15 C.B.(N.S.) 376. *cf. Rouse* v. *Gravelworks Ltd.* [1940] 1 K.B. 489.

[61] See *Leakey* v. *National Trust* [1980] Q.B. 485 (a duty of care may now exist even for dangers arising naturally on land; but *cf. Home Brewery Co.* v. *William Davies & Co. (Leicester)* [1987] Q.B. 339, *ante*, p. 400).

[62] Newark in his important article "Non-natural User and *Rylands* v. *Fletcher* (1961) 24 M.L.R. 557, 561.

[63] *Ibid.* at p. 558.

[64] [1868] L.R. 3, H.L. 330, 338.

though it may be artificial."[65] As Professor Newark has pointed out,[65] the courts now understand non-natural user in the latter sense. The most frequently quoted definition of non-natural user is that given by the Judicial Committee in *Rickards* v. *Lothian*, "It must be some special use bringing with it increased danger to others and must not merely be the ordinary use of the land or such a use as is proper for the general benefit of the community."[66]

It is suggested that the concept of non-natural user is now understood by the courts as being similar to the idea of unreasonable risk in negligence.[67] In *Read* v. *Lyons*, Lord Porter commented that "non-natural user seems to be a question of fact . . . and in deciding this question I think that all the circumstances of time and practice of mankind must be taken into consideration so that what may be regarded as dangerous or non-natural may vary according to the circumstances."[68] The courts balance the magnitude of the risk (*i.e.* the extent of the accumulation and the injury potential of the thing accumulated) with the desirability or necessity of the activity from the point of view of the defendant and the public. This equating of non-natural user with unreasonable risk in negligence seems to have been recognised by MacKenna J. in *Mason* v. *Levy Auto Parts of England Ltd.*[69] The defendants stored on their land large quantities of combustible materials which ignited in mysterious circumstances. In determining whether the defendants ought to be held liable under the rule in *Rylands* v. *Fletcher*, the learned judge considered that he ought to pay regard to (i) the quantities of combustible materials which the defendants brought onto the land; (ii) the way in which they stored them; and (iii) the character of the neighbourhood. "It may be," he concluded, "that these considerations would also justify a finding of negligence. If that is so, the end would be the same as I have reached by a more laborious, and perhaps more questionable route."[70]

As Lord Porter recognised, it is inevitable that the courts' view of what is non-natural should change in response to changing social conditions and needs. A striking illustration of such a change is afforded by a comparison of some of the dicta in *Read* v. *Lyons* and the case of *Rainham Chemical Works Ltd.* v. *Belvedere Fish Guano Co.*[71] In the former, Lord Macmillan hesitated "to hold that in these days and in an industrial community it was a non-natural use of land to build a factory on it and conduct there the manufacture

---

[65] Newark, *supra*, p. 558.
[66] [1913] A.C. 263, 279–280, *per* Lord Moulton, approved in *Read* v. *Lyons* [1947] A.C. 156, 169 *per* Viscount Simon.
[67] See Stallybrass, "Dangerous Things and the Non-Natural User of Land" (1929) 3 C.L.J. 376; Goodhart, "The Rule in *Rylands* v. *Fletcher*" (1947) 63 L.Q.R. 160, 163; Morris, "Absolute Liability for Dangerous Things" 61 Harv. L.R. ev. 515, 520–523 (1948); Fridman, "The Rise and Fall of *Rylands* v. *Fletcher*" 34 Can. Bar Rev. 810 (1956); Williams, "Non-Natural Use of Land" [1973] C.L.J. 310.
[68] [1947] A.C. 176. *cf. J.P. Porter Co. Ltd.* v. *Bell* [1955] 1 D.L.R. 62 which reviews the authorities.
[69] [1967] 2 Q.B. 530.
[70] *Ibid.* at pp. 542–543.
[71] [1921] 2 A.C. 465.

of explosives."[72] The House declined to consider itself bound by the *Rainham Chemicals case* where it seems to have been taken for granted that such an activity constituted a non-natural use of land.

The identification of non-natural user with conduct creating an abnormal risk that ought not to be borne by the public has given to the courts a device for determining liability in accordance with what they consider to be public policy. There is no objective universal test of what is non-natural. The court must make its own value judgment on the defendant's conduct, taking into account its social utility and the care with which it is carried out. Because of this some of the early cases may require consideration.[73] It may well be, for example, that courts in the future will be reluctant to hold that the use of land for the supply of power or other necessities to a great city is non-natural.[74]

The following have in the past been regarded as a natural user of land; water installations in a house or flat,[75] a fire in a domestic grate,[76] burning stubble in the normal course of agriculture,[77] electric wiring[78] and gas pipes in a house or shop,[79] the ordinary working of mines and minerals on land,[80] erecting or pulling down houses or walls,[81] trees whether planted or self-sown (if not poisonous).[82] Generating steam on a steamship is not "non-natural."[83] But the storing of water as in *Rylands* v. *Fletcher*, or industrial water under pressure,[84] or gas and electricity in bulk in mains is a non-

---

[72] [1947] A.C. 156, 174. See generally at pp. 174–175. It was a time of war. Viscount Simon expressed a similar view though more hesitantly: at pp. 169–170. Lord Uthwatt at p. 187 declined to express an opinion. See also the comments of Scott L.J. in the Court of Appeal [1945] K.B. 216, 240. Lord Macmillan's view was adopted by Lawton J. in *British Celanese Ltd.* v. *A.H. Hunt Ltd.* [1969] 1 W.L.R. 959, 963–964: "The manufacturing of electrical and electronic components in the year 1964 ... cannot be adjudged to be a special use ... The metal foil was there for use in the manufacture of goods of a common type which at all material times were needed for the general benefit of the community."

[73] *Read* v. *Lyons* [1947] A.C. 156, 169–170, 173–174, 176.

[74] In *Dunne* v. *North Western Gas Board* [1964] 2 Q.B. 806, the Court of Appeal was reluctant to hold a nationalised industry liable in the absence of fault, but the contrary argument of Windeyer J. in *Benning* v. *Wong* (1969) 122 C.L.R. 249, 301 is compelling. As to statutory authority, see *post*, p. 436.

[75] *Rickards* v. *Lothian* [1913] A.C. 263. *cf. Wei's Western Wear Ltd.* v. *Yui Holdings Ltd.* (1984) 5 D.L.R. (4th) (water installations in restaurant).

[76] *Sochacki* v. *Sas* [1947] 1 All E.R. 344; *cf.* Williams [1973] C.L.J. 310, 311, 314, pointing out that there has been considerable variation in the level of generality at which the courts define "use."

[77] *Perkins* v. *Glyn* [1976] R.T.R. ix (note); *cf.*, in the somewhat different climatic conditions of New Zealand, *New Zealand Forest Products Ltd.* v. *O'Sullivan* [1974] 2 N.Z.L.R. 80, where, however, negligence was clearly established. In *Metson* v. *De Wolfe* (1980) 117 D.L.R. (3d) 278, 283, it was said that there was no case in Nova Scotia "where the application of the rule in *Rylands* v. *Fletcher* has been in any way modified or eroded for considerations of normal agricultural husbandry." This is perhaps closer to the spirit of *Rylands* v. *Fletcher* itself than to the subsequent English case law.

[78] *Collingwood* v. *Home and Colonial Stores Ltd.* [1936] 3 All E.R. 200.

[79] *Miller* v. *Addie & Sons (Collieries) Ltd.* 1934 S.C. 150.

[80] *Rouse* v. *Gravelworks Ltd.* [1940] 1 K.B. 489.

[81] *Thomas and Evans Ltd.* v. *Mid-Rhondda Co-operative Society* [1941] 1 K.B. 381.

[82] *Noble* v. *Harrison* [1926] 2 K.B. 332.

[83] *Howard* v. *Furness, etc., Ltd.* [1936] 2 All E.R. 781; *Eastern Asia Navigation Co. Ltd.* v. *Freemantle* (1951) 83 C.L.R. 353 (dealing with oil fuel in harbour berth for oil-burning vessels, a natural user); *Smeaton* v. *Ilford Corp.* [1954] Ch. 450, 472 (collection in sewer of large volume of noxious and inherently dangerous sewage by local authority, not a natural user); *Miller Steamship Co. Pty. Ltd.* v. *Overseas Tankship (U.K.) Ltd.* [1963] 1 Lloyd's Rep. 402, 426 (ship in harbour bunkering with furnace oil, a natural user); though the court inclined to the view that the rule was not anyway applicable to an escape from a ship; *Gertsen* v. *Municipality of Metropolitan Toronto* (1973) 41 D.L.R. (3d) 646 (land-fill project using household waste which generated methane gas, not a natural user).

[84] *Charing Cross Electricity Supply Co.* v. *Hydraulic Power Co.* [1914] 3 K.B. 772; *Peters* v. *Prince of Wales Theatre Ltd.* [1943] K.B. 73, 76 (sprinkler system in theatre "ordinary and usual").

natural use of land. It has been held that keeping a motor-car in a garage with petrol in the tank,[85] and a motor-coach in a parking ground after the tank has been emptied is a non-natural use of land,[86] but the decisions have been criticised.[87]

Things naturally on the land[88]

The distinction between natural and non-natural user has at times been confused with the distinction between things naturally on the land and things artificially there.[89] The former defines the nature of the user of the land; the latter the cause of accumulation thereon. Only when it has been determined that the accumulation on the land is a deliberate one, need the court consider whether the defendant's user is non-natural. The rule in *Rylands* v. *Fletcher* applies only to things which the occupier brings onto his land and collects and keeps there. It was quickly established that the occupier could not be liable under the rule merely for permitting a spontaneous accumulation (*e.g.* of water, vegetation, birds) on his land,[90] or even for inducing a spontaneous accumulation as an undesired by-product of the normal working of the land.[91] In *Pontardawe R.D.C.* v. *Moore-Gwyn*,[92] for instance, there was no liability for the fall of rocks from an outcrop, when the fall was due to the natural process of weathering.

An occupier, therefore, is not liable to his neighbour under the rule in *Rylands* v. *Fletcher* for damage caused by ordinary trees which are self-sown because they are naturally on the land. Nor in general is he liable even if he has planted the trees because he has not used his land in an extraordinary or non-natural manner.[93] "To grow a tree is one of the natural users of the soil."[94] In contrast, in *Crowhurst* v. *Amersham Burial Board*,[95] the defendants planted on their land a yew tree which grew so as to project over onto the land of the plaintiff on which cattle were pastured. The leaves of yew trees are poisonous to cattle. The plaintiff's horse ate some leaves and died

---

[85] *Musgrove* v. *Pandelis* [1919] 2 K.B. 43; the criticism of this case by Romer L.J. in *Collingwood* v. *Home and Colonial Stores Ltd.* (1936) 155 L.T. 550, 553 was approved by Lord Porter in *Read* v. *Lyons* [1947] A.C. 156, 176. It is almost inconceivable that *Musgrove* v. *Pandelis* would be followed in this respect today. *cf. Maron* v. *Baert & Signaw* (1981) 126 D.L.R. (3d) 9.

[86] *Perry* v. *Kendricks Transport Ltd.* [1956] 1 W.L.R. 85, 92. Parker L.J. considered *Musgrove* v. *Pandelis* was binding on the C.A.

[87] Goodhart (1956) 72 L.Q.R. 184–186, pointing out that insurance companies distinguish between petrol in the tank of a car, and petrol stored in bulk which is both more dangerous and unusual. *cf. Mulholland and Tedd Ltd.* v. *Baker* [1939] 3 All E.R. 253, rule correctly applied.

[88] See Goodhart in *Essays in Jurisprudence* (1931), Chap. 8, for an illuminating discussion of this topic. It is not confined to the rule in *Rylands* v. *Fletcher* but includes nuisance. Also Noel, "Nuisances from Land in its Natural Condition" (1934) 56 Harv. L.R. 772.

[89] Stallybrass, *loc. cit.*

[90] *e.g. Giles* v. *Walker* (1890) 24 Q.B.D. 656; *Sparke* v. *Osborne* (1906) 7 C.L.R. 51; *Seligman* v. *Docker* [1948] Ch. 53.

[91] *e.g. Wilson* v. *Waddell* (1876) 2 App.Cas. 95, following *Smith* v. *Kenrick, ante.* Contrast *Fletcher* v. *Smith* (1877) 2 App.Cas. 781; *Hurdman* v. *Great North Eastern Ry.* (1878) 3 C.P.D. 168.

[92] [1929] 1 Ch. 656.

[93] *Noble* v *Harrison* [1926] 2 K.B. 332, 336, *per* Rowlatt J., and at p. 342, *per* Wright J.; *Davey* v. *Harrow Corp.* [1958] 1 Q.B. 60, 71–73, *per* Lord Goddard C.J. As to damage caused by encroachment of tree roots, see *ante*, p. 401.

[94] *Noble* v. *Harrison* [1926] 2 K.B. 332, 336, *per* Rowlatt J.

[95] (1878) 4 Ex.D. 5.

and the defendants were held liable under the rule in *Rylands* v. *Fletcher*. It was not in the circumstances a natural use of the land to plant on it a poisonous tree.

A further illustration of the application of these principles is afforded by the interesting case of *Giles* v. *Walker*.[96] Thistle-seed was blown in large quantities by the wind from the defendant's land to that of the plaintiff; it was held that "there can be no duty as between adjoining occupiers to cut the thistles, which are the natural growth of the soil,"[97] and that the defendant was not liable. Upon the facts the decision seems to have been correct so far as the rule in *Rylands* v. *Fletcher* goes, for all that the defendant had done was to plough up some forest land on which there had previously been no thistles but from which, for some unexplained reason, an immense crop of them sprang up in two successive years. But even in relation to the rule in *Rylands* v. *Fletcher*, the principle seems to have been stated too widely. If, for example, an occupier deliberately plants weeds in large quantities, he would surely be liable under the rule for damage caused by their escape, for it is not a natural use of one's land to cultivate weeds in bulk.

It must be stressed that although a natural condition cannot give rise to liability under the rule in *Rylands* v. *Fletcher* it may still constitute a nuisance for which an occupier may be liable if he has knowledge or means of knowledge of its existence and if it is reasonable to require him to take the necessary steps to abate it.[98] Moreover, an occupier may be liable if he deliberately causes the escape of things naturally on his land.[99]

DEFENCES TO THE RULE

In *Rylands* v. *Fletcher* possible defences to the rule were no more than outlined and we must look to later decisions for their development.

Consent of the plaintiff

Where the plaintiff has expressly or impliedly consented to the presence of the source of danger and there has been no negligence on the part of the defendant, the defendant is not liable.[1] The exception merely illustrates the general defence, *volenti non fit injuria*, and would not need special mention here but for the fact that the Court of Appeal and the House of Lords have considered it expedient to take particular notice of it. The main application of the principle of implied consent is found in cases where different floors in

---

[96] (1890) 24 Q.B.D. 656; Harris [1967] C.L.J. 24–27.
[97] At p. 657, *per* Lord Coleridge C.J. Goodhart, *op. cit.* at p. 154, points out that the soil was not in its natural condition as it was ploughed up forest land. This point does not seem to have been taken in the case, presumably because the accumulation was a spontaneous result of the normal working of land. See *ante*.
[98] *Goldman* v. *Hargrave* [1967] 1 A.C. 645. See *ante*, pp. 399–400.
[99] *Whalley* v. *Lancashire and Yorkshire Ry.* (1884) 13 Q.B.D. 131.
[1] *Gill* v. *Edouin* (1894) 71 L.T. 762; 72 L.T. 579; *Att.-Gen* v. *Cory Bros. Ltd.* [1921] 1 A.C. 521, 538, 543, 550. *Ross* v. *Fedden* (1872) L.R. 7 Q.B. 661 and *Kiddle* v. *City Business Properties Ltd.* [1942] 1 K.B. 269 are cases of this type.

the same building are occupied by different persons and the tenant of a lower floor suffers damage as the result of water escaping from an upper floor.[2] In a block of premises each tenant can normally be regarded as consenting to the presence of water on the premises if the supply is of the usual character, but not if it is of quite an unusual kind, or defective or dangerous, unless he actually knows of that. The defendant is liable if the escape was due to his negligence.[3]

Common benefit

Where the source of the danger is maintained for the common benefit of the plaintiff and the defendant, the defendant is not liable for its escape. This is akin to the defence of consent of the plaintiff, and Bramwell B. in *Carstairs* v. *Taylor*[4] treated it as the same thing. There A had hired from B the ground floor of a warehouse, the upper part of which was occupied by B. Water from the roof was collected by gutters into a box, from which it was discharged by a pipe into drains. A rat gnawed a hole in the box and water leaked through it and injured A's goods. There was no negligence on B's part. B was held not liable. In *Peters* v. *Prince of Wales Theatre (Birmingham) Ltd.*,[5] the Court of Appeal regarded "common benefit" as no more than an element (although an important element) in showing consent in cases of the type of *Carstairs* v. *Taylor*. In other judicial dicta the exception has been regarded as an independent one.[6] The precise ambit of "common benefit" has never been properly determined. Until recently, for example, it was not considered to apply between consumers of gas or water and the public industries which supply them.[7] If an explosion occurs owing to the escape of gas, it does not seem to have been suggested that the defences of common benefit or consent of the plaintiff would be available to the defendants, possibly because the plaintiff has no choice as to the source of his supply of gas, whereas in other cases he can decide for himself whether he will accept the arrangement offered to him by his landlord. It is submitted that this is the correct approach, but in *Dunne* v. *North Western Gas Board*[8] Sellers L.J., delivering the judgment of the Court of Appeal, considered that common benefit was an important factor. "It would seem odd that facilities so much sought after by the community and approved by their

---

[2] The doctrine has no application where the parties are *adjoining* occupants but there is no relationship of landlord and tenant between them (*Humphries* v. *Cousins* (1877) 2 C.P.D. 239); but the position is not so clear when the parties are not landlord and tenant but are occupiers of the same building: *Kiddle* v. *City Business Properties Ltd.* [1942] 1 K.B. 269, 274; *Peters* v. *Prince of Wales Theatre (Birmingham) Ltd.* [1943] 1 K.B. 73.

[3] *Prosser* v. *Levy* [1955] 1 W.L.R. 1224, 1233, C.A. (reviewing previous cases); [1956] C.L.J. 13–15, Kadirgamar, "The Escape of Water from Domestic Premises" (1973) 37 Conv.(N.S.) 179, points out that most of the difficulties arising from this and the next defence have been faced unnecessarily because in nearly all the cases (*cf. Western Engraving Co.* v. *Film Laboratories Ltd.* [1936] 1 All E.R. 106) the defendant's activity was a natural use of land. See also Law Com. No. 32 (1970), p. 19.

[4] (1871) L.R. 6 Ex. 217. So too, *Northwestern Utilities Ltd.* v. *London Guarantee, etc. Co. Ltd.* [1936] A.C. 108, 120 and *Gilson* v. *Kerrier R.D.C.* [1976] 1 W.L.R. 904.

[5] [1943] 1 K.B. 73, 78.

[6] *Gill* v. *Eduoin* (1894) 72 L.T. 579; *Anderson* v. *Oppenheimer* (1880) 5 Q.B.D. 602.

[7] *e.g. Northwestern Utilities Ltd.* v. *London Guarantee, etc. Co. Ltd.* [1936] A.C. 108.

[8] [1964] 2 Q.B. 806.

legislators should be actionable at common law because they have been brought to the places where they are required and have escaped without negligence by an unforeseen series of mishaps."[9] In addition the learned judge did not think that a nationalised industry can be said to accumulate a substance for its own purposes.

Act of stranger

If the escape was caused by the unforeseeable act of a stranger, the rule does not apply. In *Box* v. *Jubb*[10] the defendant's reservoir overflowed partly because of the acts of a neighbouring reservoir-owner and the defendant escaped liability. The plaintiff also failed in his claim in *Rickards* v. *Lothian*[11] where some third person deliberately blocked up the waste-pipe of a lavatory basin in the defendant's premises, thereby flooding the plaintiff's premises.[12] It has been suggested that the defence is limited to the "mischievous, deliberate and conscious act of a stranger,"[13] and therefore excludes his negligent acts. However, as Jenkins L.J. pointed out in *Perry* v. *Kendricks Transport Ltd.*[14] the basis of the defence is the absence of any control by the defendant over the acts of a stranger on his land and therefore the nature of the stranger's conduct is irrelevant. The onus is on the defendant to show that the escape was due to the unforeseeable act of a stranger without any negligence on his own part.

If, on the other hand, the act of the stranger could reasonably have been anticipated or its consequences prevented, the defendant will still be liable. In *Northwestern Utilities Ltd.* v. *London Guarantee and Accident Co. Ltd.*,[15] an hotel belonging to and insured by the plaintiffs was destroyed in a fire caused by the escape and ignition of natural gas. The gas had percolated into the hotel basement from a fractured welded joint in an intermediate pressure main situated below street level and belonging to the defendants, a public utility company. The fracture was caused during the construction of a storm sewer, involving underground work beneath the defendants' mains, by a third party. The Privy Council accepted that the defences of act of God and act of third party prevent a plaintiff from succeeding in a claim based on the rule in *Rylands* v. *Fletcher* but held the defendants liable for negligence. The risk involved in the defendants' operations was so great that a high degree of care was expected of them. They knew of the construction of the

---

[9] *Ibid*. at p. 832.

[10] (1879) 4 Ex. D. 76. *Wilson* v. *Newberry* (1871) L.R. 7 Q.B. 31, 33 is perhaps another instance of the rule but illustrates bad pleadings still better.

[11] [1913] A.C. 263; Weir, *Casebook on Tort*, (6th ed.), p. 395.

[12] Also *Perry* v. *Kendricks Transport Ltd.* [1956] 1 W.L.R. 85 (child threw a match into an empty petrol tank which exploded and injured the plaintiff—defendants not liable).

[13] *Perry* v. *Kendricks Transport Ltd.*, *supra*, at p. 87, *per* Singleton L.J. Similarly in *Prosser* v. *Levy* [1955] 1 W.L.R. 1224 by the same judge. The learned judge relies on *Philco, etc. Ltd.* v. *J. Spurling Ltd.* (1949) 2 All E.R. 882 and *Dominion Natural Gas Co.* v. *Collins and Perkins* [1909] A.C. 640, but these are authorities on *novus actus interveniens* and irrelevant to the different question of breach of duty.

[14] *Supra*, at p. 90. Similarly *per* Parker L.J. In *Smith* v. *Great Western Ry*. (1926) 42 T.L.R. 391 the negligent act of a third party (failing to ascertain a defect in an oil tank) was held to be a good defence, but this case was not brought to the attention of the court in *Prosser* v. *Levy*.

[15] [1936] A.C. 108. See Lord Wright, *Legal Essays*, p. 124; Goodhart (1951) 4 C.L.P. 177.

sewer, and they ought to have appreciated the possibility of damage to their mains and taken appropriate action to prevent or rectify it.

While it is clear that a trespasser is a "stranger" for this purpose,[16] we can only conjecture who else is included in the term. For the defaults of his servants[17] in the course of their employment, the occupier is of course liable; he is also liable for the negligence of an independent contractor[18] unless it is entirely collateral[19]; for the folly of a lawful visitor[20] in tampering with a potentially dangerous machine provided for his amusement[21]; and it may well be for the misconduct of any member of his family on the premises, for he has control over them. Moreover, it has been argued that he ought to be responsible for guests or licensees on his land. But perhaps a distinction ought to be taken here. It would be harsh to hold a person liable for the act of every casual visitor who has bare permission to enter his land and of whose propensities to evil he may know nothing; *e.g.* an afternoon caller who leaves the garden gate open or a tramp who asks for a can of water and leaves the tap on. Possibly the test is, "Can it be inferred from the facts of the particular case that the occupier had such control over the licensee or over the circumstances which made his act possible that he ought to have prevented it? If so, the occupier is liable, otherwise not."[22]

In connection with this exception to the rule in *Rylands* v. *Fletcher*, we must consider whether the rule applies to a danger created on the premises by the occupier's predecessor in title. It may be inferred from the decision in the *Northwestern Utilities* case[23] that if the occupier knew or might with reasonable care have ascertained, that the danger existed, he is liable for its escape. If, however, this condition is not satisfied, it is submitted that he ought not to be liable. There is no direct decision on the point, but the rule itself seems to make it essential that the defendant should "bring on his lands" the danger. It is true that this is qualified by the *Northwestern Utilities* case, but that decision does not apply to an occupier who neither knows nor could reasonably have discovered the existence of a danger created by his predecessor. Moreover, Eve J. in an obiter dictum in *Whitmores Ltd.* v. *Stanford*[24] said that the rule in *Rylands* v. *Fletcher* does not extend to making the owner of land liable for the consequences of the escape of a dangerous element brought on the owner's land by another person, not for the purposes of the owner but for the purposes of that other person.

[16] *Mandraj* v. *Texaco Trinidad Inc.* (1969) 15 W.I.R. 251.

[17] But a servant may be a stranger as in *Stevens* v. *Woodward* (1881) 6 Q.B.D. 318 (when he used a private lavatory to which he had been prohibited access and omitted to turn off the tap; employer not liable for flooding).

[18] *Balfour* v. *Barty-King* [1957] 1 Q.B. 496, 505–506, C.A., *per* Lord Goddard C.J. (the defendant has control of his independent contractor in that he chooses him, invites him to his premises to do work, can order him to leave at any moment, although it is left to the contractor how the work is to be done); [1957] C.L.J. 132–133.

[19] *Post*, p. 585.

[20] *Ante*, pp. 210–214.

[21] *Hale* v. *Jennings* [1938] 1 All E.R. 579.

[22] In Salmond and Heuston, *Torts* (19th ed.), p. 372, the same criterion is adopted. Charlesworth, *Negligence* (7th ed.), pp. 860–863. See *Holderness* v. *Goslin* [1975] 2 N.Z.L.R. 46 (farm manager's son left in control of farm).

[23] And, indeed, from *Goldman* v. *Hargrave* [1967] 1 A.C. 465 and associated cases: *ante*, p. 399.

[24] [1909] 1 Ch. 427, 438.

It is evident from the *Northwestern Utilities* case that once the defendant proves the act of a stranger, the point is reached when a claim based on the rule in *Rylands* v. *Fletcher* merges into a claim in negligence, so that if there is no fault the plaintiff will not succeed. The original basis of liability under the rule was responsibility for the creation of an exceptional risk which happened to ripen into injury. By means of the defence of act of a stranger the basis of the liability is shifted to responsibility for culpable failure to control the risk. The rule in *Rylands* v. *Fletcher* thus ceases to be available at the very moment when the plaintiff needs it. One can compare liability under the rule with the liability at common law for dangerous animals which was stricter.[25] It seems that the non-malicious act of a stranger was not a valid defence to the *scienter* action, because it was within the risk that must be accepted by anyone who knowingly chooses to keep a dangerous animal.

Statutory authority

The rule in *Rylands* v. *Fletcher* may be excluded by statute. Whether it is so or not is a question of construction of the particular statute concerned. In *Green* v. *Chelsea Waterworks Co.*,[26] for instance, a main belonging to a waterworks company, which was authorised by Parliament to lay the main, burst without any negligence on the part of the company and the plaintiff's premises were flooded; the company was held not liable. On the other hand, in *Charing Cross Electricity Co.* v. *Hydraulic Power Co.*,[27] where the facts were similar, the defendants were held to have no exemption upon the interpretation of their statute. The distinction between the cases is that the Hydraulic Power Co. were empowered by statute to supply water for industrial purposes, that is, they had permissive power but not a mandatory authority, and they were *under no obligation to keep their mains charged* with water at high pressure, or at all. The Chelsea Waterworks Co. were authorised by statute to lay mains and *were under a statutory duty to maintain a continuous supply of water*; it was an inevitable consequence that damage would be caused by occasional bursts and so by necessary implication the statute exempted them from liability where there was no "negligence."[28] Where a statutory authority is under a mandatory obligation to supply a service, whether with a saving or nuisance clause (that nothing shall exonerate it from proceedings for nuisance) or whether without such a clause, the authority is under no liability for anything expressly required by statute to be

---

[25] The new, statutory liability is similarly strict.

[26] (1894) 70 L.T. 547; applied by the House of Lords in *Longhurst* v. *Metropolitan Water Board* [1948] 2 All E.R. 834. Note, however, that since April 1, 1982 statutory water undertakers are strictly liable for damage (including personal injury) caused by an escape of water from a communication pipe or main under s.6 of the Water Act 1981. This strict liability does not avail other statutory undertakers such as gas and electricity suppliers or highway authorities.

[27] [1914] 3 K.B. 772. Where there is negligence of the sort occurring in *Northwestern Utilities Ltd.* v. *London Guarantee, etc. Co. Ltd.* [1936] A.C. 108, statutory authority will be no defence.

[28] *Smeaton* v. *Ilford Corp.* [1954] Ch. 450, 475–477. "Negligence" in this connection is not a very appropriate word for it means "adopting a method which in fact results in damage to a third person, except in a case where there is no other way of performing the statutory duty": *per* Farwell J. in *Provender Millers (Winchester) Ltd.* v. *Southampton C.C.* [1940] Ch. 131, 140.

done, or reasonably incidental to that requirement, if it was done without negligence.[29] Where the statutory authority is merely permissive, with no clause imposing liability for nuisance, the authority is not liable for doing what the statute authorises, provided it is not negligent; but it is liable when there is a clause imposing liability for nuisance, even if it is not negligent.[30] As to the escape of water from reservoirs, even express statutory authority for their construction will not by itself exonerate their undertakers since the Reservoirs (Safety Provisions) Act 1930, now replaced by the Reservoirs Act 1975.[31] The Dolgarrog Dam disaster of 1925 led to the passing of this legislation. A reservoir 1,400 feet above sea level and holding 200 million gallons of water burst and caused great devastation and loss of life.

One important question in this area awaits a final answer: if, on its proper construction, the statutory authority exempts the undertaker from *Rylands* v. *Fletcher* liability and imposes only an obligation to use due care, upon whom does the burden of proof lie? A bare majority of the High Court of Australia[32] has held that the burden lies upon the plaintiff to prove lack of such care; but the contrary arguments of the minority seem more convincing in principle and allow for the grave difficulties facing a plaintiff with the task of proving negligence against the supplier of a public utility such as gas or electricity.[33]

The question whether the rule in *Rylands* v. *Fletcher* applies in all its strictness to local authorities has been considered but not decided.[34] In *Smeaton* v. *Ilford Corporation*[35] Upjohn J. found it unnecessary to express a concluded view on the question whether a local authority exercising statutory duties is altogether outside the rule as suggested by Denning L.J., or prima facie within the rule subject only to express or implied statutory modification as tentatively suggested by Evershed M.R. in the *Pride of Derby* case.[36]

Act of God

Where the escape is caused directly by natural causes without human intervention in "circumstances which no human foresight can provide

---

[29] *Department of Transport* v. *North West Water Authority* [1984] A.C. 336.

[30] *Dunne* v. *North Western Gas Board* [1964] 2 Q.B. 806, 833–837; [1964] C.L.J. 25–27 (no negligence or breach of statutory duty, defendants not liable under *Rylands* v. *Fletcher* or in nuisance); Linden, "Strict Liability, Nuisance and Legislative Authorization" (1966) Osgoode Hall L.J. 196–221, a useful discussion of the rule of statutory authority: Law Com. No. 32 (1970), pp. 20–21. See also statutory authority in relation to nuisance, *ante*, p. 410. None of these cases seems to take the rather obvious point that the reasons for making the statutory authorisation mandatory or permissive probably have nothing to do with liability for damages.

[31] s.28, Sched. 2.

[32] *Benning* v. *Wong* (1969) 122 C.L.R. 249 (McTiernan, Menzies and Owen JJ.).

[33] Barwick C.J. and Windeyer J.; Sawer (1970), 33 M.L.R. 557; *cf. Manchester Corp.* v. *Farnworth* [1930] A.C. 171.

[34] *Pride of Derby, etc. Association Ltd.* v. *British Celanese Ltd.* [1953] Ch. 149, 172–177, *per* Evershed M.R.; at pp. 189–190, *per* Denning L.J.; *Benning* v. *Wong* (1969) 122 C.L.R. 249, 301, *per* Windeyer J.

[35] [1954] Ch. 450, 478. See *ibid.* at p. 462 as to the distinction between "discharge"—something caused or permitted—and "escape"—involuntary.

[36] See n. 34. See also the remarks on public authorities in *Dunne* v. *North Western Gas Board*.

against and of which human prudence is not bound to recognise the possibility,"[37] the defence of act of God applies. This was recognised by Blackburn J. in *Rylands* v. *Fletcher*[38] itself and was first applied in *Nichols* v. *Marsland*.[39] In this case the defendant for many years had been in possession of some artificial ornamental lakes formed by damming up a natural stream. An extraordinary rainfall, "greater and more violent than any within the memory of witnesses" broke down the artificial embankments and the rush of escaping water carried away four bridges in respect of which damage the plaintiff sued. Judgment was given for the defendant; the jury had found that she was not negligent and the court held that she ought not to be liable for an extraordinary act of nature which she could not reasonably anticipate.

Whether a particular occurrence amounts to an act of God is a question of fact, but the tendency of the courts nowadays is to restrict the ambit of the defence, not because strict liability is thought to be desirable but because increased knowledge limits the unpredictable. In *Greenock Corporation* v. *Caledonian Ry.*,[40] the House of Lords criticised the application of the defence in *Nichols* v. *Marsland*, and four of their lordships cast doubt on the finding of facts by the jury in that case.[41] The Corporation constructed a concrete paddling pool for children in the bed of the stream and to do so they had to alter the course of the stream and obstruct the natural flow of the water. Owing to a rainfall of extraordinary violence, the stream overflowed at the pond, and a great volume of water, which would normally have been carried off by the stream, poured down a public street into the town and caused damage to the plaintiffs' property. The House of Lords held that the rainfall was not an act of God[42] and that the Corporation were liable. It was their duty "so to work as to make proprietors or occupiers on a lower level as secure against injury as they would have been had nature not been interfered with."[43] Similar considerations apply to an extraordinary high wind[44] and an extraordinary high tide.[45] Lightning,[46] earthquakes, cloudbursts and tornadoes may be acts of God but there seems to be no English decision in which they have been involved.

In law, then, the essence of an act of God is not so much a phenomenon which is sometimes attributed to a positive intervention of the forces of nature, but a process of nature not due to the act of man[47] and it is this

---

[37] *Tennent* v. *Earl of Glasgow* (1864) 2 M. (H.L.) 22, 26–27, *per* Lord Westbury, approved by the House of Lords in *Greenock Corp.* v. *Caledonian Ry.* [1917] A.C. 556. Also *AMF International Ltd.* v. *Magnet Bowling Ltd.* [1968] 1 W.L.R. 1028, 1039, *per* Mocatta J.

[38] (1866) L.R. 1 Ex. 265, 280.

[39] (1876) 2 Ex.D. 1.

[40] [1917] A.C. 556.

[41] *Ibid.* at pp. 573–574, 575, 580–581.

[42] Or *damnum fatale*, the equivalent in Scottish law. But now it has been held that *Rylands* v. *Fletcher* is not part of Scots law and the suggestion that it is "is a heresy which ought to be extirpated": *R.H.M. Bakeries (Scotland) Ltd.* v. *Strathclyde Regional Council* 1985 S.L.T. 214, 217, *per* Lord Fraser.

[43] *Ibid.* at p. 579, *per* Lord Shaw. Similarly *per* Lord Finlay L.C. at p. 527; *per* Lord Dunedin at p. 577; *per* Lord Wrenbury at p. 583.

[44] *Cushing* v. *Walker & Sons* [1941] 2 All E.R. 693, 695. "Before wind can amount to an act of God . . . the wind must not merely be exceptionally strong, but must be of such exceptional strength that no one could be reasonably expected to anticipate or provide against it," *per* Hallett J.

[45] *Greenwood Tileries Ltd.* v. *Clapson* [1937] 1 All E.R. 765, 772, *per* Branson J.

[46] *Nichols* v. *Marsland* (1875) L.R. 10 Ex. 255, 260, dictum of Bramwell B.

[47] "Something in opposition to the act of man": Lord Mansfield in *Forward* v. *Pittard* (1785) 1 T.R. 27, 33.

negative side which deserves emphasis. The criterion is not whether or not the event could *reasonably* be anticipated, but whether or not human foresight and prudence could reasonably recognise the *possibility* of such an event.[48] Even in such limited form, however, this defence, like the defence of act of a stranger,[49] shifts the basis of the tort from responsibility for the creation of an exceptional risk to culpable failure to control that risk. This has been criticised on the ground that an accidental escape caused by the forces of nature is within the risk that must be accepted by the defendant when he accumulates the substance on his land.[50] As Scrutton L.J. put it in his strong dissenting judgment in *Att.-Gen.* v. *Cory Bros.*, "the fact that an artificial danger escaped through natural causes was no excuse to the person who brought an artificial danger there."[51] Nevertheless, the defence is now firmly part of the law and brings the rule in *Rylands* v. *Fletcher* closer to the tort of negligence. As Lord Greene M.R. accepted in *J. J. Makin Ltd.* v. *L.N.E.R.*, a proprietor can avoid the ordinary liability based on the rule in *Rylands* v. *Fletcher* if he can show that the water had escaped without his negligence.[52]

Default of the plaintiff

If the damage is caused solely by the act or default of the plaintiff himself, he has no remedy. In *Rylands* v. *Fletcher* itself, this was noticed as a defence.[53] If a person knows that there is a danger of his mine being flooded by his neighbour's operations on adjacent land, and courts the danger by doing some act which renders the flooding probable, he cannot complain.[54] So, too, in *Ponting* v. *Noakes*,[55] the plaintiff's horse reached over the defendant's boundary, nibbled some poisonous tree there and died accordingly, and it was held that the plaintiff could recover nothing, for the damage was due to the horse's own intrusion and, alternatively, there had been no escape of the vegetation. Had it been grown there expressly for the purpose of alluring cattle to their destruction, the defendant would have been liable,

---

[48] The former view was taken in *Nichols* v. *Marsland*, the latter in *Greenock Corp.* v. *Caledonian Ry.* [1917] A.C. 556.

[49] *Ante*, pp. 434–436.

[50] Particularly, Goodhart, "The Third Man" (1951) 4 C.L.P. 177; "*Rylands* v. *Fletcher* Today" (1956) 72 L.Q.R. 184.

[51] (1919) 35 T.L.R. 570, 574 (fall of refuse in Rhondda Valley probably caused by the saturation of its inferior strata by an extraordinary rainfall). Also *Dixon* v. *Metropolitan Board of Works* (1881) 7 Q.B.D. 418, *per* Lord Coleridge C.J.

[52] [1943] 1 K.B. 467, 470 citing counsel, seemingly with approval. See Buxton, "The Negligent Nuisance" (1966) 8 U. Malaya L.R. 7: the decision in *Nichols* v. *Marsland* "leaves very few cases where a defendant could be held liable who had not in fact been negligent." "Unless one can visualise the accumulation in circumstances which do not constitute an ordinary user of the land of something likely to do mischief if it escapes, and which does escape from the defendant's land neither by act of God nor of third party, everything that is within *Rylands* v. *Fletcher* could also be negligence": Street (1965) I.C.L.Q. 862, 870.

[53] (1868) L.R. 3 H.L. 330, 340. If the rule applies to a deliberate discharge of the thing (which is unlikely) necessity is as much a defence as in trespass: *Rigby* v. *Chief Constable of Northamptonshire* [1985] 1 W.L.R. 1242.

[54] *Lomax* v. *Stott* (1870) 39 L.J. Ch. 834; *Dunn* v. *Birmingham Canal Co.* (1872) L.R. 7 Q.B. 244. *Miles* v. *Forest Rock Granite Co. Ltd.* (1918) 34 T.L.R. 500 would be more helpful if the report had stated more exactly the finding of the jury. *Postmaster-General* v. *Liverpool Corp.* [1923] A.C. 587.

[55] [1894] 2 Q.B. 281; *cf. Cheater* v. *Cater* [1918] 1 K.B. 247.

not on the grounds of *Rylands* v. *Fletcher*, but because he would have been in the position of one who deliberately sets traps baited with flesh in order to attract and catch dogs which are otherwise not trespassing at all.[56] Where the plaintiff is contributorily negligent, the apportionment provisions of the Law Reform (Contributory Negligence) Act 1945 will apply.

If the injury due to the escape of the noxious thing would not have occurred but for the unusual sensitiveness of the plaintiff's property, there is some conflict of authority whether this can be regarded as default of the plaintiff. In *Eastern S.A. Telegraph Co. Ltd.* v. *Cape Town Tramways Companies Ltd.*,[57] an escape of electricity stored and used by the defendants in working their tramcars, interfered with the sending of messages by the plaintiffs through their submarine cable. The plaintiffs failed to recover as no tangible injury had been done to their property—no apparatus had been damaged. The defendants' operations were not destructive of telegraphic communication generally, but only affected instruments unnecessarily so constructed as to be affected by minute currents of the escaping electricity. With regard to such instruments it was said, "A man cannot increase the liabilities of his neighbour by applying his own property to special uses, whether for business or pleasure." However, in *Hoare Co.* v. *McAlpine*,[58] where vibrations from pile-driving caused structural damage to a large hotel on adjoining land, Astbury J. held it to be a bad plea that the vibrations had this effect only because the hotel was so old as to be abnormally unstable; but he found also that the evidence did not establish that it was in such a condition. Thus the question remains an open one, and it can hardly be said that the hotel proprietor had put his property to any special or unusually sensitive use.

REMOTENESS OF DAMAGE

The defendant under *Rylands* v. *Fletcher* cannot be liable *ad infinitum* and in Blackburn J.'s formulation of the rule he "is prima facie answerable for all the damage which is the natural consequence of its escape." The Privy Council in *The Wagon Mound (No. 1)*[59] stated that their Lordships had not found it necessary to consider the rule in *Rylands* v. *Fletcher* in relation to remoteness of damage and it has been suggested that the inference is that causation, not foreseeability, is the test under the rule.[60] There is no very compelling reason, however, why foreseeability should not be utilised as the test of remoteness in cases where it is irrelevant to the initial determination of liability: "granted that an escape takes place, albeit unforeseeably, what

---

[56] *Townsend* v. *Wathen* (1808) 9 East 277.
[57] [1902] A.C. 381, 393; *Western Silver Fox Ranch Ltd.* v. *Ross and Cromarty C.C.* 1940 S.C. 601, 604–606 (breeding silver foxes not a non-natural use of land).
[58] [1923] 1 Ch. 167. See Pollock's criticism of this decision in *Torts*, p. 377, n. 16, and (1923) 39 L.Q.R. 145–146; Charlesworth, *Negligence* (7th ed.), p. 843.
[59] [1961] A.C. 388, 427.
[60] McGregor, *Damages* (15th ed.), p. 81. Lawton J. in *British Celanese Ltd.* v. *A.H. Hunt Ltd.* [1969] 1 W.L.R. 959, 964, found it unnecessary to decide the issue.

would a reasonable man regard as the foreseeable consequences of such an escape?"[61] It will also be recollected that so many qualifications have been placed upon the decision in *The Wagon Mound (No. 1)* that the concept of foreseeability is now applied in a very broad and liberal manner[62] and there is unlikely to be much practical difference between an inquiry whether a consequence is foreseeable or natural. The natural or foreseeable consequences of a dam bursting are, *inter alia*, the inundation of subjacent land, damage to buildings, roads and personal injuries. If the water flows into the shaft of an adjoining mine, with the result that the mine cannot be worked for six months, the mine owner may recover damages, but the miners who lose their wages during that period probably have no remedy,[63] not because the loss is "unnatural" or "unforeseeable" but because it is a loss of a type for which the law restricts recovery.[64] Even if the escaping water flows into a carbide factory and thereby generates gas which causes a tremendous explosion it is unlikely that much will be achieved by seeking to draw distinctions between what is natural and foreseeable. As in all such cases the issue is finally one of legal policy.[65]

MODERN POSITION OF THE RULE IN RYLANDS V. FLETCHER[66]

The rule in *Rylands* v. *Fletcher*, then, had its origins in the law of private nuisance and has often been treated as a particular species of nuisance. In *Read* v. *Lyons*, for instance, Lord Simonds remarked that "the judgment of Blackburn J. in the case itself shows that the law of nuisance and the rule in *Rylands* v. *Fletcher* might in most cases be invoked indifferently."[67] The rule of course has in many senses a more restricted application than nuisance; there must be an accumulation, and it must be of a substance likely to cause injury if it escapes,[68] neither of which is essential to liability in nuisance. Moreover, the condition of non-natural user, though similar to unreasonable user in nuisance, normally involves some degree of exceptional risk which unreasonable user does not. Nevertheless in many factual situations, a plaintiff will succeed equally well either under the rule or in nuisance.[69]

Despite the original relationship of the rule to nuisance, however, the former has been developed in such a way that it provides a remedy which is

---

[61] See *ante*, p. 142. *The Wagon Mound (No. 2)* [1967] 1 A.C. 617 seems to support this view, though whether there are in fact any instances of strict liability in nuisance must be highly questionable: *ante*, pp. 380–385.

[62] *Ante*, pp. 142–144.

[63] *Cattle* v. *Stockton Waterworks Co.* (1875) L.R. 10 Q.B. 453, 457.

[64] See the cases (in negligence) on economic loss: *ante*, pp. 84–91 and *Weller* v. *Foot and Mouth Disease Research Institute* [1966] 1 Q.B. 569.

[65] See Dias, "Remoteness of Damage and Legal Policy" [1962] C.L.J. 178, 194–195.

[66] See Winfield (1931) 4 C.L.J. 194–197; Friedmann, "Modern Trends in the Law of Torts" (1937) 1 M.L.R. 49–63; "Nuisance, Negligence and the Overlapping of Torts" (1940) 3 M.L.R. 305–309; *Law and Social Change*, pp. 75–82, 93–98; Wright, "The Law of Torts, 1923–1947" (1948) 26 Can. Bar Rev. 47, 76–81; Linden, "Whatever Happened to *Rylands* v. *Fletcher*? in *Studies in Canadian Tort Law*.

[67] [1947] A.C. 156, 183.

[68] Law Com. No. 32 (1970), at p. 24.

[69] Compare *Midwood & Co. Ltd.* v. *Manchester Corp.* [1905] 2 K.B. 597 (nuisance) with *Charing Cross Electricity Co.* v. *Hydraulic Power Co.* [1914] 3 K.B. 722 (the rule in *Rylands* v. *Fletcher*).

basically quite different from nuisance. Private nuisance remains fundamentally a remedy for the infringement of a proprietary interest in land.
There are, as we have seen,[70] different types of nuisance and because of this
the burden of proof placed on the plaintiff varies. But the basic characteristic
common to all types of private nuisance is that of interference with the
plaintiff's proprietary interest in land. For this reason a non-occupier cannot
maintain a claim in nuisance and an occupier's right to damages for his
personal injuries is ancillary to his claim for compensation for damage to his
property.[71] In contrast, it now seems good law that the rule in *Rylands* v.
Fletcher protects all interests including the interest of a non-occupier, *e.g.* a
user of the highway, in his personal security.[72] As one writer has put it, the
rule provides a remedy for what is "essentially a wrong arising from occupation of land (and it is irrelevant whether the person suffering the injury
occupies land or not)."[73] This serves to distinguish it quite fundamentally
from nuisance.

At the same time as the area covered by the rule in *Rylands* v. *Fletcher* has
been enlarged, the usefulness of the rule has been reduced by the unwillingness of the courts to apply it in circumstances where the defendant could not
be said to have been at fault. In *Dunne* v. *North Western Gas Board*,[74] Sellers
L.J. asserted that in the present time the defendant's liability in *Rylands* v.
Fletcher itself "could simply have been placed on the defendant's failure of
duty to take reasonable care,"[75] and it seems a logical inference from this and
from the judgment as a whole that the Court of Appeal considered the rule
to have no useful function in modern times. Because of this policy, "the rule
in *Rylands* v. *Fletcher*, by reason of its many limitations and exceptions,
today seldom forms the basis of a successful claim in the courts"[76] and it
seems fair to remark that the rule "has hardly been taken seriously by
modern English courts."[77]

The most important restriction on any extended application of the rule is
the requirement of non-natural user. As it is now interpreted, this excludes
from the ambit of the rule those accumulations which in the judgment of the
court (there being no objective test) do not involve an unreasonable risk or
an extraordinary use of land. Such an interpretation allows the courts to hold
that a common activity such as the collection and storage of gas or water does
not constitute a non-natural use of land, even though the injury potential of
the activity is high. Moreover, in determining what is extraordinary or
unreasonable the courts can have regard not only to the interests of the
defendant but to the public interest as well. The benefit to the public
accruing from the activity in question was an important element in both

---

[70] *Ante*, p. 381.
[71] *Ante*, p. 396.
[72] *Ante*, pp. 426–427.
[73] West, (1966) 30 Con. 95, 101. He defines nuisance as "essentially a wrong to occupation of land (whether the person causing the injury does so *qua* occupier of land or not)." See *British Celanese Ltd.* v. *A.H. Hunt Ltd.* [1969] 1 W.L.R. 959, 964, *per* Lawton J.
[74] [1964] 2 Q.B. 806.
[75] *Ibid.* at p. 831.
[76] Law Com. No. 32 (1970), p. 7.
[77] *Att.-Gen.* v. *Geothermal Produce (N.Z.) Ltd.* [1987] 2 N.Z.L.R. 348, 354, *per* Cooke J.

Read v. *Lyons*[78] and *Dunne* v. *North Western Gas Board*[79] and was again emphasised in *British Celanese Ltd.* v. *A.H. Hunt Ltd.*[80] In this case the defendants, who were manufacturers of electronic components, collected on their land a large number of strips of metal foil, light enough to be blown about in the wind. Lawton J. refused to regard this as a non-natural use of land. "The manufacturing of electrical and electronic components in the year 1964 . . . cannot be adjudged to be a special use nor can the bringing and storing on the premises of metal foil be a special use in itself. . . . The metal foil was there for use in the manufacture of goods of a common type which at all material times were needed for the general benefit of the community."[81] It would seem therefore that normal industrial activities properly carried out may no longer involve a non-natural use of land and many of the older authorities on this point will need reconsidering.

Moreover, as a result of the defences of act of God, act of a third party and statutory authority, the courts must investigate not only the reasonableness of the accumulation, but also the defendant's responsibility for its actual escape. The nature and quality of the defendant's conduct are therefore factors of great importance, and although the decisional process is different from that in negligence, the result is almost always the same. We have virtually reached the position where a defendant will not be considered liable when he would not be liable according to the ordinary principles of negligence.

Unfortunately, it is precisely at the point when the plaintiff cannot succeed in a claim in negligence that he needs to have recourse to the rule in *Rylands* v. *Fletcher*. It may well be contrary to modern judicial philosophy that a defendant should be liable in the absence of fault but this involves as its consequence that an innocent plaintiff should bear the loss. The injustice that may be caused by this was clearly illustrated by the case of *Pearson* v. *North Western Gas Board*.[82] The plaintiff was seriously and her husband fatally injured by an explosion of gas which also destroyed their home. On the facts of the case, even assuming the doctrine of *res ipsa loquitur* to operate in favour of the plaintiff, Rees J. was compelled to hold that the expert evidence adduced by the defendants rebutted any prima facie case in negligence. As the plaintiff was precluded from relying on the rule in *Rylands* v. *Fletcher* by the decision in *Dunne* v. *North Western Gas Board*,[83] the action failed. It is suggested that the decline of the rule in *Rylands* v. *Fletcher* in recent times has left the individual injured by the activities of our industrial society without adequate protection. It has been said on high authority that

" . . . to regard negligence as the normal requirement of responsibility in

---

[78] [1947] A.C. 156.
[79] [1964] 2 Q.B. 806.
[80] [1969] 1 W.L.R. 959.
[81] *Ibid.* at p. 963.
[82] [1968] 2 All E.R. 669.
[83] [1964] 2 Q.B. 806.

tort, and to look upon strict liability as anomalous and unjust seems to ... mistake present values as well as past history. In an age when insurance against all forms of liability is commonplace, it is surely not surprising or unjust if law makes persons who carry on some kinds of hazardous undertakings liable for the harm they do, unless they can excuse or justify it on some recognisable ground."[84]

Judicial ideas are no more immutable than any others and it may be that the above account is too pessimistic, but it seems likely that any future extension of strict liability will come only from the legislature. Some instances of modern statutory liability are considered in a later section of this chapter[85] but a more generalised revival of the *Rylands* v. *Fletcher* idea is proposed in two modern law reform proposals. The Law Commission in its Report on Civil Liability for Dangerous Things and Activities[86] suggested the concept of "special danger"—*i.e.* activities involving "a more than ordinary risk of accidents or a risk of more than ordinary damage if accidents in fact result"—as a basis for future development of the law.[87] The problem remains, however, of how this should be implemented. One possibility would be a statutory reformulation of *Rylands* v. *Fletcher* shorn of the qualifications and defences which so emasculate it now, perhaps on the lines of the *Restatement*, which imposes strict liability on one who carries on an "abnormally dangerous activity,"[88] but this would be open to varying judicial inclinations and would give rise to considerable uncertainty for a very long period of time. Accordingly the Royal Commission on Civil Liability and Compensation for Personal Injury[89] recommended a different approach (but only for death or personal injury) in the form of a parent statute which would empower a Minister to "list" dangerous things or activities as giving rise to strict liability. Listing would be by statutory instrument made on the advice of an advisory committee. There was some disagreement in the Commission as to the scope of the admissible defences but there was a unanimous recommendation that statutory authority should not, of itself, provide immunity from strict liability. Such a scheme would undoubtedly provide a greater degree of certainty than under the present law but would be open to the objection that it would leave without redress any persons suffering injury from an unlisted activity, whether omission arose from

---

[84] *Benning* v. *Wong* (1969) 122 C.L.R. 249, 304, *per* Windeyer J. This judgment contains the most comprehensive judicial consideration of the present status of *Rylands* v. *Fletcher*.

[85] *Post*, p. 449. Strict liability under industrial safety legislation is, of course, of respectable antiquity: *ante*, Chap. 8.

[86] Law Com. No. 32 (1970).

[87] Proposals for the imposition of strict liability upon producers of goods have become generally accepted with surprising speed: *ante*, Chap. 10. One of the principal reasons advanced for change in that area is that the industry should carry the costs of compensation for the injuries produced by it, particularly when it can spread the cost among its consumers. This applies equally to the sort of situation considered in this chapter but the idea of "exceptional peril" is undoubtedly an additional reason here. It is perhaps an emotional one, but none the less powerful for that, as witness its acceptance by Parliament in, *e.g.* the Nuclear Installations Act 1965.

[88] Restatement 2d., s.519. Yet the factors which the court is directed to consider (s.520) to determine whether the activity is abnormally dangerous come very close in a number of respects to the defences to the English rule.

[89] Cmnd. 7054 (1978), Vol. 1, Chap. 31.

ignorance of the risk[90] or commercial or political pressures on the government of the day.[91] The retention of the rule in *Rylands* v. *Fletcher* as a form of "back-up" to this liability would go some way to meet this point, though the Royal Commission's preference, for reasons of certainty, was for the abolition of that rule.[92]

In conclusion it should be noted that power already exists to utilise delegated legislation to go a good deal of the way along the road proposed by the Royal Commission. The purposes of the Health and Safety at Work etc. Act 1974 go beyond the securing of safety in employment and include:

(1) "protecting persons other than persons at work against risks to health or safety arising out of or in connection with the activities of persons at work";

(2) "controlling the keeping and use of explosive or highly flammable or otherwise dangerous substances, . . . ";

(3) "controlling the emission into the atmosphere of noxious or offensive substances . . . "[93]

In order to promote these purposes the Secretary of State, normally on the advice of the Health and Safety Commission,[94] has power to make "health and safety regulations"[95] which will give rise to civil liability except in so far as they provide otherwise.[96] To the extent that these regulations impose absolute duties they may, accordingly, provide any persons injured thereby with an effective civil remedy.

FIRE

Common law

Winfield has traced the history of the earlier forms of action available as remedies for damage caused by the spread of fire.[97] The usual remedy was the special action of trespass on the case for negligently allowing one's fire to escape in contravention of the general custom of the realm which we first hear of in *Beaulieu* v. *Finglam*.[98] The allegation in the action for fire that the defendant *tam negligenter ac improvide* "kept his fire that it escaped," referred to negligence in its older sense—one mode of committing a tort. Centuries later remedies became available under the rule in *Rylands* v.

---

[90] The law reports contain numerous examples of accidents arising from previously unappreciated risks: *e.g. Roe* v. *Minister of Health* [1954] 2 Q.B. 66; *Vacwell Engineering* v. *B.D.H. Chemicals* [1971] 1 Q.B. 88.

[91] *cf.*, in a somewhat different context, the Government's insistence on the inclusion of the "development risks" defence in the Consumer Protection Act 1987: *ante*, p. 257.

[92] Para. 1670. But no recommendation was made because property damage was outside its terms of reference and "we do not think it is for us to attempt to rationalise the existing categories of strict liability."

[93] Health and Safety at Work Act 1974, s.1.

[94] See s.11.

[95] s.15, Sched. 3.

[96] s.47.

[97] Winfield (1926) 42 L.Q.R. 46–50, or *Select Essays*, pp. 25–28; and (1931) 4 C.L.J. 203–206; Newark (1945) 6 N.I.L.Q. 134–141; Ogus, "Vagaries in Liability for the Escape of Fire" [1969] C.L.J. 104.

[98] (1401) Y.B. Pasch. 2 Hen. 4, f. 18, pl. 6, translated in Fifoot, *History and Sources of the Common Law*, p. 166.

Fletcher[99] in nuisance[1] and in negligence.[2] Although it is repeatedly said that at common law a man must keep his fire "at his peril," research shows that we cannot be sure that at any period in the history of the common law a man was absolutely liable for the escape of his fire.[3] He is liable for damage done by his fire if it has been caused wilfully,[4] or by his negligence, or by the escape without negligence of a fire which has been brought into existence by some non-natural user of the land. It has been pointed out that the last type of liability is not quite the same as liability under the rule in *Rylands* v. *Fletcher* in that the thing accumulated on the land does not itself escape. The criterion of liability is: "Did the defendants ... bring to their land things likely to catch fire, and keep them there in such conditions that if they did ignite the fire would be likely to spread to the plaintiff's land?"[5] With this qualification liability is the same as under the rule in *Rylands* v. *Fletcher*.

Exactly what "*negligenter*" meant can only be conjectured, for the old authorities are confused, but it certainly excluded liability where the fire spread or occurred (*a*) by the act of a stranger[6] over whom he had no control, such as a trespasser,[7] and (*b*) by the act of nature. He is responsible for the default of his servant,[8] his wife, his guest[9] or one entering his house with his leave[10] and for his independent contractor.[11] The second exception was established in *Tuberville* v. *Stamp*[12] where it was held that liability extended

---

[99] *Jones* v. *Festiniog Ry.* (1866) L.R. 1 Ex. 265, fire included in "things likely to do mischief if they escape" and thus within *Rylands* v. *Fletcher*; *Powell* v. *Fall* (1880) 5 Q.B.D. 597; *Musgrove* v. *Pandelis* [1919] 2 K.B. 43; *Job Edwards Ltd.* v. *Birmingham Navigations* [1924] 1 K.B. 341, 351–352; *Collingwood* v. *Home and Colonial Stores Ltd.* [1936] 3 All E.R. 200, 205; *Balfour* v. *Barty-King* [1957] 1 Q.B. 496, 505, C.A. (Lord Goddard C.J. deals with the history of the action on the case from its origin to modern times).

[1] *Spicer* v. *Smee* [1946] 1 All E.R. 489.

[2] Bankes L.J. in *Musgrove* v. *Pandelis* [1919] 2 K.B. 43, 46, *per* Scrutton L.J.; *Job Edwards Ltd.* v. *Birmingham Navigations* [1924] 1 K.B. 341, 361.

[3] Winfield (1926) 42 L.Q.R. 46–50 or *Select Essays*, pp. 26–29; Jordan C.J. in *Commissioner for Railways* v. *Wise Bros. Pty.* (1946) 47 S.R.(N.S.W.) 233, on appeal Latham C.J.; (1947) 75 C.L.R. 59, as to liability in general; *Edwards* v. *Blue Mountains C.C.* (1961) 78 W.N.(N.S.W.) 864 and (1962) 35 A.L.J. 392.

[4] If the damage is intentional it is a trespass or assault, *e.g.* deliberately throwing a lighted match on a haystack or a lighted firework in a man's face.

[5] *Mason* v. *Levy Auto Parts of England Ltd.* [1967] 2 Q.B. 530, 542, *per* MacKenna J. Weir, *Casebook on Tort* (6th ed.), p. 397.

[6] *Balfour* v. *Barty-King* [1957] 1 Q.B. 496, 504; *Tuberville* v. *Stamp* (1697) 1 Ld. Raym. 264; *H.N. Emanuel Ltd.* v. *G.L.C.* [1971] 2 All E.R. 835.

[7] Unless the occupier has knowledge of the fire and fails to take steps to extinguish it within a reasonable time.

[8] But a servant acting outside the course of his employment is a stranger: *McKenzie* v. *McLeod* (1834) 10 Bing. 385.

[9] *Crogate* v. *Morris* (1617) 1 Brownl. 197; *Boulcott Golf Club Inc.* v. *Engelbrecht* [1945] N.Z.L.R. 556 (Finlay J. reviews the authorities).

[10] (1926) 42 L.Q.R. 46–50, where the authorities are examined; *Holderness* v. *Goslin* [1975] 2 N.Z.L.R. 46. In the *Emanuel* case, *supra*, Lord Denning M.R. suggested that a person on the occupier's premises with leave and licence was a stranger for this purpose if in lighting the fire he acts contrary to anything the occupier could expect him to do. However, the New Zealand case of *Eriksen* v. *Clifton* [1963] N.Z.L.R. 605, cited in support of this proposition, seems in fact to be a case of liability for personal negligence not vicarious liability.

[11] *Balfour* v. *Barty-King* [1957] 1 Q.B. 496 (defendant was held liable for a fire caused by an independent contractor whom he employed to thaw frozen pipes in an attic which contained large quantities of combustible material. Contractor used blow-lamp and caused a fire which spread and destroyed plaintiff's adjoining house. Havers J. held defendant liable for negligence of his independent contractor and also under *Rylands* v. *Fletcher*. C.A. affirmed decision but did not think it necessary to consider *Rylands* v. *Fletcher* as a separate head of liability, but had no doubt that it applied); [1957] C.L.J. 132–133; *Black* v. *Christchurch Finance Co.* [1894] A.C. 48.

[12] (1697) 1 Ld. Raym. 264. Lord Raymond gives the best report of the argument; but the record is set out in full by Salkeld (2 Salk. 726). See *Balfour* v. *Barty-King, supra*, n. 11; *Eriksen* v. *Clifton* [1963] N.Z.L.R. 705, 707.

to a fire originating in a field as much as to one beginning in a house, but if the defendant kindles it at a proper time and place and the violence of the wind carry it to his neighbour's land, that is fit to be given in evidence. The common law liability still remains in all cases which are not covered by statutory provision.

Statutes

(1) *Fires beginning accidentally on the defendant's land*

The common law liability has been modified in respect of fires spreading from the defendant's land by the Fires Prevention (Metropolis) Act 1774,[13] which provides that no action shall be maintainable against anyone in whose building or on whose estate a fire shall accidentally begin. This section of the Act is of general application and is not limited to London.[14] In *Filliter* v. *Phippard*[15] the word "accidentally" was interpreted restrictively so as to cover only "a fire produced by mere chance or incapable of being traced to any cause."[16] In other words a fire caused by negligence[17] or due to a nuisance[18] will give rise to a cause of action.

The immunity of a defendant under the statute is illustrated by *Collingwood* v. *Home and Colonial Stores Ltd.*[19] A fire broke out on the defendants' premises and spread to those of the plaintiff. It originated in the defective condition of the electrical wiring on the defendants' premises, but as there was no negligence on their part they were held not liable. Nor was the rule in *Rylands* v. *Fletcher* applicable, for the installation of electric wiring, whether for domestic or trade purposes, was a reasonable and ordinary use of premises. Even if the fire is lit intentionally, providing it is lit properly, there is no liability if it spreads without negligence and causes damage, *e.g.* a spark jumps out of an ordinary household fire and causes it to spread.[20] It would be different, of course, if the fire were made too large for the grate.

However, the statute does not confer protection on one who was not at fault so far as the origin of the fire is concerned but who was negligent in letting it spread. In *Musgrove* v. *Pandelis*,[21] the plaintiff occupied rooms over a garage and let part of the garage to the defendant who kept a car there. The defendant's servant, who had little skill as a chauffeur, started the

[13] s.86.
[14] *Filliter* v. *Phippard* (1847) 11 Q.B. 347, 355. Indeed, it even applies to New Zealand and to parts of Australia. Estate applies to land not built upon.
[15] (1847) 11 Q.B. 347.
[16] *Ibid.* at p. 357, *per* Lord Denman C.J.
[17] *e.g. Mulholland and Tedd* v. *Baker Ltd.* [1939] 3 All E.R. 253, 255, *per* Asquith J. (paper lit and inserted in drainpipe to smoke out a rat, fire spread to packing case and exploded drum of paraffin. Liable in negligence and under the rule in *Rylands* v. *Fletcher*).
[18] *e.g. Spicer* v. *Smee* [1946] 1 All E.R. 489, 495, *per* Atkinson J. (defective electric wiring negligently installed by contractor caused fire, owner liable in nuisance or negligence).
[19] (1936) 155 L.T. 550.
[20] *Sochacki* v. *Sas* [1947] 1 All E.R. 344; *cf. New Zealand Forest Products Ltd.* v. *O'Sullivan* [1974] 2 N.Z.L.R. 80, 84.
[21] [1919] 2 K.B. 43.

engine of the car and without any fault on his part the petrol in the carburettor caught fire. If he had acted like any chauffeur of reasonable competence he could have stopped the fire by turning off the tap connecting the petrol tank with the carburettor. He did not do so and the fire spread and damaged the plaintiff's property. The defendant was held liable, for the fire which did the damage was not that which broke out in the carburettor but that which spread to the car and this second or continuing fire did not "accidentally" begin.[22] The same principle applies where the fire originated as a consequence of an act of nature. In *Goldman* v. *Hargrave*,[23] a redgum tree on the defendant's land was struck by lightning and caught fire in a fork eighty feet above ground. The defendant had the tree felled the following morning, but then, instead of extinguishing the fire with water as he could have done, he left it to burn itself out. Three days later a wind came up and revived the fire which spread to and damaged the plaintiff's land. It was held in the circumstances that the defendant was negligent in not completely extinguishing the fire and that the Act of 1774 provided no defence. The burden of proving such negligence is on the plaintiff; it is not for the defendant to prove that the fire was accidental.[24] Even though a plaintiff cannot prove negligence, if the fire originated from a non-natural user of the defendant's land, the Act of 1774 does not provide a defence and the defendant will be liable.[25]

(2) *Railway engines*

Other statutes deal with the escape of sparks from railway engines. Where, as is commonly the case, a railway is constructed and worked under statutory powers, and there is no negligence in the construction or use of locomotives, there is no liability for fires caused by the escape of sparks from locomotives; such was the decision in *Vaughan* v. *Taff Vale Ry.*,[26] where the defendants had taken every precaution that science could suggest to prevent injury of this sort, and it was held that as Parliament had authorised the use of locomotives it was consistent with policy and justice that the defendants, in the absence of any negligence, should not be liable. But this view was rather hard upon farmers with crops adjacent to a railway line and a compromise was effected by the Railway Fires Acts 1905 and 1923,[27] which cast upon railways a liability not exceeding £200, even if the total damage

---

[22] Also *Sturge* v. *Hackett* [1962] 1 W.L.R. 1257 (defendant was tenant of a groundfloor flat. To destroy some birds' nests attached to the walls of the flat, he lit a paraffin rag, applied it to the nest, which caught fire; the fire spread and destroyed the entire building. Held, the fire which caused the damage was the fire that got out of control, *viz.* the fire in the birds' nests and not that started by lighting the rag).

[23] [1967] 1 A.C. 645.

[24] *Mason* v. *Levy Auto Parts of England Ltd.* [1967] 2 Q.B. 530, 538–539, *per* MacKenna J. (discussing previous authorities).

[25] *Ibid.* at pp. 540–541. MacKenna J. after reviewing the authorities felt bound to follow them but did so reluctantly: "In holding that an exemption given to accidental fires, 'any law usage or custom to the contrary notwithstanding,' does not include fires for which liability might be imposed upon the principle of *Rylands* v. *Fletcher*, the Court of Appeal (in *Musgrove* v. *Pandelis*) went very far.".

[26] (1860) 5 H. & N. 679; *Jones* v. *Festiniog Ry.* (1868) L.R. 3 Q.B. 733 (sparks from railway engine caused fire, railway not worked under statutory powers, liable under *Rylands* v. *Fletcher*); *Powell* v. *Fall* (1890) 5 Q.B.D. 997; *Mansel* v. *Webb* (1918) 88 L.J.K.B. 323 (sparks from traction engine on highway causing fire, liability under *Rylands* v. *Fletcher*).

[27] s.1 of each Act.

claimed and done is much in excess,[28] for damage caused to agricultural land or agricultural crops by fire arising from the emission of sparks or cinders from their locomotives, although the locomotive was used under statutory powers. Presumably this puts the liability of the railway company up to £200 on the same level as that fixed by the common law and, on the other hand, does not deprive it of any of the defences pleadable at common law which are discussed above, *e.g.* default of the plaintiff.[29]

STRICT LIABILITY UNDER MODERN LEGISLATION

We saw, when considering nuisance, how that branch of the common law has been supplemented (indeed, in some respects almost obliterated) by detailed statutory provisions governing pollution of the environment. Most of this legislation is of a "regulatory" nature and does not give rise to liability in damages.[30] We have also seen that for the purposes of civil liability there have been proposals for a generalised statutory scheme for exceptional risks.[31] The reader should be aware, however, that recent years have seen the enactment of a number of important statutory forms of liability in particular areas of exceptional risk which go a long way towards avoiding the likelihood of protracted litigation inherent in the ill-defined nature of the rules of strict liability at common law.[32] Full accounts of these Acts must be sought elsewhere but the following is a summary of the civil liability aspects of some of the more important of them.[33]

Nuclear incidents[34]

The major factors requiring the enactment of legislation on liability for nuclear incidents were the risk of widespread damage, possibly involving losses of millions of pounds, from a single emission of ionising radiations and the possible injustice in the Limitation Acts owing to the long periods which

---

[28] *Att.-Gen.* v. *G.W. Ry.* [1924] 2 K.B. 1; *Langlands (Swanley)* v. *British Transport Commission* [1956] 1 W.L.R. 890 (purpose of the Acts within the limit of £200 is to put the plaintiff in the position he would have been if the defendants had not been acting under statutory powers).

[29] *Groom* v. *G.W. Ry.* (1892) 8 T.L.R.253, 256. In *Parker* v. *L.N.E. Ry.* (1945) 175 L.T. 137, defendants were held liable, as they had not adopted a modern invention used by other railways. The Acts are of course of far less importance since the advent of diesel and electric traction but (*a*) British Rail sometimes operates steam "specials" as well as a number of permanent steam lines in Wales and (*b*) the numerous private steam lines operated under statutory authority, would seem to be subject to the Acts.

[30] *Ante*, pp. 375–376.

[31] *Ante*, pp. 444–445.

[32] *e.g.* had litigation ensued from the Flixborough chemical plant disaster in 1974 it would surely have been argued, citing *Read* v. *Lyons*, that the activity was "natural," though with what prospects of success the author would not like to say. Unfortunately, a situation like Flixborough is not covered by any special legislation.

[33] See also s.14 of the Gas Act 1965 which imposes virtually absolute liability for damage caused by gas in underground storage; and s.6 of the Water Act 1981 imposing strict liability for burst mains (*ante*, p. 436, n. 26). The strict liability of an aircraft operator is considered *ante*, p. 365.

[34] Street and Frame, *Law Relating to Nuclear Energy* is the leading work on this subject, and the editors of this work are indebted to them for clarifying such a complex series of statutes, statutory orders and international conventions.

might elapse between the impact of ionising radiations on the plaintiff and his suffering ascertainable damage.[35]

By the Nuclear Installations Act 1965[36] no person other than the United Kingdom Atomic Energy Authority shall use any site for the operation of nuclear plant unless a licence to do so has been granted in respect of that site by the Minister of Power.

Liability arises only when there is a nuclear incident which occurs at or in connection with certain nuclear installations, or in the course of transport of nuclear substances, and it can arise only in connection with licensed nuclear sites.[37] Section 7(1) enacts:

"It shall be the duty of the licensee to secure that—

(*a*) no such occurrence involving nuclear matter as is mentioned in subsection (2) of this section causes[38] injury to any person or damage to any property of any person other than the licensee, being injury or damage arising out of or resulting from the radioactive properties, or a combination of those and any toxic, explosive or other hazardous properties, of that nuclear matter; and

(*b*) no ionising radiations emitted during the period of the licensee's responsibility—

(i) from anything caused or suffered by the licensee to be on the site which is not nuclear matter; or

(ii) from any waste discharged (in whatever form) on or from the site, cause injury to any person or damage to any property of any person other than the licensee."[39]

The liability of the licensee under section 7(1)(*a*), once damage within the Act is proved to have resulted, is a strict one. There is no need to prove negligence on the part of anyone.[40] Any person, other than the licensee, may sue provided he can prove "injury" (which means "personal injury" and includes loss of life) or "damage to any property."[41] There is no need that the dangerous matter should "escape" from the site on which it was kept onto other land. The Act creates a statutory right of action for damages, where injury or damage has been caused in breach of a duty.[42] Where liability in respect of the same injury is incurred by two or more persons, both or all of those persons shall be treated as jointly and severally liable in respect of that

---

[35] Street and Frame, *op. cit.*, p. 38. However, after the first Nuclear Installations Act in 1959, the Limitation Act 1963 to some extent mitigated this problem in all personal injury cases and this has been carried further by the Limitation Act 1980: *post*, p. 725.

[36] This Act consolidated the law relating to nuclear installations, namely, the Nuclear Installations (Licensing and Insurance) Act 1959 and the Nuclear Installations (Amendment) Act 1965. The Act came into force on December 1, 1965, except for s.17(5) (which bars enforcement in the United Kingdom of certain foreign judgments), Nuclear Installations Act 1965 (Commencement No. 1) Order 1965 (No. 1880). Nuclear site licences are granted only to corporate bodies and are not transferable, s.3(1). Minor amendments to the scheme were made by the Nuclear Installations Act 1969.

[37] s.12

[38] Should a claim under the Act ever come to court there may be acute problems of proof of factual causation.

[39] For other occurrences liability is confined to nuclear matter which is not excepted matter. "Nuclear matter" and "excepted matter" are defined in s.26(1).

[40] Street and Frame, *op. cit.*, p. 52.

[41] *Ibid.* p. 53. The form of the definition would seem to preclude any claim for pure economic loss.

[42] ss.12, 16.

injury or damage.[43] It is a defence that the breach of duty under the Act is attributable to hostile action in the course of any armed conflict, but it is not a defence that it is attributable to a natural disaster, notwithstanding that the disaster is of such an exceptional character that it could not reasonably have been foreseen.[44] The amount of compensation payable may be reduced by reason of the fault of the plaintiff, "but only if, and to the extent that, the causing of that injury or damage is attributable to the act of [the plaintiff] committed with the intention of causing harm to his person or property or with reckless disregard for the consequences of his act."[45] Under the Law Reform (Contributory Negligence) Act 1945 both the degree of blame-worthiness and the causative potency of the act have to be considered in reducing damages.[46] But under the 1965 Act once the plaintiff is found to be intentional or reckless within the meaning of the subsection, the amount of the reduction rests solely on the extent to which the harm is caused by the plaintiff's act.[47] If after the plaintiff has been harmed his damages are increased by his failure to have proper medical attention, this failure by him to mitigate his damage would have prevented him from recovering that portion of his loss which is attributable to his omission, and it is doubtful whether section 13(6) of the 1965 Act has a different effect.[48] It may well be that in an extreme case the plaintiff's claim will fail completely by a plea of *ex turpi causa non oritur actio*.[49] Section 12(1) provides that "where any injury or damage has been caused in breach of a duty imposed" by the Act, then subject to certain exceptions "no other liability shall be incurred by any person in respect of that injury or damage."[50] Section 15(1) enacts that "notwithstanding anything in any other enactment, a claim under the Act shall not be entertained after the expiration of 30 years from the date of the occurrence which gives rise to the claim, or, where that occurrence was a continuing one, or was one of a succession of occurrences all attributable to a particular happening" on a particular site, the date of the last event in the course of that occurrence or succession of occurrences is the relevant one. The period runs from the defendant's act, not from the infliction of damage. However, the licensee's liability is in fact limited to a period of 10 years.[51] He is required to make such provision (either by insurance or some other means) as the Minister may, with the consent of the Treasury, approve for sufficient funds to be available, generally up to a total of £20m.[52] to cover

---

[43] s.17(3). *i.e.* two or more licensees, since only a licensee can be liable under the Act.
[44] s.13(4)(*a*) and (*b*). Act of God, *e.g.* earthquake, is not a defence.
[45] s.13(6).
[46] *Ante*, pp. 165–168.
[47] Street and Frame, *op. cit.*, p. 60.
[48] *Ibid.* p. 60.
[49] *Ibid.* p. 61.
[50] *Ibid.* pp. 61–66. The effect of the subsection may be summarised as follows: "Where ionising radiations are emitted as a result of defective equipment provided under contract with the licensee by a supplier, the section, it seems, prevents a person who suffers personal injury in consequence from suing the manufacturer or supplier, however negligent they might have been. It seems to prevent the supplier from being contractually liable to indemnify the licensee against damages payable to the victim by the licensee. It may prevent licensees from invoking *Lister* v. *Romford Ice and Cold Storage Co. Ltd.* (*post*, pp. 577–579) as a means of claiming an indemnity from the employee whose negligence actually caused the emission." The operation of s.12 is unaffected by Part I of the Consumer Protection Act 1987.
[51] s.16
[52] Increased from £5m. by the Energy Act 1983, Pt. II.

compensation during this period. In other cases (where the claim exceeds the statutory limit or after the expiry of 10 years) claims are to be directed to the Government, which satisfies them out of moneys provided by Parliament.[53]

The Act applies in certain circumstances to occurrences outside the United Kingdom.[54]

Oil Pollution[55]

The Merchant Shipping (Oil Pollution) Act 1971 imposes civil liability upon the owner of a ship carrying a cargo of persistent oil in bulk for escape or discharge of persistent oil[56] from the ship. From a date to be appointed the Act is amended by the Merchant Shipping Act 1988[57] and the account here is of the Act as amended. Liability extends to damage[58] caused in the United Kingdom, the cost of any measures reasonably taken for the purpose of preventing or reducing such damage, or damage caused by any measures so taken.[59] The Act provides three defences,[60] namely, that the discharge or escape—

(i) resulted from an act of war, hostilities, civil war, insurrection or an exceptional, inevitable and irresistible natural phenomenon[61] or

(ii) was due wholly to anything done or left undone by another person, not being a servant or agent of the owner, with intent to do damage[62] or

(iii) was due wholly to the negligence or wrongful act of a government or other authority in exercising its function of maintaining lights or other navigational aids.

The Act provides a complete code of liability of shipowners for such occur-

---

[53] ss.16, 18. The United Kingdom Atomic Energy Authority is not a "licensee" within the Act but the liabilities of a licensee are imposed upon it by s.8.

[54] s.13(1); Street and Frame, *Law Relating to Nuclear Energy*, pp. 74–85.

[55] Abecassis and Jarashow, *Oil Pollution from Ships*, (2nd ed.); Garner, *Control of Pollution Encyclopaedia*, Pt. IV.

[56] Not necessarily the persistent oil in the cargo.

[57] s.34, Sch. 4.

[58] "Damage" includes "loss" (s.20(1)). *Quaere* whether it extends to personal injuries (*cf.* in Animals Act 1971, s.11). Since the 1988 amendment it is clear that hoteliers or fishermen can claim loss of profits caused by environmental pollution: s.3(3).

[59] s.1(1). By s.1(2) the cost of measures taken to avert a threatened escape is recoverable.

[60] s.2.

[61] *cf.* "act of God," *ante*, p. 43.

[62] Thus the negligent act of a third party provides no defence.

rence and any common law liability is generally abolished.[63] There are also provisions for compulsory insurance[64] and for limitation of liability.[65]

The Law Reform (Contributory Negligence) Act 1945 applies to proceedings under the Act.[66]

Poisonous Waste

The Control of Pollution Act 1974[67] provides that where any damage is caused by poisonous, noxious or polluting waste which has been deposited on land, any person who deposited it or caused or knowingly permitted it to be deposited is civilly liable for the damage,[68] provided that his act constituted an offence under section 3(3) or section 18(2) of the Act.[69] To constitute an offence under those sections the waste must have been deposited on an unlicensed site or in breach of the conditions in the licence,[70] must amount to an "environmental hazard"[71] and must have been deposited in such circumstances or for such a period that whoever deposited it there may reasonably be assumed to have abandoned it there or to have brought it there for the purpose of its being disposed as waste.[72] The Act provides the following defences to a civil action[73]:

(i) that the defendant took care to inform himself, from others who were in a position to provide the information, as to whether the deposit

---

[63] s.3. This abolition extends to the liability of servants or agents of the owner and of salvors. But such persons may be liable for acts done with intent to cause damage or done recklessly in the knowledge that damage would probably result: s.3(1)(ii). Any existing common law liability would, of course, continue to apply to the owner or master of another ship colliding with the oil carrier.

[64] s.10. See Garner, *op. cit.*, Pt. IV, para. [58]. Persons suffering damage who are unable to claim under the 1971 Act may receive compensation from the International Fund for Compensation for Oil Pollution Damage under Pt. I of the Merchant Shipping Act 1974 (also amended by the Merchant Shipping Act 1988): see Garner, *op. cit.*, Pt. IV/8. There are also various voluntary compensation schemes, known by the endearing acronyms of CRISTAL, PLATO and TOVALOP (considered by the House of Lords in *Esso Petroleum Co. Ltd.* v. *Hall Russell & Co. Ltd.* [1988] 3 W.L.R. 730).

[65] s.4. The right to limit is lost if the damage "resulted from anything done or omitted to be done by the owner with intent to cause any such damage ... or recklessly and in the knowledge that any such damage ... would probably result." This is along the lines of the general maritime limitation provision in the Merchant Shipping Act 1979. The 1971 Act as enacted contained the old limitation — breaking formula of "actual fault or privity".

[66] s.1(5). See *ante*, Chap. 6.

[67] The Act replaced the Deposit of Poisonous Wastes Act 1972. Its civil liability aspects came into force on June 14, 1976: S.I. 1976 No. 731. See generally, *Encyclopaedia of Environmental Health Law and Practice*; Garner, *Control of Pollution Encyclopaedia*, Pts. II and VII. Unlike the Merchant Shipping (Oil Pollution) Act, *supra*, this Act does not abolish other forms of liability: s.88(5).

[68] s.88 "Damage" here clearly includes personal injuries, *cf. supra*, n. 58.

[69] s.3 deals with "controlled waste", s.18 with other waste.

[70] s.3(1).

[71] Defined in s.4(5) as a situation where "the waste has been deposited in such a manner or in such a quantity (whether that quantity by itself or cumulatively with other deposits of the same or different substances) as to subject persons or animals to a material risk of death, injury or impairment of health or as to threaten the pollution (whether on the surface or underground) of any water supply." The fact that waste is deposited in containers is not of itself to be taken to exclude any risk which might be expected to arise if the waste were not in containers (s.4(5)(b); and the degree of risk of the hazards mentioned is to be assessed with particular regard "(a) to the measures, if any, taken by the person depositing the waste, or by the owner or occupier of the land, or others, for minimising the risk; and (b) to the likelihood of the waste, or any container in which it is deposited, being tampered with by children or others" (s.4(6)).

[72] s.3(3).

[73] The first three defences here mentioned are also defences to a criminal charge under the Act. However, one defence provided to a criminal charge is not available in civil proceedings: ss.3(4)(d), 88(2).

would constitute an offence and had no reason to suppose that the information given to him was false or misleading[74];

(ii) that the defendant acted under instructions from his employer and neither knew nor had reason to suppose that the deposit was unlawful[75];

(iii) in the case of an action arising from making a deposit otherwise than in accordance with conditions specified in a disposal licence, that the defendant took all such steps as were reasonably open to him to ensure that the conditions were complied with[76];

(iv) the damage was wholly due to the fault of the person who suffered it[77];

(v) the damage was suffered by a person who voluntarily accepted the risk thereof.[78]

The Law Reform (Contributory Negligence) Act 1945 applies to liability arising under the Act.[79]

---

[74] s.3(3)(*a*).
[75] s.3(3)(*b*).
[76] s.3(3)(*c*).
[77] s.88(1)(*a*).
[78] s.88(1)(*b*).
[79] s.88(4)(*b*).

CHAPTER 16

ANIMALS[1]

At common law a person might be liable for damage caused by an animal on one or more of three distinct grounds, namely, ordinary liability in tort, liability under the *scienter* rule[2] and liability for cattle trespass. The law was substantially modified with regard to two of these matters by the Animals Act 1971[3]; but its structure is still in large measure the same and it is convenient to retain the common law headings for the purposes of exposition.[4]

Ordinary Liability In Tort

There are many possible ways in which one may incur tortious liability through the instrumentality of an animal under one's control, but the fact that the agent happens to be animate rather than inanimate is immaterial, for while the common law, like other legal systems,[5] developed special or additional rules of liability for animals, it did not deny the applicability to them of the general law. A good example of this is nuisance, for you can be liable for nuisance through the agency of your animals, just as you can be for nuisance through the agency of anything else you own. A man who keeps pigs too near his neighbour's house commits a nuisance, but that is not solely because they are pigs. He would commit a nuisance just as much if what he owned were a manure heap. There is no independent tort called "nuisance by pigs," or "nuisance by animals."[6] Indeed, nuisance may be the only appropriate remedy where there is no "escape" and where the animal is not dangerous, *e.g.* obstruction of the highway by large numbers of animals,[7] or

---

[1] The common law on this topic is covered by the exhaustive monograph of Glanville Williams, *Liability for Animals*. There are about six million dogs and half a million horses in the U.K.: Cmnd. 7054, Vol. 1, para. 159.
[2] This expression is properly confined to liability for animals which do not belong to a dangerous species, but is commonly used in the wider sense used here.
[3] The Act came into force on October 1, 1971. The leading study of the modern law is North, *The Modern Law of Animals*. See too Law Commission, Civil Liability for Animals, Law Com. No. 13 (1967). The Pearson Commission recommended no change in the law: Cmnd. 7054, Vol. 1, Chap. 30.
[4] For the previous law, see the eighth edition of this work, Chap. 17, and Law Com. No. 13 (1967).
[5] See Law Com. No. 13 (1967), n. 35.
[6] *Pitcher* v. *Martin* [1937] 3 All E.R. 918 illustrates negligence and nuisance committed through the agency of a dog; *Farrer* v *Nelson* (1885) 15 Q.B.D. 258 nuisance through the agency of pheasants (distinguished in *Seligman* v. *Docker* [1949] 1 Ch. 53).
[7] *Cunningham* v. *Whelan* (1917) 52 Ir.L.T. 67.

stench from pigs[8] or the crowing of cockerels.[9] Generally there is no liability for the escape of noxious animals on the defendant's land in the ordinary course of nature, such as rabbits, rats or birds.[10] But if a landowner deliberately collects rabbits or game on his land for any purpose, he is liable for damage by them to neighbouring owners if it is caused by his "extraordinary, non-natural or unreasonable action."[11]

Again, if a dog-owner deliberately sets his dog on a peaceable citizen he is guilty of assault and battery in the ordinary way just as if he had flung a stone or hit him with a cudgel. So, too, if a man teaches his parrot to slander anyone, that is neither more nor less the ordinary tort of defamation than if he prefers to say it with his own tongue rather than with the parrot's. Similarly, ordinary trespass can be committed by means of animals. Trespass by beasts so often takes the form of "cattle trespass" (with which we deal separately) that one does not meet with many ordinary actions for trespass in the reports. However an indirect example is *Paul* v. *Summerhayes*[12] where fox hunters persisted in riding over the land of a farmer in spite of his protests and were held to have committed trespass.

Liability for animals may also be based on negligence:

"Quite apart from the liability imposed upon the owner of animals or the person having control of them by reason of knowledge of their propensities, there is the ordinary duty of a person to take care either that his animal or his chattel is not put to such a use as is likely to injure his neighbour—the ordinary duty to take care in the cases put upon negligence."[13]

In an action based upon the breach of such a duty to take care, the ordinary rules in an action of negligence apply. There is abundant authority to show that the action for negligence for harm done through animals is quite distinct from both the cattle trespass rule and the *scienter* rule.[14] In one respect, however, the common law failed to extend the principles of negligence to cases involving animals. It was the rule for centuries that if animals

---

[8] *Aldred's Case* (1610) 9 Co. 57b.

[9] *Leeman* v. *Montagu* [1936] 2 All E.R. 1677. In *Clarkson* v. *Bransford* (1987, Huddersfield County Court) the plaintiff recovered damages for nervous shock in nuisance and negligence in respect of the escape of the defendant's non-dangerous snakes from his house into hers. The defendant kept 24 snakes in the attic (Kemp & Kemp, *Quantum of Damages*, June 1987 issue).

[10] *Brady* v. *Warren* [1900] 2 Ir. 636 (rabbits); *Seligman* v. *Docker* [1949] 1 Ch. 53 (wild pheasant increasing in numbers owing to favourable weather conditions). In an extreme case, however, there might be liability under the principle of *Goldman* v. *Hargrave* (*ante*, p. 399).

[11] *Farrer* v. *Nelson* (1885) 15 Q.B.D. 258, 260 (nuisance by unreasonable number of pheasants *brought* onto the land); *Peech* v. *Best* [1931] 1 K.B. 1, 14; *Seligman* v. *Docker* [1949] 1 Ch. 53, 61–63. See Williams, *op. cit.*, pp. 235–262, for nuisance by wild animals, and (1956) 73 S.A.L.J. 335 for liability for escape of wild geese).

[12] (1878) 4 Q.B.D. 9; *League against Cruel Sports* v. *Scott* [1986] Q.B. 240.

[13] *Fardon* v. *Harcourt-Rivington* (1932) 146 L.T. 391, 392, *per* Lord Atkin; *Searle* v. *Wallbank* [1947] A.C. 341, 359–360.

[14] See *Draper* v. *Hodder* [1972] 2 Q.B. 556 (where a claim based upon *scienter* failed at the trial); *Smith* v. *Prendergast, The Times,* October 18, 1984. Similarly, a claim might in some cases be founded upon the statutory variant of negligence created by the Occupiers' Liability Act 1957. See North, *op. cit.*, pp. 176 *et seq.*

(or at least, ordinary tame animals) strayed from adjacent land on to the highway neither the owner of the animals nor the occupier of the land was liable for any ensuing damage even though it could have been prevented by controlling the animal or by fencing.[15] This immunity has now been abolished by the Animals Act 1971,[16] so that where damage is caused by animals straying on the highway the question of liability is to be decided in accordance with the ordinary principles of negligence. It is provided, however, that if a person has a right to place animals on unfenced land, he is not to be regarded as in breach of a duty of care by reason only of his placing them there, so long as the land is in an area where fencing is not customary or is common land or a town or village green.[17] It is important to note that the Act does *not* require all landowners to fence against the highway: in moorland areas of Wales and the north of England this would be an intolerable burden and in such areas a motorist must be expected to be on the look out for straying livestock.[18]

LIABILITY FOR DANGEROUS ANIMALS

At common law the keeper of an animal was strictly liable, independently of negligence, for damage done by the animal if (*a*) the animal was *ferae naturae* (*i.e.* belonged to a dangerous species) or (*b*) the animal was *mansuetae naturae* (*i.e.* did not belong to a dangerous species) and he knew of its vicious characteristics.[19] These forms of strict liability have been retained by the Animals Act 1971 and, though they have been subjected to considerable modification, much of the old learning will continue to be relevant. It is, however, important to remember that the only source of the law is now the words of the Act and these must always prevail.

Animals belonging to a dangerous species

Where any damage is caused by an animal which belongs to a dangerous species, any person who is a keeper of the animal is liable for the damage.[20] A dangerous species is defined as "a species[21] (*a*) which is not commonly

---

[15] *Searle* v. *Wallbank* [1947] A.C. 341. The applicability of the rule to South Australia was confirmed by the majority of the court in *State Govt. Insurance Commission* v. *Trigwell* (1979) 26 A.L.R. 67; but the rule has been reversed by statute in most Australian jurisdictions. See Clarke (1985) 34 I.C.L.Q. 786. For other cases see the eighth edition of this work. The immunity had no application where the animal was brought on to the highway and then got out of control: *Gomberg* v. *Smith* [1963] 1 Q.B. 25.

[16] s.8, which Lord Hailsham L.C. referred to as "the only [section] which it is really worth enacting": Hansard, H.L., Vol. 312, cols. 887–888.

[17] s.8(2). Like many "by reason only" exceptions, this subsection is a fertile source of difficulties. Even without it, the owner would not be liable by reason *only* of placing his animals there, for there would have to be sufficient traffic to create a serious danger. For various problems of interpretation, see North, *op. cit.*, pp. 157–160. The subsection was applied in *Davies* v. *Davies* [1975] Q.B. 172 (see (1974) 124 N.L.J. 683, 774) but the case turned largely on the right of a commoner to license others to graze animals.

[18] For statistics on road accidents involving animals see Law Com. No. 13 (1967), paras. 49–52. Dogs are in fact the major culprits apart, of course, from car drivers.

[19] See Law Com. No. 13 (1967), paras. 4–9.

[20] s.2(1). For the definition of "keeper," see below.

[21] By s.11 "species" includes sub-species and variety: see further *infra*, n. 28.

domesticated in the British Islands and (b) whose fully grown animals normally have such characteristics that they are likely, unless restrained, to cause severe damage or that any damage they may cause is likely to be severe."[22] A number of points arise on this definition. First, it seems that as was the case at common law in classifying animals as "*ferae naturae*," the question of whether an animal belongs to a dangerous species is one of law for the court. It is therefore to be expected that where an animal had been classified as *ferae naturae* at common law it will be regarded as belonging to a dangerous species under the Act (*e.g.* a lion,[23] an elephant[24] and at least certain types of monkeys[25]). In two respects, however, the definition is wider than at common law in that the Act (a) renders a species dangerous if it poses a threat to property[26] and (b) allows for a species to be considered dangerous if it is not commonly domesticated in Britain, *even though it may be so domesticated overseas*.[27] Secondly it will remain the case that once a species has been judicially classified as dangerous, then, subject to the doctrine of precedent, there is no room for distinctions based upon the fact that some variants or individual animals within the species may not in fact be at all dangerous: in other words, the law continues to ignore "the world of difference between the wild elephant in the jungle and the trained elephant in the circus . . . [which] is in fact no more dangerous than a cow."[28] Thirdly, the Act clearly adopts as the test of danger *either* "the greater risk of harm" *or* "the risk of greater harm": an elephant may not in fact be very likely to get out of control and do damage, but *if* it does so, its bulk gives it a great capacity for harm.

For the purposes of this form of liability a person is a "keeper" of the animal if "(a) he owns the animal or has it in his possession; or (b) he is the head of a household of which a member under the age of 16 owns the animal or has it in his possession; and if at any time an animal ceases to be owned by or to be in the possession of a person, any person who immediately before

---

[22] s.6(2).

[23] *Murphy* v. *Zoological Society of London* [1962] C.L.Y. 68.

[24] *Behrens* v. *Bertram Mills Circus Ltd.* [1957] 2 Q.B. 1.

[25] Hale 1 P.C. 101; *cf. Brook* v. *Cooke* (1961) 105 S.J. 684. As to other animals see Williams, *op. cit.*, pp. 292–294. Bees are not *ferae naturae* at common law: *Stormer* v. *Ingram* (1978) 21 S.A.S.R. 93. The Dangerous Wild Animals Act 1976 provides for a system of licensing of keepers of dangerous wild animals. Such animals are those listed in the Sched. to the Act and it is thought that such listing would be almost conclusive on the issue of whether the animal belonged to a dangerous species under the 1971 Act (none of the listed animals appears to be commonly domesticated here). Omission from the list should not, however, be particularly persuasive that the animal is not dangerous under the 1971 Act. Species such as the buffalo and hippopotamus were omitted because it was not thought likely that any attempt would be made to keep them privately (H.L. Vol. 371, Col. 1180) and the same presumably applied to the elephant and the camel. Under the 1976 Act the local authority must specify, as a condition of the grant of a licence, that the keeper maintains a liability insurance policy: s.(6)(a)(iv), (v). There is also compulsory insurance under the Riding Establishments Acts 1964 and 1970.

[26] The definition of "damage" in s.11 is not exhaustive, but does, it is submitted, include damage to property: see Law Com. No. 13 (1967), para. 15(iii).

[27] Thus a camel is dangerous under the Act, though not *ferae naturae* at common law: *Tutin* v. *Chipperfield Promotions Ltd.* (1980) 130 N.L.J. 807, not following *McQuaker* v. *Goddard* [1940] 1 K.B. 687 (which probably applied the wrong test at common law, anyway).

[28] *Behrens* v. *Bertram Mills Circus Ltd.*, *supra*, at p. 14. However, it is not clear to what extent the common law was prepared to distinguish among sub-species and the same problem will arise under the Act: see North, *op. cit.*, pp. 36–38.

that time was a keeper thereof . . . continues to be a keeper of the animal until another person becomes a keeper thereof . . . "[29]

Other animals

Section 2(2)[30] provides:

"Where damage is caused by an animal which does not belong to a dangerous species, a keeper of the animal is liable for the damage . . . if:

(a) the damage is of a kind which the animal, unless restrained, was likely to cause or which, if caused by the animal, was likely to be severe; and

(b) the likelihood of the damage or of its being severe was due to characteristics of the animal which are not normally found in animals of the same species or are not normally so found except at particular times or in particular circumstances; and

(c) Those characteristics were known to that keeper or were at any time known to a person who at that time had charge of the animal as that keeper's servant or, where that keeper is the head of a household, were known to another keeper of the animal who is a member of that household and under the age of sixteen."

The purpose of this somewhat complex provision is to preserve, with some modifications, the old rule of *scienter* liability for tame animals. Paragraph (a) follows the pattern of section 2(1) in adopting likelihood of injury or likelihood that any injury that may be caused will be severe. Paragraph (b), however, is likely to give rise to difficulty with its concept of "abnormal" characteristics, if only because it may be so difficult to determine the "normal" characteristics of a species.[31] In a case like *Barnes* v. *Lucille Ltd.*,[32] where the plaintiff was bitten by a bitch with pups, he would still presumably succeed, since the "normal" bitch is aggressive only at such times. A more difficult case would be *Fitzgerald* v. *A.D. and E.D. Cooke Bourne Farms Ltd.*[33] where the plaintiff's injuries were inflicted by the frolics of a young filly, behaviour which is perfectly normal for such animals. However, it may be that the norm here is "horse" not "filly" so that the frolicsomeness would be a characteristic found only at a particular time, *viz.* during the animal's youth.[34]

The requirement of knowledge in paragraph (c) is clearly of "actual"

---

[29] s.6(3). It is provided, however, by s.6(4) that where an animal is taken into and kept in possession for the purpose of preventing it from causing damage or of restoring it to its owner, a person is not a keeper of it by virtue only of that possession.

[30] "Remarkably opaque language": Ormrod L.J. in *Cummings* v. *Grainger* [1977] Q.B. 397, 407.

[31] See North, *op. cit.*, pp. 49–54.

[32] (1907) 96 L.T. 680. See also *Cummings* v. *Grainger* [1977] Q.B. (untrained alsatian used as a guard dog in enclosed yard); Jackson (1977) 40 M.L.R. 590.

[33] [1964] 1 Q.B. 249. With respect there is room for the view that the Court of Appeal was too tender to fillies and too hard on "timorous persons, unused to horses."

[34] *Wallace* v. *Newton* [1982] 1 W.L.R. 375 where, however, the horse ("Lord Justice") was fully grown.

rather than of constructive knowledge, though a person who ought to know of his animal's vicious characteristics may, of course, still be liable for negligence. In some cases the knowledge is imputed to the keeper by process of law under paragraph (c), but this does not mean that knowledge of a person not mentioned in that paragraph will be irrelevant: if, for example, the wife of the keeper has knowledge of the animal's propensities it may be proper for the court to infer as a matter of fact that the keeper also knew of them.[35]

It should be noted with regard to both types of dangerous animals, that the Act, unlike the common law,[36] contains no requirement that the animal must escape from control, nor that there must be any sort of attack.[37] If, therefore, an elephant slips or stumbles or a sheep transmits a virulent disease to another's flock, strict liability will apply.

The definition of "keeper" for this head of liability is the same as that for animals belonging to a dangerous species.

Defences

The Act provides that it is a defence to an action brought under section 2 that the damage was wholly due to the fault of the person suffering it[38] or that he voluntarily assumed the risk thereof[39] (though a person employed as a servant by a keeper of the animal is not to be treated as accepting voluntarily risks incidental to his employment[40]). Contributory negligence, is, of course, a partial defence.[41]

There is special provision for injury to trespassers by dangerous animals. Section 5(3) provides that a person is not liable under section 2 for any damage by an animal "kept on any premises or structure[42] to a person trespassing there, if it is proved either (a) that the animal was not kept there for the protection[43] of persons or property; or (b) (if the animal was kept there for the protection of persons or property) that keeping it there for that purpose was not unreasonable." It would seem unreasonable to protect your premises with a lion or a cobra, but not, perhaps, with a fierce dog.[44] This subsection does not, of course, affect any liability for negligence which the defendant may incur *qua* occupier of the premises or keeper of the animal,

---

[35] As in *Gladman* v. *Johnson* (1867) 36 L.J.C.P. 153.
[36] *Behrens* v. *Bertram Mills Circus Ltd., supra*, at p. 19; *Fitzgerald* v. *A.D. and E.H. Cooke Bourne Farms Ltd., supra*, at p. 270; Williams, *op. cit.*, p. 341.
[37] *Wallace* v. *Newton* [1982] 1 W.L.R. 375.
[38] s.5(1).
[39] s.5(2). The Unfair Contract Terms Act 1977 does not apply to the strict liability under the 1971 Act.
[40] s.6(5). See North, *op. cit.*, pp. 73–76.
[41] s.10.
[42] Not necessarily animals owned or kept by the occupier.
[43] This probably does not have to be a dominant purpose. Thus the old lady who keeps a dog partly for companionship and partly for protection would fail on (a), though her conduct would certainly be reasonable under (b).
[44] So held in *Cummings* v. *Grainger* [1977] Q.B. 397. "True it was a fierce dog. But why not? A gentle dog would be no good. The thieves would soon make friends with him": *ibid.* at p. 405, *per* Lord Denning M.R. Since 1975 it is an offence to have a guard dog roaming about premises unless under the control of a handler: Guard Dogs Act 1975. This only gives rise to criminal liability but it has been suggested that contravention might make the keeping unreasonable under the 1971 Act: *Cummings* v. *Grainger, supra*.

but it is thought that the keeping of guard dogs is consistent with the occupier's duty to trespassers,[45] provided at least some warning of their presence is given.

LIABILITY FOR STRAYING LIVESTOCK

At common law the possessor of "cattle"[46] was strictly liable, independently of *scienter*, for damage done by them when they trespassed on the land of his neighbour.[47] Whatever may have been the original *rationale* of this form of liability, it was certainly not the same as that of *scienter*, for agricultural animals present no peculiar risk. However, the Law Commission recommend the retention of strict liability for this type of harm on the ground that it provided a simple method of allocating liability for what were usually comparatively small damages.[48] The law was, however, in need of considerable modification and the modern form of "cattle trespass" is found in section 4 of the Act, which provides:

"(1) Where livestock[49] belonging[50] to any person strays[51] on to land in the ownership or occupation of another and—

(*a*) damage is done by the livestock to the land or to any property on it[52] which is in the ownership or possession of the other person[53]; or

(*b*) any expenses[54] are reasonably incurred by that other person in keeping the livestock while it cannot be restored to the person to whom it belongs or while it is detained in pursuance of section 7 of [the] Act,[55] or in ascertaining to whom it belongs;

the person to whom the livestock belongs is liable for the damage or expenses, except as otherwise provided by [the] Act."

Defences to strict liability for straying livestock

The Act provides that there is no liability under this head for damage

---

[45] See *ante*, p. 225.

[46] "Cattle" or *avers* was a class virtually identical with livestock under the Act: see *infra*, n. 49.

[47] See Williams, *op. cit.*, 2 and 3.

[48] Law Com. No. 13 (1967), paras. 62–63.

[49] Defined in s.11 as "cattle, horses, asses, mules, hinnies, sheep, pigs, goats and poultry [which is further defined as the domestic varieties of fowls, turkeys, geese, ducks, guinea-fowls, pigeons, peacocks and quails] and also deer not in the wild state."

[50] By s.4(2) livestock belongs to the person in whose possession it is. Finance companies owning herds under hire-purchase agreements may therefore rest easy in their corporate beds.

[51] The marginal note to s.4 refers to "trespassing," but the enacting words do not. "Stray" is probably wide enough to cover the facts of *Ellis* v. *Loftus Iron Co.* [1874] L.R. 10 C.P. 10: *Wiseman* v. *Booker* (1878) 3 C.P.D. 184.

[52] Notwithstanding the general definition of "damage" in s.11, it is submitted that the words of this paragraph make it clear beyond argument that damages are not recoverable for personal injuries under this section and *Wormald* v. *Cole* [1954] 1 Q.B. 614 is no longer law.

[53] The range of potential plaintiffs and their claimable losses is, with regard to property, rather wider than at common law: see North *op. cit.*, pp. 94–96.

[54] A local authority operating a pound for animals straying on its land may properly impose a standard charge: *Morris* v. *Blaenau Gwent D.C.* (1982) 80 L.G.R. 793.

[55] See *post*, p. 462.

which is due wholly to the fault of the person suffering it[56] and that contributory negligence is a partial defence.[57] In this context default of the plaintiff is often closely bound up with fencing obligations and the Act therefore provides that damage:

" . . . shall not be treated as due to the fault of the person suffering it by reason only that he could have prevented it by fencing; but [the defendant] is not liable . . . where it is proved that the straying of the livestock on to the land would not have occurred but for a breach by any other person, being a person having an interest in the land, of a duty to fence."[58]

One other common law defence is preserved by the Act: the defendant is not liable under this form of liability if his livestock strayed on to the plaintiff's property from the highway and its presence there was a lawful use[59] of the highway.[60] An example of this principle is the decision in *Tillet* v. *Ward*.[61] X owned an ox which, while his servants were driving it with due care through a town, entered the shop of Y, an ironmonger, through an open door. It took three quarters of an hour to get it out and meanwhile it did some damage. X was held not liable to Y, for this was one of the inevitable risks of driving cattle on the streets. It would have made no difference if the ironmonger's door had been shut instead of open, and the ox had pushed its way through, or had gone through a plateglass window.[62]

Detention and sale of straying livestock

The common law provided a form of self-help remedy to a person harmed by straying livestock by way of distress damage feasant.[63] The Law Commission concluded that some remedy of this type should be retained but considered that the old remedy was so hedged about with limitations (in particular, it provided no power of sale) and obscurities that it would be better to create a new, statutory right. This is found in section 7 of the Act, which may be summarised as follows:

[56] s.5(1).
[57] s.10.
[58] s.5(6). The law relating to the obligation to fence is notoriously complex and the Law Commission thought it inappropriate to deal with it other than by providing a relatively simple rule: Law Com. No. 13 (1967), n. 98. It should be noted that there is no requirement under s.5(6) that the duty in question be owed to the defendant. For a detailed comparison of s.5(6) with the common law position, see North, *op. cit.*, Chap. 4.
[59] Hence the defence is inapplicable if the animals had been allowed to stray on to the highway: *Matthews* v. *Wicks, The Times*, May 25, 1987.
[60] s.5(5). This does not, of course, remove any liability for negligence in such a case: *Gayler and Pope Ltd.* v. *Davies & Son Ltd.* [1924] 2 K.B. 75.
[61] (1882) 10 Q.B.D. 17.
[62] *Gayler and Pope Ltd.* v. *Davies & Son Ltd.* [1924] 2 K.B. 75. The driver of beasts which stray without his fault into property adjoining the highway is entitled to enter the property in order to get them out, and for that purpose he must be allowed such time as is reasonable in the circumstances: *Goodwin* v. *Cheveley* (1895) 28 L.J. Ex. 298.
[63] See Williams, *op. cit.*, Pt. I.

(i) The right of distress damage feasant is abolished in relation to animals.[64]

(ii) The occupier of land may detain any livestock which has strayed[65] on to his land and which is not then under the control of any person.[66]

(iii) He has, within 48 hours of exercising the right of detention, to give notice to the police and, if he knows the person to whom the livestock belongs, to that person.[67]

(iv) The right to detain the livestock ceases[68] if:

    (*a*) the detainer has not complied with the provisions regarding notice; or

    (*b*) the detainer is tendered sufficient money to satisfy any claim he may have for damage and expenses in respect of the straying livestock[69]; or

    (*c*) he has no such claim and the person to whom the livestock belongs claims it.

(v) The detainer is liable for any damage caused to the livestock by failure to treat it with reasonable care and supply it with adequate food and water.

(vi) Where the livestock has been rightfully detained for not less than 14 days, the person detaining it may sell it at a market or by public auction, unless proceedings are then pending for the return of the livestock or for any claim for damages done by it or expenses incurred in detaining it.[69]

(vii) Where the net proceeds of sale exceed the amount of any claim the detainer may have for damages and expenses, the excess is recoverable from him by the person who would be entitled to the livestock but for the sale.[70]

REMOTENESS OF DAMAGE AND STRICT LIABILITY UNDER THE ACT

The Animals Act contains no provisions relating to remoteness of damage. At common law both forms of *scienter* liability and cattle trespass had close affinities with *Rylands* v. *Fletcher* and were probably governed by the remoteness principle applicable to that rule—was the consequence a "natural" one, a question of causation. There were, however, at least two exceptions to the generality of this principle. First, in the case of *scienter* liability for animals *mansuetae naturae*, the keeper was only liable if the

---

[64] The right is therefore abolished for *all* animals and the new remedy applies only to *livestock*, for the definition of which see *supra*, n. 49. The right of distress damage feasant remains in respect of other property, but it is practically moribund.

[65] The word "strayed" *may* not be wide enough to encompass livestock which have been driven on to the land, though the condition that the animals must not be under the control of any person (see *infra*, n. 66) suggests that the draftsman meant to include such a case.

[66] This was also a condition of the exercise of the common law right and is designed to prevent breaches of the peace.

[67] As to the person to whom livestock belongs, see *supra*, n. 50.

[68] In the absence of a request for the return of the livestock, however, the detainer will not necessarily be liable for conversion.

[69] *i.e.* under s.4.

[70] Presumably, if the net proceeds are *not* sufficient to meet the claim the detainer may sue for the excess. Further, the section makes no provision for the case where a detainer with no claim for damages or expenses exercises the power of sale which the section undoubtedly confers on him: the only sensible solution is to make him hold the proceeds on trust for the owner. These solutions, however, involve a fairly robust interpretation of the Act: North, *op. cit.*, pp. 119–120.

animal caused some harm of the kind to be expected from its known vicious characteristics[71]; secondly, in the case of cattle trespass, there was a rule that the damage had to be in accordance with the natural characteristics of the animal.[72] The position under the Act is to some extent speculative. The rule in *Rylands* v. *Fletcher* was not considered in *The Wagon Mound (No. 1)*, though it has been argued elsewhere in this book that there is no reason for refusing to apply the principles of foreseeability as developed since *The Wagon Mound*.[73] If this is correct, those principles should also be applicable to the Animals Act.[74] However, the form of section 2(2) means that with regard to liability for animals not belonging to a dangerous species the position will be fundamentally the same as at common law, since the damage must be of a kind made likely by the characteristics known to the keeper.[75] As for animals belonging to a dangerous species, a camel has been held to be such because it may cause severe injury by kicking and biting, but strict liability was imposed for injuries suffered by falling off the camel because of its irregular gait.[76] Whether or not any special rule survives for trespassing cattle is not likely to be of any importance now that damages for personal injuries cannot be recovered under that head.[77]

PROTECTION OF LIVESTOCK AGAINST DOGS

Liability for attacks on livestock

Section 3 of the Animals Act re-enacted, with some modification, the form of strict liability formerly found in the Dogs Acts 1906–1928 and provides that where a dog causes damage by killing or injuring livestock,[78] any person who is a keeper[79] of the dog is liable for the damage.[80] The Act provides the following defences: that the damage was wholly due to the fault of the person suffering it[81]; that that person voluntarily accepted the risk of the damage[82]; and that the livestock was killed or injured on land on which it had strayed and either the dog belonged to the occupier or its presence on the land was authorised by the occupier.[83] Contributory negligence is a partial defence.[84]

---

[71] See Williams, *op. cit.*, p. 301. If, however, the animal committed a "direct" wrong of the type to be expected, the keeper was probably liable for other losses stemming from that injury, *e.g.* a disease caught from the bite of a vicious dog: Williams, p. 320.
[72] *Wormald* v. *Cole* [1954] 1 Q.B. 614.
[73] *Ante*, p. 440.
[74] *cf.* North, *op. cit.*, pp. 47, 58, 107–108.
[75] See *ante*, p. 459.
[76] *Tutin* v. *Chipperfield Promotions Ltd.* (1980) 130 N.L.J. 807.
[77] *Supra*, n. 52.
[78] "Livestock" for this purpose is slightly wider than under s.4, including pheasants, partridges and grouse in captivity: s.11.
[79] "Keeper" has the same meaning as in s.2: see *supra*, n. 29.
[80] s.3. See North, *op. cit.*, Chap. 7.
[81] s.5(1).
[82] s.5(2).
[83] s.5(4).
[84] s.10.

Killing or injuring dogs to protect livestock

It may, in certain circumstances, be lawful for a person to kill or injure an animal belonging to another if this is necessary for the protection of his livestock or crops. The common law rule on this was laid down by the Court of Appeal in *Cresswell* v. *Sirl*[85] but this rule has been replaced, so far as the protection of livestock against dogs is concerned,[86] by section 9 of the Animals Act.

It is a defence[87] to an action for killing or injuring a dog to prove that:

(i) the defendant acted for the protection of livestock[88] and was a person entitled so to act; and

(ii) within 48 hours thereafter notice was given to the officer in charge of a police station.

A person is entitled to act for the protection of livestock if either the livestock or the land on which it is belongs[89] to him or to any person under whose express or implied authority he is acting[90]; and he is deemed to be acting for their protection if and only if,[91] either:

(a) the dog is worrying or is about to worry the livestock and there are not other reasonable means of ending or preventing the worrying; or

(b) the dog has been worrying livestock, has not left the vicinity and is not under the control of any person and there are no practicable means of ascertaining to whom it belongs.[92]

---

[85] [1948] 1 K.B. 241.

[86] The rule in *Cresswell* v. *Sirl* continues to govern in the case of animals other than dogs, *e.g.* pigeons damaging crops, as in *Hamps* v. *Darby* [1948] 2 K.B. 311. See the eighth edition of this work, pp. 761–762.

[87] But not the only defence. A defendant who fails to make out the statutory defence (*e.g.* because he has not informed the police) may presumably fall back on the common law.

[88] For the definition in this context, see *supra*, n. 78.

[89] For this purpose an animal belongs to a person if he owns it or has it in his possession and land belongs to the occupier thereof: s.9(5).

[90] But if the livestock have strayed on to the land of another, there is no right under this section to shoot a dog which is lawfully on that land: s.9(2)(*b*).

[91] But the two following conditions are satisfied by reasonable belief on the defendant's part: s.9(4).

[92] This right to take punitive action in respect of an attack which is over is the major difference between s.9 and *Cresswell* v. *Sirl*.

CHAPTER 17

INTERFERENCE WITH GOODS

ENGLISH law governing remedies for interference with goods is exceedingly technical, partly because of the long survival and overlap of a number of different heads of liability and partly because the law, though tortious in form, is largely proprietary in function.[1] The Torts (Interference with Goods) Act 1977[2] has made some simplification by abolishing one head of liability but it is only a piecemeal attempt to deal with certain deficiencies in the common law and is in no way a code governing interference with goods.[3] Accordingly, the law must still be sought mainly in the decisions of the courts and it is impossible to give an intelligible account of the developed law without a brief historical sketch.

The most obvious forms of interference, such as removing or damaging the goods, were covered in early law by trespass *de bonis asportatis*, the forerunner of the modern "trespass to goods." Trespass was (and still is) essentially a wrong to possession[4] and the defendant need not have asserted any right to deal with the goods or indulged in any "appropriation" of them.[5] Trespass was obviously unsuitable to deal with the case where the owner had voluntarily put his goods into another's possession and the other refused to re-deliver them, but this situation was covered by the remedy of detinue.[6] In neither form of action could the plaintiff be sure of recovering his goods *in specie* since the judgment in trespass was for damages and in detinue gave the defendant the option of giving up the goods or paying damages but it is unlikely that this was considered a defect[7] and it should be noted that the

---

[1] See Weir, *Casebook on Tort* (6th ed.), Pt. VI, Introduction.

[2] Parts of the Act dealing with disposal of uncollected goods came into force on January 1, 1978 (S.I. 1977 No. 1910). The parts which are the principal concern of this chapter came into force on June 1, 1978 (S.I. 1978 No. 579).

[3] The Act is based upon the Report of the Law Reform Committee, Cmnd. 4774 (1971). See Bentley (1972) 35 M.L.R. 171. The Report proposed rather more thoroughgoing reforms than the Act in fact produces.

[4] See *post*, p. 469.

[5] An alternative form of action for unlawful taking was replevin. This was originally a tenant's remedy for wrongful distress by his lord. By the fifteenth century it had become available for other forms of unlawful taking (Y.B. 19 Henry 6, 65 (Pasch. 5)) but in practice has tended to be used only for unlawful distress.

[6] Detinue was thus based upon the *right* to possession and its connection with bailment gave it a strong contractual flavour. However, "the medieval writ lay across the categories of modern analysis, and to force it into one or other of them is to be guilty of anachronism": Fifoot, *History and Sources of the Common Law*, p. 25.

[7] Pollock and Maitland, *History of English Law*, ii, pp. 181–182. The attitude of the law seems to have been based partly on the fact that medieval movables were often so perishable that the court could not undertake the responsibility of enforcing their restoration and partly on the view that all things had a legal "price": Maitland, *Forms of Action*, p. 48.

remedy of specific restitution of chattels has remained unusual right up to modern times.[8] However, detinue was open to the very serious objection from the plaintiff's point of view that the defendant could insist on the method of trial known as wager of law, *i.e.* getting compurgators to swear that they believed him to be oathworthy, although they knew nothing of the facts of the case. This was the principal reason for the remarkable development whereby detinue was all but wiped out by the encroachment of trover.[9] Trover began as an action of trespass upon the case in which it was alleged that the defendant had converted the plaintiff's goods to his own use. By the mid-sixteenth century it had emerged as a distinct species of case involving four allegations.[10] It was alleged (*a*) that the plaintiff was possessed of the goods; (*b*) that he accidentally lost them; (*c*) that the defendant found them[11]; (*d*) that the defendant converted them to his own use.[12] The losing and finding were soon treated as pure fictions and the defendant was not allowed to deny them.[13] The new remedy rapidly encroached upon the spheres of trespass and replevin so that at one time it looked as if any "asportation" or moving of the property might be regarded not only as a trespass to it but also conversion of it, but this very wide doctrine was restricted to a principle that the dealing with the goods must amount to a denial of the owner's title. Trover became a complete alternative to replevin despite the fact that it could be argued that, the goods being regarded as in the custody of the law, the distraint did not amount to a denial of the owner's title.

The difficulty in extending trover to cases covered by detinue was that conversion could only be committed by a positive act—misfeasance as opposed to nonfeasance. Detinue lay where a man was in possession of another's goods and refused to give them up but could it be said that such a mere refusal was a positive act? The line between misfeasance and nonfeasance is apt to be a fine one and the courts after some hesitation took advantage of this and held mere refusal to redeliver to be conversion.[14] Detinue, with its procedural disadvantages, wilted considerably under this treatment though it retained a place in the law because inability to redeliver as a result of loss or destruction of the goods could not amount to a positive denial of title for the purposes of conversion.[15]

Nineteenth-century legislation swept away the fictions upon which trover

---

[8] See *post*, p. 491.

[9] Another deficiency of detinue was that if the chattel had been damaged in the bailee's hands he could satisfy the judgment by opting to return the damaged chattel. This was met, however, by allowing an action on the case, the ancestor of the modern "bailee's liability." Accidental damage or destruction was never absorbed into trover.

[10] Holdsworth, *History of English Law*, iii, pp. 285–287, 350–351, 450, 581–584; vii, pp. 403–513; viii, pp. 466–468; ix, p. 42; Milsom, "Not Doing is no Trespass" [1954] C.L.J. 105, 114; Simpson, "The Introduction of The Action on the Case for Conversion" (1959) 75 L.Q.R. 364.

[11] This seems to have been borrowed from the earlier form of detinue *sur trover* which, unlike detinue *sur bailment*, "had no ancestry in debt, and no trace of contract": Milsom, *Historical Foundations of the Common Law*, p. 327.

[12] Rastell, Entries (1596) 4b–5a.

[13] *Gumbleton* v. *Grafton* (1600) Cro. Eliz. 781 (losing); *Isaack* v. *Clark* (1614) 2 Bulstrode 306 (finding).

[14] Holdsworth, *op. cit.*, vii, pp. 405–415.

[15] *Owen* v. *Lewyn* (1673) 1 Ventris 223.

was based and it became the modern action for conversion, though no change was made in the substance of the law. The abolition of the wager of law in 1833 caused some revival in detinue but in view of the expansion of conversion, detinue only really remained necessary where the defendant was *unable* to redeliver the goods. The process of simplification has now been carried a stage further by section 2 of the Torts (Interference with Goods) Act 1977[16] which abolishes detinue and provides that conversion now also covers the only case that was probably formerly the exclusive province of detinue—*i.e.* inability to redeliver goods as a result of their loss or destruction.[17] It may be questioned whether this change achieves very much of a practical nature since (*a*) one still needs to look back at the common law of detinue to determine what constitutes the new form of conversion and (*b*) there still survive two torts of interference with property which have a considerable overlap with conversion, *i.e.* trespass to goods and replevin.[18]

TRESPASS TO GOODS

Trespass to goods is a wrongful physical interference with them. It may take innumerable forms, such as scratching the panel of a coach,[19] removing a tyre from a car,[20] or the car itself from a garage,[21] or, in the case of animals, beating[22] or killing[23] them. Putting out poison for an animal to take[24] is probably not trespass since the interference is not direct, a requirement of all true forms of trespass.[25] A defendant engaging in such conduct would, of course, be liable if injury to the animals ensued but his liability would be in what was classified before the abolition of the forms of action as case rather than trespass. Despite the fact that trespass is actionable *per se*, there is some authority to the effect that trespass to goods requires proof of some damage or asportation[26] but the general view of textbook writers is to the contrary[27]

[16] For commencement see *supra*, n. 2.

[17] See *post*, p. 477.

[18] The Law Reform recommended a new, all-embracing tort of "wrongful interference with chattels" (Cmnd. 4774 (1971)). The Act does use this terminology (see s.1) but only as a convenient label for the various reforms made by it on ancillary matters; it certainly does not merge the three torts of conversion, trespass and replevin.

[19] Alderson B. in *Foulders* v. *Willoughby* (1841) 8 M. & W. 538, 549.

[20] *G.W.K. Ltd.* v. *Dunlop Rubber Ltd.* (1926) 42 T.L.R. 376, 593.

[21] *Wilson* v. *Lombank Ltd.* [1963] 1 W.L.R. 1294.

[22] *Slater* v. *Swann* (1730) 2 Stra. 872.

[23] *Sheldrick* v. *Abery* (1793) 1 Esp. 55.

[24] As opposed to forcing it down its throat.

[25] Clerk and Lindsell, *Torts* (16th ed.), para. 22–119; Street, *Torts* (8th ed.), p. 59. The American *Restatement* 2d s.217, Comment, while abandoning the distinction between direct and indirect harm, appears to accept that it represents the common law. Previous editions of this work took the contrary view but it is doubtful if the authorities cited (some of them on the different tort of cattle trespass) really carry the point. This is not, however, to say that the rule now stated in the text is a more desirable one: see the comment of the Law Reform Committee in its eighteenth Report, *loc. cit.*, para. 21. Chasing animals seems to be a borderline case: on the one hand, there is no physical contact; on the other hand, chasing *humans* has always been accepted as assault, a variety of trespass. The better view is that chasing animals probably is trespass, and this gains some support from *Farmer* v. *Hunt* (1610) 1 Brownl. 220 and *Durant* v. *Childe* (1611) 1 Brownl. 221.

[26] *Everitt* v. *Martin* [1953] N.Z.L.R. 29; *Slater* v. *Swann* (1730) 2 Stra. 872.

[27] Clerk and Lindsell, *Torts* (16th ed.), para. 22–119; Salmond and Heuston, *Torts* (19th ed.), p. 105; Street, *Torts* (8th ed.), p. 60; Pollock, *Torts* (15th ed.), pp. 264–265. See also *Leitch & Co. Ltd.* v. *Leydon* [1931] A.C. 90, 106, *per* Lord Blanesburgh.

and there must be many instances where, if mere touching of objects like waxworks or exhibits in a gallery or museum be not trespass, their possessor would be without remedy. Where, however, the touching is not intentional the law may well be otherwise. Diplock L.J. has said that actual damage is an essential ingredient in unintentional trespass to the person[28] and if this is so there is no reason for distinguishing the case of trespass to goods. Certainly, the considerations of policy which point to making intentional meddling actionable even without damage have no application to unintended contacts.

Assuming that some damage has been caused, is negligence necessary for liability for unintentional trespass to goods? The answer is clearly yes[29] but the traditional view is that once a direct injury has been proved the defendant bears the burden of proving "inevitable accident"[30] as a defence. However, since the decision in *Fowler* v. *Lanning*,[31] which held that in an action for unintentional trespass to the person the plaintiff must prove negligence on the part of the defendant the same may be true of cases of trespass to goods, though the matter cannot be regarded as finally settled. A more extreme view, but one not without its attractions, is that in the modern law trespass to goods is confined to intentional interference and that negligent interference is remediable only by the tort of negligence.[32] Trespass, however, obviously remains appropriate where one takes another's goods in the mistaken belief that he is entitled to do so, for the act is intentional towards the goods.[33] In *Wilson* v. *Lombank Ltd.*[34] the plaintiff had "purchased" a car from a person who had no title to it and had sent it to a garage for repair. The defendant, believing, wrongly, that the car was his, removed it from the garage. It was held that the defendant was liable in trespass.[35]

Possession essential

As trespass is an interference with possession, it follows that if the plaintiff were not in possession at the date of the alleged meddling, he cannot sue for trespass. He may be able to sue for conversion, but that is a different matter.

[28] *Letang* v. *Cooper* [1965] 1 Q.B. 232, 244–245, *ante*, p. 71.
[29] *National Coal Board* v. *Evans* [1951] 2 K.B. 861.
[30] See generally *post*, p. 702.
[31] [1959] 1 Q.B. 426; *ante*, pp. 70–71.
[32] In *Letang* v. *Cooper, supra*, Lord Denning at p. 240 went so far as to say that negligence is the only cause of action for unintended injury to the person and presumably his Lordship would have said the same for unintended damage to goods. Though there are clear authorities the other way on trespass to goods (*e.g.* Br. Abr. *Trespass*, 63 (A.D. 1373); *Covell* v. *Laming* (1808) 1 Camp. 497) his Lordship was not hampered by equally clear authorities in relation to trespass to the person. In truth, once it is conceded that the burden of proof of negligence lies on the plaintiff (a point on which the court in *Letang* v. *Cooper* was unanimous) the traditional distinction between trespass and negligence loses almost all its significance and a classification like Lord Denning's, directed at the defendant's state of mind, is more satisfactory. However, some support for the view that there may still be an unintentional trespass to goods is found in the Torts (Interference with Goods) Act 1977. s.1(1)(*b*) refers to "trespass to goods" but s.11(1), dealing with contributory negligence, refers only to "intentional trespass to goods."
[33] As in the case of excessive execution. Proof of malice is unnecessary—*Moore* v. *Lambeth County Court Registrar (No. 2)* [1970] 1 Q.B. 560.
[34] [1963] 1 W.L.R. 1294; *Colwell* v. *Reeves* (1811) 2 Camp. 575; Weir, *Casebook on Tort* (6th ed.), p. 428.
[35] But see *post*, p. 482 as to the possible effect of the Torts (Interference with Goods) Act 1977 on this case.

"The distinction between the actions of trespass and trover is well settled: the former is founded on possession; the latter on property."[36]

Alleged exceptions

It is said that there are exceptions to this rule and that the following persons can sue for trespass although they had not possession—(*a*) A trustee against any third person who commits a trespass to trust chattels in the hands of the beneficiary. (*b*) An executor or administrator for trespasses committed to goods of the deceased after his death but before probate is granted to the executor or before the administrator takes out letters of administration. (*c*) The owner of a franchise (*e.g.* a right to take wreck or treasure trove) against anyone who seizes the goods before he himself can take them.[37] But it is questionable whether any of these exceptions is genuine. The language used in the authorities relating to the trustee is none too clear, but it indicates that the trustee has possession of chattels in the hands of the beneficiary, and not merely the right to possess them.[38] It does not follow from this that the beneficiary himself cannot sue, for if he holds the chattels he seems to have joint possession with the trustee.[39] Again, the executor and administrator have long been regarded as having the deceased's possession continued in them; when they assume office their title relates back to his death. They have not merely the right to possess: they are in possession.[40] Similarly, in the case of the franchise, possession is deemed to be with the owner of the franchise. In *Bailiffs of Dunwich* v. *Sterry*,[41] the plaintiffs had the right to wrecks at Dunwich and the defendant took a cask of whisky from a wreck before the plaintiffs could get it. The defendant was held liable for trespass, for "the right to the possession draws after it a constructive possession, which is sufficient to support the action."[42]

In a simple bailment determinable at will the bailor does not lose possession and may sue any wrongdoer other than his bailee[43] in trespass,[44] though the bailee also probably has sufficient possession to bring trespass.[45]

CONVERSION

Conversion at common law may be committed in so many different ways

---

[36] Lord Kenyon C.J. in *Ward* v. *Macauley* (1791) 4 T.R. 489, 490. But if the goods are damaged or destroyed, the owner out of possession will have an action formerly classified as case: *Mears* v. *London & South Western Ry.* (1862) 11 C.B. (N.S.) 850. In more modern terminology, the action for negligence is available to one who has possession *or* ownership: *ante*, p. 85.

[37] Clerk & Lindsell, *Torts* (16th ed.), para. 22–120.

[38] *White* v. *Morris* (1852) 11 C.B. 1015; *Barker* v. *Furlong* [1891] 2 Ch. 172, a case of conversion, but Romer J. approved *White* v. *Morris*.

[39] Lewin, *Trusts* (16th ed.), p. 618.

[40] *Tharpe* v. *Stallwood* (1843) 5 M. & G. 760, 770; Pollock & Wright, *Possession*, pp. 146–147.

[41] (1831) 1 B. & Ad. 831.

[42] *Ibid.* at p. 842; Pollock & Wright, *op. cit.*, p. 147.

[43] If the act is licensed by the bailee it seems it is not trespass as against the bailor: Palmer, *Bailment*, p. 122.

[44] *Lotan* v. *Cross* (1810) 2 Camp. 464.; *Ancona* v. *Rogers* (1876) 1 Ex.D. 285, 292. The authorities are discussed in *Penfolds Wines Pty. Ltd.* v. *Elliott* (1946) 74 C.L.R. 204, 214–220, 226–236, 239–244; Paton, *Bailment*, Preface, ss.3, 82; *U.S.A.* v. *Dollfus Mieg et Cie* [1952] A.C. 582, 605, 611–613; *Wilson* v. *Lombank Ltd.* [1963] 1 W.L.R. 1294.

[45] *Nicolls* v. *Bastard* (1835) 2 C.M. & R. 659, 660, *per* Parke B., *arguendo*.

that any comprehensive definition is probably impossible[46] but the connecting thread running through the cases seems to be that the wrong is committed by a dealing with the goods of a person which constitutes an unjustifiable denial of his rights in them or the assertion of rights inconsistent therewith. Thus it may be committed by wrongfully taking possession of goods, by wrongfully disposing of them, by wrongfully destroying them or simply by wrongfully refusing to give them up when demanded, for in all these cases can be traced conduct by the defendant which amounts to a denial of the plaintiff's rights or the assertion of inconsistent rights.[47] But if this element was lacking there was no conversion. Thus if a bailee negligently allows goods in his charge to be destroyed the plaintiff's loss is just the same as if the bailee had wrongfully sold them to a third party but there is no conversion because the negligent (as opposed to deliberate) destruction is not an assertion of any rights in the goods. Such conduct is now conversion by statute but this is merely for the draftsman's terminological convenience and has no effect on the concept of conversion at common law: for this reason, it must be kept separate in our analysis.

What constitutes conversion at common law

(1) *Taking possession*

Taking possession of another's goods will normally be conversion as well as being trespass, but there will be no conversion where the interference is merely temporary and is unaccompanied by any intention to exercise any rights over the goods.[48] If I snatch your hat from your head with intent to steal it, that is conversion as well as trespass, but if I throw it at another person, that is trespass only, for I am not questioning your title to it.[49] So, too, if you shift my bicycle from a public stand in order to get at your own, and forget to replace mine so that it is stolen by someone, that may be trespass, but it is not conversion.[50] It is not, however, necessary that the defendant should assert rights of ownership over the goods: taking for the purposes of acquiring a lien[51] or of temporary user[52] have been held to be conversion.

---

[46] See *Howard Perry & Co. Ltd.* v. *B.R.B.* [1980] 1 W.L.R. 1375, 1380.

[47] In many cases, such as wrongful sale of the goods, it is not necessary that the defendant be aware that he is infringing the plaintiff's rights, but merely taking the goods into one's custody, *e.g.* to transport them, is not conversion without such knowledge: see *post*, p. 486.

[48] A temporary diversion of sold goods by the seller at the behest of a third party was conversion in *The Playa Larga* [1983] 2 Lloyd's Rep. 171. *cf. 384238 Ontario Ltd.* v. *R. in Right of Canada* (1984) 8 D.L.R. (4th) 676, where conversion by temporary taking was denied in the absence of user.

[49] *Price* v. *Helyer* (1828) 4 Bing. 597; *Fouldes* v. *Willoughby* (1841) 8 M. & W. 540. But it is surely conversion if I deliberately throw it into the sea so that you cannot recover it? It is certainly theft as well as criminal damage.

[50] *cf. Bushel* v. *Miller* (1718) 1 Stra. 128.

[51] *Tear* v. *Freebody* (1858) 4 C.B.(N.S.) 228.

[52] Rolle Abr. tit. *Action Sur Case*, p. 5; *Aitken* v. *Richardson* [1967] N.Z.L.R. 65. The problem is perhaps less significant than it might seem. It is true that at common law the only form of judgment for conversion was damages representing the value of the thing (*i.e.* a forced sale) but the courts have for many years stayed actions for conversion where the defendant offers to return the property in dispute. As to the present form of judgment where goods are detained, see s.3 of the Torts (Interference with Goods) Act 1977 and *post*, p. 491.

(a) **Mere reception of goods.** Where A, without lawful authority,[53] transfers B's goods to C, the mere voluntary reception of them by C is in general conversion, however innocent C may be. This is abundantly supported by decisions with respect to receipt of goods by a buyer[54] and a receipt of a cheque by a banker,[55] and there are judicial dicta that appear to regard the rule as of general application.[56] Some qualifications of it where the defendant acts *bona fide* are discussed below.[57] A more questionable exception appeared in *Spackman* v. *Foster*[58] to the effect that receipt of goods by way of pledge did not amount to conversion even though the same receipt by way of purchase would have.[59] Whether or not this decision was ever good law it was reversed by the Torts (Interference with Goods) Act 1977.[60]

(b) **"Involuntary bailee."** Involuntary reception of goods is not conversion.[61] Such is the case of an innocent person into whose pocket a thief, in order to escape detection, inserts a purse which he has stolen from a third person. Even where the receiver knows that the thing belongs to someone else,[62] he incurs no liability by having it thrust upon him.

It is no new thing for pushing tradesmen occasionally to send unsolicited goods to persons in the hope of making a sale, but this practice developed to the extent that it came to be regarded in some quarters as a serious social problem.[63] By virtue of the Unsolicited Goods and Services Act 1971[64] the recipient of unsolicited goods is entitled in certain circumstances[65] to treat them as unconditional gifts after six months from receipt, or 30 days from notice to the sender, so long as the sender does not in the meantime take possession of them and the recipient does not unreasonably refuse to permit

[53] *Souhrada* v. *Bank of New South Wales* [1976] 2 Lloyd's Rep. 444 (N.S.W. Sup. Ct.).
[54] *Wilkinson* v. *King* (1809) 2 Camp. 335; *Farrant* v. —— (1822) 3 Stark. 130 (further reported as *Farrant* v. *Thompson*, 5 B. & Ald. 826); *Dyer* v. *Pearson* (1824) 3 B. & C. 38; *Hilbery* v. *Hatton* (1864) 2 H. & C. 822. *Ingram* v. *Little* [1961] 1 Q.B. 31 and other "mistaken identity" cases are good examples. *cf. Milford Mutual Facilities* v. *H.W. Hidson* [1962] C.L.Y. 3092.
[55] *Fine Art Society* v. *Union Bank of London* (1886) 17 Q.B.D. 705; *Gordon* v. *London City & Midland Bank* [1902] 1 K.B. 242, 265; *Morison* v. *London County & Westminster Bank* [1914] 3 K.B. 356, 364; *Reckitt* v. *Barnett* [1928] 2 K.B. 244, 263; [1929] A.C. 726; *Lloyds Bank* v. *Chartered Bank* [1929] 1 K.B. 40, 69; *Orbit Mining & Trading Co. Ltd.* v. *Westminster Bank Ltd.* [1963] 1 Q.B. 794. Under the Cheques Act 1957, s.4, re-enacting and extending the Bills of Exchange Act 1882, s.82, the banker has a defence if he has acted in good faith and without negligence.
[56] "Certainly a man is guilty of a conversion who takes my property by assignment from another who has no authority to dispose of it; for what is that but assisting that other in carrying his wrongful act into effect": Lord Ellenborough C.J. in *McCombie* v. *Davies* (1805) 6 East 538; cited with approval in the first five cases in last note; distinguished in *Spackman* v. *Foster, infra*, on the ground that in *McCombie's* case there was a demand that the innocent pledgee should restore the goods and a refusal by him to do so; *sed qu.*, for demand and refusal are not the only mode in which conversion can be committed.
[57] *Post*, pp. 485–487.
[58] (1883) 11 Q.B.D. 99.
[59] The actual decision went against the pledgee: since the initial receipt was not conversion the limitation period did not start until his refusal to hand over the goods to the owner.
[60] s.11(2).
[61] See Burnett, "Conversion by an Involuntary Bailee" (1960) 76 L.Q.R. 364; Palmer, *Bailment*, Chap. 12.
[62] It seems that where one receives goods one should ensure that they do not belong to someone else before scrapping them: *A.V.X.* v. *E.G.M. Solders, The Times*, July 7, 1982.
[63] See *Which*, June 1969, 173.
[64] The Act came into force on August 12, 1971. The Act was amended by the Unsolicited Goods and Services Act 1975 but this does not affect the issues dealt with here.
[65] The goods must have been sent to the recipient with a view to his acquiring them; the recipient must not have had reasonable cause to believe that they were sent with a view to their being acquired for the purposes of a trade or business, and he must not have agreed either to acquire or to return them.

him to do so. Subject to this, the law relating to an involuntary bailee may be stated as follows—

1. He cannot, without his knowledge or consent, be made a bailee in the strict sense of that term. In *Lethbridge* v. *Phillips*,[66] L, a celebrated miniature painter, lent a miniature to B who wished to show it to the defendant. B sent it to the defendant without any previous knowledge or consent on the defendant's part. The miniature was much damaged by being placed near a large stove in the house of the defendant who was nevertheless held not liable to L.

2. Mere negligence on the part of the recipient with respect to the safe custody of the thing will not make him liable. So, in *Howard* v. *Harris*,[67] where a playwright sent the manuscript of a play to a theatrical producer who had never asked for it and who lost it, the producer was held not liable.

3. But he must not wilfully damage or destroy the thing.[68] The law has not, however, been fully explored here. It is simple enough with a small and imperishable article like a book or a fountain pen, but what of a parcel of fish or a piano which is delivered at my house in my absence? I can distrain them damage feasant, but what I want to do is to get rid of them and I am certainly not bound to incur the expense of packing and returning them. If the sender is traceable, probably the most sensible thing to do is to notify him that the goods are at his risk and to request him to fetch them; and if (as is likely with perishables) the goods become a nuisance, the recipient would surely be justified in abating the nuisance by destroying them, even without notice to the sender, if the emergency were so pressing as to leave him no time to give it. The position is rather different when the goods came into the defendant's hands by reason of a genuine, voluntary bailment for then the bailee has a statutory power of sale of the goods if the bailor fails to collect them.[69]

4. The involuntary bailee does no wrong if he acts reasonably in trying to return the goods. In *Elvin and Powell Ltd.* v. *Plummer Roddis Ltd.*,[70] X, a swindler, directed the plaintiffs to supply the defendants at Brighton with £350 worth of coats. X then forged a telegram to the defendants: "Goods dispatched to your branch in error.—Sending van to collect. Elvin and Powell." Then a confederate of X called on the defendants, who delivered the coats to him under the impression that he was the plaintiffs' agent. The confederate disappeared. The plaintiffs sued the defendants for (*a*) negligence as bailees and (*b*) conversion. The jury negatived negligence and found that there was contributory negligence on the plaintiffs' part, and

---

[66] (1819) 2 Starkie 544.

[67] (1884) Cababé & Ellis 253. Palmer, *Bailment*, pp. 382–384, argues that neither of these cases is clear enough firmly to establish the immunity of the involuntary bailee. If, however, the immunity does exist it is "more fitted to penalising unscrupulous merchandisers than to providing a universally just solution to the problem." (*Ibid.* at p. 384).

[68] "I am not bound to warehouse it, nor am I entitled to turn it into the street": Bramwell B., *obiter*, in *Hiort* v. *Bott* (1874) L.R. 9 Ex. 86, 90.

[69] See the Torts (Interference with Goods) Act 1977, ss.12, 13, replacing the narrower provisions of the Disposal of Uncollected Goods Act 1952. At common law there was no power of disposal except in cases of real necessity: *Sachs* v. *Miklos* [1948] 2 K.B. 23; *Anderson* v. *Earlanger* [1980] C.L.Y. 133. The 1977 Act does not define "bailment" but it is thought that the provisions on sale would not extend to the "involuntary bailment."

[70] (1933) 50 T.L.R. 158.

Hawke J. held that there was no conversion, for the defendants had acted reasonably.[71] Contrast with this case *Hiort* v. *Bott*,[72] where A mistakenly sent an invoice for barley to B (who had ordered none), which stated that B had bought the barley of A through G as broker; and A also sent B a delivery order which made the barley deliverable to the order of A or of B. G then told B there had been a mistake and got B to endorse the delivery order to himself. G thereby got hold of the barley, disposed of it and absconded. Here B was held liable to A for conversion. Had he merely handed the delivery order to G for return to A, the decision might have been otherwise, but by endorsing it to G he had gone far beyond what was necessary to secure the return of it to A.

(2) *Abusing possession*

Abuse of possession which the defendant already has may take many forms, such as sale accompanied by delivery of the plaintiff's goods or their documents of title to another,[73] pawning them,[74] or otherwise disposing of them. Even the use of a borrowed car for the transporting of uncustomed watches is a conversion of the car, for such conduct if discovered leads to the forfeiture of the car under the Customs and Excise Act 1952 and its consequent loss to the owner.[75] In less extreme cases of unauthorised use by a bailee the question whether his act amounts to conversion probably depends upon the degree of departure from the terms of the bailment.[76] However, at common law an omission on the part of the defendant (*e.g.* negligently allowing the goods to be stolen) would not make him liable for conversion[77] though if he were a bailee of the goods he might be liable in detinue in such circumstances.[78] Since this type of detinue is now by statute assimilated to conversion there may now be liability in conversion.[79]

A mere bargain and sale or other attempted disposition of goods by a person without a transfer of possession, *i.e.* delivery, on the other hand, is not a conversion; the act is void and does not change the property or the possession.[80] But in those cases where a person in possession of goods to

---

[71] So, too, *Batistoni* v. *Dance* (1908) 52 S.J. 202.

[72] (1874) L.R. 9 Ex. 86; Weir, *Casebook on Tort* (6th ed.), p. 430. Criticised by Burnett, *loc. cit.* Note that the defendant was not, strictly, a bailee since he never had actual possession of the barley.

[73] *Hollins* v. *Fowler* (1875) L.R. 7 H.L. 757.

[74] *Parker* v. *Godin* (1728) 2 Stra. 813.

[75] *Moorgate Mercantile Co. Ltd.* v. *Finch* [1962] 1 Q.B. 701; Weir, *Casebook on Tort* (6th ed.), p. 426. The Court of Appeal held that it was at least the probable result of such use of the car that the car would be forfeited and therefore that the defendant must be taken to have intended this result even though, no doubt, he hoped that it would not happen.

[76] Palmer, *Bailment*, pp. 753–756.

[77] *Ashby* v. *Tolhurst* [1937] 2 K.B. 242; *Tinsley* v. *Dudley* [1951] 2 K.B. 18. Both cases of theft of plaintiff's vehicle from defendant's car park. The decisions would, of course, have been different if the defendants had actually handed the vehicles over under a mistaken belief: *Hollins* v. *J. Davy Ltd.* [1963] 1 Q.B. 844 (where, however, a contractual clause protected the defendants).

[78] It is important to note that there is no bailment where a vehicle is placed in an ordinary car park: *Chappell* v. *National Car Parks, The Times*, May 22, 1987. The cases do not seem to have been affected by the Occupiers' Liability Act 1957: *ante*, p. 224. But *cf. Fairline Shipping Corp.* v. *Adamson* [1975] Q.B. 180; Diamond (1975) 38 M.L.R. 198.

[79] See *post*, p. 477. Thus a carrier who negligently allows goods to be stolen may now be liable for conversion of the goods as well as negligent breach of bailment.

[80] *Lancashire Waggon Co.* v. *Fitzhugh* (1861) 6 H. & N. 502. But it might be the crime of theft: Smith, *Theft*, (3rd ed.), pp. 11–12.

which he has no title may confer a good title on someone else by selling, pledging, or otherwise disposing of the goods,[81] then, since the true owner is deprived of his title to the goods, such a disposition constitutes conversion whether or not the goods are actually delivered.

The destruction of goods amounts to conversion and so does the alteration of their nature. If I make an omelette of your eggs or a statue out of your block of marble, that is conversion.[82] The question to whom the omelette and the statue belong is another matter, and Salmond pointed out that the attempts of the older lawyers to transplant the Roman law of *specificatio*, *confusio* and the like to our system are of small practical use at the present day. The better method of solving the question is to split it into, "Who owns the newly created thing?" and "Who is entitled to possession of it?"[83] The probable answer to the first inquiry is that ownership of material is unchanged by alteration of it; to the second, that the court will use its discretion in making an order for specific restitution and will award the thing to him whose interest is the more substantial, on condition that he pays the value of the other's interest. But if the thing is perishable, recovery of the value of the goods converted is the only remedy possible. Where the property of A is mixed with that of B which is of substantially the same nature and quality and they cannot practicably be separated (grain in a bin, oil in a tank) the mixture is owned in common in proportion to the quantity contributed by each and the law is the same whether the mixing is wrongful or by consent.[84]

Demand and refusal. Proof of a demand by the plaintiff for the return of the goods met by a refusal of the defendant is one of the common ways of producing evidence of conversion for it tends to show that the defendant's detention of them is wrongful.[85] The refusal must, however, be unconditional or, if it is conditional, the condition must be an unreasonable one. It is certainly not unreasonable to refuse to give up a bank note which you pick up in the street to the first stranger who alleges it to be his, if you tell him that you must make further inquiries or that he must produce evidence which will authenticate his claim.[86] Whether the length of time spent in making these

---

[81] *e.g.* by sale in market overt: Sale of Goods Act 1979, s.22. *Post*, p. 485.

[82] The bottling of wine entrusted to a person in cask may be evidence of conversion even if none of the wine is drunk, but much will depend on the circumstances of the bottling. If done to preserve the wine from deterioration it is not conversion. See *Philpott* v. *Kelley* (1835) 3 A. & E. 106.

[83] *Torts* (19th ed.), pp. 126–127. For a thorough examination of the law see Matthews "Proprietary Claims at Common Law for Mixed and Improved Goods" [1981] C.L.P. 159; and Matthews, "*Specificatio* in the Common Law" (1981) 10 Anglo-American L.R. 121.

[84] *Indian Oil Corp. Ltd.* v. *Greenstone Shipping S.A.* [1988] Q.B. 345. But a contract between A and B may provide for ownership: *Clough Mill Ltd.* v. *Martin* [1985] 1 W.L.R. 111, 119.

[85] A wrongful detention can sometimes be shown without proof of demand and refusal: *London Jewellers Ltd.* v. *Sutton* (1934) 50 T.L.R. 193, 194. A bailee is not, in the absence of special contract, obliged to return the chattel to his bailor; he must merely allow the bailor to collect it: *Capital Finance Co. Ltd.* v. *Bray* [1964] 1 W.L.R. 323; Weir, *Casebook on Tort* (6th ed.), p. 436. Where a bailee is in breach of his duty to return goods then, quite independently of conversion, he is strictly liable for harm befalling them: see, *e.g. Mitchell* v. *Ealing L.B.C.* [1979] Q.B. 1.

[86] *Green* v. *Dunn* (1811) 3 Camp. 215n.; *Alexander* v. *Southey* (1821) 5 B. & Ald. 247; *Clayton* v. *Le Roy* [1911] 2 K.B. 1031.

inquiries and the mode in which they are made are reasonable or not may be nice questions.[87]

Where, however, there is no question of pursuing enquiries to see whether delivery to the claimant is proper, the defendant cannot justify a refusal because compliance with the demand may have unpleasant consequences for him. In *Howard E. Perry & Co. Ltd.* v. *B.R.B.*[88] it was held that the defendants' refusal to allow the plaintiffs to enter their premises to collect goods which belonged to them could not be justified by their fear of intensified industrial action.

(3) *Residual forms of conversion*

Though most cases of conversion at common law fall within the categories of taking or abusing possession, such acts on the part of the defendant are not a necessary element in liability provided he has dealt with the goods in a way inconsistent with the plaintiff's rights, such as signing a delivery order for goods which are delivered under that order.[89] It has even been held that refusing to hand over the registration book of the plaintiff's car amounts to conversion of the *car* since the absence of the book makes it difficult to deal with the car.[90] However, dicta in *Oakley* v. *Lyster*[91] went further and suggested that a bare denial of the plaintiff's title unaccompanied by any possession of or dealing with the goods constituted conversion. The actual decision did not support such a wide doctrine,[92] which was laid to rest by the Torts (Interference with Goods) Act 1977.[93]

Where the defendant is in possession of the plaintiff's goods there is no doubt that an unjustified refusal to return them generally constitutes conversion but it has been held that where the plaintiff has possession there is no conversion if the defendant simply refuses to allow the plaintiff to remove them. In *England* v. *Cowley*[94] M. owed money to both the plaintiff and the defendant, her landlord. The plaintiff held a bill of sale over M's furniture and put a man into M's house to take charge of it. When the plaintiff then attempted to remove the furniture the defendant forbade him to do so and stationed a policeman at the gate to make sure he did not. The defendant was held not liable for conversion. Bramwell B. said:

"In order to maintain trover, a plaintiff who is left in possession of the

---

[87] *e.g. Borroughes* v. *Bayne* (1860) 5 H. & N. 296, where the court was not unanimous.

[88] [1980] 1 W.L.R. 1875; Palmer (1981) 44 M.L.R. 87.

[89] *Hiort* v. *Bott* (1874) L.R. 9 Ex. 86 (distinguished in *Kitano* v. *The Commonwealth* (1974) 129 C.L.R. 151); *Van Oppen* v. *Tredegars* (1921) 37 T.L.R. 504; *Douglas Valley Finance Co. Ltd.* v. *S. Hughes (Hirers) Ltd.* [1969] 1 Q.B. 738; see also *Ernest Scragg & Sons Ltd.* v. *Perseverance Banking and Trust Co. Ltd.* [1973] 2 Lloyd's Rep. 101.

[90] *Bryanston Leasings Ltd.* v. *Principality Finance Ltd.* [1977] R.T.R. 45; see also the *Douglas Valley* case, *supra*, n. 89.

[91] [1931] 1 K.B. 148.

[92] The defendant had in fact not only used some of the plaintiff's property himself but had interfered with the plaintiff's right to deal with it by denying, or purporting to deny, him access to it.

[93] s.11(3): "denial of title is not of itself conversion." Note that a denial of title, if accompanied by malice, may amount to the tort of injurious falsehood: Goodhart (1931) 46 L.R. 168, 171; *ante*, p. 289.

[94] (1873) L.R. 8 Exch. 126. Weir, *Casebook on Tort* (6th ed.), p. 432.

goods must prove that his dominion over his property has been interfered with, not in some particular way, but altogether; that he has been entirely deprived of the use of it. It is not enough that a man should say that *something* shall not be done by the plaintiff; he must say that *nothing* shall."[95]

Conversion under the Torts (Interference with Goods) Act 1977

Apart from one or two minor matters[96] this Act did not interfere with the concept of conversion at common law. However, the Act abolished detinue,[97] which was wrongful retention of a chattel. In most cases of detinue there would be a concurrent liability in conversion based upon a demand and refusal to return[98] but as we have seen conversion required a positive act and had never lain where the defendant once had the plaintiff's goods but was unable to return them because they had been lost or negligently destroyed.[99] Accordingly, to deal with this situation, the Act provides[1] that an "action lies in conversion for loss or destruction of goods which a bailee[2] has allowed to happen in breach of his duty to his bailor (that is to say it lies in a case which is not otherwise conversion, but would have been detinue before detinue was abolished)."[3]

Conversion and co-owners

As between co-owners there is unity of possession, each is entitled to possession and use of the chattel, and the mere enjoyment in one way or another by one co-owner cannot amount to conversion against the other. The assertion of exclusive rights will, however, be actionable in tort. By section 10 of the Torts (Interference with Goods) Act 1977 co-ownership is no defence to an action in conversion[4] where one, without the authority of the other—

---

[95] It must be pointed out that Bramwell B.'s examples of a man who hinders his friend from taking a pistol to fight a duel or who blocks the path of a horseman so that he has to turn back are somewhat removed from the facts of the case; the first act would be justifiable as an act in the prevention of crime, the second would at least allow the plaintiff to take his property in other directions.

[96] Receipt by way of pledge (*supra*, n. 60); conversion by denial of title (*supra*, n. 93); co-ownership (*infra*, n. 4).

[97] s.2(1).

[98] See *ante*, p. 467. The Law Reform Committee went so far as to say that "conversion will lie in every case in which detinue would lie, save only that detinue lies, but conversion does not lie, against a bailee of goods who in breach of his duty has allowed them to be lost or destroyed": Cmnd. 4774 (1971), para. 8. Megarry V.-C. (who had been a member of the Law Reform Committee) seems to have agreed in *Howard E. Perry & Co. Ltd.* v. *B.R.B.* [1980] 1 W.L.R. 1375, though it is not clear what attitude the learned judge would have taken to a long but not indefinite detention. Compare Palmer in (1981) 44 M.L.R. 87; "Title to Goods and Occupation of Land: A Conflict of Interests" (1980) 9 Anglo-American L.R. 279; and in "The Abolition of Detinue" [1981] Conv. 62. If Palmer is correct that there were forms of wilful detainer which were detinue but not conversion then the abolition of detinue may create a serious gap in the law.

[99] See *ante*, p. 467. In cases where before the Act there was a concurrent liability in conversion and detinue the plaintiff might claim in detinue because this might enable him to get specific restitution. See now, s.3 of the Act.

[1] s.2(2).

[2] Not, therefore, in a situation like that in *Ashby* v. *Tolhurst, supra*, n. 77.

[3] The plaintiff must, therefore, show a right to immediate possession since this was necessary for detinue at common law. As to the *jus tertii*, see *post*, p. 480.

[4] The same rules apply to trespass.

"(a) destroys the goods,[5] or disposes of the goods in a way giving a good title to the entire property in the goods[6] or otherwise does anything equivalent to the destruction of the other's interest in the goods,[7] or

(b) purports to dispose of the goods in a way which would give a good title to the entire property in the goods if he was acting with the authority of all co-owners of the goods."

Paragraph (a) is by way of restatement of the common law[8]; paragraph (b) extends it so as to make the disposition conversion even if it does not confer a good title on the disponee.[9]

Title of plaintiff

What kind of right to the goods must the plaintiff have in order that interference with it may amount to conversion? The answer is that he can maintain the action if at the time of the defendant's act he had (a) ownership and possession of the goods, or (b) possession of them; or (c) an immediate right to possess them, but without either ownership or actual possession[10]: This seems to be the law, but it can be elicited only from a great confusion of terminology in the reports. Thus it is said in several cases that the plaintiff must have "a right of property in the thing and a right of possession" and that unless both these rights concur the action will not lie.[11] If "right of property" means "ownership," this might lead one to infer that no one can sue for conversion except an owner in possession at the date of the alleged conversion. But that is not so, for a bailee has only possession and not ownership (which remains in the bailor), and yet the bailee can sue a third party for conversion.[12] And, as we shall see,[13] one who has mere possession at the date of the conversion can generally sue, and so can one who has no more than a right to possess.

[5] This does not, presumably, cover acts of normal user which change the form of the property as in *Fennings* v. *Grenville* (1808) 1 Taunt. 241 (cutting up and boiling down a whale).

[6] e.g. a sale in market overt but not a valid pledge under s.2 of the Factors Act 1889 since that does not transfer the "entire property."

[7] *Adventure Films Ltd.* v. *Tully, The Times*, October 14, 1982, (detention of television film).

[8] On which see particularly *Baker* v. *Barclays Bank Ltd.* [1955] 1 W.L.R. 822.

[9] The law as to disposition by a co-owner is now therefore closer to that governing disposition by a non-owner, where it has never been suggested that conversion does not lie if the disposition is invalid. In *Nyberg* v. *Handelaar* [1892] 2 Q.B. 202 A and B were co-owners of a gold enamel box under an agreement that A was to have possession until it was sold. A entrusted it to B for a limited purpose but B pledged it to C. In A's successful action against C, Lopes L.J. gave his opinion that A could have maintained conversion against B because of the agreement. But B's pledge would not now purport to dispose of the entire property.

[10] The definition of Atkin J. in *Lancashire and Yorks Ry.* v. *MacNicoll* (1919) 88 L.J.K.B. 601, 605 (adopted by Scrutton L.J. in *Oakley* v. *Lyster* [1931] 1 K.B. 148, 153, and by Lord Porter in *Caxton Publishing Co. Ltd.* v. *Sutherland Publishing Co. Ltd.* [1939] A.C. 178, 201–202) needs extension to include (c), *supra*. *Rogers* v. *Kennay* (1846) 9 Q.B. 594, 596: "Any person having a right to the possession of goods may bring trover in respect of the conversion of them, and allege them to be his property: and lien, as an immediate right of possession, was held to constitute such a property": *per* Patteson J. See also *Bute (Marquess)* v. *Barclays Bank Ltd.* [1955] 1 Q.B. 202.

[11] *Gordon* v. *Harper* (1796) 7 T.R. 9, 12; *Bloxam* v. *Sanders* (1825) 9 B. & C. 941, 950; *Owen* v. *Knight* (1837) 4 Bing.N.C. 54, 57; *Bradley* v. *Copley* (1845) 1 C.B. 685.

[12] *Burton* v. *Hughes* (1842) 2 Bing. 173, 175.

[13] *Post*, pp. 480–484.

Examples of right to possess

There is no need to enlarge upon (*a*) ownership and possession, or (*b*) possession, for possession was analysed in Chapter 13. But (*c*), the immediate right to possess, must be briefly examined. A reversionary owner out of possession certainly has not got it, *e.g.* a landlord of premises let together with furniture to a tenant whose term is still unexpired; if the furniture is wrongfully seized by the sheriff, it is the tenant and not the landlord who can sue for conversion.[14] Again, a servant in custody of his master's goods has not possession of them, for it is constructively in the master.[15] But if the master has made him a bailee of them so as to vest him with exclusive possession, then, like any other bailee of this sort, he has it; so, too, if goods are delivered to him to hand to his master, he has possession of them until he has done some act which transfers it to his master, *e.g.* a shop-assistant has possession of money paid to him by a customer until he puts it in the till. Up to that moment the master has only the right to possess. These examples are tolerably plain, but it must depend to a large extent on the facts of each case whether the law will attribute to a person the immediate right to possess. A bailor has it against a mere bailee at pleasure even if he never himself had actual possession of the goods and only acquired title by virtue of an illegal but completely executed contract of sale.[16] In *Manders* v. *Williams*,[17] brewers supplied porter in casks to a publican on condition that he returned the empty casks; held, they could maintain trover against a sheriff who took the casks in execution for the publican's debts, for directly they were emptied the right to immediate possession was in the brewers, the publican becoming a mere bailee at will.[18] So, too, where furniture dealers transferred furniture on hire-purchase to X with an express proviso that the hiring was to terminate without any notice if the goods were taken in execution for debt, they could sue the sheriff for conversion when he levied execution on them.[19] The wrongful sale of goods subject to a hire-purchase agreement will constitute a repudiation and hence vest a right to immediate possession in the finance company even though the agreement does not expressly provide for this.[20]

In a simple bailment, *i.e.* one which does not exclude the bailor from possession, an action for conversion against a third person is maintainable by either bailor or bailee[21]; by the bailee because he is in possession, by the bailor because it is said that his title to the goods draws with it the right to

---

[14] *Gordon* v. *Harper* (1796) 7 T.R. 9.

[15] See Holmes, *The Common Law*, pp. 227–228; Pollock and Wright, *Possession in the Common Law*, pp. 58–60.

[16] *Belvoir Finance Co. Ltd.* v. *Stapleton* [1971] 1 Q.B. 210 (plaintiff finance company buys car from dealer and lets it on H.P. to defendant's employer. Contracts of sale and H.P. both illegal. Defendant "sells" car on behalf of employer. Liable for conversion).

[17] (1849) 4 Ex. 339.

[18] Distinguish *Bradley* v. *Copley* (1845) 1 C.B. 685, where, upon the construction of a bill of sale, demand was held to be necessary to confer the immediate right to possess.

[19] *Jelks* v. *Hayward* [1905] 2 K.B. 460; applied in *North General Wagon and Finance Co. Ltd.* v. *Graham* [1950] 2 K.B. 7, C.A.; applied in *Alexander* v. *Railway Executive* [1951] 2 K.B. 882; distinguished in *Reliance Car Facilities Ltd.* v. *Roding Motors* [1952] 2 Q.B. 844, C.A. (hiring terminable on notice, but no notice given).

[20] *Union Transport Finance Ltd.* v. *British Car Auctions Ltd.* [1978] 2 All E.R. 385.

[21] *Nicolls* v. *Bastard* (1835) 2 C.M. & R. 659; 5 L.J. Ex. 7.

possession, that the bailee is something like his servant and that the possession of the one is equivalent to that of the other.[22]

A buyer of goods can sue the seller or a third party for conversion if he has
ownership of the goods even though he has not yet got possession of them[23];
but he cannot sue the third party if ownership has passed to such third person
by reason of exceptions to the rule *nemo dat quod non habet, e.g.* by bona
fide purchase for value in market overt[24]; the seller, however, is liable for
conversion to the original buyer.

A person who is entitled to the temporary possession of a chattel and who
delivers it back to the owner for a special purpose may, after that purpose is
satisfied and during the existence of his temporary right, sue the owner for
conversion of it[25]; *a fortiori* he can sue anyone else.

Jus tertii

Once a system of law accepts possession as a sufficient foundation for a
claim for recovery of personal property it is faced with the question of how
far the defendant should be allowed to raise the issue that a third party has a
better right to the property than the plaintiff—the *jus tertii*. There are
arguments either way. On the one hand, refusal to admit the *jus tertii* allows
recovery by a plaintiff who may have himself wrongfully dispossessed the
true owner and also exposes the wrongdoer to the risk of multiple liability.
On the other hand, it may be argued that a person who has dispossessed
another should have no right to raise such issues concerning the relationship
between the dispossessed and some other party having a claim over the
goods, for there is a serious risk of abuse and of the interminable prolonga-
tion of actions. The common law compromised. If the plaintiff was in
possession at the time of the conversion, the defendant could not set up the
jus tertii,[26] unless he was acting under the authority of the true owner.[27]
Where, however, the plaintiff was not in possession at the time of the
conversion but relied on his right to possession *jus tertii* could be pleaded by

---

[22] Williams, *Personal Property* (18th ed.), p. 59; *Manders* v. *Williams* (1849) 4 Ex. 339, 344, *per* Parke B. The
extension of remedies to the bailor was a gradual process (Holdsworth, H.E.L., iii, pp. 348–349), nor has
any adequate explanation been offered why he should retain the "special property" in the goods which
gives him a right to sue a third party for conversion; but, however that may be, it was recognised that he
could sue trover as early as 1471: Y.B. Mich. 12 Edw. IV, f. 12a, *per* Brian C.J., C.P. As to the avoidance of
double liability in such cases, see p. 481, *post*.

[23] e.g. *North West Securities Ltd*. v. *Alexander Breckon Ltd*. [1981] R.T.R. 518. Note that if the goods remain
in the seller's possession subject to his lien for their unpaid price, the buyer cannot sue a wrongdoer for
conversion: *Lord* v. *Price* (1874) L.R. 9 Ex. 54; Weir, *Casebook on Tort* (6th ed.), p. 425. *Bolwell
Fibreglass Pty. Ltd.* v. *Foley* [1984] V.R. 97.

[24] *Post*, p. 485.

[25] *Roberts* v. *Wyatt* (1810) 2 Taunt. 268.

[26] Assumed rather than decided in the famous case of *Armory* v. *Delamirie* (1721) 1 Stra. 505 where a
chimney-sweep's boy who had found a jewel recovered in conversion against a goldsmith who took it for
valuation and refused to return it. The rule was the same for trespass where, of course, the plaintiff's
possession was a pre-condition to his right to sue.

[27] See the tenth edition of this work, pp. 424–425. However, the fact that he had returned the property to the
owner was not of itself a defence: *Wilson* v. *Lombank Ltd.* [1963] 1 W.L.R. 1294.

the defendant.[28] To this rule there was an exception where the defendant was the plaintiff's bailee, for the defendant was regarded as being estopped from denying the plaintiff's title unless evicted by title paramount or defending the action on behalf of the true owner.[29]

These rules were fundamentally changed by the Torts (Interference with Goods) Act 1977. Since then, in an action for "wrongful interference with goods"[30] the defendant is entitled to show, in accordance with Rules of Court,[31] that a third party has a better right than the plaintiff as respects all or any part of the interest claimed by the plaintiff or in right of which he sues.[32] Rules of Court made under the Act require the plaintiff to give particulars of his title and to identify any other person whom he knows to have a claim on the goods.[33] The defendant may apply for directions as to whether any third person with a competing claim should be joined and if that third person fails to appear on such a successful application the court may deprive him of any right of action against the defendant.[34]

The general purpose of these provisions is to allow the court so far as possible to settle competing claims in one set of proceedings. Where all the claimants are before the court under section 8, then the relief granted is to be "such as to avoid double liability of the wrongdoer,"[35] which presumably means that the court is to apportion the damages representing the value of the chattel according to the respective interests of the claimants.[36] The Act is perhaps not so clear where only the claimant with a possessory title is before the court, for example, because the true owner does not appear or cannot be found. A literal interpretation of section 8 might suggest that the ability to plead the *jus tertii* provides the defendant with a defence,[37] but it is submitted that in such a case the provisions of section 7 preserve the common law rule that a claimant relying on a possessory interest may recover the full value of

---

[28] *Leake* v. *Loveday* (1842) 4 M. & G. 972. *cf.* Atiyah (1955) 18 M.L.R. 97 and Jolly's reply, (1955) 18 M.L.R. 371. The reason seems to be that conversion was a denial of title and the defendant should therefore be allowed to attack the thing upon which the plaintiff based his claim. Where, however, the plaintiff was in possession at the time of the conversion the defendant's act was also a trespass. Trespass contained a penal element of deterrence against breach of the peace, which was no doubt why the *jus tertii* was not pleadable. It was natural that the trespass rule should "infect" conversion based on possession.

[29] See Clerk and Lindsell, *Torts* (16th ed.), para. 22–77. A bailee subjected to competing claims by the bailor and a third party could escape the quandary by interpleader proceedings enabling him to drop out of the litigation and leave the other two to fight it out between themselves.

[30] Defined in s.1 as conversion, trespass, negligence so far as it results in damage to goods or to an interest in goods and "any other tort so far as it results in damage to goods or to an interest in goods." The last phrase clearly includes rescous, pound breach and replevin. *Quaere* as to injurious falsehood? How far can the change in the law on *jus tertii* be evaded by framing the claim as breach of bailment or in contract? The courts may be able to block the former (*cf. American Express Co.* v. *British Airways Board* [1983] 1 W.L.R. 701) but the latter will be more difficult to deal with. See further Palmer, "The Application of the Torts (Interference with Goods) Act 1977 to Actions in Bailment" (1978) 41 M.L.R. 629.

[31] See R.S.C., Ord. 15, r. 10A.

[32] s.8(1). This provision applies even though the third party has disposed of the alleged interest before proceedings are begun: *De Franco* v. *Metropolitan Police Comr., The Times*, May 8, 1987.

[33] But vehicle collision actions are not governed by this requirement.

[34] See also s.9, which provides machinery to deal with concurrent claims in different courts.

[35] s.7(2).

[36] As between finder and true owner, the interest of the finder would presumably be nil.

[37] Or at least reduce the plaintiff's damages to the value of his interest.

the thing converted.[38] In such a situation the true owner may have been divested of his claim against the wrongdoer under section 8(2)(*d*) but if not, he might still be entitled to sue by virtue of his title. Two provisions of the Act are aimed at this problem. By section 7(3), "on satisfaction, in whole or in part, of any claim for an amount exceeding that recoverable if subsection (2) applied [*i.e.* where both claimants are parties], the claimant is liable to account over to the other person having a right to claim to such extent as will avoid double liability"[39]; and by section 7(4), "where, as a result of enforcement of a double liability, any claimant is unjustly enriched to any extent, he shall be liable to reimburse the wrongdoer to that extent." Thus if A loses his goods, which are found by B and then converted by C, both B and A might bring successive claims against C. If B accounts to A under section 7(3), A must then reimburse C. If B does not so account, B is liable to reimburse C. A "double liability" would, however, still exist if both A and B were insolvent.[40]

It has been suggested above that where the true owner of goods cannot be involved in the proceedings the common law rule that a mere possessory interest entitles the plaintiff to recover the full value of the goods against a wrongdoer still applies. Does this mean that if there is clear evidence that the goods were stolen by P from X (who has since disappeared) P may nevertheless recover from D, who converted them? It seems that the law's answer is that notwithstanding the general rule about the *jus tertii* P's claim may be barred by public policy if to assist in recovery of the property would offend the court's conscience.[41] However, not every illegal acquisition by P will call this into play.[42]

Finding

The popular saying that "Finding is keeping" is a dangerous half-truth, which needs a good deal of expansion and qualification to make it square with the law.

---

[38] *The Winkfield* [1902] P. 42 (a strong case since the bailee plaintiff would have been under no liability to the owners for loss of the goods); *Swire* v. *Leach* (1865) 18 C.B.(N.S.) 479; *Chabbra Corp. Pte. Ltd.* v. *Jag Shakti (Owners)* [1986] A.C. 337. This was certainly the intention of the Law Reform Committee: Cmnd. 4774 (1971), para. 75.

[39] This does not in fact apply to what might be thought the most obvious case, where a bailee recovers the full value of the goods. In that situation there can be no "double liability," the rights of the bailor against the defendant being extinguished by judgment in favour of the bailee: *Nicolls* v. *Bastard* (1835) 2 C.M. & R. 659, 660; *The Winkfield* [1902] P. 42, 61. However, the bailee must account to his bailor at common law for the amount by which the damages exceed his own interest: *Eastern Construction Co. Ltd.* v. *National Trust Co. Ltd.* [1914] A.C. 197, 210; *Hepburn* v. *A. Tomlinson (Hauliers) Ltd.* [1966] A.C. 451, 467–468, 480.

[40] What is the effect of the Act upon *Wilson* v. *Lombank Ltd.* [1963] 1 W.L.R. 1294? P purchased a car from a person who had no title, the car in fact belonging to M.C. Co. While the car was at a garage after undergoing repairs, D's agents passed by and, mistakenly thinking it belonged to D, took it away. D discovered the truth and returned the car to M.C. Co. P sued D for trespass to goods and recovered the full value of the car (£470) because, in Hinchcliffe J.'s opinion, D could not set up the title of M.C. Co. against P's possessory title. Since it is inconceivable that M.C. Co. could have sued D for anything other than nominal damages it seems somewhat strained to talk of a "double liability" under s.7. *cf.* Clerk & Lindsell, *Torts* (16th ed.), para. 22–82. Could this be a case where s.8(1) is to be taken at its face value? A simple solution, suggested by Salmond, *Torts* (17th ed.), p. 109 is to equate, at common law, the person who has returned the goods to the true owner with one who acts under the true owner's authority.

[41] *Solomon* v. *Metropolitan Police Cmr.* [1982] Cr.L.R. 606; *Thackwell* v. *Barclays Bank plc* [1986] 1 All E.R. 676.

[42] *Singh* v. *Ali* [1960] A.C. 160; *Belvoir Finance Co. Ltd.* v. *Stapleton* [1971] 1 Q.B. 210.

A finder of a chattel has such a title as will enable him to keep it against everyone, with two exceptions:

1. The rightful owner. Far from getting any title against him, the finder, if he appropriates the chattel, not only commits the tort of conversion,[43] but is also guilty of the crime of theft unless he appropriates the chattel in the belief that the owner cannot be discovered by taking reasonable steps.[44]

2. The occupier[45] of the land on which the chattel is found may *in some cases* have a title superior to that of the finder. The Court of Appeal in *Parker* v. *British Airways Board*[46] took the opportunity to restate the law in a comprehensive manner and bring order to an area in which there were numerous conflicting precedents. The cases in which the occupier of the land has the superior title[47] are—

(a) Where the finder is a trespasser on the land.[48]
(b) Where the property is attached to the land, as in *South Staffordshire Water Co.* v. *Sharman*[49] where gold rings were found in mud being cleared from the plaintiff's land.
(c) Where he is the occupier of premises in or on which the chattels (not attached to the premises) are found and, before the finding "he has manifested an intention to exercise control over the [premises] and the things which may be upon it or in it".[50]

The burden of proof of this rests upon the occupier, though in some cases the matter speaks for itself:

"If a bank manager saw fit to show me round a vault containing safe deposits and I found a gold bracelet on the floor, I should have no doubt that the bank had a better title than I, and the reason is the manifest intention to exercise a very high degree of control. At the other extreme is the park to which the public has unrestricted access during daylight hours. During those hours there is no manifest intention to exercise any such control. In between these extremes are the forecourts of petrol filling stations, unfenced front gardens of private houses, the public parts of shops and supermarkets as part of an almost infinite variety of land, premises and circumstances."[51]

In *Parker's* case itself the plaintiff found a gold bracelet on the floor of the

[43] *Moffatt* v. *Kazana* [1969] 2 Q.B. 152.
[44] Theft Act 1968, ss.1, 2(1)(c).
[45] Not a non-occupying owner: *Hannah* v. *Peel* [1945] K.B. 509. For property found on local authority land, see s.41 of the Local Government Miscellaneous Provisions Act 1982.
[46] [1982] Q.B. 1004; Roberts (1982) 45 M.L.R. 683; Tettenborn [1982] C.L.J. 242. For detailed account of the law before this case, see Palmer, *Bailment*, Chap. 22.
[47] It is assumed that the finder is not employed by the possessor of the land, for a servant (and perhaps agent) who finds in the course of his employment must account to his employer.
[48] Where the finder is not a trespasser but dishonestly intends to retain the property even against the true owner, the finder "probably has some title, albeit a frail one, because of the need to avoid a free-for-all": [1982] Q.B. 1004, 1010.
[49] [1896] 2 Q.B. 44. The case can also be explained on the ground that the finders were employed by the plaintiffs: [1982] Q.B. 1004, 1013.
[50] [1982] Q.B. 1004, 1018, *per* Donaldson L.J.
[51] *Ibid.* at p. 1019.

executive lounge at Heathrow Airport and was held entitled to it as against the occupiers. The facts that they restricted entry to the lounge to certain classes of passengers and gave their staff instructions as to what to do with lost property were insufficient to manifest the intention to exercise the requisite degree of control.[52] It is, of course, open to the occupier to regulate the right to possession of lost property by contract with the entrant; it remains to be seen whether merely putting up notices at the entrance declaring that lost property is to vest in the occupier will be an effective manifestation of the intent to control required by Parker's case.[53]

DEFENCES TO CONVERSION

Licence and the exercise of a right of distress are two common defences to an action for conversion but these have already been considered in relation to trespass to land. It remains to examine the following:

Mistake

The first thing to be said about mistake is that it does not usually provide a defence, for liability in conversion is strict:

> "At common law one's duty to one's neighbour who is the owner . . . of any goods is to refrain from doing any voluntary act in relation to his goods which is a usurpation of his proprietary or possessory rights in them. Subject to some exceptions . . . it matters not that the doer of the act of usurpation did not know, and could not by the exercise of any reasonable care have known of his neighbour's interest in the goods. This duty is absolute; he acts at his peril."[54]

This rule was set solidly into our law by the House of Lords in *Hollins* v. *Fowler*.[55] B fraudulently obtained possession of cotton from Fowler. Hollins, a cotton broker who was ignorant of the fraud, bought it from B and resold it to another person, receiving only broker's commission. Hollins was held liable to Fowler for the conversion of the cotton. The justification for such a rule is not at all obvious, particularly when in the typical case the

[52] The much-battered case of *Bridges* v. *Hawkesworth* (1851) 21 L.J.Q.B. 75, in which the occupier of a shop failed against the finder of banknotes on the floor of the shop, was approved in *Parker's* case.

[53] Even if it is not, a finder who takes lost property in defiance of such a condition in his licence would seem to be a trespasser.

[54] *Marfani & Co. Ltd.* v. *Midland Bank Ltd.* [1968] 1 W.L.R. 956, 971, *per* Diplock L.J. However, an innocent converter will be in a more favourable position with regard to limitation than one who knows the facts: *post*, p. 723.

[55] (1875) L.R. 7 H.L. 757. See also *Stephens* v. *Elwall* (1815) 4 M. & S. 259, 261 *per* Lord Ellenborough C.J. Thus an auctioneer who innocently sells the goods of another is liable: *Consolidated Co.* v. *Curtis & Son* [1892] 1 Q.B. 495; *R.H. Willis & Sons* v. *British Car Auctions Ltd.* [1978] 1 W.L.R. 438, doubting *National Mercantile Bank Ltd.* v. *Rymill* (1881) 44 L.T. 767; Weir, *Casebook* (6th ed.), p. 433.

plaintiff will have handed his goods over to a rogue on some flimsy excuse while the defendant has acquired the goods not only in good faith but from some reputable dealer who has himself been deceived. One solution which has been suggested would be to apportion the loss between plaintiff and defendant in such a case[56] but this has been rejected as impracticable by the Law Reform Committee.[57] An alternative approach would have been to apply the "ready-made" system of apportionment in the Law Reform (Contributory Negligence) Act 1945 to liability in conversion.[58] There was some authority for this but the matter is now governed by section 11(1) of the Torts (Interference with Goods) Act 1977 which firmly states that contributory negligence is no defence in proceedings founded on conversion, or on intentional trespass to goods.[59]

There are, however, many exceptions to the rule that innocent mistake is no defence. The first group consists of what is sometimes known as the exceptions to the rule *nemo dat quod non habet* whereby a bona fide purchaser of goods from A commits no conversion but actually obtains a good title to them even though the goods really belonged to B and B never intended to allow A to sell them. B's remedy is against A alone. In such cases the law has sought to strike a compromise between the competing principles that ownership of property must be protected and that speedy commerce in goods should be facilitated. Details of this very large topic must be sought elsewhere[60] but the principal exceptions are briefly as follows:

(1) Sale in market overt.

(2) Estoppel by representation or by negligent conduct.[61]

(3) Sale under a voidable title.[62]

(4) Disposition in the ordinary course of business by a mercantile agent in possession of the goods or documents of title with the owner's consent.[63]

(5) Second sale by seller in possession.[64]

(6) Sale by buyer in possession.[65]

(7) Private purchaser of vehicle subject to a hire-purchase agreement.[66]

[56] By Devlin L.J. in *Ingram* v. *Little* [1961] 1 Q.B. 31, 73–74.

[57] Twelfth Report, Transfer of Title to Chattels Cmnd. 2958 (1966). See Thornely, "Transfer of Title to Chattels by Non-Owners" [1966] C.L.J. 186. The Committee's principal reasons were that a scheme of apportionment would introduce a wide judicial discretion just where predictability is particularly important and that there would be grave practical difficulties in "chain" transactions.

[58] This would not have gone so far as Devlin L.J.'s proposal since the plaintiff's damages could only have been reduced if he was at fault. Devlin L.J. had proposed that as between a completely innocent plaintiff and a completely innocent defendant the loss should be apportioned equally.

[59] However, under s.47 of the Banking Act 1979 a "defence of contributory negligence" is available to a banker converting a cheque if the circumstances are such that he would be protected by s.4 of the Cheques Act 1957 if he were not negligent. This presumably means that the 1945 Act is to apply and effectively restores the decision in *Lumsden* v. *London Trustee Savings Bank* [1971] 1 Lloyd's Rep. 114.

[60] Benjamin, *Sale of Goods* (3rd ed.), and other works on Sale.

[61] Such a plea is extremely difficult to establish, no doubt because it would soon eat up all the other exceptions. Carelessness in allowing goods to be stolen or putting the goods in the hands of a third party will not found the estoppel. See *Moorgate Mercantile Co. Ltd.* v. *Twitchings* [1977] A.C. 890.

[62] *e.g. Lewis* v. *Averay* [1972] 1 Q.B. 198.

[63] Factors Act 1889, s.2.

[64] Sale of Goods Act 1979, s.24.

[65] Sale of Goods Act 1979, s.25.

[66] Hire Purchase Act 1964, Pt. III. See also twelfth Report of the Law Reform Committee Cmnd. 2958 (1966).

Another apparent exception to the general rule that ignorance of the plaintiff's rights does not excuse was recognised by the Privy Council in *Maynegrain Pty. Ltd.* v. *Compafina Bank*.[67] The defendants were bailees of barley belonging to X which had been pledged to the Y Bank by means of warehouse receipts. Unknown to the defendants Y Bank was acting as agent for Z Bank, the plaintiff. On X's order and with Y's tacit consent the defendants dispatched some of the barley to Kuwait. This was done without Z's authority. Z's action for conversion failed: Y Bank was agent for an undisclosed principal, Z Bank, and the defendants were entitled to act on Y's consent. Though consent is undeniably a defence to an action for conversion, there are difficulties in reconciling this result, sensible as it may seem, with general principles of agency, for since Y's act was unauthorised it could only be effective if done within an ostensible authority—but that doctrine is inapplicable to undisclosed agency.[68]

The act of shipping the barley in *Maynegrain* was assumed to be sufficient to amount to conversion, but the position is different where the defendant innocently interferes with P's goods whether upon his own initiative or upon the instructions of another, when the defendant's act amounts to nothing more than transport or custody of the goods. Blackburn J. in *Hollins* v. *Fowler* said that:

> " . . . one who deals with goods at the request of the person who has the actual custody of them, in the bona fide belief that the custodian is the true owner, should be excused for what he does if the act is of such a nature as would be excused if done by the authority of the person in possession, if he was a finder of the goods or entrusted with their custody. . . . A warehouseman with whom goods have been deposited is guilty of no conversion by keeping them, or restoring them to the person who deposited them with him, though that person turns out to have had no authority from the true owner."[69]

Similarly there is no liability if a railway company, acting upon A's directions, carries B's goods, honestly believing that A has B's authority to give such directions[70] or, of course, where a finder removes them to a place of safety.[71]

It must be confessed that this test is a rather artificial one. We have first to pretend that, in the event of A wrongfully directing an innocent person X to do something to B's goods, A is in the position of a finder or custodian of the goods; and then we must ask ourselves, "Would X's acts have been excused

---

[67] (1984) 58 A.L.J.R. 389. Palmer [1986] L.M. & C.L.Q. 218. *cf. Awad* v. *Pillai, ante,* p. 83, where the defendant was liable in negligence to someone other than the person he believed to be the owner of the property. A claim in negligence in *Maynegrain* also failed.

[68] See Palmer, *loc. cit.,* p. 224.

[69] (1875) L.R. 7 H.L. 757, 766–767. *Aliter* if the warehouseman has notice of the claim of the true owner: *Winter* v. *Bancks* (1901) 84 L.T. 504.

[70] See (1875) L.R. 7 H.L. 757, 767.

[71] *Sorrell* v. *Paget* [1950] 1 K.B. 252; Weir, *Casebook on Tort* (6th ed.), p. 440.

if these were the facts?" If aye, then X committed no conversion. But allowing for this criticism, the test seems to be workable. It would protect all those persons in *Hollins* v. *Fowler* who merely handled the cotton ministerially, such as a carrier who merely received and delivered the goods in the ordinary way[72] and it would not save the man who had sold the cotton to another. A solicitor of an undischarged bankrupt who receives after-acquired property on behalf of his client and transfers it to another agent, even with knowledge that that agent has been instructed to sell, is not liable for conversion at the suit of the trustee in bankruptcy, for the solicitor's act can be described as ministerial within the test laid down by Blackburn J.[73] Unfortunately, as Blackburn J. himself admitted, it is doubtful how far it goes. Does it protect X if A wrongfully gives him B's wheat to grind into flour and he innocently does so? The learned judge thought not (and indeed a mere finder of lost wheat could not authorise the grinding of it), and yet he felt that it would be hard to hold X liable. No doubt a finder of perishable commodities would be justified in taking any reasonable steps to preserve them pending the ascertainment of their owner; *e.g.* he would not commit conversion by making jam of strawberries if that were the only mode of preserving them. But cases like these might well be based on the general defence of necessity.[74]

Retaking of goods

This is a species of self-help. If A's goods are wrongfully in B's possession or control, there is no need for A to go to the expense of litigation to recover them. He can retake them, peaceably if he can, and in any event with no more force than is commensurate with the violence of B's resistance. Indeed, retaking may be his only opportunity of doing himself justice, for delay may mean destruction or conveying away of the goods by B, who may be quite incapable of paying their value.[75] It should be noted that, while maiming or wounding are not justifiable for simple recaption of property,[76] yet they may well become justifiable for another reason—self-defence. This may occur where B, in endeavouring wrongfully to resist A's attempt to recapture the goods, commits an assault upon A and so justifies A in using violence to protect himself. And if B's violence takes the form of assault with a deadly weapon, A may even inflict death if his own life is in peril. But as the test is that A must use no more force than is necessary, and as this necessity varies with the facts of each case, self-help is likely to be just as dangerous a

---

[72] In *Hollins* v. *Fowler*, Blackburn J. speaks of the delivery as merely "changing the custody" but it is hard to see why, as he suggests, it would be "very difficult, if not impossible" to fix the carrier with knowledge that the goods had been *sold* to the consignee. Yet to impose liability on the carrier who had such knowledge would seem to be a wholly unreasonable burden. See *Re Samuel (No. 2), infra.*

[73] *Re Samuel (No. 2)* [1945] Ch. 408. "To involve conversion the act, looked at in isolation, must have the effect of depriving the true owner of his property"; at p. 411, *per* Lord Greene M.R. If A lends B's plough to C without authority and C uses it thinking it is A's, such a use is not a conversion by C: Warren, *Trover and Conversion*, p. 101. For conversion by abusing possession, see *ante*, p. 474.

[74] *Post*, pp. 706–710.

[75] Blackstone, Comm., iii, 4.

[76] cf. *Whatford* v. *Carty* [1960] C.L.Y. 3258 (a criminal case); Weir, *Casebook on Tort* (6th ed.), p. 350.

remedy here as elsewhere.[77] Moreover, there are other qualifications of A's right to retake goods.[78]

Qualifications

(a) **With respect to persons.** He can retake the goods not only from B, the original tortfeasor, but even from a third person subject to the apparent exceptions which arise where that third person has acquired a good title even against A.[79] Such exceptions are only apparent because A, having lost his right to the property, has got nothing which he can retake.

(b) **With respect to place.** There is no doubt that the person entitled to goods may enter and take them from the land of the first taker if the taker himself wrongfully put them there.[80] But it is by no means certain what the law is when the goods are on the premises of one who was not responsible for bringing them there and who has committed no tort with respect to them.[81] The only case of any real assistance is *Anthony* v. *Haney*,[82] and even there the dicta are *obiter* and, although of considerable weight, do not probe the question of recaption very deeply.[83] Tindal C.J. in that case[84] gave as examples of permissible retaking by A from the land of an innocent person, C, (*a*) where the goods have come there by accident; (*b*) where they have been feloniously taken by B and A follows them to C's land; (*c*) where C refuses to deliver up the goods or to make any answer to A's demand for them.

As to (*a*) accident, the Chief Justice's examples were A's fruit falling upon C's land, or A's tree falling upon it by decay or being blown upon it by the wind. By "accident" it seems clear that "inevitable accident" was meant. Negligent or intentional placing of goods on the land of another is a tort, *e.g.* where a cricket ball is hit by any ordinary stroke out of the ground into another person's premises or onto the highway. The occupier of the premises, far from being put under any obligation to allow the owner of the goods to enter and retake them, is entitled to distrain them damage feasant until the owner of the goods pays for such damage as they have done. Where, however, the entry of the goods was inevitable, not only is there no liability for trespass on the part of their owner, but the view that he can

---

[77] See Branston (1912) 28 L.Q.R. 262–275, and Pollock, *Torts* (15th ed.), p. 293, n. 81, on *Blades* v. *Higgs* (1861) 10 C.B.(A.S.) 713; (1865) 11 H.L.C. 621.

[78] There are also certain important statutory restrictions upon the retaking of goods, the best-known of which are in the Consumer Credit Act 1974.

[79] *Ante*, p. 485.

[80] *Patrick* v. *Colerick* (1838) 3 M. & W. 483.

[81] "The decisions tell too uncertain a story for [the owner] to be properly advised to take the law into his own hands": Lawson, *Remedies of English Law*, (2nd ed.), p. 28.

[82] (1832) 8 Bing. 186.

[83] The scraps which are selected from old authorities and cited in this connection seem to be either irrelevant or to be contradicted in the very context in which they occur, *e.g.* in Y.B. 6 Edw. 4, f. 7, pl. 17 (1466: "Case of Thorns"), Brian C.J. and other judges opposed Catesby's argument as to the right of recaption. *Millen* v. *Hawery* (1624) Latch 13 is also inconclusive. Blackstone, Comm., iii, 45, says almost in the same breath that the owner can retake his goods "wherever he happens to find them" and then that "entering on the grounds of a third person is not allowable except where the goods have been feloniously stolen."

[84] (1832) 8 Bing. 186, 192–193.

retake them seems to be right, even if there is no direct decision to that effect. It may be hard that the occupier of land should have no right to compensation for harm done by the fall of a large thing, like a tree, on his premises, but his plight is no worse than in any other instance of inevitable accident.

As to (b), the rule that if A's goods are feloniously taken by B, A may follow them onto C's land rests upon a passage in Blackstone[85] which commended itself to two of the judges in *Anthony* v. *Haney*.[86] The distinction between felonies and misdemeanours no longer exists[87] but there seems no reason why the rule, if it is a rule at all, should not apply wherever B's taking is criminal.[88]

As to (c), Tindal C.J. thought that where C refused to deliver up the goods or to answer A's demand, "a jury might be induced to presume a conversion from such silence, or at any rate the owner might in such case enter and take his property subject to the payment of any damage he might commit."[89] The learned Chief Justice had already dealt with inevitable accident, so that he was presumably contemplating a case in which the presence of A's goods on C's land was due, not to that, but to the tort of A or of someone else for whose act A was in some way or other responsible. If so, it is doubtful whether his dictum about A's right to retake the goods is law. Later dicta leave it quite uncertain whether A can do so where C's refusal to deliver up the goods amounts to conversion,[90] and they are decidedly against such a view where C's conduct in obstructing A's entry does not; and this, too, even where the goods come on C's premises without any tort on A's part. Thus in *British Economical Lamp Co. Ltd.* v. *Empire Mile End Ltd.*,[91] C let his theatre to B. B did not pay his rent, so C re-entered and thus terminated the lease. B left in the theatre some detachable electric lamps which he had hired from A. A sued C for detinue of the lamps. It was held that the facts did not show any detinue and it was also said that C had done no wrong by not allowing A to enter and remove them. Note that A had certainly committed no tort to C in leaving the lamps there.[92] Thus it is not easy to predict what

---

[85] Comm. iii, 4–5. His citation of 2 Rolle Rep. 55, 56 208 and Rolle Abr. 565, 566 are unconvincing. In *Webb* v. *Beavan* (1844) 6 M. & G. 1055, Tindal C.J. was of opinion that this was at least arguable as a defence to trespass.

[86] *Supra*, at pp. 192, 193.

[87] Criminal Law Act 1967, s.1(1).

[88] But there are practical difficulties here, too, for B's criminality might depend upon B's state of mind, of which A was ignorant: for example, B might have taken the property under a claim of right.

[89] (1832) 8 Bing. 186, 192–193. The report in 1 L.J.C.P. 81, 84 omits the passage about the right to enter, subject to payment of damages; the report in 1 Moo. & Sc. 300, 308 omits any reference to the obligation to pay for the damage done.

[90] If C distrains the goods damage feasant and refuses to return them when A pays for the damage done by them, A can sue replevin, but that throws no light on the question whether he can retake them.

[91] (1913) 29 T.L.R. 386.

[92] cf., p. 367. Maule J. in *Wilde* v. *Waters* (1855) 24 L.J.C.P. 193, 195 thought that if a former tenant of a house left a picture on the wall and the new tenant merely said "I don't want your chattel, but I shall not give myself any trouble about it," that would not be conversion; but this dictum is colourless with respect to the old tenant's right to retake the picture, and the same may be said of dicta in *Mills* v. *Brooker* [1919] 1 K.B. 555, 558, *per* Avory J. and *Ellis* v. *Noakes* [1932] 2 Ch. 98n., 104, *per* Lawrence J. In *Moffatt* v. *Kazana* [1969] 2 Q.B. 152, 156–157, Wrangham J. recognised the difficulty but found it unnecessary to deal with it. See further Palmer, "Title to Goods and Occupation of Land: A Conflict of Interests" (1980) 9 Anglo-American L.R. 279.

the law is either where the occupier of the land commits conversion by his refusal or where he is blameless. It may be argued on the one hand that where the owner of goods was under no tortious liability for their appearance on the occupier's land, he ought to be able to retake them in any event, provided he does no injury to the premises or gives adequate security for making good any unavoidable injury. On the other hand, it may be urged that self-help ought to be strictly limited even against a wrongdoer and forbidden altogether against one who is not a wrongdoer, except that retaking might be permitted in circumstances of inevitable accident or of necessity (*e.g.* where the goods are perishable or are doing considerable damage to the land and it is impossible to communicate speedily enough with the occupier or his agent). It has been held that the owner of a swarm of bees has no right to follow it onto another man's land,[93] but this is of no general assistance for, once the bees get onto that land they become again *ferae naturae* and the property of no one.

Tindal C.J. did not profess to make an exhaustive list of the cases in which recaption is permissible, but be the extent of this justification of trespass and conversion what it may, one thing is clear. The retaker, before he attempts to retake, must, if required to do so, explain to the occupier of the land or the person in possession of the goods the facts upon which his proposed action is based. A mere allegation that the goods are his, without any attempt to show how they came on the premises, will not do, for "to allow such a statement to be a justification for entering the soil of another, would be opening too wide a door to parties to attempt righting themselves without resorting to law, and would necessarily tend to breach of the peace."[94]

MEASURE OF DAMAGES FOR INTERFERENCE WITH GOODS

Defendant not in possession

Where the defendant is no longer in possession of the plaintiff's goods because, for example, he has destroyed them or disposed of them, the plaintiff's remedy is judgment for the value of the goods[95] together with any consequential loss which is not too remote. After some initial hesitation[96] it now seems to be generally accepted that the value should be assessed at the

---

[93] *Kearry* v. *Pattinson* [1939] 1 K.B. 471.

[94] Tindal C.J. in *Anthony* v. *Haney* (1832) 8 Bing. 186, 191–192.

[95] *Chubb Cash Ltd.* v. *John Crilley & Son* [1983] 1 W.L.R. 599. However, a finance company letting goods on hire purchase is limited to recovering the amount owing under the agreement: *Wickham Holdings Ltd.* v. *Brooke House Motors Ltd.* [1967] 1 W.L.R. 295. For the position of the plaintiff with a possessory interest, see *ante*, p. 481. Value is prima facie the market price; if there is no market price then it is the cost of replacement: *Hall* v. *Barclay* [1937] 3 All E.R. 620. If there is doubt as to the value of the chattel the plaintiff will get the benefit of it for *omnia praesumuntur contra spoliatorem*: *Armory* v. *Delamirie* (1721) 1 Stra. 505. See generally Street, *Principles of the Law of Damages*, Chap. 8.

[96] See, *e.g. Mercer* v. *Jones* (1813) 3 Camp. 477; *Greening* v. *Wilkinson* (1825) 1 C. & P. 625.

date of the conversion[97] (though it should be noted that in other contexts the courts show some resistance to any universal rule that damages are to be assessed at the date of the wrong[98]). The recovery of consequential loss is illustrated by *Bodley* v. *Reynolds*,[99] where a carpenter's tools were converted and he was thereby prevented from working. £10 above the value of the tools was awarded as special damage. Generally, however, loss incurred as a result of the plaintiff's inability to deliver the goods under a lucrative contract of sale is too remote unless the defendant is aware of the contract.[1] There are many cases of conversion of documents which are intrinsically valueless but have a value in that their possession confers rights on the holder. It is clear that the measure of damages for the conversion of a negotiable instrument is prima facie the face value, not the value as paper[2] but it has been held that this principle is inapplicable to non-negotiable documents such as holiday credit stamps.[3] With respect, this approach seems curiously narrow and may be inconsistent with other authorities.[4]

Defendant detaining goods

The only remedy for conversion at common law was the purely personal one of damages. However, when the defendant was in possession of the goods and refused to deliver them up on demand his act was not only conversion but also detinue and the form of judgment in detinue might include an order for the delivery up of the goods.[5] Detinue has now been abolished but the remedies for conversion where goods are detained by the defendant are now found in section 3 of the Torts (Interference with Goods) Act 1977, which is modelled on the common law remedies available for detinue.[6] The relief available is in one of the following forms[7]:

[97] *Caxton Publishing Co. Ltd.* v. *Sutherland Publishing Co. Ltd.* [1939] A.C. 178, 192, *per* Lord Roche; at p. 203, *per* Lord Porter; *Douglass Valley Finance Co. Ltd.* v. *S. Hughes (Hirers) Ltd., supra*; *Belvoir Finance Co. Ltd.* v. *Stapleton* [1971] 1 Q.B. 210; Elliott, "Damages in Detinue and Conversion" (1951) 9 N.I.L.Q. 157; McGregor, *Damages* (15th ed.), pp. 814–831. One might infer from the Civil Procedure Act 1833, s.29 of which allowed a jury to give damages in the nature of interest *over and above the value of the goods at the time of the conversion*, that the statute favoured this view of the common law, for it looks as if express legislation was necessary to make an exception to it; McGregor, *op. cit.*, p. 814, n. 83. s.29 was repealed by the Law Reform (Miscellaneous Provisions) Act 1934, s.3. Moreover, Maule J., in *Reid* v. *Fairbanks* (1853) 13 C.B. 692, 728, regarded *Greening* v. *Wilkinson, supra*, as inconsistent with modern doctrine.

[98] *Post*, p. 634.

[99] (1846) 8 Q.B. 779. *cf. Chubb Cash Ltd.* v. *John Crilley & Son* [1983] 1 W.L.R. 599.

[1] *The Arpad* [1934] P. 189. *cf. France* v. *Gaudet* (1871) L.R. 6 Q.B. 199, distinguished in *The Arpad*.

[2] *Morison* v. *London County & Westminster Bank* [1914] 3 K.B. 356.

[3] *Building and Civil Engineering Holidays Scheme Management Ltd.* v. *Post Office* [1964] 2 Q.B. 430. This decision was reversed in the Court of Appeal ([1966] 1 Q.B. 247), but the cause of action there was under the Crown Proceedings Act, not in conversion.

[4] *cf.* the conversion of title deeds, where the court may award as damages the full value of the estate if the defendant does not redeliver the deeds: *Coombe* v. *Sanson* (1822) 1 Dorn. & Ry. 201. The eighteenth Report of the Law Reform Committee, Cmnd. 4774 (1971), para. 90, points out that many valuable tokens in common use in modern life could be the subject of conversion. But in some cases (*e.g.* credit cards) the cost of replacement would be nil.

[5] See the full discussion by Diplock L.J. in *General and Finance Facilities Ltd.* v. *Cook Cars (Romford) Ltd.* [1963] 1 W.L.R. 644, 650–651. There were in fact three forms: (i) for the value of the chattel and damages for detention; (ii) for the return of the chattel *or* recovery of its value as assessed and damages for detention; (iii) for the return of the chattel and damages for detention.

[6] The section applies if the defendant ceases to be in possession between issue of proceedings and judgment: *Hillesden Securities Ltd.* v. *Ryjack Ltd.* [1983] 1 W.L.R. 959.

[7] s.3(2).

(a) an order for the delivery of the goods, and for payment of any consequential damages,[8] or

(b) an order for delivery[9] of the goods, but giving the defendant the alternative of paying damages by reference to the value[10] of the goods, together in either alternative with payment of any consequential damages, or

(c) damages.[11]

Relief under (a) is at the discretion of the court, but the plaintiff may choose between (b) and (c).[12] If the plaintiff chooses (c), the defendant cannot satisfy the judgment by returning the goods.[13]

Improvement of goods

The problem of a converter improving goods is illustrated by *Munro* v. *Willmott*.[14] The plaintiff was given a temporary licence to leave her car in the defendant's yard. After the car had been there for some years the defendant wished to convert the yard into a garage but was unable to communicate with the plaintiff. Accordingly, he "did up" the car (then worth £20) at a cost of £85 and then sold it for £100. In proceedings for conversion, Lynskey J. felt obliged to assess the value of the car at the date of judgment (£120) but he gave credit for the sum expended by the defendant, leaving £35 as the damages recoverable by the plaintiff.[15] The matter is now governed by section 6 of the Torts (Interference with Goods) Act 1977 which provides that if the improver acted in the mistaken but honest belief that he had a good title, an allowance is to be made for the extent to which the value of the

[8] As to which, see *Brandeis Goldschmidt Ltd.* v. *Western Transport Ltd.* [1981] Q.B. 864, a case of detinue before the Act. In the absence of proof that the plaintiffs had suffered any business loss in being unable to process the goods or that they would have disposed of them on the market, they were held entitled only to nominal damages notwithstanding a fall in the market before redelivery. The plaintiffs do not appear to have argued that they were entitled to interest on the capital value of the goods during detention.

[9] At common law the form of judgment for detinue was that the plaintiff 'do have delivery up" of the goods and while the defendant might have to facilitate their collection (*Metals and Ropes Co. Ltd.* v. *Tattersall* [1966] 1 W.L.R. 1500) it was up to the plaintiff to go and get his goods. *Quaere* whether the rule is the same under the Act. Manchester (1977) 127 N.L.J. 1219 suggests that the court could order an actual redelivery by virtue of its power to impose conditions (s.3(6)) and it seems to be implied in *Howard E. Perry & Co. Ltd.* v. *British Railways Board* [1980] 1 W.L.R. 1375, 1385, that a redelivery could be ordered. Nonetheless, the wording of s.3(6) seems more apt for the imposition of conditions on the plaintiff.

[10] Assessed at what time? The common law rule was probably that in detinue the value was assessed at judgment, in conversion at the time of conversion, whence the advice that detinue was apt for a rising, and conversion for a falling, market (*cf.* the views expressed in *Sachs* v. *Miklos* [1948] 2 K.B. 23). Detinue has now been abolished and it must follow that the conversion rule applies for the purposes of s.3. If, however, the market rises after the conversion the defendant cannot simply pay the value of the goods at the time of conversion under s.3(2)(b) since the increase in value would be recoverable as consequential loss: *Sachs* v. *Miklos, supra,* at p. 40. For the position where the goods have risen in value because of the defendant's improvements to them, see *post.*

[11] *i.e.* assessed by reference to the value *and* the consequential loss. Again, as under (b), rises in market value may be recoverable as consequential loss: *The Playa Larga* [1983] 2 Lloyd's Rep. 171.

[12] s.3(3)(b).

[13] s.3(5). Where there has been no fall in value it is thought that the court would still stay the action before judgment upon return of the goods: *Fisher* v. *Prince* (1762) 3 Burr. 1363.

[14] [1949] 1 KB. 295; *Reid* v. *Fairbanks* (1853) 13 C.B. 692.

[15] It is submitted that the correct approach on the conversion count (there was an alternative count for detinue) would have been to assess the value at the date of conversion. On the basis of *Greenwood* v. *Bennett* [1973] Q.B. 195 it seems that the defendant committed two acts of conversion (beginning work on the car and selling it) and that the plaintiff could rely on either. But it has been held at first instance that where a series of acts of conversion constitute a continuous course of conduct the plaintiff can only claim the value at the beginning: *Highland Leasing* v. *Paul Field* [1986] 2 C.L. 276.

goods at the time at which it falls to be assessed, is attributable to the improvement.[16] The requirement of good faith would seem to make the law somewhat narrower than it was before.[17]

Effect of judgment

Where damages for wrongful interference are assessed on the basis that the plaintiff is being compensated for the whole of his interest in the goods[18] (including a case where judgment is subject to a reduction for contributory negligence[19]) payment of the damages or of any settlement[20] in full extinguishes the plaintiff's title to that interest in the goods.[21] Until payment of the damages, however, the plaintiff retains his property in the goods and may exercise all his rights as owner even after judgment has been given in his favour. In *Ellis* v. *John Stenning & Son*[22] A sold land to B, reserving to himself the right to cut and sell the uncut timber on the land. He then sold the timber to E. B wrongfully removed some of the timber and E obtained judgment against him for conversion but took no steps to enforce his judgment, because B was insolvent. B sold the timber to S. E then sued S for conversion of the timber. It was held that S was liable because, the judgment against B not having been satisfied, title to the timber remained with E.[23]

OTHER CAUSES OF ACTION FOR WRONGFUL INTERFERENCE WITH GOODS

Replevin

As we have seen,[24] replevin is an ancient cause of action which is theoretically applicable to any trespassory taking[25] of goods but in practice is limited

---

[16] s.6(1). Under the Copyright Act 1956 a victim of copyright infringement was the notional owner of an infringing article and could sue for conversion damages based on the value of the article without deduction of the cost of production: *Infabrics Ltd.* v. *Jaytex Ltd.* [1982] A.C. 1. However, the Copyright, Designs and Patents Act 1988 abolishes conversion damages for breach of copyright.

[17] See, however, Matthews, "Freedom, Unrequested Improvements and Lord Denning" [1981] C.L.J. 340, who argues that the same result would be arrived at in *Munro* v. *Willmott* if the plaintiff founded his case upon the "doing up" of the car rather than the subsequent sale. It must also be pointed out that under s.12 of the 1977 Act the defendant in *Munro* v. *Willmott* might now have a lawful power of sale. The Act also provides for an allowance in favour of a defendant who is a bona fide purchaser of the car from the improver (who in this instance need not act bona fide), since though not an improver he will normally have paid a price reflecting the improved value (s.6(2)). See also s.6(3) (allowance in action for recovery of purchase price on total failure of consideration).

[18] *e.g.* where the defendant's trespass or negligence has destroyed them or where they have been wrongfully disposed of. A judgment in respect of mere damage has no effect upon title.

[19] As where the defendant has negligently destroyed the goods. Contributory negligence is no defence to conversion or intentional trespass: *ante*, p. 485.

[20] See s.5(2). Where a plaintiff settles with one of two or more defendants the onus is upon him to establish that the settlement was not one which compensated him for the whole of his interest in the goods: *Macaulay* v. *Screenkarn Ltd.* [1987] F.S.R. 257.

[21] s.5. This provision has no application, however, where the damages paid are limited to some lesser amount by virtue of any enactment or rule of law (*e.g.* under the Merchant Shipping Act 1979 or under the Carriage by Air Act 1961). The plaintiff's title is, therefore, presumably extinguished where there is a valid limitation of liability clause in a contract not governed by such statutory codes.

[22] [1932] 2 Ch. 81.

[23] E could not then enforce the judgment in full against both B and S: Clerk and Lindsell, *Torts* (15th ed.), p. 1086.

[24] *Ante*, p. 466.

[25] Thus it does not lie against a carrier who detains them, for he did not obtain possession by trespass though he may be liable in conversion: *Galloway* v. *Bird* (1827) 4 Bing. 299; *Mennie* v. *Blake* (1856) 6 E. & B. 842.

to taking by wrongful distress. The modern procedure in the action is for the plaintiff to apply to the registrar of the county court, who will see that the goods alleged to have been wrongfully taken are restored to the plaintiff on his giving security to prosecute an action of replevin in the county court or in the High Court. The plaintiff thus recovers his goods without having to await the outcome of the action while the defendant is protected by the security given by the plaintiff.

Replevin is therefore now a form of interlocutory relief. Section 4 of the Torts (Interference with Goods) Act 1977 adds a new and more important form of interlocutory relief, available in the county court and High Court, whereby goods the subject of present or future proceedings for wrongful interference may be ordered to be delivered up to the claimant, or a person appointed by the court, on such terms and conditions as may be specified. The procedure is particularly apt if there is a risk that the goods may be destroyed or disposed of before trial of the action but it is not confined to such situations. An order was made under it in *Howard E. Perry & Co. Ltd. v. British Railways Board*[26] even though the goods were in no danger and the defendants recognised the plaintiffs' title: the shortage of stock caused by industrial action was acute and damages would not adequately compensate the plaintiffs for the injury to their business.

Distress and related matters

Distress is a remedy given by the common law, whereby a party in certain cases is entitled to enforce a right or obtain redress for a wrong in a summary manner, by seizing chattels and retaining them as a pledge until satisfaction is obtained.[27] Illegal, irregular and excessive distress are actionable at the suit of the owner of the chattels[28] but interference by him with a distress may in its turn be actionable as rescous or pound breach.[29]

[26] [1980] 1 W.L.R. 1375.
[27] For the modern, statutory remedy replacing distress damage feasant in respect of straying livestock, see *ante*, p. 462.
[28] Clerk and Lindsell, *Torts* (14th ed.), Chap. 16. (Distress is not treated in later eds.).
[29] *Ibid*. Note the right to claim treble damages under 2 Will. & Mar. c. 5, s.3.

CHAPTER 18

INTERFERENCE WITH CONTRACT OR BUSINESS[1]

In this chapter we are concerned with a group of torts the function of which is to protect some of a person's intangible interests—those which may loosely be called his business interests—from unlawful interference. As we have already seen, the law has been less ready to protect these interests from negligently inflicted harm than it has been to protect person and tangible property,[2] but we are now concerned only with liability for intended harm. It is not possible, however, to say simply that whenever one man intentionally causes harm to another that is a tort for, as we have also seen, the mere fact that my motive in performing an otherwise lawful act is to cause damage to another will not of itself make the act tortious.[3] Provided we give a narrow meaning to "intention" the law may well for practical purposes come close to the proposition that it is tortious intentionally to cause damage by any unlawful act, but it has developed by way of distinct, nominate torts and it is necessary to retain that division for the purposes of exposition.

Three further prefatory remarks are necessary. First, a great many of the cases in this area of the law are concerned with industrial strife of one kind or another and where this is so the common law has been excluded or modified since 1906 by statutory immunities granted to persons acting in a "trade dispute." The scope of this immunity has been changed no less than six times in the last 20 years. Since the legislation assumes the existence of the common law background we must first endeavour to ascertain the general principles governing this area of tort and then see shortly how it is affected when there is a trade dispute.

Secondly, the torts considered in this chapter may also come into question in cases of alleged unlawful competition between traders,[4] but in practice they are of little significance because of the common law's refusal to adopt any principle of "fair competition" other than the prohibition of obviously unlawful acts like torts and crimes and breaches of contract. Any full study of "unfair competition" would have to take account of the legislation protecting intangible business property like trade marks and patents,[5] and of the

---

[1] Heydon, *Economic Torts* (2nd ed.); Heydon, "The Future of the Economic Torts" (1975) U.W.A.L.Rev. 1; Weir, *Casebook on Tort* (6th ed.), Chap. 15.
[2] See the discussion of "economic loss" *ante*, p. 84. *cf. ante*, pp. 291–293.
[3] *Ante*, p. 48.
[4] One of the "foundation" cases, *Mogul SS. Co.* v. *McGregor, Gow & Co.* [1892] A.C. 25 (Weir, *Casebook on Tort* (6th ed.), p. 502) arose from attempts by a cartel to monopolise the China tea trade.
[5] See specialist works, such as Kerly, *Trade Marks and Trade Names*; Terrell, *Patents*; Copinger and Skone James, *Copyright*.

statutory controls over restrictive trading agreements[6] and monopolies,[7] which have little or nothing to do with anything resembling the law of tort.[8] One of the most significant sources of competition law is the EEC Treaty, which may be directly applicable in England and override municipal law. Article 85 prohibits agreements which have the effect of restricting or distorting competition and Article 86 prohibits the "abuse of a dominant [market] position." It is virtually certain that Article 86 gives rise to a cause of action in English law at the suit of a person damnified by its contravention[9] and it does so on the basis of an action for breach of statutory duty so that the court may award damages.[10] This is a remarkable development and leads to a sharp distinction according to whether the alleged improper trading practice can be shown to be within the purview of the Treaty as affecting "trade between member states."[11] If it can, the scope of the remedy in damages is immensely wider than under pure municipal law, the modern legislation in which has generally eschewed the private action for damages as a means of enforcement.[12] However, in *Bourgoin S.A.* v. *Ministry of Agriculture, Fisheries and Food*[13] the Court of Appeal, while regarding itself as bound by the view that Article 86 gave rise to a claim for damages, held that another directly applicable provision, Article 30 (dealing with quantitative restrictions on imports) attracted only the remedy of judicial review. Further consideration of these problems belongs to the study of European law and competition.

Finally, the common law contained areas of tortious liability for interference with family and service relationships which were based upon the archaic idea that a man had a proprietary interest in the services of his family and his servants. For example, a husband whose wife[14] was incapacitated by the defendant's negligence had his own action against the defendant for the value of the domestic services which she had formerly rendered and for the loss of her "consortium" (or society)[15] and a master had a remedy for "enticement" against one who wrongfully persuaded his servant to leave his employment. Some of these causes of action were restricted by judicial

---

[6] Restrictive Trade Practices Act 1976.

[7] Fair Trading Act 1973.

[8] However, under s.35 of the 1976 Act a person affected by failure to register a registrable agreement has an action for breach of statutory duty.

[9] This point was not before the House of Lords in *Garden Cottage Foods Ltd.* v. *Milk Marketing Board* [1984] A.C. 130, which was concerned only with the scope of the remedy. However, Lord Diplock, speaking for the majority, found it "difficult to see" how the contrary could ultimately be successfully argued (*ibid.* at p. 144). Lord Wilberforce (*ibid.* at p. 152) dissenting as to the remedy, said that it can be "accepted that a private person can sue in this country to prevent an infraction of Art. 86. This follows from the fact, which is indisputable, that this article is directly applicable in member states" and from *Belgische Radio en Televisie* v. *S.V.S.A.B.A.M.* [1974] E.C.R. 51.

[10] *Garden Cottage Foods Ltd.* v. *Milk Marketing Board, supra; An Bord Bainne Co-operative Ltd.* v. *Milk Marketing Board* [1984] 2 C.M.L.R. 584.

[11] As to which see *Cutsforth* v. *Mansfield Inns* [1986] 1 W.L.R. 558.

[12] *cf.* in the U.S.A. the strong tradition of enforcement of anti-trust legislation by private action, often for multiple damages.

[13] [1986] Q.B. 716. See further, *ante*, p. 173.

[14] But a wife had no claim in respect of injury to her husband.

[15] Awards for the latter element were small.

decision[16] and by legislation in 1970.[17] The Administration of Justice Act 1982[18] swept away the remaining ones[19] without putting anything in their place.[20] The Act does not as a matter of law preclude a court from holding that an action for negligence lies in favour of a person who could formerly have brought an action based on loss of services but in view of the current law on economic loss[21] it seems most unlikely that such a development will occur.[22]

INTERFERENCE WITH A SUBSISTING CONTRACT

A commits a tort if, without lawful justification, he intentionally interferes with a contract between B and C, (*a*) by persuading B to break his contract with C, or (*b*) if by some unlawful act he directly or indirectly prevents B from performing his contract.

The existence at common law of the tort of enticement of a servant has already been noticed, but though to modern eyes it involved A persuading B to break his contract with C its historical origins lie more in status than in contract. The origin of a different approach lies in the mid-nineteenth century in *Lumley* v. *Gye*.[23] The plaintiff's declaration alleged that he was owner of the Queen's Theatre, that he had contracted with Johanna Wagner,[24] a famous operatic singer, to perform exclusively in the theatre for a certain time and that the defendant, owner of a rival theatre, wishing himself to obtain Miss Wagner's services "knowing the premises and maliciously intending to injure the plaintiff . . . enticed and persuaded [her] to

---

[16] *e.g.* a master's cause of action for loss of services of his servant was restricted to servants living as part of his household: *Inland Revenue Commissioners* v. *Hambrook* [1956] 2 Q.B. 641.

[17] Law Reform (Miscellaneous Provisions) Act 1970, ss.4, 5, abolishing most claims for loss of services of children and for "enticement" and "harbouring" of wives and for damages for adultery. See the eleventh edition of this work.

[18] s.2:
"No person shall be liable in tort . . .
    (a) to a husband on the ground only of his having deprived him of the services or society of his wife;
    (b) to a parent (or person standing in the place of a parent) on the ground only of his having deprived him of the services of a child; or
    (c) on the ground only—
        (i) of having deprived another of the services of his menial servant;
        (ii) of having deprived another of the services of his female servant by raping or seducing her; or
        (iii) of enticement of a servant or harbouring a servant."

[19] See *Brigg* v. *Brown* [1984] 1 All E.R. 997, 1008. The apparently contrary statement in *Hodgson* v. *Trapp* [1988] F.L.R. is to be explained by the fact that the events occurred before the commencement of the 1982 Act: see [1988] 3 W.L.R. 1281 (appeal on another point).

[20] The only cause of action of much significance in modern times was the husband's for loss of his wife's services, for though archaic in form, its function in enabling the recovery of the cost of substitute domestic help was perfectly reasonable. However it became virtually redundant when the courts held that the wife could recover such losses in her own claim: *Daly* v. *General Steam Navigation Ltd.* [1981] 1 W.L.R. 120.

[21] *Ante*, p. 84.

[22] Scots common law has never had the actions based on loss of services and the House of Lords in *Robertson* v. *Turnbull* 1982 S.L.T. 96 refused to allow a relative's claim for financial loss based on breach of duty to the relative.

[23] (1853) 2 El. & Bl. 216.

[24] Students of contract will be familiar with *Lumley* v. *Wagner* (1852) 1 De G. M. & G. in which the same plaintiff obtained an injunction against Miss Wagner.

refuse to perform." On demurrer it was held by the majority of the Court of Queen's Bench that while the authorities had until then confined liability for enticement to the relation between master and servant (which that between Lumley and Wagner clearly was not) yet the plaintiff's claim succeeded. The majority held that the case could be decided upon the narrow ground that the action for enticement should be extended beyond the strict relation of master and servant to embrace other contracts for personal services, but support was also given in varying degrees to a broader proposition that a plaintiff might sue for the knowing violation of the security of any type of contractual right. In *Bowen* v. *Hall*,[25] on rather similar facts, the Court of Appeal accepted the broader proposition and doubted whether *Lumley* v. *Gye* could in fact be based upon the narrower ground of enticement. The rule that inducing or procuring another to break his contract could be actionable at the suit of the other contracting party who suffered damage thereby was only accepted in the face of strong dissent,[26] but the good sense of it is clear. Commercial contractual relations had become valuable rights which could be regarded as entitled to at least some of the protection given by the law to property[27] and while it was argued that the plaintiff ought to be satisfied with his action for breach of contract against the party induced, the latter might be incapable of paying all the damages.[28]

The tort has been extended a good deal since *Lumley* v. *Gye* and in its modern form its requirements may be summarised as follows. For convenience of exposition reference will normally be made to A's having brought about a "breach" of the contract between B and C and in most of the cases this will have occurred[29] but, as we shall see, there may be liability without an actual breach.

Variants of the tort

(1) *Direct*[30] *persuasion*

This is the primary form of the tort[31] exemplified by the facts of *Lumley* v. *Gye* itself.[32] A distinction may be taken between persuasion and mere advice,[33] and advice in the sense of "a mere statement of, or drawing of the

---

[25] (1881) 6 Q.B.D. 333.
[26] By Coleridge J. in *Lumley* v. *Gye, supra,* and Lord Coleridge C.J. in *Bowen* v. *Hall, supra.*
[27] "A violation of a legal right committed knowingly is a cause of action, and . . . it is a violation of a legal right to interfere with contractual relations recognised by law if there be no sufficient justification for the interference": *Quinn* v. *Leatham* [1901] A.C. 495, 510, *per* Lord Macnaghten.
[28] Crompton J. in *Lumley* v. *Gye, supra,* at pp. 230–231. Of course, every contractor accepts the risk of insolvency in his co-contractor, but he does not accept it in combination with the procurement of a breach by a third party. Erle J. (*ibid.* at p. 234) also refers to the fact that the contractual damages may be limited by factors which ought not to avail the wilful interferer.
[29] Hence the tort is commonly called "inducing breach of contract."
[30] There need be no individual contact between A and B: *Greig* v. *Insole* [1978] 1 W.L.R. 302 (resolutions and press statement by cricket governing body).
[31] *D.C. Thomson & Co. Ltd.* v. *Deakin* [1952] Ch. 646, 694, *per* Jenkins L.J.
[32] *Supra.* See also *S. Wales Miners' Federation* v. *Glamorgan Coal Co. Ltd.* [1905] A.C. 239.
[33] *e.g. D.C. Thomson & Co. Ltd.* v. *Deakin, supra,* at p. 686, *per* Lord Evershed M.R. See Report of the Royal Commission on Trade Unions and Employers' Associations, Cmnd. 3623 (1968), para. 891.

attention of the party addressed to, the state of facts as they were,"[34] is not actionable.[35] However, it has been said that advice which is intended to have persuasive effect is not distinguishable from inducement[36] and "the fact that an inducement to break a contract is couched as an irresistible embargo rather than in terms of seduction does not make it any the less an inducement."[37] It is submitted that the issue is really one of intention and causation. If A's words were intended to cause and did cause B to break his contract with C, then they are actionable by C whatever their form.[38] If so, bearing in mind that intention in this context is not the same as motive and that the tort may be committed without any ill will towards the plaintiff,[39] it is likely to be a rare case in which A's words have had a causative effect on B's conduct and yet A escapes liability on the ground that they were only "advice."[40]

Liability under this head may arise from A's entering into a contract with B knowing that the contract is inconsistent with a prior contract of B's with C as in *B.M.T.A.* v. *Salvadori*[41] where A bought a car from B knowing that the sale constituted a breach by B of his contract with C that he would not sell the car within a year. Where the prior contract of B and C is specifically enforceable it would create an equitable interest in the subject-matter in favour of C, which C could enforce against A even if A had only constructive notice of C's rights.[42] In many cases this would render consideration of A's tort liability in a case of actual knowledge otiose, but it seems possible to assert such a claim where there is some additional loss.[43] In the case of land, statutory provisions may give priority to a later contract registered as a land charge even if entered into with knowledge of an earlier, unregistered

---

[34] *D.C. Thomson & Co. Ltd.* v. *Deakin, supra,* at p. 686.

[35] A statement of something which may be done lawfully or unlawfully cannot be said to induce wrongs committed by those who respond unlawfully: *C.B.S. Songs Ltd.* v. *Amstrad Consumer Electronics plc* [1988] A.C. 1013 (provision of machines capable of being used for breach of copyright).

[36] *Camden Nominees Ltd.* v. *Forcey* [1940] Ch. 352, 366; *D.C. Thomson & Co. Ltd.* v. *Deakin, supra,* at p. 686.

[37] *J.T. Stratford & Co. Ltd.* v. *Lindley* [1965] A.C. 269, 333, *per* Lord Pearce; *Greig* v. *Insole* [1978] 1 W.L.R. 302.

[38] The relative positions of the persons involved and the degree of anxiety to achieve his ends shown by the alleged inducer are both factors to be taken into account: *Square Grip Reinforcement Co. Ltd.* v. *Macdonald* 1968 S.L.T. 65.

[39] *S. Wales Miners' Federation* v. *Glamorgan Coal Co. Ltd.* [1905] A.C. 239; *Edwin Hill & Partners* v. *First National Finance Corp.* [1989] 1 W.L.R. 225, 234.

[40] The defence of justification (*post,* p. 507) might be relevant in a case of disinterested advice.

[41] [1949] Ch. 556. It is no answer that B needed little, if any, persuasion. *cf. Batts Combe Quarry Ltd.* v. *Ford* [1943] Ch. 51.

[42] That is to say, unless A was a bona fide purchaser for value without notice.

[43] See *Pritchard* v. *Briggs* [1980] Ch. 338, though on the facts the majority of the court rejected a claim for damages.
In *Swiss Bank Corp.* v. *Lloyds Bank Ltd.* [1979] Ch. 548 the trial judge held that (*a*) independently of specifically enforceable equitable rights a person who takes a charge on property with actual knowledge of inconsistent prior rights may be restrained by injunction from exercising his rights under the charge (*b*) that the defendants only acquired this knowledge after acquisition of the charge but (*c*) they could not rely on any defence of justification to assert their rights because the charge was illegal as contravening exchange control. In the Court of Appeal (where it was held that there was no prior equitable charge in favour of the plaintiffs and that the defendants' charge was not illegal) it was conceded that the claim based on actual knowledge was of no value to the plaintiffs in the absence of an equitable charge: [1982] A.C. 584, 598. It would seem unsafe to conclude on the basis of this that the absence of an equitable interest precludes any liability in tort: see the cases in notes 44 and 45.

transaction,[44] but it seems that this affects only proprietary rights and does not bar an action in tort based on interference with the earlier contract.[45]

The other forms of the tort require interference by unlawful means. It is sometimes argued that direct persuasion applied by A to B not to perform his contract is itself the procurement of breach by unlawful means,[46] but the argument is circular and it seems better simply to say that in this form of the tort no use of unlawful means is required.[47]

(2) *Direct intervention*

This takes the form of direct action by A on the person or property of B whereby B is disabled from performing his contract with C, as where A physically detains B[48] or steals B's specialised tools without which B cannot carry out his obligation.[49] A similar case exists where A interferes with the subject-matter of the contract in a way which if done by B would amount to a breach of the contract. In *G.W.K. Ltd.* v. *Dunlop Rubber Co. Ltd.*[50] B manufactured cars and contracted with C that all cars exhibited by B should be fitted with tyres of C's manufacture. At an exhibition, A, who also manufactured tyres, secretly removed C's tyres from B's car and substituted his own. A was held liable to B for trespass to his goods[51] and to C for unlawful interference with his contract with B. However, there must be some conduct which is "unlawful"[52] apart from the intent to injure C, so that, for example, refusing, without any breach of contract, to provide B with supplies that he needs to fulfil his contract with C is no more a tort against C than it is against B, even though A's motive is to injure C.[53]

(3) *Indirect intervention*

If, instead of persuading B to break his contract or causing him to do so by direct unlawful action against him, A brings about the breach of the contract between B and C by operating through a third party, X, A may still be liable

---

[44] *Midland Bank Trust Co. Ltd.* v. *Green* [1981] A.C. 513. For the relationship between tort and property in this context see Cohen-Grabelsky, (1982) 45 M.L.R. 241.

[45] See *Midland Bank Trust Co. Ltd.* v. *Green (No. 3)* [1982] Ch. 529 arising from the same facts as the previous case. The claim there was framed as a civil conspiracy but the point is that a personal liability may exist quite independently of the determination of the proprietary issue and, perhaps, render victory on the proprietary issue somewhat academic. By chance, the tort liability of the party to whom the land had been conveyed was statute-barred in the *Midland Bank* litigation by the now repealed s.1(3) of the Law Reform (Miscellaneous Provisions) Act 1934. On the tort liability, see also the remarks of Eveleigh L.J. in *Midland Bank Trust Co. Ltd.* v. *Green* [1980] Ch. 590, 626, 629.

[46] *e.g. per* Jenkins L.J. in *D.C. Thomson & Co. Ltd.* v. *Deakin* [1952] Ch. 646, 694.

[47] *Pete's Towing Services Ltd.* v. *N.I.U.W.* [1970] N.Z.L.R. 32, 45.

[48] *D.C. Thomson & Co. Ltd.* v. *Deakin* [1952] Ch. 646, 678, *per* Evershed M.R.; at pp. 694–696, *per* Jenkins L.J.

[49] *Ibid.* at p. 702, *per* Morris L.J.

[50] (1926) 42 T.L.R. 375, 593.

[51] This trespass is, of course, analogous to the detention of B or the theft of his property in the examples above, but the statement in the text represents Jenkins L.J.'s view of the *G.W.K.* case: *D.C. Thomson & Co. Ltd.* v. *Deakin, supra,* at p. 694.

[52] *Contra*, Heydon, *op. cit.*, p. 31.

[53] But in such a case the line between inducement and intervention may be very fine and no unlawful means are required for the former: see *Restatement* 2d., s.766, comment 1, illustrations 1 and 2.

to C,[54] provided unlawful means are used. A common example of this form of the tort, though now much restricted by the legislation governing trade disputes, has been the situation where X is B's servant, whom A induces to act in breach of his contract of employment so as to prevent B fulfilling his contract. In *J. T. Stratford & Son Ltd.* v. *Lindley*,[55] C carried on business hiring out barges to B. These were collected from C and returned to B's watermen. The defendants (A) were officials of a union to which all but a very few watermen belonged and wished to bring pressure on C in connection with a grievance at another company controlled by him. Accordingly, A instructed B's watermen (X) not to man, service or tow barges belonging to C, an embargo which soon brought C's business to a standstill as barges which were out on hire were not returned. In proceedings by C against A for an interlocutory injunction the House of Lords held that a prima facie case had been established that A was liable for procuring breaches by B of the hiring contracts, the unlawful means being the inducement of X to "black" the barges.[56] The unlawful means adopted may be considerably more remote than interference in the contractual relationship between B and his servants. In *Merkur Island Shipping Corporation.* v. *Laughton*[57] the International Transport Workers' Federation (I.T.F.) wished to bring pressure on C, owners of the *Hoegh Apapa* then docked in Liverpool under charter to B and sub-charter to N.L. N.L. had a contract with tug owners to take the *Hoegh Apapa* out, but as a result of a request from A, an official of I.T.F., the tug crews, in breach of their contracts of employment, refused to move her.[58] It was held that C had made out a prima facie case of unlawful interference with its contract with B, notwithstanding that the direct inducement was not, as in *Stratford* v. *Lindley*, one step removed from the contract but three steps removed. In principle there was no distinction between indirect interference at the first stage and such interference at a remoter stage, but the more indirect and remote the interference, the more difficult it may be to establish on the facts that A did intend to interfere with the particular contract relied on by the plaintiff and that that interference was a necessary consequence of A's wrongful act.[59]

(a) **Unlawful means.** In *D. C. Thomson & Co. Ltd.* v. *Deakin*[60] the Court of Appeal was emphatically of the opinion that unless the case was one of direct inducement of B, the tort required the use of some independently unlawful means. The difficulty with this is that it makes the question of A's liability to C turn on what may be a purely technical contravention of the law by A which is of no real concern to C.[61] Further, there are uncertainties in the

---

[54] But *cf. Dimbleby & Sons Ltd.* v. *N.U.J.* [1984] 1 W.L.R. 427, which suggests that *B* can sue A.
[55] [1965] A.C. 269.
[56] On the facts, the defendants failed to make out a prima facie case that there was a trade dispute within the Trade Disputes Act 1906. There was insufficient evidence of A's knowledge with regard to another contract between C and B2 for repair of barges.
[57] [1983] 2 A.C. 570. This point was not argued in the House of Lords: *ibid.* at p. 602.
[58] In fact, an unusually high tide allowed her escape.
[59] [1983] 2 A.C. 570, 588, *per* Dillon L.J.
[60] [1952] Ch. 646.
[61] See Lord Radcliffe's comment in *J.T. Stratford & Son Ltd.* v. *Lindley* [1965] A.C. 307, 330.

meaning of "unlawful" for this purpose.[62] Voices have sometimes been heard to question or deny the validity of this requirement[63] but, while it is probably true to say that this issue has not been central in the cases since *Thomson* v. *Deakin*, the necessity for unlawful means has been so consistently repeated in subsequent statements of the law[64] that it is now hopeless to argue the contrary. Nor, despite the arbitrary results capable of being produced by the requirement of illegality, is the law necessarily unwise in displaying this reluctance to extend liability, for if the requirement of illegality were abandoned a much greater burden would have to be placed upon the defence of justification if we were to avoid the intolerable situation that A was liable to C whenever and however he knowingly brought about a breach of a contract between B and C.

(b) Inducement by servant. If my servant, acting bona fide within the scope of his authority, procures or causes me to break a contract which I have made with you, you cannot sue the servant for interference with the contract; for he is my *alter ego* here, and I cannot be sued for inducing myself to break a contract, although I may be liable for breaking the contract. In *Said* v. *Butt*[65] the plaintiff wished to get a ticket for X's theatre. He knew that X would not sell him one because they had quarrelled. He therefore persuaded a friend to procure him a ticket without disclosing his identity. When the plaintiff presented himself at the theatre, the defendant, who was X's servant and manager of the theatre, detected the plaintiff and refused to admit him. He sued the defendant for procuring a breach of his contract with X. The action was dismissed because there was no contract, since the identity of the plaintiff was, in the circumstances, material to the formation of the alleged contract; and alternatively, even if there had been a valid contract, the principle stated above would prevent the action from lying.[66] If the servant does not act bona fide, presumably he is liable on the ground that he has ceased to be his employer's *alter ego*.[67] It is true that even then he might still be acting in the course of his employment, but we must take it that this curious piece of metaphysics exempts the employer from vicarious liability for this particular tort.

Intent of the defendant

There is no liability under this head for negligently interfering with C's rights under contract. A must have knowledge of the contract between B

---

[62] It clearly includes torts and breaches of contract but it is uncertain since the *Lonrho* case whether it includes crimes not themselves actionable as torts. See *post*, p. 524.
[63] See, *e.g.* Lord Denning M.R. in *Daily Mirror Newspapers Ltd.* v. *Gardner* [1968] 2 Q.B. 762, 782, but he recanted in *Torquay Hotel Co. Ltd.* v. *Cousins* [1969] 2 Ch. 106, 138.
[64] See, *e.g. Merkur Island Shipping Corp.* v. *Laughton* [1983] 2 A.C. 581, 586, 590, 606 (H.L.).
[65] [1920] 3 K.B. 497, 506.
[66] Approved by Greer L.J. in *Scammell Ltd.* v. *Hurley* [1929] 1 K.B. 419, 443; *cf.* Scrutton and Sankey L.JJ. *ibid.* at pp. 436, 449. This principle will protect company directors who vote to cause a breach of contract.
[67] This paragraph was adopted by Evershed M.R. in *D.C. Thomson & Co. Ltd.* v. *Deakin* [1952] Ch. 646, 681, who added, "The difficulty is avoided if the act which the servant is procured to do is not an act in accordance with or under his contract, but is in breach or violation of it."

and C or act with the intention of bringing about a breach of it. As to knowledge, however, he need not be familiar with all the details of the contract, for otherwise the tort would hardly ever be committed. In *Emerald Construction Co. Ltd. v. Lowthian*[68] the defendants knew of the existence of the contract between the plaintiffs and their co-contractors but they did not know its precise terms and said that they assumed from their experience in other cases that it could be terminated at short notice. Nevertheless, the evidence showed that the defendants were determined to bring the contractual relationship to an end if they could, regardless of whether it was done in breach or not. The Court of Appeal held that this was sufficient to entitle the plaintiffs to an interlocutory injunction.[69] Where a defendant is familiar with the trade in question he may be taken to have knowledge of the existence of a contract even though he cannot identify the other contracting party and even though he may have no direct information about any particular contract at all. In *Merkur Island Shipping Corporation v. Laughton*[70] the defendants were in fact given a copy of the charter of the trapped vessel before the application for an injunction, but the House of Lords held that they had the requisite knowledge independently of this. Commenting that no one is likely to be better informed than a seamen's union as to the terms on which vessels sailing under flags of convenience were employed, Lord Diplock adopted the words of the Master of the Rolls in the court below[71]:

"Whatever the precise degree of knowledge of the defendants at any particular time, faced with a laden ship which, as they well knew, was about to leave port, the defendants must in my judgment be deemed to have known of the almost certain existence of contracts of carriage to which the shipowners were parties. The wholly exceptional case would be that of a ship carrying the owner's own goods. Whether that contract or those contracts consisted of a time charter, a voyage charter or one or more bills of lading contracts or some or all of such contracts would have been immaterial to the defendants. Prima facie their intention was to immobilise the ship and in so doing to interfere with the performance by the owners of their contract or contracts of carriage."[72]

There is, however, no general duty actively to inquire about contracts between others.[73] If A had an honest doubt whether there was a contract at

---

[68] [1966] 1 W.L.R. 691. See also *Greig v. Insole* [1978] 1 W.L.R. 302 (where A announces an embargo in terms which appear to apply to persons who have contracts with C it is no answer for A to say that his real intention was only to apply it to those who can lawfully withdraw from their relations with C).

[69] Note that this decision does not invalidate the different proposition of Jenkins L.J. in *D.C. Thomson & Co. Ltd. v. Deakin* at [1952] Ch. 697 that where a person merely advocates an object which can be achieved by lawful means he is not to be responsible merely because others respond to that advocacy by using unlawful means.

[70] [1983] 2 A.C. 570, *ante*, p. 501.

[71] *Ibid.* at p. 591. See also *Associated Newspapers Group v. Wade* [1979] 1 W.L.R. 697.

[72] No doubt it is still true as a matter of principle that it is not enough that A must have known that the persons reached by his exhortations must have contracts of some kind or other with other persons and that his exhortations might result in some breaches of them: Jenkins L.J. in *D.C. Thomson & Co. Ltd. v. Deakin, supra*, at p. 698.

[73] *Leitch & Co. v. Leydon* [1931] A.C. 90.

all between B and C it has been held that this would provide a good defence[74] but if the doubt is whether A's rights or C's under two inconsistent agreements should prevail and A chooses to adopt a course which on one view of the law will undoubtedly interfere with C's rights, it has been said that he must at least show that he was advised and honestly believed that he was entitled to take that course.[75]

The meaning of intention gives rise to difficulty. The problem may be illustrated by the county court case of *Falconer* v. *A.S.L.E.F.*[76] The defendants called rail workers out on strike and the plaintiff, an ordinary traveller, incurred hotel expenses when he was unable to travel on the journey for which he had bought a ticket.[77] The "target" of the strike action was undoubtedly the railway undertaking but it was obviously a necessary consequence of the strike's having any effect at all that it should lead to interference in the performance of contracts of carriage. The learned judge held that the defendants "intended" to interfere with the plaintiff's contract for the purposes of this tort. However, in *Barretts & Baird (Wholesale) Ltd.* v. *I.P.C.S.*[78] Henry J. held that the intention of strikers was to put pressure on their employers to improve their conditions of service and not to disrupt the plaintiffs' contracts,[79] even though that was an unavoidable by-product of the strike. "On the evidence the desire to strike was the cause of the injury to the plaintiffs rather than the desire to injure the plaintiffs being the cause of the strike."[80] The first view would probably extend the law further than it has commonly been thought to go and would expose strikers having no immunity under trade union legislation to a very wide-ranging liability; on the other hand it is not quite accurate to describe the plaintiffs in these two cases as merely "ricochet" victims for it may be the effect of pressure on the public and customers which causes the employer to succumb to the strikers' demands. However, even on the view that the plaintiff must be the target, no malice or spite is required[81]: apart from the protection of the trade disputes legislation[82] the tort would be committed by a trade union officer calling his members out on strike and he cannot defend himself by arguing that his purpose was the increase of his members' wages: unlike the tort of conspiracy, no predominant purpose to injure the plaintiff is required.[83]

There must have been interference with performance of a contract

Though the wider wrongs of intimidation and interference with trade by

---

[74] *Smith* v. *Morrison* [1974] 1 W.L.R. 659; *cf. Pritchard* v. *Briggs* [1980] Ch. 338, 410–415.
[75] *Swiss Bank Corp.* v. *Lloyds Bank Ltd.* [1979] Ch. 549, 580. An honest mistake as to the legal effect of action was not a defence to a claim for an injunction in *Solihull M.B.* v. *N.U.T.* [1985] I.R.L.R. 211.
[76] [1986] I.R.L.R. 331.
[77] For the effect of the carriers' conditions exempting them from liability, see *post*, p. 505.
[78] [1987] I.R.L.R. 3. Freidman (1987) 104 L.Q.R. 176; Napier [1987] C.L.J. 221; Simpson (1987) 50 M.L.R. 506. The plaintiffs' primary contention in this case was the commission of the tort of interference with trade by unlawful means (see *post*, p. 521), but the judge treated intention under this tort and under the tort of interference with contract as one and the same.
[79] *cf.* "*Lonrho* intention"; see *post*, p. 518.
[80] [1987] I.R.L.R. 3, 10.
[81] *S. Wales Miners' Federation* v. *Glamorgan Coal Co.* [1905] A.C. 239; *Greig* v. *Insole* [1978] 1 W.L.R. 302, 338.
[82] See *post*, p. 526.
[83] *Lonrho p.l.c.* v. *Fayed* [1989] 2 All E.R. 65 (a case of interference with trade by unlawful means).

unlawful means may protect mere expectancies, there is no doubt that for the purposes of the tort we are now considering there must be interference with a subsisting[84] contract between B and C. Hence if the contract allegedly broken proves to be void there is no tort.[85] On the other hand, if the contract is merely unenforceable (*e.g.* for non-compliance with section 40 of the Law of Property Act 1925) then it may well be actionable to procure its breach. The action would not be an indirect method of enforcing the contract against the other contracting party because it lies against a third party and in tort.[86]

There need not in all cases be an actual breach of the contract. In *Torquay Hotel Co. Ltd.* v. *Cousins* an interlocutory injunction was issued to restrain the defendants from preventing oil companies from carrying out their contracts to deliver oil to the plaintiff's hotel notwithstanding that the contract with the principal supplier of oil contained a clause absolving it from liability if delivery was prevented by circumstances outside its control. Lord Denning M.R. said that liability extends to a case where a "third person *prevents* or *hinders*[87] one party from performing his contract, even though it be not a breach."[88] Whatever the nature of the defendant's conduct this should be so where there is "no breach" only in the sense that an exemption clause in the contract allows a contracting party to escape liability in damages for non-performance of his obligation.[89] Again, where the defendant uses unlawful means to interfere with a contractual relationship[90] there would be no point in requiring any sort of breach, because even interference with prospective, non-contractual advantages by such means may be actionable.[91] However, despite an apparent dictum to the contrary,[92] the *Torquay Hotel* principle does not, it is submitted, extend to imposing liability in a case where A has, without any unlawful act, done no more than persuade B to exercise an

---

[84] But the tort would be committed even though the contract was wholly performed on one side and the breach was of a negative covenant on the other (*e.g.* a post-employment covenant not to compete): *Rickless* v. *United Artists Corp.* [1988] Q.B. 40.

[85] *De Francesco* v. *Barnum* (1890) 45 Ch.D. 430; *Joe Lee Ltd.* v. *Dalmeny* [1927] 1 Ch. 300; *Said* v. *Butt* [1920] 3 K.B. 497. In *Greig* v. *Insole* [1978] 1 W.L.R. 302, 341, Slade J. said he was "prepared to assume" that the tort was not committed if the contract was void or voidable.

[86] *cf.* Heydon, *op. cit.*, p. 35; Clerk & Lindsell, *Torts* (16th ed.), para. 15–04. While logical, the view stated in the text could cause acute difficulties to a vendor of land subject to an unenforceable contract of sale: Smith, "The Economic Torts: Their Impact on Real Property" (1977) 41 Conv. 318. *Smith* v. *Morrison* [1974] 1 W.L.R. 659 perhaps points against liability where the contract is unenforceable. But after the enactment of the Law of Property (Miscellaneous Provisions) Bill 1988 land sale contracts will be void if not in writing.

[87] But where mass picketing by A caused B to incur expenditure in bringing C into work, C could not sue for this tort for B had performed its obligations under the contract: *Thomas* v. *N.U.M. (S. Wales Area)* [1986] Ch. 20.

[88] [1969] 2 Ch. 106, 138. *cf. Emerald Construction Co. Ltd.* v. *Lowthian* [1966] 1 W.L.R. 691, 701, where Lord Denning M.R. said that if A's efforts to bring the contract to an end within a certain time regardless of whether this will involve its breach do themselves bring about a situation in which B can lawfully terminate the contract, A remains liable to C, for he cannot rely on his own wrongful act.

[89] This was the view of the clause by Russell and Winn L.JJ. in *Torquay Hotel Co.* v. *Cousins*: [1969] 2 Ch. 106, 143, 147; *Falconer* v. *A.S.L.E.F.* [1986] I.R.L.R. 331. In *Merkur Island Shipping Corp.* v. *Laughton* [1983] 2 A.C. 570, Lord Diplock utilised the terminology of "primary" and "secondary" obligations which he had developed in cases such as *Photo Productions Ltd.* v. *Securicor* [1980] A.C. 385.

[90] In *Torquay Hotel Co.* v. *Cousins, supra*, at p. 137, Lord Denning M.R. gives the example of an opera singer poisoned by the jealous rival of the owner of the theatre at which she is contracted to sing. The singer would be excused by impossibility or frustration.

[91] *Post*, p. 521. *cf. Merkur Island Shipping Corp.* v. *Laughton* [1983] 2 A.C. 570, 588, *per* Dillon L.J.

[92] By Winn L.J. in *Torquay Hotel* v. *Cousins, supra*, at p. 147; and see *Brekkes Ltd.* v. *Cattel* [1972] Ch. 105, 114.

option open to him under his contract with C,[93] for example, to terminate it by proper notice,[94] for so to hold would be to draw an indefensible distinction between existing, but terminable, relationships and those which are merely prospective,[95] and render it necessary to fall back on the defence of justification in order, for example, lawfully to persuade an employee to change his employment for higher pay.[96] Though Lord Denning's formulation was approved in unqualified terms in *Merkur Island Shipping Corporation*. v. *Laughton* that was a clear case of unlawful means and the approval should be read with that in mind.[97]

While there may be wrongful interference with contract short of actual breach, there must be interference with *performance* of the contract. Accordingly, makers and dealers in "bootleg" recordings[98] did not commit this tort even though their activities very seriously affected the value of a contract giving a recording company the exclusive right to exploit live performances.[99]

If it is a tort wrongfully to procure a breach of contract is it also a tort to procure the commission of other legal wrongs? There is no need to call up the tort where the legal wrong procured is itself a tort against the plaintiff, for the procurer is then himself liable as a joint tortfeasor[1]; nor, it seems, is there a tort of inducing a breach of trust, because a person who procures such an act becomes himself, by the doctrines of equity, liable as a trustee.[2] Procuring the commission of a criminal offence is not a tort unless the crime also amounts to a tort against the plaintiff, in which case the procurer is a joint tortfeasor.[3]

Plaintiff must prove that he has suffered damage as a result of the interference

Damage is the gist of the action and without it the plaintiff must fail.[4]

---

[93] *Allen* v. *Flood* [1898] A.C. 1. But *cf.* Employment Act 1982, s.12; Local Government Act 1988, s.17.
[94] *Cutsforth* v. *Mansfield Inns Ltd.* [1986] 1 W.L.R. 538.
[95] In *Midland Cold Storage Ltd.* v. *Steer* [1972] Ch. 630 Megarry J. said: "I am certainly not prepared to hold on motion that, conspiracy or unlawful means apart, there is a tort of wrongfully inducing a person not to enter into a contract."
[96] *cf. Restatement* 2d ss.766–768 under which (*a*) wrongful interference with a contract cannot be justified by competitive self-interest but (*b*) persuasion not to enter into a contract or lawfully to terminate a contract is made tortious only subject to a specific defence of competitive activity without unlawful means.
[97] [1983] 2 A.C. 570. Indeed, in *Torquay Hotel* itself, while Lord Denning's formulation makes no direct reference to the point, the defendants did threaten to induce breaches by B's servants of their contracts of employment. See also Dillon L.J. in *Merkur Island* in the C.A.: [1983] 2 A.C. 570, 588.
[98] Recordings made without authorisation at live performances; see *Rickless* v. *United Artists' Corp.* [1988] Q.B. 40. But recording companies now have a right of action under the Copyright, Designs and Patents Act 1988, ss. 185–188.
[99] *R.C.A. Corp.* v. *Pollard* [1982] 3 W.L.R. 1007, 1024, *per* Slade L.J. As to the tort of interference with trade by unlawful means, see *post*, p. 521.
[1] *C.B.S. Songs Ltd.* v. *Amstrad Consumer Electronics plc* [1988] A.C. 1013, 1058; *cf. Belegging, etc., B.V.* v. *Witten Industrial Diamonds Ltd.* [1979] F.S.R. 59, 66.
[2] *Metall und Rohstoff A.G.* v. *Donaldson Lufkin & Jenrette Inc.* [1988] 3 W.L.R. 548 (on appeal, *The Times*, February 2, 1989). There are circumstances in which a person who acts in breach of contract may be treated as a *constructive* trustee for the benefit of the other party to the contract. Where he is induced so to act it is artificial to plead that the defendant induced the breach of a constructive trust when the court has not yet decided whether there is such a trust. The plaintiff should simply plead that the inducer should be regarded as a constructive trustee and liable to account accordingly: *ibid.* at p. 562.
[3] *C.B.S. Songs Ltd.* v. *Amstrad Consumer Electronics p.l.c.* [1988] A.C. 1013, 1059.
[4] The plaintiff may, of course, obtain a *quia timet* injunction to restrain a threatened interference.

Where it is clear that the contract-breaker would have taken the same steps anyway the inducement is not an effective cause of the loss.[5] Where, as will normally be the case, the breach is such as must in the ordinary course of business inflict damage on the plaintiff, he may succeed without proof of any particular damage.[6] Where loss of a pecuniary nature is inferred or proved,[7] the plaintiff may also recover damages for non-pecuniary losses such as injured feelings.[8]

Defence of justification[9]

It is certain that justification is capable of being a defence to this tort, but what constitutes justification is incapable of exact definition.[10] It has been said that regard must be had to the nature of the contract broken, the position of the parties to the contract, the grounds for the breach, the means employed to procure it, the relation of the person procuring it to the person who breaks the contract, and the object of the person procuring the breach.[11] The advancement of one's own interests will not suffice, nor will that of the interests of one's own group[12] and the defendant cannot escape by showing that his motives are impersonal, disinterested and altruistic.[13] However, in *Brimelow* v. *Casson*,[14] persuasion of theatre proprietors by a theatrical performers' protection society to break their contracts with a theatrical manager was justified on the grounds that the wage paid by the manager to chorus girls was so low that they were obliged to supplement it by resort to prostitution.[15] It has been suggested that pressure of a moral[16] obligation as justification is the basis of *Brimelow* v. *Casson*, though the case has been said to stand alone[17] and there are conflicting dicta on moral obligation.[18] Presumably there is justification when a doctor urges[19] his

---

[5] See *Jones Bros. (Hunstanton) Ltd.* v. *Stevens* [1955] 1 Q.B. 275.

[6] *Exchange Telegraph Co.* v. *Gregory* [1896] 1 Q.B. 147. *Goldsoll* v. *Goldman* [1914] 2 Ch. 603.

[7] McCardie J.'s formulation in *Pratt* v. *B.M.A.* [1919] 1 K.B. 244, 281 suggests that such loss is a necessary foundation of a claim for non-pecuniary items.

[8] *Pratt* v. *B.M.A.*, *supra*. If the defendant is the plaintiff's competitor the case may be a suitable one for the award of exemplary damages: *post*, p. 601.

[9] Heydon, *op. cit.*, pp. 38–47.

[10] *cf.* the more definite privileges in defamation.

[11] *Glamorgan Coal Co. Ltd.* v. *S. Wales Miners' Federation* [1903] 2 K.B. 545, 574–575, *per* Romer L.J.

[12] *S. Wales Miners' Federation* v. *Glamorgan Coal Co. Ltd.* [1905] A.C. 239; *Camden Nominees Ltd.* v. *Forcey* [1940] Ch. 352; *Greig* v. *Insole* [1978] 1 W.L.R. 302. However, it has been held in New Zealand that action by a trade union to avoid involvement in industrial discord provoked by the defence of justification, especially bearing in mind the reasonable offer made by the defendant union, acceptance of which by the plaintiff would have enabled the contract in question to continue: *Pete's Towing Services Ltd.* v. *N.I.U.W.* [1970] N.Z.L.R. 32.

[13] *Greig* v. *Insole, supra*; *Posluns* v. *Toronto Stock Exchange* (1964) 46 D.L.R. (2d) 210, 270 (affirmed (1968) 67 D.L.R. (2d) 165) (where, however, justification arose from the plaintiff's implied submission to the discipline of the Exchange); *Slade & Stewart Ltd.* v. *Haynes* (1969) 5 D.L.R. (3d) 736.

[14] [1924] 1 Ch. 302.

[15] *cf. Stott* v. *Gamble* [1916] 2 K.B. 504 (banning of film under statutory powers).

[16] *Pritchard* v. *Briggs* [1980] Ch. 338, 416, *per* Goff L.J.

[17] *Camden Nominees Ltd.* v. *Forcey* [1940] Ch. 352, 366, *per* Simonds J.; *Pritchard* v. *Briggs* [1980] Ch. 338, 416, *per* Goff L.J.

[18] e.g. *South Wales Miners' Federation* v. *Glamorgan Coal Co. Ltd.* [1905] A.C. 239, 245, 246, 249, 255; *Crofter Hand-Woven Harris Tweed Co.* v. *Veitch* [1942] 435, 443, where the example is given of a man inducing his daughter not to marry a "scoundrel" (but engagement is no longer a contract).

[19] It is assumed that the advice is "persuasive" in the sense explained *ante*, p. 499.

patient to give up a fixed term employment because it is a danger to his health,[20] but what of the tutor who insists that his student give up a vacation job because it will interfere with his studies?[21]

The question of justification may also arise where A seeks to assert rights under a contract with B which is inconsistent with another contract between B and C. The question here is whether A has a right equal or superior to that of C and if he has he is justified in persuading B to break his contract with C. So if B enters into a contract on Monday to sell to A for £10,000 and then next day to sell the same property to C for £15,000 A, by persuading B to perform the first contract commits no wrong against C.[22] A will also be justified in reaching an accommodation with B rather than exercising his strict legal rights under the contract. In *Edwin Hill & Partners* v. *First National Finance Corporation*[23] a finance company which had a legal charge over B's property to secure a loan came to an arrangement with B whereby they would develop the property themselves rather than exercise their power of sale under the charge. A condition in this arrangement whereby the plaintiff was to be replaced as architect for the scheme did not constitute inducing breach of contract.[24]

It has been suggested that the defence of justification can never succeed if unlawful means are used, but this is not certain.[25]

INTIMIDATION

The word "intimidation" when used in the present context signifies a threat delivered by A to B whereby A intentionally causes B to act (or refrain from acting) either to his own detriment or to the detriment of C. There are thus two forms of the tort, which will be considered separately, but first two general points must be mentioned.

(a) "Threat" when used in this connection means "an intimation by one to another that unless the latter does or does not do something the former will do something which the latter will not like."[26] It is coercive and not mere idle abuse and demands either action or abstention from action on the part of the recipient,[27] so a mere announcement by A that he proposes to strike B is not, for the purposes of the law, a "threat" and cannot of itself give rise to a claim

---

[20] But might not this give the patient lawful justification for withdrawing from the contract?

[21] The *Restatement* 2d., ss.770 and 772 treat as justification (a) unrequested advice from a person charged wth responsibility for the welfare of the other and (b) all other honest advice if requested.

[22] A may have the defence of justification even though his contract is second in time provided he did not know of the first when he made it, but the authorities (some of which may depend upon a connection with the now abolished action for harbouring a servant) are not wholly reconcilable: see Cohen-Grabelsky (1982) 45 M.L.R. 241.

[23] [1989] 1 W.L.R. 225.

[24] It appears that the plaintiff had succeeded in an action against B for breach of contract: (1984) 272 E.G. 63, 179. It was common ground that if the plaintiffs had appointed a receiver or sold the property a new architect could have been appointed.

[25] See Clerk & Lindsell, *Torts* (16th ed.), para. 15–12; Heydon (1970) 20 Univ. of Toronto L.J. 178–182.

[26] *Hodges* v. *Webb* [1920] 2 Ch. 70, 89, *per* Peterson J.

[27] *J.T. Stratford & Son Ltd.* v. *Lindley* [1965] A.C. 269, 292, *per* Pearson L.J. See *News Group Newspapers Ltd.* v. *S.O.G.A.T. '82* [1986] I.R.L.R. 337 ("Scab, we will get you" interpreted to mean "we will get you if you do not stop working for the plaintiffs").

for damages.[28] On the other hand, the fact that a threat is couched in polite and regretful language does not make it any less a threat, and there is little value in the distinction which has been suggested between a warning and a threat.[29]

(b) For a threat as thus defined to be capable of giving rise to an action for damages on the part of anyone it must be a threat of an unlawful act. Anything that I may lawfully do I may also lawfully threaten to do, whatever the motive or purpose of my threat. This is an inescapable result of *Allen* v. *Flood*,[30] however unfortunate some of its consequences may be. Accordingly in *Hardie and Lane Ltd.* v. *Chilton*,[31] the Court of Appeal held that a threat by A, a trading association, to put B, one of its members, on a "stop list" (which would prevent B from getting goods from the members of the association) unless B paid a sum of money for having broken a rule of the association was not a tort.

Three-party intimidation

Despite some earlier hesitations, it is now certain that A commits the tort of intimidation against C if he threatens B with conduct which is unlawful in relation to B and thereby intentionally causes B to act (or refrain from acting) in a way which causes damage to C.[32] It is not a requirement of this tort that B's conduct be in any way unlawful in relation to C.[33] An old illustration is *Garret* v. *Taylor*,[34] where the plaintiff was the lessee of a quarry and alleged that the defendant had "disturbed" his customers and his workmen by "threatening to mayhem and vex them with suits if they had brought any stones." It was held that on these facts the plaintiff had a good cause of action.

In *Rookes* v. *Barnard*,[35] decided by the House of Lords in 1964 and the leading authority on this tort, the plaintiff (C) was employed by B.O.A.C. (B) in their design office and the three defendants (A) were officials of the A.E.S.D. Union, two of them also being employees of B.O.A.C.[36] C had been but was no longer a member of the Union. In order to preserve 100 per cent. union membership in the design office and notwithstanding the fact

---

[28] *Ibid.* at pp. 283–284, *per* Lord Denning M.R.

[29] *Hodges* v. *Webb, supra,* at p. 87.

[30] [1898] A.C. 1; *Rookes* v. *Barnard* [1964] A.C. 1129, 1169, *per* Lord Reid.

[31] [1928] 2 K.B. 306. See also *Ware and De Freville Ltd.* v. *Motor Trade Association* [1921] 3 K.B. 40. *Hardie and Lane Ltd.* v. *Chilton* was approved by the House of Lords in *Thorne* v. *Motor Trade Association* [1937] A.C. 797. For the crime generally known as "blackmail" see the Theft Act 1968, s.21.

[32] There seems no doubt that it would also be the tort of intimidation against C if A threatened an unlawful act to B unless C acted to his detriment.

[33] *Rookes* v. *Barnard* [1964] A.C. 1129; Weir, *Casebook on Tort* (6th ed.), p. 517. Note the difference between this tort and that of interference with a subsisting contract.

[34] (1620) Cro.Jac. 567; *Tarleton* v. *M'Gawley* (1793) Peake N.P. 270.

[35] *Supra.* The decision gave rise to a substantial literature. Amongst the most important articles are: Hamson, "A Note on *Rookes* v. *Barnard*" [1961] C.L.J. 189; "A Further Note on *Rookes* v. *Barnard*" [1964] C.L.J. 1059; Weir; "Chaos or Cosmos? *Rookes, Stratford* and the Economic Torts" [1964] C.L.J. 225; Hoffmann, "*Rookes* v. *Barnard*" (1965) 81 L.Q.R. 116; Wedderburn "The Right to Threaten Strikes" (1961) 24 M.L.R. 572; "The Right to Threaten Strikes II" (1962) 25 M.L.R. 513: "Intimidation and the Right to Strike" (1964) 27 M.L.R. 257.

[36] Silverthorne, who was not employed by B.O.A.C., was a party to an unlawful conspiracy to threaten breaches of contract: *Rookes* v. *Barnard, supra,* at pp. 1210–1211.

that a strike would have involved the men in breaches of their contracts of employment,[37] A notified B of the resolution passed by members of the union that if C was not dismissed, "a withdrawal of labour of all A.E.S.D. Membership will take place." B yielded to this threat and lawfully terminated C's contract of employment. Owing to the provisions of the Trade Disputes Act 1906[38] C could not rely upon a simple conspiracy to injure but in the House of Lords it was held that he was entitled to succeed on the ground of intimidation. The House held, agreeing with the Court of Appeal,[39] that there is a tort of intimidation, but they also held, reversing the Court of Appeal, that the tort extends to threats by A to break his contract with B and is not confined to threats of criminal or tortious conduct.

The essence of the tort lies in the coercion of B, through whom A intentionally inflicts damage upon C, but obviously the law cannot hold every form of coercion to be wrongful. If A tells his grown-up son, B, that he will stop B's allowance if B marries C, A may succeed, as is no doubt his intention, in depriving C of a profitable marriage, but he commits no tort against her, for he is perfectly entitled to stop B's allowance for any reason. The law has therefore adopted the natural dividing line between what is lawful and what is unlawful as against B, the person threatened.[40] The significance of *Rookes* v. *Barnard* was that it made it clear that a threat of a breach of contract was unlawful for this purpose[41] but the criticism has been made (and this indeed was the opinion of the Court of Appeal[42]) that if intimidation is extended to threats to break contracts "it would overturn or outflank some elementary principles of contract law,"[43] notably the doctrine of privity of contract, which holds that one who is not a party to a contract cannot found a claim upon it or sue for breach of it.

Two answers have been made to the privity of contract objection. First, it can be said not merely that C does not sue for breach of contract between A and B, but that his cause of action actually depends upon the contract not having been broken. It is only because B yields to A's threat that it might be broken that C suffers damage at all. If B does not yield and the contract is broken, then A's threat has not caused C to suffer loss.[44] And if it be objected that A may act first (against B) and explain why afterwards,

[37] An unusual feature of the case is that, as the defendants admitted, the men's contracts of employment contained an express undertaking that no strike would take place.
[38] s.1.
[39] [1963] 1 Q.B. 623.
[40] *Rookes* v. *Barnard* [1964] A.C. 1129, 1207, *per* Lord Devlin.
[41] The question arises whether a threat to strike is unlawful it if is to be called with the period of notice required to terminate the contract of employment. The Court of Appeal held that such a threat did not amount to intimidation in *Morgan* v. *Fry* [1968] 2 Q.B. 710, but it is hard to support the view of Lord Denning M.R. that a threat to strike on notice is lawful because it is a threat only to *suspend* the contract: see *Simmons* v. *Hoover Ltd.* [1977] I.C.R. 61. In determining whether a threat of industrial action is unlawful it may be necessary to consider how far the terms of a collective agreement (which is not a binding contract) are incorporated in an individual contract of employment (which is): *Hadmor Productions Ltd.* v. *Hamilton* [1983] 1 A.C. 191, 225. In many cases a threat to call a strike will not be actionable in tort because of s.13(1)(*b*) of the Trade Union and Labour Relations Act 1974: *post*, p. 530.
[42] [1963] 1 Q.B. 623.
[43] *Ibid.* at p. 695, *per* Pearson L.J.
[44] This is the line of reasoning that seems to be preferred by Lords Evershed, Hodson and Devlin: [1964] A.C. 1129, pp. 1187–88; 1200–1201; 1207–1208.

whereupon B acts to C's detriment, the answer is that it is not A's act which has caused C's loss but the implied threat that it will be repeated.[45] Alternatively it may be said bluntly that in all cases of intimidation, whatever the nature of the threatened act, C's cause of action is wholly independent of B's. C founds not upon the wrong, if any, done to B but on the fact that A has set out to injure him by the use of an unlawful weapon:

> "I can see no difference in principle between a threat to break a contract and a threat to commit a tort. If a third party could not sue for damage caused to him by the former I can see no reason why he should be entitled to sue for damage caused to him by the latter. A person is no more entitled to sue in respect of loss which he suffers by reason of a tort committed against someone else than he is entitled to sue in respect of loss which he suffers by reason of breach of a contract to which he is not a party. What he sues for in each case is loss caused to him by the use of an unlawful weapon against him—intimidation of another person by unlawful means."[46]

The second approach does more than answer the privity of contract objection: it refutes its basic premise. The point is "that the 'weapon,' *i.e.* the means, which the defendant uses to inflict loss on the plaintiff, may be unlawful because it involves conduct wrongful towards a third party. There is no reason in principle why such wrongful conduct should include torts and not breaches of contract. One might argue about whether it is expedient for the law to forbid the use of such acts as a means of causing loss, but the privity doctrine is a red herring."[47] If one asks why the law should draw the line at threats of breach of contract and not include within the tort of intimidation some threats against B even though the acts threatened are not strictly unlawful, the answer can lie only in the structure of the law. There is a legal "chasm"[48] between, for example, not entering into a contract and breach of an existing contract, which will not easily be bridged.

It must, however, be admitted that the above argument, to some extent, depends upon a "general" or even expansive approach to unlawful means in intimidation and in the economic torts as a whole. As a result of the decision of the House of Lords in *Lonrho Ltd.* v. *Shell Petroleum Co. Ltd. (No. 2)*[49] it is possible (though by no means certain) that threat of a breach of a penal statute does not amount to unlawful means for the purposes of intimidation unless the statute itself gives rise to a civil remedy.[50] If so, it is perhaps

---

[45] *Ibid.* at pp. 1187–8, 1208–1209. However, there may be cases where C suffers loss intended by A even though it cannot be said that B acts in response to any implied threat by A, as where A simply fails, in breach of contract, to deliver goods to B which he knows B has sold on to C (see Wedderburn (1964) 27 M.L.R. 257, 265). Such conduct is certainly not actionable as intimidation.

[46] *Rookes* v. *Barnard* [1964] A.C. 1129, 1168, *per* Lord Reid. See also Lord Pearce at pp. 1234–1235; Hoffmann and Weir, *loc. cit. cf.* Hamson, *loc. cit.*

[47] Hoffmann, *loc. cit.* p. 125.

[48] The word is Lord Herschell's: *Allen* v. *Flood* [1898] A.C. 1, 121.

[49] [1982] A.C. 173.

[50] See *post*, p. 524. The doubt about *Lonrho* arises from the fact that the acts alleged were not aimed at causing loss to the plaintiff. *cf.* Lord Devlin in *Rookes* v. *Barnard*, *supra*, at p. 1206, who appears to assume that any threat of a crime is "unlawful means."

surprising that a threat of a mere breach of contract should give rise to liability.

Two-party intimidation

There is little direct authority on the position where A threatens B with an unlawful act[51] and thereby intentionally[52] causes B to act (or refrain from acting) in a way which causes loss to B himself.[53] Nevertheless the general opinion seems to be that A commits a tort, certainly where his threat is of violence,[54] and also, since *Rookes* v. *Barnard*, where the threat is of any unlawful act[55] within the meaning of that case.[56] On the other hand, in *J.T. Stratford & Son Ltd.* v. *Lindley*[57] Lord Reid said, "A case where a defendant presents to the plaintiff the alternative of doing what the defendant wants him to do or suffering loss which the defendant can cause him to incur is not necessarily *in pari casu* and may involve questions which cannot arise where there is intimidation of a third person." The problems centre round the effect in the two-party situation of a threat of a breach of contract.

First, in the two-party situation there is normally a remedy already available to B, while in the three-party situation, if C cannot sue for intimidation, he cannot sue at all.[58] If B is threatened with a breach of contract he may be able to treat the contract as repudiated and sue for anticipatory breach or, of course, he may await the breach and then sue for damages. In fact, the balance of advantage would seem to lie in holding that where A threatens B with a breach of his contract with B, B should be restricted to his contractual remedies. The law should not encourage B to yield to the threat but should seek to persuade him to resist it.[59] In some cases he may be able to obtain an injunction to restrain the breach and in any case he will be adequately compensated by his remedy in damages for breach of contract as his damage can scarcely be other than financial. If B is threatened with a tort it is, of course, equally true that he may bring an action for damages if the tort is committed or bring an action for a *quia timet* injunction first, but, especially

---

[51] But despite the statement in *Thomas* v. *N.U.M. (S. Wales Area)* [1986] Ch. 20, it seems there is no tort of intimidation by harassment short of unlawful threats: *News Group Newspapers Ltd.* v. *S.O.G.A.T. '82* [1987] I.R.L.R. 337, 348; *Patel* v. *Patel*, *The Times*, August 21, 1987.

[52] See *Huljich* v. *Hall* [1973] 2 N.Z.L.R. 279.

[53] There is no reason why the two-party and the three-party situations should not coexist on the same facts. In, *e.g. Rookes* v. *Barnard* itself B.O.A.C. might have wished to sue in respect of their loss of the services of Mr. Rookes.

[54] Old textbook authority cited by Pearson L.J. in *Rookes* v. *Barnard* [1963] 1 Q.B. 623, 689 regards it as a form of trespass. See, *e.g.* Finch's *Law*, edition of 1678, pp. 201–202. See also Salmond & Heuston, *Torts* (19th ed.), p. 422.

[55] Seeking to enforce legislation which is subsequently found to be *ultra vires* is not an unlawful act: *Central Canada Potash Co. Ltd.* v. *Saskatchewan* (1978) 88 D.L.R. (3d) 609.

[56] A decision based on two-party intimidation is that in *News Group Newspapers Ltd.* v. *S.O.G.A.T. '82* [1986] I.R.L.R. 337, 347, with reference to the seventh plaintiff. The various dicta include: *Allen* v. *Flood* [1898] A.C. 1, 17, *Hawkins J.*; *Rookes* v. *Barnard* [1964] A.C. 1187, *per* Lord Evershed; [1963] 1 Q.B. 663, *per* Sellers L.J.; *J.T. Stratford & Son Ltd.* v. *Lindley* [1965] A.C. 269, 285, *per* Lord Denning M.R.; 302, 305–306, *per* Salmon L.J.; 336, *per* Lord Pearce; *D. & C. Builders Ltd.* v. *Rees* [1966] 2 Q.B. 617, 625, *per* Lord Denning M.R. None of these dicta is, however, very strong, and those in the *Stratford* case are more concerned with the effect of the Trade Disputes Act 1906.

[57] [1965] A.C. 269, 325.

[58] Hoffmann, *loc. cit.*, pp. 127–128.

[59] See the example given by Hoffmann, *ibid.*

where the threat is of violence, it is perhaps less realistic to say that these legal remedies afford him adequate protection against the consequences of resistance. From the point of view of policy, therefore, there is much to be said for the view that no independent tort is committed when all that is threatened, in the two-party situation, is a breach of contract, though there is not very much authority for such a proposition.[60]

Secondly, since *Rookes* v. *Barnard* there has been considerable development in the contractual context of the doctrine of "economic duress," and in this context it is clear that although a threat to break a contract is "illegitimate" it will not amount to duress unless it goes beyond commercial pressure and amounts to "coercion of the will." In *Pao On* v. *Lau Yiu*[61] A threatened that unless B agreed to vary an existing contract between them by giving A a guarantee against loss, A would not fulfil his side of the agreement. A's action on the guarantee succeeded because, although B had acceded to the demand because of fears of delay in litigation and loss of public confidence, the pressure fell short of coercion. Though intimidation was not discussed in the case it cannot be that B could have avoided the binding nature of the contract by the simple device of counterclaiming for damages for intimidation and it seems therefore that for the purposes of intimidation the plaintiff should be required to show unlawful coercion at least of such a degree as would enable him to avoid a contract.[62] If there are any cases in which the victim of unfair pressure may avoid a contract even though the threat is not of unlawful action,[63] there seems no possibility of any concurrent tort liability.[64]

CONSPIRACY

Though our early law knew a writ of conspiracy, this was restricted to abuse of legal procedure and the action on the case in the nature of conspiracy, which came into fashion in the reign of Elizabeth I, developed into the modern tort of malicious prosecution. Conspiracy as a crime was developed by the Star Chamber during the seventeenth century and, when taken over by the common law courts, came to be regarded by them as not only a crime but also as capable of giving rise to civil liability provided damage resulted to

---

[60] In *Central Canada Potash Co. Ltd.* v. *Saskatchewan* (1978) 88 D.L.R. (3d) 609, 640, Martland J. expressed agreement with this argument as set out in a previous edition, but the following passage in his judgment suggests that he may have intended to confine his agreement to cases where A is asserting what he reasonably (but wrongly) believes to be his contractual right.

[61] [1980] A.C. 614.

[62] Another problem is that the right to avoid a contract for economic duress may be lost by affirmation: *North Ocean Shipping Co. Ltd.* v. *Hyundai Construction Co. Ltd.* [1979] Q.B. 705. It is not easy to see on what basis the right to sue for intimidation could be similarly lost: cf. *Neibuhr* v. *Gage* (1906) 108 N.W. 884.

[63] Some of the cases on "unconscionable bargains" might be regarded as at least akin to duress.

[64] In *Universe Tankships Inc. of Monrovia* v. *I.T.W.F.* [1983] A.C. 366, 400, Lord Scarman, dissenting (but on another point) said: "It is, I think, already established law that economic pressure can in law amount to duress; and that duress, if proved, not only renders voidable a transaction into which a person has entered under its compulsion but is actionable as a tort, if it causes damage or loss." cf. Lord Diplock, *ibid.* at p. 385: "The use of economic duress to induce another person to part with property or money is not a tort *per se*; the form that the duress takes may, or may not, be tortious."

the plaintiff. As a tort, however, it was little developed until the second half of the nineteenth century[65] and the law remained obscure until the decision of the House of Lords in *Crofter Hand-Woven Harris Tweed Co. Ltd.* v. *Veitch*.[66] Conspiracy remains a crime as well as a tort, but the scope of the crime has been curtailed by statute[67] so that, broadly speaking, the only conspiracies which are now indictable are those to commit a substantive criminal offence, to defraud or to corrupt public morals or outrage public decency.[68] The Act, however, has no effect on civil liability. In fact, even aside from the Act the tort and the crime have cut loose from whatever common origin they had.[69]

The tort takes two forms according to whether or not unlawful means are used, though the decision of the House of Lords in *Lonrho Ltd.* v. *Shell Petroleum Co. Ltd. (No. 2)*[70] may have greatly reduced the importance of "unlawful means conspiracy." Indeed, the Court of Appeal has indicated that the law laid down in *Lonrho* has effectively resulted in the unlawful means category no longer existing in any meaningful form;[70a] but until the law is finally clarified by the House of Lords it seems justifiable to continue to speak of two forms of the tort.

Conspiracy to injure

It was firmly established in *Crofter Hand-Woven Harris Tweed Co. Ltd.* v. *Veitch*[71] that if there is a combination of persons whose purpose is to cause damage to the plaintiff, that purpose may render unlawful acts which would otherwise be lawful. The production of Harris Tweed is an industry of the Isle of Lewis. Originally the yarn for the cloth was hand-spun from wool by the crofters of Lewis and was wholly produced in the Isle. By 1930, hand-spinning of wool had become commercially impracticable and thenceforth many weavers in Lewis imported yarn from the mainland. Five mill owners in Lewis nevertheless spun yarn woven by the crofters. These mill owners alleged that cloth woven on Lewis from mainland yarn could be sold much more cheaply than cloth made from yarn spun in Lewis. It was therefore in their interest to get a minimum price fixed for the cloth. Of the workers in their mills 90 per cent. belonged to the T.G.W.U. and the Lewis dockers were also members of it. The union, with the object of getting all mill workers to be members and of increasing wages, approached the mill owners, who replied that they could not raise the wages because of the competition of the crofters who wove imported yarn. The union officials then put an embargo on the importation of yarn by ordering Lewis dockers not to handle such yarn. They obeyed (without breaking any contract) and

---

[65] It "is a modern invention altogether": *Midland Bank Trust Co. Ltd.* v. *Green (No. 3)* [1982] Ch. 529, 539, *per* Lord Denning M.R.
[66] [1942] A.C. 435.
[67] Criminal Law Act 1977.
[68] The last two may be offences even when committed by one person.
[69] *Midland Bank Trust Co. Ltd.* v. *Green (No. 3), supra*, at p. 541.
[70] [1982] A.C. 173; Elias and Tettenborn [1981] C.L.J. 230.
[70a] *Metall und Rohstoff A.G.* v. *Donaldson Lufkin & Jenrette Inc.*, *The Times*, February 2, 1989.
[71] [1942] A.C. 435.

thus injured the trade of seven small producers of tweed who used imported yarn and who sued the officials for conspiracy.

It must be stressed at the outset, lest the importance of this form of liability be exaggerated, that the plaintiffs lost their case because the predominant purpose of the embargo was to promote the interests of the union members rather than to injure the plaintiffs,[72] but their Lordships made it clear that if the predominant purpose of a combination is to injure another in his trade or business[73] or in his other legitimate interests[74] then, if damage results, the tort of conspiracy exists. The *Crofter* principle was applied by the Court of Appeal in *Gulf Oil (Great Britain) Ltd.* v. *Page*[75] in granting an interlocutory injunction against a combination to publish a statement defamatory of the plaintiffs even though the statement was admitted to be true and there would, therefore, have been an absolute defence to an action for libel.

(1) *Purpose*

The object or purpose of the combination must be to cause damage to the plaintiff. The test is not what the defendants contemplated as a likely or even an inevitable consequence of their conduct; it is "what is in truth the object in the minds of the combiners when they acted as they did?"[76] Malice in the sense of malevolence, spite or ill will is not essential for liability[77]; what is required is that the combiners should have acted *in order that* (not *with the result that*, even the foreseeable result) the plaintiff should suffer damage. If they did not act in order that the plaintiff should suffer damage they are not liable, however selfish their attitude and however inevitable the plaintiff's damage may have been.[78]

Cases of mixed motive are common enough in individuals, and it is obvious that a combination of persons may have more than one purpose. Where this is so the question must be asked, what was the real or predominant purpose of the combination, and it is to be answered broadly as by a jury or judge of fact.[79] Difficulty may arise where the purposes of the various parties to the combination are different. If each party has his own private end to gain, but yet the joint aim is no more than a desire for prosperity or peace in industry, there is no tort.[80] On the other hand, if one of the parties is

---

[72] See also *Mogul SS. Co. Ltd.* v. *McGregor Gow* [1892] A.C. 25; *Sorrell* v. *Smith* [1925] A.C. 700.
[73] This, so their Lordships held, had really been settled in *Quinn* v. *Leathem* [1901] A.C. 495, notwithstanding earlier doubts about the meaning of that case.
[74] [1942] A.C. 435, 446–447, 451, 462, 478.
[75] [1988] Ch. 327.
[76] [1942] A.C. 435, 445, *per* Viscount Simon L.C. Nevertheless, though "purpose" is not the same as "intention," "in many cases the one is the parent of the other" (*ibid.* at p. 452, *per* Viscount Maugham) and a man's "intention" may furnish useful evidence of his "purpose."
[77] *Ibid.* at pp. 450, 463, 469–471. Proof of malevolence coupled with proof of a lack of tangible benefit to the combiners would show a combination to be wrongful, but mere malevolence does not damage anyone. "I cannot see how the pursuit of a legitimate practical object can be vitiated by glee at the adversary's expected discomfiture": *ibid.*, *per* Lord Wright.
[78] As may be expected from this, successful actions for conspiracy are rare.
[79] *Ibid.* at pp. 445, 478.
[80] *Ibid.* at pp. 453, 495. Thus in an alliance between an employer and a trade union the former might wish to keep up prices against competition, the latter to safeguard employment.

actuated merely by hatred or vindictive spite he may be liable and if the others are aware of this and lend him their assistance they too may thereby become participants in the wrong.[81] Without such knowledge, however, there can be no conspiracy, since the essence of the tort is an unlawful combination.[82]

Another way of expressing the central requirement of conspiracy to injure is to say that the law is concerned with the distinction between legitimate and illegitimate purposes, for the former will legalise the infliction of the most catastrophic and inevitable harm to the plaintiff's business. The legitimate purpose of a combination is sometimes spoken of as its justification[83] (and the expression is convenient) but this does not mean that a combination to do an act harmful to the plaintiff is necessarily actionable unless the defendants prove that it was justified. The burden of proof lies with the plaintiff throughout.[84] On the other hand, there may obviously be cases where the plaintiff establishes a prima facie case by proving that he suffered damage from acts done in combination by the defendants the natural and probable outcome of which was damage to him. The defendants may then have to meet this "provisional burden" by adducing evidence that their purpose was something else and that it was legitimate, without affecting the "legal burden" of proof.[85]

Precise definition of what is and is not a legitimate purpose is probably not possible,[86] but the fact that we live in a competitive or acquisitive society has led English law, for better or worse, to adopt the test of self-interest or selfishness as being capable of justifying the deliberate doing of lawful acts which inflict harm.[87] Acts done to forward or protect the defendants' trade or business interests are clearly justified, but it is not essential that the interest promoted be a material one.[88] In *Scala Ballroom (Wolverhampton) Ltd.* v. *Ratcliffe*[89] the plaintiffs refused to admit coloured persons to their ballroom[90] but they did allow coloured musicians to play in the orchestra. The defendants were members of the Musicians' Union, a union with many coloured members, and they gave notice to the plaintiffs that members of the union would not be permitted to play at the ballroom so long as the colour bar was in operation. An injunction to restrain them from persuading their members not to play there was refused.[91] On the other hand, in *Huntley* v. *Thornton*[92] damages were awarded against union officials whose object in keeping the plaintiff out of work was, as Harman J. found, to uphold "their

---

[81] *Ibid.* at p. 495.
[82] *Jarman & Platt* v. *Barget* (1977) 3 F.S.R. 260.
[83] See, *e.g. Sorrell* v. *Smith* [1925] A.C. 700, 712, *per* Viscount Cave L.C.; Heydon, *op. cit.*, p. 16.
[84] *Crofter* case, *supra*, at pp. 471, 495.
[85] Perhaps this is what Viscount Maugham was referring to in the *Crofter* case, *supra*, at p. 449.
[86] *Crofter* case, *supra*, at p. 446, *per* Viscount Simon L.C.
[87] *Ibid.* at p. 472, *per* Lord Wright. See *British Airways Board* v. *Laker Airways Ltd.* [1985] A.C. 58.
[88] Lord Wright (*ibid.* at p. 478) implies that a combination of parishioners to withhold subscriptions from the incumbent is not unlawful if the object is the promotion of the religious interests of the parish. *cf. Bear* v. *Reformed Mennonite Church* 341 A. (2d) 105 (1975).
[89] [1958] 1 W.L.R. 1057.
[90] See now the Race Relations Act 1976.
[91] See further, Heydon, *op. cit.*, p. 20.
[92] [1957] 1 W.L.R. 321; *Hutchinson* v. *Aitchison* (1970) 9 K.I.R. 69.

own ruffled dignity. . . . It had become a question of the district committee's prestige; they were determined to use any weapon ready to their hand to vindicate their authority, and grossly abused the quite frightening powers at their command."[93]

Other examples of unlawful objects are given by their Lordships in the *Crofter* case. "Mere busybodies" are probably not protected,[94] nor are those who are induced to join a combination by the payment of money and have no other interest to protect.[95] A combination to compel the plaintiff to pay a debt is apparently unlawful,[96] but where the object is to punish him it is necessary to distinguish between mere vindictive vengeance, which is unlawful, and the purpose of deterring others from similarly offending, which apparently is not.[97] If the object is to increase the effective strength of a trade union, it is lawful.[98] The fact that the damage is disproportionate to the purpose sought to be achieved does not itself render the conspiracy actionable[99]; nor is the court concerned with the expediency or otherwise of the policy adopted by the combiners.[1]

(2) *Combination*

There must be concerted action between two or more persons, which includes husband and wife.[2] It seems that there can be no conspiracy between an employer and his employees, at least where they merely go about their employer's business.[3] On the other hand, there might be circumstances where an employer would be vicariously liable for a conspiracy involving his servants provided the other requirements of that form of liability are met. There may be a conspiracy between a company and its directors, whose knowledge and purpose may be imputed to the company.[4]

(3) *Overt act causing damage*

In contrast with the crime of conspiracy, an overt act causing damage is an essential element of liability in tort. If, therefore, the acts relied on are incapable of being made part of any cause of action—*e.g.* evidence given by

---

[93] [1957] 1 W.L.R. 321, 341, *per* Harman L.J. Such a case was foreshadowed by Lord Wright in the *Crofter* case, *supra*, at p. 445.
[94] *cf.* Diplock J. at first instance in the *Scala* case.
[95] [1942] A.C. 435, 451, 460, 480.
[96] *Giblan* v. *National Amalgamated Labourers' Union* [1903] 2 K.B. 600. What of the case when the defendants combine to compel the plaintiff to subscribe to an extraneous charity?
[97] *Crofter* case, *supra*, at p. 475; *Eastham* v. *Newcastle United Football Club Ltd.* [1964] Ch. 413, 453–454.
[98] *Crofter* case, *supra*, at p. 493, *per* Lord Porter, citing *Hodges* v. *Webb* [1920] 2 Ch. 70; *White* v. *Riley* [1921] 1 Ch. 1.
[99] Though it may cast doubt upon the defendants' bona fides.
[1] *Ibid.* at p. 447.
[2] *Midland Bank Trust Co. Ltd.* v. *Green (No. 3)* [1982] Ch. 529. This is a clear difference between the tort and the crime.
[3] Clerk & Lindsell, *Torts* (16th ed.), para. 15–22.
[4] *Belmont Finance Corp. Ltd.* v. *Williams Furniture Ltd. (No. 2)* [1980] 1 All E.R. 393. *cf. Belmont Finance Corp. Ltd.* v. *Williams Furniture Ltd.* [1979] Ch. 250 (knowledge not to be imputed where company plaintiff).

witnesses in a court of law—then the tort cannot be made out.[5] A sufficient element of damage is shown where expenses are necessarily incurred by the plaintiff in investigating and counteracting the machinations of the defendants.[6]

"Unlawful means" conspiracy

This form of the tort involves the use of means which are independently unlawful, though not necessarily tortious. For many years its significance was thought to lie in the fact that, while the combiners had to intend to do an unlawful act,[7] it was not necessary that their purpose should be to injure the plaintiff. However, this may have been overturned by the House of Lords in *Lonrho Ltd*. v. *Shell Petroleum Co. Ltd. (No. 2)*.[8] Shell and others constructed an oil refinery in what was then Southern Rhodesia and Lonrho constructed a pipeline thereto from a port in Mozambique. In November 1965 the government of Southern Rhodesia declared unilateral independence and the United Kingdom passed legislation, the "sanctions order,"[9] making it a criminal offence to supply oil to Southern Rhodesia. No further oil was shipped through Lonrho's pipeline, causing the company loss of revenue. The facts to be assumed by the House of Lords for the purposes of the appeal[10] were that Shell and others had, in breach of the sanctions order, covertly supplied Southern Rhodesia with oil by other means and thereby prolonged the state of illegal independence *and the time during which Lonrho's pipeline was out of use*. It was clear that the breach of the sanctions order gave rise to no action in tort for breach of statutory duty[11] and a claim based on breach of the sanctions order as "unlawful means" for the purposes of the tort of interference with trade failed.[12] The case was also, however, framed as a conspiracy between Shell and others to contravene the sanctions order. This too failed, on the basis that in unlawful means conspiracy, as in conspiracy to injure, there must be an intent to injure the plaintiff, and conspiracy should not be extended "beyond acts done in execution of an agreement entered into by two or more persons for the purpose not of protecting their own interests but of injuring the interests of the plaintiff."[13] Accordingly, since the case was to be decided on the factual assumption that the purpose of Shell and others in combining to contravene the sanctions order was to forward their own commercial interests, not injure those of

---

[5] *Marrinan* v. *Vibart* [1963] 1 Q.B. 234, affirmed *ibid.* at p. 528.

[6] *B.M.T.A.* v. *Salvadori* [1949] Ch. 556.

[7] The defendants must know the facts which make the combination unlawful but they need not know that the means are legally classified as unlawful: *Belmont Finance Corp.* v. *Williams Furniture Ltd. (No. 2)* [1980] 1 All E.R. 393, 404, 414.

[8] [1982] A.C. 173; *ante*, p. 172. Weir, *Casebook on Tort* (6th ed.), p. 529 (conspiracy point).

[9] Made pursuant to the Southern Rhodesia Act 1965.

[10] The matter came before the House in the form of a case stated from an arbitration.

[11] *Ante*, Chap. 7.

[12] *Post*, p. 524.

[13] [1982] A.C. 173, 189. It is true that the question before the House only concerned conspiracy "where the acts agreed to be done . . . amount to criminal offences under a penal statute" but the formulation of the law would seem to leave no scope for the argument that a different rule applies to, *e.g.* conspiracy to commit a tort or a breach of contract.

Lonrho, no matter how likely or foreseeable such injury might be, the claim in conspiracy failed.

The meaning of the decision in *Lonrho* has produced radical differences of opinion in courts here and abroad. One view, which is supported by the judgment of Lord Denning M.R. in the Court of Appeal in *Lonrho* is that "it is sufficient if the [unlawful means] conspiracy is aimed or directed at the plaintiff and it can reasonably be foreseen that it may injure him, and does in fact injure him"[14] and the Supreme Court of Canada has since stated the law in similar terms in a decision in which *Lonrho* was considered.[15] This would allow for liability where, for example, A and B conspired by unlawful means with the purpose of driving a competitor C out of the market and thereby monopolising it. If such a case involved no unlawful means their "purpose" would be treated as the advancement of their own self-interest[16] or, to put it another way, their object in removing C from the market would be legitimate. To deny such legitimacy in the case where unlawful means were used would still leave some practical scope for this form of conspiracy. This would not mean that A and B are liable for conspiracy wherever they acted unlawfully with the foreseeable consequence that C suffered loss, for conspiracy should not extend further than the other economic torts (for example, interference with contract by unlawful means) where the predominant view[17] is that this is not sufficient. The plaintiff must be the "target" of the combination but if he is, on this view, the advancement of the defendants' own interests does not justify the use of unlawful means.

However, subject to further consideration by the House of Lords, this does not now represent English law. In *Metall und Rohstoff* v. *Donaldson Lufkin & Jenrette Inc.*[18] the allegations pleaded (which the court was required to assume to be true for the purposes of an issue as to service out of the jurisdiction) were as follows. Company A, dealers on the Metal Exchange, knowingly assisted an employee of the plaintiffs to engage in fraudulent trading, the result of which was that Company A became exposed to liabilities of more than £6.5m. To protect itself, Company A, at the instigation of Company B, its parent company, falsely asserted that these accounts were the responsibility of the plaintiffs and wrongfully seized certain metal warrants belonging to the plaintiffs. The plaintiffs obtained judgment for £50m. against Company A but recovered only £6.7m. since A was insolvent. A further claim for, *inter alia*, unlawful means conspiracy was brought against Company B but it was not alleged that the predominant purpose of the conspiracy was to injure the plaintiffs since the defendants were obviously concerned to protect their own position. The Court of

---

[14] *The Times*, March 7, 1981. In the House of Lords, Lord Diplock said, "my choice is unhesitatingly the same as . . . all the members of the Court of Appeal": [1982] A.C. 173, 189.

[15] *Canada Cement La Farge Ltd.* v. *British Columbia Lightweight Aggregate Ltd.* (1983) 145 D.L.R. (3d) (again the action failed, the conspiracy not being "directed at" the plaintiff). But the Supreme Court did not think this consistent with the law laid down for England in *Lonrho*.

[16] See the *Crofter*, case, *supra*.

[17] But see *Falconer* v. *A.S.L.E.F.*, *ante*, p. 504.

[18] *The Times*, February 2, 1989. See also *Allied Arab Bank Ltd.* v. *Hajjar* [1988] 3 W.L.R. 553 where assets were diverted to avoid liability on judgment debts.

Appeal, after a full consideration of *Lonrho*, held that the omission of an allegation of intention to injure was fatal to the claim. On this basis, it is hard to see what, if anything, a separate category of unlawful means conspiracy adds to the law and while not perhaps strictly abolished by judicial *fiat* it may be expected to fade away. *Lonrho* itself is authority for the view that pursuit of naked self-interest by criminal means can never amount to conspiracy.[19] If the wrong agreed on itself amounts to a tort against the plaintiff perhaps little has been lost by the restriction of conspiracy, for the combination must be carried into effect to cause damage and then the substantive tort is committed. Certainly, it is sometimes said[20] that a claim for conspiracy gives the plaintiff procedural advantages, but the reality of this may turn on how far it is to be held on ordinary principles that instigation or procurement suffices to make a person who does not participate in the act a joint tortfeasor.[21] The restriction of conspiracy might seem to put the plaintiff at a disadvantage if the unlawful means is a tort against a third party[22] or the breach of a contract to which the defendant is not a party[23] but this is not necessarily so, for the defendant's procurement of the commission of the tort may again expose him to liability as a joint tortfeasor, and as to a breach of contract he may anyway have committed the substantive tort of interference with an existing contract. In any event, the emergence of the generic tort of interference with trade or business by unlawful means[24] may have had the effect that most cases which were formerly regarded as unlawful means conspiracies amount to torts even without the element of combination. If there is a lacuna in the law it is probably confined to combinations to do acts which amount to crimes but to no other wrong, but the exclusion of such cases from the tort of conspiracy may be a necessary consequence of *Lonrho* whatever the mental element required for the tort.[25-26]

Place of conspiracy in the law

Conspiracy, it has been said, is a highly anomalous tort, though it has attracted more controversy among academic writers than success in practical application.[27] The central issue has been why the "magic of plurality" should make something unlawful if it is not unlawful when done by one person

[19] See the *Crofter* case, *supra*, which established that pursuit of self-interest does not amount to an intent to injure the plaintiff. In any event, an act which is a crime alone is probably not unlawful means according to *Lonrho*, though that aspect of the case concerns the different tort of interference with trade by unlawful means.

[20] As in *Metall und Rohstoff* itself.

[21] It is suggested in *Metall und Rohstoff* that the seizure of the warrants may have amounted to conversion.

[22] But in *Lonrho p.l.c.* v. *Fayed* [1988] 3 All E.R. 464, 471, at first instance, Pill J. held that where A and X combine to tell lies to B in order to cause harm to C that amounts to a *Crofter*-type conspiracy or nothing.

[23] In any event, the proposition that a breach of contract is unlawful means in conspiracy, while perhaps a logical deduction from *Rookes* v. *Barnard*, is by no means beyond argument: see Lord Devlin's remark in *Rookes* v. *Barnard* at [1964] A.C. 1210 and *Barretts & Baird (Wholesale) Ltd.* v. *I.P.C.S.* [1987] I.R.L.R. 3, 9.

[24] See p. 521, *post*.

[25-26] See n.19, *supra*. Another possible lacuna exists if a narrow meaning is given to "trade or business" in the generic unlawful means tort. It is also suggested in *Metall und Rohstoff* that Lord Diplock in *Lonrho* was speaking only of conspiracies in the "commercial sphere".

[27] *Lonrho Ltd.* v. *Shell Petroleum Co. Ltd. (No. 2)* [1982] A.C. 173, 188.

alone. Numbers may, of course, bring increased power and in the *Crofter* case Viscount Maugham said that he had never felt any difficulty in seeing "the great difference between the acts of one person and the acts in combination of two or of a multitude,"[28] but, as Viscount Simon L.C. remarked in the same case:

> "The view that the explanation is to be found in the increasing power of numbers to do damage beyond what one individual can do is open to the obvious answer that this depends on the personality and influence of the individual. In the play, Cyrano de Bergerac's single voice was more effective to drive the bad actor Montfleury off the stage than the protests of all the rest of the audience to restrain him. The action of a single tyrant may be more potent to inflict suffering on the continent of Europe than a combination of less powerful persons."[29]

The argument from numbers continues to have some appeal in the criminal law[30] but there are now few situations in which there may be an indictment for conspiracy in respect of acts which would not be criminal if done by one person.[31] One day the law may re-examine the place in our law of combination and of the "chasm" between lawful and unlawful acts which exists in the case of an individual, but the latest judicial pronouncements suggest a retreat from liability[32] rather than an advance towards a principle that the intentional infliction of harm without justification is actionable.[33]

Interference with Trade by Unlawful Means[34]

Given that the chasm referred to in the previous paragraph is now unbridgeable is there a more modest general principle that it is a tort intentionally to inflict economic harm[35] on another by use of "unlawful means?" There is now authority that, at least where the harm is interference with trade or business, there is such a tort.[36] Its principal practical impact is to fill in the gaps in the other, long-established torts involving unlawful means by imposing liability where there is no combination, no threat and no interference

---

[28] [1942] A.C. 435, 448.

[29] *Ibid.* at p. 443. See also Lord Diplock's rather less colourful example of the street-corner grocers and a chain of supermarkets in single ownership in the *Lonrho* case: [1982] A.C. 173, 189.

[30] See Law Com. No. 76.

[31] Conspiracy to commit a substantive offence has great practical significance in the criminal law because it allows the police to "nip crime in the bud."

[32] Particularly the *Lonrho* case.

[33] Compare *Bradford Corp.* v. *Pickles* [1895] A.C. 151 with *Tuttle* v. *Buck* (1909) 119 N.W. 946.

[34] Carty, "Unlawful Interference with Trade" (1983) 3 L.S. 193; Carty, "Intentional Violation of Economic Interests. The Limits of Common Law Liability" (1988) 104 L.Q.R. 250; Elias and Ewing, "Economic Torts and Labour Law: Old Principles and New Liabilities" [1982] C.L.J. 321.

[35] Where the harm is personal injury *Wilkinson* v. *Downton* [1897] 2 Q.B. 57 supports the even wider proposition that it is actionable wilfully to inflict it without justification: see *ante*, p. 68. Possibly the same principle might cover damage to property.

[36] *Merkur Island Shipping Corp.* v. *Laughton* [1983] 2 A.C. 570, 609–610, *per* Lord Diplock. Its existence was conceded in *Lonrho p.l.c.* v. *Fayed* [1989] 2 All E.R. 65, where the C.A. spoke of it as being in the course of development.

with a subsisting contract. In *J. T. Stratford & Son Ltd*. v. *Lindley*,[37] the facts of which have already been given,[38] two at least of their Lordships considered that if the defendants had used unlawful means—*i.e.* had committed against the barge hirers the tort of procuring breaches of their contract with their men—the plaintiffs would have had a cause of action not only in respect of breaches of hiring contracts but also in respect of new business they were unable to undertake. "In addition to interfering with existing contracts," said Lord Reid[39] "the defendant's action made it practically impossible for the appellants to do any new business with the barge hirers. It was not disputed that such interference with business is tortious if any unlawful means are used." Indeed, this result is an irresistible inference from the acceptance of the tort of intimidation: if it is a tort by A against C to threaten a wrong to B if B continues to deal with C it is hard to see why it should not be equally tortious to inflict harm on C by committing that wrong rather than merely threatening it. More generally, however, this tort has been said to be the genus of which the other unlawful means torts (intimidation and interference with contract and conspiracy where unlawful means are involved[40])are species.[41] If this is correct, it may be asked why it is necessary to deal with the established, nominate torts at all, to which one can only respond that until the limits of the general tort are clearly established plaintiffs are likely to rely upon as many causes of action as they can, even though from our point of view it is untidy to have two or more torts rather than one.

Mental element

Like the established economic torts, this is a tort of intention and it is thought that the conduct of the defendant must have the plaintiff as its target[42] though it need not be the predominant purpose in the sense that the defendant needs to be activated by malevolence: the pursuit of self-interest by unlawful means is actionable. Although in some branches of the law a defendant may be treated as intending the known inevitable or likely consequences of his act, that is not so here, for it would stretch the tort too far to impose liability where "the reasons which actuate the defendant to use unlawful means are wholly independent of a wish to interfere with the plaintiff's business, such interference being no more than an incidental consequence foreseen by and gratifying to the defendant."[43] It must, however, be said that it is by no means crystal clear that this forms the mental element of the "species" torts of unlawful interference with contract[44] and

---

[37] [1965] A.C. 269.
[38] *Ante*, p. 501.
[39] [1965] A.C. 269, 324; see also *ibid.* at p. 329.
[40] But not "*Crofter*-type" conspiracy nor directly inducing breach of contract by persuasion, despite the reference in *Merkur Island, supra*, at p. 610.
[41] *Merkur Island, supra*, at p. 610. This approach would also accommodate the suggestion that inducing breach of statutory duty might be a tort in its own right: see *Barretts & Baird (Wholesale) Ltd.* v. *I.P.C.S.* [1987] I.R.L.R. 3.
[42] *Barretts & Baird (Wholesale) Ltd.* v. *I.P.C.S.* [1987] I.R.L.R. 3; *Lonrho p.l.c.* v. *Fayed* [1989] 2 All E.R. 65.
[43] *Van Camp Chocolates Ltd.* v. *Aulsebrooks Ltd.* [1984] 1 N.Z.L.R. 354, 360 (defendant's purpose to make a profit for himself, effect on plaintiff's trade "super-added and inessential").
[44] See *ante*, p. 504.

unlawful means conspiracy[45] (indeed, in the case of the latter it very probably does not) and it is not easy to see how the species can differ in this respect from the genus.

Trade or business

Beyond the fact that most cases are likely to arise in the context of trade or business it is not apparent why liability should be confined to cases where those activities are interfered with. If it is actionable to use unlawful means to drive away C's prospective customers[46] why should it not equally be actionable to use such means against a person who proposes to buy his house but has not yet signed a contract to do so? If "trade or business" is to be regarded as a requirement of the tort there is a danger that the genus may be narrower than the species. However, it has been suggested that the tort protects only some identifiable legal right. In *Lonrho plc* v. *Fayed*[47] the facts which the court was required to assume to be true[48] were that the defendants had made fraudulent misrepresentations about themselves to the Secretary of State in order to influence him not to refer their bid for H.F. Co. to the Monopolies and Mergers Commission. The plaintiffs contended that they had thereby been deprived of the opportunity to bid for H.F. Co. but Pill J. rejected their claim because while the law certainly allowed a freedom to bid for property that was neither a "business asset" of the plaintiffs' nor a legal right which the law would protect.[49] The Court of Appeal, however, declined to deal with this and other points on a striking-out application.

Two-party or three-party?

As we have seen, at least one form of the established economic torts (intimidation) may exist even though the defendant uses unlawful means directly against the plaintiff rather than against a third party.[50] Is it, therefore, the law that if A steals the tools of a carpenter, B, and locks him up, B may sue for unlawful interference with trade as well as conversion and false imprisonment? Or (assuming breach of contract to be unlawful means) that A is liable in tort if, in order to bring down B, he breaches his contract with him? It is thought that the answer in each case should be "no" because, quite apart from the practical consequences of thus multiplying liability,[51] it would

---

[45] See *ante*, p. 519.

[46] *cf. Tarleton* v. *M'Gawley* (1793) Peake N.P. 270 (intimidation).

[47] [1988] 3 All E.R. 464. As to the conspiracy claim in this case, see *ante*, p. 520. The case of *National Phonographic Co. Ltd.* v. *Edison Bell* [1908] 1 Ch. 335, which contained dicta (especially at pp. 355–357) apparently supportive of the plaintiffs' claim was distinguished as being concerned with interference with a subsisting contract.

[48] It was an application to strike out the statement of claim.

[49] Alternatively, Pill J. held (i) the tort did not extend to a competitor making false statements about himself, (ii) there was no sufficient nexus between the false representations and the loss to the plaintiffs. *Quaere* whether there was the requisite intent? For the C.A., see [1989] 2 All E.R. 65.

[50] See *ante*, p. 509. But see also, as to interference with contract, *Dimbleby & Sons Ltd.* v. *N.U.J.* [1984] 1 W.L.R. 427.

[51] *e.g.* a tort liability would introduce the possibility of exemplary damages in the second example.

be a travesty of history to unify these disparate wrongs under one heading of tort.

Unlawful means

If the law of economic torts is in a mess[52] it is largely because of uncertainty over what constitutes unlawful means. This concept has played the leading role in the development of the modern law but the question of definition has tended to be passed over in the cases with little analysis.[53] Since the broad, "genus" tort is a comparatively recent growth, most of the authorities on unlawful means concern the older, nominate wrongs so that the elements of the former are to some extend rationalisations from the latter and, as we have seen, there is a regrettable element of doubt as to whether "unlawful means" bears the same meaning wherever it occurs.[54] Bearing that in mind, it is tolerably clear that conduct which is itself tortious is always unlawful means.[55] The same is probably true of breach of contract[56] but once we move outside the area of wrongs which are civilly actionable in damages the law becomes more uncertain. For example, it has been held that an arrangement void for contravention of the Restrictive Trade Practices Act 1956 constitutes unlawful means[57] but this is hard to reconcile with the clear decision in the *Mogul* case that an agreement in restraint of trade at common law did not.[58] Breach of confidence might qualify as unlawful means (assuming it not to be a tort in itself)[59] but there has been no subsequent support for Lord Denning M.R.'s suggestion that the concept might extend to "interference with the press."[60] On the other hand, a fraudulent statement to a third party is unlawful means even though the third party could not sue for tort because he suffers no damage.[60a]

It might seem self-evident that the commission of a crime amounts to unlawful means, but this is not so, at least where the crime is created by statute.[61] This was the first point dealt with by the House of Lords in *Lonrho Ltd.* v. *Shell Petroleum Co. Ltd. (No. 2),*[62] the facts of which have already been summarised, and in which it was held that the restrictions imposed on the bringing of a direct civil action for breach of a statute[63] could not be outflanked by framing the claim as one for the tort of unlawful interference

---

[52] Carty, (1988) 104 L.Q.R. at p. 278.

[53] See generally, Clerk & Lindsell, *Torts* (16th ed.), para. 15–20.

[54] See, *e.g. ante*, p. 511.

[55] But *cf. supra*, n. 26, and as to the "two-party" case, see *ante*, pp. 512 and 524.

[56] Again, an exception must probably be made for the case where the defendant acts directly against the plaintiff: *ibid.*

[57] *Daily Mirror Newspapers Ltd.* v. *Gardner* [1968] 2 Q.B. 762; see also *Brekkes* v. *Cattel* [1972] Ch. 105. As to "Eurotorts" in breach of the EEC Treaty, see *ante*, p. 496.

[58] *Mogul SS. Co.* v. *McGregor Gow* [1892] A.C. 25; *Davies* v. *Thomas* [1920] 2 Ch. 189; *British Airways Board* v. *Laker Airways Ltd.* [1985] A.C. 58.

[59] See *post*, p. 558.

[60] *Associated Newspapers Group Ltd.* v. *Wade* [1979] 1 W.L.R. 697.

[60a] *Lourho p.l.c.* v. *Fayed.* [1989] 2 All E.R. 65.

[61] *A fortiori* an act which, by statute, is merely null and void is not unlawful means. See *Dunlop* v. *Woollahra Municipal Council* [1982] A.C. 158, though the claim there was not based on this tort.

[62] [1982] A.C. 173, *ante*, p. 518. Weir, *Casebook on Tort* (6th ed.), p. 153 (unlawful means point).

[63] See Chap. 7.

with trade.[64] As a matter of strict precedent, however, this aspect of the *Lonrho* case must have been decided on the same factual assumption as that which governed the conspiracy claim, *viz.* that while injury to Lonrho's business was foreseeable it was not the defendants' *purpose* to bring it about.[65] It might, therefore, be open to a court to find liability where a defendant committed a statutory offence as the vehicle for the deliberate infliction of harm upon the plaintiff.[66]

In view of the *Lonrho* decision a similar question might arise with regard to common law crimes[67] which are not also torts in their own right.[68] The closest case on this point is probably *Chapman* v. *Honig*[69] where a landlord gave notice to quit to his tenant, the notice being in accordance with the terms of the lease. H's purpose, however, was to punish the tenant for having given evidence (under *subpoena*) in an action brought against him by another of his tenants and it followed that the landlord was guilty of a criminal contempt of court.[70] Nevertheless, the Court of Appeal held, by a majority, that the tenant had no cause of action against the landlord. In coming to this conclusion Pearson L.J. foreshadowed the "construction" approach in *Lonrho* by treating the common law criminal contempt as if it were created by a hypothetical enactment and asking what intention was to be inferred, with regard to civil liability, from the exercise of the contempt jurisdiction.[71] However, it is not easy to reconcile *Chapman* v. *Honig* with *Acrow (Automation) Ltd.* v. *Rex Chainbelt Inc.*[72] (where *Chapman* v. *Honig* was not cited). Acrow Ltd. obtained an injunction to restrain an American company, S.I., from acting in breach of contract so as to impede Acrow's manufacture of machinery under licence from S.I. S.I. purported to ignore the injunction and instructed Rex Chainbelt, suppliers of components for Acrow's process, to cease supply. This did not involve the breach of any subsisting contract between Acrow and Rex Chainbelt. The Court of Appeal granted an injunction to restrain Rex Chainbelt from obeying S.I.'s instructions: Rex Chainbelt's conduct was interference by unlawful means because it was done in obedience to the orders of S.I. which were in contempt of court. The case may be different from *Chapman* v. *Honig* in that the contempt involved was civil not criminal[73] but it is not easy to see

---

[64] *cf. Hargreaves* v. *Bretherton* [1959] 1 Q.B. 45 where it had been held that the statutory crime of perjury gave rise to no civil action.

[65] [1982] A.C. 173, 183 "The claim is put . . . as an innominate tort, committed by Shell and by B.P. severally, of causing foreseeable loss by an unlawful act . . . "

[66] This possibility is accepted in *Copyright Agency* v. *Haines* (1982) 40 A.L.R. 264, 275. See also *Associated British Ports* v. *T.G.W.U.*, *The Times*, June 9, 1989.

[67] There is, of course, no hard and fast line between the two categories—an offence may be regulated for some purposes by statute, for other purposes by common law.

[68] Some other systems have a much closer correspondence between crime and tort, *e.g.* the Italian penal code specifically enacts that every crime which has caused pecuniary or non-pecuniary damage obliges the offender to make compensation: Art. 185.

[69] [1963] 2 Q.B. 502; Weir, *Casebook on Tort* (6th ed.), p. 151.

[70] *Att.-Gen.* v. *Butterworth* [1963] 1 Q.B. 696.

[71] [1963] Q.B. 502, 521.

[72] [1971] 1 W.L.R. 1676; Wedderburn (1972) 35 M.L.R. 184.

[73] However, while it is clear that a party subject to an injunction who disobeys it (S.I.) commits a *civil* contempt, logic would seem to suggest that one who abets him (Rex Chainbelt) commits a criminal contempt.

why this should point towards tortious liability. Nor can any distinction be drawn on the basis that there were three persons involved whereas *Chapman* v. *Honig* was a "two-party" case, for a true "three-party" case only arises where A acts in a manner which is primarily unlawful in relation to B with the purpose of injuring C. In *Acrow* there *was no* B.[74]

TRADE DISPUTES

A general textbook on the law of tort is no place for an extended discussion of the specialised law relating to trade disputes but those disputes have provided most of the "raw material" for the development of the common law and their legal regulation has been so substantially modified by statute since 1906 that some account of the legislative intervention is necessary.

Trade Disputes Acts 1906 and 1965[75]

The Trade Disputes Act 1906 was of enormous importance but only the briefest summary of its provisions can be attempted here. The Act:
  (i)   made trade unions completely immune from actions in tort, though it did not affect liability of individuals;
  (ii) rendered "conspiracy to injure" (*i.e.* without unlawful means) not actionable in the context of trade disputes;
  (iii) rendered inducement of breaches of contracts of employment not actionable in the context of trade disputes.
The Trade Disputes Act 1965 reversed *Rookes* v. *Barnard* in trade dispute cases by rendering not actionable a threat to break or induce the breach of a contract of employment.

Industrial Relations Act 1971

This Act set out to enlarge the range of civil remedies for wrongful acts done in contemplation or furtherance of "industrial disputes," but through the new statutory concept of unfair industrial practices, not through the law of tort.[76] Some of these unfair industrial practices were similar to certain varieties of torts and the common law was not wholly abolished. However, the Act was a disastrous failure for political reasons and was repealed by the Trade Union and Labour Relations Act 1974.

Trade Union and Labour Relations Act 1974

This Act still forms the basis of legal immunities in trade disputes, though

---

[74] Except in the sense that B was the court or the general law, but that is equally true of *Chapman* v. *Honig*.
[75] See the ninth edition of this work.
[76] There was a voluminous literature on this ill-fated Act. For a summary of its provisions concerning industrial disputes, see Salmond, *Torts (16th ed.), Chap. 17.*

most of the relevant provisions have in fact been inserted by textual amendment by later legislation. Protection is granted, in the context of a trade dispute, to interference with contract (and not merely a contract of employment), to intimidation or conspiracy to injure and to interference with trade by unlawful means but by the Employment Act 1980 this protection was to a large extent withdrawn in case of "secondary action."

Present law

(1) *Trade unions*

It will have been observed that nearly all the cases in this chapter arising from industrial disputes have taken the form of actions against individual workers or trade union officials. This is because for many years trade unions themselves were immune from actions in tort. This was not based on the fact that a trade union was an unincorporated body, for in *Taff Vale Railway Co. v. Amalgamated Society of Railway Servants*[77] the House of Lords held that a union registered under the Trade Union Act 1871 was enough of a legal entity to be sued in tort. The *Taff Vale* case was reversed by section 4 of the Trade Disputes Act 1906. After a brief period during which a registered trade union was a corporate body under the Act of 1971, the Trade Union and Labour Relations Act 1974 restored the immunity, though liability was imposed (where there was no trade dispute) for certain torts causing personal injury or breaches of duty connected with the union's property.

It remains the law that a trade union is not, and is not to be treated as if it were, a body corporate,[78] but a much wider measure of tort liability is now imposed by the Employment Act 1982.[79] The central difficulty is that of attributing responsibility to the "centre" in such a "devolved" organisation as the typical trade union, bearing in mind the likelihood that "unofficial action" will be taken at individual plant level without prior consultation with the union's central organs. The fundamental proposition of the 1982 Act is that the immunity of trade unions in tort is totally abolished,[80] though the union enjoys the same defences as an individual where action is taken in contemplation or furtherance of a trade dispute.[81] However, the range of the union's responsibility for the acts of its officers and members differs according to the nature of the claim which is brought against it. According to section 15 of the 1982 Act, if the union is sued for inducing breach of or interfering with contract, or for intimidation by threats to interfere with contract,[82] or for conspiracy to commit these torts,[83] then the act in question

---

[77] [1901] A.C. 426.

[78] Trade Union and Labour Relations Act 1974, s.2(1). A consequence of this is that a trade union does not have sufficient personality to maintain an action for defamation: *E.E.T.P.U.* v. *Times Newspapers Ltd.* [1980] Q.B. 585.

[79] Under s.2(1) of the 1974 Act a trade union is capable of suing and being sued in its own name.

[80] s.15(1).

[81] *Post*, p. 528. However, it is not very clear whether this is so because the union is to be treated as a "person" for the purposes of s.13 of the Trade Union and Labour Relations Act 1974 or because its liability can only be truly vicarious.

[82] s.15(2)(a).

[83] s.15(2)(b). Hence intimidation by threats of violence or conspiracy to trespass are outside the section.

shall be taken to have been done by the union only if it was authorised or endorsed by a "responsible person," which means the principal executive committee, any person authorised by the rules to endorse acts of the kind in question, the president or general secretary, any other employed official,[84] or any committee to which an employed official reports, but an act by an official or a committee to which he reports shall not be taken as authorised or endorsed if the official or committee was prevented from authorising or endorsing the act by union rules or if the act has been repudiated by the president or general secretary.[85] In all other cases it would seem that the union's responsibility for the acts of an individual are to be determined by the general law of master and servant or agency.[86]

Where the union's liability arises in respect of personal injury caused by negligence, nuisance or breach of duty, or in respect of ownership or possession of property,[87] there is no limit on its amount, but in other cases there are financial limits according to the size of the union.[88] However, damages are not recoverable by enforcement against "protected property" (which includes a political fund which is not available for financing strikes and provident benefits fund).[89] Actions for damages (as opposed to injunctions) have not so far figured largely in litigation against individuals caused by industrial action; the limits to union liability set by the 1982 Act are low in relation to the loss that may be suffered[90] and the very large fines imposed for contempt by disobedience to injunctions have probably been a more powerful sanction.

(2) *Liability of individuals*

An individual (*e.g.* a shop steward) is liable for unprivileged acts in the course of a trade dispute, whether or not a trade union is liable.[91] The extent of individual immunity in this context is found in section 13 of the Trade Union and Labour Relations Act 1974, as limited, in the case of "secondary action" by the Employment Act 1980.

Section 13 in its present form reads as follows:

"(1) An act done by a person in contemplation or furtherance of a trade dispute shall not be actionable in tort on the ground only—
(a) that it induces another person to break a contract or interferes or induces any other person to interfere with its performance; or
(b) that it consists in his threatening that a contract (whether one to

---

[84] A shop steward is hardly ever an employed official of the union.
[85] See s.15(4)–(6). A repudiation is ineffective if followed by inconsistent action.
[86] Considered by the House of Lords in the context of the Industrial Relations Act 1971 in *Heatons Transport (St. Helens) Ltd.* v. *T.G.W.U.* [1973] A.C. 15.
[87] *cf.* s.14(2) of the 1974 Act, imposing liability in such cases "if not arising from an act done in contemplation or furtherance of a trade dispute."
[88] See s.16(3). From £10,000 if the union has less than 5,000 members to £250,000 if the union has 100,000 or more members.
[89] s.17(2), (3).
[90] The upper limit of £250,000 is a good deal less in real terms than the £23,000 awarded in the *Taff Vale* case. However, where industrial action is industry-wide there may be numerous plaintiffs.
[91] Employment Act 1982, s.15(8). There is no financial limit on such personal liability.

which he is a party or not) will be broken or its performance interfered with, or that he will induce another person to break a contract[92] or to interfere with its performance.

(4) An agreement or combination by two or more persons to do or procure the doing of any act in contemplation or furtherance of a trade dispute shall not be actionable in tort if the act is one which, if done without any such agreement or combination, would not be actionable in tort."

(a) **Trade dispute.** In order to gain the protection of section 13, the act done by the defendant must be "in contemplation or furtherance of a trade dispute." This concept, the so-called "golden formula," is defined in section 29 of the Trade Union and Labour Relations Act 1974, as amended by the Employment Act 1982.[93] It means a dispute[94] between workers[95] and their employer[96] which relates wholly or mainly[97] to one or more of the following: terms and conditions (including physical conditions) of employment; engagement, non-engagement, termination or suspension of employment[98] or of duties of employment; matters of discipline; membership or non-membership of a trade union; facilities for union officials; machinery for negotiation or consultation and other procedures, including recognition of unions.[99] However, by section 10 of the Employment Act 1988 the immunity is withdrawn where the reason or one of the reasons for which the act is done is the fact or belief that the employer is employing non-union labour. Action in support of the "closed shop," the source of many trade dispute cases, is no longer lawful.

A crucial amendment by the 1982 Act was the removal of section 29(4), which provided that a dispute to which a trade union was party should be treated as a dispute to which workers were parties. For this reason, union officials cannot claim the protection of section 13, if, as part of a wider dispute, they initiate industrial action against an employer who is in harmony with his workers.[1] If, however, some support for the union's policy can

---

[92] Subs. (2) was repealed by the Employment Act 1982, s.19(1) and subs. (3) by the Employment Act 1980, s.17(8).

[93] All references here are to the 1974 Act, as amended by the 1982 Act.

[94] But by s.29(5) an act, threat or demand done or made by one person or organisation against another which, if resisted, would have led to a trade dispute with that other shall, notwithstanding that because that other submits to the act or threat or accedes to the demand no dispute arises, be treated for the purposes of the Act as being done or made in contemplation of a trade dispute with that other.

[95] Including former workers whose employment was terminated in connection with the dispute or whose dismissal was one of the circumstances giving rise to the dispute: s.29(6).

[96] An inter-union dispute is not, as such, any longer within the scope of the protection, but such a dispute will very often involve the employer.

[97] Under the previous legislation the dispute had only to be "connected with" the relevant matters.

[98] Including fears of redundancy: *Hadmor Productions Ltd.* v. *Hamilton* [1983] 1 A.C. 191; Elias [1982] C.L.J. 249. *cf. Mercury Communications Ltd.* v. *Scott-Garner* [1984] Ch. 37.

[99] There can only be a trade dispute relating to matters outside the United Kingdom for the purposes of the Act if persons acting in the United Kingdom in contemplation or furtherance thereof are likely to be affected: s.29(3).

[1] *e.g.* the campaign of the International Transport Workers' Federation against "flags of convenience," which forms the basis of cases such as *N.W.L. Ltd.* v. *Woods* [1979] 1 W.L.R. 1294 and *Merkur Island Shipping Corp.* v. *Laughton* [1983] 2 A.C. 570. It seems that the remarks in *Conway* v. *Wade* [1909] A.C. 509 which are criticised in *N.W.L. Ltd.* v. *Woods* [1979] 1 W.L.R. 1294, 1304, become valid again after the 1982 Act.

be mustered among the plaintiff employer's workers the range of matters covered by section 29 is very wide. In *B.B.C.* v. *Hearn*[2] the defendants, in order to protest against apartheid, threatened to instruct the members of their union to commit breaches of contract in relation to broadcast by satellite to South Africa of the 1977 Cup Final. In proceedings for an interlocutory injunction the Court of Appeal held it unlikely that there was a trade dispute, but Roskill L.J. recognised that the situation might well have been different if, instead of the defendants simply threatening to "black" the broadcast they had gone to the B.B.C. and said "We wish it to be established as part of our conditions of employment that we are not required to work on broadcasts to South Africa." This received the approval of Lord Diplock in *N.W.L. Ltd.* v. *Woods*[3] but it has since been remarked that a "trade union cannot turn a dispute which in reality has no connection with terms and conditions of employment into a dispute connected with terms and conditions of employment by insisting that the employer inserts appropriate terms into the contracts of employment into which he enters."[4]

An act is "in furtherance" of a trade dispute when the doer genuinely believes it will assist the cause in support of which it is done: the House of Lords has emphatically rejected the addition of any requirement that the act be "not too remote" or "reasonably likely to succeed."[5]

(b) Interference with subsisting contract and intimidation. Section 13(1) protects the most obvious forms of trade union coercion, *i.e.* inducing breaches of contract and threats to do so. There would, for example, be no liability on facts such as those in *Rookes* v. *Barnard* if the threats had been made in support of a wage claim.[6] The protection is not confined to interference with contracts of employment[7] but where the contract affected is not a contract of employment, there are restrictions on the use of "secondary action."[8] The word "only" is important, for the protection is thereby confined to cases in which the defendant commits no other, incidental tort to procure the breach of contract. If, *e.g.* he uses words amounting to defamation he is not protected.

(c) Conspiracy. Section 13(4) removes "conspiracy to injure" from the

[2] [1977] 1 W.L.R. 1004.
[3] *Supra*, at p. 1304.
[4] Lord Cross in *Universe Tankships Inc. of Monrovia* v. *I.T.W.F.* [1983] 1 A.C. 366, 392. However, this was a case where there was harmony between the employer and workers and the union was an interloper. See also *Mercury Communications Ltd.* v. *Scott-Garner, supra.*
[5] *Express Newspapers Ltd.* v. *McShane* [1980] A.C. 672; *Duport Steels Ltd.* v. *Sirs* [1980] 1 W.L.R. 142. However, this point became a good deal less important with the Employment Act 1980 because an objective likelihood of success is an element under that Act of protected "secondary action": *post*, p. 532.
[6] Since the action was in fact taken to enforce a "closed shop" it would now be unlawful by s.10 of the Employment Act 1988 (*ante*, p. 529). *cf.* the provisions of s.14 of the Employment Act 1982, under which it was unlawful for A to call out B's men so as to disrupt supplies to C in order to bring pressure on C because he used non-union labour, but it was not unlawful to use such tactics for this purpose against B.
[7] "There is no essential difference between embarrassing an employer by persuading his workers to break their contracts of employment in contemplation or furtherance of a trade dispute and embarrassing him, in the same circumstances, by persuading his suppliers or his customers to break their contracts of sale or purchase": Standing Committee E, June 18, 1974, col. 489.
[8] See below.

field of trade disputes because it involves an action which would not be actionable in tort if done without agreement or combination.[9] The scope of "unlawful means" conspiracy is also restricted by the requirement that the act should be one which would be actionable *in tort* if done by one person. Thus an agreement to break a contract may not be actionable.[10] An agreement to induce a breach of contract might be thought to fall outside this protection because inducement is a tort if committed by one person, but this is not so if the inducement is protected by section 13(1).[11]

(d) **Unlawful interference with trade.** This tort is not directly referred to in section 13, except in so far as the "nominate" torts above are species of which it is the genus. Obviously it should not be possible to evade the statutory immunity by pleading the genus and relying on the species as unlawful means,[12] but there would seem to be no statutory protection if the unlawful means take any other form such as nuisance or trespass.[13] A trade union or union official calling its members out on strike is therefore protected but it has been said to be arguable that an individual striker has no protection against a claim that he uses unlawful means when he withdraws

---

[9] The protection is really unnecessary. If the defendants are acting in contemplation or furtherance of a trade dispute they have a "legitimate purpose" at common law; and they do not "intend to injure" the plaintiff: *Hadmor Productions Ltd.* v. *Hamilton* [1983] 1 A.C. 191, 228. The effect of *Lonrho Ltd.* v. *Shell Petroleum Co. Ltd. (No. 2)* [1982] A.C. 173, *ante,* may be to do much the same for "unlawful means" conspiracy.

[10] Of course, this depends upon the uncertain ambit of the tort of interference with trade by unlawful means, which *may* be committed by an individual.

[11] The matter was clearer under s.13(3) of the 1974 Act, repealed by the Employment Act 1980: "For the avoidance of doubt it is hereby declared that—(*a*) an act which by reason of subsection (1) or (2) above is itself not actionable; (*b*) a breach of contract in contemplation or furtherance of a trade dispute; shall not be regarded as an unlawful act or as the use of unlawful means for the purpose of establishing liability in tort." However, in *Hadmor Productions Ltd.* v. *Hamilton* [1983] 1 A.C. 191 the House of Lords held that an act which was "not actionable" under s.13(1) did not amount to "unlawful means" for the purposes of intimidation.

[12] Otherwise the immunity given by s.13(1) would disappear at a stroke.

[13] The whole question of immunity for this tort is now in a state of confusion. Immunity for interference by unlawful means when the means alleged is an act covered by s.13(1) was most obviously provided by s.13(3), *supra,* which was repealed in 1980, though the decision in *Hadmor Productions* v. *Hamilton, supra,* suggests that the immunity remains by virtue of s.13(1). However, in *Hadmor,* [1983] 1 A.C. 191, 229, and in *Merkur Island Shipping Corp.* v. *Laughton* [1983] 2 A.C. 570, 609, it is firmly stated by Lord Diplock (with whom all other members of the House agreed) that unlawful interference with trade is the tort referred to in s.13(2) of the 1974 Act: "For the avoidance of doubt it is hereby declared that an act done by a person in contemplation or furtherance of a trade dispute is not actionable in tort on the ground only that it is an interference with the trade, business or employment of another person, or with the right of another person to dispose of his capital or his labour as he wills." This was formerly the "second limb" of s.3 of the Trade Disputes Act 1906, which was passed at a time when it was thought that there might be a general tort of interference with trade without unlawful means—a "*Quinn* v. *Leathem* without the conspiracy" (Lord Devlin in *Rookes* v. *Barnard* [1964] A.C. 1129, 1216)—and it has long been clear that there is no such tort. It is, of course, possible that Parliament had something else in mind when re-enacting these words in 1974, but if Lord Diplock is correct the effect of s.13(2) thereafter was to render the other provisions of s.13 unnecessary and, indeed, to go a good way beyond them. This was in effect the principle stated by the Court of Session in *Plessey Co. plc* v. *Wilson* [1983] I.R.L.R. 198, when it held that s.13(2) might legitimise a trespassory sit-in on the basis that the object of the action was "interference with trade or business." s.13(2) was repealed by s.19(1) of the Employment Act 1982 and as a matter of legislative history this was done to give the quietus to *Plessey*. It seems most unlikely that the repeal of s.13(2) will lead to the emergence of a tort of improper interference with trade by lawful means. It would, however, be unfortunate if the repeal of s.13(2) *and* s.13(3) were to lead to the conclusion that there is no protection for unlawful interference with trade when the unlawful means is an act covered by s.13(1): *e.g. Merkur Island, supra,* at p. 609 (when s.13(2) was still in force).

his labour because this situation does not appear to fall within section 13(1).[14]

(e) Secondary action. The complex[15] provisions of section 17 of the Employment Act 1980 restrict the scope of the section 13 immunity for "secondary action." Nothing in section 13 is to prevent an act from being actionable in tort on a ground specified in section 13(1) where (*a*) the contract interfered with in respect of which the action is brought is *not* a contract of employment[16] and (*b*) there has been secondary action which does not satisfy the requirements of section 17.[17] Secondary action is action interfering with a contract of employment in one of the ways specified in section 13(1) where the employer under that contract is not a party to the trade dispute.[18] Hence if, in pursuance of a trade dispute between A and C, A induces the employees of B, with whom C has a contract, to break their contracts of employment with a view to bringing about a breach of the contract between B and C the action is presumptively unlawful. However, this is not the end of the matter for the scope of this withdrawal of immunity is limited by the remainder of section 17, which provides three routes through which secondary action may finally be held to be not unlawful.[19] The principal provision is section 17(3) which provides that secondary action is not unlawful if—

"(a) the purpose or principal purpose of the secondary action was directly to prevent or disrupt the supply during the dispute of goods or services[20] between an employer who is a party to the dispute[21] and the employer under the contract of employment to which the secondary action relates; and

(b) the secondary action (together with any corresponding action relating to other contracts of employment with the same employer) was likely to achieve that purpose."

This was considered by the House of Lords in *Merkur Island Shipping Corporation*. v. *Laughton*[22] where, it will be remembered, the I.T.F. union, in dispute with Merkur Island, a flag of convenience shipowner, induced tug-boat crews to refuse, in breach of their contracts of employment, to move Merkur Island's vessel, thereby interfering with the charter of the

---

[14] *Barretts & Baird (Wholesale) Ltd.* v. *I.P.C.S.* [1987] I.R.L.R. 3. The position was different under the now repealed s.13(3)(*b*): see *supra*, n. 11. See generally Wedderburn, *The Worker and the Law* (3rd ed.), p. 637.

[15] See the remarks of Sir John Donaldson M.R. in *Merkur Island Shipping Corp.* v. *Laughton* in the C.A.: [1983] 2 A.C. 570, 594, and of Lord Diplock in the H.L.: *ibid.* as p. 612.

[16] *e.g.* the charterparty in *Merkur Island*.

[17] s.17(1).

[18] s.17(2).

[19] Judgments now tend to conform to a recognisable chronological pattern: (1) Is the conduct actionable at common law? (2) Is it of a type protected by s.13? (3) Is the contract within s.17 of the 1980 Act and is there secondary action? (4) Can the secondary action follow one of the s.17 escape routes?

[20] Which means supply under a contract subsisting at the time of the secondary action: s.17(6).

[21] Because s.17(4), dealing with a different situation, contains provisions about associated companies and s.17(3) does not, the court will not lift the veil of incorporation under s.17(3). Hence in *Dimbleby & Sons Ltd.* v. *N.U.J.* [1984] 1 W.L.R. 427 T.B.F. and T.B.F. (Printers) were subsidiaries of the same holding company. The N.U.J. were in dispute with T.B.F. so disruption of supply between Dimbleby and T.B.F. (Printers) was not protected. See also *The Marabu Porr* [1979] 2 Lloyd's Rep. 331.

[22] [1983] 2 A.C. 570; *ante*, p. 503; *Marina Shipping Ltd.* v. *Laughton* [1982] Q.B. 1127.

vessel to Leif Hoegh. Having said that any removal of the immunity by section 17 enured for the benefit not only of the person against whom the secondary action was taken but also for that of the employer who was party to the trade dispute,[23] Lord Diplock held that the action by I.T.F. was not protected. Merkur Island were not parties to any contract for the supply of towage services,[24] so it was not possible to say that the purpose of the action was to prevent the supply of services between an employer who was party to the dispute (Merkur Island) and the employer under the contract of employment to which the secondary action related (the tug owners).[25]

Similar provisions are contained in the Act to govern secondary action aimed at disruption of supply between any person and an associated employer of the employer party to the dispute where the goods or services are in substitution for goods or services which but for the dispute would have fallen to be supplied to or by the employer who is party to the dispute.[26]

(f) Picketing. Picketing in various forms has shown itself to be one of the most effective forms of industrial action. At common law it may be unlawful as amounting to a trespass to the highway, or a public or private nuisance,[27] or as involving the inducement or procuring of a breach of contract. However, under section 15 of the Trade Union and Labour Relations Act 1974[28] it is lawful for a person in contemplation or furtherance of a trade dispute to attend at or near his own place of work[29] "for the purpose only of peacefully obtaining or communicating information, or of peacefully persuading any person to work or abstain from working."[30] "Secondary action" (*e.g.* persuading a supplier's lorry driver not to deliver[31] so as to disrupt a commercial contract) is protected if the attendance is lawful under the 1974 Act,[32] but there is no protection for "secondary picketing," *i.e.* attendance at the premises of the employer's supplier or customer.

(g) Ballots. Yet another basis for the removal of the immunity granted by the 1974 Act is to be found in Part II of the Trade Union Act 1984. This requires action taken by a trade union[33] to be supported by a majority in a

[23] [1983] 2 A.C. 570. After 1982, the repeal of s.29(4) of the Trade Union and Labour Relations Act 1974 would mean that there was no trade dispute in *Merkur Island*: *ante*, p. 529.
[24] In fact, the towage contract was entered into by sub-charterers, Ned Lloyd, though the result would have been the same if Leif Hoegh had been parties to it. See also n. 21, *supra*.
[25] I.T.F. had notice of the Merkur Island-Leif Hoegh contract. There is no discussion of whether they had notice of the Ned Lloyd-tug owner contract. The implication is that to determine their "purpose" under s.17(3) what counts is the actual contractual arrangements.
[26] s.17(4). The other provision on secondary action relates to picketing: *infra*.
[27] See *ante*, p. 414; Carty [1984] P.L. 600.
[28] As substituted by s.16 of the Employment Act 1980.
[29] Or, where he is a union official, at or near the place of work of a member of the union whom he is accompanying and whom he represents. Where a person's employment was terminated in connection with a trade dispute, his former place of work. s.15 does not allow entry on the employer's land without his consent: *British Airports Authority* v. *Ashton* [1983] 1 W.L.R. 1079.
[30] s.15(1). Inducing breaches of contracts of employment by means of picketing is protected only if s.15 is complied with: Employment Act 1980, s.16(2).
[31] In modern times this function of picketing is probably more important than preventing "blackleg" labour.
[32] Employment Act 1980, s.17(5).
[33] Whether the action is taken by the union is determined according to the test in s.15 of the Employment Act 1982 (*ante*, p. 527). The absence of a ballot does not remove the immunity of those who participate in unofficial action, but if the action is official and the ballot requirements are not complied with individuals as well as the union lose the protection of the 1974 Act: s.10 of the 1984 Act.

secret ballot of all those reasonably expected to take part in the action,[34] and in view of the practicalities of organising a ballot and the fact that advance approval of action is valid for only four weeks[35] puts a serious constraint upon the taking of effective action even where that has overwhelming support. Detailed modifications of the ballot procedure are to be found in sections 12 to 18 of the Employment Act 1988.

(h) Injunctions. Where an employer is the victim of industrial action his primary purpose in embarking on litigation is usually (and this is likely to remain the case notwithstanding the extension of tort liability to trade unions) to get an injunction. Since an injunction may be granted on an interlocutory basis pending trial (which may not take place for many months) and, in cases of great urgency, on an *ex parte* basis,[36] it is clear that there is a possibility of the union side being robbed of the initiative in an industrial action. To meet this point, section 17 of the Trade Union and Labour Relations Act 1974 contains two provisions. First, where an application for an injunction is made *ex parte* and the defendant claims, or in the opinion of the court would be likely to claim, that he acted in contemplation or furtherance of a trade dispute, the court shall not grant the injunction unless satisfied that all steps which in the circumstances were reasonable have been taken with a view to securing that notice of the application and an opportunity of being heard with respect to the application have been given to him. This reduces the risk of the defendants in a "labour injunction" case being taken unawares, but contains nothing about how the court should proceed when both parties are before it. At the time when the 1974 Act was passed it was thought that the issue on an application for an interlocutory injunction was whether the plaintiff had established a prima facie case, but in *American Cyanamid Ltd.* v. *Ethicon Ltd.*[37] the House of Lords held that the test was rather more favourable to the plaintiff, was there "a serious question to be tried?" To meet this development section 17(2) was inserted into the Act[38] and provides that where an application is made for an interlocutory injunction and the party against whom it is sought claims that he acted in contemplation or furtherance of a trade dispute, the court shall, in exercising its discretion whether or not to grant the injunction, have regard to the likelihood of that party's succeeding at the trial of the action in establishing the matter which would afford a defence under the Act. Under the *American Cyanamid* decision the court must ask itself whether the plaintiff has shown (*a*) a serious question to be tried and (*b*) that the "balance of convenience" is in his favour. It is not very clear whether section 17(2) adds a third element or is subsumed in (*b*), but it *is* clear that it was intended to be more difficult to obtain an interlocutory injunction in trade

---

[34] The Act applies even though the union is a federation which cannot effectively hold a complying ballot: *Shipping Company Uniform Inc.* v. *I.T.W.F.* [1985] I.R.L.R. 71.

[35] But a further ballot is not necessary to reimpose industrial action which has been suspended during negotiations: *Monsanto plc* v. *T.G.W.U.* [1987] 1 W.L.R. 617.

[36] *i.e.* in the absence of the defendant or his representative.

[37] [1975] A.C. 396.

[38] By the Employment Protection Act 1975, Sched. 16, Pt. III, para. 6.

dispute cases than in others. If the affidavits suggest that it is more likely than not that the defendant would succeed in establishing a statutory immunity that is a weighty factor in favour of refusing to grant an injunction.[39] It has been suggested that now that unions (and not merely officials) may in certain circumstances be liable in damages for unlawful industrial action[40] it is more likely that an employer will pursue his claim to a full trial and there is less reason to refuse an interlocutory injunction in trade dispute cases[41]; but it has also been said that the "right to strike" is a valuable (indeed essential) element in the system of collective bargaining and that it "should not be rendered less valuable than Parliament intended by too fanciful or ingenious a view of what might develop into a serious issue to be tried."[42]

PASSING OFF

The tort of passing off is part of a much wider canvas of legal remedies controlling unfair competitive practices and we have already said that "unfair competition" would be beyond the scope of this book, so that such matters as copyrights, trade marks and patents must be sought elsewhere. However, a brief account of passing off may be justified since it is (*a*) a tort and (*b*) entirely based on the common law.[43]

The action arose in the nineteenth century and depends upon the simple principle that a man is not to sell his goods or his services under the pretence that they are those of another man.[44] It has five elements: (1) a misrepresentation, (2) made by a trader in the course of trade, (3) to prospective customers of his or ultimate consumers of goods or services supplied by him, (4) which is calculated to injure the business or goodwill of another trader (in the sense that this is a reasonably foreseeable consequence) and (5) which causes actual damage to a business or goodwill of the trader by whom the action is brought.[45]

Varieties of passing off

The representation must be such as to cause confusion in the public mind

[39] *Hadmor Productions Ltd.* v. *Hamilton* [1982] A.C. 191, 223–224. As to the Court of Appeal's duty to defer to the judge's exercise of discretion, see *Hadmor, supra,* at p. 220; but *cf. Mercury Communications Ltd.* v. *Scott Garner* [1984] Ch. 37 where there was fresh evidence. See also *N.W.L. Ltd.* v. *Woods* [1979] 1 W.L.R. 1294 and *Associated British Ports* v. *T.G.W.U.*, *The Times*, June 9, 1989 (public interest).

[40] See *ante*, p. 524.

[41] *Dimbleby & Sons Ltd.* v. *N.U.J.* [1984] 1 W.L.R. 427, 431–432. Previously, so the argument runs, the employer would have no incentive to pursue the action and the grant of an interlocutory injunction would in effect finally decide the case against the union.

[42] *Barretts & Baird (Wholesale) Ltd.* v. *I.P.C.S.* [1987] I.R.L.R. 3, 11, *per* Henry J. However, on the facts (*a*) the judge thought there was little likelihood of the action going to trial, and (*b*) in any event the plaintiffs had failed to establish a serious question to be tried.

[43] See Drysdale and Silverleaf, *Passing Off.* The other matters mentioned above depend almost entirely upon statute. Other common law torts which may be relevant in this area include deceit and injurious falsehood.

[44] *Perry* v. *Truefitt* (1842) 6 Beav. 66, 73, *per* Lord Langdale M.R.; *Spalding & Bros.* v. *A.W. Gamage Ltd.* (1915) 84 L.J.Ch. 449, 450, *per* Lord Parker.

[45] *Erwen Warnink B.V.* v. *J. Townend & Sons (Hull) Ltd.* [1979] A.C. 731, 742, *per* Lord Diplock.

between the plaintiff's goods or business and the defendant's goods or business: false statements disparaging the plaintiff's goods are actionable as injurious falsehood and statements falsely exaggerating the worth of the defendant's wares are not, as such, actionable by a competitor even though he has suffered damage thereby.[46] However, there may be passing off without a direct representation in words—a common form of the tort is imitating the get-up or appearance of the plaintiff's goods.[47] In *White Hudson & Co. Ltd.* v. *Asian Organisation Ltd.*[48] the plaintiffs' medicated cough sweets had been sold in Singapore since 1953 bearing the word "Hacks." In 1958 the defendants began selling their cough sweets in Singapore in similar wrappers, bearing the word "Pecto." It was proved that the majority of purchasers in Singapore were unable to read English and that many of them had, by 1958, acquired the habit of asking for "red paper cough sweets." Prior to 1953 no cough sweets had been sold in red cellophane wrappers and between 1953 and 1958 only the plaintiff's had been so sold. On these facts the Privy Council held that the plaintiffs were entitled to an injunction restraining the defendants from offering cough sweets for sale in the "Pecto" wrapper without clearly distinguishing them from the plaintiffs'. In the *White Hudson* case there was a risk of confusion even though a different name was used.[49] Where, however, plaintiff and defendant are in different lines of business even then the use of the same name may not involve a risk of confusion. In *Granada Group Ltd.* v. *Ford Motor Co. Ltd.*[50] the plaintiffs, a major publishing and entertainment company, failed to restrain the defendants from attaching the name "Granada" to a new car. The requirement of a risk of confusion[51] also means that the tort is not committed merely because the defendant has deliberately exploited the plaintiff's advertising campaign so as to seize a share of a market created by the plaintiff. In *Cadbury-Schweppes Pty. Ltd.* v. *Pub Squash Co. Pty. Ltd.*[52] the plaintiffs launched a lemon drink ("Solo") supported by an extensive advertising campaign emphasising heroic masculinity and evoking an idealised memory of soft drinks of the past. The defendants then launched a lemon drink ("Pub Squash") with a get up and advertising theme closely related to that for "Solo." The dismissal of the plaintiff's claim for damages and an injunction was upheld by the Privy Council for the defendants had sufficiently dis-

---

[46] *Ante*, p. 290.
[47] A distinctive container like a bottle is not capable of being protected under the Trade Mark legislation: *Re Coca-Cola Co.* [1986] 1 W.L.R. 695.
[48] [1964] 1 W.L.R. 1466; *Lee Kar Choo* v. *Lee Lian Choon* [1967] 1 A.C. 602, where it is also pointed out that there may be passing off where the get-up of the defendant's goods is similar to that of the plaintiff, even though there is no infringement of the plaintiff's registered trade mark. *cf. My Kinda Town* v. *Soll* [1983] R.D.C. 407 (confusion probably inevitable between competing businesses of similar style).
[49] See also *Reckitt & Coleman* v. *Borden* [1987] F.S.R. 505.
[50] [1972] F.S.R. 103; *Stringfellow* v. *McCain Foods* [1984] R.P.C. 501. But *cf. Eastman Photographic Materials Co. Ltd.* v. *John Griffith Cycle Corp. Ltd.* (1898) 15 R.P.C. 105. On attempts to protect the commercial value of a name, see below.
[51] Actual confusion on the part of a member of the purchasing public need not be proved (*Lee Kar Choo* v. *Lee Lian Choon* [1967] 1 A.C. 602) but proof that it has occurred will obviously assist the plaintiff's case, especially if substantial damages are claimed and not only an injunction.
[52] [1981] 1 W.L.R. 193; Dworkin (1981) 44 M.L.R. 564.

tinguished their goods from those of the plaintiff to prevent any likely confusion in the minds of the public.[53]

If the plaintiff's case is based on similarity or identity of name, then he must show that the name used actually connotes goods manufactured by him and is not merely descriptive of those goods.[54] This is a question of fact in each case, for descriptive words may by usage have become distinctively attached to the plaintiff's goods.[55] The leading case is *Reddaway* v. *Banham*[56] where it was held that "camel hair belting," which originally signified nothing more than belting made of camel hair, had come to signify belting made by the plaintiffs.[57] A plaintiff undertakes no light burden of proof in trying to convince a court that a word in common use has become associated with his goods[58]—far heavier than in proving imitation of a device used as a trade mark. So a mere six months' use of the name "shampoomatic" for a carpet cleaner was insufficient to entitle the manufacturers to an injunction against its use by another company.[59]

Although the classic form of the tort is one trader representing his goods as those of someone else, the basis of the liability is wider: it is the injury to the plaintiff's business goodwill[60] "the benefit and advantage of the good name, reputation and connection of a business . . . the attractive force which brings in custom."[61] If, therefore, the plaintiff has ceased to trade in the line of business in question he may be deprived of the protection of passing off because the goodwill cannot subsist independently of the business.[62] A difficult (and growing) problem concerns the "location" of goodwill. It seems that the plaintiff cannot succeed unless he has goodwill in England and that involves not merely a reputation, but something which can be called

---

[53] An alternative claim based upon "unfair competition" (below), was not pursued before the Privy Council.

[54] Thus "vacuum cleaner" was held to mean simply a cleaner working by suction and not necessarily one manufactured by the British Vacuum Cleaner Co.: *British Vacuum Cleaner Co. Ltd.* v. *New Vacuum Cleaner Co. Ltd.* [1907] 2 Ch. 312.

[55] Equally, though once so attached, they may become so public and in such universal use as to be again *publici juris: Lazenby* v. *White* (1871) 41 L.J.Ch. 354; *Ford* v. *Foster* (1872) L.R. 7 Ch. 611, 628, *per* Mellish L.J.; *Gledhill* v. *British Perforated* (1911) 28 R.P.C. 429 (C.A. 714). See also *Norman Kark Publications Ltd.* v. *Odhams Press Ltd.* [1962] 1 W.L.R. 380.

[56] [1896] A.C. 199.

[57] And in 1931 it was held, upon the facts, that a Belgian manufacturer did not sufficiently distinguish his goods from the plaintiff's by describing them as "Lechat's camel hair belting": *Reddaway & Co. Ltd.* v. *Hartley* (1930) 48 R.P.C. 283.

[58] *Norman Kark Publications Ltd.* v. *Odham's Press Ltd.* [1962] 1 W.L.R. 380. The burden is lighter if the plaintiff can show that the defendant intended to produce confusion: *Office Cleaning Services Ltd.* v. *Westminster Office Cleaning Association* [1949] 2 All E.R. 269, 271. However, it is pointed out in Kerly, *Trade Marks and Trade Names*, (11th ed.), p. 362, that since most cases do not go beyond the interlocutory injunction stage the change in the law wrought by the *Cyanamid* case (*post*, p. 638) "means that relief will now be granted in many more cases than the precedents might suggest."

[59] *Countess Housewares Ltd.* v. *Addis* [1964] R.P.C. 251. It was pointed out that the word was in part, though not wholly, descriptive; and there is, of course, no clear dividing line between descriptive and imaginative names.

[60] *Spalding & Bros.* v. *A.W. Gamage Ltd.* (1915) 84 L.J.Ch. 449, 450, *per* Lord Parker.

[61] *I.R.C.* v. *Muller & Co.'s Margarine Ltd.* [1901] A.C. 217, 223–224, *per* Lord Macnaghten.

[62] *Star Industrial Co. Ltd.* v. *Yap Kwee Kor* [1976] F.S.R. 256, 268. But a temporary cesser of business will not affect the plaintiff's rights. See also *Ad-Lib Club Ltd.* v. *Granville* [1972] R.P.C. 673.

a business here.[63] Thus in *Bernadin et Cie* v. *Pavilion Properties Ltd.*[64] the plaintiffs, owners of the "Crazy Horse Saloon" in Paris, failed in an action against defendants who set up a similar establishment in London and used the same name.

Goodwill may attach to the description of a product so that it is shared by all persons making that product and they have a cause of action against a defendant who falsely attributes that description to his own goods even though he in no sense passes them off as the plaintiffs'. In *Erwen Warnink B.V.* v. *Townend & Sons (Hull) Ltd.*[65] the plaintiffs were the main producers of advocaat, a drink of Dutch origin compounded of spirits and eggs, enjoying substantial sales in England. The defendants manufactured a drink, properly known as "egg flip," made from sherry and eggs and marketed it under the name "Keeling's Old English Advocaat." Because it attracted a lower rate of duty than the spirit-based drink it could be sold more cheaply and captured an appreciable share of the English market for advocaat. On the basis of a finding of fact that advocaat was a distinct and recognisable species of beverage based on spirits,[66] the House of Lords held that the defendants were guilty of passing off. In doing so they approved the decision in *J. Bollinger* v.*Costa Brava Wine Co. Ltd.*[67] (the Champagne case) and made it clear that the principle was not confined to goods produced in a particular locality.[68]

As a general rule a person can freely use his own name, or one which he has acquired by reputation, although the use of it inflicts damage on someone else who has the same name.[69] This is, however, qualified to some extent by the law of passing off. In *Parker-Knoll Ltd.* v. *Knoll International Ltd.*,[70] both parties were manufacturers of furniture, the plaintiff being a company well known in the United Kingdom and the defendant an American company which had only recently begun to trade in England. Notwithstanding that the defendant company did no more than use its own name on its furniture, the House of Lords, by a majority, granted an injunction to restrain it from continuing to do so without distinguishing its

---

[63] See *Erwen Warnink B.V.* v. *Townend & Sons (Hull) Ltd.* 1979] A.C. 731, 755, *per* Lord Fraser. Coleman, "Protection of Foreign Business Names and Marks" (1986) 6 L.S. 70.

[64] [1967] R.P.C. 581; *Athlete's Foot* v. *Cobra* [1980] R.P.C. 343 and *Annheuser-Busch Inc.* v. *Budejovicky Budvar* [1984] F.S.R. 413 are to the same effect. *cf. Maxim's Ltd.* v. *Dye* [1977] 1 W.L.R. 1155, which relies on the EEC Treaty.

[65] [1979] A.C. 731; Weir, *Casebook on Tort* (6th ed.), p. 494.

[66] This is vital: to take an example of counsel for the defendants, the manufacturers of tomato chutney could not restrain someone from marketing "tomato chutney" containing mangoes simply because mangoes had not been used in tomato chutney before: "tomato chutney" is as vague as "brown bread."

[67] [1960] Ch. 262; *Vine Products Ltd.* v. *Mackenzie & Co. Ltd.* [1969] R.P.C. 1 (sherry); *John Walker & Sons Ltd.* v. *Henry Ost & Co. Ltd.* [1970] 1 W.L.R. 917 (Scotch whisky).

[68] There would, of course, be nothing to prevent the defendants in *Warnink* from marketing an English-made egg and spirit drink as advocaat. In the Champagne case the defendants could only have joined the class enjoying the goodwill by setting up in Champagne as well as using Champagne grapes and the "champenoise" method.

[69] *Brinsmead* v. *Brinsmead* (1913) 30 R.P.C. 493; *Jay's Ltd.* v. *Jacobi* [1933] Ch. 411. But as to nicknames, see *Biba Group* v. *Biba Boutique* [1980] R.P.C. 413. "A new company with a title of which the name 'A,' for instance, forms part has none of the natural rights that an individual born with the name 'A' would have": *Fine Cotton Spinners* v. *Cash* (1907) 24 R.P.C. 533, 538.

[70] [1962] R.P.C. 265.

goods from those of the plaintiff.[71] The plaintiff had established that its name had come to denote goods made by it alone and not goods made by anyone else possessing or adopting that name, and the use by the defendant of a similar name did, in the opinion of the majority, amount to the false representation that its goods were the plaintiff's goods.[72] The central question in each case is, therefore, whether the name or description given by the defendant to his goods is such as to create a likelihood that a substantial section of the purchasing public will be misled into believing that his goods are the goods of the plaintiff.[73] That the defendant used his own name with no intention to deceive anybody does not mean that such a likelihood has not been created, but proof that the defendant did intend to deceive, where it can be made,[74] will materially assist the plaintiff's case. As has often been pointed out, if it was the defendant's object to deceive people into thinking that his goods were the goods of the plaintiff, the court will not be reluctant to infer that he achieved his object.[75] Similarly, whatever tolerance is shown to the use of a person's own name will not be extended to altering it— "garnishing" it, as the expression is—so as to be likely to mislead; thus a firm of wine merchants, "Short's Ltd.," obtained an injunction against one, Short, who set up a similar business and styled it "Short's."[76]

Remedies

The injunction is an important remedy in this area. It may be made in qualified form, *i.e.* restraining the defendant from disposing of his goods without sufficiently distinguishing them from the plaintiff's.[77] In addition, damages may be granted in respect of losses to the plaintiff or, in the alternative, an account of profits made by the defendant from the passing off. The House of Lords in *Marengo* v. *Daily Sketch and Sunday Graphic Ltd.*[78] left open the question whether substantial damages could be recovered against an innocent defendant.[79]

---

[71] See *Parker-Knoll Ltd.* v. *Knoll International Ltd.* [1962] R.P.C. 243, 257–258, *per* Harman L.J. (proceedings subsequent to those in the House of Lords). Note the distinction, which may sometimes be difficult to draw in practice, between carrying on business in such a way as to represent that it is the business of another and describing one's goods in such a way as to represent that they are the goods of another. The rule against the former admits of the exception of the honest use of one's own name; the rule against the latter does not: *Rodgers* v. *Rodgers* (1924) 41 R.P.C. 277, 291, *per* Romer J.

[72] *cf. Habib Bank Ltd.* v. *Habib Bank A.G. Zurich* [1981] 1 W.L.R. 1265.

[73] *Parker-Knoll, supra*, at pp. 278–279, 285, 289–290; *Granada Group* v. *Ford Motor Co.* [1972] F.S.R. 103.

[74] See James L.J.'s example, in *Massam* v. *Thorley* (1880) 14 Ch.D. 748, 757, of somebody finding a man named Bass and setting up a brewery at Burton as Bass & Co.

[75] *Brinsmead & Son Ltd.* v. *Brinsmead, supra*, at p. 507, *per* Buckley L.J.; *Parker-Knoll, supra*, at p. 290, *per* Lord Devlin.

[76] *Short's Ltd.* v. *Short* (1914) 31 R.P.C. 294; *Parker & Son (Reading) Ltd.* v. *Parker* [1965] R.P.C. 323. Perhaps *Heppells Ltd.* v. *Eppels Ltd.* (1928) 46 R.P.C. is explicable on this ground.

[77] "It has been said many times that it is no part of the function of this court to examine imaginary cases of what the defendant could or could not do under this form of injunction. The best guide, if he is an honest man, is his own conscience; and it is certainly not the business of this court to give him instructions or limits as to how near the wind he can sail": *Wright, Layman & Unney* v. *Wright* (1949) 66 R.P.C. 149, 152, *per* Lord Greene M.R.

[78] (1948) 65 R.P.C. 242. *cf. Spalding & Bros.* v. *A.W. Gamage Ltd.* (1915) 84 L.J.Ch. 449, 450.

[79] There may be circumstances in which a person, *e.g.* a printer of labels, who facilitates a passing off without actual knowledge, may be liable for negligence, but such a case would be very unusual and a person who receives such orders in the ordinary course of trade is not to be expected to institute inquiries about the lawfulness of the intended use: *Paterson Zochonis* v. *Merfarken* [1986] 3 All E.R. 522.

Frontiers of passing off

The setting of the law of passing off is competition between traders. However, it certainly extends some way beyond this, though precisely how far is not easy to say. Trade in the narrow sense is not necessary, for an author may sue for the false representation that a book is his work.[80] Nor need the defendant directly take business from the plaintiff, for it seems that a professional man[81] or a professional association[82] have a cause of action in respect of unauthorised use of their names in a manner likely to cause harm to their professional activities—for example, the use of a medical man's name to promote a quack medicine.[83] In this form the tort is less passing off than "injurious association."[84] What is more doubtful is the position where there is no risk of injury to reputation and the parties are in no sense competitors and yet the defendant misappropriates the plaintiff's name[85] or claims association with him, or some licence or endorsement from him.[86] Some decisions make a common field of activity and hence competition a requirement of the tort. Thus in *McCulloch* v. *Lewis A. May Ltd.*[87] the plaintiff, a well-known children's broadcaster under the name "Uncle Mac," failed in an action in respect of the selling of a breakfast cereal under that name. However, that approach is probably too narrow, the function of the "common field of activity" point being that if it is not fulfilled it may be difficult to establish that confusion is likely to arise in the public mind about a connection between the plaintiff's and defendant's activities.[88] Bearing this in mind, some cases seem to require little more than that people may think there is an association between the businesses of the parties,[89] even though that of the defendant is in no way disreputable and hence potentially damaging in that way.[90] The high point of this is probably *Henderson* v. *Radio Corporation Pty. Ltd.*[91] where an injunction was granted to a dancing partnership whose picture had been used, without consent, to advertise a

---

[80] *Lord Byron* v. *Johnson* (1816) 2 Mer. 29; see also Copyright, Designs and Patents Act 1988, s.84. However, in *Keane* v. *McGiven* [1982] F.S.R. 119 an attempt to restrain the use of "Social Democratic Party" failed.

[81] The old case of *Clark* v. *Freeman* (1848) 11 Beav. 112 is to the contrary but has been repeatedly disapproved: *Rivière's Trade Mark*: (1884) 26 Ch.D. 48.

[82] *Society of Accountants and Auditors* v. *Goodway* [1907] 1 Ch. 489.

[83] See Smith and Williams L.JJ. in *Dockrell* v. *Douglas* (1899) 80 L.T. 556, 557, 558; Byrne J. in *Walter* v. *Ashton* [1902] 2 Ch. 282, 293.

[84] Megarry J. in *Unitex Ltd.* v. *Union Texturing Co. Ltd.* [1973] R.P.C. 119. See also *Harrod's Ltd.* v. *R. Harrod Ltd.* (1923) 41 R.P.C. 74; *Sim* v. *H.J. Heinz & Co. Ltd.* [1959] 1 W.L.R. 313; *Totalisator Agency Board* v. *Turf News Pty. Ltd.* [1967] V.R. 605; *Annabel's (Berkeley Square) Ltd.* v. *G. Schock* [1972] F.S.R. 261.

[85] It is assumed that it is not a registered trade mark. Formerly confined to goods, registration of marks in respect of services became possible under the Trade Marks (Amendment) Act 1984.

[86] *cf. Tolley* v. *Fry, ante,* p. 307, where the claim was defamatory of the plaintiff.

[87] [1947] 2 All E.R. 845.

[88] See the "Granada" case, *supra,* n. 50.

[89] See, *e.g. Treasure Cot Co. Ltd.* v. *Hamleys Bros. Ltd.* (1950) 67 R.P.C. 89; *Morny* v. *Ball and Rogers* [1978] F.S.R. 91.

[90] But it must be admitted that this element is pretty easily established. See, *e.g. Hilton Press* v. *White Eagle Youth Holiday Camps* (1951) 68 R.P.C. 126 (possibility of accident at holiday camps might damage plaintiff's reputation in connection with the comic, "The Eagle"); *Lego Systems A/S* v. *Lego M. Lemelstrich* [1983] F.S.R. 155.

[91] [1960] N.S.W.R. 576; followed in *Krouse* v. *Chrysler Canada Ltd.* (1971) 25 D.L.R. (3d) 49; reversed on the facts (1973) 40 D.L.R. (3d) 15.

record, on the basis that the partnership's future ability to earn sponsorship fees would be affected. This teeters on the edge of a new tort of "misappropriation of business reputation."[92] On the other hand, in *Lyngstadt* v. *Anabas Products*[93] the pop group ABBA failed to restrain the use of their name and likeness on goods wholly unrelated to music. Oliver J. remarked that there was "no business of the plaintiffs with which the defendants' business could possibly be confused. . . . The evidence suggests no more than that some people might think that the plaintiffs might have granted some sort of licence for the use of the name." Hence the law of passing off confers only a very limited protection upon the business known as "character merchandising" under which P, the author of a successful film, television series or book will grant licences to manufacturing companies to attach the name of the work, or characters therein, to a wide variety of products.[94] The law of copyright may be applicable where any original artistic work is reproduced,[95] but the scope of trade mark law is limited by the principle that registration will be refused to a mark which the applicant wishes to use merely as a basis for licensing others.[96] It has been argued that there *should* be a wrong of "misappropriation of business reputation"[97] but this is not the law at present. A related and more general question is whether A commits any wrong against B if he appropriates B's valuable idea, design or information and exploits it without payment.[98] The balance of authority is against any such liability[99] and the High Court of Australia has categorically rejected a general tort of "unfair competition."[1] In *Associated Newspapers Group plc* v. *Insert Media Ltd.*[2] the defendants were inserting leaflets into the plaintiffs' newspapers without the latter's approval. An interlocutory injunction pending trial was granted on the basis that this might amount to passing off but a cause of action alleging unfair competition by debasing or devaluing the plaintiffs' goods without misrepresentation was rejected.

Imitation of an address may be part of conduct amounting to a scheme of passing off, but there is no property in an address as such. In *Day* v. *Brownrigg*[3] the house of X had been known for 60 years as "Ashford

---

[92] Unauthorised use of the plaintiff's name or likeness for advertising was one of the earliest forms of the tort of invasion of privacy in the United States. See Frazer, "Appropriation of Personality" (1983) 99 L.Q.R. 281.

[93] [1977] F.S.R. 62.

[94] See, *e.g. Wombles Ltd.* v. *Wombles Skips Ltd.* [1977] R.P.C. 99; *Taverner Rutledge* v. *Trexapalm* [1977] R.P.C. 275.

[95] See, *e.g. King Features* v. *Kleeman* [1940] 1 Ch. 523 (copyright in "Popeye").

[96] *Re American Greetings Corp.'s Application* [1984] 1 W.L.R. 184.

[97] *Supra*, n. 92.

[98] The law of copyright generally protects the *form* of a work, not the idea behind it. But the author of a work who does not have the copyright may have the right to be identified as the author under s.77 of the Copyright, Designs and Patents Act 1988.

[99] *Lever Bros.* v. *Bedingfield* (1898) 16 R.P.C. 3; *Wortheimer* v. *Stewart, Cooper* (1906) 23 R.P.C. 48; *Victoria Park Racing Co.* v. *Taylor* (1937) 58 C.L.R. 479; *Conan Doyle* v. *London Mystery Magazine* (1949) 66 R.P.C. 312. See also "character merchandising" above.

[1] *Moorgate Tobacco* v. *Philip Morris* (1984) 56 A.L.R. 193. A claim for unfair competition was not pursued before the Privy Council in the *Cadbury-Schweppes* case, *supra*, n. 52. An American doctrine of unfair competition enunciated in *International News Services* v. *Associated Press* 248 U.S. 215 (1918) has never gained ascendancy in the face of what are thought to be conflicting statutory rights.

[2] [1988] 1 W.L.R. 509.

[3] (1878) 10 Ch.D. 294.

Lodge," and his neighbour Y changed the name of *his* house (previously known as "Ashford Villa") to "Ashford Lodge." This caused much inconvenience and annoyance to X, who claimed an injunction to restrain Y from such alteration of the name. It was held on demurrer that he had no cause of action.[4] Perhaps the result would have been different if the defendant had had the purpose of deceiving others and thereby causing harm to the plaintiff in his profession.[5]

---

[4] Liability was also denied, but this time in a business context, in *Street* v. *Union Bank of Spain and England* (1885) 30 Ch.D. 155.

[5] *Cf. National Phonograph Co.* v. *Edison Bell Consolidated Phonograph Co.* [1908] 1 Ch. 335 (deception as unlawful means in tort) and *Lonrho p.l.c.* v. *Fayed* [1989] 2 All E.R. 65.

CHAPTER 19

ABUSE OF LEGAL PROCEDURE[1]

MALICIOUS PROSECUTION[2]

History

THE history of this tort takes us back to the old writ of conspiracy which was in existence as early as Edward I's reign and was probably of statutory origin. It was aimed against combinations to abuse legal procedure and it fell into decay in the sixteenth century partly because of its narrow limitation to abuse by two or more persons and partly because the writ of maintenance supplanted it. Even then there was room for another remedy, for maintenance, although it applied to officious meddling in civil litigation, probably did not extend to malicious institution of criminal proceedings.[3] This gap was filled by an action upon the case in the nature of conspiracy. It was not very accurately named, for it lay against a single person as well as against those who acted in combination. Its beginnings are somewhat obscure, but it was coming into use in Elizabeth I's reign[4] and eventually became known as the action for malicious prosecution. Its progress was gradual, for it had to make its way between two competing principles—the freedom of action that every man should have in bringing criminals to justice and the necessity for checking lying accusations of innocent people.[5] For some time the judges oscillated between apprehension of scaring off a just accuser and fear of encouraging a false one; but *Saville* v. *Roberts* (1698)[6] put the action on a firm basis and indeed it is so much hedged about with restrictions and the burden of proof upon the plaintiff is so heavy that no honest prosecutor is ever likely to be deterred by it from doing his duty. On the contrary, now that in fact the enormous majority of prosecutions are brought by the state and reliance need no longer be placed upon the private citizen for this

---

[1] The law and its history are detailed in Winfield, *History of Conspiracy and Abuse of Legal Procedure*, and *Present Law of Abuse of Legal Procedure*. See too, H. Stephen, *Malicious Prosecution*.

[2] Winfield, *Present Law*, etc. Chap. 6.

[3] Winfield, *History, etc.*, p. 136; *Present Law*, etc. pp. 4–6. Maintenance as a tort survived until 1967 but has now been abolished: Criminal Law Act 1967, s.14; *post*, p. 553.

[4] Coke thought *Jerom* v. *Knight* (1587) 1 Leon. 107 was the first instance of it, but *Fuller* v. *Cook* (1584) 3 Leon. 100 is earlier: Winfield, *History*, pp. 118 *et seq.*

[5] See *Glinski* v. *McIver* [1962] A.C. 726, 741, *per* Viscount Simonds; *ibid.* at pp. 753–754, *per* Lord Radcliffe.

[6] 1 Ld.Raym. 374; 5 Mod. 394.

purpose, the law is open to the criticism that it is too difficult for the innocent to obtain redress.[7] It is notable how rarely an action is brought at all, much less a successful one, for this tort.[8]

The action for malicious prosecution being an action on the case[9] it is essential for the plaintiff to prove damage, and in *Saville* v. *Roberts*[10] Holt C.J. classified damage for the purpose of this tort as of three kinds, any one of which might ground the action; malicious prosecution might damage a man's fame, or the safety of his person, or the security of his property by reason of his expense in repelling an unjust charge. A moral stigma will inevitably attach where the law visits an offence with imprisonment,[11] but there are today innumerable offences which are punishable only by fine. In such cases the plaintiff can only rely upon damage to his fame if the offence with which he is charged is necessarily and naturally defamatory of him,[12] and in effect the question is the converse of the question of law which is involved in actions for defamation. "Is the statement that the plaintiff was charged with the offence capable of a *non*-defamatory meaning?"[13] Thus a charge of wrongly pulling the communication cord in a railway train does not necessarily affect the fair fame of the accused and will not ground an action for malicious prosecution under Holt C.J.'s first head,[14] but it is otherwise where, *e.g.* the plaintiff is charged with deliberately travelling on a train without having paid his fare.[15] On the other hand, unless the plaintiff was awarded the equivalent of the taxed costs which he incurred in defending himself, the difference between the costs awarded in the criminal proceedings, if any, and the costs actually incurred is sufficient to ground the action under Holt C.J.'s third head.[16]

Assuming there is damage as explained above, the plaintiff must prove (*a*) that the defendant prosecuted him; and (*b*) that the prosecution ended in the plaintiff's favour; and (*c*) that the prosecution lacked reasonable and probable cause; and (*d*) that the defendant acted maliciously. We can take these point by point.

---

[7] But s.133 of the Criminal Justice Act 1988 creates statutory machinery for compensation where a conviction is reversed or a pardon granted on the ground of miscarriage of justice. Formerly, *ex gratia* payments had been made.

[8] But see *White* v. *Metropolitan Police Comr. The Times*, April 24, 1982.

[9] In *Berry* v. *British Transport Commission* [1962] 1 Q.B. 306, 339, Ormerod L.J. suggested that the time may have come to consider the abolition of the distinction between actions on the case and other actions in tort.

[10] (1698) 1 Ld.Raym. 374; 5 Mod. 394.

[11] Clerk and Lindsell, *Torts* (16th ed.), para. 19–06.

[12] *Berry* v. *British Transport Commission* [1961] 1 Q.B. 149, 166, following *Wiffen* v. *Bailey and Romford U.D.C.* [1915] 1 K.B. 600. This was not the original meaning intended by Holt C.J. (*Berry* v. *British Transport Commission, supra*, at pp. 160–163, *per* Diplock J.) and it has been criticised by the Court of Appeal; *Berry* v. *British Transport Commission, supra*, at p. 333, *per* Devlin L.J.; at pp. 335–336, *per* Danckwerts L.J. See also Prichard [1960] C.L.J. 171.

[13] *Berry* v. *British Transport Commission* [1961] 1 Q.B. 149, 166, *per* Diplock J.

[14] *Ibid.*; *Wiffen* v. *Bailey and Romford U.D.C.* [1915] 1 K.B. 600.

[15] *Rayson* v. *South London Tramways Co.* [1893] 2 Q.B. 304.

[16] *Berry* v. *British Transport Commission* [1962] 1 Q.B. 306, where *Wiffen* v. *Bailey and Romford U.D.C.* [1915] 1 K.B. 600 was held not binding on this point. It is otherwise where costs incurred in a civil action are concerned: *Quartz Hill Consolidated Gold Mining Co.* v. *Eyre* (1883) 11 Q.B.D. 674.

Essentials of the tort

(1) *Prosecution*

A prosecutor has been described as "a man actively instrumental in putting the law in force,"[17] but this is too vague to be of much assistance. Certainly it is not necessary that the defendant should himself conduct the prosecution; it is sufficient that he should have signed the charge and expressed to the police his willingness to attend court and give evidence against the accused.[18] Similarly, if A goes before a magistrate and positively asserts that he suspects B of having committed a crime and the magistrate thereupon issues a warrant for B's arrest, A has commenced a prosecution.[19] The majority of prosecutions are now in the hands of the Crown Prosecution Service under the Prosecution of Offences Act 1985 but the police officer who first lays the charge is still a prosecutor for the purposes of this tort.[20] As a matter of organisation he may act upon the advice of his superiors and the final decision on a prosecution will be taken by the Service but the fact that these "filters" are interposed no more bars a claim for malicious prosecution than, say, the decision of the magistrates to commit for trial. But a person is not a prosecutor when, as an expert, he prepares a report in connection with a suspected crime and forwards it to the police or the Director of Public Prosecutions so that they may consider prosecution.[21]

(2) *Favourable termination of the prosecution*

The plaintiff must show that the prosecution ended in his favour,[22] but so long as it did so it is of no moment how this came about, whether by a verdict of acquittal, or by discontinuance of the prosecution by leave of the court,[23]

---

[17] Lopes J. in *Danby* v. *Beardsley* (1880) 43 L.T. 603. In *Mohammed Amin* v. *Jagendra Kumar Bannerjee* [1947] A.C. 322, the Judicial Committee held that in malicious prosecution the test is not whether criminal proceedings have reached a stage at which they may be correctly described as a "prosecution," but whether they have reached a stage at which damage to the plaintiff results. No English authority was cited for this meaning of "prosecution," and, in the case itself, where an Indian magistrate had taken cognisance of the complaint by the defendant that an offence had been committed by the plaintiff, the Judicial Committee held that an action for malicious prosecution would lie. It is difficult to see why the proceedings could not "correctly be described as a prosecution."

[18] *Malz* v. *Rosen* [1966] 1 W.L.R. 1008. See also *Romegialli* v. *Marceau* (1963) 42 D.L.R. (2d) 481; *Casey* v. *Automobiles Renault Canada Ltd.* (1965) 54 D.L.R. (2d) 600.

[19] *Elsee* v. *Smith* (1822) 1 D. & R. 97; *Davis* v. *Noak* (1816) 1 Stark. 377; (1817) 6 M. & S. 29 (*sub. tit. Davis* v. *Noake*); *Clarke* v. *Postan* (1834) 6 C. & P. 423; *Dawson* v. *Vasandu* (1863) 11 W.R. 516.

[20] See Clayton and Tomlinson [1985] L.S.Gaz. 3505. Difficulty will probably be avoided if we speak of *a* (not *the*) prosecutor.

[21] *Evans* v. *London Hospital Medical College* [1981] 1 W.L.R. 184. See also *Cohen* v. *Morgan* (1825) 6 D. & R. 9; *Leigh* v. *Webb* (1800) 3 Esp. 164 (merely telling story of loss to magistrate).

[22] *Parker* v. *Langly* (1713) 10 Mod. 145 and 209. This was not always the law: Winfield, *Present Law*, pp. 182–183.

[23] *Watkins* v. *Lee* (1839) 5 M. & W. 270. Under the Prosecution of Offences Act 1985 the Director of Public Prosecutions may discontinue proceedings in the magistrates' court without leave. Withdrawal of the charge, even if without prejudice to the right to recommence, has been held in Canada to be sufficient: *Romegialli* v. *Marceau* (1963) 42 D.L.R. (2d) 481; *Casey* v. *Automobiles Renault Canada Ltd.* (1965) 54 D.L.R. (2d) 600.

or by quashing of the indictment for a defect in it,[24] or because the proceedings were *coram non judice*,[25] or by nonsuit.[26] The effect of a *nolle prosequi* (staying by the Attorney-General of proceedings on an indictment) is open to question. An old case indicates that it is not a sufficient ending of the prosecution because it still leaves the accused liable to be indicted afresh on the same charge.[27] But this seems inconsistent with the broad interpretation put upon "favourable termination of the prosecution" which signifies, not that the accused has been acquitted, but that he has not been convicted.[28]

It was held in *Reynolds* v. *Kennedy*[29] that no action could lie if the plaintiff had been convicted, even if his conviction was later reversed on appeal, the reason apparently being that the original conviction showed conclusively that there was foundation for the prosecution. In a number of modern cases, however, it was the fact that the proceedings had terminated in the plaintiff's favour only as the result of an appeal, but nothing was made of this.[30] The question of reasonable and probable cause for the prosecution is an independent question and should not be regarded as finally answered in the defendant's favour on the ground only that a conviction was secured in a court of first instance. *Reynolds* v. *Kennedy* should no longer be regarded as good law.

Conviction procured by fraud. On the other hand, if a conviction stands, then the plaintiff cannot succeed in an action for malicious prosecution, and this is so even if the conviction is one against which there is no right of appeal and which has been obtained by the fraud of the prosecutor. In *Basébé* v. *Matthews*,[31] Byles J. thought that if the rule were otherwise every case would have to be retried on its merits, and Montague Smith J. feared that they would be turning themselves into a Court of Appeal where the legislature allowed none. The weight of these arguments is not easy to guage. Certainly, there must always be *some* risk that the prospect of even unsuccessful civil proceedings might deter a prosecutor from acting in a clear case[32] and it is significant that when there were signs of defamation actions being used as a form of appeal from criminal convictions Parliament immediately intervened with legislation effectively banning such actions.[33] Furthermore, there now appears to be a general rule that the court will strike out as an abuse of process a suit which is a collateral attack on the final decision of a competent criminal court.[34] Whatever the merits of the opposing arguments.

---

[24] *Jones* v. *Gwynn* (1712) 10 Mod. 148, 214.

[25] *Atwood* v. *Monger* (1653) Style 378.

[26] *Goddard* v. *Smith* (1704) 1 Salk. 21; 3 Sulk. 245; 6 Mod. 261; 11 Mod. 56.

[27] *Goddard* v. *Smith, supra.*

[28] The question has been much litigated in America, where the balance of the decisions are to the effect that *nolle prosequi* is a sufficient ending of the prosecution: Prosser, *Torts* (5th ed.), p. 874; so, too, decisions of the Supreme Courts of N.S.W. (*Gilchrist* v. *Gardner* (1891) 12 N.S.W. Law Rep. 184) and of British Guiana (*Khan* v. *Singh* (1960) 2 W.I.R. 441). See also *Romegialli* v. *Marceau, supra.*

[29] (1784) 1 Wils. 232.

[30] *Herniman* v. *Smith* [1938] A.C. 305; *Berry* v. *B.T.C.* [1962] 1 Q.B. 306; *Abbott* v. *Refuge Assurance Co. Ltd.* [1962] 1 Q.B. 432; *Blaker* v. *Weller* [1964] Crim.L.R. 311.

[31] (1867) L.R. 2 C.P. 684.

[32] *cf. Rondel* v. *Worsley, ante*, p. 105.

[33] Civil Evidence Act 1968, s.13: *ante*, p. 324.

[34] *Hunter* v. *Chief Constable of West Midlands* [1982] A.C. 529.

Basébé v. *Matthews* still represents the law. It was followed in *Everett* v. *Ribbands*[35] where the plaintiff had been bound over to find sureties to be of good behaviour. He failed in an action for malicious prosecution, for the proceedings complained of had actually been determined against him.

(3) *Lack of reasonable and probable cause*

There does not appear to be any distinction between "reasonable" and "probable." The conjunction of these adjectives is a heritage from the redundancies in which the old pleaders delighted,[36] and although it has been said that reasonable cause is such as would operate on the mind of a discreet man, while probable cause is such as would operate on the mind of a reasonable man,[37] this does not help us much, for it is difficult to picture a reasonable man who is not discreet.

The principal difficulty, and it is no minor one, in stating the law as to reasonable and probable cause arises from the division of function between judge and jury.[38] It has been recognised for centuries[39] that once a man has been acquitted by a criminal court, juries are too ready to award him damages against his prosecutor,[40] and therefore it is for the judge to decide whether the defendant had reasonable and probable cause for launching the prosecution,[41] but it is for the jury to decide any incidental questions of fact necessary for the judge's determination.[42] Moreover, this branch of the law is unusual in requiring the plaintiff to undertake the difficult task of proving a negative. It is for him to prove that the prosecutor did not have reasonable and probable cause, and not for the prosecutor to prove that he had.[43]

In *Herniman* v. *Smith*[44] the House of Lords approved and adopted the definition of reasonable and probable cause given by Hawkins J. in *Hicks* v. *Faulkner*[45] as "an honest belief in the guilt of the accused based upon a full conviction, founded upon reasonable grounds, of the existence of a state of circumstances, which, assuming them to be true, would reasonably lead any

[35] [1952] 2 Q.B. 198; *Bynoe* v. *Bank of England* [1902] 1 K.B. 467.
[36] Winfield, *Present Law*, p. 192.
[37] *Broad* v. *Ham* (1839) 5 Bing.N.C. 72, 725, *per* Tindal C.J.
[38] *Glinski* v. *McIver* [1962] A.C. 726, 742, *per* Viscount Simonds.
[39] See *Pain* v. *Rochester and Whitfield* (1599) Cro.Eliz. 871, cited by Denning L.J. in *Leibo* v. *Buckman Ltd.* [1952] 2 All E.R. 1057, 1062.
[40] *e.g. Abrath* v. *North Eastern Ry.* (1886) 11 App.Cas. 247, 252, *per* Lord Bramwell; *Leibo* v. *Buckman Ltd.*, *supra*, at p. 1063, *per* Denning L.J.; *Glinski* v. *McIver*, *supra*, at pp. 741–742, *per* Viscount Simonds; *ibid.* at pp. 777–778, *per* Lord Devlin. *cf. ibid. per* Lord Radcliffe at p. 754.
[41] *Johnstone* v. *Sutton* (1786) 1 T.R. 510; *Herniman* v. *Smith* [1938] A.C. 305; *Reynolds* v. *Metropolitan Police Comr.* [1985] Q.B. 881. It is doubtful whether the question is one of fact or law. Probably it is best regarded as a question of fact, but one which is to be treated in the same way as if it were a question of law: *Glinski* v. *McIver*, *supra*, at p. 768, *per* Lord Devlin.
[42] The judge need put to the jury only questions on the salient issues of fact, for otherwise the questions would have no end: *Dallison* v. *Caffery* [1965] 1 Q.B. 348, 368, *per* Lord Denning M.R.
[43] *Abrath* v. *N.E. Ry.* (1883) 11 Q.B.D. 440; *Stapeley* v. *Annetts* [1970] 1 W.L.R. 20. *Green* v. *De Havilland* (1968) 112 S.J. 766, to the contrary, cannot be relied on. *cf.* the rule in false imprisonment, *ante*, p. 64. If, when the principles of malicious prosecution were being laid down, the courts had been acquainted with the idea, now familiar, of a judge himself determining a disputed question of fact, the whole question of reasonable and probable cause would have been left to the judge, but it is now too late to achieve this result without legislation: *Glinski* v. *McIver*, *supra*, at p. 778, *per* Lord Devlin.
[44] [1938] A.C. 305, 316, *per* Lord Atkin.
[45] (1878) 8 Q.B.D. 167, 171; affirmed (1882) 46 L.T. 130.

ordinarily prudent and cautious man placed in the position of the accuser, to the conclusion that the person charged was probably guilty of the crime imputed." This definition may, however, be over-elaborate for some cases,[46] and has even been said not to fit the ordinary run of cases.[47] It cannot serve as a substitute for the rule of law which says that, in order to succeed in an action for malicious prosecution, the plaintiff must prove to the satisfaction of the judge that, at the time when the charge was made, there was an absence of reasonable and probable cause for the prosecution.[48] Various other definitions have been attempted, but perhaps the most helpful is that given by Lord Devlin in *Glinski* v. *McIver*.[49] Reasonable and probable cause "means that there must be cause (that is, sufficient grounds . . .) for thinking that the plaintiff was probably guilty of the crime imputed: *Hicks* v. *Faulkner*.[50] This does not mean that the prosecutor has to believe in the probability of conviction: *Dawson* v. *Vasandau*.[51] The prosecutor has not got to test the full strength of the defence; he is concerned only with the question of whether there is a case fit to be tried.[52] As Dixon J. (as he then was) put it, the prosecutor must believe that 'the probability of the accused's guilt is such that upon general grounds of justice a charge against him is warranted' *Commonwealth Life Assurance Society Ltd.* v. *Brain.*"[53]

In many cases the issue of reasonable and probable cause raises only one question, namely, whether the facts admittedly known to and believed by the prosecutor when he launched the prosecution furnished him with reasonable and probable cause for so doing, and in such cases there is no question to be left to the jury. This question is for the judge alone.[54] Moreover, if the prosecutor knew, or, rather, thought he knew, certain facts, it matters not that those facts turn out to be false. "The defendant can claim to be judged not on the real facts but on those which he honestly, and however erroneously, believes; if he acts honestly upon fiction, he can claim to be judged on that."[55]

The judge's concern is essentially with the objective aspect of the question—whether there was reasonable and probable cause in fact—but the overall question is a double one, both objective and subjective: did the prosecutor actually believe and did he reasonably believe that he had cause for prosecution?[56] Not only must there be reasonable and probable cause in

---

[46] *Abbott* v. *Refuge Assurance Co.* [1962] 1 Q.B. 432, 452, *per* Upjohn L.J.
[47] *Glinski* v. *McIver* [1962] A.C. 726, 758, *per* Lord Denning.
[48] *Ibid.*
[49] [1962] A.C. 726, 766–767; *Dallison* v. *Caffery* [1965] 1 Q.B. 348, 371, *per* Diplock L.J.; Weir, *Casebook on Tort* (6th ed. p. 536.
[50] (1878) 8 Q.B.D. 167.
[51] (1863) 11 W.R. 516, 518.
[52] On this point see also *Tempest* v. *Snowden* [1952] 1 K.B. 130, 139, *per* Denning L.J.; *Glinski* v. *McIver* [1962] A.C. 726, 759, *per* Lord Denning; *Dallison* v. *Caffery, supra,* at p. 376, *per* Diplock L.J. *cf. Glinski* v. *McIver, supra,* at p. 756, *per Lord Radcliffe; Abbott* v. *Refuge Assurance Co.* [1962] 1 Q.B. 432, 463, *per* Davies L.J. (in a dissenting judgment). For the case where the prosecution acts on advice, see *post,* p. 549.
[53] (1935) 53 C.L.R. 343, 382.
[54] *Leibo* v. *Buckman Ltd.* [1952] 2 All E.R. 1057, 1064, *per* Denning L.J.; *Glinski* v. *McIver, supra,* at pp. 743–744, *per* Viscount Simonds; *ibid.* at p. 753, *per* Lord Radcliffe; *ibid.* at p. 760, *per* Lord Denning; *ibid.* at pp. 771–772, *per* Lord Devlin.
[55] *Glinski* v. *McIver* [1962] A.C. 726, 776, *per* Lord Devlin.
[56] *Ibid.* at p. 768, *per* Lord Devlin; *Abbott* v. *Refuge Assurance Co.* [1962] 1 Q.B. 432, 453, *per* Upjohn L.J.

fact, but "it would be quite outrageous if, where a party is proved to believe that a charge is unfounded, it were to be held that he could have reasonable and probable cause,"[57] and the prosecutor himself must also honestly believe that he has reasonable and probable cause. His belief is a matter for the jury, not the judge, to determine, but the burden of proving lack of honest belief is on the plaintiff and the question should only be put to the jury "in the highly unlikely event that there is cogent positive evidence that, despite the actual existence of reasonable and probable cause, the defendant himself did not believe that it existed."[58] If there is such evidence, then it is permissible to ask the jury whether the defendant honestly believed that the plaintiff was guilty of the offence with which he was charged,[59] but questions of guilt are not really for the prosecutor,[60] and it may be better, therefore, to ask the jury whether the prosecutor honestly believed in the case he put forward.[61]

In this connection a problem may arise where the prosecutor acts upon advice, as is commonly the case, for example, where the prosecution is initiated by the police. The prosecutor, and thus the potential defendant in an action for malicious prosecution, may be the individual police officer concerned, but as a matter of police organisation he will act upon the advice or instruction of his superior officers and the final decision to prosecute may have been taken by the Crown Prosecution Service.[62] In principle the fact that the prosecutor has received advice should be regarded as no more than one of the facts to be taken into account, for if the prosecutor did not himself have an honest belief in the case he put forward it is irrelevant that he received advice before doing so.[63] In practice, however, if the prosecutor believes in the facts of the case and is advised by competent counsel before whom the facts are fairly laid that a prosecution is justified, it will be exceedingly difficult to establish lack of reasonable and probable cause.[64] An opinion of counsel favourable to the prosecutor is not conclusive, but it is a potent factor to be taken into account when deciding whether to prosecute.[65]

If there are several charges in the indictment, the rule as to reasonable and

---

[57] *Haddrick* v. *Heslop* (1848) 12 Q.B. 268, 274, *per* Lord Denman C.J.; *Broad* v. *Ham* (1839) 8 Scott 40, 50, *per* Erskine J.

[58] *Dallison* v. *Caffery* [1965] 1 Q.B. 348, 372, *per* Diplock L.J.; *ibid.* at p. 368, *per* Lord Denning M.R.; *Glinski* v. *McIver* [1962] A.C. 726, 743–744, *per* Viscount Simonds; *ibid.* at p. 745, *per* Lord Radcliffe; *ibid.* at p. 768, *per* Lord Devlin. The mere argument that the facts known to the prosecutor were so slender or unconvincing that the prosecutor could not have believed in the plaintiff's guilt is not evidence; *ibid.* at p. 754, *per* Lord Radcliffe. See also *Watters* v. *Pacific Delivery Service* (1964) 45 D.L.R. (2d) 638.

[59] *Glinski* v. *McIver, supra,* at p. 744, *per* Viscount Simonds; *ibid.* at pp. 755–756, *per* Lord Radcliffe.

[60] *Dallison* v. *Caffery* [1965] 1 Q.B. 348, 375–376, *per* Diplock L.J.

[61] *Tempest* v. *Snowden* [1952] 1 K.B. 130, 137, *per* Evershed M.R.; *ibid.* at p. 140, *per* Denning L.J.; *Glinski* v. *McIver, supra,* at 760–761, *per* Lord Denning; *ibid.* at pp. 767–768, *per* Lord Devlin, but *cf. ibid.* at pp. 770–778.

[62] See *ante*, p. 545.

[63] *Ibid.* at pp. 756–757, *per* Lord Radcliffe; *ibid.* at p. 777, *per* Lord Devlin.

[64] *Abbott* v. *Refuge Assurance Co. Ltd.* [1962] 1 Q.B. 432, where Davies L.J. dissented on the facts. See also *Ravenga* v. *Macintosh* (1824) 2 B. & C. 693, 697, *per* Bayley J.; *Glinski* v. *McIver, supra,* at pp. 744–745, *per* Viscount Simonds. A similar result will follow where a private citizen is advised by the police that the facts which he has reported constitute a particular offence: *Malz* v. *Rosen* [1966] 1 W.L.R. 1008. It is respectfully submitted, however, that Diplock L.J. overstates the strength of the defendant's position in such a case: *ibid.* at p. 1013.

[65] *Abbott* v. *Refuge Assurance Co. Ltd., supra,* at p. 450, *per* Ormerod L.J.

probable cause applies to all of them,[66] but where there is reasonable and probable cause for a prosecution on a lesser charge than that actually preferred, a question of degree may arise:

> "Where there is a charge of theft of 20s. and reasonable and probable cause is shown as regards 19s. of it, it may well be that the prosecutor, when sued for malicious prosecution, is entitled to succeed, because he was in substance justified in making the charge, even though he did so maliciously. But the contrary must surely be the case if the figures are reversed and reasonable and probable cause is shown as to 1s. only out of the 20s."[67]

Another problem may be posed as follows. Suppose the prosecutor puts forward at the criminal trial a case based upon weak evidence and without any real belief in its truth with the result that the jury acquit the accused. If the prosecutor then finds firm evidence of the accused's guilt may he use this to meet a claim for malicious prosecution? The logic of reasonable and probable cause might point to a decision in favour of the plaintiff (though perhaps not substantial damages[68]), but the law probably is that the defendant is entitled to judgment if he can prove the plaintiff's guilt.[69]

(4) *Malice*

Judicial attempts to define malice have not been completely successful. "Some other motive than a desire to bring to justice a person whom he [the accuser] honestly believes to be guilty"[70] seems to overlook the fact that motives are often mixed. Moreover, anger is not malice; indeed, it is one of the motives on which the law relies in order to secure the prosecution of criminals,[71] and yet anger is much more akin to revenge than to any desire to uphold the law. Perhaps we are nearer the mark if we suggest that malice exists unless the predominant wish of the accuser is to vindicate the law.[72] The question of its existence is one for the jury[73] and the burden of proving it is on the plaintiff.[74]

At one time malice was not always kept distinct from lack of reasonable and probable cause,[75] but a cogent reason for separating them is that,

---

[66] *Reed* v. *Taylor* (1812) 4 Taunt. 616. *cf. Johnstone* v. *Sutton* (1786) 1 T.R. 510.

[67] *Leibo* v. *Buckman Ltd.* [1952] 2 All E.R. 1057, 1071, *per* Jenkins L.J.; *ibid.* at p. 1073, *per* Hodson L.J. *cf.* the dissenting judgment of Denning L.J. *ibid.* at pp. 1066–1067.

[68] See Clerk & Lindsell, *Torts* (16th ed.), para. 19–33 and *Williams* v. *Banks* (1859) 1 F. & F. 557.

[69] Clerk & Lindsell, *op. cit.*, and the *Restatement*, 2d, which adopts the civil standard of proof.

[70] Cave J. in *Brown* v. *Hawkes* [1891] 2 Q.B. 718, 723; *Glinski* v. *McIver* [1962] A.C. 726, 766, *per* Lord Devlin.

[71] [1891] 2 Q.B. 722. But if the prosecutor's anger is aroused, not by his belief in the plaintiff's guilt but by some extraneous conduct of the plaintiff, then there may be evidence of malice: *Glinski* v. *McIver* [1962] A.C. 726 (plaintiff gave evidence for X on a criminal charge which the defendant, a police officer, believed to be perjured, and X was acquitted. If this was the reason for the plaintiff's prosecution on a charge of fraud, the prosecutor would have been malicious). See too *Heath* v. *Heape* (1856) 1 H. & N. 478.

[72] *Stevens* v. *Midland Counties Ry.* (1854) 10 Ex. 352, 356, *per* Alderson B. *cf.* H. Stephen, *Malicious Prosecution* (1888), p. 37.

[73] *Mitchell* v. *Jenkins* (1833) 5 B. & Ad. 588; *Hicks* v. *Faulkner* (1878) 8 Q.B.D. 167, 175, *per* Hawkins J.

[74] *Abrath* v. *N.E. Ry.* (1886) 11 App.Cas. 247.

[75] Winfield, *Present Law*, p. 189.

however spiteful an accusation may be, the personal feelings of the accuser are really irrelevant to its probable truth. The probability or improbability of X having stolen my purse remains the same however much I dislike X. And it has long been law that malice and lack of reasonable and probable cause must be separately proved. Want of reasonable and probable cause may be evidence of malice in cases where it is such that the jury may come to the conclusion that there was no honest belief in the accusation made.[76] If there was such an honest belief, the plaintiff must establish malice by some independent evidence, for malicious motives may co-exist with a genuine belief in the guilt of the accused.[77] If want of reasonable and probable cause is not proved by the plaintiff, the defect is not supplied by evidence of malice.[78] "From the most express malice, the want of probable cause cannot be implied."[79]

MALICIOUS PROCESS

For malicious prosecution the defendant must have "prosecuted," but there may also be liability if the defendant has maliciously and without reasonable and probable cause instituted some process short of actual prosecution, of which the most important example is the procuring of a warrant for the plaintiff's arrest. In *Roy* v. *Prior*[80] the defendant, a solicitor, was acting for the defence of a man charged with a criminal offence. The plaintiff was a doctor who had attended the accused and the defendant issued a witness summons requiring him to be present to give evidence at the trial. According to the plaintiff, this summons was never served on him, but in any case he was not present at the trial and, on the defendant's instructions, the accused's counsel applied for a warrant for his arrest. In support of the application the defendant himself gave evidence to the effect that the plaintiff had been evading service of the summons. As a result the warrant was issued and the plaintiff was arrested at 1 a.m. and kept in custody until 10.30 a.m. on the same day, when he was brought before the court. The House of Lords held that if the plaintiff could prove that the defendant had acted maliciously and without reasonable and probable cause, as he alleged, then he was entitled to succeed.[81] On similar principles a person may also be liable for procuring the issue of a search warrant.[82]

---

[76] *Brown* v. *Hawkes* [1891] 2 Q.B. 718, 722, *per* Cave J.; *Hicks* v. *Faulkner* (1878) 8 Q.B.D. 167, 175, *per* Hawkins J.

[77] *Brown* v. *Hawkes, supra,* at p. 726, *per* Lord Esher.

[78] *Turner* v. *Ambler* (1847) 10 Q.B.D. 252; *Glinski* v. *McIver, supra.*

[79] *Johnstone* v. *Sutton* (1786) 1 T.R. 510, 545; *Glinski* v. *McIver, supra,* at p. 744, *per* Viscount Simonds.

[80] [1971] A.C. 470.

[81] It matters not that the arrest was procured in the course of civil rather than criminal proceedings, though arrest on civil process is now exceptional. See, *e.g. Daniels* v. *Fielding* (1846) 16 M. & W. 200; *Melia* v. *Neate* (1863) 3 F. & F. 757. The point decided by the House of Lords in *Roy* v. *Prior, supra,* was that the immunity from suit of a witness in respect of his evidence does not protect him from an action for maliciously procuring the issue of a warrant of arrest. The plaintiff is not suing on or in respect of the evidence. He is suing because he alleges that the defendant procured his arrest by means of judicial process which the defendant instituted both maliciously and without reasonable and probable cause: [1971] A.C. 470, 477, *per* Lord Morris.

[82] *Reynolds* v. *Metropolitan Police Comr.* [1985] Q.B. 881.

MALICIOUS CIVIL PROCEEDINGS

Historically, there was no reason why the old action upon the case for conspiracy should not be extended to malicious civil proceedings as well as to malicious criminal proceedings,[83] and it was in fact held to apply (*inter alia*) to malicious procurement of excommunication by an ecclesiastical court,[84] to bringing a second writ of *fi. fa.* against a man when one had already been obtained[85] and perhaps to malicious arrest of a ship.[86] In more modern times it has been laid down that it is available whenever the civil proceedings attack a man's credit in scandalous fashion; *e.g.* malicious bankruptcy proceedings against him, or malicious winding-up proceedings against a company.[87] The same requisites must be satisfied as for malicious prosecution.[88]

But does the law go still farther and make the malicious institution of *any* civil proceeding actionable? There is no historical reason why it should not, and the reason it does not in fact do so[88a] lies not so much in any stance of principle against such liability as in the lack of legal damage to the plaintiff in the great majority of cases. As Bowen L.J. put it in *Quartz Hill Gold Mining Co.* v. *Eyre*,[89] "the bringing of an ordinary action does not as a natural and necessary consequence involve any injury to a man's property, for this reason, that the only costs which the law recognises . . . are the costs properly incurred in the action itself. For these the successful defendant has already been compensated." Now this is, of course, simply untrue, for the taxed costs will hardly ever amount to the total costs of the defence, and it is noteworthy that any deficiency in costs awarded to the accused in a criminal case does amount to damage.[90] Further, the argument does not explain why an action will not lie in respect of a civil action which blemishes the plaintiff's character, such as a charge of fraud. It will not do to say that his reputation will be cleared by his successful defence of the action,[91] for exactly the same may be said of the successful defence of a criminal charge. However, whether or not English law is deficient in this area,[92] the legislature has

---

[83] Winfield, *Present Law*, pp. 199, 202.

[84] *Hocking* v. *Matthews* (1670) 1 Vent. 86; *Gray* v. *Dight* (1677) 2 Show. 144. *cf. Fisher* v. *Bristow* (1779) 1 Doug. 215.

[85] *Waterer* v. *Freeman* (1617) Hob. 205, 266.

[86] *The Walter D. Wallet* [1893] P. 202.

[87] *Quartz Hill Gold Mining Co.* v. *Eyre* (1883) 11 Q.B.D. 674, 683, 689; *Brown* v. *Chapman* (1762) 1 W.Bl. 427. For a modern example, where, however, the plaintiff failed, see *Beechey* v. *William Hill* [1956] C.L.Y. 5442.

[88] Thus in a claim for malicious bankruptcy there is no cause of action (and hence time does not run) until the adjudication is annulled: *Radiojevic* v. *L.R. Industries Ltd.* May 14, 1982, C.A. (unreported).

[88a] In *Metall und Rohstoff A.G.* v. *Donaldson Lufkin & Jenrette Inc.*, *The Times*, February 2, 1989, the C.A., while not required to decide the point, expressed grave doubt as to whether any tort existed outside the limited categories referred to above.

[89] (1883) 11 Q.B.D. 674, 690; *cf. Corbett* v. *Burge* (1932) 48 T.L.R. 626 (though it is not possible to tell from the report if the plaintiff would have been successful if he had shown malice).

[90] *Berry* v. *B.T.C.* [1962] 1 Q.B. 306.

[91] *Quartz Hill Gold Mining Co.* v. *Eyre*, *supra*, per Bowen L.J.

[92] The rules in the *Restatement* 2d, ss.674–675 are more satisfactory than our law, but the pressure for the existence of the action in America is very great since there is generally no means by which a successful defendant can recover his costs.

intervened in outrageous cases, for litigious monomaniacs may be muzzled under the Supreme Court Act 1981.[93]

Aside from liability for malicious civil proceedings the law also recognises a related tort sometimes called "abuse of process." This lies where a legal process, not itself without foundation, is used for an improper, collateral purpose, for example as an instrument of extortion in a matter not connected with the suit.[94] But the presentation of a dishonest claim (or defence) does not of itself amount to the tort.[95]

MAINTENANCE AND CHAMPERTY[96]

Maintenance means the improper stirring up of litigation by giving aid to one party to bring or defend a claim without just cause or excuse[97] while champerty is the particular form of maintenance which exists when the person maintaining the litigation is to be rewarded out of its proceeds. At common law a person guilty of either committed both a crime and tort, but in modern times the defences became so numerous and the reasons for imposing liability so outdated that the law ceased to serve any useful purpose. As crimes and as torts, maintenance and champerty have now been abolished.[98]

---

[93] s.45, as amended by the Prosecution of Offences Act 1985, s.24. The legislation, which originated in the Vexatious Actions Act 1896, was needed, for in *Re Chaffers* (1897) 45 W.R. 365 a person had within five years brought 48 civil actions against the Speaker of the House of Commons, the Archbishop of Canterbury, the Lord Chancellor and others. 47 of them were unsuccessful. See also *Att.-Gen.* v. *Vernazza* [1960] A.C. 965; *Re Langton* [1966] 1 W.L.R. 1575.

[94] *Grainger* v. *Hill* (1838) 4 Bing.N.C. 212; *Speed Seal Products Ltd.* v. *Paddington* [1985] 1 W.L.R. 1327; *Vavawa* v. *Howard Smith Co.* (1911) 13 C.L.R. 35, 91 ("merely a stalking horse to coerce the defendant in some way entirely outside the ambit of the legal claim upon which the court is asked to adjudicate"). There are very few cases, perhaps because applications are normally made to stay the abusive process on this ground before damage is suffered. *Board of Education* v. *Farmingdale Classroom Teachers' Assoc.* 343 N.E. 2d 278 (1975) is a bizarre U.S. example.

[95] *Metall und Rohstoff A.G.* v. *Donaldson Lufkin & Jenrette Inc. The Times*, February 2, 1989.

[96] For the history and former law, see Winfield, *History of Conspiracy and Abuse of Legal Procedure*, pp. 131–160; *Present Law*, pp. 1–116; Bodkin, *Maintenance and Champerty*, and the eighth edition of this work, pp. 585–592.

[97] *Re Trepca Mines Ltd. (No. 2)* [1963] Ch. 199, 219, *per* Lord Denning M.R.

[98] Criminal Law Act 1967, ss.13(1)(*a*), 14(1). Note that a champertous agreement is still void for illegality so far as the law of contracts is concerned: *ibid.* s.14(2). As to assignment of tort claims, see *post*, p. 730.

CHAPTER 20

MISCELLANEOUS AND DOUBTFUL TORTS

THE first part of this chapter mentions some wrongs which are certainly torts but the details of which are rather outside the scope of an elementary book. The remainder briefly outlines the legal protection of (*a*) confidential information and (*b*) privacy. In the case of the first there are undoubtedly well-developed legal principles but it is uncertain how far they rest on tort. As to the second, it is clear that there is no generally protected right of privacy but tort does have some role and there is controversy over whether it should be extended.

MISCELLANEOUS TORTS

The most conspicuous of these is unlawful interference with a franchise. A franchise is a royal privilege, or branch of the Queen's prerogative, subsisting in the hands of a subject.[1] The forms of it are innumerable, but common examples are the franchise of a number of persons to be incorporated and subsist as a body politic, and franchises to have waifs, wrecks, strays, treasure trove, royal fish, to hold markets or fairs,[2] to take tolls for bridges and ferries.[3]

In another sense, "franchise" signifies the right to vote at a parliamentary or municipal election. In the famous case of *Ashby* v. *White*,[4] a returning officer was held liable in damages for wrongfully refusing to take the plaintiffs vote at a parliamentary election.[5]

Usurpation of a public office or interference with the discharge of it is a tort against the person rightly entitled to it. The remedy in tort seems to have been almost forgotten in modern legal literature[6] and the last reported

---

[1] Blackstone, Comm, ii, 37.

[2] The cause of action in the case of infringement of market rights is probably in the nature of nuisance: *Stoke City Council* v. *W. & J. Wass Ltd.* [1988] 3 All E.R. 394, 397.

[3] Details are given in Clerk and Lindsell, *Torts* (14th ed.), Chap. 26 (not in the current edition). For recent examples, see *Iveagh* v. *Martin* [1961] 1 Q.B. 232; *Wyld* v. *Silver* [1963] 1 Q.B. 169; *Sevenoaks D.C.* v. *Patullo* [1984] Ch. 211.

[4] (1703) 2 Ld.Raym. 938; 1 Bro.Parl.Cas. 62. The best account of the case for students' purposes is in *Smith's Leading Cases* (13th ed.), p. 253. *Tozer* v. *Child* (1857) 7 E. & B. 377, carries the same point as to municipal elections.

[5] The Representation of the People Act 1985 provides that no action for damages shall lie in respect of the breach by a returning officer of his official duty. This negatives the decisions in *Ashby* v. *White* and *Tozer* v. *Child*. The remedy is now criminal, not civil.

[6] Its history and the current law are developed by Winfield, "Interference with Public Office" (1940) 56 L.Q.R. 463.

English decision on it goes back to 1808.[7] The chief reason for its decline was the greater popularity of the quasi-contractual action for money had and received.[8] The chief characteristics of a "public office" (apart from any statutory definition) are that it is a post the occupation of which involves the discharge of duties towards the community or some section of it, whether the occupier of the post is or is not remunerated.[9] It is not clear from the authorities whether the defendant can successfully plead an honest but mistaken belief as to his rights, in usurping or interfering with the office.[10] Damages are probably not limited to the amount of the fees that would have been received but for the usurpation.[11]

The tort of "misfeasance in a public office" by abuse of administrative powers, for long regarded as doubtful, is now well-established and has been mentioned elsewhere.[12]

DOUBTFUL TORTS AND DOUBTFUL WRONGS

Infringement of privacy[13]

This may be described as some form of interference with another's seclusion of himself, his family or his property from the public.[14] The common law goes a good way towards protecting this interest but does so indirectly and does not recognise[15] any general "right of privacy" for breach of which there is a specific legal sanction.[16]

A good deal of protection is given against the cruder forms of intrusion on the privacy of a person's property. Where there is actual entry upon it or into the airspace above it at an unreasonably low height[17] the law of trespass covers the situation and where there is no entry the law of nuisance to some

---

[7] *Carrett* v. *Smallpage* (1808) 9 East 330. A later Irish decision is *Lawlor* v. *Alton* (1873) 9 Ir.R.C.L. 160.

[8] First applied for this purpose in *Woodward* v. *Aston* (1676) 2 Mod. 95, and not much used (if at all) since 1872. Other remedies are mandamus, injunction, action for a declaration. They, too, are not now of common occurrence, perhaps because usurpation of public office has become less easy and profitable than in time past.

[9] Winfield, *loc. cit.*, pp. 464–465.

[10] *Ibid.* pp. 468–469. It is a defence according to the *Restatement of Torts* 2d, s.865.

[11] Winfield, *loc. cit.*, pp. 469–470.

[12] See *ante*, p. 174.

[13] Wacks, *The Protection of Privacy*; Report of the Committee on Privacy, Cmnd. 5012 (1972) (which contains much factual information and an appendix on the present law).

[14] The collection of personal data (particularly by computer), even without publicity, is sometimes brought under the heading of privacy but the problems of control of collection, of security and of access can clearly only be dealt with by a statutory scheme, such as now exists under the Data Protection Act 1984. This contains civil liability for damage caused by inaccurate personal data.

[15] It is perhaps true to say that there is no *direct* decision on the point and that it would be open to the House of Lords to hold otherwise. In the most recent case, *Malone* v. *Metropolitan Police Commr.* [1979] Ch. 344 counsel for the plaintiff did not contend for a general right of privacy.

[16] The law in the U.S. is completely different and stems from a famous article, Warren and Brandeis, "The Right of Privacy" Harv.L.R. 193. See now *Restatement* 2d, s.652A–I, enumerating four forms of invasion (intrusion upon seclusion; appropriation of name or likeness; offensive publicity to private life; publicity placing a person in a false light). For continental law see Gutteridge and Walton (1931) 47 L.Q.R. 203, 219; Lipstein [1963] C.L.J. 85, 96–98.

[17] *Bernstein* v. *Skyways* [1978] Q.B. 479, *ante*, p. 364.

extent secures privacy. Persistent watching and besetting may be a nuisance[18] as may persistent harassment by telephone calls.[19] However, neither at law nor in equity will a court prevent a landowner from opening new windows which command a view of his neighbour's premises. At one time there were traces of a different doctrine, but the modern rule was clinched by the House of Lords in *Tapling* v. *Jones* in 1865.[20] It may create hardship in some cases, but in a densely populated country like England, the privacy of a man's landed property must give way to the building activities of his neighbours.[21]

The protection of the common law is deficient for two reasons. First, neither trespass nor nuisance avails someone who is not in occupation of the premises affected.[22] Secondly, neither tort is apt to deal with modern means of electronic and optical surveillance, which may be carried on from a great distance. There is no trespass in watching or listening from outside and it is difficult to see how the law of nuisance could be stretched to cover an "interference" of which the occupier was wholly unaware at the time. Thus in *Malone* v. *Metropolitan Police Commissioner*[23] the plaintiff failed in his action for a declaration that the tapping of his telephone on the authority of the Secretary of State was unlawful because, *inter alia*, there was no right to "telephonic privacy."[24]

Other actionable forms of interference with proprietary rights may indirectly involve a court in protecting privacy. Of these the most important is perhaps the law of confidence, but the law governing copyright, patents, designs, trade marks or trade names may also be relevant. In *Williams* v. *Settle*[25] the plaintiff's father-in-law had been murdered in circumstances which attracted publicity. The defendant, who had taken photographs at the plaintiff's wedding two years previously, sold one for publication in the national press. The copyright in the photographs was the plaintiff's[26] and therefore the court was able to award him very heavy damages for the defendant's "scandalous conduct" which was "in total disregard not only of the legal rights of the plaintiff regarding copyright but of his feelings and his sense of family dignity and pride."

Where there is no interference with any recognised property right of the

---

[18] *Lyons & Sons* v. *Wilkins* [1899] 1 Ch. 255. Forbes J. at first instance in *Hubbard* v. *Pitt* [1976] Q.B. 142 followed *Lyons* v. *Wilkins*. Modern legislation makes the decision inapplicable where there is a trade dispute, but in other contexts it stands, at least where there is annoyance or molestation. For the views of the C.A., see [1976] Q.B. 175–177, 180, 188–189. *cf.* the unreported case, referred to by the Committee on Privacy, *op. cit.*, p. 291, n. 19, of the dentist in Balham who failed to obtain any remedy against his neighbours who erected large mirrors to observe what was going on in his premises. In *Bernstein* v. *Skyways, supra*, Griffiths J. recognised that constant aerial surveillance and photography might be a nuisance.

[19] *Motherwell* v. *Motherwell* (1976) 73 D.L.R. (3d) 62.

[20] 11 H.L.C. 290.

[21] Nevertheless, in determining planning appeals the Minister may take a man's privacy into account. See the case cited by Neill, "The Protection of Privacy" (1962) 25 M.L.R. 393, 394, n. 7.

[22] *e.g.* the guest in a hotel bedroom.

[23] [1979] Ch. 344.

[24] The matter is now governed by the Interception of Communications Act 1985, but this is criminal, not civil.

[25] [1960] 1 W.L.R. 1072. See the observations on this case in *Rookes* v. *Barnard* [1964] A.C. 1129, 1225, *per* Lord Devlin.

[26] See also s.85 of the Copyright, Designs and Patents Act 1988 (right to privacy of photographs etc. commissioned for private and domestic purposes — actionable as breach of statutory duty).

plaintiff he may be able to rely on the law of defamation if, for example, an intrusion into his seclusion exposes him to gross ridicule from his fellows, but even here, with two exceptions,[27] truth provides an absolute defence.[28] Hence, a defeated boxer has no remedy against one who publishes an accurate photographic film of the fight in which he was beaten, for the law cannot take account of his annoyance at the result of a public competition in which he has been worsted[29] and there are no legal controls on the practice of digging up scandalous or ridiculous aspects of a person's past.[30] Even where the statement is untrue there is no defamation unless it can properly be said to reflect on the reputation of the person about whom it is made. In *Dunlop Rubber Co. Ltd.* v. *Dunlop*[31] the plaintiff succeeded in a claim for an injunction against the defendants in publishing for advertising purposes and without his consent portraits of him falsely representing him as a foppish old gentleman but this was because of the ridicule to which it exposed him, and not because of any right to restrain publication of one's portrait, good or bad, for such a right has been denied in several cases.[32]

There have been several attempts to get legislation on the subject of privacy. A Home Office Committee[33] in 1972 came out by a majority against the introduction of any general right of privacy, though proposing alteration or clarification of some existing legal rules. The majority came to this conclusion because in their view a general right would be too vague and uncertain and might interfere with free speech. There has been legislation in the special areas "bugging," telephone tapping and electronic storage of personal data,[34] but the comparatively intractable problem is the press, the views in which must inevitably be unwelcome to some of those who are its subjects. It does not seem likely that the civil law has a great deal to offer public figures who are periodically[35] pursued by offensive methods of news gathering, but what are we to say of the revelation, without breach of confidence, of damaging private information? It is easy enough to state the extremes: everyone must tolerate some publicity and nobody wishes daily newspapers to be like blue books; it is only *offensive* and *unjustified* invasions of privacy that are really objectionable. It is less easy to be confident

---

[27] (i) Under the Rehabilitation of Offenders Act 1974, dealing with "spent convictions." (ii) It seems that where there is a combination truth is not a defence to a claim for conspiracy. See *ante*, pp. 321 and 515.

[28] Some intrusions are clearly totally beyond the reach of the law of defamation because there is no form of statement about the plaintiff, *e.g.* where A thrusts his conversation or company on a total stranger in a public place.

[29] See *Palmer* v. *National Sporting Club Ltd.* (1906) in *MacGillivray's Copyright Cases* (1905–1910), p. 55; *Sports etc. Agency* v. *"Our Dogs" Publishing Co. Ltd.* [1916] 2 K.B. 880; [1917] 2 K.B. 125. *cf. Monson* v. *Tussauds Ltd.* [1894] 1 Q.B. 671 (waxwork tending to injure reputation by being placed in the company of likenesses of criminals).

[30] *cf. Melvin* v. *Reid* 297 P. 91 (1931).

[31] [1921] 1 A.C. 367. See also *Tolley* v. *Fry, ante*, p. 307.

[32] *Corelli* v. *Wall* (1906) 22 T.L.R. 532; *Dockrell* v. *Dougall* (1899) 80 L.T. 556; *Tolley* v. *Fry* [1930] 1 K.B. 467, 478, *per* Greer L.J.: "Unless a man's photograph, caricature or name be published in such a context that the publication can be defamatory within the law of libel, it cannot be made the subject-matter of complaint by action at law."

[33] See *supra*, n. 13.

[34] See *supra*, nn. 14 and 24.

[35] For an extreme case see *Galella* v. *Onassis* 353 F.Supp. 196 (1972); decree modified 487 F. (2d) 986 (1973).

that the boundary line between the two commands sufficiently widespread recognition to be the basis for legal redress.[36] The government has recently promised a further review of the whole area.

Breach of confidence

The modern law gives considerable protection against disclosure or misuse of confidential information[37] though any detailed review would be out of place here, if only because the law rests upon an amalgam of doctrines drawn from contract, and perhaps tort and equity.[38] The law of tort may be relevant in the area of confidence in two ways. First, misuse of confidential information may lead to liability for one of the nominate torts. Thus in *Ansell Rubber Co.* v. *Allied Rubber Industries*[39] the defendants were held liable in damages for inducing breach of contract[40] when they persuaded one of the plaintiffs' employees, in breach of his contractual duty of fidelity, to disclose his employer's trade secrets. Secondly, there is some support for the view that breach of confidence or unauthorised use of information given in confidence to another is an independent head of tortious liability. This view rests upon decisions where damages have been awarded in respect of such conduct even though there was no contractual nexus between the parties,[41] and in one of the cases the view has been expressed that the law has affinities with conversion.[42] However, the latest consideration of the law of confidence by the House of Lords suggests that it is based upon a broad equitable obligation of conscience.[43]

While one cannot say firmly how far, if at all, the present law of confi-

[36] A useful critical exercise is to consider the 26 illustrations to *Restatement* 2d, s.652D. If any right of privacy were to be introduced it should clearly be capable of express or implied waiver and some of the defamation heads of privilege should be applicable by analogy: see *Restatement* 2d, s.652G and Mr. Walden's Bill of November 26, 1969, printed in Appendix F to the Report of the Committee on Privacy. The private sphere of a person's life would have to be treated as diminishing as he came to occupy an increasingly public position, but it might be a difficult question to determine how long he should be thus treated: see, *e.g. Sidis* v. *F.-R. Publishing Corp.* 113 F. (2d) 806 (1940); *Street* v. *N.B.C.* 645 F. 2d 1227 (1981).

[37] Most of the cases are concerned with trade or governmental secrets, but the law of confidence may also protect personal privacy: see, *e.g. Prince Albert* v. *Strange* (1848) 2 De G. & Sm. 652; *Argyll* v. *Argyll* [1967] Ch. 302.

[38] Thus the original (and probably still the primary) remedy in this field was the injunction. For general surveys of this area of law see Turner, *The Law of Trade Secrets*; Gurry, *Breach of Confidence*; Jones, "Restitution of Benefits Obtained in Breach of Another's Confidence" (1970) 86 L.Q.R. 463; Dworkin, "Confidence in the Law," Inaugural Lecture, University of Southampton, 191; North, "Breach of Confidence: Is There a New Tort?" (1972) 12 J.S.P.T.L. 149; Law Commission Report No. 110 (1981). See also Cmnd. 7341 (1978).

[39] [1967] V.R. 37. *cf. British Industrial Plastics* v. *Ferguson* [1940] 1 All E.R. 479, where the defendants were unaware that any contract was being broken. It seems that a breach of confidence might be unlawful means for the tort of conspiracy: see *Spermolin* v. *Winter* [1962] C.L.Y. 2441.

[40] See *ante*, pp. 498–500.

[41] *Seager* v. *Copydex Ltd.* [1967] 1 W.L.R. 923; *Seager* v. *Copydex Ltd. (No. 2)* [1969] 1 W.L.R. 809; *Nicrotherm Electrical Co. Ltd.* v. *Percy* [1956] R.P.C. 252 (upheld on other grounds [1957] R.P.C. 207). It is true that damages may be awarded in lieu of an injunction under Lord Cairns' Act 1858 but these cases did not purport to exercise that power (though *cf.* Slade J. in *English* v. *Dedham Vale Properties Ltd.* [1978] 1 W.L.R. 93, 111 and Lord Goff in *Att. Gen.* v. *Guardian Newspapers Ltd. (No. 2)* [1988] 3 W.L.R. 776, 810). See generally North, *loc. cit. cf.* Jones, *loc. cit.*, p. 491, who considers that rights in confidential information are based on a broad equitable principle and that the decision in the *Nicrotherm* case is "mildly revolutionary in that, by implying that a damages claim can succeed independently of any prayer for equitable relief, it presupposes a fusion of law and equity."

[42] *Seager* v. *Copydex Ltd. (No. 2)*, *supra*, at pp. 813, 815, *per* Lord Denning M.R. and Winn L.J.

[43] *Att. Gen.* v. *Guardian Newspapers Ltd. (No. 2)* [1988] 3 W.L.R. 776. See also *Moorgate Tobacco Co. Ltd.* v. *Philip Morris Ltd.* (1984) 56 A.L.R. 193.

dence depends upon tort,[44] the Law Commission in 1981 produced a Report and Draft Bill which would replace the present law by a statutory tort of breach of confidence. Details of the proposals must be sought in the Report itself[45] but the salient features are as follows. The obligation of confidence would be applicable to information which was not "in the public domain" and which had come to the recipient in circumstances in which he could be regarded as giving an undertaking of confidence[46] or where he had come by it improperly (for example, by unauthorised interference or surveillance[47]). Damages would be available for losses already suffered, whether pecuniary or in the form of mental distress, with an account of profits as an alternative in suitable cases. In respect of a feared future breach of confidence an injunction would, as at present, be available with power to award damages in lieu, but an interesting development would be the introduction of an "adjustment order." Where a defendant was subject to an injunction in respect of confidential information which he had received innocently[48] he could receive a contribution from the person to whom the information belonged in respect of wasted expenditure incurred before he became aware that it was subject to an obligation of confidence.[49]

---

[44] See the comment of Megarry V.-C. in *Malone* v. *Metropolitan Police Commr.* [1979] Ch. 344, 360.

[45] Law Com. No. 110 (1981).

[46] Whether expressly or by inference from the relationship between him and the giver of the information.

[47] The Report also proposes the imposition of an obligation of confidence with regard to information acquired in the course of judicial proceedings in camera or, in certain cases, in chambers, but not with regard to information revealed in open court because that is the "public domain." However, it was held in *Home Office* v. *Harman* [1983] A.C. 280 that a person who obtained documents by discovery committed a contempt by using them for purposes other than the litigation even though they had been read out in open court.

[48] *e.g.* where the information was revealed to him by a person who improperly acquired it and claimed to be the owner.

[49] The Commission rejected an absolute defence of bona fide purchase for value: para. 6.53.

CHAPTER 21

VICARIOUS LIABILITY[1]

MASTER AND SERVANT[2]

THE expression "vicarious liability" signifies the liability which A may incur to C for damage caused to C by the negligence or other tort of B. It is not necessary that A shall have participated in any way in the commission of the tort nor that a duty owed in law by A to C shall have been broken. What is required is that A should stand in a particular relationship to B and that B's tort should be referable in a certain manner to that relationship. The commonest instance of this in modern law is the liability of a master for the torts of his servants done in the course of their employment. The relationship required is the specific one of master and servant and the tort must be referable to that relationship in the sense that it must have been committed by the servant in the course of his employment. It is with this instance of vicarious liability that the first part of this chapter is concerned, but there are other instances which cannot be included in a work of this kind. Such are the liability of partners for each other's torts and, perhaps, the liability of a principal for the torts of his agent.[3]

It is important that we should not confuse vicarious liability with the primary liability of A for damage caused to C by the act of B. This may arise in two ways. First, where A is at fault in selecting B for the task or allowing him to continue in employment: most of the cases concern the liability of an employer for injury caused to one of his servants by a fellow-servant.[4] Secondly, there may be a primary liability even though A is not *in fact* guilty of any negligence but is under a "non-delegable duty." Unfortunately for precision in the use of legal terms, the expression "vicarious liability" is today sometimes used to cover this case, too. Such duties arise for example, where an employer is held liable for damage caused by the act of an independent contractor, for in that case, as we shall see, the employer is not liable unless the independent contractor's act is one which has the legal result that some duty owed directly by the employer to the plaintiff has been

---

[1] Weir, *Casebook on Tort* (6th ed.), Chaps. 6 and 7; Atiyah, *Vicarious Liability in the Law of Torts*.

[2] In modern employment legislation "employer" and "worker" are the most commonly used expressions, but in the context of vicarious liability it is thought that a textbook is justified in continuing to speak of "master" and "servant." If the archaism offends, the writer can only comment that he feels no shame at being a servant. For the liability of company directors, see *post*, p. 676.

[3] Atiyah, *op. cit.*, pp. 99–115. See also *post*, p. 579.

[4] See *ante*, p. 186. For an example outside this area see *Nahhas* v. *Pier House Management (Cheyne Walk) Ltd.* (1984) 270 E.G. 328 (failure to inquire into background of porter) though there was also a true vicarious liability on the facts.

broken. Unlike the case of master and servant, nothing in particular turns on the precise relationship between the employer and the contractor. What matters is the duty owed by the employer to the plaintiff, and the employer's liability, if any, is for a breach of that duty.[5] In the law of contract, if A promises to do something for C it is generally, and always subject to the construction of the contract, no answer for A in a claim by C that the failure of performance was brought about by the act of A's agent, B, and such an assumption of personal responsibility may exist in some cases of tort but there is no general rule and the assumption must be determined from the circumstances of the case.[6]

Historical outline

Historically, the idea of vicarious responsibility is common enough. A good deal of primitive law is founded on revenge, and revenge tends to be indiscriminate. In the Mosaic Code it is significant that it was found necessary to state expressly that each man should be put to death only for his own sin and not for that of his father or son, and Plato thought it advisable to assert a similar principle in his laws.

In our own law[7] the early Anglo-Norman period is a transitional one in which the idea of complete liability for the wrongs of servants or slaves is changing to the idea of liability only where there has been command or consent on the part of the master of the servant's wrong. From 1300 onwards the change continues until by the early sixteenth century the command theory has become established. Thenceforward, during that century and the seventeenth, the master's liability was restricted to the case where he had particularly commanded the very act complained of.[8] On this basis the liability clearly is not vicarious, for a man who orders an unlawful act is a direct participant in the tort.

By the latter part of the seventeenth century so limited a form of liability had become inadequate in view of rising commercial prosperity and the increasing complexities of trade, but nothing changed until the time of Sir John Holt.[9] At last, however, Holt established the rule that the master was liable not only for acts done at his express command but also for those done by his implied command, this to be inferred from the general authority he had given his servant in his employment.[10] The new rule may appear to be but a slight extension of the old one. In truth, however, it involves a major change, for while an express command is something to be proved by direct evidence, an implied command is something which can only be inferred from

---

[5] This proposition was accepted by Eveleigh L.J. in *Rogers v. Night Riders*, [1983] R.T.R. 324, 329.

[6] See *Esso Petroleum Co. Ltd. v. Hall Russell & Co. Ltd.* [1988] 3 W.L.R. 730, 759, *per* Lord Jauncey. See the "hospital" cases *post*, p. 565 and the employer's personal duty to his workers: *ante*, p. 186.

[7] See Wigmore's article in *Select Essays in Anglo-American Legal History* (1909), iii, pp. 520 *et seq.*; Holdsworth, H.E.L., iii, 382–387, viii, 472–482.

[8] See, *e.g. Southern v. How* (1617) 2 Rolle 5.

[9] Chief Justice 1688–1710. Parliament itself intervened in some special cases. See, *e.g.* the Act for making Navigable the Rivers Aire and Calder, 1698, s.5.

[10] The new rule is stated with great clarity in *Tuberville v. Stamp* (1697) 1 Ld.Raym. 264. The old rule appears as late as *Kingston v. Booth* (1682) Skin. 288.

the general scope of the servant's employment considered as a whole. Liability is related to the scope of the employment and the foundation of the modern law is laid.[11] Nevertheless the principle of primary liability was for the time retained and in form at least the question was still whether the master could be shown to have been a direct participant in the tort as having impliedly commanded it. The relationship of master and servant was not itself a legal requirement of liability—it was merely a factual element in the case from which a command or "authority" could be implied, and other relationships might serve the same purpose equally well.[12] By the end of the eighteenth century, however, the idea began to grow up that some special importance attached to the relationship of master and servant as such,[13] and in 1849 it was finally held that the exercise of that relationship was essential.[14] Thereafter, though primary liability on the part of anyone could be established on proof of direct participation in the tort, such direct participation was not even theoretically required to make a master liable for his servant's tort. The liability is derived from the relationship and is truly vicarious. At the same time the phrase "implied authority" which had been the cornerstone of the master's primary liability gives way gradually to the modern "course of employment."[15]

Who is a servant?

Since vicarious liability generally arises from a contract of service ("servant") but not from a contract for services ("independent contractor") it is necessary to determine the indicia of a contract of service. At the outset it should be noted that this task has to be performed for purposes totally unconnected with vicarious liability[16] but it seems to be assumed that the question "who is servant?" should receive the same answer almost regardless of the context in which it is asked.[17]

It may be thought that the starting point in the inquiry should be to ask whether the parties themselves have expressly assigned their contractual relationship to one category or the other, but such a declaration can in fact never be conclusive as to the legal classification of the relationship, though it

---

[11] It can be said with some confidence that the modern law of vicarious liability can be traced back to Holt, but not beyond. See authorities cited by Glanville Williams, "Vicarious Liability and the Master's Indemnity" (1957) 20 M.L.R. 220, 228.

[12] For late examples, see *Bush* v. *Steinman* (1799) 1 Bos. & Pul. 404; *Sly* v. *Edgely* (1806) 6 Esp. 6; *Matthews* v. *West London Waterworks* (1813) 3 Camp. 403; *Randleson* v. *Murray* (1838) 8 Ad. & E. 109.

[13] See, *e.g. Stone* v. *Cartwright* (1795) 6 T.R. 411; *Brucker* v. *Fromont* (1796) 6 T.R. 659 and the cases concerning temporary servants such as *Laugher* v. *Pointer* (1826) 5 B. & C. 547; *Quarman* v. *Burnett* (1840) 6 M. & W. 499.

[14] *Reedie* v. *London and North Western Ry.* (1849) 4 Exch. 244. *Bush* v. *Steinman, supra*, was expressly overruled.

[15] Wigmore regards Lord Kenyon as chiefly responsible for the change, but the cases which he cites in support of this are tenuous, and in one of them (*Laugher* v. *Pointer* (1826) 5 B. & C. 547, 577) an opinion of Abbott C.J. is attributed to Lord Kenyon: *Essays in Anglo-American Legal History*, iii, pp. 533–534.

[16] *e.g.* the liability of an employer to pay national insurance contributions is generally dependent on the existence of a contract of service; and certain duties under industrial safety legislation operate only in favour of "persons employed." Most of the cases in the last 20 years have arisen in contexts like these.

[17] See Atiyah, *op. cit.*, pp. 32–33; *Calder* v. *H. Kitson Vickers & Sons (Engineers) Ltd.* [1988] I.C.R. 232, 254.

is one factor to be taken into account by the court.[18] Thus a building worker who rendered services on the express oral understanding that he was a "labour only sub-contractor"[19] was nonetheless held to be a party to a contract of service for the purposes of the Construction (Working Places) Regulations 1966 since the remainder of the contractual relationship was indistinguishable from that prevailing between master and servant.[20]

At one time it was generally accepted that the test of the relationship of master and servant was that of control,[21] and a contract of service was thought to be one by virtue of which the employer "can not only order or require what is to be done, but how it shall be done."[22] The control test probably retains a good deal of importance in cases to which it can be applied,[23] but in modern conditions the notion that a master has the right to control the manner of work of all his servants, save perhaps in the most attenuated form,[24] contains more of fiction than of fact. It is clearly the law that such professionally trained persons as the master of a ship, the captain of an aircraft and the house surgeon at a hospital are all servants for whose torts their masters are responsible, and it is unrealistic to suppose that a theoretical right in a master, who is as likely as not to be a corporate and not a natural person, to control how any skilled worker does his job, can have much substance.[25] It has, therefore, now been recognised that the absence of such control is not conclusive against the existence of a contract of service[26] and various attempts to find a more suitable test have been made.

In an often cited statement[27] Lord Thankerton said that there are four indicia of a contract of service, (a) the master's power of selection of his servant, (b) the payment of wages or other remuneration, (c) the master's right to control the method of doing the work, and (d) the master's right of

---

[18] *Ferguson* v. *John Dawson & Partners (Contractors) Ltd.* [1976] 1 W.L.R. 1213; *Ready Mixed Concrete (South East) Ltd.* v. *Minister of Pensions and National Insurance* [1968] 2 Q.B. 497; *Global Plant Ltd.* v. *Secretary of State for Social Services* [1972] 1 Q.B. 139; *Davis* v. *New England College at Arundel* [1977] I.C.R. 6; *Young & Woods Ltd.* v. *West* [1980] I.R.L.R. 201. Megaw L.J. in the *Ferguson* case at p. 1222 would have been prepared to go further and say that the parties' declaration ought to be wholly disregarded.

[19] This practice, known as "the lump" grew up mainly to avoid payment of income tax under the P.A.Y.E. system. Tax legislation now attempts to meet the point by special provisions for the building trade.

[20] *Ferguson* v. *John Dawson, supra; cf.* Lawton L.J., dissenting, at p. 1226: "I can see no reason why in law a man cannot sell his labour without becoming another man's servant even though he is willing to accept control as to how, when and where he will work." In *Massey* v. *Crown Life Insurance Co.* [1978] 1 W.L.R. 676. Lawton L.J. thought that the case was distinguishable from *Ferguson* because there was a written contract with detailed terms. Lord Denning M.R. was content to say that *Ferguson* "turned on its facts."

[21] For an early statement of the control test, see *Yewens* v. *Noakes* (1880) 6 Q.B.D. 530, 532–533, *per* Bramwell B. For its development see Atiyah, *op. cit.*, pp. 40–44.

[22] *Collins* v. *Hertfordshire County Council* [1947] K.B. 598, 615, *per* Hilbery J.

[23] *Argent* v. *Minister of Social Security* [1968] 1 W.L.R. 1749, 1759, *per* Roskill L.J.

[24] "What matters is lawful authority to command so far as there is scope for it. And there must always be some room for it, if only in incidental or collateral matters": *Zuijs* v. *Wirth Brothers Pty. Ltd.* (1955) 93 C.L.R. 561, 571, *per* Dixon C.J.; *Whittaker* v. *Minister of Pensions and National Insurance* [1967] 1 Q.B. 156.

[25] Kahn-Freund, "Servants and Independent Contractors" (1951) 14 M.L.R. 504. But a minister of religion will not *generally* be employed under a contract of service; his duties are spiritual and dictated by conscience: *Davies* v. *Presbyterian Church* [1986] 1 W.L.R. 323. The position of priests of the established church is governed by a separate body of ecclesiastical law.

[26] *Morren* v. *Swinton and Pendelbury Borough Council* [1965] 1 W.L.R. 576; *Whittaker* v. *Minister of Pensions and National Insurance* [1967] 1 Q.B. 156; *Ready Mixed Concrete (South East) Ltd.* v. *Minister of Pensions and National Insurance* [1968] 2 Q.B. 497; *Market Investigations Ltd.* v. *Minister of Social Security* [1969] 2 Q.B. 173.

[27] *Short* v. *J. & W. Henderson Ltd.* (1946) 62 T.L.R. 427, 429.

suspension or dismissal. It is respectfully suggested, however, that this does not carry the matter much further; the first and last, and perhaps also the second, are indicia rather of the existence of a contract than of the particular kind of contract which is a contract of service,[28] and some judges have preferred to leave the question in very general terms. Somervell L.J. thought that one could not get beyond the question whether the contract was "a contract of service within the meaning which an ordinary person would give under those words,"[29] but more helpful than this is Denning L.J.'s well-known statement[30]:

> "It is often easy to recognise a contract of service when you see it, but difficult to say wherein the distinction lies. A ship's master, a chauffeur and a reporter on the staff of a newspaper are all employed under a contract of service; but a ship's pilot,[31] a taxi-man, and a newspaper contributor[32] are employed under a contract for services. One feature which seems to run through the instances is that, under a contract of service, a man is employed as part of a business, and his work is done as an integral part of the business; whereas under a contract for services, his work, although done for the business, is not integrated into it but is only accessory to it."[33]

One of the most elaborate discussions of the matter is to be found in the judgment of MacKenna J. in *Ready Mixed Concrete (South East) Ltd.* v. *Minister of Pensions and National Insurance,*[34] where the learned judge held that three conditions must be fulfilled; a contract of service exists if (i) the servant agrees that, in consideration of a wage or other remuneration, he will provide his own work and skill in the performance of some service for his master; (ii) he agrees, expressly or impliedly, that in the performance of that service he will be subject to the other's control in a sufficient degree to make that other master; (iii) the other provisions of the contract are consistent with its being a contract of service. Although MacKenna J. gave some examples of provisions inconsistent with a contract of service, such as a requirement that the person employed should provide all necessary equip-

---

[28] *Ready Mixed Concrete (South East) Ltd.* v. *Minister of Pensions and National Insurance* [1968] 2 Q.B. 497, 524, *per* MacKenna J.

[29] *Cassidy* v. *Ministry of Health* [1951] 2 K.B. 343, 352–353; *Argent* v. *Minister of Social Security* [1968] 1 W.L.R. 1749, 1760, *per* Roskill J.

[30] But it has been said that this approach cannot be applied so as to result in an affirmative finding that the contract was one of service when the control test, whether on its own or with other indicia, yielded the conclusion that it was a contract for services: *Stevens* v. *Brodribb Sawmilling Co. Pty. Ltd.* (1986) 63 A.L.R. 573, 519.

[31] But see Pilotage Act 1987, s.16, which makes the shipowner liable even where the pilotage is compulsory.

[32] *cf. Beloff* v. *Pressdram Ltd.* [1973] 1 All E.R. 241. As to professional musicians, see *Winfield* v. *London Philharmonic* [1979] I.C.R. 726 and *Addison* v. *London Philharmonic* [1981] I.C.R. 261.

[33] *Stevenson, Jordan and Harrison Ltd.* v. *Macdonald* [1952] 1 T.L.R. 101, 111; Weir, *Casebook on Tort* (6th ed.), p. 235; *cf. Petter* v. *Metropolitan Properties Co. Ltd.* (1973) 229 E.G. 973. It is not conclusive one way or the other that the person has control over his hours of work: see *W.H.P.T. Housing Association Ltd.* v. *Secretary of State for Social Services* [1981] I.C.R. 737 and *Nethermere (St. Neots) Ltd.* v. *Taverna* [1984] I.C.R. 122.

[34] [1968] 2 Q.B. 497.

ment and materials at his own expense, it is difficult to avoid the conclusion that much of this composite test assumes what is sets out to prove. Nevertheless it is probable that no more complete general test exists; the fact is that it is not possible even to compile an exhaustive list of all the relevant considerations.[35] "The most that can be said is that control will no doubt always have to be considered, although it can no longer be regarded as the sole determining factor; and that factors which may be of importance are such matters as whether the man performing the services provides his own equipment, whether he hires his own helpers, what degree of financial risk he takes,[36] what degree of responsibility for investment and management he has, and whether and how far he has an opportunity of profiting from sound management in the performance of his task."[37]

(1) *Hospitals*

It was to a substantial extent a consequence of developments in the liability for hospitals for the negligence of their staffs that dissatisfaction with the test of control developed, for while it was originally held that a hospital authority could not be liable for negligence in matters involving the exercise of professional skills,[38] this view has not been accepted since 1942. Since then it has been held that radiographers,[39] house-surgeons,[40] whole time-assistant medical officers[41] and, probably, staff anaesthetists[42] are the servants of the authority for the purposes of vicarious liability.[43] It has also been suggested that even visiting consultants and surgeons under the National Health Service are servants for this purpose.[44] However, in many of the cases there has been a tendency to treat the question of a hospital authority's liability not as one of vicarious liability only but also as one of the primary liability of the authority for breach of its own duty to the patient.[45] This approach is made easier by the National Health Service Act.[46] However, while this may save the court the task of determining whether the negligent individual is a servant of the hospital authority it will not relieve

---

[35] *Market Investigations Ltd.* v. *Minister of Social Security* [1969] 2 Q.B. 173, 184, *per* Cooke J.
[36] An independent contractor will commonly be paid "by the job" whereas a servant will generally receive remuneration based upon time worked. But a piece worker will still be a servant; and a building contract is a contract for services notwithstanding that it may contain provisions for payment by time.
[37] *Market Investigations Ltd.* v. *Minister of Social Security, supra,* at p. 185.
[38] *Hillyer* v. *St. Bartholomew's Hospital* [1909] 2 K.B. 820. Note that the hospital in this case was a charitable body.
[39] *Gold* v. *Essex County Council* [1942] 2 K.B. 293.
[40] *Collins* v. *Hertfordshire County Council* [1947] K.B. 598; *Cassidy* v. *Ministry of Health* [1951] 2 K.B. 343.
[41] *Cassidy* v. *Ministry of Health, supra.*
[42] *Roe* v. *Minister of Health* [1954] 2 Q.B. 66.
[43] Where the hospital authority is held liable there are administrative arrangements for sharing the liability with the relevant medical defence society, but this is to be modified so that the hospital will carry full liability.
[44] *Street, Torts* (8th ed.), p. 447.
[45] See, *e.g. Gold* v. *Essex County Council, supra,* at p. 301, *per* Lord Greene M.R.; *Cassidy* v. *Ministry of Health, supra,* at pp. 362–365, *per* Denning L.J.
[46] See *Razzel* v. *Snowball* [1954] 1 W.L.R. 1382 dealing with the 1946 Act. Salmond and Heuston, *Torts* (19th ed.), p. 516; Hamson, "The Liability of Hospitals for Negligence," *The Law in Action,* I, p. 19. By s.3(1) of the National Health Service Act 1977 it is the duty of the Secretary of State to provide medical services throughout England and Wales. s.13 allows him to direct Regional and Area Health Authorities to exercise his functions.

the plaintiff of the burden of showing negligence. In most cases his complaint will be that Dr. A was negligent in his treatment and if this is so then
(assuming Dr. A to be a servant) to say that the hospital authority was in
breach of *its* duty via him is to state a proposition the practical effect of which
is the same as saying that it is vicariously liable for his negligence. If,
however, he is not negligent (because, for example, he is given a task which
is beyond the competence of a doctor holding a post of his seniority) then
there is still a possibility that the hospital authority is negligent in failing to
secure adequate staffing.[47]

(2) *Police*

Until 1964 no person or body stood in the position of "master" to a police
officer,[48] and accordingly anyone injured by the tortious conduct of the
police could have redress only against the individual officers concerned.
Now, however, it is provided by the Police Act 1964, s.48, that the chief
officer of police for any police area shall be liable for torts committed by
constables[49] under his direction and control in the performance or purported
performance of their functions. This statutory liability is equated with the
liability of a master for the torts of his servants committed in the course of
their employment, but the chief officer of police does not, of course, have to
bear the damages personally. Any damages or costs awarded against him are
paid out of the police fund.[50]

(3) *Lending a servant*

Difficult cases arise where A is the general employer of B but C, by
agreement with A (whether contractual or otherwise), is making temporary
use of B's services. If B, in the course of his employment commits a tort
against X, is it A or C who is vicariously liable to X? It seems that it must be
one or the other, but not both.[51] In *Mersey Docks and Harbour Board* v.
Coggins and Griffith (Liverpool) Ltd.,[52] A employed B as the driver of a
mobile crane, and let the crane together with B as driver to C. The contract
between A and C provided that B should be the servant of C but B was paid
by A, and A alone had power to dismiss him. In the course of loading a ship
X was injured by the negligent way in which B worked the crane. At the time

---

[47] See *Wilsher* v. *Essex Area Health Authority* [1987] Q.B. 730 where both Glidewell L.J. and Browne-
Wilkinson V.-C. accepted that there might be a direct liability in the hospital authority but differed as to
the measure to be applied to the individual doctor's conduct. But a claim that staffing is inadequate may
face a formidable obstacle in the court's refusal to interfere with the authority's discretion over the
allocation of resources: *R.* v. *Central Birmingham H.A.*, *The Times*, November 26, 1987.

[48] Under the Crown Proceedings Act 1947 the Crown is only liable in respect of persons who are paid wholly
out of moneys provided by Parliament (s.2(6)) and this excludes the police. Nor are the police servants of
the police authority: *Fisher* v. *Oldham Corp.* [1930] 2 K.B. 364.

[49] But the police authority, not the chief constable, is vicariously liable for police cadets: s.17(3); *Wiltshire
Police Authority* v. *Wynn* [1981] Q.B. 95.

[50] For the "police fund" see the Police Act 1964, s.62 and Sched. 8. If an action against a chief of police is
settled the damages are payable out of the police fund only if the settlement is approved by the police
authority: *ibid.* s.48(2)(*b*).

[51] *Esso Petroleum Co. Ltd.* v. *Hall Russell & Co. Ltd.* [1988] 3 W.L.R. 730, 758.

[52] [1947] A.C. 1; Weir, *Casebook on Tort* (6th ed.), p. 237. See the observations of Sellers L.J. on the case in
McArdle v. *Andmac Roofing Co.* [1967] 1 W.L.R. 356, 361; *Steel Structures Ltd.* v. *Rangitikei County*
[1974] 2 N.Z.L.R. 306.

of the accident C had the immediate direction and control of the operations to be executed by B and his crane, *e.g.* to pick up and move a piece of cargo, but he had no power to direct how B should work the crane and manipulate its controls. The House of Lords held that A as the general or permanent employer of B was liable to X.

In such cases, the burden of proof, which is a heavy one and can only be discharged in exceptional circumstances[53] rests on A, the general or permanent employer, to shift the prima facie responsibility for the negligence of B, on to the hirer, C, who for the time being has the advantage of B's services. A distinction is to be drawn between cases where a complicated piece of machinery and a driver are lent, and cases where labour only, particularly where it is not of a highly skilled character,[54] is lent. In the former case, it is easier to infer that the general employer continues to control the method of performance since it is his machinery and the driver remains responsible to him for its safe keeping. In the latter case it is easier[55] to infer that the hirer has control not merely in the sense of being able to tell the workman what he wants done, but also of deciding the manner of doing it.[56]

The question whether A or C is liable depends on many factors: "Who is paymaster, who can dismiss,[57] how long the alternative service lasts, what machinery is employed, have all to be kept in mind."[58] But in cases of this kind the courts have generally adhered to the view that the most satisfactory test, if it can be applied, is, who at the particular time has authority to tell B not only what he is to do, but how he is to do it. It is a question of fact involving all the circumstances of the case. C may control the particular task to be performed, but he is not liable unless he also controls the method of performing it. If C, though he has no authority to do so, expressly directs B to do the act which is negligently done and causes damage, C is generally liable with B as a joint tortfeasor, but A is not liable. A term in the contract between A and C that B shall be the servant of C on the particular occasion is not conclusive[59] but such a contract may entitle A to claim indemnity from C for the damages he has had to pay to X.[60] Beyond determining the liability of

---

[53] [1947] A.C. 1, 10, *per* Lord Simon; *Ready Mixed Concrete (East Midlands) Ltd.* v. *Yorkshire Traffic Area Licensing Authority* [1970] 2 Q.B. 397.

[54] *Brogan* v. *William Allen Smith & Co. Ltd.* 1965 S.L.T. 175; *McGregor* v. *Duthie & Sons & Co. Ltd.* 1966 S.L.T. 133. *cf. Savory* v. *Holland and Hannen and Cubitts (Southern) Ltd.* [1964] 1 W.L.R. 1158; *Ready Mixed Concrete (East Midlands) Ltd.* v. *Yorkshire Traffic Area Licensing Authority, supra.*

[55] But the task is still likely to be formidable: *Bhoomidas* v. *Port of Singapore* [1978] 1 All E.R. 956, 960.

[56] [1947] A.C. 1, 17, *per* Lord Porter; *ibid.* at p. 22, *per* Lord Uthwatt; *Garrard* v. *Southey & Co.* [1952] 2 Q.B. 174, 179, *per* Parker J.

[57] *Garrard* v. *Southey* [1952] 2 Q.B. 174, 180. Nowhere is it suggested that this is the sole or the conclusive test: *per* Parker J.

[58] *Mersey Docks* case, *supra*, at p. 17, *per* Lord Porter. "Where (does) the authority lie to direct, or delegate to the workman, the manner in which the vehicle is to be driven?" *ibid.* at p. 12, *per* Lord Simon; *ibid.* at p. 21, *per* Lord Uthwatt.

[59] It is sometimes said that this is because the servant cannot be transferred without his consent. But even in the rare cases where the presumption has been rebutted and C held liable it seems improper to talk of any actual transfer of the servant's contract. If there really were a transfer the consequences for the servant could be disastrous since many valuable rights under modern legislation governing the contract of employment depend upon continuity of service.

[60] *Herdman* v. *Walker (Tooting) Ltd.* [1956] 1 W.L.R. 209; *Spalding* v. *Tarmac Civil Engineering Ltd.* [1966] 1 W.L.R. 156. Because such a contract is not determinative of the question as against X it is not within s.2 of the Unfair Contract Terms Act 1977—the allocation of indemnity rights between A and C is not an exclusion of liability: *Thompson* v. *T. Lohan* [1987] 1 W.L.R. 649.

A and C *inter se*, "it has only an indirect bearing upon the question which of them is to be regarded as master of the workman, B, on a particular occasion."[61]

By statute, owners of hackney carriages (including taxicabs) are made responsible for the torts of the driver while he is plying for hire as if the relationship of master and servant existed between them even though it does not in fact exist,[62] but the tort must be committed in the course of the driver's employment (using the word "employment" in this fictitious sense).[63]

What is the course of employment?

Unless the wrong done falls within the course of the servant's employment, the master is not liable. It may be asked, "How can any wrong be in the course of a servant's employment? No sane or law-abiding master ever hires a man to tell lies, give blows or act carelessly." But that is not what course of employment means. A wrong falls within the scope of employment if it is expressly or impliedly authorised by the master or is an unauthorised manner of doing something which is authorised, or is necessarily incidental to something which the servant is employed to do.[64] Course of employment has supplanted scope of authority, but it contains no criteria to decide when or why an act is within or outside the scope of employment and no single test is appropriate to cover all cases.[65] It is often an extremely difficult question to decide whether conduct is or is not within the course of employment as thus defined, and it would seem that the question is ultimately one of fact to be decided in the light of general principles.[66]

The decided cases are not very amenable to any scientific classification,

---

[61] [1947] A.C. 1, 15, *per* Lord Porter. As to requisition by the government of A's vehicle, to be driven by A's servant, see *Marney* v. *Campbell, Symonds & Co. Ltd.* (1946) 62 T.L.R. 324. See, too *Bontex Knitting Works Ltd.* v. *St. John's Garage* [1943] 2 All E.R. 690. Similar questions have been raised where the borrowed servant is himself injured. While it may still be true to say that the temporary employer only owes the special duty of an employer if he would also be vicariously liable for the servant's torts (though *cf.* Diplock L.J. in *Savory* v. *Holland and Hannen and Cubitts (Southern) Ltd.* [1964] 1 W.L.R. 1158, 1165) there is no reason why he should not owe some other duty of care, *e.g.* as occupier. Indeed, in a suitable case there is no reason why both employers should not be liable: see the example given by Turner P. in *Ferguson Construction Co. Ltd.* v. *Hargreaves* [1973] 1 N.Z.L.R. 634, 643.

[62] *Keen* v. *Henry* [1894] 1 Q.B. 292; *Bygraves* v. *Dicker* [1923] 2 K.B. 585; London Hackney Carriages Act 1843 and (outside London) Town Police Clauses Act 1847.

[63] *Venables* v. *Smith* (1877) 2 Q.B.D. 279.

[64] "The expressions 'acting within his authority,' 'acting in the course of his employment,' and 'acting within the scope of his agency,' as applied to an agent, speaking broadly, mean one and the same thing. What is meant by those expressions it is not easy to define with exactitude. To the circumstances of a particular case one may be more appropriate than the other. Whichever expression is used, it must be construed liberally": *per* Lord Macnaghten, *Lloyd* v. *Grace, Smith & Co.* [1912] A.C. 716, 736; *Dyer* v. *Munday* [1895] 1 Q.B. 742, 748, *per* Rigby L.J.; *Navarro* v. *Moregrand Ltd.* [1951] 2 T.L.R. 674, 680–681, *per* Denning L.J.; and see *Heatons Transport (St Helens) Ltd.* v. *T.G.W.U.* [1973] A.C. 15, 100.

[65] *Staton* v. *National Coal Board* [1957] 1 W.L.R. 893, 895, *per* Finnemore J.; *Kay* v. *I.T.W. Ltd.* [1968] 1 Q.B. 140, 153, *per* Sellers L.J.

[66] *Marsh* v. *Moores* [1949] 2 K.B. 208, 215; "It must be a question of fact whether an unauthorised act by a servant is within the scope of his employment or outside his employment," *per* Lynskey J.; *Whatman* v. *Pearson* (1868) L.R. 3 C.P. 422; *Mitchell* v. *Crassweller* (1853) 13 C.B. 237; *Lloyd* v. *Grace, Smith & Co.* [1912] A.C. 716. A policeman is not acting in the course of employment when playing football even though the match is promoted by the police authority and he is encouraged to play: *R.* v. *National Insurance Comm., ex p. Michael* [1977] 1 W.L.R. 109 ("accident arising out of and in the course of employment" under s.5(1) of the National Insurance (Industrial Injuries) Act 1965).

and the best that can be done is to select and illustrate a few of the more conspicuous sub-rules.

(1) *Carelessness of servant*

By far the commonest kind of wrong which the servant commits is one due to unlawful carelessness, whether it be negligence of the kind which is in itself a tort, or negligence which is a possible ingredient in some other tort. It should be noted also that in some torts intention or negligence is immaterial; the doer is liable either way. In cases of this sort the master may well be responsible for conduct of the servant to which no moral blame attaches.[67] But, assuming that the tort is negligence or that it is one in which inadvertence is a possible element in its commission, it may still be in the course of employment even if the servant is not acting strictly in the performance of his duty, provided he is not "on a frolic of his own."[68] Thus a first-aid attendant at a colliery is still within the course of his employment while cycling across his employer's premises to go to an office to collect his wages,[69] and so is a man sent to work at a place away from his employer's premises who drives some distance from his place of work to get a midday meal.[70] But if a driver deviates from his proper route so extensively that he can be said to have gone on an entirely new journey,[71] or if he grossly abuses the permission given to him to use his vehicle for the purpose of going for refreshment,[72] then his master will not be liable for any negligence in the course of such journeys of which he may be guilty. In cases of this kind a question of degree is necessarily involved and no hard-and-fast rule can be laid down.

In *Century Insurance Co. Ltd.* v. *Northern Ireland Road Transport Board*,[73] the driver of a petrol lorry, employed by the defendants, while transferring petrol from the lorry to an underground tank in the plaintiff's garage, struck a match to light a cigarette and threw it on the floor and thereby caused a conflagration and an explosion which damaged the plaintiff's property. The defendants were held liable, for the careless act of their

---

[67] *Gregory* v. *Piper* (1829) 9 B. & C. 591.

[68] This famous phrase was coined by Parke B. in *Joel* v. *Morison* (1834) 6 C. & P. 501, 503.

[69] *Staton* v. *National Coal Board* [1957] 1 W.L.R. 893. While employment may begin as soon as the servant enters the factory gates (*Compton* v. *McClure* [1975] I.C.R. 378) a servant travelling between home and work will not generally be in the course of his employment; cf. *Stitt* v. *Woolley* (1971) 115 S.J. 708; *Elleanor* v. *Cavendish Woodhouse* (1972) 117 S.J. 14; *Paterson* v. *Costain and Press (Overseas)* [1979] 2 Lloyd's Rep. 204 (worker on contract in Iran; constantly on call); and *Smith* v. *Stages* [1989] N.L.J. 291 (servant travelling between normal and temporary places of work). A majority of the Pearson Commission (see Chap. 1) proposed bringing "commuting" accidents into the industrial injuries scheme.

[70] *Harvey* v. *R.G. O'Dell Ltd.* [1958] 2 Q.B. 78; *Whatman* v. *Pearson* (1868) L.R. 3 C.P. 422. cf. *Higbid* v. *Hammett* (1932) 49 T.L.R. 104; *Crook* v. *Derbyshire Stone Ltd.* [1956] 1 W.L.R. 432; *Nottingham* v. *Aldridge* [1971] 3 W.L.R. 1.

[71] *Storey* v. *Ashton* (1869) L.R. 4 Q.B. 476. cf. *A. & W. Hemphill Ltd.* v. *Williams* 1966 S.L.T. 33 and *Angus* v. *Glasgow Corp.* 1977 S.L.T. 206, where it is suggested that the real test is "has the servant departed altogether from his master's business?"

[72] *Hilton* v. *Thomas Burton (Rhodes) Ltd.* [1961] 1 W.L.R. 705.

[73] [1942] A.C. 509, approving *Jefferson* v. *Derbyshire Farmers Ltd.* [1921] 2 K.B. 281, where the facts were very similar, and for all practical purposes overruling *Williams* v. *Jones* (1865) 3 H. & C. 602; Weir, *Casebook on Tort* (6th ed.), p. 246, *Spencer* v. *Curtis Bros.* [1962] C.L.Y. 1136. cf. *Kirby* v. *National Coal Board* [1958] S.L.T. 47; *Att.-Gen.* v. *Hartley* [1964] N.Z.L.R. 785.

driver was done in the course of his employment. Lord Wright pointed out that the act of the driver in lighting his cigarette was done for his own comfort and convenience; it was in itself both innocent and harmless. But the act could not be treated in abstraction from the circumstances as a separate act; the negligence was to be found by considering the time when and the circumstances in which the match was struck and thrown down, and this made it a negligent method of conducting his work.

(2) *Mistake of servant*

So far we have been dealing with the incompetent *dilettante* and we now pass to the misguided enthusiast. *Bayley* v. *Manchester, Sheffield and Lincolnshire Ry.*[74] is an illustration. The defendants' porter violently pulled out of a train the plaintiff who said his destination was Macclesfield and who was in a train that was going there. The porter mistakenly thought it was going elsewhere. The defendants were held liable. The porter was doing in a blundering way something which he was authorised to do—to see that passengers were in the right trains and to do all in his power to promote their comfort.

Another application of the same principle is an act done in protection of the master's property. The servant has an implied authority to make reasonable efforts to protect and preserve it in an emergency which endangers it. For wrongful, because mistaken, acts done within the scope of that authority the master is liable, and it is a question of degree whether there has been an excess of the authority so great as to put the act outside the scope of authority. A carter, who suspected on mistaken but reasonable grounds that a boy was pilfering sugar from the wagon of the carter's employer, struck the boy on the back of the neck with his hand. The boy fell and a wheel of the wagon went over his foot. The employer was held liable because the blow given by the carter, although somewhat excessive, was not sufficiently so to make it outside the scope of employment.[75] But a servant has no implied authority to arrest a person whom he suspects of attempting to steal after the attempt has ceased, for the arrest is then made not for the protection of the master's property but for the vindication of justice.[76]

The existence of an emergency gives no implied authority to a servant to delegate his duty to a stranger, so as to make his employer liable for the defaults of the stranger,[77] but it may be that the servant himself was negligent in the course of his employment in allowing the stranger to do his job. In *Ilkiw* v. *Samuels*,[78] a lorry driver in the employment of the defendants

---

[74] (1873) L.R. 8 C.P. 148. The reasoning of Willes J. in (1873) L.R. 7 C.P. at p. 420 is of importance. See also *Lucas* v. *Mason* (1875) L.R. 10 Ex. 251, 253, *per* Pollock B.

[75] *Polland* v. *Parr & Sons* [1927] 1 K.B. 236.

[76] *e.g. Abrahams* v. *Deakin* [1891] 1 Q.B. 516; *Hanson* v. *Waller* [1901] 1 Q.B. 390; *Radley* v. *L.C.C.* (1913) 109 L.T. 162.

[77] *Houghton* v. *Pilkington* [1912] 3 K.B. 308; *Gwilliam* v. *Twist* [1895] 2 Q.B. 84. If the reasoning of Diplock L.J. in *Ilkiw* v. *Samuels* [1963] 1 W.L.R. 991, 1003–1006 is accepted it may be that these cases would be differently decided today.

[78] [1963] 1 W.L.R. 991; *Ricketts* v. *Thomas Tilling Ltd.* [1915] 1 K.B. 644.

permitted a stranger to drive his lorry, and an accident resulted from the stranger's negligent driving. The defendants were held liable, not for the stranger's negligence, for he was not their servant,[79] but on the ground that the driver himself had been guilty of negligence in the course of his employment in permitting the stranger to drive without even having inquired whether he was competent to do so.[80] Equally, the master may sometimes be liable even though the servant has usurped the job of another, provided that what he does is sufficiently closely connected with his master's business and is not too gross a departure from the kind of thing he is employed to do. In *Kay* v. *I.T.W. Ltd.*,[81] a storekeeper employed by the defendants needed to return a fork-lift truck to a warehouse but found his way blocked by a large lorry belonging to a third party. Although there was no urgency and without first inquiring for the driver of the lorry, he attempted to move the lorry himself, and by his negligence in doing so caused an injury to the plaintiff. The Court of Appeal considered that the case fell near the borderline, for it cannot be for every act, however excessive, that the servant may do in an attempt to serve his master's interests that the master is liable.[82] Nevertheless, taking into account the fact that it was clearly within the terms of the storekeeper's employment to move certain obstacles out of the way if they blocked the entrance to the warehouse, and since it was part of his normal employment to drive trucks and small vans, the court held that his act of trying to move the lorry was not so gross and extreme as to take it outside the course of his employment.

(3) *Wilful wrong of servant*

Next, as to the servant's wilful wrongdoing.[83] Here two rules are settled.

In the first place the act done may still be in the course of employment even if it was expressly forbidden by the master.[84] The prohibition by the master of an act or class of acts will only protect him from liability which he would otherwise incur if it actually restricts what it is the servant is employed to do[85]: the mere prohibition of a mode of performing the employment is of no avail.[86] It is a question of fact in each case whether the prohibition relates

---

[79] [1963] 1 W.L.R. 991, 996, *per* Willmer L.J.

[80] See, however, the different and more complex reasoning of Diplock L.J., *ibid.* at pp. 1003–1006.

[81] [1968] 1 Q.B. 140; *East* v. *Beavis Transport Ltd.* [1969] 1 Lloyd's Rep. 302. *cf. Beard* v. *London General Omnibus Co.* [1900] 2 Q.B. 530 and see the explanation of that case by Sellers L.J.: [1968] 1 Q.B. 140, 152.

[82] [1968] 1 Q.B. 140, 151–152, *per* Sellers L.J. It is, however, odd that the master may be vicariously liable for a fraud by the servant against the master's interests, but not liable in some cases when he is seeking to forward those interests: *Iqbal* v. *London Transport Executive* (1973) 16 K.I.R. 329, 336, *per* Megaw L.J.

[83] Wilful horseplay may be outside the course of employment: *Duffy* v. *Thanet D.C.* (1984) 134 N.L.J. 680; *Aldred* v. *Nacano* [1987] I.R.L.R. 292; *cf. Harrison* v. *Michelin Tyre Co.* [1985] 1 All E.R. 918, doubted in *Aldred* v. *Nacano*. As to the employer's personal duty in such cases, see *ante*, p. 190.

[84] *C.P.R.* v. *Lockhart* [1942] A.C. 591, 600, *per* Lord Thankerton; *Ilkiw* v. *Samuels* [1963] 1 W.L.R. 991, 998, *per* Willmer L.J.; *Stone* v. *Taffe* [1974] 1 W.L.R. 1575.

[85] The servant is outside the course of employment while performing acts of precisely the character for which he is employed by the master, if he is in fact working for someone else at the time: *Kooragang Investments Pty. Ltd.* v. *Richardson & Wrench Ltd.* [1982] A.C. 462.

[86] *Plumb* v. *Cobden Flour Mills Ltd.* [1914] A.C. 62, 67, *per* Lord Dunedin; *C.P.R.* v. *Lockhart, supra,* at p. 599, *per* Lord Thankerton; *L.C.C.* v. *Cattermoles (Garages) Ltd.* [1953] 1 W.L.R. 997, 1002, *per* Evershed M.R.; *Ilkiw* v. *Samuels, supra, per* Diplock L.J. at p. 1004; *Kay* v. *I.T.W. Ltd.* [1968] 1 Q.B. 140, 158, *per* Sellers L.J. Compare *Ruddiman* v. *Smith* (1889) 60 L.T. 708 with *Stevens* v. *Woodward* (1881) 6 Q.B.D. 318.

to the sphere of the employment or to the mode of performance, and "the matter must be looked at broadly, not dissecting the servant's task into its component activities ... by asking: what was the job on which he was engaged for his employer?"[87]

In *Limpus* v. *London General Omnibus Co.*,[88] a driver of the defendants' omnibus had printed instructions not to race with, or obstruct, other omnibuses. In disobedience to this order he obstructed the plaintiff's omnibus and caused a collision which damaged it. The defendants were held liable because what he did was merely a wrongful, improper and unauthorised mode of doing an act which he was authorised to do, namely, to promote the defendants' passenger-carrying business in competition with their rivals.[89] Again, in *L.C.C.* v. *Cattermoles (Garages) Ltd.*[90] a garage-hand was not allowed to drive vehicles, but it was part of his duty to move them by hand. His employers were held liable for his negligence while driving a vehicle. However, a fire engine crew engaging in a "go-slow" in support of a pay claim were held not to be acting in the course of their employment when they failed to arrive in time to put out a fire.[90a] The question of prohibitions by the master has given rise to particular difficulty where the servant has given a lift in the master's vehicle to an unauthorised passenger.[91] At one time there was a tendency to deny liability in the master on the basis that the unauthorised passenger was a trespasser but this will no longer do[92] and the court must rely on the prohibition against carriage of passengers limiting the scope of the servant's employment. As Lord Greene M.R. put it in *Twine* v. *Bean's Express Ltd.*,[93] giving a lift to an unauthorised passenger "was not merely a wrongful mode of performing the act of the class this driver was employed to perform but was the performance of an act of a class which he was not employed to perform at all." As always, however, this test is capable of producing divergent answers on the simplest facts and did so in *Rose* v. *Plenty*.[94] A milkman had been warned by his employer not to allow children to assist him, nor to allow passengers on his float. In breach of these

---

[87] *Ilkiw* v. *Samuels, supra*, at p. 1004, *per* Diplock L.J.

[88] (1862) 1 H. & C. 526.

[89] "The law casts upon the master a liability for the act of his servant in the course of his employment; and the law is not so futile as to allow a master, by giving secret instructions to his servant, to discharge himself from liability": *ibid.* at p. 539, *per* Willes J.; *C.P.R.* v. *Lockhart, supra*; *McKean* v. *Raynor Bros. Ltd.* [1942] 2 All E.R. 591.

[90] [1953] 1 W.L.R. 997; *Ilkiw* v. *Samuels, supra*; *cf. Iqbal* v. *London Transport Executive* (1973) 16 K.I.R. 329.

[90a] *General Engineering Services Ltd.* v. *Kingston and St. Andrew Corp.* [1988] 3 All E.R. 867.

[91] One view is that this problem is now of little significance because of the compulsory insurance provisions of the Road Traffic Act 1988 regarding passengers (*post*, p. 690): *Rose* v. *Plenty* [1976] 1 W.L.R. 141, 145, *per* Lord Denning M.R. However, with respect, it is far from clear that this is the case. In the cases where the master has been held not liable the reason has not been any antecedent agreement or assumption of risk within s.149 of the Act but the fact that the servant was outside the course of his employment. In any case, similar problems could arise in situations where the Act of 1972 is inapplicable such as use of a vehicle off the road or other forms of transport.

[92] See the Occupiers' Liability Act 1984, *ante*, p. 225. It may be that the duty to trespassers under the Act for the condition of the vehicle is lower than the ordinary duty of care in negligence, but it is hard to see how any realistic distinction could be drawn with regard to the activity of driving.

[93] (1946) 62 T.L.R. 458; *Conway* v. *George Wimpey & Co. Ltd.* [1951] 2 K.B. 266; *cf. Young* v. *Edward Box & Co. Ltd.* [1951] 1 T.L.R. 789 (driver within scope of employment because foreman gave consent; foreman's consent unauthorised but within ostensible authority).

[94] [1976] 1 W.L.R. 141; Finch (1976) 39 M.L.R. 575; Manchester (1976) 126 N.L.J. 447; Weir, *Casebook on Tort* (6th ed.), p. 242.

instructions he engaged the plaintiff, aged 13, to help him, and the plaintiff was injured, while a passenger on the float, by the milkman's negligent driving. To Lawton L.J. the situation was indistinguishable from that in *Twine* v. *Bean's Express Ltd.* but the majority of the Court of Appeal, while accepting the correctness of the decision in *Twine's* case held that the milkman was acting in the course of his employment because the engagement of the plaintiff was made to further the employer's business[95]: the milkman was employed to deliver milk, which was precisely what he was doing when he caused the accident. This decision is certainly in accord with the current tendency to apply a very broad description to "course of employment"[96] but it is questionable whether it is so easily reconcilable with the earlier passenger cases as the majority of the court asserts.[97] It may also be asked in this context whether, assuming a prohibition to limit the scope of the servant's employment, the plaintiff's knowledge of the prohibition is of any significance. In principle, it is submitted that knowledge is not necessary[98] but that in cases where the servant has ostensible authority to invite persons into his master's vehicle a passenger should not be affected by any prohibition of which he is unaware.[99]

Whatever the present status of the earlier decisions on unauthorised passengers, it remains clear that even if the servant is acting outside the scope of his employment with regard to the passenger[1] he may still be within it with regard to other road users.[2]

In the second place, it does not necessarily follow that the servant is acting outside the scope of his employment because he intended to benefit himself and not his employer. It was generally thought that Willes J. in *Barwick* v. *English Joint Stock Bank*[3] had laid down the rule that the wrong must be intended to benefit the master; but in *Lloyd* v. *Grace, Smith & Co.*[4] the

---

[95] A supposed "benefit" which he has made it very clear he does not want, presumably because his insurers have insisted upon the prohibition.

[96] See particularly *Ilkiw* v. *Samuels* [1963] 1 W.L.R. 991, 1004. *Stone* v. *Taffe* [1974] 1 W.L.R. 1575 perhaps points the same way, though in that case the employer's prohibition related not to the original entry on to their property but to the duration of the stay.

[97] Surely in *Twine* and *Conway* the servants were employed to drive the vehicles, in the course of which activity they injured the plaintiffs?

[98] See Asquith L.J. in *Conway* v. *Wimpey, supra*, but this point in his judgment is related to the issue of whether the plaintiff was a trespasser. Strictly, the issue of knowledge was irrelevant in *Rose* v. *Plenty* because of the majority decision that the prohibition did not limit the scope of the employment but in view of the differences of opinion one may assume that it would have been mentioned if it had been regarded as possessing any significance.

[99] cf. *Ferguson* v. *Welsh* [1987] 1 W.L.R. 1553. Perhaps this is the reason for the decision in *Stone* v. *Taffe, supra*, that the plaintiff could succeed in the absence of evidence of his knowledge of the prohibition. The Court of Appeal regarded the questions whether the plaintiff was a visitor and the servant was acting within the scope of his employment as one and the same thing.

[1] The servant, of course, remains personally liable to the passenger, but *his* liability is not one which is required to be covered by insurance: *Lees* v. *Motor Insurers' Bureau* [1952] 2 All E.R. 511.

[2] "In driving his van along a proper route he was acting within the scope of his employment when he ran into the omnibus. The other thing he was doing simultaneously was something totally outside the scope of his employment, namely, giving a lift to a person who had no right whatsoever to be there": *Twine* v. *Bean's Express Ltd.* [1946] 62 T.L.R. 458, 459, *per* Lord Greene M.R. See also *post*, p. 576.

[3] (1867) L.R. 2 Ex. 259, 265.

[4] [1912] A.C. 716. See, too, *Uxbridge Permanent, etc. Society* v. *Pickard* [1939] 2 K.B. 248; *British Ry., etc. Co. Ltd.* v. *Roper* (1940) 162 L.T. 217; *United Africa Co.* v. *Saka Owoade* [1955] A.C. 130; *Morris* v. *C.W. Martin & Sons Ltd.* [1966] 1 Q.B. 716. Cases such as *Century Insurance Co. Ltd.* v. *Northern Ireland Road Transport Board* [1942] A.C. 509, *ante*, p. 569, can also be regarded as involving acts done by the servant for his own benefit.

House of Lords surprised the profession by holding not only that this was not the law but also that *Barwick's* case had never been any authority for supposing that it was.[5] In *Lloyd's* case, the defendants, a firm of solicitors, employed a managing clerk who conducted their conveyancing business without supervision. The plaintiff, a widow, owned some cottages. She was dissatisfied with the money which they produced and went to the defendants' office where she saw the clerk, who induced her to give him instructions to sell the cottages and to execute two documents which he falsely told her were necessary for the sale but which in fact were a conveyance of the cottages to himself. He then dishonestly disposed of the property for his own benefit. The Court of Appeal by a majority held that the defendants were not liable for the clerk's fraud[6]; the House of Lords unanimously held that they were liable. It cannot be said, however, that as a result of *Lloyd's* case the question of benefit is invariably irrelevant, for it will still be found in some cases that it is the fact that the servant intended to benefit himself alone that prevents his tort from being in the course of his employment. This will be so, for example, in the case of a driver who takes his master's vehicle "on a frolic of his own." It is because the journey was made solely for the driver's benefit that the master is not liable to a person injured by the negligence of the driver.[6a] Similarly, if the servant has committed an assault upon the plaintiff, that will be in the course of his employment if his intention was to further his master's business,[7] but if the assault was a mere act of personal vengeance, it will not.[8]

(4) *Theft by servant*

It was at one time the view that if a servant stole goods his master could not be vicariously liable to their owner on the ground that the act of stealing necessarily took the servant outside the course of his employment.[9] This view fails to recognise, however, that theft by a servant to whom the goods stolen have been entrusted is the dishonest performance by the servant of what he was employed to do honestly, namely, to take care of the goods; and this is sufficient for liability. In *Morris* v. *C.W. Martin & Sons Ltd.*,[10] where

[5] But those who made this error were at any rate in the respectable company of Lord Bowen and Lord Davey, whose dicta in earlier cases were overruled in *Lloyd's* case.

[6] [1911] 2 K.B. 489.

[6a] See also *General Engineering Services Ltd.* v. *Kingston and St. Andrew Corp.* [1988] 3 All E.R. 867.

[7] *Dyer* v. *Munday* [1895] 1 Q.B. 742.

[8] *Warren* v. *Henlys Ltd.* [1948] 2 All E.R. 935. For criticism, see (1949) 65 L.Q.R. 26–28; *Petterson* v. *Royal Oak Hotel Ltd.* [1948] N.Z.L.R. 136; *Daniels* v. *Whetstone Entertainments Ltd.* [1962] 2 Lloyd's Rep. 1; *Keppel Bus Co. Ltd.* v. *Sa'ad bin Ahmad* [1974] 1 W.L.R. 1082. *cf. Rutherford* v. *Hawke's Bay Hospital Board* [1949] N.Z.L.R. 400; *Smith* v. *Crossley Bros. Ltd.* (1951) 95 S.J. 655. For a full review of the authorities see Rose "Liability for an Employee's Assaults" (1977) 40 M.L.R. 420. Rose argues that the courts have been too ready to classify acts as personal revenge even though they are *connected* with the employment. But the existence of the Criminal Injuries Compensation Scheme largely removes what is usually the strongest pointer to reform—the uncompensated plaintiff.

[9] See, *e.g. Cheshire* v. *Bailey* [1905] 1 K.B. 237; *Mintz* v. *Silverton* (1920) 36 T.L.R. 399. *cf. Abraham* v. *Bullock* (1902) 86 L.T. 796, where the servant negligently facilitated a theft by a stranger and his master was held liable. The master may be primarily liable as, *e.g.* where the theft can be attributed to his own negligence in employing a dishonest servant or if his own negligence led to the theft: *Williams* v. *The Curzon Syndicate Ltd.* (1919) 35 T.L.R. 475; *De Parell* v. *Walker* (1932) 49 T.L.R. 37; *Adams (Durham) Ltd.* v. *Trust Houses Ltd.* [1960] 1 Lloyd's Rep. 380.

[10] [1966] 1 Q.B. 716; *Mendelssohn* v. *Normand Ltd.* [1970] 1 Q.B. 177; *Port Swettenham Authority* v. *T.W. Wu & Co.* [1978] 3 W.L.R. 530. See Jolowicz [1965] C.L.J. 200; Weir, *Casebook on Tort* (6th ed.), p. 248.

some of the older cases were overruled, the plaintiff had sent her fur coat to X to be cleaned, and X, with her permission, sent it on to the defendants, who were specialist cleaners. The defendants handed the coat to their servant, M, for him to clean it, and M stole the coat. It was held by the Court of Appeal that on these facts the defendants were liable.

It is submitted that *Morris* v. *C.W. Martin & Sons Ltd.* could have been decided on the short ground that the servant's tort—conversion of the coat—was a wrongful mode of performing the task entrusted to him by the defendants, namely, cleaning and taking care of the coat, and was thus committed in the course of his employment. The Court of Appeal, however, placed much reliance on the duty owed to the plaintiff by the defendants themselves as bailees of the coat and, in effect, held that the theft of the coat by the servant to whom they had delegated their own duty of reasonable care in respect of it, constituted a breach of that duty. This, no doubt, is an alternative ground for holding the defendants liable, but an essential element of their liability on any ground was that they had entrusted the coat to their servant. Had this not been the case it could not have been said that they had delegated to him their own duty as bailees, nor would the theft have been committed by him in the course of his employment.[11] The result is thus the same whether the case is considered in terms of the defendants' own duty as bailees or in terms of vicarious liability. It is suggested, therefore, that unless there are specific terms in the contract of bailment which displace the general rules of vicarious liability,[12] the simplest approach to the problem of the servant's theft is to inquire whether or not the goods stolen had been entrusted to his care. If this is not the case, then, unless the primary liability of the defendant can somehow be made out, the defendant is not liable: but if it is, then the theft was committed by the servant in the course of his employment and this is sufficient to make the master liable.[13]

There may be liability where there is a no bailment to the employer and the servant is not given custody of goods but where the employer's duty is to take steps to keep property secure. Thus landlords of a block of flats were held liable when a dishonest porter employed by them used his keys to enter the plaintiff's flat and steal.[14] But the result would have been different if, say, the boilerman had stolen the keys and used them for the same purpose: it is not enough that the employment gives the opportunity to steal.[15]

(5) *Damage to goods bailed*

The same approach serves to solve the problem of damage caused by a

---

[11] "I base my decision in this case on the ground that the fur was stolen by the very servant whom the defendants as bailees for reward had employed to take care of it and clean it": *Morris'* case, *supra*, at p. 737, *per* Diplock L.J.

[12] See, *e.g. John Carter (Fine Worsteds) Ltd.* v. *Hanson Haulage (Leeds) Ltd.* [1965] 2 Q.B. 495, where it appears to be recognised that a carrier's liability for a theft by his servant is vicarious: *ibid.* at p. 524, *per* Davies L.J.; *ibid* at p. 533, *per* Russell L.J.; and see *Port Swettenham Authority* v. *T.W. Wu & Co.* [1978] 3 W.L.R. 530, 536–537; *Rustenburg Platinum Mines Ltd.* v. *South African Airways* [1977] 1 Lloyd's Rep. 564.

[13] For a similar approach, see Salmond and Heuston, *Torts* (19th ed.), p. 528. *cf. Leesh River Tea Co. Ltd.* v. *British India Steam Navigation Co. Ltd.* [1967] 2 Q.B. 250.

[14] *Nahhas* v. *Pier House Management (Cheyne Walk) Ltd.* (1984) 270 E.G. 328.

[15] And see *Heasman* v. *Clarity Cleaning Co.* [1987] I.C.R. 949.

servant to goods which are the subject of a bailment to his master. If the goods have been entrusted by the master to the care of his servant and the servant negligently damages them, his master will be vicariously liable to their owner, for the servant has done carelessly what he was employed to do carefully, namely, to look after the goods. For this purpose it makes no difference that the servant at the time of his negligence was using the goods improperly for purposes entirely of his own, as, for example, if he uses a car, bailed to his master and entrusted to his care, for taking his friends for a ride, and then negligently damages the car in an accident.[16] He is as much guilty of negligence in looking after the car as he would have been if the accident had occurred while he was using the car for an authorised purpose. Nevertheless some difficulty has been felt to exist in such a case because the servant would, in relation to a third party injured in the same accident, be held to have been "on a frolic of his own." "How can this be?" Lord Denning M.R. has asked.[17] "How can the servant, on one and the same journey, be acting both within and without the course of his employment?" The answer, it is respectfully suggested, is not, as Lord Denning proposes, to abandon the notion of vicarious liability in favour of that of the primary liability of the bailee, but to recognise that the facts relevant to the two claims—that brought by the car owner and that brought by the third party—are different. The car owner's claim is based on the fact that the servant was negligent in looking after the car, which he was employed to do.[18] The third party's claim is based upon the fact that the servant was guilty of negligent driving at the time and place in question. And if the servant was using the car for a joy-ride then he was not at that place at that time in the course of his employment.[19]

(6) *Fraud of servant*

Cases of fraud raise special problems because of the special character of fraud itself. Of its very nature, fraud involves the persuasion of the victim, by deception, to part with his property or in some other way to act to his own detriment and to the profit of the person practising the fraud. Thus in *Lloyd* v. *Grace, Smith & Co.*[20] the defendants' clerk fraudulently persuaded the plaintiff to transfer her property to him, and what is significant for the purposes of vicarious liability is that it was the position in which he had been placed by the defendants that enabled him to do this. His acts were within the scope of the apparent or ostensible authority with which he had been clothed by the defendants and it is for this reason that they were liable.[21] In

[16] *Coupe Co.* v. *Maddick* [1891] 2 Q.B. 413; *Aitchison* v. *Page Motors Ltd.* (1935) 154 L.T. 128; *Central Motors (Glasgow) Ltd.* v. *Cessnock Garage and Motor Co.* 1925 S.C. 796. *cf. Sanderson* v. *Collins* [1904] 1 K.B. 628.

[17] *Morris* v. *C.W. Martin & Sons Ltd.* [1966] 1 Q.B. 716, 724–725. See also Newark, "*Twine* v. *Bean's Express Ltd.*" (1954) 17 M.L.R. 102, 114.

[18] See also *Photo Productions* v. *Securicor* [1980] A.C. 827, 846, 852.

[19] See these ideas explained more fully in [1965] C.L.J. 200, 201–203. See also *Twine* v. *Bean's Express Ltd.* (1946) 62 T.L.R. 458, 459, *per* Lord Greene M.R., and *ante,* p. 573.

[20] [1912] A.C. 716, *ante,* pp. 573–574.

[21] "If the agent commits the fraud purporting to act in the course of business such as he was authorised, *or held out as authorised,* to transact on account of his principal, then the latter may be held liable for it": *ibid.* at p. 725, *per* Earl Loreburn (emphasis added). See also *ibid.* at pp. 738–739, *per* Lord Macnaughten; *ibid.* at p. 740, *per* Lord Shaw.

Uxbridge Permanent Benefit Building Society v. *Pickard*,[22] as in *Lloyd's* case, the clerk had full authority to conduct the business of a solicitor's office in the name and on behalf of his principal. It was not within his actual authority to commit a fraud, but it was within his ostensible authority to perform acts of the kind that come within the business conducted by a solicitor. "So long as he is acting within the scope of that class of act, his employer is bound whether or not the clerk is acting for his own purposes or for his employer's purposes."[23] But there must be some statement or conduct by the employer which leads to the plaintiff's belief that the servant was acting in the authorised course of business. It is not enough that the belief has been brought about solely by reliance on the servant's misrepresentation of the scope of his authority, however reasonable, from the plaintiff's point of view, it may have been to have acted upon it. In *Armagas Ltd.* v. *Mundogas S.A.*[24] M had authority to sell a vessel belonging to the defendants on terms that it was to be chartered back to them for 12 months. As part of a fraudulent scheme he induced the plaintiffs, the purchasers, to believe that the contract involved a 36 month charter back. Such a transaction was not within the usual class of acts which an employee in his position was entitled to do and, the plaintiffs' belief resting solely on M's statement that he had the defendants' consent for what was being done,[25] it was held that M's employers were not liable for his fraud.

MASTER'S INDEMNITY

Vicarious liability being a form of joint liability, the provisions of the Civil Liability (Contribution) Act 1978[26] may enable the master to recover from his servant some or all of the damages he has had to pay on account of the servant's tort.[27] Additionally, however, the master can in some cases recover damages from his servant at common law, and so, in effect recoup himself for the damages he has had to pay. In *Lister* v. *Romford Ice and Cold Storage Co.*[28] L. was a lorry driver employed by R. Co. who by his negligent driving

---

[22] [1939] 2 K.B. 248.

[23] *Ibid.* at p. 254, *per* Sir Wilfrid Greene M.R. "In the case of a servant who goes off on a frolic of his own, no question arises of any actual or ostensible authority upon the faith of which some third person is going to change his position. The very essence of the present case is that the actual authority and the ostensible authority to [the clerk] were of a kind which in the ordinary course of an everyday transaction were going to lead third persons, on the faith of them, to change their position": *ibid.* at pp. 254–255.

[24] [1986] A.C. 717. See also the discussion of ostensible authority in *Freeman and Lockyer (A Firm)* v. *Buckhurst Park Properties (Mangal) Ltd.* [1964] 2 Q.B. 480, 502–505.

[25] Authority was also in issue in *Kooragang Investments Pty. Ltd.* v. *Richardson & Wrench Ltd.* [1982] A.C. 462 (a case of negligence) where the servant was "moonlighting" for X. There was no actual authority to do the acts in question, the employer in no way held out the servant as having authority and, indeed, the plaintiff was unaware that the servant was in the employ of the defendants. Not liable. Murdoch (1982) 98 L.Q.R. 21; Tettenborn [1982] C.L.J. 36.

[26] *Post*, Chap. 22.

[27] For cases in which a full indemnity was awarded to the master under the previous legislation, the Law Reform (Married Women and Tortfeasors) Act 1935, see *Ryan* v. *Fildes* [1938] 3 All E.R. 517; *Semtex* v. *Gladstone* [1954] 1 W.L.R. 945; *Harvey* v. *O'Dell Ltd.* [1958] 2 Q.B. 78.

[28] [1957] A.C. 555. See also the judgment of the C.A.: [1956] 2 Q.B. 180; Jolowicz "The Right to Indemnity between Master and Servant" [1956] C.L.J. 101; [1957] C.L.J. 21; Glanville Williams, "Vicarious Liability and the Master's Indemnity" (1957) 20 M.L.R. 220, 437. *cf. Gregory* v. *Ford* [1951] 1 All E.R. 121. See also *Digby* v. *General Accident Fire and Life Insurance Co.* [1943] A.C. 121.

in the course of his employment, had caused an injury to his father, another servant of R. Co., R. Co. paid the father's damages and then sued L. It was held that L.'s negligent driving was not only a tort against his father but also a breach of an implied undertaking in his contract of service that he would exercise reasonable care,[29] for which R. Co. were entitled to damages equivalent to the amount which they had had to pay to the father.

"That an employee who is negligent and causes grave damage to his employers should be heard successfully to say that he should not make any contribution to the resulting damage, is a proposition which does not in the least commend itself to me and I do not see why it should be so. I find that justice, as we conceive justice in these courts, says that the person who caused the damage is the person who must in law be called upon to pay damages arising therefrom."[30]

However, the justice of this decision has not commended itself so strongly to others and the matter was considered by an interdepartmental committee[31] with the result that employers' liability insurers entered into a "gentleman's agreement" not to take advantage of the principle unless there was evidence of collusion or wilful misconduct. Indeed, there are strong grounds for arguing that the *Lister* principle is unjustifiable in modern conditions[32]: the employer would rarely, if ever, wish to take advantage of it because of the disastrous effect on labour relations and the real plaintiff is likely to be an insurer acting under the doctrine of subrogation.[33] If it be objected that to deny the right of indemnity against the servant is to put him above the law, it may be replied that it is sufficient that he is liable to the victim of the tort, though admittedly judgment will rarely be enforced against him.[34]

There is, however, one important limit to the principle of *Lister's* case. The decision in that case constitutes, in effect, an exception to the common law rule of *Merryweather* v. *Nixan*[35] that there can be no contribution between joint tortfeasors, for that rule was held not to apply in the case of

---

[29] See *Harmer* v. *Cornelius* (1858) 5 C.B.(N.S.) 236.

[30] *Semtex* v. *Gladstone* [1954] 1 W.L.R. 945, 953, *per* Finnemore J., cited with approval in the *Lister* case in the C.A. at [1956] 2 Q.B. 213, *per* Romer L.J. In *Harvey* v. *O'Dell Ltd.* [1958] 2 Q.B. 78 McNair J. held that a servant's implied undertaking to exercise reasonable care extended only to those acts which he was specifically employed to do and that therefore the negligent *driving* of the servant, who was employed as a store-keeper, did not constitute a breach of his contract of service. Whatever one's views of the basic principle of *Lister's* case, it is submitted that *Harvey* v. *O'Dell* is an unsound restriction on that principle: see Jolowicz, "The Master's Indemnity—Variations on a Theme" (1959) 22 M.L.R. 71, 189, at pp. 73–76. *cf.* Lord Denning M.R. in *Vandyke* v. *Fender* [1970] 2 Q.B. 292, 303.

[31] Report published in 1959. See Gardiner (1959) 22 M.L.R. 652.

[32] It has been partially abrogated by statute in New South Wales.

[33] See Parsons, "Individual Responsibility Versus Enterprise Liability" (1956) 29 A.L.J. 714; Lewis, "Insurer's Agreements Not to Enforce Strict Legal Rights" (1985) 48 M.L.R. 270. Despite the "gentlemen's agreement" referred to above, *Lister's* case is not dead: see *Morris* v. *Ford Motor Co. Ltd.* [1973] 2 W.L.R. 843, where the right was sought to be exercised by a third party who was bound to indemnify the employer; Weir, "Subrogation and Indemnity" (privately published case note, 1973).

[34] Weir, *loc. cit.*, comments, "the devices of subrogation and indemnity are not part of the law of tort at all, whose role is exhausted once the primary victim is paid."
The employer is equally "above the law" so long as his policy is valid and his insurers are solvent.

[35] (1799) 8 T.R. 186.

plaintiffs whose liability "arose solely from the fact that they were answerable for the negligence of the defendant himself."[36] If, therefore, the master has himself, or through some other servant, been guilty of culpable fault, the principle of *Lister's* case does not apply and the master can only recover, if at all, under the Act of 1978.[37]

LIABILITY FOR AGENTS: VEHICLE DRIVERS

Thus far we have spoken of the relationship of master and servant. However, many cases on vicarious liability speak in the language of agency and numerous dicta can be found equating agency with a contract of service for this purpose.[38] It has been said on high authority that in principle the law governing vicarious liability for servants and agents is the same and depends upon the question, "was the servant or agent acting on behalf of, and within the scope of the authority conferred by the master or principal?" The answer will often differ simply because the authority of a servant is usually more general.[39] Whatever the validity of this in the field of economic torts or for such matters as fraud,[40] it can hardly be true for liability for accidents, since it is clearly established that the principal is not liable (except in certain isolated instances) for accidents caused by the negligence of his independent contractors performing the tasks entrusted to them. In fact, agency in its most precise legal sense is a predominantly contractual concept and involves the idea of B, the agent, acting so as to bring his principal, A, into a legal relationship with another, C. It is not, therefore, surprising that A should bear responsibility for B's fraud in purporting to carry out a transaction between A and C. There are undoubtedly other instances in the law of tort of vicarious liability for persons who are not servants[41] and who are sometimes described as agents, but these seem to rest less on any general principle of agency than upon an *ad hoc* judgment that for one reason or another the principal ought to pay.[42] This perhaps is the basis of the decision that a master of a hunt is liable for trespasses by hunt members.[43] In addition, where liability is based upon some undertaking by the defendant he may be treated as a matter of construction or by implication of law as responsible for the negligence of persons to whom he delegates performance of his duties,

[36] [1956] 2 Q.B. 180, 210, *per* Romer L.J. This aspect of the problem was not considered by the House of Lords. See Jolowicz [1957] C.L.J. 21.
[37] *Jones* v. *Manchester Corp.* [1952] 2 Q.B. 852. "A chauffeur who, through negligence, causes damage for which his employer is held responsible, may well be liable to his master. On the other hand, if the chauffeur is young and inexperienced, and is suddenly told to drive another and bigger car or lorry, which he does not understand, and an accident follows, it is by no means certain that the employer will be entitled to an indemnity": *ibid.* at p. 865, *per* Singleton L.J.
[38] See Atiyah, *op. cit.*, Chap. 9. *cf. Holderness* v. *Goslin* [1975] 2 N.Z.L.R. 46, 50–51.
[39] *Heatons Transports (St. Helens) Ltd.* v. *T.G.W.U.* [1973] A.C. 15, 99. The judgments in the Court of Appeal in this case should also be looked at: [1973] A.C. 39. The case was not an action in tort, but for an "unfair industrial practice" under the Industrial Relations Act 1971. Lord Wilberforce disclaimed any intention to deal with tort liability: see p. 100.
[40] See *ante*, p. 576. For defamation, see *ante*, p. 331.
[41] *Post*, p. 581.
[42] See *Morgans* v. *Launchbury* [1973] A.C. 127, 135, *per* Lord Wilberforce.
[43] *League Against Cruel Sports* v. *Scott* [1986] Q.B. 240 where control is emphasised.

not on the basis of vicarious liability but because his own "primary" duty extends this far. Examples may be found in the liability of a bailee for the negligence of independent contractors employed to guard his premises[44] or of a carrier by sea for the negligence of a ship-repairer.[45] Such cases will usually involve contractual undertakings but as we have seen the principle may extend to some cases of tort.[46]

Whatever may be the correct principle as to liability for agents, it is convenient to treat here a doctrine which fits easily into no existing legal category[47] but which has developed because of the insurance position in relation to road traffic liability. The doctrine may be stated as follows. Where A, the owner[48] of a vehicle, expressly or impliedly requests or instructs B to drive the vehicle in performance of some task or duty carried out for A, A will be vicariously liable for B's negligence in the operation of the vehicle.[49] Thus in *Ormrod* v. *Crosville Motor Services Ltd.*[50] A, the owner of a car, asked B to drive the car from Birkenhead to Monte Carlo, where they were to start a holiday together. It was held that A was liable for B's negligent driving even though B might be said to be partly pursuing his own interests in driving A's car. On the other hand, liability was not imposed in *Morgans* v. *Launchbury*[51] where the husband, who normally used his wife's car to go to work, got a third person to drive him home after visits to several public houses. In no sense was the husband acting as his wife's agent in using the car for his work and still less was the third person her agent.[52] It is now clear that mere permission to drive without any interest or concern of

---

[44] *B.R.S. Ltd.* v. *Arthur V. Crutchley & Co. Ltd.* [1968] 1 All E.R. 811.

[45] *Riverstone Meat Co. Ltd.* v. *Lancashire Shipping Co. Ltd.* [1961] A.C. 807.

[46] *Ante*, p. 561. In *Rogers* v. *Night Riders* [1983] R.T.R. 324 the defendants held themselves out as a car hire firm and undertook to provide a car to take P to Euston. The defendants in fact relied on independent contractor drivers and were not much more than a booking agency. In holding that the defendants were liable for an accident caused by negligent maintenance of the car the Court of Appeal said it did not matter whether the claim was framed as contract or tort.

[47] Winfield sought to explain the doctrine in terms of "casual delegation" of the use of a chattel, but the leading case now talks in terms of agency: *Morgans* v. *Launchbury* [1973] A.C. 127. The doctrine has been applied to a boat (*The Thelma (Owners)* v. *The Endymion (Owners)* [1953] 2 Lloyd's Rep. 613) but it seems unlikely that it applies to all chattels. It *might* be possible to bring the cases within the rubric of master and servant, but only at the price of admitting that one may be a servant though rendering only a single, gratuitous service. *cf.* Lord Denning in a review (1947) 63 L.Q.R. 517; Salmond and Heuston, *Torts* (19th ed.), pp. 516–517; *Gramak Ltd.* v. *O'Connor* (1973) 41 D.L.R. (3d) 14. *Watkins* v. *Birmingham City Council, The Times,* August 1, 1975.

[48] Ownership as such is probably not necessary: *Nottingham* v. *Aldridge* [1971] 2 Q.B. 739. In *Morgans* v. *Launchbury, infra,* the husband was held liable for the negligence of the driver and there was no appeal against that decision. If an owner bails his vehicle to A and A gets B to drive it, the owner is not liable for B's negligence: *Chowdhary* v. *Gillot* [1947] 2 All E.R. 541.

[49] *Morgans* v. *Launchbury* [1973] A.C. 127.

[50] [1953] 1 W.L.R. 1120; Weir, *Casebook on Tort* (6th ed.), p. 272. See also *Samson* v. *Aitchison* [1912] A.C. 844; *Pratt* v. *Patrick* [1924] 1 K.B. 488; *Parker* v. *Miller* (1926) 42 T.L.R. 408; *The Trust Co. Ltd.* v. *De Silva* [1956] 1 W.L.R. 376; P.C.; *Vandyke* v. *Fender* [1970] 2 Q.B. 292. The germ of the doctrine, which was originally based on a "right of control," may have appeared in *Booth* v. *Mister* (1835) 7 C. & P. 66. Brooke-Smith, "Liability for the Negligence of Another—Servant or Agent" (1954) 70 L.Q.R. 253.

[51] [1973] A.C. 127.

[52] *cf.* the valiant attempt of Lord Denning M.R. and Edmund Davies L.J. in the C.A. to fit the facts into a traditional agency framework: [1971] 2 Q.B. 245.

the owner in the driving does not make the owner vicariously liable,[53] nor is there any doctrine of the "family car."[54] Where, however, the facts of the relationship between owner and driver are not fully known, proof of ownership may give rise to a presumption that the driver was acting as the owner's agent.[55]

The development of a separate head of vicarious liability for vehicle drivers has clearly been prompted by a desire to ensure a claim-worthy defendant, but the House of Lords has now denied that the courts may go on a voyage of discovery into the insurance position in these cases and has said that any alteration of the law must be left to the legislature with its superior capacity for making decisions of policy.[56] However, to confine our attention in this context to instances of vicarious liability risks giving a false impression. If there is in force a policy of insurance covering the liability of the driver[57] there will generally be no point in suing the owner. If, on the other hand, the owner has permitted an uninsured driver to drive, then, whether or not he is vicariously liable, he will be liable for breach of statutory duty under *Monk* v. *Warbey*[58] if the driver is unable to satisfy the judgment. In other words, the owner will nearly always be liable in these cases, but if the liability is of the *Monk* v. *Warbey* type he will have to meet it out of his own pocket.[59]

EMPLOYER AND INDEPENDENT CONTRACTOR

In principle an employer is not responsible for the torts of his independent contractor. It is no exception to say that he is liable (*a*) for torts authorised or ratified by him or where the contractor is employed to do an illegal act, for here they are both liable as joint tortfeasors,[60] or (*b*) for his own negligence. (*c*) Cases of strict liability are sometimes treated as exceptions, but it is doubtful if they are so in theory. (*d*) Nor is it an exception that he is liable if

---

[53] *Morgans* v. *Launchbury, supra*; *Hewitt* v. *Bonvin* [1940] 1 K.B. 188 (father permitting son to take girlfriends home in car); *cf. Carberry* v. *Davies* [1968] 1 W.L.R. 1103 (owner suggesting to driver that he take owner's son out in car). See also *Britt* v. *Galmoye* (1928) 44 T.L.R. 294; *Higbid* v. *Hammett* (1932) 49 T.L.R. 104; *Norton* v. *Canadian Pacific Steamships Ltd.* [1961] 1 W.L.R. 1957; *Nelson* v. *Raphael* [1979] R.T.R. 437; *Ansin* v. *Evans* [1982] 1 N.Z.L.R. 184. A person who has "borrowed" a car, with or without the owner's permission is not acting as his agent when driving it back to him: *Klein* v. *Caluori* [1971] 1 W.L.R. 619.

[54] *cf.* the view of Lord Denning M.R. in *Launchbury* v. *Morgans* [1971] 2 Q.B. 245. A wife is not her husband's agent because she is on a family shopping expedition: *Norwood* v. *Navan* [1981] R.T.R. 457.

[55] *Barnard* v. *Sully* (1931) 47 T.L.R. 557; *Rambarran* v. *Gurrucharan* [1970] 1 W.L.R. 556; *Morgans* v. *Launchbury, supra*, at p. 139, *per* Viscount Dilhorne.

[56] *Morgans* v. *Launchbury, supra. cf.* Jolowicz [1972A] C.L.J. 209.

[57] *e.g.* under a "named driver" clause in the policy.

[58] See *ante*, p. 177.

[59] It should be noted that at the time of the accident in *Morgans* v. *Launchbury* insurance for passengers was not compulsory. It now is, and in consequence a victim who cannot find an insured defendant may be able to recover his damages from the Motor Insurers' Bureau, subject to assignment of his judgment to that body. For the M.I.B. agreements, see Hepple and Matthews, *Tort, Cases and Materials* (3rd ed.), Chap. 10.

[60] *Ellis* v. *Sheffield Gas Consumers Co.* (1853) 2 El. & Bl. 767. The defendants, *without authority*, employed contractor to dig trench in street for gas pipes. Contractor's servants carelessly left heap of stones on footpath; plaintiff fell over them and was injured. The contract was to do an illegal act, a public nuisance, and defendants were liable.

he personally interferes with the contractor or his servants and in fact directs the manner in which the work is to be done, for he is then again liable as a joint tortfeasor.[61]

The true question in every case in which an employer is sued for damage caused by his independent contractor is whether the employer himself was in breach of some duty which he himself owed to the plaintiff.[62] Such a breach of duty may exist if the employer has not taken care to select a competent contractor or has employed an inadequate number of men.[63] It may also exist if the contractor alone has been at fault, provided that the duty cast upon the employer is of the kind commonly described as "non-delegable."[64] Strictly speaking no duty is delegable,[65] but if my duty is merely to take reasonable care, then, if I have taken care to select a competent contractor to do the work, I have done all that is required of me.[66] If, on the other hand, my duty is, *e.g.* "to provide that care is taken"[67] or is to achieve some actual result such as the secure fencing of dangerous parts of machinery,[68] then my duty is not performed unless care is taken or the machinery is fenced. It is no defence that I delegated the task to an independent contractor if he failed to fulfil his duties. For this purpose, care must be taken to avoid the conclusion that because a duty owed by A to B is non-delegable, so as also is a duty owed by A to C. A building contractor may well, as a matter of contract, be responsible to the building owner for deficiences in the completed building, but it does not follow that he is responsible to third parties for damage for which they sue in tort[69]: as far as the first is concerned his duty may be to provide a building according to specifications, but to the second he owes only a duty of care.

It is a question of law whether the duty in a given case is "non-delegable," but unfortunately, so far as common law duties are concerned, little by way of principle is to be gathered from the cases.[70] We must content ourselves, therefore, with a number of examples.

[61] *M'Laughlin* v. *Pryor* (1842) 4 Man. & G. 48; *Hardaker* v. *Idle D.C.* [1896] 1 Q.B. 335. In *Brooke* v. *Bool* [1928] 2 K.B. 578 the defendant was held liable on the basis of participation in a joint enterprise. It is respectfully submitted that *Scarsbrook* v. *Mason* [1961] 3 All E.R. 767 takes this much too far: and it was doubted in *S.* v. *Walsall M.B.C.* [1985] 1 W.L.R. 1150.
[62] *D. & F. Estates Ltd.* v. *Church Commissioners* [1988] 3 W.L.R. 368, 387, *per* Lord Bridge; *Salsbury* v. *Woodland* [1970] 1 Q.B. 324, 347, *per* Sachs L.J.
[63] *Pinn* v. *Rew* (1916) 32 T.L.R. 451.
[64] For criticism of this term, and generally, see Glanville Williams, "Liability for Independent Contractors" [1956] C.L.J. 180. See also Chapman, "Liability for the Negligence of Independent Contractors" (1934) 50 L.Q.R. 71; Barak, "Mixed and Vicarious Liability—A Suggested Distinction" (1966) 29 M.L.R. 160 (where the point is made that the liability under discussion here is neither truly vicarious nor yet truly personal, for the defendant is held liable for damage which he did not himself cause by his own act).
[65] *Cassidy* v. *Ministry of Health* [1951] 2 K.B. 343, 363, *per* Denning L.J.
[66] See *Phillips* v. *Britannia Hygienic Laundry Co.* [1923] 1 K.B. 539; *Stennett* v. *Hancock* [1939] 2 All E.R. 578; *Salsbury* v. *Woodland* [1970] 1 Q.B. 324.
[67] *The Pass of Ballater* [1942] P. 112, 117, *per* Langton J. See also *The Lady Gwendolen* [1965] P. 294, where Winn L.J. (at p. 350) described the duty owed by a shipowner to other ships and to persons who might be affected by the navigation of his own ships as a duty "that all concerned in any capacity with the navigation of those ships should exercise such care as a reasonable person would exercise in that capacity."
[68] Factories Act 1961, s.14(1).
[69] *D. & F. Estates Ltd.* v. *Church Commissioners* [1988] 3 W.L.R. 368.
[70] *cf.* Jolowicz, "Liability for Independent Contractors in the English Common Law—A Suggestion" (1957) 9 Stanford L.Rev. 690. In *Salsbury* v. *Woodland, supra,* the Court of Appeal proceeded upon the assumption that there was simply a limited number of special exceptions to the general rule of non-liability for the negligence of independent contractors.

Cases of strict liability at common law

(1) *Withdrawal of support from neighbouring land*

This furnished the earliest example of a "non-delegable" duty at common law. If A, in the course of work done on his land causes subsidence on B's adjoining land and B's land is entitled to the support of A, A is liable to B, and it is no defence that the work had been entrusted to an independent contractor.[71]

(2) *Operations affecting the highway other than normal user for the purpose of passage*[72]

In *Tarry* v. *Ashton*[73] the defendant employed an independent contractor to repair a lamp attached to his house and overhanging the footway. As it was not securely fastened the lamp fell on the plaintiff, a passer-by, and the defendant was held liable, because "it was the defendant's duty to make the lamp reasonably safe . . . the contractor has failed to do that . . . therefore the defendant has not done his duty and is liable to the plaintiff for the consequences."[74] In *Gray* v. *Pullen*[75] the defendant owned a house adjoining a highway and had statutory authority to cut a trench across the road to make a drain from his premises to a sewer. For this purpose he employed a contractor who negligently filled in the trench improperly and the plaintiff, a passenger on the highway, was injured. The defendant was held liable although he was not negligent. On the other hand, in *Salsbury* v. *Woodland*[76] the defendant had employed an apparently competent contractor to fell a tree in the front garden of his house near the highway. Done competently this would have involved no risk to anyone, but owing to the negligence of the contractor, the tree fouled some telephone wires, causing them to fall into the highway, and an accident resulted in which the plaintiff was injured. The Court of Appeal held that these facts did not bring the case within the special category comprising cases of work done on the highway[77] and that there was no equivalent category comprising cases in which work is done

---

[71] *Bower* v. *Peate* (1876) 1 Q.B.D. 321; *Dalton* v. *Angus* (1881) 6 App.Cas. 740; *Hughes* v. *Percival* (1883) 8 App.Cas. 443; *cf. Stoneman* v. *Lyons* (1975) 50 A.L.J.R. 370.

[72] The liability of a highway authority under the Highways Act 1980 involves liability for default of a contractor: *ante,* p. 418.

[73] (1876) 1 Q.B.D. 314.

[74] *Ibid.* at p. 319, *per* Blackburn J.

[75] (1864) 5 B. & S. 970; *Hole* v. *Sittingbourne Ry.* (1861) 6 H. & N. 488 (bridge obstructing navigation); *Hardaker* v. *Idle D.C.* [1896] 1 Q.B. 335 (gas main broken by failure to pack soil round it while constructing a sewer); *Penny* v. *Wimbledon U.D.C.* [1899] 2 Q.B. 72 (heap of soil left unlighted in road); *Pickard* v. *Smith* (1861) 10 C.B.(N.S.) 314 (cellar flap on railway platform left open); *Daniel* v. *Rickett, etc.* [1938] 2 K.B. 322 (cellar flap left open on pavement); *Holliday* v. *National Telephone Co.* [1899] 2 Q.B. 392 (explosion in highway caused by dipping benzoline lamp in molten solder); *Walsh* v. *Holst & Co. Ltd.* [1958] 1 W.L.R. 800 (building operations adjoining highway).

[76] [1970] 1 Q.B. 324; Weir, *Casebook on Tort* (6th ed.), p. 268.

[77] Widgery L.J. observed that the cases within this category would be found on analysis to be cases where the work done was of a character which would have been a nuisance unless authorised by statute: [1970] 1 Q.B. 324, 338. *cf. ibid.* at p. 348, *per* Sachs L.J.

near the highway. Accordingly the general principle applied and the defendant was not liable for the negligence of the independent contractor.

(3) *Other cases of strict liability*

The rule in *Rylands* v. *Fletcher*,[78] damage by fire,[79] and, in some cases, nuisance,[80] impose a liability for the default of an independent contractor. Analogous to these instances is a class of "extra hazardous acts, that is, acts which, in their very nature, involve in the eyes of the law special danger to others"[81] such as acts causing fire and explosion, where an employer cannot escape liability by delegating their performance to an independent contractor.[82] He has not merely a duty to take care, but a duty to provide that care is taken, where implements or substances dangerous in themselves, such as flame-bearing instruments or explosives are necessarily incidental to the work to be performed.[83] In *Honeywill and Stein Ltd.* v. *Larkin Bros. Ltd.*[84] it was held that the plaintiffs who procured the defendants as independent contractors to take photographs of X's cinema by flashlight were liable for the defendants' negligence is setting fire to X's cinema.

(4) *Master's common law duties*

The master's common law duties in respect of his servant's safety as laid down in *Wilsons and Clyde Coal Co.* v. *English*[85] are "non delegable." This matter has already been dealt with.[86]

Cases of statutory duty

"Where a special duty is laid by statute on an individual or class of individuals either to take care or even to ensure safety (an absolute duty in the true sense) ... they cannot in any way escape from or evade the full implication of and responsibility for that duty: *Smith* v. *Cammell Laird & Co. Ltd.*"[87] Whether the duty is absolute in this sense depends upon the true construction of the statute. Many of the duties imposed by the Factories Act

[78] (1866) L.R. 1 Ex. 265; (1868) L.R. 3 H.L. 330.

[79] *Black* v. *Christchurch Finance Co.* [1894] A.C. 48; *Spicer* v. *Smee* [1946] 1 All E.R. 489; *Balfour* v. *Barty-King* [1957] 1 Q.B. 496; *H.N. Emanuel Ltd.* v. *G.L.C., The Times,* March 10, 1971. *cf. Eriksen* v. *Clifton* [1963] N.Z.L.R. 705.

[80] *Matania* v. *National Provincial Bank* (1936) 155 L.T. 74 (nuisance by dust and noise the inevitable consequence of extensive building operations), *ante*, p. 397; *Att.-Gen.* v. *Geothermal Produce N.Z. Ltd.* [1987] 2 N.Z.L.R. 348.

[81] The existence of this class of case is confirmed by *Salsbury* v. *Woodland* [1970] 1 Q.B. 324, but see Clerk and Lindsell, *Torts* (16th ed.), para. 3–43.

[82] *Honeywill and Stein Ltd.* v. *Larkin Bros. Ltd.* [1934] 1 K.B. 191, 197, *per* Slesser L.J.; *Dodd Properties* v. *Canterbury City Council* [1980] 1 W.L.R. 433, 439.

[83] *The Pass of Ballater* [1942] P. 112, 117, *per* Langton J.; *Brooke* v. *Bool* [1928] 2 K.B. 578, 587, *per* Talbot J.

[84] [1934] 1 K.B. 191; *Municipality of County of Cape Breton* v. *Chappell's Ltd.* (1963) 36 D.L.R. (2d) 58 (Nova Scotia Supreme Court); *Peters* v. *North Star Oil Ltd.* (1965) 54 D.L.R. (2d) 364 (Manitoba Q.B.). *Bluett* v. *King Core Demolition Services* (1973) 227 E.G. 503; *Petter* v. *Metropolitan Properties Co.* (1973) 229 E.G. 973. But this forms no part of the common law in Australia: *Stevens* v. *Brodribb Sawmilling Co. Pty. Ltd.* (1986) 63 A.L.R. 513.

[85] [1938] A.C. 57.

[86] *Ante*, pp. 195–197.

[87] [1940] A.C. 242, *per* Langton J. in *The Pass of Ballater* [1942] P. 112, 117; *Donaghey* v. *Boulton and Paul Ltd.* [1968] A.C. 1.

1961, *e.g.* to guard dangerous machinery, are absolute.[88] Where a statute authorises something to be done which would otherwise be illegal, the duty is generally such that there is liability if the work is done by an independent contractor.[89] However, everything turns on the particular statute,[90] so that, for example, a local authority's duty under child care legislation was discharged by boarding a child out with foster parents and the authority was not liable for negligence by the foster parents in looking after the child.[91]

Collateral or casual negligence of independent contractor

There is a recognised exception that an employer is not liable for the collateral or casual negligence of an independent contractor, that is, negligence in some collateral respect, as distinct from negligence with regard to the very matter delegated to be done.[92] The distinction between the two kinds of negligence is difficult to draw[93] but is established by the cases. In *Padbury* v. *Holliday and Greenwood Ltd.*[94] the defendants employed a subcontractor to put metallic casements into the windows of a house which the defendants were building. While one of these casements was being put in, an iron tool was placed by a servant of the subcontractor on the window sill, and the casement having been blown in by the wind, the tool fell and injured the plaintiff in the street below. The tool was not placed on the window sill in the ordinary course of doing the work which the subcontractor was employed to do. It was held that the plaintiff's injuries were caused by an act of collateral negligence and the defendants were not liable. In *Holliday* v. *National Telephone Co.*[95] the defendants were laying telephone wires

---

[88] *Hosking* v. *De Havilland Aircraft Co. Ltd.* [1949] 1 All E.R. 540; *Galashiels Gas Co. Ltd.* v. *O'Donnell* [1940] A.C. 275; *Lochgelly Iron and Coal Co.* v. *M'Mullan* [1934] A.C. 1, 8–9, *per* Lord Atkin.

[89] Chapman, *loc. cit.*, p. 78, citing *Hardaker* v. *Idle D.C.* [1896] 1 Q.B. 335, 351, *per* Rigby L.J.; *Darling* v. *Att.-Gen.* [1950] 2 All E.R. 793 (Minister of Works having statutory *power* to do work on land liable for negligence of independent contractor in leaving heap of timber on field which injured plaintiff's horse). See Baker, "Independent Contractors and the Liability of their Principals" (1954) 27 Austr.L.J. 546.

[90] In *Rivers* v. *Cutting* [1982] 1 W.L.R. 1146 the police were held not liable for the negligence of a garage which they had procured to tow away an abandoned vehicle. The statutory power was to "remove" or "arrange for the removal" of the vehicle and since the policeman was exercising the latter no question of delegation arose.

[91] *S.* v. *Walsall M.B.C.* [1985] 1 W.L.R. 1150.

[92] *Pickard* v. *Smith* (1861) 10 C.B.(N.S.) 470, 480, *per* Williams J.: "If an independent contractor is employed to do a lawful act, and in the course of the work he or his servants commit some casual act of wrong or negligence, the employer is not answerable. . . . The rule, however, is inapplicable to cases in which the act which occasions the injury is the one which the contractor was employed to do." "It is settled law that one employing another is not liable for his collateral negligence unless the relation of master and servant exists between them": *per* Lord Blackburn, *Dalton* v. *Angus* (1881) 6 App.Cas. 740, 829; *Cassidy* v. *Ministry of Health* [1951] 2 K.B. 343, 363–364, *per* Denning L.J.

[93] See the criticism of Sachs L.J. in *Salsbury* v. *Woodland* [1970] 1 Q.B. 324, 348. Prosser, *Torts* (5th ed.), p. 516, suggests that the test of collateral negligence is not its character as a minor incident or operative detail of the work to be done, but rather its dissociation from any inherent risk created by the work itself. See also Jolowicz, *loc. cit.*, pp. 707–708.

[94] (1912) 28 T.L.R. 494.

[95] [1899] 2 Q.B. 392. *cf. Reedie* v. *L. & N.W. Ry.* (1849) 4 Ex. 244 (railway company employed contractor to build a bridge. Contractor's workman negligently caused the death of a person, passing beneath along the highway, by allowing a stone to drop on him. Railway company held not liable). "I am not liable if my contractor in making a bridge happens to drop a brick . . . but I am liable if he makes a bridge which will not open. . . . The liability of the employer depends on the existence of a duty . . . it only extends to the limit of that duty. I owe a duty with regard to the structure of the bridge; I owe a duty to see that my bridge will open; but I owe no duty with regard to the disposition of bricks and hammers in the course of construction": Chapman, *loc. cit.*, pp. 80–81.

under a street and employed an independent contractor to make certain connections. A plumber employed by the contractor dipped a blowlamp into molten solder causing an explosion which injured the plaintiff. In the court below Willes J., in no uncertain terms, treated this as an act of collateral negligence, but the Court of Appeal reversed his decision and held the defendants were liable. If an employer has a lamp which overhangs the highway, he himself is under a duty to passers-by to use reasonable care to see that it is safe. He is liable if his independent contractor fails to discover a defect which a reasonable man would have discovered, and in consequence a pedestrian is injured. He is not liable if the contractor drops a hammer on a pedestrian, because that is casual or collateral negligence, not negligence in the employer's department of duty.[96]

BASIS OF VICARIOUS LIABILITY

The theoretical basis of the rule that a master is liable for the torts of his servants committed in the course of their employment for long caused controversy.[97] As we have seen, so long as the liability was thought to depend on the fact that the master had expressly or impliedly authorised the servant's tort it was at least theoretically a primary one. The master was himself guilty of a tort against the plaintiff.[98] Once it was decided that the absence of the relationship of master and servant between the defendant and the wrongdoer was fatal to liability in certain cases, however, the liability of the master came to be treated as a case apart.[99] As was stated at the beginning of this chapter, the necessary and sufficient conditions for liability are that the relationship of master and servant should exist and that the servant should have committed the tort in the course of his employment. Nothing turns on any duty which the master may himself owe to the plaintiff. "To make a master liable for the conduct of his servant the first question is to see whether the servant is liable. If the answer is Yes, the second question is to see whether the employer must shoulder the servant's liability."[1]

Nevertheless, in *Twine* v. *Bean's Express Ltd.*,[2] Uthwatt J. said that the

---

[96] Equally, it is submitted, he is not liable if the contractor, by his negligent driving, causes an accident on the way to or from the place of work.

[97] Laski, "The Basis of Vicarious Liability" (1916) 26 Yale L.J. 105; Hughes and Hudson, "The Nature of a Master's Liability in the Law of Tort" (1953) 31 Can. Bar Rev. 18; Glanville Williams, "Vicarious Liability: Tort of the Master or the Servant" (1956) 72 L.Q.R. 522.

[98] *Ante*, pp. 561–562.

[99] *Reedie* v. *London and North Western Ry.* (1849) 4 Exch. 244.

[1] *Young* v. *Edward Box & Co. Ltd.* [1951] 1 T.L.R. 789, 793, *per* Denning L.J.; *Launchbury* v. *Morgans* [1971] 2 W.L.R. 602, 606, *per* Lord Denning M.R.
The Crown Proceedings Act 1947, s.2(1), and the Police Act 1964, s.48, adopt this view. Strictly, perhaps, liability under the Occupiers' Liability Act cannot be vicarious unless the servant is himself in occupation of his master's land, since the duty under the Act is imposed on the occupier. However, there is no very significant difference between the duty under the Act and that under *Donoghue* v. *Stevenson* (*ante*, p. 209). For consideration of the scope of employment in a case where the defendants were said to be in occupation through their servant see *Stone* v. *Taffe* [1974] 1 W.L.R. 1575.

[2] [1946] 1 All E.R. 202, *ante*, p. 572; *Norton* v. *Canadian Pacific Steamships* [1961] 1 W.L.R. 1057, 1063, *per* Pearson L.J.

law attributes to the employer the acts of a servant done in the course of his employment, that, generally, the duty of both master and servant is the same, but that that is a coincidence and not a rule of law. "The general question in an action against an employer, ... is technically: 'Did the employer in the circumstances which affected him owe a duty'—for the law does not attribute to the employer the liability which attaches to the servant."[3] These observations have led to a second view as to the basis of a master's vicarious liability, expressed as follows:

> "It is the master who owes a duty to the plaintiff, and who breaks it as a result of the acts and mental states of his servant. In discussing the liability of the master it is not necessary to consider whether the servant owes a duty to the plaintiff or had committed a tort. A master may be under a so-called vicarious liability even though the servant has not committed any tort or any actionable tort."[4]

It is submitted that neither on principle nor on the balance of authority does this view represent the law. As to principle, it is difficult, if not impossible, to reconcile insistence on the presence of the specific master and servant relationship with the view that the master is primarily liable for breach of his own duty. If the act of B has the legal result that A's duty to C is broken, then A is liable to C whatever his relationship to B. Furthermore, if the master's liability is primary, how does the law distinguish between that liability and liability for damage caused by an independent contractor? The latter is undoubtedly a primary liability based upon a breach by the employer of a duty which he himself owes to the plaintiff.[5] If this is true also of liability for servants, how are we to explain, for example, that a man is liable for the negligent driving of his chauffeur (servant) but not for that of his taxi-driver (independent contractor)?[6]

So far as authority is concerned, though Uthwatt J.'s approach can find some support in decisions in the Court of Appeal and elsewhere, its correctness has been denied on at least two occasions in the House of Lords. In *Staveley Iron and Chemical Co. Ltd. v. Jones*,[7] while recognising that a master may be liable for the breach of his own personal duty to his servants, it was held that this was something different from vicarious liability. "Cases ... where an employer's liability is vicarious are wholly distinct from cases where an employer is under a personal liability to carry out a duty imposed

---

[3] [1946] 1 All E.R. 202, 204. *cf.* Newark, "*Twine* v. *Bean's Express Ltd.*" (1954) 17 M.L.R. 102.
[4] Glanville Williams, *Crown Proceedings*, p. 43. *W.B. Anderson & Sons Ltd.* v. *Rhodes (Liverpool) Ltd.* [1967] 2 All E.R. 850. But see Dias [1967] C.L.J. 155.
[5] *Salsbury* v. *Woodland* [1970] 1 Q.B. 324, 336–337, *per* Widgery L.J.; *ibid.* at p. 345, *per* Harman L.J.; *ibid.* at p. 347, *per* Sachs L.J.
[6] See *Cassidy* v. *Ministry of Health* [1951] 2 K.B. 343, 363, *per* Denning L.J. "If I am at home while my servant is driving my car on the highway, I personally owe no duty to road users in respect of that car, but my servant does owe a duty, and if he injures someone through his negligence, I am inflicted with his liability": Chapman, "Liability for the Negligence of Independent Contractors" (1934) 50 L.Q.R. 71, 75.
[7] [1956] A.C. 627; Weir, *Casebook on Tort* (6th ed.), p. 238. See also *Harrison* v. *N.C.B.* [1951] A.C. 639; *N.C.B.* v. *England* [1954] A.C. 403. It is doubtful whether the decision in *Lister* v. *Romford Ice and Cold Storage Co. Ltd.* [1957] A.C. 555 could have been reached on the basis that the master is primarily liable.

upon him as an employer by common law or statute."[8] Again in *I.C.I.* v. *Shatwell*[9] it plainly stated that if the servant himself was not liable then the master could not be held liable either. "Since in this case the employer, if liable at all, is liable only by virtue of vicarious responsibility. I agree that the primary issue if the respondent . . . is to succeed here, is whether he could maintain an action for damages against (his fellow servant)."[10]

To deny that the master's liability rests upon a notional breach of his own duty brought about by the act of his servant is not, of course, to deny that a master may sometimes be liable for breach of his own duty even though the act causing the damage was done by his servant. Wherever the law imposes a duty of the kind known as "non-delegable" upon A and the act of B produces the result that that duty is broken, A is liable whatever his relationship with B. So in all the cases in which a defendant has been held liable for the acts of his independent contractor the result would have been exactly the same if the defendant had stood in the relation of master to the actual wrongdoer. A master may thus in some cases be liable on two separate grounds.[11] He may be primarily liable for the breach, through his servant, of his own "non-delegable" duty; and he may at the same time and on the same facts also be liable vicariously for the tort of his servant committed in the course of the employment.

REASONS FOR VICARIOUS LIABILITY

The foregoing discussion of the nature of the master's liability does nothing to explain why the master should be liable for the torts of his servants,[12] and the traditional phrases "*respondeat superior*" and "*qui facit per alium facit per se*" give no help. "The former merely states the rule baldly in two words, and the latter merely gives a fictional explanation of it."[13] Many other explanations have been put forward from time to time,[14] such as that the master must have been negligent in employing a negligent servant[15] or in failing adequately to control him, that the master has "set the whole thing in motion,"[16] that the master benefits from the servant's work and so should bear the responsibility for damage the servant may cause in its perform-

---

[8] [1956] A.C. 627, 639, *per* Lord Morton. An interesting variation on "personal" liability is to be found in *Maharaj* v. *Att.-Gen. of Trinidad and Tobago (No. 2)* [1979] A.C. 385, though the defendant was not an employer and the action was not for tort.

[9] [1965] A.C. 656.

[10] *Ibid.* at p. 676, *per* Viscount Radcliffe. See also *ibid.* at p. 670, *per* Lord Reid; *ibid.* at p. 681, *per* Lord Hodson; *ibid.* at p. 686, *per* Lord Pearce; *ibid.* at p. 694, *per* Lord Donovan.

[11] See Barak, "Mixed and Vicarious Liability—A Suggested Distinction" (1966) 29 M.L.R. 160; Street, *Governmental Liability*, p. 36, citing *R.* v. *Anthony* [1946] 3 D.L.R. 577, 585, *per* Rand J.

[12] In addition to articles already cited, see Glanville Williams, "Vicarious Liability and the Master's Indemnity" (1957) 20 M.L.R. 220, 437.

[13] *Staveley Iron and Chemical Co. Ltd.* v. *Jones* [1956] A.C. 627, 643, *per* Lord Reid.

[14] Baty, *Vicarious Liability*, p. 148, lists nine reasons, none of them, in his view, satisfactory.

[15] "The most hoary reason": Street, *Foundations of Legal Liability*, II, p. 458.

[16] *Duncan* v. *Findlater* (1839) 6 Cl. & F. 894, 910, *per* Lord Brougham; *Hutchinson* v. *York, Newcastle and Berwick Ry.* (1850) 5 Exch. 343, 350, *per* Alderson B.; *Jones* v. *Staveley Iron & Chemical Co. Ltd.* [1955] 1 Q.B. 474, 480, *per* Denning L.J.; and see *Rose* v. *Plenty* [1976] 1 W.L.R. 141, 147, *per* Scarman L.J.

ance,[17] and that the master has the deeper pocket.[18] Probably the most popular today, at least with academic writers, is the last, though in a much more sophisticated form. In short, the argument is that a "master" today is normally not an individual but a substantial enterprise or undertaking, and that, by placing liability on the enterprise, what is in fact achieved is the distribution of losses caused in the conduct of its business over all the customers to whom it sells its services or products. Knowing of its potential liability for the torts of its servants, the enterprise insures against this liability and the cost of this insurance is reflected in the price it charges to its customers. In the result, therefore, losses caused by the torts of the enterprise's servants are borne in small and probably unnoticeable amounts by the body of its customers, and the injured person is compensated without the necessity of calling upon an individual, whose personal fault may be slight or even non-existent, to suffer the disastrous financial consequences that may follow liability in tort.[19]

None of these explanations, even the last,[20] is, however, sufficient to explain all the aspects of the present law, and it is difficult not to agree with Lord Pearce when he said[21]:

"The doctrine of vicarious liability has not grown from any very clear, logical or legal principle but from social convenience and rough justice. The master having (presumably for his own benefit) employed the servant, and being (presumably) better able to make good any damage which may occasionally result from the arrangement, is answerable to the world at large for all the torts committed by his servant within the scope of it."

This may not satisfy the purist or the logician, but it probably represents the prevailing state of legal opinion on the matter and, though the future may bring further extensions of vicarious liability, it is inconceivable that a serious proposal for its abolition will be made so long as the law of tort as we know it remains alive.

---

[17] *Taff Vale Ry.* v. *Amalgamated Society of Railway Servants* [1901] A.C. 426, 439, *per* Farwell J.; *Broom* v. *Morgan* [1953] 1 Q.B. 597, 608, *per* Denning L.J.

[18] *Limpus* v. *L.G.O.C.* (1862) 1 H. & C. 526, 539, *per* Willes J.

[19] See *ante*, p. 25. Whatever the merits of the decision in *Lister* v. *Romford Ice & Cold Storage Co. Ltd.* [1957] A.C. 555, *ante*, pp. 577–579, it cannot be denied that it militates against this result.

[20] This theory proves too much. If the principle of "enterprise liability" is right then it should apply to all damage caused by the activities of the enterprise and not only to that caused by conduct which the present law regards as tortious (see *ante*, pp. 25–26). It is also difficult to use it to explain those cases in which there is liability for the negligence of independent contractors. See Glanville Williams, "Liability for Independent Contractors" [1956] C.L.J. 180, 193–198.

[21] *Imperial Chemical Industries Ltd.* v. *Shatwell* [1965] A.C. 656, 685.

CHAPTER 22

JOINT AND SEVERAL TORTFEASORS

WHERE two or more people by their independent breaches of duty to the plaintiff cause him to suffer distinct injuries, no special rules are required, for each tortfeasor is liable for the damage which he caused and only for that damage.[1] Where, however, two or more breaches of duty by different persons cause the plaintiff to suffer a *single* injury the position is more complicated. The law in such a case is that the plaintiff is entitled to sue all or any of them for the full amount of his loss,[2] which means that special rules are necessary to deal with the possibilities of successive actions in respect of that loss and of claims for contribution or indemnity by one tortfeasor against the others. It is greatly to the plaintiff's advantage to show that he has suffered the same, indivisible harm at the hands of a number of defendants for he thereby avoids the risk, inherent in cases where there are different injuries, of finding that one defendant is insolvent (or uninsured) and being unable to execute judgment against him. The question of whether there is one injury can be a difficult one.[3] The simplest case is that of two virtually simultaneous acts of negligence, as where two drivers behave negligently and collide, injuring a passenger in one of the cars or a pedestrian, but there is no requirement that the acts be simultaneous. Thus if D_1 driving too fast in icy conditions causes his lorry to "jackknife" across the motorway and D_2, also driving too fast, later comes along and, trying to avoid the obstruction, runs down P, assisting at the scene, both D_1 and D_2 are liable for P's injuries.[4] The acts of the two defendants may be separated by a substantial period of time and yet contribute to one, indivisible injury for this purpose, as where D_1 manufactures a dangerous product and D_2 uses it without due care years later. Where, however, the plaintiff's loss is the culmination of a progression, the individual stages of which are brought about by the separate acts of different defendants, each defendant is liable only for the extent to which he contributed to the final result: the second defendant (and subsequent defendants) takes over a plaintiff whose condition has already been impaired by the act of his predecessor and it would be wrong to hold him liable[5] for more

---

[1] See *Performance Cars Ltd.* v. *Abraham* [1962] 1 Q.B. 33; *Baker* v. *Willoughby* [1970] A.C. 467, *ante*, pp. 135–137.
[2] Though he cannot execute judgment so as to recover more than his loss.
[3] Fleming, *Torts* (7th ed.), pp. 178–181 contains an excellent review of the authorities.
[4] Based on *Rouse* v. *Squires* [1973] Q.B. 889, where, however, the issue was whether D_2's negligence was so extreme as to deprive D_1's of any causative effect. See also *Lloyds Bank* v. *Budd* [1982] R.T.R. 80. If, however, P's car had been damaged by a collision with D_1's lorry before the arrival of D_2 on the scene then D_1 alone would be responsible for that loss.
[5] As to the first defendant, *cf. Baker* v. *Willoughby, ante*, p. 135.

than aggravating the pre-existing damage.[6] In the last resort, however, the matter is one of proof and if the plaintiff shows that what the defendant did make a material contribution to his loss it is likely that he will recover in full unless the defendant is able to show that in fact his action was insufficient to cause the whole loss.[7] Where the court concludes that the loss must be apportioned it must do the best it can with the evidence, making the fullest allowances in the plaintiff's favour[8] but in the last resort it may be driven to using arbitrary methods, such as a rateable apportionment according to the numbers of defendants. By statute, though not at common law, one defendant may recover a contribution or indemnity from any other defendant liable in respect of the same damage, but that is a matter between the defendants and does not affect the plaintiff, who remains entitled to recover his whole loss from whichever defendant he chooses.

DISTINCTION BETWEEN JOINT AND SEVERAL LIABILITY

At common law tortfeasors liable in respect of the same damage were divided into "joint" tortfeasors and "several" tortfeasors.[9] This distinction, formerly of importance, has been largely eroded by statute, as we shall see in a moment, but it remains of significance for one purpose and some account of it is necessary.

"Persons are said to be joint tortfeasors when their separate shares in the commission of the tort are done in furtherance of a common design."[10] So, in *Brook* v. *Bool*,[11] where two men searching for a gas leak each applied a naked light to a gas pipe in turn and one of them caused an explosion, they were held to be joint tortfeasors[12] but where two ships collided because of the independent acts of negligence of each of them, and one of them, without further negligence, collided with a third, it was held that they were several tortfeasors, whose acts combined to produce a single harm, because there was no community of design.[13] It was formerly thought that all persons concerned in the publication of defamatory matter, such as the author, publisher and printer of a book, must be joint tortfeasors but it is now known that this is not necessarily the case. If the publication is made on an occasion

---

[6] *Thompson* v. *Smith's Shiprepairers (North Shields) Ltd.* [1984] Q.B. 405. (On the facts, the case concerned not successive defendants but one defendant who was in breach of duty for only part of the period during which excessive noise produced the plaintiff's deafness). *cf. Clarkson* v. *Modern Foundries Ltd.* [1957] 1 W.L.R. 1210, where the issue concerned a process which fell partly within and partly without the limitation period.

[7] *Bonnington Castings Ltd.* v. *Wardlow* [1956] A.C. 613.

[8] For an example, see *Thompson* v. *Smiths Shiprepairers, supra.*

[9] Street, *Torts,* very usefully calls the latter class *several concurrent tortfeasors,* to distinguish them from several independent tortfeasors who cause separate harms.

[10] *The Koursk* [1924] P. 140, 151, *per* Bankes L.J., at pp. 159–160, *per* Sargant L.J. For the liability of company directors, see *post,* p. 676.

[11] [1928] 2 K.B. 578. See too *Arneil* v. *Patterson* [1931] A.C. 560; *cf. Cook* v. *Lewis* [1952] 1 D.L.R. 1, *ante,* p. 124.

[12] And hence liable in respect of the damage. Note that the act of only one defendant was the physical cause of the damage. The liability of the other arises from his assistance or encouragement: *C.B.S. Songs Ltd.* v. *Amstrad Consumer Electronics plc* [1988] A.C. 1013, 1058.

[13] *The Koursk, supra.* See also *Sadler* v. *G.W. Ry.* [1896] A.C. 450; *Thompson* v. *L.C.C.* [1899] 1 Q.B. 840.

of qualified privilege, or, probably, if it is fair comment on a matter of public interest, then no person is liable unless he is himself malicious.[14] An anomalous exception to the requirement of community of design is that where a master is liable vicariously for his servant's tort, master and servant are joint tortfeasors.[15] On the other hand, the parent or custodian of a child whose personal negligence enables the child to commit a tort, though he may be liable for the resulting damage, is not a joint tortfeasor with the child. He is personally negligent and his liability is for his own independent tort.[16]

The two principal consequences at common law of the defendants' being joint tortfeasors were (a) judgment against one of them, even if it remained unsatisfied, barred any subsequent action, or even the continuance of the same action, against the others and (b) the release of one operated as the release of all. In each case the reason given was that the cause of action was single and indivisible.[17] Neither rule ever applied to several tortfeasors liable for the same damage. Now, however, the first rule has been abolished by statute[18] and the importance of the second has been much reduced by a distinction between a release and a mere covenant by the plaintiff not to sue one of the tortfeasors, which does not affect his action against the others.[19]

Successive actions

We have seen how, under the present law, an unsatisfied judgment against one of joint or several concurrent tortfeasors does not bar proceedings against others. It is, however, obviously desirable that a plaintiff should, if he reasonably can, sue in the same proceedings all the tortfeasors who are liable to him for the same damage. It is therefore provided that the plaintiff may not recover costs in any but the first action in respect of the

---

[14] *Egger* v. *Viscount Chelmsford* [1965] 1 Q.B. 248, *ante*, p. 353. Accordingly, the liability of each person concerned in the publication is dependent upon his own state of mind, and the mere fact of publication does not make all who join in it joint tortfeasors. It is not possible to hold "that a defendant C is a joint tortfeasor with defendants A and B unless it is proved, in a case where that is necessary to constitute a tort, that all three had, at the time of the common act a common state of mind such as malice": *Gardiner* v. *Moore* [1969] 1 Q.B. 55, 91.

[15] "I could never see why an employer, whose only liability is the vicarious liability of being responsible for what his servant does, should be called a joint tortfeasor, which should mean a person who took some part in the tort which is the subject of the action": *Semtex* v. *Gladstone* [1954] 1 W.L.R. 945, 949, *per* Finnemore J. In *Romford Ice and Cold Storage Co. Ltd.* v. *Lister* [1956] 2 Q.B. 180, 209, Romer L.J. expressed some sympathy with this view but regarded the matter as settled by authority. See also *ibid.* at pp. 200–201, *per* Birkett L.J.

[16] See *Bebee* v. *Sales* (1916) 32 T.L.R. 413; *Newton* v. *Edgerley* [1959] 1 W.L.R. 1031.

[17] *Brinsmead* v. *Harrison* (1872) L.R. 7 C.P. 547; *Duck* v. *Mayeu* [1892] 2 Q.B. 511; *Cutler* v. *McPhail* [1962] 2 Q.B. 292.

[18] Civil Liability (Contribution) Act 1978, s.3, replacing (with effect from January 1, 1979), s.6(1)(*a*) of the Law Reform (Married Women and Tortfeasors) Act 1935.

[19] *Gardiner* v. *Moore* [1969] 1 Q.B. 55; *Apley Estates Ltd.* v. *De Bernales* [1947] Ch. 217. The distinction is technical but would seem to depend at bottom on whether the plaintiff has made clear his intention to reserve his rights against the other defendants. The problem is less acute than in the case of judgment because in practice a release by agreement will require the defendant to make some payment in settlement and the agreement would normally not be interpreted as extinguishing the original cause of action unless the payment was made.

damage unless the court is of the opinion that there was reasonable ground for bringing the further proceedings.[20]

Contribution Between Tortfeasors

At common law the general rule was that one concurrent tortfeasor, even if he had satisfied the plaintiff's judgment in full, could not recover indemnity nor contribution towards his liability from any other tortfeasor liable. The rule was laid down with regard to joint tortfeasors in *Merryweather* v. *Nixan*[21] and was later extended to several concurrent tortfeasors.[22] The harshness of this rule was modified to a limited extent and it does not apply where the tort was not clearly illegal in itself,[23] and the person claiming contribution or indemnity acted in the belief that his conduct was lawful[24]; nor does it apply where even though the tort was clearly illegal in itself, one of the parties has been vicariously liable for another's wrong to which he gave neither his authority nor assent and of which he had no knowledge.[25]

Civil Liability (Contribution) Act 1978

The rule in *Merryweather* v. *Nixan* was for most practical purposes reversed by section 6(1)(*c*) of the Law Reform (Married Women and Tortfeasors) Act 1935.[26] The operation of the 1935 Act was examined by the Law Commission in the wider context of contribution generally (including contribution between contractors) and the product of its deliberations is the Act of 1978.[27] As far as contribution between tortfeasors is concerned the Act continues the same basic structure as its predecessor but there are some significant changes of detail.

[20] Civil Liability (Contribution) Act 1978, s.4. A similar provision appeared in s.6(1)(*b*) of the Law Reform (Married Women and Tortfeasors) Act 1935 but that Act went further in providing that the sums recoverable in later actions should not in the aggregate exceed the amount awarded by the judgment first given. The Law Commission (Report on Contribution, Law Com. No. 79 (1977)) thought the "damages sanction" an unnecessary complication and potentially unjust, *e.g.* if P suffered loss at the hands of D_1 and D_2 he might have a good practical reason for suing D_1 first but might be bound by a valid contractual provision for limitation of damages against D_1.

[21] (1799) 8 T.R. 186: criticised in *Palmer* v. *Wick, etc., Co. Ltd.* [1894] A.C. 318, 324; (1901) 17 L.Q.R. 293–301. See also *Romford Ice and Cold Storage Co.* v. *Lister* [1956] 2 Q.B. 180; affirmed [1957] A.C. 555. The rule in *Merryweather* v. *Nixan* was regarded as resting on the maxim *ex turpi causa non oritur actio*. In the extraordinary case of *Everet* v. *Williams* (1725) (1893) 9 L.Q.R. 197–199, the plaintiff and defendant were in partnership as highway robbers and "dealt with several gentlemen for divers watches, rings, swords, canes, hats, cloaks, horses, bridles, saddles and other things" at Bagshot, Salisbury, Hampstead and elsewhere. The partnership realised some £2,000. The plaintiff brought a partnership action for an account of this sum. His claim was dismissed as scandalous and impertinent, his solicitors were fined £50 each for contempt, and at later dates both plaintiff and defendant were hanged.

[22] *Horwell* v. *L.G.O. Co.* (1877) 2 Ex.D. 365, 379, *per* Kelly C.B.; *The Koursk* [1924] P. 140, 158, *per* Scrutton L.J.

[23] *Betts* v. *Gibbins* (1834) 2 Ad. & E. 57, 74, *per* Lord Denman; *Moxham* v. *Grant* [1900] 1 Q.B. 88, 93, *per* Collins L.J.

[24] See *Adamson* v. *Jarvis* (1827) 4 Bing. 66 (auctioneer innocently selling X's goods at the behest of the defendant, who represented himself as owner). This exception may hold good even where the joint enterprise proves to be criminal: *Burrows* v. *Rhodes* [1899] 1 Q.B. 816.

[25] *Romford Ice and Cold Storage Co.* v. *Lister* [1956] 2 Q.B. 180; affirmed [1957] A.C. 555 *ante*, pp. 577–579.

[26] See Cmd. 4637 (1934). Two statutory exceptions to the rule antedated the 1935 Act: Maritime Conventions Act 1911, s.3, and Companies Act 1908, s.84.

[27] Report on Contribution, Law Com. No. 79 (1977). The Act came into force on January 1, 1979.

By section 1(1) of the Act, any person liable in respect of any damage suffered by another may recover contribution from any other person liable in respect of the same damage (whether jointly or otherwise) and for this purpose a person is "liable" whatever the legal basis of his liability, "whether tort, breach of contract, breach of trust or otherwise."[28] In *Brownton Ltd.* v. *Edward Moore Inbucon Ltd.*[29] P engaged D_1 to advise on the purchase of a computer system and as a result of advice P entered into a contract of purchase with D_2. The system did not work properly. D_1 having settled P's claim, was unable to claim contribution from D_2 because the 1935 Act, which was the relevant legislation in the case, applied only between *tortfeasors* and, while D_1 was liable in contract and tort to P, D_2's liability to P was in contract only.[30] Were the facts to occur today, contribution could be ordered under the 1978 Act.[31] The amount of contribution ordered is to be "such as may be found by the court to be just and equitable having regard to the extent of that person's responsibility for the damage in question."[32] The principles would seem to be the same as for the apportionment of damages between *plaintiff* and *defendant* in the other legislation dealing with concurrent fault, the Law Reform (Contributory Negligence) Act 1945,[33] so that the court must look at both causation[34] and culpability.[35] The question is one of proportion not of principle, involving an individual exercise of discretion by the trial judge and for that reason appellate courts will be reluctant to interfere with an apportionment as determined by the judge.[36] If it considers it appropriate, the court may exempt the defendant from any liability to make contribution[37] or direct that the contribution recoverable shall amount to a complete indemnity.[38] The court's powers are, however, subject to the

---

[28] Civil Liability (Contribution) Act 1978, s.6(1). "Liability" means a liability which has been or could be established in a court in England and Wales: s.1(6). As to foreign judgments, see *SNI Aèrospatiale* v. *Lee Kiu Jak* [1987] A.C. 871.

[29] [1985] 3 All E.R. 499.

[30] Contribution between co-contractors is possible at common law (see Williams, *Joint Obligations*) but there are two serious limitations on it: first, the defendants must be liable to a common demand (not satisfied in the *Brownton* case) and, secondly, the general rule is that liability is divided equally.

[31] The problem was evaded in the case by D_1 paying P and taking from P an assignment of P's right of action against D_2. This was held not to be void for champerty: see *post*, p. 730.

[32] s.2(1). The statutory right to contribution is not in the nature of a claim in tort. It has been said to resemble a quasi-contractual claim by a person who has been constrained to discharge another's liability: *Ronex Properties Ltd.* v. *John Laing Construction Ltd.* [1983] Q.B. 398.

[33] *Ante*, pp. 165–168. Where P, D_1 and D_2 are all to blame both the 1945 and 1978 Acts are applicable. The correct approach is to consider the plaintiff's fault against the totality of the defendants' conduct. That will give a figure for which the plaintiff recovers judgment against all defendants and in respect of which they may seek contribution *inter se*: *Fitzgerald* v. *Lane* [1988] 3 W.L.R. 352.

[34] Causation of the damage is what is in issue. Hence where D_1 carries P in dangerous conditions which lead to injury in a collision, D_1 may carry a greater share of the responsibility than D_2 who was jointly responsible for the collision: *Madden* v. *Quirke, The Times*, January 2, 1989.

[35] *Randolph* v. *Tuck* [1962] 1 Q.B. 175; *Weaver* v. *Commercial Press Co.* (1947) 63 T.L.R. 466; *cf. Collins* v. *Hertfordshire C.C.* [1947] K.B. 598.

[36] For examples of apportionment see *Clay* v. *A.J. Crump & Sons Ltd.* [1964] 1 Q.B. 533; *A.M.F. International Ltd.* v. *Magnet Bowling Ltd.* [1968] 1 W.L.R. 1028; *King* v. *Sadler* (1970) 114 S.J. 192. In determining the apportionment the court must have regard only to the parties before it and cannot take into account the possibility that some other person may also have been to blame: *Maxfield* v. *Llewellyn* [1961] 1 W.L.R. 1119.

[37] Contrast the Law Reform (Contributory Negligence) Act 1945, where, once a finding has been made that the plaintiff is guilty of contributory negligence, the court is obliged to reduce the damages: *ante*, p. 168.

[38] As in *Semtex Ltd.* v. *Gladstone* [1954] 1 W.L.R. 945, where the first defendant's liability was only vicarious: *cf. Jones* v. *Manchester Corp.* [1952] 2 Q.B. 852.

overriding principle that one defendant cannot, by way of contribution proceedings, be liable for a greater sum than could be recovered from him by the plaintiff. If, therefore, P's property worth £1,000 is destroyed as a result of the combined (and equal) negligence of D_1 and D_2, there being a binding contract between P and D_2 whereby the latter's liability is limited to £300, D_2 in contribution proceedings can recover no more than this amount from D_1.[39]

It often happens that one tortfeasor may be able to recover an indemnity, or damages amounting to an indemnity or contribution, from another person by virtue of a contract between them. Nothing in the 1978 Act affects the enforceability of such an indemnity[40] and it is irrelevant to this contractual claim that the extent of a tortfeasor's liability has been determined as between himself and another tortfeasor in third party proceedings[41] for contribution. In *Sims* v. *Foster Wheeler Ltd.*[42] the plaintiff's husband was killed when defective staging collapsed, and both his employers and the constructors of the staging were liable in tort. As between these two tortfeasors it was held that the employers were 25 per cent. to blame and should bear that proportion of the damages. They were, however, entitled to recover this amount from their sub-contractors by way of damages for breach of an implied warranty that the staging should be properly constructed for safe use as scaffolding. On the other hand, the Act does not render enforceable any agreement for indemnity which would not have been enforceable had it not been passed.[43] This appears to refer to cases where the party seeking indemnity knew or may be presumed to have known that he was committing an unlawful act. In *W.H. Smith & Son* v. *Clinton*,[44] the defendants had contracted to indemnify the plaintiffs, a printing and publishing firm, against any claims made against them for libels appearing in the defendants' paper *Vanity Fair*. This indemnity was held to be irrecoverable because the plaintiffs well knew that the matter published was libellous. If the plaintiffs had been innocent they could have recovered under the indemnity clause.[45] Although they could still not recover under the express contract of indemnity,[46] the courts would probably award contribution under the Act to the printer or publisher of a libel against its more culpable author.[47]

Under the Civil Liability (Contribution) Act 1978 a defendant may seek

---

[39] See Civil Liability (Contribution) Act 1978, s.2(3). The reference in s.2(3)(*b*) to a reduction of the plaintiff's damages under the Law Reform (Contributory Negligence) Act 1945 is aimed at a situation where only one defendant could rely, as against the plaintiff, on contributory negligence, *e.g.* where the other was in breach of a strict contractual duty: see Law Com. No. 79 (1977), paras. 75–79.

[40] s.7(3) saves (i) an express contractual right to contribution, (ii) an express or implied contractual right to indemnity, (iii) an express contractual provision "regulating or excluding contribution."

[41] See *post* for an explanation of this expression.

[42] [1966] 1 W.L.R. 156; *Wright* v. *Tyne Improvement Commissioners* [1968] 1 W.L.R. 336; *cf. Lambert* v. *Lewis* [1982] A.C. 225 where the person seeking indemnity was held to be the sole cause of his own loss.

[43] s.7(3).

[44] (1908) 99 L.T. 841; (1933) 49 L.Q.R. 161–162.

[45] *Daily Mirror Newspapers Ltd.* v. *Exclusive News Agency* (1937) 81 S.J. 924.

[46] s.11 of the Defamation Act 1952 provides that agreements for indemnity against civil liability shall not be unlawful unless at the time of the publication the person claiming to be indemnified knows the matter is defamatory and does not reasonably believe there to be a good defence to any action brought upon it.

[47] Williams, *Joint Torts and Contributory Negligence*, pp. 139–145.

contribution notwithstanding that he has ceased to be liable to the plaintiff since the damage occurred,[48] provided he was so liable immediately before the judgment or compromise in the plaintiff's favour,[49] but his right to seek contribution is subject to a limitation period of two years from the time when it arises.[50] The other party likewise is liable to make contribution notwithstanding that he has ceased to be liable in respect of the damage in question,[51] unless he ceased to be liable by virtue of the expiry of a period of limitation or prescription which extinguished the right on which the claim against him in respect of the damage was based.[52] This proviso will not apply to most periods of limitation in tort since they merely bar the remedy, not the right.[53] Accordingly, suppose P is injured by the combined negligence of D_1 and D_2 on January 1, 1989. On December 1, 1991, P recovers judgment against D_1. P's cause of action against D_2 becomes statute-barred on the last day of 1991,[54] but D_1 has two years[55] from the judgment against him to seek contribution from D_2. However, conversion is an exception to the principle that the expiry of a limitation period only bars the remedy, for by section 3(2) of the Limitation Act 1980, the owner's title to his chattel is extinguished six years after the conversion.[56] Thus if P's goods are wrongfully converted by D_1 and D_2 on January 1, 1985, and P recovers judgment against D_1 on December 1, 1990, D_1 will be unable to claim contribution from D_2 unless he brings proceedings before the end of 1990.

The vast majority of tort actions are settled (or withdrawn) before the court pronounces judgment and the machinery of civil justice could not operate if this were not so. Accordingly, it is essential to ensure that a settlement does not deprive the defendant of the opportunity of seeking contribution against any other person he considers liable. Under the law before the 1978 Act a defendant who settled, with or without admission of liability, could seek contribution[57] but this involved a curious reversal of the normal roles of litigation, for in the contribution proceedings he was required to show that he was liable to the plaintiff.[58] What was more, if he failed to do this he could recover no contribution even though the evidence showed beyond any doubt that the person from whom he sought it *was* liable to the plaintiff. Section 1(4) of the 1978 Act meets this point by providing that a person who has bona fide settled a claim "shall be entitled to recover contribution . . . without regard to whether or not he himself is or ever was

[48] The judgment against the defendant will, of course, extinguish the plaintiff's right of action against him by merger.
[49] s.1(2).
[50] Limitation Act 1980, s.10.
[51] *e.g.* by a settlement with the plaintiff: *Logan* v. *Uttlesford D.C.* (1986) 136 N.L.J. 541.
[52] s.1(3).
[53] *Post,* p. 723.
[54] It is assumed that there is no question of the period being extended under the Limitation Act 1980: *post,* pp. 725–729.
[55] *Supra,* n. 50.
[56] There is an exception where the conversion amounts to theft: *post,* p. 723.
[57] *Stott* v. *West Yorkshire Road Car Co. Ltd.* [1971] 2 Q.B. 651.
[58] s.6(1)(c) of the 1935 Act provided that "any tortfeasor liable in respect of [the damage] may recover contribution from any other tortfeasor who is, or would if sued have been, liable in respect of the same damage."

liable in respect of the damage, provided, however, that he would have been liable assuming that the factual basis of the claim against him could be established." One objection to this is that it produces the possibility of a collusive settlement but this is probably not very great in tort actions where the real defendants will usually be insurers.[59]

What is the position if the plaintiff sues one defendant (D_2), fails and then successfully sues the other (D_1)? Can D_1 claim contribution from D_2 notwithstanding the determination of P's claim in D_2's favour? This would not create any issue estoppel at common law, but by section 1(5) of the 1978 Act a judgment in P's action against D_2 "shall be conclusive in the proceedings for contribution as to any issue determined by that judgment in favour of the person from whom the contribution is sought." The effect of this is that if the action against D_2 was dismissed on the merits (because P failed to make out the legal basis of his claim) D_1 cannot proceed against D_2 for contribution, but the position is otherwise if the dismissal was on procedural grounds (for example, for want of prosecution by P[60]) or because of the expiry of the limitation period.[61] In practice there will generally not be successive proceedings, and the issue of contribution will be disposed of in the main action. Either P will sue D_1 *and* D_2 or, if he does not and chooses to sue D_1 alone, D_1 may utilise the "third-party" procedure and join D_2 as a defendant in P's action.[62]

---

[59] The risk of collusion is probably considerably greater in contract actions, which are brought under the statutory contribution scheme by s.1(1) of the Act.

[60] *R.A. Lister & Co. Ltd.* v. *E.G. Thompson (Shipping) Ltd. (No. 2)* [1987] 3 All E.R. 1032, 1039.

[61] *Nottingham Health Authority* v. *Nottingham C.C.* [1988] 1 W.L.R. 903, 911–912. This is the only way to avoid a conflict between s.1(3) and s.1(5). The wording proposed by the Law Commission was clearer.

[62] See R.S.C., Ord. 16 and *Hordern-Richmond Ltd.* v. *Duncan* [1947] K.B. 545, 551–552.

CHAPTER 23

REMEDIES

In this chapter we shall consider the remedies which may be available to the victim of a tort. Of these the most important is an award of damages, and the first part of this chapter is devoted to the rules governing the action for damages and their assessment.[1] In the second part the other remedies, namely, self-help, injunction and an order for the specific restitution of property, will be discussed.

PART I. DAMAGES[2]

DAMAGES RECOVERABLE ONCE ONLY

It is a characteristic feature of the law of damages that, subject to the special classes of case mentioned below, the damages to which a plaintiff is entitled from the defendant in respect of a wrongful act must be recovered once and for all. He cannot bring a second action upon the same facts simply because his injury proves to be more serious than was thought when judgment was given. This rule was laid down in *Fetter* v. *Beale*[3]; where some rather unconvincing reasons were given for it,[4] and Winfield considered that the rule was unsound in principle and in general operated unfairly against the plaintiff.[5] It is suggested, however, that the general rule that only one action may be brought in respect of one cause of action is a sound one. The principal difficulties arise in actions for personal injuries, because there the judge has so often to base his award of damages upon an estimate of many future uncertainties, particularly the plaintiff's future from a medical point of view and for this reason the rule is modified by certain procedural devices which are outlined later.[6]

---

[1] Damages for fatal accidents are considered in the next chapter.
[2] Weir, *Casebook on Tort* (6th ed.), Chap. 18. The principal modern monographs are McGregor, *Damages* (15th ed.); Street, *Principles of the Law of Damages*; Ogus, *The Law of Damages*; Burrows, *Remedies for Torts and Breach of Contract* and, for personal injuries, Kemp and Kemp, *The Quantum of Damages*.
[3] (1701) 1 Ld.Raym. 339, 692; *Fitter* v. *Veal* (1701) 12 Mod. 542.
[4] The main reason given was, in effect, that an award of damages must be taken to cover the whole of the damage suffered by the plaintiff, but this merely states the rule in a different form. Coke's reason was *interest reipublicae ut sit finis litium*, which seems fair enough, and others have based it on *nemo bis vexari pro eadem causa*. See also *Richardson* v. *Mellish* (1824) 2 Bing. 229, 240, *per* Best C.J.
[5] See the seventh edition of this work, pp. 97–98, where Winfield's views are retained. Winfield conceded that the rule might sometimes work to the plaintiff's advantage.
[6] See *post*, p. 629.

Cases outside the rule

(1) *Where two distinct rights are violated*

Where distinct wrongful acts of the defendant cause damage to distinct rights of the plaintiff, successive actions can obviously be brought; a plaintiff is not obliged to consolidate in one action all the different causes of action he may have against the defendant. And the same is true even where there has been only one wrongful act, provided two distinct rights of the plaintiff are violated. Thus in *Brunsden v. Humphrey*[7] the plaintiff's cab was damaged by the defendant's negligence and the plaintiff himself was injured. Having recovered damages in respect of the cab alone, the plaintiff was held entitled to bring a second action for his personal injuries. This does not mean, however, that a plaintiff who has recovered damages for, say, a broken leg, can later bring fresh proceedings against the defendant in respect of the same accident on the ground that he has now discovered that the accident also caused him to suffer from some nervous illness. There is only one cause of action for personal injuries,[8] and that is the test.[9]

(2) *Continuing injury*

If I wrongfully place something on your land and leave it there, that is not simply a single act of trespass, but is a continuing trespass giving rise to a fresh cause of action *de die in diem.*[10] Similarly, a continuing nuisance gives rise to a fresh cause of action each time damage occurs as a result of it, and accordingly successive actions can be brought.[11] In fact in a case of continuing nuisance prospective damages cannot be claimed, however probable the occurrence of future damage may be; the plaintiff must await the event and then bring fresh proceedings.[12] It follows, somewhat unfortunately, that if

---

[7] (1884) 14 Q.B.D. 141; *Goldrei, Foucard & Son* v. *Sinclair and Russian Chamber of Commerce in London* [1918] 1 K.B. 180; *Sandberg* v. *Giesbrecht* (1963) 42 D.L.R. (2d) 107 (Sup.Ct. of B.C., where the plaintiff was penalised in costs for the unnecessary multiplicity of proceedings). *cf. Cahoon* v. *Franks* (1967) 63 D.L.R. (2d) 274 (Sup.Ct. of Canada, where *Brunsden* v. *Humphrey* was disapproved) and the remark in *Buckland* v. *Palmer* [1984] 1 W.L.R. 1109, 1116.

[8] *Watson* v. *Powles* [1968] 1 Q.B. 596, 603, *per* Lord Denning M.R.; *Fletcher* v. *Autocar and Transporters Ltd.* [1968] 2 Q.B. 322, 336, *per* Lord Denning M.R.

[9] Note, however, that the Court of Appeal may, under certain restrictive conditions, admit additional evidence relating to the assessment of damages if it transpires that the factual basis for the trial judge's assessment was incorrect. See, *e.g. Jenkins* v. *Richard Thomas and Baldwins Ltd.* [1966] 1 W.L.R. 476; *Murphy* v. *Stone-Wallwork (Charlton) Ltd.* [1969] 1 W.L.R. 1023 (H.L.); *Mulholland* v. *Mitchell* [1971] A.C. 666.

[10] *Hudson* v. *Nicholson* (1839) 5 M. & W. 437; *Konskier* v. *B. Goodman Ltd.* [1928] 1 K.B. 421. Distinguish the case of a single act of trespass, such as the digging of a hole on the plaintiff's land, where it is only the consequence of the trespass, not the trespass itself, which continues.

[11] *Darley Main Colliery Co.* v. *Mitchell* (1886) 11 App.Cas. 127. *cf. Alan Maberley* v. *Peabody & Co. Ltd.* [1946] 2 All E.R. 192.

[12] *cf. Toronto General Trusts Corp.* v. *Roman* (1962) 37 D.L.R. (2d) 16 (Ontario C.A.) where, notwithstanding a judgment against him in an action of detinue for the return of shares, the defendant nevertheless failed to return them for a substantial period of time. A second action claiming damages for that detention was allowed but damages were not awarded in the second action for a period of detention prior to judgment in the first. Under certain conditions damages in respect of probable future harm may be awarded in lieu of an injunction under Lord Cairns' Act, *post*, pp. 640–641. See, however, *Redland Bricks Ltd.* v. *Morris* [1970] A.C. 652.

the defendant has caused a subsidence of part of the plaintiff's land, damages can be awarded only for what has already occurred, and the plaintiff cannot recover damages for the depreciation in the value of his property attributable to the risk of further subsidence.[13]

(3) Torts actionable only on proof of damage

It has sometimes been suggested that a particular distinction falls to be taken between torts actionable *per se* and those actionable only on proof of damage; in the former case it is impossible for more than one action to be brought while in the latter a fresh action may be brought each time fresh damage occurs as a result of the wrongful act.[14] While it is probably correct that only one action can be brought in respect of a tort which is actionable *per se*, however, it is submitted that this should be seen as no more than a reflection of the general rule that only one action may be brought in respect of one cause of action, not that cases of torts actionable only on proof of damage form a special exception to that rule. Just as I have two causes of action if your negligent act causes separate damage to my property and to my person,[15] so also I have two causes of action if on quite separate occasions your single act of negligence causes me to suffer distinct personal injuries.[16] But this does not mean that if you negligently hit me on the head I can bring fresh proceedings each time I suffer from a headache; and the reason is that I have suffered only one injury, the blow upon the head, not that negligently hitting me on the head is trespass and that trespass is actionable *per se*. It is better to consider in each case whether the facts relied on by the plaintiff to establish his cause of action in subsequent proceedings are substantially identical with those on which he relied in the first, than to treat torts not actionable *per se* as constituting a special exception to the general rule.

KINDS OF DAMAGES

Ordinarily an award of damages is made in order to compensate the plaintiff for his injury, and the assessment of compensatory damages is considered in detail below. An award of damages may, however, be avowedly non-compensatory in intention. If not compensatory, damages may be: (1) contemptuous; (2) nominal; or (3) exemplary or punitive.

Contemptuous

The amount awarded here is merely derisory—formerly one farthing,

---

[13] *West Leigh Colliery Co. Ltd.* v. *Tunnicliffe and Hampson Ltd.* [1908] A.C. 27.
[14] Salmond and Heuston, *Torts* (19th ed.), p. 658. The matter is more fully discussed in the seventh edition, para. 37(10). See too Gatley, *Libel and Slander*, 8th ed., p. 598, and *Darley Main Colliery Co. Ltd.* v. *Mitchell* (1886) 11 App.Cas. 127, 145, *per* Lord Bramwell; *ibid.* at p. 151, *per* Lord Fitzgerald. *cf. ibid.* at pp. 142–143, *per* Lord Blackburn.
[15] *Brunsden* v. *Humphrey* (1884) 14 Q.B.D. 141; *ante*, p. 599.
[16] Or distinct property damage: *Mt. Albert Borough* v. *Johnson* [1979] 2 N.Z.L.R. 234.

then one halfpenny and now, presumably, one new penny—and indicates that the court has formed a very low opinion of the plaintiff's bare legal claim, or that his conduct was such that he deserved, at any rate morally, what the defendant did to him. Damages of this kind may imperil the plaintiff's chances of getting his costs, for although costs now usually follow the event of the action, yet their award is in the discretion of the judge, and although the insignificance of damages is not by itself enough to justify him in depriving the plaintiff of his costs, yet it is a material factor in the exercise of his discretion. Where there is a jury it is impermissible for it to be influenced on the quantum of damages by the likely outcome as to costs and the judge should decline to answer questions on the subject.[17] Contemptuous damages are not uncommon in libel actions.[18]

Nominal

Nominal damages are awarded when the plaintiff's legal right has been infringed but he has suffered no actual damage, as can most readily occur in the case of torts which are actionable *per se*, for example, trespass to land. In *Constantine* v. *Imperial Hotels Ltd.*[19] the defendants were guilty of a breach of their duty as common innkeepers when they unjustifiably refused accommodation in one of their hotels to the plaintiff, the well-known West Indian cricketer. Although he was given accommodation elsewhere, he was awarded nominal damages of five guineas. An award of nominal damages does not, therefore, connote any moral obliquity on the plaintiff's part, but even so the judge may in his discretion deprive the plaintiff of his costs or even make him pay the costs of both sides.[20]

Exemplary or punitive[21]

In any case in which damages are at large, that is, where they cannot be precisely quantified in money terms, the court may take into account the injury to the plaintiff's feelings and the mental distress he has suffered. Where these are increased by the bad motive or wilful conduct of the defendant it is customary to make a corresponding increase in the award

---

[17] *Pamplin* v. *Express Newspapers Ltd. (No. 2)* [1988] 1 W.L.R. 116.

[18] For an example, where the plaintiff got no costs, see *Dering* v. *Uris* [1964] 2 Q.B. 669, upon which the defendant based a successful book, *Q.B. VII.*

[19] [1944] K.B. 693. See now the Race Relations Act 1976, which expressly allows damages for injury to feelings and might therefore produce a larger award on such facts.

[20] *Anglo-Cyprian Trade Agencies Ltd.* v. *Paphos Wine Industries Ltd.* [1951] 1 All E.R. 873 (a case of contract); McGregor, *op. cit.*, pp. 252–253. But the plaintiff cannot be ordered to pay the costs of both sides if he has been completely successful and there has been no misconduct on his part: *Kierson* v. *Thompson & Sons Ltd.* [1913] 1 K.B. 587. If nominal damages are awarded in an action for waste, judgment may be entered for the defendant: *Harrow School* v. *Alderton* (1800) 2 B. & C. 86; *Doherty* v. *Allman* (1878) 3 App.Cas. 709, 725. But this rule is peculiar to waste; it is of considerable antiquity and was based upon the maxim *de minimis non curat lex*: Y.B.Mich. 19 Hen. 6, pl. 19, f. 8b; Br.Abr. Waste, 123; Coke, 2 Inst. 306.

[21] "Exemplary" is now more popular than "punitive": see Lord Devlin in *Rookes* v. *Barnard* [1964] A.C. 1129 and Lord Hailsham L.C., Viscount Dilhorne and Lords Morris and Diplock in *Cassell & Co. Ltd.* v. *Broome* [1972] A.C. 1027.

under the name of "aggravated" damages. Such awards have been made, for example, in cases of battery,[22] of trespass to land,[23] of deceit[24] and of the statutory tort of racial discrimination under the Race Relations Act 1976.[25] Aggravated damages are not, however, available for negligence even where the conduct of the defendant is "crass"[26] and, despite one decision to the contrary,[27] it is thought that they should not be available to a corporation, which has no feelings to be hurt.[28] Aggravated damages may be regarded as truly compensatory,[29] despite the difficulty in quantifying that for which they are awarded. Exemplary damages, on the other hand, are not compensatory but are awarded to punish the defendant and to deter him from similar behaviour in the future. This distinction, though clear in theory,[30] is obviously difficult to apply in practice; it was also, in the past, relatively insignificant, for it was thought that exemplary damages, like aggravated damages, could be awarded in any case of tort.[31] However, in *Rookes* v. *Barnard*,[32] the House of Lords, through Lord Devlin, restated the law regarding exemplary damages and severely limited their scope, and this restriction was affirmed by the House in *Cassell & Co. Ltd.* v. *Broome*.[33] It is true that Lord Devlin thought that this would not make a great difference to the substance of the law, for aggravated damages can do most of the work of exemplary damages,[34] but, subject to what is said below, it is now clear that, except in the rare cases where exemplary damages are still allowed, any award must be strictly justifiable as compensation for the injury sustained.[35]

In Lord Devlin's view exemplary damages are in principle objectionable because they confuse the civil and the criminal functions of the law[36] and,

---

[22] *W* v. *Meah* [1986] 1 All E.R. 935 (rape). Awards against the police for deprivation of liberty or trespass to the person may include exemplary damages (*infra*) but even without this element awards may be high. See, e.g. *Reynolds* v. *Metropolitan Police Comr.* [1982] Crim.L.R. 600, where the Court of Appeal upheld an award of £12,000 for arrest and false imprisonment even though, as the transcript reveals, there was no exemplary element in this. For a useful collection of unreported awards see Clayton and Tomlinson, *Civil Actions Against the Police.*

[23] *Jolliffe* v. *Willmett & Co.* [1971] 1 All E.R. 478. See also *Columbia Picture Industries Inc.* v. *Robinson* [1987] Ch. 38 (aggravated damages available where defendant executed an "Anton Piller order" in an excessive and oppressive manner).

[24] *Archer* v. *Brown* [1985] Q.B. 401.

[25] *Alexander* v. *Home Office* [1988] 2 All E.R. 118.

[26] *Kralj* v. *McGrath* [1986] 1 All E.R. 54.

[27] *Messenger Newspapers Group Ltd.* v. *N.G.A.* [1984] I.R.L.R. 397.

[28] So held in *Columbia Picture Industries Inc.* v. *Robinson* [1987] Ch. 38.

[29] *Rookes* v. *Barnard* [1964] A.C. 1129, 1221, per Lord Devlin; *Cassell & Co. Ltd.* v. *Broome* [1972] A.C. 1027, 1124, per Lord Diplock.

[30] See *McCarey* v. *Associated Newspapers Ltd. (No. 2)* [1965] 2 Q.B. 86, 104–105, per Pearson L.J. Perhaps the best discussion is in the judgment of McCardie J. in *Butterworth* v. *Butterworth* [1920] P. 126, a case on damages for adultery where it had long been settled that damages must be compensatory only. For a modern case on the same topic see *Pritchard* v. *Pritchard* [1967] P. 195. Claims for damages for adultery can no longer be made: Law Reform (Miscellaneous Provisions) Act 1970, *ante*, p. 497.

[31] See, e.g. *Loudon* v. *Ryder* [1953] 2 Q.B. 202.

[32] *Supra*, *Loudon* v. *Ryder, supra*, is expressly overruled: [1964] A.C. 1129, 1229.

[33] [1972] A.C. 1027.

[34] [1964] A.C. 1129, 1230.

[35] *McCarey* v. *Associated Newspapers Ltd. (No. 2), supra.*

[36] [1964] A.C. 1129, 1221.

apart from cases where they are allowed by statute,[37] exemplary damages can now be awarded in only two classes of case.[38]

The first is where there is oppressive, arbitrary or unconstitutional action by servants of the Government.[39] A well-known example of this, approved by Lord Devlin, is *Huckle* v. *Money*,[40] one of the cases deciding against the legality of the search warrants which were issued against John Wilkes and others during the latter part of the eighteenth century. The plaintiff was detained under one of these warrants for no more than six hours and the defendant "used him very civilly by treating him with beef-steaks and beer." Yet the court refused to interfere with a verdict for £300 damages, for "to enter a man's house by virtue of a nameless warrant, in order to procure evidence, is worse than the Spanish Inquisition . . . it is a more daring public attack made upon the liberty of the subject."[41] This class of case does not extend to oppressive action by private corporations or individuals and is justified in the case of servants of the Government because they "are also the servants of the people and the use of their power must always be subordinate to their duty of service."[42] There has perhaps been a tendency to treat the three adjectives used by Lord Devlin as synonymous, all carrying the idea of "high-handedness," but the Court of Appeal has pointed out that grammatically this is incorrect and there may be unconstitutional action which is neither "oppressive" nor "arbitrary."[43] On the other hand, the court was clearly unhappy with the proposition that *any* false arrest or other unauthorised conduct by a police officer should attract an exemplary award, but rather than attempt to define "unconstitutional" as a matter of law it preferred the approach of relying on the trial judge to indicate to the jury[44] that in the absence of aggravating factors they might consider the case unsuitable for exemplary damages.

Lord Devlin's second category covers cases where the defendant's conduct has been calculated by him to make a profit for himself which may well

---

[37] Lord Devlin cites the Reserve and Auxiliary Forces (Protection of Civil Interests) Act 1951, s.13(2): *ibid.* at p. 1225. As to the Copyright Act 1956 see *Williams* v. *Settle* [1960] 1 W.L.R. 1072 and Lord Devlin's comments: [1964] A.C. 1129, 1225, 1229. Lord Kilbrandon in *Cassell* v. *Broome, supra*, at p. 1133, doubted whether any existing statute contemplated the award of exemplary damages in the proper sense.

[38] A claim for exemplary damages must be pleaded in the High Court, but not, it seems, in the county court because there is no equivalent of R.S.C., Ord. 18, r. 8(3): *Alexander* v. *Home Office* [1988] 2 All E.R. 118, 123.

[39] [1964] A.C. 1129, 1226; *Att.-Gen. of St. Christopher etc.* v. *Reynolds* [1980] A.C. 637. It is now almost certain that "the Government" in this context includes local government and the police: *Cassell & Co. Ltd.* v. *Broome, supra*, at pp. 1077–1078, 1130, 1134, *per* Lord Hailsham L.C. and Lords Diplock and Kilbrandon. They were awarded against the police in *White* v. *Metropolitan Police Comr., The Times,* April 24, 1982 and in other cases collected by Clayton & Tomlinson, n. 22, *supra.* Lord Devlin's speech in *Rookes* v. *Barnard* is not to be read as if it were a statute. The malicious levying of excessive distress (*Moore* v. *Lambeth County Court Registrar (No. 2)* [1970] 1 Q.B. 560) and excessive execution of an "Anton Piller order" (*Columbia Picture Industries Inc.* v. *Robinson* [1987] Ch. 38) probably allow exemplary damages under this head.

[40] (1763) 2 Wils. 205.

[41] *Ibid.* at p. 207, *per* Pratt C.J. See also *Wilkes* v. *Wood* (1763) Lofft. 1. In *Wilkes* v. *Lord Halifax* the jury awarded John Wilkes the then phenomenal sum of £4,000 for false imprisonment: 19 State Trials 1466.

[42] [1964] A.C. 1129, 1226, *per* Lord Devlin.

[43] *Holden* v. *Chief Constable of Lancashire* [1987] Q.B. 380.

[44] Actions for trespass and false imprisonment against the police will commonly be tried by jury.

exceed the compensation payable to the plaintiff.[45] The point here is that the defendant must not be allowed to make a profit from his own deliberate wrongful act, and it is not sufficient to justify exemplary damages simply that part of the defendant's purpose in doing the act complained of was to make a profit. So the mere fact that everything published in a newspaper is published with a view to selling the newspaper and making a profit does not mean that every defamatory statement in a newspaper should be redressed with an award of exemplary damages.[46] There must be something much more calculated and deliberate, though it is unnecessary that the defendant should have indulged in any precise balancing of the chances of profit and loss.[47] The essence of the matter is that the defendant, with knowledge that his proposed act is unlawful, directs his mind to the material advantage of committing the tort and comes to the conclusion that it is worth the risk that he may have to compensate the plaintiff if he should bring an action.[48] The rationalisation that Lord Devlin's second category is aimed at preventing the defendant profiting from his wrong causes some difficulty because it opens up the possibility that exemplary damages may be *extended* to torts in respect of which they had not been awarded before *Rookes* v. *Barnard*. Deceit is an obvious example and has been described in Australia as the "paradigm case" for an award of exemplary damages[49] but there is still no decisive English authority one way or the other.[50] Exemplary damages have, however, been awarded for nuisance despite the absence of any pre-*Rookes* v. *Barnard* authority.[51]

There are arguments both for and against exemplary damages,[52] though perhaps the "noes" have marginally the best of it in logic[53] and it is unlikely that anyone now sitting down to draft a civil code would include an article providing for such damages.[54] The main arguments against them are that they confuse the purposes of the civil and criminal law, import the possibility of punishment into civil litigation without the safeguards of the criminal process and provide an unmerited windfall for the plaintiff. On the other

---

[45] *Ibid.* at pp. 1226–1227. It has been said that this is not really exemplary damages but is "merely preventing the defendant from obtaining a reward for his wrongdoing . . . the plaintiff is the accidental beneficiary of a rule of law based on public policy rather than on the reparation of private wrongs": *McCarey* v. *Associated Newspapers Ltd. (No. 2)* [1965] 2 Q.B. 86, 107, *per* Diplock L.J.

[46] *McCarey* v. *Associated Newspapers Ltd. (No. 2)* [1965] 2 Q.B. 86; *Broadway Approvals Ltd.* v. *Oldhams Press Ltd. (No. 2)* [1965] 1 W.L.R. 805; *Manson* v. *Associated Newspapers Ltd.* [1965] 1 W.L.R. 1038.

[47] *Drane* v. *Evangelou* [1978] 1 W.L.R. 455 (£1,000 for trespass to land); *Asghar* v. *Ahmed* (1984) 17 H.L.R. 25. In *Messenger Newspaper Group Ltd.* v. *N.G.A.* [1984] I.R.L.R. 397 a union attempt to close down a non-closed shop company attracted exemplary damages.

[48] *Cassell & Co. Ltd.* v. *Broome, supra,* a case which all the members of the House of Lords agreed fell clearly within Lord Devlin's second category. A case may fall within this category even though the defendant estimates the potential damages as very high if he calculates that the plaintiff, through poverty or intimidation, will not sue at all.

[49] *Musca* v. *Astle Corp.* (1987) 80 A.L.R. 251.

[50] In favour, Widgery L.J. in *Mafo* v. *Adams* [1970] 1 Q.B. 548, 558; Peter Pain J. in *Archer* v. *Brown* [1985] Q.B. 40, 423. *Dubitante,* Sachs L.J. in *Mafo* v. *Adams* at p. 555; Lord Hailsham L.C. in *Cassell & Co. Ltd.* v. *Broome* [1972] A.C. 1027, 1080; and the Court of Appeal in *Metall und Rohstoff A.G.* v. *Acli Metals (London)* [1984] 1 Lloyd's Rep. 598.

[51] *Guppys (Bridport)* v. *Brookling* (1984) 269 E.G. 846. The purpose of the nuisance was to evict the plaintiff.

[52] See particularly the speeches in *Cassell* v. *Broome, supra,* and Street, *op. cit.,* pp. 33–34. Hodgin and Veitch, "Punitive Damages Reassessed" (1972) 21 I.C.L.Q. 119.

[53] *Cassell & Co. Ltd.* v. *Broome, supra,* at p. 1114, *per* Lord Wilberforce.

[54] *Ibid.* at p. 1134, *per* Lord Kilbrandon. Any such article could hardly in logic confine exemplary damages to Lord Devlin's categories: see *ibid.* at p. 1088.

hand, exemplary damages under Lord Devlin's second category in *Rookes* v. *Barnard* may serve as a makeshift remedy to prevent the unjust enrichment of the tortfeasor.[55] Further, it is perhaps unsafe to lay too much stress on the division of function between the civil and criminal law. First, the award of exemplary damages is in practice confined to those types of case where the authorities administering the criminal law may be unwilling to act (abuse of power by the government) or where the criminal law is rarely invoked (libel). It is certainly true that as to the first category administrative law remedies for official misconduct have developed markedly since the "general warrant" cases of the eighteenth century[56] but these are little use to a plaintiff who has been assaulted or deprived of his liberty and the capacity of the state for oppression has increased rather than declined in the same period. Secondly one should not too readily assume that the boundaries between civil and criminal law are rigid and immutable.[57] As a high authority has said:

" . . . over the range of torts for which punitive damages may be given . . . there is much to be said before one can safely assert that the true or basic principle of the law of damages in tort is compensation, or, if it is, what that compensation is for, . . . or, if there is compensation, whether there is not in all cases, or at least in some, of which defamation may be an example, also a delictual element which contemplates some penalty for the defendant."[58]

The verdict on the case for abolition of exemplary damages must at the moment be not proven.[59]

Where the case is a proper one for the award of exemplary damages, the remedy is to be used with discretion.[60] In particular, awards should be

[55] *Ibid.* at p. 1129, *per* Lord Diplock; McGregor, *op. cit.*, pp. 266–268. But as far as the plaintiff is concerned, the damages still represent a windfall. The Housing Act 1988, ss.27–28 adopts the rationale of preventing enrichment by measuring the tenant's damages in cases of unlawful eviction not by his loss but by the difference between the value of the premises with and without vacant possession.

[56] See Lord Diplock in *Cassell & Co. Ltd.* v. *Broome, supra,* at p. 1130. There is also, of course, a right of private prosecution but this is inferior to a civil action in two respects: (*a*) the Attorney-General may interfere by *nolle prosequi;* (*b*) the absence of the chance of damages raises the stakes against the prosecutor, who is faced with large potential costs.

[57] See, *e.g.* the compensation provisions in the Powers of the Criminal Courts Act 1973.

[58] *Cassell & Co. Ltd.* v. *Broome, supra,* at p. 1114, *per* Lord Wilberforce; see also *Taylor* v. *Beere* [1982] 1 N.Z.L.R. 81, 90.

[59] But it should be noted that the Faulks Committee on the Law of Defamation has proposed the abolition of exemplary damages in defamation actions: Cmnd. 5909 (1975), para. 360. Exemplary damages enjoy a continuing vitality in common law jurisdictions not so far removed in social habits from our own and the courts there have rejected the restrictions of *Rookes* v. *Barnard: Uren* v. *John Fairfax & Sons Pty. Ltd.* (1966) 117 C.L.R. 118, approved by the P.C. in *Australian Consolidated Press Ltd.* v. *Uren* [1969] 1 A.C. 590 (Australia); *Taylor* v. *Beere* [1982] 1 N.Z.L.R. 81; *Donselaar* v. *Donselaar* [1982] 1 N.Z.L.R. 97 (New Zealand); as to Canada, see Fridman, "Punitive Damages in Tort" (1970) 48 Can.Bar Rev. 373; *Loomis* v. *Rohan* (1974) 46 D.L.R. (3d) 423. The logic of the second category in *Rookes* v. *Barnard* might suggest the extension of exemplary damages to breach of contract, but the contrary proposition is too firmly set into our law. In *Drane* v. *Evangelou* [1978] 1 W.L.R. 455 the plaintiff's particulars of claim in the county court referred to interference with quiet enjoyment (*i.e.* an allegation of breach of contract) but the C.A. was able to hold that the claim impliedly included an allegation of trespass to land.

[60] McGregor, *op. cit.*, p. 273 argues that the considerations here set out have no relevance where the case is in Lord Devlin's second category, for that provides a "method for extracting profits tortiously obtained by the defendant," but support for all of them can be found in *Cassell* v. *Broome,* a second category case. It is submitted that the law has not finally committed itself to a restitutionary posture.

"moderate"[61] (though the House of Lords by a bare majority in 1972 upheld an award of £25,000),[62] the conduct of the plaintiff as well as the defendant should be taken into account[63] and the jury should be directed that before they make an award of exemplary damages they should consider whether the sum they have set for compensatory (including aggravated) damages is sufficient to punish the defendant.[64] Where a plaintiff sues more than one joint defendant in the same action, the sum which may be awarded by way of exemplary damages is the lowest which the conduct of any of the defendants deserves[65]; there is probably no such constraint in the case of aggravated damages.[66] In the reverse case of multiple plaintiffs the jury should be directed to arrive at a global sum by way of punishment and that should then be divided among the plaintiffs.[67] While a defendant may deserve more punishment for libelling 10 than for libelling one, to fix a figure for the individual and multiply it by the number of plaintiffs is likely to lead to an excessive award.[68]

Where the defendant has already been prosecuted and sentenced in a criminal court for precisely[69] the conduct which forms the basis of the civil suit the punitive function is spent and no exemplary award should be made.[70] The fact that the damages will be paid not by the actual wrongdoer but by someone vicariously liable for his actions does not prevent an exemplary award being made, so perhaps the same result should follow if the defendant's liability is covered by insurance.[71]

---

[61] *Rookes* v. *Barnard, supra,* at pp. 1227–1228, *per* Lord Devlin.

[62] *Cassell & Co. Ltd.* v. *Broome, supra.* However, in the context of libel (the tort in issue in *Cassell* v. *Broome*) even "compensatory" general damages seem to have far outstripped this figure even without proof of financial loss.

[63] *Lane* v. *Holloway* [1968] 1 Q.B. 379, 391, *per* Salmon L.J. (though in this case there is perhaps some confusion between aggravated and exemplary damages); *Fontin* v. *Katapodis* (1962) 108 C.L.R. 177. In *Cassell* v. *Broome, supra,* at p. 1071 Lord Hailsham L.C. speaks of this factor in the context of aggravated damages.

[64] *Cassell & Co. Ltd.* v. *Broome, supra.* The costs system in English litigation may itself be regarded as punitive: *ibid.* at pp. 1114–1115, *per* Lord Wilberforce. If the trial judge is in any doubt as to the correctness of leaving the issue of exemplary damages to the jury he should ask them, in the event of their awarding such damages, what smaller sum they would have awarded if they had confined themselves to compensation (including aggravation), but awards should not otherwise be "split": *Cassell* v. *Broome, supra,* at pp. 1082, 1094, 1116.

[65] *Cassell & Co. Ltd.* v. *Broome, supra.* This result flows from the rule that only a single award may be made against joint tortfeasors, though it is difficult to justify in this context and it has been rejected in Australia: *XL Petroleum* v. *Caltex Oil* (1985) 57 A.L.R. 639. Where the joint tortfeasors are master and servant, it is the conduct of the servant as the actual wrongdoer that is to be taken into account: *Carrington* v. *Att.-Gen.* [1972] N.Z.L.R. 1106, *cf.* Atiyah, *Vicarious Liability in the Law of Torts*, p. 435.

[66] *Hayward* v. *Thompson* [1982] Q.B. 47; but *cf. Cassell & Co. Ltd.* v. *Broome* at [1972] A.C. 1027, 1063, 1131. See further McGregor, *op. cit.*, pp. 1153–1154.

[67] Logically, since the jury has first to consider whether the element of aggravation in the compensatory damages sufficiently punishes the defendant, they should aggregate all the compensatory awards before embarking on consideration of the exemplary damages. A case can be made for dividing the exemplary damages rateably according to the differing amounts of compensatory damages awarded to different plaintiffs but this would be too complicated: see Parker L.J. in *Riches* v. *News Group Newspapers Ltd.* [1986] Q.B. 256.

[68] *Riches* v. *News Group Newspapers Ltd., supra,* where at the trial each of the plaintiffs had been awarded £300 compensatory damages and £25,000 exemplary damages!

[69] *cf. Asghar* v. *Ahmed* (1984) 17 H.L.R. 25.

[70] *Archer* v. *Brown* [1985] Q.B. 401.

[71] So held in *Lamb* v. *Cotogno* (1987) 74 A.L.R. 188. But a policy of assurance against, *e.g.* wilful battery would be against public policy. Whether there is any such rule invalidating *any* insurance against exemplary damages was the point at the root of, but not decided in *E.I. Du Pont de Nemours & Co.* v. *Agnew* [1987] 2 Lloyd's Rep. 585.

MEASURE OF DAMAGES

Scope of subject

In theory even if not always in practice this subject is distinct from that of the chapter on Remoteness of Damage,[72] though, obviously, both topics have a direct bearing upon the amount of money the plaintiff will ultimately recover. Remoteness of damage concerns the question, "in respect of what consequences of an established breach of duty can the injured party recover?"[73] Now we must see how the law attempts to answer the different question, "how much compensation can the injured party recover for consequences of the breach of legal duty which have already been held to be not too remote?"[74]

In the case of some torts such as conversion and deceit specific rules for the assessment of damages exist, and these have been noticed in their appropriate chapters.[75] For the rest, and most notably so far as damages for personal injury are concerned, the courts were once content to leave the assessment of damages to the jury with only general guidance from the judges, and many statements can be found to the effect that the quantum of damages in each case is a question of fact.[76]

It is no doubt still true that ultimately the exact sum which the plaintiff is awarded in any case is dependent upon all the detailed circumstances of the case, but this does not mean that the topic is devoid of principle.[77] On the contrary, at least where so-called pecuniary damage is concerned, some quite firm rules have developed, and even in the case of non-pecuniary damage, such as pain and suffering and what is called "loss of amenity," where precise valuation in money terms is obviously impossible, the courts have in recent years begun to elucidate the bases of their awards. In this chapter, therefore, we shall consider some of the rules governing the assessment of damages in cases of personal injury and of loss or damage to property, acting always on the assumptions that a tort has been committed and that the damage in question is not too remote.

General and special damages[78]

We have already come across "special damage" as signifying the element

---

[72] *Ante*, Chap. 6. See Wilson and Slade, "A Re-examination of Remoteness" (1952) 15 M.L.R. 458.

[73] Wilson and Slade, *ibid.*

[74] *Ibid. cf.* Chapman (Book Review) [1964] C.L.J. 136, 138.

[75] For the measure of damages in defamation, see Gatley, *Libel and Slander*, 8th ed.; Samuels, "Problems of Assessing Damages for Defamation" (1963) 79 L.Q.R. 63; *Lewis* v. *Daily Telegraph Ltd.* [1963] 1 Q.B. 340 (for proceedings in the H.L., where the question of damages was not fully considered, see [1964] A.C. 234); *McCarey* v. *Associated Newspapers Ltd. (No. 2)* [1965] 2 Q.B. 86; *Fielding* v. *Variety Inc.* [1967] 2 Q.B. 841.

[76] *e.g. Mehmet Dogan Bey* v. *Abdeni & Co. Ltd.* [1951] 2 All E.R. 162, 165, *per* McNair J., applying the statement of Lord Haldane in *British Westinghouse Electric and Manufacturing Co. Ltd.* v. *Underground Electric Rys. Co. of London Ltd.* [1912] A.C. 673, 688.

[77] See the caustic observations of Lord Sumner in *Admiralty Commissioners* v. *SS. Chekiang* [1926] A.C. 637, 643.

[78] McGregor, *Damages* (15th ed.), pp. 13–17, Jolowicz, "The Changing Use of 'Special Damage' and its Effect on the Law" [1960] C.L.J. 214.

of particular harm which the plaintiff has to prove to sue for slander[79] or public nuisance.[80] However, in the context of pleading special damage is used, in contradistinction to "general damage," to signify "the particular damage (beyond the general damage[81]) which results from the particular circumstances of the case, and of the plaintiff's claim to be compensated, for which he ought to give warning in his pleadings in order that there may be no surprise at the trial."[82] This is a sensible distinction resulting in a rule proper to the law of pleading but unfortunately it has spawned another sub-rule which distinguishes between damages which are capable of substantially exact pecuniary assessment and those which are not,[83] which has the result that, for example, loss of earnings which has accrued by the date of the trial is regarded as special damage while future loss of earnings falls under the head of general damages.[84] This is more than a mere matter of nomenclature, for the rule is that special damage must be strictly pleaded and proved.[85]

Restitutio in integrum

The basic principle for the measure of damages in tort as well as in contract is that there should be *restitutio in integrum*. Apart from cases in which exemplary damages are awarded,[86] "where any injury is to be compensated by damages, in settling the sum of money to be given for reparation of damages you should as nearly as possible get at that sum of money which will put the party who has been injured, or who has suffered, in the same position as he would have been in if he had not sustained the wrong for which he is now getting his compensation or reparation."[87] So, in an action for deceit, the proper starting point for the assessment of damages is to compare the position of the plaintiff as it was before the fraudulent statement was made to him with his position as it became as a result of his reliance upon the statement.[88] In a case of personal injury, too, this criterion can and should be applied to the pecuniary elements of the plaintiff's loss such as his loss of

---

[79] See *ante*, p. 298.

[80] See *ante*, p. 377.

[81] Which is what the law will presume. "Every libel is of itself a wrong in regard of which the law . . . implies general damage. By the very fact that he has committed such a wrong, the defendant is prepared for the proof that some general damage may have been done": *Ratcliffe* v. *Evans* [1892] 2 Q.B. 524, 529, *per* Bowen L.J.

[82] *Ibid.* at p. 528, *per* Bowen L.J. A plaintiff who claims some specific item of loss as special damages but fails to prove it may nevertheless recover general damages: The *Hebridean Coast* [1961] A.C. 545 (damage to ship; cost of chartering a substitute claimed as special damages but this loss not proved; plaintiff nevertheless allowed general damages for loss of use).

[83] See *British Transport Commission* v. *Gourley* [1956] A.C. 185, 206, *per* Lord Goddard.

[84] *Ibid.* And see *Perestrello Ltd.* v. *United Paint Co. Ltd.* [1969] 1 W.L.R. 570, 579.

[85] Of course even as regards future loss of earnings the plaintiff must produce evidence to enable the court to calculate the amount awardable.

[86] *Ante*, pp. 601–606.

[87] *Livingstone* v. *Rawyards Coal Co.* (1880) 5 App.Cas. 25, 39, *per* Lord Blackburn; *Monarch Steamship Co. Ltd.* v. *Karlshamns Oljefabriker (A/B)* [1949] A.C. 196, 221, *per* Lord Wright; *Shearman* v. *Folland* [1950] 2 K.B. 43, 49, In *Liesbosch Dredger* v. *Edison SS.* [1933] A.C. 449, 463, Lord Wright described the principle of *restitutio in integrum* as "the dominant rule of law"; "Subsidiary rules can only be justified if they give effect to that rule." cf. *Admiralty Commissioners* v. *SS. Valeria* [1922] 2 A.C. 242, 248, *per* Lord Dunedin.

[88] *Doyle* v. *Olby (Ironmongers) Ltd.* [1969] 2 Q.B. 158. See *ante*, p. 270.

earnings,[89] but it is difficult to see that it can be applied to the non-pecuniary elements such as pain and suffering, and there the plaintiff receives compensation not restitution.[90] Indeed compensation in the literal sense is no more possible than restitution, and what is given has been described as "notional or theoretical compensation to take the place of that which is not possible, namely, actual compensation."[91]

Mitigation of damage

The victim of a tort is obliged to mitigate his loss, that is to say, he may not claim damages in respect of any part of his loss that would have been avoidable by reasonable steps on his part. Most of the authorities on mitigation[92] relate to breach of contract, but the broad principles are equally applicable to tort. What is reasonable is a question of fact in each case: while the plaintiff must not be allowed to indulge his own whims or fancies at the expense of the defendant, it must also be remembered that the defendant is a wrongdoer who has caused the plaintiff's difficulty.[93] Accordingly, the standard of reasonableness is not a high one.[94] In *Emeh* v. *Kensington Area Health Authority*[95] the plaintiff became pregnant after a sterilization operation performed by the defendants. Rejecting the contention that the plaintiff was the author of her own loss by her refusal to have an abortion, Slade L.J. remarked that "save in the most exceptional circumstances, I cannot think it right that the court should ever declare it unreasonable for a woman to decline to have an abortion . . . where there is no evidence that there were any medical or psychiatric grounds for terminating the particular pregnancy."

ACTIONS FOR PERSONAL INJURY

Heads of damage

If *restitutio in integrum* is the object of damages awarded for pecuniary loss and compensation the object of damages for non-pecuniary loss, it

---

[89] *British Transport Commission* v. *Gourley* [1956] A.C. 185; *Parry* v. *Cleaver* [1970] A.C. 1, 22, *per* Lord Morris.

[90] *British Transport Commission* v. *Gourley, supra,* at p. 208, *per* Lord Goddard.

[91] *Rushton* v. *National Coal Board* [1953] 1 Q.B. 495, 502, *per* Romer L.J.; *H. West & Son Ltd.* v. *Shephard* [1964] A.C. 326, 346, *per* Lord Morris. See too *Fletcher* v. *Autocar and Transporters Ltd.* [1968] 2 Q.B. 322, 335, *per* Lord Denning M.R.; *ibid.* at pp. 339–340, *per* Diplock L.J.; *ibid.* at p. 363, *per* Salmon L.J.; *S.* v. *Distillers Co. (Biochemicals) Ltd.* [1970] 1 W.L.R. 114 (children born deformed, having been injured *in utero* by the drug "thalidomide" used by their mothers).

[92] McGregor, *Damages,* 15th ed., Chap. 7.

[93] *Banco de Portugal* v. *Waterlow* [1932] A.C. 452, 506. For cases on refusal of medical treatment, see Hudson in (1983) 3 L.S. 50.

[94] Some examples in the area of property damage will be found *post,* p. 634. *James* v. *Woodall Duckham Construction Co.* [1969] 1 W.L.R. 903 is an unusual example for personal injuries. For mitigation and remoteness, see *ante,* p. 149.

[95] [1985] Q.B. 1012. It must, however, be pointed out that unless there *are* medical or psychiatric grounds an abortion is, at least formally, unlawful.

might have been expected that in calculating the plaintiff's total damages in a given case the court would always have drawn a clear distinction between these two aspects of damages, but even after the decline of the civil jury the practice continued for some time to be to make a global award which did not distinguish between the different aspects of damages.[96] This practice was supported partly on the ground that separate assessment and addition of individual items might lead to "overlapping" and a consequently excessive award.[97] However, the introduction by the Administration of Justice Act 1969 of a new basis for the award of interest on personal injury damages[98] and subsequent decisions that different heads of damage should be treated in different ways for this purpose[99] have meant that a judge is compelled to itemise his award at least into pre-trial pecuniary loss, future loss of earnings[1] and non-pecuniary loss.[2] The idea that there can be an overlap between the pecuniary and non-pecuniary elements of an award should probably now be discarded.[3]

Even before the provisions on interest, however, it was the case that a variety of situations, each presenting some unusual feature, had compelled the courts to work out outlines of particular "heads of damage" within the broad categories of non-pecuniary and pecuniary loss and it is to these that we must now turn.

(1) *Non-pecuniary loss*

(a) **Pain and suffering**.[4] This phrase suggests a double head of damage, but in fact it is not possible to draw a sharp line between the two concepts. Pain and suffering includes the suffering attributable to the injury itself and to any consequential medical treatment, and worry about the effects of the injury upon the plaintiff's way of life[5] and prospects, including worry attributable to "compensation neurosis" which will cease on the determination of his claim for damages.[6] No damages will be awarded under this head, however severe the injury, if the plaintiff suffered no pain because he remained

---

[96] The advice of the Privy Council in *Paul* v. *Rendell* (1981) 34 A.L.R. 569 seems to show a certain nostalgia for this state of affairs. The courts always distinguished between "special" and "general" damages in the sense of pecuniary losses accruing before trial and other losses but in the nature of things damages for the former will generally be rather low.

[97] See, *e.g. Fletcher* v. *Autocar and Transporters Ltd.* [1968] 2 Q.B. 322.

[98] *Post*, p. 628.

[99] *Ibid.*

[1] Which carries no interest.

[2] The law might have reverted to its previous pattern as a result of *Cookson* v. *Knowles* [1977] Q.B. 913, but that was disapproved by the House of Lords in *Pickett* v. *British Rail Engineering Ltd.* [1980] A.C. 136.

[3] See *Lim.* v. *Camden Area Health Authority* [1980] A.C. 174, 192, and the Pearson Report, Vol. 1, para. 759.

[4] There is no particular conventional sum for slight injuries having no permanent effect: *Parry* v. *English Electric Co. Ltd.* [1971] 1 W.L.R. 664. Disappointment (*e.g.* over a ruined holiday) is not a separate head of compensation but may be taken into account to increase general damages for the injury: *Ichard* v. *Frangoulis* [1977] 1 W.L.R. 556.

[5] At this point this head of damage becomes indistinguishable from that of loss of amenity (*post*) but it is not usual to itemise them separately.

[6] *James* v. *Woodall Duckham Construction Co. Ltd.* [1969] 1 W.L.R. 903, where it was also held that the plaintiff could not recover in respect of a period of delay in determining his claim which was due to his own dilatoriness in proceeding with it. Cretney (1970) 114 S.J. 307.

unconscious or was otherwise incapable of experiencing pain,[7] or if the pain is not attributable to the defendant's tort.[8] It has been suggested that the fact that the plaintiff is wealthy may be a reason for awarding a smaller sum by way of damages for personal injuries,[9] but this view is untenable.[10] It is irrelevant that the plaintiff will be unable to enjoy the benefits that an award of damages may bring,[11] and it seems equally irrelevant that he could, if he wished, provide those benefits from his own resources.

A person is entitled to damages under this head for the mental suffering caused by his awareness that his life expectation has been shortened by the injuries[12] but the separate head of "loss of expectation of life" was abolished by the Administration of Justice Act 1982.[13] Before that Act a claim lay for the shortening of life expectancy even though the plaintiff was unaware of the loss and, indeed, even in cases of instantaneous death,[14] but the difficulties of valuation of such an item soon persuaded the courts to adopt a modest conventional sum[15] which would rarely be departed from.[16] In fact, the principal function of this head of damage was to provide in an indirect way for damages for bereavement in certain cases. This is now done directly by statute.[17]

(b) Loss of amenity.[18] It has for long been recognised that if the plaintiff's injuries deprive him of some enjoyment, for example, if an amateur footballer loses a leg, then he is entitled to damages on this account.[19] It has become clear, however, that this is to a large extent an objective element of the plaintiff's loss and distinguishable from pain and suffering, so that even though the plaintiff never appreciates the condition to which he has been reduced, he may nevertheless recover substantial damages under this head. In *Wise* v. *Kaye*[20] the plaintiff remained unconscious from the moment of the accident and was deprived of all the attributes of life but life itself. A majority of the Court of Appeal upheld an award of £15,000[21] for loss of amenity. In *H. West & Son Ltd.* v. *Shephard*[22] the plaintiff was a married

---

[7] *Wise* v. *Kaye* [1962] 1 Q.B. 638; *West & Son Ltd.* v. *Shephard* [1964] A.C. 326.

[8] *Cutler* v. *Vauxhall Motors Ltd.* [1971] 1 Q.B. 418, *ante*, p. 134.

[9] *Phillips* v. *L.S.W. Ry.* (1879) 5 C.P.D. 280, 294, *per* Cotton L.J.

[10] *Fletcher* v. *Autocar and Transporters Ltd.* [1968] 2 Q.B. 322, 340, 361 (the dicta in fact relate to loss of amenities, but it is submitted that the same applies to pain and suffering); *West* v. *Shephard, supra*, at p. 350, *per* Lord Morris.

[11] *Wise* v. *Kaye, supra*; *H. West & Son Ltd.* v. *Shephard, supra*; *Pickett* v. *British Rail Engineering Ltd.* [1980] A.C. 136.

[12] Administration of Justice Act 1982, s.1(1)(*b*). Such damages were recoverable under this head at common law: *Davies and Davies* v. *Smith and Smith* (1958) C.A. No. 34a; *Forest* v. *Sharp* (1963) 107 S.J. 536.

[13] s.1(1)(*a*).

[14] *Rose* v. *Ford* [1937] A.C. 826. Causes of action in tort generally survive for the benefit of the estates of deceased persons under the Law Reform (Miscellaneous Provisions) Act 1934 (*post*, p. 644) and the victim was regarded as having acquired a cause of action for the shortening of his life.

[15] £200 in *Benham* v. *Gambling* [1941] A.C. 157.

[16] For an unusual example, see *Burns* v. *Edman* [1970] 2 Q.B. 541.

[17] *Post*, p. 650.

[18] Sometimes referred to as "loss of enjoyment of life" or "loss of faculty." Perhaps the latter is the most accurate description: *Andrews* v. *Freeborough* [1967] 1 Q.B. 18, *per* Davies L.J.

[19] *Heaps* v. *Perrite Ltd.* [1937] 2 All E.R. 60; *Manley* v. *Rugby Portland Cement Co. Ltd.* (1951) Kemp and Kemp, *op. cit.*, 2nd ed., pp. 624, 626, *per* Birkett L.J. (omitted from subsequent eds.).

[20] [1962] 1 Q.B. 638.

[21] At least £118,000 in 1988 values.

[22] [1964] A.C. 326; Weir, *Casebook on Tort* (6th ed.), p. 550.

woman aged 41 at the time of her accident and sustained severe head injuries resulting in cerebral atrophy and paralysis of all four limbs. There was no prospect of improvement in her condition and her expectation of life was reduced to about five years. There was evidence that she might appreciate to some extent the condition in which she was, but she was unable to speak. A majority of the House of Lords upheld an award of £17,500 for loss of amenities.[23] As Lord Morris said, "The fact of unconsciousness does not . . . eliminate the actuality of the deprivations of the ordinary experiences and amenities of life which may be the inevitable result of some physical injury."[24]

Powerful objections have been voiced against *West* v. *Shephard*.[25] The principal objection is that one can no more compensate an unconscious person than a dead one and since there can be no award of damages for non-pecuniary loss in respect of the period after death, there may be a very great difference between the total sum awarded to the estate of a deceased person and that awarded to an unconscious, living one, even though the latter will be unable to use the money for his benefit and the whole sum will probably at some future date pass to his relatives.[26] On the other hand, there is a natural reluctance to treat a living plaintiff as if he were already dead.[27] A more general argument which is not aimed at the present treatment of the unconscious plaintiff but which supports the "conceptual" or "objective" approach upon which that treatment rests is the undesirability of making compensation depend upon the individual unhappiness caused by loss of amenities. It has been argued that unhappiness is in fact the only logical basis for assessment,[28] but Lord Pearce replied:

> "It would be lamentable if the trial of a personal injury claim put a premium on protestations of misery and if a long face was the only safe passport to a large award. Under the present practice there is no call for a parade of personal unhappiness. A plaintiff who cheerfully admits that he is as happy as he ever was, may yet receive a large award as reasonable compensation for the grave injury and loss of amenity over which he has managed to triumph."[29]

[23] An increase of £2,500 over the award in *Wise* v. *Kaye*, where the plaintiff had no appreciation of her condition. The trial judge in *Shephard* said that if there had been a normal life expectation the damages would have "come up well into the twenties of thousands." See also *Andrews* v. *Freeborough* [1967] 1 Q.B. 1; *Kralj* v. *McGrath* [1986] 1 All E.R. 54 (£2,000 for infant who died eight weeks after birth with no appreciation of his condition). In *Cutts* v. *Chumley* [1967] 1 W.L.R. 742 the plaintiff, though her physical injuries were perhaps less gross than those of the plaintiff in *West*, had more awareness of her condition and her expectation of life was much greater. Willis J. made a substantially higher award.

[24] [1964] A.C. 326, 349.

[25] See the dissenting speeches of Lords Devlin and Reid in that case, the dissent of Diplock L.J. in *Wise* v. *Kaye, supra*, and the decision of the High Court of Australia in *Skelton* v. *Collins* (1966) 115 C.L.R. 94 (see also Cornish, (1966) 29 M.L.R. 570).

[26] The difference became even greater when the Administration of Justice Act 1982 abolished claims for loss of expectation of life. But against the argument based upon the ultimate destination of the damages it must be pointed out: (1) the court has never exercised any general power to control the damages awarded to the victim of an accident; (2) some victims who are conscious but unable to "use" their damages might feel compensated by being able to benefit their relatives. *cf.* Ogus, *op. cit.*, pp. 216–217.

[27] *Wise* v. *Kay, supra*; *H. West & Son Ltd.* v. *Shephard, supra*.

[28] See Diplock L.J. in *Wise* v. *Kaye, supra*.

[29] *West* v. *Shephard, supra*, at pp. 368–369.

The arguments are fairly evenly balanced.[30] The Law Commission recommended no change in the law,[31] but the Pearson Commission went the other way.[32] The House of Lords looked at the matter again in *Lim* v. *Camden Area Health Authority*[33] and refused to overrule *West* v. *Shephard*, commenting that this "should not be done judicially but legislatively within the context of a comprehensive enactment"[34] on damages, but no such enactment seems imminent. However, it would be wrong to think that *West* v. *Shephard* itself is a case of "all or nothing." The minority in that case would have awarded something for the objective loss of amenity even in a case of unconsciousness, though much less than was in fact awarded[35]; equally, the majority would accept that an award under this head would be increased if the plaintiff were conscious of his loss.[36] In other words, the disagreement was not so much about the factors making up the award as about the relative weight to be given to these factors. On this basis the *result* in *Lim* might be regarded as a modest move in the direction of the minority in *West* v. *Shephard* because, making all due allowance for the greater severity of the injuries in *Shephard*, the award of £20,000 in *Lim*[37] certainly seems a good deal lower in real terms.[38] Lord Scarman said:

"An award for pain, suffering and loss of amenities is conventional in the sense that there is no pecuniary guideline which can point the way to a correct assessment. It is, therefore, dependent only in the most general way upon the movement in money values. .... As long, therefore, as the sum awarded is a substantial sum in the context of current money values, the requirement of the law is met."[39]

Yet at the time of the House of Lords decision awards of up to £60,000 were being made to plaintiffs with some awareness of deprivation.[40] However, perhaps it would be unwise to read too much into *Lim's* case in this respect—it certainly does not mean that the objective element of awards is to be constantly held down, for in 1982 it was said that £35,000 was a suitable

---

[30] In the "living death" cases the possibility of advances in medical science bringing about some amelioration of the condition may contribute to the current judicial attitude: *Croke* v. *Wiseman* [1982] 1 W.L.R. 71, 84.

[31] Law Com. No. 56, para. 31. A fuller discussion appears in the Law Commission's Published Working Paper No. 41.

[32] Cmnd. 7054, Vol. 1, para. 398, recommending that damages for loss of amenities should no longer be recoverable in cases of permanent unconsciousness. However, it is not clear whether this would extend to the case of the plaintiff who is, literally, conscious but has suffered such severe brain damage that he is unable to appreciate his loss, or the full extent of that loss. Since the Pearson Commission's proposal was based on the premise that "when we compensate someone for non-economic loss we are essentially seeking to relieve his suffering, and suffering is by its nature an experience subjective to the victim," logic would dictate similar treatment in such cases. However, while medical science will find it fairly easy to distinguish between consciousness and unconsciousness, "consciousness of loss" will often be a much more speculative matter.

[33] [1980] A.C. 174.

[34] *Ibid.* at p. 189.

[35] See [1964] A.C. 326, 341, 363.

[36] Hence the larger award in *West* v. *Shephard*, compared with *Wise* v. *Kaye*.

[37] The trial was in 1977.

[38] In real terms the *Lim* award was not much more than a third that in *West* v. *Shepherd*.

[39] [1980] A.C. 174, 189–190.

[40] See, *e.g. Taylor* v. *Glass* (1979), Kemp and Kemp, *op. cit.*, Vol. 2, p. 1513.

figure "for cases of total loss of amenity in which the plaintiff is no more than a vegetable, with no appreciation of the catastrophe that has overcome him."[41] An "average" case of conscious quadriplegia was said in 1985 to merit an award of £75,000,[42] so in 1988 the maximum figure for the worst case is perhaps £100,000.

(c) **The injury itself.** The heads of damage so far mentioned are all consequences of the injury, and in the majority of cases the consequences are more significant to the injured person than the injury itself. It is, however, sometimes said that the injury itself is a proper subject of compensation, quite apart from pain and suffering and loss of amenity. While this may be correct as a matter of principle and while there may be injuries which will lead to no disability,[43] it is not very likely that they will be unaccompanied by pain and suffering so as to require the court to give express recognition to the injury as a head of damage. A rather different, and more important point is that where the injury is a very specific one, like the loss of an eye or a leg, there is in effect a judicial "tariff," a bracket containing the standard award for non-pecuniary loss. The judge will award as damages for loss of amenities a sum comparable to that awarded in other cases unless the effect on the plaintiff is markedly different from the norm.[44]

(d) **Basis of assessment.** It is in the nature of non-pecuniary loss that it cannot be translated directly into money,[45] but nevertheless the only form of compensation available is an award of monetary damages, and an assessment of damages has to be made.[46] Such damages have been said to be "at large" and in the past their quantification was a jury question for which "no rigid rules, or rules that apply to all cases can be laid down."[47] However, in the middle 1960s the courts practically abolished the jury in personal injury actions,[48] principally because juries were considered to be incapable of

---

[41] Griffiths L.J. in *Young* v. *Redmond* 1982 C.A. No. 147, explaining his statement in *Croke* v. *Wiseman* [1982] 1 W.L.R. 71, 80.

[42] *Housecroft* v. *Burnett* [1986] 1 All E.R. 332. This decision represents an attempt to make a "new start" and the figure is lower in real terms than earlier comparable awards. However, to some extent this is because of the modern practice of separately calculating as expenses some items (*e.g.* cost of additional transport or alternative hobbies) which formerly might have been left to take care of themselves under the undifferentiated loss of amenities award. Not all injuries may be subject to the same considerations so care should be taken in using *Housecroft* v. *Burnett* as a benchmark for wholly different cases.

[43] *e.g.* where abdominal injury requires removal of the spleen: *Forster* v. *Pugh* [1955] C.L.Y. 741. *Church* v. *M.o.D.* (1984) 134 New L.J. 623 (symptomless pleural plaques, giving rise to anxiety).

[44] For a statement of the function of the Court of Appeal in setting levels of awards for non-pecuniary loss see *Wright* v. *B.R.B.* [1983] 2 A.C. 773. Awards are summarised in *Current Law* and set out more fully in Kemp and Kemp, *op. cit.* For example, the appropriate award for loss of one eye without any complications and assuming perfect sight in the other, is now around £15,000. Obviously, the appropriate figure for total blindness is a good deal more than twice this.

[45] Street, *op. cit.*, p. 5. *cf.* Munkman, *op. cit.*, pp. 16–21, where it is contended that everything, including bodily integrity, can be given a value. Unfortunately, the economists' tests ("What would you want in return for suffering this?" or "What would you pay to avoid this?") are not of much use to a practical tribunal.

[46] *The Mediana* [1900] A.C. 113, 116, *per* Lord Halsbury L.C.

[47] *The Susquehanna* [1926] A.C. 655, 662, *per* Viscount Dunedin. But he added that "in each set of circumstances certain relevant considerations will arise which . . . it would be the duty of the judge in the case to bring before the jury."

[48] *Ward* v. *James* [1966] 1 Q.B. 273, a decision of the full Court of Appeal. See also *Hennell* v. *Ranaboldo*. [1963] 1 W.L.R. 1391; *Simms* v. *William Howard & Son Ltd*. [1964] 2 Q.B. 409. Though there is still power to order a jury in "exceptional" cases Kemp & Kemp, *op. cit.*, Vol. 1, 19009, comments that it is now difficult to envisage what such circumstances might be.

achieving a measure of uniformity in essentially similar cases.[49] Since then it has become normal for judges to have cited to them previous awards and there is a pattern for various common kinds of injury. Of course, as a technique the comparison of awards has drawbacks. How can a realistic comparison be made between cases involving different kinds of injury? If, for example, £20,000 is an appropriate figure for loss by a right-handed plaintiff of use of his right arm, what guidance does that give to the damages appropriate for the loss of an eye,[50] or for the inability to bear a child,[51] or for loss of the sense of smell?[52] Indeed, one might go further and ask, even assuming a suitable standard for comparison can be found, how we justify a particular datum figure for the injury with which the comparisons are made. Why is our figure £20,000, not £200 or £200,000?[53] As far as this latter question is concerned, one can say little more than that "the choice of the right order of figure is empirical[54] and in practice results from a general consensus of opinion of damage awarding tribunals," though one might add that that consensus has become stronger since the ousting of the jury. As for comparisons, Diplock L.J. said that the standard of comparison which the law applies, "if it is not wholly instinctive and incommunicable, is based, apart from pain and suffering, upon the degree of deprivation—that is, the extent to which the victim is unable to do those things which, but for the injury, he would have been able to do."[55] Perhaps little more can be said in general terms than that the damages awarded should be fair and reasonable, bearing in mind all the relevant heads of damage, that though awards are conventional they should not be artificial,[56] that there should be an adequate degree of consistency and—particularly important over the last few years— that awards should keep pace with the times.[57]

Since the assessment of damages for non-pecuniary loss is not an exact mathematical process the Court of Appeal should not interfere unless the

---

[49] Though one feels some sympathy for the jury, since counsel could not put previous awards before it, nor suggest a maximum or minimum figure, nor even any specific figure at all: *Bates* v. *Stone Parish Council* [1954] 1 W.L.R. 1249, 1258, *per* Birkett L.J.; *Ward* v. *James* [1966] 1 Q.B. 273, 301–303. It is interesting to note that in two cases of quadriplegia juries made identical awards of £50,000. In the earlier, *Morey* v. *Woodfield (No. 2)* [1964] 1 W.L.R. 16n., the Court of Appeal found no fault in the summing-up and felt constrained to allow the award to stand. In the second, *Warren* v. *King* [1964] 1 W.L.R. 1, a new trial was ordered. In both cases the Court of Appeal clearly regarded the awards as very high.

[50] As to which see *supra*, n. 44.

[51] £4,000 to mother of four in 1981: *Devi* v. *W. Midlands Regional Health Authority*; Kemp and Kemp, *op. cit.*, Vol. 2, p. 7722.

[52] About £6,500 if *Kearns* v. *Higgs & Hill Ltd.* (1968) 112 S.J. 252 is grossed up in line with inflation.

[53] The Supreme Court of Canada has set an upper limit of $100,000 (at 1978 values) for non-pecuniary loss: *Lindal* v. *Lindal* (1981) 129 D.L.R. (3d) 263.

[54] It is obvious that current levels of award are only tolerable against a background of liability insurance, but the interests of insurers must be borne in mind in setting figures: see Lord Denning M.R. and Diplock L.J. in *Fletcher* v. *Autocar and Transporters Ltd.* [1968] 2 Q.B. 322. *cf.* Salmon L.J., *ibid.*

[55] *Bastow* v. *Bagley & Co. Ltd.* [1961] 1 W.L.R. 1494, 1498.

[56] *Fletcher* v. *Autocar and Transporters Ltd.*, *supra*, at p. 340.

[57] In *Walker* v. *John McLean & Sons Ltd.* [1979] 1 W.L.R. 760 the Court of Appeal warned that awards for non-pecuniary loss had failed to keep pace with inflation. This warning appears to have been taken to heart by trial judges, but awards are still lower in real terms than they were in the 1960s. On the level of personal injury damages in general, Mr. Prevett has calculated that the 1982 value of the £16,000 awarded by the jury in *Phillips* v. *L.S.W. Ry.* (1879) 5 C.P.D. 280 would be £500,000. (About £660,000 in 1988 money). A handful of cases have now passed the £1 million (without interest) mark under all heads, pecuniary and non-pecuniary. Medical techniques which enable seriously injured plaintiffs to be kept alive for years will inevitably increase the expenses elements in damages claims.

judge has acted on a wrong principle of law, or misapprehended the facts or has for other reasons made a wholly erroneous estimate of the damage suffered.[58]

(2) *Pecuniary loss*

In the case of a serious accident, the greater part of the plaintiff's claim for damages will be for pecuniary loss, usually loss of earnings and expenses. In so far as these losses have been incurred before the trial or settlement[59] there is unlikely to be any difficulty about their assessment other than, perhaps, with regard to offsetting other benefits received.[60] However, it is an inveterate principle of the common law that damages may only be awarded on a lump sum, "once for all" basis[61] and the court must therefore also attempt to convert future pecuniary losses into a present capital sum, a process which is inevitably inexact because it involves a host of assumptions, including the plaintiff's future rate of earning had he not been injured, the period and extent of his disability, and the chance that his earning capacity might have been affected by some other vicissitude even if the accident had not happened. In recent years the difficulty of this task has been exacerbated by rising unemployment and inflation. A limited exception has now been introduced in the form of "provisional awards" where there is a chance that the plaintiff's condition will deteriorate as a result of the defendant's tort,[62] but it is sometimes argued that the system could be improved by radical change in the shape of awarding damages for future pecuniary loss on a periodic basis.[63]

Lump sum awards are alleged to have advantages from the point of view of both the plaintiff and the defendant (or, more usually, his insurer). The plaintiff, it is said, can concentrate his efforts on recovery from his disability without fear that in doing so he will be reducing his compensation and he is given a degree of choice as to his future financial resources (for example, he

---

[58] *Pickett* v. *British Rail Engineering Ltd.* [1980] A.C. 136. Note, however, that in this case the injury was not so susceptible of a "tariff" approach as, say, loss of a leg or an eye, and there might be less room for proper differences of opinion in such cases.

[59] In the early 1970s about three-quarters of claims for £25,000 or more were not disposed of within two years of the date of the claim: Pearson Report, Cmnd. 7054, Vol. 2, Table 115.

[60] *Post*, p. 622. Loss of earnings already incurred will normally be calculated simply by reference to the period of disability and the rate paid in the plaintiff's job during that period (including wage increases): *Cookson* v. *Knowles* [1979] A.C. 556. The validity of this calculation depends upon the assumption that but for this injury the plaintiff would have continued earning at the same rate. If the assumption is unjustified, allowance must be made accordingly: *Phillips* v. *L.S.W. Ry.* (1879) 5 C.P.D. 280, 291; *Rouse* v. *P.L.A.* [1953] 2 Lloyd's Rep. 179.

[61] See generally, *ante*, p. 598. Specific performance may be ordered of an obligation to make periodic payments of money (*Beswick* v. *Beswick* [1968] A.C. 58) but that can have no application to a case of tort.

[62] *Post*, p. 629.

[63] There is, of course, no case for periodic payments in respect of past pecuniary loss. In the case of future non-pecuniary loss the Pearson Commission remarked (Cmnd. 7054, Vol. 1, para. 61(2) that the "damages are an arbitrary acknowledgment of an essentially unquantifiable loss. . . . Indeed, there is no rational basis for saying whether a particular award represents over compensation or under compensation, except by comparison with other awards." There is, however, some precedent for payments of this broad type being made on a periodic basis in disablement benefit under the industrial injuries scheme: *ante*, Chap. 1. Assessment of damages under the Fatal Accidents Act raises the same problems as those which occur over future pecuniary loss in injury cases.

may buy a small business).[64] The defendant's insurers, on the other hand, can close their books on a claim and incur no further administrative costs. There is no doubt that there is force in these arguments,[65] but there are also powerful objections to the lump sum system. There is generally no way in which the plaintiff's use of his damages can be controlled and if he uses his capital improvidently or engages in an unsuccessful business venture the end result may be that he is supported through social security by the community at large.[66] Even where the plaintiff uses his capital wisely the present system cannot protect him against unforeseen deterioration in his medical condition or in the economic situation after the trial and it becomes difficult to adopt anything but the most arbitrary rule as to offset of social security payments (which are periodic) against tort damages.[67] A majority of the Pearson Commission[68] concluded that the benefits of periodic payments outweighed any disadvantages and recommended the adoption of such a system for future pecuniary losses in cases of serious or lasting injury or death.[69] This has not been implemented. The Commission recognised that a change to periodical payments might have only a limited effect in practice since the vast majority of claims are settled out of court and there would be no practical way of preventing plaintiffs settling for a lump sum.[70] However, some interest is now being shown even by insurers in "structured settlements" for very large claims under which payments would be made on a periodic basis.[71]

We turn now to the assessment of damages for pecuniary loss on a lump sum basis. Proposals for modification of the present system of assessment will be mentioned at relevant points.

(a) **Loss of earnings**. The normal approach of the court in converting future loss of earnings to a present capital sum is the so-called "multiplier" approach. One first determines the multiplicand in the form of the plaintiff's net annual loss. This is arrived at by deducting from the gross income the plaintiff would have received but for the accident the amount of income

---

[64] The Pearson Report, Vol. 2, Table 89, reveals that only a minority of recipients of lump sums invested any of the money, or banked it or used it to pay off a mortgage, but the average payment in the sample was only £249.

[65] The Law Commission in its report on assessment of damages came down firmly in favour of the lump sum: Law Com. No. 56.

[66] Of course, exactly the same may happen in the case of an uninjured person who wastes his periodical income.

[67] *Post,* p. 622.

[68] Cmnd. 7054, Vol. 1, Chap. 14.

[69] For details, see the twelfth edition of this work, p. 632.

[70] Evidence in jurisdictions where plaintiffs have a choice between a lump sum or a periodic payment suggests a plaintiff preference for the lump sum.

[71] See (1987) 137 N.L.J. 926; Lewis, "Pensions Replace Lump Sum Damages" (1988) 15 Jo. of Law and Society 392. An Inland Revenue concession removes the tax disadvantages which would otherwise attach to such settlements. Such settlements would not necessarily have the features of flexibility and variability which some would regard as vital attributes of a periodical payments system.

tax,[72] social security contributions[73] and other expenditure the plaintiff would have had to incur to gain the income (for example, his contribution to a company pension scheme[74]). Logically, a case could be made out for deducting under the last head the plaintiff's travelling expenses to and from work which he will no longer incur after the accident but except perhaps in very exceptional circumstances[75] this is not done.[76] The annual sum thus arrived at[77] is then multiplied by a number of years' purchase calculated upon the likely duration of the loss. In determining the multiplier, however, the court will not simply adopt the number of years from trial[78] to retirement age or death for that would be to over-compensate the plaintiff. First, some allowance must be made for the "general vicissitudes of life," that is to say, damaging events like early death or unemployment which might have affected the plaintiff even if the defendant had not injured him.[79] Secondly, account must be taken of the fact that the lump sum of damages will itself produce an investment income. A reduction of the multiplier will therefore be made to effect a discount in respect of those factors.[80] In practice, there is a maximum of about 18 as the multiplier, but there is no automatic relationship between the multiplier and the plaintiff's age: thus a multiplier of 15 or 16 would be the norm whether the plaintiff was aged 20 or 30,[81] though it would show a steady decline after that age. The theoretical aim of the process is to provide a lump sum sufficient, when invested, to produce an income equal to the lost income when the interest is supplemented by withdrawals of capital. Naturally, it is unlikely that this result is actually reached in more than a handful of cases since it involves a double exercise in the art of prophesying—not only what the future holds for the injured plaintiff, but also what the future would have held for him if he had not been injured.[82] However, it may be asked whether something like the desired result is achieved over the whole range of recipients of tort damages.

[72] *British Transport Commission* v. *Gourley* [1956] A.C. 185; McGregor, *Damages* (15th ed.), Chap. 13. (1) The damages themselves are not taxable in the plaintiff's hands, though the point has always been assumed rather than formally decided. (2) Interest on the damages awarded by the court would be taxable were it not specifically exempted by statute. (3) The *income* produced by the investment of the award is taxable in the normal way and since this has to go to cover part of the plaintiff's loss he in effect suffers tax twice over. But this illogicality is tolerated: see Lord Oliver in *Hodgson* v. *Trapp* [1988] 3 W.L.R. 1281, 1294.

[73] *Cooper* v. *Firth Brown Ltd.* [1963] 2 W.L.R. 418. As to deduction of social security receipts by the plaintiff, see *post*, p. 622.

[74] *Dews* v. *N.C.B.* [1988] A.C. 1. But if as a result of the accident the plaintiff's employment is terminated and he suffers a reduction in pension, this is itself a compensable head of damage: *Parry* v. *Cleaver* [1970] A.C. 1.

[75] Lord Griffiths in *Dews* v. *N.C.B.* suggests as a possible example the case of a wealthy man who commuted daily by helicopter from the Channel Islands to London.

[76] It can be argued that it is no concern of the defendant where the plaintiff chooses to live but a further practical reason is that such deductions would complicate the settlement and disposal of claims.

[77] Increases in the plaintiff's earnings which will be produced by inflation are ignored (see *infra*) but likely increases due to promotion, etc., are brought into the calculation. For a complicated example see *Robertson* v. *Lestrange* [1985] 1 All E.R. 950 (a fatal accident case).

[78] See *Pritchard* v. *J.H. Cobden Ltd.* [1988] Fam. 22.

[79] For the position where such a vicissitude occurs before trial, see *ante*, p. 136.

[80] The same result can be achieved by applying mathematical discount tables directly to the calculated annual loss, and this is the practice in some other jurisdictions. But it is then wrong to apply a further discount for accelerated receipt: *Lai* v. *Singapore Bus Co.* [1984] A.C. 729.

[81] See Kemp and Kemp, *op. cit.*, Vol. 1, pp. 6069–6077. For fatal accident cases, see *ibid.* at pp. 27004–27007. For the situation where the plaintiff's expectation of life is reduced by the accident, see *post*, p. 621.

[82] *Paul* v. *Rendell* (1981) 34 A.L.R. 569, 571 (P.C.) *per* Lord Diplock.

The major problem here has been the fall in the value of money caused by inflation. The law is clear, namely, that inflation is to be ignored and money treated as retaining its value at the date of the judgment.[83] This is the only practical course, for as Lord Scarman remarked in *Lim* v. *Camden Area Health Authority*,[84] "it is pure speculation whether inflation will continue at present, or higher rates, or even disappear. The only sure comment one may make upon any inflation prediction is that it is as likely to be falsified as to be borne out by the event." It has also been suggested that victims of tort who receive a lump sum award are entitled to no better protection against inflation than others who have to rely on capital for their support,[85] though it may be replied that if those who rely on capital are in an inferior position in inflationary times, is it not the defendant's fault that the plaintiff has joined that class? However, there is more to be said for the present law than the simple response that nothing more can be done. It has been estimated that the current multipliers correspond approximately to the assumption that a person who invests capital will enjoy a return of 4½ per cent. a year but there is a tendency for high inflation to be accompanied by high rates of interest[86] so that the returns on invested damages may be very much higher than the assumptions upon which the multipliers rest. In this way "inflation and the high rates of interest to which it gives rise is automatically taken into account by the use of multipliers based on rates of interest related to a stable currency. It would therefore be wrong for the court to increase the award of damages by attempting to make a further specific allowance for inflation."[87] At the time these words were spoken it was possible to obtain a gross return of 14 per cent. on gilt-edged securities.[88] Since then there has been a substantial fall in the rate of inflation accompanied, in general, by a fall in interest rates,[89] though it remains to be seen whether the relationship between the two is immutable.[90] Two points, however, seriously qualify the assumptions on which the present law is based. First, if a period of high inflation is followed by a more stable financial climate the plaintiff's income from the investment of his damages will fall along with interest rates but the price of the commodities he must buy with that income is unlikely to fall in the same way. Secondly, in *Wright* v. *British Railways Board*[91] the House of Lords proceeded upon the assumption that the "real" rate of interest (that is to say, what is left after the rate from time to time is shorn of the amount

---

[83] *Mallett* v. *McMonagle* [1970] A.C. 166; *Cookson* v. *Knowles* [1979] A.C. 556; *Lim* v. *Camden Area Health Authority* [1980] A.C. 174; *Hodgson* v. *Trapp* [1988] 3 W.L.R. 1281.

[84] [1980] A.C. 174, 193.

[85] *Ibid.* at p. 194.

[86] Because "interest" represents not merely the sum a lender charges for the *use* of his money but also his estimate of how much the value of the sum lent will have declined on repayment.

[87] *Cookson* v. *Knowles* [1979] A.C. 556, 557, *per* Lord Fraser.

[88] In the earlier cases such as *Mallett* v. *McMonagle* [1970] A.C. 166 attention has been drawn to the substantial rises in the value of equity shares which had accompanied inflation. Such investments failed to keep pace with the inflation of the 1970s, hence the shift in emphasis to gilt-edged securities. But while it may be realistic to expect the recipient of a six-figure sum to take expert, continuing investment advice, is the same true if the damages are £10,000 or £20,000?

[89] But interest rates may be raised well above inflation rates as a deliberate instrument of economic policy.

[90] See the doubts of Lord Salmon in *Cookson* v. *Knowles* at p. 574.

[91] [1983] 2 A.C. 773.

which lenders estimate to be necessary to protect their capital against inflation) is a fairly constant 2 per cent.[92] If this is so, it must follow that awards which are made (as they usually are) on the assumption that the plaintiff will get a real return of 4½ per cent. on his money are likely to be too low.[93] Certainly, the House in *Wright* was not concerned with the assessment of damages for future loss of earnings but with the proper rate of interest on damages for pre-trial non-pecuniary loss[94] but a proposition about the real rate of return on money lent must be as valid for future loss as it is for past loss.[95] However, the reluctance of the courts to accept this view is not surprising for a shift from an effective discount rate of 4½ per cent. to one of 2 per cent. would produce a dramatic increase in awards in more serious cases[96] and, for all the talk of "full compensation", these have to be paid for.

Another potential difficulty is the incidence of taxation upon the income of the plaintiff's damages fund. If we start from the position that high interest rates will tend to take care of inflation by increasing the return on the plaintiff's capital, we must also accept that if the return is high enough it will push the plaintiff into a higher income tax bracket. Is some further allowance to be made for this, perhaps by increasing the multiplier on which the plaintiff's award is based? After some hesitation, the House of Lords has decided that to make a specific addition on account of taxation would be as incorrect as to allow for future inflation.[97] Even if it were possible to surmount the formidable difficulty of estimating future tax rates the exercise would be an unreal one because the tax liability of the plaintiff will depend upon how he chooses to manage his capital, for example, whether he chooses to supplement his income by investing his damages for non-pecuniary loss or buys an annuity rather than laying out his money at interest.[98]

[92] Based partly upon the rate of return on index-linked government bonds, which carry no inflation risk.

[93] See the point developed in Kemp & Kemp, Vol. 1, pp. 7010–7023.

[94] The plaintiff is entitled to interest on non-pecuniary loss damages from the time of the injury until judgment. But since such damages are awarded on the "tariff" prevailing at the time of the trial inflation is automatically taken care of and the only concern is to compensate the plaintiff for his having been kept out of his money. Hence the need to find the "real" rate of interest if the plaintiff is not to be over-compensated.

[95] The attempt of the C.A. in *Auty* v. *N.C.B.* [1985] 1 W.L.R. 784 to treat *Wright* as irrelevant to future loss is not, with respect, convincing.

[96] See Kemp & Kemp, Vol. 2, pp. 7017–7019. The Pearson Commission also thought that current multipliers led to awards which were too low: Cmnd. 7054, Vol. 1, Chap. 15. There is a very full account of the relationship between damages and inflation in the judgments in the High Court of Australia in *Todorovic* v. *Waller* (1981) 37 A.L.R. 59.

[97] *Hodgson* v. *Trapp* [1988] 3 W.L.R. 1281. It is true that Lord Oliver (at p. 1300) leaves open the possibility of making an allowance in "very exceptional cases, where it could be positively shown by evidence that justice required it . . . although for my part I do not find it easy to envisage circumstances in which evidence could satisfactorily establish that which is inherently uncertain." A return to the penal tax rates of the 1970s might prompt reconsideration.

[98] *Ibid.* at p. 1299. Some mention should be made here of actuarial computation. Actuarial tables (which were originally designed to guide life assurance companies in granting annuities in return for a capital sum) may be used to determine the present capital value of future periodical losses—which is what assessment of lump sum damages for loss of earnings is all about. Actuarial techniques give no greater likelihood of correct assessment in an individual case than any other method, but it is argued that they are more likely to lead to a correct *overall* result. Under the present law actuarial evidence is undoubtedly admissible but there has been a tendency to discourage its use, partly on account of cost: see *Taylor* v. *O'Connor* [1971] A.C. 115 and *Mitchell* v. *Mulholland (No. 2)* [1972] 1 Q.B. 65. See further Kemp and Kemp, Vol. 1, Chap. 6; Prevett, "Actuarial Assessment of Damages: the Thalidomide Case" (1972) 35 M.L.R. 140, 257. The Law Commission recommended the increased use of actuarial techniques and the introduction of a set of official tables: Law Com. No. 56, paras. 215–230.

(b) Loss of earning capacity. In cases of continuing disability the plaintiff may be able to remain in his employment but with the risk that, if he loses that employment at some time in the future, he may then, as a result of his injury, be at a disadvantage in getting another job or an equally well-paid job. This "loss of earning capacity"[99] has always been a compensable head of damage but has come into more prominence in recent years, probably as a result of the growth of the practice of "itemising" awards.[1] Assessment of damages under this head may be highly speculative and clearly no mathematical approach is possible[2]; but the court should be satisfied that there is a "substantial" or "real" risk that the plaintiff will be subject to the disadvantage before the end of his working life. If so satisfied, the judge must then do his best to value the "chance," taking into account all the facts of the case.[3]

(c) The "lost years." In some cases the injury suffered by the plaintiff will reduce his expectation of life. For many years the rule was that while a plaintiff was entitled to damages for "loss of expectation of life" (a conventional sum)[4] he could not, according to *Oliver* v. *Ashman*,[5] recover any further damages for loss of earnings during the period when, but for the accident, he would probably have remained alive and working. For an adult plaintiff with dependants the consequences of this might be catastrophic, for his dependants might be left without compensation for a very large part of the loss they had suffered.[6] In the face of prolonged legislative inaction, the House of Lords in *Pickett* v. *British Rail Engineering Ltd.*[7] overruled *Oliver* v. *Ashman*. Damages for loss of earnings are to be assessed on the plaintiff's expectation of life before the accident, making a deduction in respect of money which the plaintiff would have spent on his own support during the lost years. The details of this have caused some judicial disagreement, but the following principles seem to have emerged (though all the case law arose from claims by estates of deceased persons, a context in which *Pickett* has

---

[99] The terminology in this area is not uniform and all loss of future earnings is sometimes included within this expression: see, *e.g.* McGregor, *Damages* (15th ed.), p. 903. On this view, all loss of earnings represents a capital loss, a point which influenced the High Court of Australia in *Atlas Tiles* v. *Briers* (1978) 21 A.L.R. 129 to refuse to follow *Gourley's* case on income tax and damages (*ante*, p. 618). However, a full court assembled in *Cullen* v. *Trappell* (1980) 29 A.L.R. 1 overruled *Atlas Tiles*. The truth appears to be that earning capacity in the broad sense is a "capital" asset but can only be valued by the income it produces and that *Gourley's* case proceeded pragmatically rather than conceptually.

[1] *Moeliker* v. *A. Reyrolle & Co. Ltd.* [1976] I.C.R. 253, 261 *per* Brown L.J.

[2] The same applies to a plaintiff who is injured before his working life has begun; it may be more appropriate to select a global figure which seems fair compensation than to seek a multiplier and multiplicand: *Joyce* v. *Yeomans* [1981] 1 W.L.R. 550.

[3] See *Ashcroft* v. *Curtin* [1971] 1 W.L.R. 1731; *Smith* v. *Manchester Corp.* (1974) 17 K.I.R. 1; *Clarke* v. *Rotax Aircraft Equipment Ltd.* [1975] I.C.R. 440; *Moeliker* v. *A. Reyrolle & Co. Ltd.* [1976]. I.C.R. 253; *Nicholls* v. *N.C.B.* [1976] I.C.R. 266; *Zielinski* v. *West* (1977) Kemp and Kemp, *op. cit.* Vol. 2, 10–651. Damages may be awarded under this head even though the plaintiff is unemployed at the date of the trial: *Cook* v. *Consolidated Fisheries Ltd.* [1977] I.C.R. 635.

[4] *Ante*, p. 611.

[5] [1962] 2 Q.B. 210. See further the 11th edition of this work.

[6] See *Gammell* v. *Wilson* [1982] A.C. 27, 64–65, *per* Lord Diplock. Where death is attributable to the defendant's tort the deceased's dependants have a cause of action under the Fatal Accidents Act (*post*, p. 647), but this cannot be brought where the victim has already recovered judgment before death.

[7] [1980] A.C. 126; *Davies* (1979) 95 L.Q.R. 187; *Rogers* [1979] C.L.J. 47. A similar decision has been reached by the High Court of Australia in *Skelton* v. *Collins* (1966) 115 C.L.R. 94. See also *Andrews* v. *Grand & Toy Alberta Ltd.* [1978] 1 W.W.R. 577.

been reversed by statute[8]). First, the claim is not confined to savings which the plaintiff can show he would have made by the end of his "normal" life, so that a deduction is not to be made in respect of expenditure that the plaintiff would have made on his dependants during the lost years.[9] However, where there are dependants for whom the plaintiff has to provide housing and heat and light and so on, a deduction must be made for the fact that a proportion of such expenditure represents the living expenses of the plaintiff.[10] This differs from the Fatal Accidents Act approach, under which such expenditure is treated as relating exclusively to the dependants.[11] It follows, of course that a very much larger deduction may have to be made where the plaintiff is single.[12] While the courts must sometimes necessarily proceed on slender evidence in assessing the loss in these cases they should not enter the realms of speculation or guesswork. Where the plaintiff is middle-aged with established commitments the task presents no particular novelty or difficulty; where the plaintiff is a teenager about to embark on a career there may be enough material to justify a moderate award; but in the case of a very young child the right figure will often[13] be nil.[14]

(d) Deductions. We have seen that prima facie the plaintiff's loss is his lost earnings net of tax, etc., but it would be a rare case in which the plaintiff did not receive some payment or benefit as a consequence of the accident and the question arises how far this has to be brought into account as reducing the amount of the loss.

(i) *Statute*.

The Law Reform (Personal Injuries) Act 1948 section 2, requires the deduction from damages for loss of earnings[15] of one half of the value of certain social security benefits receivable by the plaintiff in the five years following the accident.[16] The relevant benefits are now sickness benefit,

---

[8] *Post*, p. 645.

[9] *White* v. *London Transport Executive* [1982] Q.B. 489. The contrary view has a certain logical attraction, but as Webster J. pointed out it is fundamentally inconsistent with the basis of *Pickett's* case, that *Oliver* v. *Ashman* caused injustice to dependants.

[10] *Harris* v. *Empress Motors Ltd*. [1983] 3 All E.R. 561, overruling a number of first instance decisions.

[11] The current tendency in Fatal Accidents Act claims is towards a presumption that the deceased's personal expenses are a conventional percentage of income.

[12] Not only will less of his money be spent directly on himself when he marries, but the share of household expenses attributable to him falls as the number of dependants increases. But it would be wrong to assume that the single person who spends all his surplus on pleasure gets nothing: *Wilson* v. *Stag* (1985) 136 N.L.J. 47.

[13] In *Gammell* v. *Wilson, supra*, at p. 78, Lord Scarman put forward the case of a five year old child television star "cut short in her prime" as a possible exception. However, in *Connolly* v. *Camden Area Health Authority* [1981] 3 All E.R. 250, Comyn J. suggested the addition of cases where the child might, but for the shortening of life, have inherited a capital sum.

[14] *Croke* v. *Wiseman* [1982] 1 W.L.R. 71; Davies (1982) 45 M.L.R. 333. Note, however, that the plaintiff received £25,000 in respect of loss of earnings during the considerable life expectancy that remained to him, during which he would be insensible of his plight. Lord Denning M.R. thought this assessment just as speculative as that for the lost years.

[15] This includes the damages for loss of "earning capacity," dealt with at p. 621: *Foster* v. *Tyne and Wear C.C.* [1986] 1 All E.R. 567.

[16] Where the plaintiff fails to claim benefits (whether, it seems, through ignorance or otherwise) no deduction is to be made in respect of them: *Ely* v. *Bedford* [1972] 1 Q.B. 155. Benefit is deducted before any reduction for contributory negligence, which favours the plaintiff: s.2(3).

invalidity benefit and disablement benefit. The statute is a complete code on the deduction of these benefits (that is to say, there can be no deduction of them except as provided by it[17]) but a number of important benefits are not dealt with by the statute so their deductibility must be determined by the common law. One other benefit (though one in kind, not in cash) is, however governed by statute: by section 5 of the Administration of Justice Act 1982, where an injured person is maintained wholly or partly at public expense in a hospital, nursing home or other institution, any saving attributable thereto is to be set off against his loss of income.[18]

(ii) *Common law*

It is difficult to "articulate a single precise jurisprudential principle by which to distinguish the deductible from the non-deductible receipt"[19] but the basic rule is that receipts which have come to the plaintiff as a result of his injury are prima facie to be set against his loss of earnings and consequential expenses unless they fall within established exceptions.[20] The first of these is that voluntary payments prompted by the benevolence of third parties,[21] whether into a "disaster fund" or directly to the plaintiff, are not to be brought into account for the simple reason that otherwise there would be a risk that the springs of charity would dry up.[22] Where, however, the benevolent payments come from the defendant they would seem to be deductible, which can be supported on the ground that it encourages defendants to make early payments.[23] The other principal exception is that the court will not bring into account moneys accruing to the plaintiff under policies of insurance,[24] partly because the plaintiff is not to be disadvantaged by reason of his own foresight and thrift[25] and partly because the defendant cannot be heard to say that the plaintiff's insurance arrangements give him full compensation for his loss.[26] The latter point is also the basis of the decision in

---

[17] *Jackman* v. *Corbett* [1988] Q.B. 154.

[18] Reversing the common law rule in *Daish* v. *Wauton* [1972] 2 Q.B. 262.

[19] *Hodgson* v. *Trapp* [1988] 3 W.L.R. 1281, 1286, *per* Lord Bridge.

[20] *Ibid.*

[21] The donors of the benevolence have no claim: *Esso Petroleum Co. Ltd.* v. *Hall Russell & Co. Ltd.* [1988] 3 W.L.R. 730, 751.

[22] *Redpath* v. *Belfast County Down Ry.* [1947] N.I. 167; *Parry* v. *Cleaver* [1970] A.C. 1. *Naahas* v. *Pier House Management (Cheyne Walk) Ltd.* (1984) 270 E.G. 328 (property loss).

[23] This is the law in Scotland by virtue of s.10 of the Administration of Justice Act 1982 and it is supported for England by Lloyd L.J. in *Hussain* v. *New Taplow Paper Mills Ltd.* [1987] 1 W.L.R. 336 (the point is not touched on in the H.L.: [1988] A.C. 514). But (again by analogy with Scots law) the defendant probably cannot claim credit for his payment into a disaster fund: *Dougan* v. *Glasgow Rangers Football Club* 1974 S.L.R.(Sh.Ct.) 34, Administration of Justice Act 1982, s.10.

[24] *Bradburn* v. *G.W. Ry.* (1874) L.R.Ex. 1. *Parry* v. *Cleaver, supra.*

[25] But as Atiyah points out ((1969) 32 M.L.R. 697) there would be no question ot depriving the plaintiff of his insurance moneys. The "thrift" argument presupposes that the *plaintiff* has paid the premiums and Lord Bridge in *Hodgson* v. *Trapp* at p. 1286 speaks of this as a requirement. But it has been held that it is irrelevant that the payment is made by a third party (*The Yasin* [1979] 2 Lloyd's Rep. 45) and this seems the better view: why should the damages of a family member injured on holiday be reduced because one member of the party paid all the insurance premiums?

[26] The point is particularly obvious in the case of personal accident insurance where the insured sum bears no necessary relation to any objectively determined value or loss. But property insurance is generally on an indemnity basis (for example, a car is insured under a comprehensive policy for its value). Such insurance is no bar to an action against a tortfeasor but the insured would have to reimburse his insurers out of any damages recovered.

Parry v. *Cleaver*[27] that where the plaintiff was disabled from work as a police officer and received a disability pension this was not to be brought into account because it was not the equivalent of the wages he had lost.[28] However, the wages received from his substitute employment were deductible in arriving at his loss and the same will be true of sick pay[29] even where that takes the form of a very long-term payment which the employer has secured by an arrangement with an insurance company.[30] Where the employer pays wages *ex gratia* then, unless he is the tortfeasor, they are probably not deductible.[31]

As to state benefits other than those provided for by the 1948 Act, they are generally deductible in full for there is no analogy between the generosity of private subscribers to a disaster fund and the state providing subventions for the needy out of funds subscribed compulsorily by various classes of citizens.[32] Accordingly, courts have made deductions in respect of unemployment benefit,[33] supplementary benefit (now income support),[34] family income supplement (now family credit),[35] attendance and mobility allowances[36] and statutory sick pay.[37] A state retirement pension may still not be deductible on the analogy of *Parry* v. *Cleaver*.[38] As for redundancy payment, it normally has no connexion with the injury and is non-deductible (as where the plaintiff's place of employment closes down while he is convalescing). If, however, he is selected for redundancy because of the injury the position is different.[39]

The Pearson Commission proposed a system of full offset of virtually all social security benefits payable as a result of injury. The common law has,

---

[27] [1970] A.C. 1; Weir, *Casebook on Tort* (6th ed.), p. 553; Jolowicz [1969] C.L.J. 183; Atiyah (1969) 32 M.L.R. 697.

[28] This case is a good illustration of the problems of conceptual analysis in this area. The approach of the majority of the House of Lords is to clarify the loss as "wages" and the benefit as a "pension"; the approach of the minority is to treat both as "money."

[29] Unless paid on condition of repayment in the event of a successful claim for damages: *Doonan* v. *S.M.T. Co.* 1950 S.C. 136. The employer is not entitled to recover the wages from the wrongdoer (*Receiver for Metropolitan Police District* v. *Croydon Corp.* [1957] 2 Q.B. 154) and it seems that there is in fact no particular demand for such a right of recovery: Law Com. No. 56, paras. 142–150, 158.

[30] *Hussain* v. *New Taplow Paper Mills Ltd.* [1988] A.C. 514. It may, therefore, be critical whether the employment continues, for if it does not the continuing payment is presumably a "pension" under *Parry* v. *Cleaver*. See also *Cunningham* v. *Harrison* [1973] Q.B. 942.

[31] On the basis that they are equivalent to charitable payments. *Quaere* as to the correctness of the course adopted in *Dennis* v. *L.P.T.B.* [1948] 1 All E.R. 779 of requiring the plaintiff to give an undertaking that he would reimburse his employer out of the damages: *cf.* the law on gratuitous services, *post*, p. 626.

[32] "The concept of public benevolence provided by the state is one I find difficult to comprehend": *Westwood* v. *Secretary of State for Employment* [1985] A.C. 20, 43, *per* Lord Bridge. *cf. Tremil* v. *Ernest W. Gibson & Partners* (1984) 272 E.G. 68.

[33] *Parsons* v. *B.N.M. Laboratories Ltd.* [1964] 1 Q.B. 94; *Westwood* v. *Secretary of State for Employment* [1985] A.C. 20 (not personal injury cases).

[34] *Lincoln* v. *Hayman* [1982] 1 W.L.R. 488 (pre-trial only: as the Pearson Commission pointed out (Vol. 1, para. 494) the damages awarded will go in reduction or extinguishment of such benefit after trial).

[35] *Gaskill* v. *Preston* [1981] 3 All E.R. 427.

[36] *Hodgson* v. *Trapp* [1988] 3 W.L.R. 1281 (deductible from damages for cost of care).

[37] *Palfrey* v. *G.L.C.* [1985] I.C.R. 437. Since this replaced the former short-term sickness benefit which fell under the 1948 Act plaintiffs are worse off. An income tax rebate, though hardly a "benefit," is deductible: *Hartley* v. *Sandholme Iron Co.* [1975] Q.B. 600.

[38] *Hewson* v. *Downs* [1970] 1 Q.B. 73.

[39] *Wilson* v. *N.C.B.* 1981 S.L.T. 67 (H.L.); *Colledge* v. *Bass Mitchells & Butler Ltd.* [1988] I.C.R. 125. Note that in both cases the employer was defendant to the tort claim. The plaintiff is apparently not entitled to compensation for the fact that in a new employment he will have to build up redundancy rights from scratch. *Sed quaere?*

since *Parry* v. *Cleaver*, moved a good way towards deductibility on all fronts but the courts can do nothing about the position under the 1948 Act, which represents the compromise come to in the infancy of the welfare state. The Pearson Commission regarded this as not only inequitable but wasteful but the effect of full deductibility on plaintiffs with modest pre-accident incomes would be to sharply reduce the value of their tort claims, which puts political difficulties in the way of implementation.[40]

(e) **Expenses.** The plaintiff is entitled to the cost of medical and similar services which he reasonably incurs as a result of his injuries,[41] and it is enacted that in determining the reasonableness of any expenses the possibility of avoiding them by making use of the National Health Service is to be disregarded.[42] Damages under this head may be awarded in respect of both past[43] and prospective expenses and may include not only the cost of medical treatment and attendance but all such matters as increased living expenses if, *e.g.* the plaintiff has to live in a special institution because of his injuries[44] or to be supplied with special equipment[45] or, presumably, has to adhere to a special and expensive diet.[46] In serous cases it is now the practice to present very detailed schedules of future expenses and awards under this head can be very large indeed, often much larger than those for loss of earnings.[47] But the financial detriment of a divorce resulting from the injury is, on policy grounds too remote.[48] Transport costs to and from hospital may similarly be recovered.

Care must be taken to avoid duplication of damages where a claim for the cost of future medical care is combined with a claim for loss of earnings. The proper course is to make a full award in respect of loss of earnings but deduct from the cost of care award that element of care which may be described as "domestic"[49]: food, laundry and so on. The balance is the expense which is properly attributable to the tort.

[40] See Cmnd. 7054, Vol. 1, Chap. 13. At the time of writing a proposal is under consideration to alter the present system by requiring the tortfeasor to reimburse the state for social security payments. See *Legal Action*, May 1988, p. 3. In view of the potential administrative costs this is surprising (*cf. supra*, n. 29, and *infra*, n. 42).
[41] See *Cunningham* v. *Harrison* [1975] Q.B. 942.
[42] Law Reform (Personal Injuries) Act 1948, s.2(4). If the plaintiff in fact receives treatment under the National Health Service he cannot claim for what private treatment would have cost: *Harris* v. *Brights Asphalt Contractors Ltd.* [1963] 1 Q.B. 617, 635, *per* Slade J. There is, however, no effective means of preventing the plaintiff claiming that he intends to contract for private treatment and then utilising the N.H.S. The Pearson Commission recommended (Cmnd. 7054, Vol. 1, para. 342) that private medical expenses should only be recoverable if it was reasonable on medical grounds to incur them. During debates on the Administration of Justice Bill 1982 the government said it would consult as to the desirability of giving the National Health Service a right to claim against the tortfeasor for the cost of medical services. For a limited provision of this nature, see the Road Traffic Act 1988, s.157, 158.
[43] Past expenses constitute special damage, which should be pleaded specifically.
[44] *Shearman* v. *Folland* [1950] 2 K.B. 43; *Oliver* v. *Ashman* [1962] 2 Q.B. 210; *Cutts* v. *Chumley* [1967] 1 W.L.R. 742. For the position where the plaintiff purchases more suitable accommodation, see *George* v. *Pinnock* [1973] 1 W.L.R. 118; *Roberts* v. *Johnston, The Times*, April 15, 1988.
[45] *S.* v. *Distillers (Biochemicals) Ltd.* [1970] 1 W.L.R. 114; *Povey* v. *Governors of Royal School* [1970] 1 All E.R. 841.
[46] Munkman, *Damages for Personal Injury and Death*, p. 79.
[47] *e.g. Housecroft* v. *Burnett* [1986] 1 All E.R. 332. (£178,000); *Leon Seng Tan* v. *Bunnage* (1986) Kemp & Kemp, Vol. 2, p. 1012/2 (£287,000).
[48] *Pritchard* v. *J.H. Cobden Ltd.* [1988] Fam. 22.
[49] *Lim* v. *Camden Area Health Authority* [1980] A.C. 174.

It may happen that services for which the plaintiff would otherwise have to pay are rendered by a relative or friend to whom the plaintiff incurs no legal obligation, or such a person may incur expenses on behalf of the plaintiff, as by paying for medical treatment. The question then arises whether damages may be recovered in respect of such services or expenses. For this purpose we must draw a distinction between claims by the relative or friend and by the plaintiff himself. At one time claims by certain close relatives might be based upon the ancient actions for loss of services but these were all abolished from the beginning of 1983.[50] There may still be a basis for recovery by a relative based upon a legal duty to incur the expenses for the victim's benefit,[51] but whether this is so usually matters comparatively little in view of the generous rules which now prevail with regard to recovery by the plaintiff himself. These stem from *Donnelly* v. *Joyce*[52] where the plaintiff's mother gave up employment to nurse him. In allowing the *plaintiff* to recover in respect of her lost wages the Court of Appeal said there need be no legal[53] or "moral" obligation to reimburse the third party:

"The plaintiff's loss . . . is not the expenditure of money to . . . pay for the nursing attention. His loss is the existence of the need for . . . those missing services, the value of which for purposes of damages—for the purpose of the ascertainment of the amount of his loss—is the proper and reasonable cost of supplying these needs. . . . So far as the defendant is concerned, the loss is not someone else's loss. It is the plaintiff's loss."[54]

There is no hard-and-fast rule for the sum recoverable under this head. Where the relative has given up paid employment the lost wages should certainly be recoverable, provided they do not exceed the commercial rate for the services. In other cases the sum may be less than the commercial rate but should be enough to ensure that the relative gets a reasonable recompense and the court should bear in mind the possibility that the relative may not be able to provide care indefinitely.[55] There is no doubt that *Donnelly* v.

---

[50] Administration of Justice Act 1982, s.2. There was no requirement that the relative or his loss be foreseeable.

[51] *Best* v. *Samuel Fox & Co. Ltd.* [1952] A.C. 716, 733; *Kirkham* v. *Boughey* [1958] 2 Q.B. 338, 342. The nature of this right, whether it exists in tort or in quasi-contract, seems never to have been considered. There are difficulties in either approach, but on the whole it is thought that the quasi-contractual explanation is the better. *Receiver for Metropolitan Police District* v. *Croydon Corp.* [1957] 2 Q.B. 154 may be distinguished from the situation now under consideration on the ground that in that case the plaintiff incurred no additional expenditure as a result of the tort whereas the medical expenses incurred by the relative would not have been incurred if the victim had not been injured. *cf.* Street, *op. cit.*, p. 224.

[52] [1974] Q.B. 454; Jolowicz [1974] C.L.J. 40; *Griffiths* v. *Kerkemeyer* (1977) 15 A.L.R. 387.

[53] The device had sometimes been adopted of the plaintiff and the third party making a contract for payment by the plaintiff: *Haggar* v. *de Placido* [1972] 1 W.L.R. 76. Despite the contrary suggestion of Lord Denning M.R. in *Cunningham* v. *Harrison* [1973] Q.B. 942, it seems clear from *Donnelly* v. *Joyce* that in the absence of contract there is no way in which the victim could be compelled to reimburse his benefactor out of damages received: *Housecroft* v. *Burnett* [1986] 1 All E.R. 332.

[54] [1974] Q.B. 454, 462. See also *McAll* v. *Brooks* [1984] R.T.R. 99.

[55] *Housecroft* v. *Burnett* [1986] 1 All E.R. 332 (£3,000 p.a., against commercial rate of £3,640 p.a.).

Joyce extends to expenses reasonably incurred for the plaintiff's benefit,[56] including visits which may assist in the plaintiff's recovery.[57]

Where a person rendered unpaid household services before the accident but is disabled from doing so, there can be no recovery for loss of earnings. However, it is now the law, by a principle analogous to that in *Donnelly* v. *Joyce*, that he or she may recover as damages the value of substitute services.[58] The action for loss of services formerly allowed a *husband* to claim for loss of his wife's domestic services but the action was anachronistic in form and was abolished by the Administration of Justice Act 1982; the emergence of the principle that the victim may claim in her own right rendered any statutory substitute unnecessary.

(f) Other pecuniary loss. The heads of damage so far mentioned are not exhaustive, nor can an exhaustive list be given, for the plaintiff is entitled to damages for any item of loss he may have suffered provided only that it is not too remote. The following examples provide some indication, however, of the kinds of loss that may have to be considered in any given case. If his employer provided board and lodging[59]; or a car available for private use[60] and he has to give up his employment, the plaintiff may recover the value of those items as well as his actual loss of earnings, and if he has to give up a pensionable employment he can recover for any consequent loss of pension rights.[61] In professions where reputation is significant, damages may be awarded for loss of opportunity of enhancing that reputation.[62] On a less material level, a woman may recover damages for the reduction of her prospects of marriage, which is an item of pecuniary as well as non-pecuniary loss, but it must be borne in mind that if she had married that might have reduced her earning capacity for a time. Rather than make an addition to one side of the equation and a balancing deduction on the other[63] it may be better simply to ignore marriage altogether.[64] In cases of ineffective sterilisation it has been held that there is no objection of public policy to awarding the cost of upbringing of a normal child.[65] Even a person's hobbies have to be considered.[66] If the plaintiff had a profitable hobby which he can no longer

---

[56] [1979] Q.B. 425, 462. The mother in *Donnelly* v. *Joyce* incurred travelling expenses in visiting the plaintiff in hospital and the cost of special socks and boots for the plaintiff, but the defendant did not dispute these items.

[57] *cf. Richardson* v. *Schultz* (1980) 25 S.A.S.R. 1 (no recovery where victim unconscious).

[58] *Daly* v. *General Steam Navigation Ltd.* [1981] 1 W.L.R. 120.

[59] *Liffen* v. *Watson* [1940] 1 K.B. 556. It is immaterial that a relative provides the plaintiff with free accommodation and food: *ibid.*

[60] *Clay* v. *Pooler* [1982] 3 All E.R. 570 (a fatal accident case).

[61] *Judd* v. *Hammersmith etc. Hospital Board* [1960] 1 W.L.R. 328; *Parry* v. *Cleaver* [1970] A.C. 1.

[62] Kemp and Kemp, *op. cit.*, Vol. 1, pp. 1015–1016.

[63] As was done in *Moriarty* v. *McCarthy* [1978] 1 W.L.R. 155.

[64] *Hughes* v. *McKeown* [1985] 1 W.L.R. 963; approved in *Housecroft* v. *Burnett* [1986] 1 All E.R. 332 in so far as the loss of earnings multiplicand is reasonably equivalent to the economic support of the never-to-be spouse. *cf. Aloni* v. *Nat. West Bank*, Kemp & Kemp, Vol. 2, p. 1212. In *Lampert* v. *Eastern National Omnibus Co.* [1954] 1 W.L.R. 1047 it was accepted in principle that if a woman's husband leaves her because of disfigurement suffered in an accident this is a compensable head of damage. But it is hard to see how this can survive *Pritchard* v. *J.H. Cobden, supra*, n. 48, even though that case concerned a male plaintiff and was concerned only with the financial consequences of divorce.

[65] *Thake* v. *Maurice* [1986] Q.B. 644; *Emeh* v. *Kensington, etc., A.H.A.* [1985] Q.B. 1012.

[66] *i.e.* apart from their relevance to the claim for loss of amenities, *ante*, pp. 611–614.

pursue, or if, for example, he formerly tended his own garden and now has to employ another to do it for him, he has suffered a loss for which he is entitled to compensation.[67]

(3) *Interest on damages for personal injury*

Although there is now power in certain circumstances to order an interim payment on account of damages[68] it is obvious that there will always be a lapse of time between the injury and the payment of damages, and that frequently the plaintiff will have to wait a considerable time until his claim has been determined and the damages found due to him are paid. For many years the court had a discretionary power to award interest but this is now mandatory in an action for personal injuries in which the plaintiff recovers more than £200, unless the court is satisfied that there are special reasons why interest should not be given.[69] Guidelines to the awarding of interest were first laid down in *Jefford* v. *Gee*[70] but present practice is to be found mainly in the decisions of the House of Lords in *Cookson* v. *Knowles*[71], *Pickett* v. *British Rail Engineering Ltd.*,[72] and *Wright* v. *British Railways Board*.[73] In fatal accident claims the pecuniary loss up to the date of the trial should carry interest at half the short-term interest rates current during that period,[74] but no interest should be awarded upon future pecuniary loss because that loss has not yet been sustained.[75] In personal injury cases pecuniary loss should be treated in the same way as in fatal accident cases.[76] As to non-pecuniary loss interest is to be awarded,[77] but only at the moderate rate of 2 per cent.[78] The reason for this low rate is that damages for non-pecuniary loss will be awarded at the rates prevailing at the time of the trial, thus covering any intervening fall in the value of money. What the plaintiff has therefore lost by late receipt of his damages under this head is only that element of modern interest rates which truly represent the "use value" of money.[79]

---

[67] Street, *op. cit.*, p. 58.
[68] *Post*, p. 629.
[69] Supreme Court Act 1981, s.35A (added by Administration of Justice Act 1982) replacing s.22 of the Administration of Justice Act 1969.
[70] [1970] 2 Q.B. 130.
[71] [1979] A.C. 556. The statements in *Cookson* v. *Knowles* are not rigid rules of law, but guidelines which may be departed from in appropriate circumstances: [1979] A.C. 556, 566, 578, 579.
[72] [1980] A.C. 136.
[73] [1983] 2 A.C. 773.
[74] These were as high as 15 per cent. during 1980 and 1982.
[75] [1979] A.C. 556; *Thompson* v. *Faraoni* [1979] 1 W.L.R. 1157; *cf. Ruby* v. *Marsh* (1975) 132 C.L.R. 642.
[76] *Jefford* v. *Gee, supra*; *Cookson* v. *Knowles* [1977] Q.B. 913 (on appeal, [1979] A.C. 556). There may be cases in which the award should be at the full, not the half rate: *Ichard* v. *Frangoulis* [1977] 1 W.L.R. 556.
[77] *Pickett* v. *British Rail Engineering Ltd., supra*.
[78] *Wright* v. *B.R.B., supra*.
[79] And that is about 2 per cent., the balance of modern interest rates representing "risk" (primarily inflation). The Court of Appeal in *Birkett* v. *Hayes* [1982] 1 W.L.R. 816 would have set the use value at 4 per cent., but still arrived as a final figure of 2 per cent. because of the notional tax liability on such damages had they been awarded earlier, and the uncertainty about their amount until the court assessed them. The court may abridge the period during which interest is payable if the plaintiff unjustifiably delays bringing the case to trial. For examples of plaintiffs being deprived of interest because of delay, see *Pritchard* v. *J.H. Cobden Ltd.* [1988] Fam. 22 and *Spittle* v. *Bunney* [1988] 1 W.L.R. 847.

(4) *Provisional damages*

We have already seen that much of the difficulty surrounding the assessment of damages for personal injury stems from the principle that damages are to be assessed on a once-for-all, lump sum basis and that there are difficulties in moving to a system of reviewable periodical payments. However, the principle is not without exceptions. The issue of damages may be postponed to that of liability[80] and there is power to make an interim award of damages where the court is satisfied that the plaintiff will obtain a substantial award at trial.[81] Perhaps more fundamental are the provisions of section 32A of the Supreme Court Act 1981,[82] which came into force on July 1, 1985. This applies to an action for personal injuries in which there is proved or admitted to be a chance[83] that at some time in the future the injured person will, as a result of the defendant's tort,[84] develop some serious disease or suffer some serious deterioration in his physical or mental condition.[85] In such cases[86] the court has power to make a provisional award, *i.e.* to award damages on the assumption that the plaintiff will not suffer the disease or deterioration but with power to award further damages if and when he does. Obviously, this procedure is only of use in those cases where the risk of deterioration in the plaintiff's condition is appreciated before judgment or settlement.

LOSS OF OR DAMAGE TO PROPERTY[87]

As we have seen, the basic principle for the assessment of damages is that there should be *restitutio in integrum*,[88] and in cases of loss of or damage to property this principle can be more fully applied than in cases of personal injury. It is, in fact, the dominant rule to which the subsidiary rules which follow must conform.[89] In working out these subsidiary rules the courts have been mainly concerned with cases involving ships, but the rules are the same in Admiralty and under the common law.[90]

Loss

Where property is totally destroyed as a result of the defendant's tort the

---

[80] R.S.C., Ord. 33 and *Coenen* v. *Payne* [1974] 1 W.L.R. 984.

[81] R.S.C., Ord. 29.

[82] Introduced by s.6 of the Administration of Justice Act 1982. See Brennan, *Provisional Damages.*

[83] Presumably there is a difference between a case where there is a "chance" and one where the judge is satisfied that a consequence will probably occur, though of course it may not.

[84] The court is only relieved of the necessity of assessing a chance in this type of case. If, *e.g.* the defendant contends that the damages should be small because a pre-existing disease may cause the plaintiff to die prematurely the court must assess the risk and discount accordingly.

[85] *e.g.* where the plaintiff, as a result of blood contamination, becomes HIV positive?

[86] For procedure, see *Practice Direction* [1985] 1 W.L.R. 961; R.S.C., Ord. 37, r. 8.

[87] For the measure of damages in conversion, see *ante,* pp. 490–493.

[88] *Ante,* pp. 608–609.

[89] *Liesbosch Dredger* v. *SS. Edison* [1933] A.C. 449, 463, *per* Lord Wright.

[90] *Admiralty Commissioners* v. *SS. Susquehanna* [1926] A.C. 655, 661, *per* Viscount Dunedin. An English court in an action of tort may give judgment in the currency in which the loss was sustained: *The Despina R.* [1979] A.C. 685; *Hoffman* v. *Sofaer* [1982] 1 W.L.R. 1350 (personal injuries).

normal measure of damage is its value[91] at the time and place of the destruction, and at common law this was so even if the plaintiff had only a limited interest in the property destroyed.[92] In principle the plaintiff is entitled to such a sum of money as would enable him to purchase a replacement in the market at the prices prevailing at the date of destruction[93] or as soon thereafter as is reasonable.[94] If the plaintiff can himself manufacture a replacement at less cost than market value (as might be the case, for example, with drugs, where most of the cost is attributable to research and development) he is nevertheless entitled to recover the market value.[95] Where no precise equivalent is available the plaintiff may be allowed a recovery which exceeds the amount he could have obtained by selling the property,[96] but the cost of producing an exact replacement will be refused where it is well in excess of the value of what was destroyed and a reasonable substitute is available.[97] Merely to enable the plaintiff to acquire a replacement, however, will often be insufficient to effect a full *restitutio in integrum*, and he may recover consequential damages which are not too remote, such as the reasonable cost of hire of a substitute until a replacement can be bought.[98] When the property destroyed is used by the plaintiff in the course of his business then loss of business profits may come into the account. Speaking of destruction of a ship, Lord Wright said that the "true rule seems to be that the measure of damages in such cases is the value of the ship to her owner as a going concern at the time and place of the loss. In assessing that value regard must naturally be had to her pending engagements, either profitable or the reverse."[99] In *Liesbosch Dredger* v. *SS. Edison*[1] the plaintiff's dredger, which they were using in the course of contract work at Patras Harbour, was sunk by the negligence of the defendants. It was held that they were entitled to recover the market price of a comparable dredger, the cost of adapting the new dredger and transporting it to Patras, and compensation for disturbance in the carrying out of their contract from the date of the loss until the new dredger could reasonably have been available in Patras.

As Lord Wright pointed out in *Liesbosch Dredger* v. *SS. Edison*, in assessing the value of a ship as a going concern, care must be taken to avoid

---

[91] For the difficulties involved in the concept of value, see Street, *op. cit.*, pp. 188–203. In *Millar* v. *Candy* (1981) 38 A.L.R. 299 (Federal Court of Australia) the plaintiff failed to recover the amount by which his liability under a hire-purchase agreement exceeded the value of the property.

[92] *The Winkfield* [1902] P. 42. For the effect of the Torts (Interference with Goods) Act 1977, see p. 481, *ante*.

[93] *Liesbosch Dredger* v. *S.S. Edison* [1933] A.C. 449; Weir, *Casebook on Tort* (6th ed.), p. 563.

[94] See *post*, p. 634.

[95] *Smith Kline & French Laboratories Ltd.* v. *Long* [1989] 1 W.L.R. 1.

[96] *Clyde Navigation Trustees* v. *Bowring* (1929) 34 Ll.L.R. 319. If the destroyed article had a substantial "life expectancy" and there are no second-hand ones available, the defendant may have to pay the full cost of a new replacement: *Bacon* v. *Cooper (Metals) Ltd.* [1982] 1 All E.R. 397.

[97] *Ucktos* v. *Mazetta* [1956] 1 Lloyd's Rep. 209.

[98] *Moore* v. *D.E.R. Ltd.* [1971] 1 W.L.R. 1476; *cf. Watson Norrie* v. *Shaw* (1967) 111 S.J. 117. In a road accident case the plaintiff may recover the unused portion of his premium which he forfeits on making a claim: *Patel* v. *London Transport Executive* [1981] R.T.R. 29. See also *Ironfield* v. *Eastern Gas Board* [1964] 1 W.L.R. 1125 ("no-claim" bonus).

[99] *Liesbosch Dredger* v. *SS. Edison* [1933] A.C. 449, 463–464; *Jones* v. *Port of London Authority* [1954] 1 Lloyd's Rep. 489 (lorry).

[1] [1933] A.C. 449. See *ante*, pp. 148–150, where the case is considered from the point of view of remoteness of damage. The plaintiffs' claim for the cost of hire of a substitute dredger failed because this damage flowed from their own impecuniosity.

awarding damages twice over. The market value of a profit-earning chattel such as a ship will normally recognise that the chattel will be used in a profit-earning capacity and the actual loss of prospective freights or other profits cannot, therefore, simply be added to that market value.[2] What is needed, it may be suggested, is a recognition in the assessment of the damages of the difference between the profit-earning potential of a ship without any engagement but with the chance or probability of making a profit, which will be reflected in the market value, and the actual profits which would have been made by the plaintiff's ship had it not been destroyed.[3] Nevertheless, if a ship is actually under charter at the time of her loss or has charters which would have commenced shortly thereafter, the loss of those charters may be allowed in some cases[4] as damages for loss of use of the ship from the time of its destruction until the time when it could reasonably be replaced.[5] It is submitted that in deciding whether or not these damages may be added to the market value, the manner in which the market value itself has been determined is of critical importance. If it is determined on the basis that the ship was in any case virtually certain of profitable employment, then nothing may be added for the loss of actual charters,[6] but if the market value does not assume the full employment of the ship then the loss of actual charters must be taken into account.

The defendants cannot rely on the fact that the plaintiff is entitled to claim on an insurance policy[7], nor will gifts by third parties to relieve the plaintiff's loss reduce the defendant's liability.[8]

Damage

Where property is damaged the normal measure of damages is the amount by which its value has been diminished, and in the case of ships and other chattels this will usually be ascertained by reference to the cost of repair.[9] It does not matter that the repairs have not been carried out at the date of the trial,[10] or even that they are never carried out at all, as where a ship is lost from other causes before the repairs are done.[11] The estimated cost of the repairs can be recovered as indicating the amount by which the chattel's

---

[2] *The Llanover* [1947] P. 80.
[3] For this distinction see *The Philadelphia* [1917] P. 101, 108, *per* Swinfen Eady L.J.
[4] *The Kate* [1899] P. 165; *The Racine* [1906] P. 273; *The Philadelphia* [1917] P. 101; *The Fortunity* [1961] 1 W.L.R. 351.
[5] See the explanation of Greer L.J. in *The Arpad* [1934] P. 189, 217; *The Fortunity, supra*; Street, *op. cit.*, p. 195.
[6] *The Llanover* [1947] P. 80.
[7] *McAll* v. *Brooks* [1984] R.T.R. 99; *Dominion Mosaics and Tile Co. Ltd.* v. *Trafalgar Trucking Co. Ltd.* [1989] N.L.J. 364 and see *ante*, p. 623.
[8] *Wollington* v. *State Electricity Commission (No. 2)* [1980] V.R. 91.
[9] *The London Corporation* [1935] P. 70, 77, *per* Greer L.J.; McGregor, *op. cit.*, pp. 684–688. It is irrelevant that the value of the chattel after repair is greater than it was before the damage was caused by reason of the incorporation of new materials in place of old: *The Gazelle* (1844) 2 W.Rob.(Adm.) 279; *The Munster* (1896) 12 T.L.R. 264; *Bacon* v. *Cooper (Metals) Ltd.* [1982] 1 All E.R. 397; and the same is true for land and buildings: *Harbutt's "Plasticine" Ltd.* v. *Wayne Tank and Pump Co. Ltd.* [1970] 1 Q.B. 447; *cf. Udale* v. *Bloomsbury Health Authority* [1983] 2 All E.R. 522, 528.
[10] *The Kingsway* [1918] P. 344.
[11] *The York* [1929] P. 178, 184–185, *per* Scrutton L.J.; *The London Corporation, supra.*

value is reduced. On the other hand, if a ship is damaged while on its way to the breaker's yard it is submitted that the cost of repairing the ship could not be recovered, for that cost would not represent the true reduction in the value of the ship. All that could be recovered would be the diminution, of any, in the value of the ship as scrap.[12] Similarly, if the cost of repairing the chattel exceeds its total value, then, unless the chattel is in some way unique or irreplaceable, no more than its value can be recovered.[13]

In the majority of cases the plaintiff will not only have incurred the cost of repairing his chattel, he will also have been deprived of its use for a period of time and for this loss he is entitled to damages. In the case of a profit-earning chattel (such as a commercial ship) the normal measure of damages will be the loss of profits calculated at the freight rates prevailing during the period of detention of the ship or, where the hire of a substitute is a reasonable way of avoiding such losses, the cost of that hire.[14] However, the measure based upon prevailing freight rates may in the actual case be too high or too low. It will be too high if the ship was operating at a loss at the time of the damage[15] and too low if the damage prevented the ship from fulfilling an actual charter already entered into at favourable rates.[16]

Rather more difficulty arises in the case of non-profit-earning chattels. The weight of the case law is to the effect that the plaintiff is entitled to damages for loss of use of his chattel even though he has suffered no actual pecuniary loss. In *The Mediana*[17] a lightship belonging to the plaintiff harbour board was damaged and replaced by a standby vessel kept by the board for such an emergency but the board was, nevertheless, entitled to damages for loss of use. This principle would seem to extend to a situation where there is no evidence that the plaintiff would have used the chattel, for, as Lord Halsbury L.C. said in *The Mediana*, "supposing a person took away a chair out of my room and kept it for 12 months, could anybody say you had a right to diminish the damages by showing that I did not usually sit in that chair, or that there were plenty of other chairs in the room. The proposition so nakedly stated appears to me to be absurd."[18] There is no reason, therefore, why a person whose motor car is damaged by the negligence of the defendant should not recover damages for loss of use, even though he

---

[12] See *The London Corporation* [1935] P. 70, 77–78, where Greer L.J. seems to have been in two minds on this point. See also *C.R. Taylor (Wholesale) Ltd.* v. *Hepworths Ltd.* [1977] 1 W.L.R. 659 (land). In any event it will be for the defendant to prove that the damage he has caused to the plaintiff's ship has not reduced its value to the plaintiff.

[13] *Darbishire* v. *Warran* [1963] 1 W.L.R. 1067, distinguishing *O'Grady* v. *Westminster Scaffolding Ltd.* [1962] 2 Lloyd's Rep. 238; Weir, *Casebook on Tort* (6th ed.), p. 565.

[14] On what is a reasonable substitute in the case of a motor vehicle, see *Daily Office Cleaning Contractors* v. *Shefford* [1977] R.T.R. 361; *H.L. Motorworks* v. *Alwahbi* [1977] R.T.R. 276 and the cases, *supra*, n. 98. If a substitute is hired and the plaintiff is thereby enabled to make a greater profit than he would have done if his own chattel had never been damaged, credit for this must be given: *The World Beauty* [1969] P. 12, revd. without affecting this point: [1970] P. 144.

[15] *The Bodlewell* [1907] P. 286. See also *SS. Strathfillan* v. *SS. Ikala* [1929] A.C. 196.

[16] *The Argentino* (1889) 14 App.Cas. 519. However, it is not yet finally settled whether this rule is independent of the test of remoteness of damage, *viz.* foreseeability: *ante*, p. 131.

[17] [1900] A.C. 113; Weir, *Casebook on Tort* (6th ed.), p. 562. In *The Greta Holme* [1897] A.C. 596 and *The Marpessa* [1907] A.C. 241 the same plaintiffs recovered damages for loss of the value of the work that would have been done by the vessels, no substitutes being available.

[18] [1900] A.C. 113, 117.

only uses his car for pleasure purposes and has a second car in his garage. Damages for loss of use cannot, of course, be claimed if the loss is not due to the defendant's tort but to some extraneous cause.[19]

A decision that at first may seem to conflict with these principles is *Brandeis Goldschmidt & Co. Ltd.* v. *Western Transport Ltd.*[20] The defendants, claiming a lien, wrongfully detained 42 tons of the plaintiffs' copper. The plaintiffs, in summary proceedings, obtained possession of the copper and claimed damages based on the fall in the price of copper during the period of detention and interest on so much of their overdraft during the same period as was attributable to the purchase. However, since the plaintiffs acquired the copper for processing and not for resale, they could not rely on the fall in market price; and the claim for overdraft interest failed in the absence of evidence that the consignment would have been processed and the proceeds of sale applied to the reduction of the overdraft *during the period of detention*. In the event, therefore, the plaintiffs only recovered £5 as nominal damages. The case should probably not be taken as authority against a more substantial award for loss of use on similar facts,[21] for the plaintiffs in the proceedings leading up to the trial on damages agreed not to seek to rely on any other way of putting their claim.[22]

As to the method of assessing damages for loss of use of a non-profit-earning chattel then the cost of hiring a reasonable substitute will be taken as the measure, if one is in fact hired.[23] If there is no hire the general damages for loss of use will normally be calculated on the basis of interest on the capital value of the damaged chattel plus depreciation and expenses,[24] if any, for the period of non-use.[25] However, it has been said that interest on capital value is not an absolute rule[26] and a standing cost basis of calculation has been adopted.[27]

Land and buildings

The principles considered thus far have been worked out in the context of injuries to chattels; those governing injuries to land and buildings are not fundamentally different though their application must take account of the

---

[19] See *Carslogie SS. Co. Ltd.* v. *Royal Norwegian Government* [1952] A.C. 292, *cf. Admiralty Commissioners* v. *SS. Chekiang* [1926] A.C. 637 (damages for loss of use awarded although plaintiffs took the opportunity, when the ship was in dock, of carrying out other repairs which had not yet become necessary when the damage was caused). See McGregor, *op. cit.*, pp. 785–789.

[20] [1981] Q.B. 864; Tettenborn (1982) 132 N.L.J. 154.

[21] *e.g.* calculated as interest on the value of the goods: see below.

[22] [1981] Q.B. 864, 869. It is, of course, true that *Brandeis Goldschmidt* was an action for what is now called wrongful interference with goods, whereas *The Mediana* and associated cases were actions for negligence involving damage to goods, but it is hard to see why this should lead to a difference in damages. In any case, Lord Halsbury clearly thought the cause of action made no difference—see his example of the chair.

[23] *The Mediana* [1900] A.C. 113, 122, 123. The plaintiff may recover the full commercial cost of hire even if he does not incur that: *McAll* v. *Brooks* [1984] R.T.R. 99.

[24] Such as crew's wages in the case of a ship.

[25] *The Marpessa* [1907] A.C. 241; *Admiralty Commissioners* v. *SS. Susquehanna* [1926] A.C. 637; *The Hebridean Coast* [1961] A.C. 545.

[26] *Admiralty Commissioners* v. *SS. Chekiang, supra*, at pp. 642, 647–649. See also *Admiralty Commissioners* v. *SS. Susquehanna, supra*, at p. 661, where Viscount Dunedin said that these are jury-type questions on which no rigid rules are possible.

[27] *Birmingham Corp.* v. *Sowsbery* (1969) 113 S.J. 577 (bus).

different character of land. Thus, for example, a plaintiff is more likely to recover the cost of reinstatement where this exceeds the diminution in value of his property than he is in the case of chattel: where a factory is burned down it may well be the commercially sensible course to rebuild immediately on the same site rather than remove the business to a different location.[28] Ultimately, however, the reasonableness of the proposed expenditure is the issue so that where the cost of reinstatement is out of all proportion to the diminution in value the latter will be taken as the measure.[29] Again, the court may allow a degree of reinstatement but refuse the plaintiff the extra cost of precise and meticulous restoration which will not increase the utility of the property.[30] The plaintiff may not claim the cost of repairs which exceed diminution in value where he has no intention of having them carried out.[31]

What has been said above represents a broad principle which may be departed from in particular contexts. For example, the usual measure of damages for negligent survey (where the action will commonly lie concurrently in contract and tort) is the difference between the price paid by the plaintiff and the actual market value of the property, not the cost of putting the property in the condition described in the report[32]; and in some cases of wrongful interference with land the courts have shown signs of a restitutionary approach by assessing damages so as to deprive the defendant of the fruits of his wrong.[33]

The rapid inflation of the 1970s brought into prominence, particularly in the context of damage to buildings, the question of the date on which damages were to be assessed, for a judgment representing the cost of repair at the time of the wrong, even with interest, would be unlikely to be sufficient to cover the work when the action came on for trial.[34] While there may still be a general rule that damages for tort are to be assessed at the time when the tort is committed,[35] that rule is subject to exceptions and in a repair case the applicable principle is that the date for assessment of damages is the time when, having regard to all relevant circumstances, repairs can first

---

[28] See *Harbutt's "Plasticine" Ltd.* v. *Wayne Tank and Pump Co. Ltd.* [1907] 1 Q.B. 447, 467, 472, pointing out that the market in land and buildings is more limited and inflexible than in, *e.g.* secondhand cars; *Ward* v. *Cannock Chase D.C.* [1986] Ch. 546. Contrast *Dominion Mosaics and Tile Co. Ltd.* v. *Trafalgar Trucking Co. Ltd.* [1989] N.L.J. 364 (rebuilding impracticable; value of destroyed building £60,000; £390,000 cost of lease of new premises recoverable since this was a reasonable way of mitigating loss of profits).

[29] *Jones* v. *Gooday* (1841) 8 M. & W. 146; *Lodge Holes Colliery Co. Ltd.* v. *Wednesbury Corp.* [1908] A.C. 323; *Taylor* v. *Auto Trade Supply Ltd.* [1972] N.Z.L.R. 102; *Munnelly* v. *Calcon Ltd.* [1978] I.R. 387.

[30] *Dodd Properties Ltd.* v. *Canterbury City Council* [1980] 1 W.L.R. 433, 441 (on appeal, without affecting this point, *ibid.* at p. 447); *Ward* v. *Cannock Chase D.C.* [1986] Ch. 546.

[31] *Perry* v. *Sidney Phillips & Son* [1982] 1 W.L.R. 1297 (though it is not certain that the Court of Appeal would have upheld an award based on cost of repairs even if the plaintiff had intended to carry them out); *Hole & Son (Sayers Common)* v. *Harrisons* [1973] 1 W.L.R. 345.

[32] *Perry* v. *Sidney Phillips & Son* [1982] 1 W.L.R. 1297. But the plaintiff may recover damages for the inconvenience of living elsewhere while repair work is done.

[33] *Bracewell* v. *Appleby* [1975] Ch. 408; *Strand Electric Engineering Co. Ltd.* v. *Brisford Entertainments Ltd.* [1952] 2 Q.B. 246 (goods).

[34] In *Dodd Properties Ltd.* v. *Canterbury City Council* [1980] 1 W.L.R. 433 the cost of repair when the damage was done in 1968 was £10,817. At judgment, 10 years later, it was £30,327. Interest on a judgment at the 1968 cost would have amounted to about £5,500.

[35] *Miliangos* v. *George Frank (Textiles) Ltd.* [1976] A.C. 443, 468.

reasonably be undertaken,[36] and in determining this question it is proper to pay regard to the plaintiff's financial position.[37]

Consequential losses such as loss of rental or profits, may also be recovered.[38]

PART II. OTHER REMEDIES

SELF-HELP

Self-help is apt to be a perilous remedy, for the person exercising it is probably the worst judge of exactly how much he is entitled to do without exceeding his rights.[39] Still, it is well recognised as a remedy for certain torts. A person wrongfully imprisoned may escape. A trespasser,[40] or a trespassing animal, may be expelled with no more force than is reasonable; and it has been held that a building set up by a trespasser may be pulled down, though if it is inhabited notice is necessary.[41] By the right of distress damage feasant, chattels wrongfully on the land may be detained as a means of compelling the owner to pay damages, but the right is probably confined to cases where actual damage has been caused.[42]

Goods wrongfully taken may be peaceably retaken. This form of self-help has already been considered.[43]

Abatement of nuisance

A nuisance may be abated, *i.e.* removed. But this is a remedy which the law does not favour, because, as Sir Matthew Hale said, "this many times occasions tumults and disorders,"[44] and its exercise may destroy any right of action in respect of the nuisance.[45] In the first place, before abatement is

---

[36] *Dodd Properties Ltd.* v. *Canterbury City Council, supra.*

[37] *Ibid.* For problems caused by the supposed rule that damages may not be recovered if they are caused by the plaintiff's impecuniosity, see *ante*, p. 148.

[38] *Rust* v. *Victoria Graving Dock Co.* (1887) 36 Ch.D. 113; *Dodd Properties Ltd.* v. *Canterbury City Council, supra.*

[39] *R.* v. *Chief Constable of Devon and Cornwall, ex p. C.E.G.B.* [1982] Q.B. 458, 473. This case contains a review of the powers and duties of the police where a landowner or person with rights over land exercises the right of self-help.

[40] But if the trespasser is in a building or land ancillary to a building and the occupier uses or threatens violence to secure entry, the occupier *may* be guilty of an offence under s.6 of the Criminal Law Act 1977: see further, *ante*, p. 370.

[41] *Perry* v. *Fitzhowe* (1846) 8 Q.B. 757; *Davies* v. *Williams* (1851) 16 Q.B. 546; *Jones* v. *Jones* (1862) 1 H. & C. 1. These are cases of buildings erected on commons, but Winfield thought the law was the same whatever the nature of the land. *cf. Burling* v. *Read* (1850) 11 Q.B. 904 and see *Lane* v. *Capsey* [1891] 3 Ch. 411, 415–416. s.6 of the Criminal Law Act 1977, *supra*, could only apply if it could be said that the defendant used or threatened violence *for the purpose of securing entry* to the building, which seems a little strained.

[42] Clerk and Lindsell, *Torts* (16th ed.), para. 8–27; *Controlled Parking Systems Ltd.* v. *Sedgewick* [1980] 4 W.W.R. 425 *cf. Jamieson's Tow & Salvage Ltd.* v. *Murray* [1984] 2 N.Z.L.R. 144 (damage includes cost of removal).The right of distress over trespassing animals was abolished and replaced with a statutory remedy: *ante*, p. 462.

[43] *Ante*, pp. 487–490.

[44] *De Portubus Maris*, Pt. 2, Chap. VII.

[45] *Lagan Navigation Co.* v. *Lambeg, etc. Bleaching Co. Ltd.* [1927] A.C. 226, 244, *per* Lord Atkinson. But *cf.* Clerk and Lindsell, *Torts* (16th ed.), para. 8–19.

attempted, notice should be given to the offending party to remedy the nuisance, unless it be one of omission and the security of lives and property does not allow time for notice,[46] or unless the nuisance can be removed by the abator without entry on the wrongdoer's land: I may lop the branches of my neighbour's tree which project over or into my land without notice to him,[47] although I must not appropriate what I sever.[48] Secondly, unnecessary damage must not be done: *e.g.* tearing up a picture which is publicly exhibited and which is a libel on oneself is too drastic, even though it be a nuisance.[49] Thirdly, where there are two ways of abatement, the less mischievous should be followed, unless it would inflict some wrong on an innocent third party or on the public.[50]

INJUNCTION

An injunction is a judgment or order of the court restraining the commission or continuance of some wrongful act, or the continuance of some wrongful omission. Originally only the Court of Chancery could issue an injunction, but now any Division of the High Court may do so in any case in which it appears to the court to be "just and convenient."[51] This does not mean that the court has a free hand to restrain conduct of which it disapproves, for the plaintiff must have some cause of action (whether for a tort or in protection of some legal or equitable right[52]) against the defendant, for if the law were otherwise "every judge would need to be issued with a portable palm tree."[53] Hence, while there may be jurisdiction to restrain the dissipation of the proceeds of crime, there is none (apart from statute[54]) to restrain the dissipation of the profits of those proceeds.[55]

Injunctions are generally sought against such torts as nuisance, continuing or repeated trespass or interference with contract[56] but there is no theoretical reason why an injunction should not be issued to restrain the repetition

---

[46] *Lagan Navigation Case, supra.*

[47] *Lemmon* v. *Webb* [1895] A.C. 1. Roots of a tree projecting into one's soil from neighbouring land may be sawn off, but it is not clear whether notice to the neighbouring land occupier must first be given. *Butler* v. *Standard Telephones, etc. Ltd.* [1940] 1 K.B. 399.

[48] *Mills* v. *Brooker* [1919] 1 K.B. 555.

[49] *Du Bost* v. *Beresford* (1801) 2 Camp. 511, where the point was left open, but it may probably be regarded as settled now.

[50] Blackburn J. in *Roberts* v. *Rose* (1865) L.R. 1 Ex. 82, 89; adopted by Lord Atkinson in *Lagan Navigation Co.* v. *Lambeg, etc. Bleaching Co. Ltd.* [1927] A.C. 226, 244–246, where the abators satisfied none of these three conditions.

[51] Supreme Court Act 1981, s.37. An injunction can only be granted in a county court if it is ancillary to a claim for damages: *R.* v. *Cheshire County Court Judge* [1921] 2 K.B. 694 (for statutory exceptions see the Domestic Violence and Matrimonial Proceedings Act 1976 and the County Courts Act 1984, s.22).

[52] *e.g.* an injunction may be granted to restrain a breach of contract or a breach of confidence. For the possibility that there remains a wider jurisdiction to restrain any "unlawful injury to property," see *ante*, p. 173. An equitable right may embrace a situation where the claimant has some equitable reason (*e.g.* promissory estoppel) why the defendant should not enforce a legal right against him: *British Airways Board* v. *Laker Airways* [1985] A.C. 58.

[53] *Chief Constable of Kent* v. *V.* [1983] Q.B. 34, 45, *per* Donaldson L.J.

[54] Drug Trafficking Act 1986; Criminal Justice Act 1988.

[55] *Chief Constable of Leicestershire* v. *M.* [1988] 3 All E.R. 1015; see also *Associated Newspapers Group plc* v. *Insert Media Ltd.* [1988] 1 W.L.R. 509.

[56] For injunctions in the context of trade disputes, see *ante*, p. 534.

or continuation of a tort of any kind.[57] Like other equitable remedies, the issue of an injunction is in the discretion of the court and the remedy cannot be demanded as of right. However, in the context of prohibitory injunctions (*i.e.* those ordering the defendant to desist from wrongful conduct[58]) it would be wrong to think that a plaintiff who makes out interference with his rights will face any particular difficulty in getting one. For example, a landowner is prima facie entitled to an injunction to restrain trespass by the defendant in parking his vehicle on the land[59] or running hounds across it[60] or swinging a crane jib through the air above it[61] even though he cannot produce evidence of any particular harm. It is true that an injunction will not be granted where damages are an adequate remedy[62] but this does not mean that the defendant who is willing to pay can demand to buy out the plaintiff's rights. In *Shelfer* v. *City of London Electric Lighting Co.* the operation of the defendant's engines seriously interfered with the enjoyment of the premises of which the plaintiff was occupier. Granting an injunction, Lindley L.J. commented that the Court of Chancery had repudiated the notion that the legislature, in allowing the award of damages in lieu of an injunction "intended to turn that Court into a tribunal for legalising wrongful acts; or in other words, the Court has always protested against the notion that it ought to allow a wrong to continue simply because the wrongdoer is able and willing to pay for the injury he may inflict."[63] Where the injury to the plaintiff is trivial[64] or of a very temporary character the court may content itself with awarding nominal damages. It is not, however, enough that the grant of the injunction will inflict more harm on the defendant than the continuance of the activity will upon the plaintiff.[65] An injunction will also be refused if the plaintiff has acquiesced in the defendant's infringement of his legal rights[66] and, *a fortiori*, if he has actually misled the defendant into believing that he acquiesced.[67] A controversial matter has been the significance of the interest which the public at large may have in the continuance of the defendant's activity. While this is *relevant*[68] there has been strong reluctance to refuse an injunction on this basis. In *Shelfer's* case it was said that

---

[57] See, *e.g. Egan* v. *Egan* [1975] Ch. 218 (injunction to restrain assaults).

[58] For mandatory injunctions, see *post*, p. 639.

[59] *Patel* v. *W.H. Smith (Eziot)* [1987] 1 W.L.R. 853; and see *John Trenberth Ltd.* v. *National Westminster Bank Ltd.* (1979) 39 P. & C.R. 104.

[60] *League against Cruel Sports* v. *Scott* [1986] Q.B. 240.

[61] *Anchor Brewhouse Developments* v. *Berkley House (Docklands Developments)* (1987) 284 E.G. 625, *ante*, p. 364.

[62] *London and Blackwall Ry.* v. *Cross* (1886) 31 Ch.D. 354, 369, *per* Lindley L.J. For the statutory power to award damages in lieu of an injunction, see *post*, p. 640.

[63] [1895] 1 Ch. 287, 315–316. But *cf. Sampson* v. *Hodson-Pressinger* [1981] 3 All E.R. 710, where, on somewhat unusual facts, a *defendant* failed in his attempt to rely on this reasoning.

[64] Best illustrated by attempts to restrain use of the beach or access thereto: *Llandudno U.D.C.* v. *Woods* [1899] 2 Ch. 705; *Behrens* v. *Richards* [1905] 2 Ch. 614. See also *Armstrong* v. *Sheppard and Short Ltd.* [1959] 2 Q.B. 384.

[65] *cf.* the strange case of *Bank of N.Z.* v. *Greenwood* [1984] 1 N.Z.L.R. 525 where glare from the defendant's building amounted to a nuisance which could be abated (*a*) by major work on the building or (*b*) by the plaintiffs installing blinds. Disclaiming any power to award damages in lieu of an injunction, Hardie Boys J. intimated that the installation of blinds at the defendant's expense would satisfy the plaintiff's rights and adjourned the action *sine die*.

[66] *Gaskin* v. *Balls* (1879) 13 Ch.D. 324.

[67] *Armstrong* v. *Sheppard and Short, supra.*

[68] *Wood* v. *Sutcliffe* (1851) 2 Sim.(N.S.) 163; Spry, *Equitable Remedies* (2nd ed.), pp. 375–376.

"the circumstance that the wrongdoer is in some sense a public benefactor ... [has never] been considered a sufficient reason for refusing to protect by injunction an individual whose rights are being persistently infringed. Expropriation, even for a money consideration, is only justifiable when Parliament has sanctioned it." In *Miller* v. *Jackson*,[69] the celebrated case of the village cricket club, two members of the Court of Appeal[70] concluded that the interests of the inhabitants in recreation should prevail over those of the plaintiffs in the enjoyment of their property. Subsequently, however, the Court of Appeal has in *Kennaway* v. *Thompson*[71] reaffirmed and applied the principles of *Shelfer's* case and *Miller* v. *Jackson* should probably be regarded as wrongly decided.[72]

Interlocutory injunction

An injunction which is issued at the conclusion of a trial upon the merits is known as a perpetual injunction, but an injunction may be issued provisionally until the hearing of the case on the merits, when it is known as an interlocutory injunction. The court on an application for an interlocutory injunction does not profess to anticipate the final outcome of the action and since it is always possible that when the case actually comes to trial the defendant may be found to have been in the right after all, the plaintiff may be required, as a condition of the grant of an interlocutory injunction, to give an undertaking in damages, *i.e.* to undertake to pay damages to the defendant for any loss suffered by him while the injunction was in force, should it prove to have been wrongly issued.[73] The principles on which the court acts on an application for an interlocutory injunction are to be found in *American Cyanamid Co.* v. *Ethicon Ltd.*[74] A plaintiff need not establish a prima facie case but merely that there is a "serious question" to be tried.[75] If so, the court must then decide whether the balance of convenience lies in favour of granting or refusing interlocutory relief. The court should consider all the circumstances of the case, particularly whether damages are likely to be an adequate remedy for the plaintiff[76] whether the plaintiff's undertaking in damages gives the defendant adequate protection if the plaintiff fails at the

[69] [1977] Q.B. 966.
[70] Lord Denning M.R. and Cumming-Bruce L.J. The former in fact held the defendants' conduct not actionable at all.
[71] [1981] Q.B. 88. However, the injunction was formulated so as to allow the defendants some scope for the continuation of their noisy activities; and in *Miller* v. *Jackson*, Geoffrey Lane L.J., dissenting, would have suspended an injunction for 12 months to allow the defendants to find an alternative pitch.
[72] See further as to damages and injunctions, Tromans, "Nuisance—Prevention or Payment?" [1982] C.L.J. 87; Burrows, *op. cit.*, pp. 346–358.
[73] In practice the parties often treat the application for an interlocutory injunction as the trial of the action. In cases of great urgency the plaintiff can obtain an interim injunction *ex parte* (*i.e.* in the absence of the defendant) which will remain in force for a few days, until there can be a hearing.
[74] [1975] A.C. 396. Gray, "Interlocutory Injunctions since *Cyanamid*" [1981] C.L.J. 307. The case concerned an application for a prohibitory injunction against patent infringement. An interlocutory injunction may be in mandatory (see below) form, but a stronger case is probably required than for a prohibitory injunction.
[75] *cf. J.T. Stratford & Son Ltd.* v. *Lindley* [1965] A.C. 269, 325, 331, 338, 339, 342–243 and the remarks of Lord Denning M.R. in *Fellowes* v. *Fisher* [1976] Q.B. 122. For trade dispute cases, see *ante*, p. 534.
[76] See, *e.g. University of Oxford* v. *Pergamon Press, The Times*, October 19, 1977; *cf. Lewis* v. *Heffer* [1978] 1 W.L.R. 1061.

trial[77]; and whether the preservation of the status quo is important enough to demand an injunction.[78] Curiously, perhaps, the relative strength of each party's case on the affidavits is only to be considered when the other considerations leave the balance of convenience "even."[79]

The practice in libel cases has not been affected by the *American Cyanamid* case.[80] Interlocutory injunctions in such cases have always been exceedingly rare because of the public interest in freedom of expression[81] and the fact that the question of libel or no libel is peculiarly one for the jury.[82] It seems that the court will never in practice grant one if the defendant intends to plead justification,[83] or fair comment, or qualified privilege,[84] unless it is crystal clear that the defence will fail.[85] If the defendant contends only that the words do not have a defamatory meaning the court should grant an injunction only if it is clear that any jury verdict for the defendant would be perverse.[86] Where the defendants' conduct amounts to conspiracy to injure the special libel rule has no application.[87]

Mandatory injunction

Normally injunctions are prohibitory, they forbid the defendant from persisting in his wrongful conduct, but the court has power also to grant a mandatory injunction by virtue of which the defendant is actually ordered to take positive action to rectify the consequences of what he has already done. In *Redland Bricks Ltd.* v. *Morris*[88] the defendants' excavations on their own land had caused part of the plaintiff's land to subside and had endangered part of the remainder. In the county court the plaintiffs recovered damages in respect of the subsidence which had already occurred, and the judge also granted them a mandatory injunction requiring the defendants to restore support to their land, the estimated cost of doing which was very great, and, indeed, actually exceeded the value of the whole of the plaintiff's land. In the House of Lords the defendants' appeal against this injunction was allowed and, while emphasising that the issue of a mandatory injunction is

---

[77] See, *e.g. Laws* v. *Florinplace Ltd.* [1981] 1 All E.R. 659.

[78] See *Hubbard* v. *Pitt* [1976] Q.B. 142.

[79] "I confess that I cannot see how the 'balance of convenience' can be fairly or reasonably considered without taking *some* account as a factor of the relative strength of the parties' cases, but the House of Lords seems to have held that this is only the last resort": *Fellowes* v. *Fisher* [1976] Q.B. 122, 138, *per* Browne L.J.

[80] *Herbage* v. *Pressdram Ltd.* [1984] 1 W.L.R. 1160.

[81] But the libel practice does not override the law of contempt: *Att.-Gen.* v. *News Group Newspapers* [1986] 3 W.L.R. 365.

[82] *Coulson* v. *Coulson* (1887) 3 T.L.R. 846; *Bonnard* v. *Perryman* [1891] 2 Ch. 269. But the Faulks Committee has recommended curtailment of jury trials in defamation cases: *ante*, p. 356. The jury trial reason, however, is not a sufficient explanation because the same rule applies to injurious falsehood: *Bestobell Paint* v. *Bigg* (1975) 119 S.J. 678.

[83] *Khasshoggi* v. *I.P.C. Magazines Ltd.* [1986] 1 W.L.R. 1412.

[84] *Trevor & Sons* v. *P. R. Solomon* (1978) 248 E.G. 779. *Woodward* v. *Hutchings* [1977] 1 W.L.R. 760 (which also involves breach of confidence); *Harakas* v. *Baltic Exchange Ltd.* [1982] 1 W.L.R. 959; *Quartz Hill Consolidated Gold Mining Co.* v. *Beall* (1882) 20 Ch.D. 501.

[85] The plaintiff might be a little more likely to succeed in showing this where the defence was comment or privilege because, for example, it might be clear that the words were not comment or there was no privileged occasion. However, an injunction would still be wholly exceptional.

[86] *Herbage* v. *Times Newspapers Ltd., The Times*, May 1, 1981.

[87] *Gulf Oil* v. *Page* [1987] Ch. 327.

[88] [1970] A.C. 652.

entirely discretionary and that each case depends upon its own circumstances, Lord Upjohn laid down certain general principles.[89] These may be summarised as follows:

1. Damages will not be an adequate remedy for the harm to the plaintiff.[90]

2. If the defendant has acted wantonly or has tried to steal a march on the plaintiff or on the court,[91] then the expense which the issue of a mandatory injunction would cause the defendant to incur is immaterial, but where the defendant has acted reasonably though, in the event, wrongly, the cost of remedying his earlier activities is a most important consideration.[92]

3. If a mandatory injunction is issued, the court must be careful to see that the defendant knows as a matter of fact exactly what he has to do so that he can give proper instructions to contractors for the carrying out of the work.

Quia timet injunction

Normally injunctions are issued only when a tort has already been committed, and, in the case of torts actionable only on proof of damage, it is premature for the plaintiff to seek an injunction before any damage has actually occurred. Where, however, the conduct of the defendant is such that, if it is allowed to continue, substantial damage to the plaintiff is almost bound to occur, the plaintiff may bring a "*quia timet*" action, that is, an action for an injunction to prevent an apprehended legal wrong.[93] The existence of the court's power to grant a *quia timet* injunction is undoubted,[94] but it is not often exercised, for the plaintiff must show both a near certainty that damage will occur[95] and that it is imminent.[96] And even then an injunction will not be issued to compel the defendant to do something which he is willing to do without the intervention of the court.[97]

Damages in lieu of injunction

The Court of Chancery had no power to award damages for torts which brought no profit to the wrongdoer, but by Lord Cairns's Act 1858[98] the court was enabled to award damages either in addition to, or in substitution for, an injunction, and this jurisdiction now applies to the High Court, the power being contained in section 50 of the Supreme Court Act 1981.[99] Such damages are given in full satisfaction not only for all damage already done in

[89] *Ibid.* at pp. 665–667. The other members of the House of Lords agreed with Lord Upjohn's speech.
[90] *Taylor* v. *Auto Trade Supply Ltd.* [1972] N.Z.L.R. 102. This is a general principle applicable to *all* injunctions: [1970] A.C. 652, 655.
[91] See, *e.g. Daniel* v. *Ferguson* [1891] 2 Ch. 27.
[92] *Tollemache & Cobbold Breweries Ltd.* v. *Reynolds* (1983) 268 E.G. 52 (plaintiffs displaying extreme pettiness).
[93] *Redland Bricks Ltd.* v. *Morris* [1970] A.C. 652, 664, *per* Lord Upjohn. In his Lordship's opinion, an action is still *quia timet* even though damage has already occurred, if that damage has been redressed by an award of damages: *ibid.* at p. 665.
[94] For an example, see *Torquay Hotel Co. Ltd.* v. *Cousins* [1969] 2 Ch. 106, 120, *per* Stamp J.
[95] *Att.-Gen.* v. *Nottingham Corporation* [1904] 1 Ch. 673; *Redland Bricks Ltd.* v. *Morris, supra.*
[96] *Lemos* v. *Kennedy Leigh Developments* (1961) 105 S.J. 178; *cf. Hooper* v. *Rogers* [1975] Ch. 43 where the view is expressed that there is no fixed standard of certainty or imminence.
[97] *Bridlington Relay Ltd.* v. *Yorkshire Electricity Board* [1965] Ch. 436.
[98] s.2, Jolowicz, "Damages in Equity—A Study of Lord Cairns's Act" [1975] C.L.J. 224.
[99] The legislative history of the original provision was tortuous: see Jolowicz, *loc. cit.*, pp. 228–230.

the past, but also for all future damage which may occur if the injunction is not granted. To say that damages may be awarded "in substitution for" an injunction is apt to be misleading for it is fairly clear that the power is not confined to cases in which the Court of Chancery before the Act *would* have granted the equitable relief.[1] It may be that the power arises whenever the facts of the case are such as to call into play the exercise of the court's general equitable discretion whether or not to grant an injunction.[2] Damages may be awarded in substitution for an injunction even in a *quia timet* action.[3] This is, in effect, to allow the defendant to purchase the right to commit a tort in the future but, illogical though this may be, it is really no more illogical than the idea, inherent in Lord Cairns's Act itself, that damages can be "adequate" compensation for damage which has not yet occurred, which can be avoided, and to which the plaintiff does not consent.[4] Practical considerations must, however, be taken into account and on practical grounds there may be considerable advantage in awarding a plaintiff damages only, where his probable future damage is likely to be much less than the cost to the defendant of preventing it, provided, of course, that the defendant has acted honestly and without the deliberate intention of committing or continuing to commit an unlawful act. Otherwise there is a danger that proceedings for injunctions will be used by unscrupulous plaintiffs, not to protect their rights, but to extort from defendants sums of money greater in value than any damage that is likely to occur.[5]

Generally, it has been stated to be a "good working rule" that the jurisdiction under the Act should be exercised if it would be oppressive to the defendant to issue an injunction and if the injury to the plaintiff's rights is small, is capable of being estimated in money, and is one which can be adequately compensated by a money payment.[6]

There is little authority on the measure of damages in lieu of an injunction, but the Act also allows the grant of damages in lieu of a decree of specific performance of a contract, and in that context it has been held that the principles of assessment are those which apply generally at common law.[7] Presumably the same applies to damages in lieu of an injunction.

SPECIFIC RESTITUTION OF PROPERTY

Orders for the specific restitution of property may be for the recovery of land

[1] *Isenberg* v. *East India House Estate Co.* (1863) 3 D. & G.J. & S. 263; *City of London Brewery Co.* v. *Tennant* (1873) L.R. 9 Ch.App. 212; *Wroth* v. *Tyler* [1974] Ch. 30 (substitution for specific performance). The contrary is perhaps implied by Lord Upjohn in *Redland Bricks Ltd.* v. *Morris* [1970] A.C. 652 but see Jolowicz, *loc. cit.*, pp. 242–245.

[2] Jolowicz, *loc. cit.*, pp. 241–242; *Hooper* v. *Rogers* [1975] Ch. 43, 48.

[3] *Leeds Industrial Co-operative Society* v. *Slack* [1924] A.C. 851 (the decision was by a bare majority); *Hooper* v. *Rogers* [1975] Ch. 43. There would, of course, be no cause of action at common law.

[4] *Leeds Industrial Co-operative Society Ltd.* v. *Slack, supra*, at pp. 867–868, *per* Lord Sumner, dissenting.

[5] *Colls* v. *Home and Colonial Stores Ltd.* [1904] A.C. 179, 193, *per* Lord Macnaghten.

[6] *Shelfer* v. *City of London Electric Lighting Co.* [1895] 1 Ch. 287, 322, *per* Smith L.J.; applied in *Kennaway* v. *Thompson* [1981] Q.B. 88, *ante*, p. 638. *cf. Fishenden* v. *Higgs and Hill Ltd.* (1935) 152 L.T. 128, 141. The *Shelfer* principles were elaborately considered by the Court of Appeal in the *Redland Bricks* case [1967] 1 W.L.R. 967, but in the House of Lords it was held that no question under Lord Cairns' Act arose: [1970] A.C. 652.

[7] *Johnson* v. *Agnew* [1980] A.C. 367.

or for the recovery of chattels. But whether it is restitution of land or of goods that is sought, the remedies are confined to cases where one man is in possession of another's property and this limits them to torts infringing such possession. They have, therefore, been considered at appropriate points.[8]

[8] *Ante*, pp. 371, 492.

CHAPTER 24

DEATH IN RELATION TO TORT

CONSIDERED merely as a final catastrophe, death does not require a separate chapter in the law of tort, but it does have an important bearing on liability in tort and its legal effects are most conveniently considered in a separate chapter. The death of a person may affect tortious liability in two ways:

1. *It may possibly extinguish liability for a tort.* Here the question for discussion is: "If I have committed a tort against you (not involving your death), and either of us dies, does your right of action survive?"

2. *It may possibly create liability in tort.* Here the question is: "If I cause your death, is that a tort either (*a*) against you, so that your personal representatives can sue me for it; or (*b*) against persons who have an interest in the continuance of your life: *e.g.* your spouse or children?"

DEATH AS EXTINGUISHING LIABILITY

At common law the general rule was that death of either party extinguished any existing cause of action in tort by one against the other. This was due in part to the historical connection of the action of trespass, from which much of our law of tort is derived, with the criminal law[1] and in part to the reference often made to the maxim "*actio personalis moritur cum persona*" which, though traceable to the fifteenth century,[2] probably did no more originally than state in Latin a long-established principle concerning torts such as assault and battery of which it was neither the historical cause nor the rational explanation.[3] Actions in contract generally escaped the rule,[4] and so too did those in which property had been appropriated by a deceased person and added to his own estate,[5] but it was not until 1934 that the defects of the law were forced on the attention of the legislature by the growth of motor traffic and its accompanying toll of accidents. If a negligent driver was killed in the accident which he himself had caused, nothing was recoverable from his estate or his insurer[6] by those whom he had injured. Accordingly, the Law Reform (Miscellaneous Provisions) Act 1934 was passed to provide

---

[1] Pollock and Maitland, *History of English Law*, ii, p. 526. *cf.* Milsom, "Trespass from Henry III to Edward III" (1960) 74 L.Q.R. at p. 584. Obviously a man's liability to be punished by the criminal law for some offence is extinguished by his death.

[2] Y.B. Mich. 18 Edw. 4, f. 15, pl. 17.

[3] Winfield, "Death as Affecting Liability in Tort" (1929) 29 Col.L.Rev. 239.

[4] *Pinchon's Case* (1611) 9 Rep. 86b, 88b.

[5] *Sherrington's Case* (1582) Sav. 40. See *Phillips* v. *Homfray* (1883) 24 Ch.D. 439 and Goff and Jones, *The Law of Restitution*, pp. 431–433.

[6] Insurance against third party risks was first made compulsory in 1930 (now Road Traffic Act 1988, s.143).

generally for the survival of causes of action in tort.[7] Its main provisions may be summarised as follows:

Survival of causes of action

By section 1(1) of the Act, all causes of action subsisting against or vested in any person on his death, except causes of action for defamation,[8] now survive against, or, as the case may be, for the benefit of his estate. The Act does not create a cause of action for death itself and has no bearing on the common law rule that no such cause of action exists. What it does is to provide for the survival of causes of action subsisting when the tortfeasor or the injured person dies.

The exclusion of actions for defamation from the 1934 Act was not so much the result of a conscious decision of policy that such actions should not survive death as of a desire to avoid potentially controversial areas and deal with the urgent issue of deaths in road accidents.[9] The matter was considered further by a committee under the chairmanship of Faulks J.[10] which proposed (a) that a cause of action for defamation should survive against the estate of the deceased in the normal way; (b) that when the person defamed has started an action but has died before judgment,[11] his representatives should be entitled to carry on the action in the normal way; and (c) that where the person defamed died before starting an action the representatives should be entitled to commence one, but only for an injunction and damages for pecuniary loss.[12] A different problem is "defamation of the dead," i.e. where the defamatory words are spoken about a person who is already dead, which is clearly not actionable under the present law.[13] On the one hand, such statements can be very distressing to relatives of the deceased without being actually defamatory of them; on the other hand "if those engaged in writing history were compelled, for fear of proceedings for libel, to limit themselves to events of which they could provide proof acceptable to a court of law, records of the past would be unduly and undesirably curtailed."[14] The Faulks Committee struck a compromise by recommending a right of action, available to certain close relatives for five years after the death and limited to a claim for a declaration, injunction against repetition and costs.[15]

---

[7] The generality of the main provisions of the Act renders superfluous earlier statutory provisions concerning torts against property.

[8] Other causes of action were also excluded from the operation of the Act, but these were abolished by the Law Reform (Miscellaneous Provisions) Act 1970, ss.4 and 5.

[9] See the Faulks Committee Report, Cmnd. 5909 (1975), Chap. 15.

[10] *Ibid.*

[11] If judgment has been obtained before the death of either party it may be enforced after death because the cause of action is then the judgment itself and the 1934 Act restriction ceases to be applicable: see *Rysak* v. *Rysak and Bugajaski* [1967] P. 179.

[12] Cmnd. 5909 (1979), para. 423.

[13] See, *e.g.* the correspondence in *The Times* during 1978 concerning allegations about the evidence of the plaintiffs in the *Spectator* libel action of 1957. But it is just possible a libel on a dead person may be indictable as a crime: *De Libellis Famosis* (1605) 5 Co.Rep. 125a; Smith & Hogan, *Criminal Law*, (6th ed.), p. 824.

[14] Porter Committee, Cmd. 7536 (1948), para. 29.

[15] Cmnd. 5909 (1975), para. 423. Like the other recommendations of the Faulks Committee, these have not been implemented. See further Symmons (1980) 18 Univ. of W. Ontario L.R. 521.

"Subsisting" action

It may happen that a cause of action is not complete against a wrongdoer until after he has in fact died, as, for example, where damage is the gist of the action and no damage is suffered until after the death of the wrongdoer. In such a case no cause of action subsists against the wrongdoer at the date of his death and there is nothing to survive against his estate, so that, were there no provision in the Act to deal with the point, the person suffering the damage would be deprived of his remedy. Section 1(4) provides, however, that where damage has been suffered as a result of a wrongful act in respect of which a cause of action would have subsisted had the wrongdoer not died before or at the same time as the damage was suffered, there shall be deemed to have subsisted against him before his death such cause of action as would have subsisted if he had died after the damage had been suffered. Thus, if on facts similar to those of *Donoghue* v. *Stevenson*,[16] A, the negligent manufacturer of noxious ginger-beer, dies before the ultimate consumer, B, suffers damage from drinking it, B's cause of action against A's estate is preserved as it is regarded as arising before A's death.[17]

Damages recoverable

(i) *Where the injured party dies*, the damages recoverable for the benefit of the estate may not include any exemplary damages, nor any damages for loss of income in respect of any period after the victim's death.[18] The explanation of the latter provision lies in the problem of the "lost years."[19] Once it was held that the victim of a tort whose life had been shortened might recover damages for lost earnings during the years of life of which he had been deprived and that this principle applied equally to a person who was already dead when the action was commenced,[20] there arose problems of the relationship between the 1934 Act claim and that of the dependants under the Fatal Accidents Act. In particular, there was a possibility that the defendant could be liable twice over.[21] The above provision removes this risk.[22]

It is further provided that where death has been caused by the act or omission which gives rise to the cause of action, damages are to be calculated without reference to any loss[23] or gain[24] to the deceased's estate consequent

---

[16] [1932] A.C. 562, *ante*, p. 74.
[17] A right to claim contribution from another tortfeasor is not a claim in tort and survives death without reference to the 1934 Act: *Ronex Properties Ltd.* v. *John Laing Construction Ltd.* [1983] Q.B. 398.
[18] Law Reform (Miscellaneous Provisions) Act 1934, s.1(2)(a), as amended by the Administration of Justice Act 1982, s.4.
[19] *Ante*, p. 621.
[20] See *Pickett* v. *British Rail Engineering Ltd.* [1980] A.C. 136; *Gammell* v. *Wilson* [1982] A.C. 27.
[21] See the eleventh edition of this work.
[22] However, it may be unsafe to assume that this provision removes all possibility of a "lost years" claim by the estate. It refers only to loss of income and *Pickett's* case may extend to loss of the opportunity to inherit capital: see *Adsett* v. *West* [1983] Q.B. 826. It is important to note that the 1982 Act has no application to a claim by a living plaintiff, who may still sue for loss of earnings during the "lost years." This is essential to allow full compensation for claimants with dependants who face premature death: *ante*, p. 621. In *Gammell* v. *Wilson* [1982] A.C. 27, Lord Scarman suggested that an alternative means of solving the overlap problem was simply to repeal the Fatal Accidents Act. Some American jurisdictions have never had a Fatal Accidents Act, relying on the equivalent of the 1934 Act.
[23] *e.g.* cessation of an annuity or life interest.
[24] *e.g.* insurance money.

on his death, except that funeral expenses may be included.[25] Where, however, the death is unconnected with the act or omission which gives rise to the cause of action, it appears that substantial damages can be recovered even though the deceased himself, had he been alive when the action was brought, would only have recovered nominal damages.[26]

The damages which the estate may recover include those for non-pecuniary items (such as pain and suffering and loss of amenity) during any interval between injury and death, but death now terminates these losses for legal purposes.[27]

Damages recovered form part of the estate of the deceased, are available for payment of his debts and pass under his will or upon his intestacy. The Law Reform (Contributory Negligence) Act 1945 applies to claims by estates.[28]

(ii) *When the tortfeasor dies*, the ordinary measure of damage applies in an action brought against his estate.[29]

Time limitation

Until 1970 special rules governed the time within which proceedings in tort had to be started against a deceased person's estate.[30] However, those rules were abolished by the Proceedings Against Estates Act of that year and generally the ordinary law for the limitation of actions applies, whether the action is brought against or for the benefit of the estate.[31]

Right of action is cumulative

The rights conferred by the 1934 Act are in addition to, and not in derogation of, any rights conferred on the dependants of deceased persons by the Fatal Accidents Act 1976.[32]

DEATH AS CREATING LIABILITY

We have seen how the Act of 1934 abolished the common law rule of *actio*

---

[25] s.1(2)(c).

[26] *Otter* v. *Church, Adams, Tatham & Co.* [1953] Ch. 280. This was an action in contract for professional negligence, which survived at common law. It is submitted, however, that the result would have been the same even if the plaintiff had had to rely upon the Act of 1934. *cf.* Gray and Thompson, "The Measure and Remoteness of Damages" (1953) 16 M.L.R. 518.

[27] Until the Administration of Justice Act 1982 the conventional award for "loss of expectation of life" (*ante*, p. 611) could be regarded as representing *post mortem* loss of amenity.

[28] For contributory negligence, see *ante*, Chap. 6.

[29] Where the tortfeasor's estate is insolvent any liability can be proved in the administration notwithstanding that the liability is for unliquidated damages in tort: s.1(6).

[30] For the old law, see the eighth ed. of this work, pp. 609–610.

[31] *Post*, p. 725. But under s.11(5) of the Limitation Act 1980 a new, fixed period of limitation arises where the victim dies during the period which commenced with his injury. Provision is made, by rules of court to enable proceedings to be started against an estate where no grant or probate or administration has been made: R.S.C., Ord. 15, r. 6A.

[32] s.1(5), as amended by the Fatal Accidents Act 1976, s.6, Sched. 1, para. 2(2).

personalis moritur cum persona and allowed the survival of the cause of action of a deceased person, though it did not as such *create* any cause of action. A quite separate rule of the common law providing that the death could not give rise to a cause of action *in other persons*, although they were dependent on the deceased, which may not always have been the law,[33] is derived from the ruling of Lord Ellenborough in *Baker* v. *Bolton*[34] that, "in a civil court the death of a human being could not be complained of as an injury."[35] The plaintiff and his wife were passengers on the top of the defendants' stagecoach which was upset by the negligence of the defendants, "whereby the plaintiff himself was much bruised, and his wife was so severely hurt that she died about a month after." The plaintiff recovered £100 for his own bruises and for the loss of his wife's society up to the moment of her death, but nothing for such loss after that event.

Baker v. *Bolton* was only a ruling at Nisi Prius, not a single authority was cited and the report is extremely brief, but it was nevertheless upheld in later cases[36] and the seal of approval placed upon it by the House of Lords in *Admiralty Commissioners* v. *SS. Amerika*.[37] In that case a submarine of the Royal Navy was run into and sunk by the negligence of the steamship *Amerika*. The Admiralty Commissioners granted pensions to the relatives of those who were drowned in the submarine and then claimed the capitalised amount of the pensions from the owners of the *Amerika*. The claim failed, first, because of the rule in *Baker* v. *Bolton*; secondly, because the damages were too remote, since the pensions were not paid under any legal obligation upon the Admiralty, but were voluntary disbursements in the nature of compassionate allowances. With this second ground we are not here concerned, but why the rule in *Baker* v. *Bolton* should have been followed except on the ground of *vis inertiae* it is difficult to see.[38]

Fatal Accidents Act 1976

The development of railways in England led to a great upsurge in the number of accidents, fatal and non-fatal, and this made a change in the law imperative for, while those who survived an accident could recover substantial damages, the dependants of those who were killed could recover nothing. Accordingly, in 1846, the Fatal Accidents Act, otherwise known as Lord Campbell's Act, was passed and virtually overturned the common law so far as those dependants who were specified in the Act and in later legislation were concerned. The present statute is the Fatal Accidents Act 1976, which consolidates the earlier legislation.[39] The Act provides that

---

[33] Y.B. Mich. 43 Edw. 3, f. 23, pl. 16.

[34] (1808) 1 Camp. 493.

[35] The rule in *Baker* v. *Bolton* does not apply where the plaintiff's cause of action is founded upon contract: *Jackson* v. *Watson* [1909] 2 K.B. 193.

[36] *Osborn* v. *Gillett* (1873) L.R. 8 Ex. 88; *Clark* v. *London General Omnibus Co. Ltd.* [1906] 2 K.B. 648.

[37] [1917] A.C. 38.

[38] The historical arguments of Lord Parker ([1917] A.C. 38, 43–48) and Lord Sumner (*ibid.* at pp. 56–60) are unconvincing. See Holdsworth, H.E.L., iii, 676–677, and in (1916) 32 L.Q.R. 431–437.

[39] The Act came into force on September 1, 1976. The 1976 Act has been amended in important respects by the Administration of Justice Act 1982.

whenever the death of a person[40] is caused by the wrongful act, neglect or default[41] of another, such as would (if death had not ensued) have entitled the injured person to sue and recover damages in respect thereof, then the person who would have been liable if death had not ensued shall be liable to an action for damages on behalf of the dependants, notwithstanding the death of the person injured.[42]

(1) *Dependants*

As far as concerns financial loss caused by the death the action lies for the benefit of the deceased's dependants,[43] a class of persons which has been considerably enlarged since it was first defined in 1846, most recently by the Administration of Justice Act 1982.[44] The class now comprehends (*a*) the spouse or former spouse[45] of the deceased, or person who was living as the spouse of the deceased, in the same household, immediately before the date of the death and had been so living for at least two years[46] (*b*) any parent or other ascendant of the deceased or person treated by the deceased as his parent[47]; (*c*) any child[48] or other descendant of the deceased or any person who has been treated by the deceased as a child of the family in relation to any marriage of the deceased[49]; and (*d*) any person who is, or is the issue of, a brother, sister, uncle or aunt of the deceased.[50] Moreover, in deducing any relationship an adopted person is to be treated as the child of the persons by whom he was adopted, a relationship by affinity as one of consanguinity and a relationship of the half-blood as a relationship of the whole blood. The stepchild of any person is to be treated as his child and an illegitimate person as the legitimate child of his mother and reputed father.[51] The major change introduced by the 1982 Act was the admission of the "common law spouse"

---

[40] It is immaterial that the deceased was an alien, provided he was otherwise qualified to sue: *Davidson* v. *Hill* [1901] 2 K.B. 606. See Webb, "The Conflict of Laws and the English Fatal Accidents Acts" (1961) 24 M.L.R. 467.

[41] It is now common form in statutes imposing strict liability to provide that a situation giving rise to such liability is "fault" within the meaning of the Fatal Accidents Act: see, *e.g.* the Animals Act 1971, s.10. A breach of contract causing death is within the statute: *Grein* v. *Imperial Airways Ltd.* [1937] 1 K.B. 50.

[42] s.1.

[43] The defendant must be supplied with particulars of the persons for whose benefit the action is brought, and if a person is left out, he can apply before verdict to be named as a party to benefit. But the court cannot consider a dependant not named in the proceedings and such a person can have no claim against the defendant. He may, however, have some legal or equitable remedy against the representative plaintiff: *Avery* v. *London & N.E. Ry.* [1938] A.C. 606, 613, *per* Lord Atkin. For a dependant's ability to intervene before judgment in proceedings in which she was not named, see *Cooper* v. *Williams* [1963] 2 Q.B. 567. *cf.* *Voller* v. *Dairy Produce Packers Ltd.* [1962] 1 W.L.R. 960, where there appear to have been two distinct claims under the Fatal Accidents Acts in respect of the same death.

[44] Substituting a new s.1 in the Fatal Accidents Act 1976.

[45] Including a person whose marriage has been annulled or declared void.

[46] Compare the very much wider residual category under the Inheritance (Provision for Family and Dependants) Act 1975.

[47] "Treating as a parent" appears to be a novel legal concept.

[48] Including a posthumous child: *The George and Richard* (1871) L.R. Ad. & E. 466.

[49] This concept of "child of the family" is well established in matrimonial legislation and will presumably be given the same meaning here.

[50] Fatal Accidents Act 1976, s.1(3), as substituted by Administration of Justice Act 1982.

[51] *Ibid.* s.1(5).

to the list of dependants.[52] The Fatal Accidents Act also gives rise to a claim for damages for "bereavement," but in favour of a much narrower range of persons. This is dealt with below.

An action under the Fatal Accidents Act must normally be brought on behalf of the dependants by the executor or administrator of the deceased[53] but where there is no personal representative, or no action is brought by him within six months, any dependant who is entitled to benefit under the Act may sue in his own name on behalf of himself and the others.[54] Subject to the court's powers under the Limitation Act 1980, the action must in any case be brought within three years of the death.[55]

(2) *Nature of the action*

The right of action created by the Fatal Accidents Act is "new in its species, new in its quality, new in its principles, in every way new"[56]; it is not the deceased's own cause of action which is caused to survive, it is a new action for the benefit of his dependants. For this new cause of action to exist, however, it is necessary that the circumstances of his death should have been such that the deceased himself, had he been injured and not killed, could have sued for his injury. One must consider the hypothetical ability of the deceased to sue as at the moment of his death, with the idea fictionally that death has not taken place.[57] If, therefore, the deceased had been run over in the street through nobody's fault but his own, there will be no claim on behalf of his dependants; nor will there be such a claim if by contract with the defendant the deceased had excluded any possibility of liability to himself,[58] but if the contract merely limited the amount of the defendant's liability, then the deceased could have sued for some damages, the way is open for the dependants' claim, and that claim, being independent of the deceased's, will not be affected by the limitation of liability.[59] Similarly the dependants have no claim if the deceased before his death had accepted compensation in satisfaction of his claim,[60] or had actually obtained judgment against the

---

[52] This goes further than the Pearson Commission recommendations on the Act: Cmnd. 7054, Vol. 1, para. 404. Before the 1982 Act a reduction in the resources of an unmarried mother as a result of the death of the father might constitute a loss to the children: *K.* v. *J.M.P. Co. Ltd.* [1976] Q.B. 85. This might still be relevant where the conditions of the 1982 Act are not fulfilled.

[53] s.2. An executor's title to sue dates from the death, but an administrator must first obtain a grant of letters of administration: *Hilton* v. *Sutton Steam Laundry* [1946] K.B. 65; *Finnegan* v. *Cementation Co. Ltd.* [1953] 1 Q.B. 688. *cf. Stebbing* v. *Holst & Co. Ltd.* [1953] 1 W.L.R. 603; *Bowler* v. *John Mowlem & Co.* [1954] 1 W.L.R. 1445.

[54] s.2(2). If there is no executor or administrator, the dependants need not wait six months before suing: *Holleran* v. *Bagnell* (1879) 4 L.R.Ir. 740.

[55] *Post*, pp. 726–727.

[56] *Seward* v. *Vera Cruz* (1884) 10 App.Cas. 59, 70–71, *per* Lord Blackburn.

[57] *British Columbia Electric Ry.* v. *Gentile* [1914] A.C. 1034, 1041, *per* Lord Dunedin; *Pym* v. *G.N. Ry.* (1862) 2 B. & S. 759; 4 B. & S. 396.

[58] *Haigh* v. *Royal Mail Steam Packet Co. Ltd.* (1883) 52 L.J.Q.B. 640; *The Stella* [1900] P. 161. But since the passing of s.2 of the Unfair Contract Terms Act 1977 (*post*, p. 687) it is a good deal less likely that such a term will be binding.

[59] *Nunan* v. *Southern Ry.* [1924] 1 K.B. 223; *Grein* v. *Imperial Airways* [1937] 1 K.B. 50.

[60] *Read* v. *G.E. Ry.* (1868) L.R. 3 Q.B. 555. *cf. Re Lancaster's Application* [1977] 4 C.L. 59 (criminal injuries compensation). The view that the dependants are barred was assumed to be correct for the purposes of the appeal in *Pickett* v. *British Rail Engineering Ltd.* [1980] A.C. 136. Apparently the liability in tort is destroyed from the moment that the agreement to accept compensation is made, even before the money is actually paid; *British Russian Gazette, etc.* v. *Associated Newspapers Ltd.* [1933] 2 K.B. 616.

defendant, or if by the date of his death his claim had become statute barred.[61] But so long as the deceased's claim has not become statute barred when he dies, then the dependants have the full three years from the death (or, in certain cases, the time when they know they have a cause of action) in which to sue,[62] for their claim, which arises on the death, has no connection with the deceased's.[63] It is thus somewhat illogical, though doubtless good practical sense, that, since the Law Reform (Contributory Negligence) Act 1945,[64] if the deceased was himself partly to blame for the accident which caused his death, the damages recoverable by his dependants are reduced in proportion to his share of responsibility for the accident.[65] Before the Act of 1945, of course, the dependants could have recovered nothing for the deceased could not himself have sued. At the present time, were it not for express statutory provision to the contrary, they would be able to recover the full amount of their loss without reduction.

(3) What is recoverable[66]

The Act provides for recovery in respect of two types of loss. First, in respect of death after 1982, the spouse of the deceased or the parents[67] of a minor[68] who was never married may claim damages for "bereavement," a fixed sum[69] of £3,500.[70] English law thus now has direct,[71] though conventional, provision for the *solatium* which was long recognised by Scots common law,[72] though there is widespread feeling that the sum is far too low. More important in financial terms is the claim for loss of support provided by the deceased which is given by the Act to the much wider class of "dependants." The Act simply says that the court may give damages proportioned

---

[61] *Williams* v. *Mersey Docks and Harbour Board* [1905] 1 K.B. 804. But the court may be able to override the limitation period: Limitation Act 1980, s.33.

[62] Limitation Act 1980, s.12(2).

[63] For a striking example of the independence of the dependant's claim from that of the deceased, see *Pigney* v. *Pointer's Transport Services Ltd.* [1957] 1 W.L.R. 1121, where the deceased had committed suicide in a fit of depression caused by his injury. See further, *ante*, p. 156.

[64] *Ante*, Chap. 6.

[65] Fatal Accidents Act, 1976, s.5.

[66] The standard works mentioned *ante*, p. 598, also deal with damages under the Fatal Accidents Act.

[67] In the case of an illegitimate child, only the mother.

[68] The Act does not apply to a still-born child, though since the tort causing the still-birth will be a tort against the mother she may recover substantial damages (not necessarily limited to the statutory sum) for the effect of the loss of the child on her: *Bagley* v. *North Herts. Health Authority* (1986) 136 N.L.J. 1014. *cf. Kralj* v. *McGrath* [1986] 1 All E.R. 54, where the emphasis seems to be on the mother's grief hindering her physical recovery.

[69] Which can be raised by statutory instrument. Like other damages under the Act, this sum would seem to be subject to reduction on account of the deceased's contributory negligence.

[70] Fatal Accidents Act 1976 s.1A (inserted by Administration of Justice Act 1982, s.3). Where the claim is made by both parents the sum is to be divided equally between them. (s.1A(4), the form of which suggests that if one parent is the tortfeasor, the other receives the full £3,500). Does "spouse" cover persons who are parties to an actually polygamous marriage? If so, are there separate claims or are the damages to be divided?

[71] In effect, though not in theory, the previous law allowed a *solatium* where the deceased was a young child. The child's action for loss of expectation of life (a conventional sum not exceeding £1,750) survived for the benefit of the estate and passed to the parents, who would, since there was no dependency, generally have no Fatal Accidents Act claim from which it could be deducted.

[72] But by s.1(4) of the Damages (Scotland) Act 1976 the common law claim for *solatium* was replaced by a claim for "such non-patrimonial benefit as the relative might have been expected to derive from the deceased's society and guidance if he had not died."

to the injury resulting from the death to the dependants[73]; it does not say on what principle they are to be assessed, but Pollock C.B., in 1858, adopted the test which has been used ever since, that damages must be calculated "in reference to *a reasonable expectation of pecuniary benefit as of right, or otherwise*, from the continuance of the life."[74] If, therefore, the dependants have suffered only nominal damages, or none at all, they can recover nothing,[75] nor can they recover if the deceased had earned his living by crime, for then their claim arises *ex turpi causa*.[76] However, the courts have stretched the concept of pecuniary benefit in holding that a child may claim damages for loss of its mother's care and that in assessing this loss the court is not confined to evaluating her services as housekeeper but may take into account instruction on essential matters to do with his upbringing.[77] Where a son, who worked for his father at full wages under a contract, was killed, his father was held to have no claim; for though he had lost the son's services, he could not prove that he had lost any pecuniary benefit since he had paid full wages for them.[78] An additional reason for rejecting the father's claim in that case was that the father could not show any benefit accruing to him from his relationship with his son, but only that he had lost an advantage derived from a contract with him, and this was insufficient.[79] "The benefit, to qualify under the Act, must be a benefit which arises from the relationship between the parties."[80] In *Malyon* v. *Plummer*[81] the plaintiff widow had been in receipt of a salary of about £600 per annum for somewhat nominal services to her husband's "one-man" company. The Court of Appeal estimated the value of her services to the company at £200 per annum and held that the balance, but only the balance, was attributable to her relationship as wife to the deceased. The £200 represented payment for services rendered under her contract of employment and could not therefore be recovered. Nor is a mere speculative possibility of pecuniary benefit sufficient, as where the person killed was aged four years and his father proved nothing except that he had intended to give the child a good education.[82]

On the other hand, there may be a reasonable expectation of pecuniary

[73] s.3(1).
[74] *Franklin* v. *S.E. Ry.* (1858) 3 H. & N. 211, 213–214. Hence the dependants are entitled to recover where the deceased has been prevented from accumulating savings which they would have received from him: *Singapore Bus Co.* v. *Lim* [1985] 1 W.L.R. 1075. It has been held that where the deceased's estate is substantial and pays estate duty, that duty is recoverable by the dependants/beneficiaries from the tortfeasor: *Davies* v. *Whiteways Cyder Co. Ltd.* [1975] Q.B. 262.
[75] *Duckworth* v. *Johnson* (1859) 29 L.J.Ex. 257.
[76] *Burns* v. *Edman* [1970] 2 Q.B. 541. This decision has come in for a good deal of criticism (*e.g.* Kemp and Kemp, *op. cit.*, Vol. 1, Chap. 25) but, while the claim of the dependants is certainly separate from that of the deceased, it is hard to see how the court can countenance an award of damages in respect of loss of the benefits of criminal activity.
[77] *Hay* v. *Hughes* [1975] Q.B. 790, 802; *Regan* v. *Williamson* [1976] 1 W.L.R. 305 (doubting *Pevec* v. *Brown* (1964) 108 S.J. 210); *Mehmet* v. *Perry* [1977] 2 All E.R. 529.
[78] *Sykes* v. *N.E. Ry.* (1875) 44 L.J.C.P. 191.
[79] *Burgess* v. *Florence Nightingale Hospital for Gentlewomen* [1955] 1 Q.B. 349.
[80] *Ibid.* at p. 360, *per* Devlin J.
[81] [1964] 1 Q.B. 330.
[82] *Barnett* v. *Cohen* [1921] 2 K.B. 461. Formerly nothing could be recovered for funeral or mourning expenses: *Dalton* v. *S.E. Ry.* (1858) 4 C.B.(N.S.) 296; *Clark* v. *London General Omnibus Co. Ltd.* [1906] 2 K.B. 648. However, the Law Reform (Miscellaneous Provisions) Act 1934, s.2(3) allowed recovery of funeral expenses which had been incurred by the person for whose benefit the action is brought. See now the Fatal Accidents Act 1976, s.3(5).

benefit although the relatives had no legal claim to support by the deceased, as where a son who was killed had voluntarily assisted his father in the father's work,[83] or where he once gave him money during a period of unemployment,[84] or where a wife who was killed had gratuitously performed the ordinary household duties.[85] Indeed, it is not necessary that the deceased should have been actually earning anything or giving any help, provided there was a reasonable probability, as distinct from a bare possibility, that he would do so, as there was where the deceased was a girl of 16 who lived with her parents, was on the eve of completing her apprenticeship as a dress-maker, and was likely in the near future to earn a wage which might quickly have become substantial.[86]

In assessing whether there was a reasonable expectation of benefit in the above sense, the court is not concerned with a balance of probabilities in the same way as when it is adjudicating upon facts. Thus if a wife is separated from her husband at the time of his death, it is unnecessary for her to show that on a balance of probabilities she would have returned to live with her husband. The correct approach is for the court to determine whether there was a reasonable chance, rather than a mere speculative possibility, of reconciliation. If there was such a chance, the award should be scaled down to take account of the probability of the reconciliation taking place.[87] Where the dependant was not married to the deceased but was living with him as his wife the court is directed by statute to take into account the fact that the claimant had no enforceable right to financial support from the deceased.[88]

In a case under the Fatal Accidents Act the court is concerned with assessing what would have happened if the deceased had lived. But since the loss for which damages are awarded is pecuniary loss which will be suffered by dependants in the future, it is also inevitably concerned with the pros-pects of the dependants: for example, if the dependant himself has a short expectation of life the damages will be small.[89] Since damages can at present only be awarded as a lump sum[90] the court must inevitably speculate as to the future, using the evidence available to it. The most controversial aspect of this matter related to the dependant widow's prospects of remarriage, but there the law has undergone a fundamental alteration by statute. The common law rule was that the court had to estimate the widow's chances of

---

[83] *Franklin* v. *S.E. Ry.* (1858) 3 H. & N. 211.
[84] *Hetherington* v. *N.E. Ry.* (1882) 9 Q.B.D. 160.
[85] *Berry* v. *Humm* [1915] 1 K.B. 627. See also *Burgess* v. *Florence Nightingale Hospital for Gentlewomen* [1955] 1 Q.B. 349, 361–362.
[86] *Taff Vale Ry.* v. *Jenkins* [1913] A.C. 1; *Wathen* v. *Vernon* [1970] R.T.R. 471; *Spitalali* v. *Washbourne* (1975), Kemp & Kemp, *op. cit.*, Vol. 1, p. 31051; *Kandalla* v. *B.E.A.* [1981] Q.B. 158.
[87] *Davies* v. *Taylor* [1974] A.C. 207; Fleming [1973] C.L.J. 20; see also *Wathen* v. *Vernon* [1970] R.T.R. 471; *Gray* v. *Barr* [1971] 2 Q.B. 554. *Davies* v. *Taylor* was one of the main planks of Simon Brown J.'s decision in *Hotson* v. *E. Berks. A.H.A.*, which was reversed by the H.L. without mention of *Davies* v. *Taylor* (see *ante*, p. 133). The case remains an authority on quantification as opposed to causation.
[88] Fatal Accidents Act 1976, s.3(4), as substituted by the Administration of Justice Act 1982.
[89] Thus where the deceased's widow actually died before the trial damages were awarded to her estate in respect only of the period during which she actually survived him: *Williamson* v. *John I. Thornycroft Ltd.* [1940] 2 K.B. 658; *Voller* v. *Dairy Produce Packers Ltd.* [1962] 1 W.L.R. 960.
[90] The provisional damages mentioned at *ante*, p. 629 can have no application to these cases.

remarriage and reduce the damages accordingly,[91] but some judges tended to revolt against this "guessing game"[92] and a campaign against the rule led to its reversal by the Law Reform (Miscellaneous Provisions) Act 1971. Now, in assessing the damages payable to a widow in respect of the death of her husband in any action under the Fatal Accidents Act there shall not be taken into account the remarriage of the widow nor her prospects of remarriage.[93] As far as damages for bereavement are concerned it seems right to ignore remarriage, but with regard to the other aspect of the Act, the good intentions of this provision are more evident than its logic, for it undermines the basic principle that damages for fatal accidents are awarded for future pecuniary loss. Even if it be accepted that the courts had to be relieved of the "guessing game" of estimating the chances of future remarriage, it is remarkable that the courts must ignore a remarriage which has actually taken place, though if the law were otherwise plaintiffs might simply postpone remarriage until after trial.[94] Strangely enough, the provision has not succeeded in entirely abolishing the "guessing game." First, it only applies to a *widow's* claim under the Fatal Accidents Act, and marriage prospects may be a relevant consideration in the assessment of damages for an injured but living female plaintiff,[95] or to the claim of a "common law wife" under the Act. Secondly, damages under the Fatal Accidents Act are also payable to child dependants of the victim and since the legislation makes no reference to their claim, the court may have to take into account their mother's prospects of remarriage.[96]

(4) *Assessment of damages*

Damages for bereavement are a fixed sum. What follows concerns pecuniary loss. Although the action is normally brought by the executor or administrator of the deceased, and not by the dependants themselves, the remedy given by the statute is to individuals, not to a class.[97] In calculating the damages, therefore, the pecuniary loss suffered by each dependant should

---

[91] *Goodburn* v. *Thomas Cotton Ltd.* [1968] 1 Q.B. 845. Where the widow had actually remarried before the trial or before the time for appeal had expired the case was *a fortiori* for a reduction in the award: *Curwen* v. *James* [1963] 1 W.L.R. 748.

[92] See, *e.g.* Phillimore J. in *Buckley* v. *John Allen and Ford (Oxford) Ltd.* [1967] 2 Q.B. 637, 645.

[93] Fatal Accidents Act 1976 s.3(3).

[94] In any event, cohabitation may provide the same financial support in fact as does marriage.

[95] See *ante*, p. 627, though in some cases the courts may be able to evade the marriage prospects issue for the reason given there.

[96] *Thompson* v. *Price* [1973] Q.B. 838; *cf. Howitt* v. *Heads* [1973] Q.B. 64. In *Thompson* v. *Price* the widow *had* remarried, but Boreham J. clearly thought the same principle applied to prospects of remarriage. The sum involved here will in the case of minor children be small, because the cost of the child's "keep" will fall to be assessed as part of the widow's damages, which are not subject to reduction: *Thompson* v. *Price*, *supra*, at p. 843.
The Law Commission (Law Com. No. 56) recommended the correction of this anomaly in relation to assessment of the child's damage. With a commendable desire for symmetry, it also proposed that the new principle extended to the assessment of a widower's claim for damages for the death of his wife. But it is suggested in McGregor, *Damages* (15th ed.), pp. 1015–1016 that in both cases remarriage is to be ignored because of s.4: see *post*, p. 655.

[97] *Pym* v. *Great Northern Ry.* (1863) 4 B. & S. 396; *Avery* v. *London & N.E. Ry.* [1938] A.C. 613; *Jeffrey* v. *Kent County Council* [1958] 1 W.L.R. 926; *Dietz* v. *Lennig Chemicals Ltd.* [1969] 1 A.C. 170, 183, *per* Lord Morris.

be separately assessed.[98] In practice, however, it will frequently be necessary first of all to determine a figure for the total liability of the defendant and then to apportion the damages between the various dependants[99] and this has been said to be the more usual method.[1]

Putting aside damages for bereavement, the process of assessment is very similar to that used in assessing future loss in a personal injury action, that is to say the court determines a multiplicand representing the net annual loss and applies to that a multiplier representing the duration of the loss scaled down for contingencies and the value of accelerated receipt in the form of a lump sum. The multiplier is to be set at the date of the death, not the trial[2] and the exercise is likely to be more complicated than in a personal injury case, if only because the periods of dependency of individual dependants will differ,[3] whereas in a personal injury case it is only the plaintiff's working life expectancy which is in issue. Most cases fall into one of two broad categories. The first is where the deceased is the family breadwinner. Traditionally, the approach was to build up the multiplicand item by item by a schedule of expenditure which could be regarded as for the family benefit (mortgage payments, heating, insurance, and so on) and this may still be a valid approach in some cases but it is now more common simply to take the deceased's income, net of tax and other deductions and base the multiplicand on a standard fraction of that—66.6 per cent. where the only dependant is a widow, 75 per cent. if there are also children.[4] These figures are intended to allow for the expenditure which the deceased incurred solely for his own benefit and recognise the fact that expenditure for joint benefit (e.g. heating) is not necessarily reduced by the absence of the deceased.[5] It must, however, be stressed that the standard fractions can be varied up or down if there is evidence to justify that. The other type of case is that where the deceased provided valuable but gratuitous service in looking after the home and children. Here there may be[6] no earnings to serve as the base-line for the multiplicand and the proper approach will often be to use as a measure the cost of employing substitute domestic help, if necessary on a "live-in" basis,[7] though it may in some cases be more apt to take the earnings loss of the other

---

[98] A good example is *Williamson* v. *Thornycroft & Co.* [1940] 2 K.B. 658.

[99] *Bishop* v. *Cunard White Star Co. Ltd.* [1950] P. 240, 248, *per* Hodson J. Once the total liability of the defendant has been determined, the apportionment of that sum is no concern of the defendant: *Eifert* v. *Holt's Transport Co. Ltd.* [1951] 2 All E.R. 655n.

[1] *Kassam* v. *Kampala Aerated Water Co. Ltd.* [1965] 1 W.L.R. 668, 672, *per* Lord Guest. See Kemp and Kemp, *op. cit.*, Vol. 1, p. 21001.

[2] *Graham* v. *Dodds* [1983] 1 W.L.R. 808.

[3] See, *e.g. Kassam* v. *Kampala Aerated Water Co. Ltd.* [1965] 1 W.L.R. 668; *Whittome* v. *Coates* [1965] 1 W.L.R. 1285; *Robertson* v. *Lestrange* [1985] 1 All E.R. 950. In *Dolbey* v. *Goodwin* [1955] 1 W.L.R. 553 it was held that the damages awarded to the widowed mother of the deceased could not be assessed on the same basis as if she had been his widow, as it was likely that the deceased would have married in due course and that his contributions to his mother's upkeep would then have been reduced.

[4] *Harris* v. *Empress Motors* [1984] 1 W.L.R. 212.

[5] *cf.* the assessment in "lost years" cases, which was in issue in *Harris's* case, *ante*, p. 622.

[6] Of course, as many wives work there may also be a substantial claim for loss of earnings.

[7] *Jeffery* v. *Smith* [1970] R.T.R. 279; *Hay* v. *Hughes* [1975] Q.B. 790. Though in principle a deduction should be made in respect of the living expenses of the deceased, this may be offset because the courts recognise that a commercial provider may not be "as good as" the deceased: *Reagan* v. *Williamson* [1976] 1 W.L.R. 305.

parent who stays at home to look after the children.[8] The fact that commercial help is not engaged (as where the children are looked after by a relative) does not prevent the cost of such help being used as a measure but in this event it should be the net wage without tax and insurance contributions for those are items of expenditure which will never be incurred.[9] In any event the loss by children of the services of their mother is one which is likely to be a declining one so it cannot be valued at a constant figure for the whole of the child's dependency.[10]

As in personal injury actions no allowance is made for inflation[11] on the argument that this is already built in to the discount rate upon which the multipliers are based.[12]

(5) Deductions

The law on this is now very simple: there are none to be made, for in "assessing damages in respect of a person's death ... benefits which have accrued or will accrue to any person from his estate or otherwise as a result of his death shall be disregarded."[13] This contrasts with the complexity of the law governing deductions in actions for personal injury.[14] Where the breadwinner is killed the dependants are entitled to a full award based on loss of support from his earnings, even though as a result of an employers' pension, widow's benefit, insurance money and the devolution of the estate they may be better off than they were before his death. Care must, however, be taken to ensure that there is no confusion between deductibility and proof of loss. Thus where the deceased lived by managing his investments and these devolve on the dependants then, subject to any question of inheritance tax, there is simply no loss, for the dependants have received that out of which their support formerly came. Similary, in *Auty* v. *N.C.B.*[15] the widow was held to have suffered no loss by reason of her non-receipt of a widow's post-retirement pension when, by reason of her husband's death, she received a widow's death-in-service pension at the same rate. In such cases the above provision of the Act is irrelevant.

(6) Contributory negligence

As we have seen,[16] the contributory negligence of the deceased is taken into account and the damages awarded to the dependants are reduced in proportion. Though the Act is silent on the point, it is fairly clear that the contributory negligence of the dependants is also relevant. The point is not

---

[8] *Mehmet* v. *Perry* [1977] 2 All E.R. 529.
[9] *Spittle* v. *Bunney* [1988] 3 All E.R. 1031. By analogy with *Donnelly* v. *Joyce* (*ante*, p. 626) the damages are the dependant's, not the relative's.
[10] *Ibid.* (£47,500 reduced on this basis to £25,000).
[11] Beyond basing the multiplicand upon the deceased's wages as they would have been at the date of the trial: *Cookson* v. *Knowles* [1979] A.C. 556.
[12] See *ante*, p. 619.
[13] Fatal Accidents Act 1976, s.4, as substituted by the Administration of Justice Act 1982.
[14] *Ante*, p. 622. Even before the 1982 Act, the rules governing deductions were more favourable to plaintiffs in fatal accident cases.
[15] [1985] 1 W.L.R. 784. *cf. Pidduck* v. *E. Scottish Omnibus Co.* [1989] 1 W.L.R. 317.
[16] *Ante*, p. 650.

at all far-fetched: suppose Mrs. A is being driven in a car by her husband A and is killed in an accident caused by the combined negligence of A and B. It is submitted that in principle the damages awarded to the negligent dependant should be reduced under the Law Reform (Contributory Negligence) Act 1945, s.1(1), in proportion to his share of responsibility,[17] but that the other dependants should receive their damages in full,[18] since the remedy under the Fatal Accidents Act is given to individuals, not to the dependants as a group. In one case it was held that the damages of a non-negligent dependant were not affected by the fault of another dependant, but there the accident was held to be entirely the fault of the latter and it was conceded by counsel that she had no claim.[19]

Relationship of the Fatal Accidents Act and Law Reform Act

The rights of action under these Acts are cumulative, with damages under the Law Reform (Miscellaneous Provisions) Act 1934 going to the estate and those under the Fatal Accidents Act going to dependants. In most cases, one or more of the dependants will also be entitled to the deceased's estate. There is no longer any provision for deduction of Law Reform Act claims from those under the Fatal Accidents Act but since the Administration of Justice Act 1982 damages under the Law Reform Act will, in the case of instantaneous death, be confined[20] to funeral expenses, and since these are anyway recoverable under the Fatal Accidents Act[21] there is no point in bringing a Law Reform Act claim. Where there is an interval between injury and death and hence loss of amenity and earnings and so on, then no doubt a Law Reform Act claim will continue to be presented concurrently with one under the Fatal Accidents Act.

Miscellaneous Statutes

International Carriage

The development of organised international transport has led to the

---

[17] *Mulholland* v. *McRae* [1961] N.I. 135.

[18] Glanville Williams, *Joint Torts and Contributory Negligence*, pp. 443–444. It has been objected that the pecuniary loss suffered by a dependant is not "damage" within the meaning of the Act of 1945 (*Drinkwater* v. *Kimber* [1951] 2 All E.R. 713, 715, *per* Devlin J.; affirmed on other grounds [1952] 2 Q.B. 281) but it is submitted that this objection is unsound (Glanville Williams, *op. cit.*, pp. 443–444, n. 25). In any event, the position then would be that the common law of contributory negligence would apply and the contributorily negligent dependant would receive nothing, a result which is unlikely to commend itself.

[19] *Dodds* v. *Dodds* [1978] Q.B. 543. There seems no reason why the defendant should not claim contribution from a negligent dependant under the Civil Liability (Contribution) Act 1978, and this would be the better course where the negligent dependant is not the only dependant. It would also be the appropriate course where the executor or administrator of the deceased, *i.e.* the nominal plaintiff, has contributed to the death but is not himself the principal dependant.

[20] Unless the point made at p. 645, n. 22, is valid.

[21] s.3(5).

conclusion of a number of international conventions governing the carrier's liability. The principal English statutes implementing such conventions are the Carriage by Air Act 1961, the Carriage by Railway Act 1972, the Carriage of Passengers by Road Act 1974 and the Merchant Shipping Act 1979. Accounts of these Acts must be sought elsewhere, but three of them set a limit on the damages which may be awarded for death or personal injury.[22]

Coal-Mining (Subsidence) Act 1957

The Coal-Mining (Subsidence) Act 1957, s.12, in effect subjects the National Coal Board to liability under the Fatal Accidents Act in respect of a death caused by coal-mining subsidence, even though the subsidence was not the result of any wrongful act, neglect or default. The damages recoverable are reduced if the deceased was guilty of contributory negligence and nothing can be recovered under the Act for the death of a trespasser or if the person killed was at the time underground in a mine of coal.

---

[22] The Air, Road and Shipping statutes. The limits vary considerably. For details, see *Halsbury's Laws of England* (4th ed.), titles *Aviation*; *Carriers*; and *Shipping and Navigation*. Overall, however, the limits are much lower than the sums an English court would award at common law for major losses. The limits may cease to apply if the damage is caused recklessly. The liability of the carrier under the Acts is not generally dependent upon proof of negligence by the plaintiff, but liability is not necessarily "strict". On limitation of liability in general, see Gaskell (1987) 137 N.L.J. 383.

CHAPTER 25

CAPACITY

THE title of this chapter is a compendious abbreviation of "Variation in capacity to sue, or liability to be sued, in tort." The word "status" would have done equally well, but unluckily there is not much agreement in books on jurisprudence as to what exactly it comprises. Where it is used it is employed as equivalent to "capacity" in the sense stated above.

Every system of law and every branch of each system must recognise variations in favour of, or against, abnormal members of the community. Who are to be reckoned as abnormal is a question of policy which each country must settle for itself. The hangman had a status in some parts of Europe; he never had one with us. Further, it will often happen that even in the same country a person is counted as abnormal in one age and as normal in another. Heretics and Jews were once under disabilities in England which have now disappeared. In the law of tort the chief variations in capacity are to be found with the state and its officials, minors, persons of unsound mind, corporations and trade unions.[1] Married women were abnormal for this purpose until well into the twentieth century. That condition has now disappeared, but there are still some restrictions on actions between spouses.

THE STATE AND ITS SUBORDINATES

The Crown and state officials[2]

At common law no action in tort lay against the Crown[3] for wrongs expressly authorised by the Crown or for wrongs committed by its servants in the course of their employment.[4] Moreover, the head of the department or other superior official was not, and is not, personally liable for wrongs committed by his subordinates, unless he has expressly authorised them, for all the servants of the Crown are fellow servants of the Crown and not of one

---

[1] For the position of trade unions, see *ante*, p. 527.

[2] Hogg, *Liability of the Crown*.

[3] Or against government departments, for these enjoyed the immunity of the Crown unless a statute expressly provided otherwise. See *Minister of Supply* v. *British Thomson-Houston Co*. [1943] K.B. 478.

[4] *Canterbury (Viscount)* v. *Att.-Gen*. (1842) 1 Ph. 306. The remedy by way of petition of right was available for breach of contract, and to recover property which had been wrongfully taken and withheld. *France, Fenwick & Co. Ltd*. v. *R*. [1927] 1 K.B. 52. Proceedings by way of petition of right were abolished by the Crown Proceedings Act 1947, Sched. 1, para. 2, but only with regard to liability in respect of Her Majesty's Government in the United Kingdom. A petition of right may, therefore, still lie in certain cases, but in the common law form used prior to the Petitions of Right Act 1860: *Franklin* v. *Att.-Gen*. [1974] Q.B. 185.

another.[5] On the other hand, the actual wrongdoer could, and still can, be sued in his personal capacity.[6] In practice the Treasury Solicitor usually defended an action against the individual Crown servant and the Treasury as a matter of grace undertook to satisfy any judgment awarded against him for a tort committed in the course of his employment.[7] If the actual wrongdoer could not be identified the Treasury Solicitor would supply the name of a merely nominal defendant for the purpose of the action, *i.e.* a person who, though a government servant, had nothing to do with the alleged wrong. But in *Royster* v. *Cavey*[8] it was held that the court had no jurisdiction to try the case unless the subordinate named by the Treasury Solicitor was the person who apparently had committed the tort. Since the Crown is today one of the largest employers of labour and occupiers of property in the country, this system of providing compensation for the victims of torts committed by Crown servants in the course of their employment was plainly inadequate and, finally, some 20 years after it was mooted, the Crown Proceedings Act 1947 put an end to Crown immunity in tort.

Crown Proceedings Act 1947

Under the Act the old maxim that "the King can do no wrong" is retained to the extent that no proceedings can be instituted against the Sovereign in person,[9] and there are savings in respect of the Crown's prerogative and statutory powers,[10] but otherwise the general effect of the Act is to equate the Crown with a private person of full age and capacity for the purposes of tortious liability.[11] The Crown cannot, however, be liable in tort except as provided by the Act and this cannot be evaded by dressing up the claim as one for a declaration that the Crown is behaving wrongfully.[12] Section 2(1) provides that the Crown shall be liable[13] as if it were such a person: (*a*) in respect of torts committed by its servants or agents[14]; (*b*) in respect of any

---

[5] *Raleigh* v. *Goschen* [1898] 1 Ch. 73, 83; *Bainbridge* v. *Postmaster-General* [1906] 1 K.B. 178. See also *Lane* v. *Cotton* (1701) 1 Ld.Raym. 646.

[6] He could not, and cannot now, plead the orders of the Crown or State necessity as a defence. *Entick* v. *Carrington* (1765) 19 St.Tr. 1030; *Wilkes* v. *Wood* (1763) *ibid.* at p. 1153.

[7] Dicey, *Law of the Constitution* (9th ed.), p. 531 (omitted from 10th ed.); Crown Proceedings Report Cmd. 2842 (1927). In 1942 the Lord Chancellor appointed an independent person to certify (if the claimant should so desire) whether the subordinate was acting in the course of his employment. This was in consequence of a debate on the topic in the House of Lords, April 13, 1942. *Hansard*, Vol. 122, cols. 535–568. Previously, the decision on this point had been with the department concerned.

[8] [1947] K.B. 204, the Court of Appeal acting upon emphatic *obiter dicta* of the House of Lords in *Adams* v. *Naylor* [1946] A.C. 543.

[9] s.40(1).

[10] s.11(1).

[11] But this is not to say that duties owed by the Crown can in all respects be equated with those owed by private persons: *ante*, p. 98.

[12] *Trawnik* v. *Lennox* [1985] 1 W.L.R. 532 (where the court had no jurisdiction to hear a claim for a nuisance in Berlin because it did not arise in respect of the Crown's activities in the U.K.: s.40(2)(*b*)).

[13] The action is brought against the appropriate government department in accordance with a list published by the Treasury, otherwise the Attorney-General may be made defendant (s.17). See Bickford Smith, *The Crown Proceedings Act*; Bell, *Crown Proceedings*; Glanville Williams, *Crown Proceedings*; Street, *Governmental Liability*, pp. 25–52.

[14] "Agent" includes an independent contractor (s.38(2)) but the Crown is not on this account subject to any greater liability for the tort of an independent contractor employed by it than it would be if it were a private person: s.40(2)(*d*).

breach of those duties which a person owes to his servants or agents at common law by reason of being their employer; and (c) in respect of any breach of the duties attaching at common law to the ownership, occupation, possession or control of property.[15] Section 2(2) makes the Crown liable for breach of statutory duty, provided that the statute in question is one which binds other persons besides the Crown and its officers. Moreover, the apportionment provisions of the Civil Liability (Contribution) Act 1978 and the Law Reform (Contributory Negligence) Act 1945, as well as the analogous provisions of the Maritime Conventions Act 1911, apply to proceedings in which the Crown is a party.[16] There is a little doubt whether an action lies against the Crown on behalf of a deceased person's estate under the Law Reform (Miscellaneous Provisions) Act 1934 or on behalf of his dependants under the Fatal Accidents Act 1976, but it is submitted that on principle the Crown should be liable.[17]

There are, however, certain limitations on the Crown's general liability in tort. Until 1987 it was not possible for a member of the armed forces to sue the Crown for injuries inflicted by a fellow-member in the execution of his duty or arising from the condition of premises or equipment. There was a similar immunity for the actual wrongdoer.[18] These restrictions were removed by the Crown Proceedings (Armed Forces) Act 1987.[19] The remaining limitations are:

1. Officers, that is, servants or Ministers of the Crown,[20] who may render the Crown liable are only those appointed directly or indirectly by the Crown and paid wholly out of moneys provided by Parliament or a fund certified by the Treasury as equivalent.[21] This excludes liability for police officers who are not paid out of such funds, even in the case of the Metropolitan Police,[22] and also for public corporations which are, normally, liable themselves like any other corporation.[23]

2. The Crown cannot be made liable for an act or omission of its servant unless that act or omission would, apart from the Act, have given rise to a

---

[15] The duties owed by an occupier of premises to his invitees and licensees are now contained in the Occupiers' Liability Act 1957, which binds the Crown. The liability of the Crown under the Act thus falls under s.2(2), but s.2(1)(c) continues to apply to the other duties which attach to the ownership, occupation, possession or control of property such as those in the tort of nuisance.

[16] s.4.

[17] Clerk and Lindsell, *Torts*, 16th ed., para. 2–13, Glanville Williams, *op. cit.*, pp. 55–58; Treitel, "Crown Proceedings: Some Recent Developments" [1957] Pub.L. 321, 322–326.

[18] s.10 of the 1947 Act, which applied only to death or personal injury.

[19] s.10 may be revived by order of the Secretary of State: s.2 of the 1987 Act. While the law of negligence may be applicable to routine military activities (*Groves* v. *Commonwealth* (1982) 41 A.L.R. 193) it does not follow that there would be a duty of care in the course of active operations: *Shaw Savill Co.* v. *Commonwealth* (1940) 66 C.L.R. 344.

[20] s.38(2). The Crown is not expressly defined, but it appears to include all government departments, officers, servants and agents of the Crown.

[21] s.2(6). s.1 provides that where a petition of right was formerly available, *e.g.* for detinue, "the claim may be enforced as of right." s.2 need not be invoked for the recovery of property, and the definition of "officer" in s.2(6) is inapplicable. Street, *Government Liability*, p. 35.

[22] See now the Police Act 1964, s.48, *ante*, p. 566.

[23] *Tamlin* v. *Hannaford* [1950] 1 K.B. 18. *cf. Glasgow Corp.* v. *Central Land Board*, 1956 S.L.T. 41 (H.L.). See also *Bank Voor Handel en Scheepvaart* v. *Administrator of Hungarian Property* [1954] A.C. 584. For the special position of the Post Office, see *post*, p. 661.

cause of action against the servant himself.[24] This preserves such defences as act of state but does not, it is submitted, extend so far as to exempt the Crown from liability in those exceptional cases where the master is vicariously liable even though his servant is immune from liability himself.[25]

3. The Crown is not liable for anything done by any person in discharging responsibilities of a judicial nature vested in him or any responsibilities he has in connection with execution of the judicial process.[26]

Act of state

It is proposed to deal with this matter very shortly since it belongs much more to the realm of constitutional and international law than to the law of tort.[27] There is no doubt that no action may be brought either against the Crown or anyone else in respect of an act of state, but there is little agreement on the meaning of this phrase. Certainly an injury inflicted upon a foreigner abroad which is either authorised or ratified by the Crown is for this purpose an "act of state" and cannot be made the subject of an action in the English courts,[28] but it is doubtful whether, as an answer to a claim for tort, act of state goes any further than that. It will probably not avail a defendant to plead act of state in respect of an act done within British territory,[29] whatever the nationality of the plaintiff[30] and it may well be unavailing against a non-alien wherever he may be.[31] However, as respects acts done abroad, modern changes in nationality law may require redefinition of the categories of persons against whom the defence may not be used.[32] An act of the Crown may, of course, be lawful as an act of prerogative, and section 11 of the Crown Proceedings Act preserves the Crown's rights to exercise its statutory and prerogative powers, but there is no prerogative power to seize or destroy the property of a subject without paying compensation.[33]

Post Office

The Post Office was until 1969 a department of government, but, despite

---

[24] s.2, proviso. The Crown has the benefit of any statute regulating or limiting the liability of a government department or officer of the Crown: s.2(4).

[25] Clerk and Lindsell, *Torts* (16th ed.), para. 2–04. *Contra*, Glanville Williams, *Crown Proceedings*, pp. 44–45.

[26] s.2(5).

[27] See Hood Phillips, *Constitutional and Administrative Law*, (7th ed.), pp. 278–284.

[28] *Buron* v. *Denman* (1848) 2 Ex. 167. cf. *Carr* v. *Fracis, Times & Co.* [1902] A.C. 176.

[29] *Johnstone* v. *Pedlar* [1921] A.C. 262.

[30] With the rather obvious exception of enemy aliens present in British territory without licence.

[31] It seems that Lord Reid agreed: *Att.-Gen.* v. *Nissan, supra,* at p. 213. The other members of the House of Lords were more cautious, and reserved their opinions.

[32] When most of the cases were decided the common law recognised only the simple distinction between "British subjects" and aliens and it is in these terms that the cases speak. From 1948 onwards "British subject" became a general secondary status lying behind the individual citizenship laws of Commonwealth countries, no longer necessarily implying allegiance to the Crown. Under the British Nationality Act 1981 it is turned into a limited residual class, the general secondary status now being that of Commonwealth citizen.

[33] *Att.-Gen.* v. *De Keyser's Royal Hotel* [1920] A.C. 508; *Burmah Oil Co. Ltd.* v. *Lord Advocate* [1965] A.C. 75; *Att.-Gen.* v. *Nissan,* (*supra*) at p. 227, *per* Lord Pearce. The common law right to compensation is considerably restricted by the War Damage Act 1965, *post*, p. 710.

the general provisions of the Crown Proceedings Act 1947, no proceedings in tort lay against the Crown for any act or omission of a servant of the Crown in relation to a postal packet or telephonic communication.[34] Now the Post Office is a statutory corporation,[35] but the immunity from liability in tort is preserved.[36] However, by a provision similar to that formerly contained in the Crown Proceedings Act[37] it is enacted that the Post Office shall be liable for the loss of or damage to a *registered inland* postal packet when that loss or damage is caused by the wrongful act, neglect or default of an officer, servant or agent of the Post Office.[38] Unless the contrary is shown, it is presumed that the loss or damage was so caused,[39] but the amount recoverable is limited to the market value of the packet or the maximum available under a scheme made in accordance with the provisions of the Act, whichever is the less.[40] The cause of action thus created is a statutory cause of action of a tortious character similar to an action for breach of bailment and, subject to the limits provided for, damages should be assessed on that basis.[41]

Foreign sovereigns

English law was for long committed to the proposition that a foreign sovereign State enjoyed absolute immunity from liability before an English court unless the immunity had been waived by submission to the jurisdiction.[42] The doctrine was not confined to "acts of State" and had become a serious problem in modern times because of the practice by many countries of carrying on ordinary trading activities through organs of State. Accordingly, attempts were made to restrict the immunity, culminating in the decision of the House of Lords in *The Congreso del Partido*[43] whereby a court was required to analyse the nature of the obligation and breach in question to determine whether it was of a private law or a "governmental" character.[44] However, in respect of causes of action arising after November

[34] Crown Proceedings Act 1947, s.9(1).
[35] Post Office Act 1969. It is expressly enacted that the Post Office is not to be regarded as a servant or agent of the Crown: *ibid*. s.6(5).
[36] *Ibid*. s.29. The immunity is, if anything, more extensive than that previously provided for, and the immunity of servants or agents of the Post Office, previously contained in the Crown Proceedings Act, s.9(2), is also preserved in a more extensive form: s.29(2). No contract exists between the Post Office and the sender of a postal packet and so the provisions of s.29 cannot be avoided by basing a claim on breach of contract: *Triefus & Co. Ltd*. v. *Post Office* [1957] 2 Q.B. 352. In *American Express Co*. v. *British Airways Board* [1983] 1 W.L.R. 701 (an action against a sub-contractor) it was held that s.29 ensures immunity against claims framed in bailment or under the Carriage by Air Act. The former point had been left open in *Harold Stephen & Co. Ltd*. v. *The Post Office* [1977] 1 W.L.R. 1172.
[37] s.9(2).
[38] Post Office Act 1969, s.30(1).
[39] *Ibid*. s.30(2).
[40] *Ibid*. s.30(3). Schemes are made under s.28 of the Act and replace the old Post Office Regulations.
[41] *Building and Civil Engineering Holidays Scheme Management Ltd*. v. *Post Office* [1966] 1 Q.B. 247, a decision on the Crown Proceedings Act, s.9(2). Proceedings under s.30 must be begun within 12 months of the date of posting and, unless the court grants leave to the contrary, only the sender or addressee of the packet may claim: Post Office Act 1969, s.30(5). Telecommunications services are now governed by contracts made under the Telecommunications Scheme.
[42] *The Cristina* [1938] A.C. 485. As to the immunity of diplomatic officials see the Diplomatic Privileges Act 1964.
[43] [1983] A.C. 244.
[44] The House differed as to this issue on the conversion claim in this case.

21, 1978, the law is contained in the State Immunity Act 1978. The fundamental provision is that a state is immune from the jurisdiction of the English courts except as provided by the Act.[45] Much of the Act concerns matters of contract[46], but for our purposes the principal exceptions from sovereign immunity[47] are (*a*) an act or omission in this country causing death or personal injury (*b*) obligations arising out of the ownership possession or use of property in this country[48] and (*c*) Admiralty proceedings (whether *in rem* or *in personam*) in respect of ships used for commercial purposes.[49] The residual immunity contained in the Act does not protect an entity distinct from the executive organs of the State[50] unless the proceedings arise out of the exercise of sovereign authority and the State would have been immune.[51]

Independently of sovereign immunity, there is a principle of English law that the courts will not adjudicate on acts done abroad by virtue of the sovereign authority of foreign states. In *Buttes Gas and Oil Co.* v. *Hammer*[52] the House of Lords therefore stayed litigation between private parties when it involved an examination of allegations of conspiracy between one party and a sovereign ruler and acts of assertion of territorial sovereignty by other states in the area.

European Economic Community

Article 215(2) of the EEC Treaty renders the Community liable for damage caused by its institutions or servants, "in accordance with the general principles common to the laws of the Member States." However, this cannot be precisely equated with tort liability in English law, if only because it may extend to administrative or even legislative acts which could not be the basis of a tort action in our law. In any event, jurisdiction over such claims is vested in the European Court of Justice and the topic is a branch of law in its own right.[53]

JUDICIAL ACTS[54]

The law casts a wide immunity around acts done in the administration of justice. This has been rather infelicitously styled a "privilege." But that

---

[45] s.1(1).

[46] *cf. Amalgamated Metal* v. *D.T.I.*, *The Times*, March 21, 1989 (misrepresentation in commercial context).

[47] The State may still submit to the jurisdiction: s.2.

[48] s.5 and 6 respectively.

[49] s.10. For States parties to the Brussels Convention of 1926, see s.10(6).

[50] *cf.* C. *Czarnikow Ltd.* v. *Centrala Handler Zagranicznego "Rolimpex"* [1979] A.C. 351.

[51] But a central bank is equated with a State: s.14(4).

[52] [1982] A.C. 888. Similar considerations played some part in English law's long adherence to the rule that an English court had no jurisdiction over actions involving trespass to foreign land. That rule was abolished by s.30 of the Civil Jurisdiction and Judgments Act 1982—there is still no jurisdiction if the action is principally concerned with title to, or the right to possession of such property.

[53] See Lasok and Bridge, *Law and Institutions of the European Communities*, 4th ed. and MacKenzie Stuart, "The Non-Contractual Liability of the European Economic Community," Maccabean Lecture in Jurisprudence (1975).

[54] The topic is dealt with at length in Winfield, *Present Law of Abuse of Legal Procedure*, Chap. 7.

might imply that the judge has a private right to be malicious, whereas its real meaning is that in the public interest it is not desirable to inquire whether acts of this kind are malicious or not. It is rather a right of the public to have the independence of the judges preserved rather than a privilege of the judges themselves.[55] It is better to take the chance of judicial incompetence, irritability, or irrelevance, than to run the risk of getting a Bench warped by apprehension of the consequences of judgments which ought to be given without fear or favour.

Despite a valiant attempt by Lord Denning M.R. to rationalize the law into one, unified principle,[56] a distinction must still be drawn between a judge of the High Court and others. With respect to the former, he is immune from liability for any act of a judicial character even though he is acting in excess of jurisdiction, whether as a result of a mistake of fact or of law: it is only if he acts in bad faith, doing what he knows he has no power to do, that he is liable in damages. "If the Lord Chief Justice himself, on the acquittal of a defendant charged before him with a criminal offence, were to say, 'That is a perverse verdict,' and thereupon proceed to pass a sentence of imprisonment, he could be sued for trespass."[57] To be contrasted with this is the position of justices of the peace and other judges of inferior courts,[58] who are liable if, even without bad faith, they act outside their jurisdiction. This covers not only cases which justices have no power to try[59] but also the passing of a sentence which is beyond their powers. It may even cover the omission of a procedural step which is regarded as essential to found their jurisdiction to pass the sentence in question: in *Re McC.*[60] the justices sentenced a juvenile offender to a term of detention without first informing him of his right to apply for legal aid and this act was held to be outside their jurisdiction. It seems that the same result would follow where justices have failed to inform a defendant, before commencing a summary trial of an indictable offence, of his right to trial by jury.[61] But a procedural irregularity in achieving a result which the court has power to achieve does not necessarily take the act outside the jurisdiction. This is the true explanation of *Sirros* v. *Moore.*[62] The plaintiff had been convicted of an offence and recommended for deportation by a stipendiary magistrate, but without an order for his detention. The judge in the Crown Court,[63] wrongly thinking that he

---

[55] *Bottomley* v. *Brougham* [1908] 1 K.B. 584, 586–587, *per* Channell J.; *Nakhla* v. *McCarthy* [1978] 1 N.Z.L.R. 291.

[56] In *Sirros* v. *Moore* [1975] Q.B. 118.

[57] *Re McC.* [1985] A.C. 528, 540, *per* Lord Bridge. But if the act is in fact within his jurisdiction the fact that it is done maliciously does not take it outside that jurisdiction: *Anderson* v. *Gorrie* [1895] 1 Q.B. 668. The concept of jurisdiction is a difficult one which may vary in its meaning from one legal context to another. For example, its meaning here is narrower than that given to it in the context of judicial review: *Re McC.*, *supra*, at p. 542. Here what is involved is the power to decide an issue, not the method by which that decision is reached.

[58] *e.g.* county courts. Though *Re McC.* concerns only justices the reasoning applies to all inferior courts: see [1985] A.C. 541, 554. See also *Case of the Marshalsea* (1613) 10 Co. Rep. 68b; *Houlden* v. *Smith* (1850) 14 Q.B. 841.

[59] But an error as to a collateral matter on which the jurisdiction depends will not take the case outside the jurisdiction: *Re McC.*, *supra*, at p. 544; *Johnston* v. *Meldon* (1891) 30 L.R. Ir. 15.

[60] *Supra*, on appeal from Northern Ireland, where the law is for this purpose the same.

[61] *Ibid.* at p. 546, *per* Lord Bridge. See also *R.* v. *Manchester City JJ., ex p. Davies* [1988] N.L.J. 260.

[62] [1975] Q.B. 118.

[63] This not being a trial on indictment, the Crown Court was an inferior court.

had no jurisdiction to hear an appeal against deportation, dismissed it but ordered the plaintiff to be detained. This did not amount to trespass because he *did* have power to overrule the initial decision against detention and intended to do so, but implemented that intention by a "hopelessly irregular procedure."

The position with regard to justices of the peace is further complicated by statutory provisions. Section 44 of the Justices of the Peace Act 1979[64] provides that "if apart from this section any action lies against a justice of the peace for an action done by him in the execution of his duty . . . with respect to any matter within his jurisdiction" then an action lies at the suit of a person who has been damaged thereby and proves that the act in question "was done maliciously and without reasonable and probable cause." If such a liability ever existed[65] it is probably now obsolete.[66] Section 45 gives a cause of action to any person injured by "any act done by a justice of the peace in a matter in respect of which by law he does not have jurisdiction or in which he has exceeded his jurisdiction."[67] It is this section in particular which makes it impossible to equate the position of justices with that of judges of superior courts in respect of acts outside jurisdiction. However, the liability of justices is drastically restricted by section 52 of the 1979 Act, which provides that in any action against a justice for anything done by him in the execution of his office,[68] then if it is proved that the plaintiff was guilty of the offence charged and that his imprisonment was no greater than that assigned by law for the offence, damages are limited to one penny and he is not entitled to any costs.[69] In any event, a justice who has acted reasonably and in good faith is entitled to be indemnified out of public funds in respect of damages and costs.[70] Enough has been said to show that it will be a rare case in which a person may recover substantial damages in respect of a judicial act. An action in tort is not, however, the only route to compensation. Where a criminal conviction is reversed on the basis of a newly-discovered fact there may be a statutory right to compensation under section 133 of the Criminal Justice Act 1988.

Other exemptions connected with the administration of justice

We have already seen that an advocate enjoys immunity in respect of his conduct of the case in court or decisions closely connected therewith.[71] Similarly, no action for negligence will lie in respect of investigations carried out by a potential witness before any proceedings have been commenced,

---

[64] Re-enacting s.1 of the Justices' Protection Act 1848.

[65] Winfield thought that it "only baptised something that had never existed or had since died": *op. cit.*, p. 217.

[66] *Re McC.*, *supra*, *per* Lord Bridge and Lord Templeman; Lord Keith and Lord Brandon *dubitante*.

[67] Re-enacting s.2 of the Justices' Protection Act 1848.

[68] Which covers acts done without jurisdiction or in excess of jurisdiction: *R. v. Waltham JJ., ex p. Solanke* [1986] Q.B. 983.

[69] *cf. R. v. Manchester City JJ., ex p. Davies* [1988] N.L.J. 260 (limitation inapplicable because no power to imprison except for wilful default).

[70] Justices of the Peace Act 1979, s.53.

[71] *Ante*, p. 102.

provided they are made or carried out for the purpose of possible proceedings[72]; and there is not even a right of action for one who claims that he has suffered as a result of perjury by a witness.[73] Though the functions involved are not judicial and the decisions have no direct connection with the immunities considered here, it has also been held that a social security adjudicating officer[74] and an investigating officer under the police complaints procedure[75] owe no duty of care to the subjects of their adjudication or investigation. The principal reason is that there are statutory routes of appeal backed up by judicial review but in the case of the investigating officer there is the further reason, comparable to that for judicial immunity, namely the public interest in the "free and fearless" investigation of complaints. One of the torts most likely to be committed in the course of judicial proceedings is defamation and as we have seen,[76] the law casts the protection of absolute privilege over judges, advocates and witnesses.

Officers of the law

An officer of the law who executes process apparently regular, without knowing in fact that the person who authorised him to do so has exceeded his powers, is protected in spite of the proceedings being ill-founded.[77] Again by the Constables Protection Act 1750,[78] no action can be brought against a constable for anything done in obedience to any warrant[79] issued by a justice of the peace until the would-be plaintiff has made a written demand for a copy of the warrant and the demand has not been complied with for six days. If it is complied with, then the constable, if he produces the warrant at the trial of the action against him, is not liable in spite of any defect of jurisdiction in the justice. But if he arrests a person not named in the warrant or seizes goods of one who is not mentioned in it, he does so at his peril. His mistake, however honest, will not excuse him. In *Hoye* v. *Bush*[80] Richard Hoye was suspected of stealing a mare. A warrant was issued for his arrest, but it described him as "John Hoye," which in fact was his father's name. Richard was arrested under this warrant and subsequently sued Bush, the constable, for false imprisonment. Bush was held liable, for although Richard was the man who actually was wanted, still the warrant described

---

[72] *Evans* v. *London Hospital Medical College* [1981] 1 W.L.R. 184. Note, however, that this was a case where the plaintiff alleged that the defendant's negligence had led to the plaintiff's prosecution. It does not follow that the same considerations apply to a claim for negligence by a party against his own expert. A person who sets the law in motion may be liable for malicious prosecution: *ante*, Chap. 19.

[73] *Hargreaves* v. *Bretherton* [1959] 1 Q.B. 45; *Marrinan* v. *Vibart* [1963] 1 Q.B. 234; *cf. Roy* v. *Prior* [1971] A.C. 470.

[74] *Jones* v. *Department of Employment* [1988] 2 W.L.R. 493.

[75] *Calveley* v. *Chief Constable of Merseyside* [1989] 2 W.L.R. 624.

[76] See *ante* p. 333.

[77] *Sirros* v. *Moore* [1975] Q.B. 118; *London (Mayor of)* v. *Cox* (1867) L.R. 2 H.L. 239, 269, *per* Willes J.; see generally Clerk and Lindsell, *Torts*, 16th ed., Chap. 27, s.4.

[78] s.6.

[79] For powers of arrest without warrant, see *ante* p. 62.

[80] (1840) 1 M. & G. 775; under s.125 the Magistrates' Courts Act 1980, a warrant for the arrest of a person for an offence may be executed although it is not in the constable's possession, but it must be shown to the person arrested as soon as possible.

somebody else and it did not help Bush that John Hoye was not really wanted.

MINORS

After an early period of uncertainty, the common law adopted 21 years as the age of majority for most purposes[81] and it remained at this until 1970, when it was reduced by statute to 18.[82] So far as the law of tort is concerned, only two questions arise concerning minors, namely their capacity to sue and to be sued for tort.

Capacity to sue; unborn children

In general no distinction falls to be taken between a minor and an adult so far as their respective capacities to sue for tort are concerned, save that a minor must sue by his "next friend."

There has, however, been much doubt over whether a minor can sue for an injury done to him before he was born, as where he is born with a deformity or disability as a result of injuries suffered while *en ventre sa mère*.[83] There was no decisive English authority on the point, but there were favourable decisions in Commonwealth jurisdictions[84] and it is thought that if the matter had come before an English court[85] the decision would have been in favour of liability.[86] To put the matter beyond doubt, however, the Law Commission proposed legislation on the matter[87] and the present law[88] is to be found in the Congenital Disabilities (Civil Liability) Act 1976.[89] Its principal provisions may be summarised as follows. In the first place, an action only lies if the child, the plaintiff, is born alive and disabled.[90] Secondly, the liability to the child is "derivative," in other words it only

---

[81] Holdsworth, H.E.L. iii, pp. 510–511.

[82] Family Law Reform Act 1969, s.1.

[83] It was held at an early date that a posthumous child of a deceased father could maintain an action under the Fatal Accidents Act: *The George and Richard* (1871) L.R. 3 Ad. & E. 466. Winfield thought that if a tort were committed before a child's birth to property to which he became entitled on birth, he could sue.

[84] *Watt* v. *Rama* [1972] V.R. 353; *Duval* v. *Seguin* (1972) 26 D.L.R. 418. The American trend in favour of liability, which Prosser refers to as "up till that time the most spectacular abrupt reversal of a well-settled rule in the history of torts," began in *Bonbritz* v. *Kotz* 65 F.Supp. 138 (1946).

[85] The issue was settled by agreement in *S.* v. *Distillers Co.* [1970] 1 W.L.R. 114 and a duty was admitted by the defendant in *Williams* v. *Luff* (1978) 122 S.J. 164. In *McKay* v. *Essex Area Health Authority* [1982] Q.B. 1166 the defendants conceded the existence of a duty except in so far as the claim concerned "wrongful life."

[86] Among the voluminous writings on the topic see Winfield, "The Unborn Child" (1942) 8 C.L.J. 76; Tedeschi, "On Tort Liability for 'Wrongful Life' " (1966) 1 Israel L.R. 513; Lovell and Griffiths-Jones, "The Sins of the Fathers—Tort Liability for Pre-Natal Injuries" (1974) 90 L.Q.R. 531; Pace, "Civil Liability for Pre-Natal Injuries" (1977) 40 M.L.R. 141.

[87] See "Injuries to Unborn Children" Law Com. No. 60 (1974).

[88] The Act came into force on July 22, 1976. In respect of birth on or after that date there is no possibility of the judicial creation of liability at common law: s.4(5).

[89] Pace, *loc. cit.* The Act is short but complex in its drafting.

[90] But the *mother* may have an action in respect of a still-birth: *Bagley* v. *N. Herts. H.A.* (1986) 136 N.L.J. 1014. For definition of "disabled" see s.4(1). The damages referred to in s.4(4) for "loss of expectation of life" were abolished by the Administration of Justice Act 1982: *ante*, p. 611.

arises if the defendant was under an actual or potential tort liability[91] to either parent of the child for the act or omission which led to the disability, but for this purpose "it is no answer [to claim by the child] that there could not have been such liability because the parent suffered no actionable injury, if there was a breach of legal duty which, if accompanied by injury, would have given rise to the liability."[92] In other words, if a pregnant woman takes a drug which has been manufactured or developed negligently or in circumstances which contravene the Consumer Protection Act 1987 and this causes her child to be born disabled the child may recover damages from the manufacturer even though the mother suffers no injury herself from the drug.[93] In practice the commonest situation giving rise to liability[94] is likely to be that where the child is injured *en ventre sa mère* but the Act extends more widely than this to cover an occurrence which affects either parent in his or her ability to bear a normal, healthy child,[95] so that, for example, a negligent injury to the mother's reproductive system *before conception* could found an action by a child conceived thereafter and born disabled as a result.[96] The mother herself is not generally liable under the Act so that there is no possibility of, say, an action being brought in respect of disabilities said to have been caused by the mother smoking during pregnancy.[97] The good sense of this immunity is clear[98]: not only is the possibility of liability revolting to normal feelings but there is a risk of the liability being used as a potent weapon in husband-wife disputes. The Law Commission thought that on balance the immunity should not be extended to the father, and the Act so provides, but the Pearson Commission disagreed and proposed an amendment on this point.[99] The policy arguments in favour of immunity are nothing like so strong when the potential parental liability would be covered by insurance[1] and section 2 of the Act accordingly provides that a woman driving a motor vehicle when she knows or ought to know herself to be pregnant is to be regarded as under a duty of care towards her unborn child.

---

[91] This liability will commonly be for negligence, but there is nothing in the Act to confine it to this. S.3 extends the provisions of the Nuclear Installations Act 1965 (*ante*, p. 449) to pre-natal injury. The running of time against the parent is irrelevant: s.1(3) ("or would, if sued in time, have been so"). While the child's cause of action accrues upon birth (s.4(3)) the Limitation Act would prevent time running against him until he reached majority: *post*, p. 724.

[92] s.1(3).

[93] In many cases it would be impossible for the mother to suffer any physical injury from the drug and it then perhaps looks odd to say that there has been any breach of legal duty, but it is inconceivable that such a case falls outside the Act. Perhaps the possibility of "nervous shock" to the mother may allay doubts on this point.

[94] This is not to suggest that it will be very common for the Act to be invoked at all. The Pearson Commission estimated that no more than 0.5 per cent. of all severely disabled children would have grounds for claiming tort compensation. The British Medical Association said that "the vast majority of congenital defects and diseases are of unknown causation and the number of instances which can be unequivocally ascribed to any particular act of omission or commission are few." See Cmnd. 7054, Vol. 1, Chap. 26 and Annexes 12 and 13.

[95] s.1(2)(*a*).

[96] But in this situation there is a high likelihood that the action could be met by the defence of knowledge of the risk by the mother: s.1(4).

[97] Proving cause and effect in an individual case might be impossible, anyway.

[98] But *cf*. Pace, *loc. cit.*, pp. 154–155.

[99] Cmnd. 7034, Vol. 1, para. 1471.

[1] Though the claim is in form one against the parent, most people would regard the "real" defendant as the insurer. Under the present law, claims by children injured as passengers in cars negligently driven by parents are not uncommon.

The derivative nature of the child's action in cases other than those involving negligent driving by the mother is emphasised by the supplementary provisions of section 1, which "identify" the child with the parents for the purposes of defences. Thus in the case of an occurrence preceding the time of conception knowledge by either parent of the risk of disablement will bar the child's action[2]; where the parent affected shared responsibility for the child being born disabled, the child's damages are to be reduced according to the extent of the parent's responsibility[3]; and any contract term having the effect of excluding or restricting liability to the parent is equally effective in respect of liability to the child.[4]

Modern medicine offers a number of methods of detecting, or at least predicting the probability of, naturally occurring congenital abnormalities. Since detection of one of these conditions may lead to the provision of a lawful abortion the question arises whether the child born disabled as a result of negligence in carrying out or assessing tests of this nature may claim damages for what has been called "wrongful life." This is of course a very different matter from the complaint of the plaintiff who has been injured *en ventre sa mére* or as a result of some earlier injury to the mother: the complaint now is not that the defendant caused the plaintiff's disability but that the defendant's negligence removed the opportunity of terminating the plaintiff's existence before birth. In *McKay* v. *Essex Area Health Authority*[5] the Court of Appeal said, *obiter*, that no such claim lies under the Congenital Disabilities (Civil Liability) Act[6] because (*a*) the Act imports the assumption that but for the occurrence giving rise to the disabled birth, the child would have been born normal and healthy, not that it would not have been born at all,[7] and (*b*) it prevents the imposition of any liability at common law.[8] If this is correct it means that *McKay's* case, where liability was denied at common law,[9] is of diminishing practical importance, but the Court of Appeal's reasoning is still of interest. Various objections of a "public policy" nature are referred to in the judgments (for example, the dangers of a legal assessment of the life of a handicapped child as less valuable than that of a

---

[2] s.1(4). But not where the father is responsible for the injury to the mother and she does not know of the risk.

[3] s.1(7). *cf.* a case under s.2, which would follow the normal rule of non-identification (*ante*, p. 164), allowing the child to recover in full against either defendant and consigning the final allocation of loss to contribution proceedings between the defendants. The effect of s.1(7) might be to raise by a side-wind the very issue of maternal responsibility which had prompted the grant of immunity to the mother. Accordingly, the Pearson Commission recommended its repeal: Cmnd. 7054, Vol. 1, para. 1477. But it would still be open to that defendant to allege that the injury was *solely* the mother's fault.

[4] s.1(6). This provision is likely to be of very limited effect in view of s.2(1) of the Unfair Contract Terms Act 1977 (*post*, p. 687) and is anyway inapplicable to cases under the Consumer Protection Act 1987: see s.6(3)(*c*) of that Act.

[5] [1982] Q.B. 1166.

[6] This was the intention of the Law Commission: Law Com. No. 60, para. 89.

[7] See s.1(2)(*b*): "An occurrence . . . which . . . affected the mother . . . or the child . . . so that the child is born with disabilities which would not otherwise have been present." No such assumption is built into s.1(2)(*a*), dealing with the period before conception. Could a "wrongful life" claim be based upon negligence in pre-conception genetic assessment and counselling? Or does the reference to "ability" in s.1(2)(*a*) require that there be some physically deleterious effect on the parent?

[8] s.4(5), which seems too broadly expressed for it to be argued that it is applicable only to those situations where a liability is imposed by s.1.

[9] The birth was before the Act.

"normal" child and the prospect of a claim against the mother where, informed of the danger, she refused an abortion) but that which most strongly influenced all the members of the court was the impossibility of assessing damages on what they regarded as any sensible basis, for the court would have to "compare the state of the plaintiff with nonexistence, of which the court can know nothing."[10] In fact, however, the courts had for many years been awarding damages for "loss of expectation of life,"[11] which required at least a basic judicial assumption about the "value" of death.[12] A more convincing explanation of the result of *McKay's* case is that in the eyes of the law any existence has, or is presumed to have (save perhaps in the most exceptional cases[13]) some value greater than nonexistence. Nearly all the discussion in the English and American[14] cases has been in terms of general damages, though similar problems arise over claims by the child for, say, exceptional medical expenses caused by the disability.[15] In practice most such claims are likely to be presented by the parents, whose claim is clearly unaffected by the Congenial Disabilities (Civil Liability) Act and is based on being deprived of the opportunity to choose not to conceive the child or have an abortion, as the case may be. There is no English authority[16] but it is thought that such a claim ought to succeed.[17]

The courts have also been faced with claims by mothers following unsuccessful sterilisation operations and the birth of normal children. At first, it was held that for reasons of public policy[18] damages were not recoverable for the cost and expenses of the child's upbringing, but the Court of Appeal eventually rejected this reasoning.[19] Where the child is normal it seems that any claim by a parent for the care and trouble of upbringing (but not for the

---

[10] [1982] Q.B. 1166, 1193, *per* Griffiths L.J.

[11] *Ante*, p. 611. Such damages were abolished by the Administration of Justice Act 1982.

[12] Stephenson L.J. (at p. 1181) refers to the fact that in loss of expectation of life cases the court was at least dealing on one side with human life, of which it had some experience. But can there be any doubt that a court would have awarded *some* damages for loss of expectation of life to, *e.g.* a severely disabled person killed in an accident (*cf. Burns*. v. *Edman* [1970] 2 Q.B. 541)? In fact, the assessment in *McKay's* case and in the generality of loss of expectation of life cases were equally "impossible," but in one the courts solved the problem by awarding no damages, in the other by awarding a conventional sum.

[13] See *Re B (A Minor)* [1981] 1 W.L.R. 1421 and *McKay's* case, *supra*, at p. 1188.

[14] Some of which are discussed in *McKay's* case. See also Capron in (1979) 79 Col. L. Rev. 618 and Comment (1980) 54 Tulane L. Rev. 480.

[15] In *Turpin* v. *Sortini* 182 Cal. Rptr. 337 (1981) the plaintiff's parents alleged that they would never have conceived her but for the negligence of the defendants in their assessment. The Supreme Court of California held that a claim by the plaintiff for medical expenses in treating her condition (deafness) stated a cause of action but one for general damages did not. Should the plaintiff have been required to bring into account the benefit of life? If so, how?

[16] It was not necessary for the court to deal with these aspects of the action in *McKay's* case since the reported proceedings concern an application to strike out elements of the child's own claim.

[17] The point was adverted to but not decided by Jupp J. in *Udale* v. *Bloomsbury Area Health Authority* [1983] 2 All E.R. 522, which concerned a normal child.

[18] *e.g.*, because such a claim would offend the moral ethos of society, which recognises the preciousness of human life; and because the child might suffer psychological damage if he learned of the suit. For a full discussion see Symmons, "Policy Factors in Actions for Wrongful Birth" (1987) 50 M.L.R. 269.

[19] *Emeh* v. *Kensington etc. A.H.A.* [1985] Q.B. 1012; *Thake* v. *Maurice* [1986] Q.B. 644. The wrongdoer "takes the family as he finds it" so that in the modest circumstances of *Thake* v. *Maurice* damages were modest (on the supplementary benefit scale) but in *Benarr* v. *Kettering H.A.* [1988] N.L.J. 179 a sum was awarded for the cost of private education.

expense thereof, nor for the pain and suffering of the birth) is to be offset by the happiness derived from having the child.[20]

Liability to be sued

In the law of tort there is no defence of infancy as such and a minor is as much liable to be sued for his torts as is an adult. In *Gorely* v. *Codd*,[21] Nield J. had no hesitation in holding that a boy of 16½ had been negligent when he accidentally shot the plaintiff with an air-rifle in the course of "larking about," and it is obvious that a motorist of 17½ is as responsible for negligent driving as one six months older. Where, however, the minor is very young, then, it appears, his age is relevant if he is sued for tort involving negligence or malice. This is to be inferred from the fact that a young child may well be incapable of the necessary mental state for liability in such torts, from the English cases concerning the contributory negligence of children[22]; and from a number of decisions in other jurisdictions.[23] In an action for negligence against a young child, therefore, it is insufficient to show that he behaved in a way which would amount to negligence on the part of an adult. It must be shown that his behaviour was unreasonable for a child of his age.

Tort and contract

In general contracts entered into by minors are void and unenforceable, and the question arises, therefore, whether if the facts show both a breach of a (void) contract and a tort, the contract rule can be evaded by framing the claim against the minor in tort. The answer, unsatisfactory though it may be from a theoretical point of view,[24] seems to be that a minor cannot be sued if the cause of action against him arises substantially *ex contractu* or if to allow the action would be to enforce the contract indirectly, but if the wrong is independent of the contract, then the minor may be sued even though but for the contract he would have had no opportunity of committing the tort.[25] In *R. Leslie Ltd.* v. *Shiell*[26] a minor had fraudulently represented to the plaintiffs that he was of full age and had thereby persuaded them to lend him money. He was held not liable for deceit or on any other ground for a judgment against him would have amounted to the enforcement of the contract of loan in a roundabout way. On the other hand, in *Burnard* v.

---

[20] *Thake* v. *Maurice*, *supra*, where (*a*) there was no such claim (*b*) the parents freely admitted that they loved the child.

[21] [1967] 1 W.L.R. 19; *Buckpitt* v. *Oates* [1968] 1 All E.R. 1145, 1149, *per* John Stephenson J.; *Williams* v. *Humphrey, The Times*, February 20, 1975.

[22] *Ante.* p. 163

[23] *Walmsley* v. *Humenick* [1954] 2 D.L.R. 232 (Sup. Ct. of B.C.); *McHale* v. *Watson* (1966) 115 C.L.R. 199 (H.Ct. of Aus.); *Yokton Agriculture and Industrial Exhibition Society* v. *Morley* (1967) 66 D.L.R. (3d) 37 (Sask.C.A.).

[24] See *ante*, p. 4.

[25] Pollock, *Contract* (13th ed.) pp 62–63, approved by Kennedy L.J. in *R. Leslie Ltd.* v. *Shiell* [1914] 3 K.B. 607, 620.

[26] *Supra*. This was first established in *Johnson* v. *Pye* (1665) 1 Sid. 258. See too *Stocks* v. *Wilson* [1913] 2 K.B. 235.

Haggis,[27] the defendant, an undergraduate of Trinity College, Cambridge, and a minor, was held liable in the following circumstances. He hired from the plaintiff a mare for riding on the express stipulation that she was not to be used for "jumping or larking." He nevertheless lent the mare to a friend who, while they were galloping about fields in the neighbourhood of Cambridge, tried to jump her over a fence, on which she was staked; she died from the wound. The defendant's conduct was, as Willes J. said,[28] "as much a trespass, notwithstanding the hiring for another purpose, as if, without any hiring at all, the defendant had gone into a field and taken the mare out and hunted her and killed her. It was a bare trespass, not within the object and purpose of the hiring. It was not even an excess. It was doing an act towards the mare which was altogether forbidden by the owner."[29]

If in *R. Leslie Ltd.* v. *Shiell* the minor had still been in possession of the money lent equity would have ordered its restoration on the ground of fraud. Now, under section 3(1) of the Minors' Contracts Act 1987 the court has a discretion to order the transfer back of any property acquired under the contract (or its proceeds) even without fraud. But if the money has been spent and there is nothing to show for it, nothing can be done.

Liability of parent

A parent or guardian[30] is not in general liable for the torts of a child; but to this there are two exceptions. First, where the child is employed by his parent and commits a tort in the course of his employment, the parent is vicariously responsible just as he would be for the tort of any other servant of his. Secondly, the parent will be liable if the child's tort were due to the parent's negligent control of the child in respect of the act that caused the injury,[31] or if the parent expressly authorised the commission of the tort, or possibly if he ratified the child's act. Thus, where a father gave his boy, about 15 years old, an airgun and allowed him to retain it after he had smashed a neighbour's window with it, he was held liable for the boy's tort in injuring the eye of another boy with the gun.[32] Where, however, a boy aged 13 had promised his father never to use his air-rifle outside the house (where there was a cellar in which the rifle could be fired) and subsequently broke that promise, the Court of Appeal refused to disturb the trial judge's findings that the father had not been negligent.[33] Nor will he be liable to one who is

[27] (1863) 14 C.B.(N.S.) 45. *Cf. Jennings* v. *Rundall* (1799) 8 T.R. 335; *Fawcett* v. *Smethhurst* (1915) 84 L.J.K.B. 473.
[28] *Ibid.* at p. 53.
[29] See too *Ballett* v. *Mingay* [1943] K.B.281.
[30] Note in this connection that school authorities are under no greater duty than that of a reasonably careful parent; *Ricketts* v. *Erith B.C.* [1943] 2 All E.R. 629; *Rich* v. *London County Council* [1953] 1 W.L.R. 895, C.A.; *Nicholson* v. *Westmorland County Council* [1962] C.L.Y. 2087. *cf. Carmarthenshire County Council* v. *Lewis* A.C. 549.
[31] If a juvenile court imposes a compensation order it is to be paid by the parent or guardian unless the court considers this unreasonable: Criminal Justice Act 1982, s.27. This does not apply to a local authority having a child in care under statute (*Leeds City Council* v. *W. Yorks Police* [1983] A.C. 29) but the authority would be under a tort duty of care (see, *e.g. Vicar of Writtle* v. *Essex C.C.* [1979] 77 L.G.R. 656.
[32] *Bebee* v. *Sales* (1916) 32 T.L.R. 413; *Newton* v. *Edgerley* [1959] 1 W.L.R. 1031. See, too, the Scottish case, *Brown* v. *Fulton* (1881) 9 R. 36.
[33] *Donaldson* v. *McNiven* (1952) 96 S.J. 747; *Gorely* v. *Codd* [1967] 1 W.L.R. 19. *cf. Newton* v. *Edgerley, supra,* where Lord Parker C.J. seems to put the father in an inescapable dilemma.

bitten by a dog which belongs to his daughter who is old enough to be able to exercise control over it, and this is so even if the father knows of the dog's ferocious temper.[34] Where, however the child is under the age of 16 a different rule prevails by statute.[35]

SPOUSES

It is now over 50 years since the abolition of the special rules governing a married woman's liability in tort and making her husband liable for her torts during marriage.[36] Suffice it now to say that as far as third parties are concerned there are no special rules governing husband and wife and neither is liable for the other's torts, though he or she may of course be liable as a joint tortfeasor if this is in fact the case. As between themselves, the common law rule was that no action in tort was possible, but in modern times this was productive of serious anomalies and injustices[37] and it was abolished by the Law Reform (Husband and Wife) Act 1962.[38] Each of the parties to a marriage now has the same right of action in tort against the other as if they were not married,[39] but, in order to prevent them from using the court as a forum for trivial domestic disputes, the proceedings may be stayed if it appears that no substantial benefit will accrue to either party from their continuation.[40] The proceedings may also be stayed if it appears that the case can be more conveniently disposed of under section 17 of the Married Women's Property Act 1882, which provides a summary procedure for determining questions of title or possession of property between husband and wife.[41]

CORPORATIONS

A corporation is an artificial person created by the law. It may come into existence either by the common law, or by royal charter, or by parliamentary authority, or by prescription or by custom. Whatever their origin may be, the characteristics common to most corporations are a distinctive name, a common seal and perpetuity of existence. This existence is quite independent of the human beings who are members of the corporation. Fellows of a college and shareholders of a brewery company may perish, but the college and brewery company still continue.

---

[34] *North* v. *Wood* [1914] 1 K.B. 629.
[35] *Ante*, pp. 459–460.
[36] Law Reform (Married Women and Tortfeasors) Act 1935. For a summary of the common law see the eleventh edition of this work.
[37] See Law Reform Committee, 9th Report, Cmnd. 1268 (1961).
[38] s.1(1).
[39] This means, of course, that even if proceedings are not brought against the spouse, a co-tortfeasor with him may have a right of contribution.
[40] s.1(2)(*a*). See *McLeod* v. *McLeod* (1963) 113 L.J. 420. In *Church* v. *Church* (1983) 133 N.L.J. 317 £9,605 damages were awarded in an action for battery between spouses.
[41] s.1(2)(*b*).

Capacity to sue in tort

A corporation can sue for torts committed against it,[42] but there are certain torts which, by their very nature, it is impossible to commit against a corporation, such as assault or false imprisonment. A corporation can sue for the malicious presentation of a winding-up petition[43] or for defamation, though the precise limits of the latter are unclear. It is certain that a trading corporation may sue in respect of defamation affecting its business or property,[44] but the law probably goes further and allows any corporation to sue in respect of matter defamatory of its conduct of its affairs.[45] Thus a local government authority is entitled to sue if defamed in respect of its "governing" reputation.[46]

A rather different point is that the corporation (and not its members) is the *only* proper plaintiff in respect of a tort against the corporation. This is simply a reflection of the elementary principle that A cannot bring an action against B to recover damages for an injury done by B to C, A (the member) and C (the corporation) being different persons. A shareholder is not an owner of the company's assets but merely has a right to participate in them on winding up. Hence if the sole asset of a company is a box containing £100,000 and the plaintiff owns 99 of the 100 shares in the company he cannot sue the robber who appropriates the contents of the box.[47]

Liability to be sued

Many corporations are expressly limited by the terms of their incorporation as to the acts which they may lawfully do.[48] If they observe those restrictions they are said to be acting *intra vires*, and this is still the case even when they commit a tort, provided it is done as an incident of some act which falls within their powers. If it is not connected in this way with what they are lawfully entitled to do, the tort is said to be *ultra vires*.

---

[42] *Semble*, even if engaged in an *ultra vires* undertaking at the material time: *National Telephone Co.* v. *Constable of St. Peter Port* [1900] A.C. 317, 321, *per* Lord Davey, *obiter*, a decision of the Privy Council on appeal from the Royal Court of Guernsey.

[43] *Quartz Hill Consolidated Gold Mining* v. *Eyre* (1883) 11 Q.B.D. 674.

[44] *Metropolitan Saloon Omnibus Co.* v. *Hawkins* (1859) 4 H. & N. 87.

[45] *Bognor Regis U.D.C.* v. *Campion* [1972] 2 Q.B. 169; *D. & L. Caterers Ltd.* v. *D'Ajou* [1945] K.B. 364; *National Union of General and Municipal Workers* v. *Gillan* [1946] K.B. 81; *Willis* v. *Brooks* [1947] 1 All E.R. 191. *South Hetton Coal Co. Ltd.* v. *N.E. News Association Ltd.* [1894] 1 Q.B. 133, though inconclusive on the point, seems to support this view. Dicta in *Manchester Corporation* v. *Williams* (1891) 63 L.T. 805, 806 (the fuller report) and *Lewis* v. *Daily Telegraph Ltd.* [1964] A.C. 234, 262, seems to support the narrower view.

[46] *Bognor Regis U.D.C.* v. *Campion, supra*; see also *Church of Scientology Inc.* v. *Anderson* [1980] W.A.R. 71 (religious corporation). But defamation which reflects solely upon the individual officers or workers is not actionable by the corporation. The Faulks Committee proposed that a corporation should have to show actual or prospective financial loss: Cmnd. 5909, para. 342.

[47] *Prudential Assurance Co. Ltd.* v. *Newman Industries Ltd. (No. 2)* [1982] Ch. 204, 223. The position is apparently the same even if the plaintiff keeps the key to the box and the defendant by deceit induces him to hand it over, for the deceit causes the plaintiff no loss separate from the loss to the company. *cf. Gould* v. *Vaggelas* (1984) 56 A.L.R. 31. But where there is fraud and the wrongdoers are in control of the company a shareholder may be able to bring a "derivative" action.

[48] It is generally accepted that a chartered corporation has all the powers of a natural person: *The Case of Sutton's Hospital* (1613) 10 Co.Rep. 23a. See Gower, *Modern Company Law* (4th ed.), p. 162.

(1) *Intra vires torts*

If the tort is committed by a servant or other agent of the corporation acting in the course of his employment, then the corporation is liable on exactly the same principle that any employer is vicariously responsible in the like circumstances. In time past there were procedural difficulties in the way of suing the corporation,[49] but these have long since disappeared. In 1812, it was held that a corporation could be sued in trover,[50] in 1842 in trespass,[51] and 1858 for libel,[52] and many other decisions have made it clear that wherever it is possible for a corporation to commit a tort at all, it can be sued.[53]

In one class of torts there was a difficulty which has been dispelled in only comparatively recent times—those which require malice in the sense of actual ill will, such as malicious prosecution. It was urged that a corporation had no mind and that therefore malice could not be imputed to it. But this was a needless and fallacious metaphysical subtlety, for the reason why a corporation is liable, if at all, for tort is because it is responsible (like any other employer) for the torts of its servants committed in the course of their employment, and they have the requisite mental equipment even if the corporation has none.[54]

(2) *Ultra vires torts*

In *Poulton* v. *L. & S.W. Ry.*[55] the defendants' stationmaster wrongfully detained the plaintiff because he refused to pay the fare of his horse. The power to detain in such circumstances was quite outside the defendants' powers. It was held that they were not liable, for the stationmaster could not be said to have been impliedly authorised to do such an act. Winfield considered that it followed that a corporation could not be vicariously liable for the torts of its servants committed in the course of an *ultra vires* undertaking, but it is submitted that this is not so. When *Poulton's* case was decided the "course of employment" test of vicarious liability was in its infancy; the need for "implied authority" was still much in the judges' minds[56] and there is obvious difficulty in holding that a corporation has impliedly authorised the doing of an act which it has itself no power to perform. Today, however, so long, at least, as the view is accepted that a master's liability for his servants' torts is truly vicarious,[57] there is no need for this technical argument to succeed. It will, no doubt, be comparatively rare for an *ultra vires* tort to be committed by a servant of a corporation in the course of his

[49] Pollock, *Torts* (15th ed.), p. 51, n. 19; Holdsworth, H.E.L., iii, 488–489.
[50] *Yarborough* v. *Bank of England* (1812) 16 East 6.
[51] *Maund* v. *Monmouthshire Canal Co.* (1842) 4 Man. & G. 452.
[52] *Whitfield* v. *S.E. Ry.* (1858) E.B. & E. 115.
[53] Halsbury's *Laws of England* (4th ed.), paras. 1374–1378.
[54] *Cornford* v. *Carlton Bank Ltd.* [1899] 1 Q.B. 392; [1900] 1 Q.B. 22; *Citizens' Life Assurance Co. Ltd.* v. *Brown* [1904] A.C. 423, 426, *per* Lord Lindley.
[55] (1867) L.R. 2 Q.B. 534; *Ormiston* v. *G.W. Ry.* [1917] 1 K.B. 598.
[56] See *ante*, pp. 561–562.
[57] See *ante*, pp. 586–588.

employment, but if such a case arises there is no valid reason why the corporation should not be liable.[58]

If this is correct, then the case of a tort which is expressly authorised by the corporation, whether *ultra vires* or not, will normally present no problem. If the act, constituting the tort is done by a servant of the corporation and with its express authority, it is hard to see that it will not be done in the course of his employment. It may, however, sometimes be necessary, if the corporation is to be liable, to attribute to it the *act* of another, whether its servant or not, and where this is the case it may be thought that the *ultra vires* doctrine presents a stumbling block. How, it may be asked, can an act which the corporation has no power to perform nevertheless be the corporation's act? The answer, it is suggested, is that if a corporation acts in the only way in which a corporation, being an artificial person,[59] can act—that is, if the central governing body of the corporation orders or ratifies an act—then the act must be attributed to the corporation itself. This commonsense solution was regarded as obvious in *Campbell* v. *Paddington Corporation*[60] and it is submitted that there is no valid reason why it should not be accepted.[61] Indeed, if it is not accepted, it is difficult to see how any unlawful act can ever be regarded as the corporation's act, and yet we know that a corporation cannot only be primarily liable in tort, but can even be held guilty of "actual fault" within the meaning of the Merchant Shipping Acts.[62]

(3) *Liability of directors*

Because a company is a separate legal person its directors are not, apart from statute, personally liable on contracts made by the company, nor for torts of company servants for which the company is vicariously liable. To identify the director with the company would be too great a brake on commercial enterprise and adventure, however small the company and however powerful the control of the director. Nevertheless, where directors order an act by the company which amounts to a tort they may be liable as joint tortfeasors on the ground that they have procured the wrong to be done.[63] Where the tort in question requires a particular state of mind the director must have that, but there is no general principle that a director must

---

[58] If the employment of the servant was itself *ultra vires* the corporation, then there may be some difficulty, for an *ultra vires* contract is certainly void at common law (*Ashbury Railway Carriage and Iron Co. Ltd.* v. *Riche* (1875) L.R. 7 H.L. 653; but in certain circumstances the contract may be valid under s.9 of the European Communities Act 1972) and it can, therefore, be argued that in fact the relationship of master and servant does not exist. See Goodhart, "Corporate Liability in Tort and the Doctrine of Ultra Vires" (1926) 2 C.L.J. 350.

[59] Artificial, not fictitious. A wooden leg may be artificial: it is not a fiction.

[60] [1911] 1 K.B. 869, 875, *per* Avory J.; *ibid.* at pp. 877–878, *per* Lush J.

[61] But see Goodhart, *loc. cit.* and *cf.* Warren, "Torts by Corporations in Ultra Vires Undertakings" (1926) 2 C.L.J. 180. See also Ashton-Cross, "Suggestions regarding the Liability of Corporations for the Torts of their Servants" (1950) 10 C.L.J. 419. Other textbooks are in general agreement with the view expressed above: Salmond and Heuston, *Torts*, 19th ed., pp. 480–481; Street, *Torts* (8th ed.), p. 517; Clerk and Lindsell, *Torts*, 16th ed., para. 2–46.

[62] *Lennard's Carrying Co. Ltd.* v. *Asiatic Petroleum Co. Ltd.* [1915] A.C. 705; *The Lady Gwendolen* [1965] P. 294.

[63] See, *e.g. Mancetter Developments Ltd.* v. *Germanson Ltd.* [1986] Q.B. 1212 (waste). A company and its directors may be conspirators: *ante*, p. 517.

know that the act is tortious or be reckless as to that.[64] If a company servant were to trespass on the plaintiff's land believing it to belong to the company that would be trespass and there is no reason why a director who, with the same state of mind, instructed him to do the act should escape liability.

PARTNERS

In English law a partnership is not a legal person distinct from its members and consequently has no capacity to sue or be sued,[65] but each partner is liable jointly and severally with his co-partners for a tort committed by any of them against an outsider in the course of business.[66]

CLUBS[67]

In the case of proprietary and incorporated clubs, it would seem that the ordinary rules as to the liability of a master or principal for the torts of his servants or agents apply.[68] In the case of an unincorporated club, which is not an entity known to the law and which cannot be sued in its own name, liability involves a question of substantive law and one of procedure. The first question is, who is liable for the wrongful act or breach of duty? This depends on the circumstances of the particular case, and it may be the members of the committee, or someone such as a steward who is in control of the club or possibly the whole body of members.[69] Membership of the club and even membership of the committee does not involve any special duty of care towards other *members* of the club[70] nor, it seems, towards a *stranger*, though in the latter case the members of the committee (at the time when the cause of action arose) will be liable personally to the exclusion of other members, if they act personally, as by employing an incompetent person to erect a stand as the result of which a stranger is injured.[71] In the case of torts

---

[64] *C. Evans & Sons Ltd.* v. *Spritebrand Ltd.* [1985] 1 W.L.R. 317.

[65] But the partners may sue or be sued in the name of the firm: R.S.C., Ord. 80.

[66] Partnership Act 1890, ss.10 and 12. See Lindley, *Partnership.* The partners may, of course, also be liable for the torts of their servants or agents under ordinary principles: see, *e.g. Lloyd* v. *Grace, Smith & Co.* [1912] A.C. 716.

[67] For the position of trade unions, see *ante*, p. 527.

[68] Halsbury, *Laws of England* (4th ed.), Vol. 6, para. 277; for different kinds of clubs, see paras. 204–216. In a proprietary club the property and funds of the club belong to a proprietor, who may sue or be sued in his own name or in the name of the club. The members are in contractual relation with the proprietor, and have a right to use the club premises in accordance with the rules, but they are not his servants or agents. An incorporated club may sue or be sued in its corporate name. An unincorporated members' club has no legal existence apart from its members, who are jointly entitled to the property and funds, though usually the property is vested in trustees. It cannot sue or be sued in the club name, nor can the secretary or any other officer sue or be sued on behalf of the club.

[69] Lloyd (1953) 16 M.L.R. 359.

[70] *Prole* v. *Allen* [1950] 1 All E.R. 476; *Shore* v. *Ministry of Works* [1950] 2 All E.R. 228. In *Robertson* v. *Ridley* [1989] 2 All E.R. 474, there was a difference of opinion as to the correctness of the decision in respect of the steward in *Prole* v. *Allen*.

[71] Halsbury, *Laws of England* (4th ed.), Vol. 6, para. 233; *Brown* v. *Lewis* (1896) 12 T.L.R. 445. *Bradley Egg Farm Ltd.* v. *Clifford* [1943] 2 All E.R. 378.

involving vicarious liability, apart from the actual wrongdoer's liability, the question depends upon whose servant or agent the wrongdoer was at the material time.[72] Where liability arises out of the ownership or occupation of property, as in nuisance or under the Occupiers' Liability Act 1957, the occupiers of the premises in question will normally be the proper persons to sue.[73] If the property is vested in trustees they may be the proper persons to sue, but in the absence of trustees it is a question of fact as to who are the occupiers of the premises.[74] As to the procedural point, the need for a representative action only arises where it is desired to sue the whole body of members, and a representation order may be made, provided that the members whose names appear on the writ are persons who may fairly be taken to represent the body of club members and that they and all the other club members have the same interest in the action.[75]

Persons of Unsound Mind

There is singularly little English authority as to the liability of persons of unsound mind for torts committed by them.[76] Sir Matthew Hale thought that *dementia* was one of several other forms of incapacity which might exempt a person from criminal liability, but which ordinarily do not excuse him from civil liability, for that "is not by way of penalty, but a satisfaction of damage done to the party"[77]; and there are dicta in the older cases which regard lunacy as no defence.[78] More to the purpose is a dictum of Lord Esher M.R., in 1892,[79] that a lunatic is liable unless the disease of his mind is so great that he cannot understand the nature and consequences of his act. In *Morriss* v. *Marsden*[80] the defendant, who attacked and seriously injured the plaintiff, had been found unfit to plead in earlier criminal proceedings. He was then sued by the plaintiff for damages for assault and battery. Stable J. found that the defendant's mind was so disturbed by his disease that he did not know that what he was doing was wrong, but that the assault was a voluntary act on his part and that the defendant was therefore liable.

Unsoundness of mind is thus certainly not in itself a ground of immunity from liability in tort, and it is submitted that the true question in each case is

[72] Lloyd, *loc. cit.* p. 359.

[73] *Ibid.* at pp. 359–360.

[74] *Ibid.* at p. 360.

[75] *Campbell* v. *Thompson* [1953] 1 Q.B. 445. See Lloyd, *loc. cit.*, 360–363 and R.S.C. Ord. 15, r. 12. A representation order may also be made in favour of persons as plaintiffs. For the position as to a claim for damages see *Prudential Assurance Co. Ltd.* v. *Newman Industries Ltd.* [1981] Ch. 229 and *E.M.I. Records Ltd.* v. *Riley* [1981] 1 W.L.R. 923.

[76] See Fridman, "Mental Incompetency" (1963) 79 L.Q.R. 502; (1964) 80 L.Q.R. 84; Picker, "Tortious Liability of the Insane in Canada," 13 Osgoode Hall L.J. 193.

[77] 1 Hist. of Pleas of Crown (ed. 1778), pp. 15–16. So too, in effect Bacon (Spedding's edition of his works, vii, 348).

[78] *e.g. Weaver* v. *Ward* (1616) Hob. 134.

[79] *Hanbury* v. *Hanbury* (1892) 8 T.L.R. 559, 569. *cf. Mordaunt* v. *Mordaunt* (1870) L.R. 2 P. & D. 103, 142, *per* Kelly C.B.

[80] [1952] 1 All E.R. 925. See (1952) 68 L.Q.R. 300; Todd (1952) 15 M.L.R. 486. *Morriss* v. *Marsden* was followed in *Phillips* v. *Soloway* (1957) 6 D.L.R. (2d) 570 and in *Beals* v. *Hayward* [1960] N.Z.L.R. 131. See also *Squittieri* v. *De Sautis* (1976) 75 D.L.R. (3d) 629.

whether the defendant was possessed of the requisite state of mind for liability in the particular tort with which he is charged. In trespass to the person it is enough that the defendant intended to strike the plaintiff and the defendant in *Morriss* v. *Marsden* was therefore rightly held liable; but had his disease been so severe that his act was not a voluntary one at all he would not have been liable.[81] In defamation it is enough that the defendant published matter defamatory of the plaintiff and it would certainly be no defence that in his disturbed mental state he believed it to be true. Again, as Stable J. said, "I cannot think that, if a person of unsound mind converts my property under a delusion that he is entitled to do it or that it was not property at all, that affords a defence."[82] The tort of negligence probably creates the greatest difficulty. The standard of negligence is said to eliminate the individual characteristics of the defendant,[83] but this does not mean, for example, that a driver who suffers a sudden, unexpected[84] and disabling illness is liable for the damage he does: even the reasonable man can have a heart attack.[85] No English court appears to have been required to deal in this context with what might be called "unsoundness of mind" in any generally accepted sense but *Roberts* v. *Ramsbottom*[86] deals with temporary impairment of mental ability arising from physical causes. The defendant suffered a stroke which severely impaired his consciousness but he was still able to drive erratically for some distance, colliding with two vehicles in succession. Neill J. held the defendant liable. He retained some control, albeit imperfect control, of the vehicle and his illness would only have provided a defence if it had rendered him an automaton—an epileptic fit or total unconsciousness or something of that sort.[87] Presumably, therefore, there would be liability if an insane defendant succumbed to the delusion that his vehicle was subject to control by an outside force.[88] In the alternative the defendant was liable for the events after the first collision, since he was aware that he had been feeling ill and that the first collision had taken place, though he was unable to appreciate that he should have stopped.[89]

ALIENS

A friendly alien today[90] is under no disability and has no immunity, but if the

---

[81] *Ibid.* at p. 927, *per* Stable J.

[82] *Ibid.*

[83] *Ante*, p. 114.

[84] This is important, because if he has reason to believe that he will have an attack he may be negligent in setting out: *Jones* v. *Dennison* [1971] R.T.R. 174.

[85] See *Waugh* v. *James K. Allan Ltd.* [1964] 2 Lloyd's Rep. 1. In *Morriss* v. *Marsden*, *supra*, at p. 927, Stable J. said, "If a sleepwalker, without intention or without carelessness, broke a valuable vase, that would not be actionable." His Lordship thus evidently contemplated negligent and non-negligent sleepwalkers as legal possibilities.

[86] [1980] 1 W.L.R. 823.

[87] The judge stressed that the defendant was in no way morally to blame. *cf. Nettleship* v. *Weston*, *ante*, p. 112.

[88] *cf. Buckley* v. *Smith Transport Ltd.* (1946) 4 D.L.R. 721; *Breunig* v. *American Family Insurance Co.* 173 N.W. (2d) 619 (1970).

[89] How can the defendant be held negligent in not stopping if he could not appreciate that he should have stopped?

[90] For history, see the twelfth edition of this work, pp. 696–697.

defendant is the Crown the case may be affected by the doctrine of "act of state."[91]

An alien enemy is one whose state or sovereign is at war with the sovereign of England, or one who, whatever his nationality, is voluntarily resident or carries on business in an enemy's country. But it is possible for a subject of an enemy state, who is neither residing nor carrying on business in an enemy's country, not to be an alien enemy with regard to civil rights.[92] As thus defined, an alien enemy, unless he be within the realm by the licence of the Queen, cannot sue in the Queen's courts. He can, however, be sued and can defend an action and, if the decision goes against him, he can appeal.[93]

PERSONS HAVING PARENTAL OR QUASI-PARENTAL AUTHORITY

Parents and other persons in similar positions are necessarily immune against liability for many acts which in other people would be assault, battery or false imprisonment. They have control, usually but not necessarily, of a disciplinary character, over those committed to their charge. The nature of the control varies according to the relationship and, provided that it is exercised reasonably and moderately, acts done in pursuance of it are not tortious.

Parental authority,[94] certainly ceases when the child attains 18 years, but it is a dwindling right as the child approaches adulthood and for this purpose may well cease at an earlier age.[95] Quasi-parental authority is exemplified by the control of schoolmasters over pupils and certain related cases.

Schoolteachers

At common law a schoolteacher has power to discipline pupils and this probably rests upon the need to maintain order and discipline at the school,[96] so that a parental veto upon corporal punishment would not render its use unlawful.[97] However, since the passing of the Education (No. 2) Act 1986[98]

---

[91] *Ante*, p. 661.

[92] Halsbury's *Laws of England* (4th ed.), para. 950.

[93] *Porter* v. *Freudenberg* [1915] 1 K.B. 857. For further details as to alien enemies, see McNair, *Legal Effects of War* (4th ed.), Chaps. 2, 3, 15; W. E. Davies, *Aliens*, Chap. XI; an alien enemy interned in England cannot maintain a claim for habeas corpus: *R.* v. *Bottrill* [1947] 1 K.B. 41; it is doubtful whether he can sue for false imprisonment on the ground that statutory powers have been exceeded by those who intern him: *Hirsch* v. *Somervell* [1946] 2 All E.R. 430. *Quaere*, whether an alien enemy resident in England without the licence of the Queen can sue in tort? Winfield was inclined to agree with Rogers, *Effect of War on Contract*, pp. 127–128, that he can sue: (1947) 9 C.L.J. 129–130 (book review).

[94] It is assumed by the Children and Young Persons Act 1933, s.1(7). Eekelaar, "What are Parental Rights" (1973) 89 L.Q.R. 210. The rights and authority of father and mother of a legitimate child are equal: Guardianship Act 1973, s.1. See also the Children Act 1975, s.85. The right of a master to chastise an apprentice may well be obsolete.

[95] *Gillick* v. *West Norfolk A.H.A.* [1986] A.C. 112. See *R.* v. *Rahman* (1985) 81 Cr.App.R. 349 (false imprisonment).

[96] Street, *Torts* (8th ed.), p. 86. See also *Restatement*, 2d, s.153. *cf.* the eleventh edition of this book. Disciplinary powers are not necessarily confined to conduct on school premises: *Cleery* v. *Booth* [1893] 1 Q.B. 465; *R.* v. *Newport (Salop) JJ.* [1929] 2 K.B. 416.

[97] *cf.* the decision of the European Court of Human Rights (*Campbell and Cosans* v. *U.K.* [1982] 4 E.H.R.R.) that the European Convention on Human Rights is violated where a school administers corporal punishment against the wishes of parents.

[98] s.47.

corporal punishment in state or maintained school is no longer a defence to a civil action.[99] It remains the law, however, that reasonable force may be used to avert personal injury or damage to property.[1] The common law continues to apply in respect of fee-paying pupils in private schools but if the school rules forbid corporal punishment a teacher who inflicts it probably acts unlawfully, though such a rule would probably not render him liable if he used reasonable force in the actual prevention of disorder of, of course, in self-defence.

Former rule as to husband and wife

As to husband and wife, in the older law he had the right to beat her moderately as a method of correction.[2] "But, with us," said Blackstone in 1768, "in the politer reign of Charles the Second, this power of correction began to be doubted: and a wife may now have security of the peace against her husband; or in return a husband against his wife. Yet the lower rank of people, who are always fond of the old common law, still claim and exert their ancient privilege."[3] The right is now obsolete, nor can the husband even use force to recapture his wife if she has left him in breach of his conjugal rights.[4] It is unlikely that the husband can now restrain his wife even if she is about to leave to meet her lover.[5]

Master of ship

Authority similar to quasi-parental authority may be implied by law. Thus the master of a merchant ship can use force to preserve discipline for the safety of the ship, its crew, passengers and cargo. If he has reasonable cause to believe and does in fact believe that it is necessary for these purposes he may arrest and confine anyone on board.[6] If possible, an inquiry should precede punishment, and the accused "should have the benefit of that rule of universal justice of being heard in his own defence."[7] The punishment must of course not be excessive,[8] and it must always be a question of fact whether the occasion justifies arrest.[9]

[99] But it seems that the teacher is still not criminally liable: s.47(4).
[1] s.47(3).
[2] "For that is a poynt of an honest man,
  For to bete his wife well nowe and than."
   Johan Johan (one of Heywood's Comedies, *circa* 1533).
[3] 1 *Commentaries*, 444–445.
[4] *R.* v. *Jackson* [1891] 1 Q.B. 671; *R.* v. *Reid* [1973] Q.B. 299. If he uses force or violence for the purpose of exercising his right to intercourse he does not commit rape (unless there has been a decree of judicial separation, a *decree nisi* of divorce or an injunction against molestation or an undertaking in lieu thereof: *R.* v. *Clarke* [1949] 2 All E.R. 448; *R.* v. *O'Brien* [1974] 3 All E.R. 663; *R.* v. *Steele* [1977] Cr. L.R. 290) but he does commit a criminal assault: *R.* v. *Miller* [1954] 2 Q.B. 282. Presumably, therefore, since the prohibition against actions in tort between husband and wife has been removed (*ante*, p. 673) the wife has a cause of action in tort.
[5] *cf. R.* v. *Jackson* [1891] 1 Q.B. 671, 679–680, *per* Lord Halsbury L.C.
[6] *Hook* v. *Cunard Steamship Co.* [1953] 1 W.L.R. 682. See also *Aldworth* v. *Stewart* (1866) 4 F. & F. 957. As to aircraft commanders, see Tokyo Convention Act 1967, s.3.
[7] *The Agincourt* (1824) 1 Hagg.Ecc. 271, 174, *per* Lord Stowell.
[8] It was so in *The Agincourt, supra*, where a member of the crew was cruelly kicked and beaten.
[9] If a passenger describes the captain of a ship as the "landlord of an hotel" that does not justify the captain putting him in irons in the belief that mutiny is imminent: *King* v. *Franklin* (1858) 1 F. & F. 360; *Hook* v. *Cunard Steamship Co.* [1953] 1 W.L.R. 682.

CHAPTER 26

DEFENCES

A plaintiff who fails to prove the necessary ingredients of the particular tort or torts on which he relies will, of course, fail in his action. Even if he does prove these ingredients, however, he may still fail if the defendant shows that he is entitled to rely upon some specific defence. Some of these defences are peculiar to particular torts, as is justification to the tort of defamation, and these have been noticed in their appropriate chapters. We must now consider those defences which apply more generally throughout the law of tort.[1]

CONSENT. VOLENTI NON FIT INJURIA

There are many occasions on which harm—sometimes grievous harm—may be inflicted on a person for which he has no remedy in tort, because he consented, or at least assented, to the doing of the act which caused his harm.[2] Simple examples are the injuries received in the course of a lawful game or sport, or in a lawful surgical operation. The effect of such consent or assent is commonly expressed in the maxim "*Volenti non fit injuria*," which is certainly of respectable antiquity. The idea underlying it has been traced as far back as Aristotle,[3] and it was also recognised in the works of the classical Roman jurists,[4] and in the Canon law. In English law, Bracton in his *De Legibus Angliae* (*c.* A.D. 1250–1258) uses the maxim, though not with the technicality that attached to it later,[5] and in a Year Book case of 1305 it appears worded exactly as it is now.[6] So far as actual citation of the maxim goes, most of the modern cases use it in connection with harm to the person rather than to property. The explanation seems to be that if the assent is to the infliction of harm on, or at any rate to the use of, the plaintiff's property, such assent is more usually styled *leave and licence* of the plaintiff. But this phrase expresses much the same idea.[7] Moreover, there is no reason for

---

[1] Winfield described these as "conditions which in general negative liability."
[2] "One who has invited or assented to an act being done towards him cannot, when he suffers from it, complain of it as a wrong": *Smith* v. *Baker* [1891] A.C. 325, 360, *per* Lord Herschell.
[3] T. Beven in *Journal of Comparative Legislation* (1907), p. 185; Ingman [1981] J.R. 1.
[4] Dig. 47, 10. 1. 5: "nulla injuria est quae in volentem fiat." See, too Dig. 9. 2. 7. 4: 50. 17. 203.
[5] Ed. Woodbine (1942), Vol. 4, p. 286: "cum volenti et scienti non fiat injuria."
[6] 33–5 Edw. 1 (Rolls Series), 9 Hunt *arguendo*, "volenti non fit injuria."
[7] *e.g. Park* v. *Jobson & Son* [1945] 1 All E.R. 222. *cf. Armstrong* v. *Sheppard and Short Ltd.* [1959] 2 Q.B. 384. For a case of loss of property where *volenti non fit injuria* was pleaded, but unsuccessfully, see *Saunders (Mayfair) Furs Ltd.* v. *Chas. Wm. Davies Ltd.* (1965) 109 S.J. 922.

thinking that the maxim itself was confined in past time to injuries to the person.[8]

Though the terminology in the case law is by no means consistent, "consent" is normally the expression used in relation to intentional torts and *volenti non fit injuria* in relation to negligence, though the modern "voluntary assumption of risk" probably carries the idea better.

Consent and intentional torts

A fair blow in a boxing match, an innoculation, a welcomed embrace are not torts, because the plaintiff consents to them. Consent is commonly spoken of as a defence but in the case of trespass to the person this may not be quite accurate because a defence is something which it is incumbent on the defendant to plead and prove and it has been held in England[9] (though not in Canada[10]) that it is for the plaintiff to prove absence of consent: because an assault must be something against the will of the person assaulted, it cannot be said that a person can be assaulted by his permission.[11] As a practical matter, however, the defendant may need to lead evidence to lay a foundation from which the court will infer consent and in modern pleading he would be likely to raise consent as a specific issue in his defence to the statement of claim.[12] In this sense, therefore, it may be proper to refer to it as a "defence."

It is clear that consent may be implied from conduct as well as expressed in words so that the defendant escapes liability if he was justified in inferring that the plaintiff consented even though, secretly, he did not. The very acts of taking part in a boxing match or presenting one's arm for injection,[13] for example, clearly convey consent.[14] The consent, however, must be freely given so that one obtained by wrongful threats sufficient to overbear the plaintiff's will would not be effective.[15] Statutory authority apart, a prisoner has the same power as anyone else to give or withhold consent to medical

---

[8] Bracton, in the passage cited *supra*, note 5, uses it generally, and in the Year Book case (*supra*, note 6) it was used in a property action; Manwood J. in *Grendon* v. *Bishop of Lincoln* (1576) Plowden 493, 501 makes it of general application. In *Horne* v. *Widlake* (1607) Yelv. 141 it was the basis of the decision in a property case.

[9] *Christopherson* v. *Bare* (1848) 11 Q.B. 473, 477; *Freeman* v. *Home Office (No. 2)* [1984] Q.B. 524, 539.

[10] *Hambley* v. *Shepley* (1967) 663 D.L.R. (2d) 94, 95; *Allan* v. *New Mount Sinai Hospital* (1980) 109 D.L.R. (3d) 634.

[11] In old pleading terminology, consent could be raised by a plea of "not guilty" to the general issue.

[12] As was, indeed, done in *Freeman* v. *Home Office, supra*, n. 9. See [1984] Q.B. 524, 548.

[13] But where non-trivial medical procedures are involved it is customary to require the patient to sign a consent form.

[14] *cf. Freeman* v. *Home Office (No. 2), supra*, n. 9, at p. 557, where Sir John Donaldson M.R. suggests that "consent" applies if the plaintiff does consent, but *volenti non fit injuria* applies if he does not consent but so conducts himself as to lead the defendant to believe that he does.

[15] Obviously, a threat might vitiate the will of a child but not of an adult. *Latter* v. *Braddell* (1881) 50 L.J.Q.B. 448 (Weir, *Casebook on Tort* (6th ed.), p. 322) seems unduly narrow in insisting on threats of violence.

treatment[16] but since, in a prison setting, a doctor has power to influence a prisoner's situation and prospects, a court must be alive to the risk that what may appear, on the face of it, to be a real consent is not in fact so.[17] Children of tender years and persons of unsound mind present greater difficulty. A minor who has reached 16 years may give a valid consent to medical treatment himself under section 8 of the Family Law Reform Act 1969 and he may do so at common law even below that age if he is capable of a full understanding of the consequences.[18] The position is less clear where a 16-year-old refuses treatment which the parent wishes him to have[19]: perhaps the parent's power to *impose* treatment ceases whenever the minor acquires the capacity to consent independently to treatment. In the case of young children, however, it is generally accepted, whatever the legal basis of the rule, that the consent of a parent or guardian to treatment which is reasonably necessary[20] protects the doctor against an action for trespass to the person. In case of doubt, or where there is conflict between parents and medical advisers, it may be possible to make the child a ward of court, but this route is not open in the case of persons of unsound mind. It is true that the Mental Health Act 1983 provides a procedure for making a guardianship order in respect of a person suffering from mental disorder and the guardian may then have certain powers of consent to treatment, but in the context of the statute as a whole this means psychiatric treatment and not, as in *T.* v. *T.*,[21] an abortion and sterilisation which are indicated because the patient is incapable of coping with pregnancy and childbirth. Nevertheless, despite the fact that such treatment is prima facie a trespass it is lawful if in the patient's best interests, though the court's approval should normally be sought.[22] The intervention of the court is not necessary for directly therapeutic treatment of mentally disordered persons which, like emergency treatment of persons of full age and capacity who are temporarily incapable of expressing a wish by reason of unconsciousness, is justified by a form of necessity.[23] Nevertheless, the position of normal and mentally disordered persons cannot perhaps be entirely equated: in the case of the former,

---

[16] *cf.* the Report of the Work of the Prison Department 1979 (Cmnd. 7965): "The administration of a medicine against the wishes of a prisoner would only be defensible if, without it, his life would be endangered, serious harm to the prisoner or others would be likely, or there would be an irreversible deterioration in his condition." See generally Brazier [1982] P.L. 282. In *Leigh* v. *Gladstone* (1909) 26 T.L.R. 139 forcible feeding of a suffragette was held justified on the basis of necessity, but at that time suicide and attempted suicide were crimes. Can a hospital justify restraint of a patient who is dangerously ill and whose life is threatened unless he receives treatment? It is submitted that it cannot. But what damages would be awarded?

[17] *Freeman* v. *Home Office (No. 2)* [1984] Q.B. 524; *Barbara* v. *Home Office* (1984) 134 N.L.J. 888.

[18] *Gillick* v. *West Norfolk A.H.A.* [1986] A.C. 112.

[19] See the unhelpful s.8(3) of the Family Law Reform Act 1969.

[20] Even this probably puts the matter too high: a parent can lawfully arrange for his child's blood grouping to be tested to determine paternity (*S.* v. *McC.* [1972] A.C. 24); and it would be absurd to hold that circumcision for religious reasons was tortious.

[21] [1988] 2 W.L.R. 189. The same view was taken of ss.57 and 58. *cf. Re B* [1987] 2 W.L.R. 1213, where the patient was a minor.

[22] *Re F* [1989] N.L.J. 789.

[23] *Ibid.*; *cf.* the C.A., referring to justification by the exigencies of day-to-day life. Traditionally, emergency medical treatment has been justified by reference to implied consent, but this will not do in the case of persons suffering from mental disorder.

treatment while unconscious can only be justified if it is urgently necessary and the patient is not known to object to it.[24]

Consent to one medical procedure does not justify another, as where a condition is discovered and treated for mere convenience during the authorised treatment of another condition[25] or where an operation authorised by patient A is performed on patient B by mistake.[26] However, so long as the patient understands the broad nature of what is to be done, his consent is not vitiated by failure to explain the risks inherent in the procedure,[27] for it would be deplorable to deal with such cases under the rubric of trespass to the person.[28] In this sense English law does not require "informed consent." However, going beyond the basic duty to give sufficient information to enable understanding of the nature of the treatment, there is a further duty, sounding in negligence, to explain the procedure and its implications in the way a careful and responsible doctor would do. It is important to note that, in common with other issues of professional negligence,[29] the test is not what risks would appear material to a prudent patient but what is the normal practice of the medical profession.[30] Since the consequence of a failure to perform the duty to warn of risks is that the plaintiff may succeed, even though the operation has been carried out with all due care and skill, if he can show that he would not have consented[31] had a proper explanation been given, the House of Lords in *Sidaway's* case clearly feared the growth of a new category of medical litigation and of yet more defensive medicine by way of detailed explanations which would probably be beyond the comprehension of most patients. However, though the court will pay great deference to medical practice, the medical profession is not the final arbiter of what patients should be told: it seems that if a patient asks a specific question he is entitled to an adequate answer[32] and in the last resort it is the *court*, not the profession, that sets the standard. As Lord Bridge said, "even in a case where ... no expert witness ... condemns the non-disclosure as being in conflict with accepted and responsible medical practice ... the judge might

---

[24] See, *e.g. Murray* v. *McMurchy* [1949] 2 D.L.R. 442; *cf. Marshall* v. *Curry* [1933] 3 D.L.R. 260.

[25] But the terms of the consent may authorise such further treatment as the doctor considers necessary or desirable.

[26] *Chatterton* v. *Gerson* [1981] Q.B. 432; Weir, *Casebook on Tort* (6th ed.), p. 324.

[27] *cf. Canterbury* v. *Spence* (1972) 464 F.2d 772. Robertson, "Informed Consent to Medical Treatment" (1981) 97 L.Q.R. 102.

[28] *Chatterton* v. *Gerson* [1981] Q.B. 432; *Hills* v. *Potter* [1984] 1 W.L.R. 641; *Sidaway* v. *Bethlem Royal Hospital* [1985] A.C. 871; *Reibl* v. *Hughes* (1981) 114 D.L.R. (3d) 1 (Sup. Ct. of Canada). *cf.* Tan, "Failure of Medical Advice: Trespass or Negligence?" (1987) 7 L.S. 149. If there is no consent, the defendant's act is actionable even if the plaintiff would have consented if he had been aware of the truth.

[29] See *ante*, p. 116.

[30] *Sidaway* v. *Bethlem Royal Hospital* [1985] A.C. 871. Teff, "Consent to Medical Procedures" (1985) 101 L.Q.R. 432; Brazier, "Patient Autonomy and Consent to Treatment" (1987) 7 L.S. 169. There is no distinction for this purpose between therapeutic and non-therapeutic contexts: *Gold* v. *Haringey H.A.* [1987] 3 W.L.R. 649.

[31] But in *Reibl* v. *Hughes* (1981) 114 D.L.R. (3d) 1 the Supreme Court of Canada adopted the test of what a reasonable person would have done.

[32] [1985] A.C. 871, 898, 895, 901. But the patient cannot expect all the information at the doctor's disposal and therapeutic discretion must have a part to play even in responding to a direct question: see *Blyth* v. *Bloomsbury A.H.A., The Times*, February 11, 1987.

in certain circumstances come to the conclusion that disclosure of a particular risk was so obviously necessary to an informed choice on the part of the patient that no reasonably prudent medical man would fail to make it."[33]

What if consent to what would otherwise be a trespass is obtained by fraud? Or if the actor fails to disclose some fact (for example, that he has a contagious disease) which would have led the other party to withhold consent? Although the only relevant Anglo-Irish authority[34] was decided partly at least on the basis of the maxim *ex turpi causa non oritur actio* and is probably now unreliable in this respect, it seems that the law is that the consent is valid if the plaintiff is aware of the essential nature of the act[35]: if the defendant persuades the plaintiff to have intercourse with him by falsely representing that he is free of disease the plaintiff still consents to the act of intercourse. If this seems unduly favourable to the defendant, it must be remembered that a claim for deceit might lie,[36] though not where there was mere non-disclosure and no representation by words or conduct.[37]

Exclusion of liability and volenti non fit injuria

(1) *Express exclusion of liability*

Since, on one view at least, *volenti* is based upon an agreement between the plaintiff and the defendant that the former shall run the risk of the latter's negligence, it seems sensible to start with those cases where there is an express provision to that effect, even though most of them are probably correctly regarded as examples of a separate defence of exclusion of liability or disclaimer.[38]

At common law, in the absence of duress or some other vitiating factor, entry into a contract which exempted the defendant from liability for negligence was a complete defence and the same attitude was adopted where the plaintiff entered another's land by licence subject to a condition exempting the occupier from liability.[39] For this purpose the question was not whether the plaintiff did in fact agree to run the risk of negligence, but whether the defendant had given sufficient notice to make the excluding term part of the

---

[33] At p. 900.
[34] *Hegarty* v. *Shine* (1878) 14 Cox C.C. 145. See also *R.* v. *Clarence* (1888) 22 Q.B.D. 23, a criminal case on similar facts. In the criminal law if the consent to sexual intercourse is ineffective and this is held to be a criminal assault it must also logically be the very serious crime of rape.
[35] Hence a civil action might succeed on such facts as those in *R.* v. *Williams* [1923] 1 K.B. 340, where the defendant represented that he was performing a procedure to improve the plaintiff's voice.
[36] As in *Graham* v. *Saville* [1945] 2 D.L.R. 489 (bigamous marriage).
[37] The *Restatement* 2d, s.892B, would impose liability in *Hegarty* v. *Shine* but not where the misrepresentation goes to an inducement not connected with the nature of the invasion or the extent of the harm to be expected therefrom, *e.g.* where A consents to sexual intercourse with B for payment and B intends to pay with counterfeit money.
[38] Such cases are distinguished from *volenti* proper by Lord Denning M.R. in *Barnett* v. *British Waterways Board* [1973] 1 W.L.R. 700. It is also implicit in s.2(3) of the Unfair Contract Terms Act 1977 that the defences are separate.
[39] Similarly, where a person accepted a lift in a car which carried a prominent notice that passengers travelled at their own risk, he could not sue the driver for negligence: *Buckpitt* v. *Oates* [1968] 1 All E.R. 1145. Such notices became ineffective as a result of the Road Traffic Act 1972, s.148(3) (now s.149(3) of the Road Traffic Act 1988). Disclaimers in relation to the giving of advice are discussed *ante*, p. 286.

contract or licence: if he had done so, the plaintiff was bound even though he might not have troubled to read the terms and hence was unaware of the excluding one. This remains the basic rule, but in most cases it is now heavily qualified by the Unfair Contract Terms Act 1977. Where the defendant acts in the course of a business[40] or occupies premises for business purposes[41] he cannot, by reference to any contract term or notice,[42] exclude or restrict his liability for death or personal injury resulting from negligence,[43] and in the case of other loss or damage caused by negligence can only exclude or restrict his liability in so far as the term in the contract or notice is reasonable.[44] It is also provided that "where a contract term or a notice purports to exclude or restrict liability for negligence a person's agreement to or awareness of it is not of itself to be taken as indicating his voluntary acceptance of any risk."[45] The implication of this is that the defence of *volenti non fit injuria* is still available, but it remains to be seen what evidence of voluntary acceptance of the risk beyond the making of the agreement (which is not enough) will be required.

The defendant sometimes seeks to shelter behind an excluding term which is not in a contract between him and the plaintiff but between the plaintiff and a third party (as where a stevedore claims the protection of a provision limiting liability in a contract of carriage by sea made between the carrier and the consignor or consignee of the cargo). Details of this must be sought in works on the law of contract but the courts have generally insisted that the defendant be able to show contractual privity between himself and the plaintiff if he is to succeed in relying on the term.[46] However, in *Norwich City Council* v. *Harvey*[47] a building was damaged by fire as the result of the negligence of a sub-contractor. The main contract between the building owner and the head contractor provided that the former should bear the risk of loss by fire and the Court of Appeal concluded that this was a reason for denying any duty of care in respect of the fire between the sub-contractor and the building owner. Unfortunately, the contract cases are not referred to in *Harvey*, so it is difficult to say how far it extends beyond the context of building contracts.

(2) *Implied assumption of risk*[48]

If the circumstances warrant the inference that the plaintiff has voluntarily

---

[40] Which "includes a profession and the activities of any government department or local or public authority": s.14.

[41] s.1(3). For a modification of this restriction in relation to premises, see *ante*, p. 221.

[42] Which "includes an announcement, whether or not in writing, and any other communication or pretended communication."

[43] s.2(1).

[44] s.2(2).

[45] s.2(3).

[46] Though in *New Zealand Shipping Co. Ltd.* v. *A.M. Satterthwaite & Co. Ltd.* [1975] A.C. 154 the Privy Council made it fairly easy to establish such privity in the stevedore situation. The court declined to express an opinion on the "argument that, quite apart from contract, exemptions from, or limitations of, liability in tort may be conferred by mere consent on the part of the party who may be injured."

[47] [1989] 1 All E.R. 1180.

[48] Jaffey, "Volenti Non Fit Injuria" [1985] C.L.J. 87.

assumed the risk of the defendant's negligence he cannot sue. The question does not, however, arise until it is established that the defendant has committed a tort against the plaintiff (or has been guilty of conduct that would be a tort apart from the issue of *volenti*). This is a point of considerable importance, but it is sometimes overlooked and the maxim invoked where there is no occasion for its use. If I undertake, for example, to repair the roof of your house, and while doing so I fall off and am injured, the reason that I cannot sue you is not that I have consented to the risk (though I may have done so in fact) but that you did not in the first place owe me any duty to instruct me in how to go safely about my task.[49] Again, actual knowledge of the risk by the plaintiff is necessary for the application of *volenti* proper, but even where that knowledge is absent the defendant may have discharged his duty by giving reasonable notice of the risk.[50] Diplock L.J. even went so far as to say that "the maxim in the absence of expressed contract has no application to negligence simpliciter where the duty of care is based solely upon proximity or 'neighbourship' in the Atkinian sense,"[51] but it is respectfully submitted that this is inconsistent with many decisions where the conduct of the plaintiff has led to the conclusion that he was *volens* as to future negligence.[52] Certainly, a quite extraordinary situation would have to exist for the court to be justified in holding that the plaintiff had consented *generally* to lack of reasonable care by the defendant. So, for example, in *Slater* v. *Clay Cross Co. Ltd.* where the plaintiff was lawfully walking along a narrow tunnel on a railway track owned and occupied by the defendants where she was struck and injured by a train owing to the negligence of the driver, Denning L.J. said, "It seems to me that when this lady walked in the tunnel, although it may be said that she voluntarily took the risk of danger from the running of the railway in the ordinary and accustomed way, nevertheless she did not take the risk of negligence by the driver."[53] Nevertheless, the conclusion must sometimes be drawn that the plaintiff has expressly or impliedly consented to run the risk of the defendant's negligence or breach of duty. The conclusion was irresistible in *Imperial Chemical Industries Ltd.* v. *Shatwell.*[54] The plaintiff and his brother, James, were working in the defendants' quarry, and they agreed to disregard the defendants' orders, and also certain statutory regulations imposed upon themselves, and to test some detonators without taking the required precautions. In the result an explosion occurred which injured the plaintiff, and he sought to hold the defendants liable vicariously on the ground of James' negligence and breach of statutory duty in the course of his

---

[49] See s.2(3)(*b*) of the Occupiers' Liability Act 1957, *ante*, p. 216.

[50] *Scanlon* v. *American Cigarette Co. (Overseas) Pty. Ltd. (No. 3)* [1987] V.R. 289.

[51] *Wooldridge* v. *Sumner* [1963] 2 Q.B. 43, 69.

[52] If the tort has already been committed any waiver by the plaintiff of his right of action would require a contract supported by consideration or a promise under seal (*post*, p. 715). Jaffey in [1985] C.L.J. 87, 88–90 argues that a contract is also necessary where the plaintiff waives his rights after the negligent conduct but before damage is suffered. *Sed quaere?*

[53] [1956] 2 Q.B. 264, 271.

[54] [1965] A.C. 656; Weir, *Casebook on Tort* (6th ed.), p. 217; *Bolt* v. *William Moss & Sons Ltd.* (1966) 110 S.J. 385; *Hugh* v. *N.C.B.* 1972 S.C. 252; *McMullen* v. *N.C.B.* [1982] I.C.R. 148.

employment. It was held that the defence of *volenti non fit injuria* would have been available to James had he been sued, and therefore that the defendants were not vicariously liable. The plaintiff had consented to the very conduct which had caused his injury and, moreover, had fully appreciated the risk of injury to himself by explosion which it entailed.[55]

Is an "agreement" necessary?

In *Nettleship* v. *Weston*[56] the plaintiff agreed to give the defendant driving lessons in the defendant's car and was injured when the defendant lost control of the car because of her inexperience. All members of the Court of Appeal rejected the defence of *volenti*[57] but Lord Denning M.R. and Megaw L.J. suggested that nothing short of an agreement could found the defence, so that merely getting into a car with a driver known to be totally inexperienced could never be *volenti*,[58] though since a contract is not necessary it is not clear why such a situation should not give rise to an implied agreement.[59] It would, again, be easy to spell out an implied agreement between the brothers in *Imperial Chemical Industries* v. *Shatwell*, but it would be artificial to attempt to do so where there was no communication or even opportunity of communication between the parties, as where the plaintiff is injured while crossing the defendant's property by an activity carried out thereon, and in *Titchener* v. *British Railways Board*[60] the House of Lords assumed that *volenti* could be applicable to such a case. Of course, if the plaintiff exposes himself to a known risk without any agreement with the defendant, it may be possible to say that his damages are to be reduced on account of his contributory negligence or even that his own fault breaks the chain of causation and amounts to the sole effective cause. In *Dann* v. *Hamilton*[61] Asquith J. rejected *volenti* against a plaintiff who had taken a lift with a drunken driver, though he subsequently[62] made it plain that the decision would have been the other way had a plea of contributory negligence (at that time a complete defence) been put forward, and in *Owens* v. *Brimmell*[63] the Law Reform (Contributory Negligence) Act 1945 was applied to such a situation. Yet it would surely be hard to say that a driving instructor was guilty of contributory negligence so that in that situation the

---

[55] For other cases where the risk was obvious see *Frehlick* v. *Anderson* (1961) 27 D.L.R. (2d) 46; *Kinney* v. *Hareman* (1977) 1 W.W.R. 405. *cf. White* v. *Blackmore* [1972] 2 Q.B. 651.

[56] [1971] 2 Q.B. 691; Weir *Casebook on Tort* (6th ed.), p. 92.

[57] They also rejected another defence based on a low duty of care: see p. 112.

[58] [1971] 2 Q.B. 691, 701.

[59] See Jaffey, *loc. cit.*, p. 102, who, however, supports the view of Salmon L.J. in *Nettleship* v. *Weston* at p. 704, that the parties' prior conversation about insurance cover rebutted the inference of *volenti* and argues that the expectation of insurance cover should be assumed by the court even if not expressly mentioned by the parties.

[60] [1983] 1 W.L.R. 1427.

[61] [1939] 1 K.B. 509. Not followed in *Insurance Commissioner* v. *Joyce* (1948) 77 C.L.R. 39; *Loggenkamp* v. *Bennett* (1950) 80 C.L.R. 292. Gordon, "Drunken Drivers and Willing Passengers" (1966) 82 L.Q.R. 62.

[62] See (1953) 69 L.Q.R. 317. He had left open the possibility that *volenti* might operate where drunkenness was so extreme that to accept a lift was like "meddling with a time bomb." This was taken up in *Ashton* v. *Turner* [1981] Q.B. 137, where there was the additional factor that the parties were escaping from a burglary.

[63] [1977] Q.B. 859.

result would still have to be "all or nothing."[64] It must, however, be said that it is by no means clear that *volenti* any longer has any relevance in a claim by a passenger against a driver. Section 149 of the Road Traffic Act 1988 provides that where a person uses a motor vehicle in circumstances in which liability insurance is required (and this includes liability to passengers) then "any antecedent agreement or understanding between them (whether intended to be legally binding or not) shall be of no effect so far as it purports or might be held—

(*a*) to negative or restrict any such liability of the user in respect of persons carried in or upon the vehicle as is required . . . to be covered by a policy of insurance, or

(*b*) to impose any such conditions with respect to the enforcement of any such liability of the user."

It is further provided that "the fact that a person so carried has willingly accepted as his the risk of negligence on the part of the user shall not be treated as negativing any such liability of the user." Clearly, therefore, a notice on the dashboard excluding liability is no longer effective but it is not certain whether the Act bites on a plea of *volenti* that arises not from any "agreement or understanding" but from an inference of consent drawn from the circumstances (assuming that to be within the concept of *volenti* in the first place). The balance of authority[65] is that it does.[66]

Knowledge does not necessarily imply assent

The maxim is *volenti non fit injuria*; it is not *scienti non fit injuria*. The test of consent is objective and is not an inquiry into what the plaintiff felt or inwardly consented to,[67] but it does not follow that a person assents to a risk merely because he knows of it. The most conspicuous illustrations of this have occurred in cases of harm sustained by workers in the course of their employment. Until the latter half of the nineteenth century, very little attention was paid by the law to the safety of manual labourers, and several of the decisions on *volenti non fit injuria* went near to holding that knowledge of risk in the employment invariably implied assent to it. Protective legislation began to make notable headway from about 1860 onwards. And, quite apart from legislation, the courts, beginning with the judgment of Bowen L.J. in *Thomas* v. *Quartermaine*,[68] have declined to identify, as a matter of course, knowledge of a risk with acceptance of it.

---

[64] In *Cook* v. *Cook* (1986) 68 A.L.R. 353 a finding of contributory negligence against an amateur "instructor" was not appealed.

[65] *Gregory* v. *Kelly* [1978] R.T.R. 426; *Winnik* v. *Dick* 1984 S.L.T. 185 (Scots law); to the contrary is *Ashton* v. *Turner* [1981] Q.B. 137 (all decided under the equivalent provision of the Road Traffic Act 1972). Sym-mons, "Volenti Non Fit Injuria and Passenger Liability" (1973) 123 N.L.J. 373.

[66] But the statute would not prevent the court doing what was done by the High Court of Australia in *Cook* v. *Cooke*, *supra*, n. 64, not following *Nettleship* v. *Weston*, and finding a lower standard of care.

[67] *Bennett* v. *Tugwell* [1971] 2 W.L.R. 847, 852, *per* Ackner J., citing Gordon, "Drunken Drivers and Willing Passengers" (1966) 82 L.Q.R. 62, 71.

[68] (1887) 18 Q.B.D. 683. *cf. Bloor* v. *Liverpool, etc. Co. Ltd.* [1936] 3 All E.R. 399. The actual decision in *Thomas* v. *Quartermaine* has not escaped criticism: *Smith* v. *Baker* [1891] A.C. 325, 366–367, *per* Lord Herschell. *cf. ibid.* at pp. 368–369, *per* Lord Morris; also Pollock, *Torts* (15th ed.), pp. 119–120; Glanville Williams, *Joint Torts and Contributory Negligence*, pp. 298–299.

This doctrine was driven home by the House of Lords in *Smith* v. *Baker*,[69] where it was held that *volenti non fit injuria* had no application to harm sustained by a man from the negligence of his employers in not warning him of the moment of a recurring danger, although the man knew and understood that he personally ran risk of injury if and when the danger did recur. He worked in a cutting on the top of which a crane often jibbed (*i.e.* swung) heavy stones over his head while he was drilling the rock face in the cutting. Both he and his employers knew that there was a risk of the stones falling, but no warning was given to him of the moment at which any particular jibbing commenced. A stone from the crane fell upon and injured him. The House of Lords held that the defendants were liable. Lord Herschell admitted that:

"Where a person undertakes to do work which is intrinsically dangerous, notwithstanding that reasonable care has been taken to render it as little dangerous as possible, he no doubt voluntarily subjects himself to the risks inevitably accompanying it, and cannot, if he suffers, be permitted to complain that a wrong has been done to him, even though the cause from which he suffers might give to others a right of action"; but he added, "where . . . a risk to the employed, which may or may not result in injury, has been created or enhanced by the negligence of the employer, does the mere continuance in service, with knowledge of the risk, preclude the employed, if he suffers from such negligence, from recovering in respect of his employer's breach of duty? I cannot assent to the proposition that the maxim, 'Volenti non fit injuria,' applies to such a case, and that the employer can invoke its aid to protect him from liability for his wrong."[70]

Consent must be freely given

The main point to notice here is that "a man cannot be said to be truly 'willing' unless he is in a position to choose freely, and freedom of choice predicates, not only full knowledge of the circumstances on which the exercise of choice is conditional, so that he may be able to choose wisely, but the absence of any feeling of constraint so that nothing shall interfere with the freedom of his will."[71] The plaintiff in *Imperial Chemical Industries Ltd.* v. *Shatwell*[72] was obviously under no pressure from the defendants to adopt the dangerous method of work which caused his injury, for they had, to his knowledge, specifically forbidden it; but usually there will be economic or

---

[69] [1891] A.C. 325. Of the other cases concerning employer and workman, see in particular *Bowater* v. *Rowley Regis Corp.* [1944] K.B. 476.

[70] *Ibid.* at pp. 360, 362.

[71] *Bowater* v. *Rowley Regis Corp.* [1944] K.B. 476, 479, *per* Scott L.J., cited with approval by Lord Hodson in *Imperial Chemical Industries Ltd.* v. *Shatwell* [1965] A.C. 656, 681–682; *Merrington* v. *Ironbridge Metal Works Ltd.* [1952] 2 All E.R. 1101. For a case where constraint was put upon an employee by someone other than his employer, see *Burnett* v. *British Waterways Board* [1973] 1 W.L.R. 700.

[72] [1965] A.C. 656, *ante*, p. 688.

other pressures upon a workman which will make it unjust for an employer to say that he ran the risk with his eyes open, being fully aware of the danger he incurred.[73] In the absence of some such relationship as employer and workman between the parties it will, no doubt, be easier to establish the necessary freedom of consent, but if such consent is absent the defence of *volenti non fit injuria* cannot prevail.[74]

Consent and the standard of care

It has already been pointed out that *volenti non fit injuria* has no place unless a presumptive tort has been committed, but this is not to say that the element of consent is invariably irrelevant in the absence of a prima facie breach of duty by the defendant. The plaintiff may have consented to a certain disregard for his safety by the defendant with the result that conduct which would in other circumstances amount to negligence does not in the event involve the defendant in a breach of his duty of care. This point is obvious with regard to participants in sports. As Barwick C.J. said in *Rootes* v. *Shelton*,[75]

> "By engaging in a sport ... the participants may be held to have accepted risks which are inherent in that sport ... : but this does not eliminate all duty of care of the one participant to the other."

The same may apply to a spectator who is injured in the course of some game or sport which he is watching. A spectator does not consent to negligence on the part of the participants,[76] but "provided the competition or game is being performed within the rules and requirement of the sport and by a person of adequate skill or competence the spectator does not expect his safety to be regarded by the participant."[77]

In *Wooldridge* v. *Sumner*[78] the plaintiff, a photographer at a horse show, was struck by a galloping horse whose rider had allegedly taken the corner too fast. It was held that there was no negligence. Had the defendant acted in disregard of all safety of others so as to have departed from the standards which might reasonably be expected in anyone pursuing the competition, he might well have been liable[79]; but all he had done was to commit an error of

---

[73] *Ibid.* at p. 681, *per* Lord Hodson; *ibid.* at p. 686, *per* Lord Pearce. See also the observations of the same learned Lords on *Williams* v. *Port of Liverpool Stevedoring Co. Ltd.* [1956] 1 W.L.R. 551 ([1965] A.C. at pp. 681, 687–688) and the cases cited *supra*, n. 71.

[74] *Hambley* v. *Shepley* (1967) 63 D.L.R. (2d) 94 (Ont. C.A.) is an interesting example.

[75] [1968] A.L.R. 33, 34.

[76] See *Cleghorn* v. *Oldham* (1927) 43 T.L.R. 465 and the unreported cases referred to by Sellers L.J. in *Wooldridge* v. *Sumner* [1963] 2 Q.B. 43, 55–56. For the position of the occupier of the premises where the game or sport is taking place, see *Murray* v. *Harringay Arena Ltd.* [1951] 2 K.B. 529; *Wilks* v. *Cheltenham Home Guard Motor Cycle and Light Car Club* [1971] 1 W.L.R. 668.

[77] *Wooldridge* v. *Sumner, supra*, at p. 56, *per* Sellers L.J.; *ibid.* at p. 67, *per* Diplock L.J.

[78] *Supra*; Weir, *Casebook on Tort* (6th ed.), p. 89. For criticism, see Goodhart, (1962) 78 L.Q.R. 490; *Wilks* v. *Cheltenham, etc. Club, supra*, at pp. 670, 673–674, *per* Lord Denning M.R. and Edmund-Davies L.J.

[79] [1963] 2 Q.B. 43, 57, *per* Sellers L.J.: "There would, I think, be a difference, for instance, in assessing blame which is actionable between an injury caused by a tennis ball hit or a racket accidentally thrown in the course of play into the spectators at Wimbledon and a ball hit or a racket thrown into the stands in temper or annoyance when play was not in progress."

judgment in the course of doing his best to win. The result is summarised by Diplock L.J. in these words:

> "A person attending a game or competition takes the risk of any damage caused to him by any act of a participant done in the course of and for the purposes of the game or competition notwithstanding that such an act may involve an error of judgment or a lapse of skill, unless the participant's conduct is such as to evince a reckless disregard for the spectator's safety."[80]

In *Condon* v. *Basi*[81] the issue arose between participants in an amateur league football match and substantial damages were awarded for injuries arising from a tackle which was described by the trial judge as "made in a reckless and dangerous manner not with malicious intent towards the plaintiff but in an excitable manner without thought of the consequences." The rules of the sport are of course very relevant in determining what is a proper standard of care but they should not in all cases be decisive: contravention of a rule designed only to produce fair play should not automatically amount to negligence; equally, conduct may be dangerous even though it does not infringe any particular rule.[82] Whether one regards such cases as involving a departure from the normal duty of care on the basis of the implied consent of the participants, or as illustrating the proposition that in determining what amounts to reasonable care all the circumstances of the case must be taken into account, has been said not to make the slightest difference.[83] English courts have, however, declined to adopt a variable standard of care as between drivers of vehicles and their passengers where the latter have reason to doubt the competence of the former, probably because of the universality of insurance.[84]

Rescue cases[85]

What are called "rescue cases" deserve a separate section, for they straddle three branches of the law—*volenti non fit injuria*, remoteness of consequence and contributory negligence, and the two latter may, for the sake of convenience, be considered here as well as the former in this connection. Rescue cases are typified by A's death or injury in rescuing or endeavouring to rescue B from an emergency of danger to B's life or limb created by the negligence of C.[86] Is C liable to A? Or can C successfully plead (*a*) *volenti*

---

[80] *Ibid.* at p. 68. Contrast *Harrison* v. *Vincent* [1982] R.T.R. 8, where the negligence lay in preparation of equipment.

[81] [1985] 1 W.L.R. 866.

[82] *Affutu-Nartey* v. *Clarke, The Times*, February 9, 1984.

[83] *Condon* v. *Basi* [1985] 1 W.L.R. 866, *per* Sir John Donaldson M.R., though he stated a preference for the latter.

[84] See *ante*, p. 112.

[85] Goodhart, "Rescue and Voluntary Assumption of Risk" (1934) 5 C.L.J. 192; Allen, *Legal Duties*, pp. 217–220; Tiley, "The Rescue Principle" (1967) 30 M.L.R. 25; Linden, "Rescuers and Good Samaritans" (1971) 34 M.L.R. 241.

[86] For a case in which the rescuer himself was sued, see *Horsley* v. *McLaren* [1971] 2 Lloyd's Rep. 410 (Sup.Ct. of Canada); Spencer [1970] C.L.J. 30.

DEFENCES

non fit injuria; or (*b*) that A's conduct is a *novus actus interveniens* which makes his injury too remote a consequence of C's initial negligence; or (*c*) that A's injury was due to contributory negligence on his own part?

Until 1924, our law was almost destitute of any decision on these questions.[87] The American law reports, on the other hand, from 1871 onwards had contained numerous cases which, subject to the limitations stated below, conferred a right of action upon the rescuer or his representatives. In 1935, in *Haynes* v. *Harwood*[88] the Court of Appeal adopted a similar principle.

We can best consider the three arguable defences of C to such an action separately:

(1) *Volenti non fit injuria*

Dr. Goodhart, in summarising the American cases, said:

"The American rule is that the doctrine of assumption of risk does not apply where the plaintiff has, under an exigency caused by the defendant's wrongful misconduct, consciously and deliberately faced a risk, even of death, to rescue another from imminent danger of personal injury or death, whether the person endangered is one to whom he owes a duty of protection or is a mere stranger to whom he owes no such special duty."[89]

This was accepted as an accurate representation of English law by Greer L.J. in *Haynes* v. *Harwood*,[90] where the Court of Appeal affirmed a judgment of Finlay J. in favour of a policeman who had been injured in stopping some runaway horses with a van in a crowded street. The defendant had left the horses and van unattended on the highway and they had bolted. The policeman, who was on duty, not in the street, but in a police station, darted out and was crushed by one of the horses which fell upon him while he was stopping it. It was also held that the rescuer's act need not be instinctive in order to be reasonable, for the man who deliberately encounters peril after reflection may often be acting more reasonably than one who acts upon impulse.[91]

There are several reasons why *volenti non fit injuria* is no answer to the rescuer's claim. In the first place, it is now clear that he founds upon a duty owed directly to himself by the defendant, and not upon one derived from

---

[87] *Roebuck* v. *Norwegian Titanic Co.* (1884) 1 T.L.R. 117 seems to have been forgotten soon after it was reported.
[88] [1935] 1 K.B. 146.
[89] *Loc. cit.*, at p. 196.
[90] [1935] 1 K.B. 146, 156–157, applied in *The Gusty* [1940] P. 159; *Morgan* v. *Aylen* [1942] 1 All E.R. 489; *Baker* v. *T.E. Hopkins & Son Ltd.*, [1959] 1 W.L.R. 966.
[91] [1935] 1 K.B. 146, 158–159, *per* Greer L.J.; *ibid.* at p. 164, *per* Maugham L.J.; *Baker* v. *T.E. Hopkins & Son Ltd.*, *supra*; *Videan* v. *British Transport Commission* [1963] 2 Q.B. 650, 669, *per* Lord Denning M.R.; *Chadwick* v. *B.R.B.* [1967] 1 W.L.R. 912.

that owed to the person imperilled, so that, for example, the plaintiff has recovered damages for injury suffered in going to the rescue of a trespasser, who, as the law then stood, had no claim.[92] If the defendant ought to have foreseen an emergency and that someone would expose himself to danger in order to effect a rescue, then he owes a duty directly to the rescuer.[93] To go on to hold that the rescuer was *volens* would be flatly self-contradictory. In the second place, a rescuer acts under the impulse of duty, legal, moral or social, and does not therefore exercise that freedom of choice which is essential to the success of the defence. Thirdly, it is in the nature of a rescue case that the defendant's negligence precedes the plaintiff's act of running the risk. The plaintiff does not assent to the defendant's negligence at all, and, indeed, may be wholly ignorant of it at the time. All he knows is that someone is in a position of peril which calls for his intervention as a rescuer.[94]

(2) *Novus actus interveniens, or remoteness of consequence*

The policeman's act was that of a normally courageous man in the like circumstances, and therefore was both the direct and foreseeable consequence of the defendant's unlawful act; hence the injury which he suffered was not too remote. "The reasonable man here must be endowed with qualities of energy and courage, and he is not to be deprived of a remedy because he has in a marked degree a desire to save human life when in peril."[95] And, even if his duty to intervene were merely a moral one, still "the law does not think so meanly of mankind as to hold it otherwise than a natural and probable consequence of a helpless person being put in danger that some able-bodied person should expose himself to the same danger to effect a rescue."[96] This covers the case, not only of a policeman or a fireman, who may be expected to be involved in a rescue, but also that of any other person who makes such an attempt with any reasonable prospect of success.[97] So, in *Chadwick v. British Railways Board*[98] the defendant railway authority was held liable where the plaintiff's husband, who lived near a railway line, had gone from his home to the scene of a major railway disaster and, having played a major part in rescue operations there, subsequently became psychoneurotic as a result of his experiences.[99] On the other hand, the principle does not sanction any foolhardy or unnecessary risks, such as an attempt to stop a runaway horse on a desolate country road.[1] Here, as elsewhere in innumerable legal relations, the test is, "What is reasonable?"

---

[92] *Videan* v. *British Transport Commission* [1963] 2 Q.B. 650.

[93] *Ibid.*

[94] *Baker* v. *T.E. Hopkins & Son Ltd.* [1959] 1 W.L.R. 966, 976, *per* Morris L.J.

[95] [1935] 1 K.B. at p. 162, *per* Maugham L.J.

[96] Pollock, *Torts* (15th ed.), p. 370, adopted by Maugham L.J. in *Haynes* v. *Harwood* [1935] 1 K.B. 146, 163.

[97] It is no defence that hindsight shows the attempt to have been futile so long as it appears reasonable at the time: *Wagner* v. *International R.R.* (1921) 133 N.E. 437.

[98] [1967] 1 W.L.R. 912; *Morgan* v. *Aylen* [1942] 1 All E.R. 489; *Baker* v. *T.E. Hopkins & Son Ltd.* [1959] 1 W.L.R. 966.

[99] In *Urbanski* v. *Patel* (1978) 84 D.L.R. (3d) 650 (noted Spencer [1979] C.L.J. and Robertson (1980) 96 L.Q.R.) the first plaintiff lost her only kidney as a result of the defendant's negligence. The second plaintiff recovered damages in respect of an unsuccessful kidney donation by him.

[1] [1935] 1 K.B. 146, 163, *per* Maugham L.J.

And it is unreasonable to go to the assistance of a driver of a horse and cart merely because he shouts for help to pacify a restive horse which has bolted into a field but which is endangering nobody.[2] Furthermore the injury suffered by the rescuer must be a reasonably foreseeable consequence of his attempt to assist.[3]

The fact that members of the emergency services are in a sense employed to take risks has led some American courts to deny liability to them on the part of the person whose negligence creates the danger. This, the so-called "fireman's rule," was decisively rejected by the House of Lords in *Ogwo* v. *Taylor*.[4] Of course, some fires may present no foreseeable hazard to a trained fireman acting with skill and care but if the risk is unavoidable (as it was on the facts) he is not to be disadvantaged because of his calling.

(3) *Contributory negligence*

In *Haynes* v. *Harwood,* this was set up but was not much pressed. Indeed, the earlier case of *Brandon* v. *Osborne, Garrett & Co. Ltd.*[5] had made it improbable that it would have met with any success. There, X and his wife were in a shop as customers. Owing to the negligence of the defendants who were repairing the shop roof, some glass fell from a skylight and struck X. His wife, who was unharmed herself, but who reasonably believed X to be in danger, instinctively clutched his arm and tried to pull him from the spot, and thus injured her leg. Swift J. held that there was no contributory negligence on her part, provided, as was the fact, she had done no more than any reasonable person would have done. "Bearing in mind that danger invites rescue, the court should not be astute to accept criticism of the rescuer's conduct from the wrongdoer who created the danger."[6]

Do the rules just stated apply where the person who is rescued is the person who was negligent, instead of being some third party endangered by the negligent person's conduct? So far we have been considering a case in which A is injured in trying to rescue B from the effects of C's negligence. But is the position the same if A is injured in trying to rescue C himself from peril caused by C's negligence? Would it have made any difference in *Haynes* v. *Harwood* if the person by whose negligence the horses had bolted had been imperilled and had been saved by the policeman? On principle, it seems that there ought to be no difference, bearing in mind that the rescuer's right in the more usual three party situation is an independent one and is not derived from that of the person imperilled, and that C ought to be just as

---

[2] *Cutler* v. *United Dairies (London) Ltd.* [1933] 2 K.B. 297. That seems to be the interpretation of this case by the Court of Appeal in *Haynes* v. *Harwood,* who while they recognised the decision as sound, disapproved of some dicta of Scrutton L.J. in it *cf.* Tiley, *loc. cit.*, pp. 32–33. See, too, *Sylvester* v. *Chapman Ltd.* (1935) 79 S.J. 777; and Goodhart, *loc. cit.*, at pp. 192–203.

[3] *Crossley* v. *Rawlinson* [1982] 1 W.L.R. 369; *cf. Chapman* v. *Hearse* (1961) 106 C.L.R. 112.

[4] [1988] A.C. 431.

[5] [1924] 1 K.B. 548.

[6] *Baker* v. *T.E. Hopkins Ltd., supra,* at p. 984, *per* Willmer L.J.

much liable in the one case as in the other. It was so held at first instance in *Harrison* v. *British Railways Board.*[7]

Another question is whether a man would be justified in running risks of life or limb in order to save his own or other people's property from evil consequences threatened by the wrongful conduct of another person. In *Hyett* v. *G.W. Ry.,*[8] the plaintiff was injured in attempting such a rescue and the Court of Appeal held that, on the facts, his conduct was reasonable and that the defendants were liable; the court held that the doctrine of *Haynes* v. *Harwood* applies to rescue of property as well as to rescue of the person; and pointed out that in either case it is necessary for the court to consider the relationship of the rescuer to the property in peril, or to the person in peril, and also to consider the degree of danger.[9] Goodhart suggested that the only difference between the life and the property cases is that a rescuer would not be justified in exposing himself to as great danger in saving property as he would in saving human life.[10] In general, this seems sound in principle, though particular cases are imaginable in which the rescuer might reasonably encounter just as much danger in trying to preserve property as to preserve life; *e.g.* where documents of great national importance, and of which no copies exist, are in peril of being destroyed by a fire caused by the tortious conduct of some person other than the rescuer.[11]

PUBLIC POLICY. ILLEGALITY[12]

It is a well known principle of the law of contract that if the plaintiff has to found his claim on an illegal act or agreement he will fail: *ex turpi causa non oritur actio.* Though that maxim may be properly confined to cases involving contracts[13] there are also certainly cases of tort in which to allow recovery to a plaintiff implicated in illegality would shock the court's conscience[14]; the difficulty arises in determining when a claim will be rejected for this reason. In *National Coal Board* v. *England*[15] Lord Asquith said, "If two burglars,

---

[7] [1981] 3 All E.R. 679; Fleming [1982] C.L.J. 33; *Canadian National Ry.* v. *Bakty* (1978) 82 D.L.R. (3d) 731. Barry J. had expressed the same view *obiter* in *Baker* v. *T.E. Hopkins Ltd.* [1958] 1 W.L.R. 993, 1004. The Court of Appeal did not consider the point.

[8] [1948] 1 K.B. 345. See *Hutterly* v. *Imperial Oil and Calder* (1956) 3 D.L.R. (2d) 719; *Russell* v. *McCabe* [1962] N.Z.L.R. 392. In the Scottish decision *Steel* v. *Glasgow Iron and Steel Co.* 1944 S.C. 237, such an action was held to be maintainable subject to the conditions that (1) the rescuer's act ought reasonably to have been contemplated by the defendant, and (2) the risk undertaken must be reasonable in relation to the interests protected.

[9] [1948] 1 K.B. 345, 348, *per* Tucker L.J. Note that the Social Security Act 1975, s.54, includes in the "course of employment" steps taken by the insured person to rescue persons or property on his employer's premises.

[10] 5 C.L.J. 198.

[11] See *Russell* v. *McCabe* [1962] N.Z.L.R. 392, 404, *per* North J.

[12] Crago (1964) 4 M.U.L.R. 534; Fridman (1972) 18 McGill L.J. 275; Weinrib (1976) 26 U.T.L.J. 28; Ford (1977) 11 M.U.L.R. 32; Swanton (1981) 9 Sydney L.Rev. 304.

[13] *Smith* v. *Jenkins* (1970) 119 C.L.R. 397, 410, *per* Windeyer J.

[14] The same idea may surface in "no-fault" or social security compensation. Under the New Zealand Accident Compensation Act 1982 (see generally, *ante*, p. 34) the compensation authority may decline to give compensation where "it would be repugnant to justice for . . . such compensation to be paid." Compensation can never be *entirely* about need.

[15] [1954] A.C. 403, 429.

A and B, agree to open a safe by means of explosives, and A so negligently handles the explosive charge as to injure B, B might find some difficulty in maintaining an action for negligence against A." In *Ashton* v. *Turner*,[16] the plaintiff sued in respect of the negligence of the defendant in driving a getaway car from the scene of the burglary in which they had both participated. In dismissing the plaintiff's claim Ewbank J. held that this was a case in which the law should not recognise a duty of care owed by one participant in crime to another in relation to an act done in connection with the commission of that crime.[17] On the other hand, it is clear that the mere fact that the plaintiff is involved in some wrongdoing, whether alone or jointly with the defendant, is not of itself a defence. For example, if you stole a bottle of whisky belonging to me, I could sue you for the tort of conversion even though it appeared that I had bought the bottle during hours prohibited by the Licensing Acts. If proof is needed, one only has to point to the fact that a workman is not barred from suing for breach of his employer's duty because he is himself in breach of some statutory duty imposed directly on him[18] though that conduct may on the facts provide some other answer, in whole or in part, to the claim, such as that the damage is too remote[19] or there is contributory negligence. Even if it be argued that these cases are in a special category because the legislation was passed for the protection of the very class of which the plaintiff forms part, there must have been cases without number in which drivers have recovered damages though they were themselves exceeding the speed limit and without it having occurred to anyone that the effect of that infringement of the law could be more than to reduce damages on account of contributory negligence.

In some cases the illegality should be ignored because it is totally unconnected with the tort. To the example already given, Lord Asquith added, "But if A and B are proceeding to the premises which they intend burglariously to enter, and before they enter them, B picks A's pocket and steals A's watch, I cannot prevail upon myself to believe that A could not sue in tort."[20] Where, however, the illegality has a closer link with the loss, some means must be found of identifying those cases in which it will bar the claim. Where the plaintiff and defendant are joint wrongdoers a useful test is suggested in the important decision of the High Court of Australia in *Jackson* v. *Harrison*.[21] The plaintiff and the defendant, both of whom had, to the knowledge of each other, been disqualified from driving,[22] went for a drive in the car of one of them. An accident occurred as a result of the

---

[16] [1981] Q.B. 137; Symmons (1981) 44 M.L.R. 585.

[17] In the alternative, the judge found for the defendant on the basis of *volenti non fit injuria*, based partly on the defendant's drunkenness and partly on the fact that it was a getaway.

[18] *N.C.B.* v. *England, supra*, where it is suggested that the countrary view would be inconsistent with the Law Reform (Contributory Negligence) Act 1945; *Progress & Properties Ltd.* v. *Craft* (1976) 12 A.L.R. 59.

[19] See, *e.g. Ginty* v. *Belmont Building Supplies Ltd.* [1959] 1 All E.R. 414; *Rushton* v. *Turner Brothers Asbestos Ltd.* [1960] 1 W.L.R. 96; *Boyle* v. *Kodak Ltd.* [1969] 1 W.L.R. 661, 672–673, *per* Lord Diplock.

[20] Similarly, if A and B were knocked down on their way to a "job" by the careless driving of C they could sue C. But they might find it difficult to recover substantial damages for loss of earnings: see *Burns* v. *Edman, ante*, p. 651.

[21] (1978) 19 A.L.R. 129.

[22] There was no contributory negligence or *volenti* because the defendant, though disqualified for earlier traffic offences, had the experience and ability to drive carefully.

negligent driving of one and the other was injured. In upholding a decision in favour of the plaintiff a majority of the court[23] adopted the test of whether the court would be required to engage in a detailed examination of criminal activity in order to set a standard of care. If it would, it would refuse to do so and liability would be denied. As Jacobs J. said:

> "The two safe blowers provide the simplest illustration. What exigencies of the occasion would the tribunal take into account in determining the standard of care owed? That the burglar alarm had already sounded? That the police were known to be on their way? That by reason of the furtive occasion itself a speed of action was required which made it inappropriate to apply to the defendant a standard of care which in lawful circumstances would be appropriate? The courts will not engage in this invidious inquiry."

This approach would be consistent with the result in *Ashton* v. *Turner* (though *Jackson* v. *Harrison* was not cited in that case) because the plaintiff and defendant were in the very act of escaping from the police. Similarly, no doubt, it would lead to denial of recovery to persons actually engaged in stealing a car[24] but not perhaps where they had moved well away from the scene of the crime and were no longer under immediate pressure to avoid detection.[25] It might be argued that public policy should deny any duty when two persons go out together in a car for a drinking spree and there is some support for this,[26] but it is debatable how far the doctrine should be allowed to counter the efforts of both Parliament and the courts to exclude the defence of *volenti non fit injuria* in motor accidents.[27]

There are dicta, but not very much in the way of binding authority, on the situation where the plaintiff is engaged in criminal activity alone rather than jointly with the defendant. Lord Denning M.R. said that a person who attacks another in circumstances amounting to a criminal affray may be debarred from suing if he gets "more than he bargained for"[28]; and that a burglar may have no claim if he is unjustifiably shot by a householder[29] or bitten by a fierce dog,[30] though it is respectfully suggested that the shooting

---

[23] Strictly, a majority of the majority, for Murphy J. would have given illegality no effect in tort in the absence of express statutory provision.

[24] See *Sloan* v. *Triplett* 1985 S.L.T. 294; *Lindsay* v. *Poole* 1984 S.L.T. 269.

[25] Such was the situation in the earlier Australian case of *Smith* v. *Jenkins* (1970) 119 C.L.R. 397 which was relied on in *Ashton* v. *Turner*. Though the High Court in *Jackson* v. *Harrison* certainly did not overrule *Smith* v. *Jenkins* it is not easy to reconcile that case with the *Jackson* v. *Harrison* formula. *cf. Bond* v. *Loutit* [1979] 2 W.W.R. 154.

[26] By Megaw L.J. in *Nettleship* v. *Weston* [1971] 2 Q.B. 691, 701.

[27] See *ante*, p. 690.

[28] *Murphy* v. *Culhane* [1977] Q.B. 94. The decision, however, is only on the issue whether the plaintiff could obtain judgment on the admissions made by the defendant in his pleadings and the Court of Appeal held that he could not. The case assumes that dependants suing under the Fatal Accidents Act are barred by public policy if the deceased would have been so barred, which, it is respectfully submitted, is correct. As to contributory negligence, see *ante*, p. 159.

[29] *Ibid.* Even though the householder may be guilty of manslaughter. However, a burglar shot by a neighbour while in the act of escaping has been awarded damages reduced on account of "contributory negligence": see *The Times*, September 30, 1983.

[30] *Cummings* v. *Grainger* [1977] Q.B. 397.

example goes too far. In *Marshall* v. *Osmond*[31] where the plaintiff, a passenger in a car taken without the consent of its owner, was struck by a police car at the conclusion of a chase, no reference was made in the Court of Appeal to public policy[32] and the plaintiff's claim failed on the basis that the police officer's driving had not been negligent bearing in mind the circumstances of the chase. It seems correct that for participation in such an offence the plaintiff should not be subjected to what would amount to a sentence of outlawry for the purposes of the civil law, given the well-established principles governing the use of force in the prevention of crime[33] and the way in which the court is able to manipulate the standard of care in negligence. A decision which does rely on public policy is *Meah* v. *McCreamer (No. 2)*[34] where it was used to deny A an indemnity from B in respect of damages A had had to pay to C for a serious battery, even though injuries suffered by A as a result of B's negligence had been the cause of A's criminal behaviour. Since, however, A had in earlier proceedings recovered damages from B for the imprisonment he suffered for his crime, the result is not without difficulty.[35]

Consideration of the effect of illegality on contract is outside the scope of this book even though technically many of the "contract" cases are in fact claims for torts such as conversion or fraud which arise out of the contract between the parties. Details must be sought in the standard works on contract but as in the "joint enterprise" cases discussed above the courts have here, too, eschewed rigid rules. As Bingham L.J. said in *Saunders* v. *Edwards*[36] (where the plaintiff recovered damages for fraud notwithstanding that the contract on which it was based contained a false valuation to evade stamp duty), "on the whole the courts have tended to adopt a pragmatic approach to these problems, seeking where possible to see that genuine wrongs are righted so long as the court does not thereby promote or countenance a nefarious object or bargain which it is bound to condemn. Where the plaintiff's action in truth arises directly *ex turpi causa*, he is likely to fail. ... Where the plaintiff has suffered a genuine wrong, to which allegedly unlawful conduct is incidental, he is likely to succeed."[37]

Public policy and consent

As we have seen, consent may render lawful, for purposes of both tort and crime, what would otherwise be unlawful: an embrace which is consented to is not a battery nor is a taking with consent conversion. There are, however,

---

[31] [1983] Q.B. 1034.

[32] At first instance *Ashton* v. *Turner* was considered, but Milmo J. thought it of no assistance since the claim was not against another party to the criminal enterprise. He did, however, hold that a police officer in pursuit of a stolen vehicle did not owe the same duty to the occupants as to other roads users.

[33] *Ante*, p. 64. See also *Lynch* v. *M.o.D.* [1983] N.I. 216.

[34] [1986] 1 All E.R. 943.

[35] For the remoteness aspect of the case, see *ante*, p. 148.

[36] [1987] 1 W.L.R. 1116.

[37] A much debated question has been whether A may refuse to return B's goods because they are to be used in the commission of crime. No, said the New South Wales court in *Gollan* v. *Nugent* (1987) 8 N.S.W.L.R. 166, which contains a full discussion.

limits to this for the purposes of the criminal law where the public interest so requires and fighting (otherwise than in the course of properly conducted sport[38]) is unlawful if bodily harm is intended or caused, notwithstanding the consent of the participants.[39] However, it seems that in such a case the consent may still be effective to bar a civil action,[40] perhaps because this is thought to further the policy of the law in discouraging such conduct. Of course, saying that the plaintiff's claim is barred by public policy would lead to the same result. This is not, however, to say that an unlawful fight can never give rise to a civil action. In *Lane* v. *Holloway*,[41] after a verbal altercation, the elderly plaintiff struck the young defendant on the shoulder and the defendant replied with an extremely severe blow to the plaintiff's eye. The plaintiff recovered damages,[42] for although each party to a fight takes the risk of incidental injuries the plaintiff had not consented to the risk of a savage blow out of all proportion to the occasion.

MISTAKE[43]

Mistake, whether of law or of fact, cannot be said to be a general ground of exemption from liability in tort. There is no need to discuss the rule that ignorance of the law does not excuse, for that is not peculiar to the law of tort. As to mistake of fact one must examine the elements of whatever tort happens to be in question. There are several torts in which liability hangs upon whether a reasonable man would have done what the defendant did, and mistake becomes relevant here, because a man may quite well make one and yet be behaving reasonably. Thus the plaintiff in malicious prosecution must prove lack of reasonable and probable cause for the prosecution, and in false imprisonment the defendant may in certain circumstances be able to escape liability if he can show that he had reasonable cause to believe that the plaintiff was guilty of an offence. In defamation, mistake is relevant in some instances of publication and privilege. A mistaken belief may remove the requisite mental element for the tort of deceit, and a judicial officer may be immune from liability for his judicial acts even though he acts under a mistaken belief as to his jurisdiction. Yet there are torts which go the other way, and matters have gone too far to make mistake a general defence in the law of tort, for a good deal of the law relating to trespass, conversion and wrongs of strict liability would need recasting. Thus an auctioneer who innocently sells A's goods in the honest and reasonable belief that they

---

[38] *cf. R.* v. *Coney* (1882) 8 Q.B.D. 534 (prize fight with bare fists).

[39] *Att.-Gen.'s Reference (No. 6 of 1980)* [1981] Q.B. 715.

[40] *Murphy* v. *Culhane* [1977] Q.B. 94; *R.* v. *Coney, supra,* at p. 553; *Bain* v. *Altoft* [1967] Qd.R. 32. See also *Madalena* v. *Kuun* (1987) 35 D.L.R. (4th) 222 holding that while consent is no defence to the *crime* of having intercourse with a girl below the age of 16, her real consent is a defence to a civil claim.

[41] [1968] 1 Q.B. 379.

[42] Although the Law Reform (Contributory Negligence) Act 1945 probably applies to intentional trespass to the person (*ante,* p. 159) the disproportion between the conduct of the two parties in *Lane* v. *Holloway* prevented any reduction of the damages: see *Murphy* v. *Culhane, supra.* See, too, *Barnes* v. *Nayer, The Times,* December 19, 1986 (insufficient provocation for murderous attack with machete).

[43] Trindade (1982) 2 O.J.L.S. 211.

belong to B on whose instructions he sells them, has been held liable to A[44]; and a surgeon who, as a result of an administrative mix up, carries out the wrong operation is liable in trespass to the patient,[45] though in both cases the innocent wrongdoer would be entitled to be indemnified by the person responsible for the mistake. Sometimes such cases have been defended on the ground that, if the rule were otherwise, the courts would find it difficult to discover, as a matter of evidence, whether the belief were honest and reasonable,[46] but the mere fact that, in the case of some torts, exactly this inquiry must be undertaken, demonstrates that the reason is unconvincing. In fact, it is suggested that the cases do not need to be justified on this ground and that it is wrong even to think in terms of the desirability of a general rule about mistake. Each area of liability depends upon a proper assessment of the balance between the interests of potential plaintiffs and defendants and it is not surprising that "mistake" will vary in significance from one tort to another.

INEVITABLE ACCIDENT

Inevitable accident is defined by Sir Frederick Pollock as an accident "*not avoidable by any such precautions as a reasonable man, doing such an act then and there, could be expected to take.*"[47] It does not mean a catastrophe which could not have been avoided by any precaution whatever, but such as could not have been avoided by a reasonable man at the moment at which it occurred, and it is common knowledge that a reasonable man is not credited by the law with perfection of judgment. "People must guard against reasonable probabilities, but they are not bound to guard against fantastic possibilities."[48]

To speak of inevitable accident as a defence, therefore, is to say that there are cases in which the defendant will escape liability if he succeeds in proving that the accident occurred despite the exercise of reasonable care on his part, but it is also to say that there are cases in which the burden of proving this is placed upon him. In an ordinary action for negligence, for example, it is for the plaintiff to prove the defendant's lack of care, not for the defendant to disprove it, and the defence of inevitable accident is accordingly irrelevant[49]; and it is equally irrelevant in any other class of case in which the

[44] *Consolidated Co.* v. *Curtis* [1892] 1 Q.B. 495; see *ante*, p. 484.
[45] *Chatterton* v. *Gerson* [1981] Q.B. 432, 443.
[46] Salmond, *Torts* (7th ed.), (1928) s.3(3); not included in later editions.
[47] *Torts* (15th ed.), p. 97. *cf. The Marpesia* (1872) L.R. 4 P.C. 212, 220, *per* Sir James Colville: "An inevitable accident in point of law is this: *viz.* that which the party charged with the offence could not possibly prevent by the exercise of ordinary care, caution, and maritime skill." *The Saint Angus* [1938] P. 225; *Ryan* v. *Youngs* [1938] 1 All E.R. 522 Beven, *Negligence in Law* (4th ed.) i, pp. 697–712, gives the history of the topic.
[48] *Fardon* v. *Harcourt-Rivington* (1932) 146 L.T. 391, *per* Lord Dunedin.
[49] "I do not find myself assisted by considering the meaning of the phrase 'inevitable accident.' I prefer to put the problem in a more simple way, namely has it been established that the driver of the car was guilty of negligence?" *Browne* v. *De Luxe Car Services* [1941] 1 K.B. 549, 552, *per* Greene M.R. This should not be understood to mean that the defendant in an action for negligence need never bring any evidence to exculpate himself. The plaintiff's evidence may raise a presumption or prima facie case which, if nothing more appears, will entitle the court to infer that the defendant was negligent. But the legal burden of proof remains with the plaintiff and when all the evidence has been heard the court must decide, whether it has been discharged: *Brown* v. *Rolls-Royce Ltd.* [1960] 1 W.L.R. 210, 215–216, *per* Lord Denning.

burden of proving the defendant's negligence is imposed upon the plaintiff. It was for long thought that the burden of proof in trespass rested with the defendant and that trespass, therefore, offered scope to the defence of inevitable accident, but it has now been held that here too the burden is with the plaintiff.[50] In trespass as well as in negligence, therefore, inevitable accident has no place.

In these cases inevitable accident is irrelevant because the burden is on the plaintiff to establish the defendant's negligence, but it does not follow that it is any more relevant if the plaintiff has no such burden. If, as in *Rylands* v. *Fletcher*,[51] the defendant is liable notwithstanding that he has taken reasonable care, it can avail him nothing to prove inevitable accident, and the same is true in those cases where liability for nuisance is strict,[52] and, subject to the Defamation Act 1952, s.4, in cases of defamation.

There seems, in fact, to be only one class of case in which the conception of inevitable accident has any meaning, and even there it is in truth misleading. In cases to which the maxim *res ipsa loquitur* applies[53] the plaintiff can rely upon the mere happening of the accident as evidence of negligence, and then it is sometimes said that the defendant is liable unless he proves inevitable accident.[54] But this, it is submitted, is to over-simplify the position in cases of *res ipsa loquitur*, and perhaps to falsify it.[55] It therefore seems that the conception of inevitable accident has no longer any useful function and it is doubtful whether much advantage is gained by the continued use of the phrase.[56]

ACT OF GOD

This defence is limited to negation of liability under the rule in *Rylands* v. *Fletcher* and has already been dealt with.[57]

PRIVATE DEFENCE

Reasonable defence of oneself,[58] of one's property, and of those whom one

---

[50] *Ante*, pp. 70–71.

[51] (1868) L.R. 3 H.L. 330, *ante*, Chap. 16.

[52] *Ante*, pp. 380–385.

[53] *Ante*, pp. 125–130.

[54] *The Merchant Prince* [1892] P. 179; *Southport Corp.* v. *Esso Petroleum Co. Ltd.* [1954] 2 Q.B. 182, 200, *per* Denning L.J. (the Court of Appeal's decision was reversed by the House of Lords [1956] A.C. 218).

[55] See the observations of Devlin J. on *The Merchant Prince* in *Southport Corp.* v. *Esso Petroleum Co. Ltd.* [1956] A.C. 218, 229–232 and *ante*, pp. 129–130.

[56] See Pape, "The Burden of Proof of Inevitable Accident in Actions for Negligence" (1965) 38 A.L.J. 395. *cf.* Clerk and Lindsell, *Torts* (16th ed.), para. 1–162. It may be that a new use for "inevitable accident" exists after the Highways (Miscellaneous Provisions) Act 1961 s.1 (*ante*, p. 418), which abolished the former non-liability of highway authorities for non-feasance. If a person suffers injury from a danger resulting from the authority's failure to repair the highway, the authority is liable unless it proves that it had taken reasonable care to secure that the part of the highway in question was not dangerous to traffic: s.1(2). "It may be that if the highway authority could show that no amount of reasonable care on its part could have prevented the danger the common law defence of inevitable accident would be available to it": *Griffiths* v. *Liverpool Corp.* [1967] 1 Q.B. 374, 391, *per* Diplock L.J.

[57] *Ante*, Chap. 15.

[58] Including defence against an unlawful arrest: "If a person is purporting to arrest another without lawful warrant the person arrested may use force to avoid being arrested, but he must not use more force than necessary": *R.* v. *Wilson* [1955] 1 W.L.R. 493, 494, *per* Lord Goddard C.J.; *Kenlin* v. *Gardiner* [1967] 2 Q.B. 510.

is bound to protect negatives any liability in tort. Some authorities regard it as a species of self-help, *i.e.* as one of the remedies for tort.[59] Certainly what begins as self-defence often ends as self-help, but the better view is that private defence is allowed "not for the redress of injuries, but for their prevention,"[60] and much more injury may in certain circumstances be incidental to the expulsion of a trespasser than would ever be permissible in merely keeping him out.

Defence of the person

There is no doubt that the right extends to the protection of one's spouse and family, and, whatever the limits of this defence, almost certainly anyone can be protected against unlawful force for the independent reason that there is a general liberty, even as between strangers, for the use of such force as is reasonable in the circumstances in the prevention of crime.[61]

It must always be a question of fact, rather than of law, whether violence done by way of self-protection is proportionate to warding off the harm which is threatened. On the one hand, I am certainly not bound to wait until a threatened blow falls before I hit in self-defence; thus my blow may be justified when my assailant does no more than shake his stick at me, uttering taunts at the same time[62]; much less do I commit any assault by merely putting myself in a fighting attitude in order to defend myself.[63] On the other hand, not every threat will justify a blow in self-defence; still less can B be excused "if upon a little blow given by A to B, B gives him a blow that maims him."[64] If A uses force on B because of a mistake (*e.g.* he believes B is attacking him when in fact he is not) it is arguable that he has no defence to a civil action by B but the law probably now is that he has a defence if his mistake is a reasonable one in the circumstances.[65]

Defence of property

Actual possession (whether with a good title or not), or the right to possession of property is necessary to justify force in keeping out (or, for that matter, expelling) a trespasser. Thus, in *Holmes* v. *Bagge*,[66] the plaintiff and defendant were both members of the committee of a cricket club. During a match in which the defendant was captain and the plaintiff was a spectator, the defendant asked the plaintiff to act as substitute for one of the eleven. He did so, but being annoyed at the tone of the defendant in

---

[59] Salmond, *Torts* (7th ed.), 46; but his editors impliedly preferred the other view. See now (19th ed.), p. 142. *Turner* v. *M.G.M. Ltd.* [1950] 1 All E.R. 449, 470–471 (Lord Oaksey).
[60] Pollock, *Torts* (15th ed.), pp. 135–136.
[61] Criminal Law Act 1967, s.3; *R.* v. *Duffy* [1967] 1 Q.B. 63.
[62] *Dale* v. *Wood* (1822) 7 Moore C.P. 33.
[63] Lord Lyndhurst C.B. in *Moriarty* v. *Brooks* (1834) 6 C. & P. 684.
[64] *Cockroft* v. *Smith* (1705) 2 Salk. 642; *Lane* v. *Holloway* [1968] 1 Q.B. 379. But the law should not grade the levels of permissible response to an assault with too much nicety.
[65] Subject to the rule in *Walters* v. *W. H. Smith*, a reasonable mistake of fact is clearly a defence to an action arising from an arrest: p. 63, *ante*. *cf.* Prosser, *Torts* (5th ed.), p. 125.
[66] (1853) 1 E. & B. 782; see also *Dean* v. *Hogg* (1834) 10 Bing. 345 and *Roberts* v. *Taylor* (1845) 1 C.B. 117.

commanding him to take off his coat, he refused either to remove the garment or to leave the playing part of the field. He was then forcibly removed by the defendant's direction. The defendant, when sued for assault, pleaded possession of the ground, but the plea was held bad because possession was in the committee of the club. Note, however that a person who does not have possession of the land may use reasonable force against persons thereon who obstruct him in carrying out statutory powers,[67] and it may be that if the defendant in *Holmes* v. *Bagge* had pleaded that he removed the plaintiff for disturbing persons lawfully playing a lawful game he would have been justified.[68]

The idea that a burglar may be shot at sight or that a trespasser must always take premises as he finds them goes beyond what the law allows. The broad test here, as elsewhere in private defence, is reasonableness. One is not necessarily bound to make one's premises safe for trespassers, and if burglars fall into sawpits or are bitten by dogs, tossed by bulls or mauled by savage horses, it may be that they must put up with it.[69] But there is a difference between harm suffered from what may be called the ordinary condition of the premises and harm suffered from means of defence deliberately adopted. These means must be reasonable, *i.e.* proportionate to the injuries which they are likely to inflict. Such would be broken glass or spikes on a wall, or a fierce dog,[70] but not deadly implements like spring-guns.[71] The infliction of grave bodily harm is too high a price to demand for keeping one's property intact. Even at common law a trespasser wounded in this way could recover damages[72] unless he knew that the guns were somewhere on the land[73] and it is an offence against the Offences Against the Person Act 1861[74] to set a spring-gun or similar device except, probably, in and for the protection of a dwelling-house between sunset and sunrise. Consistently with the principle of proportion in the means of defence, more latitude is permissible in protecting premises by night than in the daytime, or when the occupier is not in the presence of the trespasser than when he is. Thus an intruder who tears himself on a spiked wall has no ground of complaint, but he certainly would have one if he, being peaceable and unarmed, had a spike thrust into him by the occupier.[75] "Presence [of the occupier] in its very

---

[67] *R.* v. *Chief Constable of Devon and Cornwall, ex p. C.E.G.B.* [1982] Q.B. 458.

[68] *Ibid., per* Lord Denning M.R.

[69] For the liability of occupiers to trespassers generally, see *ante*, p. 225. It is assumed that an element of public policy enters into such cases and that the duty towards a burglar (if it exists at all) is very much lower than that towards a non-criminal trespasser. *cf.* the more rigorous view of Lord Denning M.R. as to burglars *ante*, p. 699.

[70] *Sarch* v. *Blackburn* (1830) 4 C. & P. 297. The position is now governed by s.5(3)(*b*) of the Animals Act 1971, which is to the like effect, though the position may have been indirectly affected by the Guard Dogs Act 1975: *ante*, p. 460.

[71] It is usefully suggested in Salmond and Heuston, *Torts* (18th ed.), p. 262, that the law permits a deterrent danger but not a retributive (*i.e.* concealed) one. In the case of the latter, a "possessor of land cannot do indirectly and by a mechanical device that which, were he present, he could not do immediately and in person": *Katko* v. *Briney* 183 N.W. 2d 657 (1971).

[72] *Bird* v. *Holbrook* (1828) 4 Bing. 628.

[73] *Ilott* v. *Wilkes* (1820) 3 B. & Ald. 304.

[74] s.31, re-enacting. Spring Gun Act, 1827 *cf. Wooton* v. *Dawkins* (1857) 5 W.R. 469.

[75] In *Pickwick Papers*, Captain Boldwig's mode of ejecting Mr. Pickwick, whom he found asleep in a wheelbarrow in his grounds, was excessive. He directed his gardener first to wheel Mr. Pickwick to the devil and then, on second thoughts, to wheel him to the village pond.

nature is more or less protection . . . presence may supply means [of defence] and limit what it supplies."[76]

Injury to innocent third person

Suppose that in protecting myself from an unlawful attack by A, I injure you, an innocent passer-by. On what principles ought my liability to you to be discussed? Certainly not on those of private defence, for I cannot "defend" myself against one who has done me no unlawful harm. It would seem that the true principles applicable are that I committed no tort if I did not intend to harm and was not negligent, and that I may rely on the defence of necessity[77] if I did. But this does not mean that whatever I may do is justifiable under the one head or the other. Provided I acted reasonably I am excused, and not otherwise.

In *Scott* v. *Shepherd*,[78] A threw a lighted squib into a crowded market-house. It fell upon the gingerbread stall of Yates. A bystander, Willis, to prevent injury to himself and the wares of Yates, instantly picked up the squib and threw it away. It fell upon the gingerbread stall of Ryal, who, to save his own goods from injury threw the squib farther. It struck B in the face, exploded and blinded him in one eye. Now it was held without any difficulty, except as to the exact form of action, that A was liable to B for trespass and assault. No proceedings were taken against Willis or Ryal, but supposing that they had been sued by B, would they have been liable? Two of the judges thought not, because they acted "under a compulsive necessity for their own safety and self-preservation."[79] No exact technicality was attached by the judges to "necessity" or "self-preservation," but one difficulty is the question whether Willis and Ryal really did behave as reasonable men would have done. Willis, it will be noted, acted to prevent injury to himself as well as to the wares of Yates, and it must be recollected that a man may well act reasonably even if he shows no great presence of mind. A cooler man would have stopped the danger by putting his foot on the squib, but perhaps Willis did all that the lawyer, if not the moralist, could expect of him. Ryal, on the other hand, appears to have acted merely to preserve his goods, and we may doubt whether a man of ordinary presence of mind would throw a squib into a crowd to save his gingerbread from ruin.

NECESSITY

This negatives liability in tort, provided, of course, that the occasion of necessity does not arise from the defendant's own negligence,[80] though the

---

[76] *Deane* v. *Clayton* (1817) 7 Taunt. 489, 521, *per* Dallas J. For the defences available to the occupier of land who kills or injures a dog, see Animals Act 1971, s.9.

[77] See below.

[78] (1773) 2 W.Bl. 892.

[79] *Ibid.* at p. 900, *per* De Grey C.J.; *ibid.* at p. 898, *per* Gould J.

[80] *Southport Corp.* v. *Esso Petroleum Ltd.* [1954] 2 Q.B. 182, 194, *per* Singleton L.J.; *ibid.* at p. 198, *per* Denning L.J.; *Esso Petroleum Ltd.* v. *Southport Corp.* [1956] A.C. 218, 242, *per* Lord Radcliffe. For a case where there was no negligence in creating the occasion so that necessity applied but the defendants' conduct in responding to the necessity was negligent, see *Rigby* v. *Chief Constable of Northamptonshire* [1985] 1 W.L.R. 1242.

authority on it is scanty.[81] It differs from private defence in that in necessity the harm inflicted on the plaintiff was not provoked by any actual or threatened illegal wrong on the plaintiff's part and that what the defendant did may be entirely for the good of other people and not necessarily for the protection of himself or his property. Its basis is a mixture of charity, the maintenance of the public good and self-protection, and it is probably limited to cases involving an urgent situation of imminent peril. It does not, for example, furnish a defence to an action for trespass brought against homeless persons who enter and "squat" in unoccupied premises.[82]

Familiar examples are pulling down a house on fire to prevent its spread to other property,[83] destroying a building made ruinous by fire to prevent its collapse into the highway,[84] throwing goods overboard to lighten a boat in a storm,[85] and perhaps assistance, medical[86] or otherwise, rendered to a person unconscious at the time. So, too, the removal of the plaintiff's barge because it is frozen hard to the defendant's barge which he is lawfully moving.[87] The measures which are taken must be reasonable, and this will depend, amongst other things, upon whether there is human life or merely property in danger.[88] In *Kirk v. Gregory*,[89] X died in a state of *delirium tremens*. His servants were feasting and drinking in the house. X's sister-in-law removed X's jewellery from the room where he lay dead to another room for safety's sake. Some unknown person stole it. The sister-in-law was held liable to X's executor for trespass to the jewellery because there was no proof that her interference was reasonably necessary. On the other hand, the justification for interference depends upon the state of things at the moment at which interference takes place. Subsequent events may show that interference was not needed at all, but that will not deprive the doer of his defence. In *Cope v. Sharpe*,[90] a fire broke out on A's land. While A's servants were trying to beat it out, the gamekeeper of C (who had shooting rights over A's land) set fire to some strips of heather between the fire and

---

[81] *Esso Petroleum Ltd.* v. *Southport Corp.* [1956] A.C. 218, 228, *per* Devlin J.; *ibid.* at p. 235, *per* Earl Jowitt; *ibid.* at p. 242, *per* Lord Radcliffe; *Southwark London Borough Council* v. *Williams* [1971] 1 Ch. 734.

[82] *Southwark London Borough Council* v. *Williams, supra,* where the Court of Appeal was concerned that the defence of necessity should not become a "mask for anarchy." In *John Trenberth Ltd.* v. *National Westminster Bank* (1979) 39 P. & C.R. 104, the defendants were liable in trespass although entry to the neighbouring land was the only way of repairing their ruinous building.

[83] Shelley *arguendo* in Y.B.Trin. 13 Hen. 8, f.15, pl.1, at f.16a; Kingsmill J. in Y.B.Trin. 21 Hen. 7, f.27b, pl. 5; *Saltpetre Case* (1606) 12 Rep. 12, 13; *Sirocco* v. *Geary* (1853) 3 Cal. 69. But officious interference with a fire brigade which is adequately coping with the fire is not justified: *Carter* v. *Thomas* [1893] 1 Q.B. 673.

[84] *Dewey* v. *White* (1827) M. & M. 56 (A, whose adjoining house was inevitably damaged, had no remedy). See, however, the observations of Lord Upjohn in *Burmah Oil Co. (Burmah Trading) Ltd.* v. *Lord Advocate* [1965] A.C. 75, 164–165.

[85] *Mouse's Case* (1609) 12 Rep. 63. It should be noted that this case took place on an inland waterway. The position as to jettison at sea may be affected by the principle of general average.

[86] For the relationship of consent and necessity in these cases, see p. 684, *ante.*

[87] *Milman* v. *Dolwell* (1810) 2 Camp. 378. Defendant lost his case because he did not plead necessity. *cf. Romney Marsh* v. *Trinity House* (1870) L.R. 5 Ex. 204.

[88] "The safety of human lives belongs to a different scale of values from the safety of property. The two are beyond comparison and the necessity for saving life has at all times been considered a proper ground for inflicting such damages as may be necessary upon another's property": *Esso Petroleum Ltd.* v. *Southport Corp.* [1956] A.C. 218, 228, *per* Devlin J.; Weir, *Casebook on Tort* (6th ed.), p. 354. *cf.* Glanville Williams in (1953) 6 *Current Legal Problems* 216, 234.

[89] (1876) 1 Ex.D. 55.

[90] [1912] 1 K.B. 496.

some nesting pheasants of C. Shortly afterwards, A's servants succeeded in extinguishing the fire. A sued the gamekeeper for trespass. He was held not liable, for there was real and imminent danger to the game at the moment at which he acted, and what he did was reasonably necessary.

A landowner may defend himself against an incursion of water by erecting barricades or heightening banks on his own land even if the foreseeable result is the flooding of his neighbour's land by the diverted water.[91] The law allows a kind of reasonable selfishness in such matters.[92] Altruism is not demanded; ordinary skill and care are.[93] This applies not only to private landowners but also to any authority charged with protecting landowners from the incursion of water.[94] Nor is it material that the barriers were erected at some distance within the boundaries of the land instead of on the edge of it; for it would be illogical to allow a landowner to protect the whole of his land against floods and yet to hold him liable because he had set his embankment farther back and so had left part of his land undefended.[95]

But this repulsion of a temporary incursion must be distinguished from accumulating water on one's land and then getting rid of it by artificial means in such a way as to flood a neighbour's land. That is not lawful.[96] And this is so even if the accumulation of the water is due, not to the act of the landowner, but to an extraordinary rainfall. Thus, in *Whalley* v. *Lancashire and Yorkshire Ry.*,[97] an unprecedented storm and rainfall flooded the drains bordering on the railway embankment of the defendants so that a large quantity of water was dammed up against the embankment. The water afterwards rose so as to endanger the embankment. The defendants then pierced it with gullies and the water flowed away and flooded the plaintiff's land. The defendants were held liable, although the jury found that if they had had only the preservation of their own land to consider their act would have been reasonable. They could lawfully have turned away the flood if they had seen it coming, but "there is a difference between protecting yourself from an injury which is not yet suffered by you, and getting rid of the consequences of an injury which has occurred to you."[98]

Greyvensteyn v. *Hattingh*,[99] an appeal case from South Africa, related to a plague of locusts. They entered the plaintiff's land, and the defendants, in the reasonable belief that they were trekking towards their land, entered a strip of land belonging to third parties and turned away the locusts so that they re-entered the plaintiff's land and devoured his crops. The defendants were held not liable either because they were repelling an extraordinary misfortune or because, if locusts were to be regarded in South Africa as a normal incident of agriculture, the defendants were entitled to get rid of

[91] *Home Brewery plc* v. *William Davis & Co. (Leicester) Ltd.* [1987] Q.B. 339.
[92] *Nield* v. *L. & N.W. Ry.* (1874) L.R. 10 Ex. 4, 7, *per* Bramwell B.
[93] *Maxey Drainage Board* v. *G.N. Ry.* (1912) 106 L.T. 429.
[94] *R.* v. *Pagham* (1828) 8 B. & C. 356.
[95] *Gerrard* v. *Crowe* [1921] 1 A.C. 395, 400, *per* Viscount Cave.
[96] *Hurdman* v. *N.E. Ry.* (1878) 3 C.P.D. 168. *Maxey Drainage Board* v. *G.N. Ry.* (1912) 106 L.T. 429; *Gerrard* v. *Crowe*, *supra*.
[97] (1884) 13 Q.B.D. 131.
[98] *Ibid.* at p. 140, *per* Lindley L.J.
[99] [1911] A.C. 355.

them just as they would be allowed to scare away crows regardless of the direction they took in leaving.[1]

So far we have been dealing with harm inflicted on property. There is no reported decision that is of any real assistance on necessity as a defence for inflicting injuries to the person.[2] The dicta in *Scott* v. *Shepherd*[3] were only *obiter*. In *Gregson* v. *Gilbert*[4] where 150 negro slaves were thrown overboard owing to shortage of water, it was held in an action upon a policy of insurance for the value of the slaves that, upon the facts, no sufficient evidence of necessity had been shown for the captain's act, but the decision is obviously of little value for modern purposes. All that it is safe to hazard is that the principle of reasonableness applies here also, that more latitude would be allowed in the protection of the actor's person than of his property, and still more where he acts for the public safety and not for his own.[5]

Is compensation demandable?

Another point not free from doubt is whether, assuming that the defence of necessity has been established, the defendant must make compensation or at least restitution for the harm which he has inflicted. It is clear that no damages can be claimed in tort where the defendant's act is justified by necessity,[6] but that does not settle the question whether the defendant is liable to make restitution, *i.e.* to restore to its former condition the property of the plaintiff which has been affected by the defendant's act, or, if restoration be impossible, to pay the plaintiff equivalent compensation. Here, the basis of the plaintiff's claim would be quasi-contract, not tort, the practical difference being that compensation payable on a quasi-contractual claim may be considerably less than damages on a claim in tort. Perhaps a distinction exists between (*a*) an act done for the common weal, and (*b*) an act done simply in protection of one's person or property. As to (*a*), in the *Saltpetre Case*,[7] it was said that every man, as well as the King and his officials, may, for the defence of the realm, enter upon another man's land and make trenches or bulwarks there; "but after the danger is over, the trenches and bulwarks ought to be removed, so that the owner shall not have prejudice in his inheritance"; and in *Burmah Oil Co. (Burmah Trading) Ltd.*

---

[1] Scaring crows is a normal incident in the occupation of land; piercing a railway embankment is not an ordinary use of the embankment: *Whalley* v. *Lancs. & Yorks. Ry.* (1884) 13 Q.B.D. 131, 138.

[2] The well-known criminal cases of *R.* v. *Dudley* (1884) 15 Cox C.C. 624 and *U.S.* v. *Holmes* (1842) 1 Wall Jr. 1 hold that A is not justified in killing B to save his own life. And see *R.* v. *Abbott* [1977] A.C. 755.

[3] (1773) 2 W.Bl. 892, *ante*, p. 146.

[4] (1783) 3 Dougl. 232.

[5] The driver of a fire engine is in no privileged position; he must observe traffic signals: *Ward* v. *L.C.C.* [1938] 2 All E.R. 341. S.87 of the Road Traffic Regulation Act 1984 exempts fire engines, ambulances and police cars from speed limits, but does not affect the civil liability of the driver: *Gaynor* v. *Allen* [1959] 2 Q.B. 403.

[6] *Cope* v. *Sharpe* [1912] 1 K.B. 496. Tindal C.J. in *Anthony* v. *Haney* (1823) 8 Bing. 186, 192–193 said *obiter* that an owner who peaceably retakes his goods from the land of another who refuses to give them up, must pay for such damage as he commits. But this relates to the limits of self-help rather than to necessity. In *Southport Corp.* v. *Esso Petroleum Co. Ltd.* [1965] A.C. 218, 227, Devlin J. was not prepared to hold without further consideration that a man is entitled to damage the property of another without compensating him merely because the infliction of such damage is necessary to save his own property.

[7] (1606) 12 Rep. 12, 13, *per* the justices consulting in Serjeants Inn.

v. *Lord Advocate*[8] it was held by a majority of the House of Lords that the
Crown must pay compensation for property destroyed, by an exercise of the
Royal prerogative during the War, in order to prevent it from falling into
enemy hands. The effect of this decision was, however, removed by the War
Damage Act 1965, which provides that "No person shall be entitled *at
common law* to receive from the Crown compensation in respect of damage
to, or destruction of, property caused . . . by acts lawfully done by, or on the
authority of, the Crown during, or in contemplation of the outbreak of, a
war in which the Sovereign was, or is engaged."[9] Notwithstanding the
dictum in the *Saltpetre Case* it may be doubted whether a private person,
who, of course, does not act under the prerogative and is unaffected by the
Act of 1965, need ever have made any compensation for acts justifiably done
in defence of the realm.[10] It is, however, exceedingly difficult to conceive
that today a private citizen could justify an otherwise tortious action on the
ground that it was done in defence of the realm.[11] As to (*b*), it is suggested
that bare restitution or compensation for the use or consumption of property
might be claimed on quasi-contractual grounds: *e.g.* using a neighbour's fire
extinguisher to put out a fire in one's own house.[12]

Duress

Duress, or threatened injury to a person unless he commits a tort, was
held many years ago to be no defence if he does commit it. In *Gilbert* v.
Stone,[13] 12 unknown armed men threatened to kill the defendant unless he
entered the plaintiff's house with them, which he did. To an action for
trespass he was held to have no defence, "for one cannot justify a trespass
upon another for fear, and the defendant hath remedy against those that
compelled him." But actual physical compulsion as distinct from mere threat
of it, is a defence.[14]

[8] [1965] A.C. 75.

[9] s.1(1), italics added. On this provision see *Nissan* v. *Att.-Gen.* [1968] 1 Q.B. 286, 309–310, *per* John
Stephenson J.; *ibid.* [1970] A.C. 179, 229, *per* Lord Pearce. The normal situation is, of course, that special
statutory provisions for compensation will apply.

[10] The whole passage in 12 Rep. 12–13 is rather confused and the earlier authorities do not support Coke, who
reported the case. See, *e.g. Maleverer* v. *Spinke* (1538) Dyer 35b, 36b, para. 40.

[11] See *Burmah Oil Co. (Burmah Trading) Ltd.* v. *Lord Advocate (supra)*, at pp. 164–165 *per* Lord Upjohn.
Lord Reid, *ibid.* at p. 99, conceded that there might be occasions when a subject is entitled to act on his
own initiative in defence of the realm, particularly if there is no one in authority there to direct him, but he
thought it impossible that any subject could have been entitled to carry out the major demolitions with
which the case was concerned.

[12] There is no English decision in point, but an example put by Lord Mansfield in *Hambly* v. *Trott* (1776) 1
Cowp. 371, 375 is consistent with the suggestion. For a case the facts of which would seem to call for such a
remedy see *Esso Petroleum Ltd.* v. *Southport Corp.* [1956] A.C. 218. The American *Restatement of
Restitution*, 122, is to the like effect and applies the rule also where A harms B's property in order to
preserve C or C's property, for "a person is not entitled to be a good samaritan at the expense of another."
122, however, exempts A from any obligation to make restitution to B if A's act appeared reasonably
necessary to avert a *public* catastrophe.

[13] (1647) Aleyn 35. It may be doubted whether any absolute rule excluding duress as a defence would be
applied today (Fleming, *Torts* (7th ed.), p. 90). If not, similar issues of balancing one evil against another
and of the availability of quasi-contractual remedy might arise as in cases of necessity.

[14] *Smith* v. *Stone* (1647) Style 65; dictum in *Weaver* v. *Ward* (1616) Hob. 134.

Statutory Authority

When a statute authorises the commission of what would otherwise be a tort, then the party injured has no remedy apart from the compensation (if any) which the statute allows him. Statutory powers are not, however, charters of immunity for any injurious act done in the exercise of them. In the first place, courts will not impute to the legislature any intention to take away the private rights of individuals without compensation, unless it be proved that there was such an intention; and the burden of proving it is said to rest with those who exercise the statutory powers.[15] On the other hand, the court must beware lest it interfere with the administrative discretion which may have been granted by the statute.[16] Most of the cases have concerned liability for nuisance and the matter has been considered under that head.[17]

[15] *Farnworth* v. *Manchester Corp.* [1929] 1 K.B. 533, 556, *per* Lawrence L.J., For proceedings in the House of Lords, see [1930] A.C. 171. But the question would seem to be one purely of statutory construction and as such not to involve questions of the burden of proof at all. The point is that unless the clearest language is used it is to be assumed that Parliament did not intend an encroachment upon the liberties of the subject: *Att.-Gen.* v. *Nissan* [1970] A.C. 179, 229, *per* Lord Pearce.
[16] See *Marriage* v. *E. Norfolk Catchment Board* [1950] 1 K.B. 284 and *ante*, p. 99.
[17] *Ante*, p. 410.

CHAPTER 27

EXTINCTION OF LIABILITY IN TORT

EXTINCTION of liability in tort may take place in several ways, some of them by act of the parties, others by operation of law.[1]

WAIVER

"Waiver" is a term used in a number of different senses in the law. It may mean conduct by the plaintiff which signifies an intention to give up a right of action for a legal wrong. Subject to the doctrine of promissory estoppel (which cannot be pursued here and the applicability of which to money claims is a matter of some doubt[2]) a right of action for tort can only be "waived" in this sense by an agreement for valuable consideration or a release under seal.[3] Waiver is also used to mean election between inconsistent rights as when the plaintiff, having ratified the unauthorised act of his agent and sued a third party to judgment (which went unsatisfied) was barred from suing his agent for going beyond his authority.[4] What amounts to an election for this purpose? Certainly the obtaining of judgment in an action does; but beyond that it is a question of fact to be determined by the circumstances of the case. Once a person has committed himself unequivocally to one of two inconsistent rights he cannot afterwards resort to the other[5] but the mere commencement of an action which is not pushed to judgment is not conclusive. Similarly mere demand for payment of what is due is not a waiver of the right of action for the wrong[6] nor is receipt of part payment of what is due, unless it is accepted as full discharge.[7]

Waiver is, however, used in a rather special sense in connection with tort. This is where the plaintiff is allowed to select an action in quasi-contract (or, in more modern terminology, in restitution) in preference to suing for the tort. Historically, the particular variety of quasi-contract with which we are concerned is that which, when the old forms of action were in force, was redressed by a claim upon *indebitatus assumpsit*.[8] This was of much more

---

[1] For extinction of liability by death, now more the exception than the rule, see *ante*, p. 643.

[2] See the standard works on contract.

[3] See *post*, p. 715.

[4] *Verschures Creameries Ltd.* v. *Hull and Netherlands S.S. Co.* [1921] 2 K.B. 608.

[5] *Re United Railways of Havana and Regla Warehouses Ltd.* [1961] A.C. 1007, 1065, *per* Lord Denning M.R.; *United Australia Ltd.* v. *Barclays Bank Ltd.* [1941] A.C. 1, 30, *per* Lord Atkin.

[6] *Valpy* v. *Sanders* (1848) 5 C.B. 886; *Morris* v. *Robinson* (1824) 3 B. & C. 196.

[7] *Burns* v. *Morris* (1834) 4 Tyrw. 485; *Lythgoe* v. *Vernon* (1860) 5 H. & N. 180.

[8] "Thoughts much too deep for tears subdue the court When I *assumpsit* bring, and god-like waive a tort" *The Circuiteers*, 1 L.Q.R. 233.

Prosser, *Torts* (5th ed.), p. 672 comments that while there seems some unwritten rule compelling the citation of this jingle its peculiar merit escapes him.

general application than waiver of tort (for example, it governed recovery of money paid under a total failure of consideration or under a mistake of fact) and involved an allegation (wholly fictitious) that the defendant was indebted to the plaintiff in a certain sum and had promised, at the time of the contract or afterwards, to pay that sum to him. Like other (to us) barely comprehensible fictions in the development of English law it owed its origins to competition for business between different courts, in this case the filching by the King's Bench of the work done in the Common Pleas under the much older writ of "debt."

The details of how this process came to be applied to actions in tort must be sought elsewhere[9] but the reader will ask why should a plaintiff ever wish to waive his action in tort in preference for one in quasi-contract? His preference may seem the more remarkable in view of the fact that he has got to prove in the first instance that the tort has been committed, although the court does not insist on the establishment of mere technical ingredients in the wrong.[10] Many of the procedural and substantive advantages have gradually disappeared with the passage of time, most recently, for example, by the abolition of the rule that a claim for unliquidated damages for tort could not be proved in bankruptcy.[11] At one time there was a very short limitation period of only six months in actions against the estate of a deceased person and this was evaded in *Chesworth* v. *Farrer*[12] by suing in quasi-contract. Though this has now gone, there may still be cases where time begins to run later for the quasi-contract than for the tort claim.[13] Most important now is the point that the quasi-contract claim allows the plaintiff to escape the tort rule that damages are measured by his loss and, to some extent at least, to extract from the defendant the proceeds of his wrong-doing—for example, where a converter disposed of the plaintiff's property for more than its market value. More significantly, the victim of such wrongs as breach of copyright or patent infringement may be able to claim an account of profits, though the remedy here is given by statute. There are, however, cases where the courts seem to have had little difficulty in shaping a "restitutionary" remedy by way of the ordinary action for damages,without the plaintiff having to plead a claim in quasi-contract[14] and it may be that the pattern of future development is to recognise this as an alternative, dis-cretionary basis for the assessment of damages and abandon the concept of waiver of tort.[15] Nevertheless, until this view is expressly adopted by the courts, we must examine the scope of the doctrine of waiver of tort. The question arises, therefore, of whether there are any limits on the torts that can be waived.

[9] Jackson, *History of Quasi-Contract in English Law*, pp. 61–84; Winfield, *Province of the Law of Tort*, pp. 168–176 and *The Law of Quasi-Contracts*, pp. 91–100; Hedley, 100 L.Q.R. 653; *United Australia Ltd.* v. *Barclays Bank Ltd.* [1941] A.C. 1; Lord Wright in (1941) 57 L.Q.R. 184–202 and in his *Legal Essays and Addresses*, pp. 53–54.

[10] *Heilbut* v. *Nevill* (1870) L.R. 5 C.P. 478.

[11] See *post*, p. 732.

[12] [1967] 1 Q.B. 407; *cf. Beaman* v. *A.R.T.S. Ltd.* [1948] 2 All E.R. 89. For the present limitation period, see *ante*, p. 646.

[13] See Goff and Jones, *The Law of Restitution* (3rd ed.), p. 621.

[14] See, *e.g. Strand Electric* v. *Brisford Entertainments* [1952] 2 Q.B. 246.

[15] See Beatson (1978–1979) 17 Univ. of W.Ont.L.R. 1; Birks [1982] C.L.P. 53.

In 1831[16] Tindal C.J. thought that there was no limit except that the defendant must not be prejudiced. But it is inconceivable that it can apply to all torts. The essence of *indebitatus assumpsit* was that the plaintiff claimed that the defendant "had and received" money which belonged to the plaintiff. In the modern law the claim that has succeeded to the *indebitatus* counts may be rationalised as resting on the theory that the defendant has been unjustly enriched at the plaintiff's expense, whether or not we say, as the older cases did, that there has been a "deemed" receipt of money.[17] In this way waiver extends to cases where the defendant has received goods (or even services[18]): conversion has long been recognised as capable of waiver[19] and waiver of trespass to land, where it results in the sale of things extracted from the land[20] is permissible[21] unless the trespass was committed merely as a mode of establishing a right or unless exemplary damages are claimed.[22] So, too, is trespass to goods.[23] Deceit can be waived unless the right to rescind the underlying contract for fraud no longer exists because restitution of the property is impossible. "If you are fraudulently induced to buy a cake, you may return it and get back the price, but you cannot both eat your cake and return your cake."[24] If you have eaten it, you can sue me in tort for deceit but not for the return of the price, and it is obvious that the damages recoverable may well be less than the price paid for the article. Among the earliest cases of waiver of tort are those concerning usurpation of the fees of the plaintiff's office,[25] but they are not likely to be of much relevance today. Obviously, however, there are some torts in respect of which the defendant receives no "enrichment," even by the most generous interpretation—assault and battery, for example.[26] Whether or not defamation can be waived matters little so long as the courts are prepared to reach a similar, restitutionary result by allowing exemplary damages in some cases.[27]

One obstacle to the acceptance of a general theory of recovery where benefits are gained by the defendant from his tortious act is the decision of the majority of the Court of Appeal in *Phillips* v. *Homfray*[28] where an action in quasi-contract failed against the executors of the deceased, who had trespassed on the plaintiff's land by using roads and passages under the land for the removal of minerals. Rejecting the argument that the court could order payment for the use of the roads and passages, Bowen L.J. said, "The

[16] *Young* v. *Marshall* (1831) 8 Bing. 43, 44.
[17] *Lightly* v. *Clouston* (1808) 1 Taunt. 112; *Foster* v. *Stewart* (1814) 3 M. & S. 191 (waiver of enticing away an apprentice); *Powell* v. *Rees* (1837) 7 A. & E. 426 (conversion of goods).
[18] *Rumsey* v. *N.E. Ry.* (1863) 14 C.B.(N.S.) 641, and *supra*, n. 17.
[19] *Marsh* v. *Keating* (1834) 1 Bing.N.C. 198, 215–216. See too, *Thomas* v. *Whip* (1715) Buller N.P. 130.
[20] *cf. Phillips* v. *Homfray*, n. 29, *infra*.
[21] *Powell* v. *Rees* (1837) 7 A. & E. 426.
[22] Jackson, *op. cit.*, p. 75.
[23] *Oughton* v. *Seppings* (1830) 1 B. & Ad. 241; *Rodgers* v. *Maw* (1846) 15 M. & W. 444, *per* Pollock C.B.; *Neate* v. *Harding* (1851) 6 Ex. 349, 351, *per* Parke B.
[24] *Clarke* v. *Dickson* (1858) E.B. & E. 148, 152, *per* Crompton J.
[25] *Howard* v. *Wood* (1678) 2 Show. 21; Goff and Jones, *op. cit.*, p. 605.
[26] *Hambly* v. *Trott* (1771) 1 Cowp. 371, 376.
[27] See *ante*, p. 603. It is suggested in Goff and Jones, *op. cit.*, p. 613 that if the plaintiff is merely incidentally libelled in a book by the defendant there can be no waiver, but that the position is different where the defendant publishes a single broadsheet consisting entirely of defamatory statements about the plaintiff.
[28] (1883) 24 Ch.D. 439; Goff and Jones, *op. cit.*, pp. 608–612.

profit which equity follows into the hands of the executors must be some profit of which the plaintiff has been deprived, and not merely a negative benefit which the testator may have acquired by saving himself the expense of performing his duty." However, this view is not easy to square with a number of other decisions.[29]

ACCORD AND SATISFACTION

Tortious liability can be extinguished by agreement for valuable consideration between the injured party and the tortfeasor.[30] This is styled accord and satisfaction but is really little more than a specialised form of contract and so, to be effective, it must comply with the rules for the formation of contract.[31] "Accord" signifies the agreement, "satisfaction" the consideration which makes it operative. The satisfaction may be either executed, *e.g.* "I release you from your obligation in consideration of £100 now paid by you to me"; or it may be executory, *e.g.* "I release you from your obligation in consideration of your promise to pay me £100 in six months."[32]

Accord and satisfaction may be conditional. A person injured in an accident brought about by the negligence of the defendant may accept an offer of compensation, reserving to himself the right to renew his claim if his injuries turn out to be worse than they were at the time of the accord.[33]

Non-performance of accord and satisfaction

What is the position of the parties if the accord and satisfaction are not carried out? Are they in the same situation as if it had never been made or must the party aggrieved sue upon the broken accord and satisfaction and upon that only? The answer is that it depends upon the construction of the agreement which embodies the accord and satisfaction.[34] If the satisfaction consists of a promise on the part of the tortfeasor, the interpretation of the

---

[29] See Goff and Jones, *op. cit.*, p. 611, citing in particular *Rumsey* v. *N.E. Ry.* (1863) 14 C.B.(N.S.) 641 (quasi-contract available where free carriage of luggage obtained by fraud) and *Strand Electric Co.* v. *Brisford Entertainments* [1952] 2 Q.B. 246, *ante*, p. 713, n. 14.

[30] *Peytoe's Case* (1611) 9 Rep. 77b. It is most important to note that since the claim will be for unliquidated damages an accord and satisfaction will be effective even though a court might have awarded *more* or *less* in the way of damages. It is also possible for the parties, by an agreement falling short of full accord and satisfaction, to limit the issues between them, as in *Tomlin* v. *Standard Telephones and Cables Ltd.* [1969] 1 W.L.R. 1378, an action for damages for personal injuries, where it was agreed that the defendants would pay 50 per cent. of the plaintiff's damages, leaving only the amount of those damages to be determined. See also *S.* v. *Distillers Co. (Biochemicals) Ltd.* [1970] 1 W.L.R. 114.

[31] See *D. & C. Builders Ltd.* v. *Rees* [1966] 2 Q.B. 617.

[32] *British Russian Gazette, etc. Ltd.* v. *Associated Newspapers Ltd.* [1933] 2 K.B. 616, *per* Scrutton L.J.; *ibid.* at p. 650, *per* Greer L.J.

[33] *Lee* v. *L. & Y. Ry.* (1871) L.R. 6 Ch. 527; *Ellen* v. *G.N. Ry.* (1901) 17 T.L.R. 453; *North British Ry.* v. *Wood* (1891) 18 R. 27 (H.L.).

[34] Although the agreement will usually be contained in "without prejudice" correspondence, which means that the correspondence cannot be used in evidence, this correspondence can be produced to the court if the question is whether a binding agreement has actually been reached between the parties (*Tomlin* v. *Standard Telephones and Cables Ltd.* [1969] 1 W.L.R. 1378) and, presumably, also when a question of the interpretation of the agreement has to be decided.

agreement may be, "I accept this promise as an absolute discharge of your tortious liability"; if so, all that the injured party can sue upon in the event of the tortfeasor not carrying out his promise, is the contract which has been substituted for the tortious liability. Alternatively, the interpretation of the agreement may be, "I accept this promise as a discharge of your liability provided you carry it out"; in that case, if the promise is not fulfilled, the injured party has two alternative remedies: he can either fall back upon his original claim in tort, or he can sue upon the contract which was intended to take its place. Somewhat different considerations apply to an accord and satisfaction which is expressed to be conditional in the first instance, as in the example given above of provisional acceptance of compensation in an accident. Here the injured party cannot have recourse to his action in tort unless the condition is not fulfilled. If it is fulfilled within the time specified by the agreement or, if no time is specified, within a reasonable time, then the tortious liability is extinguished. If it is not thus fulfilled, then the injured party can either rely upon his claim in tort or sue upon the conditional agreement which was substituted for it and which has been broken.[35]

Release

Closely akin to accord and satisfaction is release of tortious liability given by the injured party. In fact, there seems to be little difference between the two except that a release is usually, but not necessarily, embodied in an instrument under seal and the necessity for consideration is thus avoided.[36] Release is apparently effective whether it is given before or after an action against the tortfeasor is commenced.[37]

JUDGMENT

Final judgment by a court of competent jurisdiction extinguishes a right of action. It has a twofold effect. First, it estops any party to the litigation from disputing afterwards the correctness of the decision either in law or in fact.[38] Secondly, it operates as a merger of the original cause of action in the rights created by the judgment; and these are either to levy execution against the defendant or to bring a new action upon the judgment (not upon the original claim, for that has perished).

The reason why judgment wipes out the plaintiff's original cause of action is put on either of two grounds. One is public policy: *interest reipublicae ut sit finis litium*; the other is private justice: *nemo debet bis vexari pro uno et*

---

[35] Salmond and Williams, *Contracts,*

[36] *Phillips* v. *Clagett* (1843) 11 M. & W. 84. See *ante*, p. 592, for the position regarding release of joint tortfeasors.

[37] *Apley Estates Co. Ltd.* v. *De Bernales* [1946] 2 All E.R. 338, 340, *per* Evershed J. The Court of Appeal affirmed his decision, but without reference to this point: [1947] Ch. 217.

[38] Provisional damages (*ante*, p. 629) are a practical, if not theoretical, qualification of this.

eodem delicto.[39] However, as we have seen,[40] judgment is no bar to another action unless the cause of action is the same.

LIMITATION

Whether a person's claim is based upon tort or upon any other form of injury, he will lose his remedy if he falls asleep upon it. The reasons for this are twofold. In the first place, no one ought to be exposed to the risk of stale demands of which he may be quite ignorant and which, owing to changed circumstances, he may be unable to satisfy. Secondly, it may have become impossible or difficult, owing to the loss of documents or the death of witnesses, to establish a defence which would have negatived the claim if it had been presented more promptly. These considerations point to a short, definite time limit for the presentation of claims, but they have always been counterbalanced by other considerations of justice to the victim of the tort—suppose, for example, he is suffering from a disability which renders him unable to pursue his claim, or he is unaware of the damage he has suffered (which may or may not be because the wrongdoer has concealed it)? Further, considerations of justice to defendants may be less compelling now than in former times since in the great majority of cases the "real" defendant will be a liability insurance company with large resources and the ability to keep extensive records. In fact, the present trend of law is towards the softening of rigid time limits and the use of greater discretion in allowing the presentation of old, but meritorious claims.

The principal Act today is the Limitation Act 1980,[41] with substantial amendments brought in by the Latent Damage Act 1986. Broadly speaking, actions founded on tort must be brought within six years from the date when the cause of action accrued. In the case of personal injuries and defamation,[42] however, the period is three years. The strictness of these rules is ameliorated in various ways, for example by postponing the running of time where the plaintiff was ignorant that he had a claim and, in personal injury cases, by giving the court a discretionary power to override the time limits altogether. Personal injury limitation will be dealt with separately.

The defendant must plead the Limitation Act if he wishes to rely on it,[43] for the court will not of its own motion take notice that the action is out of

---

[39] Bower, *Res Judicata* (1924), pp. 1–2.

[40] *Ante*, pp. 598–600. The facts of a case may be such as to enable the defendant successfully to plead *res judicata*, or to have the action dismissed as frivolous and vexatious: *Wright* v. *Bennett* [1948] 1 All E.R. 227. For previous judgments in the context of third party proceedings see *ante*, p. 597.

[41] The earliest comprehensive legislation was the Statute of Limitations 1623, discussed at length in the first edition of this book. The 1980 Act consolidated the Limitation Act 1939 with subsequent amending Acts, most notably the Limitation Act 1975 and the Limitation Amendment Act 1980. For the 1980 reforms, see the Law Reform Committee's 21st Report Cmnd. 6923 (1977). The notes to the 1980 Act in *Current Law Statutes Annotated* form a very detailed commentary on limitation. For the 1986 reforms see the Law Reform Committee's 24th Report Cmnd. 9390 (1984).

[42] The three year period for defamation was introduced with effect from December 30, 1985 by s.57(2) of the Administration of Justice Act 1985, adding a new s.4A to the 1980 Act. When the period has expired without the plaintiff's knowledge he may proceed within one year of discovery with leave of the court.

[43] R.S.C. Ord. 18, r. 8.

time,[44] but if it is pleaded, the plaintiff has the burden of showing that his claim accrued within the period.[45] A plaintiff who begins an action within the time allowed may find that the proceedings are dismissed for want of prosecution if conducted in a dilatory manner and the delay causes prejudice to the defendant or prevents a fair trial. However, if the limitation period is still unexpired when the defendant applies for dismissal the court should refuse the application except in very unusual circumstances since it would have no power to prevent the plaintiff starting a fresh action.[46]

Commencement of the period

According to the Act of 1980 the period of limitation runs "from the date on which the cause of action accrued." No further explanation of "accrued" is given, but authorities from earlier legislation are still in point. They show that the period begins to run "from the earliest time at which an action could be brought."[47] " 'Cause of action' means that which makes action possible."[48] A cause of action arises, therefore, at the moment when a state of facts occurs which gives a potential plaintiff a right to succeed against a potential defendant. There must be a plaintiff who can succeed, and a defendant against whom he can succeed,[49] subject to the qualification that a merely procedural bar to bringing a suit will not prevent time running.[50] Thus, for example, when goods belonging to a person who has died intestate have been converted after his death, the proper party to sue is the administrator and time does not begin to run until he has taken out letters of administration.[51] So, too, where the tortfeasor is entitled to diplomatic immunity, time does not run in his favour until the termination of his period of office, for until then no action will lie against him.[52] If, however, time has once begun to run, it will continue to do so even over a period during which there is no one capable of suing or of being sued.[53] The fact that the potential

---

[44] *Dunsmore* v. *Milton* [1938] 3 All E.R. 762. If the defendant decides to contest the case on its merits, it is not open to him to amend to plead limitation at a later stage when it becomes apparent that he is likely to lose on the merits: *Ketteman* v. *Hansel Properties Ltd.* [1987] A.C. 189.

[45] *London Congregational Union* v. *Harriss and Harriss* [1988] 1 All E.R. 15.

[46] *Birkett* v. *James* [1978] A.C. 297. Hence the plaintiff cannot be penalized for delay in starting proceedings within the limitation period: *Dept. of Transport* v. *Chris Smaller (Transport) Ltd.* [1989] 1 All E.R. 897.

[47] *Reeves* v. *Butcher* [1891] 2 Q.B. 509, 511, *per* Lindley L.J. The day on which the cause of action arose is excluded: *Marren* v. *Dawson, Bentley & Co. Ltd.* [1961] 2 Q.B. 135. If the last day of the period is one when court offices are closed the plaintiff has until the first following day when they are open: *Kaur* v. *S. Russell & Sons* [1973] 1 Q.B. 336.

[48] Preston and Newsom, *Limitation of Actions* (3rd ed.), p. 4, citing Lord Dunedin in *Board of Trade* v. *Cayzer, Irvine & Co. Ltd.* [1927] A.C. 610, 617. Or in terms of pleading, "Every fact which it would be necessary for the plaintiff to prove, if traversed, in order to support his right to the judgment of the court": *Read* v. *Brown* (1888) 22 Q.B.D. 128, 131, *per* Lord Esher M.R.

[49] Preston and Newsom, *op. cit.,* p. 4, referring to dicta of Vaughan Williams L.J. in *Thomson* v. *Clanmorris* [1900] 1 Ch. 718, 728–729.

[50] *Sevcon Ltd.* v. *Lucas CAV Ltd.* [1986] 1 W.L.R. 462 (sealing of patent necessary before action could be brought).

[51] *Pratt* v. *Swaine* (1828) B. & C. 285. The principle was laid down in *Murray* v. *East India Co.* (1821) 5 B. & Ald. 204, which, however, was not an action in tort.

[52] *Musurus Bey* v. *Gadban* [1894] 2 Q.B. 352.

[53] *Rhodes* v. *Smethurst* (1838) 4 M. & W. 42; (1840) 6 M. & W 351.

plaintiff is unable to identify the defendant does not, in principle, prevent a cause of action accruing,[54] though this is now qualified in many cases.[55]

Latent damage

When the tort is actionable *per se,* as in trespass and libel,[56] time begins to run, in general, at the moment the wrongful act was committed, whether the injured party knows of it or not, provided there is no fraudulent concealment.[57] This applies though the resulting damage does not occur or is not discovered until a later date, for such damage is not a new cause of action, but is merely an incident of the other.[58] On the other hand, where the tort is actionable only upon proof of actual damage, as in nuisance, deceit and negligence, time runs from the damage.[59] If, therefore, you were injured by drinking my negligently manufactured ginger beer more than three years after it was made you could bring an action against me without asking the court to exercise its special dispensing powers for personal injury cases, because no cause of action would have accrued to you until you drank.[60] This rule of negligence contrasts with that applicable to actions for breach of contract, where time runs from the date of the breach, so that a plaintiff whose contractual claim is time-barred may yet save himself by asserting a concurrent right of action for tortious negligence.[61] Much difficulty has been encountered in negligence cases over "latent damage." For example, exposure to dust may damage the plaintiff's lungs in an irreversible way but the condition may not become severe enough to bring itself to his attention for some years. On such facts it was held in *Cartledge* v. *Jopling & Sons Ltd.*[62] that the cause of action accrued when the injury was suffered, not when it was discovered, so that a man's right of action might be barred before he knew he had it. The hardship of this rule in cases of personal injury led fairly promptly to its alteration by statute[63] though the first attempt was unsatisfactory and Parliament had to try again in 1975.[64] This is dealt with later. However, the same problem came to a head in the 1970s in cases concerning defective premises and this is the origin of the current law produced by the amendments to the 1980 Act by the Latent Damage Act 1986. Section 14A

---

[54] *R.B. Policies at Lloyd's* v. *Butler* [1950] 1 K.B. 76.

[55] See *post*, p. 725.

[56] *Duke of Brunswick* v. *Harmer* (1849) 14 Q.B. 185.

[57] *Granger* v. *George* (1826) 5 B. & C. 149.

[58] *Howell* v. *Young* (1826) 5 B. & C. 259.

[59] *Backhouse* v. *Bonomi* (1861) 9 H.L.C. 503.

[60] *cf.* Scots Law under the Law Reform (Limitation of Actions etc.) Act 1954 s.6(1)(*a*), boldly interpreted in *Watson* v. *Winget* 1960 S.L.T. 321. If the Consumer Protection Act 1987 were relied upon, the position would be different: *post*, p. 729.

[61] See *Midland Bank Trust Co. Ltd.* v. *Hett, Stubbs & Kemp* [1979] Ch. 385, though the contract claim was in fact held not to be time-barred. Compare *Forster* v. *Outred & Co.* [1982] 1 W.L.R. 86 (where the plaintiff, in a claim for professional negligence, was held to have suffered damage when she executed a mortgage as surety for her son's debts, even though she was not required to pay those debts until two and a half years later).

[62] [1963] A.C. 758.

[63] Limitation Act 1963.

[64] Limitation Act 1975. See now the Limitation Act 1980, ss.11, 14.

of the 1980 Act[65] applies to any action for damages for negligence[66] (other than one which includes a claim for damages for personal injuries) and provides for two alternative limits. The first, as before, is six years from the date on which the cause of action accrued.[67] This is illustrated by the decision of the House of Lords in *Pirelli General Cable Works Ltd.* v. *Oscar Faber & Partners*[68] where cracks appeared in a negligently designed chimney soon after its construction, but were not discovered for another seven years. The plaintiffs' action in tort[69] was held to be statute-barred.[70] A latent *defect* in the building did not give rise to a tort claim, which required *damage* and this did not occur until cracks came into existence as a result of the defect,[71] even though the cracks or the defect might be undiscovered and undiscoverable.[72] It was suggested that time might begin to run even before damage had occurred where the defect was so gross that the building was "doomed from the start," in which case the cause of action would accrue as soon as it was built, but such cases were said to be likely to be exceptional, and it is not clear that the conditions for the application of this principle have been fulfilled in any subsequent case.[73] It is not enough that the damage should have been an inevitable consequence of the defect,[74] though it has been suggested[75] that it may cover extreme cases where the defects are so severe that they are likely to be disclosed almost immediately, as where a house is built without any drainage pipes at ground level. The *Pirelli* view that there was no cause of action until cracking occurred is consistent with the proposition that until then the plaintiff's loss in having a defective building was purely economic loss and hence not actionable in tort,[76] but if the claim is against a local authority for breach of its statutory functions in connection with the inspection of dwellings time does not run until later still, when the condition of the building gives rise to danger to the health or safety of its occupants, for it is to those matters that the statute is directed.[77]

The alternative period is three years from the earliest date (the "starting

---

[65] Inserted by s.1 of the Latent Damage Act 1986.
[66] But not other torts. There is no definition of negligence, and the two obvious issues are whether it covers breach of statutory duty (*cf. ante*, p. 170) and breach of a duty to take care under a contract. It probably does not, but as far as the latter is concerned, the plaintiff may in many cases be able to frame his claim in tort in the alternative: *ante*, p. 4.
[67] s.14A(4)(*a*).
[68] [1983] 2 A.C. 1; Stanton (1983) 99 L.Q.R. 175.
[69] The plaintiffs conceded that their contract claim was time-barred.
[70] Rejecting the "date of discoverability" rule put forward by the C.A. in *Sparham-Souter* v. *Town and Country Developments Ltd.* [1976] 1 Q.B. 858.
[71] The defendants were consulting engineers who approved the design of the chimney, not builders. They accordingly argued that their liability was analogous to the liability in tort of a solicitor who gives negligent advice on law, in which case time does not begin to run until the client acts on the advice (see *Forster* v. *Outred & Co.*, *supra*, n. 61). Though it was not necessary to decide the question, Lord Fraser in *Pirelli* thought the analogy ill-founded.
[72] [1983] 2 A.C. 1, 16, *per* Lord Fraser.
[73] It has been suggested that the "doomed from the start" principle was applied in *Tozer Kemsley* v. *Jarvis* (1983) 1 Const.L.J. 79 and *Chelmsford D.C.* v. *T. J. Evers* (1983) 1 Const.L.J. 65, but *cf.* Ralph Gibson L.J. in *London Congregational Union* v. *Harriss and Harriss* [1988] 1 All E.R. 15, 28. See also *Dove* v. *Banhams Patent Locks Ltd.* [1983] 1 W.L.R. 1436.
[74] *Ketteman* v. *Hansel Properties Ltd.* [1987] A.C. 189.
[75] By Neill L.J. in *Jones* v. *Stroud D.C.* [1986] 1 W.L.R. 1141.
[76] For the current view on the nature of the damage in these cases, see *ante*, p. 230.
[77] *Jones* v. *Stroud D.C.* [1986] 1 W.L.R. 1141.

date") on which the plaintiff had not only the right to sue but also knew or reasonably could have known about the damage and its attributability to the defendant's negligence.[78] This is only relevant if it expires later than the first period of six years from the cause of action. Hence suppose D completes a house in June 1988 and cracking occurs because of defective foundations in June 1990, which came to P's notice in 1991. P's claim becomes statute barred in June 1996[79] and it is irrelevant that more than three years have passed since P's discovery of the damage. However, if the cracks came to P's notice in May 1996 he would have until the equivalent time in May 1999 to bring his claim. Indeed, the alternative three year period from discovery applies even if the primary, six year period has already expired, so that if P discovered the cracks in 2000 he could still sue. However, superimposed upon *both* periods is the so-called "long-stop" provision of section 14B which bars any claim for negligence (other than in respect of personal injuries) 15 years from the date of the last act of negligence to which the damage is attributable. To continue with the same example, therefore, and assuming the negligence to have occurred immediately before the completion of the house, all potential claims would be extinguished in June 2003, even, be it noted, if no cause of action had yet arisen because of the absence of any damage.

Though we have spoken about defective buildings, the provisions apply to any type of damage other than personal injuries, for example, that arising from negligent legal advice[80] or surveying.[81]

An awkward problem about buildings is that they may be disposed of during the limitation period. In the *Pirelli* case the House of Lords introduced the novel concept of "class limitation," whereby the duty of care was owed to the owners of the property as a class and if time began to run against one owner it also ran against all his successors in title. The House was not, however, directly concerned with the question of whether successors in title who had no interest in the property when the damage occurred had a cause of action at all and in *Perry* v. *Tendring D.C.*[82] it was held that they did not. Now the matter is governed by the complicated provisions of section 3 of the Latent Damage Act 1986. Briefly, where a cause of action has accrued to the first owner and the second owner acquires the property a fresh cause of action accrues to the second owner on the date he acquires his interest in the property, provided the first owner had not before then known or had reason to know about the damage. Although the second owner only acquires his cause of action when he acquires the property, there is no risk of extension of

---

[78] This is a considerable over-simplification of complex provisions: see s.14A(5)–(10) of the Limitation Act 1980. They are modelled on those of s.11 dealing with personal injury: *post*, p. 725.

[79] *cf.* the claim under the Defective Premises Act 1972 (*ante*, p. 234) which expires six years from completion of the house.

[80] *Forster* v. *Outred & Co.* [1892] 1 W.L.R. 86; *Baker* v. *Ollard* (1982) 126 S.J. 593; *D.W. Moore & Co. Ltd.* v. *Ferrier* [1988] 1 W.L.R. 267.

[81] *Secretary of State for the Environment* v. *Essex Goodman & Suggitt* [1986] 1 W.L.R. 1432.

[82] (1984) 30 B.L.R. 118; Robertson (1983) 99 L.Q.R. 599; Jones (1984) 100 L.Q.R. 413.

the limitation period because for the purpose of section 14A of the 1980 Act it is deemed to accrue at the same time as that of the first owner.[83]

Fraud and concealment

Related to the problem of latent damage are special provisions in the Limitation Act 1980[84] dealing with fraud and concealment. First, where the plaintiff's action is based on the fraud of the defendant or his agent[85] or of any person through whom he (or his agent) claims time does not run until the plaintiff has discovered the fraud or could with reasonable diligence have discovered it.[86] This part of the section is limited to cases where the action is actually founded on fraud (*e.g.* where it is a claim for damages for deceit or to rescind a contract) and does not extend to causes of action in which "dishonest" or "fraudulent" conduct *may* figure (*e.g.* conversion),[87] but by section 32(1)(*b*) the same suspension of the running of time applies[88] where "any fact relevant to the plaintiff's right of action has been deliberately concealed from him by the defendant" and this includes a case of "deliberate commission of a breach of duty in circumstances in which it is unlikely to be discovered for some time."[89] The essence of this provision is that the defendant is penalised not simply for his breach of duty but because the breach of duty (or his effort to conceal it) was deliberate and his conduct was therefore unconscionable. Thus in *Kitchen* v. *R.A.F. Association*,[90] solicitors' negligent failure to inform the plaintiff of her possible claim against X did not bring the equivalent provision into operation but their failure to inform her about an offer by X to pay £100 (concealed because they did not wish her to discover their original breach of duty) did.[91] This paragraph of section 32(1) may apply to a cause of action for negligence which has been deliberately concealed, but it is provided that the provisions of section 14A (time running from discovery) and 14B (the 15 year long-stop) have no application to such

---

[83] That is to say, both the primary, six year period and the 15 year long-stop period will run from the time when the damage occurred when the property was in the first owner's hands. There can be no question of the running of part of the alternative three year period while the property is in the first owner's hands since it is a pre-condition of the application of s.3 that he should not have had actual or constructive knowledge of the damage.

[84] s.32, replacing Limitations Act 1939, s.26. The previous case law is of particular interest here because s.32 was intended by the Law Reform Committee to restate the 1939 Act provision as it had been interpreted in the courts: Cmnd. 6923, para. 2.22. However, the section differs somewhat from the Committee's original draft.

[85] Which includes an independent contractor: *Applegate* v. *Moss* [1971] 1 Q.B. 406.

[86] s.32(1)(*a*). On reasonable diligence, see *Peco Arts. Inc.* v. *Hazlitt Gallery Ltd.* [1983] 1 W.L.R. 1315 (a s.32(1)(*c*) case).

[87] *Beaman* v. *A.R.T.S. Ltd.* [1949] 1 K.B. 550, 558, *per* Lord Greene M.R.; at p. 567 *per* Somervell L.J.

[88] See also s.32(1)(*c*) which applies to actions "for relief from the consequences of a mistake."

[89] s.32(2). Does this cover the "turning of a blind eye?" *Beaman* v. *A.R.T.S. Ltd., supra.*

[90] [1958] 1 W.L.R. 563; *Bartlett* v. *Barclays Bank Trustee Co. Ltd.* [1980] Ch. 515. Megarry V.-C. in *Tito* v. *Waddell (No. 2)* [1977] Ch. 106, 245, said that if time has already begun to run, a supervening fraudulent concealment will not interrupt it, but this would in practice confine the section to deliberate breaches of duty. *cf.* s.32(2) of the 1980 Act which seems to be by way of example rather than definition. Perhaps there is a conflict between s.32(1)(*b*) and the words immediately following para. (*c*).

[91] In a building case, time would not run in favour of a developer who builds a house with ordinary foundations when he knows special precautions to be necessary (*King* v. *Victor Parsons & Co. Ltd.* [1973] 1 W.L.R. 658) but it would run in favour of a local authority whose building inspector carelessly failed to notice the defect in the work.

a case.[92] The first is unnecessary, since section 32 already postpones the running of time; there is no reason for the second since the defendant is guilty of wilful wrongdoing.

The principle of section 32 will prevent the running of time in many cases where there is a wrongful dealing[93] with goods by a person who has custody of, or a limited interest in, them and hence the opportunity to conceal that dealing. However, it would be hard if the running of time were also suspended against innocent purchasers. Therefore, notwithstanding that fraud or concealment will generally affect persons who claim through the actual wrongdoer, section 32(3)(b) provides that nothing in the section shall enable an action to be brought to recover property or its value[94] against the purchaser of the property or any person claiming through him, in any case where the property has been purchased for valuable consideration by an innocent third party since the fraud or concealment.[95]

Extinction of title; theft

Before 1939 it was only in cases affecting title to land that expiry of the limitation period affected title. In all other cases it merely barred the plaintiff from pursuing his remedy before the courts, so that a person wrongfully deprived of his goods whose action was time barred might recover them by extra-judicial means and have a right of action in respect of subsequent wrongful dealings with them. The Act of 1939 changed this with regard to conversion and there are further modifications in the 1980 Act.

First, it is enacted by section 3(1) that once a cause of action for conversion has occurred in respect of a chattel, no action may be brought for any subsequent conversion after the expiry of six years from the accrual of the original cause of action unless, of course, the owner has recovered possession of it in the meanwhile. Secondly, section 3(2) provides that once the period of limitation in respect of the original cause of action has expired, then the owner's title is extinguished. So, if you convert my goods wrongfully and later sell them to someone else, once six years have elapsed from the taking, not only have I lost the right to sue either you or the person who bought the goods from you, but he is in a position to deal with them as absolute owner notwithstanding that at the time of the sale to him you had no title which you could pass on to him. However, the Law Reform Committee was troubled at the prospect of time running in favour of a thief or receiver and we now have the further and rather complicated provisions of section 4 of the 1980 Act. The effect of the section is that time does not run

---

[92] s.32(5), added by s.2(2) of the Latent Damage Act 1986.

[93] It is assumed in this discussion that the wrongful dealing does not amount to theft. If it does, time does not run because of the provisions of s.4: see below. S.32 is not applicable in the normal case of theft where the thief is unknown or untraceable: *R.B. Policies at Lloyd's* v. *Butler* [1950] 1 K.B. 76.

[94] This is an extension of the previous proviso: see the remarks of Lord Denning M.R. in *Eddis* v. *Chichester Constable* [1969] 2 Ch. 345, 358.

[95] It seems, therefore, that where a custodian knowingly commits conversion by sale to innocent P and conceals this from the owner, P does not get the benefit of the proviso since his purchase is contemporaneous with the fraud or concealment.

against the owner in respect of the theft[96] of his chattel or any conversion "related to theft," which latter phrase means any subsequent conversion other than a purchase in good faith.[97] Thus if property is stolen and then sold by the thief to X (who is aware of its origin) and then given by X to Y, the owner's rights of action against the thief and X and Y continue indefinitely and his title will never be extinguished. However, the occurrence of a good faith purchase starts time running against the owner in favour of the good faith purchaser (and any converter from him). After six years the owner will no longer be able to sue the good faith purchaser or anyone who subsequently dealt with the goods[98] and his title to the goods will be extinguished. However, he retains his right to sue the original thief and other converters who preceded the good faith purchaser.[99]

Disabilities

One of the longest-standing derogations from standard limitation periods occurs where the plaintiff is under disability. If, on the date when the right of action accrued, the person to whom it accrued was under a disability, time does not begin to run until he ceases to be under a disability or dies (whichever first occurs).[1] For these purposes, the law now recognises only two forms of disability, infancy and unsoundness of mind.[2] Infancy presents no difficulty, for it means simply a person under the age of 18. A person is of unsound mind "if he is a person who, by reason of mental disorder within the meaning of the Mental Health Act 1983, is incapable of managing and administering his property and affairs,"[3] which is substantially the same as the meaning given to the phrase by the courts under the previous legislation.[4]

What is the position of a plaintiff who was of sound mind when time began to run but later becomes of unsound mind; or of a plaintiff who was an infant when his cause of action accrued and became of unsound mind before he reached the age of 18; or of a plaintiff who is under a disability at the moment when he succeeds to the title of a predecessor who was under no disability? The Act provides that unless the right of action first accrues to a person who

---

[96] Which includes obtaining by deception and blackmail: s.4(5)(*b*).

[97] Any conversion following the theft is presumed to be related to the theft unless the contrary is shown: s.4(4). A purchase in good faith may itself give the purchaser a good title, but will by no means necessarily do so: *ante.*, p. 485.

[98] If this person is a thief, all the provisions of the section will apply over again *vis-à-vis* the good faith purchaser, who is now the owner.

[99] s.4(1): "... but if his title ... is extinguished under section 3(2) ... he may not bring an action in respect of a theft preceding the loss of his title, unless the theft in question preceded the conversion from which time began to run for the purposes of section 3(2)."

[1] s.28(1).

[2] s.38(2).

[3] s.38(3). A person is conclusively presumed to be of unsound mind in the two situations described in s.38(4). Contrast *Harnett* v. *Fisher* [1927] A.C. 573, where it was held that a person who was wrongly detained as a lunatic under the Lunacy Act 1890 was not under a disability on the ground of lunacy.

[4] See *Kirby* v. *Leather* [1965] 2 Q.B. 367. The Law Reform Committee rejected the extension of disability to cover long-term physical illness, which may be as much of an obstacle to the plaintiff's asserting his rights as some forms of mental disorder.

is then disabled the disability has no effect.[5] Where, however, there are successive disabilities in the same person (unsoundness of mind supervening on infancy) time does not run until the latter of the disabilities has ended, provided that there is no interval of ability between the disabilities.[6]

Special periods of limitation

(1) *Personal injuries and death*

The law is now to be found in sections 11 to 14 and 33 of the Limitation Act 1980, re-enacting the Limitation Act 1975.[7] The provisions apply to "any action for damages for negligence, nuisance or breach of duty (whether the duty exists by virtue of a contract or of provision made by or under a statute or independently of any contract or any such provision) where the damages claimed by the plaintiff for the negligence, nuisance or breach of duty consist of or include[8] damages in respect of personal injuries to the plaintiff or any other person." These words are wide enough to include actions for trespass to the person, intentional or unintentional[9] and actions by deceased persons' estates under the Law Reform (Miscellaneous Provisions) Act 1934 but not cases where the plaintiff's complaint is that the defendant has deprived him of his cause of action against the tortfeasor who actually caused the injury, as by failing to pursue the claim with diligence.[10] The expression "personal injuries" includes any disease and any impairment of a person's physical or mental condition.[11]

Where section 11 applies the limitation period is three years from the date on which the cause of action accrued, or the date (if later) of the plaintiff's "knowledge."[12] A person has knowledge under section 11 when he knows[13] all the following facts:

  (*a*) that the injury in question was significant;
  (*b*) that the injury was attributable in whole or in part to the act or

---

[5] s.28(1), (2). If the plaintiff is immediately rendered of unsound mind by the tort itself he is disabled when the cause of action accrues, for the law takes no account of parts of a day: *Kirby* v. *Leather, supra. Aliter* if the unsoundness of mind, though caused by the tort, comes on some days later. However, that might be a pointer towards the court's exercising its discretion under s.33 of the Act: *post*, p. 727.
Nor, if the right of action accrues to disabled P:1 who then dies and it passes to disabled P:2 is any further extension of time allowed in respect of P:2's disability: s.28(3).
[6] This is the effect of s.28(1), which refers to the plaintiff's ceasing to be under *a* disability. See also *Borrows* v. *Ellison* (1871) L.R. 6 Ex. 128.
[7] The 1975 Act was based upon the 20th Report of the Law Reform Committee, Cmnd. 5630 (1974).
[8] If, therefore, the plaintiff claims damages for personal injuries *and* damage to property in the same action both claims are governed by s.11. But if the plaintiff was barred under s.11 he could bring a separate action within the longer period allowed for damage to property: *Brunsden* v. *Humphrey*, *ante*, p. 599.
[9] *Letang* v. *Cooper* [1965] 1 Q.B. 232; *Long* v. *Hepworth* [1968] 1 W.L.R. 1299; *ante*, p. 71. Before the Administration of Justice Act 1982 they also included claims for loss of services.
[10] *McGahie* v. *U.S.D.A.W.* 1966 S.L.T. 74: *Ackbar* v. *C.F. Green & Co. Ltd.* [1975] Q.B. 582. An action brought on the principle of *Monk* v. *Warbey* (see *ante*, p. 177) would not, therefore, be an action for personal injuries.
[11] s.38(1).
[12] s.11(4).
[13] But there are objective elements in this: see below.

omission which is alleged to constitute negligence, nuisance or breach of duty[14];

(c) the identity of the defendant[15]; and

(d) if it is alleged that the act or omission was that of a person other than the defendant,[16] the identity of that person and the additional facts supporting the bringing of an action against the defendant.[17]

However, the plaintiff's knowledge that any acts or omissions did or did not, as a matter of law, involve negligence, nuisance or breach of duty is irrelevant.[18] An injury is "significant"[19] if the plaintiff would reasonably have considered it sufficiently serious to justify his instituting proceedings for damages against a defendant who did not dispute liability and was able to satisfy a judgment.[20] "Knowledge"[21] is basically objective, in that it includes knowledge which the plaintiff might reasonably have been expected to acquire from facts observable or ascertainable by him or from facts ascertainable by him with the help of medical or other appropriate expert advice which it is reasonable for him to seek. However, he is not fixed with knowledge of a fact ascertainable only with the help of expert advice so long as he has taken all reasonable steps to obtain (and, where appropriate) to act on this advice.[22] Thus, where the plaintiff suffered injury by a piece of metal flying off a hammer in 1957, the failure of the expert who later conducted a hardness test to notice the defect which was in fact the cause of the accident prevented time running against the plaintiff with the result that the plaintiff's personal representative was able to bring a successful action in 1975.[23]

If the claim is under the Fatal Accidents Act 1976 in respect of a death caused by the defendant's tort the time limit is found in section 12 of the 1980 Act. First, no action can be brought under the Fatal Accidents Act unless the deceased himself could have maintained an action at the date of his death.[24]

---

[14] This means that the plaintiff knows in broad terms what the injury is capable of being attributed to the defendant's misconduct; he does not need to know all the details: *Wilkinson* v. *Ancliff (B.L.T.) Ltd.* [1986] 1 W.L.R. 1352.

[15] *Simpson* v. *Norwest Holst Southern Ltd.* [1980] 1 W.L.R. 968.

[16] *e.g.* where the defendant is an employer who is vicariously liable. Even though a claim might succeed on the basis of breach of the employer's "personal duty" (see *ante*, pp. 188–197) it may therefore be in the plaintiff's interest to allege a breach of duty by an individual employee.

[17] s.14(1).

[18] *Ibid.* Thus the advice of the plaintiff's legal advisers that he has no cause of action does not stop time running against him, (*Farmer* v. *N.C.B.*, *The Times*, May 27, 1985), though he might have a cause of action for professional negligence against them.

[19] It has been held that if the plaintiff knows that one injury is significant, time runs even in respect of another, of the significance of which he is unaware: *Bristow* v. *Grout*, *The Times*, November 3, 1986.

[20] s.14(2). It follows that even a quite minor injury may justify the institution of proceedings. In determining reasonableness under s.14(2) the test is to some extent subjective: would *that* plaintiff, with *that* plaintiff's intelligence, have been reasonable in considering that injury was sufficiently serious: *McCafferty* v. *Metropolitan Police Receiver* [1977] 1 W.L.R. 1073, 1081, *per* Geoffrey Lane L.J. The case decides that the plaintiff's desire not to disrupt his relationship with the defendant by instituting proceedings is not a factor which can be taken into account when the court is asked to exercise its discretion under s.33. Nor is the plaintiff's wholly admirable wish not to appear to "sponge" a relevant factor under s.14: *Buck* v. *English Electric Co. Ltd.* [1977] 1 W.L.R. 806.

[21] Knowledge ia not the same as belief: *Davis* v. *M.o.D.*, *Times*, August 7, 1985. But *cf. Wilkinson* v. *Ancliff (B.L.T.), Supra.*

[22] s.14(3).

[23] *Marston* v. *B.R.B.* [1976] I.C.R. 124.

[24] s.12(1).

Subject, therefore, to the court's power to override the time limit,[25] any potential right of action under the Fatal Accidents Act will disappear three years after the accident or the date of the deceased's knowledge if later.[26] If the deceased has a cause of action at the date of his death, then the dependant may bring an action, again subject to the court's power to override the time limit,[27] within three years of the date of the death or the date of the dependant's knowledge, whichever is the later.[28] In most cases of course, there is more than one dependant and in that event the provision regarding the date of knowledge is to be applied to each of them separately and anyone debarred by this is to be excluded from the action.[29]

A much more fundamental development in the law of limitation is the court's power to override the statutory time limits if it appears to the court to be equitable to do so having regard to the degree to which the primary limitation rules prejudice the plaintiff and any exercise of the power would prejudice the defendant.[30] The court is directed to have regard to all the circumstances of the case and in particular to—

(a) the length of, and reasons[31] for, the delay[32] on the part of the plaintiff;

(b) the effect of the delay upon the evidence in the case;

(c) the conduct of the defendant after the cause of action arose, including his response to the plaintiff's reasonable request for information;

(d) the duration of any disability of the plaintiff arising after the accrual of the cause of action[33];

(e) the extent to which the plaintiff acted promptly and reasonably once he knew[34] he might have an action for damages;

(f) the steps, if any, taken by the plaintiff to obtain medical, legal or other expert advice and the nature of any such advice as he may have received.[35]

A good deal of controversy quickly grew up around the question of the extent of the court's discretion. There is evidence that the Law Reform

---

[25] *Infra.* The court can override the time limit if the deceased's own claim is barred by s.11 but not if it was barred by any other statute, *e.g.* Art. 29 in Sched. 1 to the Carriage by Air Act 1961 (two years from the date of arrival at destination).

[26] s.11. By s.12(1) "where any such action by the injured person would have been barred by the time limit in section 11 . . . no account shall be taken of the possibility of that time limit being overriden under section 33." Claimants under the Fatal Accidents Act *must* therefore ask the court to override the time limit under s.33 if three years have elapsed since the injury or the deceased's knowledge.

[27] s.33(1).

[28] s.12(2). The question whether the injury was "significant" naturally has no application for the purposes of the dependant's knowledge.

[29] s.13. This is less significant than it might seem, because the dependants will normally include children, against whom time would not run until majority.

[30] s.33(1). The actual term used in the Act is "disapply." "Parliament has now decided that uncertain justice is preferable to certain injustice": *Firman* v. *Ellis* [1978] Q.B. 886, 911, *per* Ormrod L.J. For the relationship between s.33 of this Act and the power in s.33 of the Supreme Court Act 1981 to order pre-action discovery, see *Harris* v. *Newcastle-upon-Tyne H.A.* [1989] 1 W.L.R. 97.

[31] Which may include not only the express reasons given by the plaintiff, but also the subconscious factors which may have prevented him from litigating: *McCafferty* v. *Metropolitan Police Receiver* [1977] 1 W.L.R. 1073.

[32] Which means the delay after the primary limitation period has expired: *Thompson* v. *Brown* [1981] 1 W.L.R 744, 751; *Eastman* v. *London County Bus Services Ltd., The Times,* November 23, 1985.

[33] *cf. Kirby* v. *Leather, ante,* p. 724.

[34] Which means actual knowledge, not the deemed knowledge which may arise under s.14, *supra*: *Eastman* v. *London Country Bus Services, supra.*

[35] s.33(3). Legal advice is privileged, but the plaintiff may be interrogated as to whether the advice was favourable or unfavourable: *Jones* v. *G.D. Searle & Co.* [1979] 1 W.L.R. 101.

Committee intended section 33 to apply only to "exceptional" or "residual" or "difficult" cases[36] but the Court of Appeal in *Firman* v. *Ellis*[37] soon held that the words were too plain to admit of any such restrictive interpretation even if it were possible to categorise such cases, and this broader approach was upheld by the House of Lords in *Thompson* v. *Brown*.[38] However, to this there is a clear exception where the plaintiff commences an action within the normal period but he fails to serve the writ within the prescribed time or the action is dismissed for want of prosecution. The court then has no discretion[39] to allow the plaintiff to proceed in a new action because he is not prejudiced at all by the primary limitation provisions of the Act but by his dilatoriness or that of his advisors.[40] The consequence, of course, may be that a defendant is better off if a writ has been issued (but not served) within the primary limitation period than if one has not been issued at all.[41] Indeed, there may be no prejudice at all to the defendant, for there may be no dispute as to liability and he may be fully aware that a writ has been issued.[42]

It is not unlikely that the plaintiff's failure to commence proceedings or serve the writ in time will be attributable to negligence[43] on the part of his advisors. The fact that a claim for professional negligence is available does not prevent the court's application of section 33 but it is a "highly relevant"[44] consideration in the exercise of the discretion because the strength of the claim against the advisor will directly affect the degree of prejudice the plaintiff will suffer by the application of the primary period of limitation. However, even where this claim is "cast iron," one must bear in mind the difficulty, delay and expense which may be caused to the plaintiff by having to change horses in midstream.[45]

Now that *Thompson* v. *Brown* has settled the nature of the court's discretion it is probably correct to say that section 33 is operating more

---

[36] Cmnd. 5630, paras. 38, 56 and 57. What Griffiths J. (a member of the Committee) described in *Finch* v. *Francis* (July 2, 1977, unreported) as "the occasional hard case."

[37] [1978] Q.B. 886.

[38] [1981] 1 W.L.R. 744; Davies (1981) 44 M.L.R. 710.

[39] But misrepresentation by the defendant may estop him from relying on the primary limitation period: *Deerness* v. *John R. Keeble & Son (Brantham) Ltd.* [1983] 2 Lloyd's Rep. 260.

[40] *Walkley* v. *Precision Forgings Ltd.* [1979] 1 W.L.R. 606; *Thompson* v. *Brown, supra*. In *Firman* v. *Ellis* an action had been started within the primary limitation period, so the actual decision has been overruled. *cf. Wilson* v. *Banner Scaffolding Ltd., The Times,* June 22, 1982 (writ issued within primary period a nullity for non-compliance with s.231 Companies Act 1948; discretion applicable).

[41] *Thompson* v. *Brown* [1981] 1 W.L.R. 752. For the effect of the court's power to renew an unserved writ, see Morgan "Limitation and Discretion" (1982) 1 C.J.Q. 109.

[42] See the remarks of Donaldson M.R. in *Deerness* v. *John R. Keeble & Son (Brantham) Ltd.* (1982) 126 S.J. 729 (affirmed [1983] 2 Lloyd's Rep. 260) (where the defendants had in fact made a substantial interim payment without prejudice days before the time for service of the writ expired): "They must have budgeted for a heavy liability and no doubt hoped to avoid all costs of litigation by achieving a negotiated settlement. ... They may have known that occasionally solicitors will fail to issue a writ in time. ... What they can scarcely have contemplated, even in their wildest dreams, was that the plaintiff would be much less negligent and instead of failing to issue a writ at all would have issued one but failed to serve it." The "date of knowledge" variant of the primary limitation period may lead to another strange result, namely the plaintiff sometimes arguing for an early date, for if his unserved writ was issued more than three years after the date of knowledge it is presumably a nullity and the case is one for the exercise of discretion.

[43] Not every error is negligence, but the inference arising from allowing a limitation period to expire is difficult to rebut. *cf. Bradley* v. *Hanseatic Shipping* [1986] 2 Lloyd's Rep. 34.

[44] *Thompson* v. *Brown, supra*, at p. 752.

[45] *Thompson* v. *Brown, supra*, at p. 750; *Firman* v. *Ellis, supra. cf. Birkett* v. *James* [1978] A.C. 297 (dismissal for want of prosecution). As has often been pointed out the real issue in such cases is not whether the plaintiff shall recover damages, but which liability insurers shall pay them.

successfully than Ormrod L.J. thought when he remarked that yet another Parliamentary attempt at reform was necessary[46] but it is hard, as a matter of policy as opposed to statutory interpretation, to justify the present sharp distinction between cases where proceedings have and have not been issued within the primary period.[47]

(2) Maritime cases

The Maritime Conventions Act 1911[48] fixes two years as the period of limitation for damage to a vessel, her cargo, freight or any property on board her, or for damages for loss of life or personal injuries suffered by any person on board caused by the fault of another vessel. The court may, however, extend this period to such extent and upon such conditions as it thinks fit.[49] But the Act only applies to actions brought against ships other than that on which the damage actually occurred, and, accordingly, where an action was brought against shipowners in respect of the death of a seaman on their ship, it was held that the general law of limitation (the three-year period) applied.[50]

(3) Liability under the Consumer Protection Act 1987

We have seen that this Act imposes strict liability for defective products.[51] Though applying to some private property damage it is likely in practice to be overwhelmingly concerned with personal injury.[52] It adds a new section 11A to the Act of 1980 and the main rules are identical to those generally applying in personal injury cases, that is to say, a primary three year period from the damage, an alternative period running from the plaintiff's knowledge and a power to override the limitation period. However, there is one major difference: no action can be brought in any case more than 10 years from the date when the product was put into circulation. This bar is absolute, that is to say, it cannot be overridden by the court under section 33 of the 1980 Act and it applies even if the plaintiff was under a disability or there was fraud, concealment or mistake—or even if no cause of action could have arisen within the 10 year period because there was no damage.[53] None of these provisions, however, affects an action for common law negligence.

[46] In *Chappell* v. *Cooper* [1980] 1 W.L.R. 958, 967.
[47] For a general survey, arguing for abolition of the fixed primary periods, see Davies, "Limitations on the Law of Limitation" (1982) 92 L.Q.R. 249. See also Morgan "Limitation and Discretion" (1982) 1 C.J.Q. 109. It is presumably necessary to retain some (fairly short) fixed period during which the plaintiff can know that he has an *absolute* right to proceed. See also *Dept. of Transport* v. *Chris Smaller (Transport) Ltd.* [1989] 1 All E.R. 897, 903.
[48] s.8. A number of other statutes provide their own periods of limitation, *e.g.* Carriage by Air Act 1961; Nuclear Installations Act 1965; Carriage by Railway Act 1972; Carriage by Road Act 1974.
[49] *Ibid.* For a case on the exercise of the discretion, see *The Alnwick* [1965] P. 357.
[50] *The Niceto de Larrinaga* [1966] P. 80.
[51] See *ante*, Chap. 10.
[52] Where property damage alone is sued for the limitation period is three years, not the usual six: Limitation Act 1980, s.11A(4), inserted by the Consumer Protection Act 1987, Sched. 1, Pt. I, para. 1. The Latent Damage Act 1986 does not apply because this is not an action for negligence, but by s.5(5) of the 1987 Act time runs from the date when the damage occurred *or* the earliest time at which a person with an interest in the property had knowledge of the material facts (as to which see subss.(6) and (7)).
[53] See Limitation Act 1980, ss.11A(3), 28(7) and 32(4A), all inserted by the Consumer Protection Act 1987, Sched. I, Pt. I.

(4) *Cases of contribution*

Section 10 of the Limitation Act 1980 provides that a claim to recover statutory contribution[54] must be brought within two years of the date when the right to contribution first accrued.[55] If the tortfeasor claiming contribution has himself been sued by the victim of the tort, then the right to contribution accrues when judgment is given against him[56]; if he compromises the action the right accrues when the amount of the payment to be made by him to the victim is agreed.[57] In the case of claims for contribution between shipowners in respect of their liabilities for loss of life or personal injuries aboard ship, which are governed by the Maritime Conventions Act 1911, however, the period of limitation for contribution is one year from payment only.[58]

ASSIGNMENT OF RIGHT OF ACTION IN TORT[59]

This topic may conveniently be treated here, although it relates not so much to extinction of liability in tort, but to transfer of a right of action in tort.

It is a long-standing rule in the law of assignment of choses in action that, while property can lawfully be assigned, a "bare right to litigate" cannot,[60] because to allow such an assignment would be to encourage undesirable speculation in law suits.[61] Indeed, the agreement would savour of maintenance and champerty, which, formerly, were themselves torts and are still grounds for striking down a contract[62] and providing a defence to the assignee's action.[63] This is not to say, however, that there can never be a valid assignment of a right of action in tort and the basic rule must be read in the light of the following qualifications and exceptions.[64]

"Proper interest of assignee"

It has been held that if A transfers property to B he may also assign a right of action for breach of contract[65] (*e.g.* breach of covenant to repair in a lease)

---

[54] The legislation thus gives added importance to the possibility of a common law claim between tortfeasors, *e.g.* by virtue of an express contract between them (*ante*, p. 595) or under *Lister* v. *Romford Ice & Cold Storage Co. Ltd.* [1957] A.C. 555 (*ante*, p. 577) since the limitation period for such claims remains at six years.

[55] s.10(1). The provisions of the Act on disability and on fraud, concealment and mistake apply to contribution claims: s.10(5).

[56] s.10(3).

[57] s.10(4).

[58] Maritime Conventions Act 1911, s.8.

[59] Winfield, *Present Law of Abuse of Procedure*, pp. 67–69.

[60] Reaffirmed in *Trendtex Trading Corp.* v. *Credit Suisse* [1982] A.C. 679.

[61] Some reasons formerly given for the rule are either unconvincing or obsolete. Thus it was said in argument in *Anon.* (1600) Godbolt 81 that damages in the assigned action are too uncertain at the date of assignment, or that the assignee "may be a man of great power, who might procure a jury to give him greater damages."

[62] *Ante*, p. 553.

[63] *Laurent* v. *Sale & Co.* [1963] 1 W.L.R. 829.

[64] For statutory transmission on death, see Chap. 24.

[65] *Ellis* v. *Torrington* [1920] 1 K.B. 399.

in relation to that property, for then, it has been said, the assignee buys not in order to obtain a cause of action but in order to protect the property he has bought.[66] Notwithstanding certain statements denying the assignability of *any* tort claim, it is submitted that at the present day such a case should be treated in the same way if the cause of action is in tort.[67] It is more difficult to know how far there might one day be applied to a case of tort the doctrine stated in the House of Lords in *Trendtex Trading Corporation* v. *Credit Suisse*,[68] a case of assignment of a claim for breach of contract. It was said that an assignee who has a "genuine commercial interest" in the enforcement of a claim may take a valid assignment of it so long as the transaction is not champertous and it seems that a genuine commercial interest may be present simply because the assignee is a creditor of the assignor.[69] On this basis, unless an arbitrary line is to be drawn between contract and tort, it may be that, for example, an assignment to a bank of the assignor's claim for damages for negligent misstatement inducing a contract which the bank has financed, and on which it stands to lose, would be valid.[70] By contrast, it is thought that the law should still refuse to give effect to the assignment of, say, a claim for libel or for personal injuries even though the assignor was indebted to the assignee.[71]

Judgment

No such problems arise with regard to the assignment of a judgment in an action of tort. If the judgment has already been given, the rights of the creditor are assignable like any other debt.[72] Similarly, a person may assign the fruits of an action yet to be commenced for this is no more than the assignment of property to be acquired. Thus, in *Glegg* v. *Bromley*[73] an assignment *pendente lite* of the fruits of an action for slander was upheld.[74]

---

[66] *Ibid.* at pp. 412–413, *per* Scrutton L.J.

[67] See the comments of Lord Denning M.R. in the Court of Appeal in *Trendtex Trading Corp.* v. *Credit Suisse* [1980] Q.B. 657.

[68] [1982] A.C. 679; *Brownton Ltd.* v. *Edward Moore Inbucon Ltd.* [1985] 3 All E.R. 499, another contract case. But see Lloyd L.J. at p. 509, whose statement of the principle of the *Trendtex* case applies to contract and tort alike.

[69] The action was an attempt by the assignor to set aside the assignment, when a settlement of the assigned claim produced some ten times what the assignor had sold it for. The agreement was in fact champertous because its purpose was not merely to enable the assignees to recoup their losses in financing the abortive deal made by the assignors with the contract breaker, but to allow them to sell the claim to a third party and divide the spoils. On the facts, however, the proper law of the agreement was Swiss.

[70] There are essentially the facts of the *Trendtex* case with a change in the cause of action and the removal of the champertous element. But suppose the claim is for *fraudulent* misrepresentation? *cf.* Turner L.J. in *De Hoghton* v. *Money* (1866) L.R. 2 Ch.App. 164, 166.

[71] Lord Roskill in the *Trendtex* case at p. 702 refers to the principle that "causes of action which were essentially personal in their character, such as claims for defamation and personal injury, were incapable of assignment" but he is speaking in terms of the law seventy years ago and his general point is that the law of maintenance was then more severe. In the Court of Appeal in the *Trendtex* case ([1980] Q.B. 629) Lord Denning M.R. and Oliver J., who would have abandoned the "bare right of action" approach altogether, would have maintained a rule against the assignability of "personal tort" claims. It seems that if A makes a voluntary payment to B to compensate B for loss caused by C, A may take a valid assignment of B's claim in tort against C: *Esso Petroleum Co. Ltd.* v. *Hall Russell & Co. Ltd.* [1988] 3 W.L.R. 730, 738.

[72] *Carrington* v. *Harway* (1662) 1 Keb. 803; *Goodman* v. *Robinson* (1886) 18 Q.B.D. 332.

[73] [1912] 3 K.B. 474.

[74] *Cohen* v. *Mitchell* (1890) 25 Q.B.D. 262 can also be supported on this ground, although other reasons were given for the decision.

Subrogation[75]

The commonest example of subrogation in this connection is in the law of insurance. An insurance company which has compensated a policyholder under an indemnity insurance policy stands in his shoes with regard to his claims against the person who caused the injury. Hence if A by negligent driving of his car damages B's car, and the X company, with whom B is insured, compensates him, the X company can exploit B's action for negligence against A.[76]

INSOLVENCY

Insolvency of defendant

The original rule was that a claim for unliquidated damages in tort was not provable as a bankruptcy debt so that the claim remained alive against the bankrupt and liability did not pass to his trustee. A similar principle applied to the winding-up of an insolvent company.[77] Now, by the Insolvency Act 1986,[78] a liability in tort is a "bankruptcy debt"[79] so that the plaintiff may seek to share in the assets along with the other creditors and discharge from the bankruptcy[80] extinguishes this liability. To this, however, there is one very important exception for our purposes, namely that discharge does not, unless the court otherwise directs, release the bankrupt from his liability for damages for personal injuries arising from "negligence, nuisance or breach of a statutory, contractual or other duty."[81] In practice, the defendant is likely to be insured against these risks and in such a case his rights against the insurer are transferred to the plaintiff under the Third Parties (Rights Against Insurers) Act 1930, an exception to the rule of privity of contract. By the Insolvency Rules made under the authority of the Companies Act 1985 tort claims are likewise provable in the winding-up of an insolvent company but after winding-up the company ceases to exist[82] and the Third Parties (Rights Against Insurers) Act 1930 is of no assistance to a plaintiff

---

[75] For a statement of the principle, see *Castellain* v. *Preston* (1883) 11 Q.B.D. 380, 387 *et seq., per* Brett L.J.; *Burnand* v. *Rodocanachi* (1882) 7 App.Cas. 333, 339, *per* Lord Blackburn; *Morris* v. *Ford Motor Co.* [1973] Q.B. 792.

[76] But see *ante*, p. 17, for the "knock for knock" agreement. In *Lister* v. *Romford Ice and Cold Storage Co. Ltd.* [1957] A.C. 555 the action was in fact brought by the employers' insurers, and the employers themselves were not consulted about the action: [1956] 2 Q.B. 180, 185, *per* Denning L.J. Normally the action is brought in the name of the insured, but if there has been an assignment which complies with the requirements of the Law of Property Act 1925, s.136, the insurer can bring the action in his own name: *Compania Colombiana de Seguros* v. *Pacific Steam Navigation Co.* [1965] 1 Q.B. 101, 121–122, *per* Roskill J.; *Esso Petroleum Co. Ltd.* v. *Hall Russell & Co. Ltd.* [1988] 3 W.L.R. 730, 738, *per* Lord Goff.

[77] But tort claims became provable against the insolvent *estate* of a deceased person by s.1(6) of the Law Reform (Miscellaneous Provisions) Act 1934.

[78] Replacing equivalent provisions of the Insolvency Act 1985.

[79] See s.382. By subs. (2), "in determining . . . whether any liability in tort is a bankruptcy debt, the bankrupt is deemed to become subject to that liability by reason of an obligation incurred at the time when the cause of action accrued."

[80] Which may be on order of the court or, in some cases, by mere passage of time: see s.279.

[81] s.281(5).

[82] Subject to a power in the court to set aside the winding up within two years: Companies Act 1985, s.651.

who has not sued before the dissolution. That Act transfers to the plaintiff the rights of the insured against the insurer, it does not make the insurer liable for the torts of the insured: hence if there is no-one who can be sued for the tort the Act has no application.[83]

Insolvency of plaintiff

Under the Insolvency Act the bankrupt's property[84] forms, with certain exceptions, his estate available for distribution among creditors. The devolution of any tort claims he has is not directly dealt with by the Act and the law must be presumed to be as it was under previous legislation. Briefly, if the tort is a purely personal one, like assault or defamation or negligence causing personal injuries, the right of action for it remains exercisable by the injured party himself and does not pass to his trustee in bankruptcy; but when the tort is to property, *e.g.* conversion of goods, then the right to sue for it passes to the trustee, who can sell or assign it to anyone as he, in his discretion, thinks fit.[85] If the same set of facts gives rise to injuries to both the person and the property of the bankrupt, then it is probable, but not certain, that in such circumstances the claim for personal injury remains with the bankrupt while that for injury to his property passes to his trustee.[86] This view has in its favour the general principle that it is the bankrupt's *property* with which the trustee is primarily concerned and, secondly, the argument that the trustee might find it awkward to prosecute a personal claim if the bankrupt were unwilling to engage in the action at all.

---

[83] *Bradley* v. *Eagle Star Insurance*, [1989] 2 W.L.R. 568.
[84] Defined in s.436 to include "things in action."
[85] No problems arise here about "bare rights of action": *Ramsey* v. *Hartley* [1977] 1 W.L.R. 686.
[86] *Rogers* v. *Spence* (1846) 12 Cl. & F. 700, 720–721, *per* Lord Campbell. See Clark and Lindsell, *Torts* (16th ed.), para. 2–29.

INDEX